100 B.C.	B.C. A.D.	A.D. 100	A.D. 200	A.D. 300	A.D. 400

Hadrian's wall constructed

PLUTARCH

PLOTINUS

TACITUS

AUGUSTINE

Birth and death of Jesus Christ

EPICTETUS

NICOMACHUS

Books replace scrolls

LUCRETIUS

PTOLEMY

VIRGIL

MARCUS AURELIUS

GALEN

Julius Caesar assassinated

1600	1700	1800

DESCARTES

MONTESQUIEU

MILTON

VOLTAIRE

MOLIÈRE

HUME

French Revolution

PASCAL

ROUSSEAU

HUYGENS

DIDEROT

ADAM SMITH

Church bans Galileo's teaching of Copernican doctrine

KANT

GIBBON

LOCKE

MONTAIGNE

BOSWELL

SPINOZA

GILBERT

JEFFERSON

RACINE

CERVANTES

LAVOISIER

NEWTON

BACON

SWIFT

GALILEO

BERKELEY

SHAKESPEARE

KEPLER

HAMILTON

HARVEY

Industrial Revolution begins

HOBBES

GREAT BOOKS
OF THE
WESTERN WORLD

MORTIMER J. ADLER
Editor in Chief

19

DANTE
CHAUCER

DANTE ALIGHIERI
The Divine Comedy

GEOFFREY CHAUCER
Troilus and Criseyde
The Canterbury Tales

ROBERT P. GWINN,
Publisher,
Chairman, Board of Directors

PETER B. NORTON, *President*

PHILIP W. GOETZ, *Editor in Chief*

ENCYCLOPÆDIA BRITANNICA, INC.
CHICAGO

AUCKLAND GENEVA LONDON MADRID MANILA PARIS
ROME SEOUL SYDNEY TOKYO TORONTO

THE UNIVERSITY OF CHICAGO

*The Great Books is published with the editorial advice
of the faculties of The University of Chicago*

General Contents

DANTE ALIGHIERI
The Divine Comedy   1
Translated by Charles S. Singleton

GEOFFREY CHAUCER
Troilus and Criseyde 177
The Canterbury Tales 277
Translated by Nevill Coghill

DANTE

Biographical Note

DANTE, 1265–1321

Dante Alighieri was born in Florence about the middle of May, 1265. The city, then under its first democratic constitution, was sharply divided between the Papal party of the Guelphs and the Imperial party of the Ghibellines. Dante's family were adherents of the Guelph faction, and when Dante was only a few months old, the Guelphs obtained decisive victory at the Battle of Benevento. Although of noble ancestry, the Alighieri family was neither wealthy nor particularly prominent.

It seems probable that Dante received his early education at the Franciscan school of Santa Croce. He evidently owed much to the influence of Brunetto Latini, the philosopher and scholar who figured largely in the councils of the Florentine commune. Before twenty, he began writing poetry and became associated with the Italian poets of the "sweet new style," who exalted their love and their ladies in philosophical verse. Dante's "lady," whom he celebrated with singular devotion, was a certain Beatrice. According to Boccaccio's life of Dante, she was Beatrice Portinari, daughter of a Florentine citizen, who married a wealthy banker, and died when she was but twenty-four. Dante first sang of Beatrice in the *Vita Nuova* (1292), a sequence of poems with prose comment in which he recounts the story of his love, of the first meeting when they were both nine years of age, the exchange of greetings which passed between them on May Day, 1283, and of Beatrice's death in 1290.

Upon turning thirty, Dante became actively involved in Florentine politics. The constitution of the city was based upon the guilds, and Dante, upon his enrolment in the guild of physicians and apothecaries, which also included book dealers, became eligible for office. He participated in the deliberations of the councils, served on a special embassy, and in 1300 was elected one of the six priors that governed the city. The former struggle between the Guelphs and Ghibellines had appeared in new form in the conflict between the Whites and the Blacks. As one of the priors, Dante

seems to have been influential in the move to lessen factionalism by banishing from Florence the rival leaders, including among the Blacks his wife's relative, Corso Donati, and among the Whites his "first friend," the poet, Guido Cavalcanti. Despite the opposition of Dante and the White leaders to Papal interference in Florentine affairs, Pope Boniface VIII in 1301 invited Charles of Valois, brother of King Philip of France, to enter Florence to settle the differences between the two factions. Actually he assisted the Blacks to seize power, and more than six hundred Whites were condemned to exile. In 1302 Dante, with four others of the White party, was charged with corruption in office. He was condemned to pay a fine of five thousand florins within three days or lose his property, exiled for two years, and denied the right ever again to hold public office. Three months later, upon his refusal to pay the fine, Dante was condemned to be burned alive if he should come within the power of the republic.

"After it was the pleasure of the citizens of the most beautiful and most famous daughter of Rome, Florence, to chase me forth from her sweet bosom," Dante writes of his exile in the *Convivio*, "I have gone through almost every region to which this tongue of ours extends, showing against my will the wound of fortune." It is recorded that Dante attended a meeting at San Godenzo, where an alliance was formed between the Whites in exile and the Ghibellines, but he does not seem to have been present in 1304 when the combined forces were defeated at Lastra. Perhaps he had already separated himself from the "evil and foolish company" of his fellow-exiles, "formed a party by himself," and found his "first refuge and hostelry" at the court of the Della Scalas in Verona. Probably during the following years he spent time at Bologna and later at Padua, where Giotto is said to have entertained him. Toward the end of 1306 he was the guest of the Malaspinas in Lunigiana and acted as their ambassador in making peace with the Bishop of Luni. Sometime after this date he may have visited Paris and attended the university there.

During the early years of his exile Dante appears to have studied in those subjects which gained him the title of philosopher and theologian as well as poet. In the *Convivio,* probably written between 1305 and 1308, he tells how, after the death of Beatrice, he turned to Cicero's *De Amicitia* and the *Consolatio Philosophiae* of Boethius, which awoke in him the love of philosophy. To sing its praises he began his *Convivio,* which he intended to be a kind of treasury of universal knowledge in the form of poems connected by lengthy prose commentaries. At the same time he worked upon the *De Vulgari Eloquentia,* a Latin treatise in which he defended the use of Italian as a literary language.

The election of Henry of Luxemburg as emperor in 1308 stirred Dante's political hopes. When Henry entered Italy in 1310 at the head of an army, Dante in an epistle to the princes and people of Italy hailed the coming of a deliverer. At Milan he paid personal homage to Henry as his sovereign. When Florence, in alliance with King Robert of Naples, prepared to resist the emperor, Dante in a second epistle denounced them for their obstinacy and prophesied their doom. In a third epistle he upbraided the Emperor himself for his delay and urged him on against Florence. It was probably during this period that he wrote his *De Monarchia,* an intellectual defense of the emperor as the sovereign of the temporal order. The death of Henry in 1313, after a year or so of ineffectual fighting, brought an end to the political aspirations of Dante and his party. The city of Florence in 1311 and again in 1315 renewed his condemnation.

After Henry's death, Dante passed the rest of his life under the protection of various lords of Lombardy, Tuscany, and the Romagna. According to one tradition, he retired for a time to the monastery of Santa Croce di Fonte Avellana in the Appenines, where he worked on the *Divine Comedy,* which may have been planned as early as 1292. He was almost certainly for a time at the court of Can Grande della Scala, to whom he dedicated the *Paradiso.* In 1315 Florence issued a general recall of exiles. Dante refused to pay the required fine and to "bear the brand of oblation," feeling that such a return would derogate from his fame and honor. To the end of his life he appears to have hoped that his *Comedy* would finally open the gates of the city to him.

The last few years of the poet's life were spent at Ravenna, under the patronage of Guido da Polenta, a nephew of Francesca da Rimini. Dante's daughter, Beatrice, was a nun in that city, and one of his sons held a benefice there; his wife seems to have resided in Florence throughout his exile. Dante was greatly esteemed at Ravenna and enjoyed a congenial circle of friends. Here he completed the *Divine Comedy* and wrote two eclogues in Latin which indicate that a certain contentment surrounded his closing days. Returning from a diplomatic mission to Venice on behalf of his patron, he caught a fever and died September 14, 1321. He was buried at Ravenna before the door of the principal church, with the highest honors, and "in the habit of a poet and a great philosopher."

Contents

Biographical Note   ix

INFERNO   1

PURGATORIO   45

PARADISO   90

Notes   134

Illustrations   168

Inferno

CANTO I

Midway in the journey of our life I found myself in a dark wood, for the straight way was lost.[1] Ah, how hard it is to tell what that wood was, wild, rugged, harsh; the very thought of it renews the fear! It is so bitter that death is hardly more so. But, to treat of the good that I found in it, I will tell of the other things I saw there.

I cannot rightly say how I entered it, I was so full of sleep at the moment I left the true way; but when I had reached the foot of a hill, there at the end of the valley that had pierced my heart with fear, I looked up and saw its shoulders already clad in the rays of the planet[2] that leads men aright by every path. Then the fear was somewhat quieted that had continued in the lake of my heart through the night I had passed so piteously. And as he who with laboring breath has escaped from the deep to the shore turns to look back on the dangerous waters, so my mind which was still fleeing turned back to gaze upon the pass that never left anyone alive.

After I had rested my tired body a little, I again took up my way across the desert strand, so that the firm foot was always the lower. And behold, near the beginning of the steep, a leopard light-footed and very fleet, covered with a spotted hide! And it did not depart from before my eyes, but did so impede my way that more than once I turned round to go back.

It was the beginning of the morning, and the sun was mounting with the stars that were with it when Divine Love first set those beautiful things in motion, so that the hour of the day and the sweet season gave me cause for good hope of that beast with the gay skin; yet not so much that I did not feel afraid at the sight of a lion that appeared to me and seemed to be coming at me, head high and raging with hunger, so that the air seemed to tremble at it; and a she-wolf,[3] that in her leanness seemed laden with every craving and

had already caused many to live in sorrow: she put such heaviness upon me with the fear that came from sight of her that I lost hope of the height. And like one who is eager in winning, but, when the time comes that makes him lose, weeps and is saddened in all his thoughts, such did that peaceless beast make me, as, coming on against me, she pushed me back, little by little, to where the sun is silent.

While I was running down to the depth there appeared before me one who seemed faint through long silence. When I saw him in that vast desert, I cried to him, "Have pity on me whatever you are, shade or living man!"

"No, not a living man, though once I was," he answered me, "and my parents were Lombards, both Mantuans by birth. I was born *sub Julio*,[4] although late, and I lived at Rome under the good Augustus, in the time of the false and lying gods. I was a poet, and I sang of that just son of Anchises who came from Troy after proud Ilium was burned. But you, why do you return to so much woe? Why do you not climb the delectable mountain, the source and cause of every happiness?"

"Are you, then, that Virgil, that fount which pours forth so broad a stream of speech?" I answered him, my brow covered with shame. "O glory and light of other poets, may the long study and the great love that have made me search your volume avail me! You are my master and my author. You alone are he from whom I took the fair style that has done me honor. See the beast that has turned me back. Help me against her, famous sage, for she makes my veins and pulses tremble."

"It behooves you to go by another way if you would escape from this wild place," he answered when he saw me weep, "for this beast, the cause of your complaint, lets no man pass her way, but so besets him that she slays him; and she has a nature so vicious and malign that she never sates her greedy appetite and after feeding is hungrier than before. Many are the beasts with which she mates, and there will yet be more, until the Hound shall come who will deal her a painful death. He will not feed on earth or pelf, but on wisdom, love, and virtue, and his birth shall be between felt and felt. He shall be the salvation of that low-lying Italy for which the virgin Camilla and Euryalus, Turnus, and Nisus died of their wounds.[5] He shall hunt her through every town till he has thrust her back into Hell, whence envy first sent her forth. Therefore I think and deem it best that you should follow me, and I will be your guide and lead you hence through an eternal place, where you shall hear the despairing shrieks and see the ancient tormented spirits who all bewail the second death. Then you shall see those who are content in the fire[6] because they hope to come among the blessed, whensoever that may be; and to these if you would then ascend, there shall be a soul worthier than I to guide you; with her I shall leave you at my departing. For the Emperor who reigns thereabove wills not that I come into His city, because I was rebellious to His law. In all parts is His empire, in that part is His kingdom, there is His city and His lofty seat. Oh, happy he whom He elects thereto!"

And I to him, "Poet, I beseech you, by that God whom you did not know, so that I may escape this ill and worse, lead me whither you said just now, that I may see St. Peter's gate and those whom you term so woeful."

Then he set out, and I followed after him.

CANTO II

Day was departing, and the dark air was taking the creatures on earth from their labors; and I alone was making ready to sustain the strife, both of the journey and of the pity, which unerring memory shall retrace. O Muses, O high genius, help me now! O memory that wrote down what I saw, here shall your worthiness appear!

I began, "Poet, you who guide me, consider if my strength is sufficient, before you trust me to the deep way. You tell how the father of Silvius went, while still mortal, to the immortal world and was there in his bodily senses. But that the Adversary of all evil should show him such favor seems not unfitting to an understanding mind, considering the high effect that was to spring from him, and who and what he was; for in the Empyrean heaven[1]

he was chosen as father of glorious Rome and of her empire, and both, to say the truth, were established[2] as the holy place where the successor of great Peter has his seat. In this journey, which you affirm he made, he learned things that were the cause of his victory and of the papal mantle. Later, the Chosen Vessel went there, that he might bring thence confirmation of that faith which is the beginning of the way of salvation. But I, why do I come there? And who allows it? I am not Aeneas, I am not Paul; of this neither I nor others think me worthy. Wherefore, if I yield and come, I fear that the coming may be folly. You are wise; you understand better than I explain it." And like one who unwills what he has willed and with new thoughts changes his resolve, so that he quite gives up the thing he had begun, such did I become on that dark slope, for by thinking on it I rendered null the undertaking that had been so suddenly embarked upon.

"If I have well understood what you say," the shade of that magnanimous one replied, "your spirit is beset by cowardice, which oftentimes encumbers a man, turning him from honorable endeavor, as false seeing turns a beast that shies. To free you from this fear I will tell you why I came and what it was I heard when I first felt pity for you. I was among those who are suspended, and a lady called me, so blessed and so fair that I prayed her to command me. Her eyes were more resplendent than the stars, and she began to say to me, sweetly and softly, in an angelic voice, 'O courteous Mantuan spirit, whose fame still lasts in the world,[3] and shall last as long as the world, my friend—and not the friend of Fortune—finds his way so impeded on the desert slope that he has turned back in fright; and, from what I have heard of him in Heaven, I fear he may already have gone so astray that I am late in arising to help him. Go now, and with your fair speech and with whatever is needful for his deliverance, assist him so that it may console me. I am Beatrice who send you.[4] I come from a place to which I long to return. Love moved me and makes me speak. When I am before my Lord I will often praise you to Him.'

"Then she was silent; and I began, 'O Lady of virtue, through whom alone mankind rises beyond all that is contained by the heaven that circles least, your command so pleases me, that had I obeyed already it would be late. You have only to declare your will to me. But tell me the reason why you are not wary of descending to this center from that spacious region to which you long to return.'

" 'Since you wish to know so deeply,' she answered me, 'I will tell you briefly why I am not afraid to come within this place. Those things alone should be feared that have power to do one harm—not other things, for they are not fearful. I am made such by God, of His grace, that your suffering does not touch me, and no flame of this burning assails me. In Heaven there is a gracious lady[5] who has such pity of this impediment to which I send you that stern judgment is broken thereabove. She called Lucy,[6] in her request, and said, "Your faithful one has need of you now, and I commend him to you." Lucy, foe of every cruelty, arose and, coming to where I sat with ancient Rachel,[7] said, "Beatrice, true praise of God, why do you not succor him who bore you such love that for you he left the vulgar throng? Do you not hear his pitiful lament? Do you not see the death that assails him on that flood over which the sea has no vaunt?"

" 'On earth no one was ever so swift to seize advantage or to flee from harm as I was when these words were uttered, to come down here from my blessed seat—trusting in your noble speech, which honors you and all who have heard it.'

"When she had said this to me, she turned her eyes, which shone with tears, making me the more eager to come; and so, even as she wished, I came to you, and rescued you from the beast that was preventing your going the short way up the fair mountain. What, then, is this? Why, why do you hold back? Why do you harbor such cowardice in your heart? Why are you not bold and free, when in Heaven's court three such blessed ladies are mindful of you, and my words pledge you so great a good?"

As little flowers, bent down and closed by chill of night, straighten and all unfold upon their stems when the sun brightens them, such in my faint strength did I become; and so much good courage rushed to my heart that I began, as one set free, "Oh, how compassionate was she who helped me, and how courteous were you, so quick to obey the true words she spoke to you! By your words you have made me so

eager to come with you that I have returned to my first resolve. Now on, for a single will is in us both; you are my leader, you my master and my teacher."

So I said to him, and when he moved on, I entered along the deep and savage way.

CANTO III

THROUGH ME YOU ENTER THE WOEFUL CITY,
   THROUGH ME YOU ENTER ETERNAL GRIEF,
   THROUGH ME YOU ENTER AMONG THE LOST.
JUSTICE MOVED MY HIGH MAKER:
   THE DIVINE POWER MADE ME,
   THE SUPREME WISDOM, AND THE PRIMAL LOVE.
BEFORE ME NOTHING WAS CREATED
   IF NOT ETERNAL, AND ETERNAL I ENDURE.
   ABANDON EVERY HOPE, YOU WHO ENTER.

These words of obscure color I saw inscribed over a portal; whereupon I said, "Master, their meaning is hard for me." And he to me, as one who understands, "Here must all fear be left behind; here let all cowardice be dead. We have come to the place where I have told you you will see the wretched people who have lost the good of intellect." And when he had placed his hand on mine, with a cheerful look from which I took comfort, he led me among the secret things.

Here sighs, laments, and loud wailings were resounding through the starless air, so that at first they made me weep. Strange tongues, horrible outcries, utterances of woe, accents of anger, voices shrill and faint, and the beating of hands among them, were making a tumult that swirls unceasingly in that dark and timeless air, like sand when a whirlwind blows. And I, my head circled with error, said, "Master, what is this I hear? And what people are these who seem so overcome by pain?"

And he to me, "Such is the miserable condition of the sorry souls of those who lived without infamy and without praise. They are mingled with that base band of angels who were neither rebellious nor faithful to God, but stood apart. The heavens drive them out, so as not to be less beautiful; and deep Hell does not receive them, lest the wicked have some glory over them."

And I, "Master, what is so grievous to them that it makes them lament so bitterly?"

He answered, "Very briefly I will tell you. These have no hope of death, and their blind life is so abject that they are envious of every other lot. The world does not suffer that report of them shall live. Mercy and justice disdain them. Let us not speak of them, but look, and pass on."

Looking again, I saw a banner that ran so fast, whirling about, that it seemed it might never have rest, and behind it came so long a train of people that I should never have believed death had undone so many. After I had recognized some among them, I saw and knew the shade of him who from cowardice made the great refusal.[1] Straightway I understood and knew for certain that this was the sorry sect of those who are displeasing to God and to his enemies. These wretches, who never were alive, were naked and were much stung by gadflies and wasps there, which were streaking their faces with blood that mingled with their tears and was gathered by loathsome worms at their feet.

Then, directing my gaze farther on, I saw people at the shore of a great river; wherefore I said, "Master, now grant that I may know who these are, and what law makes them seem so ready to cross over, as I discern through the dim light."

And he to me, "These things will be made known to you when we stay our steps at the dismal stream of Acheron."

Then, with eyes downcast and ashamed, fearing that my words had displeased him, I refrained from speaking till we reached the river.

And behold, an old man,[2] his hair white with age, coming towards us in a boat and shouting, "Woe to you, wicked souls! Do not hope to see Heaven ever! I come to carry you to the other shore, into eternal darkness, into fire and cold. And you there, living soul, stand aside from these that are dead." But when he saw that I did not do so, he said, "By another way, by other ports, not here, you shall cross to shore. A lighter bark must carry you."

And my leader to him, "Charon, do not rage. Thus is it willed there where that can be done which is willed; and ask no more."

Thereon the grizzled cheeks of the ferryman of the livid marsh, who had wheels of flame about his eyes, were quiet. But those forlorn and naked souls changed color, their teeth chattering, as soon as they heard the cruel words. They cursed God, their parents, the human race, the place, the time, the seed of their begetting and of their birth. Then, weeping loudly, all drew to the evil shore that awaits every man who fears not God. The demon Charon, his eyes like glowing coals, beckons to them and collects them all, beating with his oar whoever lingers.

As the leaves fall away in autumn, one after another, till the bough sees all its spoils upon the ground, so there the evil seed of Adam: one by one they cast themselves from that shore at signals, like a bird at its call. Thus they go over the dark water, and before they have landed on the other shore, on this side a new throng gathers.

"My son," said the courteous master, "those who die in the wrath of God all come together here from every land; and they are eager to cross the stream, for Divine Justice so spurs them that their fear is changed to desire. No good soul ever passes this way; therefore, if Charon complains of you, you can now well understand the meaning of his words."

When he had ended, the gloomy plain shook so violently that even now the memory of my terror bathes me in sweat. The tear-soaked ground[3] gave forth a wind that flashed a crimson light which overcame all my senses, and I fell like one who is seized by sleep.

CANTO IV

A heavy thunderclap broke the deep sleep in my head, so that I started like one who is awakened by force; and, standing up, I moved my rested eyes around, gazing intently to make out the place where I was. True it is that I found myself on the brink of the chasm of pain, which holds the clamor of endless wailings. It was so dark and deep and misty that, though I peered intently down into the depth, I could make out nothing there.

"Let us descend now into the blind world here below," the poet began, all pale. "I will be first, and you second."

And I, noting his pallor, said, "How shall I come, if you are afraid, who are wont to encourage me when I hesitate?"

And he to me, "The anguish of the people

here below paints my face with the pity that you take for fear. Let us go, for the long way urges us." So he entered, and had me enter, the first circle[1] that girds the abyss.

Here there was no plaint, that could be heard, except of sighs, which caused the eternal air to tremble; and this arose from the sadness, without torments, of the crowds that were many and great, both of children and of women and men.

The good master said to me, "Do you not ask what spirits are these that you see? Now, before you go farther, I will have you know that they did not sin; but if they have merit, that does not suffice, for they did not have baptism, which is the portal of the faith you hold; and if they were before Christianity, they did not worship God aright, and I myself am one of these. Because of these shortcomings, and for no other fault, we are lost, and only so far afflicted that without hope we live in longing."

Great sadness seized my heart when I heard him, for I recognized that people of great worth were suspended in that Limbo.

"Tell me, master, tell me, sir," I began, wishing to be assured of the faith that conquers every error, "did ever anyone go forth from here, either by his own or by another's merit, who afterwards was blessed?"

And he, who understood my covert speech, replied, "I was new in this condition[2] when I saw a Mighty One come here, crowned with sign of victory. He took hence the shade of our first parent, Abel his son, and Noah, and Moses, obedient giver of laws, Abraham the patriach and David the king, Israel with his father and his children and with Rachel, for whom he did so much, and many others; and He made them blessed. And I would have you know that before these no human souls were saved."

We did not cease going on because he spoke, but all the while were passing through the wood, I mean the wood of thronging spirits; nor had we yet gone far from the place of my slumber when I saw a fire,[3] which overcame a hemisphere of darkness. We were still a little distant from it, yet not so far but that I might in part discern that honorable folk possessed this place.

"O you who honor science and art, who are these that have such honor that it sets them apart from the condition of the rest?"

And he to me, "Their honored fame, which resounds in your life above, wins grace in Heaven, which thus advances them."

Meanwhile I heard a voice which said, "Honor the great Poet! His shade, which had departed, now returns."

After the voice had ceased and was still, I saw four great shades coming to us, in semblance neither sad nor joyful. The good master began, "Note him there with sword in hand who comes before the other three as their lord. He is Homer,[4] sovereign poet; next is Horace,[5] satirist; Ovid[6] comes third, and Lucan[7] last. Since each shares with me the name the single voice has uttered, they do me honor, and in that they do well."

Thus I saw assembled the fair school of that lord of highest song who, like an eagle, soars above the rest. After they had talked awhile together, they turned to me with sign of salutation, at which my master smiled; and far more honor still they showed me, for they made me one of their company, so that I was sixth amid so much wisdom. Thus we went onward to the light, talking of things it is well to pass in silence, even as it was well to speak of them there.

We came to the foot of a noble castle,[8] seven times encircled by lofty walls and defended round about by a fair stream. This we crossed, as on solid ground, and through seven gates[9] I entered with these sages. We came to a meadow of fresh verdure, where there were people with grave and slow-moving eyes and looks of great authority; they spoke seldom and with gentle voices.

Then we drew to one side, into an open place which was luminous and high, so that we could see all of them. There before me, on the enameled green, the great spirits were shown to me, so that I glory within me for having seen them. I saw Electra[10] with many companions, among whom I knew Hector, and Aeneas, and falcon-eyed Caesar armed. I saw Camilla and Penthesilea; and on the other side I saw King Latinus, who sat with his daughter Lavinia. I saw that Brutus who drove out the Tarquin, I saw Lucretia, Julia, Marcia, and Cornelia; and by himself apart I saw Saladin.

When I raised my eyes a little higher, I

saw the Master of those who know,[11] seated in a philosophic family. All look to him, all do him honor. There, nearest to him and in front of the rest, I saw Socrates and Plato; I saw Democritus,[12] who ascribes the world to chance, Diogenes, Anaxagoras, and Thales,[13] Empedocles, Heraclitus,[14] and Zeno. I saw the good collector of the qualities of things— I mean Dioscorides[15]—and I saw Orpheus,[16] Tully, Linus, and Seneca the moralist,[17] Euclid the geometer, and Ptolemy,[18] Hippocrates,[19] Avicenna,[20] Galen, and Averroës, who made the great commentary.[21] I cannot give full account of them all, for my long theme so drives me on, that many times the telling comes short of the fact.

The company of six diminishes to two; by another way my wise guide leads me, out of the quiet, into the trembling air; and I come to a part where there is naught that shines.

CANTO V

Thus I descended from the first circle into the second, which girds less space,[1] and so much greater woe that it goads to wailing. There stands Minos,[2] horrible and snarling: upon the entrance he examines their offenses, and judges and dispatches them according as he entwines. I mean that when the ill-begotten soul comes before him, it confesses all; and that discerner of sins sees which shall be its place in Hell, then girds himself with his tail as many times as the grades he wills that it be sent down. Always before him stands a crowd of them; they go, each in his turn, to the judgment; they tell, and hear, and then are hurled below.

"O you who come to the abode of pain," said Minos to me, when he saw me, pausing in the act of that great office, "beware how you enter and in whom you trust; let not the breadth of the entrance deceive you!" And my leader to him, "Why do you too cry out? Do not hinder his fated going: thus is it willed there where that can be done which is willed; and ask no more."

Now the doleful notes begin to reach me; now I am come where much wailing smites me. I came into a place mute of all light, which bellows like the sea in tempest when it

is assailed by warring winds. The hellish hurricane, never resting, sweeps along the spirits with its rapine; whirling and smiting, it torments them. When they arrive before the ruin, there the shrieks, the moans, the lamentations; there they curse the divine power. I learned that to such torment are condemned the carnal sinners, who subject reason to desire.

And as their wings bear the starlings along in the cold season, in wide, dense flocks, so does that blast the sinful spirits; hither, thither, downward, upward, it drives them. No hope of less pain, not to say of rest, ever comforts them. And as the cranes go chanting their lays, making a long line of themselves in the air, so I saw shades come, uttering wails, borne by that strife; wherefore I said, "Master, who are these people that are so lashed by the black air?"

"The first of these of whom you wish to know," he said to me then, "was empress of many tongues. She was so given to lechery that she made lust licit in her law, to take away the blame she had incurred. She is Semiramis,[3] of whom we read that she succeeded Ninus and had been his wife: she held the land the Sultan rules.[4] The next is she who slew herself for love and broke faith to the ashes of Sichaeus;[5] next is wanton Cleopatra.[6] See Helen,[7] for whom so many years of ill revolved; and see the great Achilles,[8] who fought at the last with love. See Paris,[9] Tristan,"[10] and more than a thousand shades whom love had parted from our life he showed me, pointing them out and naming them.

When I heard my teacher name the ladies and the knights of old, pity overcame me and I was as one bewildered. "Poet," I began, "willingly would I speak with those two that go together and seem to be so light upon the wind."[11]

And he to me, "You shall see when they are nearer to us; and do you entreat them then by that love which leads them, and they will come."

As soon as the wind bends them to us, I raised my voice, "O wearied souls! come speak with us, if Another[12] forbid it not."

As doves called by desire, with wings raised and steady, come through the air, borne by their will to their sweet nest, so did these issue from the troop where Dido is, coming to us through the malignant air, such force had my compassionate cry.

"O living creature, gracious and benign, that go through the black air visiting us who stained the world with blood, if the King of the universe were friendly to us, we would pray Him for your peace, since you have pity on our perverse ill. Of that which it pleases you to hear and to speak, we will hear and speak with you, while the wind, as now, is silent for us.

"The city where I was born lies on that shore where the Po descends to be at peace with its followers. Love, which is quickly kindled in a gentle heart, seized this one for the fair form that was taken from me[13]—and the way of it afflicts me still. Love, which absolves no loved one from loving, seized me so strongly with delight in him, that, as you see, it does not leave me even now. Love brought us to one death. Caina awaits him who quenched our life."

These words were borne to us from them. And when I heard those afflicted souls I bowed my head and held it bowed until the poet said to me, "What are you thinking of?"

When I answered, I began, "Alas! How many sweet thoughts, what great desire, brought them to the woeful pass!"

Then I turned again to them, and I began, "Francesca,[14] your torments make me weep for grief and pity; but tell me, in the time of the sweet sighs, by what and how did Love grant you to know the dubious desires?"

And she to me, "There is no greater sorrow than to recall, in wretchedness, the happy time; and this your teacher knows. But if you have such great desire to know the first root of our love, I will tell as one who weeps and tells. One day, for pastime, we read of Lancelot, how love constrained him; we were alone, suspecting nothing. Several times that reading urged our eyes to meet and took the color from our faces, but one moment alone it was that overcame us. When we read how the longed-for smile was kissed by so great a lover, this one, who never shall be parted from me, kissed my mouth all trembling. A Gallehault was the book and he who wrote it;[15] that day we read no farther in it." While the one spirit said this, the other wept, so that for pity I swooned, as if in death, and fell as a dead body falls.

CANTO VI

At the return of my mind which had closed itself before the piteousness of the two kinsfolk that had quite overwhelmed me with sadness, I see about me new torments and new tormented souls, whichever way I move and turn about to gaze. I am in the third circle of the eternal, accursed, cold and heavy rain: its measure and its quality are never new; huge hail, foul water, and snow pour down through the murky air; the ground that receives it stinks. Cerberus,[1] monstrous beast and cruel, with three throats barks doglike over the people who are here submerged. His eyes are red, his beard greasy and black, his belly wide and his hands taloned; he claws the spirits, flays and quarters them. The rain makes them howl like dogs; the profane wretches often turn themselves, making of one side a screen for the other.

When Cerberus the great worm perceived us, he opened his mouths and showed his fangs; he was aquiver in every limb. And my leader, reaching out his open hands, took up earth, and with full fists threw it into the ravenous gullets. As the dog that barking craves, and then grows quiet when he snaps up his food, straining and struggling only to devour it, such became the foul faces of the demon Cerberus, who so thunders on the souls that they would fain be deaf.

We were passing over the shades whom the heavy rain subdues, and we were setting our feet upon their emptiness, which seems real bodies. All were lying on the ground, save one, who sat up as soon as he saw us pass before him.

"O you that are led through this Hell," he said to me, "recognize me if you can: you were made before I was unmade."

And I to him, "The anguish you endure perhaps take you from my memory, so that I do not seem ever to have seen you; but tell me who you are, who are set in a place so grievous and who suffer such punishment that, if any is greater, none is so loathsome."

And he to me, "Your city, which is so full of envy that already the sack runs over, held me in it, in the bright life. You citizens called me Ciacco:[2] for the ruinous fault of gluttony, as you see, I am broken by the rain; and I, in my misery, am not alone, for all these endure the same penalty for the same fault." And he said no more.

I answered him, "Ciacco, your misery so weighs upon me that it bids me weep. But tell me, if you can, what the citizens of the divided city will come to; and if any one in it is just; and tell me why such discord has assailed it."

And he to me, "After long contention they will come to blood, and the rustic party will drive out the other with much offense. Then, through the power of one who presently is temporizing, that party is destined to fall within three years, and the other to prevail, long holding its head high and keeping the other under heavy burdens, however it may lament and feel the shame. Two men are just, and are not heeded there. Pride, envy, and avarice are the three sparks that have inflamed their hearts." Here he ended his grievous words.[3]

And I to him, "I would have you instruct me further, and make me a gift of further speech: Farinata and Tegghiaio, who were so worthy, Jacopo Rusticucci, Arrigo, and Mosca, and the others who set their minds on doing good, tell me where they are and give me to know them, for great desire urges me to learn whether Heaven soothes or Hell envenoms them."

And he, "They are among the blackest souls, and different faults weigh them down toward the bottom; if you descend that far, there you can see them. But when you shall be in the sweet world I pray you recall me to men's memory. More I do not tell you, nor do I answer you more." Thereon he twisted his straight eyes asquint, looked at me for a moment, then bent his head and fell down with the other blind ones.

And my leader said to me, "He wakes no more until the angel's trumpet sounds and the hostile Power comes, when each shall find again his dismal tomb and take again his flesh and form, and hear that which resounds to all eternity."

Thus with slow steps we passed along through the foul mixture of the shades and of the rain, touching a little on the future life; wherefore I said, "Master, these torments, will they increase after the great Judgment, or will they grow less, or will they be just as burning as now?"

And he to me, "Return to your science,[4] which has it that the more a thing is perfect, the more it feels the good, and so the pain. Although this accursed folk can never come to true perfection, yet they look to be nearer it then than now."

We went round along that road, speaking much more than I repeat, and we came to the place where the descent is; there we found Plutus, the great enemy.

CANTO VII

"*Pape Satàn, pape Satàn aleppe!*"[1] Plutus[2] began with a clucking voice; and that gentle sage who knew all, said, to reassure me, "Do not let your fear harm you; for, whatever power he have, he shall not keep us from descending this rock." Then he turned back to that bloated visage and said, "Silence, accursed wolf! Consume yourself inwardly with your own rage. Not without cause is this journey to the depth; so is it willed on high, there where Michael avenged the proud rebellion." As sails swollen by the wind fall in a heap when the mainmast snaps, so fell that cruel beast to the ground.

Thus we descended into the fourth hollow, taking in more of the dismal bank which insacks all the evil of the universe.

Ah, justice of God! who crams together so many new travails and penalties as I saw? And why does our guilt so waste us? As does the wave, there over Charybdis,[3] breaking itself against the wave it meets, so must the folk here dance their round. Here I saw far more people than elsewhere, both on the one side and on the other, howling loudly, rolling weights, which they pushed with their chests; they clashed together, and then right there each wheeled round, rolling back his weight, shouting, "Why do you hoard?" and "Why do you squander?" Thus they returned along the gloomy circle on either hand to the opposite point, shouting at each other again their reproachful refrain; then, having reached that point, each turned back through his half-circle to the next joust.

And I, heart-wrung at this, said, "Master, now declare to me who are these people, and if all these tonsured ones on our left were clerics."

And he to me, "Each and all of these were so

asquint of mind in the first life that they followed there no right measure in their spending; most clearly do they bark this out when they come to the two points of the circle where opposite fault divides them. These who have no covering of hair on their head were clerics, and popes and cardinals, in whom avarice wreaks its excess."

And I said, "Master, among such as these I ought surely to recognize some who were polluted with these evils." And he to me, "You harbor a vain thought: the undiscerning life that made them foul now makes them dim to all discernment. They will come forever to the two buttings; these will rise from the grave with closed fist, and these with cropped hair. Ill-giving and ill-keeping have robbed them of the fair world and set them to this scuffle— what that is, I spend no fair words to say. Now can you see, my son, the brief mockery of the goods that are committed to Fortune, for which humankind contend with one another; because all the gold that is beneath the moon, or ever was, would not give rest to a single one of these weary souls."

"Master," I said, "now tell me further: this Fortune which you touch on here, what is it, which has the goods of the world so in its clutches?"

And he to me, "O foolish creatures, how great is the ignorance that besets you! I would have you receive my judgment on this now. He whose wisdom transcends all, made the heavens and gave them guides, so that every part shines to every part, equally distributing the light. In like manner, for worldly splendors He ordained a general minister and guide who should in due time transfer the vain goods from race to race, and from one to another blood, beyond the prevention of human wit, so that one race rules and another languishes, pursuant to her judgment, which is hidden like the snake in the grass. Your wisdom cannot withstand her: she foresees, judges, and pursues her reign, as theirs the other gods. Her changes know no truce. Necessity compels her to be swift, so fast do men come to their turns. This is she who is much reviled even by those who ought to praise her, but do wrongfully blame her and defame her. But she is blest and does not hear it. Happy with the other primal creatures she turns her sphere and rejoices in her bliss.

"Now let us descend to greater wretchedness: already every star sinks that was rising when I set out, and to stay overlong is forbidden."

We crossed the circle to the other edge, above a fount that boils and pours over by a trench leading from it. The water was far darker than perse; and we, in company with the murky waves, entered down through a strange way. This dismal little stream, when it has descended to the foot of the malign gray slopes, flows into the marsh that is named Styx;[4] and I, who was standing intent to gaze, saw a muddy people in that bog, all naked and with looks of rage. They were smiting each other not with hand only, but with head and chest and feet, and tearing each other piecemeal with their teeth.

The good master said, "Son, you see now the souls of those whom anger overcame; and I would also have you know for certain that down under the water are people who sigh and make it bubble at the surface, as your eye tells you wherever it turns. Fixed in the slime they say, 'We were sullen in the sweet air that is gladdened by the sun, bearing within us the sluggish fumes; now we are sullen in the black mire.' This hymn they gurgle in their throats, for they cannot speak it in full words."

Thus we compassed a great arc of that foul pond between the dry bank and the slough, with eyes turned on those that swallow the mire; and we came at length to the foot of a tower.

CANTO VIII

I say, continuing, that long before we had come to the foot of the high tower, our eyes went upward to its summit because of two little flames we saw set there, while yet another returned the signal from so far off that the eye could hardly catch it. And I turned to the sea of all wisdom and said, "This one, what does it mean? And that other fire, what does it answer? And who are they that have made it?" And he to me, "Over the foul waves you can already make out what is expected, if the fumes of the marsh do not hide it from you."

Bowstring never drove arrow from itself that coursed so swiftly through the air as a little bark I saw come towards us then through the water, piloted by a single boatman, who cried, "Now you are caught, fell spirit!"

"Phlegyas, Phlegyas,[1] this time you shout in vain," said my lord. "You shall not have us longer than while crossing the mire." As one who listens to some great deception that has been practiced on him, and then repines at it, such Phlegyas became in his gathered wrath.

My leader got into the bark, then had me enter after him—and only when I was in it did it seem laden.

As soon as he and I had embarked, the ancient prow moves off, cutting more of the water than it is wont with others. While we were running through the dead channel, there rose before me one covered with mud, and said, "Who are you that come before your time?"

And I to him, "If I come, I do not remain. But you, who are you that have become so foul?"

He answered, "You see that I am one who weeps."

And I to him, "In weeping and in sorrow do you remain, accursed spirit, for I know you, even if you are all filthy."

Then he stretched both his hands to the boat, whereat the wary master thrust him off, saying, "Away there with the other dogs!" Then he put his arms about my neck, kissed my face, and said, "Indignant soul, blessed is she who bore you! He was an arrogant one in the world. No goodness whatever adorns his memory; so is his shade furious here. How many up there now account themselves great kings, that here shall lie like swine in mire, leaving behind them horrible dispraises."

And I, "Master, I should like well to see him soused in this soup, before we quit the lake."

And he to me, "Before the shore comes into view you shall be satisfied. It is fitting that in such a wish you should be gratified."

A little after this I saw such rending of him by the muddy folk that I still praise and thank God for it. All cried, "At Filippo Argenti!"—and the irascible Florentine spirit turned on himself with his teeth.

Here we left him, and I tell no more of him; but on my ears smote a sound of wailing, at which I bend my eyes intently forward. The good master said, "Now, my son, the city that is named Dis[2] draws near, with its grave citizens, with its great garrison."

And I, "Master, already I distinctly discern its mosques there within the valley, red as if they had come out of the fire."

And he to me, "The eternal fire that blazes there within makes them show red, as you see, in this nether Hell."

We came at last into the deep moats entrenching that doleful city. The walls seemed to me to be of iron, and not until we had made a great circuit did we come to a place where the boatman loudly cried, "Out with you here! This is the entrance."

Above the gates I saw more than a thousand of those rained down from Heaven, who cried angrily, "Who is this that without death goes through the kingdom of the dead?" And my wise master made a sign that he wished to speak with them apart. Then they restrained somewhat their great disdain, and said, "You come alone, and let that one depart, who has entered so daringly into this kingdom. Let him retrace alone his foolish way; try, if he can!—for you shall stay here, who have escorted him through so dark a country."

Judge, reader, if I did not lose heart at the sound of the accursed words, for I did not think I should ever return here.

"O my dear leader, who seven times and more have restored my confidence and drawn me from great peril confronting me, do not leave me thus undone," I said. "And if going farther is denied us, let us quickly retrace our steps together."

And that lord who had led me thither said to me, "Do not fear, for no one can take from us our passage, by such a One is it granted us; but wait for me here, and comfort your weary spirit and feed it with good hope, for I will not forsake you in the nether world." So he goes away and leaves me there, the gentle father, and I remain in doubt, as yes and no contend within my head.

I could not hear what he proposed to them; but he was not long there with them when they all scrambled to get back in. These our adversaries shut the gates in the face of my lord, who remained without and turned back to me with slow steps. He had his eyes upon the ground, and his brows were shorn of all boldness, and he was saying with sighs, "Who has denied me the abodes of pain?" And to me he said, "Be not dismayed because of my vexation, for I shall prevail in this, whatever be contrived within to hinder us. This insolence of theirs is nothing new, for they showed it once at a less secret gate, which still stands without a bolt.[3] Over it you saw the dead inscription;[4] and already, on this side of it, there comes down the steep, passing the circles without escort, one by whom the city shall be opened to us."

CANTO IX

That color which cowardice painted outwardly on me when I saw my leader turn back, repressed more speedily his own new color. He stopped attentive, like a man that listens, for his eye could not lead him far through the dark air and the dense fog.

"Yet we must win this fight," he began, "or else . . . such did she offer herself to us! Oh, how long to me it seems till someone come!" I saw well how he covered up the beginning with the rest that came after, which were words different from the first; but none the less his speech gave me fear, because I drew his broken phrase perhaps to a worse meaning than it held.

"Into this depth of the dismal hollow does any ever descend from the first circle where the sole punishment is hope cut off?" I asked; and he answered, "It seldom happens that any of us makes the journey on which I go. It is true that once before I was down here, conjured by that cruel Erichtho[1] who was wont to call back shades into their bodies. My flesh had been but short while divested of me, when she made me enter within that wall to draw forth a spirit from the circle of Judas. That is the lowest place, and the darkest, and farthest from the heaven that encircles all. Well do I know the way, so reassure yourself. This marsh, which exhales the mighty stench, girds round the sorrowful city, wherein now we cannot enter without anger."

And more he said, but I have it not in memory, for my eye had wholly drawn me to the high tower with the glowing summit, where all at once three hellish blood-stained Furies had instantly risen up. They had the limbs and bearing of women, and they were girt with greenest hydras. For hair they had little serpents and cerastes[2] bound about their savage temples. And he, who well rec-

ognized the handmaids of the queen of eternal lamentation,[3] said to me, "See the fierce Erinyes! That is Megaera on the left; she that wails on the right is Alecto; Tisiphone is in the middle"; and with that he was silent. Each was tearing her breast with her nails; and they were beating themselves with their hands, and crying out so loudly that in fear I pressed close to the poet.

"Let Medusa[4] come and we'll turn him to stone," they all cried, looking downward. "Poorly did we avenge the assault of Theseus."[5]

"Turn your back, and keep your eyes shut; for should the Gorgon show herself and you see her, there would be no returning above." Thus said the master, and he himself turned me round and, not trusting to my hands, covered my face with his own hands as well.

O you who have sound understanding, mark the doctrine that is hidden under the veil of the strange verses!

And now there came over the turbid waves a crash of fearful sound, at which both shores trembled: a sound as of a wind, violent from conflicting heats, which strikes the forest and with unchecked course shatters the branches, beats them down and sweeps them away, haughtily driving onward in its cloud of dust and putting wild beasts and shepherds to flight.

He loosed my eyes, and said, "Now direct your sight across that ancient scum, there where that fume is harshest."

As the frogs before their enemy the snake all vanish through the water, till each cocks itself on the bottom, I saw more than a thousand ruined souls flee before one that strode dry-shod over Styx. He was clearing that gross air from before his face, often moving his left hand before him, and only with that annoyance did he seem weary. Well did I perceive that he was a messenger from Heaven; and I turned to the master, who signed to me that I should stand quiet and bow down to him. Ah, how full of disdain he seemed to me! He came to the gate, and with a little wand he opened it, and there was no resistance.

"O outcasts from Heaven, race despised," he began upon the horrible threshold, "why is this insolence harbored in you? Why do you kick against that Will which can never be thwarted of its end, and which many times has increased your pain? What does it avail to butt against the fates? Your Cerberus, if you well remember, still bears his chin and his throat peeled for doing so."[6] Then he turned back on the filthy way, and spoke not a word to us, but looked like one whom other care urges and incites than that of those who stand before him.

Then we moved our steps toward the city, secure after the holy words. We entered it without any strife; and I, who was eager to behold the condition which such a fortress encloses, cast my eye round about, as soon as I was in; and on every hand I see a great plain full of woe and of cruel torment. As at Arles,[7] where the Rhone slackens its course, and as at Pola,[8] near the Quarnero, which shuts Italy in and bathes her borders, the sepulchers make all the place uneven, so they did here on every side, save that the manner here was more bitter; for among the tombs flames were scattered, whereby they were made to glow all over, hotter than iron need be for any craft. Their covers were all raised up, and such dire laments were issuing forth from them as truly seemed to come from people wretched and suffering.

And I, "Master, what are these people who, buried within these chests, make themselves heard by their woeful sighs?"

And he to me, "Here are the heresiarchs with their followers of every sect, and the tombs are laden far more than you think. Like with like is buried here, and the monuments are more and less hot."

Then, after he had turned to the right hand, we passed between the tortures and the high battlements.

CANTO X

Now, along a solitary path between the wall of the city and the torments my master goes on, and I follow after him.

"O supreme virtue," I began, "who lead me round as you will through the impious circles, speak to me and satisfy my desires. Might these people who lie within the sepulchers be seen? Indeed, the covers are all raised, and no one keeps guard."

And he to me, "All shall be closed when from Jehoshaphat[1] they return here with the bodies which they have left above. In this part

Epicurus[2] with all his followers, who make the soul die with the body, have their burial-place. Therefore, to the question which you ask me you shall soon have satisfaction here within, and also to the wish which you hold from me."

And I, "Good leader, I do not keep my heart hidden from you except in order to speak little, and to this you have before now disposed me."

"O Tuscan, who go alive through the city of fire speaking thus modestly, may it please you to stop in this place. Your speech clearly shows you a native of that noble fatherland to which I perhaps did too much harm." Suddenly this sound issued from one of the coffers, whereat in fear I drew a little nearer to my leader. And he to me, "Turn round! what are you doing? See there Farinata[3] who has risen erect: from the waist upwards you will see him all."

Already I had fixed my eyes on his, and he rose upright with chest and brow thrown back as if he had great scorn of Hell; and the bold and ready hands of my leader pushed me between the tombs to him, and he said, "Let your words be fitting."

When I was at the foot of his tomb, he looked at me for a moment, then, as if in disdain, asked me, "Who were your ancestors?"

And I, who was eager to obey, concealed nothing, but made all plain to him; whereupon he raised his brows a little; then he said, "They were fiercely adverse to me and to my forebears and to my party, so that twice over I scattered them."[4]

"If they were driven forth, they returned from every quarter, both times," I answered him, "but yours have not learned that art well."

Then there arose to sight alongside of him a shade, visible to the chin: I think he had raised himself on his knees. He looked round about me as though he wished to see whether someone was with me, but when his expectation was quite spent, he said, weeping, "If you go through this blind prison by reason of high genius, where is my son, and why is he not with you?"

And I to him, "I come not of myself. He who waits yonder, whom perhaps your Guido[5] had in disdain, is leading me through here."

Already his words and the manner of his

punishment had read his name to me: hence was my answer so full.

Suddenly straightening up, he cried, "How? Did you say 'he had'? Does he not still live? Does the sweet light not strike his eyes?" And when he perceived that I made some delay in answering, he fell supine again and showed himself no more.

But the other, that great soul at whose instance I had stopped, changed not his aspect, nor moved his neck, nor bent his side. "And if," he said, continuing his first discourse, "they have ill learned that art, that fact torments me more than this bed. But the face of the Lady who rules here[6] will not be kindled fifty times before you shall know how much that art weighs. And, so may you return some time to the sweet world, tell me, why is that people so fierce against my kindred in all its laws?" Whereon I to him, "The havoc and the great slaughter, which dyed the Arbia red, cause such prayers to be made in our temple."

He sighed, and shook his head, then said, "I was not alone in that, nor surely without cause would I have moved with the others; but I was alone there where all agreed to make an end of Florence, the one who defended her before them all."

"Ah, so may your seed sometime find peace," I prayed him, "solve the knot which has here entangled my judgment. It seems, if I hear aright, that you see beforehand what time brings with it,[7] but have a different manner with the present."

"Like one who has bad light, we see the things," he said, "which are remote from us: so much does the Supreme Ruler still shine on us; but when they draw near, or are, our intelligence is wholly vain, and unless others bring us word, we know nothing of your human state; wherefore you can comprehend that all our knowledge will be dead from that moment when the door of the future shall be closed."

Then, compunctious for my fault, I said, "Will you, now, tell him who fell back that his son is still among the living? And let him know that, if I was silent in response to him before, it was because my thoughts were already in that error which you have resolved for me."

And now my master was recalling me; wherefore with more haste I begged the spirit to tell me who were there with him; and he said to me, "Here I lie with more than a thousand. Here within is the second Frederick,[8] and the Cardinal;[9] and of the rest I do not speak."

With that he hid himself; and I turned my steps to the ancient poet, thinking on the words that seemed hostile to me. He set out, and then, as we went, he said to me, "Why are you so disturbed?" And I satisfied him in his question.

"Let your memory preserve what you have heard against yourself," that sage bade me, "and now give heed here—" and he raised his finger; "when you are before her sweet radiance whose fair eyes see all, from her you shall know of your life's journey."

Then he turned his steps to the left and, leaving the wall, we made our way toward the middle by a path that strikes into a valley which even up there annoyed us with its stench.

CANTO XI

On the edge of a high bank, formed by huge broken rocks in a circle, we came above a more cruel pen; and here, because of the horrible excess of the stench which the deep abyss throws out, we drew back to the cover of a great tomb, on which I saw an inscription that said, "I hold Pope Anastasius,[1] whom Photinus drew from the right path."

"We must delay our descent, that the sense may first accustom itself a little to the vile breath, and then we shall not heed it." Thus my master; and I said to him, "Pray find some compensation, that the time may not be lost." And he, "Know that I am so minded."

"My son, within these rocks," he then began, "are three lesser circles, one below another, like those you are leaving. All are full of accursed spirits; but in order that hereafter the sight alone may suffice you, hear how and why they are impounded.

"Of every malice that gains hatred in Heaven the end is injustice; and every such end, either by force or by fraud, afflicts another. But because fraud is an evil peculiar to man, it more displeases God, and therefore the fraudulent are the lower, and more pain assails them.

"All the first circle[2] is for the violent: but because violence is done to three persons, it is divided and constructed in three rings. To

God, to one's self, and to one's neighbor may violence be done: I say to them and to their things, as I shall make plain to you.

"By violence death and grievous wounds may be inflicted upon one's neighbor; and on his substance, ruins, burnings, and injurious extortions; wherefore the first ring torments all homicides and every one who smites wrongfully, despoilers and plunderers, in various troops.

"A man may lay violent hand upon himself, and upon his own property; and therefore in the second ring must every one repent in vain who deprives himself of your world, gambles away and dissipates his substance, and weeps there where he should be joyous.

"Violence may be done against the Deity, by denying and blaspheming Him in the heart, and despising Nature and her goodness; and therefore the smallest ring seals with its mark both Sodom and Cahors,[3] and all who speak contemning God in their heart.

"Fraud, which gnaws every conscience, a man may practice upon one who trusts in him, or upon one who reposes no confidence. This latter way seems to sever only the bond of love which nature makes; wherefore in the second circle hypocrisy, flatteries, sorcerers, falsity, theft, simony, panders, barratry, and like filth have their nest.

"By the other way both that love which Nature makes is forgotten, and that also which is added to it and which creates a special trust; therefore, in the smallest circle, at the center of the universe and the seat of Dis, every traitor is consumed eternally."

And I, "Master, your discourse proceeds most clearly, and full well distinguishes this chasm and the people that it holds; but tell me: they of the fat marsh, and they whom the wind drives, and they whom the rain beats, and they who clash with such rough tongues, why are they not punished within the ruddy city, if God's anger is upon them? And if it is not, why are they in such plight?"

And he said to me, "Why does your wit so wander beyond its wont? Or your mind, whither does it gaze? Do you not remember the words with which your *Ethics* treats the three dispositions which Heaven wills not: incontinence, malice, and mad bestiality? and how incontinence less offends God and incurs less blame? If you consider well this doctrine,

and bring to mind who they are that suffer punishment above, outside, you will see clearly why they are divided from these wicked spirits, and why the divine vengeance smites them with less wrath."

"O sun that heal every troubled vision, you do content me so, when you solve, that questioning, no less than knowing, pleases me; but turn back a little," I said, "to where you say that usury offends the divine Goodness, and loose the knot."

"Philosophy, for one who understands it," he said to me, "points out, not in one place alone, how Nature takes her course from divine Intellect and from Its art; and if you note well your *Physics,* you will find, after not many pages, that your art, as far as it can, follows her, as the pupil does his master; so that your art is as it were grandchild of God. By these two, if you remember Genesis at the beginning, it behooves man to gain his bread and to prosper. But because the usurer takes another way, he contemns Nature in herself and in her follower, for he puts his hope elsewhere.

"But follow me now, for it pleases me to go: the Fishes[4] are quivering on the horizon, and all the Wain lies over Caurus, and there, farther on, is the descent of the cliff."

CANTO XII

The place where we came for the descent of the bank was alpine, and such, because of what was there, that every eye would shun it.

Like the ruin which struck the Adige in its flank, on this side of Trent, either by earthquake or through failure of support, where, from the top of the mountain whence it started, to the plain, the rock is so tumbled down as to give some passage to anyone above—such was the descent of that ravine; and on the edge of the broken chasm was outstretched the infamy of Crete[1] that was conceived in the false cow.[2] And when he saw us he bit himself, like one whom wrath rends inwardly.

My sage cried out toward him, "Perhaps you believe that here is the Duke of Athens,[3] who dealt you your death up in the world. Get you gone, beast, for this man does not come tutored by your sister, but journeys here to see your punishments."

As a bull that breaks loose in the moment when it has received the mortal blow, and cannot go, but plunges this way and that, so I saw the Minotaur do.[4] And my wary guide cried, "Run to the passage: while he is in fury it is well that you descend."

So we took our way down over that rocky debris, which often moved under my feet with the new weight. I was going along thinking, and he said, "Perhaps you are thinking on this ruin, guarded by that bestial wrath which I quelled just now. Know then that the other time I came down here into the nether Hell this rock had not yet fallen. But certainly, if I reckon rightly, it was a little before He came who took from Dis[5] the great spoil of the uppermost circle, that the deep foul valley trembled so on all sides that I thought the universe felt love, whereby, as some believe, the world has many times been turned to chaos;[6] and at that moment this ancient rock, here and elsewhere, made such downfall. But fix your eyes below, for the river of blood draws near, in which boils everyone who by violence injures others."

O blind cupidity and mad rage, which in the brief life so goad us on, and then, in the eternal, steep us so bitterly!

I saw a wide ditch bent in an arc, as one embracing all the plain, according as my guide had said, and between it and the foot of the bank were centaurs running in a file, armed with arrows, as in the world they were wont to go to the chase. Seeing us coming down they all stopped and from the band three came forward, with bows and shafts which they first selected; and one cried from a distance, "To what torment do you come, you who descend the slope? Tell us from there; if not, I draw my bow!"

My master said, "Our answer we will make to Chiron[7] there beside you; to your own hurt was your will ever thus hasty." Then he nudged me and said, "That is Nessus,[8] who died for the beautiful Dejanira and himself wrought vengeance for himself; and the one in the middle, who gazes on his own breast, is the great Chiron, he who brought up Achilles; the other is Pholus,[9] who was so full of rage. Around the ditch they go by thousands, piercing with their arrows whatever spirit lifts itself out of the blood more than its guilt has allotted to it."

We drew near to those fleet beasts; and Chiron took an arrow and, with the notch of it, brushed back his beard upon his jaws; and when he had uncovered his great mouth, he said to his companions, "Have you observed that the one behind moves what he touches? The feet of the dead are not wont to do so."

And my good leader, who was now at his breast, where the two natures are consorted, replied, "Indeed he is alive, and thus alone have I to show him the dark valley: necessity brings him to it, and not sport. From singing halleluiah, came one who gave me this new office. He is no robber, nor I a thievish spirit; but by that Power by which I move my steps on so wild a road, give us one of your band whom we may keep beside, that he may show us where the ford is, and carry this one on his back, who is not a spirit that can go through the air."

Chiron bent round on his right breast and said to Nessus: "Go back and guide them, then; and if another troop encounters you, make it give way."

We moved on then with the trusty escort, along the edge of the crimson boiling, in which the boiled were uttering piercing shrieks. I saw people in it, down even to the eyebrows, and the great centaur said, "These are tyrants who took to blood and plunder. Here they lament their merciless crimes: here is Alexander,[10] and cruel Dionysius[11] who made Sicily have woeful years; and that brow with the hair so black is Azzolino,[12] and that other blond one is Opizzo of Este[13] who up in the world was indeed slain by his stepson." Then I turned to the poet, and he said, "Let him be first guide to you now, and me second."

A little farther on the centaur stopped beside a people who seemed to issue from that boiling stream as far as the throat. He showed us a spirit[14] on one side alone and said, "That one clove, in God's bosom, the heart[15] which on the Thames still drips with blood."

Then some I saw who had their heads, and even all their chests, out of the stream; and of these I recognized many. Thus more and more that blood sank down till it cooked only the feet; and here was our passage of the ditch.

"As on this hand you see that the boiling stream continually diminishes," said the centaur, "so I would have you believe that on this other it lowers its bed more and more, until it comes round again to the place where tyranny must groan. Divine justice there goads that Attila who was a scourge on earth, and

Pyrrhus[16] and Sextus;[17] and forever milks the tears, unlocked by the boiling, from Rinier of Corneto and Rinier Pazzo,[18] who made such warfare upon the highways."

Then he turned back and crossed the ford again.

CANTO XIII

Nessus had not yet reached the other side when we moved forward through a wood which was not marked by any path. No green leaves, but of dusky hue; no smooth boughs, but gnarled and warped; no fruits were there, but thorns with poison. Those wild beasts that hate tilled lands between Cecina and Corneto[1] do not have thickets so rough or dense. Here the foul Harpies[2] make their nests, who drove the Trojans from the Strophades with dismal announcement of future ill; they have broad wings, and human necks and faces, feet with claws, and their great bellies are feathered; they make lament on the strange trees.

And the good master began to say to me, "Before you enter farther, know that you are in the second ring, and shall be, until you come to the horrible sand. Look well, therefore, and you shall see things that would make my words incredible."

I heard wailings uttered on every side, and saw no one who made them; wherefore, all bewildered, I stopped. I believe that he believed that I believed that all those voices from amid the trunks came from people who were hidden from us. Therefore the master said, "If you break off a little branch from one of these plants, the thoughts you have will all be cut short." Then I stretched my hand a little forward and plucked a twig from a great thornbush, and its stub cried, "Why do you break me?" And when it had become dark with blood, it began again to cry, "Why do you tear me? Have you no spirit of pity? We were men, and now are turned to stocks. Truly your hand ought to be more merciful had we been souls of serpents."

As from a green brand that is burning at one end, and drips from the other, hissing with the escaping air, so from that broken twig came out words and blood together; whereon

I let fall the tip, and stood like one who is afraid.

"If he, O wounded spirit, had been able to believe before," replied my sage, "what he had never seen save in my verses, he would not have stretched forth his hand against you; but the incredible thing made me prompt him to a deed that grieves me. But tell him who you were, so that by way of some amends he may refresh your fame in the world above, whither it is allowed him to return."

And the stub said,[3] "You so allure me with your sweet words that I cannot keep silent; and may it not burden you that I am enticed to talk a little. I am he who held both the keys of Frederick's[4] heart, and turned them, locking and unlocking, so softly that from his secrets I kept almost every one. So faithful was I to the glorious office that for it I lost both sleep and life. The harlot[5] that never turned her whorish eyes from Caesar's household[6]—the common death and vice of courts—inflamed all minds against me; and they, inflamed, did so inflame Augustus that my glad honors were changed to dismal woes. My mind, in scornful temper, thinking by dying to escape from scorn, made me unjust against my just self. By the new roots of this tree I swear to you that I never broke faith with my lord, who was so worthy of honor. And if one of you returns to the world, let him comfort my memory which still lies prostrate from the blow that envy gave it."

The poet waited a little, then said to me, "Since he is silent, do not lose time, but speak and ask of him, if you would know more."

To which I answered, "Do you ask him further of what you think may satisfy me, for I cannot, such pity fills my heart."

Therefore he began again, "So may this man do freely what you ask of him, imprisoned spirit, may it please you to tell us further how the soul is bound in these knots; and tell us, if you can, whether from such members any soul is ever loosed."

Then the stub puffed hard, and soon that breath was changed into this voice, "You shall be answered briefly. When the fierce soul quits the body from which it has uprooted itself, Minos sends it to the seventh gullet. It falls into the woods, and no part is chosen for it, but wherever fortune flings it, there it sprouts like a grain of spelt; it shoots up to a sapling, and to a wild growth; the Harpies, feeding then upon its leaves, give pain and to the pain an outlet. Like the rest we shall come, each for his cast-off body, but not, however, that any may inhabit it again; for it is not just that a man have what he robs himself of. Hither shall we drag them, and through the mournful wood our bodies will be hung, each on the thornbush of its nocuous shade."

We were still attentive to the stub, believing it might wish to say more to us, when like one aware of the wild boar and the chase approaching his post, who hears the beasts and the branches crashing, we were surprised by an uproar. And behold, two on the left hand, naked and torn, fleeing so hard that they were breaking every tangle of the wood. The one in front was shouting, "Now come, come quickly, death!" and the other, thinking himself too slow, "Lano,[7] your legs were not so nimble at the jousts of the Toppo!" and perhaps because breath was failing him, he made one knot of himself and of a bush. Behind them the wood was full of black bitches, eager and fleet, like greyhounds loosed from the leash. On him who had squatted they set their teeth and tore him piecemeal, then carried off those woeful limbs.

My escort then took me by the hand and led me to the bush, which was lamenting in vain through its bleeding fractures. "O Jacopo da Santo Andrea,"[8] it cried, "what have you gained by making a screen of me? What blame have I for your sinful life?"

When my master had stopped beside it, he said, "Who were you, that through so many wounds blow forth with blood your doleful speech?"

And it to us, "O souls, who have arrived to see the shameful havoc that has thus torn my leaves from me, collect them at the foot of the wretched bush. I was of the city that changed her first patron for the Baptist, on which account he with his art will ever make her sorrowful; and were it not that at the passage of the Arno some semblance of him still remains, those citizens who afterwards rebuilt it on the ashes left by Attila[9] would have labored in vain.[10] I made me a gibbet of my own house."

CANTO XIV

Because the love of my native place constrained me, I gathered up the scattered twigs and gave them back to him who was already faint of voice. Thence we came to the confine, where the second ring is divided from the third and where a horrible mode of justice is seen.

To make these new things clear, I say we reached a plain which rejects all plants from its bed. The woeful wood is a garland round about it, as round the wood the dismal ditch. Here we stayed our steps at the very edge. The ground was a dry deep sand, not different in its fashion from that which once was trodden by the feet of Cato.[1]

O vengeance of God, how much should you be feared by all who read what was revealed to my eyes! I saw many herds of naked souls, who were all lamenting very miserably; and different laws seemed to be imposed upon them. Some were lying supine upon the ground, some sitting all crouched up, and others were going about incessantly. Those who moved about were far more numerous, and those who were lying in the torment were fewer, but they gave more tongue to their pain.

Over all the sand huge flakes of fire were falling slowly, like snow in the mountains without a wind. As the flames which Alexander, in those hot regions of India, saw fall upon his army, entire to the ground, whereat he had his legions tramp the soil, because the flakes were better extinguished before they spread, so did the eternal burning descend there, and the sand was kindled by it like tinder under the flint, to redouble the pain. The dance of the wretched hands was ever without repose, now here, now there, as they beat off the fresh burning.

I began, "Master, you who overcome all things except the obdurate demons that came out against us at the entrance of the gate, who is that great one[2] who seems not to heed the fire, and lies disdainful and scowling, so that the rain seems not to ripen him?"

And that same one, who had perceived that I was asking my leader about him, cried out, "What I was living, that am I dead. Though Jove weary out his smith, from whom in anger he took the sharp bolt by which on my last day I was smitten; and though he weary out the others, turn by turn, in Mongibello[3] at the black forge, crying, 'Good Vulcan, help, help!' even as he did at the fight of Phlegra,[4] and hurl at me with all his might, he would not have thereby glad vengeance."

Then my leader spoke with such force as I had not heard him use before, "O Capaneus! in that your pride remains unquenched you are punished the more: no torment save your own raging would be pain to match your fury." Then he turned round to me with gentler look, saying, "That was one of the seven kings who besieged Thebes,[5] and held, and seems to hold, God in disdain and prize Him little; but as I said to him, his revilings are quite fitting adornments to his breast. Now come along behind me, and see that you do not set your feet upon the burning sand, but keep them back ever close to the woods."

In silence we came to where there spurts forth from the forest a little stream[6] whose redness makes me shudder yet. As issues from the Bulicame a rivulet which then the sinful women share among themselves, so this ran down across the sand. Its bottom and both its banks were made of stone, as were the margins on the side; wherefore I perceived that our passage was there.

"In all that I have shown to you since we entered through the gate whose threshold is denied to no one, nothing has been discerned by your eyes so notable as the present stream, which quenches every flame above it." These were the words of my leader; wherefore I prayed him to bestow on me the food for which he had bestowed the appetite.

"In the middle of the sea there lies a wasted country," he then said, "which is named Crete, under whose king the world once was chaste. A mountain is there, called Ida, which once was glad with waters and with foliage; now it is deserted like a thing outworn. Rhea chose it of old for the faithful cradle of her son and, the better to conceal him when he cried, made them raise shouts there.[7] Within the mountain stands the great figure of an Old Man,[8] who holds his back turned toward Damietta,[9] and gazes on Rome as on his mirror: his head is fashioned of fine gold, his arms and breast are pure silver, then down to the fork he is of brass, and down from there is all of choice iron, except that the right foot is baked clay, and he rests more on this than on the other. Every part except the gold is cleft by a fissure that drips with tears which, collected, force a passage through the cavern there. Their course is from rock to rock into this valley: they form Acheron, Styx, and Phlegethon;[10] then their way is down by this narrow channel until, there where there is no more descending, they form Cocytus—and what that pool is, you shall see; here therefore I do not describe it."

And I to him, "If the present stream flows down thus from our world, why does it appear to us only at this border?"

And he to me, "You know that the place is circular; and though you have come far, always to the left in descending to the bottom, you have not yet turned through the whole circle; wherefore if aught new appears to us, it should not bring wonder to your face."

And I again, "Master, where are Phlegethon and Lethe[11] found? for about the one you are silent, and the other you say is formed by this rain."

"Truly you please me in all your questions," he answered, "but the boiling of the red water should well solve one that you ask. Lethe you shall see, but out of this abyss, there where the souls go to wash themselves, when the fault repented of has been removed."

Then he said, "Now it is time to quit the wood; see that you come behind me: the margins, which are not burning, form a path, and over them every flame is quenched."

CANTO XV

Now one of the hard margins bears us on, and the vapor from the stream overshades, so that it shelters the water and the banks from the fire. As the Flemings between Wissant[1] and Bruges,[2] fearing the tide that rushes in on them, make the bulwark to drive back the sea; and as the Paduans do along the Brenta,[3] to protect their towns and castles before Carentana[4] feels the heat; in like fashion were these banks made, except that the builder, whoever he was, made them neither so high nor so thick.

We were already so far removed from the wood that I should not have seen where it was had I turned to look back, when we met a troop of souls that were coming alongside the bank, and each looked at us as men look at one another under a new moon at dusk; and they knit their brows at us as the old tailor does at the eye of his needle.

Eyed thus by that company, I was recognized by one who took me by the hem, and cried, "What a marvel!" And I, when he reached out his arm to me, fixed my eyes on his scorched face, so that the baked features did not prevent my knowing him, and reaching down my hand toward his face, I answered, "Are you here, ser Brunetto!"

And he, "O my son, let it not displease you if Brunetto Latino[5] turns back a little with you, and lets the train go on."

"I beg it of you with all my heart," I said to him, "and if you wish me to sit with you, I will, if it please him there with whom I go."

"O son," he said, "whoever of this flock stops even for an instant must then lie a hundred years without brushing off the fire when it strikes him. Therefore go on: I will come at your skirts, and then will rejoin my band who go lamenting their eternal woes."

I dared not descend from the path to go on a level with him, but I kept my head bowed like one who walks in reverence. He began, "What chance or destiny brings you down here before your last day, and who is this that shows the way?"

"There above, in the bright life," I answered him, "I went astray in a valley, before my age was at the full. Only yesterday morning I turned my back on it. He appeared to me, as I was returning into it, and by this path he leads me home."

And he to me, "If you follow your star you cannot fail of a glorious port, if, in the fair life, I discerned aright; and if I had not died so soon, seeing heaven so kind to you, I would have cheered you in your work. But that thankless, malignant people, who of old came down from Fiesole,[6] and still smack of the mountain and the rock, will make themselves an enemy to you because of your good deeds; and there is cause: for among the bitter sorb-trees it is not fitting that the sweet fig should come to fruit. Old report in the world calls them blind; it is a people avaricious, envious and proud: look that you cleanse yourself of their customs. Your fortune holds for you such honor that the one

party and the other shall be ravenous against you, but the grass shall be far from the goat. Let the Fiesolan beasts make fodder of themselves, and not touch the plant (if any spring yet upon their dungheap) in which survives the holy seed of those Romans who remained there when it became the nest of so much wickedness."

"If my prayer were all fulfilled," I answered him, "you would not yet be banished from human nature, for in my memory is fixed, and now saddens my heart, the dear, kind, paternal image of you, when in the world hour by hour you taught me how man makes himself eternal; and how much I hold it in gratitude it behooves me, while I live, to declare in my speech. That which you tell me of my course I write, and keep with a text to be glossed by a lady who will know how, if I reach her. This much I would have you know: so conscience chide me not, I am prepared for Fortune as she wills. Such earnest is not strange to my ears; therefore let Fortune whirl her wheel as pleases her, and the yokel his mattock."

Thereon my master turned round on his right and looked at me, then said, "He who notes it listens well."

None the less I go on speaking with ser Brunetto, and ask him who are the most noted and most eminent of his companions.

And he to me, "It is well to know of some of them; about the rest it is well that we be silent, as the time would be too short for so much talk. In brief, know that all were clerks, and great men of letters and of great fame, in the world defiled by one same sin. Priscian[7] goes on with that wretched crowd, and Francesco d'Accorso[8] too; and you could also have seen there, had you hankered for such scurf, him who was transferred by the Servant of Servants[9] from Arno to Bacchiglione,[10] where he left his sinfully distended muscles. I would say more, but my going and my speech must not be longer, for I see yonder a new smoke rising from the sand: people are coming with whom I must not be. Let my *Treasure*,[11] in which I yet live, be commended to you, and I ask no more."

Then he turned back, and seemed like one of those who run for the green cloth in the field at Verona,[12] and of them seemed he who wins, not he who loses.

CANTO XVI

Already I was in a place where the resounding of the water which was falling into the next circle was heard, like the hum which beehives make, when three shades set out together running, from a troop that was passing under the rain of the fierce torment. They came towards us, each crying, "Stop, you who by your dress seem to us to be from our degenerate city!" Ah me, what wounds old and new I saw in their members, burnt in by the flames! It pains me yet, only to remember it.

My teacher gave heed to their cries, then turned his face to me and said, "Now wait: to these one should show courtesy; and were it not for the fire which the nature of this place darts, I should say that haste befitted you more than them."

As we stopped, they resumed their ancient wail, and when they reached us, all three made of themselves a wheel. As champions,[1] naked and oiled, are wont to do, eying their grip and vantage before exchanging thrusts and blows; thus each, wheeling, directed his face on me so that his neck kept turning in a direction contrary to his feet.

And, "If the wretchedness of this sandy place and our blackened and hairless faces," one of them began, "bring us and our prayers into contempt, let our fame move you to tell us who you are, that thus securely move living feet through Hell. He whose tracks you see me trample, though he goes naked and peeled, was of greater degree than you think: grandson of the good Gualdrada,[2] his name was Guido Guerra,[3] and in his lifetime he did much with counsel and with sword. This other, who treads the sand behind me, is Tegghiaio Aldobrandi,[4] whose voice should have been prized up in the world; and I who am placed with them in torment was Jacopo Rusticucci,[5] and truly my fierce wife more than aught else has wrought me ill."

Had I been sheltered from the fire I would have thrown myself down among them, and I think my teacher would have permitted it; but since I should have been burnt and baked, fear overcame my good will which made me greedy to embrace them. Then I began, "Not contempt, but sorrow, your condition fixed within me, so deeply that it will not leave me

soon, when this my lord said to me words by which I felt that such men as you might be coming. I am of your city, and always have I rehearsed and heard with affection your deeds and honored names. I am leaving the gall, and I go for sweet fruits promised me by my truthful leader; but first I must go down to the center."

"So may your soul long direct your limbs, and your fame shine after you," he then replied, "tell us if courtesy and valor abide in our city as once they did, or if they are quite gone from it, for Guiglielmo Borsiere,[6] who has been but short while in pain with us and goes yonder with our company, greatly afflicts us with his words."

"The new people and the sudden gains have engendered pride and excess in you, O Florence, so that already you weep for it!" This I cried with uplifted face; and the three, who understood this to be my answer, looked at each other as men look on hearing the truth.

"If at other times it costs you so little to satisfy others," they all replied, "happy you if you can speak thus at will. Therefore, if you escape from these dark regions and return to see again the beautiful stars, when you shall rejoice to say, 'I was there,' see that you speak of us to others." Then they broke their wheel and in their flight their nimble legs seemed wings; an "Amen" could not have been uttered so quickly as they vanished; wherefore it seemed well to my master to depart. I followed him; and we had gone but a little way when the sound of the water was so near that we could scarcely have heard each other speak. As that river[7] which is first to hold its own course from Mount Viso eastward, on the left slope of the Apennine—called the Acquacheta above,[8] before it descends into its low bed, and at Forlì loses that name—roars there over San Benedetto dell'Alpe, falling in one cataract when there might well have been a thousand; thus, down from a precipitous bank we found that dark water resounding, so that in short while it would have hurt our ears.

I had a cord girt round me,[9] and with it I once thought to take the gay-skinned leopard. After I had quite loosed it from me, as my leader bade, I passed it to him knotted and coiled. Whereon he, turning to the right, flung it some distance out from the edge, down into the depth of that abyss.

"Surely," I said to myself, "something strange will answer the strange signal which the master so follows with his eye."

Ah, how careful one should be with those who not only see the deed, but have the wit to read one's thoughts! "Soon will come up what I look for and what your mind dreams of," he said to me; "soon must it be discovered to your sight."

To that truth which has the face of a lie a man should always close his lips so far as he can, for through no fault of his it brings reproach; but here I cannot be silent; and, reader, I swear to you by the notes of this Comedy[10]—so may they not fail of lasting favor—that I saw, through that thick and murky air, come swimming upwards a figure amazing to every steadfast heart, even as he returns who sometimes goes down to loose the anchor that is caught on a reef or something else hidden in the sea, who stretches upwards his arms and draws in his feet.

CANTO XVII

"Behold the beast with the pointed tail,[1] that passes mountains and breaks walls and weapons! Behold him that infects all the world!" Thus my leader began to speak to me; and he beckoned him to come to shore near the end of our rocky path. And that foul image of fraud came onward, and landed his head and his bust, but he did not draw his tail onto the bank. His face was the face of a just man, so benign was its outward aspect, and all his trunk was that of a serpent; he had two paws, hairy to the armpits; his back and breast and both his sides were painted with knots and circlets. Tartars or Turks never made cloth with more colors of groundwork and pattern, nor were such webs laid on the loom by Arachne.[2]

As sometimes boats lie at the shore, part in the water and part on land, and as there among the guzzling Germans the beaver settles himself to wage his war, so lay that worst of beasts upon the edge of stone which bounds the sand. All his tail was quivering in the void, twisting upward its venomous fork, which had the point armed like a scorpion's.

My leader said, "Now we must bend our way a little, as far as that evil beast which is couching yonder." We descended, therefore, on the right hand side and took ten steps upon the verge, so as to keep well away from the sand and the flames. And when we had come to him, I see upon the sand, a little farther onwards, people sitting near the empty space.

Here the master said to me, "That you may carry away full experience of this ring, go and see their condition. Let your talk there be brief. Till you return I will speak with this beast, that he may lend us his strong shoulders."

So I went by myself still farther along the extreme margin of that seventh circle, where the woeful people were seated. Their grief was bursting forth through their eyes; with their hands they defended themselves, now here, now there, sometimes from the flames, sometimes from the burning ground; not otherwise do the dogs in summer, now with muzzle, now with paw, when they are bitten by fleas, or flies, or gadflies. When I set my eyes on the faces of some of these on whom the grievous fire descends, I did not recognize any of them, but I perceived that from the neck of each hung a pouch, which had a certain color and a certain device, and thereon each seems to feast his eyes. And when I came among them, looking about, I saw, upon a yellow purse, azure that had the form and bearing of a lion.[3] Then, gazing farther, I saw another, red as blood, display a goose whiter than butter. And one, who had his white wallet marked with an azure and gravid sow,[4] said to me, "What are you doing in this ditch? Now get you gone! And since you are still alive, know that my neighbor Vitaliano[5] shall sit here at my left side. With these Florentines am I, a Paduan; often they din my ears, shouting, 'Let the sovereign knight[6] come who will bring the pouch with three goats!' "[7] Then he twisted his mouth and stuck out his tongue, like an ox that licks its nose; and I, fearing lest a longer stay should anger him who had admonished me to stay but little, turned back from the weary souls.

I found my leader already mounted on the croup of the fierce beast, and he said to me, "Now be strong and bold: henceforward the descent is by such stairs as these. Mount in front, for I wish to be between, so that the tail may not harm you." As one who has the shivering-fit of the quartan so near that his nails are already pale, and he trembles all over at the mere sight of shade, such I became at these words of his; but shame rebuked me, which makes a servant brave in the presence of a good master. I seated myself on those ugly shoulders, and I wanted to say (but the voice did not come as I thought), "See that you embrace me!" But he who at other times had succored me in other peril clasped me in his arms and steadied me as soon as I was mounted up, then said, "Geryon, move on now; let your circles be wide, and your descending slow: remember the new burden that you have."

As the bark backs out little by little from its place, so Geryon withdrew thence; and when he felt himself quite free, he turned his tail to where his breast had been, and, stretching it out, moved it like an eel, and with his paws gathered the air to himself. I do not think that there was greater fear when Phaëthon[8] let loose the reins, whereby the sky, as yet appears, was scorched, nor when the wretched Icarus[9] felt his loins unfeathering by the melting wax, and his father cried to him, "You go an ill way!" than was mine when I saw that I was in the air on every side, and saw extinguished every sight, save of the beast. He goes swimming slowly on, wheels and descends, but I perceive it only by a wind upon my face and from below. I heard now on our right the whirlpool making a horrible roaring below us, wherefore I stretch forth my head and look down. Then I became more terrified at the descent, for I saw fires and heard laments, whereat, trembling, I cling the closer. And I saw then—for I had not seen it before—the descending and the circling, by the great evils which were drawing near on every side.

As the falcon that has been long on the wing—that, without seeing lure or bird, makes the falconer cry, "Ah, ah, you're coming down!"—descends weary, with many a wheeling, to where it set out swiftly, and alights disdainful and sullen, far from its master: so, at the very foot of the jagged rock, did Geryon set us down at the bottom, and, disburdened of our persons, vanished like an arrow from the string.

CANTO XVIII

There is a place in Hell called Malebolge,[1] all of stone which is the color of iron, like the wall that goes round it. Right in the middle of this malign field yawns a pit very wide and deep, of whose structure I shall tell in its place. That belt, therefore, which remains between the pit and the foot of the high hard bank is circular, and it has its bottom divided into ten valleys. Such a figure as where, for guard of the walls, successive ditches encircle castles, the place where they are presents, such an image did these make here. And as in such strongholds from their thresholds to the outer bank are little bridges, so from the base of the cliff ran crags which traversed the embankments and the ditches as far as the pit, which cuts them off and collects them.

In this place we found ourselves dropped from the back of Geryon, and the poet held to the left, and I came on behind. On the right hand I saw new woe, new torments, and new scourgers, with which the first ditch was replete. At its bottom were the sinners, naked; on our side of the middle they came facing us, and, on the other side, along with us, but with greater strides: thus the Romans, because of the great throng, in the year of the Jubilee,[2] have taken measures for the people to pass over the bridge, so that on one side all face toward the Castle and go to St. Peter's, and on the other they go toward the Mount.[3] Along the dark rock, on this side and on that, I saw horned demons with large scourges, who smote them fiercely from behind. Ah, how they made them lift their heels at the first blows! Truly none waited for the second or the third!

While I was going on, my eyes were met by one of them, and instantly I said, "This fellow I've certainly seen before"; wherefore I paused to make him out, and my gentle leader stopped with me and gave me leave to go back a little. And that scourged soul thought to hide himself, lowering his face, but it availed him little, for I said, "You there, casting your eye on the ground, if the features you wear are not false, are Venedico Caccianemico.[4] But what brings you to such pungent sauces?"

And he to me, "Unwillingly I tell it, but your plain speech, which makes me remember the former world, compels me. I was he who brought Ghisolabella[5] to do the will of the Marquis, however the vile story may be reported. And I am not the only Bolognese who laments here; nay, this place is so full of them, that so many tongues are not now taught, between Savena and Reno, to say *sipa*;

and if of this you wish assurance or testimony, recall to mind our avaricious nature." As he spoke thus, a demon smote him with his lash, and said, "Off, pander! There are no women here to coin."

I rejoined my escort; then, with but a few steps, we came to where a reef went out from the bank. This we very easily ascended and, turning to the right upon its jagged ridge, we quitted those eternal circlings.

When we were at the place where it yawns beneath to give passage to the scourged, my leader said, "Stop, and let the sight of these other ill-born souls strike on you, whose faces you have not seen, for they have been going along with us."

From the old bridge we viewed the train that was coming towards us on the other side, likewise driven by the scourge. The good master, without my asking, said to me, "Look at that great one who comes, and seems to shed no tear for pain. What a regal aspect he yet retains! That is Jason,[6] who by courage and by craft despoiled the Colchians of the ram. He passed by the isle of Lemnos when the bold and pitiless women had given all their males to death. There, with tokens and with fair words, he deceived the young Hypsipyle who first had deceived all the rest. He left her there pregnant and forlorn: such guilt condemns him to such torment; and Medea[7] too is avenged. With him go all who practice such deceit; and let this suffice for knowledge of the first valley and of those it holds in its fangs."

We were now where the narrow path intersects with the second embankment and makes of that the abutment to another arch. From there we heard people whining in the next pouch, and puffing with their muzzles and smiting themselves with their palms. The banks were crusted over with a mold from the vapor below that sticks on them and that did battle with the eyes and with the nose. The bottom is so deep that we could nowhere see it without mounting to the crown of the arch where the ridge rises highest. Hither we came, and thence I saw down in the ditch a people plunged in filth that seemed to have come from human privies.

And while I was searching down there with my eyes, I beheld one whose head was so befouled with ordure that it did not appear whether he was layman or cleric. He bawled to me, "Why are you so greedy to look more at me than at the other filthy ones?" And I to him, "Because, if I rightly recall, I have seen you before with your hair dry, and you are Alessio Interminei of Lucca;[8] therefore do I eye you more than all the rest." And he, then, beating his pate, "Down to this the flatteries wherewith my tongue was never cloyed have sunk me."

Hereupon my leader said to me, "Now push your look a little further forwards, so that your eye may fully reach the face of that foul and disheveled wench who is scratching herself there with her filthy nails, now squatting, now standing. She is Thaïs[9] the whore, who answered her paramour when he said, 'Have I great favor with you?'—'Nay, wondrous!' And therewith let our sight be satisfied."

CANTO XIX

O Simon Magus![1] O you his wretched followers that, rapacious, prostitute for gold and silver the things of God which ought to be the brides of righteousness! now must the trumpet sound for you, since you are in the third pouch.

We were now at the next tomb, having climbed to that part of the reef which hangs directly over the middle of the ditch. O Supreme Wisdom, how great is the art which Thou showest in heaven, on earth, and in the evil world! and how justly does Thy Power dispense!

Upon the sides and upon the bottom I saw the livid stone full of holes, all of one size and each was round. They seemed to me not less wide or larger than those that are made for the baptizings in my beautiful San Giovanni;[2] one of which, not many years ago, I broke to save one who was drowning in it—and let this be the seal to undeceive all men.

From the mouth of each projected the feet of a sinner and his legs as far as the calf, and the rest was within. They all had both their soles on fire, because of which their joints were twitching so hard that they would have snapped ropes and withes. As flame on oily things is wont to move only on their outer surface, so it did there, from the heels to the toes.

"Master, who is that who writhes himself, twitching more than all his fellows," I said, "and who is sucked by a ruddier flame?" And he to me, "If you will have me carry you down there by that more sloping bank, from himself you shall learn of him and of his wrongs."

And I, "Whatever pleases you is to my liking: you are my lord and you know that I depart not from your will; and you know that which is left unsaid."

Then we came onto the fourth dike, turned and descended on our left, down to the perforated and narrow bottom; and the good master did not set me down from his side till he had brought me to the hole of him who was lamenting with his shanks.

"O wretched soul, whoever you are that, planted like a stake, have your upper part down under!" I began, "speak if you can."

I was standing there like the friar who confesses the perfidious assassin who, after he is fixed, recalls him in order to delay his death; and he[3] cried, "Are you already standing there, are you already standing there, Bonifazio?[4] By several years the writ has lied to me. Are you so quickly sated with those gains for which you did not fear to take by guile the beautiful Lady,[5] and then to do her outrage?"

I became like those who stand as if bemocked, not comprehending what is answered them and unable to reply. Then Virgil said, "Tell him quickly, 'I am not he, I am not he whom you think!' and I answered as I was bidden; whereat the spirit writhed hard both his feet; then, sighing, and with tearful voice, he said to me, "Then what is it you ask of me? If to know who I am concerns you so much that you have for that come down the bank, know that I was vested with the great mantle;[6] and I was truly a son of the she-bear,[7] so eager to advance the cubs that up there I pursed my gains, and here I purse myself. Beneath my head are the others that preceded me in simony, mashed down and flattened through the fissures of the rock. I shall be thrust down there in my turn when he comes for whom I mistook you when I put my sudden question. But longer already is the time that I have cooked my feet and stood inverted thus than he shall stay planted with glowing feet, for after him shall come a lawless shepherd[8] from the west, of uglier deeds, one fit to cover both him and me. A new Jason[9] he will be, like him we read of in Maccabees, but even as to that one his king was pliant, so to this one shall be he who governs France."

I do not know if here I was overbold, in answering him in just this strain, "Pray now tell me how much treasure did our Lord require of Saint Peter before he put the keys into his keeping? Surely he asked nothing save: 'Follow me.' Nor did Peter or the others take gold or silver of Matthias[10] when he was chosen for the office which the guilty soul had lost. Therefore stay right here, for you are justly punished; and guard well the ill-got gain that made you bold against Charles.[11] And were it not that reverence for the Great Keys which you held in the glad life even now forbids it to me, I would use yet harder words, for your avarice afflicts the world, trampling down the good and exalting the bad. It was shepherds such as you that the Evangelist had in mind when she that sitteth upon the waters was seen by him committing fornication with the kings: she that was born with the seven heads, and from the ten horns had her strength,[12] so long as virtue pleased her spouse. You have made you a god of gold and silver; and wherein do you differ from the idolators, save that they worship one, and you a hundred? Ah, Constantine, of how much ill was mother, not your conversion, but that dowry which the first rich Father took from you!"[13] And while I intoned these notes to him, whether anger or conscience stung him, he kicked hard with both his feet. And indeed I think it pleased my guide, with so satisfied a look did he keep listening to the sound of the true words uttered. Thereupon he took me in his arms, and when he had me quite on his breast, remounted by the path where he had descended; nor did he tire of holding me clasped to himself, but carried me up to the summit of the arch which is the crossway from the fourth to the fifth dike. Here he gently set down his burden, gently because of the rugged and steep crag, which would be a hard passage for goats; and from there another valley was disclosed to me.

CANTO XX

Of new punishment I must make verses, and give matter to the twentieth canto of the first canzone, which is of the submerged.

I was now all prepared to look into the depth disclosed to me, which was bathed with tears of anguish, and through the circular valley I saw a people coming, silent and weeping, at the pace made by litanies in this world. As my sight went lower on them, each seemed to be strangely distorted between the chin and the beginning of the chest, for the face was turned toward the loins, and they had to come backwards, since seeing forward was denied them. Perhaps some time by stroke of palsy a man has been thus twisted right around, but I have not seen it, nor do I believe it possible.

Reader, so God grant you to take profit of your reading, think now for yourself how I could keep my cheeks dry when near at hand I saw our image so contorted that the tears from the eyes bathed the buttocks at the cleft. Truly I wept, leaning on one of the rocks of the hard crag, so that my guide said to me, "Are you even yet among the other fools? Here pity lives when it is altogether dead. Who is more impious than he who sorrows at God's judgment?[1]

"Raise, raise your head, and see him for whom the earth opened before the eyes of the Thebans, whereat they all cried, 'Whither are you rushing, Amphiaraus?[2] Why are you leaving the war?' And he stopped not from falling headlong down to Minos, who seizes every one. See how he has made a breast of his shoulders: because he wished to see too far before him, he looks behind and makes his way backwards.

"See Tiresias,[3] who changed semblance when from male he became female, transforming all his members; and afterwards he had to strike again the two entwined serpents with his rod before he could resume his manly plumes.

"He that backs up to the other's belly is Aruns[4] who, in the hills of Luni[5] where grubs the Carrarese[6] who dwells beneath, had a cave for his abode among the white marbles, from which he could observe the stars and the sea with unobstructed view.

"And she that covers her bosom, which you cannot see, with her loose tresses, and has on that side all her hairy parts was Manto,[7] who searched through many lands, then settled in the place where I was born[8]—and on this I would have you hear me for a little. After her father had departed from life and the city of Bacchus[9] had become enslaved, she wandered for a long time about the world. Up in fair Italy, at the foot of the mountains that bound Germany above Tirol,[10] lies a lake which is called Benaco. By a thousand springs, I think, and more, the region between Garda and Val Camonica and Pennino is bathed by the water which settles in that lake, and in the middle of it is a spot where the pastors of Trent and Brescia and Verona, if they went that way, might give their blessing. Peschiera, a beautiful and strong fortress to confront the Brescians and the Bergamese, sits where the shore around is lowest. There all the water that in the bosom of Benaco cannot stay must descend and make itself a river, down through green pastures. Soon as the water starts to run, it is no longer named Benaco, but Mincio, as far as Govèrnolo, where it falls into the Po; and after a short course it comes to a level where it spreads and makes a marsh that sometimes in summer is unwholesome. The cruel virgin, passing that way, saw land in the middle of the fen, untilled and without inhabitants. There, to shun all human fellowship she stopped with her servants to practice her arts, and lived, and left there her empty body. Afterwards the people who were scattered round about gathered to that place, which was strong because of the marsh it had on all sides. They built the city over those dead bones, and for her who first chose the place they called it Mantua, without other augury. Once the people within it were more numerous, before the folly of Casalodi was tricked by Pinamonte.[11] Therefore I charge you, if you ever hear other origin given to my city, let no falsehood defraud the truth."

And I, "Master, your words are to me so certain and do so hold my confidence, that all others would be to me as dead coals. But tell me, of the people who are passing, if you see any that are worthy of note, for to that alone does my mind revert."

Then he to me, "That one, who from the cheek spreads his beard over his swarthy shoulders, was augur when Greece was left so empty of males that they scarcely remained for the cradles, and with Calchas he gave the moment for cutting the first cable at Aulis.[12] Eurypylus was his name, and thus my high Tragedy sings of him in a certain passage—as you know well, who know the whole of it. That other who is so spare in the flanks was Michael Scot,[13] who truly knew the game of magic frauds. See Guido Bonatti;[14] see Asdente,[15] who now would fain have attended to his leather and his thread, but too late repents. See the wretched women who left the needle, the spool, and the spindle, and became fortunetellers; they wrought spells with herbs and with images.

"But now come, for already Cain with his thorns[16] holds the confines of both the hemispheres, and touches the wave below Seville; and already last night the moon was round. You must remember it well, for it did you no harm sometimes in the deep wood."

Thus he spoke to me, and we went on the while.

CANTO XXI

Thus from bridge to bridge[1] we came along, talking of things of which my Comedy is not concerned to sing, and we had reached the summit, when we stopped to see the next cleft of Malebolge and the next vain lamentations: and I saw it strangely dark.

As in the Arsenal of the Venetians,[2] in winter, the sticky pitch for caulking their unsound vessels is boiling, because they cannot sail then, and instead, one builds his ship anew and another plugs the ribs of his that has made many a voyage, one hammers at the prow and another at the stern, this one makes oars, that one twists ropes, another patches jib and mainsail; so, not by fire but by divine art, a thick pitch was boiling there below, which overglued the bank on every side. It I saw, but in it I saw nothing save the bubbles raised by the boiling, and all of it swelling up and settling down together. While I was gazing fixedly down on it, my leader, saying, "Watch out, watch out!" drew me to himself from the place where I was standing. Then I turned round like one who is eager to see what he must shun, and who is dismayed by sudden fear, so that he looks back but does not delay his flight to look, and behind us I saw a black devil come running up along the crag. Ah, how savage he was in aspect and how fierce he seemed in act, with outspread wings and light on his feet. His shoulder, which was sharp and high, was laden by both haunches of a sinner, and he held him grasped by the tendons of the feet.

He spoke from our bridge, "O Malebranche,[3] here's one of Saint Zita's[4] Elders! Thrust him under, while I go back for more, to that city where there's a fine supply of them:

every man there is a barrator, except Bonturo;[5] there they make Ay of No, for cash."

Down he hurled him, and turned back on the hard crag, and never was an unleashed mastiff so swift in pursuit of a thief. The sinner sank under and rose again, rump up; but the devils, who were under cover of the bridge, cried, "Here's no place for the Holy Face![6] Here you'll swim otherwise than in the Serchio![7] And so, unless you want to feel our grapples, do not come out above the pitch."

Then they struck him with more than a hundred prongs, and said, "Here you'll have to dance under cover, so grab on secretly, if you can." Just so cooks make their scullions plunge the meat down into the cauldron with their forks, that it may not float.

The good master said to me, "That it may not be seen that you are here, squat down behind a jag, so that you may have some screen for yourself; and whatever outrage be done to me, be not afraid, for I know about things here and was in a like fray once before."

Then he passed on beyond the head of the bridge, and when he arrived upon the sixth bank he had need to show a steadfast front. With the fury and uproar of dogs that rush out upon some poor beggar who straightway begs from where he stops, these rushed out from under the little bridge and turned all their hooks against him. But he cried, "Let none of you be savage! Before you touch me with your forks, let one of you come forward to hear me, and then decide about grappling me."

All cried, "Let Malacoda[8] go"; whereon, while the rest stood still, one moved and came up to him, saying, "What will it avail him?"

"Do you think, Malacoda, to see me come here," said my master, "secure thus far against all your defenses, without divine will and propitious fate? Let us pass, for it is willed in Heaven that I show another this savage way." Then was his pride so fallen, that he let the hook drop at his feet, and said to the others, "Now let no one strike him."

And my leader to me, "Oh you that sit asquat among the splinters of the bridge, securely now return to me." Wherefore I moved and quickly came to him; and the devils all pressed forward, so that I feared they might not keep the pact. Thus I once saw the soldiers afraid who were coming out of Caprona under pledge,[9] seeing themselves among so many enemies. I drew near to my leader, pressing in close to him, and did not turn my eyes from their looks, which were not good. And they lowered their forks, one of them saying, "Shall I touch him on the rump?" and another answering, "Yes, see that you nick it for him." But that demon who was speaking with my leader turned round instantly, saying, "Hold, hold, Scarmiglione!"

Then he said to us, "To go farther by this crag will not be possible, for the sixth arch lies all shattered at the bottom; but if it is still your pleasure to go forward, then proceed along this ridge: nearby is another crag that affords a way. Yesterday, five hours later than now, completed one thousand two hundred and sixty-six years since the road was broken here. I am sending some of my company that way, to see if any is out taking the air. Go with them, for they will not harm you."

"Come forward, Alichino and Calcabrina," he began to say, "and you, Cagnazzo; and let Barbariccia lead the ten. Let Libicocco come too, and Draghignazzo, and tusked Ciriatto and Graffiacane and Farfarello and crazy Rubicante.[10] Search around the boiling glue. Let these two be safe as far as the next crag that all unbroken goes across the dens."

"O me! master, what is this I see?" I said. "Ah, let us go alone without escort, if you know the way, for, as for myself, I want none! If you are as wary as you are wont, do you not see how they grind their teeth and with their brows threaten harm to us?" And he to me, "I would not have you be afraid; let them grind on as they please, for they do it at the boiled wretches."

They wheeled round by the bank on the left, but first each pressed his tongue between his teeth at their leader for a signal, and he had made a trumpet of his arse.

CANTO XXII

Ere now have I seen horsemen moving camp, and beginning an assault and making their muster, and sometimes retiring to escape; I have seen coursers over your land, O Aretines,[1] and I have seen the starting of raids, the onset of tournaments, and the running of jousts, now with trumpets and now with bells, with drums and castle-signals, with native things and foreign—but never to so strange a pipe have I seen horsemen or footmen set forth, or ship by sign of land or star!

We were going along with the ten demons: ah, savage company! but "in church with saints and with guzzlers in the tavern!" My attention was all on the pitch, in order to see every condition of the pouch, and of the people who were burning in it. Like dolphins when with their arching backs they give sign to mariners that they should prepare to save their ship, so from time to time one of the sinners would show his back to alleviate his pain, and hide it again, quicker than a lightning-flash. And as at the edge of the water of a ditch the frogs lie with only their muzzle out, so that they hide their feet and the rest of their bulk, so were the sinners on every side; but as Barbariccia approached, so would they draw back under the boiling.

I saw—and my heart still shudders at it— one waiting, just as it happens that one frog stays and another jumps. And Graffiacane, who was nearest to him, hooked him by his pitchy locks, and haled him up so that to me he seemed an otter. I already knew all their names, having noted them well when they were chosen, and then observed what they called each other.

"O Rubicante, see that you set your claws on him and flay him," shouted all the accursed crew together. And I, "Master, pray learn, if you can, who is the hapless wretch that has fallen into the hands of his enemies."

My leader drew up to his side, and asked him whence he came; and he replied, "I was born in the kingdom of Navarre. My mother placed me as servant of a lord, for she had borne me to a ribald destroyer of himself and of his substance. Then I was of the household of the good King Thibaut:[2] there I set myself to practice barratry, for which I render reckoning in this heat."

Then Ciriatto, from whose mouth on either side protruded a tusk, as of a boar, made him feel how one of them could rip. The mouse had come among evil cats; but Barbariccia locked him in his arms and said, "Stand back while I enfork him," then turned to my master and said, "Ask on, if you would learn more from him before another mangles him."

My leader therefore, "Tell us, then: of the other sinners under the pitch, do you know any who are Italian?" And he, "I parted just now from one who was a neighbor of theirs. Would I were still under cover with him, for I should not fear claw or hook." And Libicocco cried, "We have endured too much!" and seized his arm with the grapple so that, tearing, he ripped out a muscle of it. Draghignazzo also made as if to hook him in the legs, at which their captain wheeled round on them all with an ugly look.

When they were a little quieted, my leader straightway asked him who was still gazing at his wound, "Who was that from whom you say you made an ill departure to come ashore?"

And he answered, "That was Fra Gomita,[3] he of Gallura,[4] vessel of every fraud, who had his master's enemies in his hand, and did so deal with them that they all praise him for it. He took the cash and dismissed them smoothly, as he says; and in his other affairs too he was no petty barrator, but sovereign. Don Michel Zanche of Logodoro[5] keeps company with him, and in talking of Sardinia their tongues are never weary. O me! see that other one grinding his teeth! I would tell more, but I fear he's preparing to scratch my itch." And the great marshal, turning to Farfarello, who was rolling his eyes to strike, said, "Get back there, villainous bird!"

"If you would see or hear Tuscans or Lombards," the frightened one then began again, "I will make some of them come. But let the Malebranche stand back a bit, so that they may not fear their vengeance; and I, sitting in this same place, for one that I am, will make seven come when I whistle, as is our custom when any of us gets out."

Cagnazzo at these words raised his muzzle and said, shaking his head, "Hear the cunning trick he has contrived to throw himself down in." Whereon he, who had artifices in great store, replied, "I am indeed cunning when I contrive greater sorrow for my companions!" Alichino held in no longer and, in opposition to the others, said to him, "If you plunge, I won't follow you at a gallop, but I'll beat my wings above the pitch. Let the ridge be left, and let the bank be a screen, to see if you alone are more than a match for us."

Now, reader, you shall hear new sport. All turned their eyes toward the other side, he first who had most opposed it. The Navarrese chose well his time, planted his feet firmly on the ground, and in an instant leaped and broke away from their marshal. Thereat each was stung with his fault, but he most who was the cause of the blunder; wherefore he started and cried out, "You're caught!" But it availed him little, for wings could not outspeed the terror: the one went under, and the other, flying, turned his breast upward; not otherwise the wild duck that suddenly dives down, when the falcon approaches, and he returns upward, vexed and defeated. Calcabrina, furious at the trick, went flying after him, eager for the sinner to escape, so as to have a scuffle; and, when the barrator had disappeared, he turned his claws on his fellow and grappled with him above the ditch; but the other was indeed a full-grown hawk to claw him well, and both fell into the middle of the boiling pond. The heat at once unclutched them, but there was no getting out, they had so beglued their wings. Barbariccia, lamenting with the rest, made four of them fly to the other bank, each with his fork; and very quickly, on this side and on that, they descended to their posts and stretched their hooks toward the belimed ones, who were already cooked within their crust; and we left them thus embroiled.

CANTO XXIII

Silent, alone, without escort, we went on, one before and the other behind, as Friars Minor go their way. My thought was turned by the present brawl on the fable of Aesop[1] where he told of the frog and the mouse; for Ay and Yea are not more alike than the one case is to the other, if we compare the beginning and the end attentively. And just as one thought springs from another, so from that another was born which redoubled my first fear. I thought: they have been fooled because of us, and with such hurt and mockery as I believe must vex them greatly. If rage be added to their malice, they will come after us, fiercer than the dog to the leveret he snaps up. Already I felt my hair all bristling with fear as I went along intent on what was behind us, and I said, "Master, unless you quickly hide yourself and me, I dread the Malebranche. We have them after us already: I so imagine them that I hear them now."

And he, "If I were of leaded glass, I should not draw to me your outward semblance more quickly than I receive your inward. Even now came your thoughts among mine, with like action and like look, so that of both I have made one counsel. If it be that the slope on the right lies so that we can descend into the next ditch, we shall escape the imagined chase."

He had not yet finished telling me his plan when I saw them coming with outstretched wings, not very far off, bent on taking us. My leader instantly took me up, like a mother who is awakened by the noise and sees beside her the kindled flames, and catches up her child and flies, and, more concerned for him than for herself, does not stay even to put on a shift; and, down from the ridge of the hard bank he gave himself supine to the sloping rock that closes one side of the next pouch. Never did water run so fast through a sluice to turn the wheel of a landmill when it approaches nearest to the paddles, as my master went down that bank, carrying me along upon his breast, not as his companion but as his child. Scarcely had his feet reached the bed of the depth below when they were on the height directly over us; but there was nothing to fear, for the high Providence which willed to set them as ministers of the fifth ditch deprives them all of power to leave it.

There below we found a painted people who were going round with very slow steps, weeping and in their looks tired and overcome. They wore cloaks with cowls down over their eyes, of the cut that is made for the monks of Cluny,[2] so gilded outside that they dazzle, but within, all of lead, and so heavy that those Frederick[3] imposed were of straw. O toilsome mantle for eternity!

We turned, ever to the left, along with them, intent on their dreary weeping. But, because of the load, that tired folk came on so slowly that our company was new at every step we took; wherefore I said to my guide, "Pray find someone who may be known by deed or name, looking round as we go." And one who caught the Tuscan speech cried after us, "Stay your steps, you who run thus through the dusky air! Perhaps you shall obtain from

me what you ask." At which my leader turned to me and said, "Wait, and then proceed at his pace." I stopped, and saw two show by their look great haste of mind to be with me, but their load and the narrow way retarded them. When they came up, with eye askance they gazed at me awhile without uttering a word; then, turning to each other, they said, "This man seems alive, by the action of his throat; and if they are dead, by what privilege do they go divested of the heavy stole?" Then they said to me, "O Tuscan, who are come to the assembly of the sad hypocrites, do not disdain to tell us who you are."

And I to them, "I was born and grew up on the fair stream of Arno, at the great town, and I am in the body that I have always had; but you, who are you, down whose cheeks distils such woe as I see? And what penalty is this upon you that glitters so?" And one of them replied to me, "The orange cloaks are of lead so thick that the weight thus causes their scales to creak.[4] We were Jovial Friars,[5] and Bolognese: I named Catalano,[6] and he Loderingo,[7] and by your city chosen together, as one man alone is usually chosen, to maintain the peace; and we were such, that it still appears around the Gardingo."[8]

I began, "O Friars, your evil . . ."—but I said no more, for there caught my eye one crucified on the ground with three stakes. When he saw me he writhed all over, blowing in his beard with sighs; and Fra Catalano, observing this, said to me, "That transfixed one you are gazing at counseled the Pharisees that it was expedient to put one man to torture for the people. He is stretched out naked across the way, as you see, and needs must feel the weight of each that passes; and in like fashion is his father-in-law racked in this ditch, and the others of that council which was a seed of evil for the Jews." Then I saw Virgil wonder over him who was thus outstretched, as on a cross, so vilely in the eternal exile.[9] Then he directed his words to the friar, "May it not displease you, if it be permitted, to tell us if there lies any passage on the right by which we two can get out of here, without requiring some of the black angels to come to deliver us from this bottom."

He then replied, "Nearer than you hope is a ridge of rock that starts from the great encircling wall and spans all the savage valleys, save that at this one it is broken down and does not cover it; you will be able to mount up by the ruin[10] that lies against the side and piles up at the bottom."

My leader stood for a moment with bowed head, then said, "He that hooks the sinners back yonder gave a poor account of the matter." And the friar, "At Bologna once I heard it said that the devil has many vices, among which I heard that he is a liar and the father of lies."

Then my guide went on with great strides, somewhat disturbed with anger in his look; and I departed from those burdened souls, following the prints of the beloved feet.

CANTO XXIV

In that part of the youthful year when the sun tempers his locks beneath Aquarius, and the nights already wane towards half the day, when the hoarfrost copies on the ground the image of his white sister, but the temper of his pen lasts but short while—the peasant, whose fodder fails, rises and looks out and sees the fields all white; at which he smites his thigh, returns indoors and grumbles to and fro, like the poor wretch who knows not what to do; then comes out again and recovers hope when he sees how in but little time the world has changed its face, and taking his crook, drives forth his sheep to pasture. Thus my master caused me dismay when I saw his brow so troubled, and thus quickly came the plaster to the hurt. For when we came to the ruined bridge my leader turned to me with that sweet look which I saw first at the foot of the mountain. After taking some counsel with himself, looking first well at the ruin, he opened his arms and laid hold of me. And like one who works and reckons, always seeming to provide beforehand, so, while lifting me up toward the top of one great rock, he was looking out another crag, saying, "Grapple next on that, but try first if it will bear you." It was no road for anyone wearing the mantle, for we—he light and I pushed on—could scarcely mount from jag to jag. And had it not been that on that dike the slope was shorter than on the other, I know not about him, but I should have been quite vanquished. But because all Malebolge

inclines toward the mouth of the nethermost well, the site of each valley is such that one side is higher and the other lower. We, however, came at length to the point where the last stone is broken off. The breath was so spent from my lungs, when I was up, that I could go no farther, but sat down as soon as I got there.

"Now it behooves you thus to cast off sloth," said my master, "for sitting on down or under coverlet, no one comes to fame, without which whoso consumes his life leaves such vestige of himself on earth as smoke in air or foam on water. Rise, therefore; conquer your panting with the soul that wins every battle, if with its heavy body it sinks not down. A longer ladder must be climbed; it is not enough to have left these spirits. If you understand me, now act that it may profit you." I then rose, showing myself better furnished with breath than I felt, and said, "Go on, for I am strong and resolute."

We took the way up the ridge, which was rugged, narrow, and difficult, and far steeper than the last; and I talked as I went, so as not to seem exhausted, when a voice, ill-suited for forming words, came out from the next ditch. I do not know what it said, though I was already on the crown of the arch that crosses there, but he who was speaking seemed to be moving. I had turned my eyes downward, but because of the darkness my keen gaze could not reach the bottom; wherefore I said, "Master, pray go on to the next belt, and let us descend the wall, for from this point not only do I hear without understanding, but I look down and make out nothing."

"Other reply," he said, "I do not give you than the doing, for a fit request should be followed by the deed in silence."

We descended at the end of the bridge where it joins the eighth bank, and then the ditch was manifest to me: I saw within it a fearful throng of serpents, of kinds so strange that the memory of it still chills my blood. Let Libya[1] with her sands vaunt herself no more! for though she bring forth chelydri, jaculi, and phareae, and cenchres with amphisbaena, she never, with all Ethiopia,[2] nor with the land that lies on the Red Sea, showed plagues so numerous or malignant. Amid this cruel and most dismal swarm were people running naked and terrified, without hope of hiding-place or heliotrope. They had their hands bound behind with serpents: these thrust through their loins the head and tail, which were knotted in front.

And lo! at one who was near our bank darted a serpent that transfixed him there where the neck is joined to the shoulders, and never was *o* or *i* written so fast as he took fire and burned, and must sink down all turned to ashes; and when he was thus destroyed on the ground, the dust drew together of itself and at once resumed the former shape; thus by great sages it is affirmed that the Phoenix[3] dies and is born again when it approaches its five-hundredth year.

In its life it feeds not on herb or grain, but only on tears of incense and amomum; and nard and myrrh are its last winding-sheet.

And as one who falls and knows not how, by force of some devil dragging him to the ground, or by some other obstruction that binds a man, who, when he rises, stares about him, all bewildered by the great anguish he has suffered and, looking, sighs: such was that sinner when he rose.

Oh power of God! how severe it is, that showers down such blows for vengeance!

My leader then asked him who he was; to which he answered, "Short while ago I rained down from Tuscany into this fierce gullet. A bestial life, not human, pleased me, mule that I was. I am Vanni Fucci,[4] beast, and Pistoia was my fitting den." And I to my leader, "Tell him not to slip away, and ask what sin thrust him down here, for I have seen him a man of blood and rage." And the sinner, who heard, did not dissemble, but directed toward me his mind and look, and colored with dismal shame, then said, "It grieves me more that you have caught me in the misery where you see me than when I was taken from the other life. I cannot refuse you what you ask. I am put down so far because I was a thief in the sacristy of the fair adornments: a deed that was once falsely put upon another. But that you may not rejoice in this sight, if ever you escape from these dark regions, open your ears and hear what I announce: Pistoia first strips herself of Blacks; then Florence renews her people and her ways. Mars draws a vapor from Val di Magra which is wrapt in turbid clouds, and with impetuous and bitter storm there shall be fighting on Campo Piceno, whence suddenly it shall rend the mist, so that every White shall

be struck by it. And I have said this that it may grieve you."[5]

CANTO XXV

At the end of his words the thief raised up his hands with both the figs,[1] crying, "Take them, God, for I aim them at you!" From this time forth the serpents were my friends, for one then coiled itself about his neck, as if it said, "You shall say no more," and another about his arms and bound him again, so riveting itself in front that he could not give a jog with them.

Ah, Pistoia, Pistoia![2] why do you not decree to turn yourself to ashes and to last no longer, since you surpass your own seed in evil-doing? Through all the dark circles of Hell I saw no spirit so proud against God, not him who fell from the walls at Thebes.[3]

He fled, speaking no more; and I saw a centaur full of rage come shouting, "Where is he, where is the unripe one?" Maremma,[4] I do believe, has not so many snakes as he upon his croup up to where our form begins; and on his shoulders behind the nape lay a dragon with outstretched wings that sets on fire whomever it encounters. My master said, "That is Cacus,[5] who beneath the rock of Mount Aventine full often made a lake of blood. He goes not with his brothers on one same road, because of the cunning theft he made of the great herd that lay near him; and for this his crooked ways were ended under the club of Hercules, who dealt him perhaps a hundred blows and he felt not ten of them."

While he thus spoke, the centaur ran past, and there came below us three spirits whom neither I nor my guide perceived till they cried out, "Who are you?" whereon we broke off our talk and gave heed to them alone. I did not know them; but it happened, as often happens by some chance, that one had occasion to name another, saying, "Where can Cianfa[6] be?" Wherefore, in order that my leader might remain attentive, I placed my finger upwards from my chin to my nose.

If, reader, you are now slow to credit that which I shall tell, it will be no wonder, for I who saw it do scarcely admit it to myself.

While I kept my eyes on them, lo! a serpent with six feet darts up in front of one and fastens on him all over. With the middle feet it clasped the belly, and with its fore feet took his arms, then struck its teeth in one and the other cheek; its hind feet it spread upon his thighs, and put its tail between them, and bent it upwards on his loins behind. Ivy was never so rooted to a tree as the horrid beast entwined its own limbs round the other's; then, as if they had been of hot wax, they stuck together and mixed their colors, and neither the one nor the other now seemed what it was at first: even as in advance of the flame a dark color moves across the paper, which is not yet black and the white dies away. The other two were looking on, and each cried, "Oh me, Agnello,[7] how you change! Lo, you are already neither two nor one!"

Now the two heads had become one, when we saw the two shapes mixed in one face, where both were lost. Two arms were made of the four lengths; the thighs with the legs, the belly and the chest, became members that were never seen before. Each former feature was blotted out: the perverse image seemed both and neither, and such, with slow pace, it moved away.

As the lizard under the great scourge of the dog days, darting from hedge to hedge, seems a lightning-flash, if it cross the way, so appeared, making for the bellies of the other two, a small fiery serpent,[8] livid and black as a peppercorn; and it transfixed in one of them that part by which we first receive our nourishment, then fell down before him, stretched out. The transfixed one gazed at it, but said nothing, only standing there yawning as if sleep or fever had come upon him. He eyed the reptile, the reptile him; the one from his wound, the other from its mouth, smoked violently, and their smoke met.

Let Lucan now be silent, where he tells of the wretched Sabellus[9] and of Nasidius,[10] and let him wait to hear what now comes forth. Concerning Cadmus[11] and Arethusa[12] let Ovid be silent, for if he, poetizing, converts the one into a serpent and the other into a fountain, I envy him not; for two natures front to front he never so transmuted that both forms were prompt to exchange their substance. They mutually responded in such a way that the reptile cleft its tail into a fork, and the wounded one drew his feet together. The legs and thighs so stuck together that soon no mark of the juncture could be seen; the cloven tail took on the shape that was lost in the other; and its skin grew soft, the other's hard. I saw the arms drawing in at the armpits, and the brute's two feet, which were short, lengthening out in proportion as the other's arms were shortening. Then the hind paws, twisted together, became the member that man conceals, and from his the wretch had put forth two feet. While the smoke veils the one and the other with a new color, and generates hair on the one part and strips it from the other, the one rose upright and the other fell down, but neither turned aside the baleful lamps beneath which each was changing his muzzle. He that was erect drew his in toward the temples, and from the excess of matter that came in there the ears issued from the smooth cheeks; that which did not run back, but was retained, made of that excess a nose for the face and thickened the lips to due size. He that lay prone drives the snout forward and draws the ears back into the head as the snail does its horns; and the tongue, which before was whole and fit for speech, divides, and in the other the forked tongue joins up; and the smoke stops. The soul that was become a brute flees hissing along the valley; and the other, speaking, spits[13] after it. Then he turned on it his new shoulders, and said to the third, "I'll have Buoso[14] run on all fours along this road, as I have done!"

Thus I saw the seventh ballast change and transmute—and here let the novelty be my excuse, if my pen goes aught astray. And though my eyes were somewhat confused and my mind bewildered, these could not flee so covertly but that I clearly distinguished Puccio Sciancato,[15] and it was he alone, of the three companions that came first, who was not changed; the other was he whom you, Gaville,[16] lament.

CANTO XXVI

Rejoice, O Florence, since you are so great that over sea and land you beat your wings, and your name is spread through Hell! Among the thieves I found five of your citizens, such that shame comes to me—and you rise thereby to no great honor. But if near morning our dreams are true, you shall feel ere long what Prato,[1] as well as others, craves for you. And if it were already come, it would not be too soon.

Would it were, since indeed it must, for it will weigh the more on me the more I age.

We departed thence, and by the stairs which the jutting rocks had made for our descent before, my leader remounted and drew me up; and pursuing the solitary way among the jags and rocks of the ridge, the foot could not advance without the hand.

I sorrowed then, and sorrow now again, when I turn my mind to what I saw; and I curb my genius more than I am wont, lest it run where virtue does not guide it; so that, if a kindly star or something better has granted me the good, I may not grudge myself that gift.

As many as the fireflies which the peasant, resting on the hill—in the season when he that lights the world least hides his face from us, and at the hour when the fly yields to the mosquito—sees down along the valley, there perhaps where he gathers the grapes and tills: with so many flames the eighth ditch was all agleam, as I perceived as soon as I came where the bottom could be seen. And as he who was avenged by the bears saw Elijah's chariot at its departure, when the horses rose erect to heaven—for he could not so follow it with his eyes as to see aught save the flame alone, like a little cloud ascending: so each flame moves along the gullet of the ditch, for not one shows its theft, and each steals away a sinner.

I was standing on the bridge, having risen up to see, so that if I had not laid hold of a rock I should have fallen below without a push; and my leader, who saw me so intent, said, "Within the fires are the spirits: each swathes himself with that which burns him."

"Master," I replied, "I am the more certain for hearing you, but already I thought it was so, and already I wanted to ask: who is in that fire which comes so divided at its top that it seems to rise from the pyre where Eteocles[2] was laid with his brother?"

He answered me, "Therewithin are tormented Ulysses[3] and Diomedes,[4] and they go together thus under the vengeance as once under the wrath; and in their flame they groan for the ambush of the horse[5] which made the gate by which the noble seed of the Romans went forth; within it they lament the craft, because of which the dead Deidamia[6] still mourns Achilles, and there for the Palladium[7] they bear the penalty."

"If they can speak within those sparks," I said, "master, I earnestly pray you, and pray again, that my prayer avail a thousand, that you deny me not to wait until the horned flame comes hither: you see how with desire I bend towards it."

And he to me, "Your prayer deserves much praise and therefore I accept it; but do you restrain your tongue: leave speech to me, for I have understood what you wish—and perhaps, since they were Greeks, they would be disdainful of your words."

After the flame had come where it seemed to my leader the time and place, I heard him speak in this manner: "O you who are two within one fire, if I deserved of you while I lived, if I deserved of you much or little when in the world I wrote the lofty lines, move not; but let the one of you tell where he went, lost, to die."

The greater horn of the ancient flame began to wag, murmuring, like one that is beaten by a wind; then carrying to and fro its tip, as if it were a tongue that spoke, it flung forth a voice and said, "When I departed from Circe,[8] who had detained me more than a year there near Gaeta,[9] before Aeneas had so named it, neither fondness for my son, nor reverence for my aged father, nor the due love which would have made Penelope glad, could conquer in me the longing that I had to gain experience of the world, and of human vice and worth. But I put forth on the deep open sea with one vessel only, and with that small company which had not deserted me. The one shore and the other I saw as far as Spain, as far as Morocco, and Sardinia, and the other islands which that sea bathes round. I and my companions were old and slow when we came to that narrow outlet[10] where Hercules set up his markers,[11] that men should not pass beyond. On the right hand I left Seville, on the other I had already left Ceuta.[12] 'O brothers,' I said, 'who through a hundred thousand dangers have reached the west, to this so brief vigil of our senses that remains to us, choose not to deny experience, following the sun, of the world that has no people.[13] Consider your origin: you were not made to live as brutes, but to pursue virtue and knowledge.'

"With this little speech I made my companions so keen for the voyage that then I could hardly have held them back. And turning our stern to the morning, we made of our oars wings for the mad flight, always gaining on the left. The night now saw the other pole and all its stars, and ours so low that it did not rise from the ocean floor. Five times the light beneath the moon had been rekindled and as many quenched, since we had entered on the passage of the deep, when there appeared to us a mountain dark in the distance, and to me it seemed the highest I had ever seen. We rejoiced, but soon our joy was turned to grief, for from the new land a whirlwind rose and struck the forepart of the ship. Three times it whirled her round with all the waters, and the fourth time it lifted the stern aloft and plunged the prow below, as pleased Another, till the sea closed over us."

CANTO XXVII

The flame was already erect and quiet, having ceased to speak, and, with the consent of the gentle poet, now went away from us, when another that came on behind it made us turn our eyes to its tip for a confused sound that came from it. As the Sicilian bull[1] (which bellowed first with the cry of him—and that was right—who had shaped it with his file) was wont to bellow with the voice of the victim, so that, though it was of brass, yet it seemed transfixed with pain: thus, having at first no course or outlet in the fire, the doleful words were changed into its language. But after they had found their way up through the tip, giving it the same vibration that the tongue had given in their passage, we heard it say, "O you to whom I direct my voice and who just now spoke Lombard, saying, 'Now go your way, I do not urge you more,' although I have come perhaps somewhat late, let it not irk you to stop and speak with me: you see it irks not me, and I am burning. If you are but now fallen into this blind world from that sweet land of Italy whence I bring all my guilt, tell me if the Romagnoles[2] have peace or war; for I was of the mountains[3] there between Urbino and the chain from which the Tiber springs."[4]

I was still bent down and intent when my leader touched me on the side and said, "You speak: he is Italian." And I, who was already prepared to answer, began without delay, "O soul that are hidden down there, your Romagna is not, nor ever was, without war in the hearts of her tyrants; but no open war have I left there now.[5] Ravenna is as it has been for many a year: the eagle of Polenta[6] broods over it so that he covers Cervia[7] with his wings. The city that once bore the long siege and made of the French a bloody heap, finds itself again under the green claws. And the old mastiff and the new of Verrucchio, who made the ill disposal of Montagna,[8] ply their teeth where they are wont. The cities on Lamone and Santerno[9] are ruled by the young lion[10] of the white lair, who changes side from summer to winter. And that city whose flank the Savio bathes,[11] even as it lies between the plain and the mountain, so does it live between tyranny and freedom. Now I pray you tell us who you are; be not more grudging than another has been to you, so may your name endure in the world!"

After the flame had roared for a while in its own fashion, the sharp point moved to and fro, and then gave forth this breath, "If I thought that my answer were to one who might ever return to the world, this flame would shake no more; but since from this depth none ever returned alive, if what I hear is true, I answer you without fear of infamy.

"I was a man of arms, and then a corded friar,[12] trusting, so girt, to make amends; and certainly my hope would have come full, but for the High Priest[13]—may ill befall him!— who set me back in my first sins: and how and wherefore I would have you hear from me. While I was the form of the flesh and bones my mother gave me, my deeds were not those of the lion, but of the fox. I knew all wiles and covert ways, and plied the art of them so well that to the ends of the earth their sound went forth. When I saw myself come to that part of my life when every man should lower the sails and coil up the ropes, that which before had pleased me grieved me then, and with repentance and confession I turned friar, and—woe is me!—it would have availed.

"The Prince of the new Pharisees, having war near the Lateran[14]—and not with Saracens or with Jews, for his every enemy was Christian, and none had been to conquer Acre,[15] nor been a merchant in the Soldan's land[16]—regarded neither the supreme office and holy orders in himself, nor, in me, that cord which used to make its wearers leaner; but as Constantine sought out Sylvester[17] within Soracte[18] to cure his leprosy, so this one sought me out as the doctor to cure the fever of his pride. He asked counsel of me, and I kept silent, for his words seemed drunken. Then he spoke again, 'Let not your heart mistrust. I absolve you here and now, and do you teach me how I may cast Penestrino[19] to the ground. I can lock and unlock Heaven, as you know; for the keys are two, which my predecessor did not hold dear.' Thereon the weighty arguments pushed me to where silence seemed to me the worst, and I said, 'Father, since you do wash me of that sin into which I now must fall, long promise with short keeping will make you triumph on the High Seat.'

"Then, when I died, Francis came for me; but one of the black Cherubim said to him, 'Do not take him, wrong me not! He must come down among my minions because he gave the fraudulent counsel, since which till now I have been at his hair; for he who repents not cannot be absolved, nor is it possible to repent of a thing and to will it at the same time, for the contradiction does not allow it.'

"O wretched me! how I started when he seized me, saying, 'Perhaps you did not think that I was a logician!' He bore me to Minos, who coiled his tail eight times round his rough back, and then, biting it in great rage, said, 'This is a sinner for the thievish fire'; wherefore here where you see me I am lost, and go, thus robed, in bitterness."

When he had thus ended his words the sorrowing flame departed, twisting and tossing the pointed horn.

We passed onward, I and my guide, along the reef as far as the next arch which spans the ditch where they pay the fee who acquire their load by sundering.

CANTO XXVIII

Who could ever fully tell, even in unfettered words, though many times narrating, the blood and the wounds that I now saw? Surely every tongue would fail, because of our speech and our memory which have little capacity to comprehend so much.

Were all the people assembled again who once in the fateful land of Apulia[1] bewailed their blood shed by the Trojans,[2] and those of the long war that made so vast a spoil of rings—as Livy writes, who does not err—together with those who felt the pain of blows in the struggle with Robert Guiscard,[3] and those others whose bones are still heaped up at Ceperano,[4] where every Apulian was false, and there by Tagliacozzo where old Alardo conquered without arms;[5] and one should show his limb pierced through, and another his cut off, it would be nothing to equal the foul fashion of the ninth pouch.

Truly a cask, through loss of mid-board or side-piece, gapes not so wide as one I saw, cleft from the chin to the part that breaks wind; his entrails were hanging between his legs, and the vitals could be seen and the foul sack that makes ordure of what is swallowed. While I was all absorbed in gazing on him, he looked at me and with his hands pulled open his breast, saying, "Now see how I rend myself, see how mangled is Mohammed![6] In front of me goes Ali[7] weeping, cleft in the face from chin to foreclock; and all the others whom you see here were in their lifetime sowers of scandal and of schism, and therefore are thus cleft. A devil is here behind that fashions us thus cruelly, putting again to the edge of the sword each of this throng when we have circled the doleful road; for the wounds are closed up before any of us pass again before him. But who are you that are musing on the ridge, perhaps to delay going to the punishment pronounced on your own accusations?"

"Neither has death yet reached him, nor does guilt bring him for torment," replied my master, "but in order to give him full experience, it behooves me, who am dead, to lead him down here through Hell from circle to circle; and this is as true as that I speak to you."

More than a hundred there were who, when they heard him, stopped in the ditch to look at me, forgetting their torment in their wonder.

"Tell Fra Dolcino,[8] then, you who perhaps will see the sun before long, if he would not soon follow me here, so to arm himself with victuals that stress of snow may not bring victory to the Novarese, which otherwise would not be easy to attain."

After he had raised one foot to go on, Mohammed said this to me, then set it on the ground to depart.

Another[9] who had his throat pierced through and his nose cut off up to the eyebrows, and only one ear left, stopped with the rest to gaze in astonishment, and before the others opened his gullet, which was all red outside, and said, "O you whom guilt does not condemn and whom I saw above in the land of Italy, if too great likeness does not deceive me, if ever you return to see the sweet plain that slopes from Vercelli to Marcabò,[10] remember Pier da Medicina. And make it known to the two best men of Fano, to messer Guido and to Angiolello,[11] that unless our foresight here is vain, they will be thrown out of their vessel and sunk near La Cattolica, through the treachery of a fell tyrant. Between the islands of Cyprus and Majorca Neptune never saw so great a crime, not of the pirates nor of the Argolic people. That traitor who sees with but one eye,[12] and holds the city from sight of which one who is here with me would wish he had fasted, will make them come to parley with him, then will so deal with them that for the wind of Focara they will not need vow or prayer."

And I to him, "Show me and explain, if you would have me carry news of you above, who he is to whom that sight was bitter." Then he laid hold of the jaw of one of his companions and opened the mouth, saying, "This is he, and he does not speak: being banished, he quenched the doubt in Caesar, affirming that to a man prepared delay was always harmful." Ah, how aghast appeared to me, with tongue cut off in his throat, Curio[13] who was so daring in his speech!

And one who had both hands lopped off, raising the stumps through the murky air so that the blood befouled his face, cried, "You will recall Mosca[14] too who said, alas! 'A thing done has an end!' which was seed of ill to the Tuscan people"—"and death to your own stock," I added then; whereat he, heaping sorrow on sorrow, went off as one crazed with grief.

But I stayed to view the troop, and saw a thing that I should be afraid even to relate without more proof, but that conscience, the good companion that emboldens a man under the hauberk of feeling itself pure, reassures me. Truly I saw, and seem to see it still, a trunk without the head going along as were the others of that dismal herd, and it was holding the severed head by the hair, swinging it in hand like a lantern, and it was

gazing at us and saying: "O me!" Of itself it was making a lamp for itself, and they were two in one and one in two—how this can be, He knows who so ordains. When he was right at the foot of the bridge he raised high his arm with the head, in order to bring near to us his words, which were, "See now my grievous penalty, you who, breathing, go to view the dead: see if any other is so great as this! And that you may carry news of me, know that I am Bertran de Born,[15] he who to the young king[16] gave the evil counsels. I made the father and the son rebel against each other. Ahithophel[17] did not more with Absalom and David by his wicked instigations. Because I parted persons thus united, I carry my brain parted from its source, alas! which is in this trunk. Thus is the retribution observed in me."

CANTO XXIX

The many people and the strange wounds had made my eyes so drunken that they longed to stay and weep; but Virgil said to me, "What are you still gazing at? Why does your sight still rest down there among the dismal mutilated shades? You have not done so at the other pits. Consider, if you think to count them, that the valley circles two and twenty miles; and already the moon is beneath our feet. The time is now short that is allowed us, and there is more to see than you see here."

"If you had given heed to my reason for looking," I answered then, "perhaps you would have granted me a longer stay."

Meanwhile my leader was going on, and I was following after him, making my reply, and adding, "Within that hollow where I was but now holding my eyes so fixedly, I believe a spirit of my own blood laments the guilt that costs so dear down there." Then said the master, "Do not let your thought distract itself on him henceforth; attend to somewhat else, and let him stay there; for I saw him there below the bridge point at you and fiercely threaten with his finger, and I heard them call him Geri del Bello.[1] You were then so wholly occupied with him who once held Hautefort[2] that you did not look that way till he was gone."

"O my leader," I said, "the violent death which is not yet avenged for him by any who is partner in the shame made him indignant; wherefore, as I judge, he went on without speaking to me, and thereby has he made me pity him the more."

Thus we spoke, up to the first place on the crag which shows the next valley, had there been more light, right to the bottom. When we were above the last cloister of Malebolge, so that its lay brothers could be seen by us, strange lamentations assailed me which had their shafts barbed with pity; at which I covered my ears with my hands. Such suffering as there would be if, between July and September, the sick from the hospitals of Valdichiana and of Maremma and of Sardinia[3] were all in one ditch together, such was there here; and such a stench issued thence as is wont to come from festered limbs. We descended onto the last bank of the long crag, keeping ever to the left, and then my sight was clearer down into the depth, where the ministress of the High Lord, infallible Justice, punishes the falsifiers whom she registers here.

I do not believe it was a greater sorrow to see the whole people in Aegina[4] sick, when the air was so full of corruption that every animal, even to the little worm, fell dead, and afterwards, as the poets hold for certain, the ancient peoples were restored from seed of ants, than it was to see, through that dark valley, the spirits languishing in divers heaps. One lay on his belly, one lay on the shoulders of another, and one shifted on all fours along the dismal way. Step by step we went in silence, watching and listening to the sick, who were unable to raise themselves.

I saw two sitting propped against each other, as pan is leaned against pan to warm, spotted from head to foot with scabs; and never did I see currycomb plied by stableboy whose master waits for him, nor by one who unwillingly stays awake, as each of these plied thick the clawing of his nails upon himself, for the great fury of the itch which has no other succor; and the nails were dragging down the scab, as a knife does the scales of bream or of other fish that has them larger.

"O you who with your fingers dismail yourself," my leader began to one of them, "and who sometimes make pincers of them, tell us if there is any Italian among these who are here within, so may your nails suffice you eternally in this work."

"We are Italians, both of us, whom you see so disfigured here," replied the one, weeping, "but who are you that inquire of us?"

And my leader said, "I am one who with this living man descend from ledge to ledge, and I mean to show him Hell."

Then their mutual support was broken, and each turned toward me trembling, with others who overheard him. The good master drew quite close to me, saying, "Tell them what you will." And I began, as he desired, "So may memory of you in the first world not fade away from the minds of men, but may it live under many suns, tell me who you are and of what people; let not your ugly and disgusting punishment make you fear to declare yourselves to me."

"I was of Arezzo,"[5] one of them replied, "and Albero of Siena[6] had me burned; but what I died for does not bring me here. True it is, I said to him, speaking in jest, 'I would know how to raise myself through the air in flight'; and he, who had a lively desire and little wit, would have me show him the art; and only because I did not make him a Daedalus, he had me burned by one who held him as a son. But, for the alchemy I practiced in the world, Minos, to whom it is not allowed to err, condemned me to this last pouch of the ten."

And I said to the poet, "Now was ever a people so vain as the Sienese? Surely not so the French by far."

Whereat the other leper, who heard me, responded to my words, "Except for Stricca, who knew how to spend in moderation; and except for Niccolò,[7] who first devised the costly use of the clove, in the garden where such seed takes root; and except for the company[8] in which Caccia d'Asciano[9] squandered the vineyard and the great purse, and Abbagliato[10] showed his wit. But, that you may know who thus seconds you against the Sienese, sharpen your eye toward me, that my face may answer well to you, and you will see that I am the shade of Capocchio,[11] who falsified the metals by alchemy; and you must recall, if I rightly eye you, how good an ape of nature I was."

CANTO XXX

In the time when Juno was wroth for Semele against the Theban blood,[1] as she showed more than once, Athamas[2] became so insane that, seeing his wife go carrying their two children on either hand, he cried, "Let us spread the nets to take the lioness and the whelps at the pass!" and then stretched out his pitiless claws, grasping the one that was named Learchus, and whirled him round and dashed him on a rock; and she drowned herself with her other burden. And when Fortune brought low the all-daring pride of the Trojans, so that the king together with his kingdom was blotted out, Hecuba, sad, wretched and captive, after she had seen Polyxena slain and, forlorn, discerned her Polydorus on the seastrand,[3] she, driven mad, barked like a dog, so had the sorrow wrung her soul. But no fury of Thebes or of Troy was ever seen so cruel against any, in rending beasts, much less human limbs, as were two pallid shades that I saw biting and running like the pig when it is let out of the sty. The one came at Capocchio and fixed its tusks on his neckjoint, so that, dragging him, it made his belly scratch along the solid bottom. And the Aretine, who was left, trembling said to me, "That goblin is Gianni Schicchi, and he goes rabid mangling others thus."

"Oh," said I to him, "so may the other not fix its teeth on you, be pleased to tell who it is, before it breaks away from here."

And he to me, "That is the ancient spirit of infamous Myrrha,[4] who became loving of her father beyond rightful love. She came to sin with him by falsifying herself in another's form, even as the other, who goes off there, ventured, that he might gain the lady of the herd, to counterfeit in himself Buoso Donati,[5] making a will and giving it due form."

And when the furious two on whom I had kept my eyes had passed on, I turned to look at the other ill-born shades, and I saw one shaped like a lute, if only he had been cut short at the groin from the part where a man is forked. The heavy dropsy which, with its ill-digested humor, so unmates the members that the face does not answer to the paunch, made him hold his lips apart, like the hectic who, for thirst, curls the one lip toward his chin and the other upwards.

"Oh you who are without any punishment, and I know not why, in this dismal world," he said to us, "behold and consider the misery of Master Adam.[6] Living, I had in plenty all that I wished, and now, alas! I crave one drop of water! The little brooks that from the green hills of Casentino run down into the Arno, making their channels cool and moist, are always before me, and not in vain, for the image of them parches me far more than the malady that wastes my features. The rigid justice that scourges me draws occasion from the place where I sinned, to give my sighs a quicker flight; there is Romena,[7] where I falsified the currency stamped with the Baptist,[8] for which on earth I left my body burnt. But if I could see here the miserable soul of Guido or of Alessandro[9] or of their brother, I would not give the sight for Fonte Branda.[10] One of them is here within already, if the raging shades who go around speak true; but what does it avail me whose limbs are tied. If I were only still so light that I could move one inch in a hundred years, I would have set out already on the road to seek him among this disfigured people, for all it is eleven miles around and not less than half a mile across. Because of them am I in such a family: they induced me to strike the florins that had three carats of alloy."

And I to him, "Who are the two wretches that are smoking like wet hands in winter, lying close to your confines on the right?"

"Here I found them when I rained down into this trough," he answered, "and since then they have not given a turn, nor do I think they will, to all eternity. The one is the false woman who accused Joseph;[11] the other is the false Sinon,[12] Greek from Troy. Burning fever makes them reek so strongly."

And one of them, who took offense perhaps at being named so darkly, with his fist struck him on his stiff paunch; it sounded like a drum; and Master Adam struck him in the face with his arm, which seemed no less hard, saying to him, "Though I am kept from moving, by the weight of my limbs, which are heavy, I have an arm free for such a need."

To which he replied, "When you were going to the fire you didn't have it thus ready; but you did have it as ready, and more, when you were coining."

And the dropsied one, "You speak the truth in this; but you were not so true a witness there at Troy where you were questioned about the truth."

"If I spoke falsely, you falsified the coin," said Sinon, "and I am here for a single sin, and you for more than any other demon."

'Remember, perjurer, the horse," he of the swollen paunch replied, "and may it torture you that all the world knows of it."

"And to you be torture the thirst that cracks your tongue," said the Greek, "and the foul water that makes your belly thus a hedge before your eyes."

Then the coiner, "Thus for fever your jaws gape wide, as usual; for if I have thirst and if humor stuffs me, you have the burning and an aching head, and to lick the mirror of Narcissus[13] you would not want many words of invitation."

I was standing all intent to listen to them, when the master said to me, "Now just you keep on looking a little more and I will quarrel with you!"

When I heard him speak to me in anger, I turned to him with such shame that it circles through my memory even yet. And as is he who dreams of something hurtful to him and, dreaming, wishes that it were a dream, so that he longs for that which is, as if it were not, such I became that, unable to speak, I wanted to excuse myself, and did excuse myself all the while, not thinking I was doing it.

"Less shame washes away a greater fault than yours has been," said the master, "therefore disburden yourself of all sadness; and do not forget that I am always at your side, should it again fall out that fortune find you where people are in a similar dispute, for the wish to hear that is a base wish."

CANTO XXXI

One and the same tongue first stung me, so that it tinged both my cheeks, and then it supplied the medicine to me; thus I have heard that the lance of Achilles[1] and of his father was wont to be the cause, first of a sad and then of a good gift.

We turned our backs to the wretched valley, going up by the bank that girds it round, crossing over it in silence. Here it was less than night and less than day, so that my sight went little ahead, but I heard a blast from a horn so loud that it would have made any thunderclap seem faint, and it directed my eyes, following back on its course, wholly to one place. After the dolorous rout when Charlemagne lost the holy gest, Roland[2] did not sound a blast so terrible.

I had not long kept my head turned in that direction when I seemed to see many lofty towers; whereon I, "Master, say, what city is this?" And he to me, "It is because you pierce the darkness from too far off that you stray in your imagining; and when you reach the place you will see plainly how much the sense is deceived by distance; therefore, spur yourself on somewhat more." Then lovingly he took me by the hand and said, "Before we go further forward, in order that the fact may seem less strange to you, know that these are not towers, but giants, and every one of them is in the pit, round about the bank from the navel downward."

As when a mist is vanishing, the sight little by little shapes out that which the vapor hides that fills the air; so, as I pierced the thick and murky atmosphere and came on nearer and nearer to the brink, error fled from me and fear grew upon me; for, as on its round wall Montereggione[3] crowns itself with towers, so here the horrible giants, whom Jove still threatens from heaven when he thunders, betowered with half their bodies the bank that encompasses the pit.

And already I discerned the face of one of them, his shoulders and his breast, and great part of his belly, and down along his sides both arms. Nature assuredly, when she gave up the art of making creatures such as these,[4] did right well to deprive Mars of such executors; and though she repents not of elephants and whales, he who looks subtly holds her therein more just and more discreet, for where the instrument of the mind is added to an evil will and to great power, men can make no defense against it. His face seemed to me as long and huge as the pine cone of St. Peter's at Rome,[5] and his other bones were in proportion with it; so that the bank, which was an apron to him from his middle downward showed us fully so much of him above, that three Frieslanders[6] would have made ill vaunt to have reached to his hair; for I saw thirty great spans of him down from the place where a man buckles his cloak.

"*Raphèl maὺ amecche zabì almi,*"[7] the fierce mouth, to which sweeter psalms were not fitting, began to cry. And my leader towards him, "Stupid soul, keep to your horn and with that vent yourself when rage or other passion takes you. Search at your neck and you will find the belt that holds it tied, O soul confused: see how it lies across your great chest." Then he said to me, "He is his own accuser: this is Nimrod,[8] through whose ill thought one sole language is not used in the world. Let us leave him alone and not speak in vain, for every language is to him as his is to others, which is known to none."

Then, turning to the left, we went farther on and, at the distance of a crossbow shot, we found the next, far more savage and bigger. Who had been the master to bind him I do not know, but he had his right arm shackled behind, and the other in front, by a chain which held him clasped from the neck downward, so that upon his uncovered part it was wound as far as the fifth coil.

"This proud one chose to try his strength against supreme Jove," said my guide, "wherefore he has such requital. Ephialtes[9] he is called, and he made the great endeavors when the giants put the gods in fear. The arms he plied he moves no more."

And I to him, "If it were possible, I should wish my eyes might have experience of the immense Briareus."[10] To which he replied, "Hard by here you shall see Antaeus,[11] who speaks and is unfettered, and he will put us down into the bottom of all guilt. He whom you wish to see is much farther on, and he is bound and fashioned like this one, except that he seems more ferocious in his look."

Never did mighty earthquake shake a tower so violently as Ephialtes forthwith shook himself. Then more than ever did I fear death, and nothing else was wanted for it but the fear, had I not seen his bonds. We then proceeded farther on and came to Antaeus, who stood full five ells, not reckoning his head, above the rock.

"O you that, in the fateful valley[12] which made Scipio heir of glory, when Hannibal with his followers turned his back, did once take for prey a thousand lions, and through whom, had you been at the high war of your brothers, it seems that some still believe the sons of earth would have conquered, set us down below—and disdain not to do so— where the cold locks up Cocytus.[13] Do not make us go to Tityus[14] nor to Typhon:[15] this man can give of that which is longed for here. Bend down, therefore, and do not curl your lip. He can yet restore your fame on earth, for he lives and expects long life yet, if grace does not untimely call him to itself."

Thus spoke my master; and the other in haste stretched out those hands of which Hercules once felt the mighty grip, and took my leader; and Virgil, when he felt their grasp, said to me, "Come here, that I may take you," and then of himself and me he made one bundle.

Such as the Garisenda[16] seems to one's view, beneath the leaning side, when a cloud is passing over it against the direction in which it leans, such did Antaeus seem to me as I watched to see him stoop—and it was such a moment that I should have wished to go by another road! But he set us down gently on the bottom that swallows Lucifer with Judas, nor did he linger there thus bent, but raised himself like the mast of a ship.

CANTO XXXII

If I had harsh and grating rhymes, as would befit the dismal hole on which all the other rocks converge and weigh, I would press out more fully the juice of my conception; but since I do not have them, it is not without fear that I bring myself to speak; for to describe the bottom of the whole universe is not an enterprise to be taken up in sport, nor for a tongue that cries mamma and daddy. But may those ladies[1] aid my verse who aided Amphion to wall in Thebes,[2] so that the telling may not be diverse from the fact. O you beyond all others misbegotten crowd who are in the place whereof it is hard to speak, better had you here been sheep or goats!

When we were down in the dark pit beneath the feet of the giant, far lower, and I was still gazing up at the high wall, I heard a voice say to me, "Look how you pass: take care not to tread on the heads of the wretched weary brothers." At this I turned and saw before me, and under my feet, a lake which through frost had the semblance of glass and not of water. Never did the Danube in Austria, nor the far-off Don under its cold sky, make in winter so thick a veil for their current as there was here: for had Tambernic[3] fallen on it, or Pietrapana,[4] it would not have given a creak, even at the edge. And as the frog lies to croak with muzzle out of the water, when the peasant girl dreams often of her gleaning, so, livid up to where the hue of shame appears, were the doleful shades within the ice, setting their teeth to the note of the stork. Each held his face turned downwards; by the mouth their cold, and by the eyes the misery of their hearts, is testified among them.

When I had looked round me awhile, I glanced down at my feet and saw two who were pressed so close together that they had the hair of their heads intermixed. "Tell me, you who thus press your breasts together," I said, "who are you?" And they bent back their necks, and when they had raised their faces towards me, their eyes, which before were moist only within, welled up with tears, which ran down over the lips, and the frost bound each to each and locked them even tighter; clamp never bound board on board so strongly; whereupon they butted together like two goats, such anger overcame them.

And one who had lost both ears from the cold, with his face still downwards said, "Why do you gaze so much on us? If you would know who these two are, the valley whence the Bisenzio descends belonged to their father Albert and to them.[5] They issued from one body; and all Caina[6] you may search and not find a shade more fit to be fixed in ice; not him whose breast and shadow were pierced with a single blow from Arthur's hand;[7] not Focaccia;[8] not this one, who so obstructs me with his head that I see no farther, and who was named Sassol Mascheroni[9]—if you are Tuscan you now know well who he was. And that you may not put me to further speech, know that I was Camiscion de' Pazzi,[10] and I await Carlino[11] to exculpate me."

After that I saw a thousand faces made purple by the cold, whence a shuddering comes over me, and always will, at frozen fords. And while we were going toward the center to which all gravity collects, and I was shivering in the eternal chill, whether it was will or fate or chance I do not know, but, walking among the heads, I struck my foot hard in the face of one.[12]

Wailing he railed at me, "Why do you trample on me? If you do not come to increase the vengeance of Montaperti,[13] why do you molest me?" And I, "Master, now wait here for me, that I may rid me of a doubt respecting this one, then you shall make me hasten as much as you wish." My leader stopped; and I said to the shade who was still cursing bitterly, "Who are you that thus reproach another?" "Nay, who are you," he answered, "that go through Antenora[14] smiting the cheeks of others, so that, were you alive, it would be too much."

"Alive I am," was my reply, "and if you crave fame, it may be worth much to you that I note your name among the rest." And he to me, "The contrary is what I crave. Take yourself hence and trouble me no more, for ill do you know how to flatter in this depth." Then I seized him by the hair of the nape and said, "Either you'll name yourself, or not a hair will be left on you here."

Whereon he to me, "Though you strip me bald, I will not tell you or show you who I am, though you should fall a thousand times upon my head."

I had already twisted his hair in my hand and had yanked out more than one tuft, he barking and with his eyes kept close down, when another cried, "What ails you, Bocca? Is it not enough for you to make noise with your jaws, but you must bark? What devil is at you?"

"Now," said I, "I do not wish you to speak more, accursed traitor, for to your shame will I carry true news of you." "Go away," he answered, "and tell what you will, but if you get out from here do not be silent about him that just now had his tongue so ready. He is lamenting here the silver of the French. 'I saw,' you can say, 'him of Duera,[15] there where the sinners are put to cool.' Should you be asked who else was there, you have at your side him of the Beccheria[16] whose gullet was slit by Florence. Gianni de' Soldanieri[17] I think is farther on, with Ganelon,[18] and with Tebaldello[19] who opened Faenza while it slept."

We had already left him when I saw two

frozen in one hole so close that the head of the one was a hood for the other; and as bread is devoured for hunger, so the upper one set his teeth upon the other where the brain joins with the nape. Not otherwise did Tydeus gnaw the temples of Menalippus[20] for rage than this one was doing to the skull and the other parts.

"O you who by so bestial a sign show hatred against him whom you devour, tell me the wherefore," I said, "on this condition, that if you with reason complain of him, I, knowing who you are and his offense, may yet requite you in the world above, if that with which I speak does not dry up."

CANTO XXXIII

From his savage repast the sinner raised his mouth, wiping it on the hair of the head he had spoiled behind, then began, "You will have me renew desperate grief, which even to think · of wrings my heart before I speak of it. But if my words are to be seed that may bear fruit of infamy to the traitor whom I gnaw, you shall see me speak and weep together. I do not know who you are, nor by what means you have come down here; but truly you do seem to me Florentine when I hear you. You have to know that I was Count Ugolino,[1] and this is the Archbishop Ruggieri. Now I will tell you why I am such a neighbor to him. How, by effect of his ill devising, I, trusting in him, was taken and thereafter put to death, there is no need to tell; but what you cannot have heard, that is, how cruel my death was, you shall hear and you shall know if he has wronged me.

"A narrow hole in the Mew which because of me has the title of Hunger, and in which others are yet to be shut up, had, through its opening, already shown me several moons, when I had the bad dream that rent for me the veil of the future. This man appeared to me as master and lord, chasing the wolf and the whelps upon the mountain[2] for which the Pisans cannot see Lucca. With trained hounds, lean and eager, he had put in front of him Gualandi with Sismondi and with Lanfranchi,[3] and after a short run the father and the sons seemed to me weary, and it seemed to me I saw their flanks ripped by the sharp fangs.

"When I awoke before the dawn I heard my children, who were with me, crying in their sleep and asking for bread. You are cruel indeed if you do not grieve already, to think what my heart was foreboding; and if you weep not, at what do you ever weep?

"They were awake now, and the hour approached when our food was usually brought to us, and each was apprehensive because of his dream. And below I heard them nailing up the door of the horrible tower; whereat I looked in the faces of my children without a word. I did not weep, so was I turned to stone within me. They wept, and my poor little Anselm said, 'You look so, father, what ails you?' I shed no tear for that, nor did I answer all that day, nor the night after, until the next sun came forth on the world. As soon as a little ray made its way into the woeful prison, and I discerned by their four faces the aspect of my own, I bit both my hands for grief. And they, thinking I did it for hunger, suddenly rose up and said, 'Father, it will be far less painful to us if you eat of us; you did clothe us with this wretched flesh, and do you strip us of it!'   ·

"Then I calmed myself in order not to make them sadder. That day and the next we stayed all silent: Ah, hard earth! why did you not open? When we had come to the fourth day Gaddo[4] threw himself outstretched at my feet, saying, 'Father, why do you not help me?' There he died; and even as you see me, I saw the three fall, one by one, between the fifth day and the sixth; whence I betook me, already blind, to groping over each, and for two days I called them after they were dead. Then fasting did more than grief had done."

When he had said this, with eyes askance he again took hold of the wretched skull with his teeth, which were strong on the bone like a dog's. Ah, Pisa! shame of the peoples of the fair land[5] where the sì is heard, since your neighbors are slow to punish you, let Capraia and Gorgona[6] shift, and make a hedge for Arno at its mouth, so that it drown every soul in you! For if Count Ugolino had the name of betraying you of your castles, you ought not to have put his children to such torture. Their youthful years, you modern Thebes, made Uguiccione and Brigata innocent,[7] and the other two that my song names above.

We went farther on, where the frost

roughly swathes another people, not bent downwards, but with faces all upturned. The very weeping there prevents their weeping, and the grief, which finds a barrier upon their eyes, turns inward to increase the agony, for the first tears form a knot and, like a crystal visor, fill all the cup beneath the eyebrow. And although, as in a callus, all feeling, because of the cold, had departed from my face, it now seemed to me as if I felt some wind, wherefore I, "Master, who moves this? Is not every vapor extinguished here below?"

And he to me, "Soon shall you be where your eye itself, seeing the cause that rains down the blast, will make answer to you in this."

And one of the wretches of the cold crust cried out to us, "O souls so cruel that the last station is given to you, lift from my face the hard veils, so that, before the weeping freezes again, I may vent a little the misery that stuffs my heart." Wherefore I to him, "If you would have me help you, tell me who you are, and if I do not relieve you, may I have to go to the bottom of the ice."[8]

He replied then, "I am Fra Alberigo;[9] I am he of the fruits from the evil garden, and here I am paid date for fig."

"Oh," I said to him, "are you then dead already?"

And he to me, "How my body may fare in the world above I have no knowledge. Such vantage has this Ptolomea[10] that oftentimes the soul falls down here before Atropos[11] sends it forth; and that you may more willingly scrape the glazen tears from my face, know that as soon as the soul betrays as I did, its body is taken from it by a devil who thereafter rules it until its time has all revolved. The soul falls headlong into this cistern, and perhaps the body of the shade that is wintering here behind me still appears above on earth: you must know if you are but now come down. He is ser Branca d'Oria,[12] and many years have passed since he was shut up thus."

"I believe you are deceiving me," I said to him, "for Branca d'Oria is not yet dead, and eats and drinks and sleeps and puts on clothes."

"In the ditch of the Malebranche[13] above," he said, "where the sticky pitch is boiling, Michel Zanche had not yet arrived when this one left a devil in his stead in his own body, as did also a near kinsman of his who commit-

ted the treachery together with him. But now reach out your hand here: open my eyes"; and I opened them not for him—and to be rude to him was courtesy!

Ah Genoese! men strange to all good custom and full of all corruption, why are you not driven from the earth? For with the worst spirit of Romagna I found one of you who for his deeds even now is in soul bathed in Cocytus, and in body appears still alive on earth!

CANTO XXXIV

"*Vexilla regis prodeunt*[1] *inferni* towards us; look forward therefore," said my master, "see if you discern him." As, when a thick fog breathes, or when our hemisphere darkens to night, a mill which the wind turns appears from afar, such an edifice did I now seem to see; then, because of the wind, I drew back behind my leader, for there was no other shelter there. I was now (and with fear I do put it into verse!) where the shades were wholly covered, showing through like straw in glass. Some are lying, some are erect, this with the head, that with the soles uppermost; another, like a bow, bends his face to his feet. When we had gone so far forward that it pleased my master to show me the creature who was once so fair, he took himself from before me and made me stop, saying, "Lo Dis!—and lo the place where you must arm yourself with fortitude."

How frozen and faint I then became, ask it not, reader, for I do not write it, because all words would fail. I did not die and I did not remain alive: now think for yourself, if you have any wit, what I became, deprived alike of death and life!

The emperor of the woeful realm stood forth from mid-breast out of the ice; and I in size compare better with a giant than giants with his arms: see now how huge that whole must be to correspond to such a part. If he was once as beautiful as he is ugly now, and lifted up his brows against his Maker, well may all sorrow proceed from him. Oh how great a marvel it was to me when I saw three faces on his head:[2] one in front and it was red, and the other two joined to this just over the middle of each shoulder, and all were joined at the crown. The right one seemed between white and yellow, and the left one was such in appearance as are those who come from whence the Nile descends. From under each there came forth two mighty wings,[3] of size befitting such a bird—sails at sea I never saw so broad. They had no feathers, but were like a bat's. And he was flapping them, so that three winds went forth from him, whereby Cocytus was all congealed. With six eyes he was weeping, and down over three chins dripped tears and bloody foam. In each mouth he champed a sinner with his teeth, as with a heckle, and thus he kept three of them woeful. To the one in front the biting was nothing compared with the clawing, for sometimes his back remained all stripped of skin.

"The soul up there that has the greatest punishment," said the master, "is Judas Iscariot, who has his head within and plies his legs outside. Of the other two who have their heads below, the one that hangs from the black muzzle is Brutus:[4] see how he writhes and utters not a word; the other is Cassius, who seems so stark of limb. But night is rising again, and now we must depart, for we have seen the whole."

As was his pleasure, I clasped him round the neck, and he took advantage of time and place, and when the wings were opened wide he caught hold on the shaggy flanks; down from shag to shag he descended between the matted hair and the frozen crusts. When we had come to where the thigh turns just on the thick of the haunch, my leader with labor and strain brought round his head to where his shanks had been and grappled on the hair like one who is climbing, so that I thought we were returning into Hell again.

"Cling fast," said the master, panting like a man forspent, "for by such stairs as these we must depart from so much evil." Then he issued forth through the opening of a rock and placed me upon its edge to sit, then reached toward me his cautious step. I raised my eyes and thought to see Lucifer as I had left him, and saw him with his legs held upwards—and if I became perplexed then, let the dull crowd

judge who do not see what is the point that I had passed.[5]

"Rise to your feet," said the master. "The way is long and the road is hard, and already the sun returns to mid-tierce."[6]

It was no palace hall where we were, but a natural dungeon which had a bad floor and want of light. "Before I tear myself from the abyss, my master," I said, when I had risen, "speak to me a little, to draw me out of error. Where is the ice? And he there, how is it that he is fixed thus upside down? And how, in so brief a time, has the sun made transit from evening to morning?"

And he to me, "You imagine that you are still on the other side of the center, where I caught hold on the hair of the evil worm that pierces the world. As long as I descended you were on that side; when I turned myself you passed the point to which all weights are drawn from every part. And you are now come beneath the hemisphere opposite to that which canopies the great dry land and underneath whose zenith the Man was slain who was born and lived without sin, and you have your feet upon a little sphere which forms the other face of the Judecca. Here it is morning when it is evening there, and this one who made a ladder for us with his hair is still fixed as he was before. On this side he fell down from Heaven; and the earth, which before stood out here, for fear of him made a veil of the sea and came to our hemisphere; and perhaps in order to escape from him that which appears on this side left here the empty space and rushed upwards."[7]

Down there, from Beelzebub as far removed as his tomb extends, is a space not known by sight, but by the sound of a rivulet descending in it along the hollow of the rock which it has eaten out in its winding and gently sloping course.[8] My leader and I entered on that hidden road to return into the bright world; and caring not for any rest, we climbed up, he first and I second, so far that through a round opening I saw some of the beautiful things that Heaven bears; and thence we issued forth to see again the stars.

Purgatorio

CANTO I

To course over better waters the little bark of my genius now hoists her sails, leaving behind her a sea so cruel; and I will sing of that second realm where the human spirit is purged and becomes fit to ascend to Heaven. But here let dead poetry rise again, O holy Muses, since I am yours; and here let Calliope[1] rise up somewhat, accompanying my song with that strain whose stroke the wretched Pies felt so that they despaired of pardon.

Sweet hue of oriental sapphire which was gathering in the serene face of the sky, pure even to the first circle, to my eyes restored delight, as soon as I issued forth from the dead air that had afflicted my eyes and breast. The fair planet that prompts to love was making the whole East smile, veiling the Fishes that were in her train. I turned to the right and gave heed to the other pole, and saw four stars never seen before save by the first people. The heavens seemed to rejoice in their flames. O northern widowed clime, that are deprived of beholding them![2]

When I had withdrawn my gaze from them, turning a little to the other pole, there whence the Wain[3] had already disappeared, I saw close to me an old man[4] alone, worthy in his looks of so great reverence that no son owes more to his father. His beard was long and streaked with white, like his locks of which a double tress fell on his breast.[5] The rays of the four holy lights so adorned his face with brightness that I saw him as if the sun were before him.

"Who are you that, against the blind stream, have fled the eternal prison?" said he, moving those venerable plumes. "Who has guided you, or what was a lamp to you issuing forth from the deep night that ever makes the infernal valley black? Are the laws of the abyss thus broken? Or is some new counsel changed in Heaven that though damned you come to my rocks?"

My leader then laid hold on me, and with speech and hand and sign made reverent my legs and brow. Then he answered him, "Of myself I came not. A lady descended from Heaven through whose prayers I succored this man with my company. But since it is your will that more of our condition be unfolded to you as it truly is, mine it cannot be that to you this be denied. This man has not seen his last evening, but by his folly was so near to it that very little time was left to run. Even as I said, I was sent to him to rescue him, and there was no other way than this along which I have set myself. I have shown him all the guilty people, and now I intend to show him those spirits that purge themselves under your charge.[6] How I have brought him would be long to tell you: from on high descends power that aids me to conduct him to see you and to hear you. Now may it please you to approve his coming. He goes seeking freedom,[7] which is so precious, as he knows who renounces life for it; you know it, for death for its sake was not bitter to you in Utica,[8] where you did leave the raiment which on the great day will be so bright.[9] The eternal edicts are not violated by us, for this one is alive and Minos does not bind me; but I am of the circle where are the chaste eyes of your Marcia,[10] who in her look still prays you, O holy breast, that you hold her for your own. For love of her, then, incline yourself to us: let us go on through your seven realms. I will report to her your kindness, if you deign to be mentioned there below."

"Marcia so pleased my eyes while I was yonder," he then said, "that every kindness she wished of me I did. Now that she dwells beyond the evil stream no more may she move me, by the law which was made when I came forth from there. But if a lady of Heaven moves and directs you, as you say, there is no need of flattery: let it fully suffice that for her sake you ask me. Go, then, and see that you gird him with a smooth rush, and that you bathe his face so that you remove all defilement from it, for with eye dimmed by any mist it would not be fitting to go before the first minister of those of Paradise. This little island, round about its very base, down there where the wave beats it, bears rushes on its soft mud. No other plant which would put forth leaf or harden can live there, because it yields not to the buffetings. Then let not your return be this way. The sun, which is now rising, will show you where to take the mountain at an easier ascent." So he vanished; and I rose up, without speaking, and drew all close to my leader and turned my eyes to him. "Son," he began, "follow my steps: let us turn back, for this plain slopes that way to its low limits."

The dawn was vanquishing the matin hour which fled before it, so that I recognized from afar the trembling of the sea. We were making our way across the solitary plain, like a man who returns to the road he has lost and, till he comes to it, seems to go in vain. When we came there where the dew strives with the sun, for being in the place where, in the breeze, it is little dispersed, my master gently laid both hands outspread on the grass. I therefore, aware of his purpose, reached toward him my tear-stained cheeks, and on them he wholly disclosed that color of mine which Hell had hidden.

Then we came on to the desert shore, that never saw any man navigate its waters who afterwards had experience of return. There, even as pleased another, he girded me. O marvel! that such as he plucked the humble plant, even such did it instantly spring up again, there whence he had uprooted it.

CANTO II

The sun had now reached the horizon whose meridian circle covers Jerusalem with its highest point; and night, circling opposite to him, was issuing forth from Ganges with the Scales, which fall from her hand when she exceeds,[1] so that there where I was the white and rosy cheeks of fair Aurora[2] were turning orange through too great age.

We were alongside the ocean yet, like folk who ponder on their road, who go in heart and linger in body; and lo, as when, suffused by dawn, Mars glows ruddy[3] through the thick vapors low in the west over the ocean floor, so

to me appeared—may I see it again!—a light coming over the sea so swiftly that no flight is equal to its motion; from which when I had taken my eyes for a little in order to question my leader, I again saw it grown brighter and bigger. Then on each side of it appeared to me a something white, and from beneath it, little by little, came forth another whiteness. My master still said not a word, until the first whitenesses appeared as wings; then, when he clearly discerned the pilot, he cried, "Bend, bend your knees! Behold the angel of God! Clasp your hands: henceforth you shall see such ministers. Look how he scorns all human instruments, and will have no oar, nor other sail than his own wings between such distant shores; see how he holds them straight toward heaven, fanning the air with his eternal feathers that are not changed like mortal plumage."

Then, as the divine bird came nearer and nearer to us, the brighter did he appear, so that close up my eyes could not endure him and I cast them down; and he came on to the shore with a vessel so swift and light that the water took in naught of it. At the stern stood the celestial steersman, such, that blessedness seemed to be inscribed upon him: and within sat more than a hundred spirits. "*In exitu Israel de Aegypto*"[4] all of them were singing together with one voice, with the rest of that psalm as it is written. Then he made the sign of holy cross upon them, whereon they all flung themselves upon the strand, and he went away swift as he had come.

The crowd which remained there seemed strange to the place, gazing about like those who essay new things. The sun was shooting forth the day on all sides and with his deft arrows had chased Capricorn from midheaven, when the new people raised their faces towards us, saying to us, "If you know, show us the way up the mountain."

And Virgil answered, "Perhaps you think we are acquainted with this place; but we are pilgrims, like yourselves. We came but now, a little while before you, by another road which was so rough and hard that henceforth the climb will seem but play to us."

The souls, who had perceived from my breathing that I was yet alive, marveling grew pale; and as to a messenger who bears an olive-branch the people crowd to hear the news, and no one shows himself shy of trampling, so did all of these fortunate souls fix their eyes on my face, as though forgetting to go to make themselves fair.

I saw one of them[5] with such great affection drawing forward to embrace me that he moved me to do the same. O empty shades except in aspect! Three times I clasped my hands behind him and as often brought them back to my breast. Wonder, I think, was painted in my looks, whereat the shade smiled and drew back, and I, following him, pressed forward. Gently he bade me stand; then I knew who it was, and begged him that he would stay a little and talk with me.

He answered me, "Even as I loved you in my mortal body, so do I love you freed from it; therefore I stay. But you, why do you go?"

"My Casella, to return here once again where I am I make this journey," I said, "but how has so much time been taken from you?"

And he to me, "No wrong is done me if he who takes up whom and when he will has denied me this passage many times, for of a just will his own is made. Truly, for three months now he has taken with all peace whoever would embark. I, therefore, who was now turned to the seashore where the water of Tiber grows salt, was kindly gathered in by him. To that river-mouth he has now set his wings, for there the souls are always gathering that sink not down to Acheron."

And I, "If a new law does not take from you memory or practice of the songs of love which used to quiet in me all my longings, may it please you therewith to comfort my soul somewhat, which coming hither with its body is so wearied."

"*Love that discourses in my mind,*"[6] he then began so sweetly that the sweetness still within me sounds. My master and I and that folk who were with him appeared content as if naught else touched the mind of any. We were all rapt and attentive to his notes, when lo, the venerable old man, crying, "What is this, you laggard spirits? What negligence, what stay is this? Haste to the mountain to strip off the slough that lets not God be manifest to you."

As doves, when gathering wheat or tares, assembled all at their repast and quiet, without their usual show of pride, if something appears that frightens them, suddenly leave their food because they are assailed by a greater care; so I saw that new troop leave the song and hasten toward the hillside, like one who goes, but knows not where he may come forth; nor was our departure less quick.

CANTO III

Although their sudden flight was scattering them over the plain, turned to the mountain where justice probes us, I drew close to my faithful companion. And how should I have sped without him? Who would have brought me up the mountain? He seemed to me smitten with self-reproach. O pure and noble conscience, how bitter a sting is a little fault to you!

. When his feet left off haste, which takes seemliness from every act, my mind, which at first had been restrained, widened its scope as in eager search, and I turned my face to the hill that rises highest heavenward from the sea. The sun, which was flaming red behind, was broken in front of me by the figure which was formed by the staying of its rays upon me. I turned to my side, fearing that I was abandoned, when I saw the ground darkened before me only. And my comfort, turning full round, began to say to me, "Why do you still distrust? Do you not believe that I am with you and that I guide you? It is now evening in the place where the body is buried within which I made shadow: Naples has it, and it was taken from Brindisi.[1] If in front of me now there is no shadow, do not marvel more than at the heavens, that one obstructs not the light from the other. To suffer torments, heat, and frost, bodies such as these that Power ordains, which wills not that the way of Its working be revealed to us. Foolish is he who hopes that our reason may compass the infinite course taken by One Substance in Three Persons. Be content, human race, with the *quia;* for if you had been able to see everything, no need was there for Mary to give birth; and you have seen desiring fruitlessly men such that their desire would have been satisfied which is given them for eternal grief: I speak of Aristotle and of Plato and of many others."[2] And here he bent his brow and said no more, and remained troubled.

We came meanwhile to the foot of the mountain. Here we found the cliff so steep that in vain would legs be nimble there. Between

Lerici and Turbia[3] the most deserted, the most broken landslip is a stairway easy and free compared with that.

"Now who knows on which hand the hillside slopes," said my master, staying his step, "so that he can ascend who goes without wings?" And while he held his face low, searching his mind about the road, and I was looking up around the rock, on the left appeared to me a company of souls who were moving their feet towards us and yet seemed not to approach, they came on so slowly.

"Master," said I, "lift up your eyes: behold yonder those who will give us counsel, if you cannot find it in yourself."

Then he looked, and with an air of relief replied, "Let us go thither, for they come slowly; and do you make firm your hope, dear son."

As yet that people were still as far (I mean, after a thousand paces of ours) as a good thrower would cast with his hand, when they all pressed close to the hard rocks of the steep cliff and stood still and close together, as men stop to look who are in doubt.[4]

"O you who have made a good end, spirits already elect." Virgil began, "by that peace which, I believe, awaits you all, tell us where the mountain slopes so that it is possible to go up, for time lost irks him most who knows most."

As sheep come forth from the fold by one and two and three, and the rest stand timid, bending eyes and muzzle to the ground; and what the first does the others also do, huddling themselves to it if it stops, simple and quiet, and know not why; so saw I then the head of that happy flock move to come on, modest in countenance, in movement dignified.

When those in front saw the light broken on the ground at my right side, so that my shadow was from me to the cliff, they halted and drew back somewhat; and all the others that came after did the same, not knowing why. "Without your asking I confess to you that this is a human body which you see, whereby the light of the sun is cleft on the ground. Do not marvel, but believe that not without power which comes from Heaven does he seek to scale this wall." Thus my master. And that worthy company said, "Turn back then and go on before us," with the backs of their hands making sign. And one

of them began, "Whoever you are, turn your face as you thus go: consider if ever you saw me yonder." I turned to him, and looked at him fixedly: blond he was, and handsome, and of noble mien, but a blow had cloven one of his eyebrows. When I had humbly disclaimed ever to have seen him, he said, "Look now," and showed me a wound high on his breast, then said smiling, "I am Manfred,[5] grandson of the Empress Constance.[6] Therefore I beg of you that when you return you go to my fair daughter,[7] mother of the pride of Sicily and of Aragon,[8] and tell her the truth, if aught else be told. After I had my body pierced by two mortal stabs I gave myself weeping to Him who pardons willingly; horrible were my sins, but the Infinite Goodness has such wide arms that It receives all who turn to It. If Cosenza's pastor,[9] who was then sent by Clement to hunt me down, had well read that page in God, the bones of my body would yet be at the bridgehead near Benevento, under the guard of the heavy cairn. Now the rain washes them and the wind stirs them, beyond the Kingdom,[10] hard by the Verde,[11] whither he transported them with tapers quenched. By curse of theirs none is so lost that the Eternal Love cannot return, so long as hope keeps aught of green. True it is that whoso dies in contumacy of Holy Church, even though he repent at the last, must stay outside upon this bank thirtyfold for all the time that he has lived in his presumption, if such decree is not made shorter by holy prayers. See now if you can make me glad by revealing to my good Constance how you have seen me, as well as this ban: for much is gained here through those who are yonder."

CANTO IV

When through impression of pleasure, or of pain, which some one of our faculties receives, the soul is wholly centered thereon, it seems that it gives heed to no other of its powers; and this is contrary to that error which holds that one soul above another is kindled within us; and therefore when aught is heard or seen which holds the soul strongly bent to it, the time passes away and we perceive it not, for one faculty is that which notes it, and another that which possesses the entire soul, the latter as it were bound, the former free. Of this I had true experience as I listened to that spirit and marveled; for fully fifty degrees the sun had climbed and I had not perceived it, when we came to where those souls with one voice cried out to us, "Here is what you ask."

A bigger opening many a time the man of the farm hedges up with a little forkful of his thorns, when the grape is darkening, than was the gap by which my leader mounted, and I after him, we two alone, when that troop had parted from us. One can walk to San Leo and descend to Noli,[1] one can mount Bismantova[2] to the summit, with feet alone; but here a man must fly, I mean with the swift wings and the plumes of great desire, behind that leader, who gave me hope and was a light to me. We were climbing within the cleft rock, and the surface on either side pressed close on us, and the ground beneath required both feet and hands.

After we were upon the upper edge of the high bank, out on the open slope, "My master," I said, "what way shall we take?" And he to me, "Let no step of yours descend, but ever up the mountain win your way behind me until some wise escort appear to us."

So high was the top that it surpassed my sight, and the slope was steeper far than a line from mid-quadrant to center. I was weary when I began, "O sweet father, turn and look how I remain alone if you do not stop!"

"My son," he said, "drag yourself up as far as here," pointing out to me a ledge a little higher up, which on that side circles all the mountain. His words so spurred me on that I forced myself to creep after him until the ledge was beneath my feet. There we both sat down, turned towards the East whence we had climbed, for to look back that way is wont to encourage a man. I first directed my eyes to the shores below, then raised them to the sun, marveling that we were struck by it on the left side. Right well the poet perceived that I was all amazed[3] at the chariot of the light where it was entering between us and Aquilo; wherefore he to me, "If Castor and Pollux[4] were in company of that mirror which conducts its light up and down, you would see the ruddy Zodiac[5] revolve yet closer to the Bears,[6] unless it strayed from its old road. If you would conceive how this can be, concentrate within you and imagine Zion[7] and this mountain to be so placed

on the earth that they have one sole horizon and different hemispheres; then you will see that the way which Phaëthon, unhappily for him, knew not how to drive, must needs pass this mountain on the one side when it passes that mountain on the other, if your mind right clearly apprehends."

"Surely, my master," I said, "never did I see so clearly as I now discern, where my wit seemed lacking, that the mid-circle of the celestial motion, which is called the Equator in a certain science, and which lies always between the sun and the winter, for the reason that you tell, departs here toward the north, as far as the Hebrews used to see it toward the hot climes. But, if it please you, I would fain know how far we have to go, for the hillside rises higher than my eyes can reach."

And he to me, "This mountain is such that ever at the beginning below it is toilsome, but the higher one goes the less it wearies. Therefore, when it shall seem to you so pleasant that the going up is as easy for you as going downstream in a boat, then will you be at the end of this path: hope there to rest your weariness; no more I answer, and this I know for true."

And when he had spoken these words, there sounded a voice close by, "Perhaps before then you'll need to sit!" At the sound of it each of us turned, and we saw on our left a great boulder which neither he nor I had noticed before. We went over to it, and there were persons lounging in the shade behind the rock, even as men who settle themselves to rest for laziness; and one of them, who seemed to me weary, was sitting and clasping his knees, holding his face low down between them.

"O my sweet lord," said I, "set your eye on that one who shows himself lazier than if sloth were his sister!"

Then he turned to us and gave heed, barely moving his look up along his thigh, and said, "Then you go on up who are so sturdy!"

Then I knew who he was, and that toil which still quickened my breath a little did not hinder my going to him; and when I had got to him, he scarcely lifted his head, saying, "Have you truly seen how the sun drives his chariot on your left side?"

His lazy actions and his brief words moved my lips to smile a little, then I began, "Belacqua,[8] I am not grieved for you now; but tell me, why are you sitting here? Are you

waiting for an escort? Or have you only resumed your old ways?"

And he, "O brother, what's the use of going
up? For God's angel who sits at the gate would
not let me pass to the torments. First must the
heavens revolve around me outside it, so long
as they did during my life, because I delayed
good sighs until the end—unless prayer first
aid me which rises from a heart that lives in
grace. What avails the other, which is not
heard in Heaven?"

And now the poet was climbing before me
and saying, "Come on now: see, the meridian
is touched by the sun, and on the shore night
now sets its foot on Morocco."

CANTO V

I had now parted from those shades and was
following in the steps of my leader, when one
behind me, pointing his finger, cried, "See, the
rays do not seem to shine on the left of him
below, and he seems to bear himself like one
who is alive!"

I turned my eyes at the sound of these
words, and saw them gazing in astonishment
at me alone, at me alone, and the light that
was broken.

"Why is your mind so entangled," said the
master, "that you slacken your pace? What
matters to you what is whispered here? Follow me and let the people talk. Stand as a
firm tower which never shakes its summit for
blast of winds; for always the man in whom
thought wells up on thought sets back his
mark, for the one thought weakens the force
of the other." What could I answer if not, "I
come"? I said it, overspread somewhat with
that color which sometimes makes a man worthy of pardon.

And meanwhile across the mountain slope
came people a little in front of us, singing the
Miserere[1] verse by verse. When they perceived
that I gave no place to the passage of the rays
through my body, they changed their song
into an "Oh!" long and hoarse; and two of
them, as messengers, ran to meet us, and asked
of us, "Let us know of your condition."

And my master said, "You may go back and
report to those who sent you that this man's
body is true flesh. If they stopped for seeing
his shadow, as I suppose, they have sufficient

answer. Let them do him honor, and it may be
dear to them."

Never did I see kindled vapors cleave the
bright sky at early night, or August clouds at
sunset, so swiftly as these returned above; and,
arrived there, they with the others wheeled
round towards us, like a troop that runs without curb.

"These people that press to us are many,
and they come to entreat you," said the poet;
"but do you continue on your way and, while
going, listen."

"O soul that go to your bliss with those
members with which you were born," they
came crying, "stay your steps for a little; look
if you have ever seen any of us, so that you
may carry news of him yonder. Ah, why do
you go? Ah, why do you not stay? We were
all done to death by violence, and sinners up to
the last hour. Then light from Heaven made us
mindful, so that, repenting and pardoning, we
came forth from life at peace with God, who
fills our hearts with sad longing to see Him."

And I, "Although I gaze upon your faces, I
do not recognize any; but if aught that I can do
be pleasing to you, spirits well-born, speak, and
I will do it, by that peace which, following in
the steps of such a guide, makes me pursue it
from world to world."

And one began, "Each of us trusts in your
good offices without your oath, if only lack of
power thwart not the will; wherefore I, who
speak alone before the others,[2] do beg of you,
if ever you see that country which lies between
Romagna and that of Charles,[3] that you be
courteous to me with your prayers in Fano,[4] so
that holy orison be made for me, that I may
purge away my grievous sins. Thence I sprang;
but the deep wounds whence flowed the blood
in which I had my life were dealt me in the
bosom of the Antenori, there where I thought
to be most secure: he of Este[5] had it done, who
held me in wrath far beyond what justice war-
ranted; but if I had fled toward La Mira[6] when I
was surprised at Oriaco[7] I should yet be yonder
where men breathe. I ran to the marsh, and the
reeds and the mire so entangled me that I fell,
and there I saw form on the ground a pool from
my veins."

Then said another, "Ah, so may that desire be fulfilled which draws you up the lofty
mountain, do you with gracious pity help my
own. I was of Montefeltro, I am Buonconte.[8]

Giovanna,[9] or any other, has no care for me, so that I go among these with downcast brow."

And I to him, "What force or what chance so carried you astray from Campaldino[10] that your burial-place was never known?"

"Oh!" he answered, "at the foot of the Casentino[11] a stream crosses, named the Archiano,[12] which rises in the Apennines above the Hermitage.[13] To the place where its name is lost I came, wounded in the throat, flying on foot and bloodying the plain. There I lost my sight and speech. I ended on the name of Mary, and there I fell, and my flesh remained alone. I will tell the truth, and do you repeat it among the living. The Angel of God took me, and he from Hell cried, 'O you from Heaven, why do you rob me?[14] You carry off with you the eternal part of him for one little tear which takes him from me; but of the rest I will make other disposal!'

"You know well how in the air is condensed that moist vapor which turns to water soon as it rises where the cold seizes it. Evil will that seeks only evil he joined with intellect, and, by the power his nature gave, stirred the mists and the wind;[15] then when day was spent, he covered with clouds the valley from Pratomagno[16] to the great mountain chain and so charged the sky overhead that the pregnant air was turned to water. The rain fell, and that which the ground refused came to the gulleys and, gathering in great torrents, so swiftly rushed toward the royal river[17] that nothing stayed its course. The raging Archiano found my frozen body at its mouth and swept it into the Arno and loosed the cross on my breast which I had made of me when pain overcame me. It rolled me along its banks and along its bottom, then covered and wrapped me with its spoils."

"Pray, when you have returned to the world and have rested from your long journey," the third spirit followed on the second, "remember me, who am la Pia.[18] Siena made me, Maremma unmade me, as he knows who with his ring had plighted me to him in wedlock."

CANTO VI

When the game of hazard breaks up, the loser is left disconsolate, repeating the throws and sadly learns. With the other all the people go along: one goes in front, one plucks him from behind, and at his side one brings himself to mind. He does not stop, but listens to this one and that one; each to whom he reaches forth his hand presses on him no longer, and thus from the throng he defends himself. Such was I in that dense crowd, turning my face to them this way and that and, by promising, I got free from them. Here was the Aretine[1] who met his death at the fierce hands of Ghino di Tacco;[2] and the other who was drowned[3] as he fled in the rout; here Federigo Novello[4] was imploring with outstretched hands, and he of Pisa who made the good Marzucco[5] show fortitude. I saw Count Orso;[6] and the soul severed from its body by spite and by envy, as it said, and not for fault committed, Pierre de la Brosse,[7] I mean: and let the Lady of Brabant[8] look to it, while she is here, so that for this she be not of the worse flock.

As soon as I was free of all those shades, whose one prayer was that others should pray, so that their way to blessedness may be sped, I began, "It seems to me, O my light, that you deny expressly in a certain passage that prayer bends the decree of heaven; and these people pray but for this—shall then their hope be vain, or are your words not rightly clear to me?"

And he to me, "My writing is plain and the hope of these souls is not fallacious, if with sound judgment you consider well; for the summit of justice is not lowered because the fire of love fulfil in a moment that which he must satisfy who sojourns here; and there where I affirmed that point, default could not be amended by prayer, because the prayer was disjoined from God. But do not rest in so profound a doubt, except she tell you who shall be a light between the truth and the intellect. I know not if you understand: I speak of Beatrice. You will see her above, smiling and happy, on the summit of this mountain."

And I, "My lord, let us go on with greater haste, for now I do not weary as before, and see how the hill now casts its shadow."

"We will go forward with this day," he answered, "as far as yet we may, but the fact is quite other than you suppose. Before you are there above you will see him return that is now hidden by the slope, so that you do not break his beams. But see yonder a soul seated all alone, who is looking towards us; he will point out to us the quickest way."

We came to him: O Lombard soul, how lofty and disdainful was your bearing, and the movement of your eyes how grave and slow! He said nothing to us, but let us go on, watching only after the fashion of a couching lion; but Virgil drew on towards him, asking him to show us the best ascent; and he did not reply to his question, but inquired of our country and condition. And the gentle leader began, "Mantua—"; and the shade, all in himself recluse, rose toward him from his place there, saying, "O Mantuan, I am Sordello[9] of your city!"— and they embraced each other.

Ah, servile Italy, hostel of grief, ship without pilot[10] in great tempest, no mistress of provinces, but brothel! So eager was that noble soul, only at the sweet name of his city, to give glad welcome there to his fellow-citizen—and now in you your living abide not without war, and of those whom one wall and one moat shut in, one gnaws at the other! Search, wretched one, round the shores of your seas, and then look within your bosom, if any part of you enjoy peace! What avails it that Justinian should refit the bridle, if the saddle is empty? But for that the shame were less!

Ah, people that ought to be obedient[11] and let Caesar sit in the saddle, if you rightly understand what God notes to you! See how this beast has grown vicious, through not being corrected by the spurs, since you did put your hand to the bridle!

O German Albert,[12] who do abandon her that is become wanton and wild and who should bestride her saddle-bows, may just judgment fall from the stars upon your blood, and be it so strange and manifest that your successor[13] may have fear thereof! For you and your father,[14] held back yonder by greed, have suffered the garden of the Empire to be laid waste. Come to see Montecchi[15] and Cappelletti,[16] Monaldi and Filippeschi,[17] you man without care, those already wretched and these in dread. Come, cruel one, come and see the distress of your nobles, and heal their hurts; and you will see Santafiora,[18] how forlorn it is. Come see your Rome that weeps, widowed and alone, crying day and night, "My Caesar, why do you abandon me?" Come see your people, how they love one another; and if no pity

for us moves you, come to be shamed by your own renown!

And if it be lawful for me, O Jove supreme that on earth wast crucified for us, are Thy just eyes turned elsewhere, or is it preparation Thou makest in the depths of Thy counsel for some good quite cut off from our perception? For all the cities of Italy are full of tyrants, and every yokel who comes to play the partisan becomes a Marcellus.[19]

O my Florence, you may indeed rejoice at this digression which does not touch you, thanks to your people who are so resourceful. Many others have justice at heart, but slowly it is let fly, because the shaft does not come without counsel to the bow; but your people has it ever on its lips! Many others refuse the public burden; but your people answers eagerly without being called, crying, "I'll shoulder it!" Now make you glad, for you have good cause: you rich, you at peace, you so wise! If I speak the truth, the result does not conceal it. Athens and Lacedaemon,[20] that framed the laws of old and were so grown in civil arts, offered but the merest suggestion of right living, compared with you that make such subtle provisions that what you spin in October lasts not to mid-November. How many times within your memory have you changed laws, coinage, offices, and customs, and renewed your members! And if you well bethink you, and see clear, you will see yourself like the sick woman who cannot find repose upon the down, but with her tossing seeks to ease her pain.

CANTO VII

After the courteous and joyful greetings had been repeated three and four times, Sordello drew back and said, "But who are you?"

"Before the souls worthy to ascend to God were turned to this mountain, my bones were buried by Octavian; I am Virgil, and for no other fault did I lose Heaven than for not having faith." Thus answered my leader then.

As one who of a sudden sees a thing before him that he marvels at, who believes and believes not, saying, "It is, it is not,"—such seemed the other, and then he bent down his brow and humbly approached him again and embraced him where the inferior embraces.

"O glory of the Latins," said he, "through whom our tongue showed forth its power, O eternal praise of the place whence I sprang, what merit or what favor shows you to me? If I am worthy to hear your words, tell me if you come from Hell, and from which cloister?"

"Through all the circles of the woeful kingdom," he answered him, "I have come hither. A power from Heaven moved me, and by its help I come. Not for doing, but for not doing, have I lost the sight of the high Sun that you desire and that was known by me too late. A place there is below, not sad with torments but with darkness only, where the lamentations sound not as wailings, but are sighs. There I abide with the little innocents, seized by the fangs of death before they were exempted from human guilt; there I abide with those who were not clothed with the three holy virtues,[1] and without sin knew the others and followed all of them. But if you know and can, give us some direction whereby we may come more speedily to where Purgatory has its true beginning."

He answered, "No fixed place is set for us; it is permitted me to go up and round, and as far as I may go I will accompany you as guide. But see now how the day declines, and to go up by night is not possible, therefore it is well to take thought of a good resting-place. There are souls on the right here, apart: with your consent I will lead you to them, and not without delight will they be known to you."

"How is that?" was answered; "he who wished to climb by night, would he be hindered by others, or would he not climb because he had not the power?" And the good Sordello drew his finger on the ground, saying, "Look, even this line you would not cross after the sun is set. Not that aught else save the nocturnal darkness hinders the going up: that hampers the will with impotence. Truly by night one might return downwards, and walk wandering around the mountainside while the horizon holds the day closed."

Then my lord, as though marveling, said, "Lead us therefore whither you say we may have delight in tarrying."

We had gone from there but a little way when I perceived that the mountain was hollowed out, even as valleys hollow out mountains here. "Thither will we go," said the shade, "to where the slope makes a lap of itself, and wait there for the new day." There was a slanting path, between steep and level, which brought us to the side of that hollow, there where its edge more than half dies away. Gold and fine silver, cochineal and white lead, Indian wood bright and clear, fresh emerald at the moment it is split, would all be surpassed in color, if placed within that valley, by the grass and by the flowers growing there, as the less is surpassed by the greater. Nature had not only painted there, but of the sweetness of a thousand scents she made there one unknown to us and blended. From there I saw, seated upon the green grass and the flowers, singing "*Salve, Regina,*"[2] souls who because of the valley were not visible from without.

"Before the lessening sun sinks to its nest," began the Mantuan who had brought us thither, "do not ask me to lead you among them there. From this bank you will distinguish better the acts and countenances of all of them, than if you were received among them on the level below. He who sits highest and has the look of having neglected what he ought to have done, and does not move his lips with the others' song, was Rudolf the Emperor,[3] who might have healed the wounds that were the death of Italy, so that through another[4] she is succored too late. The other, who appears to be comforting him, ruled the land where the waters spring that the Moldau carries to the Elbe,[5] and the Elbe to the sea: his name was Ottokar,[6] and in swaddling-bands he was better far than bearded Wenceslaus,[7] his son, who is fed by lust and idleness. And he with the small nose,[8] who seems close in counsel with him that has so kindly a mien, died in flight and disflowering the lily: look there how he beats his breast. See the other[9] that, sighing, has made a bed for his cheek with the palm of his hand. They are the father and the father-in-law of the plague of France;[10] they know his wicked and foul life, and hence comes the grief that pierces them so. He that seems so stout of limb[11] and who accords his singing with him of the virile nose[12] was begirt with the cord of every worth; and if the youth[13] who is sitting behind him had followed him as king, then indeed his worth had passed from vessel to vessel, which cannot be said of the other heirs; James[14] and Frederick[15] have the realms; the better heritage no one possesses. Rarely does human worth rise through the branches, and this He wills who gives it, in order that it may be asked from Him. My words apply also to the large-nosed one no less than to the other, Peter, who is singing with him, wherefore Apulia and Provence[16] are now in grief; as much is the plant inferior to its seed as Constance yet boasts of her husband more than Beatrice and Margaret of theirs. See the king of the simple life sitting there alone, Henry of England:[17] he in his branches has a better issue. He that sits on the ground lowest among them, looking up, is William the marquis,[18] because of whom Alessandria and its war make Montferrat and the Canavese mourn."[19]

CANTO VIII

It was now the hour[1] that turns back the longing of seafaring folk and melts their heart the day they have bidden sweet friends farewell, and that pierces the new pilgrim with love if he hears from afar a bell that seems to mourn the dying day, when I began to annul my hearing and to gaze on one of the souls, uprisen, who was signing with his hand to be heard. He joined and lifted both his palms, fixing his eyes on the East, as if he said to God, "For naught else do I care." "*Te lucis ante*" came from his lips so devoutly and with such sweet notes that it rapt me from myself. Then the rest joined him sweetly and devoutly through the whole hymn, keeping their eyes fixed on the supernal wheels.

Reader, here sharpen well your eyes to the truth, for the veil is now indeed so thin that certainly to pass within is easy.

Then I saw that noble army silently gaze upward as if expectant, pallid and humble; and I saw come forth from above and descend two angels with flaming swords, broken short and deprived of their points. Their robes were green as newborn leaves, which they trailed behind them, smitten and fanned by their green wings. One came and took his stand a little above us, and the other alighted on the opposite bank, so that the company was contained in the middle. I clearly discerned their blond heads, but in their faces my sight was dazzled, like a faculty confounded by excess.

"Both come from Mary's bosom," said Sordello, "to guard the valley, because of the serpent that will presently come." Whereat I, who knew not by what path, turned round all chilled and pressed close to the trusty shoulders. And Sordello continued, "Let us go down into the valley among the great shades, and we will speak with them: it will be well pleasing to them to see you."

I believe I descended but three steps and was below, and saw one who was gazing only at me, as if he would recognize me. It was now the time when the air was darkening, yet not so dark that it did not make plain between his eyes and mine what it had shut off before. He moved toward me and I toward him: noble Judge Nino,[2] how I rejoiced to see you there, and not among the damned! No fair salutation was silent between us; then he asked, "How long is it since you came to the foot of the mountain over the far waters?"

"Oh," I said to him, "from within the woeful places I came this morning, and I am in my first life, albeit by this my journeying I gain the other." And when they heard my answer, Sordello and he drew back like folk suddenly bewildered, the one to Virgil and the other turned to one who was seated there, crying, "Up, Currado, come see what God, of His grace, has willed!" Then, turning to me, " By that singular gratitude you owe to Him who so hides His primal purpose that there is no fording thereunto, when you are beyond the wide waters, tell my Giovanna[3] that she pray for me there where the innocent are heard. I do not think her mother[4] loves me longer since changing her white wimples which she, in her wretchedness, needs must yet long for. By her right easily may be known how long the fire of love lasts in woman, if eye or touch do not often kindle it. The viper that leads afield[5] the Milanese will not make her so fair a tomb as Gallura's cock[6] would have done." Thus he spoke, his aspect stamped with the mark of that righteous zeal which in due measure glows in the heart.

My greedy eyes kept going to the sky just where the stars are slowest, as in a wheel nearest the axle. And my leader, "Son, what are you gazing at up there?" And I to him, "At those three torches with which the pole here is all aflame." And he to me, "The four bright stars you saw this morning are low on the other side, and these are risen where those were."

As he was speaking, lo! Sordello drew him to himself, saying, "See there our adversary!" and pointed with his finger that he should look that way. At that part where the little valley has no rampart was a snake, perhaps such as gave to Eve the bitter food. Through the grass and the flowers came the evil streak, turning from time to time its head and licking its back like a beast that sleeks itself. I did not see and therefore cannot tell how the celestial falcons moved, but well did I see both one and the other in motion. Hearing the green wings cleave the air, the serpent fled; and the angels wheeled round, flying alike back up to their posts.

The shade that had drawn close to the judge when he exclaimed, through all that assault had not for an instant loosed his gaze from me. "So may the light that leads you on high find in your will as much wax as is needed up to the enamelled summit," he began, "if you know true news of Val di Magra[7] or of the neighboring region, tell it to me, who once was great there. I was called Currado Malaspina:[8] I am not the old Currado,[9] but from him I am descended. To my own I bore the love that is refined here."

"Oh," said I to him, "through your lands I have never been, but where do men dwell in all Europe that they are not renowned? The fame that honors your house proclaims alike its lords and its district, so that he knows of them who has never been there; and I swear to you, so may I go above, that your honored race does not strip itself of the glory of the purse and of the sword. Custom and nature so privilege it, that though the wicked head turn the world awry, it alone goes right and scorns the evil path."

And he, "Now go, for the sun shall not lie seven times in the bed that the Ram covers and bestrides with all four feet before this courteous opinion will be nailed in the midst of your head, with stronger nails than men's talk, if course of judgment be not stayed."

CANTO IX

The concubine of old Tithonus[1] was now showing white on the balcony of the East, forth from her sweet lover's arms; her forehead was glittering with gems, set in the form of the cold animal that strikes men with its tail. And in the place where we were night had taken two of the steps with which she climbs, and already the third was bending down its wings when I, who had somewhat of Adam with me, being overcome with sleep, lay me down on the grass there where all five of us were already seated.

At the hour near morning when the swallow begins her sad lays, perhaps in memory of her former woes, and when our mind, more a pilgrim from the flesh and less captive to thoughts, is in its visions almost divine,[2] I seemed to see, in a dream, an eagle poised in the sky, with feathers of gold, its wings outspread, and prepared to swoop.[3] And I seemed to be in the place where Ganymede[4] abandoned his own company, when he was caught up to the supreme consistory; and I thought within myself, "Perhaps it is wont to strike only here, and perhaps disdains to carry anyone upward in its claws from any other place." Then it seemed to me that, having wheeled a while, it descended terrible as a thunderbolt and snatched me upwards as far as the fire: there it seemed that it and I burned; and the imagined fire so scorched me that perforce my sleep was broken.

Even as Achilles started up, turning his awakened eyes about him and not knowing where he was, when his mother carried him off, sleeping in her arms, from Chiron to Skyros,[5] whence later the Greeks took him away; so did I start, as soon as sleep fled from my face, and I grew pale, like one who is chilled with terror. My comfort was alone beside me, and the sun was already more than two hours high, and my face was turned to the sea.

"Have no fear," said my lord, "take confidence, for all is well with us; do not hold back, but put forth all your strength. You are now arrived at Purgatory: see the cliff there that encloses it about; see the entrance there where it appears cleft. A while ago, in the dawn that precedes the day, when your soul was sleeping within you, upon the flowers that adorn the place down there, came a lady who said, 'I am Lucy;[6] let me take this man who is sleeping, so will I speed him on his way.' Sordello remained, and the other noble souls. She took you, and when the day was bright she went on upwards and I in her steps. Here she laid you down; but first her beautiful eyes showed me that open entrance; then she and slumber together went away."[7]

Like a perplexed man who is reassured,

whose fear changes to confidence when the truth is revealed to him, so I was changed; and when my leader saw me free from care he moved on up the slope, and I behind him, toward the height.

You see well, reader, that I uplift my theme: do not wonder, therefore, if I sustain it with greater art.

We drew near and came to a point from which, where at first there appeared to be merely a break, like a fissure that divides a wall, I saw a gate, with three steps beneath for going up to it, of different colors, and a warder who as yet spoke not a word. And as I looked more and more intently I saw that he was seated upon the topmost step, and in his face he was such that I endured it not. In his hand he had a naked sword, which so reflected the rays on us that often in vain I directed my eyes upon it.

"Say from there, what is it you seek?" he began to say; "Where is the escort? Take care lest the coming upward be to your hurt."

"A heavenly lady who knows these things well," my master answered him, "said to us just now: 'Go that way, there is the gate.' "

"And may she speed your steps to good!" began again the courteous doorkeeper; "Come forward, then, to our stairs."

We then came on, and the first step was white marble so polished and clear that I mirrored myself in it in my true likeness; the second was darker than perse and was of a stone rugged and burnt, cracked in its length and in its breadth. The third, which lies massy above, seemed to me of porphyry as flaming red as blood that spurts from a vein. Upon this step the angel of God held both his feet, seated upon the threshold that seemed to me to be of adamant.[8] Up by the three steps, with my good will, my leader drew me, saying, "Beg him humbly that he withdraw the bolt."

I threw myself devoutly at the holy feet; I besought for mercy's sake that he would open to me, but first I smote three times upon my breast. Seven P's[9] he traced on my forehead with the point of his sword and said, "See that you wash away these wounds when you are within."

Ashes, or earth that is dug out dry, would be of one color with his vesture, and from beneath it he drew two keys, the one of gold and the other of silver. First with the white and then with the yellow he did so to the gate that I was content.

"Whenever one of these keys fails so that it does not turn rightly in the lock," he said to us, "this passage does not open. The one is more precious; but the other requires great skill and wisdom before it will unlock, for this is the one that disentangles the knot. From Peter I hold them, and he told me to err rather in opening than in keeping shut, if but the people prostrate themselves at my feet." Then he pushed open the door of the sacred portal, saying, "Enter; but I bid you know that he who looks back returns outside again."

When the pivots of that sacred portal, which are of metal resounding and strong, were turned within their hinges, Tarpea roared not so loud nor showed itself so stubborn, when the good Metellus[10] was taken from it, leaving it lean thereafter. I turned attentive to the first note, and "*Te Deum laudamus*"[11] I seemed to hear in a voice mingled with the sweet music. What I heard gave me the same impression we sometimes get when people are singing with an organ, and now the words are clear and now are not.

CANTO X

When we were within the threshold of the gate which the souls' wrong love disuses, making the crooked way seem straight, I heard by its resounding that it was closed again; and if I had turned my eyes to it, what would have been a fitting excuse for my fault?

We were climbing through a cleft in the rock, which kept bending one way and the other, like a wave that goes and comes. "Here must we use a little skill," my leader began, "in keeping close, now here, now there, to the side that recedes." And this made our steps so scant that the waning orb of the moon had regained its bed to sink to rest before we came forth from that needle's eye. But when we were free and out in the open above, where the mountain draws back, I weary and each of us uncertain of our way, we stopped on a level place more solitary than roads through deserts. From its edge, bordering the void, to the foot of the high bank which rises sheer, a human body would measure in three lengths; and as far as my eye could make its flight, now on the left and now on the right, such this terrace seemed to me. Not yet had we moved our feet on it when I perceived that the encircling bank (which, being vertical, lacked means of ascent) was of pure white marble, and was adorned with such carvings that not only Polycletus[1] but Nature herself[2] would there be put to shame.

The angel who came to earth[3] with the decree of peace, wept for since many a year, which opened Heaven from its long ban,[4] before us there appeared so vividly graven in gentle mien that it seemed not a silent image: one would have sworn that he was saying, "*Ave*," for there she was imaged who turned the key to open the supreme love,[5] and these words were imprinted in her attitude: "*Ecce ancilla Dei*,"[6] as expressly as a figure is stamped on wax.

"Do not keep your mind on one part only," said the sweet master, who had me on the side where people have their heart; wherefore I moved my eyes and saw beyond Mary, on the same side as was he who prompted me, another story set in the rock; wherefore I went past Virgil and drew near to it, that it might be displayed before my eyes. There, carved in the same marble,[7] were the cart and the oxen drawing the holy ark, because of which men fear an office not given in charge.[8] In front appeared people, and all the company, divided into seven choirs, made two of my senses say, the one "No," the other, "Yes, they are singing." In like manner, by the smoke of the incense that was imaged there my eyes and nose were made discordant with *yes* and *no*. There, preceding the blessed vessel, dancing girt up, was the humble Psalmist, and on that occasion he was both more and less than king. Opposite, figured at a window of a great palace, was Michal looking on, like a woman vexed and scornful.

I moved my feet from where I was to examine close at hand another story which I saw gleaming white beyond Michal. There storied was the high glory of the Roman prince whose worth moved Gregory to his great victory: I mean the Emperor Trajan.[9] And a poor widow was at his bridle in attitude of weeping and of grief. Round about him appeared a trampling and throng of horsemen, and above them the eagles in gold moved visibly in the wind. Among all these the poor woman seemed to say, "My lord, do me vengeance for my son who is slain, wherefore my heart is pierced."

And he seemed to answer her, "Wait now till I return." And she, "My lord," like one whose grief is urgent, "and if you do not return?" And he, "He who shall be in my place will do it for you." And she, "What shall another's well-doing avail you, if you forget your own?" He then, "Now take comfort, for I must discharge my duty before I go: justice requires it, and pity bids me stay."

He who never beheld any new thing wrought this visible speech, new to us because here it is not found.

While I was taking delight in gazing on the images of humilities so great, and for their Craftsman's sake precious to behold, "Lo, here are many people," murmured the poet, "but they come with slow step: they will direct us on to the high stairs." My eyes, which were content to behold novelties whereof they are fain, were not slow in turning towards him.

But, reader, I would not have you turned from good resolution for hearing how God wills the debt shall be paid. Heed not the form of the pain: think what follows, think that at the worst beyond the great Judgment it cannot go.

"Master," I began, "what I see moving towards us does not seem to me persons, but what it is I do not know, my sight wanders so." And he to me, "The grievous condition of their torment doubles them to the ground, so that my own eyes at first had contention therewith. But look closely there and with your sight disentangle that which comes beneath those stones: already you may discern how each beats his breast."

O proud Christians, wretched and weary, who, sick in mental vision, put trust in backward steps: are you not aware that we are worms, born to form the angelic butterfly that flies unto judgment without defenses? Why does your mind soar up aloft, since you are as it were imperfect insects, even as the worm in which full form is wanting?

As for corbel to support a ceiling or a roof, sometimes a figure is seen to join the knees to the breast—which, unreal, begets real distress in one who sees it—so fashioned did I see these when I gave good heed. They were truly more or less contracted according as they had more and less upon their backs; and he who showed the most suffering in his looks, seemed to say, weeping, "I can no more."

CANTO XI

"Our father, who art in Heaven, not circumscribed, but through the greater love Thou hast for Thy first works[1] on high,

"Praisèd be Thy name and Thy worth by every creature, as it is meet to render thanks to Thy sweet effluence.

"May the peace of Thy kingdom come to us, for we cannot reach it of ourselves, if it come not, for all our striving.

"As Thine angels make sacrifice to Thee of their will, singing Hosanna, so let men make of theirs.

"Give us this day our daily manna, without which he backward goes through this harsh desert who most labors to advance.

"And as we forgive everyone the wrong we have suffered, even do Thou in loving-kindness pardon, and regard not our desert.

"Our strength, which is easily overcome, put not to trial with the old adversary, but deliver us from him, who so spurs it.

"This last petition, dear Lord, we make not now for ourselves, for there is no need, but for those who remain behind us."

Thus, praying good speed for themselves and for us, those shades were going under the burden, like that of which one sometimes dreams, unequally anguished all of them, wearily making their rounds on the first terrace, purging away the mists of the world. If there they always ask good for us, what for them can here be said or done, by those who have their will rooted in good? Truly we ought to help them wash away the stains they have borne hence, so that pure and light they may go forth to the starry wheels.

"Ah, so may justice and pity soon disburden you, that you may spread your wing which may uplift you according to your desire, show us on which hand we may go most quickly to the stair; and if there is more than one passage, show us that which is least steep, for he who comes with me here, for the burden of Adam's flesh wherewith he is clothed, against his will is slow at climbing up."

It was not plain from whom came the words that were returned to these my leader had spoken, but they were, "Come with us to the right along this bank, and you will find the opening where it is possible for a living man to climb. And were I not hindered by the stone that subdues my proud neck, so that I must hold my face down, I would look at this man who is yet alive and is not named, to see if I know him, and make him piteous of this burden. I was Italian,[2] the son of a great Tuscan: Guiglielmo Aldobrandesco[3] was my father; I know not if his name was ever with you. The ancient blood[4] and the gallant deeds of my ancestors made me so arrogant that, not thinking of our common mother,[5] I held all men in such exceeding scorn that it was the death of me, as the Sienese know and every child in Campagnatico knows. I am Omberto; and not only to me does pride work ill, but it has dragged all my kinsfolk with it into calamity; and for this I must bear this weight, until God is satisfied, here among the dead, since I did it not among the living."

Listening, I bent down my face; and one of them, not he who spoke, twisted himself beneath the weight that encumbers them, and saw me and knew me, and was calling out, trying hard to keep his eyes fixed on me who all stooping went along with them.

"Oh," I said to him, "are you not Oderisi,[6] the honor of Gubbio[7] and the honor of that art which in Paris is called 'illumination'?"

"Brother," he said, "more smiling are the pages that Franco Bolognese[8] paints: the honor is now all his—and mine in part. Truly I should not have been so courteous while I lived, because of the great desire for excellence whereon my heart was set. For such pride the fee is paid here; nor should I yet be here, were it not that, having power to sin, I turned to God. O empty glory of human powers! how briefly lasts the green upon the top, if it is not followed by barbarous times! Cimabue thought to hold the field in painting, and now Giotto[9] has the cry, so that the other's fame is dim; so has the one Guido taken from the other the glory of our tongue—and he perchance is born that shall chase the one and the other from the nest. Earthly fame is naught but a breath of wind, which now comes hence and now comes thence, changing its name because it changes quarter. What greater fame will you have if you strip off your flesh when it is old than if you had died before giving up *pappo* and *dindi,* when a thousand years shall have passed, which is a shorter space compared to the eternal than the movement of the eyelids to that circle which is slowest turned in heaven? With him who moves so slowly[10] along the way in front of me all Tuscany resounded, and now there is scarcely a whisper of him in Siena,[11] whereof he was lord when the rage of Florence was destroyed,[12] which was as proud then as it is prostitute now. Your repute is as the hue of grass, which comes and goes, and he discolors it through whom it springs green from the ground."

And I to him, "Your true words fill my heart with good humility and abate in me a great swelling; but who is he of whom you just now spoke?"

"He is Provenzan Salvani," he answered, "and he is here because, in his presumption, he thought to bring all Siena into his grasp. Thus has he gone and thus he goes without rest, since he died: such coin does he pay in satisfaction who yonder is too daring."

And I, "If the spirit that awaits the verge of life before he repents abides there below and mounts not up here, unless holy prayers assist him, until as much time passes as he has lived, how was it granted him to come up here?"

"When he was living with greatest glory," said he, "he stationed himself of his own free will in the marketplace of Siena, putting away all shame; and there, to deliver his friend from the pains he was suffering in Charles' prison, he brought himself to tremble in every vein. No more will I say, and I know that I speak darkly; but, short time will pass before your neighbors shall so act that you will be able to interpret this: such a deed released him from those confines."

CANTO XII

Side by side, like oxen that go yoked, I went on beside that burdened soul, as long as the gentle teacher allowed it; but when he said, "Leave him and press on, for here it is well that with sail and oars each urge his bark along with all his might," I raised my body erect again as one should walk, though my thoughts remained bowed down and shrunken.

I had set out and was gladly following in my master's steps and both of us were now showing how light of foot we were, and he said to me, "Turn down your eyes: it will be well for you to solace your way by seeing the bed beneath your feet."

As, in order that there be memory of them, the stones in the church floor over the buried dead bear figured what they were before; wherefore many a time men weep for them there, at the prick of memory that spurs only the faithful: so I saw sculptured there, but of better semblance in respect of skill, all that for pathway juts out from the mountain.

I saw, on the one side, him who was created nobler than any other creature fall as lightning from heaven.

I saw Briareus, on the other side, pierced by the celestial bolt, lying heavy on the ground in mortal chill.

I saw Thymbraeus,[1] I saw Pallas[2] and Mars, still armed, around their father, gazing on the scattered limbs of the giants.[3]

I saw Nimrod[4] at the foot of his great labor, as if bewildered; and there looking on were the people who were proud with him in Shinar.

O Niobe,[5] with what grieving eyes did I see you traced on the roadway between seven and seven children slain!

O Saul,[6] how upon your own sword did you appear there dead on Gilboa,[7] which never thereafter felt rain or dew!

O mad Arachne,[8] so did I see you already half spider, wretched on the shreds of the work which to your own hurt was wrought by you!

O Rehoboam,[9] there your image does not seem to threaten now, but a chariot bears it off full of terror, and no one is in pursuit!

It showed also, that hard pavement, how Alcmaeon[10] made the luckless ornament seem costly to his mother.

It showed how his sons fell upon Sennacherib[11] within the temple, and how they left him there slain.

It showed the destruction and the cruel slaughter which Tomyris wrought when she said to Cyrus, "You did thirst for blood, and with blood I fill you."[12]

It showed how the Assyrians fled in the rout, when Holofernes[13] was slain, and also the remains of that slaughter.

I saw Troy in ashes and in caverns: O Ilion, how cast down and vile it showed you—the sculpture which is there discerned!

What master was he of brush or of pencil who drew the forms and lineaments which there would make every subtle genius wonder? Dead the dead, and the living seemed alive. He who saw the reality of all I trod upon, while I went bent down, saw not better than I!

Now wax proud, and on with haughty visage, you children of Eve,[14] and bend not down your face to see your evil path!

Already more of the mountain was circled by us and much more of the sun's course was sped than my mind, not free, had reckoned, when he who was always looking ahead as he went began, "Lift up your head, there is now no more time for going thus absorbed. See there an angel who is making ready to come towards us. See how the sixth handmaiden is returning from the service of the day. Adorn with reverence your bearing and your face, that it may please him to send us upward. Remember that this day will never dawn again."

Right well was I used to his admonitions never to lose time, so that in that matter his speech could not be dark to me.

The fair creature came towards us, clothed in white and such in his face as seems the tremulous morning star. He opened his arms and then spread his wings and said, "Come: the steps are at hand here, and henceforth the climb is easy. To this bidding there are very few that come: O race of men, born to fly upward, why do you fall so at a breath of wind?"

He brought us where the rock is cleft: there he struck his wings across my forehead and then promised me safe journeying. As on the right hand, for climbing the hill where stands the church above Rubaconte[15] that dominates the well-guided city[16] the bold scarp of the ascent is broken by the stairs which were made in a time when the record and the stave were safe,[17] so the bank that falls there very steeply from the other circle is made easier, but the high rock presses close on this side and on that.

As we were turning our steps there, "*Beati pauperes spiritu*"[18] was sung so sweetly as no words would tell. Ah, how different these passages from those of Hell, for here the entrance is with songs, and down there with fierce laments.

Now we were mounting by the holy stairs, and it seemed to me I was far lighter than before, on the level; wherefore I said, "Master, tell me, what weight has been lifted from me that I feel almost no weariness as I go on?" He answered, "When the P's that are still left on your brow[19] all but effaced shall be, as one is, quite erased, your feet shall be so conquered by good will that not only will they not feel fatigue, but it will be a delight to them to be urged upwards."

Then did I like those who go with something on their head unknown to them, save that the signs of others make them suspect, so that the hand lends its aid to make sure, and searches and finds, fulfilling the office which sight cannot accomplish; and with the spread fingers of my right hand I found only six of the letters that he of the keys had traced on my temples: and observing this my leader smiled.

CANTO XIII

We were now at the top of the stairway where a second time the mountain is cut away which, by our ascent of it, frees us from evil. There a terrace girds the hill around, like the first, except that its arc makes a sharper curve. No figure is there, nor any image that may be seen, but only the bank and the bare road and the livid color of the stone.

"If to inquire one waits for people here," the poet was saying, "I fear that perhaps our choice may be delayed too long." Then he set his eyes fixedly on the sun, made of his right side a center for his movement, and brought round his left. "O sweet light, by trust in which I enter on this new road, do you guide us," he said, "with the guidance that is needful in this place. You warm the world, you shed light upon it: if other reason urge not to the contrary, your beams must ever be our guide."

As far as here is counted for a mile, even so far there had we now gone, in but short time, because of ready will; and flying towards us were heard, but not seen, spirits uttering courteous invitations to the table of love.[1] The first voice that passed flying, called out loudly, "*Vinum non habent*," and passed on behind us repeating it; and before it had become wholly inaudible through distance, another passed, crying, "I am Orestes,"[2] and also did not stay.

"O father," said I, "what voices are these?" and even as I was asking, lo! the third voice saying, "Love them from whom you have suffered wrong." And my good master, "This circle scourges the sin of envy, and therefore from love the cords of the whip are drawn. The curb must be of the opposite sound: I think you will hear it, as I judge, before you come to the pass of pardon. But fix your eyes full steadily through the air and you will see people sitting there in front of us, and each is seated against the rock." Then more than before I opened my eyes: I looked in front of me and saw shades with cloaks not different in color from the stone. And when we were a little farther on, I heard cries of, "Mary, pray for us!" then "Michael" and "Peter" and "All Saints."

I do not believe there goes on earth today a man so hard that he would not have been pierced with pity at what I saw then, for when I had come so near that their condition came to me distinct, great grief was wrung from my eyes. They appeared to be covered with coarse haircloth, and one supported the other with his shoulder, and all were supported by the bank. Even so the blind who are destitute take their place at pardons to beg for their needs;[3] and one sinks his head on the other, so that pity may quickly be awakened in others, not only by the sound of their words, but by their appearance, which pleads not less. And even as the sun profits not the blind, so to the shades in the place I speak of, heaven's light denies its bounty, for all their eyelids an iron wire pierces and stitches up, even as is done to an untamed hawk because it stays not quiet.

It seemed to me that I did them wrong as I went my way, seeing others, not being seen myself; wherefore I turned to my wise counsel. Well knew he what the dumb would say, and therefore did not wait for my question, but said, "Speak, and be brief and to the point."

Virgil was coming with me on that side of the terrace from which one could fall, since no parapet surrounds it; and on the other side of me were the devout shades that through the horrible seam were pressing out the tears that bathed their cheeks. I turned to them, and began, "O people assured of seeing the light on high which alone is the object of your desire, so may grace soon clear the scum of your conscience that the stream of memory may flow down through it pure, tell me, for it will be gracious and dear to me, if there is any soul here among you that is Italian—and perhaps it will be well for him if I know of it."

"O my brother, each one here is a citizen of a true city: but you mean one that lived in Italy while a pilgrim." This I seemed to hear for answer somewhat farther on from where I was, wherefore I made myself heard yet more that way; and among the rest I saw a shade that looked expectant, and if any would ask how, it was lifting up its chin in the manner of the blind.

"Spirit," I said, "who subdue yourself in order to ascend, if it be you who answered me, make yourself known to me either by place or name."

"I was of Siena,"[4] it replied, "and with these others here I mend my sinful life, weeping to Him, that He may grant himself to us. Sapient I was not, although Sapia was my name; and at others' hurt I rejoiced far more than at my own good fortune. But lest you think that I deceive you, hear if I was not mad, as I tell you, when I was already descending the arc of my years. My townsmen had joined battle near Colle[5] with their adversaries, and I prayed God for that which He had willed: there were they routed and turned back in the bitter steps of flight; and, seeing the chase, I was filled with joy beyond all bounds, so much that I turned upwards my impudent face, crying out to God, 'Now I fear Thee no more,' as the blackbird did for a little fair weather. I sought peace with God on the brink of my life, and my debt would not yet be reduced by penitence, had not Pier Pettinaio[6] remembered me in his holy prayers, who in his charity did grieve for me. But who are you that go asking of our condition and bear your eyes unsewn, as I believe, and breathing do speak?"

"My eyes," I said, "will yet be taken from me here, but for short time only, because they have little offended with looks of envy. Far greater is the fear that holds my soul in suspense, of the torment below, so that already the load down there is heavy upon me."

And she to me, "Who then has led you up here among us, if you think to return below?"

And I, "He that is with me here and is silent; and I am alive, and do you therefore ask of me, spirit elect, if you would that yonder I should yet move my mortal feet for you."

"Oh, this is so strange a thing to hear," she answered, "that it is a great token of God's love for you. Therefore help me sometimes with your prayers. And I pray you by all you most desire that, if ever you tread the soil of Tuscany, you restore my name among my kindred. You will see them among that vain people who put their trust in Talamone,[7] and will lose more hope there than in finding the Diana[8]— but there the admirals will lose the most."

CANTO XIV

"Who is this that circles our mountain before death has given him flight, and opens and shuts his eyes at will?"[1]

"I know not who he is, but I know he is not alone. Question him, since you are nearer, and greet him kindly, that he may speak."

Thus two spirits, leaning towards each other, were discoursing of me there on my right; then they turned up their faces to speak to me, and one of them said, "O soul that, still fixed in your body, go on toward Heaven, for charity console us and tell us whence you come and who you are: for you make us marvel so greatly at the grace that is given you as needs must something that never was before."

And I, "Through mid-Tuscany there winds a little stream that rises in Falterona,[2] and a course of a hundred miles does not suffice for it. From its banks I bring this body. To tell you who I am would be to speak in vain, for my name as yet makes no great sound."

"If I rightly penetrate your meaning," he that had spoken first then answered me, "you speak of the Arno."

And the other said to him, "Why did he conceal that river's name, even as one does some horrible thing?"

And the shade that was questioned acquitted himself thus, "I do not know, but it is fitting indeed that the name of such a valley should perish, for from its source (where the rugged mountain-chain from which Pelorus is cut off so teems with water that in few places is it surpassed)[3] down to where it yields itself to replace that which the sky draws up from the sea, whence rivers have that which flows in them, virtue is fled from as an enemy by all, as if it were a snake, either through some misfortune of the place or from evil habit that goads them; wherefore the dwellers in the wretched valley

have so changed their nature that it seems as though Circe[4] had them at pasture. Among filthy hogs,[5] fitter for acorns than for any food made for human use, it first directs its feeble course. Then, coming lower, it finds curs more snarling than their power warrants, and from them it scornfully turns away its snout. It goes on falling, and the more it swells the more does the accursed and ill-fated ditch find the dogs turned to wolves.[6] Then, after descending through many a deep gorge, it finds foxes so full of fraud that they have no fear that any trap may take them. Nor will I refrain from speech because another hears me (and it will be well for him if he keep in mind that which true prophecy discloses to me). I see your grandson[7] who becomes a hunter of those wolves on the bank of the savage stream, and he strikes them all with terror; he sells their flesh still living, then slaughters them like worn-out cattle: many he deprives of life, himself of honor. Bloody he comes forth from the dismal wood: he leaves it such that in a thousand years from now it will not rewood itself as it was before."

As at the announcement of grievous ills the face of him who listens is troubled, from whatsoever side the danger may assail him, so I saw the other soul, who had turned to hear, become disturbed and sad, when it had taken in these words.

The speech of the one and the look of the other made me desire to know their names, and urgently I questioned them; wherefore the spirit who had spoken to me before began again, "You would have me consent to do for you what you will not for me; but since God wills that so much grace of His shine forth in you, I will not be chary with you; know therefore that I was Guido del Duca.[8] My blood was so inflamed with envy that if I had seen a man become glad you would have seen me suffused with lividness. Of my sowing I reap such straw: O human race, why do you set your hearts where there must be exclusion of partnership?

"This is Rinieri,[9] this is the glory and the honor of the house of Calboli, where none since has made himself heir to his worth. And not his blood alone, between the Po and the mountains and the sea and the Reno,[10] has been stripped of the virtues required for earnest and for pastime, for within these bounds the land is so choked with poisonous growths that tardily would they now be rooted out by tillage. Where is the good Lizio and Arrigo Mainardi,[11] Pier Traversaro and Guido di Carpigna?[12] O men of Romagna turned to bastards! When will a Fabbro[13] take root again in Bologna? when in Faenza a Bernardin di Fosco,[14] noble scion of a lowly plant? Marvel not, Tuscan, if I weep when I remember Guido da Prata,[15] and Ugolin d'Azzo[16] who lived among us, Federigo Tignoso[17] and his company, the Traversaro[18] house and the Anastagi[19]—the one family and the other now without an heir—the ladies and the knights, the toils and the sports to which love and courtesy moved us, there where hearts have become so wicked! O Bretinoro,[20] why do you not flee away, now that your family has departed, with many another, in order to escape corruption? Bagnacaval[21] does well that gets no sons; and Castrocaro[22] ill, and Conio[23] worse, that yet troubles to beget such counts. The Pagani[24] will do well, when their Devil[25] takes himself off, but not so that unsullied witness shall ever be left of them. O Ugolin de' Fantolini,[26] your name is safe, since no more are looked for who might blacken it by degeneracy. But, Tuscan, go on your way now, for it now pleases me far more to weep than to talk, so has our discourse wrung my heart."

We knew that those dear souls heard us go, therefore by their silence they made us confident of the way. After we were left alone and were journeying on, a voice like lightning when it cleaves the air came counter to us, saying, "Everyone that finds me shall slay me," and fled like thunder that rolls away, if suddenly the cloud is rent. As soon as our hearing had respite from it, lo, the other with so loud a crash that it was like a thunderclap that follows quickly, "I am Aglauros[27] that was turned to stone"; and then, to draw close to the poet I made a step to the right, not forward.

The air was now quiet on every side; and he said to me, "That was the hard bit which should hold man within his bounds: but you take the bait, so that the old adversary's hook draws you to him, and therefore little avails curb, or lure. The heavens call to you and circle about you, displaying to you their eternal splendors, and your eyes gaze only on the earth: wherefore He smites you who sees all."

CANTO XV

As much as between the end of the third hour and the beginning of the day appears of the sphere that is always playing like a child, so much now appeared to be left of the sun's course toward nightfall: it was evening there and here it was midnight. And the beams were striking us full in the face, for the mountain was now so far circled by us that we were going straight toward the sunset, when I felt my brow weighed down by the splendor far more than before, and the things not known were a wonder to me. Wherefore I lifted my hands above my eyebrows and made for me the shade that lessens excess of light.

As when the beam leaps from the water or the mirror to the opposite quarter, rising at the same angle as it descends, and at equal distance departs as much from the line of the falling stone, even as experiment and science show; so it seemed to me that I was struck by light reflected there in front of me, from which my sight was quick to flee.

"What is that, gentle father," I said, "from which I cannot screen my eyes so that it may avail me, and which seems to be moving towards us?"

"Do not marvel if the family of Heaven still dazzles you," he answered me; "this is a messenger that comes to invite to the ascent. Soon will it be that the seeing of these will not be hard for you, but as great a delight as nature has fitted you to feel."

When we had reached the blessed angel, with a glad voice he said, "Enter here to a stairway far less steep than the others."

We were mounting, having already departed thence, and "Beati misericordes"[1] was sung behind, and "Rejoice, you that overcome."

My master and I, we two alone, were journeying upward, and I thought as we went to gain profit from his words, and I turned to him and asked, "What did the spirit of Romagna mean when he spoke of 'exclusion' and 'partnership'?" Whereupon he to me, "Of his own worst fault he knows the harm, and therefore it is little wonder if he reprove it, that it may be less mourned for. Because your desires are centered there where the portion is lessened by partnership, envy moves the bellows to your sighs. But if the love of the highest sphere turned upwards your desire, that fear would not be at your heart. For there, the more they are who say 'ours,' the more of good does each possess, and the more of charity burns in that cloister."[2]

"I am more hungering to be satisfied," I said, "than if I had at first been silent, and more of doubt do I assemble in my mind. How can it be that a good distributed can make more possessors richer with itself than if it is possessed by a few?"

And he to me, "Because you still set your mind on earthly things, you gather darkness from true light. That infinite and ineffable Good that is there above speeds to love as a ray of light comes to a bright body. So much it gives of itself as it finds of ardor, so that how far soever love extends, the more does the Eternal Goodness increase upon it; and the more souls there are that are enamored there above, the more there are for loving well, and the more love is there, and like a mirror one reflects to the other. And if my discourse does not appease your hunger, you shall see Beatrice and she will deliver you wholly from this and every other longing. Strive only that soon may be erased, as are the other two already, the five wounds, which are healed by being painful."

As I was about to say, "You satisfy me," I saw that I had reached the next circle, so that my eager eyes held me silent. There I seemed suddenly to be caught up in an ecstatic vision and to see persons in a temple, and a woman about to enter, with the tender attitude of a mother, saying "My son, why have you done so to us? Behold your father and I sought you, sorrowing"; and as she was silent, that which first appeared was there no more.

Then there appeared to me another woman, with those waters streaming down her cheeks that grief distills when it arises from great resentment against another,[3] and she was saying, "If you are lord of the city for whose name was so great strife among the gods, and whence all knowledge sparkles, avenge you of those daring arms which embraced our daughter, O Pisistratus!" And her lord seemed to me kindly and gently to answer her, with placid mien, "What shall we do to one who desires ill to us, if he who loves us is condemned by us?"

Then I saw people, kindled with the fire of anger, stoning a youth to death, and ever crying out loudly to each other, "Kill, kill!" and him I saw sink to the ground, for already death was heavy upon him, but of his eyes he ever made gates unto heaven, praying to the high Lord in such torture, with that look which unlocks pity, that He would forgive his persecutors.[4]

When my mind returned outwardly to the things that are real outside of it, I recognized my not false errors. My leader, who could see me acting like one who frees himself from sleep, said, "What ails you, that you cannot control yourself, but have come more than half a league veiling your eyes and with staggering legs, like a man overcome by wine or sleep?"

"O my sweet father," I said, "if you will listen to me I will tell you what it was that appeared to me when my legs were so taken from me."

And he, "If you had a hundred masks upon your face, your thoughts however slight would not be hidden from me. That which you saw was shown you in order that you might not refuse to open your heart to the waters of peace, which are poured from the eternal fountain. I did not ask 'What ails you?' for the reason of one who looks only with unseeing eyes when another's body lies insensible, but I asked in order to give strength to your feet. So must the sluggish be spurred who are slow to use their waking hour when it returns."

We were journeying on through the evening, straining our eyes forward as far as we could against the bright late beams, when lo, little by little, a smoke dark as night, rolling towards us; nor was there room there to escape from it: this took from us our sight and the pure air.

CANTO XVI

Gloom of hell, or night bereft of every planet under a barren sky obscured by clouds as much as it can be, never made a veil to my sight so thick nor of stuff so harsh to the sense, as that smoke which covered us there, so that it did not let the eye stay open; wherefore my wise and trusty escort drew to my side and offered me his shoulder. Even as a blind man goes behind his guide that he may not stray or knock against what might injure or perhaps kill him, so I went through that bitter and foul air, listening to my leader, who kept saying, "Take care that you are not cut off from me."

I heard voices, and each one seemed to pray for peace and for mercy to the Lamb of God that takes sins away.[1] Their beginnings were always "*Agnus Dei*"; one word was with them all, and one measure, so that full concord seemed to be among them.

"Are these spirits, master, that I hear?" I said; and he answered me, "You judge aright, and they go loosening the knot of anger."

"Who then are you that cleave our smoke and speak of us even as if you still measured time by calends?" Thus spoke a voice; wherefore my master said, "Answer, and ask if by this way one goes up." And I, "O creature that are cleansing yourself to return fair to Him who made you, you shall hear a marvel if you follow me."

"I will follow you as far as is allowed me," it replied, "and if the smoke does not let us see, hearing will keep us together instead."

Then I began, "With those swaddling-bands which death unbinds I am journeying upwards, and I came here through the anguish of Hell; and since God has received me so far into His grace that He wills that I see His court[2] in a manner wholly outside modern usage, do not hide from me who you were before death, but tell me, and tell me if I am on the right way to the passage; and your words shall be our escort."

"I was Lombard and was called Marco;[3] I knew the world and loved that worth at which all now have unbent the bow. For mounting up you are going aright." Thus he replied, then added, "I pray you that you pray for me when you are above."

And I to him, "I pledge my faith to you to do what you ask of me. But I am bursting from a doubt within if I do not free myself from it. At first it was simple, and now it is made double by your statement, which makes certain to me, both here and elsewhere, that with which I couple it. The world is indeed as utterly deserted by every virtue as you declare to me, and pregnant and overspread with iniquity, but I beg you to point out to me the cause, so that I may see it and show it to men, for one places it in the heavens and another here below."

He first heaved a deep sigh which grief wrung into "Ah me!" then began, "Brother, the world is blind, and truly you come from it! You who are living refer every cause upward to the heavens alone, as if they of necessity moved all things with them. If this were so, free will would be destroyed in you, and there would be no justice in happiness for good or grief for evil. The heavens initiate your movements: I do not say all of them, but supposing I did say so, a light is given you to know good and evil, and free will, which if it endure fatigue in its first battles with the heavens, afterwards, if it is well nurtured, it conquers completely. You lie subject, in your freedom, to a greater power and to a better nature, and that creates the mind in you which the heavens have not in their charge. Therefore, if the present world goes astray, in you is the cause, in you let it be sought: and I will now be a true scout to you in this.

"From His hands, who fondly loves it before it exists, comes forth after the fashion of a child that sports, now weeping, now laughing, the simple little soul, which knows nothing, save that, proceeding from a glad Maker, it turns eagerly to what delights it. First it tastes the savor of a trifling good: there it is beguiled and runs after it, if guide or curb bend not its love. Wherefore it was needful to impose law as a bridle, it was needful to have a ruler who could discern at least the tower of the true city. Laws there are, but who puts his hand to them? None, because the shepherd that leads may chew the cud but has not the hoofs divided. Wherefore the people, who see their guide snatch only at that good whereof they are greedy, feed upon that, and seek no further. Well can you see that ill-guidance is what has made the world wicked, and not nature that is corrupt in you. Rome, which made the world good,[4] was wont to have two Suns, which made visible both the one road and the other, that of the world and that of God. The one has quenched the other, and the sword is joined to the crook: and the one together with the other must perforce go ill—since joined, the one does not fear the other. If you do not believe me, look well at the ear, for every plant is known by the seed.

"On the land that is watered by the Adige and the Po[5] valor and courtesy were once to be found, before Frederick met with strife.[6] Now anyone may safely pass there who out of shame would avoid speaking with the good or coming near them. There are yet indeed three old men in whom the ancient times rebuke the new, and it seems to them long till God remove them to a better life: Currado da Palazzo[7] and the good Gherardo[8] and Guido da Castel,[9] who is better named, in the French fashion, the simple Lombard. Tell henceforth that the Church of Rome, by confounding in itself two governments, falls in the mire and befouls both itself and its burden."[10]

"O Marco mine," I said, "you reason well; and now I perceive why the sons of Levi were excluded from inheritance.[11] But what Gherardo is this who, you say, remains for sample of the extinct people, in reproach of the barbarous age?"

"Either your speech beguiles me, or it makes trial of me," he answered, "for you, speaking to me in Tuscan, seem to know nothing of the good Gherardo. I know him by no other added name, unless I took it from his daughter Gaia.[12] May God be with you, for I come with you no farther. Behold the brightness that rays through the smoke already whitening, and I must go—the angel is there—before I am seen by him."

So he turned back and would not hear me more.

CANTO XVII

Recall, reader, if ever in the mountains a mist has caught you, through which you could not see except as moles do through the skin, how, when the moist dense vapors begin to dissipate, the sphere of the sun enters feebly through them, and your fancy will quickly come to see how, at first, I saw the sun again, which was now at its setting. So, matching mine to the trusty steps of my master, I came forth from such a fog to the rays which were already dead on the low shores.

O imagination, that do sometimes so snatch us from outward things that we give no heed, though a thousand trumpets sound around us, who moves you if the sense affords you naught? A light moves you which takes form in heaven, of itself, or by a will that downward guides it.

Of her impious deed who changed her form into the bird that most delights to sing,[1] the impress appeared in my imagination, and at this my mind was so restrained within itself, that from outside came naught that was then received by it. Then rained down within the high fantasy one crucified, scornful and fierce in his mien, and so was he dying. Round about him were the great Ahasuerus, Esther his wife, and the just Mordecai who was in speech and deed so blameless.[2] And when this imagination burst of itself, like a bubble for which the water fails beneath which it was made, there rose in my vision a maiden, weeping sorely, and she was saying, "O Queen, why through anger have you willed to be naught? You have killed yourself in order not to lose Lavinia: now you have lost me! I am she who mourns, mother, at yours, before another's ruin."[3]

As sleep is broken, when on a sudden new light strikes on the closed eyes, and being broken, quivers before it wholly dies away, so my imagining fell down from me as soon as a light, brighter by far than that to which we are accustomed, smote on my face. I was turning to see where I was when a voice said, "Here is the ascent," which removed me from every other intent; and it gave to my desire to behold who it was that spoke such eagerness as never rests till it sees face to face. But, as the sun which oppresses our sight, and veils its own form by excess, so was my power failing me.

"This is a divine spirit that directs us to the way of the ascent without our asking, and hides itself by its own light. It does with us as one man with another, for he that waits for the asking and sees the need already sets himself unkindly toward denial. Now let us accord our steps to such an invitation; let us strive to ascend before it grows dark, for then it would not be possible until the day returns." Thus spoke my leader, and together we turned our footsteps to a stairway; and as soon as I was on the first step, near me I felt as it were the motion of a wing fanning my face, and I heard the words, "*Beati pacifici,* who are without evil wrath."[4]

Already the last rays before nightfall were lifted so high above us that the stars were appearing on many sides. "O my strength, why do you so melt away?" I said within myself, for I felt the power of my legs suspended. We stood where the stair went no higher and we were stopped there, even as a ship that arrives at the shore; and I listened a little if I might hear anything in the new circle. Then I turned to my master, and said,

"My sweet father, say what offense is purged here in the circle where we are: if our feet are stayed, do not stay your speech."

And he to me, "The love of good which comes short of its duty is here restored: here the ill-slackened oar is plied anew.[5] But that you may understand yet more clearly, turn your mind to me, and you shall gather some good fruit from our stay."

He began: "Neither Creator nor creature, my son, was ever without love, either natural or of the mind,[6] and this you know. The natural is always without error; but the other may err either through an evil object,[7] or through too much or too little vigor. While it is directed on the Primal Good, and on secondary goods observes right measure, it cannot be the cause of sinful pleasure. But when it is turned awry to evil, or speeds to good with more zeal, or with less, than it ought, against the Creator works His creature. Hence you can comprehend that love must needs be the seed in you of every virtue and of every action deserving punishment.

"Now, inasmuch as love can never turn its sight from the weal of its subject, all things are secure from self-hatred; and since no being can be conceived of as severed from the First, and as standing by itself, every creature is cut off from hatred of Him. It follows, if I distinguish rightly, that the evil we love is our neighbor's, and this love springs up in three ways in your clay. There is he that hopes to excel by the abasement of his neighbor, and solely for this desires that he be cast down from his greatness. There is he that fears to lose power, favor, honor, and fame, because another is exalted, by which he is so saddened that he loves the contrary. And there is he who seems so outraged by injury that he becomes greedy of vengeance, and such a one must needs contrive another's hurt. This threefold love is wept for down here below.[8]

"Now I would have you hear of the other, which hastens toward the good in faulty measure. Each one apprehends vaguely a good wherein the mind may find rest, and this it desires; wherefore each one strives to attain thereto. If lukewarm love draws you to see it

or to gain it, this terrace after due repentance torments you for it.

"Another good there is which does not make man happy, it is not happiness, it is not the good essence, the fruit and root of every good. The love which abandons itself to that is wept for above us in three circles, but how it is distinguished as threefold I do not say, that you may search it out for yourself."

CANTO XVIII

The lofty teacher had made an end of his discourse and was looking intently in my face to see if I was satisfied; and I, whom a fresh thirst was already goading, was silent outwardly, and within was saying, "Perhaps I irk him with too much questioning." But that true father, who was aware of the timid desire which did not declare itself, by speaking gave me courage to speak. Therefore I said, "Master, my sight is so quickened in your light that I discern clearly all that your discourse distinguishes or declares; wherefore, dear and gentle father, I pray that you expound love to me, to which you reduce every good action and its opposite."

"Direct on me the keen eyes of your understanding," he said, "and the error will be manifest to you of the blind who make themselves guides.

"The mind, which is created quick to love, is responsive to everything that pleases, as soon as by pleasure it is roused to action. Your faculty of apprehension draws an image from a real existence and displays it within you, so that it makes the mind turn to it; and if, thus turned, the mind inclines toward it, that inclination is love, that inclination is nature which is bound in you anew by pleasure. Then, even as fire moves upwards by reason of its form, being born to ascend thither where it lasts longest in its matter, so the captive mind enters into desire, which is a spiritual movement, and never rests until the thing loved makes it rejoice. Now it may be apparent to you how far the truth is hidden from the people who aver that every love is praiseworthy in itself, because perhaps its matter appears always to be good: but not every imprint is good, although the wax be good."

"Your discourse and my understanding which has followed it," I replied, "have revealed love to me; but that has made me more full of doubt; for if love is offered to us from without, and if the soul walks with no other foot, it has no merit whether it go straight or crooked."

And he to me, "As far as reason sees here I can tell you; beyond that wait only for Beatrice, for it is a matter of faith.

"Every substantial form that is both distinct from matter and united with it, holds within itself a specific virtue, which is not perceived except through operation nor ever shows itself save by its effect, as life in a plant by the green leaves. Therefore, whence comes the intelligence of the first cognitions man does not know, nor whence the affection for the first objects of desire, which exist in you even as zeal in the bee for making honey; and this primal will admits no deserving of praise or blame. Now, in order that to this will every other will may be conformed, there is innate in you the faculty that counsels and that ought to hold the threshold of assent. This is the principle wherefrom is derived the reason of desert in you, according as it garners and winnows good and evil loves. They who in their reasoning went to the root of the matter took note of this innate liberty, and accordingly bequeathed ethics to the world. Wherefore, suppose that every love which is kindled in you arises of necessity, the power to arrest it is in you. This noble virtue Beatrice understands as the free will: and therefore look that you have it in mind if she should speak of it to you."

The moon, retarded almost to midnight, shaped like a bucket that continues to glow, made the stars appear scarcer to us, and her course against the heavens was on those paths which the sun inflames, when they in Rome see it between the Sardinians and the Corsicans at its setting. And that noble shade, through whom Pietola[1] is more renowned than any Mantuan town, had put off the burden I had laid upon him; wherefore I, who had garnered clear and plain reasons to my questions, remained like one who rambles drowsily. But this drowsiness was taken suddenly from me by people who had now come round to us behind our backs. And even as Ismenus and Asopus saw of old a fury and a throng along their banks by night, if but the Thebans had need of Bacchus,[2] suchwise, by what I saw of them, bending their way around that circle, were coming those whom right will and a just love bestride. Soon were they upon us, because all that great throng was moving at a run; and two in front were shouting in tears, "Mary ran with haste to the hill country," and "Caesar, to subdue Lerida, thrust at Marseilles and then ran on to Spain."[3] "Swift, swift! let no time be lost through little love," cried the others following, "that zeal in doing well may renew grace."

"O people in whom keen fervor now perhaps makes good the negligence and delay used by you through lukewarmness in well-doing, this one who lives—and indeed I do not lie to you—would go up as soon as the sun shines to us again; therefore tell us where the opening is at hand."

These were my leader's words; and one of the spirits said, "Come behind us, and you shall find the gap. We are so filled with desire to keep moving that we cannot stay; forgive therefore, if you take our penance for rudeness. I was Abbot of San Zeno at Verona[4] under the rule of the good Barbarossa, of whom Milan still talks with sorrow.[5] And one there is that has already a foot in the grave[6] who soon will lament on account of that monastery, and will be sad for having had power there, because his son,[7] deformed in his whole body and worse in mind, and who was born in shame, he has put there in place of its lawful shepherd."

If he said more, or if he was silent, I do not know, so far already had he raced beyond us, but this much I heard and was pleased to retain. And he that was my succor in every need said, "Turn round here, see two of them who come giving a bite to sloth." Behind all the rest they were saying, "The people for whom the sea opened[8] were dead before Jordan saw its heirs; and those who did not endure the toil to the end with Anchises' son gave themselves to a life without glory."

Then when those shades were so far parted from us that they could no more be seen, a new thought arose within me, from which others many and diverse were born; and I so rambled from one to another that, wandering thus, I closed my eyes, and transmuted my musing into a dream.

CANTO XIX

At the hour when the day's heat, overcome by Earth and at times by Saturn,[1] can no more warm the cold of the moon—when the geomancers see their *Fortuna Major*[2] rise in the East before dawn by a path which does not long stay dark for it—there came to me in a dream a woman,[3] stammering, with eyes asquint and crooked on her feet, with maimed hands, and of sallow hue. I gazed upon her: and even as the sun revives cold limbs benumbed by night, so my look made ready her tongue, and then in but little time set her full straight, and colored her pallid face even as love requires. When she had her speech thus unloosed, she began to sing so that it would have been hard for me to turn my attention from her. "I am," she sang, "I am the sweet Siren who leads mariners astray in mid-sea, so full am I of pleasantness to hear. Ulysses, eager to journey on, I turned aside to my song; and whosoever abides with me rarely departs, so wholly do I satisfy him."[4] Her mouth was not yet shut when a lady, holy and alert, appeared close beside me to put her to confusion. "O Virgil, Virgil, who is this?" she said sternly; and he came on with his eyes fixed only on that honest one. He seized the other and laid her bare in front, rending her garments and showing me her belly: this waked me with the stench that issued therefrom. I turned my eyes, and the good master said, "I have called you at least three times: arise and come, let us find the opening by which you may enter."

I rose up; and all the circles of the holy mountain were already filled with the high day, and we journeyed with the new sun at our back. Following him, I was bearing my brow like one that has it burdened with thought, who makes of himself a half-arch of a bridge, when I heard, "Come, here is the passage," spoken in a tone gentle and kind, such as is not heard in this mortal region. With open wings that seemed like a swan's he who thus had spoken to us turned us upward between the two walls of hard rock, then moved his feathers and fanned us, declaring "*Qui lugent*"[5] to be blessed, for they shall have their souls possessed of consolation.

"What ails you that you keep gazing on the ground?" my guide began to say to me, when we had both climbed a little above the angel. And I, "In such apprehension I am made to go by a new vision, which bends me to itself so that I cannot leave off thinking on it."

"You have seen," he said, "that ancient witch who alone is now wept for above us: you have seen how man is freed from her. Let it suffice you, and strike your heels on the ground: turn your eyes to the lure which the eternal King spins with the mighty spheres." Like the falcon that first looks down, then turns at the cry and stretches forward, through desire of the food that draws him thither, such I became, and such, so far as the rock is cleft to afford a way to him who mounts, I went, up to where the circling is begun.[6]

When I had come forth on the fifth round, I saw people upon it who were weeping, lying on the ground all turned downward. "*Adhaesit pavimento anima mea*," I heard them saying with sighs so deep that the words could hardly be distinguished.

"O elect of God, whose sufferings both justice and hope make less hard, direct us toward the high ascents."[7]

"If you come exempt from lying prostrate, and would most quickly find the way, let your right hand be ever to the outside." Thus the poet asked, and thus came the answer from a little way ahead; wherefore, by this speech, I marked what was concealed, then turned my eyes on the eyes of my lord: at which with a glad sign he gave assent to what the look of my desire was craving. And when I was free to do as I wished, I drew forward above that soul whose words before had made me take note of him, saying, "Spirit in whom weeping matures that without which there is no returning to God, suspend a little for me your greater care. Tell me who you were; and why you have your backs turned upwards, and whether you will have me obtain aught for you yonder whence I set out alive."

And he to me, "Why heaven turns our backs to itself you shall know; but first *scias quod ego fui successor Petri*.[8] Between Sestri and Chiavari[9] descends a fair river[10] and of its name the title of my blood makes its top. One month, and little more, I learned how the great mantle weighs on him who keeps it from the mire, so that all other burdens seem a feather. My conversion, ah me! was tardy; but when I was made Roman Shepherd, then I found how false life is. I saw that there[11] the heart was not at rest; nor was it possible to mount higher in that life, wherefore the love of this was kindled in me. Up to that time I had been a wretched soul, parted from God and wholly avaricious. Now, as you see, I am here punished for it. What avarice does is displayed here in the purging of the down-turned souls, and the mountain has no more bitter penalty. Even as our eyes, fixed upon earthly things, were not lifted on high, so justice here has sunk them to the earth; even as avarice quenched all our love of good, so that our works were lost, so justice here holds us fast, bound and captive in feet and hands; and so long as it shall be the pleasure of the just Lord, so long shall we lie here outstretched and motionless."

I had kneeled, and wished to speak; but when I began, and he became aware, by the sound alone, of my reverence, "What cause," said he, "has thus bent you down?" And I to him, "Because of your dignity my conscience smote me for standing."

"Straighten your legs, rise up, brother," he replied, "do not err: I am fellow-servant with you and with the others unto one Power. If ever you have understood that holy gospel sound which says *'Neque nubent,'* you may well see why I speak thus. Go your way now: I would not have you stop longer, for your stay hinders my weeping, whereby I ripen that which you have spoken of. A niece I have yonder who is named Alagia,[12] good in herself if only our house make her not wicked by example; and she alone remains to me yonder."

CANTO XX

Against a better will the will fights ill: wherefore against my pleasure, to please him, I drew from the water the sponge unfilled. I moved on, and my leader moved on, keeping to the free spaces alongside the rock, as one goes on a wall close to the battlements; for the people who pour from their eyes drop by drop the evil that fills the whole world approach too near the edge on the other side.

Accursed be you, ancient wolf, who have more prey than all the other beasts, because of your hunger endlessly deep! O heaven, in whose revolution it seems conditions here below are thought to be changed, when will he come through whom she shall depart?

We were going on with slow and scant steps and I attentive to the shades whom I heard piteously weeping and complaining, and by chance I heard one ahead of us crying out in his lament, "Sweet Mary,"[1] even as a woman does who is in travail; and continuing, "How poor you were may be seen from that hostelry where you laid down your holy burden." And following this I heard, "O good Fabricius,[2] you chose to possess virtue with poverty rather than great riches with iniquity." These words so pleased me that I pressed forward to have aquaintance with that spirit from whom they seemed to come, and he went on to tell of the bounty which Nicholas[3] gave to the maidens, to lead their youth to honor.

"O spirit that do discourse of so much good, tell me who you were," I said, "and why you alone renew these worthy praises. Your words shall not be without reward, if I return to complete the short way of that life which flies to its end."

And he, "I will tell you, not for any solace that I expect from yonder, but because such grace shines in you before you are dead. I was the root of the evil plant that overshadows all the Christian land so that good fruit is seldom plucked therefrom; but if Douai, Lille, Ghent, and Bruges had the strength, there would soon be vengeance on it:[4] and this I implore of Him who judges all things. I was called Hugh Capet yonder;[5] of me were born the Philips and the Louises, by whom of late France is ruled.[6] I was the son of a butcher of Paris. When the ancient kings[7] had all died out, save one, a gray-clad monk,[8] I found tight in my hands the reins of the government of the realm, and with so much power from new possessions and with friends in such abundance that to the widowed crown my son's head was promoted, from whom began their consecrated bones.

"So long as the great dowry of Provence[9] had not taken the sense of shame from my race, it was of little account, but still it did no evil. There by force and by fraud its rapine began; and then, for amends, it seized Ponthieu[10] and Normandy and Gascony;[11] Charles came into Italy[12] and, for amends, made a victim of Conradin;[13] and then, for amends, thrust Thomas[14] back to Heaven. A time I see not long from this present day which brings another Charles[15] out of France, to make both himself and his own the better known. Forth he comes unarmed save only with the lance with which Judas tilted, and he so couches it that he bursts the paunch of Florence; from this he shall gain, not land, but sin and shame, so much the heavier for him the lighter he reckons such wrong. The other,[16] who once came forth a captive from a ship, I see selling his own daughter[17] and haggling over her as do the corsairs with female slaves. O Avarice, what more can you do to us, since you have so drawn my race to yourself that it has no care for its own flesh? In order that the past and the future ill may seem less, I see the fleur-de-lis enter Alagna,[18] and in His Vicar Christ made captive. I see Him mocked a second time; and I see renewed the vinegar and the gall, and Him slain between living thieves. I see the new Pilate so cruel that this does not sate him, but without decree he directs his greedy sails against the Temple.[19] O my Lord, when shall I rejoice to see the vengeance which, concealed, makes sweet Thine anger in Thy secrecy?

"What I was saying of that only bride of the Holy Ghost, and which made you turn toward me for some gloss, so much is the answer to all our prayers, as long as the day lasts; but when the night comes, we take up a contrary sound instead: then we recall Pygmalion,[20] whom insatiate lust of gold made traitor, thief, and parricide; and the misery of the avaricious Midas[21] which followed on his greedy demand, whereat men must always laugh. Each then remembers the foolish Acan,[22] how he stole the spoils, so that the wrath of Joshua seems to sting him here again. Then we accuse Sapphira[23] with her husband; we celebrate the kicks which Heliodorus had;[24] and in infamy the name of Polymestor who slew Polydorus circles all the mountain.[25] Last, the cry here is, 'Tell us, Crassus, for you know, what is the savor of gold?'[26] Sometimes we discourse, the one loud, the other low, according to the ardor that spurs us to speak, now with greater, now with lesser force; therefore, in the good we tell of here by day I was not alone before, but here nearby no other soul was raising his voice."

We were already parted from him and were striving to go forward as fast as we were able, when I felt the mountain shake like something that is falling; at which a chill seized me such as seizes one who goes to his death. Assuredly Delos was not shaken so violently before Latona made her nest therein to give birth to the two eyes of Heaven.[27] Then began such a cry on all sides that my master drew toward me saying, "Do not fear while I guide you." "*Gloria in excelsis, Deo*" all were saying, by what I understood from those nearby, where the cry could be heard.

We stood motionless and in suspense, like the shepherds who first heard that song, until the quaking ceased and it was ended. Then we took up our holy way again, looking at the shades that lay on the ground, already returned to their wonted plaint. No ignorance—if my memory err not in this—did ever with so great assault make me desirous of knowing as it seemed I then experienced in thought. Nor, for our haste, did I dare ask, nor of myself could I see aught there. So I went on, timid and pensive.

CANTO XXI

The natural thirst[1] which is never quenched, save with the water whereof the poor Samaritan woman asked the grace, was tormenting me, and our haste was urging me along the encumbered way behind my leader, and I was grieving at the just vengeance; and lo, as Luke writes for us that Christ, new-risen from the sepulchral cave, appeared to the two who were on the way, a shade appeared to us, and he was coming on behind us while were watching the crowd that lay at our feet, and we were not aware of him till he first spoke, saying "O my brothers, may God give you peace."

We turned quickly and Virgil answered him with the greeting that is fitting thereto; then he began, "May the true court which binds me in the eternal exile bring you in peace to the assembly of the blest."

"How," he said—and meanwhile we hastened on—"if you are shades whom God deigns not on high, who has brought you so far along His stairs?"[2]

And my teacher, "If you look at the marks which this man bears and which are traced by the angel, you will clearly see that he is to reign with the good. But since she who spins day and night had not yet drawn off for him the distaff which Clotho loads and compacts for everyone,[3] his soul, which is your sister and mine, could not make the ascent alone, because it sees not after our fashion. Wherefore I was brought forth from Hell's wide jaws to guide him, and I will guide him onward as far as my school can lead him. But tell me, if you can, why the mountain quaked so just now, and why all seemed to shout at once, down to its moist base?"

Thus asking did he thread the needle's eye of my desire, and with hope alone my thirst was made less craving; and the other began, "The holy rule of the mountain suffers nothing that is without order or is outside its custom. This place is free from every change. That which heaven receives into itself from itself may here operate as cause, and naught else: wherefore neither rain, nor hail, nor snow, nor dew, nor hoarfrost falls any higher than the short little stairway of three steps. Clouds dense or thin do not appear, nor lightning-flash, nor Thaumas's daughter who often changes her region yonder;[4] nor does dry vapor rise beyond the highest of the three steps of which I spoke, where the vicar of Peter has his feet. It trembles perhaps lower down, little or much, but up here, from wind that is hidden in the earth, it never trembles, I know not how. It trembles here when some soul feels itself pure so that it may rise or set out for the ascent, and that shout follows. Of its purity the will alone gives proof, which takes by surprise the soul, wholly free now to change its convent, and avails it to will. It wills indeed before, but the desire consents not, which Divine Justice sets, counter to the will, toward the penalty, even as it was toward the sin. And I,[5] who have lain in this pain five hundred years and more, only now felt free volition for a better threshold. Therefore you felt the earthquake and heard the pious spirits about the mountain give praises to that Lord— soon may He send them above!"

Thus he spoke to us; and since we enjoy more the draught in proportion as our thirst is great, I could not tell how much he profited me. And the wise leader, "Now I see the net that entangles you here, and how it is unmeshed, why it trembles here, and at what you rejoice together; and now be pleased to make me know who you are, and why you have lain here so many centuries let me gather from your words."

"In the time when the good Titus,[6] with help of the Highest King, avenged the wounds whence issued the blood sold by Judas, I was famous enough yonder with the name which lasts longest and honors most," replied that spirit, "but not yet with faith. So sweet was my vocal spirit that me, a Toulousan, Rome drew to itself, where I was deemed worthy to have my brows adorned with myrtle. Men yonder still speak my name, which is Statius. I sang of Thebes, and then of the great Achilles, but I fell on the way with my second burden. The sparks which warmed me from the divine flame whereby more than a thousand have been kindled were the seeds of my poetic fire: I mean the *Aeneid,* which in poetry was both mother and nurse to me—without it I had achieved little of worth; and to have lived yonder when Virgil lived I would consent to one sun more than I owe to my coming forth from exile."

These words turned Virgil to me with a look that, silent, said, "Be silent." But the power that wills cannot do everything; for smiles and tears are such close followers on the emotion from which each springs, that in the most truthful they least follow the will. I only smiled, like one who makes a sign; at which the shade was silent, and looked into my eyes, where the expression is most fixed, and, "So may your great labor end in good," he said, "why did your face just now show me the flash of a smile?"

Now am I caught on the one side and the other: the one makes me keep silence, the other conjures me to speak, so that I sigh and am understood by my master, and, "Do not fear to speak," he says to me, "but speak and tell him what he asks so earnestly." Wherefore I, "Perhaps you wonder, ancient spirit, at my smiling; but I would have yet more wonder seize you. This one who guides my eyes on high is that Virgil from whom you derived the strength to sing of men and of the gods; and if you did believe other cause for my smile, dismiss it as untrue, and believe it was those words which you spoke of him."

Already he was stooping to embrace my teacher's feet; but he said to him, "Brother, do not so, for you are a shade and a shade you see."

And he, rising, "Now you may comprehend the measure of the love that burns in me for you, when I forget our emptiness and treat shades as solid things."

CANTO XXII

Now the angel who had directed us to the sixth circle was left behind us, having erased a stroke from my face, and he had declared to us that they whose desire is for righteousness are blessed, his words completing this "*sitiunt*," without the rest.[1] And I, lighter than at the other passages, went on so that without any toil I was following the fleet spirits upwards, when Virgil began, "Love, kindled by virtue, has ever kindled other love, if but its flame appear outwardly; wherefore, from the hour when Juvenal[2] descended among us in the Limbo of Hell and made your affection known to me, my good will toward you has been such as never yet did bind to an unseen person, so that these stairs will now seem short to me. But tell me—and as a friend pardon me if too great confidence slackens my rein, and talk with me now as with a friend—how could avarice find place in your breast, amid wisdom so great as that wherewith you were filled by your zeal?"

These words first made Statius begin to smile a little, then he replied, "Every word of yours is a dear token to me of love; but truly things oftentimes do so appear, their true reasons being hidden, that they give false matter for doubting. Your question makes plain to me your belief, perhaps because of that circle where I was, that I was avaricious in the other life. Now know that avarice was too far parted from me, and this want of measure thousands of courses of the moon have punished; and were it not that I set right my care, when I gave heed to the lines where you exclaim, angered as it were against human nature: 'To what do you not drive the appetite of mortals, O accursèd hunger of gold?'[3] at the rolling I should feel the grievous jousts. It was then that I perceived that our hands could open their wings too wide in spending, and I repented of that as well as of other sins. How many will rise again with shorn locks, through ignorance, which takes away repentance of this sin, during life and at the last hour! Know, too, that the fault which rebuts any sin with direct opposition dries up its verdure here along with it. Therefore, if I, to purge me, have been among that people who bewail their avarice, it is because of its contrary that this has befallen me."

"Now, when you sang of the cruel strife of Jocasta's twofold sorrow,"[4] said the singer of the Bucolic songs, "it does not appear, from that which Clio[5] touches with you there, that the faith, without which good works suffice not, had yet made you faithful. If that is so, then what sun or what candles dispelled your darkness,[6] so that thereafter you set your sails to follow the Fisherman?"[7]

And he to him, "You it was who first sent me toward Parnassus[8] to drink in its caves, and you who first did light me on to God. You were like one who goes by night and carries the light behind him and profits not himself, but makes those wise who follow him, when you said, 'The ages are renewed; Justice returns and the first age of man, and a new progeny descends from heaven.' Through you I was a poet, through you a Christian; but that you may see better what I outline, I will set my hand to color it. Already the whole world was big with the true faith, sown by the messengers of the eternal realm, and those words of yours I have just spoken were so in accord with the new preachers that I began to frequent them. They came then to seem to me so holy that when Domitian persecuted them,[9] their wailing was not without my tears, and while I remained yonder I succored them and their righteous lives made me scorn all other sects. And before I had led the Greeks to the rivers of Thebes in my verse, I received baptism; but, for fear, I was a secret Christian, long making show of paganism, and this lukewarmness made me circle round the fourth circle for more than four centuries. You, therefore, that did lift for me the covering that was hiding from me the great good I tell of, while we still have time to spare on the ascent, tell me, where is our ancient Terence,[10] and Caecilius[11] and Plautus[12] and Varius,[13] if you know; tell me if they are damned, and in which ward."

"These, and Persius[14] and I and many others," replied my leader, "are with that Greek whom the Muses suckled more than any other, in the first circle of the dark prison; oftentimes we talk of that mountain which has our nurses ever with it. Euripides[15] is with us there, and Antiphon,[16] Simonides,[17] Agathon,[18] and many other Greeks who once decked their brows with laurel. There of your own people are seen Antigone, Deiphyle, Argia,[19] and Ismene[20] sad still as she was. There is seen who showed Langia;[21] there is the daughter of Tiresias and Thetis[22] and Deidamia[23] with her sisters."

Now were both poets silent, intent now on gazing round, freed from the ascent and the walls, and already four handmaids of the day were left behind and the fifth was at the chariot-pole, directing yet upward its flaming horn, when my leader said, "I think it behooves us to turn our right shoulders to the outer edge and to circle the mountain as we are wont." Thus usage was our guide there, and we went our way with less doubt because of the assent of that worthy soul.

They were going on in front, and I solitary behind, and I was listening to their speech which gave me understanding in poetry. But soon the pleasant converse was broken by a tree which we found in the midst of the way, with fruit sweet and good to smell. And as a fir-tree tapers upward from branch to branch, so downwards did that—I think so that none may climb it. On the side where our way was bounded there fell from the high rock a clear water which spread itself over the leaves above. The two poets approached the tree, and a voice from within the leaves cried, "Of this food you shall have want." Then it said, "Mary thought more how the wedding-feast might be honorable and complete, than of her own mouth, which now answers for you; and the Roman women of old were content with water for their drink; and Daniel despised food and gained wisdom. The first age was fair as gold: with hunger it made acorns savory, and with thirst made every streamlet nectar. Honey and locusts were the viands that nourished the Baptist in the desert; wherefore he is in glory and so great, as in the Gospel is revealed to you."

CANTO XXIII

While I was peering thus intently through the green foliage, even as he is wont to do who wastes his life after the birds, my more than father said to me, "Son, come on now, for the time that is allotted us must be more usefully apportioned."

I turned my face, and my steps no less quickly, following after the sages whose talk was such that it made the going of no cost to me, when lo, in tears and song was heard: "*Labïa mëa Domine,*"[1] in such manner that it gave birth to joy and to grief. "O sweet father, what is this I hear?" I began; and he, "Shades who go perhaps loosening the knot of their debt."

Even as pilgrims who go absorbed in thought and, if they overtake strangers on the road, turn to them without stopping, so a crowd of souls, silent and devout, which came on behind us with greater speed and passed on, gazed at us in wonder. Each was dark and hollow in the eyes, pallid in the face and so wasted that the skin took its shape from the bones. I do not believe that Erysichthon[2] became thus withered to the utter rind by hunger when he had most fear of it. I said to myself in thought, "Behold the people who lost Jerusalem, when Mary struck her beak into her son!"[3] The sockets of their eyes seemed rings without gems: he who reads *OMO* in the face of man[4] would there surely have recognized the *M*. Who, not knowing how, would believe that the scent of a fruit and that of a water, begetting desire, would have wrought thus?

I was now wondering what so famishes them, the cause of their leanness and their wretched scurf being unknown to me as yet, when lo, from the depths of his head a shade turned his eyes on me and looked at me fixedly, then cried loudly, "What a grace is this to me!" I should never have known him by his appearance, but in his voice was plain to me that which his countenance had suppressed in itself: this spark rekindled in me all my knowledge of the changed features, and I recognized the face of Forese.[5]

"Ah, strive not with the dry scab that discolors my skin," he begged, "nor with my lack of flesh, but tell me the truth about yourself, and tell me who are those two souls yonder that give you escort. Delay not to speak to me!"

"Your face, which once I wept for dead," I answered him, "now gives me no less cause for tears when I see it so disfigured. Therefore tell me, in God's name, what strips you so? Make me not talk while I am marveling, for ill can he speak who is full of other desire."

And he to me, "From the eternal counsel virtue descends into the water and into the tree left behind, whereby I waste away thus. All this people who weeping sing, sanctify themselves again in hunger and thirst, for having followed appetite to excess. The scent which comes from the fruit, and from the spray that is diffused over the green leaves, kindles within us a craving to eat and to drink; and not once only, as we circle this road, is our pain renewed—I say pain and ought to say solace: for that will leads us to the trees which led glad Christ to say '*Elì*,' when He delivered us with His blood."

And I to him, "Forese, from that day on which you changed the world for a better life, not five years have revolved till now. If power to sin more came to an end in you before the hour supervened of the good sorrow that weds us anew to God, how is it you are come up here already? I had thought to find you down there below, where time is repaid for time."

And he to me, "Thus soon has led me to drink the sweet wormwood of the torments my Nella with her flood of tears; by her devout prayers and by her sighs she has brought me from the slope where they wait, and set me free from the other circles. So much more precious and beloved of God is my widow, whom I loved so well, as she is the more alone in good works: for the Barbagia of Sardinia[6] is far more modest in its women than the Barbagia where I left her. O sweet brother, what would you have me say? Already in my vision is a future time, to which this hour shall not be very old, when the brazen-faced women of Florence shall be forbidden from the pulpit to go displaying their breasts with the paps. What Barbarian, what Saracen women were there ever, who required either spiritual or other discipline to make them go covered? But if the shameless creatures were assured of what swift heaven is preparing for them, already would they have their mouths open to howl; for if our foresight here beguiles me not, they shall be sorrowing before he shall cover his cheeks with hair who is now consoled with lullabies. Ah, brother, now no longer conceal yourself from me! You see how not only I, but all these people are gazing there where you veil the sun."

Wherefore I to him, "If you bring back to mind what you have been with me and what I have been with you, the present memory will still be grievous. From that life he who goes before me turned me the other day, when the sister of him," and I pointed to the sun, "showed full to you. He it is that has led me through the profound night of the truly dead, in this true flesh which follows him. From there his counsels have drawn me up, ascend-ing and circling this mountain, which makes you straight whom the world made crooked. So long he says that he will bear me company until I shall be there where Beatrice will be: there must I remain bereft of him. Virgil is he who tells me this," and I pointed to him, "and this other is that shade for whom just now your realm shook all its slopes, releasing him from itself."

CANTO XXIV

Speech made not the going, nor did the going make that more slow; but, talking, we went on apace even as a ship driven by a fair wind. And the shades, that seemed things twice dead, darted wonder at me from the depths of their eyes, perceiving that I was alive. And I, continuing my discourse, said, "He goes up perchance for another's sake more slowly than he would do. But, tell me, if you know, where is Piccarda;[1] and tell me if I see any person of note among this folk that so gazes at me."

"My sister, who whether she was more fair or good I do not know, triumphs already on high Olympus, rejoicing in her crown." So he said first, and then, "Here it is not forbidden to name each other, since our features are so wrung by the fast. This," and he pointed with his finger, "is Bonagiunta, Bonagiunta of Lucca;[2] and that face beyond him, more drawn than the others, had Holy Church in his arms: he was from Tours;[3] and by fasting he purges the eels of Bolsena[4] and the Vernaccia wine." Many others he named to me, one by one, and at their naming all appeared content, so that for this I saw not one dark look. I saw, plying their teeth on the void for very hunger, Ubaldin da la Pila[5] and Bonifazio[6] who shepherded many people with his staff. I saw Messer Marchese,[7] who once had leisure for drinking at Forlì with less thirst, and yet was such that he felt not sated. But as he does who looks, and then esteems one more than another, so did I to him of Lucca, who seemed to have most knowledge of me. He was murmuring, and I know not what, save that I heard "Gentucca"[8] there where he felt the pang of the justice which so strips them.

"O soul," said I, " that seem so eager to talk with me, speak so that I may hear you, and satisfy both yourself and me by your speech."

"A woman is born and wears not yet the veil," he began, "who shall make my city pleasing to you, however men may blame it. You shall go hence with this prophecy; if you have taken my murmuring in error, the real events will yet make it clear to you. But tell me if I see here him who brought forth the new rhymes, beginning: 'Ladies that have understanding of love'?"[9]

And I to him, "I am one who, when Love inspires me, takes note, and goes setting it forth after the fashion which he dictates within me."

"O brother," he said, "now I see the knot which kept the Notary, and Guittone,[10] and me, short of the sweet new style that I hear. Clearly I see how your pens follow close after him who dictates, which certainly befell not with ours—and he who sets himself to seek farther can see no other difference between the one style and the other." And, as if satisfied, he was silent.

As the birds that winter along the Nile sometimes make a flock in the air, then fly in greater haste and go in file, so all that people there, light both through leanness and through desire, turning away their faces, quickened again their pace. And as one who is weary of running lets his companions go on, and walks until the panting of his chest be eased, so Forese let that holy flock pass by, and came on behind with me, saying, "When shall it be that I see you again?"

"I do not know how long I may live," I answered him, "but truly my return here will not be so speedy that in desire I shall not be sooner at the shore, because the place where I was put to live is, day by day, more stripped of good and seems doomed to wretched ruin."

"Now go," said he, "for him who is most in fault[11] I see dragged at the tail of a beast,[12] toward the valley where there is no absolving. The beast at every step goes faster, increasing ever till it dashes him and leaves his body hideously disfigured. Those wheels have not long to revolve"—and he lifted his eyes up to the heavens—"before that will be clear to you which my speech cannot further declare. Now do you remain behind, for time is precious in this realm, so that I lose too much by coming with you thus at equal pace."

As a horseman sometimes issues forth from a troop that is riding and goes to win the honor of the first encounter, so he parted from us with greater strides, and I remained on the way with those two who were such great marshals of the world. And when he had gone on so far ahead of us that my eyes became such followers of him, as my mind was of his words, the laden and verdant branches of another tree appeared to me, and not far distant, because only then had I come round there. Beneath it I saw people lifting up their hands and crying I know not what toward the leaves, like eager and fond little children, who beg, and he of whom they beg answers not, but to make their longing full keen, holds aloft what they desire and hides it not. Then they departed, as if undeceived. And now we came to the great tree which rejects so many prayers and tears.

"Pass farther onward, without drawing near. A tree is higher up that was eaten of by Eve, and this plant was raised from it." Thus among the branches I know not who spoke; wherefore Virgil and Statius and I, drawing close together, went onward along the side that rises.

"Remember," the voice was saying, "the accursèd ones[13] that were formed in the clouds who, when gorged, fought Theseus with their double breasts; and the Hebrews[14] who at the drinking showed themselves soft, wherefore Gideon would not have them for comrades when he came down the hills to Midian."[15]

Thus, keeping close to one side of the way, we passed by, hearing sins of gluttony, once followed by woeful gains. Then, spread out along the solitary way, full a thousand paces and more bore us onward, each of us in meditation without a word.

"Why go you thus in thought, you three alone?" said a sudden voice; whereat I started as do frightened and skittish beasts. I raised my head to see who it was, and never in a furnace was glass or metal seen so glowing and red as one I saw who said, "If it please you to mount up, here must you make the turn: this way he goes who desires to go for peace." His countenance had bereft me of sight, wherefore I turned and followed my teachers like one who goes according as he hears.

And as, heralding the dawn, the breeze of May stirs and smells sweet, all impregnate with grass and with flowers, such a wind I felt strike full on my brow, and right well I felt the pinions move, which wafted ambrosial fragrance to my senses; and I heard say, "Blessed are they who are so illumined by grace that the love of taste kindles not too great desire in their breasts, and who hunger always so far as is just."

CANTO XXV

It was now an hour when the ascent brooked no impediment, for the meridian circle had been left by the sun to the Bull, and by the night to the Scorpion. Therefore, like one that does not stop but, whatever may appear to him, goes on his way, if the goad of necessity prick him, so did we enter through the gap, one before the other, taking the stairway which by its straitness unpairs the climbers. And as the little stork that lifts its wing through desire to fly and, not venturing to abandon the nest, drops it again, even so was I, with desire to ask, kindled and quenched, going as far as the movement he makes who is preparing to speak. Nor, though our gait was swift, did my sweet father forbear, but said, "Discharge the bow of your speech which you have drawn to the iron."

Then I opened my mouth confidently and began, "How can one grow lean there where the need of nourishment is not felt?"

"If you would call to mind how Meleager[1] was consumed at the consuming of a fire-brand," he said, "this would not be so difficult to you; and if you would think how, at your every movement, your image moves within the mirror, that which seems hard would seem easy to you. But, in order that you may find rest in your desire, here is Statius, and I call on him and pray that he be now the healer of your wounds."

"If I explain to him the eternal view," replied Statius, "where you are present, let my excuse be that I cannot deny you."

Then he began, "If, son, your mind regards and receives my words, they will enlighten you on the 'how' of what you ask. The perfect blood, which never is drunk by the thirsty veins and is left behind as it were food which one removes from the table, acquires in the heart an informing power for all the bodily members, like the blood which flows through the veins to become those members. Digested yet again, it descends there whereof to be silent is more seemly than to speak; and thence afterwards drops upon other's blood, in natural vessel. There the one is mingled with the other, one designed to be passive, the other to be active, by reason of the perfect place whence it springs; and, conjoined with the former, the latter begins to operate, first by coagulating, then by quickening that to which it has given consistency to serve as its material. The active virtue having become a soul, like that of a plant (but in so far different that this is on the way, and that has already arrived) so works then that now it moves and feels, like a sea-fungus; then it proceeds to develop organs for the powers of which it is the germ. Now, son, expands, now distends, the virtue which proceeds from the heart of the begetter, where nature makes provision for all the members. But how from animal it becomes a human being you do not see yet: this is such a point that once it made one wiser than you[2] to err, so that in his teaching he separated the possible intellect from the soul because he saw no organ assumed by it.

"Open your breast to the truth which is coming, and know that, so soon as in the foetus the articulation of the brain is perfect, the First Mover turns to it with joy over such art of nature, and breathes into it a new spirit replete with virtue, which absorbs that which is active there into its own substance, and makes one single soul which lives and feels and circles on itself. And that you may marvel less at my words, look at the sun's heat, which is made wine when combined with the juice that flows from the vine.

"And when Lachesis has no more thread, the soul is loosed from the flesh and carries with it, in potency, both the human and the divine; the other faculties all of them mute, but memory, intellect, and will far more acute in action than before. Without staying, it falls of itself marvelously to one of the banks. Here it first knows its own roads. As soon as space encompasses it there, the formative virtue radiates around, in form and quantity as in the living members. And as the air, when it is full of moisture, becomes adorned with various colors by another's rays which are reflected in it, so here the neighboring air shapes itself in that form which is virtually imprinted on it by the soul that stopped there; and then, like the flame which follows the fire wheresoever it moves, the spirit is followed by its new form. Inasmuch as therefrom it has its semblance, it is called a shade, and therefrom it forms the organs of every sense, even to the sight. By this we speak and by this we laugh, by this we make the tears and sighs which you may have heard about the mountain. According as the desires and the other affections prick us, the shade takes its form; and this is the cause of that at which you marvel."

And now we had come to the last circuit and had turned to the right and were intent on other care. Here the bank flashes forth flames, and the edge of the terrace sends a blast upwards which bends them back and sequesters a path from them; wherefore it behooved us to go on the side that was free, one by one, and on the one side I feared the fire, and on the other I feared I might fall off. My leader said, "Along this place the rein must be kept tight on the eyes, for one might easily take a false step."

"*Summae Deus clementiae*" I then heard sung in the heart of the great burning, which made me no less eager to turn; and I saw spirits going though the fire, wherefore I looked at them and at my steps, with divided gaze from time to time. After the end which is made to that hymn, they cried aloud, "*Virum non cognosco,*" then softly began the hymn again. When it was finished, they further cried, "Diana kept to the woods and chased Helice forth, who had felt the poison of Venus."[3] Then they returned to their singing; then they cried wives and husbands who were chaste, even as virtue and marriage enjoin upon us. And this fashion, I believe, suffices them for all the time the fire burns them: with such treatment and with such diet must the last wound of all be healed.

CANTO XXVI

While we were advancing thus along the brink, one before the other, the good master often saying to me, "Take heed: let my warning avail you," the sun was striking me on my right shoulder, for now its beams were changing the whole face of the West from azure to white. And with my shadow I made the flame appear more glowing, and merely at this slight sign I saw many shades, as they went on, give heed. This it was that first brought them to speak of me, and they began to say to each other, "That one does not seem a shadowy body"; then certain of them came as far as they could toward me, ever careful not to come out where they would not be burned.

"O you who go behind the others, not from tardiness but perhaps from reverence, answer me who burn in thirst and in fire; nor to me alone is your answer needful, for all these others have greater thirst thereof than Indian or Ethiopian for cold water. Tell us how it is that you make a wall of yourself to the sun, quite as if you had not yet entered into death's net." Thus one of them spoke to me, and now I should have made myself known, had I not been intent on another strange thing which then appeared: for through the middle of the burning road people were coming with their faces opposite to these, and made me gaze in suspense. There on every side I see all the shades making haste and kissing one another, without stopping, content with brief greeting: thus within their dark band one ant touches muzzle with another, perhaps to spy out their way and their fortune.

As soon as they end the friendly greeting and before the first step there speeds onward, each one tries to shout the loudest: the newcome people "Sodom and Gomorrah," and the other, "Pasiphaë[1] enters into the cow, that the bull may hasten to her lust." Then, like cranes that should fly, some to the Riphaean mountains[2] and others toward the sands,[3] these shy of the frost, those of the sun, the one people passes on, the other comes away, and they return weeping to their former chants and to the cry that most befits them. And those same who had entreated me drew near to me as before, by their looks eager to listen.

Having twice seen their desire, I began, "O souls, certain of gaining, whensoever it may be, a state of peace, my limbs have not remained yonder green or ripe, but are here with me, with their blood and their joints. I go up hence in order to be blind no longer. A lady is above who wins grace for me,[4] whereby I bring my mortal part through your world. But—so may your greatest longing soon be satisfied, so that the heaven harbor you which is full of love and widest spreads[5]—tell me, so that

I may yet trace it on paper, who you are, and what is that throng that is going away behind your backs."

Not otherwise is the astonished mountaineer overawed, and gazing round is dumb, when rude and rustic he enters the city, than was each shade in his looks; but when they were unburdened of amazement, which in lofty hearts is quickly stilled, "Blessed are you," he began again who had questioned me before, "who in order to die better do ship experience of our regions! The people who do not come with us offended in that for which Caesar in his triumph once heard 'Queen' cried out against him;[6] therefore they go off crying 'Sodom,' reproving themselves as you have heard, and they help the burning with their shame. Our sin was hermaphrodite:[7] but because we observed not human law, following appetite like beasts, when we part from them, the name of her who bestialized herself in the beast-shaped planks is uttered by us, in opprobrium of ourselves. Now you know our deeds, and of what we were guilty; if perchance you wish to know by name who we are, there is no time to tell, nor could I. Concerning me I will indeed satisfy your wish: I am Guido Guinizzelli,[8] and already I make my purgation because of good repentance before the end."

As in the sorrow of Lycurgus[9] two sons became on beholding their mother again, so I became, but I do not rise to such heights, when I hear name himself the father of me and of others my betters who ever used sweet and gracious rhymes of love; and without hearing or speaking, I went pondering, gazing a long time at him; nor did I draw nearer to him, because of the fire. When I had fed my sight on him, I offered myself wholly ready for his service, with the oath that compels another's belief.

And he to me, "You leave, by that which I hear, traces so deep and clear in me that Lethe cannot take them away or make them dim; but if your words just now swore truth, tell me for what reason you show yourself, by speech and look, to hold me dear."

And I to him, "Your sweet verses, which so long as modern use[10] shall last, will make dear their very ink."

"O brother," he said, "he there whom I point out to you"—and he pointed to a spirit ahead[11]—"was a better craftsman of the mother tongue: verses of love and tales of romance he surpassed them all—and let the fools talk who think that he of Limoges excels.[12] They give heed to rumor rather than to truth, and thus settle their opinion before listening to art or reason. Thus did many of our fathers with Guittone, from cry to cry giving the prize to him alone, until with most the truth prevailed. Now, if you have such ample privilege that you are permitted to go to the cloister wherein Christ is abbot of the college, say there a paternoster for me, so far as is needful to us of this world where power to sin is no more ours." Then, perhaps to give place to another following close behind, he vanished through the flames like a fish that goes through the water to the bottom.

I moved forward a little towards him that had been pointed out to me, and said that for his name my desire was making ready a grateful place. He began graciously to say, "So does your courteous request please me that I neither can nor would conceal myself from you. I am Arnaut, who weep and sing as I go; contritely I see my past folly, and joyously I see before me the joy that I await. Now I pray you, by that power which guides you to the summit of the stair, in due time be heedful of my pain." Then he hid himself in the fire that purifies them.

CANTO XXVII

As when it darts forth its first beams there where its Maker shed His blood, while Ebro falls beneath the lofty Scales[1] and the waves in the Ganges are scorched by noon, so stood the sun, so that the day was departing when the glad angel of God appeared to us. He stood outside the flames on the bank and sang "*Beati mundo corde*" in a voice far more living than ours. Then, "No farther may you go, holy souls, if first the fire sting not; enter into it, and to the singing beyond be not deaf," he said to us, when we were near him; whereat I became such, on hearing him, as is he who is put into the pit. I bent forward over my clasped hands, gazing at the fire and vividly imagining human bodies once seen burned. The good escorts turned to me, and Virgil said to me, "My son, here may be torment, but not death. Remember, remember . . . and if on Geryon I

guided you safely, what shall I do now nearer
to God? Be well assured that if within the belly
of this flame you should stay full a thousand
years, it could not make you bald of one hair.[2]
And if perchance you think that I deceive you,
go close to it and try it with your own hands
on the edge of your garment. Put away now,
put away all fear, turn hitherward, come, enter with confidence." And I still adamant and
against my conscience.

When he saw me stand there unmoved and
stubborn, he said, a little vexed, "Now see,
son, between Beatrice and you is this wall."

As at the name of Thisbe, Pyramus, at the
point of death, opened his eyelids[3] and looked
at her, when the mulberry turned red, so, my
stubbornness being softened, I turned to the
wise leader when I heard the name which ever
springs up in my mind; at which he shook his
head and said, "What? Do we desire to stay on
this side?" then smiled as one does to a child
that is won with an apple.

Then he entered into the fire in front of
me, asking Statius, who for a long way had
been between us, to come behind. As soon as
I was in it I would have flung myself into
molten glass to cool me, so without measure
was the burning there. My sweet father, to encourage me, went on discoursing of Beatrice,
saying, "Already I seem to behold her eyes."
A voice was guiding us, which was singing
on the other side; and we, ever attentive to
it, came forth where the ascent began. "*Veni-
te, benedicti Patris mei,*"[4] sounded from within
a light that was there, such that it overcame
me and I could not look on it. "The sun is
sinking," it added, "and the evening comes; do
not stop, but hasten your steps before the west
grows dark."

The way went straight up through the rock
in such a direction that I was intercepting before me the rays of the sun, which was now
low. And of few steps had we made assay when
I and my sages perceived, by the shadow which
had vanished, that the sun had set behind us.
And before the horizon in all its vast range
had become of one hue, and night held all
her dominions, each of us made his bed of a
step, for the law of the mountain took from
us the strength as well as the desire to climb
farther.

As goats, which have been swift and way-
ward on the peaks before they are fed, become

tranquil as they ruminate, silent in the shade
while the sun is hot, guarded by the shepherd
who leans upon his staff and tends their repose;
and as the herdsman, who lodges out of doors,
passes the night beside his quiet flock, watching lest a wild beast scatter it, such were we
then all three, I as a goat and they as shepherds,
bounded by the high rock on this side and on
that. Little of the outside could be seen there,
but through that little I saw the stars brighter
and larger than their wont. As I was thus rumi-
nating, and thus gazing at them, sleep fell on
me, sleep which often knows the news before
the event.

In the hour, I think, when Cytherea,[5] who
seems always burning with the fire of love,
first shone on the mountain from the east, I
seemed to see in a dream a lady young and
beautiful going through a meadow gathering
flowers and, singing, she was saying, "Whoso
asks my name, let him know that I am Leah,
and I go moving my fair hands around to make
myself a garland. To please me at the glass
I adorn me here, but my sister Rachel never
leaves her mirror and sits all day. She is fain to
behold her fair eyes, as I am to deck me with
my hands: she with seeing, I with doing am
satisfied."[6]

And now before the splendors which precede the dawn, and rise the more welcome to
pilgrims as, returning, they lodge less far from
home, the shades of night fled away on every
side, and my sleep with them; whereupon I
rose, seeing the great masters already risen.

"That sweet fruit which the care of mortals
goes seeking on so many branches, this day
shall give your hungerings peace." Such were
Virgil's words to me, and never were there
gifts that could be equal in pleasure to these.
Such wish upon wish came to me to be above,
that at every step thereafter I felt my feathers
growing for the flight.

When all the stair was sped beneath us and
we were on the topmost step, Virgil fixed his
eyes on me and said, "The temporal fire and
the eternal you have seen, my son, and are
come to a part where I of myself discern no
farther onward. I have brought you here with
understanding and with art. Take henceforth
your own pleasure for your guide. Forth you
are from the steep ways, forth from the narrow. See the sun that shines on your brow,
see the tender grass, the flowers, the shrubs,

which here the earth of itself alone produces: till the beautiful eyes come rejoicing which weeping made me come to you, you may sit or go among them. No longer expect word or sign from me. Free, upright, and whole is your will,[7] and it would be wrong not to act according to its pleasure; wherefore I crown and miter you over yourself."

CANTO XXVIII

Eager now to search within and round about the divine forest green and dense, which tempered the new day to my eyes, without waiting longer I left the bank, taking the level ground very slowly over the soil that everywhere gives forth fragrance. A sweet breeze that had no variation in itself was striking on my brow with the force only of a gentle wind, by which the fluttering boughs all bent freely toward the quarter where the holy mountain casts its first shadow; yet were they not so deflected from their upright state that the little birds among the tops ceased practicing all their arts, but singing they greeted the morning hours with full joy among the leaves, which kept such burden to their rhymes as gathers from branch to branch through the pine forest on Chiassi's shore[1] when Aeolus lets forth Sirocco.[2]

Now my slow steps had carried me on into the ancient wood so far that I could not see back to where I had entered it, when lo, a stream took from me further progress, which with its little waves was bending leftwards the grass that grew on its bank. All the waters which here are purest would seem to have some defilement in them, compared with that, which conceals nothing, although it flows quite dark under the perpetual shade, which never lets sun or moon beam enter there.

With feet I stayed and with my eyes I passed to the other side of the rivulet to look at the great variety of the fresh-flowering boughs; and there appeared to me there, as appears of a sudden a thing that for wonder drives away every other thought, a lady all alone, who went singing and culling flower from flower, with which all her path was painted.

"Pray, fair lady, who do warm yourself at love's beams, if I may believe outward looks which are wont to be testimony of the heart," I said to her, "may it please you to draw forward to this stream so near that I may understand what you sing. You make me recall where and what Proserpine[3] was at the time her mother lost her, and she the spring."

As in a dance a lady turns with feet close to the ground and to each other, and hardly sets foot before foot, she turned upon the red and yellow flowerlets toward me, like a virgin that lowers her modest eyes, and gave satisfaction to my prayer, drawing so near that the sweet sound reached me with its meaning. As soon as she was there where the grass was just bathed by the waves of the fair stream, she bestowed on me the gift of lifting her eyes. I do not believe that so great a light shone forth under the eyelids of Venus, transfixed by her son against all his custom.[4] She was smiling as she stood there on the opposite bank, arranging in her hands the many colors which that high land brings forth without seed. The river kept us three paces apart, but Hellespont where Xerxes[5] passed it—ever a curb on all human pride—did not suffer more hatred from Leander[6] for its swelling waters between Sestos and Abydos[7] than that from me because it did not open then.

"You are newcomers," she began, "and, perhaps, why I am smiling in this place chosen for nest of the human race some doubt holds you wondering; but the psalm *Delectasti* gives light that may dispel the cloud from your minds. And you that are in front, and did entreat me, say if you would hear more, for I have come ready to all your questions till you are satisfied."

"The water," I said, "and the sound of the forest contend in me with a recent belief in a thing I have heard contrary to this." Whereon she, "I will tell you how that which makes you wonder proceeds from its cause, and I will clear away the mist that offends you.

"The highest Good, who Himself alone does please Himself, made man good, and for good, and gave him this place as an earnest of eternal peace. Through his fault he had short stay here; through his fault he exchanged honest joy and sweet sport for tears and toil. In order that the disturbance which the exhalations of the water and of the earth (which follow so far as they can the heat) produce below might do no hurt to man, this mountain rose thus high toward heaven, and stands clear of them from where it is locked. Now, because all the air revolves in a circuit with the first circling,[8] if its revolution is not interrupted at any point, such movement strikes upon this height, which is wholly free in the pure air, and this motion causes the forest, because it is dense, to resound; and the plant, being struck thus, has such potency that with its virtue it impregnates the breeze, and this then in its whirling scatters it abroad; and the rest of the earth, according to its fitness in itself and in its sky, conceives and brings forth from diverse virtues diverse growths. It should, then, not seem a marvel on earth, this being heard, when some plant takes root there without visible seed. And you should know that the holy plain, where you are, is full of every seed, and has in it fruit that yonder is not plucked.

"The water you see springs not from a vein that is restored by vapor which cold condenses, like a stream that gains and loses force, but issues from a fountain constant and sure which by the will of God regains as much as it pours forth freely on two sides. On this side it descends with virtue that takes from one the memory of sin; on the other side it restores the memory of every good deed. Here Lethe,[9] so on the other side Eunoe[10] it is called; and it works not if first it be not tasted on this side and on that. Its savor surpasses every other sweetness. And notwithstanding that your thirst might be fully satisfied even if I disclosed no more to you, I will yet give you a corollary for grace, nor do I think my speech will be less welcome to you if it reaches beyond my promise.

"They who in olden times sang of the Age of Gold and its happy state perhaps in Parnassus[11] dreamed of this place. Here the root of mankind was innocent; here is always spring, and every fruit; this is the nectar of which each tells."

I turned then right round to my poets, and saw that with a smile they had heard these last words; then to the fair lady I turned my face.

CANTO XXIX

Singing like a lady enamored,[1] she continued, at the end of her words, "*Beati quorum tecta sunt peccata!*"[2] and, like nymphs who used to wend alone through the woodland shades, this one desiring to see and that to avoid the sun, she moved on, then, counter to the stream, going along the bank, and I abreast of her, matching her little steps with mine. We had not taken a hundred between us when the banks made an equal bend in such a way that I faced the East again; nor yet was our way thus very far when the lady turned full round to me, saying, "My brother, look and listen!" And lo! a sudden brightness flooded the great forest on all sides, such that it put me in doubt if it were lightning; but since lightning ceases even as it comes, and this, lasting, became more and more resplendent, in my thought I said, "What thing is this!" And a sweet melody ran through the luminous air; wherefore good zeal made me reprove Eve's daring, that, there where earth and heaven were obedient, a woman, alone and but then formed, did not bear to remain under any veil, under which, if she had been devout, I should have tasted those ineffable delights before, and for a longer time.[3] While I went on among so many first-fruits of the eternal pleasure, all enrapt, and still desirous of more joys, in front of us the air under the green boughs became like a flaming fire to us, and the sweet sound was now heard as a song.

O most holy Virgins, if hunger, cold, or vigils I have ever endured for you, the occasion spurs me to claim my reward. Now it is meet that Helicon stream[4] forth for me, and Urania[5] aid me with her choir to put in verse things difficult to think.

A little farther on, a delusive semblance of seven trees of gold was caused by the long space still intervening between us and them; but when I had come so near that the common object, which deceives the sense, lost not by distance any of its features, the faculty that prepares matter for reason made them out to be candlesticks, even as they were, and in the words of the chant "Hosanna." Above flamed the splendid array, brighter by far than the moon in a clear midnight sky in her midmonth. I turned round full of wonder to the good Virgil, and he answered me with a look no less charged with amazement; then I turned my face again to the high things, which moved towards us so slowly that they would have been outstripped by new-made brides. The lady chid me, "Why are you so eager only for the sight of the living lights, and do not heed that which comes after them?" Then I saw people, following as after their leaders, clad in white, and a whiteness so pure never was here. The water was taking in my image on the left, and like a mirror reflected to me my left side if I looked in it. When I was at a point on my bank where only the stream separated me, I held my steps in order to see better, and I saw the flames advance, leaving the air behind them painted, and they looked like moving paint brushes, so that overhead it remained streaked with seven bands in all those colors whereof the sun makes his bow, and Delia[6] her girdle. These banners went back farther than my sight and, as well as I could judge, the outermost were ten paces apart. Beneath so fair a sky as I describe came four and twenty elders, two by two, crowned with lilies; all were singing, "Blessed art thou among the daughters of Adam, and blessed forever be thy beauties."[7]

When the flowers and the other fresh herbage opposite me on the other bank were left clear of those chosen people, even as star follows star in the heavens, four living creatures came after them, each crowned with green leaves; and each of them was plumed with six wings, the plumes full of eyes, and the eyes of Argus,[8] were they alive, would be such. To describe their forms, reader, I do not lay out more rhymes, for other spending constrains me so that I cannot be lavish in this; but read Ezekiel who depicts them as he saw them come from the cold parts, with wind and cloud and fire; and such as you shall find them on his pages, such were they here, except that, as to the wings, John is with me, and differs from him.

The space within the four of them contained a triumphal chariot on two wheels, which came drawn at the neck of a griffin;[9] and he stretched upwards one wing and the other between the middle and the three and three bands so that he did harm to none by cleaving. So high they rose that they were lost to sight; he had his members of gold so far as he was bird, and the rest was white mixed with red. Not only did Rome never gladden an Africanus[10] or an Augustus[11] with a chariot so splendid, but even that of the Sun would be poor to it—that of the Sun which, going astray, was consumed at devout Earth's prayer, when Jove in his secrecy was just.[12]

Three ladies came dancing in a round at the right wheel, one of them so ruddy that she would hardly have been noted in the fire;[13] another was as if her flesh and bones had been of emerald;[14] the third seemed new-fallen snow;[15] and they seemed to be led, now by the white, now by the red, and from this one's song the others took their movement fast and slow. By the left wheel four other ladies made festival, clothed in purple, following the measure of one of them that had three eyes in her head.[16]

Behind the whole group I have described I saw two old men, unlike in dress but alike in bearing, venerable and grave: the one showed himself of the household of that great Hippocrates[17] whom nature made for the creatures she holds dearest; the other showed the contrary care, with a sharp and shining sword, such that on this side of the stream it made me afraid. Then I saw four of lowly aspect; and behind them all an old man coming alone, asleep, with keen visage. And these seven were clad like the first band, but they had no garland of lilies around their heads, rather of roses and of other red flowers: one who viewed them from short distance would have sworn that all were aflame above their eyebrows. And when the chariot was opposite to me, a thunderclap was heard: and those worthy folk seemed to have their further march forbidden, stopping there along with the banners in front.

CANTO XXX

When the Wain of the first heaven, which never knew setting or rising, or veil of other cloud than of sin, and which there made each one aware of his duty, even as the lower wain guides him who turns the helm to come into port, had stopped still, the truthful people, who had come first between the griffin and it, turned to the chariot as to their peace, and one of them, as if sent from Heaven, singing cried thrice, "*Veni, sponsa de Libano,*" and all the others after.[1]

As the blessed at the last Trump will rise ready each from his tomb, singing Hallelujah with reclad voice, so upon the divine chariot, *ad vocem tanti senis,* rose up a hundred ministers and messengers of life eternal, who all cried, "*Benedictus qui venis*"[2] and, scattering flowers up and around, "*Manibus, oh, date lilia plenis.*"[3]

Sometimes I have seen at the beginning of the day the eastern region all rosy, while the rest of the heaven was adorned with fair clear sky, and the face of the sun rise shaded, so that through the tempering of vapors the eye sustained it a long while: so within a cloud of flowers, which rose from the angelic hands and fell down again within and without, olive-crowned over a white veil a lady appeared to me, clad, under a green mantle,[4] with hue of living flame; and my spirit, which now for so long a time trembling with awe in her presence had not been overcome, without having more knowledge by the eyes, through occult virtue that proceeded from her, felt old love's great power. As soon as on my sight the lofty virtue smote that had already pierced me before I was out of my boyhood, I turned to the left with the confidence of a little child that runs to his mother when he is frightened or in distress, to say to Virgil, "Not a drop of blood is left in me that does not tremble: I know the tokens of the ancient flame." But Virgil had left us bereft of himself, Virgil sweetest father, Virgil to whom I gave myself for my salvation; nor did all that our ancient mother lost keep my dew-washed cheeks from turning dark again with tears.

"Dante,[5] because Virgil leaves you, do not weep yet, do not weep yet, for you must weep for another sword!"

Like an admiral who goes to stern and bow to see the men that are serving on the other ships, and encourages them to do well, so on the left side of the chariot—when I turned at the sound of my name, which of necessity is registered here—I saw the lady, who first appeared to me veiled under the angelic festival, direct her eyes to me beyond the stream. Although the veil that fell from her head, encircled with Minerva's leaves,[6] did not let her be seen distinctly, royally and ever stern in her mien, she continued, like one who speaks and keeps back the hottest words till the last, "Look at me well: indeed I am, indeed I am Beatrice! How did you deign to climb the mountain? Did you not know that here man is happy?" My eyes fell down to the clear fount, but, seeing myself in it, I drew them back to the grass, so great shame weighed on my brow; so does the mother seem harsh to her child as she seemed to me, for bitter tastes the savor of stern pity.

She was silent; and the angels of a sudden sang, "*In te, Domine, speravi,*" but beyond "*pedes meos*" they did not pass. Even as the snow, among the living rafters upon the back of Italy, is congealed, blown and packed by Slavonian winds,[7] then melting, trickles through itself, if only the land that loses shadow breathes,[8] so that it seems a fire that melts the candle; so was I without tears or sighs before the song of those who ever sing in harmony with the eternal spheres. But when I heard how in their sweet notes they took my part, quite as if they had said, "Lady, why do you so confound him?" the ice that was bound tight around my heart became breath and water, and with anguish poured from my breast through my mouth and eyes.

She, still standing motionless on the aforesaid side of the chariot, then turned her words to the pitying angels thus: "You watch in the everlasting day, so that nor night nor slumber steals from you one step which the world makes along its ways; wherefore my answer is more concerned that he who weeps yonder should understand me, so that fault and grief may be of one measure. Not only through the working of the great wheels, which direct every seed to some end according as the stars are its companions, but through largess of divine graces, which have for their rain vapors so lofty that our sight goes not near thereto, this man was such in his new life, virtually, that every right disposition would have made marvelous proof in him. But so much the more rank and wild becomes the land, ill-sown and untilled, as it has more of good strength of soil. For a time I sustained him with my countenance: showing him my youthful eyes I led him with me turned toward the right goal. So soon as I was on the threshold of my second age and had changed life, this one took himself from me and gave himself to others. When from flesh to spirit I had ascended, and beauty and virtue were increased in me, I was less dear and less pleasing to him and he turned his steps along a way not true, following false images of good, which pay no promise in full. Nor did it avail me to obtain inspirations with which, both in dream and otherwise, I called him back, so little did he heed them. He fell so low that all means for his salvation were now short, save to show him the lost people. For this I visited the gate of the dead, and to him who has conducted him up hither my prayers were offered with tears. The high decree of God would be broken if Lethe were passed and such viands were tasted without some scot of penitence that may pour forth tears."

CANTO XXXI

"O you who are on that side of the sacred river,"[1] she began again, turning against me the point of her speech, which even with the edge had seemed sharp to me; and continuing without pause, "Say, say, if this is true: to such an accusation your confession must be joined."

My power was so confounded that my voice moved and became extinct before it was set free from its organs. She forebore but little, then said, "What are you thinking? Answer me, for the sad memories in you are not yet destroyed by the water." Confusion and fear, together mingled, drove forth from my mouth a *Yes* such that the eyes were needed to hear it.

As a crossbow breaks its cord and the bow when it shoots with too great tension, and the shaft hits the mark with less force, so did I burst under that heavy load, pouring forth tears and sighs, and my voice failed along its passage. Wherefore she to me, "Within your desires of me that were leading you to love that Good beyond which there is nothing to which man may aspire, what pits did you find athwart your path, or what chains, that you had thus to strip you of the hope of passing onward? And what attractions or what advantages were displayed on the brow of others, that you were obliged to dally before them?"

After drawing a bitter sigh, I barely had the voice to make answer, and my lips shaped it with difficulty. Weeping I said, "The present things, with their false pleasure, turned my steps aside, as soon as your countenance was hidden."

And she, "Had you been silent, or had you denied that which you confess, your fault would not be less noted, by such a Judge is it known. But when accusation of the sin bursts from one's own cheek, in our court the grindstone turns itself back against the edge. Still, that you may now bear shame for your error, and another time, hearing the Sirens, may be

stronger, lay aside the seed of tears and listen: so shall you hear how in opposite direction my buried flesh ought to have moved you.

"Never did nature or art present to you beauty so great as the fair members in which I was enclosed and now are scattered to dust. And if the highest beauty thus failed you by my death, what mortal thing should then have drawn you into desire for it? Truly, at the first arrow of deceitful things you ought to have risen up, following me who was no longer such. Young damsel or other novelty of such brief enjoyment should not have weighed down your wings to await more shots. The young bird waits two or three, but before the eyes of the full-fledged in vain is net spread or arrow shot."

As children stand ashamed and dumb, with eyes on the ground, listening conscience-stricken and repentant, so stood I. And she said, "Since you are grieved through hearing, lift up your beard and you will receive more grief through seeing."

With less resistance is the sturdy oak uprooted, whether by wind of ours or by that which blows from Iarbas' land,[2] than at her command I raised my chin; and when by the beard she asked for my face, well I knew the venom of the argument. When my face was lifted up, my sight perceived those primal creatures resting from their strewing; and my eyes, still little assured, saw Beatrice turned toward the animal that is one person in two natures. Beneath her veil and beyond the stream she seemed to me to surpass more her former self than she surpassed the others here when she was with us; and the nettle of remorse so stung me there that of all other things, that which had most turned me to love of it became most hateful to me. Such contrition stung my heart that I fell overcome; and what I then became she knows who was the cause of it.

Then when my heart had restored my outward sense I saw above me the lady I had found alone[3] and she was saying, "Cling, cling to me!" She had brought me into the river up to the throat and, drawing me behind her, was moving over the water as light as a shuttle. When I was close to the blessed shore, I heard "*Asperges me*"[4] sung so sweetly that I cannot remember it, far less write it. The fair lady opened her arms, clasped my head and dipped me under, where it behooved me to swallow of the water. Then she drew me forth and led me bathed into the dance of the four fair ones, and each of them covered me with her arm. "Here we are nymphs and in heaven we are stars: before Beatrice descended to the world we were ordained to her for her handmaids. We will bring you to her eyes; but in the joyous light which is within them the three on the other side, who look deeper, shall quicken yours." Thus they began to sing, then brought me with them to the breast of the griffin, where Beatrice stood turned towards us. "See that you spare not your gaze," they said, "we have placed you before the emeralds from which Love once shot his darts at you."

A thousand desires hotter than flame held my eyes on the shining eyes that remained ever fixed on the griffin. As the sun in a mirror, so was the twofold animal gleaming therewithin, now with the one, now with the other bearing.⁵ Think, reader, if I marveled when I saw the thing stand still in itself, and in its image changing.

While my soul, full of amazement and gladness, was tasting of that food which, sating of itself, causes hunger for itself, the other three, showing themselves by their bearing to be of a higher order, came forward, dancing to their angelic roundelay. "Turn, Beatrice, turn your holy eyes upon your faithful one," was their song, "who has moved so many steps to see you. For grace do us the grace to unveil to him your mouth, that he may discern the second beauty which you conceal." O splendor of living light eternal! Who has ever grown so pale under the shade of Parnassus⁶ or drunk so deep at its well, that he would not seem to have his mind encumbered, on trying to render you as you appeared, when in the free air you did disclose yourself, there where in its harmony that heaven overshadows you!

CANTO XXXII

So fixed and intent were my eyes in satisfying their ten-year thirst, that every other sense was quenched in me; and they themselves had a wall of indifference, on one side and on the other, so did the holy smile draw them to itself with the old net, when my face was turned perforce to my left by those goddesses,¹ for I heard

from them a "Too fixedly!" And the condition of the sight that is in eyes just smitten by the sun left me for a time without vision. But after my sight had adjusted itself to the lesser object—lesser, I mean, with regard to the greater from which I was forced to withdraw—I saw that the glorious army had wheeled on its right and was returning with the sun and the seven flames in its face.

As under their shields a troop wheels about to save itself and turns with its standard before it can completely face round, that soldiery of the celestial realm which was in advance had wholly gone past us before the chariot bent round its pole. Then the ladies returned to the wheels and the griffin moved his blessed burden,² on such wise however that no feather of him was ruffled. The fair lady who had drawn me at the ford, and Statius³ and I, were following the wheel that made its turn with the smaller arc, and as we passed through the lofty wood, empty through fault of her who believed the serpent,⁴ an angelic song set the time to our steps. Perhaps three flights of an arrow loosed from the string would cover such distance as we had advanced, when Beatrice descended. I heard "Adam" murmured by all, then they encircled a tree stripped of its flowers and of its foliage in every bough. Its branches, which so much the wider spread the higher up they are, would be marveled at for height by the Indians in their woods.⁵

"Blessed art thou, Griffin, that dost not pluck with thy beak from this tree, sweet to the taste, for the belly is ill racked thereby." Thus around the sturdy tree cried the others; and the animal of two natures, "So is preserved the seed of all righteousness"; and turning to the pole which he had pulled, he drew it to the foot of the widowed trunk and that which was of it he left bound to it.

As our plants, when the great light falls downward mingled with that which shines behind the celestial Carp, begin to swell, and then renew themselves, each in its own color, before the sun yokes his coursers under other stars; so, disclosing a hue less than of roses and more than of violets,⁶ the tree was renewed that first had its branches so bare. I did not understand the hymn, and it is not sung here, which that company then sang, nor did I bear to hear the music to the end.

If I could portray how the pitiless eyes sank

to slumber,[7] hearing of Syrinx, the eyes whose long vigil cost so dear, like a painter who paints from a model I would picture how I fell asleep: but whoso would, let him be one that can depict slumber well. I pass on, therefore, to when I awoke, and tell that a splendor rent the veil of my sleep, and a call, "Arise, what are you doing?"

As when brought to see some of the blossoms of the apple tree that makes the angels greedy of its fruit and holds perpetual wedding feasts in Heaven, Peter and John and James were overpowered,[8] and came to themselves again at the word by which deeper slumbers were broken, and saw their company diminished alike by Moses and Elias, and their Master's raiment changed, so I came to myself, and saw standing over me that compassionate lady who first had been my guide along the stream; and all in doubt I said, "Where is Beatrice?" And she, "See her beneath the new foliage, seated upon its root; see the company that encircles her: the rest are rising on high behind the griffin, with sweeter song and more profound." And if her speech continued longer I do not know, for already in my eyes was she who had shut me off from every other care. She was sitting there alone on the bare ground, like a guard left there of the chariot which I had seen bound by the bi-formed animal. In a circle the seven nymphs were making of themselves an enclosure for her, with those lights in their hands that are safe from Aquilo and from Auster.[9]

"Here shall you be short time[10] a forester, and you shall be with me forever a citizen of that Rome whereof Christ is Roman. Therefore, for profit of the world that lives ill, hold your eyes now on the chariot, and what you see, mind that you write it when you have returned yonder." Thus Beatrice; and I, who at the feet of her commands was all devout, gave my mind and my eyes whither she willed.

Never with so swift a motion[11] did fire descend from dense cloud, when it falls from the confine that stretches most remote, as I saw the bird of Jove swoop downward through the tree, rending the bark as well as the flowers and the new leaves, and it struck the chariot with all its force, so that it reeled like a ship in a tempest, driven by the waves, now to starboard, now to larboard. Then I saw leap into the body of the triumphal vehicle a fox that seemed starved of all good nourishment; but my lady, rebuking it for its foul offenses, turned it to such flight as its fleshless bones allowed. Then, from there whence it had come before, I saw the eagle descend into the body of the chariot and leave it feathered with its plumage. And a voice such as issues from a heart that is afflicted came from Heaven, and it said, "O little bark of mine, how ill are you laden!" Then it seemed to me that the earth opened between the two wheels, and I saw a dragon issue therefrom, which drove its tail upward through the chariot, and, like a wasp that retracts its sting, drawing to itself its malignant tail, tore out part of the bottom and made off, all content. What was left was covered again, as live soil with grass, with the plumage, offered perhaps with sincere and kind intent, and both one and the other wheel were covered with it in less time than a sigh keeps open the mouth. Thus transformed, the holy structure put forth heads upon its parts, three on the pole and one on each corner: the three were horned like oxen, but the four had a single horn on the forehead. Such a monster was never seen before. Secure, like a fortress on a high mountain, there apppeared to me an ungirt harlot sitting upon it, with eyes quick to rove around; and, as if in order that she should not be taken from him, I saw standing at her side a giant, and they kissed each other again and again. But because she turned her lustful and wandering eye on me, that fierce paramour beat her from head to foot. Then, full of jealousy and fierce with rage, he loosed the monster and drew it through the wood so far that only of that he made a shield from me for the harlot and for the strange beast.[12]

CANTO XXXIII

"*Deus, venerunt gentes,*"[1] the ladies began, alternating, now three now four, a sweet psalmody, and weeping. And Beatrice, sighing and compassionate, was listening to them, so moved that little more did Mary change at the Cross. But when the other virgins gave place to her to speak, uprisen erect on her feet, she answered, colored like fire, "*Modicum et non videbitis me, et iterum,* my beloved sisters, *modicum et vos videbitis me.*"[2] Then she set all the seven in front of her; and behind her, merely beckoning, she placed me and the lady and the sage who remained. Thus she went on, and I do not think she had taken the tenth step on the ground when with her eyes she smote on mine, and with tranquil look said to me, "Come more quickly, so that if I speak with you, you be well placed to listen to me." As soon as I was with her, as it was my duty to be, she said to me, "Brother, why, coming now with me, do you not venture to ask of me?"

As with those who with excessive reverence are speaking in the presence of their superiors so that they do not bring the voice whole to their lips, so it was with me, and without full utterance I began, "My lady, my need you know and that which is good for it." And she to me, "From fear and from shame I wish that you henceforth divest yourself, so that you may no more speak like one who is dreaming. Know that the vessel which the serpent broke was, and is not: but let him whose fault it is[3] believe that God's vengeance fears no hindrance. Not for all time shall be without an heir the eagle that left its feathers on the chariot, whereby it became a monster and then a prey: for I see surely, and therefore I tell of it, stars already close at hand, secure from all check and hindrance, that shall bring us a time wherein a Five Hundred, Ten, and Five, sent by God,[4] shall slay the thievish woman, with that giant who sins with her. And perhaps my prophecy, obscure as Themis[5] and Sphinx,[6] persuades you less because, after their fashion, it darkens your mind; but soon the facts shall be the Naiads[7] that will solve this hard enigma, without loss of flocks or of harvest. Do you note, and even as these words are uttered by me, so teach them to those who live the life that is a race to death; and have in mind, when you write them, not to hide what you have seen of the tree which has now twice over been despoiled here. Whosoever robs that tree, or rends it, offends with blasphemy of act against God, who for His own sole use created it holy. For tasting of that tree the first soul longed in pain and in desire five thousand years and more for Him who punished on Himself that taste. Your wit sleeps if it deem not that for a special reason it is of such loftiness and thus inverted at its top; and if your vain thoughts had not been as water of Elsa[8] round about your mind, and their pleasantness as Pyramus[9] to the mulberry, by so many circumstances only you would recognize, in the moral sense, the justice of God in the interdict on the tree. But since I see you turned to stone in your mind, and stonelike, such in hue that the light of my word dazes you, I would also have you bear it away within you—and if not written, at least depicted—for the reason that the pilgrim's staff is brought back wreathed with palm."[10]

And I, "Even as wax under the seal, that does not change the imprinted figure, my brain is now stamped by you; but why do your longed-for words soar so far beyond my sight, that the more it strains the more it loses them?"

"In order that you may know," she said, "that school which you have followed, and may see if its teaching can follow my word, and see your way so far distant from the divine way, as the heaven that highest spins is remote from earth."

Whereon I answered her, "I do not remember that I ever estranged me from you, nor have I conscience thereof that gnaws me."

"And if you cannot remember it," smiling she replied, "bethink you now how you have drunk of Lethe[11] this very day; and if from smoke fire is argued, this forgetfulness clearly proves fault in your will elsewhere intent. But henceforth my words shall be as simple as may be needful to make them plain to your rude sight."

Now more refulgent and with slower steps the sun held the meridian circle, which shifts here and there with the point of view, when, just as one going before a company for escort, stops if he comes on some strange thing or traces thereof, the seven ladies stopped at the edge of a pale shade, such as beneath green leaves and dark boughs the mountains cast over their cold streams. In front of them it seemed to me I saw Euphrates and Tigris[12] issue from one fountain, and, like friends, slowly part from one another.

"O light, O glory of the human race, what water is this that pours here from one source and from itself withdraws itself?" To my question she replied, "Ask Matelda[13] to tell you." And here the beautiful lady answered, as one freeing herself from blame, "This and other things I have told him, and I am certain that Lethe's water did not hide it from him."

And Beatrice, "Perhaps some greater care, which often robs the memory, has darkened the eyes of his mind. But see Eunoe that flows forth there: bring him thereto, and, as you are wont, revive his weakened faculties."[14]

As a gentle spirit that makes no excuse, but makes its will of another's will, as soon as that is disclosed by outward sign, so the fair lady, after I was taken by her, moved on, and with womanly grace said to Statius, "Come with him."

If, reader, I had greater space for writing, I would yet partly sing the sweet draught which never would have sated me; but since all the pages ordained for this second canticle are filled, the curb of art lets me go no further. I came forth from the most holy waves, renovated even as new trees renewed with new foliage, pure and ready to rise to the stars.

Paradiso

CANTO I

The glory of the All-Mover penetrates through the universe and reglows in one part more, and in another less. I have been in the heaven that most receives of His light, and have seen things which whoso descends from up there has neither the knowledge nor the power to relate, because, as it draws near to its desire, our intellect enters so deep that memory cannot go back upon the track. Nevertheless, so much of the holy kingdom as I could treasure up in my mind shall now be the matter of my song.

O good Apollo, for this last labor make me such a vessel of your worth as you require for granting your beloved laurel.[1] Thus far the one peak of Parnassus[2] has sufficed me, but now I have need of both, as I enter the arena that remains. Enter into my breast and breathe there as when you drew Marsyas from the sheath of his limbs.[3] O divine Power, if you do so lend yourself to me that I may show forth the image of the blessed realm which is imprinted in my mind, you shall see me come to your beloved tree and crown me with those leaves of which the matter and you shall make me worthy. So rarely, father, are they gathered, for triumph of caesar or of poet—fault and shame of human wills—that the Peneian[4] frond ought to beget gladness in the glad Delphic deity whenever it causes anyone to long for it. A great flame follows a little spark: perhaps, after me, prayer shall be offered with better voices, that Cyrrha[5] may respond.

The lamp of the world rises to mortals through different passages; but through that which joins four circles with three crosses it issues with a better course and conjoined with better stars, and tempers and stamps the wax of the world more after its own fashion.[6] Almost such an outlet had made morning there and evening here, and all the hemisphere there was white, and the other dark, when I saw Beatrice turned to her left side and looking at the sun:

never did eagle so fix his gaze thereon. And even as a second ray is wont to issue from the first, and mount upwards again, like a pilgrim who would return home: thus of her action, infused through the eyes into my imagination, mine was made, and I fixed my eyes on the sun beyond our wont. Much is granted to our faculties there that is not granted here, by virtue of the place made for humankind as its proper abode. I did not endure it long, nor so little that I did not see it sparkle round about, like iron that comes molten from the fire. And suddenly day seemed added to day, as if He who has the power had adorned heaven with another sun.

Beatrice was standing with her eyes all fixed upon the eternal wheels, and I fixed mine on her, withdrawn from there above. Gazing upon her I became within me such as Glaucus became on tasting of the grass that made him sea-fellow of the other gods.[7] The passing beyond humanity may not be set forth in words: therefore let the example suffice any for whom grace reserves that experience.

Whether I was but that part of me which Thou didst create last, O Love that rulest the heavens, Thou knowest, who with Thy light didst lift me. When the revolution which Thou, by being desired, makest eternal turned my attention unto itself by the harmony which Thou dost temper and distinguish, so much of the heaven seemed to me then to be kindled by the sun's flame that rain or river never made a lake so wide. The novelty of the sound and the great light kindled in me a desire to know their cause, never before felt with such keenness. Whereupon she who saw me as I saw myself, to quiet my perturbed mind, opened her lips before I opened mine to ask, and began, "You make yourself dull with false imagining, so that you do not see what you would see had you cast it off. You are not on earth, as you believe; but lightning, fleeing its proper site, never darted so fast as you are returning to yours."

If by these brief words which she smiled to

me I was freed from my first perplexity, within a new one I became the more enmeshed; and I said, "I was already content concerning one great wonder; but now I marvel how it can be that I should pass through these light bodies."

Whereupon, after a pitying sigh, she turned her eyes on me with the look that a mother casts on her delirious child. And she began, "All things have order among themselves, and this is the form that makes the universe like God.[8] Herein the high creatures behold the imprint of the Eternal Worth, which is the end wherefore the aforesaid ordinance is made. In the order whereof I speak all natures are inclined by different lots, nearer and less near unto their principle; wherefore they move to different ports over the great sea of being, each with an instinct given it to bear it on: this bears fire upwards toward the moon; this is the motive force in mortal creatures; this binds together and unites the earth. And not only does this bow shoot those creatures that lack intelligence, but also those that have intellect and love. The Providence which ordains all this, with Its light makes ever quiet that heaven within which revolves the sphere that has the greatest speed; and thither now, as to a place decreed, the virtue of that bowstring bears us on, which aims at a joyful target whatsoever it shoots.

"To be sure, even as a shape often does not accord with the intention of the art, because the material is deaf to respond, so the creature sometimes departs from this course, having the power, thus impelled, to swerve toward some other part; and even as the fire from a cloud may be seen to fall downwards, so the primal impulse, diverted by false pleasure, is turned toward earth. You should not wonder more at your rising, if I deem aright, than at a stream that falls from a mountain top to the base. It would be a marvel if you, being freed from hindrance, had settled down below, even as stillness would be in living fire on earth."

Then she turned her gaze heavenwards again.

CANTO II

O you that are in your little bark, eager to hear, following behind my ship that singing makes her way, turn back to see again your shores.

Do not commit yourselves to the open sea, for perchance, if you lost me, you would remain astray. The water which I take was never coursed before. Minerva breathes and Apollo guides me, and nine Muses point out to me the Bears.

You other few who lifted up your necks betimes for bread of angels, on which men here subsist but never become sated of it, you may indeed commit your vessel to the deep brine, holding to my furrow ahead of the water that turns smooth again. Those glorious ones who crossed the sea to Colchis, when they saw Jason turned plowman, were not as amazed as you shall be.[1]

The inborn and perpetual thirst for the deiform realm bore us away, swift almost as you see the heavens. Beatrice was gazing upward, and I on her; and perhaps in that time that a bolt strikes, flies, and from the catch is released, I saw myself arrived where a wondrous thing drew my sight to it. She, therefore, from whom my thoughts could not be hidden, turned toward me, as glad as she was fair, and "Direct your mind to God in gratitude," she said, "who has united us with the first star."[2]

It seemed to me that a cloud had enveloped us, shining, dense, solid and polished, like a diamond smitten by the sun. Within itself the eternal pearl received us, as water receives a ray of light, itself remaining uncleft. If I was body (and if here we conceive not how one bulk could brook another, which must be if body enters body), the more should longing enkindle us to see that Essence wherein we behold how our nature and God united themselves. There that which we hold by faith shall be seen, not demonstrated, but known of itself, like the first truth that man believes.

I answered, "My Lady, devoutly as I most may, I do thank Him who has removed me from the mortal world. But tell me, what are the dusky marks of this body which there below on earth cause folk to tell the tale of Cain?"[3]

She smiled a little, and then said to me, "If the judgment of mortals errs where the key of sense does not unlock, truly the shafts of wonder should not prick you henceforth, since even when following after the senses you see that reason's wings are short. But tell me what you yourself think of it."

And I, "That which appears to us diverse

here above I suppose to be produced by rare and dense matter."

And she, "Verily you shall see that your belief is plunged deep in error, if you listen well to the argument I shall make against it.

"The eighth sphere[4] displays to you many lights which both in quality and in magnitude can be seen to be of diverse countenances. If rarity and density alone produced this thing, one single virtue, more or less or equally distributed, would be in all. Different virtues must needs be fruits of formal principles, the which, save only one, would be destroyed, according to your reckoning. Further, were rarity the cause of that darkness whereof you make question, either this planet would thus be lacking in its matter quite through and through, or else, just as fat and lean are distributed in a body, it would alternate the pages in its volume. If the first were the case, this would be manifest in the eclipse of the sun, by the shining through of the light, as it does when it is poured upon any rare matter. This is not so; therefore we must look at the other supposition, and if it chance that I quash that, your opinion will be refuted.

"If it be that this rarity does not pass throughout, needs must there be a limit at which its contrary intercepts its passing farther, and thence that other's ray would be cast back, just as color returns from the glass that hides lead behind itself. Now you will say that the ray shows itself dimmer there than in other parts, because it is reflected there from farther back. From this objection experiment, which is wont to be the fountain to the streams of your arts, may deliver you, if ever you try it. You shall take three mirrors, and set two of them equally remote from you, and let the other, even more remote, meet your eyes between the first two. Turning toward them, cause a light to be placed behind your back which may shine in the three mirrors and return to you reflected from all three. Although the more distant image may not reach you so great in quantity, you will there see it must needs be of equal brightness with the others.

"Now—as beneath the blows of the warm rays the substrate of the snow is left stripped both of the color and the coldness which it had—you, left thus stripped in your intellect, will I inform with light so living that it shall quiver as you look on it.

"Within the heaven of the divine peace revolves a body in whose power lies the being of all that it contains. The following heaven, which has so many things to show, distributes this being through diverse essences, distinct from it and contained by it. The other circles, by various differentiatings, dispose the distinctions which they have within themselves unto their ends and their sowings. These organs of the universe proceed,[5] as you now see, from grade to grade, for they receive from above and operate downwards. Observe well now how I advance through this pass to the truth which you seek, so that hereafter you may know how to take the ford alone. The motion and the virtue of the holy spheres, even as the hammer's art by the smith, must needs be inspired by the blessed movers; and the heaven which so many lights make beautiful takes its stamp from the profound mind that turns it, and of that stamp makes itself the seal. And as the soul within your dust is diffused through different members and conformed to different potencies, so does the Intelligence deploy its goodness, multiplied through the stars, itself circling upon its own unity. Divers virtues make divers alloy with the precious body it quickens, wherein, even as life in you, it is bound. Because of the glad nature whence it flows, the mingled virtue shines through the body, as gladness does through a living pupil. Thence comes what seems different between light and light, not from density and rarity. This is the formal principle which produces, comformably with its own excellence, the dark and the bright."

CANTO III

That sun which first had heated my breast with love, proving and refuting had uncovered to me the sweet aspect of fair truth, and, to confess me corrected and assured, I raised my head more erect to speak, in measure as was meet; but a sight appeared which held me so fast to itself, to look on it, that I bethought me not of my confession.

As through smooth and transparent glass, or through clear and tranquil waters, yet not so deep that the bottom be lost, the outlines of our faces return so faint that a pearl on a white brow comes not less boldly to our eyes, so did I behold many a countenance eager to speak; wherefore I fell into the contrary error to that which kindled love between the man and the fountain.[1] No sooner was I aware of them than, taking them for mirrored faces, I turned round my eyes to see of whom they were, and saw nothing; and I turned them forward again, straight into the light of the sweet guide, whose holy eyes were glowing as she smiled.

"Do not wonder," she said to me, "that I smile at your childish thought, since it does not yet trust itself upon the truth, but turns you, after its wont, to vacancy. These that you see are real substances, assigned here for failure in their vows. Wherefore speak with them and hear and believe, for the true light that satisfies them does not suffer them to turn their steps aside from it."

And I directed myself to the shade who seemed most eager to speak, and I began like a man whom excessive desire confuses, "O well-created spirit, who in the rays of life eternal do taste the sweetness which, if not tasted, is never understood, it would be a kindness to me if you satisfied me with your name and with your lot."

Whereon she, eager and with smiling eyes, "Our charity does not shut the doors against right will any more than that which wills that all Its court be like Itself. In the world I was a virgin sister, and if your memory be searched well, my being more beautiful will not conceal me from you, but you will recognize that I am Piccarda,[2] who, placed here with these other blessèd ones, am blessèd in the slowest sphere. Our affections, which are kindled solely in the pleasure of the Holy Ghost, rejoice in being conformed to His order. And this lot, which appears so lowly, is given to us because our vows were neglected and void in some particular."

Whereon I said to her, "In your wondrous aspects a something divine shines forth that transmutes you from recollection of former times; therefore I was not quick in calling you to mind, but now that which you tell me helps me so that I more clearly recall your features. But tell me, you who are happy here, do you

desire a more exalted place, to see more, and to make yourselves more dear?"

With those other shades she first smiled a little, then answered me so glad that she seemed to burn in the first fire of love, "Brother, the power of love quiets our will and makes us wish only for that which we have and gives us no other thirst. Did we desire to be more aloft, our longings would be discordant with His will who assigns us here: which you will see is not possible in these circles if to exist in charity here is of necessity, and if you well consider what is love's nature. Nay, it is the essence of this blessed existence to keep itself within the divine will, whereby our wills themselves are made one; so that our being thus from threshold to threshold throughout this realm is a joy to all the realm as to the King, who draws our wills to what He wills; and in His will is our peace. It is that sea to which all moves, both what It creates and what nature makes."

Then was it clear to me how everywhere in Heaven is Paradise, even if the grace of the Supreme Good does not there rain down in one same measure. But as it happens when of one food we have enough and the appetite for another still remains, that this is asked for and thanks are returned for that, so I did with gesture and with speech, to learn from her what was the web through which she had not drawn the shuttle to the end.

"Perfect life and high merit enheaven a lady[3] more aloft," she said to me, "according to whose rule, in your world below, are those who take the robe and veil themselves that they, even till death, may wake and sleep with that Spouse who accepts every vow which love conforms unto His pleasure. From the world, to follow her, I fled while yet a girl, and in her habit I clothed me and promised myself to the way of her order. Then men, more used to evil than to good, snatched me from the sweet cloister: and God knows what then my life became.

"And this other splendor which shows itself to you at my right side, and which is enkindled with all the light of our sphere, understands of herself that which I say of me. She was a sister, and from her head in like manner was taken the shadow of the sacred veil. Yet, turned back as she was into the world, against her will and against right custom, from her heart's veil she was never loosed. This is the light of the great Constance,[4] who bore to the second blast of Swabia the third and final power."

Thus did she speak to me, and then began to sing *Ave Maria,* and, singing, vanished, as through deep water some heavy thing. My sight, which followed her so far as was possible, after it lost her, turned to the mark of greater desire and wholly reverted to Beatrice; but she so flashed upon my gaze that at first my sight endured it not; and this made me the slower with my questioning.

CANTO IV

Between two foods, distant and appetizing in equal measure, a free man would die of hunger before he would bring one of them to his teeth. So would a lamb stand between two cravings of fierce wolves, in equal fear of both; so would a hound stand still between two hinds. Wherefore, if I was silent, urged in equal measure by my doubts, I neither blame nor commend myself, since it was of necessity.

I was silent, but my desire was depicted on my face, and my questioning with it, in warmer colors far than by distinct speech. Beatrice did what Daniel did, when he lifted Nebuchadnezzar out of the wrath that had made him unjustly cruel, and she said, "I see well how one and another desire so draw you on that your eagerness entangles its own self and therefore breathes not forth. You reason, 'If right will endures, by what justice can another's violence lessen the measure of my desert?' Further, that the souls appear to return to the stars, in accordance with Plato's teaching, gives you occasion for doubt. These are the questions that thrust equally upon your will. And therefore I will first treat that which has the most venom.

"Of the Seraphim he who is most in God, Moses, Samuel, and whichever John you will—I say, even Mary—have not their seats in any other heaven than these spirits which have now appeared to you, nor have they more or fewer years for their existence; but all make the first circle beautiful, and have sweet life in different measure, by feeling more and less the eternal breath. These showed themselves here, not because this sphere is allotted to them, but to afford sign of the celestial grade that is least exalted. It is needful to speak thus to your faculty, since only through sense perception does it apprehend that which it afterwards makes fit for the intellect. For this reason Scripture condescends to your capacity, and attributes hands and feet to God, having other meaning; and Holy Church represents to you with human aspect Gabriel and Michael and the other who made Tobit whole again. What Timaeus[1] argues about the souls is not like this which is seen here, for seemingly he holds what he says for the truth. He says the soul returns to its own star, believing it to have been severed thence when nature gave it for a form. But perhaps his opinion is other than his words sound, and may be of a meaning not to be derided. If he means that the honor of their influence and the blame returns to these wheels, perhaps his bow hits some truth. This principle, ill-understood, once misled almost the entire world, so that it ran astray in naming Jove and Mercury and Mars.

"The other perplexity that troubles you has less of poison, for its malice could not lead you away from me elsewhere. For our justice to seem unjust in mortal eyes is argument of faith, not of heretical iniquity. But since your understanding can well penetrate to this truth, I will make you content as you desire.

"If it be violence when he who suffers contributes nothing to what forces him, these souls would not be excused on that account. For will, if it will not, is not quenched, but does as nature does in fire, though violence wrest it aside a thousand times. For should it bend itself much or little, it follows force: and thus did these when they had power to return to the holy place. If their will had remained whole, such as held Lawrence[2] on the grid and made Mucius[3] severe to his own hand, it would have urged them back, so soon as they were loosed, by the road along which they had been dragged—but such sound will is all too rare. And by these words, if you have gathered them up as you should, is the argument quashed that would have troubled you yet many times.

"But now across your path another strait confronts your eyes, such that you would not get through it by yourself before you would be exhausted. I have put it in your mind for certain that a soul in bliss cannot lie, since it is always near the Primal Truth; and then you could hear from Piccarda that Constance kept her love for the veil, so that here she seems to contradict me. Many a time ere now, brother, has it happened that unwillingly, in order to escape from danger, that was done which ought not to have been done; even as Alcmeon who, urged thereto by his father, slew his own mother, and, so as not to fail in piety, became pitiless. At this point I would have you realize that force mixes with the will, and they so act that the offenses cannot be excused. Absolute will does not consent to the wrong, but the will consents thereto in so far as it fears, by drawing back, to fall into greater trouble. Therefore, when Piccarda says this, she means it of the absolute will, and I of the other; so that we both speak truth together."

Such was the rippling of the holy stream which issued forth from the Fount from which springs every truth, and such it set at rest one and the other desire.

"O beloved of the First Lover, O divine one," said I then, "whose speech overflows me and warms me so that it quickens me more and more, not all the depth of my affection is sufficient to render to you grace for grace; but may He who sees and can answer thereto. Well do I see that never can our intellect be wholly satisfied unless that Truth shine on it, beyond which no truth has range. Therein it rests, as a wild beast in his lair, so soon as it has reached it; and reach it it can, else every desire would be in vain. Because of this, questioning springs up like a shoot, at the foot of the truth; and this is nature which urges us to the summit, from height to height. It is this, Lady, that invites and emboldens me to question you with reverence of another truth which is obscure to me. I wish to know if man can so satisfy you for broken vows, with other goods, as not to weigh too short upon your scales."

Beatrice looked on me with eyes so full of the sparkling of love and so divine that my power, vanquished, took flight, and I almost lost myself with eyes downcast.

CANTO V

"If I flame on you in the warmth of love beyond the measure that is seen on earth and so vanquish the power of your eyes, do not marvel, for it comes from perfect vision which, according as it apprehends, so does it move its foot to the apprehended good. Well do I note how in your intellect already is shining the eternal light which, seen, alone and always kindles love; and if aught else seduce your love, it is naught save some vestige of that light, ill-recognized, which therein shines through. You wish to know if for an unfulfilled vow so much can be paid with other service as may secure the soul from suit."

So Beatrice began this canto, and as one who does not interrupt his speech, she thus continued her holy discourse, "The greatest gift which God in His bounty bestowed in creating, and the most conformed to His own goodness and that which He most prizes, was the freedom of the will, with which the creatures that have intelligence, they all and they alone, were and are endowed. Now, if you argue from this, the high worth of the vow will appear to you, if it be such that God consents when you consent; for in establishing the compact between God and man, this treasure becomes the sacrifice, such as I pronounce it, and that by its own act. What then can be given in compensation? If you think to make good use of that which you have offered, you seek to do good with ill-gotten gains.

"You are now assured as to the greater point; but since Holy Church gives dispensation in this matter, which seems contrary to the truth I have declared to you, it behooves you to sit a while longer at table, for the tough food which you have taken requires still some aid for your digestion. Open your mind to that which I reveal to you, and fix it therewithin; for to have heard without retaining makes not knowledge.

"Two things constitute the essence of this sacrifice: the first is that in respect to which it is made, and the other is the covenant itself. This last is never canceled save by being kept, and concerning this was my preceding speech so precise. Therefore it was imperative upon the Hebrews to offer sacrifice in any case, though the thing offered might sometimes be changed, as you should know. The other, which is known to you as the matter, may indeed be such that there is no fault if it be exchanged for other matter. But let no one shift the load upon his shoulder at his own judgment, without the turning of both the white and the yellow key; and let him hold all changing folly unless the thing laid down be not contained in that which is taken up, as four in six. Therefore, whatever thing weighs so much through its own worth as to tip every scale cannot be made good by any other outlay.

"Let mortals never take the vow in sport. Be faithful, and with that be not perverse, as was Jephthah in his first offering,[1] who ought rather to have said 'I did amiss,' than, by keeping his vow, to do worse. And you can find the great leader of the Greeks in like manner foolish, wherefore Iphigenia[2] wept that her face was fair, and made weep for her both the simple and the wise who heard the tale of such a rite. Be graver, you Christians, in moving. Be not like a feather to every wind, and think not that every water may cleanse you. You have the New Testament and the Old, and the Shepherd of the Church, to guide you: let this suffice for your salvation. If evil greed cry aught else to you, be you men, and not silly sheep, so that the Jew among you may not laugh at you. Be not like the lamb that leaves its mother's milk and, silly and wanton, fights with itself at its own pleasure."

Thus Beatrice to me, even as I write; then she turned full of longing to that part where the universe is most alive. Her silence and her changed look imposed silence on my eager mind, which already had new questionings before it. And as an arrow that strikes the target before the bowcord is quiet, so we sped into the second realm.[3] Here I beheld my lady so glad, when she passed into that heaven's light, that the planet itself became the brighter for it; and if the star changed and smiled, what did I become, who by my very nature am subject to every kind of change?

As in a fish-pool that is still and clear the fish draw to that which comes in such manner from without that they deem it something they can feed on, so did I see full more than a thousand splendors draw towards us, and in each was heard, "Lo one who shall increase our loves!" And, as each came up to us, the shade was seen full of joy, by the bright effulgence that issued from it.

Think, reader, if this beginning went no further, how you would feel an anguished craving to know more, and by yourself you will see what my desire was, to hear of their conditions from them, as soon as they became manifest to my eyes.

"O happy-born, to whom Grace concedes to see the thrones of the eternal triumph before you leave your time of warfare, we are enkindled by the light that ranges through all heaven; therefore, if you desire to draw light from us, sate yourself at your own pleasure." Thus was it said to me by one of those devout spirits; and by Beatrice, "Speak, speak securely, and trust even as to gods."

"I see well how you do nest yourself in your own light, and that you dart it from your eyes, because it sparkles when you smile; but I know not who you are, nor why, O worthy spirit, you have your rank in the sphere that is veiled to mortals by another's rays." This I said, turned toward the light which first had spoken to me; whereon it glowed far brighter than before. Even as the sun, which, when the heat has consumed the tempering of the dense vapors, conceals itself by excess of light, so, by reason of more joy, the holy figure hid itself from me within its own radiance and, thus close enclosed, it answered me in such fashion as the next canto sings.

CANTO VI

"After Constantine turned back the Eagle counter to the course of the heavens which it had followed behind the ancient who took Lavinia to wife,[1] a hundred and a hundred years and more the bird of God abode on Europe's limit, near to the mountains from which it first had issued; and there it governed the world beneath the shadow of its sacred wings, from hand to hand, until by succeeding change it came into mine. I was Caesar, and am Justinian,[2] who, by will of the Primal Love which I feel, removed from among the laws what was superfluous and vain. And before I had put my mind to this work, one nature and no more I held to be in Christ, and with that faith I was content; but the blessed Agapetus,[3] who was the supreme pastor, directed me to the true faith by his words. I believed him, and what he held by faith I now see as clearly as you see that every contradiction is both false and true. So soon as with the Church I moved my feet, it pleased God, of His grace, to inspire me with this high task, and I gave myself entirely to it, committing arms to my Belisarius,[4] with whom Heaven's right hand was so joined that it was a sign for me to rest from them.

"Here ends, then, my answer to the first question; but its condition constrains me to add a certain sequel to it, in order that you may see with how much reason they move against the sacred standard, both those that take it for their own and those that oppose it.[5] See what great virtue made it worthy of reverence, beginning from the hour when Pallas died to give it sway. You know that it made its stay in Alba for three hundred years and more, till at the end, when the three fought against the three for it still. And you know what it did, through seven kings, from the wrong of the Sabine women down to the woe of Lucretia, conquering the neighboring peoples round about. You know what it did when borne by the illustrious Romans against Brennus, against Pyrrhus, and against the rest, princes and governments; whence Torquatus and Quinctius, named from his neglected locks, the Decii and the Fabii, acquired the fame which I gladly embalm. It cast down the pride of the Arabs[6] that followed Hannibal across the Alpine rocks whence, Po, you do fall. Under it, Scipio and Pompey triumphed, while yet in their youth, and to that hill beneath which you were born it showed itself bitter.[7] Afterward, near the time when all Heaven willed to bring the world to its own state of peace, Caesar,[8] by the will of Rome, laid hold of it; and what it did from the Var[9] even to the Rhine, the Isere beheld, and the Loire and the Seine beheld, and every valley whence Rhone is filled. What it did after it came forth from Ravenna and leaped the Rubicon was of such flight as no tongue nor pen might follow. Towards Spain it wheeled the host, then towards Durazzo, and did so smite Pharsalia[10] that grief was felt on the burning Nile. It saw again Antandros and the Simois,[11] whence it had set forth, and there where Hector lies;[12] and then it shook itself again—the worse for Ptolemy. From there it fell like lightning on Juba,[13] then turned to your west,[14] where it heard Pompey's trumpet. Of what it wrought with the succeeding marshal, Brutus and Cassius howl in Hell, and Modena and Perugia were doleful.[15] Because of it sad Cleopatra is still weeping who, fleeing before it, took from the viper sudden and black death.[16] With him it coursed far as the Red Sea Shore; with him it set the world in such peace that Janus's temple was locked.[17]

"But what the standard that makes me speak had done before, and after was to do throughout the mortal realm subject unto it, becomes in appearance little and obscure if it be looked on in the hand of the third Caesar with clear eye and pure affection; because the living Justice which inspires me granted to it, in his hand of whom I speak, the glory of doing vengeance for Its own wrath. Now marvel here at what I unfold to you: afterwards it sped with Titus to do vengeance for the vengeance of the ancient sin.[18] Then, when the Lombard tooth bit Holy Church, under its wings Charlemagne, conquering, succored her.[19]

"Now you may judge of such as I accused but now, and of their offenses, which are the cause of all your ills. The one opposes to the public standard the yellow lilies, and the other claims it for a party, so that it is hard to see which offends the most. Let the Ghibellines, let them practise their art under another ensign, for this one he ever follows ill who cleaves justice from it. And let not this new Charles strike it down with his Guelphs,[20] but let him fear talons which have stripped the hide from a greater lion. Many a time ere now the sons have wept for the sin of the father; and let him not believe that God will change arms for his lilies.

"This little star is adorned with good spirits who have been active in order that honor and fame might come to them. And when desires, thus deviating, tend thitherward, the rays of true love must needs mount upwards less living. But in the equal measure of our rewards with our desert is part of our joy, because we see them neither less nor greater. Hereby the living Justice makes our affection so sweet within us that it can never be bent aside to any evil. Diverse voices make sweet music, so diverse ranks in our life render sweet harmony among these wheels.

"And within this present pearl shines the light of Romeo, whose noble and beautiful work was ill rewarded; but the Provençals who wrought against him have not the laugh, and indeed he takes an ill path who makes harm for himself of another's good work. Raymond Berenger had four daughters, each of them a queen, and Romeo, a man of lowly birth and a pilgrim, did this for him. And then crooked words moved him to demand a reckoning of this just man, who had rendered him seven and five for ten.[21] Thereon he departed, poor and old, and if the world but knew the heart he had while begging his bread morsel by morsel, much as it praises him it would praise him more."

CANTO VII

"Hosanna, sanctus Deus sabaòth,
superillustrans claritate tua
felices ignes horum malacòth!"[1]

—so, revolving to his melody I saw that substance sing, on whom a double light is twinned; and he and the others moved in their dance, and like swiftest sparks veiled themselves from me by sudden distance. I was in doubt, and was saying to myself, "Speak to her, speak to her," I was saying, "speak to her, to my lady who slakes my thirst with her sweet distillings!" But that reverence which is wholly mistress of me, only by *Be* and by *ice*, bowed me like one who drowses. Short while did Beatrice suffer me thus, and she began, irradiating me with a smile such as would make a man happy in the fire, "By my judgment, which cannot err, how just vengeance could be justly avenged, has set you pondering; but I will quickly free your mind, and do you listen, for my words will make you the gift of a great doctrine.

"By not enduring for his own good a curb upon the power that wills, that man who never was born, in damning himself damned all his progeny; wherefore the human race lay sick down there for many centuries in great error, until it pleased the word of God to descend where He, by the sole act of His eternal love, united with Himself in person the nature which had estranged itself from its Maker.

"Turn your sight now to that which now I say: this nature, which was thus united to its Maker, was, when it was created, pure and good; but by its own self it had been banished from Paradise, because it turned aside from the way of the truth and its proper life. The penalty therefore which the Cross inflicted, if it be measured by the nature assumed—none ever so justly stung; also none was ever of such great wrong, if we regard the Person who suffered it, with whom that nature was bound up. Therefore from one act issued things diverse, for one same death was pleasing to God and to the Jews; thereat the earth trembled and Heaven was opened. No longer, now, should it seem hard to you when it is said that just vengeance was afterwards avenged by a just court.

"But now I see your mind from thought to thought entangled in a knot, from which, with great desire, it awaits release. You say, 'I follow clearly what I hear, but why God willed this sole way for our redemption is hidden from me.' This decree, brother, is buried from the eyes of everyone whose understanding is not matured within love's flame. But inasmuch as at this mark there is much aiming and little discernment, I shall tell why that way was the most fitting.

"The Divine Goodness, which spurns all envy from itself, burning within itself so sparkles that It displays the eternal beauties. That which immediately derives from it thereafter has no end, because when It seals, Its imprint may never be removed. That which rains down from it immediately is wholly free, because it is not subject to the power of the new things. It is the most conformed to it and therefore pleases It the most; for the Holy Ardor, which irradiates everything, is most living in what is most like Itself.

"With all these gifts the human creature is advantaged, and if one fails, it needs must fall from its nobility. Sin alone is that which disfranchises it and makes it unlike the Supreme Good, so that it is little illumined by Its light; and to its dignity it never returns unless, where fault has emptied, it fill up with just penalties against evil delight. Your nature, when it sinned totally in its seed, was removed from these dignities, even as from Paradise; nor could it recover them, if you consider carefully, by any way except the passing of one of these fords: either that God alone, solely by His clemency, had pardoned; or that man should of himself have given satisfaction for his folly. Fix your eyes now within the abyss of the Eternal Counsel, as closely fastened on my words as you are able. Man, within his own limits, could never make satisfaction, for not being able to descend in humility, by subsequent obedience, so far as in his disobedience he had intended to ascend; and this is the reason why man was shut off from power to make satisfaction by himself. Therefore it was needful for God, with His own ways, to restore man to his full life—I mean with one way, or else with both. But because the deed is so much the more prized by the doer, the more it displays of the goodness of the heart whence it issued, the divine Goodness which puts its imprint on the world, was pleased to proceed by all Its ways to raise you up again; nor between the last night and the first day has there been or will there be so exalted and so magnificent a procedure, either by one or by the other; for God was more bounteous in giving Himself to make man sufficient to uplift himself again, than if He solely of Himself had remitted; and all other modes were scanty in respect to justice, if the Son of God had not humbled himself to become incarnate.

"Now, to give full satisfaction to your every wish, I go back to explain to you a certain place, that you may see it as clearly as I do. You say, 'I see water, I see fire and air and earth, and all their mixtures come to corruption and endure but little, and yet these things were created things; so that, if what I have said to you be true, they ought to be secure against corruption.'

"The angels, brother, and the pure country in which you are, may be said to be created even as they are, in their entire being; but the elements which you have named, and all things that are compounded of them, are informed by created power. Created was the matter that is in them, created was the informing virtue in these stars that wheel about them. The soul of every beast and of the plants is drawn from a potentiate compound by the shining and the motion of the holy lights; but your life the Supreme Beneficence breathes forth without intermediary, and so enamors it of Itself that it desires It ever after. And hence you further can infer your resurrection, if you reflect how was the making of human flesh then when the first parents were both formed."

CANTO VIII

The world was wont to believe, to its peril, that the fair Cyprian,[1] wheeling in the third epicycle, rayed down mad love; wherefore the ancient people in their ancient error not only to her did honor with sacrifice and votive cry, but they honored Dione and Cupid, the one as her mother, the other as her son, and they told that he had sat in Dido's lap;[2] and from her

with whom I take my start they took the name of the star which the sun woos, now behind her, now before. I was not aware of rising into it, but of being within it my lady gave me full assurance when I saw her become more beautiful.

And as we see a spark within a flame, and as a voice within a voice is distinguished when one holds the note and another comes and goes, I saw within that light other lamps moving in a circle more and less swift according to the measure, I believe, of their internal sight. From a cold cloud winds, whether visible or not, never descended so swiftly that they would not seem impeded and slow to one who had seen those divine lights come to us, leaving the circling first begun among the high Seraphim; and within those that appeared most in front *Hosanna* sounded in such wise that never since have I been without the desire to hear it again.

Then one drew nearer to us, and alone began, "We are all ready at your pleasure, that you may have joy of us. With one circle, with one circling and with one thirst we revolve with the celestial Princes to whom you in the world did once say, '*You who move the third heaven by intellection*'; and we are so full of love that, in order to please you, a little quiet will not be less sweet to us."

After my eyes had been raised with reverence to my lady, and she had satisfied them with assurance of her consent, they turned back to the light which had promised so much; and "Say who you are" was my utterance, stamped with great affection; and, how much I saw it increase in size and brightness, through the new joy which was added to its joys when I spoke! Thus changed, it said to me, "The world held me below but little time;[3] and had it been more, much ill shall be that would not have been. My joy, which rays around me, holds me concealed from you and hides me like a creature swathed in its own silk. Much did you love me, and had good cause; for had I remained below, I would have shown you of my love more than the leaves. That left bank which is bathed by the Rhone, after it has mingled with the Sorgue, awaited me in due time for its lord; so did that corner of Ausonia, down from where Tronto and Verde discharge into the sea, which is skirted by Bari and Gaeta and Catona.[4] Already was shining on my brow the crown of that land which the Danube waters after it has left its German banks. And the fair Trinacria (which between Pachynus and Pelorus, on the gulf most vexed by Eurus, is darkened not by Typhoeus, but by nascent sulphur)[5] would yet have looked to have its kings born through me from Charles and Rudolph,[6] if ill lordship, which ever embitters the subject people, had not moved Palermo to shout, 'Die! Die!'[7] And if my brother foresaw this, he would already shun the rapacious poverty of Catalonia,[8] lest it make trouble for him; for truly it is needful for him or for some other to look to it, lest upon his laden bark a heavier load be laid. His nature—mean descendant from a generous forebear—would need a knighthood that gave not its care to the filling of coffers."

"Because I believe that the deep joy which your words infuse in me is, even as I see it, seen by you, my lord, there where every good has its end and its beginning, it is the more welcome to me; and this also I hold dear, that you discern it gazing upon God. You have made me glad; and so now do you make clear to me (since in speaking you have raised the question in my mind) how from sweet seed may come forth bitter."

Thus I to him; and he to me, "If I can make one truth plain to you, you will hold your face toward that which you ask, as you now hold your back. The Good which revolves and contents all the realm that you are climbing makes its providence become a power in these great bodies; and not only is the nature of things provided for in the Mind which by itself is perfect, but, along with that nature, their well-being; so that whatever this bow shoots falls disposed to a foreseen end, even as a shaft directed to its mark. Were this not so, the heavens which you are traversing would produce their effects in such wise that they would be not works of art but ruins—and that cannot be, unless the Intelligences that move these stars be defective, and defective also the Primal Intelligence in that it did not make them perfect. Do you wish this truth to be made still clearer to you?"

And I, "No, truly; for I see it to be impossible that Nature should weary in that which is needful."

Whereupon he again, "Now say, would it be worse for man on earth if he were not a citizen?"

"Yes," I replied, "and here I ask for no proof."

"And can that be, unless men below live in diverse ways for diverse duties? Not if your master writes well of this for you." Thus he came deducing far as here, then he concluded, "Therefore the roots of your works must needs be diverse, so that one is born Solon and another Xerxes, one Melchizedek and another he who flew through the air and lost his son.[9] Circling nature, which is a seal on the mortal wax, performs its art well, but does not distinguish one house from another. Whence it happens that Esau differs in the seed from Jacob, and Quirinus comes from so base a father that he is ascribed to Mars. The begotten nature would always make its course like its begetters, did not Divine provision overrule.

Now that which was behind you is before you; but, that you may know that I delight in you, I will have a corollary cloak you round. Ever does Nature, if she find fortune discordant with herself, like any kind of seed out of its proper region, come to ill result. And if the world there below would give heed to the foundation which Nature lays, and followed it, it would have its people good. But you wrest to religion one born to gird on the sword, and you make a king of one that is fit for sermons;[10] so that your track is off the road."

CANTO IX

After your Charles, fair Clemence,[1] had enlightened me, he told me of the frauds that his seed was destined to suffer,[2] but he added, "Keep silence, and let the years revolve"; so that I can say nothing except that well-deserved lamentation shall follow on the wrongs done you.

And now the life of that holy light had turned again to the Sun which fills it, as to that Good which is sufficient to all things. Ah, souls deceived and creatures impious, who from such Good turn away your hearts, directing your brows to vanity!

And lo! another of those splendors made toward me and by brightening outwardly was signifying its wish to please me. Beatrice's eyes, fixed on me as before, made me assured of dear assent to my desire.

"Pray, blessed spirit," I said, "afford speedy fulfillment to my wish, and give me proof that what I think I can reflect on you." Whereon the light which was still new to me, from out of its depth where it first was singing, continued, as one rejoicing to do a kindness: "In that region of the depraved land of Italy that lies between the Rialto and the springs of the Brenta and the Piave there rises a hill of no great height,[3] whence once descended a fire-brand that made a great assault on the country round. I and he sprang from the same root. I was called Cunizza,[4] and I am refulgent here because the light of this star overcame me. But I gladly pardon in myself the reason of my lot, and it does not grieve me—which might per-haps seem strange to your vulgar herd. Of this resplendent and precious jewel of our heaven which is nearest to me great fame has re-mained, and before it dies away this centennial year shall yet be fived. See if man should make himself excel, so that the first life may leave another after it! And this the present crowd which the Tagliamento and the Adige[5] shut in considers not; nor yet, though it be scourged, does it repent. But soon it shall come to pass that, because her people are stubborn against duty, Padua at the marsh will stain the wa-ters that bathe Vicenza.[6] And where Sile joins Cagnano,[7] one lords it and goes with his head high, for catching whom the web is already being made. Feltre shall yet bewail the crime of its impious shepherd, which will be so foul that for the like nobody ever entered Malta.[8] Great indeed would be the vat that should re-ceive the blood of the Ferrarese and weary him that should weigh it ounce by ounce, which this courteous priest will offer to show himself a member of his party—and such gifts will suit the country's way of life. Aloft are mirrors—you name them Thrones—whence God in judgment shines upon us, so that these words approve themselves to us." Here she was silent, and had to me the semblance of being turned to other heeding, by the wheel in which she set herself as she was before.

The other joy, which was already known to me as precious, became to my sight like a fine ruby on which the sun is striking. Through rejoicing, effulgence is gained there on high, even as a smile here; but below, the shade dark-ens outwardly as the mind is sad.

"God sees all, and into Him your vision sinks, blessed spirit," I said, "so that no wish may steal itself from you. Why then does your voice, which ever gladdens Heaven—together with the singing of those devout fires that make themselves a cowl with the six wings—not satisfy my longings? Surely I should not wait for your request, were I in you, even as you are in me."

"The greatest valley in which the water spreads from the sea that encircles the world,"[9] he then began, "extends its discordant shores so far counter to the sun that it makes meridian of the place where before it made horizon. I was a dweller on that valley's shore, between the Ebro and the Magra, which with short course divides the Genoese from the Tuscan; and with almost the same sunset and sunrise lie Bougie and the city whence I came, which with its own blood once made its harbor warm. Folco[10] the people called me to whom my name was known, and this heaven is imprinted by me, as I was by it: for the daughter of Belus, wronging both Sichaeus and Creusa,[11] burned not more than I, as long as it befitted my locks; nor yet the Rhodopean maid who was deluded by Demophoön,[12] nor Alcides[13] when he had enclosed Iole in his heart. Yet here we repent not, but we smile, not for the fault, which returns not to mind, but for the Power that or-dained and foresaw. Here we contemplate the art which so much love adorns, and we discern the good by reason of which the world below again becomes the world above.

"But in order that you may bear away with you all your desires fulfilled which have been born in this sphere, I must proceed yet further. You wish to know who is within this light which so sparkles here beside me as a sunbeam on clear water. Now know that therewithin Rahab[14] is at rest, and being joined with our or-der, it is sealed by her in the highest degree. By this heaven—in which the shadow that your earth casts comes to a point—she was taken up before any other soul of Christ's triumph. And it was well-befitting to leave her in some heaven as a trophy of the lofty victory which was achieved by the one and the other palm, because she favored Joshua's first glory in the Holy Land—which little touches the memory of the Pope.

"Your city—which was planted by him who first turned his back on his Maker,[15] and whose envy has been so bewept—produces and scatters the accursed flower[16] that has caused the sheep and the lambs to stray, because it has made a wolf of the shepherd. For this the Gospel and the great Doctors are deserted, and only the Decretals are studied, as may be seen by their margins. Thereon the Pope and Cardinals are intent. Their thoughts go not to

Nazareth whither Gabriel spread his wings.[17] But the Vatican and the other chosen parts of Rome which have been the burial place for the soldiery that followed Peter shall soon be free from this adultery."[18]

CANTO X

Looking upon His Son with the love which the One and the Other eternally breathe forth, the primal and ineffable Power made everything that revolves through the mind or through space with such order that he who contemplates it cannot but taste of Him. Lift then your sight with me, reader, to the lofty wheels, straight to that part where the one motion strikes the other;[1] and amorously there begin to gaze upon that Master's art who within Himself so loves it that His eye never turns from it. See how from there the oblique circle which bears the planets branches off, to satisfy the world which calls on them: and were their pathway not aslant, much virtue in the heavens would be vain, and well-nigh every potency dead here below; and if it parted farther or less far from the straight course, much of the order of the world, both above and below, would be defective.

Now remain, reader, upon your bench, reflecting on this of which you have a foretaste, if you would be glad far sooner than weary. I have set before you; now feed yourself, because that matter of which I am made the scribe wrests to itself all my care.

The greatest minister of nature, which imprints the world with heavenly worth and with its light measures time for us, being in conjunction with the part I have noted, was wheeling through the spirals in which it presents itself earlier every day. And I was with him, but of my ascent I was no more aware than is a man, before his first thought, aware of its coming. It is Beatrice who thus conducts from good to better, so swiftly that her act does not extend through time.

How shining in itself must have been that which was within the sun where I entered it, showing not by color but by light! Though I should call on genius, art, and practice, I could not tell it so that it could ever be imagined; but one may believe it—and let him long to see it. And if our fantasies are low for such a loftiness,

it is no marvel, for our eyes never knew a light brighter than the sun. Such was here the fourth family of the exalted Father who ever satisfies it, showing how He breathes forth, and how He begets. And Beatrice began, "Give thanks, give thanks to the Sun of the Angels who of His grace has raised you to this visible one."

Never was heart of mortal so disposed unto devotion and so ready, with all its gratitude, to give itself to God, as I became at those words. And all my love was so set on Him that it eclipsed Beatrice in oblivion; nor did this displease her, but she so smiled thereat that the splendor of her smiling eyes divided upon many things my mind intent on one.

I saw many flashing lights of surpassing brightness make of us a center and of themselves a crown, more sweet in voice than shining in aspect. Thus girt we sometimes see Latona's daughter[2] when the air is so impregnate that it holds the thread which makes her zone. In the court of Heaven, whence I have returned, are many gems so precious and beautiful that they may not be taken out of the kingdom, and of these was the song of those lights. Let him who does not wing himself so that he may fly up thither await tidings thence from the dumb.

When, so singing, those blazing suns had circled three times round about us, like stars neighboring the fixed poles, they seemed as ladies not released from the dance, but who stop silent, listening till they have caught the new notes. And within one I heard begin, "Since the ray of grace, by which true love is kindled and which then grows by loving, shines so multiplied in you that it brings you up that stair which none descends but to mount again, he who should deny to you the wine of his flask for your thirst would no more be at liberty than water that flows not down to the sea. You wish to know what plants these are that enflower this garland, which amorously circles round the fair lady who strengthens you for heaven. I was of the lambs of the holy flock which Dominic leads on the path where there is good fattening if they do not stray. He that is next beside me on the right was my brother and my master, and he is Albert of Cologne, and I Thomas of Aquino.[3] If thus of all the rest you would be informed, come, following my speech with your sight, going round the blessed wreath. That next flaming comes from the smile of Gratian[4] who served the one and the other court so well that it pleases in Paradise. The other who next adorns our choir was that Peter[5] who, like the poor widow, offered his treasure to Holy Church. The fifth light,[6] which is the most beautiful among us, breathes with such love that all the world there below thirsts to know tidings of it. Within it is the lofty mind to which was given wisdom so deep that, if the truth be true, there never rose a second of such full vision. At its side behold the light of that candle which, below in the flesh, saw deepest into the angelic nature and its ministry.[7] In the next little light smiles that defender of the Christian times, of whose discourse Augustine made use.[8] If now you are bringing your mind's eye from light to light after my praises, you are already thirsting for the eighth. Therewithin, through seeing every good, the sainted soul rejoices who makes the fallacious world manifest to any who listen well to him. The body from which it was driven lies down below in Cieldauro, and he came from martyrdom and exile to this peace.[9] See, flaming beyond, the glowing breath of Isidore, of Bede, and of Richard who in contemplation was more than man.[10] This one from whom your look returns to me is the light of a spirit to whom, in his grave thoughts, it seemed that death came slow. It is the eternal light of Siger[11] who, lecturing in Straw Street, demonstrated invidious truths."

Then, like a clock which calls us at the hour when the Bride of God rises to sing her matins to her Bridegroom, that he may love her, in which the one part draws or drives the other, sounding *ting! ting!* with notes so sweet that the well-disposed spirit swells with love, so did I see the glorious wheel move and render voice to voice with harmony and sweetness that cannot be known except there where joy is everlasting.

CANTO XI

O insensate care of mortals! how false are the reasonings that make you beat your wings in downward flight. One was following after the laws, another after the *Aphorisms*,[1] one was pursuing priesthood, and one dominion by

force or craft, and another plunder, and another civil business, one was moiling, caught in the pleasures of the flesh, and another was giving himself to idleness, the while, free from all these things, I was high in heaven with Beatrice, thus gloriously received.

After each had come to the point of the circle where it was before, it stayed itself, as the taper in its stand. And within that light which first had spoken to me I heard begin, while it smiled and grew brighter, "Even as I glow with its beams, so, gazing into the Eternal Light, I perceive your thoughts and the cause of them. You are perplexed and would fain have my words made clearer, in plain and explicit language leveled to your understanding, where I said just now 'where there is good fattening,' and again where I said, 'there never rose a second'; and here is need that one distinguish well.

"The Providence that governs the world with that counsel in which every created vision is vanquished before it reaches the bottom, in order that the Bride of Him who, with loud cries, espoused her with the blessed blood, might go to her Delight, secure within herself and also more faithful to Him, ordained on her behalf two princes, who on this side and that might be her guides. The one was all seraphic in ardor,[2] the other, for wisdom, was on earth a splendor of cherubic light.[3] I will speak of one, because in praising one, whichever be taken, both are spoken of, for their labors were to one same end.

"Between the Topino[4] and the stream that drops from the hill chosen by the blessed Ubaldo, a fertile slope hangs from a lofty mountain wherefrom Perugia feels cold and heat through Porta Sole, while behind it Nocera and Gualdo grieve under a heavy yoke. From this slope, where most it breaks its steepness a sun rose on the world, even as this is wont to rise from Ganges. Therefore let him who talks of this place not say *Ascesi*,[5] which would be to speak short, but *Orient*, if he would name it rightly. He was not yet very far from his rising when he began to make the earth feel, from his great virtue, a certain strengthening; for, while still a youth, he rushed into strife against his father for such a lady,[6] to whom, as to death, none willingly unlocks the door; and before his spiritual court *et coram patre* he was joined to her, and thereafter, from day to day, he loved her ever more ardently. She, bereft of her first husband, for eleven hundred years and more, despised and obscure, remained unwooed till he came; nor had it availed to hear that he who caused fear to all the world found her undisturbed with Amyclas at the sound of his voice;[7] nor had it availed to have been constant and undaunted so that, where Mary remained below, she wept with Christ upon the Cross.

"But, lest I should proceed too darkly, take now Francis and Poverty for these lovers in all that I have said. Their harmony and joyous semblance made love and wonder and tender looks the cause of holy thoughts; so that the venerable Bernard[8] first bared his feet, following such great peace, and running, it seemed to him that he was slow. Oh wealth unknown, oh fertile good! Egidius bares his feet, Silvester bares his feet, following the spouse, so does the bride delight them.[9] Then that father and master goes his way, with his lady and with that family which was already girt with the lowly cord. Nor did abjectness of heart weigh down his brow that he was Pietro Bernardone's son,[10] nor for appearing marvelously despised; but royally he opened his stern resolve to Innocent,[11] and had from him the first seal upon his Order.

"After the poor folk had increased behind him, whose wondrous life were better sung in Heaven's glory, then was the holy will of this chief shepherd circled with a second crown by the Eternal Spirit through Honorius. And when, in thirst for martyrdom, he, in the proud presence of the Sultan, had preached Christ and them that followed him, and, finding the people too unripe for conversion and in order not to stay in vain, had returned to the harvest of the Italian fields, then on the harsh rock between Tiber and Arno he received from Christ the last seal, which his limbs bore for two years. When it pleased Him, who had allotted him to such great good, to draw him up to the reward that he had gained in making himself lowly, to his brethren as to rightful heirs he commended his most dear lady and bade them love her faithfully; and from her bosom the glorious soul chose to set forth, returning to its own realm, and for its body would have no other bier.

"Think now what he was that was a wor-thy colleague to keep Peter's bark on the right course in the high sea; and such was our Patriarch;[12] wherefore you can see that whoever follows him as he commands freights good merchandise. But his flock has grown so greedy of new fare that it cannot but be scattered through wild pastures; and the farther his sheep, remote and vagabond, go from him, the more empty of milk do they return to the fold. Some of them indeed there are who fear the harm, and keep close to the shepherd, but they are so few that little cloth suffices for their cowls.

"Now if my words have not been faint, if your listening has been intent, if you recall to mind what I have said, your wish will be content in part, for you will see the plant which is whittled away, and you will see what is intended by the correction 'where there is good fattening if they do not stray.' "

CANTO XII

As soon as the blessed flame took to speaking its last word the holy millstone began to turn, and it had not yet made a full circle when a second enclosed it round and matched motion with motion and song with song: song which, in those sweet pipes, as much surpasses our Muses, our Sirens, as a first splendor that which it throws back. As two bows, parallel and like in color, bend across a thin cloud when Juno gives the order to her handmaid[1]— the one without born of the one within, like the voice of that wandering nymph[2] whom love consumed as the sun does vapors—and make the people here presage, by reason of the covenant that God made with Noah, that the world shall never again be flooded; so the two garlands of those sempiternal roses circled round us, and so did the outer correspond to the inner.

When the dance and all the great festival of both song and flames, light with light, gladsome and benign, stopped together at one instant and with one consent (even as the eyes which, at the pleasure that moves them, must needs be closed and lifted in accord), from the heart of one of the new lights there came a voice which made me seem as the needle to the star in turning me to where it was; and it began,[3]

"The love that makes me beautiful draws me to speak of the other leader on whose account such fair utterance is made here concerning mine. It is fit that where one is, the other be brought in, so that, as they warred for one same end, so together may their glory shine.

"Christ's army, which cost so dear to rearm, was moving behind the standard, slow, mistrustful and scanty, when the Emperor who reigns eternally took thought for His soldiery that was in peril, of His grace only, not that it was worthy, and, as has been said, succored His bride with two champions by whose deeds, by whose words, the scattered people were rallied.

"In that region where sweet Zephyr rises to open the new leaves wherewith Europe sees herself reclad, not far from the smiting of the waves, behind which the sun, after his long course, sometimes hides himself from every man, sits fortunate Calaroga[4] under the protection of the mighty shield whereon the lion is subject and sovereign. Therein was born the ardent lover of the Christian faith, the holy athlete, benignant to his own and harsh to his foes. And his mind, as soon as it was created, was so full of living virtue that in his mother's womb he made her a prophetess.[5] When the espousals were completed at the sacred font between him and the faith, where they dowered each other with mutual salvation, the lady who gave the assent for him saw in a dream the marvelous fruit destined to issue from him and from his heirs, and, that he might in very construing be what he was, a spirit from up here went forth to name him by the possessive of Him whose he wholly was. Dominic he was named, and I speak of him as of the husbandman whom Christ chose to help Him in His garden. Well did he show himself a messenger and familiar of Christ; for the first love manifested in him was for the first counsel that Christ gave. Oftentimes his nurse found him silent and awake upon the ground, as though he would say, 'I am come for this.' Oh father of him, Felice indeed! Oh mother of him, Giovanna indeed, if this, being interpreted, means as is said![6]

"Not for the world for whose sake men now toil after him of Ostia and after Thaddeus,[7] but for love of the true manna, in short time he became a mighty teacher, such that he set himself to go round the vineyard, which soon turns gray if the vine-dresser is negligent. And of the seat which once was more benign to the righteous poor—not in itself, but in him who sits on it and degenerates—he asked, not to dispense two or three for six, not for the fortune of the first vacancy, not for *decimas quae sunt pauperum Dei,*[8] but for leave to fight against the erring world for that seed of which four and twenty plants surround you. Then both with doctrine and with will, together with the apostolic office, he went forth like a torrent which a lofty vein presses out, and on the heretical stocks his force struck with most vigor where the resistances were most obstinate. From him there sprang then various streamlets whereby the catholic garden is watered, so that its bushes are more living.

"If such was the one wheel of the chariot in which Holy Church defended herself and won in the field her civil strife, surely the excellence of the other must be very plain to you, concerning whom, before I came, Thomas[9] was so courteous. But the track made by the topmost part of its rim is derelict; so that there is mould where the crust was. His household, which set out aright with their feet upon his footprints, is so turned about that the forward foot moves to that behind; and soon shall be seen some harvest of the bad tillage, when the tare will complain that the bin is taken from it. Nevertheless, I say, he who should search our volume leaf by leaf might still find a page where he would read, 'I am as I always was'; but it will not be from Casale or from Acquasparta,[10] whence come such to the writing that one shuns it and the other contracts it.

"I am the living soul of Bonaventura of Bagnorea,[11] who in the great offices always put the left-hand care behind. Illuminato and Augustine are here,[12] who were of the first unshod poor brethren that with the cord made themselves God's friends. Hugh of St. Victor[13] is here with them, and Peter Comestor, and Peter of Spain,[14] who down below shines in twelve books; Nathan the prophet,[15] and the Metropolitan Chrysostom,[16] and Anselm,[17] and that Donatus[18] who deigned to set his hand to the first art;[19] Rabanus is here, and beside me shines the Calabrian[20] abbot Joachim,[21] who was endowed with prophetic spirit.

"The glowing courtesy and the well-judged

discourse of Brother Thomas has moved me to celebrate so great a paladin, and with me has moved this company."

CANTO XIII

Let him imagine, who would rightly grasp what I now beheld (and, while I speak, let him hold the image firm as a rock), fifteen stars which in different regions vivify the heaven with such great brightness that it overcomes every thickness of the air; let him imagine that Wain[1] for which the bosom of our heaven suffices night and day so that with the turning of the pole it does not disappear; let him imagine the mouth of that Horn[2] which begins at the end of the axle on which the first wheel revolves—all to have made of themselves two signs in the heavens like that which the daughter of Minos made when she felt the chill of death;[3] and one to have its rays within the other, and both to revolve in such manner that one should go first and the other after; and he will have as it were a shadow of the true constellation, and of the double dance, which was circling round the point where I was; for it is as far beyond our experience as the motion of the heaven that outspeeds all the rest is beyond the motion of the Chiana.[4] There they sang not Bacchus, and not Paean, but Three Persons in the divine nature, and it and the human nature in one Person. The singing and the circling completed each its measure, and those holy lights gave heed to us, rejoicing as they passed from care to care.

Then the light[5] within which the wondrous life of the poor man of God had been narrated to me broke the silence among the concordant souls, and said, "Since one straw is threshed, since its grain is now garnered, sweet charity bids me beat out the other. You believe that into the breast from which the rib was drawn to form her beautiful cheek whose palate costs dear to all the world, and into that which, pierced by the lance, made such satisfaction, both after and before, that it turns the scale against all fault, whatever of light it is allowed human nature to have was all infused by that Power which made the one and the other; and therefore you wonder at what I said above, when I declared that the excellence which is

enclosed in the fifth light never had a second. Now open your eyes to that which I answer you, and you will see your belief and what I say become in the truth as the center in a circle.

"That which dies not and that which can die are naught but the splendor of that Idea which in His love our Sire begets;[6] for that living light which so streams from its Lucent Source that It is not disunited from It, nor from the Love which is intrined with them, does of Its own goodness collect Its rays, as though reflected, in nine subsistences, Itself eternally remaining One. Thence It descends to the ultimate potentialities, downward from act to act becoming such that finally it makes but brief contingencies; and these contingencies I understand to be the generated things which the moving heavens produce with seed and without it. The wax of these and that which molds it are not always in the same condition, and therefore under the ideal stamp it then shines now more, now less; hence it comes that one same plant, in respect to species, fruits better or worse, and that you are born with diverse dispositions. If the wax were exactly worked, and the heavens were at the height of their power, the light of the whole seal would be apparent. But nature always gives it defectively, working like the artist who in the practice of his art has a hand that trembles. Yet, if the fervent Love disposes and imprints the clear Vision of the primal Power, complete perfection is there acquired. Thus was the dust once made fit for the full perfection of a living creature, thus was the Virgin made to be with child; so that I approve your opinion that human nature never was, nor shall be, what it was in those two persons.

"Now, if I went no further, 'How, then, was that other without an equal?' would your words begin. But in order that that which is not apparent may clearly appear, consider who he was and the cause which moved him to make request when it was said to him, 'Ask.' I have not so spoken that you cannot plainly see that he was a king, who asked for wisdom, in order that he might be a worthy king; not to know the number of the mover spirits here above, nor if *necesse* with a contingent ever made *necesse*;[7] nor *si est dare primum motum esse*;[8] nor if in a semicircle a triangle can be so constructed that it shall have no right angle.

Wherefore, if you note this along with what I said, kingly prudence is that peerless vision on which the arrow of my intention strikes. And if to 'rose' you turn your discerning eyes, you will see it has respect only to kings—who are many and the good are rare. Take my words with this distinction, and they can stand thus with what you believe of the first father and of our Beloved.

"And let this ever be as lead to your feet, to make you slow, like a weary man, in moving either to the *yes* or the *no* which you see not; for he is right low down among the fools, alike in the one and in the other case, who affirms or denies without distinguishing; because it happens that oftentimes hasty opinion inclines to the wrong side, and then fondness for it binds the intellect. Far worse than in vain does he leave the shore (since he returns not as he puts forth) who fishes for the truth and has not the art. And of this Parmenides, Melissus, Bryson,[9] are open proofs to the world, as are the many others who went on but knew not whither. Thus did Sabellius, and Arius,[10] and those fools who were to the Scriptures like swords, in rendering straight countenances distorted.

Moreover, let folk not be too secure in judgment, like one who should count the ears in the field before they are ripe; for I have seen first, all winter through, the thorn display itself hard and stiff, and then upon its summit bear the rose. And I have seen ere now a ship fare straight and swift over the sea through all her course, and perish at the last as she entered the harbor. Let not dame Bertha and squire Martin,[11] if they see one steal and one make offering, believe to see them within the Divine Counsel: for the one may rise and the other may fall."

CANTO XIV

From the center to the rim, and so from the rim to the center, the water in a round vessel moves, according as it is struck from without or within. This which I say fell suddenly into my mind as the glorious life of Thomas became silent, because of the likeness which was born of his speech and that of Beatrice, who was pleased to begin thus after him, "This man has need, and does not tell you of it, either by word or as yet in thought, to go to the root of another truth. Tell him if the light wherewith your substance blooms will remain with you eternally even as it is now; and, if it does remain, tell how, after you are made visible again, it can be that it will not hurt your sight."

As when urged and drawn on by increasing delight, those who are dancing in a ring from time to time raise their voices and gladden their motions, so at that prompt and devout petition the holy circles showed new joy in their revolving and in their marvelous melody. Whoso laments because we die here to live there on high has not seen there the refreshment of the eternal rain.

That One and Two and Three which ever lives, and ever reigns in Three and Two and One, uncircumscribed, and circumscribing all things, was thrice sung by each of those spirits with such a melody as would be adequate reward for every merit. And I heard in the divinest light of the lesser circle a modest voice, perhaps such as was that of the Angel to Mary, make answer, "As long as the feast of Paradise shall be, so long shall our love radiate around us such a garment. Its brightness follows our ardor, the ardor our vision, and that is in the measure which each has of grace beyond his merit. When the flesh, glorious and sanctified, shall be clothed on us again, our persons will be more acceptable for being all complete; wherefore whatever of gratuitous light the Supreme Good gives us will be increased, light which fits us to see Him; so that our vision needs must increase, our ardor increase which by that is kindled, our radiance increase which comes from this. But even as a coal which gives forth flame, and with its white glow outshines it, so that its visibility is maintained, so shall this effulgence which already surrounds us be surpassed in brightness by the flesh which the earth still covers; nor will such light have power to fatigue us, for the organs of the body will be strong for everything that can delight us."

So sudden and eager both the one and the other chorus seemed to me in saying "Amen," that truly they showed desire for their dead bodies—perhaps not only for themselves, but also for their mothers, for their fathers, and for the others who were dear before they became eternal flames.

And lo! round about and of equal brightness rose a lustre beyond that which was there, like a brightening horizon. And as, at rise of early evening, new lights begin to show in heaven, so that the sight does, and yet does not, seem real, it seemed to me that there I began to perceive new subsistences making a ring beyond the other two circumferences. Oh true sparkling of the Holy Spirit! how suddenly glowing it became to my eyes, which, vanquished, endured it not. But Beatrice showed herself to me so beautiful and smiling that it must be left among those sights which followed not my memory. Therefrom my eyes regained power to raise themselves again, and I saw myself, alone with my lady, translated to a more exalted blessedness. That I was more uplifted I perceived clearly by the fiery smile of the star which seemed to me ruddier than its wont. With all my heart, and with that speech which is one in all men, I made a holocaust to God such as befitted the new grace; and the burning of the sacrifice was not yet completed in my breast when I knew the offering to be accepted and propitious, for with such a glow and such a ruddiness splendors appeared to me within two rays that I said, "O Helios, who dost so adorn them!"[1]

As, pricked out with greater and lesser lights, between the poles of the Universe, the Milky Way so gleams as to cause even the wise to question, so did those beams, thus constellated, make in the depth of Mars the venerable sign which joinings of quadrants make in a circle. Here my memory outstrips my wit, for that Cross so flashed forth Christ that I can find for it no fit comparison; but he that takes up his cross and follows Christ shall yet forgive me for what I leave untold when he sees Christ flash in that dawn.

From horn to horn and between the top and the base, lights were moving that sparkled brightly as they met and passed; so we see here, straight and athwart, swift and slow, changing appearance, the motes of bodies, long and short, moving through the ray that sometimes streaks the shade which men with skill and art contrive for their defense. And as viol and harp, strung with many cords in harmony, chime sweetly for one who does not catch the tune, so from the lights that appeared to me there a melody gathered through the cross

which held me rapt, though I followed not the hymn. Well I discerned it to be of lofty praise, for there came to me: "Rise" and "Conquer," as to one who understands not, but hears; by which I was so moved to love that till then nothing had bound me with such sweet bonds. Perhaps my word appears too daring, as though slighting the pleasure of the beautiful eyes, gazing into which my longing has repose. But he who considers that the living seals of every beauty have more effect the higher they are, and that I there had not yet turned to them, may excuse me for that whereof I accuse myself in order to excuse myself, and may see that I speak truth; for the holy pleasure is not excluded here, because it becomes the purer as one mounts.

CANTO XV

Gracious will, wherein right-breathing love always resolves itself, as cupidity does into grudging will, imposed silence on that sweet lyre and quieted the holy strings which the right hand of the Heaven slackens and draws tight. How shall those beings be deaf to righteous prayers, who, in order to prompt me to beg of them, became silent with one consent? Right it is that he should grieve without end who, for the love of what does not endure forever, robs himself of that love.

As, through the still and cloudless evening sky a sudden fire shoots from time to time, moving the eyes that were at rest, and seeming a star that changes place, save that from where it kindles no star is lost, and it lasts but short while; so, from the horn that extends on the right, there darted a star of the resplendent constellation that is there, down to the foot of that cross; nor did the gem depart from its ribbon, but coursed along the radial strip, and seemed like fire behind alabaster. With like affection did the shade of Anchises stretch forward (if our greatest Muse merits belief), when in Elysium he perceived his son.

"*O sanguis meus, O superinfusa gratia Dei, sicut tibi cui bis unquam celi ianua reclusa?*"[1] Thus that light; wherefore I gave my heed to it, then I turned back my sight to my lady, and on this side and that I was amazed, for in her eyes was blazing such a smile that I thought with mine I had touched the limit both of my beatitude and of my paradise.

Then, a joy to hearing and to sight, the spirit added to his first words things I did not comprehend, so deep was his speech; nor did he conceal himself from me by choice, but of necessity, for his conception was set above the mark of mortals. And when the bow of his ardent affection was so relaxed that his speech descended toward the mark of our intellect, the first thing I understood was, "Blessed be Thou, Three and One, who show such favor to my seed." And he continued, "Happy and long-felt hunger, derived from reading in the great volume where white or dark is never changed, you have relieved, my son, within this light in which I speak to you, thanks to her who clothed you with plumes for the lofty flight. You believe that your thought flows to me from Him who is First, even as from the unit, if that be known, ray out the five and the six; and therefore who I am, and why I seem to you more joyous than another in this festive throng, you do not ask me. You believe the truth, for the lesser and the great of this life gaze into that mirror in which, before you think, you display your thought. But in order that holy love, in which I watch with perpetual vision, and which makes me thirst with sweet longing, may be the better fulfilled, let your voice, confident and bold and glad, sound forth the will, sound forth the desire, whereto my answer is already decreed."

I turned to Beatrice, and she heard before I spoke, and smiled to me a sign that made the wings of my desire increase. And I began thus, "Love and intelligence, as soon as the first Equality became visible to you, became of one weight for each of you, because the Sun which illumined you and warmed you is of such equality in its heat and light that all comparisons fall short. But will and faculty in mortals, for the reason that is plain to you, are not equally feathered in their wings, so that I, who am mortal, feel myself in this inequality, and therefore can only give thanks with the heart for your paternal welcome. But I beseech you, living topaz who are a gem in this precious jewel, that you satisfy me with your name."

"O my branch, in whom I took delight only expecting you, I was your root." Thus he began his answer to me,[2] then said, "He from whom your family has its name[3] and who a hundred years and more has circled the mountain on the first ledge, was my son and was your grandfather's father. Truly it is fitting that you should shorten his long toil with your good offices.

"Florence, within her ancient circle from which she still takes tierce and nones,[4] abode in peace, sober and chaste. There was no necklace, no coronal, no embroidered gowns, no girdle that was more to be looked at than the person. Not yet did the daughter at her birth cause fear to the father, for the time and the dowry did not outrun due measure on this side and that. Houses empty of family there were none, nor had Sardanapalus[5] arrived yet to show what could be done in the chamber. Not yet was Montemalo surpassed by your Uccellatoio,[6] which, as it has been passed in the uprising, so shall it be in the fall. Bellincion Berti[7] have I seen go girt with leather and bone, and his wife come from her mirror with unpainted face. I have seen de' Nerli and del Vecchio[8] content in unlined skin, and their wives at the spindle and the distaff. O happy they! each one of them sure of her burial place, and none as yet deserted in her bed because of France. The one kept watch in minding the cradle, and, soothing, spoke that speech which first delights fathers and mothers. Another, as she drew the threads from the distaff, would tell her household about the Trojans, and Fiesole, and Rome.[9] Then a Cianghella or a Lapo Salterello[10] would have been as great a marvel as Cincinnatus and Cornelia would be now.

"To so reposeful, to so fair a life of citizens, to such a trusty community, to so sweet an abode, Mary, called on with loud cries, gave me, and in your ancient Baptistery[11] I became at once a Christian and Cacciaguida. Moronto was my brother, and Eliseo.[12] My wife came to me from the valley of the Po, and thence was derived your surname. Afterward I followed the Emperor Conrad,[13] who girt me with his knighthood, so much did I win his favor by good work. I went, in his train, against the iniquity of that law[14] whose people, through fault of the Pastors, usurp your right. There by that foul folk was I released from the deceitful world, the love of which debases many souls, and I came from martyrdom to this peace."

CANTO XVI

O our petty nobility of blood! if you make folk
glory in you here below where our affections
languish, it will nevermore be a marvel to me,
since there where appetite is not warped, I
mean in Heaven, I myself gloried in you. Truly
you are a mantle that soon shrinks, so that if
naught be added from day to day, time goes
round about you with its shears.

With that *You*[1] which was first used in
Rome and in which her family least perseveres,
my words began again; at which Beatrice, who
was a little withdrawn, smiled and seemed to
me like her who coughed at the first fault
that is written of Guinevere.[2] I began, "You
are my father, you give me full boldness to
speak, you so uplift me that I am more than
I. By so many streams my mind is filled with
gladness that it rejoices in itself that it can bear
this and not burst. Tell me then, dear stock
from which I spring, what was your ancestry
and what were the years that were reckoned in
your boyhood. Tell me of the sheepfold of St.
John,[3] how large it was then, and who were
the folk within it worthy of the highest seats."

As a coal quickens into flame at the breathing of the winds, so did I see that light glow
at my blandishments; and as it became more
beautiful to my eyes, so with a voice more
sweet and gentle, but not in this our modern
speech, he said to me, "From that day on
which *Ave* was uttered, to the birth in which
my mother, who now is sainted, was lightened
of me with whom she had been burdened, this
fire had come to its Lion five hundred, fifty,
and thirty times to rekindle itself beneath his
paw.[4] My ancestors and I were born at the place
where the furthest ward is first reached by the
runner in your annual game.[5] Let it suffice to
hear thus much of my forebears; as to who they
were and whence they came hither, silence is
more becoming than speech.

"All those able to bear arms who at that time
were there, between Mars and the Baptist,[6]
were the fifth of the number now living;
but the citizenship, which is now mixed with
Campi, with Certaldo, and with Figline, saw
itself pure down to the humblest artisan.[7] Oh,
how much better it would be that those folk
of whom I speak were neighbors, and to have
your boundary at Galluzzo and at Trespiano,[8]
than to have them within and to endure the
stench of the churl of Aguglione,[9] and of him
of Signa,[10] who already has his eye sharp for
jobbery.

"If the folk who are the most degenerate in
the world had not been a stepmother to Caesar,
but, like a mother, benignant to her son, there
is one who has become a Florentine and is a
money-changer and trader, who would have
lived on at Simifonti[11] where his own grandfather went a-begging. Montemurlo[12] would
still belong to its Counts, the Cerchi would
be in the parish of Acone,[13] and perhaps the
Buondelmonti in Valdigreve.[14] The intermin-
gling of people was ever the beginning of harm
to the city, as to you the food which is loaded
on is to the body. And a blind bull falls more
headlong than the blind lamb, and oftentimes
one sword cuts better and more than five.

"If you regard Luni and Urbisaglia,[15] how
they have perished, and how are following
after them Chiusi and Senigallia,[16] it will not
appear to you a strange thing or a hard, to
hear how families are undone, since cities have
their term. Your affairs all have their death,
even as have you; but it is concealed in some
things that last long, whereas lives are short.
And as the revolution of the heaven of the
moon covers and uncovers the shores without
pause, so Fortune does with Florence; wherefore it should appear no wondrous thing which
I shall tell of the great Florentines whose fame
is hidden by time. I saw the Ughi[17] and I saw
the Catellini, Filippi, Greci, Ormanni, and Al-
berichi, illustrious citizens, already in decline;
and I saw, great as they were ancient, dell'Arca
with della Sannella, and Soldanieri and Ard-
inghi and Bostichi.[18] Over the gate which at
present is laden with new felony of such great
weight that there will soon be jettison from
the bark, were the Ravignani of whose line
the Count Guido is descended[19] and whosoever has since taken the name of the high
Bellincione.[20] Della Pressa[21] knew already
how to rule, and Galligaio[22] had already in his
house the hilt and the pommel gilded. Great
already were the Vair column,[23] the Sacchetti,
Giuochi, Fifanti, Barucci, and Galli,[24] and
those that blush for the bushel. The stock from
which the Calfucci[25] sprang was already great,
and already the Sizii and Arrigucci[26] had been
raised to the highest seats. Oh, how great have
I seen those now undone by their pride! and

the balls of gold adorned Florence in all her great doings.[27] So did the fathers of those who, whenever your church is vacant, fatten themselves by staying in consistory.[28] The insolent breed[29] that plays the dragon behind him that flees, and to whoever shows his teeth— or else his purse—becomes mild as a lamb, was already on the rise, but of humble stock, so that it did not please Ubertin Donato[30] that his father-in-law afterward should make him their kinsman. Already had Caponsacco descended into the market-place down from Fiesole, and already was Giuda a good citizen, and Infangato.[31] One thing I will tell, incredible and true: the little circuit was entered by a gate named after the Della Pera.[32] Everyone who bears the fair ensign of the great Baron[33] whose name and whose worth the feast of Thomas keeps fresh, from him had knighthood and privilege, although he who fringes it round[34] is siding now with the people. Already there were Gualterotti and Importuni;[35] and the Borgo[36] would still be quiet if they had gone fasting of new neighbors. The house of which was born your weeping, by reason of its just resentment which has slain you and put an end to your glad living, was honored, both itself and its consorts. O Buondelmonte,[37] how ill for you that you did fly from its nuptials at the promptings of another. Many would be happy who now are sad if God had committed you to the Ema[38] the first time you came to the city! but it was fitting that Florence, in her last peace, should offer a victim to that mutilated stone which guards the bridge.

"With these families, and with others with them, I saw Florence in such repose that she had no cause for wailing. With these families I saw her people so glorious and so just, that the lily was never set reversed upon the staff, nor made vermilion by division."[39]

CANTO XVII

As he who still makes fathers chary toward their sons came to Clymene[1] to be reassured about that which he had heard against himself, such was I, and such was I perceived to be both by Beatrice and by the holy lamp which already, for my sake, had changed its place. Wherefore my lady said to me, "Put forth the flame of your desire, so that it may issue imprinted well by the internal stamp; not in order that our knowledge may increase through your speech, but that you may learn to tell your thirst, so that one may pour out drink for you."

"O dear root of me, who are so uplifted that, even as earthly minds see that two obtuse angles can not be contained in a triangle, so you, gazing upon the Point to which all times are present, do see contingent things before they exist in themselves; while I was in Virgil's company, up the mountain that heals the souls, and while descending through the dead world, heavy words were said to me about my future life, though I feel myself truly foursquare against the blows of chance; so that my will would be well content to hear what fortune is drawing near me, because an arrow foreseen comes slower." Thus said I to that same light which had spoken to me before, and, as Beatrice willed, my wish was confessed.

In no dark sayings, such as those in which the foolish folk of old once ensnared themselves, before the Lamb of God who takes away sins was slain, but in clear words and with precise discourse that paternal love replied, hidden and revealed by his own smile, "Contingency, which does not extend beyond the volume of your material world, is all depicted in the Eternal Vision. Yet thence it takes not necessity, any more than from the eyes in which it is mirrored does a ship which is going down the stream. Therefrom, even as sweet harmony comes from an organ to the ear, comes to my sight the time that is in store for you. As Hippolytus departed from Athens, by reason of his pitiless and perfidious stepmother,[2] so from Florence must you depart. So is it willed, so already plotted, and so shall be accomplished soon by him who ponders upon it[3] in the place where every day Christ is bought and sold. The blame, as always, will follow the injured party, in outcry; but vengeance shall bear witness to the truth which dispenses it. You shall leave everything beloved most dearly; and this is the arrow which the bow of exile shoots first. You shall come to know how salt is the taste of another's bread, and how hard the path to descend and mount by another man's stairs. And that which shall most weigh your shoulders down will be the evil and senseless company with which you shall fall into this vale; which shall then become all ungrateful, all mad and malevolent against you, but, soon after, their brows, not yours, shall redden for it. Of their brutish folly their own conduct shall afford the proof, so that it will be for your fair fame to have made you a party by yourself.

"Your first refuge and first inn shall be the courtesy of the great Lombard who bears the holy bird upon the ladder,[4] and he will have for you such benign regard that, in doing and in asking, between you two, that will be first which between others is the slowest. With him you shall see one who, at his birth, was so stamped by this strong star, that notable shall be his deeds.[5] Not yet have folk taken due note of him, because of his young age, for these wheels have revolved around him only nine years; but before the Gascon deceives the lofty Henry,[6] some sparks of his virtue shall appear, in his caring naught for money or for toils. His magnificence shall hereafter be so known, that his very foes will not be able to keep silent tongues about him. Look you to him and to his benefits. By him shall many folk be changed, the rich and the beggarly altering their condition. And you shall bear hence written of him in your mind, but you shall not tell it";—and he told things past the belief even of those who shall see them. Then he added, "Son, these are the glosses on what was said to you; behold the snares which are hidden behind but a few circlings. Yet I would not have you envious of your neighbors, since your life shall be prolonged far beyond the punishment of their perfidies."

When by his silence the holy soul showed he had finished setting the woof across the warp I had held out in readiness to him, I began, as he who, in doubt, craves counsel of one who sees and rightly wills and loves, "I see well, my father, how time spurs toward me to give me such a blow as is heaviest to whosoever is most heedless; wherefore it is good that I arm myself with foresight, so that if the dearest place be taken from me, I lose not all the rest by reason of my songs. Down in the world endlessly bitter, and upon the mountain from whose fair summit my lady's eyes uplifted me, and after, through the heavens from light to light, I have learned that which, if I tell again, will have for many a savor of great bitterness;

and if I am a timid friend to the truth, I fear to lose life among those who shall call this time ancient."

The light wherein was smiling the treasure I had found there first became flashing as a golden mirror in the sun, then it replied, "A conscience dark, either with its own or with another's shame, will indeed feel your speech to be harsh. But none the less, all falsehood set aside, make manifest all that you have seen; and then let them scratch where the itch is. For if at first taste your voice be grievous, yet shall it leave thereafter vital nourishment when digested. This cry of yours shall do as does the wind, which smites most upon the loftiest summits; and this shall be no little cause of honor. Therefore only the souls known of fame have been shown to you within these wheels, upon the mountain, and in the woeful valley; for the mind of him who hears rests not nor confirms its faith by an example that has its roots unknown or hidden, nor for other proof that is not manifest."

CANTO XVIII

Already that blessed mirror was enjoying only its own thoughts, and I was tasting mine, tempering the bitter with the sweet, when the lady who was leading me to God said, "Change your thought: consider that I am in His presence who lightens the burden of every wrong."

I turned round at the loving sound of my Comfort, and what love I then saw in the holy eyes I leave here untold; not only because I distrust my own speech, but because of memory, which cannot return on itself so far unless Another guide it. This much of that moment can I retell, that as I gazed upon her my affection was freed from every other desire so long as the Eternal Joy that shone direct on Beatrice satisfied me from the fair eyes with its reflected aspect. Overcoming me with the light of a smile, she said to me, "Turn and listen, for not only in my eyes is Paradise."

As sometimes here the affection is seen in the countenance if it be such that all the mind is taken up by it, so in the flaming of the holy glow to which I turned I recognized his wish to have some further speech with me; and he began, "In this fifth tier of the tree,[1] which has life from its top and is always in fruit and never sheds its leaves, are blessed spirits which below, before they came to heaven, were of such great renown that every Muse would be rich with them. Look, therefore, upon the horns of the cross: he whom I shall name there will do as in a cloud its swift fire does."

At the naming of Joshua, even as it was done, I saw a light drawn along the cross, nor was the word noted by me before the fact; and at the name of the great Maccabeus[2] I saw another move, wheeling, and gladness was the whip of the top. So for Charlemagne and Roland[3] my intent gaze followed two of them, as the eye follows its falcon as he flies; next William, and Renouard and Duke Godfrey drew my sight along that cross, and Robert Guiscard too.[4] Then, moving and mingling among the other lights, the soul which had spoken with me showed me how great an artist it was among the singers of that heaven.

I turned to my right side, to see in Beatrice my duty, signified either by speech or by gesture, and I saw her eyes so clear, so joyful, that her aspect surpassed all it had been at other times, even the last. And as from feeling more delight in doing well, a man from day to day becomes aware that his virtue makes advance, so did I perceive that my circling round with the heaven had increased its arc, when I saw that miracle even more adorned. And such change as comes in a moment over the face of a pale lady, when her countenance frees itself from a burden of modest shame, was presented to my eyes when I turned, because of the whiteness of the temperate sixth star which had received me within itself.[5]

I saw in that torch of Jove[6] the sparkling of the love that was there, trace out our speech to my eyes; and as birds, risen from the shore, as if rejoicing together at their pasture, make of themselves now a round flock, now some other shape, so within the lights holy creatures were singing as they flew, and in their figures made of themselves now D, now I, now L. At first, as they sang, they moved to their own notes; then, as they became one of these characters, they stopped a little and were silent.

O divine Pegasea,[7] who give glory unto men of genius and render them long-lived, as they, through you, the cities and the kingdoms, illumine me with yourself that I may set forth their shapes, as I have them in conception; let your power appear in these brief lines.

They displayed themselves then, in five times seven vowels and consonants; and I took note of the parts as they appeared in utterance to me. DILIGITE IUSTITIAM were the first verb and substantive of all the design; QUI IUDICATIS TERRAM were the last.[8] Then, ordered in the M of the fifth word they stayed, so that Jove seemed silver in that place, pricked out with gold; and I saw other lights descending where the top of the M was, and become quiet there, singing, I believe, the Good that draws them to Itself. Then, as on the striking of burning logs there rise innumerable sparks, wherefrom the foolish are wont to draw auguries, so thence there seemed to rise again more than a thousand lights, and mount, some much, some little, even as the Sun which kindles them allotted them; and when each had rested in its place, I saw the head and the neck of an eagle represented by that patterned fire. He who there paints has none to guide Him, but He Himself does guide, and from Him is recognized that virtue which shapes nests. The rest of the blessed spirits, which at first seemed content to form a lily on the M, with a slight motion completed the design.

O sweet star, how many and how bright were the gems which made it plain to me that our justice is the effect of the heaven which you engem! Wherefore I pray the Mind, in which your motion and your virtue have their beginning, that It look on the place whence issues the smoke that dims your radiance, so that once again It may be wroth at the buying and the selling in the temple which made its walls of miracles and martyrdoms. O soldiery of Heaven whom I look upon, pray for all those who have gone astray on earth, following the ill example. Of old it was the wont to make war with swords, but now it is made by taking away, now here now there, the bread which the tender Father bars from none.

But you that write only to cancel, bethink you that Peter and Paul, who died for the vineyard that you are laying waste, are still alive. Though you indeed may say, "I have my desire so set on him[9] who willed to live alone, and who, for a dance, was dragged to martyrdom, that I know not the Fisherman nor Paul."

CANTO XIX

With outstretched wings appeared before me the beautiful image which those interwoven souls, joyful in their sweet fruition, were making. Each of them seemed a little ruby on which a ray of sun should glow so enkindled as to reflect it into my eyes. And that which I must now tell, never did voice report nor ink record, nor was it ever comprised by phantasy; for I saw and also heard the beak speaking, and uttering with its voice *I* and *Mine* when in conception it was *We* and *Our*. And it began, "For being just and duteous am I here exalted to that glory which cannot be surpassed by desire; and upon earth have I left such a memory that the wicked people there commend it, but follow not its story." Thus one sole heat makes itself felt from many embers, even as from many loves one sole sound issued from that image.

And I then, "O perpetual flowers of the eternal bliss, who make all your odors seem to me but one, breathe forth and deliver me from the great fast which has long held me hungering, not finding any food for it on earth. Well do I know that if the Divine Justice makes another realm in heaven Its mirror, yours does not apprehend It through a veil. You know how eager I prepare myself to listen; you know what is that question which is so old a fast to me."

As the falcon which, issuing from the hood, moves his head and flaps his wings, showing his will and making himself fine, such did I see that ensign which was woven of praises of the Divine Grace become, with songs such as he knows who thereabove rejoices. Then it began, "He that turned His compass round the limit of the world, and within it marked out so much both hidden and revealed, could not so imprint His power on all the universe that His word should not remain in infinite excess; and this is certified by that first proud one, who was the highest of all creatures[1] and who, through not awaiting light, fell unripe; from which it is plain that every lesser nature is too scant a vessel for that Good which has no limit and measures Itself by Itself. Thus your vision, which must needs be one of the rays of the Mind with which all things are replete, cannot of its own nature be of such power that it should not perceive its origin to be far beyond all that is apparent to it. There-fore the sight that is granted to your world penetrates within the Eternal Justice as the eye into the sea; which, though from the shore it can see the bottom, in the open sea it sees it not, and none the less it is there, but the depth conceals it. There is no light unless it comes from that serene which is never clouded, else is it darkness, either shadow of the flesh or its poison.

"Now is laid well open to you the hiding-place which concealed from you the living Justice concerning which you have made question so incessantly. For you said, 'A man is born on the bank of the Indus,[2] and none is there to speak, or read, or write, of Christ, and all his wishes and acts are good, so far as human reason sees, without sin in life or in speech. He dies unbaptized, and without faith. Where is this justice which condemns him? Where is his sin if he does not believe?' Now who are you who would sit upon the seat to judge at a thousand miles away with the short sight that carries but a span? Assuredly, for him who subtilizes with me, if the Scriptures were not set over you, there would be marvelous occasion for questioning. O earthly animals! O gross minds! The primal Will, which of Itself is good, has never moved from Itself, which is the supreme Good. All is just that accords with It; no created good draws It to itself, but It, raying forth, is the cause of it."

As the stork circles over her nest, when she has fed her young, and as the one which she has fed looks up to her, such became (and I so raised my brows) the blessed image which, impelled by so many counsels, moved its wings. Wheeling it sang and said, "As are my notes to you who understand them not, such is the Eternal Judgment to you mortals."

After those glowing flames of the Holy Spirit became quiet, still in the sign which made the Romans reverend to the world, it began again, "To this realm none ever rose who believed not in Christ, either before or after he was nailed to the tree. But behold, many cry Christ, Christ, who, at the Judgment, shall be far less near to Him than he who knows not Christ; and the Ethiop will condemn such Christians when the two companies shall be separated, the one forever rich, and the other poor. What may the Persians say to your kings, when they shall see that volume open in which are recorded all their dispraises? There shall be seen, among the deeds of Albert, that which will soon set the pen in motion, by which the Kingdom of Prague shall be made a desert.[3] There shall be seen the woe which he who shall die by a boarskin blow is bringing upon the Seine by falsifying the coin.[4] There shall be seen the pride that quickens thirst, which makes the Scot and the Englishman mad, so that neither can keep within his own bounds.[5] It will show the lechery and effeminate life of him of Spain, and him of Bohemia,[6] who never knew valor nor wished it. It will show the Cripple of Jerusalem,[7] his goodness marked with an *I*, while an *M* will mark the opposite. It will show the avarice and cowardice of him who has in ward the Isle of Fire where Anchises ended his long life;[8] and to give to understand how paltry he is, the writing for him shall be in contractions that will note much in little space. And plain to all shall be revealed the foul deeds of his uncle and his brother,[9] which have dishonored so eminent a lineage and two crowns.[10] And he of Portugal and he of Norway[11] shall be known there, and he of Rascia,[12] who, to his harm, has seen the coin of Venice.

"Oh happy Hungary, if she no longer allow herself to be maltreated![13] and happy Navarre,[14] if she arm herself with the mountains which bind her round! And all should believe that, for earnest of this, Nicosia and Famagosta[15] are now lamenting and complaining because of their beast who departs not from the side of the others."

CANTO XX

When he who illumines all the world descends from our hemisphere so that day on every side is spent, the heaven, which before is kindled by him alone, suddenly shows itself again with many lights wherein one alone is shining; and this change in the sky came to my mind when the ensign of the world and of its leaders became silent in the blessed beak; because all those living lights, shining far more brightly, began songs that have lapsed and fallen from my memory.

O sweet Love, that mantlest thyself in a smile, how glowing didst thou appear in those pipes that were filled only with the breath of holy thoughts!

When the bright and precious jewels wherewith I saw the sixth luminary engemmed had imposed silence on these angelic chimes, I seemed to hear the murmuring of a river which falls down clear from rock to rock, showing the abundance of its high source. And as the sound takes its form at the neck of the lute, and the wind at the vent of the pipe it fills, so, without keeping me waiting longer, that murmuring of the Eagle rose up through the neck, as if it were hollow. There it became voice, and thence it issued through the beak in the form of words such as the heart whereon I wrote them was awaiting.

"That part in me which in mortal eagles sees and endures the sun you must now gaze on intently," it began to me, "because, of the fires whereof I make my shape, those with which the eye in my head is sparkling are of all their ranks the chiefs. He that shines midmost, as the pupil, was the singer of the Holy Ghost, who bore the ark about from town to town.[1] Now he knows the merit of his song, so far as it was the effect of his own counsel, by the reward which is proportioned to it. Of the five which make an arch for my brow, he who is nearest to my beak consoled the poor widow for her son. Now he knows, by experience of this sweet life and of the opposite, how dear it costs not to follow Christ.[2] And he who follows on the circumference whereof I speak, upon the upward arc, by true penitence delayed death.[3] Now he knows that the eternal judgment is not changed when worthy prayer there below makes tomorrow's that which was today's. The next who follows, with a good intention which bore bad fruit, made himself Greek, together with the laws and me, in order to give place to the Pastor.[4] Now he knows how the evil derived from his good action does not harm him, even though the world should be destroyed thereby. And him you see in the downward arc was William,[5] for whom that land mourns that weeps on account of the living Charles and Frederick.[6] Now he knows how Heaven is enamored of the righteous king, as by the effulgence of his aspect he yet makes this evident. Who would believe, down in the erring world, that Ripheus the Trojan[7] was the fifth of the holy lights in this circle? Now he knows much of the divine grace that the world cannot see, even though his sight discerns not the bottom."

Like the lark that soars in the air, first singing, then silent, content with the last sweetness that satiates it, so seemed to me the image of the imprint of the Eternal Pleasure, by whose will everything becomes that which it is. And albeit there I was to my questioning like glass to the color that it clothes, yet would it not endure to bide its time in silence, but by its weight and pressure forced from my lips, "How can these things be?" At which I saw a great festival of flashing lights. And then, its eye kindling yet more, the blessed sign, not to keep me in suspense and amazement, replied, "I see that you believe these things because I tell them, but you see not the *how,* so that, though believed in, they are hidden. You do as one who well apprehends a thing by name, but may not see its quiddity unless another explain it. *Regnum celorum*[8] suffers violence from fervent love and from living hope which vanquishes the Divine will: not as man overcomes man, but vanquishes it because it wills to be vanquished, and vanquished, vanquishes with its own benignity. The first soul of the eyebrow and the fifth make you marvel, because you see the region of the Angels decked with them. They came forth from their bodies not as you think, Gentiles, but Christians, with firm faith, the one in the Feet that were to suffer, the other in the Feet that had suffered. For the one came back to his bones from Hell, where none ever returns to right will; and this was the reward of living hope, of living hope that gave power to the prayers made to God to raise him up, that it might be possible for his will to be moved. The glorious soul I tell of, having returned to the flesh for a short time, believed in Him that was able to help him; and, believing, was kindled to such a fire of true love that on his second death he was worthy to come to this rejoicing. The other, through grace that wells from a fountain so deep that never did creature thrust eye down to its first wave, set all his love below on righteousness; wherefore, from grace to grace, God opened his eye to our future redemption, so that he believed in it, and thenceforth endured not the stench of paganism, and reproved the perverse peoples for it. Those three ladies[9] whom you saw by the right wheel stood for baptism to him more than a thousand years before baptizing.

"O predestination, how remote is thy root from the vision of those who see not the First Cause entire![10] And you mortals, keep yourselves restrained in judging; for we, who see God, know not yet all the elect. And to us such defect is sweet, because our good in this good is refined, that what God wills we also will."

Thus, to make my short sight clear, sweet medicine was given to me by that divine image. And as a good lutanist makes the vibration of the string accompany a good singer, by which the song gains more pleasantness, so I remember that, while it spoke, I saw the two blessed lights, just as the winking of the eyes concords, making their flames quiver to the words.

CANTO XXI

Already my eyes were fixed again on the face of my lady, and with them my mind, and from every other intent it was withdrawn; and she did not smile, but, "Were I to smile," she began to me, "you would become such as was Semele when she turned to ashes;[1] for my beauty which, along the steps of the eternal palace, is kindled the more, as you have seen, the higher the ascent, were it not tempered, is so resplendent that your mortal powers at its flash would be like the bough shattered by a thunderbolt. We have risen to the seventh splendor which beneath the breast of the burning Lion rays down now mingled with its power.[2] Fix your mind after your eyes, and make of them mirrors to the figure which in this mirror shall be shown to you."

He who should know what was the pasture of my sight in her blessed aspect, when I transferred me to another care, would recognize how much it rejoiced me to be obedient to my heavenly guide, weighing the one with the other side.

Within the crystal which bears the name, circling round the world, of its beloved leader beneath whom every wickedness lay dead, I saw, of the color of gold on which a sunbeam is shining, a ladder rising up so high that my sight might not follow it.[3] I saw, moreover, so many splendors descending along the steps, that I thought every light which appears in heaven had been poured down from it.

And, as by their natural custom, the daws move about together, at the beginning of the day, to warm their cold feathers, then some fly away not to return, some wheel round to whence they had started, while others wheeling make a stay; such movements, it seemed to me, were in that sparkling, which came in a throng, as soon as it smote upon a certain step.

And that one which stopped nearest to us became so bright that in my thought I said, "I clearly perceive the love which you are signaling to me. But she from whom I await the how and the when of speech and of silence pauses, and therefore I, counter to desire, do well not to ask." Whereupon she, who saw my silence in His sight who sees all, said to me, "Loose your warm desire." And I began, "My own merit does not make me worthy of your answer, but for her sake who gives me leave to ask, O blessed life that are hidden within your own joy, make known to me the cause that has placed you so near me; and tell why in this wheel the sweet symphony of Paradise is silent, which below through the others so devoutly sounds."

"You have the hearing as the sight of mortals," it replied to me, "wherefore here is no song, for that same reason for which Beatrice has not smiled. Down by the steps of the sacred ladder I descended so far only to give you glad welcome with my speech and with the light that mantles me; nor was it greater love that made me swifter; for love as much and more is burning up there, even as the flaming manifests to you; but the high charity which makes us prompt servants of the counsel which governs the world allots here as you perceive."

"I see well," said I, "O holy lamp, how free love suffices in this Court for following the eternal Providence; but this is what seems to me hard to discern, why you alone among your consorts were predestined to this office." Nor had I come to the last word when the light made a center of its middle, and spun round like a rapid millstone. Then answered the love that was therein, "A divine light is directed on me, penetrating through this wherein I embosom myself, the virtue of which, conjoined with my vision, lifts me above myself so far that I see the Supreme Essence from which it is drawn. From this comes the joy with which

I am aflame, for to my sight, in the measure of its clearness, I match the clearness of my flame. But that soul in heaven which is most enlightened, that Seraph who has his eye most fixed on God, could not satisfy your question; for that which you ask lies so deep within the abyss of the eternal statute that it is cut off from every created vision. And when you return to the mortal world, carry this back, so that it may no longer presume to move its feet toward so great a goal. The mind, which shines here, on earth is smoky, and therefore think how it can do below that which it cannot do, though heaven raise it to itself."

His words so restrained me that I left the question and drew me back to ask it humbly who it was. "Between the two shores of Italy, and not very far from your native land, rise crags so high that the thunders sound far lower down; and they make a hump whose name is Catria,[4] beneath which a hermitage is consecrated, which once was wholly given to worship." Thus it began again to me with its third speech; then continued, "There in the service of God I became so steadfast that with food seasoned only with olive-juice I passed easily through heats and frosts, content in contemplative thoughts. That cloister used to yield abundant harvest to these heavens, and now it is become so barren that soon it needs must be revealed. In that place was I Peter Damian,[5] and in the House of Our Lady on the Adriatic shore[6] I was Peter the Sinner. Little of mortal life was left to me when I was sought for and dragged to that hat which ever passes down from bad to worse. Cephas[7] came, and the great vessel of the Holy Spirit came, lean and barefoot, taking their food at whatsoever inn. Now the modern pastors require one to prop them up on this side and one on that, and one to lead them, so heavy are they, and one to hold up their trains behind. They cover their palfreys with their mantles, so that two beasts go under one hide. O patience, that do endure so much!"

At these words I saw more flamelets from step to step descending, and whirling; and every whirl made them more beautiful. Round about this one they came, and stopped, and uttered a cry of such deep sound that nothing here could be likened to it; nor did I understand it, so did the thunder overcome me.

CANTO XXII

Overwhelmed with amazement, I turned to my guide, like a little child who always runs back to where it has most confidence; and she, like a mother who quickly comforts her pale and gasping son with her voice which is wont to reassure him, said to me, "Do you not know that you are in heaven, do you not know that heaven is all holy, and that whatever is done here comes of righteous zeal? How the song, and I by smiling, would have transmuted you, you can now conceive, since this cry has so much moved you; wherein, had you understood their prayers, already would be known to you the vengeance which you shall see before you die. The sword of here on high cuts not in haste nor tardily, save to his deeming who in longing or in fear awaits it. But turn now to the others, for you shall see many illustrious spirits, if you direct your sight as I say."

As was her pleasure, I turned my eyes, and I saw a hundred little spheres which together were making themselves beautiful with their mutual rays. I was standing as one who within himself represses the prick of his desire, who does not make bold to ask, he so fears to exceed. And the greatest and most shining of those pearls came forward to satisfy my desire concerning itself. Then within it I heard, "If you could see, as I do, the charity which burns among us, you would have uttered your thoughts; but lest you, by waiting, be delayed in your lofty aim, I will make answer to the thought itself about which you are so circumspect.[1]

"That mountain on whose slope Cassino lies[2] was of old frequented on its summit by the folk deceived and perverse, and I am he who first bore up there His name who brought to earth that truth which so uplifts us; and such grace shone upon me that I drew away the surrounding towns from the impious worship that seduced the world. These other fires were all contemplative men, kindled by that warmth which gives birth to holy flowers and fruits. Here is Macarius, here is Romualdus, here are my brethren who stayed their feet within the cloisters and kept a steadfast heart."[3]

And I to him, "The affection you show in speaking with me, and the good semblance which I see and note in all your ardors, have expanded my confidence as the sun does the rose when it opens to its fullest bloom. Therefore I pray you—and do you, father, assure me if I am capable of receiving so great a grace, that I may behold you in your uncovered shape."

Whereon he, "Brother, your high desire shall be fulfilled up in the last sphere, where are fulfilled all others and my own. There every desire is perfect, mature, and whole. In that alone is every part there where it always was, for it is not in space, nor has it poles; and our ladder reaches up to it, wherefore it steals itself from your sight. All the way thither the patriarch Jacob saw it stretch its upper part, when it appeared to him so laden with Angels. But no one now lifts his foot from earth to ascend it, and my Rule remains for waste of paper. The walls, which used to be an abbey, have become dens, and the cowls are sacks full of foul meal. But heavy usury is not exacted so counter to God's pleasure as that fruit which makes the heart of monks so mad; for whatsoever the Church has in keeping is all for the folk that ask it in God's name, not for kindred, or for other filthier thing. The flesh of mortals is so soft that on earth a good beginning does not last from the springing of the oak to the bearing of the acorn. Peter began his fellowship without gold or silver, and I mine with prayer and with fasting, and Francis his with humility; and if you look at the beginning of each, and then look again whither it has strayed, you will see the white changed to dark. Nevertheless, Jordan driven back, and the sea fleeing when God willed, were sights more wondrous than the succor here."

Thus he spoke to me, then drew back to his company, and the company closed together; then like a whirlwind all were gathered upward. My sweet lady, with only a sign, thrust me up after them by that ladder, so did her power overcome my nature; nor ever here below, where we mount and descend by nature's law, was motion so swift as might match my flight. So may I return, reader, to that devout triumph for the sake of which I often bewail my sins and beat my breast, you would not have drawn out and put your finger into the fire so quickly as I saw the sign which follows the Bull, and was within it.[4]

O glorious stars, O light impregnated with mighty power, from which I derive all my genius, whatsoever it may be, with you was rising and with you was hiding himself he who is father of every mortal life when I first felt the air of Tuscany; and then, when the grace was bestowed on me to enter the lofty wheel that bears you round, your region was assigned to me! To you my soul now devoutly sighs, that it may acquire virtue for the hard pass which draws it to itself.

"You are so near to the final blessedness," Beatrice began, "that you must have your eyes clear and keen. And therefore, before you enter farther into it, look back downward and behold how great a world I have already set beneath your feet, in order that your heart may present itself, joyous to its utmost, to the triumphant throng which comes glad through this round ether."

With my sight I returned through all and each of the seven spheres, and saw this globe such that I smiled at its paltry semblance; and that counsel I approve as best which holds it for least, and he whose thought is turned elsewhere may be called truly upright. I saw the daughter of Latona⁵ glowing without that shade for which I once believed her rare and dense. The aspect of your son, Hyperion,⁶ I there endured, and saw how Maia and Dione⁷ move around and near him. Then appeared to me the tempering of Jove between his father and his son, and then was clear to me the varying they make in their position. And all the seven were displayed to me, how great they are and swift, and how distant each from other in location. The little threshing-floor which makes us so fierce was all revealed to me from hills to river-mouths, as I circled with the eternal Twins. Then to the beauteous eyes I turned my eyes again.

CANTO XXIII

As the bird, among the beloved leaves, having sat on the nest of her sweet brood through the night which hides things from us, who, in order to look upon their longed-for aspect and to find the food wherewith to feed them, wherein her heavy toils are pleasing to her, foreruns the time, upon the open bough, and with glowing love awaits the sun, fixedly gazing for the dawn to break; so was my lady standing, erect and eager, turned toward the region beneath which the sun shows less haste. I, therefore, seeing her in suspense and longing, became as he who in desire would fain have something else, and in hope is satisfied. But short was the time between the one and the other *when,* of my waiting, I mean, and of my seeing the heavens become more and more resplendent. And Beatrice said, "Behold the hosts of Christ's triumph and all the fruit garnered from the circling of these spheres!" It seemed to me her face was all aflame, and her eyes were so full of joy that I must needs pass it by undescribed.

As in the clear skies at the full moon Trivia¹ smiles among the eternal nymphs that deck heaven through all its depths, I saw, above thousands of lamps, a Sun which kindled each one of them as does our own the things we see above; and through its living light the lucent Substance² outglowed so bright upon my vision that it endured it not.

O Beatrice, sweet guide and dear! She said to me, "That which overcomes you is power against which naught defends itself. Therein are the wisdom and the power that opened the roads between Heaven and earth, for which of old there was such long desire."

Even as fire breaks from a cloud, because it dilates so that it has not room there, and contrary to its own nature, falls down to earth, so my mind, becoming greater amid those feasts, issued from itself, and of what it became has no remembrance.

"Open your eyes and look on what I am; you have seen things such that you are become able to sustain my smile." I was as one that wakes from a forgotten dream, and who strives in vain to bring it back to mind, when I heard this proffer, worthy of such gratitude that it can never be effaced from the book which records the past.

Though all those tongues which Polyhymnia and her sisters³ made most rich with their sweetest milk should sound now to aid me, it would not come to a thousandth part of the truth, in singing the holy smile, and how it lit up the holy aspect; and so, depicting Paradise, the sacred poem must needs make a leap, even as one who finds his way cut off. But whoso thinks of the ponderous theme and of the mortal shoulder which is laden therewith, will not blame it if it tremble beneath the load. It is no voyage for a little bark, this which my daring prow cleaves as it goes, nor for a pilot who would spare himself.

"Why does my face so enamor you that you turn not to the fair garden which blossoms beneath the rays of Christ? Here is the Rose[4] wherein the Divine Word became flesh; here are the lilies[5] by whose odor the good way was taken."

Thus Beatrice; and I who to her counsels was all eager, again gave myself up to the battle of the feeble brows.

As under the sun's ray, which streams pure through a broken cloud, ere now my eyes, sheltered by shade, have seen a meadow of flowers, so saw I many hosts of splendors glowed on from above by ardent rays, though I saw not whence came the glowings. O benign Power, which doth so imprint them, Thou didst ascend so as to yield place there for the eyes that were powerless before Thee!

The name of the fair flower which I ever invoke, both morning and evening, absorbed all my mind as I gazed on the greatest flame. And when on both of my eyes had been depicted the quality and the greatness of the living star which conquers up there even as down here it conquered, there descended through the heaven a torch which formed a circle in the likeness of a crown that girt her and wheeled about her. Whatever melody sounds sweetest here below and most draws to itself the soul, would seem a cloud which, being rent, thunders, compared with the sound of that lyre wherewith was crowned the beauteous sapphire by which the brightest heaven is ensapphired.

"I am angelic love, who circle the supreme joy that breathes from out the womb which was the hostelry of our Desire; and I shall circle, Lady of Heaven, until thou shalt follow thy Son, and make the supreme sphere more divine by entering it." Thus the circling melody sealed itself, and all the other lights made Mary's name resound.

The royal mantle of all the world's revolving spheres, which most burns and is most quickened in the breath of God and in His workings, had, above us, its inner shore so distant that sight of it, there where I was, was not yet possible to me. Therefore my eyes had not power to follow the crowned flame which mounted upward after her offspring. And as

an infant which, when it has taken the milk, stretches its arms toward its mother, its affection glowing forth, each of these splendors stretched upward with its peak, so that the deep love they had for Mary was made plain to me. Then they remained there in my sight, singing *Regina celi*[6] so sweetly that never has the delight departed from me. Oh, how great is the abundance which is heaped up in those rich coffers, who were good sowers here below! Here they live and rejoice in the treasure which was gained with tears in the exile of Babylon,[7] where gold was scorned. Here, under the exalted Son of God and Mary, together with both the ancient and the new council, he triumphs in his victory who holds the keys of such glory.[8]

CANTO XXIV

"O Fellowship elect to the great supper of the blessed Lamb, who feeds you so that your desire is ever satisfied, since by the grace of God this man foretastes of that which falls from your table before death appoint his time to him, give heed to his immense longing and bedew him somewhat: you drink ever of the fountain whence flows that which he thinks." Thus Beatrice; and those glad souls made themselves spheres upon fixed poles, flaming like comets, as they whirled. And as wheels within the fittings of clocks revolve, so that to one who gives heed the first seems quiet and the last to fly, so did those carols, dancing severally fast and slow, make me judge of their riches. From the one I noted as the richest I saw issue a fire so joyful that it left there none of greater brightness; and it revolved three times round Beatrice with a song so divine that my phantasy does not repeat it to me; wherefore my pen leaps and I do not write it, for our imagination, not to say our speech, is of too vivid color for such folds.

"O holy sister mine, who do so devoutly pray to us, by your ardent affection you loose me from that fair sphere"; after it had stopped, the blessed fire breathed forth these words to my lady as I have told them.

And she, "O eternal light of the great man with whom our Lord left the keys, which He bore below, of this marvelous joy, test this man on points light and grave, as pleases you, concerning the Faith by which you did walk upon the sea. Whether he loves rightly and rightly hopes and believes is not hidden from you, for you have your vision where everything is seen depicted. But since this kingdom has made its citizens by the true faith, it rightly falls to him to speak of it, that he may glorify it."

Even as the bachelor arms himself—and does not speak until the master propounds the question—in order to adduce the proof, not to decide it, so, while she was speaking, I was arming myself with every reason, to be ready for such a questioner and for such a profession.[1]

"Speak, good Christian, and declare yourself: Faith, what is it?" Whereon I raised my brow to that light whence this was breathed forth, then I turned to Beatrice, who promptly signaled to me that I should pour the water forth from my inward fountain.

"May the grace that grants me to confess to the Chief Centurion," I began, "cause my conceptions to be well expressed." And I went on, "As the veracious pen of your dear brother wrote of it, who with you, father, put Rome on the good path, Faith is the substance of things hoped for and the evidence of things not seen; and this I take to be its quiddity."

Then I heard, "Rightly do you deem, if you understand well why he placed it among the substances and then among the evidences."

And I thereon, "The deep things which grant to me here the sight of themselves are so hidden to eyes below that there their existence is in belief alone, upon which the lofty hope is founded; and therefore it takes the designation of substance. And from this belief needs must we reason, without seeing more: therefore it receives the designation of evidence." Then I heard, "If all that is acquired below for doctrine were thus understood, the wit of sophist would have no place there." These words were breathed forth from that enkindled love; and it continued, "Now the alloy and the weight of this coin have been well enough examined; but tell me if you have it in your purse?" And I, "Yes, I have it so shining and so round that in its stamp nothing is doubtful to me."

Then issued from the deep light that was shining there, "This precious jewel whereon

every virtue is founded, whence did it come to you?"

And I, "The plenteous rain of the Holy Spirit which is poured over the old and over the new parchments is a syllogism that has proved it to me so acutely that, in comparison with this, every demonstration seems obtuse to me."

Then I heard, "That old and that new proposition which are so conclusive to you, why do you hold them for divine discourse?"

And I, "The proof which discloses the truth to me are the works that followed, for which nature never heats iron nor beats anvil."

"Tell me," came the reply, "who assures you that these works ever were? The very thing itself which requires to be proved, and naught else, affirms them to you."

"If the world turned to Christianity without miracles," I said, "that one is such that the rest are not the hundredth part; for you entered the field poor and hungry, to sow the good plant which was once a vine and is now become a thorn."

This ended, the high and holy court resounded a "Te Deum laudamus" through the spheres, in the melody which up there is sung.

And that Baron[2] who, thus from branch to branch examining, had now drawn me on so that we were approaching the last leaves, began again, "The Grace that holds amorous discourse with your mind, till now has opened your lips aright, so that I approve what has come from them; but now you must declare what you believe and whence it was offered to your belief."

"O holy father, spirit who see that which you did so believe that you, toward the sepulchre, did outdo younger feet," I began, "you would have me declare here the form of my ready belief, and also you have asked the cause of it. And I reply: I believe in one God, sole and eternal, who, unmoved, moves all the heavens with love and with desire; and for this belief I have not only proofs physical and metaphysical, but it is given to me also in the truth that rains down hence through Moses and the Prophets and the Psalms, through the Gospel, and through you who wrote when the fiery Spirit had made you holy. And I believe in three Eternal Persons, and these I believe to be one essence, so one and so threefold as to comport at once with *are* and *is*. With the profound divine state whereof I now speak, the evangelic doctrine many times sets the seal upon my mind. This is the beginning, this is the spark which then dilates to a living flame and like a star in heaven shines within me."

Even as the master who listens to that which pleases him, then embraces his servant, rejoicing in his news, as soon as he is silent; so, singing benedictions on me, the apostolic light at whose bidding I had spoken encircled me three times when I was silent, I so pleased him by my speech.

CANTO XXV

If ever it come to pass that the sacred poem to which heaven and earth have so set hand that it has made me lean for many years should overcome the cruelty which bars me from the fair sheepfold where I slept as a lamb, an enemy to the wolves which war on it, with changed voice now and with changed fleece a poet will I return, and at the font of my baptism will I take the crown; because there I entered into the Faith that makes souls known to God; and afterward Peter, for its sake, thus encircled my brow.

Then a light moved towards us from that circle whence has issued the first-fruit which Christ left of His vicars; and my lady, full of gladness, said to me, "Look! look! Behold the Baron for whose sake, down below, folk visit Galicia."[1]

As when the dove alights beside its mate, and the one lavishes its affection on the other, circling it and cooing, so did I see the one great and glorious prince received by the other, praising the food which feeds them thereabove. But when the joyful greeting was completed, each stopped silent *coram me*,[2] so aflame that it overcame my sight. Then Beatrice, smiling, said, "Illustrious life, by whom the bounty of our Court was chronicled,[3] make hope resound in this height; you can, who did figure it all those times when Jesus showed most favor to the three."[4]

"Lift up your head and see that you reassure yourself, for that which comes up here from the mortal world must be ripened in our beams." This assurance came to me from the second fire; whereon I lifted up my eyes unto the hills which had bent them down before with excess of weight.

"Since, of His grace, our Emperor wills that you, before your death, come face to face with His Counts in His most secret hall,[5] so that, having seen the truth of this Court, you may strengthen in yourself and others the Hope which there below rightly enamors, say what it is, and how your mind blossoms with it, and say whence it came to you." Thus the second light continued further.

And that compassionate one, who had guided the feathers of my wings to such lofty flight, anticipated my reply thus, "The Church Militant has not any child possessed of more hope, as is written in the Sun which irradiates all our host; therefore is it granted him to come from Egypt to Jerusalem, that he may see, before his term of warfare is completed. The other two points which are asked, not for sake of knowing, but that he may report how greatly this virtue is pleasing to you, I leave to him, for they will not be difficult to him, nor of vainglory; and let him answer thereto, and may the grace of God concede this to him."

As the pupil who answers the teacher, ready and eager in that wherein he is expert, so that his worth may be disclosed, "Hope,"[6] I said, "is a sure expectation of future glory, which divine grace produces, and preceding merit. From many stars this light comes to me, but he first instilled it into my heart who was the supreme singer of the Supreme Leader. 'Let them hope in Thee who know Thy name,' he says in his divine song, and who knows it not, if he have my faith. You afterwards in your Epistle did instill it into me, together with his instilling, so that I am full, and pour again your shower upon others."

While I was speaking, within the living bosom of that fire trembled a flash, sudden and frequent, like lightning; then it breathed forth, "The love whereof I am still aflame toward that virtue which followed me even to the palm and the departure from the field wills that I breathe again to you, who do delight in it; and it is my pleasure that you tell that which Hope promises to you."

And I, "The new and the old Scriptures set up the token of the souls that God has made

His friends, and this points it out to me. Isaiah says that each one shall be clothed in his own land with a double garment, and his own land is this sweet life; and your brother, where he treats of the white robes, makes manifest this revelation to us far more expressly."

At first, close on the end of these words, "*Sperent in te*" was heard above us, to which all the carols made answer; then one light among them shone out so bright that if the Crab had one such crystal, winter would have a month of one unbroken day. And as a glad maiden rises and goes and enters into the dance, only to do honor to the bride, not for any failing, so did I see the brightened splendor approach the two who were wheeling to such a song as befitted their burning love. It joined there in the singing and the wheeling, and my lady kept her gaze upon them, even as a bride silent and motionless. "This is he who lay upon the breast of our Pelican, and this is he who was chosen from upon the Cross for the great office." Thus my lady; but no more after than before her words did she move her gaze from its fixed attention.

As is he who gazes and strains to see the sun a little eclipsed, and who through seeing becomes sightless, so did I become in respect to that last fire, till it was said, "Why do you dazzle yourself in order to see that which has here no place? On earth my body is earth, and there it shall be with the rest, until our number equals the eternal purpose. With the two robes in the blessed cloister are those two lights only which ascended; and this you shall carry back into your world."

At these words the flaming circle fell silent, together with the sweet mingling made within the sound of the trinal breath, even as, to avoid fatigue or danger, oars till then struck through the water, stop all at once at the sound of a whistle.

Ah! how greatly was I stirred in my mind when I turned to see Beatrice, at not being able to see, although I was near her, and in the world of bliss.

CANTO XXVI

While I was apprehensive because of my quenched sight, there issued forth from the effulgent flame that quenched it a breath that made me attentive, and it said, "Until you have again the sense of sight which you have consumed in me, it is well that you compensate it by discourse. Begin then, and say on what aim your soul is set; and be assured that your sight in you is confounded, not destroyed; for the lady who guides you through this divine region has in her look the power which the hand of Ananias had."[1]

And I said, "At her good pleasure, soon or late, let succor come to the eyes which were the doors when she did enter with the fire wherewith I ever burn. The good which satisfies this Court is Alpha and Omega of all the scripture which Love reads to me, either low or loud."

The same voice that had delivered me from my fear at the sudden dazzlement gave me concern to speak again; and it said, "Assuredly you must sift with a finer sieve: you must tell who directed your bow to such a target."

And I, "By philosophic arguments,[2] and by authority that descends from here, such love must needs imprint itself on me; for the good, inasmuch as it is good, kindles love in proportion as it is understood, and so much the more the more of good it contains in itself. Therefore, to that Essence wherein is such supremacy that whatsoever good be found outside of It is naught else save a beam of Its own radiance, more that to any other must the mind be moved, in love, of whoever discerns the truth on which this proof is founded. Such a truth he makes plain to my intelligence who demonstrates to me the first love of all the eternal substances. The voice of the veracious Author makes it plain where, speaking of Himself, He says to Moses, 'I will make you see all goodness.' You also set it forth to me in the beginning of your sublime proclamation, which more than any other heralding, declares below the mystery of this place on high."

And I heard, "On the ground of human reason and of the authorities concordant with it, the highest of all your loves looks to God; but tell me also if you feel other cords draw you toward Him, so that you declare with how many teeth this love grips you."

The holy intention of the Eagle of Christ was not hidden, indeed it was plain to me whither he would direct my profession.

Therefore I began again, "All those things whose bite can make the heart turn to God have wrought together in my love; for the being of the world and my own being, the death that He sustained that I might live, and that which every believer hopes, as do I, with the living assurance of which I spoke, have drawn me from the sea of perverse love and placed me on the shore of right love. The leaves wherewith all the garden of the Eternal Gardener is enleaved I love in measure of the good borne unto them from Him."

As soon as I was silent a most sweet song resounded through the heaven, and my lady sang with the rest, "Holy, Holy, Holy!" And as sleep is broken by a piercing light when the visual spirit runs to meet the splendor that goes from tunic to tunic, and he who awakens shrinks from what he sees, so ignorant is his sudden wakening, until his judgment comes to his aid; thus Beatrice chased away every mote from my eyes with the radiance of her own, which shone more than a thousand miles; so that I then saw better than before; and as one amazed I asked concerning a fourth light which I saw with us. And my lady, "Within those rays the first soul which the First Power ever created gazes with love upon its Maker."

As the bough which bends its top at passing of the wind, and then uplifts itself by its own virtue which raises it, so did I, in amazement, while she was speaking, and then a desire to speak, wherewith I was burning, gave me assurance again, and I began, "O fruit that were alone produced mature, O ancient father of whom every bride is daughter and daughter-in-law, devoutly as I can, I implore you that you speak to me: you see my wish, and that I may hear you sooner I do not tell it."

Sometimes an animal that is covered so stirs that its impulse must needs be apparent, since what envelops it follows its movements: in like manner that first soul showed me, through its covering, how joyously it came to do me pleasure. Then it breathed forth, "Without its being told to me by you, I discern your wish better than you whatever is most certain to you, for I see it in the truthful Mirror which makes of Itself a reflection of all else, while of It nothing makes itself the reflection. You wish to know how long it is since God placed me in the lofty garden wherein this lady prepared you for so long a stair; and how long it

was a delight to my eyes; and the true cause of the great wrath; and the idiom which I used and shaped. Now know, my son, that the tasting of the tree was not in itself the cause of so long an exile, but solely the overpassing of the bound. In the place whence your lady dispatched Virgil, I longed for this assembly during four thousand three hundred and two revolutions of the sun; and while I was on earth I saw him return to all the lights of his path nine hundred and thirty times. The tongue which I spoke was all extinct before the people of Nimrod attempted their unaccomplishable work;[3] for never was any product of reason durable forever, because of human liking, which alters, following the heavens. That man should speak is nature's doing, but whether thus or thus, nature then leaves you to follow your own pleasure. Before I descended to the anguish of Hell the Supreme Good from whom comes the joy that swathes me was named *I* on earth; and later He was called *El:* and that must needs be, for the usage of mortals is as a leaf on a branch, which goes away and another comes. On the mountain which rises highest from the sea I lived pure, then guilty, from the first hour to that which follows, when the sun changes quadrant, next upon the sixth.[4]

CANTO XXVII

"Glory be to the Father, to the Son, and to the Holy Spirit!" all Paradise began, so that the sweet song held me rapt. What I saw seemed to me a smile of the universe, so that my rapture entered both by hearing and by sight. O joy! O ineffable gladness! O life entire of love and of peace! O wealth secure without longing!

Before my eyes the four torches stood enkindled, and that which had come first began to make itself more vivid, and in its aspect became as would Jupiter if he and Mars were birds and should exhange plumage. The Providence which there assigns turn and office had imposed silence on the blessed choir on every side, when I heard, "If I change color, marvel not, for, as I speak, you shall see all these change color. He who on earth usurps my place, my place, my place, which in the sight of the Son of God is vacant,[1] has made my burial-ground a sewer of blood and of stench, so that the Perverse One² who fell from here above takes comfort there below."

With that color which, by reason of the opposite sun, paints the cloud at evening and at morning, I then saw the whole heaven overspread. And as a chaste lady who is sure of herself, and at another's fault, only hearing of it, becomes timid, so did Beatrice change her semblance; and such, I believe, was the eclipse in heaven when the Supreme Power suffered.

Then his words continued, in a voice so altered from itself that his looks were not more changed, "The spouse of Christ was not nurtured on my blood and that of Linus and of Cletus,³ to be employed for gain of gold; but for gain of this happy life Sixtus and Pius and Calixtus and Urban⁴ shed their blood after much weeping. It was not our purpose that one part of the Christian people should sit on the right of our successors, and one part on the left; nor that the keys which were committed to me should become the ensign on a banner for warfare on the baptized; nor that I should be made a figure on a seal to sold and lying privileges, whereat I often blush and flash. Rapacious wolves, in shepherd's garb, are seen from here above in all the pastures: O defense of God, wherefore dost thou yet lie still? Cahorsines and Gascons make ready to drink our blood.⁵ O good beginning, to what vile ending must you fall! But the high Providence, which with Scipio⁶ defended for Rome the glory of the world, will succor speedily, as I conceive. And you, my son, who, because of your mortal weight will again return below, open your mouth and do not hide what I hide not."

Even as our air, when the horn of the heavenly Goat is touched by the sun, flakes down frozen vapors, so I saw the ether thus adorned, flaking upwards triumphal vapors which had made sojourn with us there. My sight was following their semblances, and followed, till the intermediate space became so great that it took from it the power of passing farther onward. Whereon my lady, who saw me freed from gazing upwards, said to me, "Cast your sight down and see how far you have revolved."

From the time when I had looked before, I saw that I had moved through the whole arc which the first climate makes from its middle to its end; so that, on the one hand, beyond Cadiz, I saw the mad track of Ulysses, and on the other nearly to the shore where Europa

made herself a sweet burden;⁷ and more of the space of this little threshing-floor would have been disclosed to me, but the sun was proceeding beneath my feet and was a sign and more away.

My enamored mind, which ever pays court to my lady, was more than ever burning to bring back my eyes to her; and if nature or art ever made baits to take the eye so as to possess the mind, in human flesh or in its portraiture, all these together would seem as nothing beside the divine delight that glowed upon me when I turned to her smiling face. And the power which her look granted me drew me forth from the fair nest of Leda⁸ and thrust me into the swiftest of the heavens.

Its parts, most living and exalted, are so uniform that I cannot tell which of them Beatrice chose as a place for me. But she, who saw my longing, began, smiling so glad that God seemed to rejoice in her countenance, "The nature of the universe which holds the center quiet and moves all the rest around it, begins here as from its starting-point. And this heaven has no other *Where* than the divine mind, wherein is kindled the love that revolves it, and the virtue which it rains down. Light and love enclose it in a circle, as it does the others, and this engirdment He alone who girds it understands. Its motion is not determined by another's, but the others are measured by this, just as ten by its half and its fifth. And how time should have its roots in such a flowerpot, and in the others its leaves, may now be manifest to you.

"O greed, who do so plunge mortals in your depths that none has power to lift his eyes from your waves! The will blossoms well in men, but the continual rain turns the sound plums into blighted fruit. Faith and innocence are found only in little children; then each flies away before the cheeks are covered. One, so long as he lisps, keeps the fasts, who afterward, when his tongue is free, devours any food through any month; and one, while he lisps, loves his mother and listens to her, who afterward, when his speech is full, longs to see her buried. Thus the white skin turns black at the first sight of the fair daughter of him that brings morning and leaves evening. That you marvel not at this, consider that on earth there is no one to govern, wherefore the human family goes thus astray. But before January be all unwintered,[9] because of the hundredth part that is neglected below, these lofty circles shall so shine forth that the storm which has been so long awaited shall turn round the sterns to where the prows are, so that the fleet shall run straight; and good fruit shall follow on the flower."

CANTO XXVIII

After she who imparadises my mind had declared the truth counter to the present life of wretched mortals, as one who sees in a mirror the flame of a torch which is lighted behind him before he has it in sight or in thought, and turns round to see if the glass tells him the truth, and sees that it accords with it as a song with its measure, so my memory recalls that I did, gazing into the beautiful eyes wherewith Love made the cord to capture me. And when I turned and my own were met by what appears in that revolving sphere whenever one gazes intently on its circling, I saw a point which radiated a light so keen that the eye on which it blazes needs must close because of its great keenness; and whatever star seems smallest from here would seem a moon if placed beside it like a star with neighboring star.

Perhaps as near as a halo seems to girdle the light which paints it, when the vapor that bears it is most dense, at such distance around the point a circle of fire was whirling so rapidly that it would have surpassed that motion which most swiftly girds the universe; and this was girt around by another, and that by a third, and the third by a fourth, by a fifth the fourth, then by a sixth the fifth. Thereon the seventh followed, now spread so wide that the messenger of Juno entire would be too narrow to contain it. So the eighth and the ninth; and each was moving more slowly according as it was in number more distant from the unit. And that one had the clearest flame from which the pure spark was least distant, because, I believe, it partakes more of its truth.

My lady, who saw me eager and in great suspense, said, "On that point the heavens and all nature are dependent. Look on that circle which is most conjoined to it, and know that its motion is so swift because of the burning love whereby it is spurred."

And I to her, "If the universe were disposed in the order which I see in those wheels, that which is set before me would have satisfied me. But in the world of sense the revolutions may be seen so much the more divine as they are more remote from the center. Wherefore if my desire is to attain to its end in this wondrous and angelic temple which has only love and light for its confine, needs must I further hear why the model and the copy go not in one fashion, for by myself I contemplate this in vain."

"If your fingers are insufficient for such a knot, it is no wonder, so hard has it become by not being tried." So said my lady, then she continued, "Take that which I shall tell you, if you would be satisfied, and sharpen your wits about it. The material spheres are wide or narrow according to the more or less of virtue which is diffused through all their parts. Greater goodness must needs work greater weal; and the greater body, if it has its parts equally complete, contains the greater weal. Hence this sphere, which sweeps along with it all the rest of the universe, corresponds to the circle which loves most and knows most. Wherefore, if you draw your measure round the virtue, not the semblance, of the substances which appear to you in circles, you will see a wondrous correspondence of greater to more and of smaller to less, in each heaven with respect to its Intelligence."

As the hemisphere of the air remains splendid and serene when Boreas blows from his milder cheek, whereby the obscuring mist is cleared and dissolved, so that the heaven smiles to us with the beauties of its every region, so I became after my lady had provided me with her clear answer, and like a star in heaven the truth was seen.

And when she had paused in her speech, not otherwise does molten iron throw out sparks than the circles sparkled. Each spark kept to its fiery ring, and they were so many that their number stretches to more thousands than the doubling of the chessboard.[1] I heard Hosannah sung from choir to choir to the fixed point that holds them, and will forever hold them at the *Ubi*[2] in which they have ever been. And she, who saw the questioning thoughts within my mind, said, "The first circles have shown to you the Seraphim and the Cherubim. Thus swiftly they follow their bonds, in order to liken themselves to the point as most they can, and they can in proportion as they are exalted in vision. Those other loves who go round them are called Thrones of the divine aspect, because they terminated the first triad. And you should know that all have delight in the measure of the depth to which their sight penetrates the Truth in which every intellect finds rest; from which it may be seen that the state of blessedness is founded on the act of vision, not on that which loves, which follows after; and the merit, to which grace and good will give birth, is the measure of their vision; thus, from grade to grade the progression goes.

"The next triad that thus flowers in this eternal spring which nightly Aries does not despoil perpetually sings Hosannah with three melodies which sound in the three orders of bliss that form the triad. In this hierarchy are the next divinities, first Dominions, then Virtues; and the third are Powers. Then in the two penultimate dances, the Principalities and Archangels circle; the last is wholly of Angelic sports. These orders all gaze upward and prevail downward, so that toward God all are drawn, and all do draw. And Dionysius with such great desire set himself to contemplate these orders that he named and distinguished them, as I: but Gregory afterward differed from him,[3] wherefore, as soon as he opened his eyes in this heaven, he smiled at himself. And if a mortal declared on earth so much of secret truth, I would not have you wonder, for he who saw it here on high disclosed it to him, with much else of the truth about these circles."

CANTO XXIX

When the two children of Latona, covered by the Ram and by the Scales,[1] make the horizon their belt at one same moment, as long as from the instant when the zenith holds them balanced till the one and the other, changing hemispheres, are unbalanced from that belt, for so long, her face illumined with a smile, was Beatrice silent, looking fixedly at the point which had overcome me. Then she began, "I tell, not ask, what you wish to hear, for I have seen it there where every *ubi* and every *quando* is centered. Not for gain of good unto Himself, which cannot be, but that His splendor might, in resplendence, say, "*Subsisto*"—in His eter-

nity beyond time, beyond every other bound, as it pleased Him, the Eternal Love opened into new loves. Nor before, as if inert, did He lie, for neither before nor after did the moving of God upon these waters proceed. Form and matter, conjoined and simple, came into being which had no defect, as three arrows from a three-stringed bow; and as in glass, in amber, or in crystal, a ray shines so that there is no interval between its coming and its pervading all, so did the triform effect ray forth from its Lord into its being, all at once, without distinction of beginning. Therewith order was created and ordained for the substances; and those in whom pure act was produced were the summit of the universe. Pure potentiality held the lowest place; in the middle such a bond tied up potentiality with act that it is never unbound. Jerome wrote for you of the angels as being created a long stretch of ages before aught else of the universe was made; but the truth I tell is written on many a page of the scribes of the Holy Spirit, and you shall be aware of it if you look well; and also reason sees it somewhat, which would not admit that the movers could be so long without their perfection. Now you know where and when these Loves were created, and how; so that three flames of your desire are already quenched.

Then, sooner than one might count to twenty, a part of the Angels disturbed the substrate of your elements. The rest remained and with such great delight began this art which you behold that they never cease from circling. The origin of the fall was the accursed pride of him whom you have seen constrained by all the weights of the universe. Those whom you see here were modest to recognize their being as from the Goodness which had made them apt for intelligence so great: wherefore their vision was exalted with illuminating grace and with their merit, so that they have their will full and established. And I would not have you doubt, but be assured that to receive grace is meritorious, in proportion as the affection is open to it.

"By now, if you have taken in my words, you may contemplate much in regard to this consistory without more help. But since it is taught in your schools on earth that the angelic nature is such that it understands and remembers and wills, I will speak further, in order that you may see in purity the truth that down there is confounded by the equivocation in such like teaching. These substances, since first they were gladdened by the face of God, have never turned their eyes from It, wherefrom nothing is concealed; so that their sight is never intercepted by a new object, and therefore they have no need to remember by reason of interrupted concept. Thus down there men dream while awake, believing or not believing that they speak truth—but in the one case is the greater blame and shame. You mortals do not proceed along one same path in philosophizing, so much does the love of show and the thought of it carry you away; and even this is borne with less anger up here than when the Divine Scripture is set aside or when it is perverted. They think not there how much blood it costs to sow it in the world, nor how much he pleases who humbly keeps close to it. Each one strives for display and makes his own inventions, and these are treated of by the preachers, and the Gospel is silent. One says that at Christ's passion the moon turned back and interposed itself, so that the light of the sun did not reach below—and he lies, for the light itself hid itself, so that this eclipse took place for the Spaniards and the Indians, as well as for the Jews. Florence has not so many Lapos and Bindos[2] as fables such as these that are shouted the year long from the pulpits on every side; so that the poor sheep, who know naught, return from the pasture fed with wind—and not seeing the harm does not excuse them. Christ did not say to his first company, 'Go and preach idle stories to the world,' but he gave to them the true foundation; and that alone sounded on their lips, so that to fight for kindling of the faith they made shield and lance of the Gospel. Now men go forth to preach with jests and with buffooneries, and so there be only a good laugh, the cowl puffs up and nothing more is asked. But such a bird nests in the hood's tail that if the people saw it, they would see what pardons they are trusting in; from which such folly has grown on earth that without proof of any testimony they would flock to every promise. On this the pig of St. Anthony[3] fattens, and others also, who are far more pigs, paying with money that has no stamp of coinage.

"But since we have digressed enough, turn back your eyes now to the true path, so that the way be shortened with the time. This nature extends so exceedingly in number that never was there speech or mortal concept that might advance so far; and if you look at that which is revealed by Daniel, you will see that in his thousands no definite number is to be found. The Primal Light that irradiates them all is received by them in as many ways as are the splendors to which It joins Itself. Wherefore, since the affection follows upon the act of conceiving, the sweetness of love glows variously in them, more and less. Behold now the height and breadth of the Eternal Goodness, since it has made itself so many mirrors wherein it is reflected, remaining in itself One as before."

CANTO XXX

The sixth hour is glowing perhaps six thousand miles away, and this world already slopes its shadow almost to a level bed, when the midst of heaven deep above us begins to grow such that a star here and there is lost to sight at this depth; and as the brightest handmaid of the sun advances, the heaven then shuts off its lights one by one, till the fairest is gone; not otherwise the triumph that plays forever round the Point which overcame me, seeming enclosed by that which it encloses, was gradually extinguished to my sight, wherefore seeing nothing and love constrained me to return with my eyes to Beatrice. If what has been said of her so far as here were all included in a single praise, it would be too slight to serve this present turn. The beauty I beheld transcends measure not only beyond our reach, but I truly believe that He alone who made it can enjoy it all. At this pass I concede myself defeated more than ever comic or tragic poet was defeated by a point in his theme; for, as the sun does to the sight which trembles most, even so remembrance of the sweet smile shears my memory of its very self. From the first day when in this life I saw her face, until this sight, the continuing of my song has not been cut off, but now my pursuit must desist from following her beauty further in my verses, as at his utmost reach must every artist.

Such as I leave her to a greater heralding than that of my trumpet, which draws its arduous subject to a close, with the act and voice of a leader whose task is accomplished she began again, "We have issued forth from the greatest body to the heaven which is pure light: light intellectual full of love, love of true good full of joy, joy that transcends every sweetness. Here you shall see the one and the other soldiery of Paradise, and the one in those aspects which you shall see at the last judgment."

As a sudden flash of lightning which scatters the visual spirits so that it robs the eye of the sight of the clearest objects, so round about me there shone a vivid light and left me so swathed in the veil of is effulgence that nothing was visible to me.

"Ever does the love which quiets this heaven receive into itself with such like salutation, in order to prepare the candle for its flame." No sooner had these brief words come within me than I comprehended that I was surmounting beyond my own power, and such new vision was kindled in me that there is no light so bright that my eyes could not have withstood it. And I saw a light in form of a river glowing tawny between two banks painted with marvelous spring. From out this river issued living sparks and dropped on every side into the blossoms, like rubies set in gold. Then, as if inebriated by the odors, they plunged again into the wondrous flood, and as one was entering another was issuing forth.

"The high desire which now inflames and urges you to have knowledge concerning that which you see pleases me the more the more it swells; but first you must needs drink of this water before so great a thirst in you be slaked." So spoke the sun of my eyes to me, then added, "The stream and the topazes which enter and issue, and the smiling of the grasses, are the shadowy prefaces of their truth; not that these things are defective in themselves, but on your side is the defect, in that you do not yet have vision so exalted."

No infant, on waking far after its hour, so suddenly rushes with face toward the milk, as then did I, to make yet better mirrors of my eyes, stooping to the wave which flows there that we may be bettered in it. And even as the eaves of my eyelids drank of it, so it seemed to me out of its length to have become round. Then, as folk who have been under masks seem other than before, if they do off the semblances

not their own wherein they were hid, so into greater festival the flowers and the sparks did change before me that I saw both the courts of Heaven made manifest. O splendor of God whereby I saw the high triumph of the true kingdom, give to me power to tell how I beheld it!

A Light is thereabove which makes the Creator visible to every creature that has his peace only in beholding Him. It spreads so wide a circle that the circumference would be too large a girdle for the sun. Its whole expanse is made by a ray reflected from the summit of the Primum Mobile, which therefrom takes its life and potency; and as a hillside mirrors itself in water at its base, as if to look upon its own adornment when it is rich in grasses and in flowers, so above the light round and round about in more than a thousand tiers I saw all that of us have won return up there. And if the lowest rank encloses within itself so great a light, how vast is the spread of this rose in its outermost leaves! My sight lost not itself in the breadth and in the height, but took in all the extent and quality of that joy. There, near and far neither add not take away, for where God governs without intermediary, the law of nature in no way prevails.

Into the yellow of the eternal Rose, which rises in ranks and expands and breathes forth odor of praise unto the Sun which makes perpetual spring, Beatrice drew me as one who is silent and wishes to speak, and she said, "Behold how great the assembly of the white robes! See our city, how wide is its circuit! See our seats so filled that few souls are now wanted there!

"And in that great chair whereon you fix your eyes because of the crown that already is set above it, before you sup at these nuptials shall sit the soul, which on earth will be imperial, of the lofty Henry,[1] who will come to set Italy straight before she is ready. The blind cupidity which bewitches you has made you like the little child who dies of hunger and drives away his nurse. And such a one will then be prefect in the divine forum who openly and secretly will not go with him along one same road.[2] But not for long shall God then suffer him in the holy office; for he shall be thrust down where Simon Magus is for his deserts, and shall make him of Alagna go deeper still."

CANTO XXXI

In form then of a pure white rose the saintly host was shown to me, which with His own blood Christ made His bride. But the other host—who, as it flies, sees and sings His glory who enamors it and the goodness which made it so great—like a swarm of bees which one moment enflower themselves, and the next return to where their work acquires savor— was descending into the great flower which is adorned with so many petals, and thence re-ascending to where its love abides forever. They had their faces all of living flame, and their wings of gold, and the rest so white that no snow reaches such a limit. When they descended into the flower, from rank to rank they proffered of the peace and the ardor which they had acquired as they fanned their sides. Nor did the interposing of so great a flying plenitude, between what was above and the flower, impede the vision or the splendor; for the divine light so penetrates through the universe, in measure of its worthiness, that naught can be an obstacle to it. This secure and joyful kingdom, thronged with ancient and with modern folk, had look and love all directed on one mark.

O threefold Light, which, in a single star sparkling on their sight, dost so satisfy them, look down upon our tempest here below!

If the Barbarians, coming from such region as is covered every day by Helice, wheeling with her son whom she delights in, when they beheld Rome and her mighty work, when Lateran[1] rose above all mortal things, were wonder-struck, I, who to the divine from the human, to the eternal from time had come, and from Florence to a people just and sane, with what amazement must I have been full! Truly, what with it and with the joy, I was content to hear naught and to stand mute. And as a pilgrim who is refreshed within the temple of his vow as he looks around, and already hopes to tell again how it was, so, taking my way upwards through the living light, I led my eyes along the ranks, now up, now down, and now circling about. I saw faces all given to love, adorned by the light of Another, and by their own smile, and movements graced with every dignity.

My look had now taken in the general form of Paradise as a whole, and on no part as yet had my sight paused; and I turned with rekindled will to ask my lady about things as to which my mind was in suspense. One thing I purposed, and another answered me: I thought to see Beatrice, and I saw an elder, clad like the folk in glory. His eyes and cheeks were suffused with benign gladness, his mien kindly such as befits a tender father. And, "Where is she?" I said at once; whereon he, "To terminate your desire Beatrice urged me from my place; and if you look up to the circle which is third from the highest tier, you will see her again, in the throne her merits have allotted to her."

Without answering I lifted up my eyes and saw her where she made for herself a crown as she reflected the eternal rays. From the region which thunders most high no mortal eye is so far distant, where it plunged most deep within the sea, as there from Beatrice was my sight. But to me it made no difference, for her image came down to me unblurred by aught between.

"O lady, in whom my hope is strong, and who for my salvation did endure to leave in Hell your footprints, of all those things which I have seen acknowledge the grace and the virtue to be from your power and your excellence. It is you who have drawn me from bondage into liberty by all those paths, by all those means by which you had the power so to do. Preserve in me your great munificence, so that my soul, which you have made whole, may be loosed from the body, pleasing unto you." So did I pray; and she, so distant as she seemed, smiled and looked on me, then turned again to the eternal fountain.

And the holy elder said, "In order that you may consummate your journey perfectly, whereto prayer and holy love dispatched me, fly with your eyes throughout this garden; for gazing on it will better prepare your sight to mount through the divine ray. And the Queen of Heaven, for whom I am all afire with love, will grant us every grace, since I am her faithful Bernard."[2]

As is he who comes perchance from Croatia to look on our Veronica,[3] and whose old hunger is not sated, but says in thought so long as it is shown, "My Lord Jesus Christ, true God, was then your semblance like to this?" such was I, gazing on the living charity of him who, in this world, in contemplation tasted of that peace.

"Son of grace, this joyous being," he began, "will not be known to you if you hold your eyes only down here at the base; but look upon the circles, even to the most remote, until you see upon her seat the Queen to whom this realm is subject and devoted."

I lifted up my eyes; and as at morning the eastern parts of the horizon outshine that where the sun declines, so, as if going with my eyes from valley to mountain-top I saw a part on the extreme verge surpass with its light all the rest of the rim. And as the point where we await the pole that Phaethon misguided is most aglow, and on this side and on that the light diminishes, so was that pacific oriflamme[4] quickened in the middle, on either side in equal measure tempering its flame. And at the midpoint, with outstretched wings, I saw more than a thousand Angels making festival, each one distinct in effulgence and in ministry. I saw there, smiling to their sports and to their songs, a beauty which was gladness in the eyes of all the other saints. And had I equal wealth in speech as in conception, yet would I not dare to attempt the least of her delightfulness.

Bernard, when he saw my eyes fixed and intent on the object of his own burning glow, turned his own with such affection to her, that he made mine more ardent in their gazing.

CANTO XXXII

With his love fixed on his Delight, that contemplator freely assumed the office of a teacher, and began these holy words, "The wound which Mary closed and anointed, that one who is so beautiful at her feet is she who opened it and pierced it. Below her, in the order which the third seats make, sits Rachel with Beatrice, as you see. Sarah, Rebecca, Judith, and she who was great-grandmother of the singer who, through sorrow for his sin, cried 'Miserere mei,'[1] you may see, thus from rank to rank in gradation downward, as with the name of each I go downward through the rose from petal to petal. And from the seventh row downwards, even as down to it, Hebrew women follow in succession, dividing all the tresses of the flower; because, according to the look which their faith turned to Christ, these are the wall by which the sacred stairway is divided. On this side, wherein the flower is mature in all its petals, are seated those who believed in Christ yet to come. On the other side, where the half-circles are broken by vacant places, sit those who turned their faces toward Christ already come. And as on this side the glorious seat of the Lady of Heaven, and the other seats below it, make so great a partition, thus, opposite, does the seat of the great John[2] who, ever holy, endured the desert and martyrdom, and then Hell for two years;[3] and beneath him Francis and Benedict and Augustine[4] and others were allotted thus to divide, as far down as here, from circle to circle. Now behold the depth of the divine foresight, for one and the other aspect of the faith shall fill this garden equally. And know that, downward from the row which cleaves midway the two dividing lines, they are seated for no merit of their own, but for that of others, under certain conditions; for all these are spirits absolved before they had true power of choice. Well can you perceive it by their faces and by their childish voices, if you look well upon them and if you listen to them.

"Now you are perplexed, and in perplexity are silent; but I will loose the hard knot wherein your subtle thoughts are binding you. Within the amplitude of this realm a casual point can have no place, any more than can sorrow, or thirst, or hunger; for whatever you see is established by eternal law, so that the correspondence is exact between the ring and finger. And therefore this company, hastened to true life, is not sine causa more or less excellent here among themselves. The King, through whom this realm reposes in such great love and in such great delight that no will dares for more, creating all the minds in His glad sight, at His own pleasure endows with grace diversely—and here let the fact suffice. And this is clearly and expressly noted for you in Holy Scripture in those twins[5] whose anger was stirred within their mother's womb. Therefore, according to the color of the locks, of such grace needs must the lofty light crown them according to their worth. Wherefore, without merit of their own works, they are placed in different ranks, differing only in the primal keenness of vision. In the early ages, their parents' faith alone, with their own innocence, sufficed for their salvation; After those first ages were complete, it was needful for males, through circumcision, to acquire power for their innocent wings; but after the time of grace had come, without perfect baptism in Christ such innocence was held there below.

"Look now upon the face which most resembles Christ, for only its brightness can prepare you to see Christ."

I saw such gladness rain down upon her, borne in the holy minds created to fly through that height, that all I had seen before had not held me in suspense of such great marveling, nor showed me such likeness to God. And that Love which first descended there,[6] singing "*Ave Maria, gratia plena*," now spread his wings before her. On all sides the blessed Court responded to the divine song, so that every face became the brighter therefor.

"O holy father, who for my sake endure to be here below, leaving the sweet place in which by eternal lot you have your seat, who is that angel who with such joy looks into the eyes of our Queen, so enamored that he seems afire?" Thus did I again recur to the teaching of him who drew beauty from Mary, as the morning star from the sun.

And he to me, "Confidence and grace, as much as there can be in angel and in soul, are all in him, and we would have it so, for it is he who bore the palm down to Mary, when the Son of God willed to load Himself with the burden of our flesh.

"But come now with your eyes, as I proceed in speaking, and note the great patricians of this most just and pious empire. Those two who sit there above, most happy for being nearest to the Empress, are, as it were, two roots of this rose: he who is beside her upon the left is that Father because of whose audacious tasting the human race tastes such bitterness. On the right you see that ancient Father of Holy Church to whom Christ entrusted the keys of this beauteous flower. And he who saw,[7] before he died, all the grievous times of the fair Bride who was won with the spear and the nails sits at his[8] side; and beside the other rests that leader,[9] under whom the thankless, fickle, and stubborn people lived on manna. Opposite Peter you see Anna[10] sitting, so content to gaze upon her daughter that she moves not her eyes as she sings Hosannah. And opposite the greatest father of a family sits Lucy,[11] who moved your lady when you were bending your bows downward to your ruin.

"But because the time flies that brings sleep upon you, we will stop here, like a good tailor that cuts the garment according to his cloth, and we will turn your eyes to the Primal Love, so that, gazing toward Him, you may penetrate, as far as that can be, into His effulgence. But lest, perchance, you fall back, moving your wings and thinking to advance, grace must be obtained by prayer, grace from her who has power to aid you; and do you follow me with your affection so that your heart depart not from my words."

And he began this holy prayer:

CANTO XXXIII

"Virgin Mother, daughter of thy Son, humble and exalted more than any creature, fixed goal of the eternal counsel, thou art she who didst so ennoble human nature that its Maker did not disdain to become its creature. In thy womb was rekindled the Love under whose warmth this flower in the eternal peace has thus unfolded. Here thou art for us the noonday torch of charity, and below among mortals thou art the living fount of hope. Lady, thou art so great and so availest, that whoso would have grace and has not recourse to thee, his desire seeks to fly without wings. Thy lovingkindness not only succors him who asks, but oftentimes freely foreruns the asking. In thee is mercy, in thee pity, in thee munificence, in thee is found whatever of goodness is in any creature. Now this man, who from the lowest pit of the universe even to here has seen one by one the spiritual lives, implores thee of thy grace for power such that he may be able with his eyes to rise still higher toward the last salvation. And I, who never for my own vision burned more than I do for his, proffer to thee all my prayers, and pray that they be not scant, that with thy prayers thou wouldst dispel for him every cloud of his mortality, so that the Supreme Pleasure may be disclosed to him. Further I pray thee, Queen, who canst do whatsoever thou wilt, that thou preserve sound for him his affections, after so great a vision. Let thy protection vanquish human impulses. Behold Beatrice, with how many saints, for my prayers clasping their hands to thee."

The eyes beloved and reverenced by God, fixed upon him who prayed, showed us how greatly devout prayers do please her; then they were turned to the Eternal Light, wherein we may not believe that any creature's eye finds its way so clear.

And I, who was drawing near to the end of all desires, raised to its utmost, even as I ought, the ardor of my longing. Bernard was signing to me with a smile to look upward, but I was already of myself such as he wished; for my sight, becoming pure, was entering more and more through the beam of the lofty Light which in Itself is true.

Thenceforward my vision was greater than speech can show, which fails at such a sight, and at such excess memory fails. As is he who dreaming sees, and after the dream the passion remains imprinted and the rest returns not to the mind; such am I, for my vision almost wholly fades away, yet does the sweetness that was born of it still drop within my heart. Thus is the snow unsealed by the sun; thus in the wind, on the light leaves, the Sibyl's oracle was lost.

O Light Supreme that art so far uplifted above mortal conceiving, relend to my mind a little of what Thou didst appear, and give my tongue such power that it may leave only a single spark of Thy glory for the folk to come; for, by returning somewhat to my memory and by sounding a little in these lines, more of Thy victory shall be conceived.

I believe that, because of the keenness of the living ray which I endured, I should have been lost if my eyes had been turned from it. I remember that on this account I was the bolder to sustain it, until I united my gaze with the Infinite Goodness.

O abounding grace whereby I presumed to fix my look through the Eternal Light so far that all my sight was spent therein.

In its depth I saw ingathered, bound by love in one single volume, that which is dispersed in leaves throughout the universe: substances and accidents and their relations, as though fused together in such a way that what I tell is but a simple light. The universal form of this knot I believe that I saw, because, in telling this, I feel my joy increase.

A single moment makes from me greater oblivion than five and twenty centuries have wrought upon the enterprise that made Nep-

tune wonder at the shadow of the Argo.[1] Thus my mind, all rapt, was gazing, fixed, motionless and intent, ever enkindled by its gazing. In that Light one becomes such that it is impossible he should ever consent to turn himself from it for other sight; for the good, which is the object of the will, is all gathered in it, and outside of it that is defective which is perfect there.

Now will my speech fall more short, even in respect to that which I remember, than that of an infant who still bathes his tongue at the breast. Not because more than one simple semblance was in the Living Light wherein I was gazing, which ever is such as it was before; but through my sight, which was growing strong in me as I looked, one sole appearance, even as I changed, was altering itself to me.

Within the profound and shining subsistence of the lofty Light appeared to me three circles of three colors and one magnitude; and one seemed reflected by the other, as rainbow by rainbow, and the third[2] seemed fire breathed forth equally from the one and the other.

O how scant is speech, and how feeble to my conception! and this, to what I saw, is such that it is not enough to call it little.

O Light Eternal, who alone abidest in Thyself, alone knowest Thyself, and, known to Thyself and knowing, lovest and smilest on Thyself!

That circling which, thus begotten, appeared in Thee as reflected light, when my eyes had dwelt on it for a time, seemed to me depicted with our image within itself and in its own color, wherefore my sight was entirely set upon it.

As is the geometer who wholly applies himself to measure the circle, and finds not, in pondering, the principle of which he is in need, such was I at that new sight. I wished to see how the image conformed to the circle and how it has its place therein; but my own wings were not sufficient for that, save that my mind was smitten by a flash wherein its wish came to it. Here power failed the lofty phantasy;[3] but already my desire and my will were revolved, like a wheel that is evenly moved, by the Love which moves the sun and the other stars.

Notes

CANTO I

1. The action of the poem begins on the night before Good Friday of the year 1300; cf. *Inf.* XXI. Dante was thirty-five years old. The dark wood is the forest of the world of sense.

2. In the astronomy of Dante's time, the sun was one of the planets that circle the earth.

3. The wolf is the type of avarice. Cf. Jeremiah, 5. 6. These three beasts correspond with the triple division of sins into those of incontinence, of violence, and of fraud (see *Inf.* XI).

4. In the time of Julius Caesar.

5. Of the four slain warriors named by Dante here, two fought on the side of the Trojan Aeneas and two fought against him.

6. The purifying fire of Purgatory.

CANTO II

1. The Empyrean heaven, the tenth and outermost sphere, God's abode and "kingdom," as it is called in *Inf.* I.

2. For Dante, the Roman Empire is directly ordained by God as part of His providential plan for man's redemption and was established in order to prepare the way for the Advent of the Saviour and the foundation of His Church on earth.

3. We may note here the first of the many appeals in the *Inferno* to enduring fame in the world of the living—a survival after death that is desired by many of the damned of Hell, as if it were their only "immortality."

4. Virgil had referred to Beatrice in the preceding canto as a soul worthier than he to take over as guide and lead the wayfarer to Paradise, but he did not explicitly name her.

5. As is made clear later (but may well be taken for granted), the blessed Virgin Mary is "our advocate" in Heaven.

6. This doubtless is St. Lucy of Syracuse, the third-century virgin martyr regarded as patron saint of those who suffer from eye ailments. Early commentators consider her as the symbol of illuminating grace.

7. Rachel was adopted by the Church as the type of the contemplative life, in which the soul devotes itself to the consideration of the things of God and so has a foretaste of the felicity of heaven. Beatrice, the type of instruction in the divine mysteries, is therefore rightly at Rachel's side.

CANTO III

1. Pope Celestine, according to most of the early commentators. Celestine V was elected pope at the age of nearly eighty, in July 1294, and abdicated some five months later.

2. Charon, son of Erebus, is the ferryman who transports the shades of the dead across the rivers of the lower world.

3. It was thought that earthquakes were caused by windy vapors imprisoned within the earth.

CANTO IV

1. Limbo (Lat. *limbus*, edge, hem, border).

2. Virgil died in 19 B.C. and therefore was newly come to Limbo when Christ harrowed Hell.

3. This fire is said to drive back the darkness and form a (celestial) hemisphere of light, symbol of the natural light of reason. Natural reason was accessible to the worthy pagans, and it was through this reason or intellect that they won honor in their endeavors. In the darkness before the Advent of Christ, these pagans had no other light than this.

4. Dante did not know Greek and had no direct knowledge of Homer, since no complete or direct translation of Homer's works existed in the Middle Ages.

5. Horace (Quintus Horatius Flaccus), the Roman poet, was born at Venusia (mod. Venosa) in 65 B.C. and died in 8 B.C.

6. Ovid (Publius Ovidius Naso) was born in 43 B.C. and died in exile in A.D. 17 or 18. His chief work, the *Metamorphoses*, was Dante's main authority for mythology.

7. Lucan (Marcus Annaeus Lucanus), born in Córdoba, Spain, in A.D. 39, was educated in Rome. Of his works there is extant only the epic called *De bello civili*, or *Pharsalia*, whose subject is the civil war between Caesar and Pompey.

8. The castle is the symbol of the abode of Philosophy, or human wisdom unenlightened by revelation; its seven high walls may perhaps signify the four moral and three intellectual virtues—prudence, temperance, fortitude, and justice; understanding, knowledge, and wisdom, all which could be attained by the virtuous heathen. Cf. Aquinas, *Summa Theologica*, Part I–II, Q65, A2.

9. The seven gates may typify the seven liberal arts of the *trivium* and the *quadrivium*, by which names the courses of instruction in them were known in the schools of the Middle Ages. The *trivium* included grammar, logic, and rhetoric; the *quadrivium*, music, arithmetic, geometry, and astronomy.

10. Electra—daughter of Atlas and mother of Dardanus, the founder of Troy.

11. This is Aristotle, whose influence in Dante's time was so pervasive that he was called simply "the Philosopher."

12. Democritus, a contemporary of Socrates, was born in Thrace, *ca.* 460 B.C., and died *ca.* 370. He adopted and extended the atomistic theory.

13. According to the early commentators, this is Diogenes the Cynic, born *ca.* 412 B.C. in Asia Minor, and died 323. Anaxagoras, philosopher of the Ionian school, was born *ca.* 500 B.C. and died *ca.* 428. Thales of Miletus, one of the Seven Wise Men, was born *ca.* 640 B.C. and died *ca.* 546.

14. Empedocles, philosopher and statesman of Acragas (Agrigentum), Sicily. Knowledge of his dates is uncertain except that he was active at Acragas after 472 B.C. and died later than 444. Heraclitus, philosopher of Ephesus who flourished *ca.* 500 B.C., held that fire was the primary form of all matter.

15. Pedanius Dioscorides, of Anazarba, in Cilicia, was a Greek physician of the first or second century A.D.

134

16. Orpheus was the mythical Greek poet who, according to the legend, played so divinely on the lyre given him by Apollo that he charmed not only the wild beasts, but even the trees and rocks on Olympus so that they moved from their places and followed him.

17. Marcus Tullius Cicero, the great Roman orator, philosopher, and statesman (106–43 B.C.), is often alluded to and quoted by Dante, who characteristically refers to him as "Tully." Linus, a mythical Greek poet. Lucius Annaeus Seneca, Roman philosopher and tragedian, was born at Córdoba, ca. 4 B.C. He was appointed tutor to the youthful Domitius Nero, and was for a time practically the administrator of the Empire. He committed suicide by command of Nero, who charged him with being involved in the conspiracy of Piso, A.D. 65.

18. Euclid, the Greek mathematician, lived in Alexandria ca. 300 B.C. The most famous of his extant works is the *Elements of Geometry*. Ptolemy (Claudius Ptolemaeus), the Alexandrian mathematician, astronomer, and geographer, was born near the end of the first century A.D. He is known to have observed at Alexandria between the years 127 and 151. His two most famous works are the *Geography*, in eight books, and his mathematical treatise, in thirteen books, commonly known as the *Almagest* (a hybrid name derived from the Arabic article *al* and the Greek superlative μεγίστη). The *Almagest* lays out a system of astronomy and geography according to the theory that the sun, stars, and planets revolve around the earth. Dante's concept of the cosmos derives from this Ptolemaic system.

19. Hippocrates, the most famous physician of antiquity, known as the father of medicine and thought to be a descendant of Asclepius.

20. Avicenna (abu-'Ali al-Ḥusayn ibn-Sīna)—also known as ibn-Sina—was an Arab philosopher and physician of Isfahan in Persia.

21. Averroës, also known as ibn-Rushd, was a Spanish-Arabian scholar of the twelfth century whose commentaries on Aristotle had tremendous influence on the history of Western philosophy.

CANTO V

1. Since Hell is funnel-shaped, each successive circle in the descent is smaller in circumference than the one above it.

2. Minos in legend and myth was a king of ancient Crete, son of Zeus and Europa, and brother of Rhadamanthus. In assigning to Minos the office of judge in Hell, Dante imitates Virgil (*Aen.* VI, 432–33).

3. Semiramis is the Greek name of a queen of ancient Assyria. She was famous for her beauty and licentiousness as well as for her prowess in war.

4. Egypt, in Dante's time, was under the Sultan's rule.

5. Dido, also called Elissa, was a daughter of Belus, king of Tyre, and the sister of Pygmalion. She married Sichaeus, who later was murdered by Pygmalion for his wealth.

6. Cleopatra, queen of Egypt, mistress of Julius Caesar and of Mark Antony.

7. Helen, wife of Menelaus, the Spartan king. Her abduction by Paris led to the long Trojan War.

8. Achilles, Greek hero of the Trojan War.

9. Paris, son of Priam and Hecuba, known in Greek mythology as most handsome of all mortal men, was appointed umpire to decide who was the fairest of the three goddesses, Juno, Minerva, or Venus. He chose Venus, who had promised to reward him with Helen, most beautiful woman in the world. His abduction of Helen led to the Trojan War.

10. Tristan, lover of Isolde. There are several medieval

versions of the Tristan story in both poetic and prose forms dating from the late twelfth and early thirteenth centuries.

11. This suggests that these two spirits are more violently tossed by the wind than the others are. According to the principle of just punishment, the heightened violence of the wind signifies that the love, which led them in life and leads them now, was, and is, most passionate.

12. In Hell the name of God is avoided, or is uttered only in blasphemy.

13. Paolo Malatesta, said to have been handsome and attractively mannered, was married in 1269 to Orabile Beatrice, by whom he later had two sons.

14. She is named only now, and her lover is not named at all—true indications that the poet is presenting a *cause célèbre*.

15. During Gallehault's residence at King Arthur's court a warm friendship developed between him and Lancelot, who confided his love for Queen Guinevere. Gallehault arranged for the two to meet. In the course of this interview, Gallehault urged the queen to kiss Lancelot—and so began the guilty love between those two.

CANTO VI

1. Again Dante has drawn one of the guardians of Hell's circles from classical sources but has transformed him to suit the requirements of the creature's infernal office.

2. Ciacco, an abbreviation of Jacopo, seems, in popular speech, to have been the term for *hog*.

3. This prophecy relates to the dissensions of the Whites and the Blacks by which Florence was rent. The "sylvan party" was that of the Whites, who were mainly Ghibellines. By the "one who just now is tacking" Dante probably refers to Pope Boniface VIII. In the overthrow of the Whites Dante's own fortunes were involved.

4. This "science" is Aristotelian philosophy as developed in the scholastic teachings.

CANTO VII

1. If we may assume that Virgil understands Plutus' angry words, we must conclude that these words have some meaning and are not simply a senseless expression of rage. Yet, the exact meaning of the strange words remains obscure.

2. Dante may have meant his "Pluto" to be Pluto, the god of the netherworld (who, in Greek mythology, was also called Hades, son of Cronus and Rhea and brother of Zeus and Poseidon), or Plutus, the god of wealth (son of Iasion and Demeter).

3. Charybdis, the famous whirlpool in the Strait of Messina, was regarded by navigators as peculiarly dangerous because in their endeavor to avoid it they risked being wrecked upon Scylla, a rock on the Italian coast.

4. In classical mythology, Styx is one of the five rivers that surround Hades.

CANTO VIII

1. The "oarsman" of Styx, whom Virgil soon addresses by name, is Phlegyas. According to the ancient myths, Phlegyas was the son of Mars and Chryse. He was the father of Ixion and of Coronis, who was violated by Apollo and became the mother of Aesculapius. Phlegyas in fury set fire to the temple of Apollo at Delphi, and for this sacrilege was slain by the god and condemned to eternal punishment in Tartarus, the region in the lower world reserved for those who sin against the gods.

2. Dis is one of the names of Satan in the *Commedia*, but here it is assigned to the city which looms in the distance with its fiery ramparts.

3. Christ broke down the first and outer portal of Hell when He came to Limbo (see *Inf.* IV), for Satan and his band tried to oppose Him at the outer entrance. That "less hidden gate" was never bolted again and is always open.

4. The inscription over the portal of Hell (*Inf.* III), "dead" because it is over the door to the world of the dead and to the "second death" (*Inf.* I).

CANTO IX

1. Erichtho, a Thessalian sorceress, who, according to Lucan, was employed by Pompey's son Sextus to conjure up the spirit of one of his dead soldiers on the eve of the battle of Pharsalia, so that he could learn what was to be the outcome of the campaign.

2. Cerastes, horned snakes.

3. This is Hecate or Persephone, also known as Proserpina, the wife of Pluto, king of the netherworld.

4. Youngest of the three sisters known as the Gorgons, Medusa alone was mortal and was at first a beautiful girl. According to Ovid, after she was ravished by Neptune in one of Minerva's temples, her hair was changed into serpents by the goddess. This gave Medusa's head so fearful an appearance that everyone who looked upon it was changed to stone.

5. Theseus, legendary hero of Athens, accompanied by his friend Pirithoüs descended to the underworld and tried unsuccessfully to abduct Proserpina, Pluto's queen. According to the version of the story accepted by Dante, Pirithoüs and Theseus were kept prisoners in Hell until Theseus alone was released through the efforts of Hercules.

6. The last and most difficult of the twelve labors of Hercules was to bring Cerberus into the upper world, which he accomplished by putting a chain on the monster and hauling him forth.

7. The reference is to the ancient Roman cemetery at Arles in Provence, near the place where the Rhone forms its delta ("stagna") before entering the Mediterranean Sea. Many sarcophagi are still to be seen there.

8. A fortified seaport near the southern tip of the Istrian peninsula, Pola (now Pulj, Yugoslavia) is celebrated for its Roman remains.

CANTO X

1. The Valley of Jehoshaphat, a common name for the Kidron Valley, source of the stream that separates Jerusalem from the Mount of Olives. According to a tradition common both to Jews and Moslems, it is in this valley that the Last Judgment is to take place.

2. Epicurus, the famous philosopher, born *ca.* 342 B.C., died 270. The philosophical school named after him taught that pleasure, i.e., the absence of pain, is the highest good.

3. This is the great Ghibelline leader of Florence— Manente, son of Jacopo degli Uberti. Known as Farinata, he was inquired about by the wayfarer previously (see *Inf.* VI) among the worthy Florentines.

4. The Guelphs were expelled from Florence for the first time in 1248 with the aid of the Emperor Frederick II, and again in 1260 following the battle of Montaperti.

5. Guido Cavalcanti, famous Florentine poet, was born probably *ca.* 1255, but not later than 1259. His friendship with Dante dates from 1283; the *Vita nuova* (see III) is dedicated to him as Dante's "first friend."

6. Hecate, also called Proserpina, goddess of the moon and queen of Hades. See *Inf.* IX.

7. Since both Farinata and Ciacco (see *Inf.* VI) have predicted events to come, the wayfarer has good reason to believe that souls in Hell can see the future.

8. The Emperor Frederick II was head of the Holy Roman Empire from 1215 until his death in 1250. In placing Frederick among the Epicurean heretics, Dante followed the contemporary estimate.

9. This is Cardinal Ottaviano degli Ubaldini.

CANTO XI

1. A certain tradition seems to have confused Anastasius II, pope from 496 to 498, and his namesake and contemporary Anastasius I, emperor from 491 to 518. Emperor Anastasius is said to have been led by Photinus, a deacon of Thessalonica, into the heresy of Acacius, patriarch of Constantinople (d. 488). Acacius denied the divine origin of Christ.

2. The seventh circle, the next ahead of the two wayfarers at this point.

3. Cahors, a town in southern France, on the river Lot. It was famous in the Middle Ages as a great center of usurers.

4. The sign of the Fishes precedes that of the Ram, and, as the Sun was in the latter sign, the time indicated is about 4, or from 4 to 5 A.M. Caurus, the northwest wind, here stands for that quarter of the heavens.

CANTO XII

1. Dante has so far failed to identify what "every eye would shun." He continues to withhold the Minotaur's name, designating it here only by the infamy it witnesses. Dante imagined the Minotaur as having a bull's body and a human head, rather than a human body and a bull's head in accordance with another tradition.

2. The legendary wooden cow by means of which the Minotaur was conceived. According to the legend, Pasiphaë, wife of King Minos of Crete, was inspired with an unnatural passion for a snow-white bull. The artisan Daedalus built her a wooden cow covered with cowhide and placed it over her. The bull mounted the "counterfeit cow," and from this intercourse Pasiphaë later gave birth to the Minotaur.

3. Theseus (see *Inf.* IX), to whom Dante, like other writers, anachronistically gives a medieval title.

4. At last the monster is named. The Minotaur was kept in a labyrinth constructed by Daedalus. Every year it devoured a tribute of seven youths and seven maidens, whom Minos exacted from the Athenians in satisfaction for their murder of his son, Androgeos. The monster eventually was slain by Theseus with the assistance of Ariadne—Minos' daughter by Pasiphaë—who supplied him with a sword and a clew to the labyrinth.

5. Here Satan himself, not Satan's city, which constitutes the entire area of lower Hell.

6. The reference is to Empedocles' theory of the alternate supremacy of hate and love as the cause of periodic destruction and construction in the scheme of the universe.

7. Saturn, enamored of Philyra and fearing the jealousy of his wife, Rhea, changed himself into a horse and in this shape begat Chiron, who took the form of a centaur. Chiron educated Achilles, Aesculapius, Hercules, and many other famous Greeks, and Virgil knows at once that, because he is the wisest, he must be the leader of the band.

8. Deianira was the wife of Hercules, whose death she unwittingly caused. Hercules killed the centaur Nessus with a poisoned arrow for having attempted to violate her; but before Nessus died, he gave Deianira a robe dipped in his blood, telling her it would act as a charm to preserve her husband's love. Later, jealous of Hercules' love for Iole, Deianira gave him the robe; and when he put it on,

the poison in Nessus' blood maddened him. To put an end to his agony, he burned himself on a funeral pyre, and Deianira in remorse hanged herself.

9. While Pholus, one of the centaurs, was entertaining Hercules during the latter's expedition against them, he met his death when he accidentally dropped one of his guest's poisoned arrows on his own foot.

10. This might be either Alexander the Great of Macedonia (356–323 B.C.) or Alexander of Pherae, a tyrant of Thessaly (ruled ca. 368–359 B.C.). Alexander of Pherae was famed for his cruelty, one of his amusements being to dress up men in the skins of wild beasts and to set dogs to worry them.

11. There is little doubt that Dante intends Dionysius the Elder, tyrant of Syracuse, who ruled 405–367 B.C.

12. Ezzelino III da Romano (1194–1259), son-in-law of the Emperor Frederick II and chief of the Ghibellines in Upper Italy. During his long lordship over the March of Treviso, the city of Padua, and part of Lombardy, he committed one atrocity after another.

13. Obizzo II d'Este (1247–93). As lord of Ferrara and later of Modena and Reggio, he was an ardent Guelph and a supporter of Charles of Anjou. He is said to have wielded his power with pitiless cruelty.

14. The soul of Guy de Montfort (ca. 1243–98), son of Simon de Montfort, earl of Leicester (who was killed at the battle of Evesham, August 4, 1265). In revenge for his father's death and for the indignities offered his corpse, Guy murdered his first cousin, Prince Henry of Cornwall, in the church of San Silvestro at Viterbo in March 1271, during the assembly of the cardinals to elect a successor to Pope Clement IV.

15. The heart of Prince Henry. Henry's body was brought to England and interred in the Cistercian abbey at Hales in Gloucestershire, which had been built by his father.

16. There has been some controversy over the identity of this murderer; Dante may refer either to Pyrrhus, son of Achilles, or to Pyrrhus, king of Epirus. The first Pyrrhus, also grandson of Lycomedes, king of Skyros, was brought by Ulysses to take part in the Trojan War. He is reported to have slain the aged Priam when the city fell, killed Priam's son, Polites, and sacrificed his daughter Polyxena to the shade of Achilles (*Inf.* XXX). His violence and cruelty are recorded by Virgil. Pyrrhus, king of Epirus (ca. 318–272 B.C.), whom Dante mentions several times elsewhere, made war against the Romans but was eventually defeated in 275 B.C.

17. Probably Sextus Pompeius Magnus, younger son of Pompey the Great and a notorious pirate.

18. Two noted highway robbers.

CANTO XIII

1. The Cecina River flows into the Mediterranean Sea about twenty miles south of Leghorn. The town of Corneto (see Rinier da Corneto, *Inf.* XII) is situated on the Marta River, about ten miles north of Civitavecchia.

2. The Harpies were loathsome monsters in the shape of birds, with clawed hands and the faces of women.

3. The spirit who speaks is Pier delle Vigne, the private secretary and confidential minister of Frederick II. (see *Inf.* X).

4. The Emperor Frederick II.

5. Envy.

6. The imperial court.

7. Lano was slain in flight at the defeat of the Sienese by the Aretines, near the Pieve del Toppo. He and Jacomo were notorious spendthrifts.

8. This is Jacopo da Santo Andrea of Padua, reported to have inherited a considerable fortune which he squandered in the most senseless acts of prodigality.

9. Legend had it that Attila had destroyed Florence. This tradition doubtless arose from a confusion of Attila with Totila, king of the Ostrogoths (541–52), by whose forces Florence was besieged in 542.

10. Under these words lies a satirical reference to the devotion of the Florentines to money-making. Dante means, says Benvenuto da Imola, "that after Florence gave up Mars, that is, fortitude and valor in arms, and began to worship the Baptist alone, that is, the florin, on which is the figure of the Baptist, they met with misfortune in their wars."

CANTO XIV

1. Cato the Younger of Utica (95–46 B.C.), whose march through the Libyan desert shortly before his death is recounted in Lucan's *Pharsalia* (IX).

2. Capaneus, depicted as a towering giant by Statius, was one of the seven legendary kings who besieged Thebes. As he was scaling the walls of the city, Capaneus defied Jupiter, and the god struck him dead with a thunderbolt.

3. Another name for Mount Etna, in Sicily. In the interior of Mount Etna and on one of the Lipari Islands, according to myth, Vulcan had his workshops and with the help of the Cyclopes forged Jupiter's thunderbolts.

4. In the battle of Phlegra Jupiter, with the help of Hercules, defeated the giants who attempted to storm Olympus.

5. Thebes, city of Boeotia. As a result of the dispute between Eteocles and Polynices, sons of Oedipus, over the sovereignty of Thebes, an expedition against the city on behalf of Polynices, known as the war of the Seven against Thebes, was undertaken by Adrastus, king of Argos, accompanied by his son-in-law Capaneus, Amphiaraus, Hippomedon, Parthenopaeus, Polynices, and Tydeus.

6. A famous hot sulphurous spring near Viterbo, noted since Roman times.

7. To prevent Saturn from hearing the cries of the infant Jupiter, whom, had he known him to be alive, he would have sought to devour, in order to avert the fulfillment of the prophecy that he would be dethroned by one of his children.

8. This image is taken directly from the dream of Nebuchadnezzar (Daniel, 2. 31–33). It is the type of the historic life of man, with its back to the past, its face toward Rome—the center of the actual world. Its upper parts of metal represent the Golden, Silver, Bronze, and Iron ages, according to the fancy of the poets. The two legs are generally interpreted as the symbols of the Empire and the Church; the right leg, on which the image rests the most, being the type of the Church. Its foot of baked earth; possibly may refer to the element of weakness in the papacy from the earthly character of the Popes. The tears of the sinful and suffering generations of man form the rivers of Hell.

9. The old town of Damietta in Egypt, situated at the mouth of the easternmost of the two principal branches formed by the Nile at its delta. During the Middle Ages Damietta seems to have been identified with the ancient Memphis.

10. Acheron, Styx, Phlegethon, and Cocytus all belong to the classical conception of the underworld.

11. The wayfarer will find Lethe at the top of Purgatory.

CANTO XV

1. Wissant, a Flemish town between Calais and Cape

Gris-Nez, in medieval times the usual embarkation point for England.

2. Bruges, a town about twenty-five miles northwest of Ghent, capital of the modern province of West Flanders.

3. A river of northern Italy that rises in the Tirolese Alps above Trent and flows southeast and then south past Bassano.

4. Carinthia forms the mountainous southwestern province of modern Austria and consists largely of the upper valley of the Drava, which runs east to the Danube.

5. Brunetto Latini, philosopher and public servant, was born in Florence *ca.* 1220 and died there *ca.* 1294.

6. A city of Tuscany, situated on a hill about four miles northeast of Florence, and commanding a view of that city and of the valley of the Arno.

7. Priscian, the celebrated Latin grammarian (fl. *ca.* A.D. 500), was born at Caesarea in Mauretania and taught grammar at Constantinople.

8. Francesco d'Accorso (1225–93) was the son of a famous Florentine jurist and law professor, Accorso da Bagnolo. Born at Bologna, where his father taught at the university, Francesco also became a celebrated lawyer and professor of civil law.

9. The person indicated is Andrea de' Mozzi, member of the noble Florentine family of that name (they were Guelphs and Bianchi) and bishop of Florence 1287–95.

10. A river of northern Italy, which rises in the Alps above Vicenza, through which it passes, and flows in a southeasterly direction as far as Padua, where it divides into three streams.

11. His great encyclopedia, *Li livres dou Tresor.*

12. This foot race, known as the *palio,* was run annually on the first Sunday in Lent on a course outside Verona.

CANTO XVI

1. Many commentators, both early and late, understand the "champions" here to be those who took part in the ancient Greek and Roman pugilistic games.

2. Gualdrada was the daughter of Bellincione Berti de' Ravignani of Florence. Through her marriage with Guido Guerra IV, the Conti Guidi traced their descent from the great Ravignani family.

3. A member of the illustrious Conti Guidi of the Dovadola line. He was a leader of the Guelphs, although his family before him appears to have belonged to the Imperial party.

4. This Florentine Guelph of the powerful Adimari family was at one time (1256) *podestà* of Arezzo.

5. According to the early commentators, Jacopo Rusticucci was socially inferior to his two companions. He was a close neighbor, in the Porta San Piero quarter of Florence, of Tegghiaio Aldobrandi.

6. Guglielmo Borsiere, according to Benvenuto, a Florentine pursemaker who grew tired of his trade and left it to become a man of society, spending his time traveling and visiting the houses of noblemen.

7. The river to which Dante refers is the Montone, which rises as a torrent in the eastern Apennines, about six miles from the Benedictine monastery of San Benedetto dell'Alpe, near which it is joined by the torrents of the Acquacheta and Riodestro.

8. The Acquacheta, the upper part of the river in question, runs across a high plateau that is almost level, so that the water is relatively quiet (*cheta, quieta*) or slow in its course.

9. The cord serves, therefore, as a belt or girdle. A girdle was a symbol of strength, enabling the wearer to accomplish something, such as capturing a leopard.

10. Here, for the first time, Dante indicates the title of his poem.

CANTO XVII

1. Whereas Dante's monster has three natures—those of man, beast, and serpent—the monster Geryon of classical literature, after whom he is named, had three bodies and three heads. Thus Virgil refers to *tergeminus Geryon.* For Geryon's treacherous nature Dante apparently drew on the medieval tradition according to which he lured strangers into his power and then slew them.

2. In Greek mythology Arachne, who excelled in weaving, challenged Minerva to a competition. Unable to find fault with Arachne's work, Minerva tore it to pieces. In despair Arachne hanged herself, but the goddess loosened the rope and changed her into a spider.

3. The arms of the Gianfigliazzi of Florence were "on a field or a lion azure."

4. The arms of the Florentine Ubbriachi (or Obriachi) were "on a field gules a goose argent." The arms of the Scrovegni family of Padua were "on a field argent a sow azure."

5. The early commentators state that this sinner still among the living was Vitaliano del Dente, who appears to have been an important person in Padua, where he was *podestà* in 1307. He is mentioned as a moneylender in several documents of the late thirteenth century.

6. This is the Florentine usurer Giovanni (or Gianni) Buiamonte of the Becchi family.

7. Several of the early commentators say that the arms of the Becchi family were "on a field or three goats sable."

8. In classical mythology Phaëthon was the son of Helios, god of the Sun, and Clymene. He persuaded Helios to let him drive the chariot of the Sun for one day; but he was too weak to hold the horses and they rushed out of their usual course, approaching so near to Earth that they almost set her on fire. Jupiter, then, in answer to the prayer of Earth, killed Phaëthon with a thunderbolt and hurled him down into the Po.

9. Icarus was the son of Daedalus, the famous artisan. Father and son were attempting to fly from Crete on wings made by Daedalus, when Icarus fell into the sea and was drowned.

CANTO XVIII

1. In the Eighth Circle the sinners are punished who belong to the first of the two classes of the fraudulent (see *Inf.* XI), that is, those who practised deceit upon persons who had no ground for special confidence in them. Its bed, which slopes gradually from the wall that environs it to the central pit of Hell, is occupied by ten deep concentric valleys, called *bolge. Bolgia* signifies, literally, a budget, or pouch; and *Malebolge,* evil pouches.

2. This first Jubilee of the Roman church was proclaimed by Boniface VIII in his bull *Antiquorum habet fidem,* dated February 22, 1300, but with retroactive force to the previous Christmas (1299).

3. The Ponte Sant'Angelo, a bridge over the Tiber at Rome, was built by the Emperor Hadrian to connect his tomb (the present Castel Sant'Angelo) with the city. The Castel Sant'Angelo, on the right bank of the Tiber at Rome, originally the Moles Hadriani, was erected by Hadrian as a mausoleum for himself and his successors.

4. Venedico de' Caccianemici dell'Orso, of Bologna, was the son of Alberto de' Caccianemici, head of the Geremei, or Guelph party of Bologna.

5. Sister of Venedico de' Caccianemici, who is said to have accepted a bribe to betray her to the marquis of Este.

The marquis reportedly took his pleasure and abandoned the fair lady, who nevertheless later (in or before 1270) married Niccolò da Fontana of Ferrara.

6. Jason was the leader of the Argonauts on their celebrated expedition to the land of Colchis in quest of the golden fleece. In the course of this adventure the Argonauts visited Lemnos, where Jason seduced and abandoned Hypsipyle. At length they arrived in the land of the Colchians, where Medea, the daughter of Aeëtes, king of Colchis, having fallen in love with Jason, helped him secure the golden fleece. When Jason and his companions sailed away, they took Medea with them. Jason married Medea, but afterward deserted her for Creusa.

7. Daughter of Aeëtes, king of Colchis. With the help of Medea, Jason secured the golden fleece. As the condition of her assistance Jason promised to marry her. He did take her with him as his wife when he sailed from Colchis, but afterward abandoned her for Creusa (sometimes called Glauce), daughter of Creon, king of Corinth. In revenge Medea caused the death of Creusa and murdered her own two children by Jason.

8. Of this Alessio, member of the prominent Interminei or Interminelli family of Lucca, little is known beyond the fact that he lived during the latter half of the thirteenth century.

9. Thaïs, a courtesan in *Eunuchus,* a play by Terence. In the episode referred to, Thraso, her lover, has sent her a gift of a slave through a soldier named Gnatho.

CANTO XIX

1. In the Bible, Simon Magus was a sorcerer of Samaria who was converted by the preaching of Philip the evangelist (see Actus 8:9–13). When he subsequently attempted to buy the power of conferring the Holy Ghost, he was severely rebuked by the apostle Peter for thinking that the gift of God might be purchased with money (see Actus 8:14–24). From the name Simon is derived the word "simony," which is applied to all traffic in sacred things, especially the buying or selling of ecclesiastical offices.

2. The famous Baptistery of Florence, in which Dante, like most Florentine children of his time, was baptized.

3. The speaker, as we learn (though not explicitly), is Pope Nicholas III. He thinks he is addressing Pope Boniface VIII.

4. Boniface VIII (Benedetto Caetani), born at Anagni *ca.* 1235, was created cardinal by Martin IV in 1281; elected pope at Naples in succession to Celestine V on December 24, 1294; and crowned at Rome on January 23, 1295. He died at Rome, October 11, 1303. Since Boniface died three years after the assumed date of Dante's journey through Hell, the poet by anticipation has assigned Boniface his place among the simonists.

5. The Church, Bride of Christ and of His Vicar on earth.

6. The speaker, Pope Nicholas III (Giovanni Gaetano Orsini), was a nobleman of Rome. He was created cardinal-deacon of San Nicola in Carcere Tulliano by Innocent IV in 1244; and was elected pope at Viterbo on November 25, 1277.

7. Nicholas was of the Orsini family, whose cognizance was a she-bear, *orsa.*

8. Clement V (Bertrand de Got) was born in Gascony *ca.* 1264. He was archbishop of Bordeaux before his election to the papacy on June 5, 1305.

9. Jason (born Joshua), second son of the high priest Simon, wrested the office of high priest from his own brother by promising the king, Antiochus IV Epiphanes, 360 talents of silver.

10. Matthias the Apostle was chosen by lot ("sortito") to fill the place of Judas Iscariot.

11. This probably refers to Nicholas' part in an intrigue against Charles of Anjou, brother of St. Louis and king of Naples and Sicily, who had refused to marry Nicholas' niece.

12. The Seven Gifts of the Holy Spirit. The ten horns symbolize the Ten Commandments, from which the Church derived strength as long as the pope governed virtuously.

13. According to a legend universally accepted in the Middle Ages as historical fact, Constantine the Great (Roman Emperor 306–37), before he removed his government to Byzantium, abandoned to the Church his temporal power in the West. This so-called Donation of Constantine is said to have been made by the emperor in return for his having been cured of leprosy by Pope Sylvester I. Lorenzo Valla, who flourished more than a century after Dante's death, proved the Donation to be a forgery; it is now thought to have been composed at the papal court or in France in the second half of the eighth century.

CANTO XX

1. Cf. Aquinas, *Summa Theologica,* Part III, Suppl. Q 94, A 3, citing Psalms, 58. 10. Virgil has not rebuked Dante for feeling compassion for individual sinners suffering the penalty of sin (see *Inf.* V; XV; XVI), but he rebukes him here for shedding tears at the mere sight of the punishment, which, being the evidence of the justice of God, ought not to awaken pity.

2. This is Amphiaraus, a great prophet and hero of Argos. He was one of the seven kings who joined Adrastus, king of Argos, in the expedition against Thebes (see *Inf.* XIV). Foreseeing that he would perish in the war of the Seven against Thebes, Amphiaraus concealed himself to avoid going to battle; but his hiding place was revealed by his wife Eriphyle, sister of Adrastus, who had been bribed with a necklace. Amphiaraus met his death at Thebes when he and his chariot were swallowed up by the earth as he attempted to flee from his pursuers.

3. Tiresias, famous soothsayer of Thebes, once separated with his staff two serpents that he found coupled in a wood, whereupon he was changed into a woman for seven years. At the end of this period he found the same two serpents and struck them again, whereupon he was changed back into a man. Subsequently, when Jupiter and Juno differed as to which of the two sexes experienced the greater pleasure in love, the question was referred to Tiresias, because he had belonged to both sexes. He decided in favor of woman, which coincided with the opinion of Jupiter. Juno in anger struck him with blindness, but Jupiter, by way of compensation, endowed him with the gift of prophecy.

4. Aruns, Etruscan soothsayer who, according to Lucan (*Phars.* I), foretold the civil war that was to end in the death of Pompey and the triumph of Caesar.

5. Ancient Luna, maritime town in Etruria on the left bank of the Magra, on the boundary between Liguria and Etruria.

6. The inhabitant "who lives below" and comes into the mountains to engage in whatever meager farming he can in the difficult terrain of these hills of marble.

7. Theban prophetess, daughter of Tiresias. According to some accounts, this Manto went to Italy and married the god of the Tiber, by whom she had a son, Ocnus, who founded a town named Mantua in his mother's honor. According to others, the Italian Manto, mother of Ocnus, was a local nymph with the gift of prophecy.

8. Mantua, Virgil's birthplace.

9. According to tradition, Thebes, the capital of Boeotia, was the birthplace of Bacchus.

10. Tirol, but the reference in this case is almost certainly not to the Tirol as a region (as understood today), but to the castle known as Tiralli, which was built in the twelfth century by the counts of Venosta and in fact gave its name to the region—that is, the *contea*.

11. The Brescian counts of Casalodi, a family of Guelphs, made themselves masters of Mantua in 1272, incurring the hostility of the people. In order to appease the populace, Count Alberto da Casalodi, on what proved to be the treacherous advice of Pinamonte, expelled great numbers of the nobles, including his own adherents. When Alberto thus was left defenseless, Pinamonte, who wished to seize the government of Mantua, suddenly, and with the aid of the populace, compelled him to leave the city, confiscated all his possessions, and put to the sword or drove out nearly every remaining family of note in Mantua.

12. Aulis, port in Boeotia, on the Euripus (modern Evripos), where the Greek fleet assembled before sailing for Troy.

13. Michael Scot, scholar and necromancer, probably was born at Balwearie, Scotland, *ca.* 1175 and died probably *ca.* 1235.

14. This famous astrologer and soothsayer of Forlì (he may have been born in Florence), was a tiler by trade. He appears to have served as domestic astrologer to Guido da Montefeltro.

15. Maestro Benvenuto, nicknamed Asdente ("Toothless"), was a shoemaker of Parma who was famed as a prophet and soothsayer during the latter half of the thirteenth century.

16. Cain, eldest son of Adam and Eve and murderer of his brother, Abel, is here mentioned in connection with the old popular belief that the man in the moon was Cain with a bundle of thorns.

CANTO XXI

1. From the bridge over the fourth *bolgia* to that which spans the fifth.

2. The Arsenal at Venice (built in 1104 and greatly enlarged in 1303–4 and 1325) was one of the most important shipyards in Europe in Dante's time.

3. "Evil-claws." The name suggests one of the more grotesque and terrifying features of these devils.

4. St. Zita (born 1218, died *ca.* 1278), the patron saint of Lucca, is also the patron saint of domestic servants, since she herself was a servant.

5. The jeering sarcasm of this touch is evident. Bonturo is actually the worst barrator of all; and in Lucca every public official is corrupt, it seems. Bonturo Dati, the head of the popular party in Lucca at the beginning of the fourteenth century, appears to have bought and sold public offices on so grand a scale that he controlled nearly all such traffic in the city.

6. The "Volto Santo" ("Sacred Face") of Lucca is an ancient crucifix of great sanctity, carved in dark wood. According to tradition, this relic was carved by Nicodemus, who, while attempting to portray the divine features, fell asleep and on awaking found the work had been miraculously completed for him.

7. A river of Tuscany.

8. "Evil-tail."

9. A castle in the territory of Pisa, about five miles from that city, on a hill close to the Arno. In August 1289, shortly after the death of Count Ugolino, head of the Guelph party in Pisa, and the expulsion of the Guelphs from that city, the Tuscan Guelphs, headed by the Lucchese and Florentines, invaded Pisan territory and captured several forts, including that of Caprona.

10. Some of the names of these demons have as plain a significance as *Malacoda;* for example, *Cagnazzo* for *Cagnaccio,* "wretched dog"; *Barbariccia,* "crisp beard"; *Graffiacane,* "scratch dog"; while others suggest a meaning by their composition or their sound, as *Alichino,* "bent wing"; *Rubicante,* "rubicund"; *Scarmiglione,* "dishevelled," and so on.

CANTO XXII

1. Dante probably saw such cavalry in the campaign against Arezzo that ended in the battle of Campaldino on June 11, 1289, between the Florentine Guelphs and the Aretine Ghibellines, in which the Ghibellines were totally defeated.

2. Thibaut II, king of Navarre from 1253 to 1270.

3. Fra Gomita, a Sardinian friar (the order is not known) who, having been appointed chancellor or deputy of Nino Visconti of Pisa, judge of the judicial district of Gallura in Sardinia, abused his position in order to traffic in the sale of public offices.

4. One of the four judicatures into which Sardinia was divided at the time.

5. Logodoro, another of the judicatures of Sardinia. Zanche was murdered about 1290, by his son-in-law Branca d' Oria; see *Inf.* XXXIII.

CANTO XXIII

1. During the Middle Ages, Aesopean fables circulated in various Latin and French prose and verse collections. The fable of the mouse and the frog, to which Dante here alludes, was a favorite with medieval writers.

2. Cluny, the famous Benedictine abbey in Burgundy.

3. "The second Frederick" of *Inf.* X. No incontrovertible evidence has been found to prove that Frederick actually employed such a method of torture, but the reference here reflects the widespread belief that he did.

4. The scales called "balances," which have a bar supported in the middle and two pans of equal weight suspended from the extremities, resemble the human figure, particularly the neck and shoulders. Such scales, if overweighted, as these sinners are in their heavy cloaks, do indeed creak, especially at the point of juncture of the crossbeam and its support, which in the comparison would be the necks of the hypocrites.

5. The members of a military and conventual order called the Ordo Militiae Beatae Mariae ("Knights of the Blessed Virgin Mary") were popularly known as Frati Gaudenti, or Jovial Friars. The order was founded in 1261 by certain citizens of Bologna.

6. Catalano di Guido di Ostia was born in Bologna *ca.* 1210 (for this form of his name see R. Davidsohn, 1908, pt. I, p. 590). He served as *podestà* of various cities of Emilia and Lombardy; and in 1249 he commanded a division of the Bolognese infantry at the battle of Fossalta, in which King Enzio of Sardinia (the illegitimate son of Frederick II) was defeated and captured.

7. Loderingo degli Andalò (born *ca.* 1210) belonged to a Ghibelline family of Bologna. His career paralleled that of Catalano.

8. A part of Florence in the neighborhood of the Palazzo Vecchio.

9. The crucified figures upon the floor of the ditch, Caiaphas, Annas, and the others, were not there when Virgil passed this way before. Virgil can marvel also at the particular form of their punishment and wonder what the reason for it may be, since he died before he could know that Christ was crucified.

10. Like the other *ruine* of Hell ("ruina" has an em-

phatic position in this verse), this one was caused by the quake that shook the earth when Christ died on the Cross.

CANTO XXIV

1. In ancient Greek geography, Libya was the name for North Africa, outside of Egypt. Later, divided into Marmarica and Cyrenaica, Libya became part of the Roman colony of Africa.

2. Ancient Ethiopia was a country west of the Red Sea, in northeast Africa, which included that part of Africa south from Egypt as far as Zanzibar.

3. The phoenix is a mythical Arabian bird. Every five hundred years it burned itself on a pyre of incense and rose again from the ashes in the shape of a small worm, which on the third day developed into the full-grown bird.

4. That is, a bastard; one of the Lazzari, a noble family of Pistoia. In 1293, he with two companions broke into the sacristy of San Zeno, at Pistoia. They carried off what silver and jewels they could lay hands on. At length, when an innocent man was about to be punished for the crime, Fucci revealed the name of the receiver of the plunder, who was hanged, while he himself escaped punishment.

5. Vanni Fucci hastens to predict the downfall of the Bianchi, Dante's own party, foretelling how, after helping to expel the Neri from Pistoia, they will themselves be driven out of Florence and finally be defeated at Campo Piceno. The expulsion of the Neri from Pistoia came about in May 1301. On All Saints' Day 1301, Charles of Valois arrived in Florence, having been allowed to enter the city unopposed, on the strength of his promise to hold the balance between the two parties and to maintain peace. However, no sooner had he obtained command of the city than he treacherously espoused the cause of the Neri and threw the whole of Florence into confusion. In the midst of the panic Corso Donati, the exiled leader of the Neri, made his way back into the city ("Florence renovates her people"), broke open the prisons, and released the prisoners, who, together with his own adherents, attacked and pillaged the houses of the Bianchi for five days. Charles of Valois, meanwhile, in spite of his promises, made no attempt to interfere. During the following year, in a series of orders of banishment, the Bianchi were expelled from Florence, Dante being among those who were condemned to exile.

CANTO XXV

1. An obscene gesture made by thrusting out (up, at God, in this case) the fist with the thumb between the fore and middle finger. Apparently the gesture was often made with both hands.

2. It was near Pistoia that Catiline was defeated in 62 B.C. According to legend the town was founded by the survivors of Catiline's forces.

3. Capaneus, who is brought to mind by Vanni Fucci's irreverence (see *Inf.* XIV). Though punished in Hell for entirely different crimes, both Capaneus and Vanni Fucci are seen as *superbi*, or "proud."

4. This region has been referred to already in the *Inferno* as a haunt of wild beasts (see *Inf.* XIII).

5. Cacus, the son of Vulcan and Medusa, was a fire-breathing, half-human monster who lived in a cave on the Aventine hill and preyed on the inhabitants of the district.

6. According to the early commentators, Cianfa was a member of the Donati family of Florence.

7. According to the early commentators, this first spirit is Agnello or Agnolo de' Brunelleschi (a Ghibelline family of Florence), who first joined the Bianchi and then went over to the Neri.

8. This proves to be the soul of Francesco Guercio de' Cavalcanti.

9. Sabellus, a Roman soldier of Cato's army in Africa. Lucan relates that in the desert of Libya he was stung by a venomous serpent called a "seps," whose bite caused his body to putrefy and fall into a mass of corruption.

10. Nasidius, another Roman soldier who served with Cato in Africa. According to Lucan, in the desert of Libya he was stung by a poisonous serpent called a "prester," whose bite caused his body to swell up till his corselet burst and he died.

11. Cadmus, son of Agenor, king of Phoenicia, and brother of Europa, was the founder of Thebes. As a penalty for slaying a dragon sacred to Mars, he was transformed into a serpent.

12. Arethusa, one of the Nereids, was nymph of the fountain of Arethusa in the island of Ortygia near Syracuse; while bathing in the stream she was seen by the god Alpheus, who pursued her; on appealing to Diana she was changed into the fountain of the same name, but Alpheus continued to pursue her under the sea and to mingle his stream with the waters of the fountain.

13. Torraca observes that in antiquity and during the Middle Ages, it was believed that human saliva had power against serpents.

14. The identity of this Buoso, the second of the three spirits, is uncertain.

15. The third spirit is Puccio Galigai, nicknamed Sciancato ("lame"), of the Galigai family of Florence. As a Ghibelline he was banished with his children in 1268; in 1280, along with others of his party, he entered into a peace pact with the Guelphs.

16. This spirit, who first came on the scene as a little snake, now, by the reference to Gaville, is identifiable as Francesco de' Cavalcanti, nicknamed Guercio ("squinting"). He was murdered by the inhabitants of Gaville, a village in the Upper Val d'Arno not far from Figline; the death was speedily avenged by the Cavalcanti, who in their fury are said to have almost dispeopled Gaville.

CANTO XXVI

1. Prato is a town in Tuscany, about eleven miles northwest of Florence, on the road to Pistoia.

2. Eteocles was the son of Oedipus, king of Thebes, and Jocasta, and twin brother of Polynices. When the brothers compelled Oedipus to abdicate and leave Thebes, Oedipus prayed to the gods that the twins might be eternally at enmity with each other. Eteocles and Polynices agreed to reign in Thebes alternately year by year; but when Eteocles' term had expired, he refused to resign the throne to his brother. Polynices consequently invoked the aid of Adrastus, king of Argos, and thus originated the famous war of the Seven against Thebes (see *Inf.* XIV). The prayer of Oedipus was now answered, for in the course of the war Polynices and Eteocles killed each other in single combat. Their bodies were burned on the same funeral pyre, but so intense was the hatred between them, even after death, that the flame from the pyre divided in two as it ascended.

3. Ulysses of Ithaca, son of Laertes and father by Penelope of Telemachus, was one of the principal Greek heroes in the Trojan War and the hero of Homer's *Odyssey*.

4. Diomedes, son of Tydeus and Deipyle, was king of Argos and one of the famous Greek heroes who fought against Troy.

5. The famous wooden horse which the Greeks constructed as a pretended atonement for the Palladium which Ulysses and Diomedes had stolen from Troy.

6. Daughter of Lycomedes, king of Skyros, with whom Thetis left her son Achilles, disguised in woman's clothes, in order that he might not take part in the expedition against Troy. After Deidamia had become the mother of Pyrrhus (or Neoptolemus) by Achilles, the latter, yield-

ing to the persuasion of Ulysses, who together with Diomedes had penetrated his disguise, abandoned her and sailed to Troy.

7. The Palladium was a wooden image of Pallas Athena, said to have been sent from heaven by Jupiter to Ilus, the legendary founder of Troy, as a gift. On its preservation within the walls of Troy was believed to depend the safety and prosperity of the city.

8. The enchantress Circe was the daughter of Helios, god of the Sun, and Perse, a nymph. According to legend, she dwelt on the island of Aeaea. She had the power to transform men into beasts. When Ulysses was cast up on her island she changed his men into swine. But Ulysses, protected against enchantment by a magic root, forced her to change them back. He then lived with Circe (by whom he had a son, Telegonus) for a year before continuing on his voyage.

9. Gaeta, ancient Caieta, seaport of central Italy in the south of Latium, is situated on a promontory at the head of the Gulf of Gaeta, on the Tyrrhenian coast, about forty-five miles northwest of Naples.

10. The Strait of Gibraltar.

11. The Pillars of Hercules usually are considered to be the promontory of Abyla (in Arabic, Jebel Musa) in North Africa and that of Calpe (Gibraltar) in Spain, so called from the tradition that they were originally one mountain, which was torn asunder by Hercules.

12. Ceuta (Latin Septa), city in North Africa, in Morocco, opposite Gibraltar.

13. In the geography of Dante's *Commedia,* Jerusalem is at the center of the northern hemisphere, which is of land and has India at its eastern limit and Gibraltar at its western. The other, southern hemisphere is composed entirely of water, except for the mountain-island of Purgatory, which rises directly opposite Jerusalem on the orb of the earth (as will be made clear in the poem).

CANTO XXVII

1. The victims of Phalaris, tyrant of Agrigentum in Sicily, are said to have been shut up and roasted alive in a brazen bull invented by the Athenian artisan Perillus. The contrivance was so fashioned that the shrieks of those inside sounded like the bellowing of a bull. According to legend, Perillus was the first to perish by his own invention.

2. The people of the Romagna. See *Purgatory,* XIV.

3. The Apennines, where the Tiber rises, at the foot of Mount Fumaiolo.

4. The spirit who speaks is that of the Ghibelline count, Guido da Montefeltro, the ablest and most famous warrior of his time in Italy.

5. At this time, spring 1300, there was peace, or at least no open warfare, in Romagna.

6. Polenta was a castle near Brettinoro (modern Bertinoro), a few miles south of Forlì, from which the Guelph Polenta family took its name. The Polenta acquired authority over Ravenna toward the end of the thirteenth century and relinquished it to Venice in 1441.

7. Cervia, a town on the Adriatic, about fourteen miles southeast of Ravenna, was a place of some importance in the Middle Ages because of its salt monopoly, which appears to have yielded a considerable revenue.

8. Malatesta de Verrucchio (died 1312), who, after defeating Montagna de' Parciati and the Ghibelline party of Rimini in 1295, became the first Malatesta lord of Rimini. Montagna de' Parciati was head of the Ghibelline party in Rimini. When Malatesta overpowered Montagna and the Ghibellines of the city in 1295, Montagna was taken prisoner and entrusted to the charge of Malatestino.

9. Faenza, nineteen miles southwest of Ravenna, is on the Lamone River; and Imola, about twenty-one miles southeast of Bologna, is on the Santerno River.

10. Maghinardo, or Mainardo, Pagano da Susinana, head of the Pagani family in Dante's time, was lord of Faenza in 1290, of Forlì in 1291, and of Imola in 1296. Dante's designation of him as the "Little Lion" refers to his coat of arms, "on a field argent a lion azure." Although a Ghibelline by birth and a staunch supporter of that party in Romagna, Maghinardo was loyal to the Florentine Guelphs, in gratitude for the care they had taken of him and his property when his father, at his death, entrusted him to their protection as a minor.

11. This is Cesena, on the Savio River, midway between Forlì and Rimini, at the foot of the hills belonging to the Tuscan Apennine range.

12. In 1296 Guido, past seventy years old, entered the Franciscan Order, girding himself with its cord.

13. Boniface VIII.

14. The war between Boniface VIII and the Colonna family and faction, who contested the validity of the abdication of Celestine V and charged that Boniface had entered the papacy by fraud.

15. Acre, now a city and seaport of Israel, is situated on a low promontory of Mount Carmel on the northern extremity of the Bay of Acre.

16. On receiving news of the fall of Acre, Pope Nicholas IV at once attempted to organize a crusade for the recovery of the city and called on all Christians under pain of excommunication to abstain from any further commerce with Egypt, the seat of Moslem power.

17. It was for this service that Constantine was supposed to have made Pope Sylvester I "the first rich Father" (*Inf.* XIX) by the famous "Donation" conveying to the Pope the sovereignty over Italy and the whole Western Empire. Sylvester, to escape from Constantine's previous persecution of the Christians, had taken refuge on Mount Soracte.

18. Soracte, a mountain near the Tiber about twenty-four miles north of Rome, where Pope Sylvester I is said to have taken refuge in a cave during the persecutions of Constantine. On its summit now stands the church of San Silvestro.

19. The ancient Praeneste, now Palestrina, a town situated on a steep hill about twenty miles southeast of Rome. It was the stronghold of the Colonna, who managed to hold out there against the papal forces until September 1298, when it was surrendered on a promise from the pope of complete amnesty. No sooner did Boniface get possession of Palestrina than he razed it to the ground.

CANTO XXVIII

1. Modern Apulia is the compartment of southeast Italy that forms the heel of the peninsula and extends along the coast of the Adriatic Sea to Abruzzi e Molise; but in the Middle Ages the name was often used to indicate the whole of the southern extremity of continental Italy.

2. The Romans, descendants of Aeneas and his men. The Trojans are referred to as the "noble seed" of the Romans in *Inf.* XXVI.

3. The Norman adventurer Robert Guiscard, duke of Apulia and Calabria, fought the Greeks and Saracens in southern Italy and Sicily during the last half of the eleventh century.

4. Modern Ceprano; a town in southeast Latium on the banks of the Liri. The allusion is to the betrayal of Manfred by the Apulians just before the fatal battle of Benevento, February 26, 1266.

5. Near Tagliacozzo, town of central Italy in Abruzzi e Molise, about twenty-one miles south-southwest of

Aquila. Érard (or Érart) de Valéry, lord of Saint-Valérien and of Marolles and constable of Champagne, was born about 1200 and died in 1277. Charles of Anjou, being engaged in a battle with Conradin, nephew of Manfred and grandson of Frederick II, at Tagliacozzo, was advised by Érard to keep his reserves in the background until Conradin's troops, who at the beginning of the day had routed his opponents, were disordered by pursuit and scattered over the field in search of plunder. Charles then advanced with fresh troops and completely routed the enemy. It is to Charles' victory by means of this stratagem of Érard's that Dante alludes here.

6. Mohammed, founder of the Mohammedan religion.

7. 'Ali ibn-abi-Talib, fourth of the caliphs, or successors of Mohammed, was born at Mecca *ca*. 600.

8. Dolcino Tornielli of Novara, born in the second half of the thirteenth century, was known as Fra Dolcino because of his connection with the sect of the Apostolic Brothers, founded in Parma by Gherardo Segarelli with the object of bringing the Church back to the simplicity of apostolic times. Following the promulgation in 1305 of a bull of Clement V for the extirpation of his sect, Fra Dolcino with thousands of followers in the hills between Novara and Vercelli defied the repeated attack of the church authorities. They finally were reduced by starvation, large numbers were massacred on the mountains, and others were burned. Fra Dolcino and his companion, the beautiful Margaret of Trent, who was said to be his mistress, were taken prisoner and burned alive in June 1307.

9. One Piero da Medicina, about whom little or nothing is known.

10. *Vercelli:* Town in Piedmont, about forty miles northeast of Turin. *Marcabò:* A castle built by the Venetians in the territory of Ravenna on the Po di Primaro.

11. Guido del Cassero and Angiolello di Carignano, two noblemen of Fano, of opposite parties, were invited by Malatestino, lord of Rimini, to a conference at La Cattolica on the Adriatic coast. On their way to the rendezvous (or perhaps as they were returning) they were surprised in their boat by Malatestino's men, thrown overboard, and drowned.

12. Malatestino had only one eye, and he was therefore known as Malatestino dell'Occhio.

13. Gaius Scribonius Curio the Younger originally was an adherent of the Pompeian party, and by its influence was made tribune of the plebs in 50 B.C. But he was bought over by Caesar, and employed his power as tribune against his former friends.

14. Mosca de' Lamberti was a passionate Ghibelline at whose instigation the Amidei murdered Buondelmonte de' Buondelmonti, a crime that led to the beginning of the Guelph and Ghibelline feuds in Florence.

15. Bertran de Born, lord of Hautefort near Périgueux, was a soldier and one of the earliest and most famous of the troubadours.

16. Prince Henry of England, second son of Henry II, was born in 1155 and died in 1183. Because he was crowned twice during his father's lifetime (at Westminster in June 1170 and at Winchester in August 1172), he was known at home and abroad as the "Young King."

17. In the Bible Ahithophel (Achitophel) the Gilonite encouraged Absalom in his rebellion against his father, King David. When Ahithophel's counsel was overthrown by David's emissary, Ahithophel hanged himself.

CANTO XXIX

1. Geri del Bello degli Alighieri, the grandson of Alighiero I, was first cousin to Dante's father, Alighiero II.

2. Hautefort, a castle in the Limousin belonging to Bertran de Born and his brother.

3. Both Sardinia and the Maremma were marshy and malarial in Dante's time.

4. Aegina is an island off the coast of Greece in the Saronic Gulf between Argolis and Attica.

5. The speaker, not otherwise named, is identified by the early commentators as one Griffolino, an alchemist of Arezzo, but little is known of him beyond what they report. According to the commentators, Griffolino pretended that he could teach Albero da Siena how to fly, in order to get money from him.

6. Albero is said to have been the son or protégé of a bishop of Siena.

7. Niccolò de' Salimbeni (or, according to some, de' Bonsignori) of Siena, was said by the early commentators to have been a member of the Brigata Spendereccia, or "Spendthrift Club," of Siena.

8. The Brigata Spendereccia of Siena, an organization of extravagant young men that flourished for a short time during the second half of the thirteenth century.

9. Caccia of Asciano, or Caccianemico, was the son of Messer Trovato of Asciano.

10. The nickname (literally, "dazed") of a spendthrift who has been identified as one Meo (i.e., Bartolommeo), son of Rainieri de' Folcacchieri of Siena.

11. Capocchio was a Florentine (or, according to some, a Sienese) who was burned alive at Siena in 1293 as an alchemist.

CANTO XXX

1. Semele was the daughter of Cadmus, king of Thebes, and Harmonia and the sister of Ino, Agave, Autonoë, and Polydorus. She was beloved by Jupiter, by whom she became the mother of Bacchus. Juno, in order to avenge herself upon Jupiter for his unfaithfulness to her, appeared to Semele in the guise of her aged nurse Beroë and induced her to ask Jupiter to show himself to her in the same splendor and majesty in which he appeared to Juno. Jupiter, knowing the danger, reluctantly complied with Semele's request and appeared before her as the god of thunder, whereupon she was struck by lightning and consumed to ashes.

2. Athamas, king of Orchomenus in Boeotia, was the son of Aeolus and Enarete. At the command of Juno, Athamas married Nephele; but he was secretly in love with Semele's sister, the mortal Ino, by whom he had two sons, Learchus and Melicertes. Possibly because he was unfaithful to Nephele, or because Ino was the nurse of Bacchus, son of Semele and Jupiter, Athamas incurred the wrath of Juno, who afflicted him with madness. He mistook Ino and her two sons for a lioness and cubs and, seizing Learchus, dashed him against a rock. Ino flung herself with Melicertes into the sea.

3. After the fall of Troy, Hecuba, widow of Priam, king of Troy, and her daughter Polyxena were taken captive by the Greeks. On their way to Greece, Polyxena was torn from Hecuba and sacrificed on the tomb of Achilles; and soon after, the lifeless body of Hecuba's son Polydorus, who had been murdered by Polymestor, king of Thrace, was washed up on the shore. Mad with grief, Hecuba was changed into a dog and in this state leaped into the sea at a place thenceforward called Cynossema, or "tomb of the dog."

4. Myrrha was the daughter of Cinyras, king of Cyprus. Seized with a fatal passion for her father, she contrived, with the aid of her nurse, to introduce herself in disguise into his chamber during the absence of her mother. When Cinyras discovered the deception, he attempted to slay

Myrrha, but she escaped and wandered to Arabia, where she was transformed into a myrrh tree and gave birth to Adonis.

5. The Buoso Donati whom Gianni Schicchi is said to have impersonated was probably the son of Vinciguerra di Donato del Pazzo.

6. At the instigation of the Conti Guidi of Romena, Master Adam counterfeited the gold florin of Florence, in coins containing twenty-one carats of gold instead of the legal standard of twenty-four carats. The fraud was soon detected, and the Florentines, jealous of the purity of their coinage, which had become a standard throughout Christendom, caused the false coiner to be burned alive in 1281.

7. A castle in the village of Romena in the Casentino, near Pratovecchio, which in Dante's time belonged to the Conti Guidi.

8. The Florentine gold florin was stamped on one side with the flower of the lily (the name *fiorino*, "florin," comes from *fiore*, "flower") and on the other with the image of John the Baptist, patron saint of Florence.

9. Guido II da Romena, his brother Alessandro, and—since the brothers were four—either Aghinolfo or Ildebrandino.

10. Perhaps the reference here is to the celebrated fountain at Siena situated at the foot of the hill upon which the church of San Domenico stands; the fountain was so called after the Brandi family, to whom the site at one time belonged.

11. The wife of Potiphar, who, after trying in vain to seduce Joseph, made the false accusation that he had sought to lie with her. See Gen. 39:6–20.

12. Sinon, the treacherous Greek who during the siege of Troy allowed himself to be taken prisoner by the Trojans and then by a lying tale persuaded them to admit within their walls the famous wooden horse.

13. Narcissus, Greek youth, of whom the nymph Echo became enamored. Finding him insensible to love, she pined away in grief and was reduced to nothing but a voice. To punish Narcissus for his insensibility, the goddess Nemesis caused him to see his own image reflected in a fountain, whereupon he became so enamored of it that he too pined away gradually, until he was changed into the flower that bears his name.

CANTO XXXI

1. According to legend, Achilles' spear could heal the wounds it inflicted.

2. Charlemagne, or Charles the Great (742–814), king of the Franks, was crowned Emperor of the West on Christmas Day 800, by Pope Leo III in Rome. In the year 1165 Charlemagne was canonized. In the traditional account, preserved in the OFr *Chanson de Roland* (late eleventh or early twelfth century), Roland is betrayed by his stepfather Ganelon, to the Saracen king Marsile, whose vast army annihilated the French forces at Roncesvalles.

3. Dante likens the giants to the towers of Montereggioni (*castrum Montis regionis*), a strongly fortified castle, situated on the crown of a low hill about eight miles northwest of Siena.

4. By ceasing to produce giants, Nature takes them out of warfare.

5. Dante compares the face of the giant Nimrod to the huge bronze pine cone which is said to have stood originally near the Campus Martius in Rome.

6. Frisians or Frieslanders (the inhabitants of Friesland) were noted for their great stature. This giant—Nimrod—is so tall that three Frisians standing on one another's shoulders would not have reached from his waist to his hair.

7. Numerous unsuccessful attempts have been made to interpret this jargon. But Dante, doubtless alluding to the confusion of tongues which struck the builders of the Tower of Babel, expressly states that Nimrod's language is intelligible to no one.

8. Nimrod, the son of Cush, was, according to Gen. 10:9 "a mighty hunter before the Lord"; hence he is equipped in Hell with a hunter's horn. According to a medieval and patristic tradition that probably arose from Genesis, Nimrod was the deviser of the Tower of Babel on the plain of Shinar. Nothing in the Bible suggests that Nimrod was a giant.

9. Ephialtes, the son of Neptune and Iphimedia. He and his brother Otus were known as the Aloidae. At the age of nine the two brothers, who were marvelously strong, made war upon the Olympian gods and attacked Olympus itself, but according to the Homeric account of the legend were killed during the attempt.

10. Briareus, or Aegaeon, son of Uranus and Earth, was one of the giants who warred against Olympus.

11. Antaeus, the son of Neptune and Earth, was a mighty giant and wrestler of Libya, invincible as long as he remained in contact with his mother, Earth.

12. The "fateful valley" of the Bagradas River (modern Medjerda River), in north central Tunisia, near Zama, where Scipio won the decisive victory over Hannibal in 202 B.C.

13. Cocytus, the frozen lake of the ninth circle of Hell.

14. According to legend the giant Tityus was the son of Jupiter and Elara. For having attempted to violate Latona, he was killed by her children Apollo and Diana and hurled down to Tartarus, where he lay outstretched on the ground covering nine acres. Vultures eternally preyed on his liver.

15. Typhon, or Typhoeus, the son of Earth (Gaea) and Tartarus, was a tremendous monster, who is sometimes described as having a hundred heads, sometimes as breathing fire, and sometimes as having a body made of snakes from the hips down and arms with serpents' heads instead of hands. Incited by his mother, Typhon attacked the Olympian gods, but was eventually defeated by Jupiter.

16. The Garisenda, one of the leaning towers of Bologna, was built in 1110 by Filippo and Oddo dei Garisendi. It is 163 feet high and ten feet out of the perpendicular.

CANTO XXXII

1. Dante's appeal to the Muses for help in describing the bottom of Hell amounts to a fresh invocation and marks, as it were, a new beginning, serving to set off the ninth circle as a new area, now entered upon.

2. Amphion, son of Jupiter and Antiope, with the help of the Muses built the walls of Thebes; charmed by the magic skill with which he played the lyre, the stones came down from Mount Cithaeron and placed themselves of their own accord.

3. There is considerable uncertainty as to which mountain is intended.

4. Commonly identified with one of the peaks, known as Pania della Croce, of the Apuan Alps, a group of peaks in the northwest corner of Tuscany.

5. This, along with the foregoing mention of the Bisenzio Valley, is enough to identify the father as Alberto degli Alberti, count of Mangona, and the two sons as Alessandro and Napoleone, who killed each other in a dispute over their inheritance.

6. Caina, as we are soon to understand, is the first subdivision of Cocytus, where those are punished who betrayed (and murdered) their kinsmen—and so it is well named after Cain, the first such murderer.

7. Mordred, the traitorous nephew (or son, according

to some versions), of King Arthur, whom he slew and by whom he was slain.

8. Vanni de' Cancellieri, nicknamed Focaccia, of Pistoia, was guilty of murdering (October 1293), not his uncle, as many early commentators have it, but a cousin, one Detto di Sinibaldo Cancellieri.

9. A Florentine, said by the commentators to have belonged to the Toschi family, who murdered a kinsman (variously recorded as brother, nephew, uncle, or cousin), for the sake of his inheritance.

10. Alberto (or Uberto) Camicione de' Pazzi of Val d'Arno, of whom nothing is known except that he treacherously killed his kinsman Ubertino.

11. Carlino de' Pazzi of Val d'Arno, who, while the Neri of Florence and the Lucchese were besieging Pistoia in 1302, held the castle of Piantravigne in the Val d'Arno for the Bianchi of Florence, but for a bribe betrayed it into the hands of the Neri.

12. This shade proves to be Bocca degli Abati, who, while ostensibly fighting on the side of the Florentine Guelphs at the battle of Montaperti, at the moment when the latter were hard pressed by Manfred's German cavalry, treacherously cut off the hand of the Florentine standard-bearer, thus creating a panic, which ended in the disastrous defeat of the Guelphs.

13. Montaperti is a village in Tuscany, a few miles east of Siena.

14. The name of the second of the four subdivisions of the ninth circle of Hell, in which are punished those who betrayed their country or their party—political traitors—is derived from the Trojan Antenor, who in the Middle Ages was believed to have betrayed Troy to the Greeks.

15. Buoso da Duera was a Ghibelline leader of Cremona.

16. Tesauro de' Beccheria of Pavia, abbot of Vallombrosa and legate in Tuscany of Alexander IV. After the expulsion of the Ghibellines from Florence in 1258, he was seized by the Florentines on a charge of intriguing with the Ghibellines, and beheaded in the same year.

17. A Florentine Ghibelline.

18. Ganelon, the traitor who brought about the destruction of Charlemagne's rear guard at Roncesvalles, where Roland, Oliver, and the rest of the twelve peers were slain.

19. Tebaldello was a member of the Ghibelline Zambrasi family of Faenza.

20. Tydeus, king of Calydon, was one of the seven kings who joined Adrastus, king of Argos, in the expedition against Thebes. In this war Tydeus was mortally wounded by the Theban, Menalippus (or Melanippus), whom, however, he managed to slay in turn.

CANTO XXXIII

1. Ugolino della Gherardesca, Conte di Donoraticio, also known as Ugolino da Pisa, was born ca. 1220 and belonged to a noble and traditionally Ghibelline family that controlled vast territories in the Pisan Maremma and in Sardinia. In 1275, he conspired with the Guelph leader Giovanni Visconti to seize control of Pisa, traditionally a Ghibelline city, but when the plot was discovered he was banished and his property was confiscated. He returned to Pisa the following year and in a short time again acquired great power and prestige. After the defeat of Pisa in the battle of Meloria (1284), a defeat which some accounts accuse him of contriving, he was made *podestà* of Pisa and the next year entered into the negotiations referred to by his opponents as the "tradimento de le castella." For this supposed treachery he was put in prison, where he died of starvation in 1289.

2. Monte San Giuliano, a long flat mountain northeast of Pisa.

3. All prominent Ghibelline families of Pisa, who joined the archbishop in the uprising against the count.

4. Count Ugolino's fourth son. The exact date of Gaddo's birth is unknown, but he was surely a grown man by 1288.

5. "Of the peoples of Italy," in the sense of those belonging to this or that city or state.

6. Two small islands in the Mediterranean, east of the northern tip of Corsica.

7. *Uguiccione:* The fifth and youngest son of Count Ugolino and brother of Gaddo. *'l Brigata:* Nino, known as "il Brigata," was the son of Guelfo, eldest son of Ugolino and brother of Anselmuccio.

8. The wayfarer does not yet know that he will actually go to the bottom of the ice in the sense that he will climb down the body of Satan and pass through the center of the earth. Here the phrase "to go to the bottom of the ice" seems to suggest that the ice of Cocytus slopes toward the center.

9. Friar Alberigo belonged to the order of the Frati Gaudenti ("Jovial Friars"), which he joined in or before 1267. He was a member of the Manfredi family, the Guelph lords of Faenza. Manfred, a close relative, plotted against Alberigo to obtain the lordship of Faenza. In the consequent dispute, Manfred struck Alberigo, who pretended to forgive the insult as an act of impetuous youth. A reconciliation took place, and later when he thought the matter had been forgotten, Alberigo invited Manfred and one of his sons to a banquet (at his house at Cesate). When dinner was finished, he called out, "Bring the fruit," and at this signal assassins, concealed behind the tapestry, rushed out and dispatched father and son before Alberigo's eyes.

10. Ptolomea. The name of this division of Cocytus, in which are punished those who murdered their guests and friends, is derived, according to some, from Ptolemy XII, king of Egypt (51–47 B.C.), who murdered Pompey.

11. Atropos, one of the three Fates (Parcae). At the birth of every mortal, Clotho, the spinning Fate, was supposed to wind a certain amount of yarn on the distaff of Lachesis, the allotting Fate; the duration of the life of the individual was the length of time occupied in spinning the thread, which, when complete, was severed by Atropos, the inevitable Fate.

12. Member of the famous Ghibelline house of Doria (or d'Oria) at Genoa (born ca. 1233, died ca. 1325). With the aid of a relative, either a nephew or cousin, he treacherously murdered his father-in-law, Michel Zanche, governor of Logudoro in Sardinia, at a banquet to which he had invited him.

13. The fifth *bolgia* of the eighth circle, where the souls guilty of barratry are confined.

CANTO XXXIV

1. "The banners of the King of Hell advance": *Vexilla regis prodeunt* are the first words of a hymn.

2. The gradual disclosure of the monstrous figure continues, and creates considerable suspense. Satan's three faces are the grotesque counterpart of the triune god. The three faces exhibit the devilish counterpart of the attributes of the three persons of the Godhead, Impotence, Ignorance, and Hate (cf. *Inf.* III); Hate scarlet with rage, Ignorance black with its own darkness, Impotence pale yellow with jealousy and envy.

3. Lucifer has kept the six wings which he had as a seraph, but now they are monstrously joined to the three necks instead of being as Isaiah had seen them. These wings, like huge sails, are the "banners" of the "Emperor" who is stuck in the ice and who cannot possibly advance.

4. Marcus Junius Brutus (ca. 85–42 B.C.), the so-called tyrannicide. After the battle of Pharsalia (48 B.C.), in

which Pompey was defeated, Brutus was pardoned by Caesar and admitted into confidence and favor; he was made governor of Cisalpine Gaul (46 B.C.) and then praetor (44 B.C.). But in spite of his obligations to Caesar, he was persuaded by Cassius to murder him for the good of the republic.

5. The center of the earth and of gravity.

6. Time references in the descent through Hell have always been given with reference to night and to nocturnal bodies, never with respect to the position of the sun. Thus the present reference to the sun is most striking, since it signals that the two wayfarers, having passed the center, must now be under the southern celestial hemisphere. Henceforth in their journey in this hemisphere, time will be told with respect to positions of the sun; the specific point of reference will be the mountain directly opposite Jerusalem on the globe, where they will soon find themselves. "Tierce" was the name either for the third hour of the day or for the period of the first three hours, 6:00 A.M. to 9:00 A.M.

7. Myth on the grandest scale thus continues. Before Satan's fall, dry land stood forth ("si sporse") from the waters of the hemisphere opposite the future site of Jerusalem; but the land, shrinking to avoid being touched by the arch-sinner as he fell, removed itself to the other hemisphere, causing the land there to rise higher above the waters than it had done previously. Thus the earth which flees to form Satan's "grave" as he falls forms the mountain of Purgatory.

8. All continues to be dark and mysterious. We are never told what this "little stream" is. Does it flow down from Purgatory, perhaps from the river Lethe? Nothing of the sort is anywhere affirmed. All we are ever told is that this is a stream which, having worn away by erosion a winding and gently sloping course, offers a passageway through which the two wayfarers can climb from Satan's "tomb" to the surface of the earth, a way which nobody except just such a pilgrim as Dante would ever use.

PURGATORIO

CANTO I

1. The verses allude to the contest between the Muses and the nine daughters of Pierus, a king of Macedonia, to whom Pierus had given the names of the nine Muses. They presumptuously challenged the Muses to a singing contest and, being defeated, were transformed into magpies.

2. Only Adam and Eve, in their brief time in Eden before the Fall, were privileged to see these stars. Then, having sinned, Adam and Eve were (somehow) removed to the "northern clime," with the sad result that they and all their descendants were deprived of the sight of these four stars. Hence the northern region is said to be "widowed" of these stars.

3. The Wain, or Ursa Major, is now below the northern horizon, a notable fact since in "our" northern hemisphere it never sinks out of sight.

4. Marcus Porcius Cato Uticensis (Cato the Younger), great-grandson of Cato the Censor, was born in 95 B.C. Brought up as a devoted adherent of the Stoic school, he became conspicuous for his rigid morality. He was one of the chief leaders of the aristocratic party and vehemently opposed the measures of Caesar, Pompey, and Crassus. On the outbreak of the civil war in 49 B.C. he sided with Pompey. After the battle of Pharsalia he joined Metellus Scipio in Africa, but when the latter was defeated at Thapsus, and all of Africa, with the exception of Utica, submitted to Caesar, he resolved to die rather than fall into his hands. In 46 B.C. he therefore put an end to his own life.

We should expect to find Cato, as a suicide and a pagan and as the bitter opponent of Caesar, founder of the Roman Empire, in Hell. Dante, however, regards Cato not in his relation to the Roman Empire, but as the devoted lover of liberty.

5. Lucan tells that from the outbreak of the civil war Cato ceased to shave or trim his beard or to cut his hair.

6. Cato is thus said to be the custodian or guardian of all seven circles of Purgatory.

7. Liberty, freedom, is thus declared to be the goal of the purgatorial journey, liberation from the slavery of sin, both original and actual.

8. Utica, the most important city after Carthage in ancient North Africa, was a Phoenician colony more ancient than Carthage herself.

9. Virgil's words leave no doubt about the ultimate salvation of Cato, which makes for a special problem since he was both a pagan and a suicide. Apparently he is appointed to serve as custodian of Purgatory until Judgment Day, after which there will no longer be a Purgatory.

10. Marcia, daughter of Lucius Marcius Philippus and second wife of Cato of Utica. Lucan relates that Cato, after the birth of their third child, ceded her to his friend Hortensius. After the death of Hortensius, Marcia persuaded Cato to remarry her.

CANTO II

1. Here night, as that point which revolves opposite to the sun, means midnight. Since it is sunset at Jerusalem, it is midnight on the Ganges.

2. The cheeks of Aurora, the rosy dawn (i.e., the eastern sky), are said to be gradually growing orange as the sun rises and Aurora grows older.

3. Mars was thought to be accompanied by vapors, which were sometimes dense and sometimes rare and which at times became ignited of themselves and burned with the color of fire.

4. "When Israel went out of Egypt." Psalms, 114.

5. This proves to be the soul of Casella, musician of Florence (or, according to some, of Pistoia) and friend of Dante, who finds him here in Antepurgatory among those who disembark on the shore of Purgatory. Casella is said to have set to music some of Dante's verses.

6. In this way the initial verse of one of Dante's *canzoni—canzone* II, 1 (*Conv.* III)—becomes a verse of the *Comedy.* This is simply a love song, set to such sweet music that it can quiet the longings of both the living and the dead.

CANTO III

1. Virgil died at Brundusium (or Brundisium), modern Brindisi, a town on the Adriatic, in Apulia, on his return from Greece, September 21, 19 B.C. The reference here is to the transference of his body from Brindisi to Naples by order of Augustus.

2. Virgil speaks of pagans such as Aristotle, Plato, and others, including himself, who desired to know God, who is the Truth. If they could have known Christ as He was revealed in His Advent and could have believed in Him, they would have been taken from Limbo by Christ in the harrowing of Hell and would now be among the elect who have their every desire quieted in the beatific vision.

Instead they are confined to Limbo, where their only torment is to live in desire.

3. Lerici, a seaport in Liguria on the eastern shore of the Gulf of La Spezia, was in Dante's day a fortified town (*castello*). La Turbie, a village near the coast in the present department of Alpes-Maritimes in southeastern France, above Monaco.

4. The souls, perceiving that Virgil and Dante are coming toward them, are astounded, since the two now move in the wrong direction on Mount Purgatory as they go toward these souls, who are of course proceeding in the right direction. All movement here ought to be counterclockwise.

5. The natural son of the Emperor Frederick II, and king of Sicily, Urban IV and Clement IV offered the throne of Sicily to Charles of Anjou, the brother of St. Louis. Charles, crowned king of Sicily at Rome, routed Manfred at Benevento. Manfred himself was slain in the battle.

6. Constance (1154–98), daughter of Roger II, king of Naples and Sicily, and wife of Henry VI, by whom she became the mother of Frederick II.

7. Constance, daughter of Manfred and Beatrice of Savoy.

8. The "honor" of Sicily is Frederick, the third son of Constance and Pedro. The "honor" of Aragon could be either Alfonso, their eldest son, or James, their second son, who, when Alfonso died in 1291, succeeded him in Aragon, leaving the government of Sicily in the hands of his younger brother, Frederick, who became king of Sicily in 1296.

9. Town in northern Calabria about twelve miles inland from the Tyrrhenian Sea. The bishop ("pastor") in question was probably not Bartolomeo Pignatelli, archbishop of Cosenza, as many commentators affirm, but Tommaso d'Agni, his successor.

10. The name often used to indicate the kingdom of Naples (which included the whole of the southern extremity of Italy extending as far north as the Tronto on the Adriatic and, roughly, the Garigliano on the Mediterranean), as well as the island of Sicily.

11. Green is the color of hope, hence the phrase may in this way refer to hope itself, by its own color.

CANTO IV

1. San Leo, chief town of the mountainous district of Montefeltro in the ancient duchy of Urbino, not far from San Marino, in the northern part of the modern region of the Marches. Noli: Town in Liguria, on the Gulf of Genoa, about ten miles southwest of Savona on the Riviera di Ponente.

2. Former hamlet in Emilia on a steep mountain of the same name about twenty miles south of Reggio and not far distant from Canossa. In the Middle Ages it was strongly fortified and was a place of some importance.

3. Dante now dramatizes his puzzlement and wonder over the fact that the sun at midmorning is not in the southeast, where an observer in Europe would see it at this season, but in the northeast quarter of the sky.

4. Castor and Pollux, the Dioscuri. According to one version of the myth, Leda, having been visited by Jupiter in the form of a swan, brought forth two eggs, from one of which issued Helen, and from the other Castor and Pollux. At their death Jupiter placed the twin brothers among the stars to form the constellation of Gemini.

5. The zodiac is a zone or belt of the heavens eighteen degrees in breadth, extending nine degrees on either side of the ecliptic (the great circle apparently described by the sun in the course of a year), within which, according to the

Ptolemaic system, the moon, Mercury, Venus, the sun, Mars, Jupiter, and Saturn perform their annual revolutions. It is divided into twelve equal parts of thirty degrees each, called signs, which are named from the constellations lying within them.

6. Since "the Bears" serve merely to designate the north in general, Virgil means that Dante, in that case, would see the sun circling even farther north, if the time were nearer the summer season.

7. Mount Zion, name of one of the two hills upon which is situated the old city of Jerusalem, here serves to indicate the city itself.

8. Little or nothing is known of this acquaintance of Dante's. The early commentators say that he was a maker of musical instruments, noted for his indolence.

CANTO V

1. The fiftieth psalm, one of the seven penitential psalms.

2. This soul who speaks "before the others" is not named, but from the details of the story he tells of his own violent death he can readily be identified as Jacopo del Cassero, member of a noble family of Fano, who was born *ca.* 1260. He incurred the enmity of Azzo VIII d'Este by his opposition to the designs of the latter upon Bologna, of which city Jacopo was *podestà* in 1296. In revenge Azzo had him assassinated.

3. The March of Ancona (Marca Anconitana), a former province of Italy situated between Romagna and the kingdom of Naples. It corresponds roughly to the *compartimento* now known as the Marches.

4. In the territory of the Paduans. The phrase suggests the great treachery on the part of the Paduans, called Antenori for being, according to the legend, the descendants of the Trojan Antenor, who was said to have founded Padua and who in the Middle Ages was believed to have betrayed Troy to the Greeks.

5. Azzo VIII d'Este, who in 1293 succeeded his father, Obizzo II, as marquis of Este.

6. Small town between Padua and Venice on the banks of the Brenta canal.

7. Now Oriago, a village between Padua and Venice, close to the lagoons.

8. "Montefeltro" is here meant as part of a famous family name, not as a statement of geographical origin. Buonconte da Montefeltro was the son of Guido da Montefeltro (*Inf.* XXVII) and like his father a leader of the Ghibelline party. In June 1287 he helped the Ghibellines to expel the Guelphs from Arezzo, an event which was the beginning of the war between Florence and Arezzo.

9. The widow of Buonconte.

10. Small plain in the Casentino, between Poppi and Bibbiena, which was the scene of the battle, fought June 11, 1289, in which Buonconte was slain.

11. District in Tuscany comprising the upper valley of the Arno and the slopes of the Tuscan Apennines.

12. Torrent which rises in the Apennines above Camaldoli and, traversing the Casentino valley at its "foot," falls into the Arno just above Bibbiena.

13. "The Hermitage" is the monastery of Camaldoli, perched high in the mountains above the Casentino not far from the peak of Falterona, about thirty miles from Florence, founded in the early eleventh century by Romuald for his order of reformed Benedictines.

14. It was a common belief that angels and devils would come for the soul at death and would struggle for possession of it.

15. It was generally acknowledged that devils and angels had power over the elements.

16. The mountain ridge which forms the southwestern barrier of the Casentino.

17. The Arno. This was an established term for rivers that flow into the sea and not merely one used by "poets."

18. Pia was a lady of Siena who, according to some accounts, was the daughter of Buonincontro Guastelloni and wife, first of Baldo di Ildobrandino de' Tolomei (who died in 1290) and secondly of Nello or Paganello de' Pannocchieschi by whom she was put to death.

CANTO VI

1. This is a reference to Benincasa da Laterina (Laterina is in the upper Val d'Arno), a judge who, while acting as assessor for the *podestà* of Siena, sentenced to death a brother (or uncle) of Ghino di Tacco. In revenge Ghino murdered him while he was sitting in the papal audit office at Rome.

2. Famous highwayman. Although the date of his death is uncertain, he is thought to have died *ca.* 1303.

3. This soul is identified by the early commentators as Guccio de' Tarlati of the Tarlati of Pietramala in the territory of Arezzo.

4. One of the Conti Guidi, son of Guido Novello (hence he is Frederick junior of Guido junior). He is said to have been killed near Bibbiena in 1289 or 1291 by one of the Guelph Bostoli of Arezzo, while helping the Tarlati of Pietramala against the latter.

5. This personage was of an ancient noble family originally from Scorno, and like his father, Scornigiano, he held the title of judge and was charged with many delicate offices within and without the city of Pisa.

6. Orso degli Alberti della Cerbaia, son of Count Napoleone degli Alberti. According to Benvenuto he was killed by his cousin Alberto, son of Count Alessandro degli Alberti.

7. Although according to tradition Pierre de la Brosse was a surgeon of low birth, he was actually a gentleman of Touraine of honorable extraction, who was chamberlain and, for a time, favorite of Philip III of France.

8. Brabant, ancient duchy of the Netherlands, covering the territory of what is now the southern Netherlands and central and northern Belgium; now the name of a province in central Belgium. Dante thus urges Marie to repent of having caused Pierre's death while she yet has time.

9. Sordello, one of the most distinguished among the Italian poets.

10. The helmsman is the emperor.

11. In denouncing the cause of Italy's woeful plight the poet turns first to the "people" of the Church, popes and ecclesiastics in power, who ought to be "devout."

12. Albert I of Austria, son of Rudolf I of Habsburg, was emperor (but never crowned), 1298–1308.

13. Albert's successor was Henry VII, emperor from 1308 to 1313.

14. Rudolf I, emperor from 1273 to 1291.

15. The Montecchi family gave its name to the imperial party, or faction of the Monticoli (Dante has Tuscanized the name), which was headed, from *ca.* 1235 to 1259, by Ezzelino III da Romano in his attempt to conquer Lombardy.

16. A Guelph party of Cremona (not, as has commonly been supposed, a Cremonese family). There is frequent mention of this party in the chronicles, between 1249 and 1266, and of their struggles against the Monticoli party for political supremacy in Lombardy.

17. Guelph family of Orvieto, otherwise known as Monaldeschi. Filippeschi: Ghibelline family of Orvieto.

These two families were the leaders, respectively, of the Ghibellines and Guelphs in Orvieto, and were in consequence continually at variance.

18. Santafiora, county and town in Sienese territory, just under Monte Amiata, at the head of the river Fiora, which from the ninth century down to 1300 belonged to the powerful Ghibelline family of the Aldobrandeschi, who thence took their title of counts of Santafiora.

19. Marcellus, Roman consul and determined opponent of Julius Caesar.

20. Lacedaemon, or Sparta, was the capital of ancient Laconia and chief city of the Peloponnesus. The allusion is to the legislation of Lycurgus there, and to that of Solon at Athens.

CANTO VII

1. The three theological virtues—faith, hope, and charity—which are *infused* virtues given only with sanctifying grace.

2. This well-known antiphon, which is a prayer to the Virgin Mary, our advocate in Heaven, is recited at dusk and is thus appropriately sung here, since now it is that time of evening in Purgatory. Moreover, as a prayer it is addressed to Mary by those who are exiles in this "vale of tears"—and indeed these souls in Purgatory have in fact gathered in a vale for the night.

3. Rudolf I, emperor from 1273 to 1291. He was born in 1218 and was the son of Albert IV, count of Habsburg, and the founder of the imperial house of Austria.

4. Ottokar, who in life was Rudolf's enemy, now appears to comfort him here.

5. Bohemia, in the southwest part of which rises the river Moldau (Czech Vltava), which, after flowing southeast for some distance, turns north and, passing through Prague, enters the Elbe (Czech Labe), about twenty miles north of Prague.

6. Ottokar II was king of Bohemia from 1253 to 1278. He refused to recognize Rudolf I as emperor, and the latter in consequence made war on him and defeated him at Marchfeld near Vienna, Ottokar being slain in the battle, on August 26, 1278.

7. Wenceslaus II, son and successor of Ottokar and son-in-law of the Emperor Rudolf, was king of Bohemia from 1278 to 1305.

8. This "small-nosed" one is Philip III, the Bold, born in 1245 and king of France from 1270 until his death in 1285. He was the son and successor of Louis IX and nephew of Charles of Anjou.

9. Henry of Navarre.

10. Philip IV, the Fair, king of France from 1285 to 1314, was the son of Philip III, whom he succeeded, and brother of Charles of Valois. Philip is not mentioned by name in the *Divine Comedy*.

11. Pedro III, king of Aragon from 1276 to 1285. He married (in 1262) Constance, daughter of King Manfred of Sicily, and thus had a claim on the crown of Sicily, which he assumed after the massacre of the Sicilian Vespers in 1282 and retained until his death in 1285, in spite of all the efforts of Charles of Anjou.

12. Charles I, king of Naples and Sicily, count of Anjou and Provence, son of Louis VIII of France and Blanche of Castile, and brother of Louis IX (St. Louis), was born in 1226. In 1246 he married Beatrice, youngest daughter of Count Raymond Berenger IV of Provence, in whose right he became count of Provence; after the death of Beatrice in 1267, he married Margaret of Burgundy, daughter of Eudes, duke of Burgundy, in 1268. In 1266, after the defeat of Manfred at Benevento, he became king of Naples and Sicily; he died January 7, 1285. Charles and Pedro of

Aragon were bitter foes in life, but now sing in harmony together in Purgatory.

13. The reference is probably to Pedro, the last-born son of Pedro III of Aragon.

14. James II, the Just, king of Sicily from 1285 to 1295 and king of Aragon from 1291 to 1327, was the second son of Pedro III of Aragon.

15. Frederick II, king of Sicily from 1296 to 1337, was born in 1272, the third son of Pedro III of Aragon.

16. Apulia and Provence are said to lament having passed under the rule of Charles' son, Charles II, who on his father's death (in 1285) became king of Naples (Apulia) and count of Provence ("Proenza").

17. Henry III, who was king of England from 1216 to 1272, succeeded his father John and reigned for fifty-six years.

18. Guglielmo VII (or V), surnamed Spadalunga ("Longsword"), was marquis of Montferrat from 1254 to 1292. Shortly after his accession to power Guglielmo took advantage of internal dissensions in several of the independent Lombard cities to reduce them to subjection. In 1264 he made an alliance with Charles of Anjou and aided him in his descent into Italy.

19. Montferrat, extending from the Ligurian Apennines to the river Po, and Canavese, stretching from the Pennine and Graian Alps to the Po, constituted the marquisate of Guglielmo VII.

CANTO VIII

1. The hour of dusk, of Compline, when the "Salve, Regina" (*Purg.* VII) and the "Te lucis ante" are sung.

2. Nino (i.e., Ugolino) de' Visconti of Pisa, judge of the district of Gallura in Sardinia, was the son of Giovanni Visconti. In 1285, Nino was called to share with the count, his grandfather, the office of *podestà* and *capitano del popolo* of Pisa in a government then dominantly Guelph.

3. Daughter (born *ca.* 1291) of Nino Visconti of Pisa and Beatrice d'Este. In 1296, while still an infant, she was entrusted by Boniface VIII to the guardianship of the town of Volterra, as the daughter of a Guelph who had deserved well of the Church, but she was deprived of all her property by the Ghibellines, and, after living with her mother at Ferrara and Milan, was married to Rizzardo da Camino, lord of Treviso. After the death of her husband in 1312, she seems to have been reduced to poverty; in 1323, she was living in Florence, where a grant of money was made her in consideration of the services of her father.

4. Beatrice, daughter of Obizzo II d'Este and sister of Azzo VIII. She was married first to Nino Visconti of Pisa, by whom she had a daughter, Giovanna, and afterwards (at Modena in June 1300) to Galeazzo Visconti of Milan. Beatrice, after her marriage, came to reside in Milan, but within two years (in 1302) the Visconti were expelled thence by the Torriani (aided by Alberto Scotto, who thus avenged the slight passed upon him). Although Galeazzo died in 1328, Beatrice lived to return to Milan, her son Azzo having regained the lordship, and died there in 1334.

5. The heraldic device of the Visconti of Milan was a blue viper swallowing a red Saracen.

6. The emblem of the Visconti of Pisa was a cock.

7. The valley of the river Magra, which flows through Lunigiana, the territory of the Malaspina family.

8. Corrado II, called "il Giovane," son of Federigo I, marquis of Villafranca, and grandson of Corrado I, "l'antico." He died *ca.* 1294.

9. Corrado I, called "l'antico," member of the Spino Secco branch of the Malaspina family. He was the son of Obizzone and the grandfather of Franceschino, who was

Dante's host in Lunigiana in 1306, as well as of Corrado II. Corrado, who was a warm supporter of his father-in-law, the Emperor Frederick II, died about the year 1255.

CANTO IX

1. Tithonus, son of Laomedon, was loved by Aurora and by her intercession was made immortal. Since he neglected to ask for him eternal youth, he shriveled up in his old age, until at last Aurora changed him into a grasshopper.

2. It was generally believed that dreams which come in the early morning hours at or just before dawn are likely to be prophetic.

3. Dante alludes here to the legend of Philomela and Procne. Procne, having been married to Tereus, to whom she bore a son, was desirous of seeing her sister Philomela, from whom she was parted. At her request, therefore, Tereus set out for Athens to fetch Philomela. On the way back to Thrace he ravished her and, to prevent her revealing what had happened, cut out her tongue and abandoned her, informing Procne on his return that her sister was dead. Philomela, however, contrived to weave her story into a piece of cloth and thus conveyed the truth to Procne. The latter in fury killed her son and served up his flesh to his father Tereus, who partook of it, unconscious that he was feeding on his own child. Learning from Procne what she had done, Tereus pursued her and Philomela with an axe and was about to slay them, when in answer to the prayers of the two sisters all three of them were metamorphosed into birds, Procne becoming a nightingale, Philomela a swallow, and Tereus a hoopoe. According to some versions, Procne became a swallow, Philomela a nightingale, and Tereus a hawk.

4. Ganymede was the son of Tros and Callirrhoe and brother of Assaracus, who was one of the forefathers of Aeneas. He was the most beautiful of mortals and, according to one version of the story, was carried off by an eagle while hunting with his companions on Mount Ida in Mysia, so that he might take his place among the immortals as the cup-bearer of Jupiter.

5. In his youth Achilles was instructed by Chiron the centaur, from whose charge he was withdrawn by his mother, who conveyed her son in his sleep to the island of Skyros to prevent his going to the Trojan War. After Achilles' mother had taken her son to the island of Skyros, he remained there in hiding, dressed like a woman, among the daughters of Lycomedes, until Ulysses visited the island, disguised as a merchant, and offered women's dresses for sale, among which he had concealed some arms. The arms were eagerly seized by Achilles, who, having thus disclosed his sex, was persuaded by Ulysses to accompany him to the Greek army, which was on its way to Troy.

6. St. Lucy, who, according to the well-known legend, plucked out her eyes when they were admired by a noble suitor. They were then restored to her more beautiful than before, and she became thereby the special patroness of those who suffer from ailments of the eyes.

7. Lucy vanishes as suddenly and mysteriously as she appeared.

8. Since this is the threshold of the entrance to Purgatory, upon which the vicar of Peter sits as the symbol of ecclesiastical authority, "pietra" here brings to mind Christ's words to Peter (Matt. 16:18): "Thou art Peter, and upon this rock I will build my Church."

9. The seven P's (from the Latin *peccatum*, "sin") stand for the sins that are somehow to be purged on the seven terraces of Purgatory.

10. Tarpeia, the Tarpeian Rock (Tarpeius mons) at Rome on which, in the temple of Saturn, was placed

the Roman treasury. The reference is to the violation of the treasury by Julius Caesar in 49 B.C. after the vain attempt of the tribune Metellus, an adherent of Pompey, to defend it.

11. *Te Deum laudamus:* A hymn which has been traditionally ascribed to Ambrose and Augustine, who were said to have uttered it extemporaneously on the occasion of the latter's baptism, but it is now thought to have been composed in the early fifth century by Nicetas.

CANTO X

1. Polycletus was a celebrated Greek sculptor (*ca.* 452–412 B.C.), a contemporary of Phidias, but somewhat younger.

2. Nature looks up to the eternal ideas of God in practicing her art, and the human artist looks to Nature in practicing his (thus human art is as grandchild to God, as stated in *Inf.* XI).

3. The first *intaglio* represents the familiar scene of the angel Gabriel's announcement of the Incarnation to the Virgin Mary.

4. With Adam's sin, the door to Heaven was closed to mankind. Those who were one day to enter Heaven went to Limbo, there to await the Redeemer (see *Inf.* IV). This was the long "ban."

5. Heaven was "opened" at the Annunciation; hence Mary can be said to have turned the key that opened God's love, which then descended to mankind.

6. "Behold the handmaid of the Lord!" Luke, 1:38.

7. The second of the "images of humilities so great" shows King David, "the humble Psalmist," dancing before the ark of the covenant.

8. The reference is to Uzzah (Oza), one of the sons of Abinadab, in whose house the ark had rested for twenty years. Uzzah and his brother Ahio accompanied the ark when David undertook its removal to Jerusalem. On the way, the oxen of the cart in which it was being borne stumbled, and Uzzah, who was walking by the side, put out his hand and steadied the ark to prevent its falling, whereupon for his presumption and profanation he was struck dead.

9. Gregory I, the saint, called Gregory the Great, was born in Rome, of a noble family, *ca.* 540 and was pope from 590 to 604. The legend, alluded to by Dante (here and in *Par.* XX), that the Emperor Trajan was recalled to life from Hell, through the intercession of Gregory the Great, in order that he might have room for repentance, was widely believed in the Middle Ages.

CANTO XI

1. The "first works" of God, are the angels and the heavens.

2. The speaker is Omberto Aldobrandeschi, the second son of Guglielmo and lord of the stronghold of Campagnatico, one of the many fortified castles of the Aldobrandeschi. The Sienese, with whom the Aldobrandeschi were constantly at war, sent an expedition against Omberto in 1259, and Omberto was slain.

3. Count of Santafiora in the Sienese Maremma. Owing to his animosity against the Sienese, Guglielmo apparently abandoned the Ghibelline principles of his house and allied himself with the Florentines and Tuscan Guelphs.

4. The Aldobrandeschi were an ancient and powerful Ghibelline family, counts of Santafiora in the Sienese Maremma, where they had been settled since the ninth century.

5. Mother earth, to which we all return at death.

6. Oderigi or Oderisi da Gubbio, miniature-painter and illuminator of whom little is known.

7. Gubbio, town of central Italy on the slopes of the Apennines in northern Umbria, about twenty miles northeast of Perugia.

8. Very little is known of this Franco of Bologna. It would appear from this reference to him that he was still living in 1300.

9. Cenni di Pepo, known as Giovanni Cimabue, the great Florentine painter and mosaicist and master of Giotto, commonly regarded because of his departure from the Byzantine tradition as the regenerator of painting in Italy. He was born *ca.* 1240 and died, not in 1300, as Vasari states in his *Life* of Cimabue, but probably *ca.* 1302.

10. This shade is Provenzan Salvani, a prominent Ghibelline of Siena who was born *ca.* 1220.

11. Siena was a republic, and Provenzan was a private citizen, but he had become chief in authority.

12. The reference is to the battle of Montaperti, disastrous defeat for the Florentines (see *Inf.* X).

CANTO XII

1. Thymbraeus, epithet of Apollo, derived from Thymbra in the Troad, where there was a celebrated temple dedicated to him.

2. Pallas, surname of the Greek goddess Athena, whom the Romans identified with Minerva.

3. The giants of mythology, who, according to Hesiod, were said to have sprung from the blood that fell from Heaven (Uranus) upon the earth, whence Earth (Gaea) was regarded as their mother. They made an attack upon Olympus, the abode of the gods, armed with huge rocks and trunks of trees, but the gods with the aid of Hercules destroyed them all and buried them under Etna and other volcanoes.

4. Nimrod, who according to Gen. 10:8–9 was the son of Cush, was commonly supposed to have been the builder of the Tower of Babel, on the plain of Shinar.

5. Niobe was the daughter of Tantalus and Dione and the wife of Amphion, king of Thebes. Being proud of the number of her children, she boasted herself superior to Latona, who had only two, Apollo and Diana, whereupon Latona persuaded Apollo and Diana to slay with their arrows Niobe's seven sons and seven daughters. Although Niobe was transformed into stone and carried away to her native Mount Sipylus in Lydia, tears continued forever to trickle down her marble cheeks.

6. Saul, the son of Kish of the tribe of Benjamin, was the first king of Israel.

7. Gilboa, mountain in Samaria.

8. Arachne (i.e., "spider") was the daughter of Idmon of Colophon, a dyer in purple. She excelled in the art of weaving and, proud of her skill, ventured to challenge Minerva to compete with her. Arachne produced a piece of cloth in which the amours of the gods were woven; and Minerva, unable to find fault with it, tore it in pieces. In despair Arachne hanged herself, but the goddess loosened the rope and saved her life, the rope being changed into a cobweb, and Arachne herself into a spider.

9. Rehoboam was the son of Solomon by the Ammonite princess Naamah. He succeeded his father as king of Israel, but, owing to his haughty refusal of the demand of the people for a remission of the heavy burdens imposed by Solomon, ten of the tribes revolted from him and acknowledged Jeroboam as their king, Judah and Benjamin alone remaining faithful to Rehoboam, who fled to Jerusalem.

10. Alcmaeon was the son of Amphiaraus the seer and Eriphyle. Amphiaraus, foreseeing that the expedition against Thebes would prove fatal to him, concealed himself in order to avoid joining it; but his wife Eriphyle, bribed by Polynices with the necklace of Harmonia, re-

vealed his hiding-place, so that he went and met his death. Before he left Argos, however, he had enjoined Alcmaeon to slay Eriphyle in punishment for her betrayal of him; accordingly, Alcmaeon put his mother to death.

11. Sennacherib, king of Assyria from 705 to 681 B.C., was the son of Sargon, whom he succeeded.

12. Tomyris (or Thamyris) was queen of the Massagetae, a Scythian people, by whom Cyrus was defeated and slain in 529 B.C. Tomyris had Cyrus' head cut off and thrown into a skin of human blood, and she mocked it, because she had treacherously slain her son.

13. Holofernes was the general of the armies of Nebuchadnezzar, king of the Assyrians, and was slain by Judith.

14. Eve was the first to sin in pride (Gen. 3:5–6). She was often opposed to Mary, in her humility, and the *Ave* spoken by Gabriel was read in reverse as *Eva*.

15. The reference here is to the church of San Miniato al Monte, which dates mainly from the eleventh century and is situated on a hill, the Monte alle Croci, to the east of Florence beyond the Arno just above the bridge formerly known as the Rubaconte.

16. That is, Florence. This is said in bitter irony.

17. This is an allusion to an incident involving one Niccola Acciaiuoli, a Florentine Guelph who, in 1299, together with Baldo d'Aguglione (*Par.* XVI), in order to destroy the evidence of a fraudulent transaction in which, with the connivance of the *podestà*, he had been engaged, defaced a sheet of the public records of Florence.

18. This is the first of the beautitudes of the Sermon on the Mount (Matt. 5:3) and the antithesis of pride.

19. We now understand from Virgil's explanation how the P's which were inscribed on Dante's forehead (*Purg.* IX) will be removed. In a token sort of way, Dante has now purged himself of pride, and the removal of the P registers that fact.

CANTO XIII

1. The metaphor anticipates the "vinum non habent" ("They have no wine," John 2:3) of Mary's words at the table, as it were, of the wedding feast of Cana, the first example of charity.

2. When Orestes, the son of Agamemnon and Clytemnestra, was in danger of being slain for having avenged the murder of his father, his friend Pylades pretended that he was Orestes in order to save his life. Orestes, however, would not allow Pylades to risk his life for him and persisted in declaring who he was.

3. In Dante's time it was a familiar sight to see the blind begging at churches and shrines on the days when crowds gathered for special indulgences (pardons) granted to the faithful. Fairs, also attracting many people, were held in these places on those occasions.

4. Sienese lady of the Salvani family, aunt of Provenzan Salvani, and wife of Ghinibaldo Saracini.

5. Town (modern Colle di Val d'Elsa) in Tuscany, in the Val d'Elsa, situated on a hill near San Gimignano, on the left bank of the Elsa, about fourteen miles northwest of Siena. It was the scene of a battle (June 17, 1269) in which the Sienese Ghibellines, with a mixed force of Germans and Spaniards, under Provenzan Salvani and Count Guido Novello, were defeated by the Florentine Guelphs with the help of some of the French troops of Charles of Anjou.

6. Peter the comb-maker (or comb-seller) was a native of Campi in the Chianti district northeast of Siena. According to the commentators he was a hermit of the Franciscan order and dwelt in Siena, where he was renowned for his piety and miracles.

7. Small seaport on the Tyrrhenian Sea, situated on a promontory in the southwestern extremity of the Sienese Maremma, in Tuscany, about ten miles southeast of the mouth of the Ombrone.

8. The name of a river which the Sienese believed to exist beneath their city and in the search for which they spent large sums of money.

CANTO XIV

1. These words are spoken by Guido del Duca and answered by Rinieri da Calboli; both of them men of note in the Romagna during the thirteenth century. Guido was a Ghibelline, Rinieri a Guelph.

2. The Arno is a great river, for Dante and all Tuscans, since it is the principal river of Tuscany, which, rising among the spurs of Monte Falterona in the Apennines, flows southeast through the Casentino, past Poppi, Bibbiena, Rassina, and Subbiano, to within four or five miles of Arezzo, where it makes a sudden sweep away to the northwest.

3. The entire range of the Apennines viewed as one chain. Pelorus (modern Punta del Faro or Cape Faro) is the promontory at the northeastern extremity of Sicily.

4. The enchantress Circe, daughter of Helios, god of the Sun, and Perse.

5. The inhabitants of Arezzo.

6. As the river swells, the little dogs, the Aretines, become wolves, i.e., the Florentines.

7. We learn that the soul being addressed, to whom the following prophecy will cause grief, is Rinieri da Calboli. Rinieri's grandson, here referred to, is the degenerate and corrupt Fulcieri da Calboli, who was *podestà* of Florence in 1303, after the return of the Neri through the influence of Charles of Valois, and he proved himself a bitter foe of the Bianchi.

8. Gentleman of Bertinoro. Our information concerning Guido del Duca is uncertain. He may have been the son of Giovanni del Duca of the Onesti family of Ravenna, who had settled in Bertinoro.

9. Rinieri de' Paolucci da Calboli (pronounced Càlboli), member of an illustrious Guelph family of Forlì, was born probably at the beginning of the thirteenth century and was *podestà* of Faenza in 1247, of Parma in 1252, and of Ravenna in 1265 (the year of Dante's birth).

10. This is a reference to Romagna, a former province of northern Italy, corresponding roughly to the eastern portion of the modern Emilia.

11. Lizio da Valbona, nobleman of Romagna, was born in the first half of the thirteenth century and was a contemporary of Rinieri. Arrigo Mainardi, or Manardi, was a gentleman of Bertinoro. Little is known of him beyond the fact that he was a contemporary of Guido del Duca and Pier Traversaro and that he was taken prisoner with the latter by the Faentines in 1170.

12. Member of the powerful Traversari family of Ravenna, Piero was born *ca.* 1145 and died, at the age of 80, in 1225. The Carpigna family, who boasted descent from one of the comrades of Odoacer (the Herulian king who extinguished the Roman Empire in the West, A.D. 476, and called himself king of Italy), appear to have been established in Romagna in the neighborhood of Montefeltro as early as the tenth century. Two members of the family bore the name of Guido, of whom the elder was already dead in 1221, while the younger, who was grandson of the other, died toward the end of the thirteenth century.

13. The reference is to Fabbro de' Lambertazzi, Ghibelline of Bologna. Benvenuto, who was well acquainted with Bologna, and who takes this opportunity of singing its praises.

14. This Bernardo, son of Fosco, of Faenza, is said by

the early commentators to have been of humble origin, but to have so distinguished himself as to be received on terms of equality by the nobles of his native city.

15. Lana and several other early commentators state that Guido was a native of Forlì, while the *Ottimo Commento* and others make him a native of Prata, a village near Faenza.

16. Probably Ugolino degli Ubaldini, son of Azzo degli Ubaldini da Senno, a member of the powerful Tuscan family of that name.

17. A noble of Rimini.

18. The Traversari family, powerful Ghibelline house of Ravenna, where they first came into prominence about the middle of the tenth century.

19. Noble Ghibelline family of Ravenna, next in importance to the Polentani and Traversari.

20. Now Bertinoro, small town in Romagna.

21. Bagnacavallo, town in Romagna.

22. Formerly a strong castle, now a village, in Romagna.

23. Cunio, castle in Romagna, near Imola, now totally destroyed.

24. The Pagani, noble Ghibelline family of Faenza.

25. Maghinardo (or Mainardo) Pagano da Susinana, head of the Pagani family in Dante's time.

26. Ugolino de' Fantolini, gentleman of Faenza.

27. Aglauros was the daughter of Cecrops, king of Athens. According to one legend, she was changed into a stone by Mercury, because she through envy tried to prevent him from visiting her sister Herse, whom he loved.

CANTO XV

1. The fifth beatitude of the Sermon on the Mount.

2. The Empyrean is a heaven of fire, the fire being love. The Empyrean is called a cloister perhaps because perfect charity is the model of what a cloister ought to be.

3. The reference is to the contest between the Greek goddess Athena and Poseidon as to who should give a name to the capital of Cecropia, the original name of Athens.

4. The third ecstatic vision is of the stoning of St. Stephen, protomartyr, who was slain outside the gates of Jerusalem by the Jews on a charge of blasphemy.

CANTO XVI

1. The voices are reciting, perhaps chanting, the "Agnus Dei," a prayer in the sacrifice of the Mass. Addressed to the "Agnus Dei" ("Lamb of God"), it implores the mercy and peace of God.

2. Paul was caught up to Heaven and saw God's "court," and other contemplatives also had that experience in some measure, as the reader will learn in *Paradiso*.

3. Marco was a Lombard (or Venetian) gentleman.

4. Rome "made the good world" by bringing it to universal peace and justice under Augustus.

5. This, in a general way, designates Lombardy, which, in the old sense, meant most of northern Italy, that part specifically referred to as watered by the Adige being the March of Treviso (Marca Trevigiana or Marca Trivigiana).

6. In the struggle of the papacy against Frederick II, last of the emperors according to Dante, the papacy took up the sword, which it should not have done.

7. Corrado, a member of an old family of Brescia, was a Guelph and acted as vicar for Charles of Anjou in Florence in 1276.

8. The son of Biaquino da Camino and India da Camposampiero, Gherardo was born *ca.* 1240. He was a citizen

of Padua and held vast estates around Belluno and Cadore, was captain of Belluno and Feltre, and in 1283 became captain-general of Treviso, an office he held until his death in March 1306.

9. A gentleman of Reggio nell'Emilia, Guido was born in 1235 and was still living in 1315.

10. The Church has confounded (that is, confused in the sense of fused) two rules by usurping that of the emperor, and this is too great a burden for her, so that she falls in the mire and sullies not only herself (i.e., in her own proper function) but also the burden of temporal guidance which she has taken on.

11. The Levites, members of the tribe of Levi, served as subordinate ministers of the temple and are often spoken of as priests, although, strictly speaking, they were distinct from the "sons of Aaron," who were priests.

12. Gaia was the daughter of Gherardo da Camino by his second wife, Chiara della Torre of Milan, and sister of Rizzardo (*Par.* IX).

CANTO XVII

1. The first of three examples of wrath and its punishment, which correspond to the examples of pride and envy of the two preceding terraces, is that of Procne, daughter of King Pandion of Athens, wife of Tereus, and sister of Philomela.

2. The second example of wrath and its punishment is that of Haman (Aman), chief minister of Ahasuerus, who was enraged that the Jew Mordecai did not bow down to him and obtained from Ahasuerus a decree that all the Jews in the Persian Empire should be put to death. After the failure of this attempt to compass the destruction of the Jews, Haman, through the intervention of Esther and Mordecai, was hanged on the gibbet he had prepared for Mordecai.

3. For the third example of wrath and its ill consequences, Dante returns to a non-biblical case, in the usual alternation. Amata, wife of Latinus and mother of Lavinia, believing mistakenly that Turnus, to whom Lavinia had been betrothed, had been killed in battle, hanged herself in fury and despair, fearing that Lavinia would then marry Aeneas, a match to which Amata was opposed.

4. See Matt. 5:9: "Blessed are the peacemakers, for they shall be called children of God."

5. The sin ("offense") of sloth.

6. There are two kinds of love, however, natural and elective.

7. Elective love can err, since it involves choice, as natural love does not. Natural love is of the end, but elective love is of the means to the end.

8. The three modes of the love of evil manifest themselves in the sins of pride, envy, and anger, and each has an evil object, which is harm to one's neighbor.

CANTO XVIII

1. This village, now known as Pietole, is about three miles south of Mantua and is commonly identified with the ancient Andes, the birthplace of Virgil.

2. The reference is to the famous Bacchic orgies, invoking the god. Ismenus and Asopus are small rivers of Boeotia; the first flows through Thebes, the second near the city. According to tradition Thebes was the birthplace of Bacchus, whose mother, Semele, was a Theban.

3. On his way to Lérida (ancient Ilerda) in Catalonia in Spain, Caesar besieged Marseilles and then left part of his army there under Brutus to complete the task and hurried on.

4. Nothing is actually known of this abbot, though he has been identified with a certain Gherardo II, who was

abbot of the church of San Zeno in Verona in the time of the Emperor Frederick I and who died in 1187.

5. Milan was destroyed by the Emperor Frederick Barbarossa in 1162.

6. The veiled reference is to Alberto della Scala, who was an old man in 1300, the fictional date of this encounter, and died on September 10, 1301. Besides Giuseppe, the illegitimate son now referred to, whose tenure of the abbacy of San Zeno (1292–1313) coincided in part with Dante's sojourn at Verona, he had three legitimate sons who succeeded him one after the other in the lordship of Verona, among whom was Can Grande, Dante's host at Verona.

7. Giuseppe was born in 1263 and died in 1313.

8. The Israelites, who were sluggish and recalcitrant in crossing the desert after the Lord had caused the waters of the Red Sea to divide so that they marched across it as on dry land, while the Egyptians perished in it.

CANTO XIX

1. The reference is to the natural cold of the earth and the cold that was believed to be shed by the planet Saturn.

2. Geomancy is the art of divination by means of figures constructed on points set down at random, which can then be seen to correspond to the configuration of certain stars. One of these figures, called *fortuna maior* ("greater fortune"), is based on the last stars of Aquarius and the first of Pisces, constellations that would be seen in the east, in the northern hemisphere as well as the southern, just before sunrise at the time of Dante's journey, since they immediately precede Aries, in which the sun appears at this time of the year (see *Inf.* I).

3. This woman, symbolizing the sins of the flesh, the *malo amor* that is purged in the three upper circles of Purgatory, could not be more ugly or deformed than this tercet suggests, defective as she is in speech and vision, lame, her hands maimed, her complexion sickly pale.

4. Dante did not know the *Odyssey* directly and so may not have known that the hero, in Homer's account, resisted the Sirens by having himself tied to the mast.

5. "They that mourn." Cf. Matt. 5:5[4]: "Blessed are they who mourn, for they shall be comforted." The beatitude here applies to those who have purged themselves of the sin of sloth.

6. God whirls the great wheels of the heavens to call us up there, even as the falconer whirls a lure to call the falcon down.

7. The soul who speaks assumes that the "souls" who have asked the way to the exit are newly arrived on this terrace (otherwise they would know where the stairway is) and that they do not have to remain there, but may proceed at once on their upward way. This is the first glimpse we have of the fact that this can happen in Purgatory.

8. "Know that I was a successor of Peter." This soul, who was a pope, appropriately declares that fact in the language of the Church. This is Adrian V, who was elected pope, in succession to Innocent V, on July 11, 1276, and died at Viterbo thirty-eight days later on August 18 before he had been crowned. No historical evidence has been found to bear out either Pope Adrian's avarice or his conversion in so brief a time in office.

9. Sestri Levante (so called to distinguish it from Sestri Ponente, a few miles west of Genoa) and Chiavari (formerly also Chiaveri), pronounced Chiàvari, are towns in Liguria on the Riviera di Levante east-southeast of Genoa.

10. The beautiful river (actually a *torrente* which is dry part of the year) is the Lavagna, which falls into the Gulf of Genoa between the two towns named.

11. In the papal chair, the supreme office. The promise of the Siren is false, for she does not quiet the heart as she claims to do.

12. Alagia de' Fieschi was the daughter of Niccolò de' Fieschi, imperial vicar in Italy, the niece of Pope Adrian V, and the wife of Dante's friend Moroello Malaspina, by whom she had three sons.

CANTO XX

1. As usual, Mary serves as the first example of the virtue that opposes the vice in question, in this case exemplifying the largess that opposes avarice.

2. The usual alternation between a biblical and non-biblical example is now observed, the second example of largess being Gaius Fabricius Luscinus, famous Roman hero, consul in 282 and 278 B.C., and censor in 275. During the invasion of Italy by Pyrrhus, king of Epirus, he was sent to the latter to negotiate an exchange of prisoners. Pyrrhus used every effort, including rare gifts, to gain him over, but Fabricius refused all his offers.

3. The third example of largess, the proper and laudable use of riches, as opposed to the ways of grasping avarice, is Nicholas, bishop of Myra in Lycia, Asia Minor, who is supposed to have lived in the fourth century under Constantine and to have been present at the Council of Nicaea (325). He is venerated as a saint by both the Greek and Roman Churches and is regarded as the patron saint of Russia and of virgins, sailors, travelers, merchants, thieves, and (as Santa Claus) of children.

4. Flanders is now indicated by this mention of Douai, Lille, Ghent, and Bruges, four of its principal cities. In 1297, Guy of Dampierre, count of Flanders, having by his alliance with Edward I of England excited the suspicions of Philip the Fair of France, was decoyed by the latter under a lying pretext to Corbeil, where he was kept prisoner until he had sworn to renounce all communication with Edward. No sooner, however, did Guy regain his liberty than he broke his oath. Philip thereupon proceeded to make war upon him, and sent his brother, Charles of Valois, into Flanders to subject the country. Guy, having been abandoned by his ally, the king of England, who through the mediation of Boniface VIII had made peace with Philip (March 1298), was compelled to come to terms with Charles.

5. The statements put by Dante into the mouth of Hugh Capet as to the origin of the Capetian dynasty are in several respects at variance with the historical facts and can be explained only on the supposition that Dante (as common tradition before him) has confused Hugh Capet with his father, Hugh the Great.

6. The kings of France and of the Capetian line who bore the name of Philip and Louis.

7. The Carolingians. Perhaps, owing to Dante's having confused the last of that line with the last of the Merovingians, it is the latter who are meant.

8. Charles, duke of Lorraine, son of Louis IV, who was king of France from 936 to 954, and brother of Lothair, who reigned from 954 to 986.

9. On the division of the Carolingian empire in 843, Provence fell to Lothair, who left it with the title of king to his son Charles (855). It afterwards became a part of the kingdom of Arles as a feudal fief and was reunited to the Empire in 1033 by Conrad II; but the union remained almost nominal, the counts of Provence claiming to be independent. In 1246, through the marriage of Charles of Anjou, brother of Louis IX of France, with Beatrice, heiress of Raymond Berenger IV of Provence, Provence became a dependency of the royal house of France, and it remained in the possession of the house of Anjou until

1486, when it was formally annexed to the French crown by Charles VIII.

10. Ponthieu, former district of France, consisting of a "county," and comprising part of the province of Picardy, is included in the modern department of Somme and was situated at the mouth of the river of that name, with Abbeville for its capital. It belonged to the English crown, having been ceded to Edward I by Philip III in 1279.

11. Normandy, ancient duchy in the north of France. Gascony, a historical region in southwest France.

12. Charles of Anjou, having been invited by Urban IV to assume the crown of Naples and Sicily, in response to the entreaties of the new pope, Clement IV, came into Italy in 1265 and in little more than three years, by his defeat of Manfred at Benevento (February 26, 1266) and of Conradin at Tagliacozzo (August 23, 1268), completely and finally crushed the power of the Hohenstaufen in Italy.

13. Conradin, son of the Emperor Conrad IV, was the last legitimate representative of the Swabian line and the last scion of the Hohenstaufen line.

14. The Thomas referred to by Dante here is Thomas Aquinas.

15. This other Charles is Charles of Valois, who was born in 1270 and died in 1325, the third son of Philip III of France (by his wife Isabella of Aragon). Charles was summoned to Italy by Boniface VIII for the twofold purpose of helping Charles II of Naples in his war against Frederick II of Sicily in Sicily and of making peace between the contending factions of the Bianchi and Neri in Tuscany.

16. Yet another Charles. This one, Charles II, king of Naples, was born in 1248, the son of Charles of Anjou. After the Sicilian Vespers (in 1282) Charles, who was then prince of Salerno, set out from Provence to join his father in his attempt to recover the island of Sicily and was entrusted by him with the command of the fleet at Naples, but with strict injunctions not to engage the enemy. Incensed, however, by the taunts of the Sicilian admiral, Ruggiero di Loria, who was in command of the fleet of Pedro III of Aragon, Charles came out and attacked him, but was totally defeated (June 1284) and himself taken prisoner on board his ship and conveyed to Sicily.

17. Beatrice, youngest daughter of Charles II of Naples, was married in 1305 to Azzo VIII, marquis of Este, in consideration, it was said, of a large sum of money.

18. Anagni, town in Latium, situated on a hill about forty miles southeast of Rome, was celebrated as the birthplace of Pope Boniface VIII and as the scene of his imprisonment by Philip the Fair of France.

19. The reference is to the persecution and destruction of the Knights Templars by Philip. The Knights Templars were one of the three great military orders founded in the twelfth century for the defense of the Latin kingdom of Jerusalem (the other two being the Knights Hospitalers or Knights of St. John, and the Teutonic Knights).

20. Pygmalion was the son of Belus, king of Tyre, whom he succeeded, and brother of Dido, whose husband, Sichaeus, he murdered for the sake of his wealth. Dido, being made aware of the murder by the appearance of Sichaeus to her in a dream, secretly sailed from Tyre with the treasure and landed in Africa, where she founded the city of Carthage.

21. Midas, a king of Phrygia, who, in return for his kindness to Silenus, the companion and instructor of Bacchus, was allowed by Bacchus to make a request of him, which the god promised to grant. Midas, in his greed for wealth, desired that everything he touched should be turned to gold. Bacchus fulfilled his desire, but Midas, finding that even the food which he touched turned to gold, soon implored him to take his favor back.

22. Achan, son of Carmi, of the tribe of Judah, who took goods that were under the ban in appropriating part of the spoil of Jericho, contrary to the commands of Joshua. After the defeat of the Israelites in their attack on Ai, Achan confessed his guilt, and the booty was discovered. Thereupon he and his whole family were stoned to death by command of Joshua, and their remains and property were burned.

23. Ananias, a disciple at Jerusalem, and his wife Sapphira, having sold their goods for the benefit of the Church, kept back part of the price, bringing the remainder to the apostles, as if it had been the whole. Being rebuked by Peter for their hypocrisy, they both fell dead at his feet.

24. Heliodorus, treasurer of Seleucus IV Philopator, king of Syria (187–175 B.C.), by whom he was commissioned to remove the treasures from the temple at Jerusalem.

25. Just before Troy fell into the hands of the Greeks, Priam entrusted his son Polydorus, with a large sum of money, to Polymestor, a Thracian king; but after the destruction of Troy, Polymestor killed his ward for the sake of the treasure and cast his body into the sea.

26. Marcus Licinius Crassus, surnamed Dives ("the wealthy"), was born ca. 112 B.C. and was consul with Pompey in 70 B.C. and triumvir with Caesar and Pompey in 60. His ruling passion was the love of money, which he set himself to accumulate by every possible means.

27. The island of Delos, smallest of the Cyclades, was said to have been raised from the deep by Neptune, but it was a floating island until, according to one version, Jupiter fixed it with adamantine chains to the bottom of the sea in order that Latona might have a refuge from the wrath of Juno. Here Latona gave birth to Apollo and Diana (hence their epithets Delius and Delia), her offspring by Jupiter.

CANTO XXI

1. Aristotle states that all men naturally desire to know.

2. The mountain of Purgatory is God's stairway: it leads to Him.

3. The reference is to Lachesis, the second of the three Fates, on to whose distaff Clotho, the first of the Fates, was supposed to place a certain quantity of wool at the birth of every mortal, the length of time it took to spin being the duration of the individual's life.

4. The reference is to Iris, the daughter of Thaumas and Electra and the personification of the rainbow, which, since it is always opposite the sun, is seen in many different quarters of the sky.

5. The soul is the Roman poet Statius, as it will soon declare. Publius Papinius Statius, who was born in Naples ca. A.D. 45 and died ca. A.D. 96, was the most eminent poet of the Silver Age of Latin literature.

6. Titus, son and successor of Vespasian, was Roman Emperor from A.D. 79 to A.D. 81. He served under his father in the Jewish wars, and when Vespasian was proclaimed emperor and returned to Italy in 70, he remained in Palestine in order to carry on the siege of Jerusalem, which he captured, after a siege of several months, in September of that year.

CANTO XXII

1. That is, the Angel had not recited all the words of the Beatitude, which are as follows in the Vulgate: *Beati qui esuriunt et sitiunt justitiam: quoniam ipsi saturabuntur.* He had omitted *esuriunt,* and said only, "Blessed are they which do *thirst* after righteousness."

2. Juvenal (Decimus Junius Juvenalis), the great Roman satirist, was born probably (ca. A.D. 60) in the reign of

Nero (A.D. 54–68) and died (ca. A.D. 140) in the reign of Antoninus Pius (A.D. 138–61).

3. These verses from the *Aeneid* concern the episode involving the tomb of Polydorus (already referred to by Dante in *Inf.* XIII) where the cruel murder for gold of the youth by Polymestor is remembered (cf. *Purg.* XX). Clearly, in such a context the words represent a vehement denunciation of avarice.

4. Jocasta, wife of Laius, king of Thebes, was the mother of Oedipus, whom she afterwards married without knowing his true identity and by whom she became the mother of Eteocles and Polynices (as well as of Antigone and Ismene, mentioned below). The fratricidal strife of Polynices and Eteocles, culminating in their killing each other in single combat during the war of the Seven against Thebes, was their mother's double sorrow.

5. Clio, the Muse of History.

6. The time of paganism was commonly called a time of darkness.

7. Peter, first a fisherman, then a fisher of men.

8. Parnassus (modern Liákoura), mountain of about 8,060 feet in Greece, north of the Gulf of Corinth and about 83 miles northwest of Athens. Mount Parnassus was sacred to Apollo and the Muses.

9. Domitian (Titus Flavius Domitianus Augustus), third of the Flavian emperors of Rome, second son of Vespasian, and successor of his brother, Titus, was born at Rome in A.D. 51, became emperor in 81, and was murdered in 96. Among the many crimes imputed to him was relentless persecution of the Christians.

10. Terence (Publius Terentius Afer), celebrated Roman comic poet, was born at Carthage ca. 195 B.C. and died in Greece in 159 B.C.

11. Caecilius Statius, Roman comic poet, contemporary of Ennius and immediate predecessor of Terence.

12. Plautus (Titus Maccius Plautus), the Roman comic playwright, was born at Sarsina in Umbria ca. 250 B.C. and died in 184 B.C.

13. Lucius Varius Rufus, Roman poet of the Augustan age, intimate friend of both Virgil and Horace and one of the editors of the *Aeneid* after the death of the author.

14. Persius (Aulus Persius Flaccus), Roman satirist, lived from A.D. 34 to A.D. 62.

15. Euripides, Greek playwright, was probably born in 485 B.C.; he died in 406. Eighteen of his tragedies in more or less complete form and fragments of about sixty others are extant.

16. Antiphon, Greek tragic poet. Plutarch includes him among the greatest of the tragic authors.

17. Simonides, Greek lyric poet who lived from ca. 556 B.C. to 467 B.C.

18. Agathon, Greek tragic poet, was born ca. 448 B.C. and died ca. 402.

19. Antigone, daughter of Oedipus and Jocasta. Deipyle was the daughter of Adrastus, king of Argos, and sister of Argia, wife of Polynices of Thebes, from whom she received the fatal necklace of Harmonia, with which Eriphyle was bribed to betray the hiding-place of her husband, Amphiaraus (see *Purg.* XII).

20. Ismene, daughter of Oedipus and Jocasta, is here spoken of as being "sad still as she was" on account of the terrible tragedies she witnessed—the violent death of her betrothed, the blinding of her father, Oedipus, by his own hand, the suicide of her mother, Jocasta, the deaths at each other's hands of her brothers, Eteocles and Polynices, and the total ruin and downfall of her father's kingdom.

21. Hypsipyle, daughter of Thoas, king of Lemnos (she is mentioned in *Inf.* XVIII). Langia was a fountain near Nemea in the Peloponnesus, to which Hypsipyle conducted Adrastus and his companions; during her absence

on this errand her charge, Archemorus, son of Lycurgus, king of Nemea, whom she had laid on the grass, was attacked and slain by a serpent, whereupon Lycurgus determined to put her to death, but was prevented by the opportune arrival of her two sons.

22. The only daughter of Tiresias who is mentioned in the *Thebaid*, Manto, was placed by Dante among the soothsayers in the fourth *bolgia* of the eighth circle of Hell, but by an oversight the poet here mentions her as being among those who are in Limbo. Many attempts have been made to exculpate Dante from this momentary nodding, which is unique in the entire poem, in fact, but none has proved persuasive. Thetis, one of the Nereids, daughter of Nereus and Doris, was wedded to Peleus, by whom she became the mother of Achilles and as such is frequently mentioned in the *Achilleid*.

23. Deidamia was the daughter of Lycomedes, king of Skyros, with whom Thetis left her son Achilles. Achilles remained hidden, dressed like a woman, among the several daughters of Lycomedes, until Ulysses persuaded him to accompany him to Troy.

CANTO XXIII

1. These words are from the Miserere (Ps. 50 [51]), which souls in Antepurgatory were singing (*Purg.* V). ("O Lord, open my lips, and my mouth shall proclaim your praise.")

2. Erysichthon was the son of the Thessalian King Triopas. Having cut down trees in a grove sacred to Ceres, he was afflicted by the goddess with a fearful hunger, which drove him finally to devour his own flesh.

3. According to Flavius Josephus, during the siege of Jerusalem by Titus a certain Jewess named Mary was driven by famine to kill and eat her own infant son.

4. There was a belief popular in Dante's time that the word *omo* (i.e., *homo,* "man") could be seen in a human face, the eyes forming the two o's, and the nose and outline of the eye sockets forming the *m*; it was also believed that *dei* ("of God") could be seen there.

5. Forese Donati, who was nicknamed Bicci Novello, was a contemporary and friend of Dante.

6. A mountainous district in the central part of Sardinia, the inhabitants of which are said to have descended from a settlement of prisoners planted by the Vandals. They were proverbial in the Middle Ages, according to the early commentators, for the laxity of their morals and their loose living.

CANTO XXIV

1. Dante will meet Piccarda, the sister of Forese, in the heaven of the moon (*Par.* III), among those who failed to keep their religious vows.

2. Bonagiunta Orbicciani degli Overardi, the son of Perfetto di Orbicciano of Lucca, was a notary and poet of the latter half of the thirteenth century.

3. This pope is not named, but is easily recognized as Martin IV (Simon de Brie or Brion), who was born ca. 1210 and was a native of Montpincé in Brie.

4. Lake Bolsena, in Latium, a few miles north-northwest of Viterbo, is one of the largest lakes in central Italy.

5. Ubaldino degli Ubaldini dalla Pila (La Pila is a castle in the Mugello, or upper valley of the Sieve, a tributary of the Arno, north of Florence) was a member of the powerful Ghibelline family of the Ubaldini, to which belonged the famous Cardinal Ottaviano degli Ubaldini (mentioned in *Inf.* X) and Ugolino d'Azzo (see *Purg.* XIV). Ubaldino was the father of Archbishop Ruggieri degli Ubaldini of Pisa (see *Inf.* XXXIII). It seems that he died in 1291.

6. A bishop who is identified by modern commenta-

tors with Bonifazio de' Fieschi of Genoa, archbishop of Ravenna from 1274 to 1295 and nephew of Innocent IV.

7. The reference to Messer Marchese here is to his having been an insatiable winebibber during his lifetime.

8. According to the most probable interpretation, Gentucca is the name of a Lucchese lady who befriended Dante in exile.

9. The first verse of the first *canzone* of the *Vita nuova,* a canzone which represents a new beginning and new style in Dante's poem to and about Beatrice.

10. Giacomo da Lentini, commonly called "the Notary," of Lentini, in Sicily. He belonged, in the first half of the thirteenth century, to the Sicilian school of poetry that flourished under the Emperor Frederick II (encountered in *Inf.* X) and his son Manfred (see *Purg.* III). Fra Guittone d'Arezzo, one of the early Italian poets, was born *ca.* 1230 at Santa Firmina, near Arezzo.

11. Corso Donati, Forese's and Piccarda's brother, who became the leader of the Neri faction in Florence.

12. I.e., dragged at the tail of a beast toward the valley of Hell. Some, taking the words literally, think Dante means that Corso was dragged to death at his horse's heels. This, however, does not agree with the account of his death given by Villani.

13. Centaurs, a mythical race of creatures, half horse and half man. With the exception of Chiron, they are said to have been the offspring of Ixion, king of the Lapithae, and Nephele, a cloud-born woman—hence Dante refers to them as "formed in the clouds."

14. The Hebrews of Gideon's army who, not being able to restrain their desire for water, "showed themselves weak at the drinking," i.e., bowed down on their knees to drink.

15. Gideon, one of the judges of Israel who delivered the Jews from the Midianites.

CANTO XXV

1. Meleager, son of Oeneus, king of Calydon in Aetolia, took part in the expedition of the Argonauts under Jason and afterwards was leader of the heroes who slew the Calydonian boar. He gave the skin of the boar to Atalanta, whom he loved, but his mother's brothers, the sons of Thestius, took it from her, whereupon Meleager in fury slew them. He thus unwittingly brought about his own death. When he was seven days old the Fates had declared that his life would last as long as the piece of wood which was burning on the hearth should remain unconsumed. His mother, Althaea, hearing this, extinguished the firebrand and kept it carefully concealed; but now, to avenge the death of her brothers, she threw it into the fire and it was consumed, whereupon Meleager expired. Althaea then, in despair at what she had done, put an end to herself.

2. This wiser one is Averroës.

3. Helice or Callisto, daughter of Lycaon, king of Arcadia, was one of Diana's nymphs, but was dismissed when Diana discovered that she had been seduced by Jupiter, by whom she became the mother of Arcas.

CANTO XXVI

1. Pasiphaë became the mother of the monstrous Minotaur through intercourse with a bull, by concealing herself within a wooden cow made for her by Daedalus.

2. The Riphaean Mountains were supposed by the ancient Greeks to be a lofty range at the extreme north of the world.

3. The sands of the Libyan desert.

4. Beatrice.

5. The Empyrean is the tenth and outermost of the heavens, hence it has the largest circumference.

6. Sodomy. The reference is to an incident which is said to have taken place during one of Caesar's triumphs, when he was greeted by the crowd with shouts of "Regina," in allusion to the common belief that while in Bithynia he had committed sodomy with King Nicomedes.

7. Hermaphroditus was the son of Mercury (Hermes) and Venus (Aphrodite), as his name witnesses. Having inherited the beauty of both his parents, he excited the love of the nymph of the fountain of Salmacis, near Halicarnassus, who tried in vain to win his affections. One day as he was bathing in the fountain she embraced him and prayed to the gods that she might be united with him forever. The gods granted the request, and the bodies of the two became united together, but retained the characteristics of both sexes.

8. Guido Guinizzelli (or Guinizelli—the spelling with double *zz* is now the more commonly accepted) was the most illustrious of the Italian poets prior to Dante.

9. Lycurgus, king of Nemea, whose son Archemorus, while under the charge of Hypsipyle, was killed by a snake.

10. The practice of writing poetry in the vernacular, on which Dante wrote his treatise *De vulgari eloquentia.*

11. The spirit pointed out by Guido is Arnaut Daniel, who flourished as a poet between 1180 and *ca.* 1210 and belonged to a noble family of Ribérac in Périgord (in the modern department of Dordogne).

12. The reference is to the troubadour Giraud de Borneil, who came from the vicinity of Excideuil near Limoges.

CANTO XXVII

1. The river Ebro (the ancient Iberus) in Spain. The river Ebro is said to fall under the Scales, the constellation opposite Aries. It is midnight at the Strait of Gibraltar.

2. The concept of fire having the supernatural power of burning spiritually without burning materially connects with the flaming sword of the Cherubim placed to guard the way to the tree of life in Eden (Gen 3:24) after Adam and Eve had been expelled.

3. The two lovers Pyramus and Thisbe dwelt in adjoining houses at Babylon and used to converse together secretly through a hole in the wall, since their parents would not sanction their marriage. On one occasion they agreed to meet at the tomb of Ninus, and when Thisbe, who arrived first, was waiting for Pyramus, she perceived a lioness which had just torn in pieces an ox. In terror she fled, in her flight dropping her garment, which the lioness soiled with blood. In the meantime Pyramus came to the tomb and, finding Thisbe's garment covered with blood, supposed that she had been killed. In despair he stabbed himself at the foot of a mulberry tree.

4. The words that Christ will speak to the just souls on His right hand at the Last Judgment. See Matt. 25:34: "Then the king will say to those on his right hand, 'Come, blessed of my Father, take possession of the kingdom prepared for you from the foundation of the world.'"

5. Cytherea, epithet of Venus, who was so called from Cythera (now Cerigo), an island off the southeast coast of the Peloponnesus, near which she is said to have risen from the foam of the sea.

6. In three highly condensed tercets the prophetic (and clearly allegorical) dream is recounted. Laban's daughters Leah and Rachel, of the Old Testament, were long established allegorical figures of the active and contemplative life respectively. Leah was the first wife of Jacob; Rachel was his second wife.

7. Free will, the central subject of the *Purgatorio* (*Purg.* XVI–XVIII), is finally in the central focus at the end. Dante, who was said by Virgil at the beginning (*Purg.* I) to be seeking liberty, has now attained it. His will is free, straight (straightened), and whole again, like man's will before original sin (he having now returned to Eden, as we soon learn).

CANTO XXVIII

1. The famous pine forest that extended (as it still does) along the shore of the Adriatic for several miles near Ravenna.

2. Aeolus, god of the winds, which he was supposed to keep shut up in a mountain and release at will. He is here said to let out the sirocco, the southeast wind that blows across to Italy from the African coast.

3. Proserpina, daughter of Jupiter and Ceres, was gathering flowers in a meadow near Enna in Sicily, when Pluto suddenly appeared and carried her off to be the queen of the lower world.

4. While Venus was kissing her son Cupid, she was unintentionally wounded by him and fell madly in love with Adonis.

5. Xerxes, son of Darius, was king of Persia from 486 B.C. to 465 B.C. In the spring of 480 B.C. he set out from Sardis at the head of a countless host on his memorable expedition against Greece, crossed the Hellespont, and marched on Athens, But he was defeated, and his fleet was dispersed at the battle of Salamis, and he was obliged to retreat.

6. Leander, a youth of Abydos, used to swim across the Hellespont every night to visit Hero, the priestess of Venus at Sestos.

7. Abydos, in Asia Minor, on the narrowest part of the Hellespont, is opposite Sestos in Thrace.

8. The "primal revolution" is that of the Primum Mobile, which in its diurnal revolution sweeps the other spheres or heavens with it around the earth and at the same time causes the atmosphere to circle the earth with it.

9. While in Hell Dante asked about the location of this river and was told (*Inf.* XIV) that he would see it in Purgatory where the souls bathe when their guilt is removed.

10. From the Greek εὔνους, "well-minded," a name coined by Dante. It is said to restore the memory of good deeds (just as Lethe, which must be drunk first, takes away the memory of sinful deeds), and a draught from it will be said to be surpassingly sweet (*Purg.* XXXIII).

11. The mountain of Parnassus was sacred to Apollo and the Muses, and was celebrated as an inspiring source of poetry and song.

CANTO XXIX

1. The advent and triumph of Beatrice, which is the central event of *Purg.* XXIX, XXX, and XXXI. It is most important for the reader to understand that in broadest outline Beatrice's advent and Dante's attaining to her complete a pattern of justification so broad as to reach back, in its beginning, to the start of this journey (*Inf.* I).

2. "Blessed are they whose transgressions are forgiven." Ps. 32:1.

3. Adam and Eve, before sin, were endowed with original justice, which gave them immortality, and we, their progeny, were each to receive such a gift at birth.

4. Helicon, famous mountain range of Boeotia believed sacred to Apollo and the Muses.

5. Muse of Astronomy.

6. Surname of Diana, goddess of the Moon, who was born on the island of Delos; hence the moon.

7. The words of Gabriel to Mary are clearly echoed here. See Luke 1:28: "And when the angel had come to her, he said, 'Hail, full of grace, the Lord is with thee. Blessed art thou among women.'"

8. Argus, surnamed Panoptes ("all-seeing") because he had a hundred eyes, was, according to one account, the son of Arestor. Juno, jealous of Jupiter's love for Io, set Argus to watch over her after she had been metamorphosed into a cow, but Jupiter commanded Mercury to slay him. Mercury therefore descended to earth in the guise of a shepherd and, having beguiled Argus to sleep with stories and songs, cut off his head. Juno thereupon transplanted his eyes into the tail of her favorite bird, the peacock.

9. The griffin symbolizes Christ in His two natures, human and divine (see *Purg.* XXXI and XXXII). Isidore of Seville describes the animal, half eagle and half lion, and compares Christ both to a lion and to an eagle.

10. Publius Cornelius Scipio Aemilianus Africanus Numantinus, known as Scipio the Younger, was born *ca.* 185 B.C. and died in 129 B.C. He was the adopted son of Publius Cornelius Scipio, the son of Scipio Africanus the Elder, the conqueror of Hannibal. He took and burned Carthage, for which he was honored with a triumph at Rome and with the surname Africanus, which he had already inherited, by adoption, from the conqueror of Hannibal.

11. Augustus, the first Roman Emperor.

12. Because Phaëthon was too weak to hold the horses, they rushed out of their usual track and approached so near the Earth that they almost set her on fire. Jupiter, thereupon, in answer to the prayer of Earth, killed Phaëthon with a thunderbolt.

13. Charity, named first because she is the highest virtue of the three and the leader of the others. Fire and the color of fire further point up the fact that this is charity or love.

14. Hope, symbolized by her emerald color.

15. Faith, who is pure white.

16. This is prudence, acknowledged to be the chief of the moral virtues. The rather grotesque feature of three eyes set in her head symbolizes her vision of past, present, and future.

17. Wearing the robes of a physician, one of the men shows himself to be a follower of Hippocrates, the most famous physician of antiquity, already named as being among the virtuous pagans of Limbo (see *Inf.* IV).

CANTO XXX

1. "Come from Lebanon, my bride, come from Lebanon, come and you shall be crowned." Thus not only is the call "veni" uttered thrice in the verses of the Canticle of Canticles, as echoed here, but that call is followed there by the promise of a crowning, and this in turn enters appropriately into the figure of a triumph in which someone yet to appear is to be exalted.

2. The welcoming cry in the masculine is remarkable in view of the fact that it is Beatrice who comes. It serves, in fact, to guide the reader yet farther along the line of a deliberate ambiguity. Is it Christ who comes now? But Christ is already on the scene, in the figure of the griffin. Is it Beatrice who comes as the bride from Lebanon? Then why not "benedicta quae venis"? The cry, in any event, brings immediately to mind Christ's entry into Jerusalem on Palm Sunday and the strewing of fronds.

3. "Oh, give lilies with full hands"; words from the *Aeneid*, vi, 883.

4. Since the olive is the tree of Minerva, the goddess of wisdom, olive green may be said to be her color. Thus, when it becomes clear in the allegory that one of Beatrice's names is Sapientia, or Wisdom, the symbolism of her crown will be evident.

5. The first word Beatrice addresses to Dante is his own name. This is the more striking in that it is the only place in the poem (and, for that matter, in all Dante's works, except in certain letters and in one lyric) where his name appears.

6. Crowned with the olive. The olive was sacred to Minerva, the Greek goddess Athena, who was known as the goddess of wisdom.

7. Northeast winds blowing from Slavonia.

8. The hot regions of Africa, in which the sun is vertically overhead at times, and no shadow is cast by any object.

CANTO XXXI

1. The adjective signals the act of a sacrament which Dante is now undergoing, the act of penance.

2. Iarbas, or Hiarbas, was king of the Gaetulians in North Africa at the time Dido founded Carthage; he was among those who sued in vain for her hand.

3. This lady, whom Dante first met alone (Purg. XXVIII), has been on the scene for some time now, but still has not been named, and she is not to be named until quite near the end of this cantica (Purg. XXXIII). Her name, Matelda, leaves serious problems of interpretation, as will be noted. For the moment, it appears that it is Matelda's function to administer the water of the two streams Lethe and Eunoe to all souls reaching this summit as well as to Dante in this most exceptional case of a living man's presence here.

4. See Ps. 50:9 ("Cleanse me of sin with hyssop, that I may be purified; wash me, and I shall be whiter than snow."). The angels presumably sing this.

5. Through the mirror of Revelation Christ's two natures can be glimpsed, not *together* in one person, but alternately, now one, now the other.

6. Castalia, the spring of Parnassus.

CANTO XXXII

1. The divinities to which this reference is made are the three theological virtues.

2. Christ sets the Church in motion again, by means of the Cross, without disturbing in any way His divine (eagle) part.

3. Statius has been on the scene all the while, but his presence has been completely overlooked since the disappearance of Virgil (the last explicit notice taken of him being in Purg. XXVIII).

4. The Garden of Eden would still be inhabited by the human race, were it not for the sin of our first parents.

5. India was famous for high trees.

6. The color between red and violet is purple and signifies Christ's sacrifice.

7. The hundred eyes of Argus, the guardian of Io (cf. XXIX), were put to sleep by Mercury's song of the nymph Syrinx, loved by Pan; Mercury then slew the over-vigilant guardian.

8. In the *Paradiso* Peter, James, and John, as representatives of the three theological virtues faith, hope, and charity, conduct Dante's examination in these virtues in Heaven (Par. XXIV–XXVI).

9. The north wind and the south wind. These two winds are mentioned together here as being typically boisterous.

10. This must not be understood as a prediction that Dante is not to live a long time yet in the world.

11. Here begins the dumb show or series of tableaux enacted around the tree of justice, which prove to represent seven principal calamities that have successively befallen the Church and are an offense to God's justice as represented by the tree.

12. The harlot and the giant stand respectively for the Pope and the king of France. The dragging of the car, transformed into a monster, through the wood, so far as to hide it from the poet, may be taken as typifying the removal of the seat of the Papacy from Rome to Avignon, in 1305.

CANTO XXXIII

1. These are the opening words of Ps. 78[79].

2. With these words Beatrice joins her handmaids as if part of a chorus, as in Greek tragedy, commenting on the spectacle of the corrupted Church and particularly on the final scene, in which the giant dragged the chariot (the Church) off through the woods until it could no longer be seen. Thus, as in such choral utterances, Beatrice can speak in the first person, and she uses the prophetic words uttered by Christ to his disciples in John 16:16 and by such projection speaks for the Church, without identifying herself with it. Her prophecy, in such a focus, means that the corrupt Church will return and be saved from its corruption some day in the not too distant future.

3. Those who are chiefly to blame are Pope Clement and Philip the Fair.

4. The one who is to come will be God-sent and, as has been suggested, will be a temporal monarch. But the problem of the DXV (to put the five hundred, ten, and five into Roman numerals, as is commonly done) remains one of the most debated in Dante studies.

5. Themis was a daughter of Heaven (Uranus) and Earth (Gaea). She was regarded as a prophetic divinity and was supposed to have been Apollo's predecessor at Delphi. When Deucalion and Pyrrha asked how they were to repeople the earth after the deluge, Themis told them to cast their mother's bones behind them, the meaning being that they were to throw stones behind their backs.

6. The Sphinx was a she-monster who appeared in the neighborhood of Thebes and, seated on a rock, put a riddle to every Theban who passed by, slaying all those who could not supply the answer. The riddle—a creature with four feet has two feet and three feet and only one voice, but its feet vary, and when it has most, it is weakest—was solved by Oedipus, who replied that the creature was a man: in infancy he crawls upon all fours, in manhood he stands erect upon two feet, and in old age he supports his tottering steps with a staff. The Sphinx, on hearing the solution of the riddle, flung herself down from the rock and was killed.

7. Ovid relates that this son of Laius (Oedipus) had cleared up the riddles which had never been understood before. Dante, however, evidently read the passage in a faulty text, which substituted *Naiades* for *Laiades* and *solvunt* for *solverat,* and was thus led to believe that Naiads, or water-nymphs, were the successful guessers.

8. The Elsa is a river of Tuscany which rises in the hills to the west of Siena and, flowing northwest, joins the Arno a few miles west of Empoli.

9. In mentioning Pyramus here, the poet is referring to the change of color in the mulberry, which is said to have turned from white to crimson when Pyramus stabbed himself at the foot of a mulberry tree. Beatrice is saying that Dante's vain thoughts have stained his mind even as the blood of Pyramus stained the mulberry.

10. It was customary for a pilgrim to bring back his staff "wreathed with palm" from the Holy Land, to show where he had been and what he had seen.

11. Lethe was the traditional river of the lower world from which the shades drank and thereby were granted forgetfulness of the past.

12. River of southwest Asia, which rises in Turkey and

flows across Syria and Iraq into the Persion Gulf, after being joined by the Tigris. Of the four rivers mentioned in Genesis as being in the earthly Paradise, it is the last named (Gen. 2:10).

13. This is the only mention of Matelda's name, but it has left us with what has proved to be an insoluble problem. The historical Matelda (if Dante intended one) remains shrouded in mystery.

14. The fact that Matelda (now specifically named) has the office of drawing each and every soul that reaches the summit through the two streams of Lethe and Eunoe only compounds the mystery of her full meaning and of her (possible) historical identity! But for all the mystery surrounding her, one thing is clear: Matelda performs this office for all souls, like Statius, that are liberated from Purgatory.

PARADISO

CANTO I

1. Daphne, loved and pursued by Apollo, was changed to a laurel.

2. See Aquinas, *Summa Theologica*, Part I–II, Q 3, A 8.

3. Marsyas, a satyr of Phrygia, who, having found a flute which Minerva had thrown away in disgust because it distorted her features, discovered that it emitted of its own accord the most beautiful strains. Elated with his discovery he was rash enough to challenge Apollo to a musical contest, the conditions of which were that the victor should do what he pleased with his vanquished rival. The trial took place before the Muses as umpires, Apollo playing on the cithara, Marsyas on the flute. The decision being given in favor of the god, Apollo, to punish Marsyas for his presumption, bound him to a tree and flayed him alive. Dante here prays to Apollo to inspire him to sing as sweetly as the god played when he vanquished the satyr.

4. Peneus, son of Oceanus and Tethys and river god of the Peneus, the chief river in Thessaly and one of the most important in Greece, was the father of Daphne, who was pursued by Apollo for her beauty.

5. Cirrha was a town on the Gulf of Corinth southwest of Delphi, the seat of the oracle of Apollo. It was intimately connected with Delphi and so was sometimes used as a synonym of either Apollo or Delphi.

6. At the vernal equinox the sun rises from a point on the horizon where the four great circles, namely, the horizon, the zodiac, the equator, and the equinoctial colure, meet, and, cutting each other, form three crosses. The sun is in the sign of Aries "a better star," because the influence of this constellation was supposed to be benignant.

7. Glaucus was a fisherman of Boeotia who sat down one day on a grassy spot where no one had ever been before, to count his catch. The fish began to move about on the grass and made their way back into the sea. Thinking it must be due to some magic property in the grass, Glaucus chewed some and immediately began to yearn for the ocean. Bidding farewell to the earth, to which he would never return, he plunged into the sea and was changed into a sea god by Oceanus and Tethys.

8. There is a total order and harmony in this universe created by God, and this is the form (the essential informing and governing principle) which makes God's handiwork, the universe, resemble its Maker.

CANTO II

1. The Argonauts, who crossed to Colchis in quest of the golden fleece, were astonished to see Jason, their leader, plowing with fire-breathing oxen and sowing dragon's teeth which grew into men.

2. The moon. As will now be made clear, Beatrice and Dante enter into the planet itself, and the poet is concerned to report the effects of so exceptional an experience.

3. Fancying the dark spaces on the surface of the moon to represent Cain carrying a thorn-bush for the fire of his sacrifice.

4. The heaven of the fixed stars, the eighth heaven counting out or upwards from that of the moon.

5. There is hierarchy and degree in a universe so conceived, and the transmission of the power is through degree (each higher heaven being nobler than the next lower heaven contained by it). This principle of hierarchy will be all the clearer when the transmission (downwards only) is referred to the Intelligences, or nine orders of angels that direct the nine spheres of the material cosmos.

CANTO III

1. Narcissus took his reflection in the fountain to be a real person.

2. Piccarda was the daughter of Simone Donati and the sister of Corso and Forese and was related by marriage to Dante. She entered a convent but was forced thence by her brother Corso so that he might marry her to a Florentine named Rossellino della Tosa.

3. The reference is to St. Clare, who, with St. Francis, founded a Franciscan conventual institution for women, the Clarisse.

4. Constance (1154–98) was the daughter of Roger II, king of Naples and Sicily, and wife of the Emperor Henry VI, by whom she became the mother of the Emperor Frederick II. She was the last heir of the Norman dynasty.

CANTO IV

1. Timaeus is the chief interlocutor in the Platonic dialogue which bears that name, and it is he who expounds the opinion referred to by Beatrice.

2. St. Lawrence, a deacon of the Church of Rome, said to have been a native of Huesca in Spain, suffered martyrdom under the Emperor Valerian in 258.

3. Gaius Mucius Scaevola, a Roman citizen who, when Lars Porsena of Clusium was besieging Rome, made his way into the enemy's camp with the intention of killing Porsena; by mistake, however, he stabbed the king's secretary instead of the king himself. Being seized, Mucius was ordered by the king to be burned alive, whereupon he thrust his right hand into a fire, which was already lighted for a sacrifice, and held it in the flames without flinching. Porsena, struck with admiration at his fortitude, ordered him to be set free.

CANTO V

1. Jephthah, the Gileadite, was a judge of Israel (*ca.* 1143–1137 B.C.). He sacrificed to Jehovah his only daughter in fulfillment of a vow that if he returned victorious over the Ammonites he would sacrifice whatever first came to meet him.

2. According to one version of the story of the sacrifice of Iphigenia, as a consequence of Agamemnon's having killed a stag in the sacred grove of Diana, the goddess in anger sent a pestilence on the Greek army and caused a calm which prevented the Greek fleet in Aulis from sailing against Troy. On the advice of Calchas the seer, Agamemnon proceeded to sacrifice his daughter Iphigenia, in order to appease the wrath of

the goddess. However, Iphigenia disappeared just as the fatal blow was to fall, and in her place a beautiful deer appeared.

3. The heaven of Mercury, which symbolizes the degree of beatitude enjoyed by the souls of the ambitious.

CANTO VI

1. Aeneas, who brought the imperial eagle from Troy.

2. Justinian I, surnamed the Great, was emperor of Constantinople from 527 to 565. Justinian is best known by his legislation.

3. Dante's reference here is to Agapetus I, who was pope from 535 to 536, a time when the Ostrogothic power in Italy was being destroyed by Belisarius.

4. Belisarius, the famous general of the Emperor Justinian, died in 565. His great achievements were the overthrow of the Vandal kingdom in Africa, the reconquest of Italy from the Goths, and the foundation of the exarchate of Ravenna upon the ruins of the Gothic dominions.

5. The Ghibelline and the Guelph, respectively.

6. "Arabs" is a term applied by an anachronism to the Carthaginians, whose territory in Dante's day was occupied by the Arabs, the reference being to their passage of the Alps under Hannibal and their subsequent defeat by Scipio Africanus.

7. According to an old tradition, Fiesole, which lies on a hill overlooking Florence, had been the headquarters of Catiline's army, and was destroyed by the Romans after his defeat and death.

8. Caesar was regarded by Dante as the first of the Roman emperors—a popular misconception in the Middle Ages.

9. The Var is a river of southern France.

10. Dyrrachium, the ancient Epidamnus, a seaport in Illyria; it is the modern Durrës. Pharsalia is the district in eastern Thessaly in which Pharsalus is situated. This was the scene of the decisive battle between Pompey and Julius Caesar, which made the latter master of the Roman world in 48 B.C.

11. It was from the town of Antandros, near the river Simoïs, that the Eagle first set forth with Aeneas. When Caesar was pursuing Pompey, he stopped to visit the Troad.

12. Hector was buried at Troy.

13. Juba, king of the Numidians, was an ally of Pompey.

14. Spain, where the followers of Pompey were defeated in the battle of Munda.

15. Mark Antony was beaten near Modena, his brother Lucius at Perugia.

16. After the final defeat of Mark Antony at Actium, Cleopatra, fleeing before the imperial eagle, is said to have killed herself with an asp.

17. The temple of Janus—of which the doors were closed only in time of peace—had been locked up but twice during the whole life of the Roman Republic. But under Augustus they were closed three times.

18. The Emperor Titus, as the destroyer of Jerusalem (in A.D. 70), was the avenger of the death of Christ.

19. In 773 Pope Adrian I invoked the aid of Charlemagne against Desiderius, king of the Longobards or Lombards. Charlemagne came to the aid of the Church under the pinions of the Eagle.

20. "This younger Charles" is Charles II of Naples, son of Charles of Anjou. The Guelphs were supporters of the Church, as opposed to the Ghibellines, who were supporters of the Empire.

21. Romeo, a pilgrim to Rome, came to the court of Raymond Berenger IV, Count of Provence (who died in 1245), and winning the count's favor, served him with such wisdom and fidelity that by his means his master's revenues were greatly increased, and his four daughters married to four kings. The Provençal nobles, jealous of Romeo, procured his dismissal, and he departed, with his mule and his pilgrim's staff and scrip, and was never seen again.

CANTO VII

1. Hail, holy God of hosts, doubly illumining with thy brightness the happy fires of these kingdoms.

CANTO VIII

1. Venus, so called from her birth in Cyprus.

2. Daughter of Oceanus and Tethys, Dione was the mother of Venus, whence Venus is sometimes called Dionaea. Cupid was the well-known son of Venus. The allusion is to the account given by Virgil of how Cupid in the form of Ascanius sat in Dido's lap and inspired her fatal passion for Aeneas.

3. The spirit amply identifies himself as Charles Martel. The eldest son of Charles II of Naples and Mary of Hungary, he was born in 1271 and died in 1295 at the age of twenty-four.

4. Dante uses the towns of Bari, Gaeta, and Catona to indicate the eastern, western, and southern confines of the kingdom of Naples, won by Charles of Anjou. The rivers Tronto, on the east side, and Verde (now called the Liri or Garigliano), on the west, separate the kingdom of Naples from the Papal States at the north. Trinacria: Sicily, conquered by Charles of Anjou. Cape Passero (Pachynus) is at the southeast point of the island of Sicily, and Cape Faro (Pelorus) is at the northeast extremity of the island. Eurus was the name given by the ancients to the east or southeast wind.

5. Sicily; the gulf darkened by sulphurous fumes is the Bay of Calabria, which, lying between Cape Pachynus, the extreme southeastern point of the island, and Cape Pelorus, the extreme northeastern, is exposed to the full violence of Eurus, or the east wind. Clouds of smoke from Etna sometimes darken it. The eruptions of Etna were ascribed by Ovid to the struggles of Typhoeus, one of the Giants who make war upon the Gods, and who, being overthrown by Zeus, was buried under Mount Etna.

6. From his father, Charles II, or his grandfather, Charles of Anjou, and from the Emperor Rudolph of Habsburg, his wife's father.

7. By the insurrection which began at Palermo in 1282—the famous Sicilian Vespers—the French were driven from the island, and the rule over it of Charles of Anjou was brought to an end. The sovereignty was conferred by the people on Peter III of Aragon, the husband of the daughter of Manfred, the illegitimate son of the Emperor Frederick II.

8. Robert, the third son of Charles II. He had been kept as a hostage in Catalonia from 1288 to 1295, and when he became king of Naples in 1309 he introduced into his service many Catalonian officials.

9. Daedalus and Icarus.

10. This seems a clear reference to Robert, Charles' brother, who was much given to writing sermons.

CANTO IX

1. The Clemence whom the poet apostrophizes here may be either the wife or the daughter of Charles Martel of Hungary, and there is considerable doubt among commentators as to which Clemence the poet is addressing.

2. Frauds by which his son Caroberto was deprived of his rights of succession to the throne of Naples.

3. The March of Treviso, in the northeast corner of Italy, lies between Venice (indicated here by the Rialto, the largest of the islands on which the city is built) and the Alps, where the rivers Brenta and Piave have their source.

4. A sister of the Ghibelline Ezzelino III da Romano and youngest daughter of Ezzelino II and Adelaide di Mangona, Cunizza was born *ca.* 1198 and in 1222 was married, for political reasons, to the Guelph captain Count Riccardo di San Bonifazio of Verona. Shortly after her marriage she became enamored of the troubadour Sordello, by whom (*ca.* 1226), with the connivance of her brother, she was abducted from Verona and conveyed back to Ezzelino's court. Her intrigue with Sordello did not last long, and she then abandoned herself to a knight named Bonio, with whom, according to the old chronicler Rolandino she wandered about the world, leading a life of pleasure.

After the death of Bonio, Cunizza was married to Aimerio, count of Breganze; after his death, she married a gentleman of Verona; and subsequently she married a fourth husband in the person of Salione Buzzacarini of Padua, Ezzelino's astrologer. In or about 1260, both Ezzelino and Alberico being dead, and the fortunes of her house being at a low ebb, Cunizza went to reside in Florence, where in 1265, she executed a deed granting their freedom to her father's and brothers' slaves, with the exception of those who had been concerned in the betrayal of Alberico.

5. The March of Treviso is designated by the two rivers which bound it on east and west respectively, the Tagliamento and the Adige.

6. Padua claims to be the oldest city in Italy and to have been founded shortly after the fall of Troy. On February 12, 1237, Ezzelino IV da Romano, with the help of Frederick II and the Ghibellines, obtained possession of the city, but, on the proclamation of the crusade against him by Pope Alexander IV in 1256, he was expelled by the Paduan Guelphs and the Venetians. After the death of Ezzelino in 1259, the Guelphs of Padua asserted their independence and conquered Vicenza (1265), whence, however, they were driven out, in 1314, by Can Grande della Scala, who was at that time imperial vicar in Vicenza.

7. The Sile and the Cagnano (which is now known as the Botteniga) are two small rivers in upper Italy in Venetia. They unite at Treviso.

8. An act of treachery in 1314 on the part of Alessandro Novello, Bishop and Lord of Feltre, in delivering up certain Ghibelline refugees from Ferrara. Some of them were beheaded; others hanged. Malta was a prison.

9. The Mediterranean, which was thought to extend from west to east 90° or a quarter of the earth's circumference.

10. Folquet de Marseille, famous Provençal troubadour who flourished as a poet from 1180 to 1195, was born *ca.* 1160 and died in 1231. After the deaths of the princes whose favor he had enjoyed, Folquet retired from the world and became (*ca.* 1195) a Cistercian monk; he persuaded his wife to enter a convent with their two sons. In 1201 he became an abbot in the diocese of Toulon and in 1205 was appointed bishop of Toulouse. In the latter capacity he was deeply implicated in the sanguinary persecution of the Albigensian heretics (1208–29).

11. Dido, by her passion for Aeneas, wronged her dead husband, Sichaeus, and Aeneas' dead wife, Creusa.

12. The Thracian princess Phyllis, thinking herself forsaken by her lover Demophoön, son of Theseus, hanged herself. Rhodope is the name of a mountain range on the edge of Thrace near which Phyllis lived.

13. Alcides was Hercules, grandson of Alcaeus and son of Jupiter and Alcmene. He lost his life as a result of his infatuation for the Thessalian princess Iole.

14. The story of Rahab is related in Joshua ii. When Joshua was trying to take Jericho, he sent to the city two spies, who lodged in the house of "an harlot named Rahab." Their presence becoming known to the enemy, their hostess saved them by sending the pursuers on a false clue, hiding her guests on the roof of the house, and, when the coast was clear, letting them "down by a cord through the window, for her house was upon the town wall." In return, they promised safety for her and her relatives when Jericho should fall; as a token, she was to "bind" a "line of scarlet thread in the window." Her service resulted in the victory of the Children of Israel.

15. Satan was the first creature to turn away from God, and in his fallen and evil condition he envied Adam and Eve, causing them to sin—with such lamentable consequences for humankind.

16. The florin, coined by Florence, which was imprinted on one side with the lily.

17. Avidity for riches has turned the pope and ecclesiastics generally into greedy wolves, and they thus set an example for their flock. The decretals are the papal decrees or epistles, usually written in reply to some question of general ecclesiastical law.

18. The Vatican hill, as having been the reputed scene of the martyrdom of Peter and of numbers of the early Christians, is held to be the most sacred quarter of all Rome.

CANTO X

1. The "two motions" are the diurnal and the annual revolutions of the sun. They "strike," or cross, each other at Aries, in which constellation the sun is at the time of Dante's journey.

2. Latona's daughter is Diana, the Moon.

3. The speaker, St. Thomas Aquinas, who belonged to the Dominican order, declares that St. Dominic led his flock over a road where the sheep "fatten well, if they do not stray," i.e., they have abundance of spiritual food, as long as they adhere to his rule. Albert of Cologne, now St. Albert (canonized 1932), better known as Albertus Magnus. Named Doctor Universalis on account of his vast learning, he was born in Swabia between 1193 and 1206.

4. Gratian (Franciscus Gratianus), founder of the science of canon law, was born about the end of the eleventh century at Chiusi in Tuscany.

5. Peter Lombard, otherwise known as Magister Sententiarum (from the title of his work *Sententiarum libri quatuor*).

6. The "fifth light," that of Solomon, is the "most beautiful" of all the circle, since it comes from the love which phrased the Song of Solomon (Canticle of Canticles), the epithalamium of Christ and Church. He revealed truth in Proverbs and Ecclesiastes.

7. Dionysius the Areopagite, the disciple of St. Paul (Acts 17:34), to whom was ascribed a book of great repute, written probably in the fifth or sixth century, *On the Celestial Hierarchy*.

8. Paulus Orosius, who lived in the fourth and fifth centuries, and wrote, at the request of St. Augustine, his *History against the Pagans*.

9. Boethius, put to death in Pavia, in 525, was buried in the church of S. Pietro in Cielo d' Oro—St. Peter's of the Golden Ceiling.

10. Isidore, bishop of Seville, died 636; the Venerable Bede, died 735; Richard, prior of the Monastery of St. Vic-

tor, at Paris, a mystic of the twelfth century; all eminent theologians.

11. Siger de Brabant was professor of the University of Paris in the thirteenth century.

CANTO XI

1. The study of medicine, so referred to because the *Aphorisms* of Hippocrates served as a textbook of medicine.

2. St. Francis of Assisi.

3. St. Dominic.

4. These verses locate Assisi, where Francis was born. Assisi is situated between the river Topino and the Chiascio, which runs into it below. The Topino empties into the Tiber.

5. So the name of Assisi was sometimes spelled, and here with a play on *ascesi* "I rose."

6. Francis was about twenty-four when he began to woo Poverty.

7. Amyclas, who had nothing to lose, was not afraid when Caesar knocked at his door.

8. Francis' first disciple was Bernardo da Quintavalle, a wealthy merchant of Assisi.

9. Aegidius of Assisi (Blessed Giles), one of Francis' three earliest followers, was the author of a book called *Verba aurea*. He died at Perugia in 1262. One of Francis' earliest followers, Sylvester is said to have been a priest and to have supplied Francis with stone for church-building.

10. Francis' father was a wool-merchant, therefore of the middle class and not noble.

11. In 1210, Innocent III verbally, and with some reluctance, sanctioned St. Francis's Rule.

12. St. Dominic, whose life is recounted in *Par.* XII.

CANTO XII

1. Iris, the rainbow. Daughter of Thaumas and Electra, Iris was the personification of the rainbow.

2. The "wanderer" is the nymph Echo, who used to keep Juno engaged by incessantly talking to her, while Jupiter sported with the nymphs.

3. It is St. Bonaventura, the biographer of St. Francis, who speaks.

4. Compared with Italy, Caleruega, in Old Castile, is "not very far" from the Atlantic.

5. His mother dreamed that she gave birth to a dog, black and white in color, with a lighted torch in its mouth, which set the world on fire; symbols of the black and white robe of the Order, and of the flaming zeal of its brethren.

6. His father's name, "Felice," means "happy." His mother's name, "Giovanna," signifies in Hebrew "the grace of the Lord."

7. Henry of Susa, cardinal of Ostia, who wrote a much studied commentary on the Decretals, and Taddeo d' Alderotto of Bologna, called "the greatest physician in Christendom."

8. The tithes which belong to God's poor.

9. Thomas Aquinas.

10. A town of northern Italy in Piedmont, on the right bank of the Po, about thirty miles east of Turin. The allusion is to Ubertino da Casale, leader of the so-called Spirituals in the Franciscan order, who opposed the relaxations of discipline introduced by Matteo d'Acquasparta as general of the order.

11. St. Bonaventura (Giovanni di Fidanza) was born at Bagnoregio, near Orvieto, in 1221, the year of St. Dominic's death. As a child he was attacked by a dangerous disease, which miraculously cured by St. Francis of Assisi. When the latter heard that the child had recovered, he is said to have exclaimed "buona ven-

tura," whereupon the boy's mother changed his name to Bonaventura.

12. Illuminato da Rieti, one of the earliest followers of St. Francis of Assisi. He accompanied St. Francis into Egypt. Augustine, another of the earliest followers of St. Francis of Assisi, whom he joined in 1210.

13. Hugh of St. Victor, celebrated mystic and theologian of the beginning of the twelfth century.

14. Petrus Comestor (i.e., Peter the Eater, so called because he was an insatiable devourer of books), priest, and afterwards dean, of the cathedral of Troyes in France, where he was born in the first half of the twelfth century. Petrus Hispanus (Petrus Juliani) was born at Lisbon *ca.* 1225, where he at first followed his father's profession of medicine. He studied at Paris, probably under Albertus Magnus; subsequently he was ordained and became (1273) archbishop of Braga. In 1274 he was created cardinal bishop of Tusculum (Frascati) by Gregory X. On September 13, 1276, he was elected pope, under the title of John XXI.

15. Nathan, the prophet, who was sent by God to reprove David for his sin in causing the death of Uriah the Hittite in order that he might marry Bathsheba.

16. The reference is to St. John Chrysostom, celebrated Greek father of the Church.

17. Anselm, archbishop of Canterbury from 1093 to 1109.

18. Aelius Donatus, Roman scholar and rhetorician of the fourth century, who is said to have been the tutor of Jerome.

19. Grammar is the first of the seven liberal arts of the trivium and quadrivium.

20. Rabanus Maurus, Archbishop of Mainz in the ninth century; a great scholar and writer.

21. Joachim of Floris, the Calabrian abbot.

CANTO XIII

1. The Big Dipper.

2. The last two stars of the hornlike Little Dipper (Ursa Minor), the mouth of which is formed by the two stars farthest from the polestar.

3. The daughter of King Minos was Ariadne, whose crown was turned into a constellation.

4. River in east Tuscany and southwest Umbria.

5. The "light" of Thomas Aquinas.

6. Thus all creation, corruptible and incorruptible, is said to be merely a reflection ("splendor") of God's idea. The idea is the Word, second person of the Trinity, which God the Father ("il nostro Sire") contemplates and through which, in His love, He produces, in His eternity, all things.

7. "Or whether an absolute premise with a conditional premise has ever produced an absolute conclusion." This is a scholastic problem in logic, also touched upon by Plato and Aristotle. The answer is "no."

8. "Not, whether a prime motion is to be admitted," i.e., a motion independent of any cause.

9. Parmenides, an early Greek philosopher, was born at Elea in Italy *ca.* 513 B.C. He is the chief representative of the Eleatic philosophy. Melissus, a philosopher of Samos who flourished *ca.* 441 B.C., was a follower of Parmenides. Bryson was a Greek philosopher mentioned by Aristotle as having attempted to square the circle, a problem which apparently he tried to solve dishonestly by non-geometrical methods.

10. Sabellius, heresiarch of the third century, refused to accept the received doctrine of the Trinity and held that the terms Father, Son, and Holy Ghost were merely different names for the One God. Arius, who died in 336, was the originator of the Arian heresy that the Father and

the Son are not "one substance," a doctrine which the Athanasian creed was designed to controvert.

11. *Berta* and *Martino* were equivalent to our "Tom, Dick, and Harry."

CANTO XIV

1. Helios, here used as the name of God, the spiritual sun. The word represents a fusion of the Greek word *helios* (ἥλιος), meaning "sun," and the Hebrew *Ely*, meaning "God."

CANTO XV

1. "O blood of mine, O lavish grace of God! To whom was Heaven's gate ever twice opened, as to thee?" Heaven receives Dante now, and will receive him again after his death; such a thing has never happened since the days of St. Paul.

2. In reply to Dante's question concerning the name and identity of this soul, the soul will require many verses to make his answer, and he will not name himself until vs. 135 as Cacciaguida, who, from what he first tells, proves to be the great-great-grandfather of Dante.

3. Alighiero (or Allagherius), son of Cacciaguida, was the first male member of the family to bear this name, which, as we learn presently, he derived from his mother.

4. The bell of the church called the Badìa, or Abbey, measured the time for the Florentines. Tierce is the first division of the canonical hours of the day, from six to nine; nones, the third, from twelve to three.

5. Sardanapalus, king of Assyria, was notorious in antiquity for his luxury and effeminacy.

6. Montemalo (or Montemallo), now Montemario, is a hill that affords the approaching traveler a view of Rome; similarly the height called Uccellatoio offers the stranger, as he draws near on the north, an outlook on Florence.

7. Florentine of the ancient Ravignani family, father of "la buona Gualdrada" (see *Inf.* XVI), through whose marriage with Guido Guerra IV the Conti Guidi traced their descent from the Ravignani.

8. Ancient noble family of Florence which received knighthood from the Marquis Hugh of Brandenburg, "il gran barone" (*Par.* XVI). del Vecchio: Ancient noble family of Florence (otherwise known as the Vecchietti).

9. Legends of the founding of Rome by the Trojans, and of the founding of Fiesole and then of Florence by the ancient Romans. Such legends enjoyed a considerable popular diffusion in Dante's day and long before.

10. Cianghella: Florentine lady of ill repute, contemporary of Dante. She is said to have been the daughter of Arrigo della Tosa and to have died *ca.* 1330. Lapo Salterello: Florentine lawyer and judge, a relative and adherent of the Cerchi, the leaders of the Bianchi faction in Florence.

11. The Baptistery of Florence, in which in early times most children born in Florence received baptism.

12. Of these two brothers, named (as was Cacciaguida) by their first names only, nothing is known, though it is thought possible that the family of the Elisei, or one branch of it, may have descended from Eliseo. They were Ghibellines and noble, and they were exiled from Florence several times.

13. Conrad III (1093–1152) was the son of Frederick, duke of Swabia.

14. Law: "Religion," the Mohammedan, the followers of which are usurping the Holy Land—which rightly belongs to you—because the popes care nothing about the reconquest of it.

CANTO XVI

1. "With the *you*." According to tradition, the plural *vos* was first used, in addressing one person, when Julius Caesar made himself emperor. In the entire *Commedia* Dante uses the honorific plural to address only Farinata and Cavalcante (*Inf.* X), Brunetto Latini (*Inf.* XV), Pope Adrian V, when he learns that it is he (*Purg.* XIX), and—always—Beatrice until the very end of the poem, where he very strikingly addresses her with the singular form *tu* (see *Par.* XXXI). Thus, his shifting to "voi" here is significant.

2. In the Old French romance of *Lancelot du Lac,* the Dame de Malehaut, watching the first clandestine interview of Guinever and Lancelot, coughed on hearing the impassioned speech of the Queen.

3. John the Baptist is the patron saint of Florence.

4. Mars returned 580 times to the constellation of Leo, which, being of like disposition to Mars, reinforces the influence of that planet. As Mars completes its revolution in 687 days, we shall get the year of Cacciaguida's birth by multiplying 687 by 580 and dividing by 365: 1091. He was therefore 56 when he followed the crusade.

5. The races were run on June 24 (St. John's day).

6. Between the old statue of Mars, on the river, and the Baptistery (cf. *Inf.* XIX). The ancient city was measured thus from south to north.

7. These three villages, all in Tuscany, are named as typical of the many small towns situated in the vicinity of Florence.

8. Ancient villages of Tuscany.

9. A castle (now destroyed), formerly called Aquilone, in the Florentine territory in the Val di Pesa to the south of the city.

10. Village of Tuscany, near the Arno, about ten miles west of Florence.

11. Semifonte was a strong fortress in the Val d'Elsa, southwest of Florence and east of Certaldo, which belonged originally to the Conti Alberti.

12. A castle on a hill between Prato and Pistoia which belonged to the Conti Guidi, who were finally (1254) obliged to sell it to the Florentines since they could not hold it against the Pistoians.

13. Wealthy Florentine family of low origin, who originally came from Acone, a small village in the neighborhood of Florence.

14. The valley of the Greve, a small river of Tuscany, which rises about twenty miles south of Florence and flows north, joining the Ema close to Galluzzo, about three miles from the Porta Romana of Florence. Buondelmonti: The leaders of the Guelph party in Florence, whose family left the country and took up their residence in Florence in 1135, on account of the destruction of their castle of Montebuono in the Valdigreve close to Florence.

15. Ancient Luna, a maritime town in Etruria on the left bank of the Magra, not far from Sarzana, on the boundary between Liguria and Etruria. Urbisaglia, the ancient Urbs Salvia, was once an important town, but in Dante's day the ancient city was a collection of ruins.

16. The ancient Clusium, formerly one of the twelve great Etruscan cities. It is situated in the Val di Chiana, close to the lake of the same name. Now Senigallia, the ancient Sena Gallica, called Senagallia by Pliny so named to distinguish it from Sena Julia (Siena). It is situated on the Adriatic at the mouth of the Misa.

17. Ughi: Ancient noble family of Florence. Catellini: Another ancient noble family of Florence mentioned by Villani.

18. All these old families have declined or disappeared.

19. The Ravignani were another of the older families extinct in Dante's day. The several lines of the Conti Guidi descended from them.

20. The descendants of Ubertino Donati, son-in-law of Bellincione Berti, took the name of Bellincioni.

21. Villani includes this family among the old families who lived in the neighborhood of the Duomo.

22. Galigaio de' Galigai was a member of an ancient noble family of Florence.

23. A representation of a strip of vair (ermine) traversed longitudinally the escutcheon of the Pigli family.

24. Sacchetti: Villani speaks of this ancient family as Guelph (V, 39) and as having been among those who fled from Florence to Lucca after the great Ghibelline victory of Montaperti (VI, 80). Giuochi: According to Villani (V, 39; VI, 33) this family was Ghibelline and, though originally noble, had suffered a decline by his time. Fifanti: Villani mentions this family as being among the early inhabitants of Florence. He records that they were Ghibelline (V, 39) and as such were expelled from the city in 1258 (VI, 65). Barucci: The Barucci family was also Ghibelline and according to Villani (IV, 10) extinct in his time. Galli: Villani states that the Galli were Ghibellines (V, 39) who lived in the Mercato Nuovo and in his time had become of no account (IV, 13).

25. A Guelph family.

26. Ancient noble families of Florence. The two families are frequently mentioned together by Villani.

27. The Lamberti family, to which Mosca (Inf. XXVIII) belonged, had golden balls on their shield. Both the Lamberti and the Uberti were of German origin.

28. The Visdomini and the Tosinghi, patrons of the bishopric of Florence, administered the episcopal revenues whenever the see was vacant, until a successor was chosen.

29. The reference is to the Adimari family. They were among those who took refuge in Lucca after the Ghibelline victory at Montaperti in 1260.

30. Ubertino Donati, who had married one daughter of Bellincione Berti, was displeased when another daughter was given in marriage to one of the humble stock of the Adimari.

31. Giuda: Again the singular is used for the plural, referring to the Giudi family of Florence. Infangato: Name, again in the singular, used to represent the Infangati family. Villani mentions them among the ancient families of note in Florence and says they were Ghibellines.

32. Ancient noble family of Florence.

33. The great baron is the Marquis Hugh of Brandenburg. He is said to have come to Florence from Germany with Emperor Otto III. This marquis of Brandenburg appears to be identical with Ugo, marquis of Tuscany from 961 to 1001.

34. This is Giano della Bella, who introduced, in 1293, severe reform measures directed against the nobles, and was banished in 1295.

35. These old families had also fallen from high estate by Dante's time.

36. The quarter called Borgo Santi Apostoli, where the Gualterotti and Importuni lived.

37. The indignation of the Amidei against Buondelmonte de' Buondelmonti, who, on his wedding day, in 1215, forsook his betrothed—one of the Amidei—for a daughter of the Donati. To avenge this insult, the Amidei murdered him, and this was the beginning of the feud.

38. Small stream in Tuscany, which rises in the hills south of Florence and falls into the Greve a few miles from the city.

39. In 1251, after the expulsion of the Ghibellines, the Guelphs altered the Florentine standard from a white lily in a red field to a red lily in a white field. The Ghibellines kept the old colors.

CANTO XVII

1. Dante compares himself to Phaëthon, who, having been told by a comrade that the god of the Sun was not really his father, went to his mother, Clymene, to find out the truth. Clymene swore to Phaëthon that he was truly the son of the god and urged him to ask his father in person. The result was that Phaëthon induced his father to let him drive his chariot, an enterprise that proved fatal to him.

2. Hippolytus was a son of Theseus by Hippolyte, a queen of the Amazons. Theseus later married Phaedra, who fell in love with her stepson Hippolytus; on his rejecting her shameful proposals, she accused him to his father of having attempted her dishonor. Theseus thereupon cursed his son, who was obliged to flee from Athens. He subsequently met his death in fulfillment of his father's curse. When Theseus afterwards discovered that Phaedra's accusation was false, Phaedra killed herself in despair.

3. Apparently the exile of Dante and other opponents of the papal policy was planned in Rome in April 1300, two months before Dante's priorate. Specifically the reference seems to be to the fact that Boniface VIII and the Roman curia were already plotting to turn the city of Florence over to the faction of the Neri, an event which did indeed lead finally to Dante's exile.

4. Apparently, after separating himself from the exiled Bianchi, Dante took refuge at Verona, with one of the Scaligers (probably Bartolomeo della Scala). The coat of arms of the Scaliger family was a ladder surmounted by the imperial eagle.

5. Can Francesco della Scala, called Can Grande, third son of Alberto della Scala (lord of Verona, 1277-1301), was born on March 9, 1291. To Can Grande Dante dedicated the Paradiso.

6. Before 1312, when the Gascon pope, Clement V, after promising to support the emperor, Henry VII, in his expedition to Italy, promoted opposition to it.

CANTO XVIII

1. The "tree" of the heavens, which derives all its sustenance from above, is conceived as a fir, whose branches grow in rings or "tiers" around the trunk. The fifth ring is the heaven of Mars.

2. Judas Maccabaeus, the great Jewish warrior.

3. Charlemagne (Charles the Great), restorer of the Empire of the West. Roland, the French epic hero who was represented as the nephew of Charlemagne and one of the twelve peers.

4. William, count of Orange, is the hero of a group of Old French epics, of which the best known is the Aliscans. Godfrey of Bouillon, leader of the first Crusade (1096), battled with the Saracens in the Holy Land and became first Christian king of Jerusalem. Robert Guiscard, a Norman conqueror of the second half of the eleventh century, took a large part of southern Italy and Sicily from the Saracens.

5. The change from the red light of Mars to the whiteness of Jupiter is compared to the change in a pale lady's face when a blush suddenly passes from it.

6. "Torch of Jove," the planet Jupiter, but in "giovial" there is doubtless a play on the adjective in its more common sense of "jovial," since the planet Jove (Jupiter) was thought to make those born under it to be of joyful and merry disposition.

7. The Muses are associated with the winged horse, Pegasus. It is not clear whether Dante had in mind any special Muse; nor is it clear, if he was thinking of a particular Muse, whether the one invoked is Cal-

liope, Urania, or Euterpe (who presided over the sphere of Jupiter). This brief invocation here serves to indicate that some most remarkable thing is about to be recounted.

8. "Diligite iustitiam qui iudicatis terram" ("Love justice, you who judge the earth") is from the first verse of the book of Wisdom. Justice is a product of the heaven of Jupiter, and the souls of the just appear in this planet.

9. John the Baptist.

CANTO XIX

1. Lucifer was the most beautiful of all the angels, who are at the very summit of creation.

2. The river Indus, in northern India, is used to indicate India itself, as the eastern limit of the habitable world.

3. Prague, on the Moldau (now Vltava), the capital of Bohemia. The allusion is to the invasion of the dominions of Wenceslaus II, king of Bohemia, in 1304 by his brother-in-law, Albert I.

4. Philip the Fair, to supply himself with money after the battle of Courtrai in 1302, debased the coinage of the realm, causing great misery.

5. The first part of the fourteenth century saw the wars of Edward I and Edward II against the Scots under Wallace and Bruce.

6. Ferdinand IV of Castile, king of Castile and León from 1295 to 1312.

7. Charles II of Naples, titular king of Jerusalem, was called "the Cripple" on account of his lameness.

8. Frederick II, king of the volcanic island of Sicily.

9. The reference is to James, second son of James I of Aragon and brother of Pedro III.

10. Of Majorca and of Aragon.

11. Diniz (also known as Dionysius), king of Portugal from 1279 to 1325, was the son of Alfonso III, whom he succeeded, and Beatrice, daughter of Alfonso X of Castile and León. Norway, an independent kingdom until the Union of Kalmar in 1397, when the three kingdoms of Norway, Sweden, and Denmark were united. Since only living sovereigns are in question here, the reference is probably to Haakon V Magnusson, king from 1299 to 1319.

12. Name by which the former kingdom of Serbia was known in the Middle Ages, from the name of its capital, Raska or Rashka, the modern Novi Pazar.

13. The throne of Hungary, which belonged to Charles Martel, was usurped by Andrew III.

14. Navarre would be happy if she could protect herself with the mountain chains that enfold her.

15. Dante here alludes to the sufferings of Cyprus under the unsettled rule of the house of Lusignan.

CANTO XX

1. David, as the light which he is here, is the very pupil of the eye, therefore the highest of all that are to be named as forming eye and eyebrow. The psalms written by him were inspired by the Holy Ghost, as were all the canonical books of the Bible. As king of Israel, he had the ark of the covenant moved to Jerusalem.

2. The just emperor Trajan lived in Christian times but died a pagan; however, in response to the prayers of Gregory the Great, he was allowed to return from the lower world (probably from Limbo), where conversion is impossible, and to resume his body long enough for him to embrace the true faith and thus win to a place in Heaven.

3. King Hezekiah, who, when Isaiah told him of his impending death, prayed and had his life prolonged for fifteen years.

4. The Emperor Constantine occupies thus the central

and highest part of the arch. The reference is to his ceding Rome to the pope and transferring the capital to Byzantium, thus making himself, the imperial eagle, and the laws Greek.

5. William II, the Good, king of Naples and Sicily in the Norman line from 1166 to 1189.

6. The kings of Naples and of Sicily who are rebuked in *Par.* XIX.

7. Ripheus was a Trojan hero who was slain during the sack of Troy.

8. The kingdom of heaven has been enduring violent assault.

9. The three theological virtues.

10. The two exceptional cases of Trajan and Ripheus support the exclamation over God's predestination, hidden from the sight of all creatures.

CANTO XXI

1. Semele, daughter of Cadmus and mother of Bacchus, having insisted on beholding her lover, Jupiter, in all his heavenly majesty, was burned to ashes by his splendor.

2. The planet Saturn.

3. The god Saturn, dear to the earth for having ruled there during the Golden Age, reminds the reader all was perfect.

4. Monte Catria, one of the peaks of the Apennines.

5. San Pietro Damiani (St. Peter Damian), proclaimed doctor of the Church by Leo XII in 1828.

6. The monastery of Santa Maria in Porto, near Ravenna.

7. St. Peter.

CANTO XXII

1. When the reader learns that this is none other than the great St. Benedict, he will understand these superlatives, and just why this flame is so.

2. The mountain referred to is that of Monte Cassino.

3. St. Macarius. It is uncertain which of the several saints of the name of Macarius is the one intended by Dante. The two best known, between whom perhaps Dante did not very clearly distinguish, are St. Macarius the Elder, called the Egyptian, and St. Macarius the Younger of Alexandria—both disciples of St. Anthony. St. Romuald, founder of the order of Camaldoli or reformed Benedictines, belonged to the Onesti family of Ravenna, where he was born *ca.* 950.

4. God's providence has seen to it that the pilgrim Dante "lands" precisely in the constellation under which he was born, Gemini, or the Twins.

5. The moon shows her spots only on the side toward the earth.

6. Hyperion is often called by ancient poets the father of the Sun.

7. Maia is the mother of Mercury; Dione, the mother of Venus.

CANTO XXIII

1. "The goddess at the three ways," a term applied by Virgil and other Latin poets to Diana (whose temple was frequently placed where three roads met), and hence by Dante to the moon, Diana being goddess of the Moon.

2. With this term the stress is rather on the human Christ. The whole vision is symbolic, however—a point not to be forgotten.

3. Polyhymnia, the Muse of the Sublime Hymn. "With her sisters," the other Muses. The Muses nourish (or "fatten") the tongues of poets.

4. Mary, the "Mystic Rose" of the liturgy. Cf. *rosario*, rosary, a series of prayers to the Virgin.

5. The apostles.

6. "Regina coeli," antiphon in praise of the Virgin Mary, Queen of Heaven, which is sung in the Office at Easter.

7. The "exile of Babylon" is the earthly life.

8. St. Peter.

CANTO XXIV

1. To understand the simile the modern reader needs to know that in the medieval examination, or *disputatio,* leading to the degree of doctor of theology, a time was appointed for the discussion of a given question. On this occasion the master or doctor examining the candidate would state the question, whereupon the "bachelor" was expected to adduce proofs (*approvare*), that is, bring arguments to bear on it (both *pro* and *con*), but he did not presume to settle or decide the question (*terminare*), since this privilege belonged only to the examining doctor and was called the *determinatio.*

2. "Lord," i.e., Peter.

CANTO XXV

1. This is James the Apostle, also known as St. James the Great and St. James of Compostela. According to tradition, James preached the Gospel in Spain. He later returned to Jerusalem, and after his death his body was miraculously transferred to Santiago de Compostela, then the capital of Galicia.

2. Latin, meaning "before me."

3. The reference is to the Epistle of James, which Dante wrongly attributes to St. James the Greater. See James 1:5, 17.

4. Three of the disciples (Peter, James, John) were chosen by Jesus to be present, and to receive the clearest revelation of his character, on three different occasions: at the Transfiguration (Matt. 17, 1–8), in the Garden of Gethsemane (Matt. 26, 36–38), and at the raising of the daughter of Jairus (Luke 8, 50–56). On these three occasions Peter, James and John stand respectively for Faith, Hope, and Love.

5. The counts in the imperial court of Heaven are the saints.

6. The definition of hope given by Dante here is that of Peter Lombard.

CANTO XXVI

1. Ananias, the disciple at Damascus, cured St. Paul of his blindness by "laying his hands upon him."

2. This amounts to a statement of what human reason can see, what an Aristotle could teach in this regard, as distinguished from divine revelation.

3. The "unaccomplishable task" which Nimrod's people attempted was the building of the Tower of Babel: Gen. 11, 4–9.

4. Adam now replies to the second question, and many readers (especially readers of Milton) will be surprised to learn how brief a time our first parents sojourned in the Garden of Eden: only a little more than six hours!

CANTO XXVII

1. The reference is to Boniface VIII, and Peter's denunciation of him. Some commentators would take this to mean that Boniface's very election to the supreme office was invalid.

2. This is Satan, of course.

3. St. Linus, generally considered the immediate successor to Peter as pope. St. Cletus (or Anacletus), pope from *ca.* A.D. 79 to *ca.* A.D. 90, was the successor of St. Linus.

4. Sixtus I was pope (*ca.* 115–125) during the reign of the Emperor Hadrian. Pius I, pope from *ca.* 140 to *ca.* 155 or 157, was contemporary with the Emperor Antoninus Pius. Callistus I, pope from 217 to 222, was succeeded by Urban I as pope from 222 to 230. All four were known as early martyrs.

5. Cahors, capital of the ancient province of Quercy in southern France. John XXII, pope from 1316 to 1334, came from that town. The predecessor of John XXII, Clement V, was a Gascon. The Gascons had generally the reputation of being avaricious and grasping.

6. Scipio Africanus the Elder, who conquered Hannibal and thus saved Rome.

7. The Phoenician shore, where Europa mounted the back of Jupiter disguised as a bull.

8. "Leda's nest" is the constellation of Gemini, in which Dante has been while in the sphere of the stars; it is so called because the twins Castor and Pollux were the children of Leda.

9. Through an inaccuracy in the Julian calendar, which made the year of 365 days and 6 hours, the solar year gained over the standard year about one day in a century; in the course of something less than 90 centuries, then, January would have been pushed into the spring, if the error had not been corrected (as it was in 1582 under Gregory XIII, when the present calendar was adopted).

CANTO XXVIII

1. This alludes to the story that the inventor of the game asked, as his reward from the King of Persia, a grain of wheat for the first square of the board, two for the second, four for the third, and so on with successive duplication to the last or sixty-fourth square, the number reached by this process extending to twenty figures.

2. Latin adverb meaning "where."

3. Pope St. Gregory differed slightly from Dionysius in his arrangement of the Orders of the Heavenly Host.

CANTO XXIX

1. "Latona's children" are Apollo and Diana, the Sun and the Moon. The sun is in Aries (the Ram, "Montone"), the moon is in Libra (the Scales).

2. Lapo and Bindo seem to have been very common names in Florence.

3. This is St. Anthony the Great, the Egyptian hermit (not to be confounded with his namesake of Padua), who was born in Upper Egypt (*ca.* 250) and died at the age of 105. He is regarded as the founder of monastic institutions. His symbol is a hog (perhaps as a type of the temptations of the devil, or possibly as a token of the power ascribed to him of warding off disease from cattle), which is generally represented lying at his feet.

CANTO XXX

1. Dante is speaking here of the Emperor Henry VII. Henry, count of Luxemburg (born *ca.* 1275), was at the instance of Clement V unanimously elected emperor on November 27, 1308, in opposition to Charles of Valois, the candidate of the French king, Philip the Fair.

2. The pope, or "prefect," is Clement V. The poet has already denounced Clement and assigned him to the circle of the simonists in Inferno (*Inf.* XIX).

CANTO XXXI

1. The Lateran was the old papal palace in Rome, first the residence of emperors, then of popes down into Dante's time.

2. St. Bernard, the great abbot of Clairvaux and preacher of the disastrous second Crusade.

3. The Veronica is the true image (*vera icona*) of the Saviour, left on a kerchief which a holy woman had handed him, on his way to Calvary, to wipe the sweat from his face. It was shown at St. Peter's in Rome on certain days.

4. This oriflamme is the part of the rose of Paradise where the Virgin is seated; its mid-point is the Virgin herself. It is called "pacific" in contrast with the warlike oriflamme, the banner given by the archangel Gabriel to the ancient kings of France, which bore a flame on a field of gold (*aurea flamma*).

CANTO XXXII

1. Ruth, the Moabitish wife of Boaz, by whom she became the great-grandmother of David (Matt. 1:5–6), the "cantor" here referred to.

2. The poet's choice of John the Baptist finds ample support in the Gospels. See Matt. 2:11.

3. In Limbo, where John, after his death, had to wait some two years for the descent of Christ to the harrowing of Hell.

4. It will be noted that St. Francis is given the highest place after John the Baptist and that this is not on any chronological principle, as in the Hebrew women, but solely, it would seem, on the principle of excellence. This being the case, it is interesting to note that St. Benedict rates a higher seat than St. Augustine.

5. Jacob and Esau "struggled together" in their mother's womb (Gen. 25:22–25 [22–26]).

6. The angel Gabriel.

7. This is St. John, the author of the Apocalypse, who prophesied the difficult times and the calamities of the Church.

8. Peter.

9. Moses.

10. St. Anna, the mother of Mary.

11. St. Lucy, who twice came to Dante's aid, first in the relay of grace that took place in Heaven, as recounted by Beatrice in Limbo (see *Inf.* II), then in carrying Dante up the steep mountain to the gate of Purgatory proper (*Purg.* IX).

CANTO XXXIII

1. The expedition of the Argonauts, under Jason, in search of the golden fleece (*Inf.* XVIII; *Par.* II) was thought to have occurred in the thirteenth century B.C.

2. This is the third person of the Trinity, the Holy Ghost, who is, by definition, the love of the Father for the Son, and the Son for the Father.

3. *Fantasia* is an image-receiving faculty, not image-making. Hence, to affirm that the high "fantasia" failed in its power at this point is equivalent to saying that the wayfarer reaches the limit of his capacity for vision, for the reception of images.

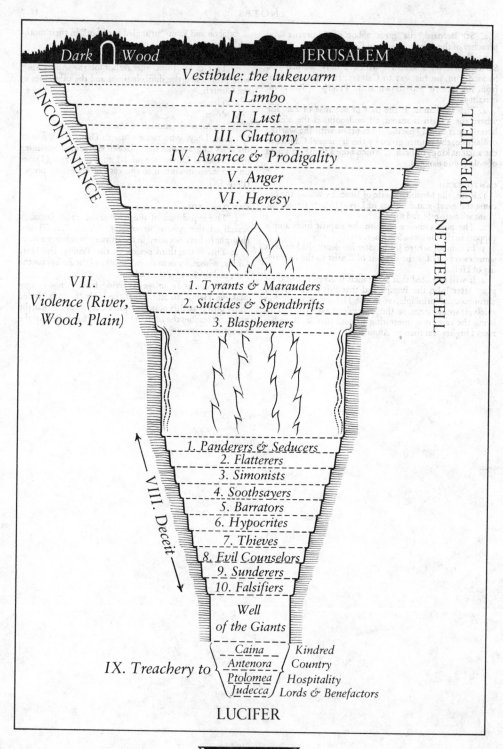

Dark Wood — JERUSALEM

INCONTINENCE — UPPER HELL — NETHER HELL

Vestibule: the lukewarm

I. Limbo

II. Lust

III. Gluttony

IV. Avarice & Prodigality

V. Anger

VI. Heresy

VII. Violence (River, Wood, Plain)

1. Tyrants & Marauders

2. Suicides & Spendthrifts

3. Blasphemers

VIII. Deceit

1. Panderers & Seducers

2. Flatterers

3. Simonists

4. Soothsayers

5. Barrators

6. Hypocrites

7. Thieves

8. Evil Counselors

9. Sunderers

10. Falsifiers

Well of the Giants

IX. Treachery to

Caina — Kindred

Antenora — Country

Ptolomea — Hospitality

Judecca — Lords & Benefactors

LUCIFER

HELL

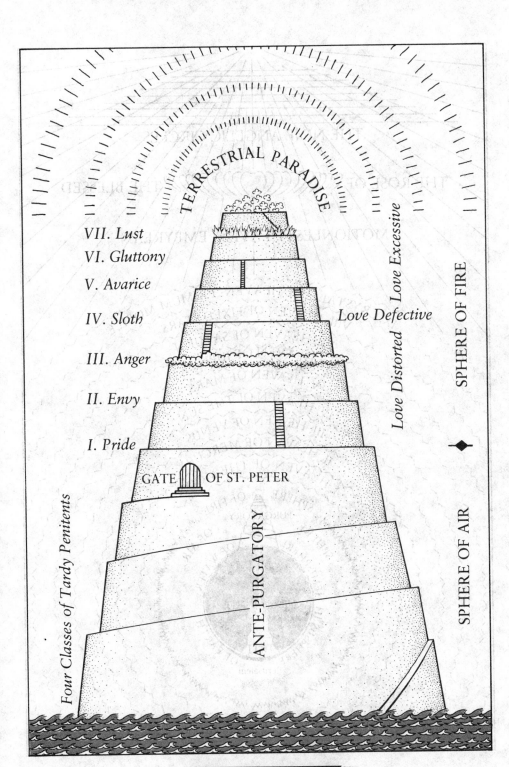

TERRESTRIAL PARADISE

VII. *Lust*
VI. *Gluttony*
V. *Avarice*
IV. *Sloth*
III. *Anger*
II. *Envy*
I. *Pride*

Love Excessive

Love Defective

Love Distorted

SPHERE OF FIRE

GATE OF ST. PETER

Four Classes of Tardy Penitents

ANTE-PURGATORY

SPHERE OF AIR

◆ · PURGATORY · ◀

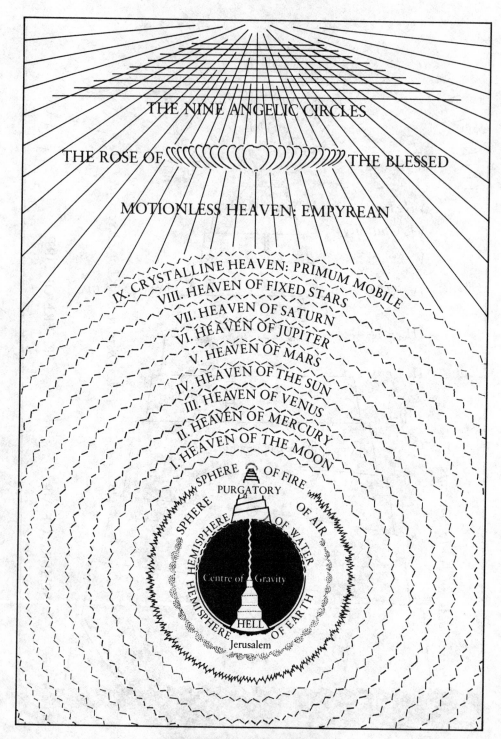

THE NINE ANGELIC CIRCLES

THE ROSE OF))))))))))(((((((((THE BLESSED

MOTIONLESS HEAVEN: EMPYREAN

IX. CRYSTALLINE HEAVEN: PRIMUM MOBILE
VIII. HEAVEN OF FIXED STARS
VII. HEAVEN OF SATURN
VI. HEAVEN OF JUPITER
V. HEAVEN OF MARS
IV. HEAVEN OF THE SUN
III. HEAVEN OF VENUS
II. HEAVEN OF MERCURY
I. HEAVEN OF THE MOON

SPHERE OF FIRE
PURGATORY
SPHERE OF AIR
HEMISPHERE OF WATER
Centre of Gravity
HELL
HEMISPHERE OF EARTH
Jerusalem

>>• THE UNIVERSE •<<

CHAUCER

Biographical Note

GEOFFREY CHAUCER, c. 1340–1400

Chaucer was born when Edward III was achieving his first victories in the Hundred Years' War against France. The history of the Chaucer family to some extent mirrors the rise of the burgher class during these years. His father and grandfather were prosperous wine-merchants who had obtained some standing at court and were beginning to engage in public service. The poet for most of his life held government offices, and Thomas Chaucer, who was almost certainly the poet's son, rose to wealth and influence in the fifteenth century.

The extant records of Chaucer's life show that he was a busy and versatile man of affairs, but they disclose almost nothing of his personal life or of his literary career. Even the exact date of his birth is a matter of conjecture. From evidence he gave in a law-suit in 1386 it is known that he was then "forty years old and more and had borne arms for twenty-seven years." From an early age he evidently had intimate knowledge of the court; he served successively in the households of Lionel, Duke of Clarence, Edward III, and John of Gaunt, Duke of Lancaster. In 1359 he was a member of Lionel's division in the largest army which Edward III had so far led into France. Chaucer was taken prisoner and ransomed by the King. The following year he seems to have acted as diplomatic courier in the negotiations resulting in the Peace of Calais. He may then have been chosen to receive special training for government service, perhaps education at the Inns of Court, for by 1367 he had become a servant to the King with a pension for life.

Chaucer's social position was advanced by his marriage, perhaps in 1366, to Philippa de Roet, a lady in waiting on the Queen and sister of Katherine Swynford, afterwards the third wife of John of Gaunt, from whose issue the Tudors traced their descent. Chaucer had already begun to win some reputation as a poet and on the death of Gaunt's first wife in 1369, he wrote, supposedly at the Duke's request, the *Book of the Duchess,* in which he shows an intimate knowledge of the French court poetry.

During the first ten years of his service as a King's esquire Chaucer was frequently employed for diplomatic missions to the continent, "on the King's secret affairs." He went several times to France and the Low Countries, but perhaps the most important for his literary development were the two missions that he made to Italy in 1372 and 1378. The first of these took him to Genoa on a commercial assignment, but he also visited Florence and was there when the city was arranging for Boccaccio's lectures on Dante. On his second journey to Italy, regarding "certain affairs touching the expedition of the King's war," he visited Milan, where Petrarch had lived and worked the last twenty years of his life.

Even before his second Italian mission Chaucer had begun to receive offices at home. In 1374 he had been appointed Comptroller of Customs and Subsidy of Wools, Skins, and Hides. That same year he obtained rent-free the house above the city gate of Aldgate and was awarded by the King a daily pitcher of wine. A few years later he was also given charge of the customs on wines. In his position in the Custom House, which he held for almost twelve years, Chaucer came into close association with the great merchants who were then beginning to come into prominence, and seems to have been particularly intimate with the merchants who actually controlled the city government of London. Yet there is little indication that he ever became strongly partisan in politics. He received his first appointment under Edward III, when John of Gaunt was the power behind the throne; it was confirmed by Richard II, and Chaucer received several preferments from him; yet he also continued to receive favors from Henry IV after Richard's deposition.

The twelve years passed in the tower above Aldgate were among the most productive for Chaucer as a writer. Besides the two court poems, the *House of Fame* and the *Parliament of Fowls,* Chaucer, as the result of his Italian journeys and reading of Boccaccio and Petrarch, was inspired to work upon "the sto-rye of Palamon and Arcyte" and the *Troilus and Criseyde.* The dedication of the *Troilus* to "moral Gower" and "philosophical Strode" disclose something of his intellectual friend-ships. He seems to have been rather intimate with Gower, for that poet acted as his deputy at the Custom House during one of his missions. Strode, who was known for his work in logic at Oxford, was also associated with Chaucer in a business transaction. Chaucer's interest in philosophy is particularly shown in his trans-lation of the *De Consolatione Philosophiæ* of Boethius, which provided the inspiration for several of his shorter poems. In the *Legend of Good Women* Chaucer proposed to atone to Love for his portrayal of the "false Cressida" by celebrating the lives of nineteen of "Cupid's saints," nine of which he completed.

In 1385, having obtained deputies for his comptrollerships, Chaucer appears to have re-tired to the country, perhaps to Greenwich. He became justice of the peace for Kent and the following year was elected to parliament as one of the knights of the shire. By the end of that year, however, Chaucer had ceased to work at the customs, perhaps because of the hostility of the Duke of Gloucester to the King's ap-pointments, and for three years he was without employment. During this period of leisure it is probable that he began the *Canterbury Tales.*

Chaucer entered upon a new series of gov-ernmental posts in 1389 when Richard II as-sumed direct control of the government. As Clerk of the King's Works, he supervised the maintenance and repair of the royal buildings and parks, including the construction of scaf-folds for the tournaments at Smithfield. In this office he was obliged to travel constantly and was twice robbed by highwaymen on the same day. His clerkship ceased in 1391, and he be-came administrative director of North Pether-ton forest in Somerset. This was his last regular office, and although he spent some time in Somerset, he was frequently in London, where he continued to enjoy royal favor. His pensions were somewhat irregular, for as was common at the time it was difficult to exact payment from the Exchequer, but there is little evidence that he suffered any real want. During his last years he presumably continued to work on the *Canterbury Tales,* and wrote a few minor poems and the *Treatise on the Astrolabe,* written for "litel Lowis my son."

In 1399, shortly after the coronation of Henry IV, Chaucer leased for fifty-three years a house in the garden of Westminster Abbey. He had previously received several gifts from Henry, and his pensions were approved and increased by the new King. Chaucer lived for less than a year in the Abbey garden. He died on October 25, 1400, and as a tenant of the grounds, was buried in Westminster Abbey in the place now known as the Poet's Corner.

Contents

TROILUS AND CRISEYDE

Biographical Note   173

BOOK I   177

BOOK II   190

BOOK III   210

BOOK IV   232

BOOK V   252

Troilus and Criseyde

BOOK I

1

Before we part my purpose is to tell
Of Troilus, son of the King of Troy,
And how his love-adventure rose and fell
From grief to joy, and, after, out of joy,
In double sorrow; help me to employ
My pen, Tisiphone, and to endite
These woeful lines, that weep even as I write.

2

To thee I call, whose joy is to torment,
O cruel Fury, in thy drear domain!
Help me, that am the sorrowful instrument
Of help to lovers, for I sing their pain
As best I can; and it is true and plain
That a sad fellow suits a sorry mate,
And sorrowing looks a tale of sorrowful fate.

3

Serving the servants of the god of love,
Not daring love in my ungainliness,
Though I should die for it I look above,
And pray, far off in darkness, for success;
But if this bring delight or ease distress
For any lover that may read this story,
Mine be the labour and be love's the glory!

4

But all you lovers bathing in delight,
If any drop of pity in you be,
Remember the despair of some past night
You have endured, and the adversity
Of other folk; you too have bitterly
Complained when love has ventured to displease
You—or you won him with too great an ease.

5

And pray for those who now are in the case
Of Troilus, which you shall later hear,
That love may bring them to his heaven of grace;
And also pray for me to God so dear
That I may show, or at the least come near
To show the pain of lovers suffering thus,
In the unhappy tale of Troilus.

6

And also pray for those that have despaired
In love and look for no recovery;

7

Also for those maliciously ensnared
By wicked tell-tales, whether he or she;
Pray thus to God in His benignity
To grant them soon their passing from earth's face
That have despaired of love and of his grace,

7

Pray also for all those that are at ease,
That God may grant them long continuance
And perseverance in the will to please
Their ladies, for love's honour and romance;
And I will pray, the better to advance
My soul, for all love's servants that may be,
And write their woes and live in charity,

8

And have a true compassion for their pain,
As though I were their brother, close and dear;
Now listen to me in a friendly vein.
For I shall go straight on, as shall appear,
To my main matter now, and you shall hear
The double sorrow of Troilus and Criseyde,
And how that she forsook him ere she died.

* * *

9

It is well known the Greeks in all their
    strength
Of arms, and with a thousand ships, set out
For Troy and they besieged it at great length
—Ten years it was before they turned about—
With one design (by many means, no doubt)
To take revenge upon the ravishment
Of Helen by Paris; that was why they went.

10

Now it fell out that living in Troy town
There was a lord of great authority,
Calkas by name, a priest of high renown
And learned in the art of prophecy;
He, by the answer of his deity,
Phoebus Apollo, whom they also call
Apollo Delphicus, knew Troy must fall.

11

And so when Calkas knew by calculation,
And by the answer this Apollo made,
The Greeks would mount so great a prepa-
    ration
That Troy must burn and be in ruin laid,
He sought to flee the city, to evade

The doom he knew she was to undergo,
To be destroyed whether she would or no.

12

And so this wise, foreknowledgeable man
Took purpose quietly to slip away,
And, to the Greek host, following his plan,
He stole in secret from the town, and they
Received him courteously, with great display
Of reverence; they trusted to the skill
Of his advice to ward off every ill.

13

When this was known, noise of it far and wide
Spread through the town and it was freely
    spoken
"Calkas has fled, the traitor, and allied
With those of Greece!" Their vengeance was
    awoken
Against a faith so treacherously broken.
"He and his family and all he owns
Ought to be burnt," they shouted, "skin and
    bones!"

14

Calkas had left behind, in these mischances,
One who knew nothing of his wicked deed,
A daughter, whose unhappy circumstances
Put her in terror for her life indeed,
Not knowing where to go or whom to heed,
For she was both a widow and alone,
Without a friend to whom she might make
    moan.

15

Criseyde this lady's name; and, as for me,
If I may judge of her, in all that place
There was not one so beautiful as she,
So like an angel in her native grace;
She seemed a thing immortal, out of space,
As if a heavenly, perfected creature
Had been sent down to earth, in scorn of
    nature.

16

This lady, having daily at her ear
Her father's shame and treason to the town,
Out of her mind, almost, with grief and fear,
Dressed in her widow's weeds of silken brown,
Sought Hector out and on her knees went
    down,
Tenderly weeping, and in piteous fashion
Excused herself and begged for his compas-
    sion.

17

This Hector was by nature full of pity
And saw she was in misery and dread,

One of the fairest, too, in all the city;
So, in his kindness cheering her, he said
"Your father's treason—put it from your head!
A curse upon it! You yourself in joy
Shall stay among us while you please, in Troy.

18

"All shall be done to honour and respect you,
As much as if you had your father here;
I'll see that there are people to protect you,
And I shall try to keep an open ear."
She gave him humble thanks and, drawing
    near,
Began her thanks again, but he prevented her;
Then she went quietly home, he had con-
    tented her.

19

So in her house, with such in her employ
As it concerned her honour to uphold,
She stayed, and, long as she remained in Troy,
Held her high rank, was loved by young
    and old,
And was well spoken of; I am not told
Whether she had children; if she had or no
My author does not say. I let it go.

20

And things fell out, as often in a war,
With varying chance for Trojan and for
    Greek;
At times the men of Troy paid dearly for
Their city, but at others nothing weak
Their enemies found them; upwards to
    the peak
Then down and under Fortune whirled
    them fast
Upon her wheel, until their anger passed.

21

But how this city came to its destruction
Is not my present purpose to relate,
For it would make too long an introduction
So to digress, and you would have to wait;
But, of the Trojan war and Trojan fate,
All those who can may study the vagaries
In Homer and in Dictys and in Dares.

22

Though shut within their city by the might
Of the Greek host, which was encamped
    about,
The men of Troy gave up no ancient rite
Due to their gods; they were indeed devout,
And their most sacred relic, beyond doubt,
Highest in honour, was named, as I recall,
Palladion, which they trusted above all.

23

And so it happened when there came the time
Of April, when the meadows all are spread
In newest green, when Spring is at its prime
And sweetly smell the flowers, white and red,
In various ways the Trojans, it is said,
Did their observance, as they long had done,
To grace the feast of this Palladion.

24

And to the temple in their Sunday-best
They crowded generally, to hear the rite
Of their Palladion, and with the rest
There came, more prominently, many a
knight
And many a lady fresh and maiden bright,
In fine array, the greatest and the least,
In honour of the season and the feast.

25

And among these, in widow's black, and yet
Unequalled in her beauty, came Criseyde;
Just as an A now heads our alphabet,
She stood unmatchable; she glorified
And gladdened all that crowded at her side;
Never was seen one to be praised so far,
Nor in so black a cloud, so bright a star

26

As was Criseyde; so all were glad to own
That saw her there, gowned in her widow's
grace;
And yet she stood there, humble and alone
Behind the others in a little space
Close to the door, for modesty; her face
Was cheerful, and the dress that she was
wearing
Simple; there was composure in her bearing.

27

This Troilus, whose custom was to guide
His younger knights, now led them up
and down
Through the great temple, and from side to
side;
He studied all the ladies in the town,
Bestowing here a smile and there a frown,
Servant to none—none troubled his repose,
And so he praised or slighted whom he chose.

28

And as he walked he was for ever glancing
To note if any squire of his or knight
Began to sigh, or let his eye go dancing
Towards some woman who had come in sight;
Then he would say "God knows, it serves you
right!

Softly she lies asleep for love of you,
Who turn in restless pain the whole night
through!

29

"I've heard, God knows, of how you lovers
live,
Your mad observances and superstitions,
The pains you take, the services you give
To win your love; when won, what dread
suspicions!
And when your prey is lost, what exhibitions
Of woe, fools that you are—and blind, dear
brothers!
Not one of you takes warning from the others."

30

And with that word he puckered up his look,
As if to say "Was that not wisely spoken?"
At which the god of love arose and shook
His angry head, revenge in him awoken,
And showed at once his bow was yet unbroken;
He smote him suddenly and with a will;
And he can pluck as proud a peacock still.

31

O blind-eyed world! O blindness of intention!
How often counter to the boasts we air
Fall the effects of arrogant invention!
Caught is the proud, and caught the debonair.
This Troilus has climbed a slippery stair
And little thinks he must come down again;
The expectations of a fool are vain.

32

As when proud Dobbin starts to shy and skip
Across the road, pricked on by too much corn,
Until he feels the lash of the long whip,
And then he thinks "Although I may be born
To lead the team, all fat and newly shorn,
Yet I am but a horse, and horse's law
I must endure as others do, and draw."

33

So was it with this proud and fiery knight,
Son of a famous king though he might be;
He had supposed that nothing had the might
To steer his heart against a will as free
As his; yet, at a look, immediately,
He was on fire, and he, in pride above
All others, suddenly was slave to love.

34

And therefore take example, from this man,
You wise ones, proud ones, worthy ones
and all;
Never scorn love, for love so quickly can
Put all the freedom of your heart in thrall;

It has been ever thus and ever shall,
For love can lay his bonds on every creature,
And no one can undo the law of Nature.

35

Now this has long proved true, and proves so
    still.
It is a thing that everybody knows;
None, we are told, has greater wit or skill
Than they whom love most powerfully
    throws;
The strongest men are overcome, and those
Most notable and highest in degree;
This was and is and yet again shall be.

36

And truly it is well it should be so;
In love the very wisest have delighted,
And they that most of all have felt its woe
Most have been comforted and most requited;
It softens hearts by cruelty excited,
And to the noble gives a nobler name,
And most it teaches fear of vice and shame.

37

Now since it is not easily withstood
And is a thing of virtue, in its kind,
Forbid love not to bind you as he would,
Since, as he pleases, he has power to bind.
The twig that bends is better, to my mind,
Than that which breaks; and so I would advise
You let love lead you, who is proved so wise.

38

But to proceed with what I have to say,
And more especially of this king's son,
Leaving collateral matters by the way,
It is of him I mean to speak or none,
Both in his joy, and his cold cares begun,
And all he did, as touching this affair;
Having begun, let me return to where

39

This Troilus and his knights were gallivanting
About the temple, quizzing and pointing out
This or that lady, all the while descanting
On where she lived, within town or without,
And it so fell that, looking through the rout,
His eye pierced deeply and at last it struck
Criseyde where she was standing, and there
    stuck.

40

And suddenly he felt himself astounded,
Gazing more keenly at her in surprise,
"Merciful god! O where" he said, confounded,
"Have you been hiding, lovely to my eyes?"
He felt his heart begin to spread and rise,

And he sighed softly, lest his friends should
    hear,
And he recaptured his accustomed sneer.

41

Now she was not among the least in stature,
But all her limbs so answerable were
To womanhood, there never was a creature
Less mannish in appearance standing there;
And when she moved, she did so with an air
Of ease and purity, so one could guess
Honour and rank in her, and nobleness.

42

To him her look and movements, all in all,
Were wonderfully pleasing, with her clear
Semblance of light disdain, when she let fall
A sidelong glance, as one who might appear
To put the question "What! May I not stand
    here?"
And then her face unclouded and shone bright;
Never had he seen so beautiful a sight.

43

And as he looked at her his pulses thickened;
Such passion, such desire, began to race
That at the bottom of his heart there
    quickened
The deeply printed image of her face;
His insolent staring now had given place
To drawing in his horns, and gladly too!
Whether to look or not he hardly knew.

44

He who had thought his cleverness so telling
And lovers' anguish something to despise,
Was now aware that love had made his
    dwelling
Within the subtle currents of her eyes;
Now, suddenly, at a mere look, there dies
The spirit in his heart, all is laid low;
Blessed be love that can convert us so!

45

She in her black, so deeply to his liking,
Above all else he lingered to behold;
But why he stayed and what desire was striking
Upon his sense he neither showed nor told,
And, to maintain his manner as of old,
He looked at other things, or so pretended,
Then back at her, until the service ended.

46

And after that, not wholly in confusion,
Out of the temple casually he pressed,
Repenting every cynical allusion
That he had made to love, for fear the jest
Might turn against himself; he did his best

To hide his misery, lest the world should
    know it,
Dissimulating, so as not to show it.

47

When from the temple he had thus departed,
Back to his palace instantly he turned;
While through and through her image shot
    and darted
Within him; trying not to seem concerned,
He burnished up his looks, and gaily spurned
At all love's servants in his speech the while,
To cover up his feelings with a smile;

48

"Lord! What a happy life," he said, "how blest,
A lover leads! The cleverest of you, now,
Who serves love most attentively and best,
Comes to more harm than honour, you'll
    allow;
Your service is requited god knows how,
Not love for love, but scorn for service true;
There's a fine rule to bind an Order to!

49

"All your observances are quite unsure
Of their result, save in a point or so;
No other Order claims so great, so pure
A servitude as yours, and that you know;
But you have worse than that to undergo.
Were I to tell you, though it made good
    sense,
What the worst is, you all would take offence.

50

"Yet notice this: what you refrain from doing,
Or indeed do, but with the best intention,
Your lady will be ever misconstruing,
Deem it an injury and start dissension;
If, for some reason of her own invention,
She's angry, you will get a scolding too;
Dear Lord! How lucky to be one of you!"

51

For all this, when he judged it time, he duly
Fell into silence; what was there to gain?
For love had limed his feathers, and so truly,
He scarce had strength enough in him to feign
That he had work to do, and would detain
His followers no longer; sunk in woe,
And at an utter loss he bid them go.

52

When he was in his chamber and alone,
At his bed's foot he sank in indecision;
At first he sighed, and then began to groan,
Till, thinking of her thus without remission
As there he sat, he had a waking vision;

His spirit dreamed he saw her, as before,
There in the temple, and he gazed once more.

53

And thus he made a mirror of his mind
In which he saw her image all entire,
And was well able in his heart to find
That it was high adventure to desire
One such as her; and if he did not tire
In serving her, he well might win to grace
Or be accepted in a servant's place.

54

In his imagination neither pain
Nor toil in service ever could be thrown
Away on one so beautiful; again
His passion was no shame, though it were
    known;
Rather, an honour, as lovers all would own,
Greater than all before; he argued so
In utter ignorance of his coming woe.

55

He settled then to learn the craft of lover,
And thought to work at it in secrecy;
First he must keep his passion under cover
From every living creature, utterly,
Unless there was some hope of remedy,
Remembering that a love too widely blown
About yields bitter fruit, though sweetly sown.

56

On, on he thought, and, over and above
All this, what he should speak and what
    keep in,
What he could do to kindle her to love,
And with a song decided to begin
At once, and so he sang aloud to win
Himself from grief, and gave his full assent
To love Criseyde and never to repent.

57

And not the gist alone of what was sung
By him, as says my author, Lollius—
But also—bar the difference of tongue—
The very phrases used by Troilus
I shall repeat; they went exactly thus;
He who would hear them as the text rehearses
Will find them all set down in the next verses.

58

The Song of Troilus

"If there's no love, O God! What am I feeling?
If there is love, who then, and what, is he?
If love be good, whence comes this sorrow stealing?
If evil, what a wonder it is to me
When every torment and adversity

That comes of him is savoury, to my thinking!
The more I thirst, the more I would be drinking.

59

And if so be I burn at my own pleasure,
Whence comes my wailing, whence my sad complaint?
Why do I weep, if suffering be my treasure?
I know not. Nothing weary, yet I faint!
O quickening death, sweet harm that leaves no taint,
How do I find thee measurelessly filling
My heart, unless it be that I am willing?

60

And yet, if I am willing, wrongfully
I make complaint! Buffeted to and fro,
I am a rudderless vessel in mid-sea,
Between the double-winded storms that blow
From ever-contrary shores; alas, for woe!
What is this wondrous malady that fills me
With fire of ice and ice of fire, and kills me?"

61

And after that "O god of love," said he
In piteous tones, "dear lord, my spirit is
For ever yours, as yours it ought to be;
I thank you, lord, that I am brought to this.
If she be woman or goddess out of bliss
That you have made me serve, I know not, I;
But as her man I mean to live and die.

62

"You in her eyes are standing mightily,
As in a place worthy of your divine
Virtue; if I, or if my service be
Acceptable to you, be you benign!
And all my royalty I here resign
Into her hand, as humbly as I can,
As to my lady, and become her man."

63

The fire of love—which God preserve me from—
Deigned not to spare in him his royal blood,
But held him like a thrall in martyrdom
And did not pay the high respect it should
Have paid his virtue or his soldierhood,
But burnt him in so many ways anew
That sixty times a day his face changed hue.

64

His thought of her so much began to mount
From day to day, to quicken and increase
In passion, that he held of no account
His other duties; often to release
Himself from torment and in hope of peace
He pressed for glimpses of her, but the flame
More fiercely burnt, the nearer that he came.

65

"The nearer to the flame, the hotter 'tis,"
As everyone among you is aware;
But were he far or near, I can say this:
By night or day, in wisdom or despair,
His heart—the eye within his breast—was there,
Fixed upon her, more lovely in his view
Than was Polyxena, and Helen too.

66

There never passed an hour of the day
But that at least a thousand times he cried
"Lovely and good, to thee, as best I may,
I give my service; would to God, Criseyde,
You would take pity on me before I died!
Dear heart, alas! my health, prosperity
And life are lost unless you pity me!"

67

So all his other troubles left his head,
Fears for the siege, his safety, they all went;
There were no other fawns of fancy bred
In him by passion: all his argument
Was for her pity, all his good intent
Was to be hers—her man—while life gave breath:
That would be life indeed, his cure from death.

68

The deadly showers that are the proof of arms,
Where Hector and his brothers showed their zest,
Never once moved him now, though these alarms
Still found him, as before, among the best
On horse or foot; and longer than the rest
He stayed where danger was, and, as to that,
He did such work as must be wondered at,

69

But not to show his hatred of the Greek,
Nor even for the rescue of the town;
What made him battle-mad was just to seek
A single end, namely to win renown
And please his lady better; up and down
And day by day in arms, he beat the life
Out of the Greeks, went through them like a knife.

70

And from then on love robbed him of his sleep
And made an enemy of his food; his sorrow
Increased and multiplied, he could not keep
His countenance and colour, eve or morrow,
Had anyone noticed it; he sought to borrow
The names of other illnesses, to cover
His hot fire, lest it showed him as a lover.

71

He said he had a fever and was ill.
I cannot say whether his lady knew
And feigned an ignorance, or if she still
Knew nothing—one or other of the two;
But I am well assured that it is true
It did not seem that she so much as thought
About him, or his griefs, or what he sought.

72

And knowing this, the fever in him ran
Almost to madness, for his fear was this,
That she already loved some other man
And had no care for any love of his.
His heart was bleeding into an abyss,
And yet, to win the world, in all his woe,
He could not bring himself to tell her so.

73

Yet he, in moments of release from care,
Scolded himself, and over and again
Would say "O fool! now you are in the snare,
Who used to mock at lovers and their pain;
Now you are caught, go on and gnaw your
   chain!
You lectured lovers, saying they were senseless,
For just those things in which you are de-
   fenceless.

74

"And what will lovers say, do you suppose,
Should this be known? Ever, behind your back,
There will be scornful laughter: 'There he
   goes,
Our man of wisdom, bold in his attack
And his irreverent scorn for us who lack
His judgement! Now, thank God, he'll join
   the dance
Of those whom love hastes slowly to advance!'

75

"But O thou woeful Troilus, would to God,
Since thou must love by force of destiny,
Thy heart were set on one that understood
Thy sorrow, though she lacked in sympathy!
But she, thy lady, is as cold to thee
As is the frost under a winter moon,
And thou art snow in fire, and lost as soon.

76

"Ah, would to God that I had reached the
   harbour
Of death, to which my miseries must lead!
Lord, what a comfort to me, what an arbour!
I should be quit of languishing indeed!
For if it's blown abroad how much I bleed
In secret, I'll be mocked a thousand times
Worse than the fools they pillory in rhymes.

77

"Ah, help me, God! And help me, sweetest
   heart!
Yes, I am caught—none ever caught so fast!
Dear love, have mercy on me, take my part,
Save me from death; and, until life is past,
More than myself I'll love you, to the last!
Gladden me, sweetheart, with a friendly
   glance,
Though I may never hope for better chance!"

78

These words and many another he let flow;
And all his lamentations would resound
With her dear name, to tell her of his woe,
Till in salt tears he very nearly drowned.
But all for nought, she never heard a sound;
And to reflect a little on that folly
A thousand times increased his melancholy.

79

Bewailing in his chamber thus alone,
To him there came a friend called Pandarus;
He slid in unperceived and heard him groan,
And, seeing his distress, addressed him thus:
"Good gracious! What's the reason for this
   fuss?
Merciful God, whatever can it mean?
Is it the Greeks have made you look so lean?

80

"Is it some fit of conscience or remorse
That now has brought you round to your
   devotions?
Ah, you are weeping for your sins, of course;
The dread of punishment has bred these
   oceans.
God save the Greeks if they and their commo-
   tions
Can wring our jolliest fellows in a mangle
And give the lustiest life a holy angle!"

81

These words he rattled off in the belief
They would convert his sorrows to vexation;
Anger, for once, might overmaster grief,
And rouse his heart to sudden indignation;
He knew of course, by common reputation,
There was no braver soldier in the war
Than he, or one who cherished honour more.

82

"What mischief brings you here, or has se-
   lected
This moment to intrude upon my care,"
Said Troilus, "who am by all rejected?
For love of God, and at my earnest prayer,
Take yourself off; for how are you to bear

Seeing me die? And therefore go away,
For die I must; there is no more to say.

83

"But if you think me ill because of fear,
You may take back your scorn; for I am one
Whom other cares oppress and hold me here,
Greater than anything the Greeks have done,
Which it is death for me to think upon;
But though I will not tell you, or reveal it,
Do not be angry, for I must conceal it."

84

Pandarus, almost melting with compassion,
Kept saying "O alas! What can it be?
Dear friend, are love and friendship out of
    fashion?
If ever truth, as between you and me,
Existed, never show such cruelty
As not to share your miseries with candour!
Don't you know well that it is I? It's Pandar!

85

"Come, let me have a part in your despair,
And even if I cannot comfort you
One of the rights of friendship is to share
Not only in pleasure, but in sorrow too;
I have and ever shall, in false and true,
In right and wrong, backed you and loved
    you well,
So do not hide your grief from me, but tell."

86

This sorrowful Troilus began to sigh
And said "God grant it may be for the best
To tell you everything and satisfy
Your longing, though it burst my very breast;
And yet I know you cannot give me rest.
Still, lest you think I do not trust a friend,
Here's how it stands; now listen and attend.

87

"Love, against whom he who would most
    securely
Seek a defence will find it least availing,
So grievously assails me, that he surely
Is teaching me despair; my heart is sailing
Straight into death, so burning, so prevailing
Are my desires, and it were greater joy
To die than to be King of Greece or Troy.

88

"Dear Pandar, best of friends, I've said enough;
I've told you the whole secret of my woe.
For God's love, think my cares are dangerous
    stuff
And keep them hidden; only you must know,
For great would be the evils that could flow

From them if they were known; be happy,
    friend,
Leave me in grief unknown to meet my end."

89

"What could be more unnatural or dafter
Than hiding this, you fool?" said Pandarus,
"Perhaps the very one you're pining after
Is placed where my advice could profit us."
"A wonder that would be!" said Troilus,
"In your own love-affairs you seldom shine,
So how the devil can you help in mine?"

90

"Now listen, Troilus," said Pandar, "Yes,
Fool though I be, it happens every day
That one whose life is ruined by excess
Can save his friend from going the same way;
I saw a blind man go, the other day,
Where others tumbled down who had their
    eyes;
Besides, the fool may often guide the wise.

91

"A whetstone is no instrument for cutting,
Yet it can put an edge on cutting tools;
I may have lost my way when I went rutting,
But my mistakes should teach you all the rules,
The wise, I say, may take advice from fools;
If you'll take warning, you'll improve your wits.
Things are defined best by their opposites.

92

"How ever could one know what sweetness is
If one had never tasted bitterness?
For inward happiness was never his
Who never was in sorrow or distress.
Set white by black, and shame by worthiness,
Each seems the more so by its opposite;
So say the wise, and so we all admit.

93

"And, as this law of contraries will show,
I who have often striven with immense
Troubles in love, ought all the more to know
How to advise you and to talk good sense
About what staggers you; take no offence
If I should wish to help you, and to share
Your heavy load. So much the less to bear!

94

"I am well aware that things are much with me
As with Oenone, the fair shepherdess,
Who wrote to your good brother, Paris—she
Made a lament out of her wretchedness;
You saw the letter that she wrote, I guess?"
"No, not as yet, I think," said Troilus.
"Indeed?" said Pandar, "Listen, it went thus:

95

" 'Phoebus, who was the first to find the art
Of medicine, knew, for everybody's care,
What herbs to give, he knew them all by heart;
But in his own case found his wits were bare,
For love had caught and bound him in a snare;
And it was all for King Admetus' daughter;
His potions did him no more good than water.'

96

"It's just the same, unhappily, with me;
I love one best, and oh my heart is sore!
And yet perhaps I know the remedy
For you, if not for me; then say no more.
I have no cause—I know it well—to soar
Like a young falcon, up and off to play,
Still, to help you, there's something I can say.

97

"One thing there is of which you can be
      certain;
Though I should die in torture, for no pain
Would I betray you; I will draw the curtain
Upon your secret; nor will I restrain
You, were it Helen's love you would obtain,
Your brother's lady, were it known to me;
Love whom you like, whoever she may be!

98

"Tell me straight out what was the origin,
Since you must trust me fully as a friend—
The cause of all this fever you are in;
And have no fear to speak, I don't intend
Or not just now, to scold or reprehend;
No one can wean a lover from the cup
Of love, until he choose to give it up.

99

"Let me inform you there are these two
      vices,
Trusting in everyone, and trusting none.
But there's a happy mean, and that suffices;
For it's a proof, if you can trust to one,
Of constancy and truth; and therefore shun
Excess, and give your trust to somebody
And tell your grief; and, if you like, tell me.

100

" 'Woe to the man,' they say, 'who is alone,
For when he falls there's none to help him
      rise,'
But since you have a friend, tell him your
      moan!
The best way, certainly, to win the prize
Of love is not—according to the wise—
To wallow and weep like Niobe the Queen
Whose tears (in marble) still are to be seen.

101

"Let be your weeping and your dreariness
And let's have lighter topics for relief;
Your time of sorrow then will seem the less,
Do not delight in grief to seek more grief,
As do those fools, who, when they strike a reef,
Egg misery on with misery, resolved
To lend no ear or have their problem solved.

102

"People have said it is a consolation
To find a fellow-sufferer in woe;
A view that ought to have our approbation
Since we are both of us tormented so
By love; I feel so wretched, as you know,
That surely there could be no heavier doom
Upon my shoulders. Why? There isn't room!

103

"I hope to God you do not think me shady,
One who would trick you of her by a wile?
You know yourself I love a certain lady
As best I can—it's gone on a long while.
And since you know I do it for no guile,
And trust me better than to think me double,
Tell me a little; for you know my trouble."

104

Yet, for all this, no word said Troilus,
But lay there long, like one upon a bier;
Then he broke out in sighing, and he thus
Turned round, and lent to Pandar's voice
      an ear.
His eyes rolled up, and Pandar was in fear
Some frenzy had taken him and he might fall
Into a fit and die, and end it all.

105

"Wake up!" cried Pandarus; his voice was sharp.
"Are you asleep? Is this a lethargy?
Or are you like some ass that hears a harp,
And gets the sound of strings in harmony,
But in his mind there sinks no melody,
He finds no pleasure to be had in it,
So dull and bestial is his donkey-wit?"

106

Pandarus stopped with that, and silence fell,
For still no answer came from Troilus,
Whose fixed intention was never to tell
A soul for whom it was he suffered thus;
The wise have told us it is dangerous
To cut a stick, for he who cuts it may
Live to be beaten with it, one fine day.

107

And this is specially true, they say, in love;
What touches love is secret, or should be.

Rumours of love spring out and spread
   enough,
Unless it's governed very carefully.
And there are times when one should seem
   to flee
The thing pursued; it is the hunter's art.
Troilus turned this over in his heart.

108

Nevertheless, on hearing Pandar's shrill
"Wake up!" he gave a sigh that seemed to
   come
With anguish, and he said "Though I lie still,
Dear friend, I am not deaf; could you be dumb
A little? I have heard your rules of thumb;
So leave me to my wretchedness and grief;
Truly your proverbs bring me no relief.

109

"And they are all the cure you have for me:
I do not want a cure, I want to die.
What do I care about Queen Niobe?
Drop your old parallels, they don't apply."
"No?" Pandarus retorted, "That is why
I said just now it is a fool's delight
To hug his grief, rather than put things right.

110

"I see that you are losing hold on reason;
But answer me, if she you hold so dear
Were known to me, might not a word in
   season,
If you permit it, whispered in her ear
By me—the things you dare not speak, for
   fear—
Draw forth her pity for a certain youth?"
"Never, by God," he said, "and by my truth!"

111

"What, not if I went earnestly about it,
As if my life depended on the need?"
"No," Troilus said, "I'd rather die without it."
"And why?" "Because you never could
   succeed."
"Are you so sure of that?" "I am indeed,"
He said, "however skilful you may be,
She'll ne'er be won by such a wretch as me."

112

Said Pandarus: "Alas! How can this be,
Despairing, without reason, of your case?
What! She's alive—your lady—isn't she?
How do you know that you are out of grace?
Such troubles, if you look them in the face,
Aren't without remedy; do not think your cure
Impossible! The future's never sure.

113

"I grant you're suffering from as sharp a pain

As Tityus does—the fellow down in Hell,
Whose stomach birds tear out and tear again,
Vultures, they call them, so the old books tell;
But for all that I cannot have you dwell
In an opinion so ridiculous
As that there cannot be a cure for us.

114

"But just because you have a coward heart
And angry ways, and foolish, wilful scares
About not trusting me, you won't impart,
You will not stir to mend your own affairs
So much as to give reasons for your airs,
But lie there dumb for hours at a stretch;
What woman could feel love for such a
   wretch?

115

"What else will she suppose about your death,
If you should die, and she not know the cause,
Save that in fear you yielded up your breath
Because the Greeks besiege us. You should
   pause
And think what thanks she'll give you, what
   applause,
For that! She'll say, and so will all the town,
'The wretch is dead, the devil drag him
   down!'

116

"Here you may weep alone, cry out and kneel,
But, love a woman when she doesn't know it
And she'll requite in ways you cannot feel;
Unknown, unkissed; 'unsought-for' means
   'forgo it.'
Many a one who loved and did not show it
Has bought love dear, a twenty-winter drouth
Of knowing her, that never kissed her mouth.

117

"What! Should he therefore fall into despair,
Turn infidel in love—for grief, I mean?
Or kill himself although she still seems fair?
No, no! But ever constant, fresh and green,
To love and serve his lady, his heart's queen,
And think himself rewarded that he serves her,
More by a thousand times than he deserves
   her."

118

And of these words young Troilus took heed,
And saw at once the folly he was in;
What Pandarus had said was true indeed;
To kill himself was not the way to win,
For it was both unmanly and a sin,
Nor would his lady ever know the fashion
Of his death, not knowing of his pain and
   passion.

119

And at the thought he sorrowfully sighed
And said "Alas! What then is best to do?"
"If you are willing," Pandarus replied,
"The best would be to tell, and tell me true;
And, on my honour, I will see you through;
If I seem slow, or find no remedy,
Drag me in pieces, hang me on a tree."

120

"Yes, so you say," said Troilus, plunged in care,
"God knows it will be none the better so;
Help will be hard indeed in this affair,
For—well I know it—Fortune is my foe;
Not one of all the men that come and go
On earth can set at naught her cruel wheel;
She plays with us and there is no appeal."

121

Said Pandar, "You blame Fortune for your fall
Because you're angry; yes, at last I see.
Don't you know Fortune is the same for all,
Common to everyone in some degree?
Yes, there's this comfort for you; goodness me,
Just as her joys pass over and are gone,
So come her tribulations, and pass on.

122

"For if her wheel should ever cease to turn
Fortune would then no longer Fortune be;
But since her wheel is always on the churn,
Perhaps her very mutability
May bring about what you desire to see;
She may be going to help you in this thing;
For all you know, you have good cause to sing.

123

"Accordingly I make it my petition,
Give up this grief, stop looking at the ground!
For he that seeks a cure from his physician
Will have to take the bandage off his wound.
May I be chained to Cerberus, Hell's Hound,
Though it be for my sister—your love-
  sorrow—
If, by my will, she is not yours tomorrow!

124

"Look up, I say, and tell me who she is
At once, that I may go about your need;
Come, do I know her? Can't you tell me this?
For if I do, there's hope I may succeed.'
A vein in Troilus began to bleed,
For he was hit, and reddened up in shame.
"Aha!" said Pandar, "here we start the game!"

125

And on the word, he gave him a good shaking,
And said "Her name, you thief! You've got to
  tell!"

And foolish Troilus then started quaking,
As if some fiend were taking him to Hell,
And said "The fountain of my woe, my well
Of grief, my sweetest foe, is called Criseyde."
He trembled at the word, he almost died.

126

When Pandar heard the name that he had
  given,
Lord, he was glad, and said "My dearest friend,
I wish you joy, by Jupiter in Heaven!
Love has done well for you! O happy end!
Be cheerful; wisdom and good name attend
Upon her, she has gentle breeding too;
Whether she's beautiful I leave to you.

127

"I never have known one of her position
So generous, so happy in her mood,
So friendly in her speech and disposition,
Or one that had more grace in doing good,
And how to do it better understood;
And, to cap all, as far as honour stretches,
Compared to such as she is, kings are wretches.

128

"And so, take heart; the first point, certainly,
In noble natures, truly apprehended
And properly established, is to be
At peace within themselves, division ended;
So should you be, for what is there but splendid
In loving well and in a worthy place?
You should not call it Fortune; call it Grace.

129

"Then think of this, and let it gladden you;
Your lady has great virtues, as you know;
It follows that she has compassion too,
Where goodness is so general; and so
Be specially attentive to forgo
Any demand that injures her good name,
For virtue does not stretch itself to shame.

130

"Happy indeed the day that I was born,
To see you settled in so fair a place!
Upon my word I truly could have sworn
You never would have won to such a grace
In love! Do you know why? You used to chase
And chaff the god of love, and in your spite
Called him 'Saint Idiot, Lord of Fools' De-
  light'!

131

"And many a sly, sophisticated prod
You gave, and said that people who were prone
To serve in love were very Apes of God;
And some, you said, would munch their meat
  alone,

Lying in bed and heaving up a groan;
'White-fevered ones,' you called them,
     'shivering lovers.'
'Pray god,' you said, 'not one of them recovers.'

132

"And some of them took on about the cold
Rather too much—so you asserted roundly—
And others were pretending when they told
Of sleepless nights, when they were sleeping
     soundly.
That's how they hoped to rise, but were
     profoundly
Mistaken, so you said, for they would fall;
That's how you went on jesting at them all.

133

"You also said that far the greater part
Of lovers spoke in general, and took care,
If they should fail with one, to learn the art
Of finding compensation otherwhere.
Now I could jest at you, if jest it were;
Nevertheless I'd stake my life, God knows,
And swear that you were never one of those.

134

"Now beat your breast, and say to him above
'Have mercy on me, Lord, for I repent,
If I said ill; I am myself in love.'
Speak from your heart, let it be truly meant."
Said Troilus, "Lord Cupid, I consent;
Pardon my mockeries! If thou forgive,
I never more will mock thee while I live."

135

"Well said, indeed," said Pandar, "that
     should stop
The god's displeasure; he should feel appeased.
And now that you have wept so many a drop,
And said those things whereby a god is pleased,
I hope to God your sorrow will be eased,
And think that she, the cause of all your grief,
Hereafter may be cause of its relief.

136

"A soil that nurtures weeds and poisonous stuff
Brings forth these herbs of healing just as oft.
Next to the foulest nettle, thick and rough,
Rises the rose in sweetness, smooth and soft;
And next the valleys rise the hills aloft,
And next the dark of night the glad tomorrow;
And joy is on the borderland of sorrow.

137

"So, lay a temperate hand upon the bridle;
Wait for the tide in patience, for the best,
Or otherwise our labour will be idle;
More haste, less speed; the faster for a rest.
Be diligent, true, secret, self-possessed,

But gay and open-hearted; persevere
In serving love, and then you need not fear.

138

" 'The heart divided over many places
Is nowhere firm in any,' say the wise.
Such hearts can never gain a lady's graces;
And some who love are like the man who tries
To plant a herb or tree, and then will rise
And pull it up, to see if it's alive
Next day; no wonder if it does not thrive.

139

"And since the god of lovers has bestowed
A worthy place upon you, stand you fast!
Into a happy harbour you have rowed,
And so I say, in spite of sorrows past,
Hope for the best; because unless you blast
Our work by over-haste, or by despair,
There's hope for a good end to your affair.

140

"Do you know why I feel the less dismay
In thinking how this matter might be tendered
In treating with my niece? The learned say
That never man or woman was engendered
Unapt to suffer love; we're all surrendered
To a celestial or a natural kind,
One or the other, and so I hope to find

141

"Some grace in her; and in regard to her,
In the young beauty of her womanhood,
It would not be becoming to prefer
A love celestial, even if she could.
Not yet at least; it's clearly for her good
To love and cherish some distinguished
     knight;
Not to would show a vicious appetite.

142

"So I am ready, and shall always be,
To go to work for you in this affair
—For both of you—I have a hope in me
To please you later; you're a sage young pair
And know how to keep counsel. Take
     good care
That no one is the wiser of it; thus
We shall be happy—all the three of us.

143

"And on my honour, at this moment too,
I have been struck by quite a happy thought;
And what it is I shall impart to you.
I think since Love, in goodness, has not
     brought
You out of all your wicked ways for nought;
He'll make you the best pillar, I suppose,
Of his whole cult, the more to grieve his foes!

144

"Example why: think of those learned men
Who most have erred against God's holy law,
And whom He has converted back again
From heresy, because He wished to draw
Them back to Him; and they stand most
    in awe
Of God, strongest in faith, it is confessed;
I understand they combat error best."

145

When Troilus heard Pandarus consenting
To help him in the loving of Criseyde,
His grief, as one might say, was less tor-
    menting,
But hotter grew his love, and he replied
With sobered look (although his heart inside
Was dancing), "Blessed Venus from on high
Help me to earn your thanks before I die!

146

"Is there a means to make my suffering less
Till this be done, dear friend? Can you
    achieve it?
What will you say of me and my distress?
I dread her anger—how will she receive it?
Suppose she will not listen or believe it?
I dread it all; and then, that it should spring
From you, her uncle! She'll hear no such
    thing."

147

And Pandarus retorted "I should worry.
Afraid the Man will fall out of the Moon?
Lord, how I hate your foolishness and flurry!
Mind your own business! Let me beg a boon
Of you: leave everything to me, and soon
You'll find I've acted in your interest."
"Well, friend," he answered, "do as you think
    best,

148

"But listen to me, Pandar, just a word!
I would not have you think me so demented
As to desire—in all that you have heard—
Anything shameful, or to be repented;
I'd rather die. So let her be contented,
I mean no villainy; make it understood
That every thought I have is for her good."

149

Pandarus gave a laugh, and he replied
"With me for surety? That's what they all say.
I shouldn't care if she had stood beside
And heard it all! Farewell! I must away.
Adieu! Take heart! God speed us both today!
Give me this work, hand me this job to do;
Mine be the labour, and the sweets to you!"

150

This Troilus fell down upon his knees,
Seized Pandar in his arms and held him fast;
"Death to the Greeks! Down with our ene-
    mies!"
He cried, "and God will help; the worst is past!
You may be sure, if life in me will last,
With God's good help, there's some of them
    will smart!
Pardon this boast; it comes from a full heart.

151

"Now, Pandarus, here's all that I can say:
O wise, O wonderful, O man of skill!
O all-in-all! My life and death I lay
In your good hands; help me!" "Of course
    I will."
"God bless you; whether it is cure or kill,
Commend me to her; say her lightest breath,"
He added, "may command me to the death."

152

This Pandarus, in eagerness to serve
This his full friend, smiled back and gave his
    views:
"Farewell, and think I'm trying to deserve
Your thanks;" he said, "I promise you good
    news."
He turned and off he wandered, in a muse,
Thinking how best to win to her good graces;
What were the proper times, the likely places?

153

For nobody who has a house to build
Goes dashing out to work and make a start
With a rash hand; he waits, if he is skilled,
And sends a line with caution from his heart
To win his purpose, first of all by art;
So Pandar inwardly prepared his plan
And wisely gave it shape ere he began.

154

Then Troilus no longer laid him down,
But sallied out at once upon his bay
And played the lion to defend the town;
Woe to the Greek who met with him that day!
From that time on so winning was his way
With everyone in Troy, he gained in grace;
They loved him that but looked upon his face.

155

For he became the friendliest of men,
The noblest, the most generous and free,
The sturdiest too, one of the best that then,
In his own times, there were, or that could be.
Dead were his jesting and his cruelty;
His loftiness, the arrogance that hurt you,
Yielded their place, exchanging with a virtue.

156

Of Troilus I now shall say no more
Awhile; he is like one that's gravely wounded,
Who finds the wound no longer is so sore,
But knows the corner has not yet been
    rounded;
An easy patient, with his faith well founded
On the physician's skill who is attending,
He faces the adventure now impending.

BOOK II

1

Out of these black waves, let us at last make sail;
O wind, O wind, the day begins to clear!
In such a sea my boat is like to fail,
It is in travail and I scarce can steer.
This sea is the tempestuous career
Of black despair that Troilus was in;
But now the calends of his hope begin.

2

O lady mine, Clio, be thou the one
Henceforth to speed me; O be thou my Muse!
Rhyme this book well for me till I have done;
Here there's no other art for me to use.
And so I ask all lovers to excuse
My story, not of my own feeling sung,
But taken from Latin into my own tongue.

3

Therefore I wish for neither thanks nor blame
In all this work; meekly, I beg you try
To overlook it if a word be lame,
For just as said my author, so say I.
And though I speak of love unfeelingly
That's nothing new; no wonder I am duller
Than he; a blind man is no judge of colour.

4

And then, you know, the forms of language change
Within a thousand years, and long ago
Some words were valued that will now seem strange,
Affected, even; yet they spoke them so,
And fared as well in love, for all I know,
As we do now; in various lands and ages
Various are the ways to win love's wages.

5

And therefore, should it happen by some chance
That one of you, some lover, listening here
To what I tell you of the slow advance
Troilus made to gain his lady's ear,
Thinks 'I would never buy my love so dear!'
Or marvels at this phrase, or at that blunder,
I do not know; to me it is no wonder.

6

Not all who find their way to Rome will trace
The self-same path, or wear the self-same gear,
And in some lands they'd count it a disgrace
Were they to act in love as we do here,
With open doings, looks that make all clear,
Visits, formalities and tricks of phrase;
To every land its own peculiar ways.

7

For there are scarcely three among you all
Who have said alike in love, or done the same;
What pleases one of you (it may befall)
Won't suit another; but on goes the game.
Some choose a tree on which to carve a name,
And some a stone; and I, as I began,
Will follow on my author, if I can.

* * *

8

Now in that mother of happy months, in
    May,
When the fresh flowers, blue and white
    and red,
Quicken again and every meadow-way
Is full of balm, that winter left for dead,
When blazing Phoebus with his beams out-
    spread
Stands in the milk-white Bull, it so occurred
—As I shall sing—I say, on May the third,

9

This Pandarus, for all his crafty speech,
Felt in himself the shafts of love so keenly
That, notwithstanding all his gift to preach,
His colour came and went a little greenly;
For love, that day, had treated him so meanly
He went in woe to bed, and there he lay
Tossing and turning till the break of day.

10

The swallow Progne, with her mournful
    song,
When morning came, began on that embit-
    tering
Tale of her change of shape, while Pandar long
Lay half asleep in bed. When dawn was
    glittering,
She, close beside him, started on her twittering
About her sister, Philomela, taken
And raped by Tereus; Pandar began to waken;

11

He called his servants and began to rise,
Remembering his errand and the boon
Promised to Troilus—his enterprise.
He made a calculation by the moon,
And found her favourable for journeys. Soon

He reached his niece's palace, close beside;
Now Janus, god of entry, be his guide!

12

When, as I say, he reached his niece's place,
He knocked: "Where is her ladyship?" said he;
And when they told him, in he strode apace,
And found two ladies in her company.
They sat in a paved parlour, and all three
Were listening to a girl reading a measure
Out of *The Siege of Thebes,* to give them pleasure.

13

"Madam," said Pandar, "Blessings on your
    head,
And on the book, and all the company!"
"Ey, uncle, welcome! Welcome indeed!" she
    said,
And up she rose at once and cordially
Captured his hand; "Three times last night,"
    said she,
"I dreamt of you; good fortune come of it!"
She showed him to a bench and made him sit.

14

"You'll be the better of it all this year,
Dear niece, if God is good," said Pandarus,
"But I have interrupted you, I fear;
What book is it that you are praising thus?
For God's love, what does it say? Impart to us;
Is it of love? Give me good news, my dear!"
"Uncle!" she said, "Your mistress isn't here."

15

And they all laughed; and after that she said
"It is *The Siege of Thebes* that we are reading;
I think we just had left King Laius dead,
Murdered by Oedipus, that sad proceeding;
We stopped at the next chapter; it is leading
On to Amphiaräus, how he fell
—He was the Bishop—through the ground,
    to Hell."

16

"I know all that" said Pandarus "myself,
And all the siege of Thebes, unhappy place;
There are twelve books about it on my shelf,
But let's forget it. Let me see your face,
Come on, take off that wimple and uncase!
Down with that book, get up and let us dance
And give the month of May some counte-
    nance!"

17

"I? God forbid!" she answered, "Are you mad?
Heavens! Is that how widows are behaving?
You frighten me! It really is too bad
To say such crazy things; you must be raving!
I should be sitting in a cave, and saving

My soul by reading holy martyrs' lives;
Let girls go out to dances, or young wives."

18

"As ever I hope to thrive," said Pandarus,
"I know a reason why you should be gay."
"Now, uncle dear," she answered, "tell it us,
Is the siege over? Have they gone away?
Those Greeks! They frighten me to death, I
    say."
"No, no," said he, "and I can tell you flat,
My secret is a thing worth five of that!"

19

"Heavenly gods!" said she, "What can you
    have got?
Worth five of that? No, no, it can't be so.
But for the world I can't imagine what
It could be; it's some joke of yours, I know,
You'll have to tell us; we are all too slow;
And my poor wit in any case is lean,
For, by the Lord, I don't know what you
    mean."

20

"And never shall," he said, "depend on that!
Secrets there are I may not bring to birth."
"But why not, uncle? What are you hinting at?"
"By God, I'll tell you this, for what it's worth;
There'd be no prouder woman on the earth
If you but knew, or in the town of Troy;
No, I'm not joking, as I may have joy!"

21

And she began to wonder more than ever
A thousand times, and lowered her eyes a
    touch,
For since the day she had been born, she never
Had wanted to know anything so much;
She sighed and answered, "If your news is such,
Dear Uncle, I will promise not to tease you,
And ask no more about it than will please you."

22

So after that, with many happy rallies,
Gay looks and gossip, talk began to range;
They joked on this and that, and there were
    sallies
On many matters, pleasant, deep, and strange,
Such as good friends together will exchange,
When newly met; and then she asked of
    Hector,
Scourge of the Greeks, the town's wall and
    protector.

23

"He's very well, thank God," said Pandarus,
"Save for a slight arm-wound—not to be
    reckoned

As serious; and then there's Troilus,
His fresh young brother, Hector, indeed, the
    Second;
There's one who has followed virtue where
    she beckoned,
A man all truth, as noble as his birth,
Wise, honoured, generous—a man of worth."

24

"O I'm so glad! And Hector's better since?
God save them both and keep them from all
    harms!
How nice it is, how fitting to a Prince
To be so valiant in the field of arms!
And to be so well-natured! That's what
    charms
Me most; such goodness and such strength,
    I mean,
So royally combined are seldom seen."

25

"That's true, that's very true," said Pandarus,
"My word! The King has two such sons today
—Hector, I mean, of course, and Troilus—
And I would stake my life on it that they
Are free of vices, freer, I dare say,
Than any man alive under the sun;
Their strength and worth are known to ev-
    eryone.

26

"Of Hector there is nothing need be said;
In all the world there is no better knight;
Indeed he is the very fountainhead
Of valour, and more in virtue than in might;
Experienced soldiers say so, and they're right.
I'll say the same of Troilus, but then
I don't know any two such fighting men."

27

"By God," she said, "of Hector that is true,
And it is true of Troilus, I agree:
Everyone talks of what they've seen him do
In arms, day after day—so gallantly!
And then at home he is all courtesy
And gentleness, in fact he wins attention
From everyone whose praise is worth a men-
    tion."

28

"You certainly are right in what you say,"
Said Pandar, "anybody's heart would warm
To see him as I saw him yesterday!
Never fled bees in such a mighty swarm
As fled the Greeks; he was in fighting form,
And through the battlefield, in every ear,
There ran no cry but 'Troilus is here!'

29

"Now here, now there, he hunted them and
    coursed them;
Nothing but Greek blood! There was Troilus
Dealing out doom; he wounded and un-
    horsed them
And everywhere he went it happened thus;
He was their death, but shield and life to us;
That was a day! Not one dared make a stand
Against him, with his bloody sword in hand.

30

"Added to that, he is the friendliest fellow,
Considering his rank, I ever knew,
And, if he chooses, can be warm and mellow
To anybody that he thinks will do."
And then, abruptly, Pandarus withdrew,
Taking his leave and saying "I must fly!"
"Uncle! I hope I'm not to blame, am I?

31

"What's wrong with you to weary of our
    chatter?
Especially a woman's! Must you go?
Now do sit down, I have a business matter
Which needs your wisdom, Uncle; don't
    say no."
And those who were about her were not slow
To move away, so that she might discuss
The run of her affairs with Pandarus.

32

When they had finished all they had to say
About her household and its maintenance,
He said "Well now I really must away;
But still I say stand up and let us dance,
Throw off your widow's habit, now's your
    chance!
Why make yourself look ugly? I'll prevent you
When such a glad adventure has been sent
    you."

33

"Ah, well remembered! Now, for heaven's
    sake,
May I not know the meaning of all this?"
"No, for it asks some leisure; it would make
Me most unhappy, if some prejudice
Should lead you into taking it amiss;
It's better I should hold my tongue in patience
Than tell a truth against your inclinations.

34

"For, by divine Minerva, dearest niece,
And Jupiter who thunders from afar,
And blissful Venus—whom I never cease
To serve—you, of all earthly women, are

The one I love the best—I'll go so far,
(Not counting mistresses); I will not grieve
   you,
As well you know yourself; and so I leave you."

35

"I know," she said, "dear Uncle, all my thanks!
You've always been a friend, I must admit.
And there is nobody I know who ranks
So high with me—and so ill-paid for it!
But by the grace of God and by my wit,
You shall be one I never will offend;
And if I did before, I will amend.

36

"But I beseech you, for the love of God,
You that I trust," she said with emphasis,
"To drop your distant speech that sounds
   so odd,
And tell your niece whatever is amiss."
On hearing that, her uncle, with a kiss,
Said to her "Gladly, little niece, I will;
And what I say—try not to take it ill."

37

She lowered her eyelids, ready to attend,
And Pandarus began to cough a bit
And said "Well, dearest, always, in the end,
Though story-tellers like to show their wit
By adding on embellishments to fit,
Yet in reality they all intend,
For all their artifice, to reach an end.

38

"And since the end is every story's strength,
And this one so befitting, and so fine,
Why should I paint or draw it out in length
For you, who are so true a friend of mine?"
Speaking, he sought some answering inward
   sign,
And long beheld her, gazing in her face,
And said "In such a mirror, be there grace!"

39

Thinking "To make a business of my tale
And tease it out, will make it none the fresher;
She'd take no pleasure in it, and could not fail
To think it was my purpose to enmesh her;
Sensitive minds distrust a form of pressure
They do not understand; I'll have to sense
Some way of touching her intelligence."

40

He went on staring in his busy way,
And she, aware that he beheld her so,
Said "Did you never see me till today?
Lord, how you stare! Answer me, yes or no!"
"Yes, yes, I'm staring, and before I go

I shall stare more; I'm wondering," said he
"If you are lucky; well, we soon shall see.

41

"For every creature there is shaped a time
Of high adventure, if he can receive it;
Should he be careless of it, then his crime
Is wilfulness, disdaining to achieve it;
It is not accident, you may believe it,
Nor fortune that's to blame, but his demerit,
His very sloth and wretchedness of spirit.

42

"A fair adventure into happiness,
My lovely niece, is yours if you can take it;
And for the love of God, for mine no less,
Catch hold of it at once, lest luck forsake it;
What need of a long speech? I will not make it;
Give me your hand; no one, if you but knew
—And if you cared—has had such luck as you!

43

"And since what I shall say you must put
   down
To good intentions, as I said before,
And since I love your honour and renown
As much as any one, and maybe more,
I swear by all the oaths I ever swore
That if it angers you, I tell you plain,
I never will set eyes on you again.

44

"Why, look! You're all a-tremble! Don't be
   frightened!
You've changed your colour; fear has made
   you pale!
The worst is over! There, the skies have
   brightened!
Of course it's a surprise; my little tale
Is new to you. But you won't find me fail.
Always trust me! Would I be one to shame you
With tales of anything that misbecame you?"

45

"Good Uncle, for the love of heaven, pray
Come off it, tell me what it's all about!
I'm terrified of what you're going to say,
And, at the same time, longing to find out.
O do say on! Don't leave me in this doubt,
Do tell me, whether it be good or ill!"
"Well, listen, then," he said, "for so I will.

46

"Now, little niece of mine, the King's dear son,
Good, wise, and open-hearted, fresh and true,
Who bears himself so well to everyone,
Prince Troilus, is so in love with you
That you must help; he'll die unless you do.

Well, there it is. What more am I to say?
Do what you like; but you can save or slay.

47

"But if you let him die, I'll take my life
—And that's the truth, I'm telling you no
      lies—
I'll cut my throat, ay with this very knife!"
At that the tears came bursting from his eyes;
"And when you've killed us both, you'll realize
Just what a fine day's fishing you've enjoyed;
What good is it to you if we're destroyed?

48

"Alas that he, who is my own dear lord,
That true man, ay, that gentle, noble knight,
Who asks for nothing but your friendly
      word . . .
I see him dying as he walks upright,
And hurrying desperately out to fight
Seeking his death, seeking his fate, on duty.
Alas that God has sent you so much beauty!

49

"But if indeed you prove yourself so cruel,
So careless of his death, that you would fetch
No deeper sigh in losing such a jewel
Of honour than a trickster or a wretch,
If you are such, your beauty cannot stretch
To justifying such a cruel deed;
So, with a choice before you, take good
      heed.

50

"Woe to the gem that has no native force!
Woe to the herb that has no healing shoot!
Woe to the beauty that knows no remorse
Or pity, but treads others underfoot!
And you, the crop of beauty and its root,
If, in such beauty, pity cannot thrive,
Then it is pity you should be alive.

51

"You may be sure this is no trick or fraud;
For I would rather you and I and he
Were hanged than I should live to be his
      bawd,
Hanged high enough for everyone to see;
I am your uncle; it were shame to me
As well as to yourself, if I should let him
Despoil you of your honour, or abet him!

52

"Now understand, my dear; I do not ask you
To bind yourself to him in any way;
No pledge is wanted, but I gently task you
To smile at him, to be more kind, more gay,
Friendlier than before; and so you may
To save his life, and that's my whole intent;
God help me, that is all I ever meant.

53

"Look, this request is purely reasonable,
There is no reason to distrust it, none.
And what you fear—the worst you would
      be able
To say against it—is that everyone
Would think his visits rather overdone;
But I reply none but a fool would find
More in it than pure friendship of the mind.

54

"Who would suppose, were he to see a man
Going to church, that he was on his way
To desecrate the images? He can
Govern himself; reflect, and you will say
He's wise and forgets nothing; every day
His praises mount; besides, he'll come so
      seldom,
What would it matter if all the town be-
      held him?

55

"Such friendly loves are quite the rule in Troy;
So wrap that cloak well round you; it's a cover.
And surely, as the Lord may give me joy,
It's best to do so, as you will discover.
And, niece, to ease the anguish of a lover,
Sugar your cold aloofness with a breath
Of kindness; don't be guilty of his death!"

56

Criseyde, who heard him broach this enterprise
Thought "Well, I'll feel for what he's lead-
      ing to."
And said, "Now, Uncle, what would you
      advise?
What would you think it best for me to do?"
"That is well said," he answered; "best for you
Would be to love him of your own accord,
Since love for love's a reasonable reward.

57

"Think that in each of you, from hour to hour,
There is some part of beauty laid to waste
By the advance of age; ere Time devour
You, *love!* When you are old, there's none
      will haste
To love you; there's a proverb to my taste:
' *"Aware too late," said Beauty, as she passed.*'
And age will cure disdain in you at last.

58

"The King's Fool has a trick, to cry aloud
On seeing a woman hold herself too high,
'May you live long enough, and all the proud,
To see the crow's foot walk about your eye;
Send for a mirror then, in which to pry
Into the face that you will bear tomorrow!
I cannot wish you any greater sorrow.' "

59

With that he ceased to speak, and hung his
  head,
And she burst out in tears as she replied
"Alas, for grief! O why am I not dead,
Since all good faith on earth has surely died?
What would a stranger do to me," she cried,
"When one I thought my friend, the best of
  them,
Bids me to seek a love he should condemn?

60

"I could have trusted you to play your part
If I had fallen, by some calamity,
In love with him, or Hector, lost my heart
To fierce Achilles, or some other he;
You would have shown no mercy then to me.
Imagine the rebukes you would have hurled!
But O, there's no believing this false world.

61

"What! Is this all the joy, is this the pleasure?
This your advice? And this my blissful case?
Is this the true reward and promised treasure?
Is all your painted argument in place?
Was this your object? Pallas, Queen of
  Grace,
Provide for me, protect me from on high!
For I am so astonished, I could die!"

62

She sighed in sorrow and she ceased to speak.
"Is that the best that you can do?" said he,
"By God, I shan't come here again this week,
Since I am so mistrusted; I can see
That you make light enough of him and me
And of our death, alas. O wretched pair!
If only he might live I would not care.

63

"O cruel god, O Mars the merciless!
O Furies Three of Hell, to you I call!
Let me not leave this house if I profess
The slightest villainy or harm at all!
But as I see my lord is doomed to fall,
And I with him, I wash my hands and say
Your wickedness has slain us both today.

64

"And since you would be glad to see me dead,
By Neptune, that is god of the salt sea,
From this time forth I never will eat bread
Until my own heart's blood flows out of me;
Certainly I can die as soon as he."
And up he jumped and made as if to leave,
But she was quick, and caught him by the
  sleeve.

65

Criseyde indeed was almost dead with fear,

Being the timidest, most shrinking creature
That ever was; not only could she hear,
But see his earnestness in every feature;
And she sensed nothing evil in the nature
Of what he asked her for; there might
  be harm
If she refused; she melted in alarm.

66

She thought "Misfortunes happen thick
  and fast
All the day long for love; in such a case
Men can be cruel, of a wicked cast,
And if this man, here, in this very place,
Should kill himself, it's more than I could face.
What would they say? Should I not be to
  blame?
I'll need to play a very subtle game."

67

Three times she murmured with a sorrow-
  ful sigh
"O heaven, how unfortunate for me!
For my good name and my position lie
In danger—and my Uncle's life, maybe.
But, by God's guidance, I shall presently
Think how to keep my honour, and to keep
My Uncle too!" and then she ceased to weep.

68

"Well, of two evils one should choose the
  less;
I'd rather show him some encouragement
Than risk my Uncle's life, I must confess.
There's nothing more to which I must con-
  sent?"
"No, dearest niece." "O well, I am content;
I'll do my utmost in the situation,
And force my heart against my inclination.

69

"But do not think I mean to lead him on,
For love a man I neither can nor may
Against my will; be certain thereupon.
But pleasant I will be, from day to day;
'No' is a thing that I would never say
(My honour safe)—save from timidity.
But 'kill the cause and cure the malady.'

70

"And here I make a solemn protestation:
Go any deeper into this affair,
And certainly no thought of your salvation
—Though both of you should die in your
  despair,
And though the world should hate me then
  and there—
Will get him any pity out of me."
"Of course, of course," said Pandar, "I agree,

71

"But may I really trust you on this head?
And to the promise you have given here,
That you will truly keep to what you said?"
"Why, certainly," she answered "Uncle
    dear."
"And I shall have no reason—is this clear?—
To scold or lecture you on any score?"
"Why no indeed," she promised, "say no
    more."

72

And then they fell to other pleasant chatter,
Till, at the last "Good Uncle," she said,
    wheeling
Back to his news, "do tell me, in this matter,
How did you come to know what he was
    feeling?
Does anyone know of it?" "No." "Is he ap-
    pealing?
Can he speak well of love? As if he cared?
Do tell me that I may be well prepared."

73

Pandar began to smile a little then
And answered "Well, it happened, truth to tell,
The other day—I can't remember when—
Down in the palace garden, by a well,
We spent the day together, so it fell;
We met to talk about a stratagem
Against the Greeks, that should embarrass
    them.

74

"And not long after, we began to leap
About and try our javelins for a throw
Or two; at last he said he wished to sleep
And down he lay upon the grass; and so
I wandered off, and, roaming to and fro,
I overheard him, as I walked alone,
Give utterance to a miserable groan.

75

"And so I stalked him softly from behind,
And this, to tell you truly, was the main
—As far as I can call it now to mind—
Of what he said. He started to complain
To the god of love; 'Have pity on my pain,
Lord, though I have rebelled in my intent
Against thee; *Mea culpa*! I repent!

76

" 'O God, that leadest, at thy disposition,
Thy creatures, each to his appointed end,
Justly foreseen by thee, my true contrition
Accept with favour, and, as may please
    thee, send
My penance, Lord; yet shield me and defend

Me from despair, dividing me from thee;
Be thou my shield for thy benignity!

77

" 'So sorely she that stood in black, apart,
Has wounded me—the beauty in her eye
Has sounded to the bottom of my heart;
By which I know that I must surely die
And, worst of all, I may tell no one why;
And hotter grow the embers when they're
    spread
With covering ashes that are pale and dead.'

78

"With that he smote his head to earth and lay
Muttering there—I really don't know what.
And I, in turn, went tiptoeing away
From his distress, as if I knew it not;
Then I came back; 'Wake up, you sleep a
    lot!'
I said, gazing upon him from above,
'It's obvious you cannot be in love,

79

" 'If you can sleep so that there's no awaking
You! Was there ever such a dull young man?'
'Go on,' he said, 'enjoy your own head-
    aching
For love, and let me live as best I can.'
And though his griefs had left him pale
    and wan,
He gave himself as fresh a countenance
As if he had been leading a new dance.

80

"Well, this passed over, till, the other day,
It happened that I wandered all alone
Into his bed-chamber; and there he lay
Flat on his bed; I never heard man groan
More sorrowfully; the reason for this moan
I did not know; as I came in, and went
Towards him, he abandoned his lament.

81

"As that gave rise in me to some suspicion,
I neared and found him in a flood of tears;
And, as the Lord may save me from perdition,
I felt more pity than I've felt for years;
My ingenuity, my tricks and fleers
Could barely keep him from his death! I vow
My heart is weeping for him even now.

82

"And never, heaven knows, since I was born
Have I so preached! I preached with might
    and main:
Never to secrecy have been so sworn
Before he told me who could cure his pain;
Don't ask me to rehearse his speech again,

His woeful words, his melancholy tune,
Or not unless you want to see me swoon.

83

"It is indeed to save his life—no less—
And do no harm to you, I am thus driven;
That we may live, show him some friendliness;
Be gentle with him, for the love of heaven!
Now I have told you flat; my heart is shriven;
And since you know that my intention's clean,
Take heed of it; no evil do I mean.

84

"And now good luck; dear God, that's all I
care;
You who have caught your fish without a net,
(And such a fish!) be wise as you are fair;
The ruby in the ring will then be set.
Never were two so fortunately met
As you, when you are wholly his, will be;
Almighty God! May I be there to see!"

85

"No, I said nothing about that!" she cried,
"Aha! God help me, you will spoil it all!"
"Dear niece, forgive me," he at once replied,
"I meant it well whatever I let fall
By Mars, his helmet and his battle-call!
Do not be angry, we are one blood, dear
niece."
"Well, all's forgiven," she answered, "and at
peace."

86

With that he took his leave and, well content,
Went home in high good humour on his own;
Criseyde arose and, never pausing, went
Straight to her private chamber, all alone,
And there she sat, as still as any stone,
And every word he had said began to wind
And echo up and down within her mind.

87

And there was some amazement in her
thought,
At this new situation; but when she
Had taken stock, she did not find it fraught
With danger—not as far as she could see;
A man—it is a possibility—
May love a woman till his heart will crack;
But she is not obliged to love him back.

88

But as she sat and meditated thus,
The clamour of a skirmish rose without,
Men in the street were shouting "Troilus!
He has just put a horde of Greeks to rout!"
At that her servants all began to shout
"Ha! Come and see! Open the lattice wide!
This is the street through which he'll have
to ride

89

"To reach the palace—the only way, of course,
From Dardanus Gate, that's where the chain
is down."
With that he came, leading his little force
In file, at ease; and so they entered town.
It was his lucky day, without a frown
On Fortune's face; nothing, they say, can be
Hindered that happens by necessity.

90

This Troilus sat high on his bay steed,
Fully and richly armed, showing his face.
His horse, being wounded, had begun to bleed;
He rode him homeward at a gentle pace,
And truly such a sight of knightly grace,
As seen in him, was never seen before,
Even in Mars, who is the god of war.

91

So like a man of arms, so like a knight
He seemed, so full of high courageousness,
For he had both the body and the might
For gallantry, as well as hardiness;
And then to see him in his fighting dress,
So fresh, so young, so thoroughbred, so trim,
It was a very heaven to look at him.

92

His helmet, which was hewn in twenty places,
Hung by a tissue down behind his back;
His shield was battered in by swords and
maces,
With arrows lodged in it in many a crack
That had pierced horn and rind and sinewy
pack;
And still the shout went up "Here comes
our joy,
And, next his brother, holder up of Troy!"

93

This made him blush a little, out of shame,
To hear his praises sung with such a din,
And it was sport to notice, as he came,
How modestly he dropped his eyes and chin.
Criseyde could take his whole appearance in;
Down to her heart she let it softly sink,
Saying to herself "O who has given me
drink?"

94

For her own thoughts she started to blush red,
As she remembered "Heavens! This is he,
The man my uncle swears may soon be dead,
If he should get no mercy out of me."
And in pure shame at such a notion, she

Pulled in her head and made the window fast,
While he and all the shouting crowd went
    past.

95

She began casting, rolling up and down
Within her thought, his excellence in war,
His royal state, his widely-spread renown,
His wit, his shape, his reputation for
Nobility; and yet what moved her more
Was that he pined for *her*, that such a youth
Should die for her—if he intended truth!

96

Now envious souls might quarrel with me
    thus:
"This was a sudden love! For how could she
So lightly give her love to Troilus,
And at first sight of him! Can such things be?"
Those who say that will get no good of me.
For everything must needs have a beginning
Ere all is done, and when it comes to winning

97

Her love, I do not say she suddenly
Gave it to him; but she began to incline
To like him first, and I have told you why.
His manhood and the thought that he
    would pine
On her account invited love to mine
Within her; but long service and devotion
Got him her love; it was no sudden motion.

98

And also blissful Venus, well arrayed,
Sat in her seventh house in heaven, and so
Was well disposed, with other stars in aid,
To cure the foolish Troilus of his woe;
And, to tell truth, she was not wholly foe
To Troilus in his nativity,
But somewhat favoured him, the luckier he.

99

And now no more of Troilus, let him go
Riding along, and let us turn as fast
Back to Criseyde, who sat with head hung low
All by herself, beginning to forecast
What course to set her mind upon at last,
If it should happen that her uncle's voice
Continued to press Troilus on her choice.

100

Lord! In her mind what arguments deployed
About this matter of which you have been told!
What it was best to do, and what avoid,
She turned them back and forth in fold on fold;
And now her heart was warm and now was
    cold,
And I shall write some part of this debate,
Which it has pleased my author to relate.

101

Prince Troilus in person well she knew
By sight, and also knew his gentle birth;
And so she thought "Though it would
    never do
To grant him love, yet, seeing his great worth,
To be on terms of friendliness and mirth
With him would be an honour, and might be
Some ease to him and a support to me.

102

"I know, moreover, he is my King's son;
Since he now looks on me with such delight,
To flee him utterly would be to run
The risk, perhaps, of rousing him to spite,
And then I should be standing in worse plight;
Would it be wise for me, in such a case,
To purchase hate where I may stand in grace?

103

"Measure and temperance lie in all endeavour,
I know; if one prohibits drunkenness,
That does not mean that everyone for ever
Is doomed to drinklessness, or so I guess!
Knowing myself the cause of his distress,
Can I despise him? I don't think I should,
Since it seems certain that he means my good.

104

"And more than that, I've known for
    many a day
That he's no fool, his character is good;
Certainly, he's no boaster, so they say,
He's too intelligent, that's understood.
Nor will I cherish him, suppose I could,
Enough for him to boast, or have good cause
To boast; for I will sign to no such clause.

105

"Let us suppose the worst that could befall:
People might know he was in love with me.
Would that dishonour me? Why, not at all!
Can I prevent him? Not that I can see.
One hears about such cases constantly;
A man will love a woman without permission
From her; is she the worse for that condition?

106

"Think, too, that he is able to pick out—
Out of the whole of Troy—the loveliest
To be his love (her honour not in doubt);
For he is out and out the worthiest
Except for Hector, who is still the best;
And yet, to save his life now lies in me!
But such is love, and such my destiny.

107

"It is no wonder if he love me, though;
Heaven help me, well I know it—by the bye,
This is a thought I must let no one know—
I am among the loveliest, it's no lie,
For anyone, at least, that has an eye;
And so they say through all the town of Troy;
What wonder then if I should give him joy?

108

"I'm my own mistress, happily at ease,
Thank God for it, according to my state,
Young and untethered, where the pastures
    please,
I fear no jealousy, have no debate;
I have no husband now to say 'Checkmate!'
Husbands are always full of jealousy,
Or masterful, or hunting novelty.

109

"What shall I do? What have I ever done?
Shall I not love—were I to think that best?
What! Heaven knows I could not be a nun.
And if I were to set my heart to rest
Upon this knight, who is the worthiest,
Keeping my honour safe and my good name,
By rights it should not do me any shame."

110

But just as when the sun is shining bright
In March, a month which often changes face,
A gust of wind will set a cloud in flight
To overspread him in the blue of space,
A sudden, cloudy thought began to chase
Across her soul and overspread them all,
Those happy thoughts; fear almost made her
    fall.

111

The fear was this: "Alas, since I am free,
Am I to love and put myself in danger?
Am I to lose my darling liberty?
Am I not mad to trust it to a stranger?
For look at others and their dog-in-manger
Loves, and their anxious joys, constraints and
    fears!
She who loves none has little cause for tears.

112

"For love is still the stormiest way of life,
In its own kind, that ever was begun;
There's always some mistrust, some silly
    strife
In love, some cloud that covers up the sun;
We wretched women! What is to be done
In all our grief? We sit and weep and think;
Our grief is this, that it's our grief we drink.

113

"And then there are these wicked tongues
    whose fashion
Is to speak harm; and men are so untrue;
Immediately they cease to feel their passion,
They cease to love; they're off to love anew;
But harm that's done is done, that's cer-
    tain too:
Those are the very ones that passion rends;
But violent delights have violent ends.

114

"How many are the times when we must own
That treachery to woman has been done!
Can any purpose in such love be shown?
And what becomes of it when it is gone?
No one can say, the answer is not known;
It has no substance, nothing solid in it;
Nothing to end with, nothing to begin it.

115

"How busy, if I love, I'll have to be,
Wooing the gossips! What a time I'll spend
Cajoling them, lest they speak harm of me!
For, without reason for it, they pretend
That it is very wrong to please one's friend.
But who can silence every wicked tongue,
Or stop the sound of bells while they are rung?"

116

But after that her thought began to clear;
She said "Well, nothing venture, nothing win,
Like it or not!" Then a return to fear
Came with some other thought to hem her in;
Fear set her quaking, hope turned pale and
    thin,
Now hot, now cold; with these two to con-
    fuse her,
She rose and looked for something to amuse her.

117

And down the stairs immediately she went,
Into the garden with her nieces three,
And up and down they wandered in content,
Flexippe, Tarba and Antigone,
In play together there, a joy to see,
And other of her women, a great rout
Followed her round the garden and about.

118

It was a wide, walled garden of pleached alleys,
And shadowy with blossom and with green,
All newly benched and sanded; little valleys
And little hills there were, and in between
They walked enlaced; Antigone, serene,
Antigone the Bright, began to sing
A Trojan song. It was a heavenly thing.

119
The Song of Antigone

O love, to whom I am, and ever shall
Be humble subject, and of purpose true,
To Thee, as best I may, I offer all
My heart's desire for ever, in revenue!
For never did thy heavenly grace endue
Any with blessedness so much as me;
I live secure in joy, from all fear free.

120

O blissful god, thou hast me sweetly fettered
In love; there surely is no creature living
Who could imagine how it might be bettered!
For, Lord, with neither quarrel nor misgiving,
The one I love is wholly bent on giving
Me tireless service true; a more unfeigned
There never was, nor less by evil stained.

121

He is the well of honour, and the ground
Of truth, the mirror of all goodliness,
Apollo-thoughted, Lord of new pleasures found,
Rock of my safety, very rootedness
Of virtue, and the slayer of distress;
And, sure, I love him best, as he loves me;
Good fortune follow him, where'er he be!

122

Whom should I thank but Thee, O god above,
For all this bliss in which I now begin
To bathe? Ah, Lord, I give Thee thanks for love!
This is the life, the right life, to be in,
To banish every form of vice and sin;
This turns me so to virtue, I intend
In heart and spirit daily to amend.

123

And whosoever says that love is vice,
Or servitude, through feeling its distress,
Is either envious or overnice,
Or is unable out of brutishness
To love at all; such are the folk, I guess,
Who defame love; nothing of him they know;
They talk, but never yet have bent his bow.

124

What, is the sun, which nature made so bright,
The worse because mere man has not the power
To look upon it with his feeble sight?
Is love the worse, because some wretch is sour?
No happiness that cannot face an hour
Of sorrow has any worth; let those whose bones
Are made of glass, beware of throwing stones!

125

But I, with all my heart and all my might,
As I have said, will love, unto my last,

My dearest heart, my own beloved knight,
In whom my soul has verily grown fast
As his in me, and shall till Time is past.
I feared love once, and dreaded to begin it;
Now I know well there is no peril in it.

126

The song was over and she ceased to sing;
After a moment, "Niece," inquired Criseyde,
"Who made that song? It is a charming thing,
And well-intentioned." And her niece replied
"Madam, the loveliest girl, and best allied,
Of highest rank in all the town of Troy;
She leads her life in greatest honour and joy."

127

"It certainly would seem so, by her song."
Criseyde replied, and sighed in her delight.
"Lord! And can so much happiness belong
To lovers? Can they love as they can write?"
"Yes, truly," said Antigone the White,
"And better; none that ever lived can tell
The bliss of loving, or describe it well.

128

"But never think that every wretch and sot
Knows the true bliss of love; it is not so.
They think it's love if one of them feels hot;
But not at all! It is their ignorance, though.
You have to ask the saints if you would know
If it is fair in Heaven; they can tell.
And ask a fiend if it is foul in Hell."

129

Criseyde said nothing; then, from a world
    away,
She answered "Yes . . . Evening has come at
    last."
But every word that she had heard her say
She printed in her heart. The daylight passed.
Her fear of love lessened and faded fast;
Love sank into her heart and, terror fleeing,
Began on the conversion of her being.

130

The day's bright honour, and the eye of
    heaven,
Night's enemy—all this I call the sun—
Was westering swiftly as his car was driven
Downwards to earth; his daily course was run,
And all things white were growing dim
    and dun
For lack of light; the stars began to show;
She and her folk went in; and time to go.

131

And later when she wished to go to rest,
Being inclined to sleep, or so she said,
When gone were every visitor and guest,

Her womenfolk attended her to bed.
When all was hushed, she lay there still;
   her head
Was filled with everything she could recall
Of the day's doings; you have heard them all.

132

A nightingale upon a cedar green
Under the chamber window where she lay
Sang loudly out against the moony sheen,
And it may well have been, in its bird's way,
A lay of love; her heart grew light and gay.
And long she listened, but at last could keep
Awake no longer, and fell dead asleep.

133

At once a dream descended on her rest;
There came an eagle, feathered white as bone,
Who set his curving talons to her breast
And tore her heart out, giving her his own
Into her body, left her there alone
—And yet she suffered neither fear nor
   smart—
And flew away, leaving her heart for heart.

134

So let her sleep, and let us turn once more
To Troilus riding back in bravery,
After the skirmish I described before;
There in his room he sits, while two or three
Messengers he had sent ran off to see
If Pandar could be found; and in the end
They came on him, and brought him to his
   friend.

135

This Pandarus came leaping in at once
And said "Who's this that's taken such a
   beating
With swords and slings today? Is it that dunce
Young Troilus, who has a fever heating?"
And he began to joke, after this greeting,
"Lord how you sweat! Jump up, let's have
   a dish
Of dinner, and so to bed." "Well, as you wish."

136

And off they went in haste, for they were bent
On supper and a quick return to bed;
Then their attendants closed the doors
   and went
Wherever private inclination led;
And Troilus, whose heart till then had bled
For woe, not knowing what news his friend
   would bring,
At last could say "Well, do I weep or sing?"

137

Said Pandarus "Lie still, and let me sleep;

It's all arranged; you can put on your hat;
And please yourself whether you sing or weep.
You'll have to trust me, but I tell you flat
She will do well by you, be sure of that,
And love you best, by God and on my oath,
Unless you fail in the pursuit, from sloth.

138

"I've got thus far in handling your affair—
From day to day, up to this happy morrow—
I've won her love—her friendship—for you;
   there!
For she has pledged herself; and you can
   borrow
On my security; I've lamed your sorrow,
I've cut its legs away." As you have heard
It all, I needn't say another word.

139

And just as flowers in the chill of night,
Closed in themselves, will stoop upon their
   stalk,
Then hold their heads up to the morning's
   light
And spread their natural beauty where we
   walk,
So Troilus, on hearing Pandar talk,
Threw up his eyes, and cried with upturned
   face,
"O Venus, blessed be thy power and grace!"

140

To Pandar then he held up both his hands;
"Dear Lord, all that I have is yours!" said he,
"I'm free! You've burst my cruel iron bands;
A thousand Troys, though they were given me
One at a time, by God, could never be
So welcome or so gladdening to my heart;
It spreads for joy, O it will burst apart!

141

"Lord, what am I to do? How live? O when
Shall I next see her? Sweetest heart! My dear!
How drive away the long, long time till then?
How soon will you be going again to see her?
You will say 'Wait, be patient, there's no
   fear,'
But felons hanging, fighting for their breath,
Wait in the greatest agony for death."

142

"Now, take it easy, for the love of Mars!
There is a time for everything, just wait
At least till night is over and the stars
Have disappeared, for it's as sure as Fate
I shall be there a little after eight;
Do as I tell you, then, as I implore you;
Or get some other man to do it for you.

143

"And God's my judge that always up till now
I've served you readily until tonight;
And this is no pretence, as you'll allow;
I've always done my best for your delight.
Do as I say, and you will be all right;
And if you won't, then seek your own relief,
And don't blame me if you should come to
    grief.

144

"I know you are a wiser man than I,
A thousand times; but still, if I were you
(God help me so!), the thing for you to try
Would be to write to her, this moment too,
In your own hand; a letter. That should do,
Begging her pity, saying you were ill;
Now don't give in to sloth, but show your will.

145

"I'll take it to her early in the day
And when you know that I am with her there,
Ride past upon a courser right away
In your best armour—but as if there were
Nothing particular happening. I'll take care
That she and I are in a window-seat;
We shall be looking down into the street.

146

"Salute us, if you like, but make it plain,
However, that your look is aimed at me;
And on your life be careful to refrain
From lingering there; God save us, that
    would be
Disaster! Just ride on with dignity;
We shall be talking of you, and I know
That when you have gone by, your ears will
    glow.

147

"As to your letter, you have sense enough
Not to be formal, or to show your wit
By being argumentative or tough;
Your handwriting should not be exquisite
Or clerkly; blot it with your tears a bit;
And if you hit on something good to soften
Her heart, avoid repeating it too often.

148

"For if the greatest harpist now alive,
Having the finest-toned, most glorious harp
That ever was, with all his fingers five,
And finger-nails that never were so sharp,
Kept warbling on one string, we all would carp
At his performance, for we should be bored
By those full strokes on that repeated chord.

149

"Don't jumble up discordant things together,
Medical terms, for instance, do not strike
The proper note in love; and take care whether
Your matter fits your form; they should be
    like;
For if a painter were to paint a pike
With donkey feet and headed like an ape,
It would not do; it would be just a jape."

150

Now this advice appealed to Troilus
But still, he answered with a lover's sense
Of apprehension "O, but Pandarus,
I'd be ashamed to write—it's no pretence—
For I might innocently give offence,
Or she refuse the letter, or resent it,
Then I should die and nothing could pre-
    vent it."

151

Pandar replied "You do as I suggest,
And let me take it to her, as I say;
For, by the Lord that made the east and west,
I hope to bring an answer right away,
Straight from her hand; and if you won't obey,
Well, let it go, and bitter be his pill
Who tries to give you help against your will."

152

Said Troilus "All right, then; I agree,
Since it's your wish; I will get up and write;
And I pray God in all sincerity
To speed the letter which I shall indite,
And your delivery of it. O White
Minerva, send me wit to write it well!"
And he sat down and wrote as I shall tell.

153

He called her his true lady, life and joy,
His sorrow's cure, his bliss, his heart's desire.
And all the other phrases they employ,
These lovers, as their cases may require;
Humbly at first he wrote, and, taking fire,
He tried to earn his way into her grace;
To tell it all would ask no little space.

154

And next he begged her with all lowliness,
Because he wrote in madness, not to chide
The audacity; he wrote under duress;
Love made him do it, or he would have died;
He begged her piteously to take his side,
And after that he said (and lied like thunder)
He was worth nothing, he was no great
    wonder,

155

And she must make allowance for his skill,
Which was but little; and he feared her so,
And argued his unworthiness until

He turned from that to dwell upon his woe,
But that was endless, it would never go;
His truth was sworn to her and he would
	hold it.
He read it over and began to fold it.

156

And as he did his tears fell salt and wet
Upon the ruby signet which he wore;
He set it neatly to the wax, and yet
He kissed the letter a thousand times before
He made an end, and, folding it once more,
Said "Letter, what a blissful destiny
Awaits thee now, since she will look on thee!"

157

On the next day this Pandar took the letter
Off to his niece; he made an early start.
He swore it must be nine o'clock, or better,
And joked away and said "Oh my poor heart!
How fresh it is! But how I feel it smart!
I never can sleep in May, I shan't tomorrow!
I have a jolly woe, a lusty sorrow!"

158

Now when she heard her uncle's voice,
	Criseyde,
With breathless heart, all eagerness to hear
The reason for his coming, thus replied
"Now tell me, on your honour, Uncle dear,
Whatever kind of wind has blown you here?
Tell us about your 'lusty sorrow,' do!
Where in love's dance can they have fitted
	you?"

159

"By God," he said, "I hop along behind!"
She laughed so much she thought her heart
	would burst.
"Mock on," said Pandarus, "that's right, be
	kind!
But I've some news for you, so listen first;
A stranger's come to town, and I conversed
With him, a Grecian spy, with something new
To say; I've come to pass it on to you.

160

"Let's go into the garden—lovely weather—
And be in private, it's a long affair."
So off they sauntered, arm in arm together,
Down from her room and out into the air,
Far enough off for none to hear and stare;
And then he stopped, turned round and looked
	about,
And said to her, drawing the letter out,

161

"Look, he that is all yours, and at your free
Disposal, recommends himself to you,

Humbly, and sends this letter here by me;
When you have time, think it well over, do,
And try to find a kindly answer too,
For otherwise, God help me, to speak plain,
He cannot live much longer in such pain."

162

She stood stock still at this, in sudden dread,
Not taking it; the meekness in her face
Began to change. "Letters and notes!" she said
"Bring none of them to me, for heaven's grace;
And, dearest Uncle, in the present case,
I beg you put my interests before
His needs and pleasures. What can I say more?

163

"Consider now if it is reasonable—
And do not spare from favour or from sloth
To tell the truth—would it be suitable
To my condition—tell me on your oath—
To take it, or to pity him, or both,
Laying myself so open to attack,
Harming myself? For heaven's sake, take it
	back!"

164

On hearing this, Pandar began to stare
And answered "Well! This is the greatest
	wonder
That ever I saw! Stop putting on this air
Of affectation; strike me dead with thunder
If I would stoop, to save the city yonder,
To bringing you a letter that could harm you,
Or one to him! What is there to alarm you?

165

"That's how you all behave, or almost all;
He who most longs to serve you, in your eyes,
Is least to be considered, let him fall!
It doesn't matter if he lives or dies.
By all I may deserve of you, be wise,
Take it, and don't refuse!" He caught her
	gown,
And in her bosom thrust the letter down.

166

"Throw it away, or tear it up, I say,
Let them all stare," he said, "we're in full
	view!"
"Well, I can wait till they have gone away."
She answered, smiling, "Uncle, I beg you, do
Take him whatever answer pleases you;
I will write nothing to him, let me state."
"No? Well, I will" he said, "if you'll dictate."

167

At that she laughed and said "Let's go to
	dinner."
He fell to jesting at himself, and passed

To other matters: "Niece, I'm getting thinner;
It's love; and every other day I fast,
I suffer so!" All his best jokes at last
Came tumbling out, until his crazy chaffing
Made her afraid that she would die of
    laughing.

168

And when they had returned into the hall
She said "Let us have dinner right away,
Uncle." Her women answered to her call,
And to her room she went without delay;
But of her business there I have to say
That one thing which, for sure, she went to do
Was privately to read this letter through.

169

She conned it word by word, and line by line,
And found no lack of it; she thought it good,
Put it away and then went down to dine,
And came unseen on Pandarus, who stood
In a brown study, and caught him by the hood;
"Aha! You're caught!" she said, "You didn't
    see!"
"Yes, I surrender! What's the penalty?"

170

They washed their hands and then sat down
    to eat,
And, about noontime, Pandar had the wit
To draw towards the window next the street,
And said "Whose is that house just opposite?
The one out there, who decorated it?"
"Which house?" she said, and moved across
    to see,
And told him whose it happened then to be.

171

They fell in converse upon slender themes,
Both sitting by the window, in the splay,
Till Pandar saw the moment for his schemes
Had come, her servants having gone away.
"Now niece," said he, "Come out with it,
    I say!
That letter that you wot of, did he show
Up well in it? Of course, I wouldn't know."

172

She didn't answer but began to hum,
But in the end she murmured "So I think."
"Well, for God's love, repay him for it, come!"
Her cheeks began to flame a rosy pink.
"I'll do the sealing, you shall do the ink!"
He knelt to her, "A small reward, maybe,
But leave the sealing of it, do, to me!"

173

"Yes, I could write, of course," she said,
    "but then
The trouble is, I don't know what to say."

"Now, niece," said Pandar, "don't say that
    again;
At least you're bound to thank him, anyway,
For his goodwill—unless you wish to slay!
And so, my little niece, for love of me,
On this occasion, don't refuse," said he.

174

"Kind heaven, may all be well when all is
    done."
She said, "God help me, this is the first letter
That ever I wrote, or any part of one."
And to her room she went alone, the better
To commune with herself and to unfetter
Her heart a little from its prison-plight
In her disdain, and set herself to write.

175

Of what she wrote him I shall only mention
The substance (if my grasp of it is sound);
She gave him thanks for every good intention
Towards her, but declined to give him ground
For greater hope; she never would be bound
In love, save as a sister; this, to please him,
She gladly would allow, if that could ease him.

176

She folded it, returned to where, alone,
Pandarus sat and stared into the street,
And on a golden cushion, on a stone
Of jasper, next to him she took her seat,
And said, "I never had a harder feat
As God's my witness, to accomplish. You
Have made me write it; you constrained
    me to."

177

She gave it him; he thanked her and replied
"God knows that things unwillingly begun
Can often turn out well, dear niece Criseyde;
That you have been with difficulty won
Should gladden him, by God and yonder
    sun!
Because they say 'Impressions lightly made
Are commonly among the first to fade.'

178

"But you have played the tyrant far too long,
Your hard heart has resisted the engraver;
Now hesitate no longer, but be strong,
And though you still may wish to keep the
    flavour
Of cold formality, O give him savour
Of joy, and soon! Too studied a disdain
Can breed an answering scorn, to ease the
    pain."

179

And just as they were arguing, just then,
Troilus turned the corner of the street

On horseback, with a company of ten,
Quietly riding like a little fleet,
Beneath his lady at her window-seat,
Towards the palace. Pandar, first aware,
Said "Look at that! You see who's riding
   there?"

180

"Now don't run in, he's seen us, I suppose
And he may think you're trying to avoid him."
"No, no," she answered, turning red as rose;
And he saluted her (though fear destroyed
   him)
With humble looks; and yet it overjoyed him.
His colour came and went, and up he cast
A nod at Pandarus, and on he passed.

181

God knows whether he sat his horse aright,
Or looked his best on that eventful day!
God knows if he was like a manly knight!
Why should I drudge to tell you his array?
Criseyde, who saw it, I will briefly say,
Liked what she saw thus gathered in a glance,
His person, his array, his countenance,

182

His goodly manner and his gentle breed,
So much that never yet since she was born
Had she felt such compassion in his need
Of her, for all the hardness of her scorn.
I hope to God she now can feel the thorn;
She shall not pull it out this week, or next,
God send her more such thorns would be my
   text!

183

Now Pandar, standing close beside her there,
Sensing the iron hot, began to smite.
"Niece, let me ask you, if the question's fair,
Would you suppose a girl was doing right
If, for a lack of pity in her, in spite
Of innocence in him, she gave no heed
And brought his death upon him?" "No, in-
   deed!"

184

"God knows that's true, if ever truth there was!
You feel I am not lying, that is plain;
Look, there he goes a-riding!" "So he does!"
"Well, as I've told you over and again,
Give up this foolishness of mad disdain
And speak to him—if but to ease his heart;
Don't let a scruple keep you so apart."

185

He had to heave to make her grant the boon;
All things considered, it was not to be;
Why not? From shame. Besides it was too soon
To offer him so great a liberty.

It was her whole intention, argued she,
To love him unbeknown, if she so might,
And only gratify his sense of sight.

186

Pandar was thinking "That will never do,
Not if I know it! Fantasies like these
Must not be entertained a year or two."
Why make a sermon of his niceties?
He saw he must agree as one agrees
For the time being; and when evening fell
He rose and took his leave, and all was well.

187

He hurried homeward then, and as he sped
Upon his way, his heart was in a dance.
And Troilus he found alone in bed,
Like all these lovers, in a kind of trance;
Between dark desperation and the chance
Of hope he lay, and Pandar came in singing,
As if to say "Just look at what I'm bringing!"

188

And said "Who's taken to his bed so soon
And buried himself?" "Friend, it is I," said he.
"Why, if it isn't Troilus, by the moon!
You must get up at once; and you shall see
A charm that has been sent to you, through me,
To cure your ecstasy of sigh and sob,
If you've the strength to finish off the job."

189

"Yes, with the help of God," said Troilus,
And took the letter of Criseyde's inditing.
Said Pandar, laughing, "God is good to us;
Here, take a light, and look at all this writing!"
Racing with joy, quaking with fear, a fighting
Rose in the heart of Troilus as he read,
And every word inspired hope or dread.

190

But in the end he took it for the best,
This letter of hers; for his attention lit
Upon a passage where his heart could rest;
Though she had veiled her meaning quite a bit,
He held to the more hopeful part of it;
So what with hope and Pandar's promised care,
He freed himself at least from sheer despair.

191

But, as we all can notice every day,
The more the wood and coal, the more the fire;
Increase of hope, be it for what it may,
Will very often bring increased desire,
Or, as an oak springs from a little spire,
So this same letter that she had returned him
Served to increase the passion that so
   burned him.

192

Therefore I have to say that day and night

This Troilus now hankered for her more
Than at the first, through hope; with all his
     might
He pressed ahead, and, helped by Pandar's lore,
He wrote to her of what he suffered for
Her sake, and, not to let the matter cool,
Sent word, by Pandar, daily as a rule.

193

All the observances that in these cases
A lover must perform, he also kept;
And, as the chance of fortune threw him aces
Or not, so he exulted or he wept;
Such throws as he received he must accept.
According to such answers as he had
His day was miserable, or was glad.

194

But it was always Pandarus to whom
He turned, in his complaining, for relief,
Begging advice and succour in his gloom,
And Pandarus, who saw his crazy grief,
Would nearly die of pity, and, in brief,
Busily searched his wits for what to do
To put an end to it, and quickly too,

195

And said "Dear lord and brother, and dear
     friend,
God knows that when you suffer I feel woe,
If you could bring yourself to make an end
Of these sad faces! I can shape things, though,
With God's good help, within a day or so,
So as to bring you to a certain place
Where you can speak to her and beg for
     grace.

196

"And certainly—perhaps you mayn't have
     heard—
The experts in the arts of love do say
One of the things that makes a man preferred
Is if he finds the leisure time to pray
For grace, and some safe corner where he may.
Given a kindly heart, it must impress,
To see and hear the guiltless in distress.

197

"Perhaps you're thinking 'Even were it so,
Supposing Nature move her to begin
To have some sort of pity on my woe,
Disdain would answer "You can never win
The spirit in her heart that rules within;
Though she may bend, she stands upon her
     stem."
Alas, my griefs! What help is that to them?'

198

"But then remember that the sturdy oak,
When all the heavy hacking has been done,

Receives at last the happy felling-stroke;
There's a great rush and down it comes in one,
As do these rocks or mill-stones, at a run;
For heavy things will fall with greater force
And speed than will a lighter thing, of course.

199

"Now take a reed that bends to every blast
Quite easily; lull wind, and it will rise;
Not so an oak, which lies when it is cast
To ground; perhaps I need not moralize.
People are glad when a great enterprise
Is well achieved, stands firm, and none can
     doubt it;
And all the more if they took long about it.

200

"But, Troilus, putting these thoughts away,
I have a question for you, a request:
Which, of your many brothers, would you say
In your heart's privacy you loved the best?"
"Deiphebus, of course, above the rest."
"Deiphebus? Well, in a day or so,
He'll ease your heart for you, and yet not
     know.

201

"Leave all to me; I'll work it if I can."
And off he went to see Deiphebus,
Whom he had always loved as Prince and man,
And was his best friend, next to Troilus.
And, to be brief, Pandar addressed him thus:
"Sir, let me beg of you to take my part
In a small matter which I have at heart."

202

"Why, certainly! Whatever I can do,
God willing, shall be done without delay;
There's no one I would rather help than you,
Except my brother Troilus. In what way?
How can I help? You only have to say.
I don't remember ever taking part
Against a project that you had at heart."

203

Pandarus thanked him, and in turn replied,
"Well, sir, there is a lady in this town
Who is my niece, and she is called Criseyde;
Now there are some who want to drag her
     down,
To steal her property and good renown,
And this is what has led me to beseech
Your help and friendship, Sir, without more
     speech."

204

"O, is she not—this lady in distress,
Of whom you speak in such a distant way—
My friend Criseyde?" Pandarus answered:
     "Yes."

"Why, then, there's nothing more you need to
    say,"
Deiphebus said, "believe it—and you may—
I'll be her champion too with spur and spear,
And if they hear of it, well let them hear.

205

"But, tell me, since you know what has
    occurred,
How should we act?" "My Lord, if I may
    borrow
On your good nature, deign to send her word
To come and see you, say, some time to-
    morrow,
When she can privately unfold her sorrow.
Were she to bring her griefs to you, why then,
It would strike fear into these wicked men.

206

"And if I might make bolder still with you,
And burden you with something more than
    this,
Could you invite your brothers—one or two
To give her case a certain emphasis?
Then, I am sure, nothing could go amiss
In helping her, what with your interest
And that of other friends, as I suggest."

207

Deiphebus, whose breed was of a kind
To do as honour and as bounty bade,
Replied "It shall be done, and I can find
Still greater help; you need not be afraid.
Suppose for instance that I could persuade
Helen herself to minister to her needs?
Paris will follow too when Helen leads.

208

"For Hector, my Commander and my
    brother,
There is no need to beg for his support;
For I have heard him, one time and another,
Speak of Criseyde with praise of every sort
—He couldn't have spoken better; and, in
    short,
She has his good opinion. It's no task,
Getting his help; it's ours before we ask.

209

"And speak yourself, will you, to Troilus
On my behalf? Ask him to come and dine."
"Sir, this shall all be done," said Pandarus;
He took his leave, intent on the design,
And to his niece's house, in a straight line,
He went and found her rising from her table,
And down he sat himself, and spoke, when
    able:

210

"O blessed Lord, O God, how I have run!

Look, little niece! You see how I am sweating?
I doubt if you will thank me when I've done;
That wretched Poliphetes—you're forgetting?
Aren't you aware?—is at this moment setting
About new means to have you put on trial."
"I? No!" she said, and paled in her denial.

211

"What is he after? Why does he so hound me?
It's very wrong. O what am I to do?
He's not alone in trying to confound me,
For there is Ántenor, Aeneas too,
Who are his friends in this—they make a crew.
But, for God's love, dear uncle, let it go;
If they take everything, well, be it so!

212

"Without all that, I have enough for us."
"No!" answered Pandarus, "it shall not be!
I've just been talking to Deiphebus,
Hector, and other lords, some two or three,
And made each one of them his enemy.
If I can help it he shall never win,
Whatever he does, whenever he may begin."

213

And as they cast about for what was best
To do, Deiphebus in courtesy
Came personally to make it his request
To have the pleasure of her company
At dinner the next day, and willingly
She told him she was happy to obey;
He thanked her then, and went upon his way.

214

Then (to be brief) Pandar went off alone
To Troilus, to tell him what had passed,
And found him sitting, still as any stone.
He told him everything from first to last
And of the subtle dust that he had cast
In his brother's eyes; "And now," he said, "it's
    done.
Behave yourself tomorrow and she's won!

215

"Speak, beg, implore her, piteously bewail,
Have no compunction, slackness, shame or
    fear,
Sooner or later one must tell the tale,
Believe it, and she'll lend a kindly ear;
You will in fact be saved by faith, my dear.
I know you feel afraid and in distress,
And what it is I bet you I can guess.

216

"You're thinking: 'How am I to do all this?
From my sad face people are bound to see
I'm sick for love of her; they could not miss;
I'd rather die unknown in misery.'
Don't think like that, it's imbecility.

I know you are afraid; if you look sick
We can make use of that; I have a trick.

217

"Go overnight, and sooner if you may,
Stay with your brother—as a relaxation,
As if to drive your malady away;
You do look ill, it's no exaggeration.
And then go off to bed in desperation
And say you can't endure a moment more;
Then lie right there and wait for what's in
    store.

218

"Say that your fevers usually take
A regular course and last until the morrow;
And let me see how nicely you can fake.
God knows that 'sick is he that is in sorrow.'
Now, off with you! Farewell! If I can borrow
The help of Venus, and you stay the pace,
She shall confirm you fully in her grace."

219

"Alas," said Troilus, "there is no need
To counsel me to feign that I am sick,
For I am sick in earnest, sick indeed,
Sick unto death. I'm wounded to the quick."
"All the less need," said Pandar, "for a trick;
The more you sweat, the less you're a deceiver;
People expect a man to sweat in fever.

220

"Keep close beside the trysting-place, and see
How well I drive the deer towards your bow."
Then Pandarus departed equably,
And Troilus went homeward in a glow
Of joy, for never had he gloried so
In all his life; giving his whole assent
To Pandar, to his brother's house he went.

221

What need to tell you of the care and fuss
Of welcome that Deiphebus displayed,
Or of the fevered looks of Troilus,
Or of the pile of blankets that they laid
Upon him, or the entertainment made
To cheer him up? But it was all for naught;
He played his part as Pandarus had taught.

222

Before he slept (it cannot be denied)
Deiphebus had begged of him that night
To be a friend and helper to Criseyde.
God knows he granted this without a fight,
To be her friend entire, with all his might;
This was indeed no more to beg of him
Than if you were to ask a duck to swim.

223

The morning came, and time was draw-
    ing near

For dinner; fair Queen Helen took the street
Towards Deiphebus; her thoughts were clear;
This was a homely visit, just to meet
And gossip with her brother, and then eat
A quiet meal; and that was why she went;
God alone knew—and Pandar—what it
    meant.

224

Criseyde came too, as innocent as she.
Antigone and Tarba came as well.
But it is best to shun prolixity;
Let us speed on, for heaven's sake, to dwell
Upon the main effect; I have to tell
Why all these folk assembled for this meeting;
Let us pass over what they said in greeting.

225

Deiphebus did them honour, filled their
    glasses,
And fed them well with what could please; but
    still
He interjected plentiful "alases,"
Saying "Dear brother Troilus is ill,
He's still in bed." And, having sighed his fill,
He took great pains to gladden them again,
As best he could, happy to entertain.

226

Helen commiserated in his sickness
So faithfully, her pity seemed to flow,
And everyone with a surprising quickness
Became a doctor: "This is how to go
About a cure . . . ." "There is a charm I
    know . . ."
But there sat one, silent among the rest,
And she was thinking "I could cure him best."

227

And after pitying, they began to praise him,
As folk still do; when someone has begun
To praise a man, others will quickly raise him
A thousand times yet higher than the sun:
"He is . . . he can . . . he'll do what few have
    done."
Pandar gave ear to all their approbation
And did not fail to add his confirmation.

228

Criseyde heard every word of this and gave
It deep attention, not without delight;
Her heart was laughing, though her looks
    were grave,
For who would not feel glory if she might
Command the life or death of such a knight?
But I'll pass on without delaying you;
All that I tell has but one end in view.

229

The moment came to rise from where they sat

At dinner; so they did, and everyone
Talked for a little while of this and that
Till Pandar, breaking in upon their fun
Said to Deiphebus, "May it be done
As I requested? Would you, if you please,
Say something of Criseyde's necessities?"

230

Helen, who held her hand, took up the phrase
And said "We are all eager, if you would."
Looked at Criseyde and, with a friendly gaze,
Added "Jove never let him come to good
Who does you harm! We'll help you as we
    should;
Sorrow on us, and all true folk, I say,
If we don't make this fellow rue the day!"

231

"You know the story," said Deiphebus
To Pandarus, "you be the one to tell."
"My lords and ladies, then, the case stands thus;
Why should I keep you waiting? Very
    well . . ."
He rang out the indictment like a bell,
And made this Poliphetes sound so grim
And heinous that they would have spat at him.

232

And each more violently than the other
On Poliphetes heaped his bitterest curse;
"He deserves hanging, though he were my
    brother,
And hanged he certainly shall be, or worse!"
Why drag the story out another verse?
Plainly at once all swore to be her friend
In all they could; on that she might depend.

233

Helen remarked to Pandar presently
"Touching this matter, does my brother know,
Hector, I mean? And Troilus, does he?
Yes; and now listen: shouldn't we make
    her go
—Since he is here—to Troilus, and show
Her troubles to him now? If you consent,
She could explain them all before she went.

234

"For he would have her grief the more at heart,
Because she is a lady in distress;
And, by your leave, I'll pop in for a start,
And tell you in a minute, even less,
If he's asleep; it might be a success."
And in he leapt and whispered in his ear
"The Lord receive thy soul! I've brought the
    bier."

235

This sally won a smile from Troilus,
And Pandar, with no more manoeuvring,

Went out to Helen and Deiphebus
And said "So long as there's no lingering,
And not too many people, you may bring
Criseyde to see him, and he gives assurance
He'll hear her to the best of his endurance.

236

"But, as you know, the room is very small,
Even a few would make it rather warm;
I won't be answerable—listen, all!—
If you come thronging in you'll do him harm
And injure him; I'd rather lose my arm!
Whether it's better to postpone her visit
Let those decide who know; not easy, is it?

237

"I think it best, as far as I can tell,
For no one to go in but just you two,
Or me, perhaps; that would be just as well,
She doesn't know the details as I do;
I can present them quickly, she renew
Her plea for patronage, and slip away.
That cannot much disturb him, I dare say.

238

"And then, as she's a stranger, he'll forgo
His rest a little, as he never would
For you; another thing: I chance to know
He wants to tell you something for the good
Of Troy—a secret, so I understood."
Neither of them suspecting his intent,
There was no further parley; in they went.

239

And Helen, in her soft and lovely way,
Saluted him, with all her womanly charm
Saying playfully "You must get up, I say,
My handsome brother must not come to
    harm!"
And round his shoulders then she slipped
    an arm
And tried with all her wit to do him good,
Amuse and comfort him, as best she could.

240

And after that she said "We beg of you,
I, and your brother, who is here with me,
Deiphebus—and Pandar begs you too—
Be friend and patron, give your sympathy
To poor Criseyde, for she is certainly
The victim of great wrongs, as Pandar
    knows;
He'll tell you how the case against her goes."

241

This Pandarus began to file his tongue
To state her case; it slipped into the groove.
After a little, when his song was sung,
Troilus said "As soon as I can move,
I gladly will be one of you, to prove

The justice of her cause with all my might."
Queen Helen said "And fortune speed the
  right!"

242

Pandarus asked him "Would you mind if she
Took leave of you before she has to go?"
"Why, God forbid that she should not,"
  said he,
"If she will honour me by doing so."
And after saying this, he added "Oh
Deiphebus, and you, my sister dear,
I have to talk to you—I've something here,

243

"In which I certainly should be the better
For your advice," and found beside his bed
(It happened so) a document or letter
Hector had sent him, asking advice, he said,
Whether some man deserved to lose his head,
I don't know who. And with the gravest air,
He begged of them to study it with care.

244

Deiphebus began unfolding it
In serious thought with Helena the Queen,
And out they roamed to read it, bit by bit,
Down the great stairway to an arbour green,
Studying it to see what they could glean;
And, roughly speaking, for about an hour
They read and pored upon it in their bower.

245

Now let them read; turn we to the event
And Pandar, prying like a man in haste,
To see if all was well; and out he went
Into the larger room, indeed, he raced;
"God bless this company!" he said, "Make
  haste,
Dear niece, Queen Helen is awaiting you
Outside, my lady and their lordships too.

246

"Come, rise and bring your niece Antigone,
Or whom you will, no matter. I would say
The fewer of you the better; come with me
And see you thank them humbly for today,
All three of them, before you go away;
Seize the right moment for departure, lest
We stay too long and rob him of his rest."

247

All innocent of Pandarus' intent,
Criseyde gave answer, in her ignorance,
"Let's go, dear Uncle." Arm in arm they went,
And while she framed her words and counte-
  nance,
Pandarus, with a very earnest glance,
Said "For God's love, you others, keep away,

Amuse yourselves; think of some game
  to play.

248

"Think where you are and who we have within
And in what state he is—God send a cure!"
Then, in an undertone, "Come on, begin,
Go softly, little niece; and I adjure
You in the name of God to make all sure,
And by the Crown of Love to ease the pain
That you have caused; don't kill him with
  disdain.

249

"Shame on the devil! Think of who he is,
Think of him lying there in pain! have done!
Time lingered is Time lost, remember this;
You both will find that true, when two are one.
Secondly, all is safe; for there are none
Who yet have guessed; come off it, if you can,
While they are hoodwinked; on, and win
  your man!

250

"Titterings and pursuings and delays
Are feathers in the wind for folk to see;
Though you may later wish for happy days,
You will not dare, and why? For she and she
Exchanged a certain word, or he and he
A look. Lest *I* lose time, I dare not deal
With this at length; come, bring your man to
  heel!"

251

Now all you lovers that are listening here,
Think what a terrible predicament
For Troilus, who heard them drawing near!
He thought "O Lord . . . O what has Fortune
  sent?
Am I to die, or shall I have content?"
He was to sue for love—his first assay!
Great God Almighty, what is he to say?

BOOK III

1

O blissful light, whose beams in clearness run
Over all Third Heaven, adorning it with splen-
  dour,
O daughter of Jove and darling of the Sun,
Pleasure of Love, O affable and tender,
The ready guest of noble hearts, defender
And cause of all well-being and delight,
Worshipped by thy benignity and might!

2

In heaven, in hell, in earth and the salt sea

Thy power is felt and is in evidence,
Since man, bird, beast, fish, herb and greening tree
Feel thee in season, eternal effluence!
God Himself loves, nor turns His countenance
   thence,
And there's no creature in this world alive
That without love has being or can thrive.

3

Thou first didst move Jove to those glad effects
Through which it comes that all things live and are,
Madest him amorous and, lo, he elects
His mortal loves; thou givest him, as far
As pleases thee, his pleasure, or dost bar,
Sending him in a thousand shapes to look
For love on earth; and whom thou wouldest, he took.

4

Yes, and fierce Mars for thee has slaked his ire;
Thou canst ennoble every heart and face
As it may please thee; those thou wilt set on fire
Learn to dread shame and shun whatever is base.
Courteous thou makest them, and fresh in grace,
And high or low, as his intent may be,
The joys a man may have are sent by thee.

5

Thou holdest realm and home in unity,
And art the steadfast cause of friendship too,
Thou knowest all that covered quality
Of things that makes us wonder what or who
It is that makes them tick; where is the clue
Why she loves him, or he loves there or here,
And why this fish, not that, comes to the weir.

6

Thy law is set upon the universe;
And this I know, for lovers told it me,
That he who strives against thee fares the worse.
Now, lady bright, of thy benignity,
In reverence to those that worship thee,
Whose clerk I am, O teach me how to show
Some of the joy that, serving thee, they know.

7

Into my naked heart a sentience pour
With power, to show thy sweetness and delight!
Caliope, be present; I implore
Thy voice, for now is need! Thou seest my plight;
How shall I tell of Troilus' joy, or write
That all may honour Venus as they read it?
And to such joy, may God bring those who need it!

* * *

8

He lay there all this meanwhile, Troilus,
Learning the lesson suited to his case;
"By Jove," he thought, "I shall say thus and
   thus,

And thus entreat my darling for her grace;
That's a good phrase, and thus I'll set my face;
This I must not forget." Unhappy man,
Pray God all goes according to his plan!

9

Lord, how his heart began to quake and thrum,
Hearing her step! His sighs came short and
   quick;
Pandar had led her in, and then had come
Closer, and twitched the curtain, by a trick
To peek inside, and said "God help the sick!
Just look who's come to see you! There she
   stands,
The one who has your murder on her hands!"

10

He spoke as if he were about to weep.
"Ah! Ah!" cried Troilus, with a pitiful sigh,
"God knows if I am ill! I cannot sleep;
I cannot see—who is it standing by?"
"Sir," said Criseyde, "it's Pandarus and I."
"You, sweetheart? O alas I cannot kneel
Or rise to show the reverence I feel."

11

He raised himself a little, but she came
At once and softly laid her hands on his.
"You must not kneel to me; in heaven's name,
What do you mean?" she said; "Two purposes
I have in coming, Sir; the first one is
To thank you; next to beg continuance
Of your protection, and your countenance."

12

This Troilus, hearing his lady pray
For his support, lay neither quick nor dead:
Bashfulness left him not a word to say,
Not even if they'd come to take his head.
But, Lord, to see him suddenly turn red!
And, gentlemen, his lesson, learned so neatly,
To beg her favour, disappeared completely.

13

All this Criseyde had noticed well enough,
For she was wise, and loved him never the less,
Though he was not self-confident or tough,
Nor tried to fool her with some fine address;
But what he said, as soon as his distress
Began to lessen, if my rhyme will hold,
I'll tell you, as my ancient authors told.

14

With a changed voice, changed by his very
   dread,
Troilus answered. In a manner bare
Of all assurance, and now blushing red,
Now paling, to Criseyde, his lady fair,
With downcast, humble and surrendered air,

Twice he burst forth; one word was all his art,
And it was, "Mercy, mercy, sweetest heart!"

15

Silent awhile, when he could speak again,
The next word was "God knows that when
   I gave
Myself to you, as far as it has lain
In me to do so, and as God may save
My soul, I became yours, and to the grave,
Poor wretch, I shall be—not that I complain
Of suffering; none the less I suffer pain.

16

"This is as much, O sweet and womanly one,
As I may now bring forth; if it displease you,
I will revenge it on me and have done,
Soon, soon, and take my life, if that will
   ease you,
And death shall stay your anger and ap-
   pease you;
Since you have heard me say somewhat, or try,
I do not care how soon I am to die."

17

To see the manful sorrow that he felt
Might well have touched a heart of very stone,
Pandarus stood in tears, about to melt,
Nudging his niece anew at every moan;
"True are the hearts" he sobbed "that weep
   alone!
O for the love of heaven, end our woe,
Or kill us both together, ere you go!"

18

"I? What?" she said, "By heaven and in truth
I do not know what you would have me say."
"Not know?" said he, "Have pity on his
   youth!
For God's love, would you have him pass
   away?"
"Well then," she said, "I'll ask him, if I may,
What is the aim and end of his intent?
I never have truly gathered what he meant."

19

"What I have meant? Ah, sweetest heart, my
   dear,"
Said Troilus, "my lovely, fresh and free,
Let but the rivers of your eyes stream clear
In friendliness, once in a while, on me,
And give me your consent that I may be
He that, without a touch of vice, may ever
Offer his whole, true service and endeavour,

20

"As to his lady and his chief resource,
With all my heart and mind and diligence,
And to be comforted, or feel the force

Of your displeasure equal to my offence,
As death for any disobedience;
Deign me the honour, too, to use your power,
Commanding me in all, at any hour,

21

"And I to be your ever-humble, true,
Secret in service, patient in distress,
And in desire constant, fresh and new
Servant, to serve you in all eagerness,
In every inclination you express,
All it may cost accepting in good part,
See, that is what I mean, my sweetest heart."

22

Said Pandarus "Well! There's a hard request,
Reasonable for a lady to deny!
Now, by the Feast of Jupiter the Blest,
Were I a god, you should be marked to die,
You, that can hear this man lay all else by
To serve you until death, he is so fervent,
Yet you refuse to take him for your servant!"

23

Now fully at her ease, she turned her eyes
To look at him, serenely debonair,
And thought she need not hurry her replies;
But in the end she answered him with care,
And softly said "My honour safe and fair,
And in such form as you have heard him
   proffer,
I will receive his service, at his offer,

24

"Beseeching him, for heaven's love, that he
Will, in all honour and without pretence,
As I mean well by him, mean well by me,
And guard my honour with all diligence.
If I can make him happy in this sense
Henceforward, then I will; this is no feigning;
And now be whole again, no more com-
   plaining.

25

"Nevertheless I warn you all the same,
Prince as you are, King's son and famous
   knight,
You shall have no more sovereignty or claim
On me in love than in such case is right;
And if you do amiss, I shall requite
It, though it anger you; but while you
   serve me,
Then I will cherish you as you deserve me.

26

"So in a word, dear heart, my chosen man,
Be happy; draw towards your strength again
And I will truly give you all I can
To pay you back in sweetness for your pain;

If I am she you need, you shall obtain
For every grief a recompense in bliss."
And then she took him in her arms to kiss.

27

And down fell Pandarus upon his knees;
Casting his eyes and hands to heaven, he cried
"Immortal god, O deathless deity
—Cupid I mean—by this be glorified!
Venus, make melody! And, hark! outside
I seem to hear the bells of Troy a-ringing
For joy, without a hand to set them swinging!

28

"But ho! No more of this—and anyhow
They'll soon be coming back, when they
    have done
Reading that letter; there! I hear them now.
Criseyde, let me adjure you now, for one,
And you, for another, Troilus, my son;
Be ready at my house when I shall call—
You may be sure I shall arrange for all—

29

"To ease your hearts in practising your craft,
And let us see which of you wins the prize
For talking feelingly of love!" He laughed;
"You shall have leisure there to theorize."
"How soon can this be done?" "You must be
    wise,"
Said Pandarus, "and wait till you are well;
It all will happen, just as you heard me tell."

30

Deiphebus and Helen on their own
Started that moment to ascend the stair,
And, lord, how Troilus began to groan,
To blind his brother and his sister there.
Said Pandarus, "It's time we went elsewhere;
Now, little niece, take leave of them, all three;
Leave them to talk, and come along with me."

31

She took her leave of them most mannerly,
As well she could, and in return they bowed
And joined in doing her full courtesy;
When she had gone they sang her praises loud,
Spoke wonders of her excellence, and vowed
Her manners were enchanting, and her wit;
It was a joy to hear them praising it.

32

Now let her wend her way to her own place,
While we return to Troilus again;
He set at naught the letter and the case
Deiphebus had studied (but in vain).
From Helen and his brother, to be plain,
He longed to be delivered; it were best,
He said, to let him sleep; he needed rest.

33

So Helen kissed him and to where she dwelt
Set off, the others too; it all went right,
And Pandarus, as fast as he could pelt,
Came back to Troilus, in bee-line flight,
And on a pallet all that happy night
At blissful ease by Troilus he lay
Happy to talk until the break of day;

34

Yet, when they all had gone except these two,
And the great doors had shut away the town,
(To tell it shortly and without ado)
This Pandarus got up and sat him down
Freely on Troilus' bed, and with a frown,
Began to speak in a more serious way,
And I shall tell you what he tried to say.

35

"My dearest lord and brother, as God knows
—And so do you—it touched me to the quick
So long to see you languish in the woes
Of love, ever more desperately sick.
By every ingenuity and trick
Since then, I have been busy, ploy by ploy,
To bring you out of suffering into joy.

36

"And I've so managed matters, as you know,
That, thanks to me, you stand in a fair way
To prosper well. I say this not to crow;
Do you know why? I am ashamed to say;
To pleasure you I have begun to play
A game I'll never play for any other,
Not though he were a thousand times my
    brother.

37

"For you I have become since I began,
Half earnest, half in game, a *go-between*,
The kind that brings a woman to a man;
You know yourself what thing it is I mean.
For I have made my niece—and she is clean—
Place her whole trust on what is fine in you;
She will do all that you would have her do.

38

"God, who knows all, bear witness here
    for me!
There was no greed of gain in what I sought;
I only wished to abridge the misery
That was destroying you—or so I thought.
Good brother, now do everything you ought,
For God's dear love, to keep her out of blame;
As you are wise and good, protect her name.

39

"As well you know, people now think of her
As one enshrined and sainted, so to say.

The man is still unborn who could prefer
A charge that she had ever gone astray;
And woe is me that set her in the way
—My own dear niece—of what is yet to do!
I am her uncle and her traitor too.

40

"And were it known that I, by cunning
   measures,
Had put into her head the fantasy
Of being wholly yours to do your pleasures,
Why, all the world would cry out shame
   on me,
And say it was the foulest treachery
This deed of mine, that ever had been done.
She would be lost, and what would you
   have won?

41

"And so, before I take the step ahead,
Let me again beseech you, let me pray
For secrecy; we would be better dead
Than be betrayed in this, I mean to say;
Do not be angry with me for the way
I harp on secrecy; this high affair,
As you well know, demands as high a care.

42

"Think of the sorrows brought about ere this
By those who boast their conquests! One
   may read
Of many a sad mischance, of things amiss,
Day after day, just for this wicked deed;
And therefore ancient writers are agreed
And they have written, as we teach the young,
'The first of virtues is to hold your tongue.'

43

"And were it now my purpose to engage
In a diffuse discussion, I could name
Almost a thousand from our heritage
Of ancient tales, of women brought to shame
By foolish boasters; you could do the same,
And proverbs too, against the vice of blabbing;
Even if it's the truth, it still is gabbing.

44

"O tongue, alas, that has so often torn,
And from so many a lady fair of face,
The cruel cry 'Alas that I was born!'
And has kept fresh so many a girl's disgrace,
When what is boasted of in any case
Is oftenest a lie, when brought to test;
Braggarts are natural liars at the best.

45

"A braggart and a liar is all one;
As thus: suppose a woman granted me
Her love, and said that others there were none;

If I were sworn to this in secrecy,
And, after, went and blabbed to two or three,
I'd be a braggart, and, by the same token,
A liar too, because my word was broken.

46

"Look at such people! Are they not to blame?
What should I call them? What? What are
   they at,
These men that boast of women, and by name,
Who never promised either this or that,
And knew no more of them than my old hat?
God bless us all! It's little wonder then
Women are shy of dealing with us men.

47

"I do not say this as distrusting you,
Or any man of sense; but for the sot,
And for the mischief in the world now due
To folly as often as to wicked plot;
This blabbing vice—a woman fears it not
In men of sense, if she has been to school;
The man of sense takes warning from the fool.

48

"But to the point, my brother; to speak plain,
Keep everything that I have said in mind,
And keep it close! And now, cheer up again,
For when your moment comes, you then
   will find
Me true; I'll do your business in such kind
As will suffice you, if the Lord is good,
For all will happen as you wish it would.

49

"I know you mean her well, by Heaven I do!
And that is why I dared to undertake
Your business; what she now has granted you
You understand; the day is set to make
The contract. Well, I cannot keep awake,
Good night! Since you're in Heaven, say a
   prayer
To send me death, or let me join you there."

50

Who could express the joy, the very bliss
That pierced the soul of Troilus when he felt
The effect of Pandar's promised help in this?
For all his former sorrows that had dealt
His heart so many a blow, began to melt
In joy; the luxury of sigh and tear
He felt no more, it seemed to disappear.

51

But just as all these woodlands and these
   hedges
That winter-long are dead and dry and grey,
Revest themselves in green and are May's
   pledges

To every lusty lad that likes to play,
So, to speak truth, and in the self-same way,
His heart grew suddenly so full of joy,
There never was a gladder man in Troy.

52

Turning to Pandar, upon whom he cast
An earnest look, a friendly one to see,
He said, "Dear friend, it was in April last
As well you know (consult your memory)
You found me almost dead for misery
And worked on me, to bring me to confess
The secret cause of my unhappiness.

53

"You know how long it was that I forbore
To tell you, though I trust you best, and
    though
I knew there was no danger on that score.
Then tell me if you will, since this was so,
If I was loth that even you should know,
How would I dare tell others, in my fear
—I who am quaking now, lest someone hear?

54

"Nevertheless I swear, and by that Lord
Who as He pleases governs all whatever,
(And if I lie, Achilles with his sword
Cleave through my heart!)—swear, should I
    live for ever,
Who am but mortal man, that I could never
Dare—could, nor would—make boast to
    anyone
Of this, for all that's good beneath the sun.

55

"For I would rather die, and I determine
To do so, in the stocks, in prison, down
In foulest filth and wretchedness and vermin,
Captive of cruel King Agámenoun;
And this in all the temples in the town
Aye, and by all the gods too, I will swear
To you tomorrow morning, if you care.

56

"And as to all that you have done for me,
That is a thing I never can repay,
I know that well, not if I were to be
Killed for your sake a thousand times a day!
And there is nothing more that I can say
Except that from now on I'll be your slave
Wherever you go, and serve you to the grave.

57

"But here, with all my heart, I beg of you
Never to think I could be so insane
As to imagine—for you seemed to do—
That what you did in friendship for my pain
Was done in bawdry, like a pimp, for gain;

I'm not a madman, though I be a clod;
I know full well it wasn't that, by God!

58

"If there are men whose business in such
    dealings
Is done for money, call them what you must;
What you have done was done with noble
    feelings,
Done with compassion, fellowship and trust;
Distinguish love from what is done for lust.
There's a diversity to be discerned
Between things similar, so I have learned.

59

"And that you may be sure I could not blister
Your services by thinking them a jest,
Or shameful, there's Polyxena, my sister,
Or there's Cassandra, Helen and the rest,
Any of them, the fairest and the best
In the whole pack; just tell me which may be
The one you want, and leave the rest to me.

60

"And since this service has been done by you
To save my life, not for reward or fee,
I beg you, for God's love, to see me through
This great adventure; if it is to be
It needs you now; whatever you decree;
You make the rules, which, high and low
    I'll keep.
And now, good night, and let us go to sleep."

61

Content in one another and at rest,
The world could hardly add a joy to theirs;
And in the morning they arose and dressed
And each went off upon his own affairs;
But Troilus who felt the burning airs
Of sharp desire and hope and promised
    pleasure
Did not forget wise Pandar's rule and
    measure,

62

And in a manlier way restrained his youth,
The reckless action, the unbridled glance,
And not a living soul, to tell the truth,
Could have imagined from his countenance,
Or what he said, a single circumstance;
Far as a cloud he seemed from everyone,
So well was his dissimulation done.

63

During the time of which I now am writing,
This was his life; with all his fullest might
By day he was in Mars' high service, fighting
The enemy in arms and as a knight;
And through the darkness to the early light,

He mostly lay, wondering how to serve
His lady better, and her thanks deserve,

64

And, soft as was his bed, I will not swear
There was no strain upon his mind; in fact
He turned and turned upon his pillows there,
Wishing himself possessed of what he lacked;
But in such cases, often men react
With as disturbed a pleasure as did he;
At least, this seems a possibility.

65

Certain it is, returning to my matter,
That all this meanwhile, so the story goes,
He saw her now and then, and, which was
     better,
She spoke to him, whenever she dared and
     chose,
And by agreeing then, beneath the rose,
(Ever the best way) settled, in their need,
How upon all occasions to proceed.

66

So hurried were their questions and replies
Anxiously spoken on the watch, (in fear
Lest anyone imagine or surmise
Something about it, reaching out an ear),
That there was nothing in the world so dear
To them as was their hope that love would send
A time to bring their speech to a right end.

67

But in the little that they did or said,
His prudent spirit took such careful heed
He knew by instinct what was in her head,
So that to her it seemed there was no need
To tell him what to do, still less, indeed,
What to avoid; love that had come so late
Had opened joy before her, like a gate.

68

And, to be brief (for I must mend my pace),
His actions and his words were so discreet,
He stood so highly in his lady's grace
That twenty thousand times she would repeat
Her thanks to God for having let them meet;
So schooled to do her service to the letter
He was, the world could not have shown a
     better.

69

She found him so dependable in all,
So secret, so obedient to her will,
That she could truly feel he was a wall
Of steel to her, a shield from every ill;
To trust in his good management and skill
She was no more afraid; he seemed inspired.
(No more afraid, I mean, than was required.)

70

And Pandarus was stoking up the fire,
Ready and punctual and diligent,
His only thought to speed his friend's desire;
So on he shoved, and back and forth he went
With letters from the city to the tent
Of Troilus; surely no one could attend
More carefully the wishes of a friend.

71

By some it is perhaps anticipated
That every word and message, look or smile
Of Troilus is now to be related
Just as they reached his lady all this while;
But it would make a long and tedious file
To read, of anyone in his position,
And have his words and looks on exhibition.

72

I have not heard of any writer who
Has tried it, nor, I think, has anyone;
I could not do it if I wanted to.
There was a deal of letter-writing done;
The matter, says my author, well might run
Another hundred verses; he ignored it.
How then should I be able to record it?

73

But to the great effect; I put it thus:
It was a concord quiet and complete
They now enjoyed (Criseyde and Troilus)
As I have said, and at this time was sweet;
Save only that they could not often meet
Or have the leisure to fulfil their speeches.
There came a time, which now my story
     reaches,

74

When Pandar, always doing what he might
To gain those ends of which you are aware,
(To bring together in his house, some night,
His lovely niece and Troilus, that there
They might talk over all this high affair
And bind it up to both their satisfaction)
Had, as he thought, discerned a time for action.

75

For he, acting with great deliberation,
Had forecast everything; his commonsense
Had given effect to this premeditation;
He had spared for neither trouble nor expense.
Come, if they liked, to have their conference,
Nothing should fail them; as for being caught
By spies, that was impossible, he thought.

76

No fear; he was down wind from every kind
Of chattering pie or spoilsport in the game;
So all was well, for the whole world was blind

To their affair, the wild bird and the tame;
The timber's there, all ready for the frame,
And we need nothing now but to be clear
As to the hour when she should appear.

77
And Troilus, to whom these careful schemes
Were fully known, waited as best he might;
He too had made arrangements, as it seems,
And found a pretext that would set things right
Should any note his absence, day or night,
While he was in the service of his love
—That he was sacrificing to the gods above,

78
Keeping a lonely vigil under vow
To hear Apollo's answer, and to see
The quivering of the holy laurel-bow
Before Apollo spoke out of the tree,
To tell him when the Greeks would turn and
     flee;
Let no one therefore—God forbid!—pre-
     vent him,
But pray Apollo's answer might be sent him.

79
Now there was little more to do, and soon
Pandar was up, for, briefly to explain,
Immediately upon the change of moon,
When earth, a night or two, was dark again,
And all the skies were gathering for rain,
Off in the morning to his niece he went,
And all of you have heard with what intent.

80
When he arrived, he started making fun
As usual, beginning with a jape
Against himself, and swore before he had
     done,
By this and that that she should not escape,
Or keep him running round her like an ape;
Certainly, by her leave, she was to come
That very night to sup with him at home.

81
She laughed at that and looked for an excuse,
And said "It's raining, look! How can I go?"
"You must; don't stand there musing, it's
     no use;
And don't be late. It's got to be, you know."
And they at last agreed it should be so,
"Or else—" he swore it softly in her ear
"If you don't come to me, I shan't come here."

82
And then she asked him, keeping her voice
     down,
Whether he knew if Troilus would be there.
He swore he wouldn't, he was out of town;

"But all the same," he said, "suppose he were,
Surely that need not weigh you down with
     care?
Rather than have him seen there, I would die
A thousand deaths; you need not fear a spy."

83
My author has not cared to set it down
What she was thinking when he told her so,
(I mean that Troilus was out of town)
Or if she thought it was the truth or no;
At least she granted him that she would go
Without suspicion, being so besought,
And, as his niece, obeyed him as she ought.

84
Nevertheless she pressed her point on Pandar;
Although to dine with him would start no
     scare,
One must beware of many a goose and gander
Who love to dream up things that never were,
So let him choose his other guests with care;
"Uncle," she urged him, "since I trust you
     best,
Make sure that all is well; I'll do the rest."

85
He swore to this by all the stocks and stones,
By all the gods that are in heaven as well,
On pain of being taken, skin and bones,
And cast as deep as Tantalus in Hell,
King Pluto's place. What more is there to
     tell?
When all was settled, Pandar took his leave;
She came to supper at the fall of eve,

86
Accompanied by certain of her men,
And by her lovely niece, Antigone,
And other of her women, nine or ten.
Who do you think was happy, answer me,
But Troilus? He stood where he could see
Out of a window in a closet-store,
Cooped there since midnight on the night
     before,

87
Unknown to anyone, save Pandarus,
Who, to resume, now met her in the hall
With every mark of joy and friendly fuss,
Embracing her, and then, as to a ball,
He led them in to supper, one and all,
When the time came and sat them softly
     down,
Needing, God knows, no dainties fetched
     from town!

88
And after supper they began to rise,

Eased and refreshed and happier by half;
Lucky the man best able to devise
Something to please her, or to make her laugh;
He sang; she played; he told a tale of chaff.
All things, however, have an end, and so
At last she took her leave, meaning to go.

89

O Fortune, O Executrix of Dooms,
O heavenly influences in the sky!
Truth is you are our herdsmen and our grooms,
And we your cattle, though we question why,
And think your reasoning has gone awry;
So with Criseyde, I mean: against her will,
The gods had their own purpose to fulfil.

90

Bent was the moon in Cancer, silver-pale,
And joined with Saturn and with Jupiter,
And such a rain from heaven, such a gale
Came smoking down that all the women there
Were terrified, quite overcome with fear;
Pandar made comment, laughing up his sleeve,
"Fine time, your ladyship, to take your leave!

91

"But, my dear niece, if ever in any way
I may have pleased you, let me beg of you
To do me a small favour; why not stay
And spend the night here? I implore you to.
It is as much your house as mine. Now, do!
It's not a joke, I really mean it so;
It would be a disgrace to let you go."

92

She, knowing her advantage just as well
As half the world does, listened to his prayer;
The streets were flooding and the rain still fell.
It seemed as good a bargain to stay there
And grant the little favour with an air
And then be thanked, as grumble and then
    stay;
Going home now was not the better way.

93

"I will indeed," she answered, "Uncle dear,
If that is what you'd like, it shall be so;
I shall be very happy to stay here,
And I was joking when I said I'd go."
"Thank you, dear niece," he answered, "joke
    or no,
To tell the truth you put me in a fright;
I am delighted you will stay the night."

94

Thus all is well; and joy began to flower
All over again, the party warmed and spread;
But Pandar, if he'd had it in his power,
Would gladlier have hurried her to bed,

And so "What a tremendous rain!" he said,
"Such weather is only fit for sleeping in,
That's my advice to you, so let's begin.

95

"Now, niece, you know where I am going
    to put you,
So that we shan't be lying far asunder,
And so you shall not hear (if that will suit you)
The noise of all this downpour and the
    thunder?
By God, right in my little closet yonder!
And I'll be in the outer room, alone,
And guard your women for you, on my own.

96

"Here in this central chamber, which you see,
Your women can sleep comfortably soft;
And right in there is where you are to be;
If you lie well tonight, 'come once, come oft,'
And never care what weather is aloft.
Some wine, now! Presently, when you think
    best,
It will be time for us to go and rest."

97

And that was all; soon if I may pursue,
Dessert was served, the traverse thereupon
Was drawn, and those with nothing
    more to do
About the room, departed and were gone,
And meanwhile it was raining, on and on
Amazingly; the wind blew loud and bleak;
People could hardly hear each other speak.

98

Then Pandarus, her uncle, as he should,
With certain of her women—three or four—
Escorted her to bed and, when he could,
He took his leave, and, bowing to the floor,
He said, "Just here, outside this closet-door,
Across the way, your women will be near you;
You only have to call and they will hear you."

99

Once she was in her closet and in bed,
With all her waiting-women ordered out
And sent to bed themselves, as I have said,
No one was left to skip or lounge about;
They had been scolded off, you needn't doubt,
(Such as were still astir) and told to keep
Their chambers and let other people sleep.

100

But Pandarus, who knew the ancient dance
At every step, and every point therein,
Saw all was well, with nothing left to chance,
And judged it was the moment to begin
His work, and from the door he took the pin;

Still as a stone, and with no more delay
He sat him down by Troilus right away.

101

To reach the point as quickly as I can,
He told him all the cunning artifice
Of the affair, and said "Get ready, man,
You are about to enter Heaven's bliss."
"O blessed Venus, send me grace for this!
I never had more need of it," he cried,
"Nor ever have felt half so terrified."

102

Said Pandarus "Don't be at all afraid;
It will all happen just as you desire.
I promise you the gruel is well made,
If it is not I'll throw it in the fire."
"Yet, blessed Venus," Troilus prayed, "inspire
My heart this night, as constantly as I
Serve, and shall serve thee better, till I die!

103

"And if it chanced the hour of my birth
Was governed by unfavourable stars,
If thou wert quenched, O Venus full of mirth,
By Saturn, or obstructed by fell Mars,
O pray thy Father to avert such jars
And give me joy, by him that in the grove,
Boar-slain Adonis, tasted of thy love.

104

"O Jove, by fair Europa's love and rape,
Whom, in a bull's form, thou didst bear away,
Help now! O Mars, thou with the bloody cape,
For Cypris' sake, hinder me not today!
O Phebus, think how Daphne in dismay
Clothed her in bark, and was a laurel tree;
Yet, for her love, send thou thy help to me!

105

"Mercury also, for the love of Hersé,
Cause of the rage of Pallas with Aglauros,
Now help, and O Diana, in thy mercy,
Be not offended by the road before us!
And you, O Fatal Three, the sister-chorus,
That, ere my shirt was shaped for me,
     have spun
My destiny, O help this work begun!"

106

Said Pandarus "You wretched mouse's heart,
Are you afraid that she is going to bite you?
Throw on this fur-lined mantle for a start
And follow me; allow me to invite you!
Wait, let me go in front of you, to light you."
And on the word, he lifted up the latch
And drew in Troilus after him, like a catch.

107

The stern wind snored so loudly round about

The house, no other noises could be heard;
Those that lay sleeping at the door without
Slept on securely there; they never stirred.
On sober tiptoe and without a word
Pandarus then, unhindered, crossed the floor
To where they lay, and softly closed the door.

108

As he came back towards her, quietly,
His niece awoke and called out "Who is there?"
"My dearest niece," he answered, "only me;
Nothing to wonder at, you needn't fear."
Then he came close and whispered in her ear
"For God's love, I beseech you, not a word!
Wake no one up; we might be overheard."

109

"What? How did you come in? In heaven's
     name!
Didn't they hear you? But they must have
     done!"
"No, there's a little trap-door—that's how I
     came."
Criseyde replied "Then let me call someone."
"What? God forbid! What foolish notions run
Into your little head! Speak softly, do,
Or else they'll think things they've no busi-
     ness to.

110

"A sleeping dog is better left alone;
No one will guess a thing, unless you make
     them;
Your women are asleep, as still as stone.
Why, you could blow the house up and not
     wake them!
They'll sleep till dawn and daylight overtake
     them.
And when I've finished what I've got to say,
As quietly as I came, I'll go away.

111

"Now, my dear niece, you surely understand,
For on this point you women think the same,
That when you've taken any man in hand
And called him 'sweetheart' (it's a lover's
     name)
To play at blind-man's-buff with him—
     the game
Of having another lover all along—
Will do yourself a shame and him a wrong.

112

"Why do I say all this? You know quite well,
Better than any, that your love is plighted
To Troilus, who, as anyone can tell,
Is one of the finest fellows ever knighted;
You made him feel his feelings were requited

And that, except for fault in him, you never
Would play him false, though you should
    live for ever.

113

"Now this is how things stand; I have to say
That since I left, this Troilus, to be plain,
Has got into my room the secret way
—That's by the gutter—and in all this rain,
—Unknown to anyone, I must explain—
Except to me, as I may hope for joy,
And by the faith I owe the King of Troy.

114

"He is in frantic pain, in such distress
That if he isn't fully mad by this,
He may run mad quite suddenly, unless
The Lord is good to him; the reason is
It has been told him by a friend of his
That you have promised love to one Horaste;
For grief of which this night will be his last."

115

Amazed to hear him saying this, Criseyde
Suddenly felt the heart in her turn cold,
And, with a sigh, impulsively replied
"Alas, I would have thought, whoever told
Such tales of me, my sweetheart would
    not hold
Me false so easily! Ah, wretched stuff
Of lying tales! I have lived long enough.

116

"Horaste, alas? I false to Troilus!
I've never even heard of him!" said she,
"What wicked spirit has maligned me thus?
Well, anyhow tomorrow he will see,
For I can clear myself as totally,
As ever woman did, if he will hear."
And she began to sigh, and shed a tear.

117

"O God," she said, "that worldly happiness,
Called by the learned 'false felicity,'
Is intermingled with such bitterness;
A deep anxiety, God knows," said she
"Gnaws at the root of vain prosperity!
For joys come rare and singly, perhaps never,
And no one has them always and for ever.

118

"O brittle happiness, unstable joy,
No matter whose you are, or how you spring,
Either one knows you for a transient toy
Or knows it not—one or the other thing;
How then can he who does not know it, sing
His joy in having joy? Does he not mark
His ignorance of the oncome of the dark?

119

"But if one knows that joy is transitory,
And every joy in worldly things must flee,
He that remembers this will lose the glory;
The very dread of losing it must be
Enough to ruin his felicity.
If then one sets no store on joy so brittle,
It follows surely that it's worth but little.

120

"And so I will conclude the matter thus,
That honestly, as far as I can tell,
There's no true happiness on earth for us;
But jealousy, thou Serpent out of Hell,
Thou envious madness, wicked infidel,
Why hast thou made my love mistrust
    me so,
Who never have offended, that I know?"

121

Said Pandar "That's what's happened, any-
    how."
Said she "But Uncle, who has told you this?
Why has my dear heart done this to me now?"
"You know, dear niece," he answered, "how
    it is;
I hope all will be well that is amiss,
For you can quench it; set his heart at rest,
And do so now, for that will be the best."

122

"Why, then, tomorrow so I will," said she,
"And then, God willing, he'll be satisfied."
"Tomorrow? That would be a joke!" said he,
"No, that will never do, my dear Criseyde;
The learned say 'It cannot be denied
That danger ever battens on delay.'
Delays aren't worth a blackberry anyway.

123

"Niece, there's a time for everything, that's
    certain,
And, when the room's on fire, it's a flaw
To argue if the candle caught the curtain
Or how the devil they dropped it on the straw;
Far better put it out than hum and haw;
God bless us, while such talk is going on
The harm has happened and the bird is gone.

124

"And little niece—now do not be offended—
If all night long you leave him in this woe,
God help me, I shall think your love pretended
And that you never cared. I dare say so
Since we're alone, we two; but I well know
You are too sensible for such a crime
As leaving him in danger all that time."

125

"*I never cared?* By God, I'd like to know
When you have cared for anyone," said she,
"As I for him!" "Indeed? Well, time will
    show;
But since for your example you take me,
Were I to leave him in this misery
For all the treasure in the town of Troy,
I pray God I may never come to joy.

126

"Now just reflect; if you, who are in love,
Can leave his life in dangerous distress,
And all for nothing, then by God above
It's worse than folly, it's sheer wickedness,
Straight malice, I should call it, nothing less.
What! Leave him in his present state of mind?
It's foolish, it's ungenerous, it's unkind."

127

"Well," said Criseyde, "then will you do a
    thing
For me, and put an end to this upset?
Take this to him; it is my own blue ring;
There's nothing he would so much like to get,
Except myself. It is an amulet
To ease his heart; and tell him that his sorrow
Is groundless, as it shall appear tomorrow."

128

"A ring? What next! Good gracious!" Pandar
    said,
"My dearest niece, that ring will need a stone
With power in it to awake the dead,
And such a ring I cannot think you own;
Where is your commonsense? It must have
    flown
Out of your head," he said, "to ruin you both;
O time, lost time! It is the curse of sloth.

129

"Do you not know a high and noble nature
Is neither moved to sorrow, nor consoled
By trifles? If a fool, or some low creature,
Fell in a jealous rage, I would not hold
His feelings worth a mite. He could be told
A few white lies some other day, you see;
But this is in a very different key.

130

"This is so noble and so tender a heart
He will choose death to give his griefs
    their due;
You may believe, however much they smart,
He will not speak his jealousies to you;
And therefore, lest his heart should break
    in two,

Speak to him now yourself of what's occurred,
For you can steer him with a single word.

131

"I've told you of the danger he is in;
His coming has been secret; none had sight
Of his arrival; where's the harm or sin
In seeing him? I shall be here all right;
But more than that, he is your chosen knight;
By rights you ought to trust him most of all,
And I am here to fetch him, at your call."

132

So touching was this accident to hear,
So like a truth, moreover, on the face
Of it, and Troilus to her so dear,
His coming secret, and so safe the place,
Although she would be doing him a grace,
All things considered, as the matter pressed,
No wonder if she acted for the best,

133

And said "As God may bring my soul to peace,
I feel for him, I grieve about his woe,
And I would do my best for his release
From pain, had I the grace; but even so
Whether you stay with me, or whether you go
To fetch him, till God clears my mind for me,
I'm in a dire dilemma, as you can see."

134

" '*Dilemma!*' Now, you listen to me in turn;
That means *The Donkeys' Bridge;* it beats a fool,
For it seems hard to wretches who won't learn,
From sloth or wilful ignorance, at school
—Not worth a bean, such fellows, as a rule.
But you are wise, and what we have on hand
Is neither hard, nor easy to withstand."

135

"Well," she said, "Uncle, do as you think just;
But I must first get up, you realize,
Before you bring him in; and since my trust
Is in you two, and you are both so wise,
Do everything discreetly and devise
A way to guard my honour and ease his soul;
For I am here as one in your control."

136

Pandar replied "That is well said, my dear,
A blessing on your wise and gentle heart!
But don't get up; you can receive him here,
There is no need to move, just play your part
And each will ease the other of all smart,
Please God! Venus, I worship thee! And very
Soon, as I dare to hope, we'll all be merry."

137

Then Troilus went down upon his knees

At once, and reverently, beside her bed;
He greeted her with loving courtesies;
But, Lord! How suddenly she blushed
    deep red,
And not if they had come to take her head
Could she have said a word; she was
    struck dumb
Seeing him there, so suddenly had he come.

138

And Pandarus, who was so good at feeling
The mood of things, at once began to jest;
"Look, niece," he said, "see how this lord is
    kneeling!
Now there's a gentleman, by any test."
He ran and fetched a cushion from the chest
"Now kneel away as long as you may please,
And may the Lord soon set your hearts at ease."

139

I cannot say—she did not bid him rise—
If grief had put the matter from her mind,
Or if she simply took it in the guise
Of an observance, of a lover's kind;
And yet she did him favours, as I find;
She kissed him, sighing, and at last entreated
Him not to kneel, but rise up and be seated.

140

Said Pandarus "Well, now you can begin;
Make him sit down, dear niece, a little higher
Beside you on the bed, up there within
The curtains, to hear better; I'll retire."
And with that word he drew towards the fire
And took a light, and framed his countenance
As if to gaze upon an old romance.

141

She, being Troilus' lady as by right,
Stood on the clear ground of her faithfulness,
And though she thought her servant and her
    knight
Was one who never should so much as guess
At any untruth in her, yet his distress
Touched her—love-maddened, he had lost his
    head;
So, to rebuke his jealousy, she said;

142

"Look, dearest heart, because love's excellence,
Which no one may resist, would have it so;
Also because I know the innocence
Of your pure truth, and saw your service grow
From day to day, I came indeed to know
Your heart all mine; these things have
    driven me
To have compassion on your misery.

143

"And for your goodness, which to this
    very hour
I have found in you, dear heart and chosen
    knight,
I thank you to the best of my poor power,
Though that is less than you deserve of right,
And I, with all my heart and soul and might,
Swear that I am, and ever shall be, true
Whatever it may cost me, love, to you.

144

"This shall prove true, as you may well believe;
But, sweetest heart, what this is leading to
Has to be said, although you must not grieve
That I should say it and complain of you;
For finally the thing I hope to do
Is slay the heaviness and pain that fill
Our hearts, and bring redress to every ill.

145

"I cannot think, my darling, how or why
This jealousy, this wicked cockatrice,
Has crept into your heart so causelessly.
How gladly would I save you from that vice!
Alas that it—or even a small slice
Of it—should refuge in so fair a place!
May Jove uproot it, may it leave no trace!

146

"But O thou Jove, O Author of all Nature,
Is this an honour to thy deity
That there should fall on many a guiltless
    creature
Such injury, when guilty ones go free?
O were it lawful to complain to Thee,
For sanctioning unwarrantable pain
Through jealousy, how loud I would com-
    plain!

147

"A further grief is this, that people say
Nowadays 'Jealousy is the soul of love.'
A bushel of poison is excused today
By one small grain of fondness, which they
    shove
Into the mixture; God that sits above
Knows if it's more like love, or more like
    shame,
Or hatred; things should bear their proper
    name.

148

"Certain it is one kind of jealousy
Is more excusable than some I know,
As when there's cause; and some such fantasy,
So well repressed by pity, will not show;

It scarce does harm or speaks it—better so;
And bravely it drinks up its own distress
And I excuse it for its nobleness.

149

"Then there's a jealousy that comes from spite,
A furious, irrepressible intrusion;
But your dear heart is not in such a plight,
And I thank God for it; for your confusion,
So I would call it, is a mere illusion,
Of the abundance of your love for me,
Which makes your heart endure this misery.

150

"Sorry I am for it, but angry not;
Yet, for my duty and for your heart's rest,
Let me be judged on oath, or else by lot,
Or by ordeal; you shall choose the test,
And, for the love of God, may this prove best!
If I be guilty, take my life away;
What is there more that I can do or say?"

151

A few, bright, newly-gathered tear-drops fell
Then from her eyes, and suddenly she cried
"In thought or deed, O God, thou knowest
      well,
To Troilus was never yet Criseyde
Untrue!" And down she laid her head to hide
Under the sheet, at which she tugged and tore,
Then sighed and held her peace, said no word
      more.

152

And now God send me help to quench this
      sorrow!
—And so I hope He will, for He best may—
For I have often seen a misty morrow
That turned into a merry summer's day;
And after winter follows greening May;
We see it all the time, and read in stories
How bitter battles win to sudden glories.

153

This Troilus, on hearing what she urged,
You may imagine, had no thought of sleep;
It was not with a sense of being scourged
That he had heard and seen his lady weep,
But of the cramp of death; he felt it creep
About his heart at every tear she shed;
It wrung his soul in anguish by her bed.

154

Deep in his spirit, he began to curse
His coming there, to curse the very day
That he was born, for bad had turned to worse;
Lost was the service he had sought to pay
His lady; he too lost, a castaway;

"O Pandarus," he thought "your cunning wile
Is worthless to me . . . O, alas for guile!"

155

And loaded down with shame he hung his
      head,
Fell on his knees and sorrowfully sighed.
What could he say in answer, all but dead?
And she was angry that could best provide
The comfort he most needed. He replied
When he could speak, "God knows that in
      this game,
When all is known, I shall not be to blame."

156

And, as he spoke, his sorrow was compacted
And shut into his heart, without relief
Of tears; he felt his spirits so contracted,
Stunned, stupefied, by such excess of grief,
Oblivion came upon him like a thief,
His fears and feelings all fled out of town
And in a swoon he suddenly fell down.

157

This was no small calamity to see;
But all was hushed, and Pandarus moved fast;
"O niece, keep quiet, or we're lost!" said he,
"Don't be afraid." But anyhow at last
In spite of all, he picked him up and cast
Him into bed, with "Wretch! You can't be
      hurt?
Are you a man?" and stripped him to his shirt

158

And "Niece," he said, "if you don't help us now
Your Troilus is lost, and all's forlorn!"
"I would indeed, if only I knew how,"
She said, "And gladly; O that I was born!"
"Yes, niece, you should be pulling out the
      thorn
That's sticking in his heart," said Pandarus,
"Say 'All forgiven,' dear, and stop this fuss."

159

"That would be dearer to me, far more dear,"
She said "than all the good under the sun!"
And then she stooped and whispered in his ear
"I am not angry with you, love; have done!
I swear it, not with you or anyone,
O speak to me, for it is I, Criseyde!"
In vain; he neither wakened nor replied.

160

They felt his pulse and she began to soften
His hands and temples with her tender touch,
Sought to deliver him and kissed him often
To loose his bonds, recall him from the clutch
Of bitter swooning; and they did so much

That, at long last, he started to draw breath,
Seeming to dawn out of the dark of death.

161

Reason took back her power on his mind,
Deeply abashed and humbled by her kiss,
And, with a sigh, as he began to find
Himself awake, he said "O what's amiss?
Merciful God! You wrong yourself in this!"
And she gave answer, calling him by name,
"Are you a man? O Troilus, for shame!"

162

And then she laid her arm across his breast
Forgave him all, and kissed him where he lay
Many a time; he thanked her with the best
Of all that welled into his heart to say,
And she gave answer in as kind a way
As came to her, to cheer him and delight,
And do away the sorrows of the night.

163

Said Pandarus "For aught I can surmise,
I and this candle serve no purpose here;
When folk are sick a light may hurt their eyes;
So, for the love of God, since you appear
To be in happy plight, let no more fear
Hang in your hearts, and may all discord cease."
He bore the candle to the mantelpiece.

164

Soon after that, though there was little need,
She took his oath and forced him to unsay
His jealousy; and after that, indeed,
She saw no cause for sending him away;
For trifles lighter than an oath will sway
On many occasions; as I dare to guess,
He that loves well means no ungentleness.

165

But still she taxed him with the charge of
    treason,
Questioning him of whom, and where,
    and why
He had been jealous, since there was no reason,
And what the sign he had been prompted by.
She pressed him busily for a reply,
Or else (she let him think) she had no doubt
It was a plot designed to find her out.

166

And, briefly, that the matter might be mended,
He felt obliged to answer when she ceased;
And, to avoid more trouble, he pretended
She had not smiled at such and such a feast;
Surely she might have looked at him, at least!
And so on. Almost everyone produces
Rubbish like that when fishing for excuses.

167

Criseyde replied "But, sweet, if it were so,

What harm was there in that? I did not mean
You any harm. By heaven, you should know
My very thoughts are yours, and clear and
    clean!
None of your arguments are worth a bean!
Are these your childish jealousies? I thank you!
You're like a little boy; I ought to spank you!"

168

Troilus sorrowfully began to sigh,
The fear that she was angry grew so strong;
He seemed to feel the heart within him die;
"Alas," he said, "I have been ill so long,
Have mercy on me if I did you wrong!
I promise never to offend you more;
I am in your hands, with much to answer for."

169

"For guilt, a mercy flows to take your part";
She answered, "and I have forgiven you;
Yet keep this night recorded in your heart,
Lest you should fall again, if tempted to;
Promise me this." "My dearest heart, I do."
"And now that I have punished you for this,
Forgive it me, my darling, with a kiss."

170

This Troilus, by sudden bliss surprised,
Put all into God's hand, as one who meant
Nothing but well, and, suddenly advised
By impulse, took her in his arms and bent
Her to him; Pandarus with kind intent
Went off to bed, saying "If you are wise,
No fainting now, lest other people rise."

171

What is there for the hapless lark to do
When taken in the sparrowhawk's fierce foot?
I can say nothing more; but, of these two,
For those to whom my story may be soot
Or sugar—I follow what my author put,
And must, though I delayed a year, express
Their joy, as I have told their heaviness.

172

Criseyde, on feeling herself taken thus,
As says my author in his ancient book,
In the enfolding arms of Troilus
Lay trembling, like an aspen leaf she shook.
And Troilus with glory in his look
Gave thanks to the bright gods and all their
    train.
So we may come to Paradise through pain.

173

And then this Troilus began to strain
Her in his arms and whispered, "Sweetest, say,
Are you not caught? We are alone, we twain,
Now yield yourself, there is no other way."
And soon she answered him, as there she lay,

"Had I not yielded long ago, my dear,
My sweetest heart, I should not now be here."

174

O true it is that he who seeks a cure,
As of a fever or a long disease,
Must, as we see all day, perforce endure
To drink the bitterest medicines to the lees;
And so we drink down pain to bring us ease,
As did these lovers in their fresh adventure;
They found their cure through pain, and long
    indenture.

175

And now the sweetness seemed to be more
    sweet
Because they had endured the bitter thorn;
For out of woe and into bliss they fleet,
Such as they had not known since they were
    born.
And better so than both to be forlorn!
For love of God, let women all take heed
And do as did Criseyde, if there be need.

176

Criseyde unloosed from care or thought of
    flight,
Having so great a cause to trust in him,
Made much of him with welcoming delight,
And, as the honeysuckle twists her slim
And scented tendrils over bole and limb
Of a tall tree, so, free of all alarms,
They wound and bound each other in their
    arms.

177

And as a nightingale that is abashed
And holds her peace, having begun to sing,
Because she may have heard the hedges crashed
By cattle, or the shout of shepherding,
Then, reassured, will let her music ring,
Just so Criseyde, now that her fears were still,
Opened her heart to him and showed her will.

178

Like one who sees his death is taking shape,
And die he must for all that he can see,
Whom suddenly a rescue and escape
Bring back from death to new security,
For all the world, to such new ecstasy
With his sweet lady won, came Troilus;
God grant no worse a fortune fall to us!

179

Her delicate arms, her back so straight and soft,
Her slender flanks, flesh-soft and smooth and
    white
He then began to stroke, and blessed as oft
Her snowy throat, her breasts so round and
    slight,

And in this heaven taking his delight,
A thousand, thousand times he kissed her too,
For rapture scarcely knowing what to do.

180

And then he said "O Love, O Charity,
Who, with thy mother, Cytherea the sweet,
After thyself is to be worshipped, she,
Venus, the planet of all kindly heat,
And next to you, Hymen I also greet,
For never to the gods was man beholden
As I, from cold care brought, to grace so
    golden!

181

"Benignest Love, thou holy bond of things,
Who seeks thy grace but renders thee no
    praise,
Lo! His desire would fly, but has no wings;
And were it not thy bounty deigns to raise
Those that best serve thee, labouring many
    days,
All would be lost, for what could they inherit
Unless thy grace were greater than their merit?

182

"Since thou hast helped me that could least
    deserve thee
Among the many numbered in thy grace,
And, when I was near death, hast let me
    serve thee
And hast bestowed me in so high a place
There is no bliss beyond it in all space,
What can I say but 'Praise and reverence
Be to thy bounty and thy excellence!' "

183

And having spoken thus, he kissed Criseyde,
At which she felt, be certain, no displeasure;
"Ah, would to God that I but knew," he cried
"How I might please you best, my heart, my
    treasure!
For was there ever man had such a measure
Of joy as I, on whom the loveliest
I ever saw has deigned her heart to rest?

184

"Here mercy is proved greater than deserving,
And every feeling proves it so in me,
For I, bright lady, whom I live in serving,
Cannot deserve your generosity;
Yet think, although I serve unworthily,
Needs must I shall learn better to deserve you
In virtue of the honour it is to serve you.

185

"And, for the love of God, my lady dear,
Since He created me to serve your will
—I mean, it is His will that you should steer
My course of life, to save me or to kill—

Teach me to earn your thanks and to fulfil
Your wishes, so that I may never chance
On your displeasure, through my ignorance.

186

"O fresh and womanly love, I dare to give
This certain promise: truth and diligence,
These you will find in me, and while I live
I will be perfect in obedience;
And should I fail you, in presence or absence,
Let me be killed for it, if it seems good
To you, my darling, in your womanhood."

187

"Indeed," said she, "dear heart of my desire,
Ground of my joy, my garner and my store,
I thank you for it with a trust entire
As it is thankful; let us say no more,
It is enough; for all was said before.
And, in a word that asks for no release,
Welcome, my lover, my sufficing peace."

188

Of all their ecstasies and joys, the least
Was more than I have power to convey;
But you, if you have tasted, judge the feast
Of their delight, the sweetness of their play;
I can say little, but at least I say
In safety, yet in dread, with night above,
They learnt the honour and excellence of love.

189

O blissful night, that they so long had sought,
How wert thou kindly to them both, how fair!
Would that my soul could such a night have
    bought,
Yes, or the least among the joys were there!
Away with coldness and away with care
And in this bliss of heaven let them dwell,
Surpassing all that tongue of man can tell.

190 (192)

These very two, in their embraces left,
So loath a moment to be disentwined,
Lest in their parting they should be bereft
Each of the other, or awake to find
It was a dream, a fancy of the mind,
Each to the other whispered in their kiss
"Can this be true? Or am I dreaming this?"

191 (193)

Lord, how he gazed at her, how blissfully!
His hungry eyes now never left her face,
And still he said "Dear heart, O can it be
That you are truly in this very place?"
"Yes, yes, indeed I am, by heaven's grace."
Criseyde gave answer with so soft a kiss
His spirit knew not where it was, for bliss.

192 (194)

With many kisses Troilus again
Touching her fluttered eyelids made reply
"Clear eyes, you were the cause of all my pain,
The humble nets my lady caught me by!
Though mercy may be written in her eye,
God knows the text was difficult to find;
How was I bound without a thong to bind?"

193 (195)

Then in his arms he took and held her close,
And sighs welled up in him and took their
    flight
A hundred times, nor were they such as those
Men sigh in grief or sickness, but the right
And easy sighs of passion and delight,
Sighs on the quickening pulse of love within,
That none will wish away when they begin.

194 (196)

Soon after this they spoke of many things
Seeking their great adventure to unfold,
And made a playful interchange of rings,
Though what the posy was we are not told;
Yet well I know there was a brooch of gold
And blue, set with a ruby heart, she took
And pinned upon his shirt, so says the book.

195 (197)

Lord! Do you think some avaricious ape
Who girds at love and scorns it as a toy,
Out of the pence that he can hoard and scrape,
Had ever such a moment of pure joy
As love can give, pursuing his foul ploy?
Never believe it! For, by God above,
No miser ever knew the joy of love.

196 (198)

Misers would answer "Yes"; but, Lord, they're
    liars!
Busy and apprehensive, old and cold
And sad, who think of love as crazed desires;
But it shall happen to them as I told;
They shall forgo their silver and their gold
And live in grief; God grant they don't re-
    cover,
And God advance the truth of every lover!

197 (199)

I wish to God those wretches that dismiss
Love and its service sprouted ears as long
As Midas did, that man of avarice;
Would they were given drink as hot and strong
As Crassus swallowed, being in the wrong,
To teach such folk that avarice is vicious
And love is virtue, which they think perni-
    cious.

198 (200)

These very two whose tale I have to tell,
Deep in the new assurance that was theirs,
Played in their talk and found it joy to dwell
On every detail, all the whens and wheres
And hows of their first meetings, and the cares
That now were passed, their heavy hearts,
    their sadness,
Which, I thank God, had all been turned to
    gladness.

199 (201)

And ever more in speaking of some pain
Or woe remembered, but now past and done,
They broke into their tale to kiss again,
And so another rapture was begun;
They yielded all their strength, since they
    were one,
Recapturing their bliss to feel at ease,
And weigh their joys with former miseries.

200 (202)

I will not speak of sleep, for reason swears
That sleep is nothing to my purpose here;
And heaven knows it was not much to theirs.
But lest this night that they had bought so dear
Escape them vainly—which was not to fear—
They packed its moments up with all the
    treasure
Of tenderness and gentle-natured pleasure.

201 (190)

However, though I cannot tell it all
As excellently as my author can,
Yet I have given—and, with God's help,
    shall—
The gist and substance of that learned man;
And if, in reverence of love, my plan
Has added more, it was my simple wit
Intending well; do what you like with it.

202 (191)

For these my words, here and in every part
Of this, are spoken under the correction
Of you that have a feeling for love's art,
And I submit them all to your reflection;
Add or diminish, make your own selection
Of my poor language; let it be your care,
I beg you! To return to where we were,

203

When the first cock, common astrologer,
Began to beat his breast and then to crow,
And Lucifer, the morning's messenger
And star of day, began to rise and show,
And eastwards there appeared (for those who
    know)

Fortuna Major, she, with stricken heart
Spoke thus to Troilus, that they should part:

204

"Life of my heart, my trust, and my delight,
Alas that I was born, alas, I say,
That day should part the lovers of the night!
But it is time to go; you must away,
Else I am lost for ever and a day;
Couldst thou not, night, have hovered on us,
    and kept
All dark, as when with Jove Alcmena slept?

205

"O dark of night, since books and learned folk
Affirm that God created thee to hide
This world, at certain times, in thy black cloak,
That rest to men should never be denied,
The beasts should bellow at thee, and men
    chide,
Since, broken with labour all the heavy day,
They get no rest from thee, that fleest away.

206

"Alas, too briefly is thy business done,
Swift night! May God, the Lord of Nature,
    hear,
And, for the malice of thy downward run,
Curse thee, and bind thee to our hemisphere,
Never beneath the earth to reappear!
For through thy reckless hurrying out of Troy
I have as hastily forgone my joy."

207

This Troilus, who at these sayings felt
(As then it seemed to him in his distress)
His heart in tears of blood begin to melt,
Like one that never yet such bitterness
Had tasted out of joy so measureless,
Enfolding his dear lady, his Criseyde,
In straining arms, lamentingly replied;

208

"O cruel day, denouncer of the joy
That love and night have stolen and made
    their prize,
Accursèd by thy coming into Troy,
For every chink has one of thy bright eyes!
Envious day! Wherefore so many spies?
What hast thou lost? What dost thou seek
    of us?
God quench the light in thee for doing thus!

209

"How has love injured thee, or been at fault,
Pitiless Day? Thine be the pains of Hell!
Many a love lies slain by thy assault,
For where thou pourest in they cannot dwell.

Is this the place to proffer light? Go sell
Thy merchandise to such as carve or paint;
We do not need thee, source of our complaint!"

210

And he began to chide the titan sun:
"Fool that thou art! No wonder men de-
    ride thee
To lie all night with Dawn, as thou hast done,
And yet to let her slip from close beside thee
To trouble other lovers; off! and hide thee
In bed again, thou and thy precious Morrow!
A curse upon you both, God give you sorrow!"

211

He sighed profoundly, turning to continue
To her, and said "Lady of weal and woe,
Lovely Criseyde, their very root and sinew,
Shall I arise, alas, and let you go?
I feel my heart will break and overflow;
How shall I live a moment if I do,
Since all the life I have is lived in you?

212

"What shall I do? Indeed I know not how,
Or when, alas, if ever, we shall see
A time to be again as we are now;
And, for my life, God knows what that can be
Since even now desire is biting me
And I shall die unless I may return!
How can I keep away from you and burn?

213

"Nevertheless my own, my lady bright,
If I could but be certain it was true
That I, your humblest servant and your knight,
Was set as firmly in your heart, as you
Are set in mine—if this I only knew,
It would mean more to me than Troy and
    Greece
Together, and I could endure in peace."

214

To which Criseyde made answer straight away
Sighing profoundly; this was her reply:
"The game has gone so far since yesterday,
That Phoebus first shall tumble from on high,
And doves be one with eagles in the sky,
And every rock in earth shall break apart,
Ere Troilus be sundered from my heart.

215

"For in my heart you are so deeply graven
That though it were my wish to turn you out,
As sure as God may bring my soul to haven,
Were I to die in torture, have no doubt,
I could not do it; therefore be without
These creeping fancies of the brain, I say,
For God's dear love, or I shall pine away.

216

"That you should hold me ever fast in mind,
As I hold you, is all that I beseech;
And if I knew that I was sure to find
It so, it were as far as joy could reach;
But dearest heart, with no more waste of
    speech,
Be true to me, or pity on us both,
For I am yours, by God and this true oath.

217

"And so feel sure of me, and no more sadness!
This is a thing I never said before
Nor shall to any; should it give you gladness
To come again and visit me once more,
I long for it as much as you, be sure,
As God may comfort me; I give you this."
She took him in her arms with many a kiss.

218

Against his will (but still it had to be)
This Troilus rose up and left their bed,
Put on his clothes and kissed her tenderly
A hundred times; and on his way he sped,
And with the voice of one whose spirit bled
He said "Farewell my dearest heart, my
    sweet,
And may God grant us safe and soon to meet."

219

Her grief had left her not a word to say,
So bitter did their parting seem, so dire;
And to his palace Troilus made way
As woebegone as she, yet still on fire
(To tell the truth), still wrung by the desire
To be again where he had been in bliss;
Nothing effaced the memory of this.

220

Back at his royal palace, quickly too,
He softly stole to bed, hoping to slink
Into long sleep, as he was wont to do;
But all for nought, he couldn't sleep a wink;
Into his fevered heart no sleep would sink.
He burned with passion for her now, who
    seemed
Worth more, a thousand fold, than he had
    dreamed.

221

Within him up and down began to wind
Her every word and gesture, stored with
    treasure,
Firmly impressed for ever on his mind,
To the least point of the remembered pleasure;
And at the memory, in no small measure,
Desire would blaze again, and longing grew
More than before, yet nothing could he do.

222

Criseyde herself, in the same manner, nursed
Within her heart the thought of his affection,
His sovereign worth, how she had met him
    first,
His gentle breeding and his circumspection,
And gave her thanks to love for this protection,
Longing to have him with her as before
And entertain her dearest heart once more.

223

Now Pandarus, when day had come again,
Went in to see his niece, and up he stepped
And said "I am afraid this dreadful rain
Left you but little leisure . . . Have you slept?
Did you have happy dreams? Now *I* was kept
Awake all night, yes, many were kept waking,
And some of us there are whose heads are
    aching."

224

He came in close and said "Well, how do
    you do
This merry morning? How are you feeling,
    niece?"
"Never the better," she replied "for you,
Fox that you are! May all your cares increase!
God knows you are the author of this piece.
For all your outward shows and words so
    white,
Little they know, who know you but by sight."

225

And, saying this, she made a move to hide
Under the sheet, for she was blushing red;
But Pandar, lifting up a corner, pried
Within, remarking "Well now, strike me
    dead!
Where is that sword of mine? Chop off my
    head!"
And, with a sudden thrust, his hand
    slipped past
Under her neck; he kissed her then at last.

226

I will pass over all that needs no saying;
God let him off his death, and so did she;
There they were, laughing happily and
    playing,
There was no reason why they should not be.
But to my purpose in this history;
When the time came, home to her house she
    went;
Pandarus had accomplished his intent.

227

Now let us turn again to Troilus;
In bed he lay, long, in a restless mood.

He had sent secretly for Pandarus
To come to him as quickly as he could;
He came at once, as may be understood;
Not once did he say "no"; gravely instead
He greeted him and sat beside his bed.

228

This Troilus, with all the force of feeling
That ever in the heart of friendship dwelt,
Threw himself down in front of Pandar,
    kneeling,
And would not rise again from where he knelt
Till he had poured the gratitude he felt
Forth in a thousand thanks, and blessed the
    morrow
Pandar was born to bring him out of sorrow.

229

"O friend of friends," he said, "the very best
That ever was or will be, truth to tell,
Who brought my soul to Heaven and to rest
From Phlegethon, the fiery flood of Hell,
Though I should serve you, though I were
    to sell
My life for you a thousand times a day,
That were a mote of what I ought to pay.

230

"The sun above, with all the world to see,
Has never yet, my life on it, set eye
On one so inly good and fair as she,
Whose I now am, and shall be till I die;
That I am hers I thank and glorify
Love that appointed me to this high end;
And I thank you for your kind office, friend.

231

"It was no little thing for you to give;
Yours is a debt I never can repay;
I owe my life to you—and why? I *live*,
Dead but for you and buried, many a day!"
And having spoken, back in bed he lay.
And Pandar listened with a sober eye
Till he had done, and then he made reply:

232

"Dear friend, if I've done anything for you,
It was a pleasure to me; in God's name
Believe it, I was very glad to do
Whatever I could for you—but all the same,
(Don't be offended!) I should be to blame
Unless I warned you; you are now in joy;
Beware, for it is easy to destroy.

233

"Think that of Fortune's sharp adversities
The most unfortunate of all, at last,
Is to have known a life of joy and ease,
And to remember it when it is past.

Therefore be careful; do not go too fast;
Never be rash, though you are sitting warm,
For if you are you'll surely come to harm.

234

"You are at ease; that is a good beginning;
But it's a certainty, as sure as fire
Is red, that keeping is as hard as winning
And needs as great a skill; bridle desire,
For worldly joy hangs only by a wire
As one can see; day after day it snaps;
And so go softly, there is need perhaps."

235

"I hope, God helping me in my design,"
Said Troilus, "I shall bear myself in such
A way as not to risk, through fault of mine,
The loss of anything, by too rash a touch;
Nor do you need to speak of this so much;
If you but knew my heart and its intention,
You would not think this matter worth a
mention."

236

He told him of the gladness of the night,
Why he had dreaded it at first, and how,
And said "O friend, as true as I'm a knight,
And by the faith I owe the gods, I vow
I never had it half as hot as now;
But this I know, the more desire bites me
To love her best, the better it delights me.

237

"And I can hardly tell you how it is,
But now I feel full of fresh quality,
Quite unlike anything I felt ere this."
Pandar replied to this judiciously:
"One who has known what heaven's bliss
can be
Will feel quite differently, I do not doubt it,
From what he did when first he heard about
it."

238

To sum things in a word, this Troilus
Could never tire of speaking in her praise,
And would asseverate to Pandarus
The bounty of his lady and her ways,
And thank and welcome him with cheerful
phrase;
The tale was ever freshly spun with wonder,
Till night came down and put the friends
asunder.

239

Soon after this—for Fortune still was steady—
There came the blessed moment of sweet news
When Troilus had warning to be ready
To meet Criseyde again; they were to use

The self-same means; he felt his heart suffuse
Itself in joy of sweet anticipation
And gave the gods all thanks and adoration.

240

The form and manner of the thing was
treated
Just as before; she came, with him ahead;
Therefore I think it need not be repeated,
And, to go plainly to the point instead,
In joy and safety they were put to bed
By Pandar, when the moment suited best;
And thus they were in quiet and at rest.

241

You needn't ask of me, since they are met,
Whether they were as happy as before;
Blissful as was their first encounter, yet
Their second was a thousandfold the more;
Gone were the sorrows and the fears of yore,
And both of them, indeed, if truth be told,
Knew as much joy as human heart can hold.

242

This is no little thing for me to say;
It stuns imagination to express.
For each began to honour and obey
The other's pleasure; happiness, I guess,
So praised by learned men, is something less.
This joy may not be written down in ink,
For it surpasses all that heart can think.

243

But cruel day would make them catch their
breath
At its approach; it signed to them again,
And what they felt was like the stroke of death;
The colour in their faces showed the strain,
And they began once more in their disdain
To call day traitor, envious and worse,
Laying the daylight under bitter curse.

244

"Alas!" said Troilus, "now I, for one,
Can see how Pyrois, and those other three
Swift steeds, that draw the chariot of the sun
Have used some by-path, out of spite to me,
And day has come so soon and suddenly;
The sun has hastened; he shall pay the price;
I never more will do him sacrifice."

245

Soon, of necessity, the daylight bid
Them part; and then, all speech and greet-
ing done,
They separated as before they did
And set a time to meet and be at one.
Many a night renewed their love begun,
And Fortune led them for a time in joy,

Criseyde and this King's son, this Prince of
   Troy.

246
Deeply fulfilled, in happiness and song,
Troilus led his life from day to day;
He jousted, spent and feasted with the throng,
Gave presents, decked himself in fine array,
And was surrounded by a world as gay
And fresh in heart as any he could find,
Fitting the natural temper of his mind.

247
His fame rose up, and with a voice so great
Throughout the world, for generosity
And honour that it rang at heaven's gate;
Being in love for him was ecstacy,
And in his inmost heart, it seems to me,
He thought there was no lover upon earth
So happy as he; love had declared its worth.

248
No loveliness that nature might allot
To any other lady that he met
Was able to undo one little knot
About his heart in her enchanted net,
He was so close-enmeshed, was so beset
By it, to loosen him or set him free
Was quite impossible, or seemed to be.

249
And often taking Pandar by the arm
Into the garden, in a joyous mood,
He fashioned feasts of language on her charm,
Praising Criseyde, praising her womanhood,
Praising her beauty; it was more than good,
It was a heaven, to hear his praises ring,
And in this manner then he used to sing:

250
"Love that is ruler over earth and sea,
Love whose commandment governs heaven on high,
Love that has made a wholesome amity
In neighbour states to join and guide them by,
That couples lovers in a holy tie,
And gives the law of love to friends as well,
Bind thou this harmony of which I tell!

251
"How that the universe, of faith so stable,
Varies its seasons with harmonious sway,
So that the elements, for all their babel,
Hold a perpetual bond that lasts for aye,
So Phoebus can bring forth his rosy day,
And so the moon has lordship over night;
This is love's doing; worshipped be his might!

252
"So that the sea, so greedy in its flowing,
Constrains his floods within a certain bound,

To hold them well in check at their fierce growing,
Lest earth and all for ever should be drowned:—
Were love to drop the bridle, then the ground
Of all that lives in love would burst apart,
And lost were all that Love now holds in heart.

253
"For so God willed, the Author of all Nature,
To circle every heart in His great bond
Of love, whose power not a single creature
Should know how to escape or go beyond,
And which can twist cold hearts to make them
   fond,
Able to love, and to feel pity too
For the unhappy heart, and help the true."

254
In all the dangers of the town's defence
He was the first to arm him as a knight,
And certainly, to trust the evidence,
Was the most dreaded soldier in a fight,
Except for Hector; hardiness and might
Came to him out of love—the wish to win
His lady's thanks had changed him so within.

255
In time of truce, out hawking he would ride,
Or else out hunting—lion, boar, or bear—
(For lesser beasts than these he left aside);
And riding back would often be aware
That she was standing at her window there,
Fresh as a falcon coming from her pen,
And she was ready with a greeting then.

256
Of love and virtue chiefly was his speech
And he despised all baseness; you may guess
There never was occasion to beseech
Him to do honour to true worthiness,
Or bring relief to any in distress.
And glad he was if any man fared well
Who was a lover too, when he heard tell.

257
He thought a man was lost, to tell the truth,
Unless on love's high service he was bent
—I mean such folk as had the right of youth;
And he had language for the sentiment
Of love, and was so strangely eloquent
About love's ordinances, lovers thought
He always spoke and acted as he ought.

258
And though of royal blood, he showed no
   pride
And harassed no one set in lower place;
To each and all benign, on every side
He earned the thanks of every smiling face;
This was love's will, all honour to love's grace!

Pride, avarice, envy, anger, in a trice
Were rooted out, and every other vice.

259

O my bright lady, thou, Dioné's daughter,
And thou, Sir Cupid, blind and wing'd,
    her son,
And O ye Nine, by Helicon's fair water,
That on Parnassus hill have loved to run,
You that have guided all that I have done,
Since it's your will to leave me, and we sever,
What can I do but honour you for ever?

260

Through you I have accomplished in my song
The full effects of love in Troilus,
His joys and griefs—for certain griefs belong
Among them, as the story comes to us.
My third book therefore is concluded thus,
With Troilus in happiness, at rest
In love, with his Criseyde, his own and best.

BOOK IV

1

How short a time, lament it as we may,
Such joy continues under Fortune's rule,
She that seems truest when about to slay,
And tunes her song, beguiling to a fool,
To bind and blind and make of him her tool,
The common traitress! From her wheel she throws
Him down, and laughs at him with mops and mows.

2

For she began to turn her shining face
Away from Troilus, took of him no heed,
And cast him clean out of his lady's grace,
And on her wheel she set up Diomede,
A thought for which my heart begins to bleed;
The very pen with which I now am writing
Trembles at what I soon must be enditing.

3

For how she left him, how Criseyde forsook
Her Troilus, or was at least unkind,
Must henceforth be the matter of my book,
For so they write who keep the tale in mind.
Alas, alas, that ever they should find
Cause to speak harm of her! And if they lie,
On them should fall the infamy, say I.

4

O Daughters of Old Night, you Furies Three,
In endless lamentation, endless pain,
Megaera, Alecto and Tisiphone,
And Roman Mars, the slayer of the slain,
Help me to write the Books that still remain

Of Troilus and Criseyde, and of the strife
In which he lost his love, and lost his life.

* * *

5

There, in a mighty host, as I have said,
The Greeks were ranged, encamped about
    Troy town;
It happened that when Phoebus' golden head
Laid on the Lion's breast, was shining down,
Hector and many a noble of renown
Fixed on a day to sally forth and fight
And do the Greeks what injury they might.

6

I do not know how long it was between
This, their decision, and the day they chose,
But came the day when, armoured bright and
    clean,
Hector and many a gallant man arose,
With spear in hand, or carrying great bows;
And out they went to battle and appeared
Before their foes, and met them beard to beard.

7

All the long day, with weapons sharply
    ground,
Arrows and darts and swords and dreadful
    maces,
They battled; many a horse and man were
    downed,
Their axes hacked away at brains and faces;
But in their last encounter (so the case is)
The night came down, the Trojans were
    misled,
And, having had the worst of it, they fled.

8

And on that day the Greeks took Ántenor,
Despite Polydamas or Monesteo,
Xantippus, Sarpedon, Polynestor,
Polites, and the Trojan lord, Ripheo.
And other lesser folk, like Phebuseo;
The day's disaster, for the folk of Troy,
Bred fear in them, a heavy loss in joy.

9

Nevertheless a truce was then arranged
(The Greeks requested it) and they began
To treat of prisoners to be exchanged
And paid great sums in ransom, man for man;
And soon through every street the rumour ran
In town and out; it came to every ear,
And Calkas was among the first to hear.

10

When Calkas knew for certain these awards
Would hold, he joined the Greeks at inter-
    view,

Thrusting himself among the older lords,
And took his seat as he was wont to do;
Then, changing countenance, he begged
　　them to
Be silent for the love of God, and pay
Respect to him and what he had to say.

11

And thus he said: "My lords and masters all,
I was a Trojan, everybody knows;
And Calkas is my name, if you recall.
Twas I who first brought comfort to your woes,
Foretelling your success against your foes.
Your work will soon and certainly be
　　crowned;
Troy will be burnt and beaten to the ground.

12

"And in what form and manner, in what way,
To blot this city out and gain your ends,
Often enough you all have heard me say,
As each, I think, among you apprehends.
I held the Greeks my very special friends
And so I came to you in person here,
And what was best to do I then made clear,

13

"Without considering my loss in treasure,
Weighed with your comfort—loss of in-
　　come too—
Thinking, my lords, in this to give you
　　pleasure,
I left my goods behind and came to you.
The loss was nothing, though, with that in
　　view;
For I surrender, as I hope for joy,
On your behalf, all that I have in Troy,

14

"Save for my daughter, whom I left, alas,
Sleeping at home when out of Troy I crept;
O stern, O cruel father that I was!
Hard-hearted resolution to have kept!
Would I had brought her naked as she slept!
For grief of which I may not reach tomorrow,
Unless you lords take pity on my sorrow.

15

"Because I saw no moment until now
For her deliverance, I held my peace;
But now or never; if you will allow,
I very soon may joy in her release.
O help, be gracious to me, Lords of Greece!
Pity a poor old wretch, and take his part!
It was to comfort you he broke his heart.

16

"You now have captured, chained, and may
　　condemn

Plenty of Trojans; if you willed it, she
My child, could be exchanged for one of them;
Now, in the name of generosity,
Out of so many, give up one to me!
And why refuse this prayer? Troy will fall
And you will conquer people, town and all.

17

"Upon my life it's true, believe you me;
Apollo told me faithfully about it,
And I have checked it by astronomy,
By lot and augury, you needn't doubt it;
The time is near when you, who stand with-
　　out it,
Shall witness flame and fire as they flash
Above the town, and Troy shall turn to ash.

18

"For Phœbus certainly and Neptune, too,
Who made the walls of this accursed town,
Are in high wrath against it and will do
Vengeance on all its folk, and bring it down,
And on Laomedon who wore the crown
In times gone by, but would not pay their hire;
And so these gods will set the town on fire."

19

Telling his story on, this old, grey man,
Humble in speech and in his look as meek,
(While the salt tears from either eyelid ran
And left their stain upon his grizzled cheek,)
Went on imploring succour from the Greek
So long that they, to cure him of these sore
Lamentings, handed over Ántenor

20

To Calkas; who so glad of it as he?
Pressing his needs upon them then, he plied
All those appointed for the embassy,
Begging that Ántenor should now provide
The offset for King Thoas and Criseyde.
And when King Priam's safeguard had been
　　sent,
At once to Troy the emissaries went.

21

Told of the reasons for this embassy,
King Priam, issuing a general writ,
Assembled Parliament immediately,
With the result—I give the gist of it—
The embassy were told they would permit
The exchange of prisoners, and what else was
　　needed;
They were well pleased; and so the plan
　　proceeded.

22

This Troilus was present in his place
When Ántenor was asked against Criseyde;

It brought a sudden change into his face,
To hear those words was almost to have died.
But he said nothing, for his tongue was tied;
Were he to speak, they might spy out his
  passion;
So he endured his grief in manly fashion.

23

And full of anguish and of grisly dread,
He waited for what other lords might tend
To say of it; two thoughts were in his head:
First, if they granted it, which heaven forfend,
Was how to save her honour? and how
  contend
Against the exchange? What could he do
  or say?
He wildly cast about to find a way.

24

Love drove him fiercely to oppose her going,
Rather to die, indeed, than let her go;
But reason said "What? Speak without her
  knowing?
You cannot think of it, as well you know;
Gain her consent, or she will be your foe,
And say it was your meddling had revealed,
Your love, so long and carefully concealed."

25

So he began to think it might be best,
If parliament decided she be sent,
To acquiesce in what they might suggest
And be the first to tell her their intent,
And leave her then to tell him what she meant
To do, which he would make his whole
  ambition,
Though all the world should be in opposition.

26

Hector, on hearing how the Greeks suggested
Taking Criseyde instead of Ántenor,
Gave them a sober answer; he protested:
"Sirs, she is not a prisoner of war,
Who ordered this? What do they take us for?
For my part, I would wish it were made clear
It's not our practice to sell women here."

27

A noise of people started up at once,
As violent as the blaze of straw on fire
(Though, as misfortune willed it, for the nonce
Their own destruction lay in their desire)
"Hector!" they cried, "What evil spirits in-
  spire
You thus to shield this woman, and to lose
Prince Ántenor? That is no way to choose!

28

"He is a wise commander and a bold,

And we have need of men, as one can see.
One of the greatest, worth his weight in gold;
Hector have done with all this fantasy!
Hear us," they said, "King Priam! We agree.
We give our voices to forgo Criseyde;
Let them deliver Ántenor!" they cried.

29

O Juvenal, how true your saying, master,
That men so little know what they should
  yearn
To have, that their desire is their disaster;
A cloud of error lets them not discern
What the best is, as from this case we learn:
These people were now clamouring to recall
Prince Ántenor, who brought about their fall.

30

It was his treason gave the Greeks possession
Of Troy; alas, too soon they set him free!
O foolish world, look, there is your discretion!
Criseyde, who never did them injury,
Shall now no longer bathe in ecstasy,
But Ántenor—"he shall come home to town,
And she shall go" they shouted up and down.

31

And so, deliberately, Parliament
Took Ántenor and yielded up Criseyde
By the pronouncement of the President,
With many a "No!" from Hector, who still
  tried
To save her; he and others were denied,
They spoke in vain; she was obliged to go,
For the majority would have it so.

32

Then all departed out of Parliament;
And Troilus—there is no more to say—
Went swiftly to his room; alone he went
Save for a man or two of his, but they
Were quickly told to take themselves away,
Because he wished to sleep, or so he said,
And down he flung himself upon his bed.

33

And as the leaves are torn by winter's theft
Each after other till the tree is bare,
And nothing but the bark and branch are left,
So Troilus lay bereft of comfort there,
Fast bound within the blackened bark of care,
And on the brink of madness, being tried
So sorely by the exchanging of Criseyde.

34

First he rose up and every door he shut
And window too; and then this sorrowful man
Sat himself down upon his bedside, but
More like a lifeless image, pale and wan,

And from his breast the heaped-up woe began
To burst in fury forth, under the spell
Of madness, and he did as I shall tell.

35

As a wild bull that lunges round and reels
Hither and thither, wounded to the heart,
And roars remonstrance at the death he feels,
So Troilus with violent fit and start
Lunged round his room, fists battering his
    heart,
Head beating wall and body flung to ground,
In utter self-confusion round and round.

36

His eyes in pity lent his heart relief,
Swift as twin wells, in tears they streamed
    away,
The high, convulsive sobs of bitter grief
Reft him of speech, and he could barely say
"O death! Alas, dost thou not hear me pray?
Wilt thou not let me die? Accursed be
The day when Nature formed and fash-
    ioned me!"

37

But after, when the fury and the rage
By which his heart was twisted and oppressed,
In time began a little to assuage
Themselves, he lay upon his bed to rest,
The tears gushed forth again and shook his
    breast;
The wonder is a body can sustain
The pain I speak of, aye, or half the pain.

38

And then he said "Fortune, alas for woe!
What have I done? In what have I offended?
Have you no pity, to deceive me so?
Is there no grace to save me? Is all ended?
Must Criseyde go because you so intended?
How can you find it in your heart to be
So cruel, Fortune, so unkind to me?

39

"Have I not, Fortune, ever held you high
Above all other gods? You know it well.
Will you deprive me thus of joy? Ah, why?
O Troilus, of thee what will they tell
Save that, a wretch of wretches, down he fell
From honour into misery; thence to wail
Criseyde, alas, until his breath should fail?

40

"Alas, O Fortune, if my life in joy
Roused your foul envy and displeasure, then
Why did you not take Priam, King of Troy,
My father, or let die my brethren?
Or have me killed, the wretchedest of men,

Cumbering earth, useless to all, and lying
Like one not fully dead, yet ever dying?

41

"Though all were taken, if Criseyde were
    left me,
I should not care whither you chose to steer;
But it is she of whom you have bereft me;
Aye, that has been your style for many a year,
To rob a man of what he holds most dear,
To prove thereby your fickle violence;
So I am lost and there is no defence.

42

"O very Lord of Love! Alas, O Lord,
Who best do know my heart, my every
    thought,
What sorrowful future can my life afford
If I forgo what was so dearly bought?
And since Criseyde and I by you were brought
Into your grace, and there our hearts were
    sealed,
How can you suffer this to be repealed?

43

"What shall I do? As long as I am master
Of my poor life of care and cruel pain,
I will cry out against this great disaster;
Alone as I was born, I will complain.
I'll never see the sunshine or the rain;
Like Oedipus, in darkness I shall end
My sorrowful life and die without a friend.

44

"O weary spirit ranging to and fro
Why fleest thou not out of the woefullest
Of bodies that were ever friend to woe?
O soul, lurking within me, leave thy nest,
Take wing out of my heart, and break! my
    breast;
Follow Criseyde, follow thy lady dear,
Thy rightful place is now no longer here!

45

"Sorrowful eyes that found their happiness
In gazing into hers that were so bright,
What are you good for now in my distress?
For nothing but to weep away your sight,
Since she is quenched that was your only light!
In vain it is I have you, eyes of mine,
Since she is gone that gave you power to
    shine.

46

"O my Criseyde, O sovereign excellence,
Who shall give comfort to the sorrowful soul
That cries his pain with such a vehemence?
Alas, there's no one; death will take his toll,
And my sad ghost, enamoured of its goal,

Will seek thee out to serve thee; O receive it!
What does the body matter, since I leave it?

47

"And O you lovers high upon the wheel
Of happy Fortune in your great endeavour,
God send you find a love as true as steel
And may your life in joy continue ever!
And when you pass my sepulchre, ah never
Forget your fellow who is resting there;
He also loved, unworthy though he were.

48

"O old, unwholesome, evil-living man,
Calkas I mean, alas, what ailed you, Sir,
To turn into a Greek, since you began
A Trojan? You will be my murderer;
Cursed was your birth for me! May Jupiter
Grant this to me, out of his blissful joy,
To have you where I want you, back in Troy!"

49

A thousand sighs that burnt like a live coal
One, then another, issued from his breast,
And mingled with the sorrows of his soul
Feeding his grief, giving his tears no rest;
He was so lacerated, so oppressed,
So utterly checkmated by this chance,
He felt no joy or grief, but lay in trance.

50

Pandarus, who had heard in Parliament
What every lord and burgess had replied,
And how they all had given their consent
To have back Ántenor and yield Criseyde,
Went nearly mad, he was so mortified;
Not knowing, in his misery, for the nonce,
What he was doing, he rushed away at once

51

To Troilus; the Squire at his door
On duty opened it anon for him,
And Pandarus, though weeping more and
   more,
Into the chamber, that was dark and dim,
Pressed onward silently; he seemed to swim
In his confusion, knew not what to say;
For very woe his wits were half astray.

52

All lacerated both in looks and mood,
In grief, with folded arms, a little space
Before this woeful Troilus he stood,
And gazed upon his pitiable face.
His heart turned chill to see his sorry case,
It slew his heart to see his friend in woe
And misery, or he imagined so.

53

And the unhappy Troilus who felt

The presence of his friend instinctively,
Like snow on sunny days began to melt,
While sorrowing Pandarus, in sympathy,
Was weeping too as tenderly as he.
So speechlessly they gazed, without relief;
Neither of them could speak a word, for grief.

54

But in the end the woeful Troilus
Near dead with suffering, burst into a roar,
A sorrowful noise indeed, and spoke him thus,
Through sighs and sobs that shook him to the
   core,
"O Pandar, I am dead; there's nothing more.
Did you not hear in Parliament" he cried
"They've taken Ántenor for my Criseyde!"

55

And Pandarus, dead-pale, could only nod
And answer, very miserably, "Yes;
I've heard—I know about it all. O God,
Who ever would have thought it? Who could
   guess?
If only it were false! It is a mess
Which, in a moment—how was one to
   know?—
Fortune has planned, to be our overthrow.

56

"In all the world no creature, I suppose,
Ever saw ruin stranger than have we,
Whether by chance or accident who knows?
Who can avoid all evils, who foresee?
Such is this world; in my philosophy
No one should think that Fortune is at call
For him alone; for she is common to all.

57

"But tell me, Troilus, why are you so mad,
Taking it all to heart, the way you do?
What you desired you at least have had;
By rights that ought to be enough for you.
What about me? I've never had my due
For my love-service, never a friendly eye
Or glance! It is for me to wail and die.

58

"Besides all this—and you must know as much
As I do here—the town and roundabout
Is full of ladies, fairer than twelve such
In my opinion; I will search them out
And find you one or two, you needn't doubt;
Be happy then, again, my own, dear brother;
If she is lost, we can procure another.

59

"What! God forbid our pleasures all should
   spring
From one sole source, or only in one way;

If one can dance, another girl can sing,
One is demure, another light and gay,
One knows her way about and one can play;
Each is admired for her special grace;
Both heron-hawk and falcon have their place.

60

"As Zeuxis wrote (so wise and full of phrases)
'New love will often chase away the old.'
Remember, circumstances alter cases.
Self-preservation, we are always told,
Comes first; the fires of passion will turn cold
By course of nature; since it was casual plea-
    sure,
You can forget about it at your leisure.

61

"For just as sure as day will follow night,
New love, or work, or other predilection,
Or the mere fact of seldom having sight
Of someone, can obliterate affection.
One of these ways, to sever the connexion,
And shorten what you suffer, shall be sought;
Absence will surely drive her from your
    thought."

62

He spoke whatever came into his head
To help his friend, and, following his brief,
He did not care what foolishness he said,
So long as it might bring him some relief.
But Troilus, so nearly dead for grief,
Paid little heed, whatever it was he meant;
In at one ear and out the other it went.

63

At last he stirred and answered as he leaned
Upon his elbow, "Friend, your remedy
Would suit me well enough, were I a fiend.
What! to betray one that is true to me?
Shame on the thought of all such villainy!
Better to have me killed before your eyes
At once, than have me do as you advise.

64

"She that I love, whatever you reply,
To whom my heart is given as to none,
Shall have me wholly hers until I die;
I have sworn truth to her and that is done.
I will not be untrue for anyone;
I live and die her man, I will not swerve;
No other living creature will I serve.

65

"And where you tell me you can find a creature
As fair as she, have done with it! Take care,
For there's no other being in all nature
To equal her, and so make no compare,
For your opinion I will never share

Touching all this, and you can spare your
    breath;
To listen to you is a kind of death.

66

"You tell me solemnly to love some other,
To start afresh and let my lady go;
It isn't in my power, my dear brother,
And if it were I would not have it so.
Can you play racquets with it, to and fro,
Nettle in, dock out, and shift from here to
    there?
Bad luck to her that takes you in her care!

67

"The way you are behaving, Pandarus,
Is like when someone sees a man in woe
And saunters up to him, and argues thus:
'Don't think about it and the pain will go.'
You'll have to turn me into granite though,
Strip me and rifle me of every passion,
Before you cure me in that easy fashion.

68

"Death well may drive the life out of my breast,
Which a long grief will surely undermine,
But never shall my soul be dispossessed
Of her love's dart, but down to Proserpine,
When I am dead, I'll go, and there resign
Myself to live in pain, and broken-hearted,
Eternal grief, that she and I are parted.

69

"You made an argument along the line
That it should prove a lesser misery
To lose Criseyde, because she once was mine,
And I had had a full felicity.
Why gab like that? Haven't you said to me
Often enough that it was worse to fall
From joy, than not to have known joy at all?

70

"But tell me, since you think it is so easy
To change in love, and wander to and fro,
How comes it that your feelings are too queasy
To change the one that causes you such woe?
Empty your heart of her and let her go,
Exchange her for some other, sweeter diet,
Some lady that will cause you no disquiet.

71

"If you, whose love is dogged by unsuccess,
Still cannot drive that love out of your mind,
I that have lived in joy and happiness
With her, as much as any man could find,
Could I so soon forget her? Are you blind?
Where have you been mewed up so long,
    how spent
Your time, who are so good at argument?

72

"No, no. God knows that everything you've
    said
Is worthless; for, befall what may befall,
I mean to die; would I indeed were dead
And no more words; come, Death, the end
    of all
Our sorrows, come, O hear me when I call!
Happy the death that's called for not in vain,
And, often called, will come to end all pain.

73

"I know that when I lived my life in quiet
To keep thee off I would have paid thee hire;
Thy coming now would be my sweetest diet;
There's nothing in the world I more desire,
O Death! My griefs have set my heart on fire,
Drown me in tears at once, or take thy dart
And with thy cold stroke quench both heat
    and heart.

74

"And since thou slayest so many of the best
Against their will, unasked for, day and night,
Do me this service now at my request,
Deliver the world of me and do me right,
The wretchedest of men that Fortune's spite
Ever struck down; it's time for me to die,
Since in this world I serve no purpose, I."

75

The tears welled up into his eyes, distilling
Like drops from an alembic, and as fast;
And Pandar held his tongue and stood un-
    willing
To venture further, with his eyes downcast.
The thought however came to him at last
"By heaven, rather than my friend should die,
I'll say a little more to him, or try."

76

"Dear friend," he said, "you are in great
    distress,
And since you think my arguments at fault,
Why don't you help yourself and take redress,
Using your manhood now to call a halt
To all these tears? Carry her by assault!
These niceties are nothing but self-pity;
Get up and take Criseyde and leave the city!

77

"Are you a Trojan? Where's your resolution?
Not take a woman who's in love with you
And who would say it was the best solution?
What foolish scruples are you listening to?
Get up at once, and stop this weeping, do,
Show us your manhood and within the hour
I'll die for it, or have her in our power."

78

And Troilus, whose voice began to soften,
Replied "You may be certain, brother dear,
That I have thought of this, and very often,
And more than what you have suggested here;
But why I haven't done it will appear
When you have heard what I have got to say;
Then, if you wish to lecture me, you may.

79

"First, as you know, this city is at war
Just for a woman carried off by force;
I'm one there could be no allowance for,
As things stand now, in such a wicked course;
I should be blamed by all and be a source
Of trouble to the town, if I withstood
My father's word; she leaves for the town's
    good.

80

"And I have also thought—should she con-
    sent—
To beg her of my father, as a grace;
That would accuse her, to her detriment.
Nor can I offer purchase in this case,
For since my father, in so high a place
As Parliament, has given it his seal,
He could not now consider my appeal.

81

"Yet most I dread her heart might be perturbed
By violence, were I to play that game,
For if the town were openly disturbed
It must result in slander on her name,
Which I would rather die for, than defame;
And God forbid that ever I prefer
Saving my wretched life to saving her.

82

"So I am lost, for all that I can see,
For it is certain, since I am her knight,
Her honour is a dearer thing to me
Than I myself, it must be, as of right.
Desire and reason tear me in their fight;
Desire counsels 'ravish her!', but reason,
So fears my heart, forbids me such a treason."

83

And still he wept away with tears unceasing
And said "Alas, what will become of us?
I feel my love increasing and increasing
And hope diminishing, my Pandarus,
For reasons ever more calamitous!
Alas, alas, why will my heart not burst?
There's little rest in love, from last to first."

84

"As for myself," said Pandarus "you're free,
Do as you like; but if I had it hot

And were a Prince, I'd take her off with me,
Though all the city shouted I should not;
I wouldn't give a penny for the lot.
When all the shouting's over and the thunder,
It ends in whispers and a nine-days'-wonder.

85

"You're so considerate, you go so deep;
Think of yourself! The time is past and done
For weeping now; better if others weep!
Especially since you and she are one.
Get up and help yourself, for, by the sun,
It's better to be blamed and pointed at
Than to lie here and perish like a gnat.

86

"It's not a vice in you, there is no shame
In holding back the woman you love most;
Maybe she'll think it's foolish of you, tame,
To let her go and join the Grecian host;
Fortune favours the brave! It is her boast
To help the hardy in a thing like this,
And thwart all wretches for their cowardice.

87

"And if Criseyde turns peevish, should she
    grieve
A little, you may make your peace at will
Hereafter; as for me, I can't believe
That even now she'd take it very ill;
Fear nothing! Let your quaking heart be still;
Remember Paris; Paris is your brother;
He has a love, and why not you another?

88

"And, Troilus, there's one thing I can swear;
If she—Criseyde—your darling and your
    bliss—
Loves you as truly now as you love her,
God knows that she will never take amiss
What you may do to remedy all this;
And if she leaves you, if she thinks it fit,
Then she is false; love her the less for it.

89

"And so take heart! Remember, you're a
    knight;
For love the laws are broken every day;
So show your courage, show your strength
    and right,
Have pity on yourself and throw away
This awe you feel; don't let this wretched day
Gnaw out your heart; set all at six and seven,
And if you die a martyr, go to heaven.

90

"And I will stand beside you. No retreat!
Even if I, and all my kith and kin,
Lie dead as dogs for it upon the street

Thrust through with bloody wounds. So count
    us in!
You'll find me friend, whether you lose
    or win.
But if you'd rather die in bed upstairs,
Good-bye! To Hell with anyone who cares!"

91

These words brought Troilus to life again
And he replied "Well, thanks for that, dear
    friend;
You needn't goad me so; I suffer pain
Greater than you can give. Now, hear the end:
Whatever happens I do not intend
To carry her off, except by her consent,
Not if it kills me. That was what I meant."

92

"Why, so did I! And I've been saying so
All day," said Pandar, "have you asked her yet?
Is that why you are sad?" He answered "No."
"Then what dismays you, if you haven't met?
How can you know that she would be upset
If you should carry her off? Why should you
    fear?
Has Jove come down and whispered in
    your ear?

93

"Get up and wash your face; and see it's clean.
Pretend that nothing's happened; see the
    King,
Or he may wonder where you can have been;
Throw dust into his eyes—yes, that's the
    thing,
For even now he may be ordering
Someone to fetch you, ere you are aware;
Cheer up, and let me deal with this affair.

94

"For I am certain that I can contrive it
Somehow, somewhere, some time tonight,
    for you
To see your lady where you can be private;
Then by her words, and her appearance too,
You'll soon perceive what she would have
    you do,
And all her mind; talk over what is best;
Farewell for now, for on this point I rest."

95

Impartial rumour that is wont to bring
A false report as swiftly as a true,
Had darted through all Troy on eager wing
From man to man, telling the tale anew,
How Calkas' daughter, she, the bright of hue,
In Parliament, not even argued for,
Had been delivered up for Antenor.

96

And very soon the rumour reached Criseyde;
She, for her part, had never given thought
To Calkas, cared not if he lived or died;
She called down curses on the man who
    brought
The treaty of exchange, but never sought
To question it, for fear it might be true;
She dared not ask of anyone she knew.

97

As one who long had set her heart and mind
On Troilus, and who had there made fast,
So that the world itself could not unbind
Such ties of love, or Troilus be cast
Out of her heart as long as life should last,
She burned with love and terror, to and fro;
What would be best to do she did not know.

98

But, as one sees in town and roundabout,
Women like visiting their friends to chatter;
Criseyde was soon the centre of a rout
Supposing her delighted at the matter;
So gossip and congratulating patter,
Dear at a penny, full of bright regret,
Poured from these city ladies when they met.

99

Said one "I am as happy as could be
On your account; you'll see your father, dear!"
Another said "Indeed? I can't agree!
We have seen all too little of her here."
Then said a third "Let's hope that she will clear
The air and bring us peace on either side,
And may the Lord Almighty be her Guide!"

100

These femininities and gossipings
She heard as one whose thoughts are far away;
God knows her heart was set on other things;
Her body sat and heard them say their say,
But the attention of her spirit lay
On Troilus; she sought him with the whole
Speechless desire and passion of her soul.

101

These women, fancying that they could
    please her
Expended all their tales on her for naught,
For no such vanities had power to ease her,
Since all the while she listened she was caught
In flames of other passions than they thought;
She felt her heart would die of misery
And weariness in such a company.

102

She was no longer able to restrain
The tears within her, they began to well
And give their signal of the bitter pain

In which her spirit dwelt and had to dwell,
Remembering from what Heaven to
    what Hell
She now had fallen, since she must forgo
The sight of Troilus; she sighed for woe.

103

And every fool of those who sat about her
Supposed that she was weeping for the pain
Of having to depart and do without her
And never be amused by her again;
Her older friends were ready to explain,
Seeing her weep, that it was human nature,
And they wept too for the unhappy creature.

104

And so these women busily consoled her
For things of which she had not even thought,
Believing she was cheered by what they
    told her;
"She ought to be more cheerful, yes she
    ought,"
They urged her; and the comfort that they
    brought
Was such as, with a headache, one might feel,
If someone came and clawed one by the heel.

105

But after all this foolish vanity
They took their leave, and home they hur-
    ried all.
Criseyde, invaded by her misery,
Went up into her chamber from the hall,
Fell on her bed for dead, and to the wall
She turned, intending never thence to rise,
As I shall tell you, and, with countless cries,

106

Her rippled hair, the colour of the sun,
She tore, and wrung her fingers long and
    slender,
Calling on God for pity upon one
Who only wished for death to save and
    end her;
Her cheeks that once were bright, now pale
    and tender
With tears, bore witness to her sad constraint,
And sobbing thus, she spoke in long com-
    plaint:

107

"Alas!" she said, "That I must leave this
    nation,
Wretched, unfortunate and full of woe,
Born under an accursèd constellation,
And, parted from my knight, compelled to go!
Sorrow upon the daylight, in the glow
Of which these eyes first saw him riding there,
Causing me, and I him, so much despair!"

108

And upon that there started from her eyes
Tears like an April shower, and as fast,
She beat her white breast, and a thousand cries
She gave for death to come to her at last,
Since he that eased her sorrow in the past
Must be forgone; and in this grief and need
She felt herself a creature lost indeed.

109

"What shall I do?" she said, "And what
　　will he?
How shall I live if we are thus divided?
And O dear heart I love so faithfully,
Who will console your misery as I did?
Calkas, on your head be the sin, misguided
Father! O Argyve, his wife,
Sorrow upon the day you gave me life!

110

"To what end should I live and sorrow thus?
Can a fish live out of its element?
What is Criseyde without her Troilus?
How should a plant or creature find content
Or live, without its natural nourishment?
There is a proverb, I have heard it said,
'The green that has least root is soonest dead.'

111

"Thus I resolve to do: since sword and dart
I dare not handle, for their cruel pain,
From the dread day on which I must depart,
Unless I die of grieving, sorrow-slain,
I never shall touch meat or drink again
Till I unsheathe my soul and end my breath,
And in this way I'll do myself to death.

112

"My dresses, Troilus, shall be unpearled,
They shall be black, my dearest heart and best,
In token, love, I have forgone the world,
Who once was wont to set your heart at rest;
And in my Order, till by death possessed,
I shall observe, you being absent thence,
The rule of grief, complaint and abstinence.

113

"The sorrowing soul that harbours in my heart
I leave to you—with yours it shall complain
Eternally, for they shall never part.
For though on earth we parted, once again
In the far field of pity, out of pain,
Known as Elysium, we shall meet above,
Like Orpheus and Eurydice, his love.

114

"Thus, dearest heart, for Ántenor, alas,
I soon shall be exchanged, is that not sure?
What will you do? Can such a sorrow pass?
How shall your tenderness of heart endure?

Forget your grief, my love! Be that your cure,
Forget me also, for I tell you true
I'll gladly die if all be well with you."

115

Could they be ever written, said, or sung,
Her words of lamentation and distress?
I do not know; but if my simple tongue
Should venture to describe her heaviness,
I should but make her sorrow seem far less
Than what it was, and childishly deface
Her high complaint; here it shall have no
　　place.

116

Pandar, who had been sent by Troilus
To see Criseyde, when, as you heard me say,
It was agreed it would be better thus
(And he was glad to serve in such a way)
Came to Criseyde in secret, where she lay
Upon her bed, in torment and in rage,
As he came in upon his embassage.

117

And this was how he found her when
　　they met;
Her tears fell salt upon her bed of care,
And bathed her breast and countenance
　　with wet;
The mighty tresses of her sunnish hair,
Hanging about her ears unbraided there,
Were a wild symbol of her martyrdom
And death; her spirit longed for it to come.

118

And, seeing him, she started thereupon
To hide her teary face and turn away,
And this made Pandar feel so woebegone,
That he could hardly bring himself to stay,
It was too much for him. And I must say
That if Criseyde had made lament before,
She did so now a thousand times the more.

119

In bitterest complaining, thus she cried:
"O Pandarus, first cause, as well I know,
Of many a cause of joy to me, Criseyde,
That is transmuted now to cruel woe,
Tell me, am I to welcome you, or no?
You were the first to bring me to the bliss
Of serving love; and must it end like this?

120

"Ends love in sorrow? Yes, or people lie;
Aye, and all worldly bliss, it seems to me.
Bliss has a goal that sorrows occupy,
And whosoever thinks this cannot be,
Wretch that I am, let him but look at me
That hate myself, and ever more shall curse
My birth, and feel I move from bad to worse.

121

"Whoever sees me, sees all grief in one,
Pain, torment, lamentation, bitterness,
None but inhabits my sad body, none!
Anguish and languishment and woe, distress,
Vexation, smart, fear, fury, giddiness . . .
Indeed I think the very heavens rain
Down tears in pity of my cruel pain."

122

"Ah my dear niece, my sister in dejection,"
Said Pandarus, "what do you mean to do?
Have some regard, some thought for your
    protection;
Will you let sorrow make an end of you?
Stop it! Here's something you must listen to:
I have a word for you, so pay attention,
Sent you by me from Troilus, I may mention."

123

Criseyde then turned towards him in a grief
So great, it was a very death to see.
"Alas," she said, "what word can bring relief?
What has my dearest heart to say to me
Whom I may never see again? Does he
Lack tears upon my going? Should he care
To send for them, I have enough to spare."

124

The visage that she showed had paid the price;
She looked like one that they had come to bind
Upon her bier; her face, once Paradise,
Had changed and seemed as of another kind;
The fun and laughter one was wont to find
In her, and all her joyfulness, had flown
From poor Criseyde, and there she lay alone.

125

About her eyes there was a purple ring
That circled them in token of her pain
And to behold her was a deadly thing,
And Pandar was unable to restrain
Tears that came gushing from his eyes like
    rain.
Nevertheless, as best he could, he tried
To give these words from Troilus to Criseyde:

126

"Niece, I suppose you've heard of the to-do;
The King, and others, acting for the best,
Have made exchange of Ántenor and you,
The cause of all this trouble and unrest.
But how these fatal doings have oppressed
Your Troilus no earthly tongue can say;
For very grief his wits have gone astray.

127

"Ah, we have been so wretched, he and I,
It nearly killed us both; but thanks to keeping

To my advice, he has made shift to dry
His eyes and somewhat to withdraw from
    weeping;
And I am sure that he would fain be sleeping
By you tonight. Together you may find
Some remedy, of one or other kind.

128

"This, short and plain, is all I have to say
—As far as I can gather, anyhow;
And you, in all this tempest of dismay,
Cannot attend to lengthy prologues now;
Send him an answer, if your tears allow,
And, for the love of God, I beg you, dear,
Stop weeping before Troilus comes here."

129

"Great is my grief," she answered, as before,
Sighing like one in deadly, sharp distress,
"But yet to me his sufferings weigh still more;
I love him better than myself, I guess.
Is it for me, alas, this heaviness
Of heart, of which he piteously complains?
Indeed this sorrow doubles my own pains.

130

"Grievous to me, God knows, it is to part,"
She said, "yet it is harder still for me
To look into the sorrow of his heart,
For that will be my death, as I foresee.
Yes, I shall surely die. And yet," said she
"Bid him to come, ere threatening death
    may sack
The city of my soul in its attack."

131

Having said this, she buried her face flat
Upon her forearms, shedding many a tear.
Pandarus said, "Alas! Ah, why do that?
You must get up, you know the time is near;
Rise up and quickly, he will soon be here!
You must not let him find you blubbered red,
Unless you wish to send him off his head.

132

"If he could see you making this to-do,
He'd kill himself; and if I had expected
This fuss, I'd not have let him visit you
For all the wealth King Priam has collected;
Since to what end his course would be directed
I know too well; and therefore you must try
To stop this woe, or, flatly, he will die.

133

"Prepare yourself, dear niece, to render aid,
To mitigate his sorrows, not to heat;
And touch him with the flat and not the blade;
Use all your wisdom, set him on his feet.
How would it help, were you to fill a street

With tears, though both of you should drown
    in them?
No time for tears; but time for stratagem.

134

"Here's what I mean: I'll bring him here, and,
    knowing
You'll be at one in what you fix upon,
I trust you'll find a way to stop your going,
Or to return soon after you have gone.
Women are quick to see a long way on;
Let's see if you can make your wit prevail,
And if you want my help it shall not fail."

135

"Go," said Criseyde, "and, Uncle, honestly,
With all the power I have I will refrain
From weeping in his sight; and eagerly
I'll work to make him happy once again;
I will explore my heart in every vein,
For there shall lack no salve to heal his sore
In anything that I'm to answer for."

136

So off went Pandar seeking Troilus.
He found him in a temple all alone,
Like one whose life had lost its impetus
And who cared nothing for it; at the throne
Of every pitying god he made his moan
Imploring to be taken from earth's face,
Sure as he was to find no better grace.

137

And, to speak briefly, it would be no lie
To say he was so overcome by care
As utterly to have resolved to die
That day; all argument had led him there,
Telling him he was lost, and to despair;
"Since all that comes, comes by necessity,
Thus to be lost is but my destiny.

138

"And certainly, I know it well," he cried,
"That, in His foresight, Providence Divine
Forever has seen me losing my Criseyde,
(Since God sees everything) and things
    combine
As He disposes them in His design
According to their merits, and their station
Is as it shall be, by predestination.

139

"But all the same, whom am I to believe?
Though there are many great and learned men,
And many are the arguments they weave,
To prove predestination; yet again
Others affirm we have free choice; but then
Those ancient men of learning are so sly:
On whose opinion am I to rely?

140

"Some say 'If God sees everything before
It happens—and deceived He cannot be—
Then everything must happen, though you
    swore
The contrary, for He has seen it, He.'
And so I say, if from eternity
God has foreknowledge of our thought and
    deed,
We've no free choice, whatever books we
    read.

141

"No other thought, no other action either,
Could ever be but such as Providence
(Which cannot be deceived about it neither)
Has long foreseen, without impediments.
If there could be a variation thence,
A wriggling out of God's foreseeing eye,
Then there would be no Providence on high.

142

"God then would have no more than an
    opinion,
With nothing steadfastly foreseen or sure;
It were absurd to say of His dominion
That it would lack a knowledge clear and pure,
Or had the doubtful knowing men endure;
To guess such errors into Deity
Were false and foul, a wicked blasphemy.

143

"Yet there's another view maintained by some
Who wear their tonsures very smooth and dry;
And they would say 'A thing is not to come
Because divine foreknowledge from on high
Foresaw it; rather, that the reason why
It was foreseen was that it had to be,
Which Providence foresaw, presumably.'

144

"So, in this manner, this Necessity
Just crosses back onto the other side
Of the debate; things do not have to be
Because foreseen, that has to be denied.
But if they are to be they cannot hide
From Providence; things certain to befall
Must be foreseen for certain, one and all.

145

"I mean—and I am labouring in this—
To question which is cause of which, and see
Whether the fact of God's foreknowledge is
The certain cause of the necessity
By which things come about eventually,
Or if the fact that they must come about
Is what makes God foresee them; there's the
    doubt.

146

"Yet I won't strive to show, nor have I shown,
How causes stand in order, but infer
That, of necessity, a thing foreknown
For certain, will most certainly occur,
Whether or not we seem to register
That God's foreknowledge made it come to
    pass;
Yet it will come, for good or ill, alas!

147

"If there's a man there, sitting on the seat,
Then, of necessity, it follows fair
Enough that your opinion is no cheat
When you conjecture he is sitting there;
And yet again, as I am well aware,
The contrary opinion stays as strong,
As thus—now listen, for I won't take long—

148

"I say, if the opinion you declare
Is true (that he is sitting there), I say
That of necessity he's truly there;
And so necessity goes either way:
Necessity that he be on display
Necessity in you to see him so,
And that's necessity in both, you know.

149

"But you may say 'He is not sitting there
Because the fact you think he is is true,
But rather, he was sitting on that chair
From long before, and so was seen by you.'
And I say, though indeed it may be due
To his being there, yet the necessity
Is common to you, interchangeably.

150

"In just this way (it makes undoubted sense)
I can construct—or so it seems to me—
My argument about God's providence
And about all the things that come to be;
And by this reasoning we all can see
That whatsoever things on earth befall
Come of necessity, predestined all.

151

"Although whatever comes about, I mean,
Must therefore be foreknown—as who can
    doubt?—
And though it does not come because fore-
    seen,
Yet it still follows, and one can't get out
Of this, that things which are to come about
Must be foreseen; or, if foreseen, take shape
Inevitably; there is no escape.

152

"And this is quite sufficient anyway
To prove free choice in us a mere pretence;
What an absurdity it is to say
That temporal happenings—the things of
    sense—
Are causes of eternal prescience!
Now truly, it's as false as it is odd
To say things cause the Providence of God!

153

"What might I think, had I such thought in
    store,
Except that God foresees what is to come
Because it is to come, and nothing more?
So might I think that all things, part and sum,
That once had being, but are dead and dumb,
Caused providence, ere they were in the
    making,
To know them, and to know without mis-
    taking.

154

"Above all this, I have yet more to show,
That just as, when I know a thing to be,
That thing must of necessity be so,
So, when a thing that I can know and see
Is coming, come it will; necessity
Of things to come, foreknown before their day,
Can never be evaded any way."

155

Then said he thus: "Almighty Jove on high,
That knowest our sad case infallibly,
Have pity on my sorrow, let me die,
Or from our trouble bring Criseyde and me."
And as he knelt there in his misery,
With all these thoughts debating in his head,
Pandar came in, and (you shall hear it) said:

156

"Almighty God enthroned in heaven above!
Whoever saw a man behaving so?
Why, Troilus, what are you thinking of?
Always your own worst enemy, as though
Criseyde had gone already! Don't you know
We have her still? Why kill yourself with
    dread?
The very eyeballs in your skull look dead.

157

"Haven't you lived for many years, dear
    brother,
Without her, happily and well at ease?
And were you born for her and for no other?
Did nature only fashion you to please
Criseyde? You should be thinking thoughts
    like these;
Just as with dice chance governs every throw,
So too with love; its pleasures come and go.

158

"Yet of all wonders this I find most strange,
Why you should weep so, when, as you'll
    admit,
You have no notion what they will arrange,
Or whether she has ways of stopping it.
You haven't yet made trial of her wit;
It's time enough to stick your neck out when
Your head's to be cut off; start weeping then!

159

"You pay attention, then, to what I say;
I've spent some time with her; she spoke to me
(As was agreed between us, by the way),
And all the time I kept on thinking, she
Had something locked in her heart's privacy
By which she hopes—if I have any ear—
To find a means to hinder what you fear.

160

"So I'd advise you, at the fall of night,
To go and see her and to make an end
Of this; and Juno in her splendid might
Will, as I hope, send grace and be our friend.
My heart is saying 'They shall never send
Criseyde away!' So set your heart at rest;
Hold to your purpose, for it is the best."

161

"You have said well, that's just what I will do,"
Said Troilus, and yet he sighed for woe,
Then stammered out another word or two,
And when he saw that it was time to go
He went alone, and secretly, as though
All was as usual, and took his way
To where she was, and did as I shall say.

162

The truth is this, that when at first they met
Pain in their hearts gave them so sharp a
    twist
Neither could say a word in greeting, yet
They fell into each other's arms and kissed.
Which was the sorrier at such a tryst
Neither could say; grief has a way of robbing
The soul of words; they could not speak for
    sobbing.

163

The tears that in their sorrow they let fall
Bitter beyond all tears of nature's kind,
Smarted as wood of aloes does, or gall;
Tears bitterer than these I do not find
The woeful Myrrha wept through bark and
    rind;
In all the world there's none so hard of heart
But would have felt compassion for their
    smart.

164

But when the weary spirits of these twain
Returned to them, to where they ought to
    dwell,
And felt a little lessening of pain
By long lament and ebbing of the well
Of tears, their hearts beginning to unswell,
At last, and with a broken voice, Criseyde,
Hoarse from her sobbing, looked at him and
    cried:

165

"O Jove, have mercy on me, I am dying!
Help, Troilus!" And then she laid her face
Upon his breast, and speechless from her
    crying,
She felt her soul was gliding into space
Leaving for ever its appointed place;
She lay, a greenish pallor in her features,
That once had been the loveliest of creatures.

166

And he began with passion to behold her
Calling her name; but there she lay for dead,
Speechless and cold, her head upon his
    shoulder,
Her eyes thrown back and upward in her
    head.
He, at a loss what should be done or said,
Kissing her cold mouth over and again,
Suffered, God alone knew—and he—what
    pain!

167

He roused himself, and laid her on the bed;
No sign of life she gave that he could see,
Stretched out in length she lay there, seem-
    ing dead,
"Alas!" his heart was sighing, "woe is me!"
And when he saw her lying speechlessly,
He said, all bare of bliss, and heavy-hearted,
That she was gone, her spirit had departed.

168

When he had long lamented and complained,
Had wrung his hands and said what was to say,
And his salt tears upon her breast had rained,
He brought himself to wipe those tears away
And pitifully he began to pray,
Saying "O Lord, that sittest on Thy throne,
Pity me too, that follow her alone!"

169

Lifeless she lay, cold and insentient,
There was no breath in her, for all he knew;
This was for him a pregnant argument
That she had left the world, and left him too;
And when he saw there was no more to do,

He dressed her limbs and body in the way
They use for those that wait their burial day.

170

And after this, sternly and cruelly,
Out of its sheath he drew his naked sword
To kill himself, sharp though the pain
    might be,
That soul might follow soul in one accord
Whithersoever Minos gave the word,
Since, by the will of Fortune and of Love,
He must no longer live on earth above.

171

And then he said, filled with a high disdain,
"O cruel Jove, O Fortune so adverse,
This is the sum of all, since you have slain
Criseyde, by treachery, and can do no worse
To me; fie on your double dealings, curse
Your cowardly power that cannot break
    my vow!
No death can part me from my lady now.

172

"I'll leave this world, since you have slain her
    thus,
And follow her below, or else above;
Never shall lover say that Troilus
Dared not, for fear, to die beside his love;
I'll join her, that I can be certain of.
Since you forbid our love for one another
Here, yet allow our souls to find each other.

173

"And O thou city that I leave in woe,
And Priam, thou, and all my brethren here,
Farewell! Farewell my mother, for I go;
And, Atropos, make ready thou my bier.
And thou, Criseyde, ah, sweetheart, ah, my
    dear,
Receive my spirit!" So he thought to cry
With sword at heart, in readiness to die.

174

But, as God willed, her spirit was restored;
She broke from swoon, and "Troilus!" she
    cried,
And he gave answer, letting fall his sword,
"Are you alive, O lady mine, Criseyde?"
"Yes, sweetest heart," she sighingly replied,
"Thanks be to Cypris"; he in new delight
Began to comfort her as best he might.

175

He took her in his arms with kisses soft,
And strove to comfort her by every art,
So that her spirit, flickering aloft,
Came back again into her woeful heart,
When, glancing somewhat downward and
    apart,

She saw the naked sword where it was lying;
Fear came upon her and she started crying,

176

And asked what made him draw it; he replied
By telling her the cause that now had passed,
And how he would have stabbed himself and
    died;
She gazed at him again, and then she cast
Her arms about his body, firm and fast;
"O what a deed!" she said beneath her breath,
"Merciful God, how near we were to death!

177

"And if I hadn't spoken, by God's grace,
You would have killed yourself?" "Yes, cer-
    tainly."
"Alas, alas," she said "O heavy case!
For by the Lord above that fashioned me,
I wouldn't live a moment more," said she
"After your death—not to be crowned the
    Queen
Of all the countries that the sun has seen!

178

"But with that very weapon—there it is—
I also would have killed myself," she said,
"But O, no more! We've had enough of this;
Let us rise up at once and go to bed
And talk about the woes that lie ahead;
For, by that night-light which I see there
    burning,
I know that daylight will be soon returning."

179

They lay in bed, but, though their arms were
    lacing,
It was not thus that they had lain before;
Now they looked misery in their embracing,
Lost was the bliss that they had known of yore;
Why were they born? Ah, would they were
    no more!
So they bewailed, until a thought awoke
Within her, and to Troilus she spoke:

180

"Listen, my sweetheart, well you know"
    said she
"That if a man does nothing but complain
About his griefs, and seeks no remedy,
It is mere folly and increase of pain;
And since we came together here again
To find some remedy out, or make a plan
To cure our woes, it's time that we began.

181

"I am a woman, as you know full well,
And sudden intuitions come to me
Which, while they still are hot, I have to tell.
Neither of us, as far as I can see,

Ought to give way to half this misery;
Surely we have the cunning to redress
What is amiss, and end this heaviness.

182

"The truth is that our misery of heart
(For all I know) comes from no more than
   this:
Only that you and I are forced to part;
Considered well, there is no more amiss.
If that be all, it's not a precipice!
For though we part, there may be ways to
   meet,
And that is all there is to it, my sweet.

183

"I'm positive of bringing things about
So that, once gone, I can return to you;
Of that I have no shadow of a doubt,
And certainly, within a week or two,
I shall be here again; that this is true
I can convince you in a word or so,
For there are heaps of ways, as I can show.

184

"I won't take long—no sermon, no confusion,
For time once lost one never can recall;
I promise to go straight to my conclusion,
Which is, it seems to me, the best of all;
And yet forgive me if my choice should fall
Upon a scheme that causes you unrest,
For, honestly, I'm speaking for the best.

185

"However, let me make the protestation
That, in the words that I am going to say,
I'm only showing my imagination
Of means to help ourselves the easiest way;
And do not take it otherwise, I pray,
For in effect I'll do as you decide;
That's no demand, and shall not be denied.

186

"Now listen: as you well have understood,
My going is agreed by Parliament
So firmly, to withstand it is no good,
As far as I can judge; that's evident.
Since no consideration can prevent
The course of things, banish it from your
   mind,
And see what other measures we can find.

187

"I know the separation of us two
Will cruelly distress us, and annoy:
Those who serve love have painful things to do
From time to time, if they would have the joy.
That I shall be no further out of Troy
Than half a morning's ride is a relief,
And ought to lessen the effect of grief.

188

"If they don't mew me up but leave me loose,
My own and best, then day by day, my dear,
Since, as you know, it is a time of truce,
You shall have news of me, you need not fear,
And long before it's over I'll be here;
You'll then have Ántenor, your chosen man,
And me as well; be happy if you can!

189

"Think of it this way: 'My Criseyde has gone;
But what of that? She'll come back right
   away.'
'And when, alas?' 'A little later on,
Ten days at most, that I can safely say.'
How happy shall we be that golden day,
To live together, evermore, in Troy!
Why, the whole world could never tell
   our joy!

190

"And, as things are, I often notice, too,
To keep our secret, (which we have to hide),
You do not speak to me, nor I to you,
For a whole fortnight; you go out to ride
But I don't see you; can you not abide
Ten days to save my honour, and make all sure
In our adventure; is that much to endure?

191

"Then, as you know, my family is here,
That is, except my father; only he
Has gone; and all the things I hold most dear
Are here together, you especially,
Whom, above all, I would not cease to see
For all the world—wide as it is to rove;
Else let me never see the face of Jove.

192

"Why do you think my father should so
   prize me,
Or long for me, unless he fears the spite
Of people in this town who may despise me
Because of him and his unhappy flight?
What does he know about my present plight?
If he but knew how happy I am here,
My going would be nothing we need fear.

193

"You see how every day, and more and more,
They treat of peace; there is some indication
That we are almost ready to restore
Queen Helen, if the Greeks make reparation;
And, if there were no other consolation,
The fact they purpose peace on either part
Is one that should a little ease your heart.

194

"If it be peace, my dearest, then the tidings
Will, of their nature, force us to contrive

Intercommunication; there'll be ridings
Thither and back, the place will be alive
All day, as thick as bees about a hive,
And everyone will be in a position
To come and go, and will not need permission.

195

"And if no peace should follow, even so,
If never such a peace or treaty were,
I *must* come back; for where am I to go?
And how in heaven should I stay out there
Among those men-at-arms, in constant fear?
And so, as God may guide the soul He made,
I see no cause for you to be afraid.

196

"And here's another way that may unfold,
If you're not satisfied to leave things thus;
My father, as you know, is getting old;
Old men are usually covetous,
And I've just thought of a fine trick for us
To catch him by—and all without a net!—
If you agree; so listen to me yet.

197

"It often has been said that, in the end,
To keep the wolf at bay you kill a sheep;
That is to say, you often have to spend
A part of what you have, if you would keep
The rest of it; now gold is graven deep
Upon the heart of every covetous man;
So let me tell you how I mean to plan.

198

"The valuables here in town with me
I'll take to give my father, and will say
They're sent in trust and for security
By certain of his former friends, and they
Desire him fervently without delay
To send for more, and send most speedily
While the town still remains in jeopardy.

199

"It shall be an enormous quantity
(So I shall say) but, lest the news get out,
It can be sent by no one but by me.
I'll show him, too, if peace should come about,
That I have friends at Court, and they, no
    doubt,
Will soften Priam's rage and plead his case,
So that he soon will be restored to grace.

200

"So, what with one thing and another, sweet,
I shall enchant him with my words, and cause
Him to suppose all heaven is at his feet:
As for Apollo's servants and their saws,
Their calculations are not worth three straws;

Gold and his lusts shall blind him, and with
    these
I'll shape him to whatever ends I please.

201

"And if by auguries, as I believe
He will, he tries to show that I am lying,
I will find means to pluck him by the sleeve
And so disturb him in the act of trying
His sortilege, or say he's falsifying;
(Gods are ambiguous in their replies,
And for one truth they'll tell you twenty lies.)

202

"And 'Fear first made the gods, so I suppose'
I'll say to him; it was his coward heart
That made him misinterpret, when he chose
To run away from Delphi, for a start,
So I shall say to him; and if my art
Doesn't convert him in a day or two,
Then you may kill me: I will force you to."

203

And truly it is written, as I find,
That all she said was said with good intent,
And that her heart was true as it was kind
Towards him, and she spoke just what she
    meant
And almost died of sorrow when she went;
She purposed to be true, as she professed,
Or so they write who knew her conduct best.

204

But he, all ears and heart to what she said,
And hearing her devisings to and fro,
Truly believed the notions in his head
Were much like hers; but yet . . . to let her go!
The heart within misgave him and said *no;*
Yet in the end he saw he had to force
Himself to trust her, as the surest course.

205

And so the anguish of his circumstance
Was quenched in hope, and so, at last, the
    night
Was softened in the joy of amorous dance;
And as the birds, whenever sun is bright,
Sing high in the green leaves and take delight,
So these two took their joy, and made com-
    munion
Of loving speech, and cleared their hearts in
    union.

206

Nevertheless Criseyde was going to leave him;
The dreadful thought was ever in his mind,
And, fearful that her promises deceived him,
He begged her piteously "Be true and kind!

Keep to your day and do not lag behind
Among the Greeks! Come quickly back to
  Troy,
Or I shall lose all honour, health and joy.

207

"As sure as that the sun will rise tomorrow,
(And O God, guide Thou me upon my way,
Wretch as I am, out of this cruel sorrow),
I mean to kill myself if you delay.
But though my death means little, still I say
Before you cause me so much misery,
My own dear heart, stay here in Troy with me.

208

"For truly lady, truly my Criseyde,
Whatever cunning shifts you may prepare
Likely enough will fail when they are tried;
There is a saying 'He who leads the bear
Has many a thought which Bruin doesn't
  share.'
The wisdom of your father is admitted;
The wise may be outrun, but not outwitted.

209

"It's difficult to limp and not be spied
By cripples, for it is a trick they know;
Your father's subtleties are Argus-eyed,
And though his goods were taken long ago
His subtleties are with him still, I know.
You won't deceive him with your woman's
  wile,
And that is all my fear; you lack the guile.

210

"I do not know if peace will ever be;
But, peace or no, in earnest or in game,
Calkas went over to the enemy,
He joined the Greeks, and foully lost his
  name;
He never would return to us, for shame.
And so that way, as far as I can see,
Cannot be trusted; it's a fantasy.

211

"Then you will find your father will cajole
You into marriage; he knows how to preach.
He will commend some Greek, and charm
  your soul
With praises of him, ravish you with speech,
Or force you into it; it's in his reach.
And Troilus, whom you will never pity,
Firm in his truth, will perish in this city.

212

"Over all this, your father will dispraise
Us all, and say we cannot save the town;
He'll tell you that the Greeks will never raise

The siege; that they have sworn, for their
  renown,
To slay us all; our walls shall be torn down.
Thus he will say: I dread that he may scare
You with his reasons into staying there.

213

"And you will see so many a lusty knight
Among the Greeks, distinguished, sure to
  please,
Each with intelligence and heart and might
To do his best to put you at your ease,
And you will tire of the rusticities
Of us fool-Trojans (though remorse may
  hurt you)
Unless true constancy should prove your virtue.

214

"And this is so unbearable to think
It rends the soul out of my breast; for O,
There could no good opinion of it sink
Into my heart, should you decide to go.
Your father's cunning will destroy us, though,
And if you leave me, as I said before,
Then think of me as dead and nothing more.

215

"So, with a humble, true and piteous heart,
I beg you to be merciful, and pray
A thousand prayers out of my bitter smart
And misery to do as I shall say:
Let us steal off together right away!
For think what folly it is, when we can choose,
To grasp a shadow, and a substance lose!

216

"I mean there is a chance for us, ere dawn,
To steal away, and be together so;
What sense is there in seeing it withdrawn
So as to join your father? Risk to go,
Uncertain if you can return or no?
It would be madness, as it seems to me
To court such danger, when you could be free.

217

"And to speak vulgarly, we both have treasure
That we can take with us, and it will spread
To let us live in honour, and in pleasure,
Until the time will come when we are dead.
By this we can avoid our present dread;
To every other way you can invent,
My heart, most certainly, will not consent.

218

"And you need have no fear of taking hurt
Through poverty, for I have friends elsewhere,
And kindred; though you came in your bare
  shirt,

You would not lack for gold and things to
    wear;
We would be honoured if we settled there.
Let us go now, for it is plain to me
This is the best, if you will but agree."

219

Criseyde gave answer, sighing, "As you say,
All this, my true love, we could surely do;
As you imagine, we could steal away,
Or have a dozen other means in view
That later we'd regret, and sorely too.
As God may help me in my greatest need,
Your fears are groundless, yes, they are indeed.

220

"For when my father's cherishing of me,
Or when my fear of him, or other fear,
Pleasure, estate, marriage, or anything
Makes me untrue to you, my dearest dear,
May Saturn's daughter, Juno the Severe,
Drive me as mad as Athamas, to dwell
Eternally in Styx, the pit of Hell!

221

"And this I swear by every god supernal,
And every goddess too and patroness,
Terrestrial nymph and deity infernal,
Satyr and faun, the greater and the less,
Rough demi-gods that haunt the wilderness;
Cut, Atropos, my thread of life and kill
If I be false! Now trust me if you will.

222

"O Simois, like an arrow running clear
Through Troy and ever downward to the sea,
Bear witness to the words I utter here,
And on the day when I shall prove to be
Untrue to Troilus, O turn and flee
Back on thy course, flow upward to thy well,
And let me sink, body and soul, to Hell!

223

"As for the thing you spoke of—thus to go,
Abandon all your friends and steal away,
May God forbid you ever should do so
For any woman! Troy has need today
Of all her men; and there is this to say:
If this were known, my life and your good
    name
Would lie in balance. Save us, Lord, from
    shame!

224

"And if so be that peace should come again
—One sees it daily, anger giving place
To amity—how could you bear the pain,
Not daring to return and show your face?
Do not expose yourself to such disgrace;

Do not be hasty in this hot affair,
For hasty men are men who suffer care.

225

"What do you think the people round about
Would make of it? That's very easily said;
They'd think, and they would swear to it
    no doubt,
It was not love that drove you, but you fled
Out of voluptuous lust and coward dread.
Then all your honour would be lost, my dear,
That honour which has ever shone so clear.

226

"And think a little of my own good name,
Still in its flower; how I should offend,
What filth it would be spotted with, what
    shame,
Were we to run away, as you intend!
For though I were to live to the world's end
What justice could I ever hope to win?
I should be lost; that would be grief and sin.

227

"And therefore let your reason cool your dish;
It's said they win who suffer patiently.
To have a wish one must give up a wish,
And make a virtue of necessity
By exercising patience; think that he
That would be lord of Fortune must ig-
    nore her;
Only a wretch will fear and fall before her.

228

"And believe this, my sweetheart; sure I am
That ere the moon, Lucina the Serene,
Has entered Leo, passing from the Ram,
I will return; and what I say I mean,
As ever help me Juno, Heaven's Queen!
On the tenth day; if death should not prevail
Against me, I'll be with you, without fail."

229

"Provided this is true," said Troilus,
"Well, I'll endure it, up to the tenth day,
Since I can see that things must needs be thus;
But for the love of heaven, still I say
Let us at once steal secretly away,
Ever together, as now, and be at rest;
My heart keeps saying that will be the best."

230

"Merciful God! What life is this?" said she,
"Ah! Do you wish to kill me in my woe?
I see it now; you have no trust in me,
Your words show well enough that this is so.
Now for the love of Cynthia white as snow,
Mistrust me not without a cause, unheard,
Untried, for pity's sake! You have my word.

231

"Think, it is sometimes wiser to forget
Time present for a better time in view;
Heavens above, you haven't lost me yet!
What's to be parted for a day or two?
Drive out the fantasies that lurk in you,
Have trust in me and lay aside your sorrow,
Or else I will not live until tomorrow.

232

"For if you knew how bitterly it smarts,
You would abandon this. Dear God!
  You know
How the pure spirit in my heart of hearts
Weeps when I see you weep, I love you so!
Also because I shall be forced to go
Among the Greeks; and if I knew not how
To come back here again, I should die now.

233

"Am I so foolish that I never could
Imagine anything, or find a way
Of coming back the day I said I would?
Who can hold back a thing that will not stay?
My father? No! for all his subtle play.
And if I should succeed, my leaving Troy
Will turn some other day to greater joy.

234

"So I beseech you from my very heart,
If there is anything that at my prayer
You would consent to do before we part,
And for the love I love you with, my dear,
O let me see you cheerful, free of care,
A happy face—for that will ease the aching
About my heart, which is at point of breaking.

235

"And there is one thing more," she said
  "my own,
I beg of you, my heart's sufficiency,
Since I am wholly yours and yours alone,
While I am absent, let no gallantry
With other ladies take your thoughts from me!
I never cease to fear it; it is said
Love is a thing of jealousy and dread.

236

"There lives no lady underneath the sun,
If you—which God forbid—should prove un-
  true,
That would be so betrayed, or so undone
As I, who think of truth as lodged in you;
Were I to find it other than I do,
It would be death; therefore, unless you see
Good reason, do not be unkind to me."

237

"As God, from whom no secret can be hidden,
May give me joy, since first you caught my eye
No taint of falsehood, bidden or unbidden,
Has ever crossed my heart," he made reply,
"And never shall until I come to die.
And well you may believe that this is so,
Though more I cannot say; but time will
  show."

238

"Most loving thanks, my dearest," an-
  swered she,
"May blissful Lady Venus, whom I serve,
Keep me from death until, in some degree,
I can requite you well, who well deserve;
And while I have my wits, which God
  preserve,
I shall do so, for I have found you true,
And honour will rebound to me from you.

239

"It was no royal state, or high descent,
No vain delight, nor any worthiness
In war or military tournament,
Pomp, riches, or magnificence of dress
That led me on to pity your distress,
But moral virtue, grounded in truth of heart,
That moved me to compassion from the start.

240

"Your noble heart, the manhood that you had,
And the contempt for all that was not right,
(It seemed to me)—all that was base and bad,
Like rudeness, or a vulgar appetite—
And that your reason bridled your delight;
These things, so far above what others give,
Have made me yours, and shall do, while I live.

241

"For this the length of years shall not undo,
Nor Fortune the Inconstant shall deface;
And Jupiter, whose power can renew
The sorrowful in gladness, send us grace
That we may meet together in this place
Within ten nights, and ease our hearts of woe;
And now farewell, for it is time to go."

242

At last their long lamenting reached its close
With many kisses as they lay embraced,
The dawn came on, and Troilus arose
And, looking at her, felt the bitter taste
Of death's cold cares; and then, in troubled
  haste,
He took his leave of her and went away;
Whether he was sad, I need not say;

243

For the imagination hardly can
Grasp, or perception feel, or poet tell

The cruel pains of this unhappy man,
For they were greater than the pains of Hell.
He saw that she must leave the citadel;
His heart was of its very soul bereft;
Without a word, he turned away and left.

BOOK V

1

And there approached that fatal destiny
Which lies in the disposal of Jove's frown
And to you angry Furies, sisters three,
Is, for its execution, handed down;
Because of which Criseyde must leave the town
And Troilus live on in pain and dread
Till Lachesis no longer spin his thread.

2

Now golden-headed Phoebus, high aloft,
Had three times melted in his sunny sheen
The winter snows, and Zephyrus as oft
Had brought the leaves again in tender green
Since Troilus, son of Hecuba the Queen,
First fell in love with her, for whom his sorrow
Was all for this: she was to leave that morrow.

* * *

3

At prime of day the sturdy Diomede
Stood ready at the gates; he was to lead
Criseyde to join the Greeks, but she indeed
Was at a loss, she felt her spirit bleed.
And, truly, not in all the books we read
Can there be found a woman so cast down
Nor ever one so loth to leave a town.

4

And Troilus with neither plan of war,
Nor counsel, lost to joy for ever more,
Now waited desolate at his lady's door,
She that had been the root and flower before
Of all his happiness and joys of yore.
Now, Troilus, farewell to all your joy,
For you will never see her back in Troy!

5

It's true that while he waited in this trance
He laboured, in a manly way, to hide
His grief; it barely changed his countenance;
But at the gate whence she was due to ride
With certain folk, he hovered on the side;
He was so woebegone, (although of course
He did not speak), he scarce could sit his horse.

6

He shook with rage, his heart began to gnaw
Within, when Diomede prepared to mount;

He muttered to himself at what he saw
"O baseness, shame, to suffer this affront!
Why not redress or bring it to account?
Were it not better die in the endeavour
Than to endure this misery for ever?

7

"Why don't I fall on them, give rich and poor
Something to do before I let her go?
Why don't I bring all Troy into a roar?
Why don't I kill this Diomede, and show
Some courage? Why not, with a man or so,
Steal her away? What more must I endure?
Why don't I help myself to my own cure?"

8

But why he would not do so fell a deed
I have to tell you, why he chose and willed
It not to be; he feared that it would breed
A battle, and Criseyde might well be killed;
And that is why his wish was unfulfilled,
Otherwise certainly, as you have heard,
It had been done without another word.

9

At last Criseyde was ready for the ride
Sighing "Alas!" with sorrow in her face;
But go she must, whatever might betide;
There is no remedy in such a case.
She rode out at a melancholy pace;
What wonder if she felt a bitter smart
Forgoing Troilus, her own dear heart!

10

And he, by way of showing courtesy,
With hawk on hand, and with a splendid rout
Of knights, rode forth and kept her company.
They passed the distant valley far without
And would have ridden further yet, no doubt,
Most gladly; it was grief to turn so soon,
But turn he had to, that unhappy noon.

11

Just at that moment Ántenor appeared
Out of the Grecian host, and every knight
Was glad and gave him welcome as he neared;
And Troilus, though very far from light
Of heart, obliged himself, as best he might,
At least to hold his tears; his eyes were dim
As he kissed Ántenor and welcomed him.

12

And here at last he had to take his leave;
He cast his eyes upon her piteously
And, riding closer, took her by the sleeve
To plead his cause, and touched her soberly;
Ah, Lord! She started weeping tenderly.
Softly and slyly he contrived to say
"Now do not kill me, darling, keep your day."

13

With that he turned his courser round about;
His face was very pale. To Diomede
He spoke not, nor to any of his rout;
This Greek, the son of Tideus, took good heed;
Here was a craft in which he knew his Creed,
And more than that; he took her leading-rein,
And Troilus to Troy rode home again.

14

This Diomede who led her by the bridle,
Now that the Trojans could no longer stay,
Thought "Well, this is no moment to be idle;
I have the work, so I should get the pay;
I'll talk to her; it will beguile the way.
As I was taught a dozen times at school
'He who forgets to help himself's a fool.' "

15

Nevertheless he understood enough
To think "It will for certain come to naught
If I should speak of love, or make it tough,
For doubtless, if she treasures in her thought
Him I suspect, she cannot well be brought
To let him go so soon; I'll try to find
A means, and yet not let her know my mind."

16

This Diomede, who knew his way about,
Chose the right moment when to fall in speech
With her of this and that, and ask right out
Why she was in distress, and to beseech
Her to command him—were it in his reach
To put her at her ease; if she but knew it,
She only had to ask and he would do it.

17

For truly, and he swore it as a knight,
There was not anything to give her pleasure
He would not do with all his heart and might,
If it could ease her heart in any measure;
He begged her to allay and not to treasure
Her grief, and said "We Grecians will take joy
In honouring you, as much as folk in Troy."

18

He also said "I know you find it strange
—No wonder either, it is new to you—
To drop these Trojan friendships in exchange
For ours of Greece, people you never knew.
But God forbid there should not be a few
Among the Grecian hosts that you will find
As true as any Trojan, and as kind.

19

"And as, a moment since, I made a vow
To be your friend, helpfully if I might,
Since I have more acquaintance with you now
Than other strangers, I will claim a right;

From this time on, command me, day or night;
And though it should be painful, I will do
Whatever may delight your heart and you.

20

"And I would have you treat me as your
          brother
And do not hold my friendship in disdain;
And though you grieve for some great thing
          or other
—I know not what—I know my heart
          would fain
Relieve you, had we leisure, of your pain;
If it be more than I can well redress,
I am right sorry for your heaviness.

21

"You Trojans and we Greeks have long
          been loth
To love each other, and many a day will be;
Yet there's one god of love we worship both;
So, for the love of God, my lady free,
Hate whom you will, but have no hate for me;
No one could serve you, trust me this is true,
That would be half so loth to anger you.

22

"And were it not that we are near the tent
Of Calkas (who can see us, by the way)
I would go on to tell you all I meant;
This must be sealed up for another day.
Give me your hand; I am and shall be aye,
God helping me, while life shall last, alone
Above all other men, your very own.

23

"And that's a thing I never said before
To any woman born; and I can vow
I never yet have had a paramour
And never loved a woman, up till now;
So do not be my enemy! Allow
For lack of eloquence in me, and spurn
Me not for it, for I have much to learn.

24

"Though it may seem a wonder, lady bright,
To hear me speak of love so quickly, yet
I have heard tell that many at first sight
Have loved, who up till then had never met;
Nor do I have in me the power to set
Myself against the god, whom I obey,
And ever will; have mercy, then, I say.

25

"Such admirable knights are in this place
And you so beautiful—that one and all
Will strain in rivalry to stand in grace
With you; but should such happiness befall
Me as to be the one that you will call

Your servant, there's not one of them so true
As I shall be, till death, in serving you."

26

Criseyde made slight rejoinder, though she
   heard,
Oppressed with grief and wondering what
   to do,
But in effect she hardly caught a word,
A sentence here and there, a phrase or two.
She thought her sorrowing heart would burst
   right through
Her breast; and when she saw her father there
She sank upon her saddle in despair.

27

Nevertheless, to Diomede she proffered
Her thanks for all his pains, and his display
Of welcome, and the friendship he had of-
   fered,
Which she accepted in a civil way;
She would be glad to do what he would say
And she would trust him, as indeed she might,
Or so she said, beginning to alight.

28

Her father took her in his arms and cried,
As twenty times he kissed her on the cheek,
"Welcome, my own dear daughter!" She
   replied
That she was glad to see him, ceased to speak
And stood before him, mute and mild and
   meek.
And here I leave her with her father thus,
And I turn back to tell of Troilus.

29

To Troy this woeful Troilus returned
In sorrow, above all other sorrows' force,
With felon look, a face where fury burned.
Abruptly he dismounted from his horse
And through his palace took his angry course,
Heedless of everything, to seek his room,
And no one dared break in upon his gloom.

30

There to the griefs till then within him pent
He gave large issue; "Death!" he cried at first,
Then, in the frantic throes he underwent,
Cursed Jove, Apollo, Cupid, said his worst
Of Ceres, Bacchus, Cypris, and he cursed
His birth, himself, his fortune and his nature
And, save his lady, every earthly creature.

31

To bed he went and wallowed, turned and lay
In fury, as Ixion does in Hell,
And so continued until nearly day;
His heart began a little to unswell

Relieved by tears that issued from their well;
And piteously he called upon Criseyde,
Crying aloud, and this is what he cried;

32

"Where is my own, my lady loved and dear?
And where is her white breast? Where is it?
   Where?
Where are her arms? And where her eyes so
   clear,
That this time yesternight were with me here?
Now I may weep alone, full many a tear!
And wildly grasp about, but in her place
I only find a pillow to embrace.

33

"How shall I do? When will she come again?
Alas, I know not! Why did I let her go?
Ah! would to God that I had then been slain!
My sweetest heart, Criseyde, my darling foe,
My lady, only love and only woe,
To whom I give my heart for ever! See,
See, I am dying, will you not rescue me?

34

"Who gazes on you now, my guiding star?
Who in your presence sits? Or who stands
   near?
Who now can comfort you in your
   heart's war?
Since I am gone, to whom do you give ear?
Who speaks for me, for me in absence here?
No one, alas! I grieve and that is why;
I know you fare as evilly as I.

35

"How am I to endure for ten whole days,
When, the first night, I suffer so much pain?
How will she do, sad creature? In what ways,
Seeing her tenderness, will she sustain
Her grief for me? O, ere you come again,
Piteous and pale and green your face will be
With longing hither to return, to me."

36

And when he fell in fitful slumberings,
After a little he began to groan,
For dreams would visit him of dreadful things
That well might be: dreaming he was alone
In some appalling place and making moan,
Or dreaming he was prisoner to bands
Of enemies; his life was in their hands.

37

His body thereupon would give a start
And with that start he found himself awake
With such a tremor felt about his heart
The terror of it made his body quake;
And there were sudden noises he would make

And he imagined he had fallen deep
From a great height; and then he had to
　　weep,

38

And spend such pity on his misery;
Wonder it was to hear his fantasies;
Then, in a moment, he would mightily
Console himself—a madness, a disease,
He said it was, to have such fears as these;
Again his bitter sorrows overbore him,
And any man would have felt sorry for him.

39

Who could have told, or fully have unfurled
His torment, his lament, his flow of brine?
No one alive or dead in all the world!
I leave you, gentle reader, to divine
That grief like his, for such a wit as mine,
Is far too great, and I should work in vain;
To think about it cuts me to the brain.

40

In heaven still the stars were to be seen,
Although the moon was paling, quickly too,
As the horizon whitened with a sheen
Far to the east, as it is wont to do
When Phoebus with his rosy car is due;
He was preparing for his journey thus
When Troilus sent word for Pandarus.

41

This Pandarus, who all the previous day
Had been unable, even for an hour,
To see him, though he'd sworn to get away
—For he was with King Priam in the Tower,
And so it simply wasn't in his power
To make a move—now, with the morn-
　　ing, went
To Troilus, who, as I say, had sent.

42

He found it easy in his heart to guess
That Troilus had lain awake in woe
And needed now to talk of his distress;
He did not need a book to tell him so.
And to his chamber he made haste to go
The shortest way, greeted and gravely
　　eyed him,
And then sat down upon the bed beside him.

43

"My Pandarus," said Troilus, "the sorrow
I undergo I cannot long endure.
I feel I shall not live until tomorrow,
So I would lay my plans, to make all sure,
And fix my funeral and sepulchre.
As for my property and all the rest,
Dispose of it for me as you think best.

44

"But for the fire and for the burial flames
In which my body shall be burned and freed,
And for the feasting and the funeral games
To grace my wake, I beg of you, take heed;
See that all's well; and offer Mars my steed,
My sword and helmet; also, brother dear,
My shield to Pallas, she that shines so clear.

45

"The powdery ash to which my heart
　　will burn
I beg of you to gather and preserve
In such a vessel as they call an urn,
A golden one; give it to her I serve,
For love of whom I die; I did not swerve.
So give it her; do me this courtesy
And beg her keep it in my memory.

46

"I know it from my malady, and by
My present dreams and some from long ago,
That I am certainly about to die.
Besides, the owl they call Escaphilo
These two nights past has shrieked for me,
　　and so
I pray for Mercury, if he please, to fetch
This soul of mine and guide a sorrowful
　　wretch!"

47

Pandarus answered "Listen, Troilus;
Dear friend, as I have often said before,
It is mere madness in you, sorrowing thus
Without a reason; I can say no more.
He that to all advice will close the door
Is one for whom I know no remedy;
Leave him to stew in his own fantasy.

48

"But, Troilus, I beg you; tell me, do,
Whether you think that ever anyone
Loved with so passionate a love as you?
God knows they have, and many so have
　　done;
Many have had to let a fortnight run
Without their ladies, and have made no fuss;
What need is there? It's quite ridiculous.

49

"For, day by day, as you yourself can see,
A man may part from lover or from wife,
When they are sundered by necessity,
Aye, though he loves her better than his life;
But all the same he will not be at strife
Within himself; for, as you know, dear
　　brother,
Friends cannot always be with one another.

50

"What do they do who see their lovers
    wedded
Because of powerful friends, as happens oft,
And in their spouses' bed behold them
    bedded?
God knows they take it wisely—fair and soft,
Because good hope will keep their hearts aloft;
And if they can endure a time of grief,
As time has hurt them, time will bring relief.

51

"That is the way to take it; let it slide!
Try to enjoy yourself, have no concern;
Ten days are not so long for you to bide;
For since she gave her promise to return,
No one will make her break it; she will learn
Some way of coming back, so fear no ill;
I'll lay my life upon it that she will.

52

"As for those dreams of yours and all such
    folly,
To Hell with them! Imagination teems
With stuff like that; it's from your melan-
    choly
That troubles you in sleep, or so it seems.
A straw for the significance of dreams!
I wouldn't give a bean for them, not I!
No one can tell you what they signify.

53

"The temple priests incline to tell you this,
That dreams are sent as Heaven's revelations;
They also tell you, and with emphasis,
They're diabolical hallucinations;
The doctors say that glandular liquations
Engender them, by fast—or gluttony;
How can the truth be contradictory?

54

"Others will say they come from an obsession;
Some fixed idea a fellow has, a theme;
And this will cause a vision-like impression.
Others report from books that it would seem
A thing quite natural for men to dream
At certain times of year, according to
The moon; believe no dream. It will not do.

55

"All very well, these dreams, for poor old
    wives,
Who trust in birds and auguries and howls
That send them all in terror of their lives!
—Ravens foreboding death and screeching
    owls—
Belief in them is false and it befouls;
O that a creature with a noble mind
Like man, should trust in garbage of the kind!

56

"Let me beseech you, then, with all my heart,
Forgive yourself for all that's gone astray.
Let's talk no more; get up and make a start.
Let's think how we may drive the time away
And how our lives will freshen on the day
When she comes back—and soon it will be
    too!—
For that's the best, God help us, we can do.

57

"Rise up, recall the lusty life in Troy
That we have led! And so we shall contrive
To fleet the time until our time for joy
Shall bring us back again our bliss alive;
The languors of a day or two—twice five—
We shall forget about, or somehow stifle,
So that the whole affair shall seem a trifle.

58

"I've seen a lot of gentlefolk about,
And we are meanwhile in a state of truce.
Let's have some fun and join the lusty rout
At Sárpedoun's, a mile away; get loose,
And cheat the time by putting it to use!
Drive it along to meet that blissful morrow
When you will see her, cause of all your
    sorrow!

59

"Rise up, I say, dear brother Troilus;
It does no honour to you, don't you see,
To weep and linger in your bedroom thus.
One thing is absolutely sure, trust me,
If you lie here a day or two, or three,
People will say it is a coward's trick,
You daren't rise up and fight, you're feigning
    sick."

60

And Troilus replied "O brother dear,
As anyone that ever suffered pain
Will know, it is no wonder to appear
In sorrow, or to weep, or to complain,
For one who feels the smart in every vein;
Though I complain and weep, I have the
    right,
Since I have lost my cause of all delight.

61

"Forced by necessity to make a start,
I will get up, as soon as ever I may,
And God, to whom I sacrifice my heart,
Send us in haste the tenth, the happy day!
There never was a bird so glad of May
As I shall be when she returns to Troy,
The cause of all my torment, and my joy.

62

"But what do you advise," said Troilus,

"Where we can best amuse ourselves in
    town?"
"Well, my advice, by God," said Pandarus,
"Is to ride out and see King Sárpedoun."
This for a while they argued up and down,
Till, in the end, Troilus gave consent
And rose; and off to Sárpedoun they went.

63

He was a man whose life had been a fable
Of honour, liberality and worth;
And all that could be offered on a table
And that was dainty, though it cost the earth,
He gave them day by day; there was no dearth,
So people said, the greatest and the least;
The like was never seen at any feast.

64

Nor could you hope to find an instrument
Delicious by the use of wind or string
In all the world, however far you went,
That tongue can tell of or that heart can bring
To mind, but blended at their banqueting;
And never was a company so fair
To look on as the ladies dancing there.

65

Of what avail was this to Troilus
In his despondency? It went for nought.
For all the while his heart, so dolorous,
Sought for Criseyde; insistently it sought.
Ever and only she was all his thought,
Now this, now that, in his imagination;
What banqueting could bring him consola-
    tion?

66

Since, of these ladies at the feast, the gem
Was lacking for him, with Criseyde away,
It was a grief for him to look at them,
Or listen to the instruments in play;
She being absent in whose hand there lay
The key of his heart, it was his fantasy
That no one had a right to melody.

67

There was no hour of the day or night,
When there was nobody to overhear,
But that he said "My darling, my delight,
How has it been with you since you were
    here?
How I would welcome you again, my dear!"
Fortune had caught him in her maze, alas!
And fitted him a helmet made of glass.

68

The letters she had written him moreover,
In former days, that now were gone for good,
A hundred times a day he read them over,
Refiguring her lovely womanhood

Within his heart, and every word and mood
Out of the past, and thus he battled on
Till the fourth day; then said he must be gone.

69

"Is it a firm intention, this of yours,
Pandar, for us to linger, you and I,
Till Sárpedoun has turned us out of doors?
Were it not better now to say good-bye?
For heaven's sake this evening let us try
To take our leave of him and disappear
For home, for honestly I won't stay here."

70

Said Pandarus: "What did we come here for?
To borrow a light and then run home again?
I don't know where we could have found
    a more
Delightful host, gladder to entertain
Than Sárpedoun; and isn't it quite plain
He likes us? Don't you see that if we fled
So suddenly, it would be most ill-bred?

71

"We told him we were paying him a visit
For a whole week; so suddenly to change
And take our leave is hardly proper, is it?
After four days! He'd think it very strange.
Let's stick by what we've chosen to arrange.
And since you've promised him that you
    would stay,
Stand by your word; we then can ride away."

72

Thus Pandar, with much trouble and persua-
    sion,
Forced him to stay awhile and show his face;
But when the week-end came, they took oc-
    casion
To bid the King farewell and leave the place;
Said Troilus: "Now Heaven send me grace
That I may find, upon my homecoming,
Criseyde returned!" And he began to sing.

73

"Nuts!" muttered Pandar softly to himself,
Who, in his heart of hearts, was thinking thus:
"All this hot stuff will cool upon a shelf
Ere Calkas sends Criseyde to Troilus!"
But still he swore "She will come back to us,
What your heart says is right," he japed away,
"She will come back as soon as ever she may!"

74

When they had reached the palace of his
    friend
There they dismounted in the evening light
And to his chamber took their way, to spend
The time in talking on into the night;
And all their talk was of Criseyde the Bright.

And, later, when it pleased them, having fed,
They rose from supper and they went to bed.

75

When morning came and day began to clear,
This Troilus stirred and awoke, and cried
To Pandarus "Dear brother, do you hear?
For heaven's sake let us get up and ride;
Let us go see the palace of Criseyde;
For since we are not yet to have the feast,
There is the palace to be seen at least."

76

To lull suspicions in his followers,
He made pretence that he had work to do
In town, and to the house that still was hers
They started off—how sad he alone knew;
It seemed to him his heart would break in two;
And when he found the doors were sparred
      across
He almost fell to earth, so great the loss.

77

And taking in all that his eyes now told
—For barred was every window in the
      place—
He felt as if a frost had fallen cold
Upon his heart; the colour of his face
Changed to a deadly pallor; quickening pace,
Without a word, he rode ahead so fast
That no one saw his countenance as he passed.

78

Then said he thus: "O palace desolate,
O house of houses that was once so bright,
O palace, empty and disconsolate,
O lantern quenched, from which they stole
      the light,
Palace that once was day and now is night,
Ought not you to fall, and I to die,
Since she is gone that we were guided by?

79

"O palace, crown of houses, now forsaken,
But once illumined by the sun of bliss,
O ring from which the ruby has been taken,
Cause of a joy that now has come to this,
Since I may do no better, I would kiss
Your cold, cold doorway, but for all this rout
Of people; farewell shrine, whose saint is
      out!"

80

He turned and cast his eyes on Pandar then;
His face was changed and pitiful to see;
As he rode on with him he spoke again,
As far as he had opportunity
Of his old joys and his new misery,
So sadly, with a face so dead and grim
That anybody would have pitied him.

81

So he went onward, riding up and down,
And memories poured in at every glance,
Passing the very places in the town
That once had had such power to entrance:
"Look, it was there I saw my lady dance!
And in that temple with her shining eyes
She took me first, my darling, by surprise.

82

"And yonder, once, I heard her lovely
      laughter,
I heard her laughter and I saw her play,
And it was blissful; then, a little after,
Just there, she once came up to me to say
'O love me, sweetheart, love me well today.'
And it was there she gazed at me so sweetly
That until death my heart was hers com-
      pletely.

83

"And at that corner, in the house you see,
I heard my loveliest of ladies sing,
So womanly, and how melodiously!
How well, how clear, with what a pleasing
      ring!
Still in my soul I hear it echoing,
That blissful sound; and there's the very
      place
In which she first received me into grace!"

84

And then he thought: "Ah, Cupid, blessed
      Lord,
When I recall the past, the purgatory
I have endured, how fiercely thou hast warred
Against me, it would make a book, a story.
What need was there to add unto thy glory
By this poor victory on me and mine,
What joy in slaying what is wholly thine?

85

"Well hast thou wreaked upon me, Lord,
      thine ire,
Thou mighty god, so fearful to annoy!
Have mercy, Lord, thou knowest I desire
Thy favour more than any other joy,
And will profess Thy faith, in whose employ
I mean to live and die, and ask no boon
Save that Thou send me back Criseyde, and
      soon!

86

"Constrain her heart with longing to return,
As, to behold her, thou constrainest me!
Then it will surely be her whole concern,
And she'll not tarry! Ah, Cupid, do not be
As cruel to our blood and monarchy
As Juno to the blood of Thebes, for whom,

And for her rage, the Thebans met their
    doom!"

87

And after this he visited the gate
Through which, at such a lively pace,
    Criseyde
Had ridden out, and he began to wait
In restless hope; and up and down he plied
His horse, and said "Alas, I saw her ride
Away from here; O God, in Heaven's joy,
Let me but see her riding into Troy!

88

"To think I guided her to yonder hill,
Alas! And it was there I took my leave.
I saw her ride away, I see her still;
The sorrow of it is enough to cleave
My heart! And hither I came home at eve,
And here must linger on, cast out from joy,
And shall, until I see her back in Troy."

89

Often enough he thought himself undone,
Defeated, pale, shrunken to something less
Than what he was, imagined everyone
Was saying "What has happened? Who can
    guess
Why Troilus is in such deep distress?"
All this was nothing but his melancholy;
A fantasy about himself, a folly.

90

Another time he would imagine—weighing
What people whispered as they cast an eye
Upon him—they were pitying him, saying
"I am right sorry Troilus will die."
And in these thoughts a day or two went by
As you have heard; such was the life he led,
Like one who halted between hope and dread.

91

It gave him pleasure in his songs to show
The reason of his grief, as best he might;
He made a song of just a word or so,
To ease his heart and make his sorrow light,
And when he was alone and out of sight
He softly sang about his lady dear
In absence, and he sang as you shall hear:

92

"O star of love, since I have lost thy light,
Shall not my heart lament thee and bewail
In darkening torment, moving night by night
Towards my death; the wind is in my sail.
If the tenth night should come, and if it fail,
Thy guiding beam, if only for an hour,
My ship and me Charybdis will devour."

93

But after singing it, he very soon

Fell once again to sighing, as of old,
And every night rose up to see the moon
As was his habit, and to her he told
His sorrows all, and yet he would make bold
To say "Yet moon, the night your horns
    renew
I shall be happy—if all the world is true!"

94

"Old were the horns I saw you wear that
    morning
When my dear lady rode away from here
Who is my cause of torment and of mourning
And therefore, O Lucina, bright and clear,
For love of God, run swiftly round thy sphere;
For when thy horns begin again to spring
Then she will come who has my bliss to
    bring."

95

Longer the day and longer still the night
Than they were wont to be, or so he thought;
The course the sun was taking was not right,
It made a longer journey than it ought;
"Phaeton is not dead, as I was taught,"
Said Troilus, "I fear he is alive
And has his father's cart, but cannot drive."

96

Fast up and down the walls he used to walk
Gazing towards the Grecian armaments,
And thus would commune with himself
    and talk
"Yonder my lady lies, at all events,
Or, maybe, yonder, where I see those tents!
And thence must come this air so sweet and
    soft,
Touching my soul and raising it aloft!

97

"Surely this breath of wind, that more and
    more,
Moment by moment, comes to fan my face,
Is of her sighing, for her heart is sore;
I prove it thus, that in no other place
In the whole city but this little space
Feel I a wind whose sound is like a pain,
And says 'Alas! When shall we meet again?' "

98

Through this long time of waiting drove he
    thus,
Till the ninth day and night had fully passed;
And always at his side was Pandarus,
Busily finding comfort to the last;
He did his best to lend a lighter cast
To all his thoughts, gave hope that on the
    morrow
She would return to him and end his sorrow.

99

Upon the other hand there was Criseyde
With her few women in the Grecian throng,
And many times a day "Alas!" she cried,
"That ever I was born! Well may I long
For death! Alas that I have lived too long!
What can I do that things may turn to good?
All is far worse than I had understood.

100

"Nothing will bring my father to relent
Or let me go; I cannot find a way
To wheedle him; when the ten days are spent,
Deep in his heart my Troilus will say
That I am false to him—and well he may.
No one will thank me for it, either side;
Alas that I was born! Would I had died!

101

"And if I were to put myself in danger,
Stealing away by night, might I not fall
Into some sentry's hand, and, as a stranger,
Be taken for a spy? But, worst of all,
Some ruffian Greek, fresh from a drunken
   brawl
Might come on me and, true as is my heart,
I should be lost. Dear Heaven, take my part!"

102

Now waxen-pale her once so shining face,
Wasted her limbs, as one who day by day
Stood, when she dared, to gaze upon the place
Where she was born, where she had longed to
   stay,
All the night long in tears, alas, she lay;
Thus she despaired of comfort or relief,
And led her life, a creature full of grief.

103

Many a time she sighed in her distress,
In her imagination picturing
Her Troilus in all his worthiness,
And all his golden words remembering,
From when her love had first begun to spring;
And so she set her woeful heart on fire
By the remembrance of her lost desire.

104

In all the world there is no heart so cruel,
Had it but heard her thus lament her sorrow,
But would have also wept at the renewal
Of tender tears; she wept both eve and
   morrow;
Many her tears; she had no need to borrow.
And yet, sharper than any grief beside,
There was no soul in whom she dared confide.

105

How ruefully she stood and stared at Troy,

Saw the tall towers and the lofty hall,
"Alas," she said, "the happiness and joy,
That once I had beyond that very wall,
But now is turned to bitterness and gall!
Troilus! What are you doing now?" she cried,
"Lord! Do you still give thought to your
   Criseyde?

106

"Alas, had I but trusted your advice
And run away with you! If we had run,
I should not now be sighing bitter sighs.
And who is there could say that I had done
Amiss to steal away with such a one?
But all too late the medicine comes to save
The corpse that they are bearing to the grave.

107

"For it is now too late to speak of it;
Prudence, one of thine eyes—for thou hast
   three—
I ever lacked, as now I must admit;
Time past I safely stored in memory,
Time present also I had eyes to see;
Time future, till it caught me in the snare,
I could not see, and thence has come my care.

108

"Nevertheless, betide what may betide,
Tomorrow night, be it by east or west,
I'll steal away, on one or other side,
And go wherever Troilus thinks best,
And in this firm intention I will rest.
Who cares what scandal wicked tongues un-
   cover?
Wretches are always envious of a lover.

109

"He who takes heed of every uttered word,
Or will be ruled by others, in the end
Will never come to good, so I have heard.
For there are things which some will rep-
   rehend
That many other people will commend;
And various as may their reasons be,
My own felicity suffices me.

110

"So, without any further argument,
I'll make for Troy; let me conclude it thus."
And yet, God knows, two whole months came
   and went
And still her purposes were dubious.
For both the town of Troy and Troilus
Shall knotless slide away out of her heart;
She never will take purpose to depart.

111

This Diomede of whom I have made mention

Now went about imagining a way,
With all the cunning of a swift invention,
How to enmesh Criseyde with least delay
And bring her heart into his net; by day
And night he worked, perfecting his design
For fishing her; he laid out hook and line.

112

Nevertheless he had the secret thought
That she was not without a love in Troy;
For never, since the moment he had brought
Her thence had he beheld her laugh for joy;
He knew not what might prove the sub-
    tlest ploy
To coax her heart, "But trying will be fun,"
He said, "nothing attempted, nothing won."

113

And yet he argued with himself one night
"Now am I not a fool, well knowing how
Her grief is for another, to invite
Her fancies my way, and attempt her now?
It may not do me good, I must allow;
And grave authorities have held the view
'A time of woe is not a time to woo.'

114

"Yet, if a man should win so sweet a flower
From him for whom she mourns so con-
    stantly,
Might he not say he was a man of power?"
So, ever bold, he thought "Well, as for me,
Happen what may, I'll try, and we shall see;
If I'm to die for it, I'll try to reach
Her heart; I shall lose nothing but my
    speech."

115

This Diomede, or so the books declare,
To serve his needs, kept ever in good fettle;
His voice was stern, his mighty limbs were
    square;
Chivalrous, hardy, headstrong, quick to settle
For action—of his father Tideus' mettle.
He was a boaster, so the stories run,
And heir to Argos and to Caledon.

116

Criseyde herself was of a modest stature,
And as to shapeliness, and face, and air,
There never can have been a fairer creature;
Often enough it was her way to wear
The heavy tresses of her shining hair
Over her collar, down her back, behind.
These with a thread of gold she used to bind.

117

Save for the fact her eyebrows joined together,
There was no fault that I can recognize;

Her eyes, they say, were clear as summer
    weather,
For everyone who saw her testifies
That paradise was seated in her eyes;
Her love and her rich beauty ever strove
Which was the greater—beauty in her, or
    love.

118

She was discreet and simple and demure,
And the most kindly-nurtured there could be;
And she was pleasant-spoken, to be sure,
Stately and generous and joyous; she
Had a free nature, having the quality
Of pity; but she had a sliding heart.
I cannot tell her age, I lack the art.

119

Troilus was well-grown, for he was tall,
Shapely, and in proportion strong and fleet;
Nature could not have bettered it at all.
Young, fresh, a lion-hardy man to meet,
He was as true as steel from head to feet,
Dowered with excellence of such a cast
As none will equal while the world will last.

120

And certainly historians have reckoned
That, in his time, no other was in sight
To whom he could have been considered
    second
In daring deeds, such as become a knight.
Although a giant may have greater might,
His heart, among the first, among the best,
Stood equal in its daring and in zest.

121

But, to go back again to Diomede,
It happened afterwards, on the tenth day
After she left the city as agreed,
That Diomede, as fresh as a branch in May,
Came visiting the tent where Calkas lay;
On a pretence of business in he went,
But I shall tell you of his true intent.

122

Now, to be brief, Criseyde on this occasion
Gave him a welcome and sat down beside him,
Nor did it seem he needed much persuasion
To make him stay; and presently she plied him
With wine and spices, seeking to provide him
Some entertainment with a dish or two,
And so they fell in speech, as old friends do.

123

And then he started speaking of the war
Between his people and the folk of Troy,
And he discussed the siege and begged her for
Her own opinion, which he would enjoy;

Descending thence, he then began to toy
With whether she had found the Grecian style
Of doing things quite foreign for a while,

124

And why her father had delayed so long
In marrying her off to a leading light.
Criseyde, who felt her suffering grow strong
For love of Troilus, her chosen knight,
Summoned her sorrowing thoughts as best she
    might,
And gave some answer; as to his intent,
She seemed to have no notion what he meant.

125

Nevertheless this fellow Diomede
Began to feel assured, and he replied
"If my impressions are not wrong, indeed,
It seems to me, dear lady, dear Criseyde,
That since I took your bridle on our ride
From Troy—do you recall that happy mor-
    row?—
I never yet have seen you but in sorrow.

126

"I cannot guess at what the cause may be,
Unless it is the love of someone dear
To you in Troy; it would much trouble me
Were you to spill so much as half a tear
For any fancied Trojan cavalier.
Do not deceive yourself; it's not the style;
You may be sure it isn't worth your while.

127

"The Trojans, one and all, are, so to speak,
In prison; if you think, you must agree;
Not one among them shall escape the Greek
For all the gold between the sun and sea;
And you can count on that, believe you me.
No mercy will be shown, not one shall live,
Though he had twice five conquered worlds
    to give.

128

"Such vengeance will be taken by our legions
For Helen's ravishing before we go
That all the gods of the infernal regions
Will stand aghast, outdone by such a show,
And men on earth, to the world's end,
    will know
The bitter cost of ravishing a Queen,
So cruel the revenge that will be seen.

129

"Unless your father's doubling on his traces,
Using equivocations and those sly
Words that are sometimes said to have two
    faces,
You will discover that I do not lie,

Yes, you will see it with your very eye,
And soon enough; you won't believe the speed
At which it all will happen, so take heed.

130

"What! Do you think your reverend father
    could
Have given Ántenor to ransom you,
Unless he knew full well the city would
Be utterly destroyed? Why, no! He knew,
And knew for certain, no one would come
    through
Who was a Trojan; having that to fear,
He dare not leave you there, so brought you
    here.

131

"What would you have, my loveliest of crea-
    tures?
Let Troy and Trojan in your heart give place;
Drive out that bitter hope and cheer those fea-
    tures,
Call back the beauty to that saddened face,
On which salt tears have left so deep a trace.
Troy is in jeopardy and Troy will bow;
There is no remedy to save it now.

132

"Among the Greeks, believe me, you may find
A love more perfect, ere the fall of night,
Than any Trojan love, and one more kind,
Ready to serve you with a better might;
And if you would vouchsafe it, lady bright,
I would be happier to be your lover
Than to be King of Argos twelve times over."

133

And on the word he turned a little red,
And in his speech his voice a little shook,
A little to one side he cast his head,
Then he fell silent. Presently he took
A glance at her and said, with sober look,
"I am—although it be to you no joy—
As nobly born as any man in Troy.

134

"For if my father Tideus had not died,
I should by now be King of many a city
In Caledon, and Argos too, Criseyde!
Indeed I hope to be so yet, my pretty;
But he was killed at Thebes, and, more's the
    pity,
So Polynices was, and many more,
Too soon, unhappily. It was the war.

135

"But, sweetheart, since I am to be your man,
And since you are the very first to whom
I ever knelt, to serve as best I can,

And ever shall, whatever be my doom,
Let me have leave, before I quit the room,
To visit you tomorrow in this fashion,
And, at more leisure, to reveal my passion."

136

Why should I tell you all the things he said?
He spoke enough, at least for the first day.
It proved successful, for Criseyde was led
To grant him his petition and to say
That she would see him, if he kept away
From certain subjects, which, as she made
    clear,
He must not touch, speaking, as you shall
    hear,

137

Like one whose heart was set on Troilus
As firmly as upon its very base;
She gave a distant answer, saying thus
To him "O Diomed, I love the place
Where I was born. Ah, Jove, in heavenly
    grace,
Soon, soon, dear Lord, deliver it from care,
For Thy great glory, keep it strong and fair!

138

"I know the Greeks would like to have
    their way
And wreak their wrath on Troy, our citadel;
But yet it will not happen as you say,
God willing; and I know my father well;
He's wise and has his plans; if, as you tell,
He bought me dearly, let me argue rather
That I'm the more beholden to my father.

139

"And that the Greeks are men of high con-
    dition
I'm well aware; but certainly they'll find
Young men in Troy as worthy of position,
As able and as perfect and as kind,
As, East or West, a man may call to mind.
That you could serve your lady, I believe you,
To earn the thanks with which she would re-
    ceive you.

140

"But—if we are to speak of love—" she said,
"I had a wedded lord, to whom, I mean,
My heart was wholly given; he is dead.
No other love, so help me Heaven's Queen,
Was ever in my heart, nor since has been.
That you are noble, and of high descent,
I've often heard, and it is evident.

141

"And so it seems an even greater wonder
That one like you should scorn a woman so.

God knows that love and I are far asunder;
I am the more disposed, as you should know,
To grieve until my death and live in woe.
What I shall later do I cannot say;
As yet I have no fancy for such play.

142

"I am in tribulation and cast down;
You are in arms, busy day in day out.
Hereafter, should you ever win the town,
Then, peradventure, it may come about
That when I see what never was seen, no
    doubt
I then may do what I have never done;
And that should be enough for anyone.

143

"I'll talk to you tomorrow if it's plain
That you are not to speak of this affair.
And, when you care to, you may come again;
This much, before you go, I will declare,
As help me Pallas of the Golden Hair,
If ever I took pity on a Greek,
It would be you, and it's the truth I speak.

144

"I am not saying I will be your love,
Nor am I saying no; but, in conclusion,
I mean well, by the Lord that sits above."
Then she let fall her eyelids in confusion,
And sighed "O God, let it be no illusion
That I shall see Troy quiet and at rest,
And if I see it not, then burst my breast!"

145

But in effect—let it be briefly spoken—
This Diomede, with freshened appetite,
Pressed on and begged her mercy, asked a
    token,
And after that, to tell the story right,
He took her glove, which gave him great de-
    light.
And when the day was over and night fell,
He rose and took his leave, for all was well.

146

Bright Venus, following her heavenly
    courses,
Showed the way down for Phoebus to alight,
And Cynthia laid about her chariot-horses
To whirl her out of Leo, if they might;
The candles of the Zodiac shone bright,
And to her bed Criseyde that evening went,
Within her father's shapely, shining tent,

147

Ever in soul revolving up and down
The sayings of this sudden Diomede,
His high position and the sinking town,

Her loneliness, the greatness of her need
Of friends and helpers; thus began to breed
The reason why—and I must make it plain—
She made it her intention to remain.

148

In sober truth, when morning came in glory,
This Diomede returned to see Criseyde,
And, shortly, lest you interrupt my story,
He spoke so ably and he justified
Himself so well that she no longer sighed;
At last, to tell the truth, I must confess
He took from her the weight of her distress.

149

And then—so it is handed down to us—
She made him present of the fine bay steed
Which he had taken once from Troilus,
Also a brooch—what can have been the
　　need?—
That had been his, she gave to Diomede
And, to console his passion, they believe
She made him wear a pennon of her sleeve.

150

From other histories it would appear
That once, when Troilus gave Diomede
A body-thrust that hurt him, many a tear
She wept upon his wound, to see it bleed,
And nursed him carefully with tender heed,
And, in the end, to ease the bitter smart,
They say—I know not—that she gave her
　　heart.

151

But we have this assurance given us
That never woman was in greater woe
Than she, when she was false to Troilus;
"Alas!" she said "that I must now forgo
My name for truth in love, for ever! Oh,
I have betrayed the gentlest and the best
That ever was, finest and worthiest.

152

"No good, alas, of me, to the world's end,
Will ever now be written, said, or sung.
Not one fair word! No book will be my friend,
I shall be rolled about on many a tongue;
Throughout the world my bell, and knell, is
　　rung;
And womenfolk will hate me most of all;
Alas, that I should suffer such a fall!

153

"And they will say 'As far as she was able,
She has dishonoured us.' Alas the day!
Though I am not the first to be unstable,
What help is that to take my shame away?
Since there is nothing better I can say,

And grieving comes too late, what shall I do?
To Diomede at least I will be true!

154

"Since I can do no better, Troilus,
And since for ever you and I have parted,
Still I shall pray God's blessing on you, thus,
As the most truly noble, faithful-hearted
Of all I ever saw, since first we started,
That ever had lady's honour in his keeping!"
And having spoken thus, she burst out
　　weeping.

155

"Certainly I shall never hate you, never!
But a friend's love, that you shall have of me;
I'll speak your praise, though I should live for
　　ever;
And O believe how sorry I should be
If I should see you in adversity.
And you are guiltless, as I well believe;
But all shall pass, and so I take my leave."

156

But honestly, how long it was between
Forsaking him and taking Diomede
I cannot say; no author I have seen
Has told us; take the volumes down and read,
You'll find no dates, for none are given in-
　　deed.
Though he was quick to woo, before he won
He found there was still more that must be
　　done.

157

I cannot find it in my heart to chide
This hapless woman, more than the story will;
Her name, alas, is punished far and wide,
And that should be sufficient for the ill
She did; I would excuse her for it still,
She was so sorry for her great untruth;
Indeed I would excuse her yet, for ruth.

158

This Troilus, as I've already told,
Went driving on and on, as best he might,
And many a time his heart went hot and cold,
And more especially upon the night
—The ninth—before the day he had the right
To hope for her—she had her word to keep.
That night he had no rest, nor thought of
　　sleep.

159

Now laurel-crowned Apollo, with his heat,
Began his course and up the sky he went
To warm the eastern waves, on which he beat
In brilliance; and the lark with fresh intent
Began to rise and sing. And Troilus sent

For Pandar, and they walked the city wall
Seeking Criseyde, or sign of her at all.

160

Till it was noon, they stood about to see
Any who came; whenever one appeared
From far away, they said that it was she,
Until a little later when he neared;
And now his heart was dull, and now it
  cleared,
Mocked at so often, they stood staring thus
At nothing, Troilus and Pandarus.

161

Then Troilus said to Pandar with a frown,
"For all I know, it will be noon for sure
Before Criseyde will come into the town;
She has enough to do and to endure
To win her father over, nothing truer.
For the old man will force her to have dinner
Before she goes—God torture the old sinner!"

162

Said Pandar "That may be, indeed, it's plain;
And therefore let us have our dinner too,
And after dinner you can come again."
So they went homeward without more to-do
And then returned. But long will they pursue
Before they find the thing they're gaping
  after,
Fortune had planned to dupe them, for her
  laughter.

163

Said Troilus: "I now can see she might
Be forced to stay with Calkas very late;
Before she comes it may be nearly night;
Come on! I'm going down to watch the gate.
These stupid porters get in such a state.
Make them keep open till she comes along;
I'll pass it off as if there's nothing wrong."

164

Day dwindled fast, night fell, and the
  moon hove
Into the sky. Still there was no Criseyde.
Troilus peered at hedge and tree and grove,
He craned his head over the wall, he spied;
And in the end he turned about and cried
"By God, I get her meaning! It's quite plain.
Why, I was nearly in despair again.

165

"She knows what's good for her, and what
  she's at!
She means to ride back secretly, of course;
And I commend her wisdom too; my hat!
She can't have people gathered in a force
To stare at her! She'll quietly take horse

When it is dark. Then she can reach the gate.
Patience, dear friend; it can't be long to wait.

166

"We've nothing else to do, and anyhow—
Look! There she is, I see her! Yes, it's she!
O Pandarus, will you believe me now?
Heave up your eyes, look there, man! Can't
  you see?"
Pandar replied: "It's not like that to me.
All wrong again. You gave me such a start;
The thing I see there is a travelling cart."

167

"Alas, you're right again!" said Troilus,
"Yet it is not for nothing, certainly,
That I should feel my heart rejoicing thus;
My thought holds presage of some good
  to me;
I don't know how, but all my life," said he
"I've never felt such comfort, such delight;
My life upon it, she will come tonight."

168

Pandar replied "It may be, like enough,"
Agreeing with his friend in all he said,
But, laughing softly at his foolish stuff,
He kept this sober thought inside his head
"It is as likely Robin Hood will tread
The path to Troy as she you wait for here;
Ah me! Farewell the snows of yester-year."

169

The Warden of the Gates began to call
To those outside the city, left and right,
Bidding them drive their cattle, one and all,
Inside, or stay without till morning light.
With many a tear, far on into the night,
Troilus turned his horse; he understood,
And home he rode; waiting would do no
  good.

170

Nevertheless he cheered himself along,
Thinking he had miscounted to the day;
He said "I must have understood it wrong,
For, on the very night when last I lay
With her, she promised 'Sweetheart, if I may,
I shall be here with you as now I am
Before the moon has passed out of the Ram.'

171

"She still may keep her promise; she knows
  best."
Early next day he went back to the gate
And up and down he wandered, east and west
Upon the walls with many a weary wait,
But all for nothing—he was blind to fate,
Blinded by hope; and sighing as before,

He went back home, for there was nothing
   more.

172

And clean out of his heart all hope had fled;
Nothing was left for him to hang upon;
Pain throbbed within his heart as if it bled
In sharp and violent throes—for she was gone.
And when he saw that she stayed on and on,
He could not judge of what it might betoken,
Since she had given her word and it was
   broken.

173

The third, the fourth, the fifth, the sixth
   ensued
After those ten long days of which I told;
His heart, between his fears and hope re-
   newed,
Half trusted to her promises of old;
But when at last he saw they would not hold
And there was nothing left for him to try,
He knew he must prepare himself to die.

174

Then came that wicked spirit that we know
(God save us all!) as manic jealousy
And crept into his heart of heavy woe;
Because of which, since dead he wished to be,
He neither ate nor drank for misery,
And from all human company he fled;
During this time, that was the life he led.

175

For so defeated and so woebegone
He was, that those with whom he came in
   touch
Could scarcely know him; he was lean
   and wan,
As feeble as a beggar on a crutch,
His jealousy had punished him so much;
To those who asked him where he felt the
   smart
He said he had a pain about his heart.

176

Priam his father, and his Mother too,
His brothers and his sisters, asked in vain
Why he looked sorrowful, to what was due
So much unhappiness, what caused his pain?
But all for nothing, he would not explain,
But that his heart was injured by a blow
And if death came he would be glad to go.

177

And then, one evening, he lay down to sleep;
It happened so that in his sleep he thought
He had gone out into the woods to weep
For her and for the grief that she had brought,
And up and down the forest as he sought

His way, he came upon a tusky boar
Asleep upon the sunny forest floor.

178

And close beside it, with her arms enfolding,
And ever kissing it, he saw Criseyde;
The grief he suffered as he stood beholding
Burst all the bonds of sleep, and at a stride
He was awake and in despair, and cried
"O Pandar, now I know it through and
   through,
I am but dead, there is no more to do.

179

"She has betrayed me, has not played me fair,
She that I trusted more than all creation,
For she has left me, given her heart elsewhere;
The blessed gods have made their revelation,
I saw it in a dream, a divination;
It was Criseyde, and I beheld her thus!"
He told the whole of it to Pandarus.

180

"O my Criseyde, alas, what subtle word,
What new desire, what beauty, or what art,
What anger justly caused, by me incurred,
What fell experience, what guilt of heart
Has torn me from you, set us far apart?
O trust, O faith, assurance deeply tried!
Who has bereft me of my joy, Criseyde?"

181

"Why did I let you leave me, when the pain
Of parting nearly drove me off my head?
O who will ever trust an oath again?
God knows, my brightest lady, I was led
To take for gospel every word you said!
But who is better able to deceive
Than one in whom we hunger to believe?

182

"What shall I do, my Pandarus? Alas!
So sharp, so new, so desperate the ache!
No remedy for what has come to pass!
Were it not better with these hands to take
My life than thus to suffer for her sake?
For death would end my grief and set me free,
While every day I live disgraces me."

183

Pandarus answered him "Alas the day
That I was born! have I not said ere this
Dreams can deceive a man in many a way?
Why? Their interpretation goes amiss.
How dare you speak so to her prejudice,
Calling her false because you dreamt of her
And are afraid? You're no interpreter!

184

"Perhaps this boar that figures in your story
(It well may be) is there to signify

Her father Calkas who is old and hoary;
He struggles out into the sun to die
And she in grief begins to weep and cry
And kiss him, as he wallows there con-
    founded.
That is the way your dream should be ex-
    pounded."

185

"But what am I to do," said Troilus,
"To know for certain, how am I to tell?"
"Ah, now you're talking!" answered Pan-
    darus,
"Here's my advice; since you can write so
    well,
Sit down and write to her, and you can spell,
Or at least try to spell her answer out,
And know the truth where you are now in
    doubt.

186

"And now, see why; for this I dare maintain,
Supposing she is faithless; if she be,
I cannot think she will write back again,
And if she writes, you very soon will see,
If she has any sort of liberty
To come back here; some phrase of hers
    will show
Why she's prevented. She will let you know.

187

"You haven't written to her since she went.
Nor she to you; and I will take my oath
She may have reasons that would win consent
Even from you (though now you may be loth)
To say it would be better for you both
For her to stay; so make her write to you;
Feel for the truth, that's all there is to do."

188

And so it was they came to a conclusion,
These same two lords, and that without delay;
And Troilus in haste and some confusion
Of heart sat down, revolving what to say
And how to tell her of his disarray
And misery; so to his lady dear,
His own Criseyde, he wrote as you shall hear:

189
Troilus' Letter

"Freshest of flowers, whose I am for ever,
Have been, and shall be, elsewhere never
    swerving,
Body and soul, life, thought, desire, en-
    deavour
All being yours, in humble undeserving
More than my tongue can tell of, since, in
    serving,

My service fills my being, as matter space,
I recommend me to your noble grace.

190

"Please you, my love, to think; have you re-
    flected
How long a time it is—ah, well you know!—
Since you departed, leaving me dejected
In bitter grief; and nothing yet to show
By way of remedy, but greater woe
From day to day? And so I must remain,
While it shall please my well of joy and pain.

191

"Humbly, and from a heart that's torn in
    pieces,
(As write he must when sorrow drives a man)
I write my grief, that every hour increases,
With such complaining as I dare, or can
Make in a letter, wet with tears that ran
Like rain, as you can see; and they would
    speak
Remonstrance, were there language on a
    cheek.

192

"First I beseech it of your clear, sweet eyes
Not to consider what is fouled in it;
But more than this, dear love, not to despise
But read it well; and if it be unfit,
Cold care in me, alas, has killed my wit;
And so if a wrong thought should seem to start
Out of my head, forgive me, sweetest heart.

193

"Could any lover dare, or have the right
To make a sad remonstrance, at the last,
Against his lady, it is I who might,
Considering this, that for these two
    months past
You have delayed, whereas you promised fast
Only to stay ten days among the Greeks;
Yet you have not returned, after eight weeks.

194

"But inasmuch as I must needs assent
To all that pleases you, I will complain
No more, but will sigh out my discontent
Humbly, and write to you in restless pain;
Day in, day out, and over and again
I long to hear from you and how you fare
And all that you have done since you were
    there,

195

"Whose happiness and welfare God increase
In honour; so that upward it may go
Ever and always; may it never cease;
And as your heart would have it, may it grow
And prosper; I pray God it may be so.

And grant that you may soon have pity on me
As I am true to you and true shall be.

196

"And if it please you hear of how I fare
Whose sorrow there is no one could contrive
To paint, I am a garner stored with care,
And, when I wrote this letter, was alive,
But hold my soul in readiness to drive
It sorrowing forth; I hold it in delay
In hope your messenger is on the way.

197

"And these two eyes, with which I see in vain,
Are turned by tears into a double well,
My song into adversity and pain,
My good to grief, my ease of heart to hell,
My joy to woe; what more is there to tell?
And every joy—curse on my life for it!—
And every ease are now their opposite.

198

"Which with your coming back again to Troy
You can redress, and, more than ever I had
A thousand times, you can increase my joy;
For there was never yet a heart so glad
As mine will then be; if you are not sad
To think of me, and feel no kind of ruth
At what I suffer, think of keeping truth.

199

"If, for some fault of mine, I have deserved
To die, or if you care no more for me,
Still, to repay me, in that I have served
You faithfully, I beg of you be free
And generous, and write immediately;
Write, for God's love, my lode-star in the
    night,
That death may make an end of my long fight.

200

"If any other reason makes you stay,
Write to console and bring me some relief;
Though it be Hell for me with you away,
I will be patient and endure my grief;
Of all my hopes a letter is the chief;
Now, sweetheart, write, don't leave me to
    complain;
With hope, or death, deliver me from pain.

201

"Indeed, indeed, my own dear heart and true,
I cannot think, when next you see my face,
Since I have lost all health and colour too,
Criseyde will know me, such is now my case.
My heart's dear daylight, lady full of grace,
The thirst to see your beauty, like a knife,
Cuts at my heart; I scarce hold on to life.

202

"I say no more, although I have to say

Many more things than I have power to tell;
Whether you give me life, or do away
My life, God give you many a happy spell!
My beautiful, my fresh-as-May, farewell!
You that alone command my life or death;
I count upon your truth at every breath.

203

"I wish you that well-being which, unless
You wish it me, I shall have none. You gave
It once, and now it lies in you no less
To name the day to clothe me in my grave.
In you my life; in you the power to save
Me from all misery, all pain, all smart!
And now farewell, my own, my sweetest
    heart!

Your T."

204

This letter was delivered to Criseyde
And in effect she answered as she should;
She wrote with greatest pity, and replied
That she would come as soon as ever she could
To mend what was amiss and make all good,
And so she finished it, but added then
That she would come for sure, but knew not
    when.

205

Her letter fawned on him and sang his praises
She swore she loved him best; but, to be brief,
He could find nothing there but empty
    phrases.
Now, Troilus, away and pipe your grief,
Be it east or west, upon an ivy leaf!
Thus goes the world; God shield us from mis-
    chance,
And all that mean true dealing, God advance!

206

So misery increased by night and day
For Troilus, his hopes began to sink,
His strength to lessen at her long delay;
He took to bed, but could not sleep a wink,
He did not speak, he did not eat or drink,
Imagining that she had proved unkind,
A thought that drove him almost out of his
    mind.

207

This dream of his I spoke about before
Haunted his soul, he could not drive it thence;
He felt for certain she was his no more,
And Jove, of his eternal providence,
Had shown him, sleeping, the significance,
Of her untruth and of his own sad story,
And that the boar contained an allegory.

208

And so to fetch his sister then he sent,

A Sibyl, called Cassandra round about,
Told her his dream and asked her what it
    meant,
And he implored her to resolve his doubt
About this boar with tusks so strong and stout;
And finally, after a little while,
Cassandra gave her answer with a smile,

209

Saying, as she expounded, "Brother dear,
If it's the truth of this you wish to know,
There are a few old tales you'll have to hear,
Concerning Fortune and her overthrow
Of certain lords of old, and they will show
At once what boar this is, and whence he took
His origin; it's written in the book.

210

"Diana being angry—and her ire
Turned on the Greeks who would not sac-
    rifice
To her, or at her altar set the fire
To the incense—had recourse to this device
For her revenge; they paid a cruel price;
She sent a boar, large as an ox in stall,
To root their crops up, corn and vines and all.

211

"To kill this boar the countryside was raised;
Now, among those who came to see it slain,
There was a maiden, one of the best praised;
And Meleager, King of that domain,
Fell so in love with her he swore again
To show his manhood; so he plied the spur,
And killed the boar and sent the head to her.

212

"And out of this, as ancient books record,
Envy arose and the dispute ran high;
Tideus is descended from this lord
Directly, or those ancient volumes lie;
But how this Meleager came to die
(It was his mother's fault, she did the wrong)
I will not tell you; it would take too long."

213

But of Tideus (ere she made an end)
She did not spare to tell, and how he came
To claim the city of Thebes and help his
    friend
Called Polynices; by a wrongful claim
It was defended in his brother's name,
Eteocles, who held the place in strength.
All this Cassandra told him at great length.

214

And how Haemonides had had the art
To get away when fifty knights were slain
By fierce Tideus; prophecies by heart
She told, of seven kings and all their train

That had encircled Thebes in this campaign,
And of the holy serpent, and the well,
And of the Furies; she went on to tell

215

Of Archemorus and his funeral game
And of Amphiaraüs swallowed down
Into the earth: the death that overcame
Tideus: how Hippomedon came to drown:
Parthenopaeus dead of wounds: renown
All shorn from Campaneus, called the Proud,
Slain by a thunderbolt; he cried aloud.

216

She told him how Eteocles, the brother
Of Polynices (celebrated pair)
Met in a skirmish and they slew each other,
And how the Greeks had wept in their de-
    spair,
And how the town was burnt and looted
    there.
So she descended from the days of old
To Diomed; and this is what she told:

217

"Now this same boar betokens Diomede,
Tideus' son, descended as he is
From Meleager, who had made it bleed;
Your lady, wheresoever now she is,
Diomede has her heart and she has his;
Weep if you will, or not, for out of doubt
This Diomede is in, and you are out."

218

"You're telling lies," he said "you sorceress,
You and your spirit of false prophecy!
You hope to be a famous prophetess;
Just look at her, this fool of fantasy!
One who takes pains in her malignity
To slander ladies! Off with you! God's sorrow
Light upon you! I'll prove you false tomorrow!

219

"You might as well lay slanders on Alceste,
Who, of all creatures—if it be no lie—
That ever lived was kindliest and best;
She, when her husband was condemned to die
Unless she took his place, immediately
Made choice to die for him and go to Hell;
And die she did, as all the stories tell."

220

Cassandra left; his rage at what she'd said
Made him forget the grief he had endured;
And suddenly he started out of bed
As though some doctor had completely cured
His illness; day by day, to be assured,
He sought to find the truth with all his force,
And thus endured his doomed adventure's
    course.

221

Fortune, to whom belongs the permutation
Of things under the moon, to her committed
By Jove's high foresight and adjudication,
When nations pass and kingdoms are uncitied
And peoples perish sullied and unpitied,
Fortune, I say, began despoiling Troy
Of her bright feathers, till she was bare of joy.

222

And, among all these things, the end and goal
Of Hector's life was now approaching fast,
When Fate, after unbodying his soul,
Would find a means to drive it forth at last;
And who can strive with Fate? His lot was
cast.
So, going into battle, he was caught,
And death came down upon him as he fought.

223

It therefore seems to me that it is right
For all who follow arms and soldiering
To mourn the death of such a noble knight;
For, as he dragged the helmet from a king,
Achilles with an unexpected swing
Shore through his armour, and his body then;
And thus was killed the worthiest of men.

224

For whom, so it is handed down to us,
The general grief was more than tongue can
tell,
And above all the grief of Troilus,
Who, next to him, was deemed to be the well
Of honour; so it was his spirit fell
What with his love, his sorrow and unrest;
He wished the heart would burst within his
breast.

225

And yet, although beginning to despair,
And dreading that his lady was untrue,
His heart returned to her and lingered there,
As hearts of lovers will, and sought anew
To get her back, Criseyde the bright of hue.
And in his heart he would excuse her, saying
That Calkas was the cause of her delaying.

226

Many a time he planned for them to meet
By wearing pilgrim kit for his disguise
And visiting her, but could not counterfeit
So well as to conceal him from sharp eyes;
Moreover, what excuse could he devise
Supposing he were recognized and caught?
Many a tear he shed as thus he thought.

227

Many a time he wrote to her anew
And piteously—he showed no sign of sloth—

Beseeching her that, since he had been true,
She would return again and keep her oath;
And so, one day, in pity (I am loth
To take it otherwise) she took her pen
And—you shall hear it all—wrote back again:

228

Criseyde's Letter

"Dear son of Cupid, mirror of perfection,
O sword of knighthood, fount of nobleness,
How may a soul in terror and dejection
Send word of joy when she is comfortless?
I heartbroken, I sick, I in distress;
Since neither with the other may have dealing
I cannot send you either heart or healing.

229

"Your long, complaining letter has ac-
quainted
My pitying heart with all your misery,
And I have noted, too, that tears have painted
Your papers, and that you require of me
To come to you; as yet that cannot be.
Lest it be intercepted, it is better
Not to say why, in writing you this letter.

230

"Grievous to me, God knows, is your unrest,
Your urgent haste; you should observe more
measure.
It seems you have not taken for the best
What Heaven has ordained, and what you
treasure
Most in your memory is your own pleasure.
Do not be angry, please, or out of humour;
What keeps me waiting here is wicked ru-
mour.

231

"For I have heard far more than I expected
Of how things stand between us; I am staying
In order that report may be corrected
By my dissimulation; and they're saying
(Now, don't be angry) you were only playing
With me; no matter for that! In you I see
Nothing but truth and pure nobility.

232

"Come back I will; but in the disarray
In which I stand just now, what day or year
This is to happen, I can hardly say.
Yet, in effect, I beg you persevere
In your affection, speak me well, my dear,
For truly, and as long as life may last,
You may be sure my friendship will hold fast.

233

"Again I beg you not to take it ill
If what I write is short; for things are such

Where now I am, I dare not write; but still
Letters are things for which I have no touch.
Moreover one short sentence can say much.
The intention is what counts and not the
     length.
And now, farewell; God give you grace and
     strength!

Your C."

234

Poor Troilus thought this letter very strange
When he had read it, and was sadly stirred;
He sighed; it seemed the calends of a change.
But finally, for all that had occurred,
He could not think she would not keep her
     word;
And easier for those who love so well
It is to trust, though trusting be a Hell.

235

Nevertheless they say that at long last
In spite of all, a man will finally
Perceive the truth; this happened, and quite
     fast,
To Troilus; she was—he came to see—
Less kindly-natured than she ought to be;
And in the end he knew beyond all doubt
That all was lost which he had been about.

236

Standing one day in melancholy mood,
With his suspicions clouded in a frown
Thinking of her, he heard a multitude
Of Trojans clamouring about the town,
Bearing, as was their fashion, up and down
A fine piece of coat armour (says my story)
Before Deiphebus, to show his glory.

237

This coat, as says my author, Lollius,
Deiphebus had rent from Diomede
That very day, and when this Troilus
Beheld it there, he gave it sudden heed
—The length—the breadth—the pattern in
     the bead
And all the worked embroidery in gold—
And suddenly he felt his heart turn cold.

238

There, on the collar, could he not perceive
The brooch he'd given her when they had to
     sever,
Yes on the very day she took her leave,
In memory of his grief and him for ever?
Had she not pledged her faith that she would
     never
Part with that brooch? But that was long be-
     fore;
He knew he could not trust her any more.

239

Homewards he took himself and soon he sent
For Pandarus, and told him from the start
About the brooch and of this new event,
Clamoured against her variable heart,
Mourned his long love, his truth to her, the
     smart
Of this new anguish, cried for the release
Of death without delay, to bring him peace.

240

And thus he spoke: "O lady bright, Criseyde,
Where is your faith to me? And where
     your vow?
Where is your love? Where is your truth?" he
     cried,
"And is it Diomede you are feasting now?
Alas, I would have thought that, anyhow,
Had you intended not to stand upon
Your truth to me, you'd not have led me on.

241

"Who now will trust an oath? Ah, let
     them go!
Alas, I never would have thought ere this
That you, my own Criseyde, could alter so!
Nay, were I guilty, had I done amiss,
Could there have been the cruel artifice
In you to slay me thus? And your good name
Is now destroyed; there lies my grief and
     shame.

242

"Was there no other brooch you had in
     keeping
To fee some newer lover with?" said he,
"Except the brooch I gave you, wet with
     weeping,
For you to wear in memory of me?
There was no reason why this had to be,
Unless it were for spite and that you meant
To make an open show of your intent.

243

"Cast from your mind, I see I have no part
In you, and yet I neither can, nor may,
For all the world, find it within my heart
To un-love you a quarter of a day!
Born in an evil hour, still I say
That you, for all the grief that you are giving,
I still love best of any creature living."

244

And then "O God Almighty, send me grace
That I may meet again with Diomede!
For truly, if I have the fighting-space
And power, I shall hope to make him bleed!
O God," he said, "that shouldest take
     good heed

To foster truth, and make wrong pay the
    price,
Why wilt thou not do vengeance on this vice?

245

"O Pandarus, so ready to upbraid me,
Who mocked me for believing in a dream,
See for yourself! Has not your niece be-
    trayed me?
How stands the bright Criseyde in your es-
    teem?
And many are the ways, or so I deem,
In which the gods reveal our joy and woe
In sleep; my dream has proved that it is so.

246

"Certainly now, without more waste of
    breath,
Henceforward and as truly as I may,
I will bear arms and I will seek my death;
Little I care how soon will be the day.
Truly, Criseyde my sweetest, let me say
To you, whom I have wholly loved and served,
What you have done to me was not deserved."

247

This Pandarus, who stood the while and heard,
Knew it was true, and he had known it long;
He made no answer to him, not a word,
Sad for his friend and for a grief so strong,
And shamed because his niece had done a
    wrong.
Stunned by these things, he stood in deep
    dismay,
Still as a stone, without a word to say.

248

But at the last he spoke, and thus he cried:
"O my dear brother, I can do no more;
What should I say to you? I hate Criseyde;
God knows that I shall hate her evermore!
As for the thing which you besought me for,
Having no true regard to my own honour
Or peace of mind, I worked your will
    upon her.

249

"If I did anything that gave you pleasure
I am glad of it; as for this treason now,
God knows that I am sorry beyond measure!
Would I could ease your heart of it; I vow
I would most gladly do so, knew I how;
Almighty God, deliver her, I pray,
Out of this world; there's no more I can say."

250

Great was the grief and plaint of Troilus;
But on her course went Fortune, as of old.
Criseyde consoles the son of Tideus,

And Troilus may weep in care and cold.
Such is the world for those who can behold
The way it goes; there's little of heart's rest;
God grant we learn to take it for the best.

251

The knighthood and the prowess, do not
    doubt it,
Of Troilus, this very gallant knight
—As you can read in all the books about it—
Were plain to see in many a cruel fight;
And certainly his anger, day and night,
Fell savagely upon the Greeks, I read;
And most of all he sought out Diomede.

252

And many a time, my author says, they met
With bloody strokes, and mighty words were
    said;
The spears that they had taken care to whet
They tried on one another, fought and bled,
And Troilus rained down blows upon his
    head.
In vain, however; Fortune had not planned
That either perish at the other's hand.

253

And had I undertaken to relate
The feats in arms of this distinguished man,
It is his battles I would celebrate;
Seeing, however, that I first began
To tell his love, I've done the best I can.
As for his deeds, let those who would recall
Them, read in Dares, he can tell them all.

254

Beseeching every lady bright of hue
And gentle woman whosoe'er she be,
That though, alas, Criseyde was proved un-
    true,
She be not angry for her guilt with me;
Her guilt is there in other books to see,
And I will gladlier write, to please you best,
Of true Penelope and good Alceste.

255

Nor am I only speaking for these men,
But most of all for women so betrayed
By treacherous folk—God give them sorrow,
    Amen!
Who by their subtlety and wit have played
On your affections in their faithless trade,
Which moves me to speak out; be careful,
    then,
Listen to what I say: beware of men.

256

Go little book, go little tragedy,
Where God may send thy maker, ere he die,

The power to make a work of comedy;
But, little book, it's not for thee to vie
With others, but be subject, as am I,
To poesy itself, and kiss the gracious
Footsteps of Homer, Virgil, Ovid, Statius.

257

And since there is such great diversity
In English, and our writing is so young,
I pray to God that none may mangle thee,
Or wrench thy metre by default of tongue;
And wheresoever thou be read, or sung,
I beg of God that thou be understood!
And now to close my story as I should.

258

The wrath of Troilus, I began to say,
Was cruel, and the Grecians bought it dear,
For there were thousands that he made away,
Who, in his time, had never any peer
Except his brother Hector, so I hear.
But O alas, except that God so willed,
He met with fierce Achilles and was killed.

259

And, having fallen to Achilles' spear,
His light soul rose and rapturously went
Towards the concavity of the eighth sphere,
Leaving conversely every element,
And, as he passed, he saw with wonderment
The wandering stars and heard their harmony,
Whose sound is full of heavenly melody.

260

As he looked down, there came before his eyes
This little spot of earth, that with the sea
Lies all embraced, and found he could despise
This wretched world, and hold it vanity,
Measured against the full felicity
That is in Heaven above; and, at the last,
To where he had been slain his look he cast,

261

And laughed within him at the woe of those
Who wept his death so busily and fast,
Condemning everything we do that flows
From blind desire, which can never last,
When all our thought on Heaven should be
    cast;
And forth he went, not to be long in telling,
Where Mercury appointed him his dwelling.

262

Lo, such an end had Troilus for love!

Lo, such an end his valour, his prowess!
Lo, such an end his royal state above,
Such end his lust, such end his nobleness!
And such an end this false world's brittleness!
And thus began his loving of Criseyde
As I have told it you, and thus he died.

263

Oh all you fresh young people, he or she,
In whom love grows and ripens year by year,
Come home, come home from worldly
    vanity!
Cast the heart's countenance in love and fear
Upwards to God, who in His image here
Has made you; think this world is but a fair
Passing as soon as flower-scent in air.

264

And give your love to Him who, for pure love,
Upon a cross first died that He might pay
Our debt, and rose, and sits in Heaven above;
He will be false to no one that will lay
His heart wholly on Him, I dare to say.
Since He is best to love, and the most meek,
What need is there a feigning love to seek?

265

Behold these old accursèd pagan rites!
Behold how much their gods are worth to you!
Behold these wretched worldly appetites!
Behold your labour's end and guerdon due
From Jove, Apollo and Mars, that rascal crew!
Behold the form in which the ancients speak
Their poetry, if you should care to seek.

266

O moral Gower, I dedicate this book
To you, and you, my philosophical Strode,
In your benignity and zeal to look,
To warrant, and, where need is, to make good;
And to that truthfast Christ who died on rood,
With all my heart for mercy ever I pray,
And to the Lord right thus I speak and say:

267

Thou One and Two and Three and Never-ending,
That reignest ever in Three and Two and One,
Incomprehensible, all-comprehending,
From visible foes, and the invisible one,
Defend us all! And Jesu, Mary's Son,
Make us in mercy worthy to be thine,
For love of her, mother and maid benign!

Amen.

Contents

THE CANTERBURY TALES

THE PROLOGUE 277
THE KNIGHT'S TALE 286
Words between the Host and the Miller 309
THE MILLER'S TALE 310
The Reeve's Prologue 317
THE REEVE'S TALE 318
The Cook's Prologue 323
THE COOK'S TALE 324
Introduction to the Man of Law's Tale 324
The Man of Law's Prologue 325
THE MAN OF LAW'S TALE 326
Epilogue to the Man of Law's Tale 338
THE SHIPMAN'S TALE 338
Words of the Host to the Shipman
    and the Prioress 343
The Prioress's Prologue 343
THE PRIORESS'S TALE 344
Words of the Host to Chaucer 346
CHAUCER'S TALE OF SIR TOPAZ 347
The Host stops Chaucer's Tale
    of Sir Topaz 349
CHAUCER'S TALE OF MELIBEE
    (in synopsis) 349
Words of the Host to the Monk 350
THE MONK'S TALE
    (Lucifer, Adam, Samson, Hercules,
    Nebuchadnezzar, Belshazzar, Zeno-
    bia, King Peter of Spain, King Peter
    of Cyprus, Bernabo Visconti of Lom-
    bardy, Count Ugolino of Pisa, Nero,
    Holofernes, King Antiochus the Il-
    lustrious, Alexander, Julius Caesar,
    Croesus) 351
Words of the Knight and the Host 360
THE NUN'S PRIEST'S TALE 361
Words of the Host to the Nun's Priest 368

THE PHYSICIAN'S TALE 368
Words of the Host to the Physician
    and to the Pardoner 371
The Pardoner's Prologue 372
THE PARDONER'S TALE 373
The Wife of Bath's Prologue 379
Words between the Summoner
    and the Friar 388
THE WIFE OF BATH'S TALE 388
The Friar's Prologue 392
THE FRIAR'S TALE 393
The Summoner's Prologue 397
THE SUMMONER'S TALE 398
The Clerk's Prologue 404
THE CLERK'S TALE 405
Chaucer's Envoy to the Clerk's Tale 418
The Merchant's Prologue 418
THE MERCHANT'S TALE 418
Epilogue to the Merchant's Tale 431
The Squire's Prologue 431
THE SQUIRE'S TALE 431
Words of the Franklin to the Squire
    and of the Host to the Franklin 438
The Franklin's Prologue 438
THE FRANKLIN'S TALE 439
The Second Nun's Prologue 448
THE SECOND NUN'S TALE 450
The Canon's Yeoman's Prologue 455
THE CANON'S YEOMAN'S TALE 457
The Manciple's Prologue 465
THE MANCIPLE'S TALE 466
The Parson's Prologue 469
THE PARSON'S TALE (in synopsis) 470
Chaucer's Retractions 471
NOTES 472

The Canterbury Tales

THE PROLOGUE

When in April the sweet showers fall
And pierce the drought of March to the root,
   and all
The veins are bathed in liquor of such power
As brings about the engendering of the flower,
When also Zephyrus with his sweet breath
Exhales an air in every grove and heath
Upon the tender shoots, and the young sun
His half-course in the sign of the *Ram* has run,
And the small fowl are making melody
That sleep away the night with open eye
(So nature pricks them and their heart en-
   gages)
Then people long to go on pilgrimages
And palmers long to seek the stranger strands
Of far-off saints, hallowed in sundry lands,
And specially, from every shire's end
Of England, down to Canterbury they wend
To seek the holy blissful martyr,[1] quick
To give his help to them when they were sick.

   It happened in that season that one day
In Southwark, at *The Tabard,* as I lay
Ready to go on pilgrimage and start
For Canterbury, most devout at heart,
At night there came into that hostelry
Some nine and twenty in a company
Of sundry folk happening then to fall
In fellowship, and they were pilgrims all
That towards Canterbury meant to ride.
The rooms and stables of the inn were wide:
They made us easy, all was of the best.
And, briefly, when the sun had gone to rest,
I'd spoken to them all upon the trip
And was soon one with them in fellowship,
Pledged to rise early and to take the way
To Canterbury, as you heard me say.

   But none the less, while I have time and
   space,
Before my story takes a further pace,
It seems a reasonable thing to say
What their condition was, the full array
Of each of them, as it appeared to me,
According to profession and degree,
And what apparel they were riding in;
And at a Knight I therefore will begin.
There was a *Knight,* a most distinguished man,
Who from the day on which he first began
To ride abroad had followed chivalry,
Truth, honour, generousness and courtesy.
He had done nobly in his sovereign's war
And ridden into battle, no man more,
As well in Christian as in heathen places,
And ever honoured for his noble graces.

   When we took Alexandria,[2] he was there.
He often sat at table in the chair
Of honour, above all nations, when in Prussia.
In Lithuania he had ridden, and Russia,
No Christian man so often, of his rank.
When, in Granada, Algeciras sank
Under assault, he had been there, and in
North Africa, raiding Benamarin;
In Anatolia he had been as well
And fought when Ayas and Attalia fell,
For all along the Mediterranean coast
He had embarked with many a noble host.
In fifteen mortal battles he had been
And jousted for our faith at Tramissene
Thrice in the lists, and always killed his man.
This same distinguished knight had led
   the van
Once with the Bey of Balat, doing work
For him against another heathen Turk;
He was of sovereign value in all eyes.
And though so much distinguished, he
   was wise
And in his bearing modest as a maid.
He never yet a boorish thing had said
In all his life to any, come what might;
He was a true, a perfect gentle-knight.

   Speaking of his equipment, he possessed
Fine horses, but he was not gaily dressed.
He wore a fustian tunic stained and dark
With smudges where his armour had left
   mark;
Just home from service, he had joined our
   ranks
To do his pilgrimage and render thanks.
   He had his son with him, a fine young
   Squire,

277

A lover and cadet, a lad of fire
With locks as curly as if they had been pressed.
He was some twenty years of age, I guessed.
In stature he was of a moderate length,
With wonderful agility and strength.
He'd seen some service with the cavalry
In Flanders and Artois and Picardy
And had done valiantly in little space
Of time, in hope to win his lady's grace.
He was embroidered like a meadow bright
And full of freshest flowers, red and white.
Singing he was, or fluting all the day;
He was as fresh as is the month of May.
Short was his gown, the sleeves were long and
      wide;
He knew the way to sit a horse and ride.
He could make songs and poems and recite,
Knew how to joust and dance, to draw and
      write.
He loved so hotly that till dawn grew pale
He slept as little as a nightingale.
Courteous he was, lowly and serviceable,
And carved to serve his father at the table.
      There was a *Yeoman* with him at his side,
No other servant; so he chose to ride.
This Yeoman wore a coat and hood of green,
And peacock-feathered arrows, bright
      and keen
And neatly sheathed, hung at his belt the
      while
—For he could dress his gear in yeoman style,
His arrows never drooped their feathers low—
And in his hand he bore a mighty bow.
His head was like a nut, his face was brown.
He knew the whole of woodcraft up and
      down.
A saucy brace was on his arm to ward
It from the bow-string, and a shield and sword
Hung at one side, and at the other slipped
A jaunty dirk, spear-sharp and well-equipped.
A medal of St. Christopher he wore
Of shining silver on his breast, and bore
A hunting-horn, well slung and burnished
      clean,
That dangled from a baldrick of bright green.
He was a proper forester, I guess.
      There also was a *Nun,* a Prioress,
Her way of smiling very simple and coy.
Her greatest oath was only "By St. Loy!"
And she was known as Madam Eglantyne.
And well she sang a service, with a fine
Intoning through her nose, as was most
      seemly,

And she spoke daintily in French, extremely,
After the school of Stratford-atte-Bowe;
French in the Paris style she did not know.
At meat her manners were well taught withal;
No morsel from her lips did she let fall,
Nor dipped her fingers in the sauce too deep;
But she could carry a morsel up and keep
The smallest drop from falling on her breast.
For courtliness she had a special zest,
And she would wipe her upper lip so clean
That not a trace of grease was to be seen
Upon the cup when she had drunk; to eat,
She reached a hand sedately for the meat.
She certainly was very entertaining,
Pleasant and friendly in her ways, and
      straining
To counterfeit a courtly kind of grace,
A stately bearing fitting to her place,
And to seem dignified in all her dealings.
As for her sympathies and tender feelings,
She was so charitably solicitous
She used to weep if she but saw a mouse
Caught in a trap, if it were dead or bleeding.
And she had little dogs she would be feeding
With roasted flesh, or milk, or fine white
      bread.
And bitterly she wept if one were dead
Or someone took a stick and made it smart;
She was all sentiment and tender heart.
Her veil was gathered in a seemly way,
Her nose was elegant, her eyes glass-grey;
Her mouth was very small, but soft and red,
Her forehead, certainly, was fair of spread,
Almost a span across the brows, I own;
She was indeed by no means undergrown.
Her cloak, I noticed, had a graceful charm.
She wore a coral trinket on her arm,
A set of beads, the gaudies tricked in green,[3]
Whence hung a golden brooch of brightest
      sheen
On which there first was graven a crowned A,
And lower, *Amor vincit omnia.*
      Another *Nun,* the secretary at her cell,
Was riding with her, and *three Priests* as well.
      A *Monk* there was, one of the finest sort
Who rode the country; hunting was his sport.
A manly man, to be an Abbot able;
Many a dainty horse he had in stable.
His bridle, when he rode, a man might hear
Jingling in a whistling wind as clear,
Aye, and as loud as does the chapel bell
Where my lord Monk was Prior of the cell.
The Rule of good St. Benet or St. Maur

As old and strict he tended to ignore;
He let go by the things of yesterday
And took the modern world's more spa-
cious way.
He did not rate that text at a plucked hen
Which says that hunters are not holy men
And that a monk uncloistered is a mere
Fish out of water, flapping on the pier,
That is to say a monk out of his cloister.
That was a text he held not worth an oyster;
And I agreed and said his views were sound;
Was he to study till his head went round
Poring over books in cloisters? Must he toil
As Austin bade and till the very soil?
Was he to leave the world upon the shelf?
Let Austin have his labour to himself.
    This Monk was therefore a good man to
      horse;
Greyhounds he had, as swift as birds, to
    course.
Hunting a hare or riding at a fence
Was all his fun, he spared for no expense.
I saw his sleeves were garnished at the hand
With fine grey fur, the finest in the land,
And on his hood, to fasten it at his chin
He had a wrought-gold cunningly fash-
ioned pin;
Into a lover's knot it seemed to pass.
His head was bald and shone like looking-
glass;
So did his face, as if it had been greased.
He was a fat and personable priest;
His prominent eyeballs never seemed to settle.
They glittered like the flames beneath a kettle;
Supple his boots, his horse in fine condition.
He was a prelate fit for exhibition,
He was not pale like a tormented soul.
He liked a fat swan best, and roasted whole.
His palfrey was as brown as is a berry.
    There was a *Friar,* a wanton one and merry,
A Limiter,[4] a very festive fellow.
In all Four Orders[5] there was none so mellow,
So glib with gallant phrase and well-turned
speech.
He'd fixed up many a marriage, giving each
Of his young women what he could af-
ford her.
He was a noble pillar to his Order.
Highly beloved and intimate was he
With County folk within his boundary,
And city dames of honour and possessions;
For he was qualified to hear confessions,
Or so he said, with more than priestly scope;

He had a special licence from the Pope.
Sweetly he heard his penitents at shrift
With pleasant absolution, for a gift.
He was an easy man in penance-giving
Where he could hope to make a decent living;
It's a sure sign whenever gifts are given
To a poor Order that a man's well shriven,
And should he give enough he knew in verity
The penitent repented in sincerity.
For many a fellow is so hard of heart
He cannot weep, for all his inward smart.
Therefore instead of weeping and of prayer
One should give silver for a poor Friar's care.
He kept his tippet stuffed with pins for curls,
And pocket-knives, to give to pretty girls.
And certainly his voice was gay and sturdy,
For he sang well and played the hurdy-gurdy.
At sing-songs he was champion of the hour.
His neck was whiter than a lily-flower
But strong enough to butt a bruiser down.
He knew the taverns well in every town
And every innkeeper and barmaid too
Better than lepers, beggars and that crew,
For in so eminent a man as he
It was not fitting with the dignity
Of his position, dealing with a scum
Of wretched lepers; nothing good can come
Of commerce with such slum-and-gutter
dwellers,
But only with the rich and victual-sellers.
But anywhere a profit might accrue
Courteous he was and lowly of service too.
Natural gifts like his were hard to match.
He was the finest beggar of his batch,
And, for his begging-district, paid a rent;
His brethren did no poaching where he went.
For though a widow mightn't have a shoe,
So pleasant was his holy how-d'ye-do
He got his farthing from her just the same
Before he left, and so his income came
To more than he laid out. And how he
romped,
Just like a puppy! He was ever prompt
To arbitrate disputes on settling days
(For a small fee) in many helpful ways,
Not then appearing as your cloistered scholar
With threadbare habit hardly worth a dollar,
But much more like a Doctor or a Pope.
Of double-worsted was the semi-cope
Upon his shoulders, and the swelling fold
About him, like a bell about its mould
When it is casting, rounded out his dress.
He lisped a little out of wantonness

To make his English sweet upon his tongue.
When he had played his harp, or having sung,
His eyes would twinkle in his head as bright
As any star upon a frosty night.
This worthy's name was Hubert, it appeared.

There was a *Merchant* with a forking beard
And motley dress; high on his horse he sat,
Upon his head a Flemish beaver hat
And on his feet daintily buckled boots.
He told of his opinions and pursuits
In solemn tones, he harped on his increase
Of capital; there should be sea-police
(He thought) upon the Harwich–Holland
    ranges;
He was expert at dabbling in exchanges.
This estimable Merchant so had set
His wits to work, none knew he was in debt,
He was so stately in administration,
In loans and bargains and negotiation.
He was an excellent fellow all the same;
To tell the truth I do not know his name.

An *Oxford Cleric,* still a student though,
One who had taken logic long ago,
Was there; his horse was thinner than a rake,
And he was not too fat, I undertake,
But had a hollow look, a sober stare;
The thread upon his overcoat was bare.
He had found no preferment in the church
And he was too unworldly to make search
For secular employment. By his bed
He preferred having twenty books in red
And black, of Aristotle's philosophy,
Than costly clothes, fiddle or psaltery.
Though a philosopher, as I have told,
He had not found the stone for making gold.
Whatever money from his friends he took
He spent on learning or another book
And prayed for them most earnestly, returning
Thanks to them thus for paying for his
    learning.
His only care was study, and indeed
He never spoke a word more than was need,
Formal at that, respectful in the extreme,
Short, to the point, and lofty in his theme.
A tone of moral virtue filled his speech
And gladly would he learn, and gladly teach.

A *Serjeant at the Law* who paid his calls,
Wary and wise, for clients at St. Paul's[6]
There also was, of noted excellence.
Discreet he was, a man to reverence,
Or so he seemed, his sayings were so wise.
He often had been Justice of Assize
By letters patent, and in full commission.

His fame and learning and his high position
Had won him many a robe and many a fee.
There was no such conveyancer as he;
All was fee-simple to his strong digestion,
Not one conveyance could be called in ques-
    tion.
Though there was nowhere one so busy as he,
He was less busy than he seemed to be.
He knew of every judgement, case and crime
Ever recorded since King William's time.
He could dictate defences or draft deeds;
No one could pinch a comma from his screeds
And he knew every statute off by rote.
He wore a homely parti-coloured coat,
Girt with a silken belt of pin-stripe stuff;
Of his appearance I have said enough.

There was a *Franklin*[7] with him, it ap-
    peared;
White as a daisy-petal was his beard.
A sanguine man, high-coloured and benign,
He loved a morning sop of cake in wine.
He lived for pleasure and had always done,
For he was Epicurus' very son,
In whose opinion sensual delight
Was the one true felicity in sight.
As noted as St. Julian was for bounty
He made his household free to all the County.
His bread, his ale were finest of the fine
And no one had a better stock of wine.
His house was never short of bake-meat pies,
Of fish and flesh, and these in such supplies
It positively snowed with meat and drink
And all the dainties that a man could think.
According to the seasons of the year
Changes of dish were ordered to appear.
He kept fat partridges in coops, beyond,
Many a bream and pike were in his pond.
Woe to the cook unless the sauce was hot
And sharp, or if he wasn't on the spot!
And in his hall a table stood arrayed
And ready all day long, with places laid.
As Justice at the Sessions none stood higher;
He often had been Member for the Shire.
A dagger and a little purse of silk
Hung at his girdle, white as morning milk.
As Sheriff he checked audit, every entry.
He was a model among landed gentry.

A *Haberdasher,* a *Dyer,* a *Carpenter,*
A *Weaver* and a *Carpet-maker* were
Among our ranks, all in the livery
Of one impressive guild-fraternity.
They were so trim and fresh their gear
    would pass

For new. Their knives were not tricked out
    with brass
But wrought with purest silver, which
    avouches
A like display on girdles and on pouches.
Each seemed a worthy burgess, fit to grace
A guild-hall with seat upon the dais.
Their wisdom would have justified a plan
To make each one of them an alderman;
They had the capital and revenue,
Besides their wives declared it was their due.
And if they did not think so, then they ought;
To be called "*Madam*" is a glorious thought,
And so is going to church and being seen
Having your mantle carried, like a queen.

    They had a *Cook* with them who stood
    alone
For boiling chicken with a marrow-bone,
Sharp flavouring-powder and a spice for
    savour.
He could distinguish London ale by flavour,
And he could roast and seethe and broil
    and fry,
Make good thick soup and bake a tasty pie.
But what pity—so it seemed to me,
That he should have an ulcer on his knee.
As for blancmange, he made it with the best.

    There was a *Skipper* hailing from far west;
He came from Dartmouth, so I understood.
He rode a farmer's horse as best he could,
In a woollen gown that reached his knee.
A dagger on a lanyard falling free
Hung from his neck under his arm and down.
The summer heat had tanned his colour
    brown,
And certainly he was an excellent fellow.
Many a draught of vintage, red and yellow,
He'd drawn at Bordeaux, while the trader
    snored.
The nicer rules of conscience he ignored.
If, when he fought, the enemy vessel sank,
He sent his prisoners home; they walked the
    plank.
As for his skill in reckoning his tides,
Currents and many another risk besides,
Moons, harbours, pilots, he had such dispatch
That none from Hull to Carthage was his
    match.
Hardy he was, prudent in undertaking;
His beard in many a tempest had its shaking,
And he knew all the havens as they were
From Gottland to the Cape of Finisterre,
And every creek in Brittany and Spain;

The barge he owned was called *The Maude-
layne.*

    A *Doctor* too emerged as we proceeded;
No one alive could talk as well as he did
On points of medicine and of surgery,
For, being grounded in astronomy,
He watched his patient closely for the hours
When, by his horoscope, he knew the powers
Of favourable planets, then ascendent,
Worked on the images[8] for his dependent.
The cause of every malady you'd got
He knew, and whether dry, cold, moist or
    hot;[9]
He knew their seat, their humour and condi-
tion.
He was a perfect practising physician.
These causes being known for what they
    were,
He gave the man his medicine then and there.
All his apothecaries in a tribe
Were ready with the drugs he would prescribe
And each made money from the other's guile;
They had been friendly for a goodish while.
He was well-versed in Aesculapius[10] too
And what Hippocrates and Rufus knew
And Dioscorides, now dead and gone,
Galen and Rhazes, Hali, Serapion,
Averroes, Avicenna, Constantine,
Scotch Bernard, John of Gaddesden, Gilber-
tine.
In his own diet he observed some measure;
There were no superfluities for pleasure,
Only digestives, nutritives and such.
He did not read the Bible very much.
In blood-red garments, slashed with
    bluish grey
And lined with taffeta, he rode his way;
Yet he was rather close to expenses
And kept the gold he won in pestilences.
Gold stimulates the heart, or so we're told.
He therefore had a special love of gold.

    A worthy *woman* from beside *Bath* city
Was with us, somewhat deaf, which was a
    pity.
In making cloth she showed so great a bent
She bettered those of Ypres and of Ghent.
In all the parish not a dame dared stir
Towards the altar steps in front of her,
And if indeed they did, so wrath was she
As to be quite put out of charity.
Her kerchiefs were of finely woven ground;
I dared have sworn they weighed a good ten
    pound,

The ones she wore on Sunday, on her head.
Her hose were of the finest scarlet red
And gartered tight; her shoes were soft
    and new.
Bold was her face, handsome, and red in hue.
A worthy woman all her life, what's more
She'd had five husbands, all at the church
    door,
Apart from other company in youth;
No need just now to speak of that, forsooth.
And she had thrice been to Jerusalem,
Seen many strange rivers and passed over
    them;
She'd been to Rome and also to Boulogne,
St. James of Compostella and Cologne,
And she was skilled in wandering by the way.
She had gap-teeth, set widely, truth to say.
Easily on an ambling horse she sat
Well wimpled up, and on her head a hat
As broad as is a buckler or a shield;
She had a flowing mantle that concealed
Large hips, her heels spurred sharply under
    that.
In company she liked to laugh and chat
And knew the remedies for love's mischances,
An art in which she knew the oldest dances.
    A holy-minded man of good renown
There was, and poor, the *Parson* to a town,
Yet he was rich in holy thought and work.
He also was a learned man, a clerk,
Who truly knew Christ's gospel and would
    preach it
Devoutly to parishioners, and teach it.
Benign and wonderfully diligent,
And patient when adversity was sent
(For so he proved in much adversity)
He hated cursing to extort a fee,
Nay rather he preferred beyond a doubt
Giving to poor parishioners round about
Both from church offerings and his property;
He could in little find sufficiency.
Wide was his parish, with houses far asunder,
Yet he neglected not in rain or thunder,
In sickness or in grief, to pay a call
On the remotest, whether great or small,
Upon his feet, and in his hand a stave.
This noble example to his sheep he gave
That first he wrought, and afterwards he
    taught;
And it was from the Gospel he had caught
Those words, and he would add this fig-
    ure too,

That if gold rust, what then will iron do?
For if a priest be foul in whom we trust
No wonder that a common man should rust;
And shame it is to see—let priests take stock—
A shitten shepherd and a snowy flock.
The true example that a priest should give
Is one of cleanness, how the sheep should live.
He did not set his benefice to hire
And leave his sheep encumbered in the mire
Or run to London to earn easy bread
By singing masses for the wealthy dead,
Or find some Brotherhood and get enrolled.
He stayed at home and watched over his fold
So that no wolf should make the sheep mis-
    carry.
He was a shepherd and no mercenary.
Holy and virtuous he was, but then
Never contemptuous of sinful men,
Never disdainful, never too proud or fine,
But was discreet in teaching and benign.
His business was to show a fair behaviour
And draw men thus to Heaven and their
    Saviour,
Unless indeed a man were obstinate;
And such, whether of high or low estate,
He put to sharp rebuke, to say the least.
I think there never was a better priest.
He sought no pomp or glory in his dealings,
No scrupulosity had spiced his feelings.
Christ and His Twelve Apostles and their lore
He taught, but followed it himself before.
    There was a *Plowman* with him there, his
        brother;
Many a load of dung one time or other
He must have carted through the morn-
    ing dew.
He was an honest worker, good and true,
Living in peace and perfect charity,
And, as the gospel bade him, so did he,
Loving God best with all his heart and mind
And then his neighbour as himself, repined
At no misfortune, slacked for no content,
For steadily about his work he went
To thrash his corn, to dig or to manure
Or make a ditch; and he would help the poor
For love of Christ and never take a penny
If he could help it, and, as prompt as any,
He paid his tithes in full when they were due
On what he owned, and on his earnings too.
He wore a tabard smock and rode a mare.
    There was a *Reeve*, also a *Miller*, there,
A College *Manciple* from the Inns of Court,

A papal *Pardoner* and, in close consort,
A Church-Court *Summoner,* riding at a trot,
And finally myself—that was the lot.

   The *Miller* was a chap of sixteen stone,
A great stout fellow big in brawn and bone.
He did well out of them, for he could go
And win the ram at any wrestling show.
Broad, knotty and short-shouldered, he would
   boast
He could heave any door off hinge and post,
Or take a run and break it with his head.
His beard, like any sow or fox, was red
And broad as well, as though it were a spade;
And, at its very tip, his nose displayed
A wart on which there stood a tuft of hair
Red as the bristles in an old sow's ear.
His nostrils were as black as they were wide.
He had a sword and buckler at his side,
His mighty mouth was like a furnace door.
A wrangler and buffoon, he had a store
Of tavern stories, filthy in the main.
His was a master-hand at stealing grain.
He felt it with his thumb and thus he knew
Its quality and took three times his due—
A thumb of gold, by God, to gauge an oat!
He wore a hood of blue and a white coat.
He liked to play his bagpipes up and down
And that was how he brought us out of town.

   The *Manciple* came from the Inner Temple;
All caterers might follow his example
In buying victuals; he was never rash
Whether he bought on credit or paid cash.
He used to watch the market most precisely
And got in first, and so he did quite nicely.
Now isn't it a marvel of God's grace
That an illiterate fellow can outpace
The wisdom of a heap of learned men?
His masters—he had more than thirty then—
All versed in the abstrusest legal knowledge,
Could have produced a dozen from their
   College
Fit to be stewards in land and rents and game
To any Peer in England you could name,
And show him how to live on what he had
Debt-free (unless of course the Peer were mad)
Or be as frugal as he might desire,
And make them fit to help about the Shire
In any legal case there was to try;
And yet this Manciple could wipe their eye.

   The *Reeve*[11] was old and choleric and thin;
His beard was shaven closely to the skin,
His shorn hair came abruptly to a stop

Above his ears, and he was docked on top
Just like a priest in front; his legs were lean,
Like sticks they were, no calf was to be seen.
He kept his bins and garners very trim;
No auditor could gain a point on him.
And he could judge by watching drought
   and rain
The yield he might expect from seed and
   grain.
His master's sheep, his animals and hens,
Pigs, horses, dairies, stores and cattle-pens
Were wholly trusted to his government.
He had been under contract to present
The accounts, right from his master's earliest
   years.
No one had ever caught him in arrears.
No bailiff, serf or herdsman dared to kick,
He knew their dodges, knew their every trick;
Feared like the plague he was, by those be-
   neath.
He had a lovely dwelling on a heath,
Shadowed in green by trees above the sward.
A better hand at bargains than his lord,
He had grown rich and had store of treasure
Well tucked away, yet out it came to pleasure
His lord with subtle loans or gifts of goods,
To earn his thanks and even coats and hoods.
When young he'd learnt a useful trade and still
He was a carpenter of first-rate skill.
The stallion-cob he rode at a slow trot
Was dapple-grey and bore the name of Scot.
He wore an overcoat of bluish shade
And rather long; he had a rusty blade
Slung at his side. He came, as I heard tell,
From Norfolk, near a place called Baldeswell.
His coat was tucked under his belt and splayed.
He rode the hindmost of our cavalcade.

   There was a *Summoner*[12] with us at that Inn,
His face on fire, like a cherubin,[13]
For he had carbuncles. His eyes were narrow,
He was as hot and lecherous as a sparrow.
Black scabby brows he had, and a thin beard.
Children were afraid when he appeared.
No quicksilver, lead ointment, tartar creams,
No brimstone, no boracic, so it seems,
Could make a salve that had the power to bite,
Clean up or cure his whelks of knobby white
Or purge the pimples sitting on his cheeks,
Garlic he loved, and onions too, and leeks,
And drinking strong red wine till all was hazy.
Then he would shout and jabber as if crazy,
And wouldn't speak a word except in Latin

When he was drunk, such tags as he was
    pat in;
He only had a few, say two or three,
That he had mugged up out of some decree;
No wonder, for he heard them every day.
And, as you know, a man can teach a jay
To call out "Walter" better than the Pope.
But had you tried to test his wits and grope
For more, you'd have found nothing in
    the bag.
Then *"Questio quid juris"* was his tag.[14]
He was a noble varlet and a kind one,
You'd meet none better if you went to
    find one.
Why, he'd allow—just for a quart of wine—
Any good lad to keep a concubine
A twelvemonth and dispense him altogether!
And he had finches of his own to feather:
And if he found some rascal with a maid
He would instruct him not to be afraid
In such a case of the Archdeacon's curse
(Unless the rascal's soul were in his purse)
For in his purse the punishment should be.
"Purse is the good Archdeacon's Hell," said he.
But well I know he lied in what he said;
A curse should put a guilty man in dread,
For curses kill, as shriving brings salvation.
We should beware of excommunication.
Thus, as he pleased, the man could bring
    duress
On any young fellow in the diocese.
He knew their secrets, they did what he said.
He wore a garland set upon his head
Large as the holly-bush upon a stake
Outside an ale-house, and he had a cake,
A round one, which it was his joke to wield
As if it were intended for a shield.

    He and a gentle *Pardoner*[15] rode together,
A bird from Charing Cross of the same
    feather,
Just back from visiting the Court of Rome.
He loudly sang *"Come hither, love, come home!"*
The Summoner sang deep seconds to this
    song,
No trumpet ever sounded half so strong.
This Pardoner had hair as yellow as wax,
Hanging down smoothly like a hank of flax.
In driblets fell his locks behind his head
Down to his shoulders which they overspread;
Thinly they fell, like rat-tails, one by one.
He wore no hood upon his head, for fun;
The hood inside his wallet had been stowed,
He aimed at riding in the latest mode;
But for a little cap his head was bare

And he had bulging eye-balls, like a hare.
He'd sewed a holy relic on his cap;
His wallet lay before him on his lap,
Brimful of pardons come from Rome, all hot.
He had the same small voice a goat has got.
His chin no beard had harboured, nor would
    harbour,
Smoother than ever chin was left by barber.
I judge he was a gelding, or a mare.
As to his trade, from Berwick down to Ware
There was no pardoner of equal grace,
For in his trunk he had a pillow-case
Which he asserted was Our Lady's veil.
He said he had a gobbet of the sail
Saint Peter had the time when he made bold
To walk the waves, till Jesu Christ took hold.
He had cross of metal set with stones
And, in a glass, a rubble of pigs' bones.
And with these relics, any time he found
Some poor up-country parson to astound,
In one short day, in money down, he drew
More than the parson in a month or two,
And by his flatteries and prevarication
Made monkeys of the priest and congregation.
But still to do him justice first and last
In church he was a noble ecclesiast.
How well he read a lesson or told a story!
But best of all he sang an Offertory,
For well he knew that when that song
    was sung
He'd have to preach and tune his honey-
    tongue
And (well he could) win silver from the
    crowd.
That's why he sang so merrily and loud.
    Now I have told you shortly, in a clause,
The rank, the array, the number and the cause
Of our assembly in this company
In Southwark, at that high-class hostelry
Known as *The Tabard,* close beside *The Bell.*
And now the time has come for me to tell
How we behaved that evening; I'll begin
After we had alighted at the Inn,
Then I'll report our journey, stage by stage,
All the remainder of our pilgrimage.
But first I beg of you, in courtesy,
Not to condemn me as unmannerly
If I speak plainly and with concealings
And give account of all their words and deal-
    ings,
Using their very phrases as they fell.
For certainly, as you all know so well,
He who repeats a tale after a man
Is bound to say, as nearly as he can,

Each single word, if he remembers it,
However rudely spoken or unfit,
Or else the tale he tells will be untrue,
The things pretended and the phrases new.
He may not flinch although it were his
    brother,
He may as well say one word as another.
And Christ Himself spoke broad in Holy
    Writ,
Yet there is no scurrility in it,
And Plato says, for those with power to read,
"The word should be as cousin to the deed."
Further I beg you to forgive it me
If I neglect the order and degree
And what is due to rank in what I've planned.
I'm short of wit as you will understand.

Our *Host* gave us great welcome; everyone
Was given a place and supper was begun.
He served the finest victuals you could think,
The wine was strong and we were glad to
    drink.
A very striking man our Host withal,
And fit to be a marshal in a hall.
His eyes were bright, his girth a little wide;
There is no finer burgess in Cheapside.
Bold in his speech, yet wise and full of tact,
There was no manly attribute he lacked,
What's more he was a merry-hearted man.
After our meal he jokingly began
To talk of sport, and, among other things
After we'd settled up our reckonings,
He said as follows: "Truly, gentlemen,
You're very welcome and I can't think when
—Upon my word I'm telling you no lie—
I've seen a gathering here that looked so spry,
No, not this year, as in this tavern now.
I'd think you up some fun if I knew how.
And, as it happens, a thought has just occurred
To please you, costing nothing, on my word.
You're off to Canterbury—well, God speed!
Blessed St. Thomas answer to your need!
And I don't doubt, before the journey's done
You mean to while the time in tales and fun.
Indeed, there's little pleasure for your bones
Riding along and all as dumb as stones.
So let me then propose for your enjoyment,
Just as I said, a suitable employment.
And if my notion suits and you agree
And promise to submit yourselves to me
Playing your parts exactly as I say
Tomorrow as you ride along the way,
Then by my father's soul (and he is dead)
If you don't like it you can have my head!
Hold up your hands, and not another word."

Well, our opinion was not long deferred,
It seemed not worth a serious debate;
We all agreed to it at any rate
And bade him issue what commands he
    would.
"My lords," he said, "now listen for your good,
And please don't treat my notion with disdain.
This is the point. I'll make it short and plain.
Each one of you shall help to make things slip
By telling two stories on the outward trip
To Canterbury, that's what I intend,
And, on the homeward way to journey's end
Another two, tales from the days of old;
And then the man whose story is best told,
That is to say who gives the fullest measure
Of good morality and general pleasure,
He shall be given a supper, paid by all,
Here in this tavern, in this very hall,
When we come back again from Canterbury.
And in the hope to keep you bright and merry
I'll go along with you myself and ride
All at my own expense and serve as guide.
I'll be the judge, and those who won't obey
Shall pay for what we spend upon the way.
Now if you all agree to what you've heard
Tell me at once without another word,
And I will make arrangements early for it."

Of course we all agreed, in fact we swore it
Delightedly, and made entreaty too
That he should act as he proposed to do,
Become our Governor in short, and be
Judge of our tales and general referee,
And set the supper at a certain price.
We promised to be ruled by his advice
Come high, come low; unanimously thus
We set him up in judgement over us.
More wine was fetched, the business being
    done;
We drank it off and up went everyone
To bed without a moment of delay.

Early next morning at the spring of day
Up rose our Host and roused us like a cock,
Gathering us together in a flock,
And off we rode at slightly faster pace
Than walking to St. Thomas' watering-place;
And there our Host drew up, began to ease
His horse, and said, "Now, listen if you please,
My lords! Remember what you promised me.
If evensong and mattins will agree
Let's see who shall be first to tell a tale.
And as I hope to drink good wine and ale
I'll be your judge. The rebel who disobeys,
However much the journey costs, he pays.
Now draw for cut and then we can depart;

The man who draws the shortest cut shall
    start.
My Lord the Knight," he said, "step up to me
And draw your cut, for that is my decree.
And come you near, my Lady Prioress,
And you, Sir Cleric, drop your shamefastness,
No studying now! A hand from every man!"
Immediately the draw for lots began
And to tell shortly how the matter went,
Whether by chance or fate or accident,
The truth is this, the cut fell to the Knight,
Which everybody greeted with delight.
And tell his tale he must, as reason was
Because of our agreement and because
He too had sworn. What more is there to say?
For when this good man saw how matters lay,
Being by wisdom and obedience driven
To keep a promise he had freely given,
He said, "Since it's for me to start the game,
Why, welcome be the cut in God's good
    name!
Now let us ride, and listen to what I say."
And at the word we started on our way
And in a cheerful style he then began
At once to tell his tale, and thus it ran.

THE KNIGHT'S TALE

PART I

Stories of old have made it known to us
That there was once a Duke called Theseus,
Ruler of Athens, Lord and Governor,
And in his time so great a conqueror
There was none mightier beneath the sun.
And many a rich country he had won,
What with his wisdom and his troops of
    horse.
He had subdued the Amazons by force
And all their realm, once known as Scythia,
But then called Femeny. Hippolyta,
Their queen, he took to wife, and, says the
    story,
He brought her home in solemn pomp and
    glory,
Also her younger sister, Emily.
And thus victorious and with minstrelsy
I leave this noble Duke for Athens bound
With all his host of men-at-arms around.
    And were it not too long to tell again
I would have fully pictured the campaign
In which his men-at-arms and he had won
Those territories from the Amazon

And the great battle that was given then
Between those women and the Athenian men,
Or told you how Hippolyta had been
Besieged and taken, fair courageous queen,
And what a feast there was when they were
    married,
And after of the tempest that had harried
Their home-coming. I pass these over now
Having, God knows, a larger field to plough.
Weak are my oxen for such mighty stuff;
What I have yet to tell is long enough.
I won't delay the others of our rout,
Let every fellow tell his tale about
And see who wins the supper at the Inn.
Where I left off, let me again begin.
    This Duke I mentioned, ere alighting down
And on the very outskirts of the town
In all felicity and height of pride
Became aware, casting an eye aside,
That kneeling on the highway, two by two,
A company of ladies were in view
All clothed in black, each pair in proper
    station
Behind the other. And such lamentation
And cries they uttered, it was past conceiving
The world had ever heard such noise of
    grieving,
Nor did they hold their misery in check
Till they grasped bridle at his horse's neck.
    "Who may you be that, at my coming, so
Perturb my festival with cries of woe?"
Said Theseus. "Do you grudge the celebration
Of these my honours with your lamentation?
Who can have injured you or who offended?
And tell me if the matter may be mended
And why it is that you are clothed in black?"
    The eldest of these ladies answered back,
Fainting a little in such deadly fashion
That but to see and hear her stirred compas-
    sion,
And said, "O Sir, whom Fortune has made
    glorious
In conquest and is sending home victorious,
We do not grudge your glory in our grief
But rather beg your mercy and relief.
Have pity on our sorrowful distress!
Some drop of pity, in your nobleness,
On us unhappy women let there fall!
For sure there is not one among us all
That was not once a duchess or a queen,
Though wretches now, as may be truly seen,
Thanks be to Fortune and her treacherous
    wheel

That suffers no estate on earth to feel
Secure, and, waiting on your presence, we,
Here at the shrine of Goddess Clemency,
Have watched a fortnight for this very hour.
Help us, my Lord, it lies within your power.
I, wretched Queen, that weep aloud my woe,
Was wife to King Capaneus long ago
That died at Thebes, accursed be the day!
And we in our disconsolate array
That make this sorrowful appeal to pity
Lost each her husband in that fatal city
During the siege, for so it came to pass.
Now old King Creon—O alas, alas!—
The Lord of Thebes, grown cruel in his age
And filled with foul iniquity and rage,
For tyranny and spite as I have said
Does outrage on the bodies of our dead,
On all our husbands, for when they were slain
Their bodies were dragged out onto the plain
Into a heap, and there, as we have learnt,
They neither may have burial nor be burnt,
But he makes dogs devour them, in scorn."

    At that they all at once began to mourn,
And every woman fell upon her face
And cried, "Have pity, Lord, on our disgrace
And let our sorrow sink into your heart."
    The Duke, who felt a pang of pity start
At what they spoke, dismounted from his
        steed;
He felt his heart about to break indeed,
Seeing how piteous and disconsolate
They were, that once had been of high estate!
He raised them in his arms and sought to fill
Their hearts with comfort and with kind good
        will,
And swore on oath that as he was true knight,
So far as it should lie within his might,
He would take vengeance on this tyrant King,
This Creon, till the land of Greece should ring
With how he had encountered him and served
The monster with the death he had deserved.
Instantly then and with no more delay,
He turned and with his banners in display
Made off for Thebes with all his host beside,
For not a step to Athens would he ride,
Nor take his ease so much as half a day,
But marched into the night upon his way.
But yet he sent Hippolyta the Queen
And Emily her sister, the serene,
On into Athens, where they were to dwell,
And off he rode; there is no more to tell.
    The figure of red Mars with spear and targe
So shone upon his banners white and large,

That all the meadows glittered up and down,
And close by them his pennon of renown
Shone rich with gold, emblazoned with that
        feat,
His slaying of the Minotaur in Crete.
Thus rode this Duke, thus rode this con-
        queror
And led his flower of chivalry to war,
Until he came to Thebes, there to alight
In splendour on a chosen field to fight.
And, to speak briefly of so great a thing,
He conquered Creon there, the Theban king,
And slew him manfully, as became a knight,
In open battle, put his troops to flight,
And by assault captured the city after
And rent it, roof and wall and spar and rafter;
And to the ladies he restored again
The bones belonging to their husbands slain,
To do, as custom was, their obsequies.
    But it were all too long to speak of these,
Or of the clamorous complaint and yearning
These ladies uttered at the place of burning
The bodies, or of all the courtesy
That Theseus, noble in his victory,
Showed to the ladies when they went
        their way;
I would be brief in what I have to say.
    Now when Duke Theseus worthily
        had done
Justice on Creon and when Thebes was won,
That night, camped in the field, he took his
        rest,
Having disposed the land as he thought best.
    Crawling for ransack among heaps of slain
And stripping their accoutrements for gain,
The pillagers went busily about
After the battle on the field of rout.
And so befell among the heaps they found,
Thrust through with bloody wounds upon the
        ground,
Two pale young knights there, lying side by
        side,
Wearing the self-same arms in blazoned pride.
Of these Arcita was the name of one,
That of the other knight was Palamon;
And they were neither fully quick nor dead.
By coat of arms and crest upon the head
The heralds knew, for all the filth and mud,
That they were Princes of the Royal Blood;
Two sisters of the House of Thebes had borne
        them.
Out of the heap these pillagers have torn them
And gently carried them to Theseus' tent.

And he decreed they should at once be sent
To Athens, and gave order they be kept
Perpetual prisoners—he would accept
No ransom for them. This was done, and then
The noble Duke turned homeward with
    his men
Crowned with the laurel of his victory,
And there in honour and felicity
He lived his life; what more is there to say?
And in a tower, in grief and anguish lay
Arcite and Palamon, beyond all doubt
For ever, for no gold could buy them out.

    Year after year went by, day after day,
Until one morning in the month of May
Young Emily, that fairer was of mien
Then is the lily on its stalk of green,
And fresher in her colouring that strove
With early roses in a May-time grove
—I know not which was fairer of the two—
Ere it was day, as she was wont to do,
Rose and arrayed her beauty as was right,
For May will have no sluggardry at night,
Season that pricks in every gentle heart,
Awaking it from sleep, and bids it start,
Saying, "Arise! Do thine observance due!"
And this made Emily recall anew
The honour due to May and she arose,
Her beauties freshly clad. To speak of those,
Her yellow hair was braided in a tress
Behind her back, a yard in length, I guess,
And in the garden at the sun's uprising,
Hither and thither at her own devising,
She wandered gathering flowers, white
    and red,
To make a subtle garland for her head,
And like an angel sang a heavenly song.

    The great, grim tower-keep, so thick and
    strong,
Principal dungeon at the castle's core
Where the two knights, of whom I spoke
    before
And shall again, were shut, if you recall,
Was close-adjoining to the garden wall
Where Emily chose her pleasures and adorn-
    ings.
Bright was the sun this loveliest of mornings
And the sad prisoner Palamon had risen,
With licence from the jailer of the prison,
As was his wont, and roamed a chamber high
Above the city, whence he could descry
The noble buildings and the branching green
Where Emily the radiant and serene
Went pausing in her walk and roaming on.

    This sorrowful prisoner, this Palamon,
Was pacing round his chamber to and fro
Lamenting to himself in all his woe.
"Alas," he said, "that ever I was born!"
And so it happened on this May day morn,
Through a deep window set with many bars
Of mighty iron squared with massive spars,
He chanced on Emily to cast his eye
And, as he did, he blenched and gave a cry
As though he had been stabbed, and to the
    heart.
And, at the cry, Arcita gave a start
And said, "My cousin Palamon, what ails you?
How deadly pale you look! Your colour
    fails you!
Why did you cry? Who can have given of-
    fence?
For God's love, take things patiently, have
    sense,
Think! We are prisoners and shall always be.
Fortune has given us this adversity,
Some wicked planetary dispensation,
Some Saturn's trick or evil constellation
Has given us this, and Heaven, though we had
    sworn
The contrary, so stood when we were born.
We must endure it, that's the long and short."

    And Palamon in answer made retort,
"Cousin, believe me, your opinion springs
From ignorance and vain imaginings.
Imprisonment was not what made me cry.
I have been hurt this moment through
    the eye,
Into my heart. It will be death to me.
The fairness of the lady that I see
Roaming the garden yonder to and fro
Is all the cause, and I cried out my woe.
Woman or Goddess, which? I cannot say.
I guess she may be Venus—well she may!"
He fell upon his knees before the sill
And prayed: "O Venus, if it be thy will
To be transfigured in this garden thus
Before two wretched prisoners like us,
O help us to escape; O make us free!
Yet, if my fate already is shaped for me
By some eternal word, and I must pine
And die in prison, have pity on our line
And kindred, humbled under tyranny!"

    Now, as he spoke, Arcita chanced to see
This lady as she roamed there to and fro,
And, at the sight, her beauty hurt him so
That if his cousin had felt the wound before,
Arcite was hurt as much as he, or more,

And with a deep and piteous sigh he said:
"The freshness of her beauty strikes me dead,
Hers that I see, roaming in yonder place!
Unless I gain the mercy of her grace,
Unless at least I see her day by day,
I am but dead. There is no more to say."
   On hearing this young Palamon
      looked grim
And in contempt and anger answered him,
"Do you speak this in earnest or in jest?"
"No, in good earnest," said Arcite, "the best!
So help me God, I mean no jesting now."
   Then Palamon began to knit his brow:
"It's no great honour, then," he said, "to you
To prove so false, to be a traitor too
To me, that am your cousin and your brother,
Both deeply sworn and bound to one another,
Though we should die in torture for it, never
To loose the bond that only death can sever,
And when in love neither to hinder other,
Nor in what else soever, dearest brother,
But truly further me in all I do
As faithfully as I shall further you.
This was our oath and nothing can untie it,
And well I know you dare not now deny it.
I trust you with my secrets, make no doubt,
Yet you would treacherously go about
To love my lady, whom I love and serve
And ever shall, till death cut my heart's nerve.
No, false Arcite! That you shall never do!
I loved her first and told my grief to you
As to the brother and the friend that swore
To further me, as I have said before,
So you are bound in honour as a knight
To help me, should it lie within your might;
Else you are false, I say, your honour vain!"
Arcita proudly answered back again:
"You shall be judged as false," he said, "not me;
And false you are, I tell you, utterly!
I loved her as a woman before you.
What can you say? Just now you hardly knew
If she were girl or goddess from above!
Yours is a mystical, a holy love,
And mine is love as to a human being,
And so I told you at the moment, seeing
You were my cousin and sworn friend. At
      worst
What do I care? Suppose you loved her first,
Haven't you heard the old proverbial saw
'Who ever bound a lover by a law'?
Love is law unto itself. My hat!
What earthly man can have more law than
      that?

All man-made law, all positive injuction
Is broken every day without compunction
For love. A man must love, for all his wit;
There's no escape though he should die for it,
Be she a maid, a widow or a wife.
   "Yet you are little likely, all your life,
To stand in grace with her; no more shall I.
You know yourself, too well, that here we lie
Condemned to prison both of us, no doubt
Perpetually. No ransom buys us out.
We're like two dogs in battle on their own;
They fought all day but neither got the bone,
There came a kite above them, nothing loth,
And while they fought he took it from them
      both.
And so it is politics, dear brother,
Each for himself alone, there is no other.
Love if you want to; I shall love her too,
And that is all there is to say or do.
We're prisoners and must endure it, man,
And each of us must take what chance he can."
   Great was the strife for many a long spell
Between them had I but the time to tell,
But to the point. It happened that one day,
To tell it you as briefly as I may,
A certain famous Duke, Perotheus,
Friend and companion of Duke Theseus
Since they were little children, came to spend
A holiday in Athens with his friend,
Visiting him for pleasure as of yore,
For there was no one living he loved more.
His feelings were as tenderly returned;
Indeed they were so fond, as I have learned,
That when one died (so ancient authors tell)
The other went to seek him down in Hell;
But that's a tale I have no time to treat.
Now this Perotheus knew and loved Arcite
In Theban days of old for many years,
And so, at his entreaty, it appears,
Arcita was awarded his release
Without a ransom; he could go in peace
And was left free to wander where he would
On one condition, be it understood,
And the condition, to speak plain, went thus,
Agreed between Arcite and Theseus,
That if Arcite were ever to be found
Even for an hour, in any land or ground
Or country of Duke Theseus, day or night,
And he were caught, it would to both seem
      right
That he immediately should lose his head,
No other course or remedy instead.
   Off went Arcite upon the homeward trek.

Let him beware! For he has pawned his neck.
What misery it cost him to depart!
He felt the stroke of death upon his heart,
He wept, he wailed. How piteously he cried
And secretly he thought of suicide.
He said, "Alas the day that gave me birth!
Worse than my prison is the endless earth,
Now I am doomed eternally to dwell
Not in Purgatory, but in Hell.
Alas that ever I knew Perotheus!
For else I had remained with Theseus.
Fettered in prison and without relief
I still had been in bliss and not in grief.
Only to see her whom I love and serve,
Though it were never granted to deserve
Her favour, would have been enough for me.
O my dear cousin Palamon," said he,
"Yours is the victory in this adventure.
How blissfully you serve your long indenture
In prison—prison? No, in Paradise!
How happily has Fortune cast her dice
For you! You have her presence, I the loss.
For it is possible, since your paths may cross
And you're a knight, a worthy one, and able,
That by some chance—for Fortune is un-
    stable—
You may attain to your desire at last.
But I, that am an exile and outcast,
Barren of grace and in such deep despair
That neither earth nor water, fire nor air,
Nor any creature that is made of these
Can ever bring me help, or do me ease,
I must despair and die in my distress.
Farewell my life, my joy, my happiness!
    "Alas, why is it people so dispraise
God's providence or Fortune and her ways,
That oft and variously in their scheme
Includes far better things than they could
    dream?
One man desires to have abundant wealth,
Which brings about his murder or ill-health;
Another, freed from prison as he'd willed,
Comes home, his servants catch him, and he's
    killed.
Infinite are the harms that come this way;
We little know the things for which we pray.
Our ways are drunkard ways—drunk as a
    mouse;
A drunkard knows quite well he has a house,
But how to get there puts him in a dither,
And for a drunk the way is slip and slither.
Such is our world indeed, and such are we.
How eagerly we seek felicity,

Yet are so often wrong in what we try!
Yes, we can all say that, and so can I,
In whom the foolish notion had arisen
That if I only could escape from prison
I should be well, in pure beatitude,
Whereas I am an exile from my good,
For since I may not see you, Emily,
I am but dead and there's no remedy."
    Now, on the other hand, poor Palamon,
When it was told him that Arcite had gone,
Fell in such grief, the tower where he was kept
Resounded to his yowling as he wept.
The very fetters on his mighty shins
Shine with his bitter tears as he begins,
"Alas, Arcite, dear cousin! In our dispute
And rivalry God knows you have the fruit.
I see you now in Thebes, our native city,
As free as air, with never a thought of pity
For me! You, an astute, determined man
Can soon assemble all our folk and clan
For war on Athens, make a sharp advance,
And by some treaty or perhaps by chance
She may become your lady and your wife
For whom, needs must, I here shall lose my
    life.
For, in the way of possibility,
As you're a prisoner no more, but free,
A Prince, you have the advantage to engage
In your affair. I perish in a cage,
For I must weep and suffer while I live
In all the anguish that a cell can give
And all the torment of my love, O care
That doubles all my suffering and despair."
    With that he felt the fire of jealousy start,
Flame in his breast and catch him by the heart
So madly that he seemed to fade and fail,
Cold as dead ashes, or as box-wood pale.
He cried, "O cruel Gods, whose government
Binds all the world to your eternal bent,
And writes upon an adamantine table
All that your conclave has decreed as stable,
What more is man to you than to behold
A flock of sheep that cower in the fold?
For men are slain as much as other cattle,
Arrested, thrust in prison, killed in battle,
In sickness often and mischance, and fall,
Alas, too often, for no guilt at all.
Where is right rule in your foreknowl-
    edge, when
Such torments fall on innocent, helpless men?
Yet there is more, for added to my load,
I am to pay the duties that are owed
To God, for Him I am to curb my will

In all the lusts that cattle may fulfil.
For when a beast is dead, he feels no pain,
But after death a man must weep again
That living has endured uncounted woe;
I have no doubt that it may well be so.
I leave the answer for divines to tell,
But that there's pain on earth I know too well.

"I have seen many a serpent, many a thief
Bring down the innocent heart to grief,
Yet be at large and take what turn they will.
But I lie languishing in prison still.
Juno and Saturn in their jealous rage
Have almost quelled our Theban lineage;
Thebes stands in waste, her walls are broken
    wide.
And Venus slays me on the other side
With jealous fears of what Arcite is doing."

Now I will turn a little from pursuing
Palamon's thoughts, and leave him in his cell,
For I have something of Arcite to tell.

The summer passes, and long winter nights
Double the miseries and appetites
Of lover in jail and lover free as air.
I cannot tell you which had most to bear.
To put it shortly, Palamon the pale
Lies there condemned to a perpetual jail,
Chained up in fetters till his dying breath;
Arcita is exiled on pain of death
For ever from the long-desired shore
Where lives the lady he will see no more.

You lovers, here's a question I would offer,
Arcite or Palamon, which had most to suffer?
The one can see his lady day by day,
But he must dwell in prison, locked away.
The other's free, the world lies all before,
But never shall he see his lady more.
Judge as you please between them, you
    that can,
For I'll tell on my tale as I began.

PART II

Now when Arcita got to Thebes again
Daylong he languished, crying out in pain
"Alas!" for never could he hope to see
His lady more. To sum his misery,
There never was a man so woe-begone,
Nor is, nor shall be while the world goes on.
Meat, drink and sleep—he lay of all bereft,
Thin as a shaft, as dry, with nothing left.
His eyes were hollow, grisly to behold,
Fallow his face, like ashes pale and cold,
And he went solitary and alone,
Wailing away the night and making moan;

And if the sound of music touched his ears
He wept, unable to refrain his tears.
So feeble were his spirits and so low,
And changed so much, one could not
    even know
Him by his voice; one heard and was in doubt.
And so for all the world he went about
Not merely like a lover on the rack
Of Eros, but more like a maniac
In melancholy madness, under strain
Of fantasy—those cells that front the brain.
Briefly, his love had turned him upside-down
In looks and disposition, toe to crown,
This poor distracted lover, Prince Arcite.

But I shall take all day if I repeat
All that he suffered for the first two years,
In cruel torment and in painful tears
At Thebes, in his home-country, as I said.
Now as he lay one night asleep in bed
The winged god Mercury, he thought,
    came near
And stood before him, bidding him have good
    cheer.
His sleep-imbuing wand he held in air,
He wore a hat upon his golden hair,
Arrayed (Arcita noticed) in the guise
He wore when closing up the hundred eyes
Of Argus, and he said, "You are to go
To Athens. There shall be an end to woe."
He spoke; Arcita started and woke up.
"Truly, however bitter be my cup,
To Athens I will go at once!" he said,
"Nor will I change my purpose for the dread
Of death, for I will see her. I can die
Gladly enough, if she be standing by."

He rose and snatched a mirror from its place
And saw what change had come upon his face,
The colour gone, the features redesigned,
And instantly it came into his mind
That being so disfigured and so wan
From the long sickness he had undergone,
He might, if he assumed a humble tone,
Live out his life in Athens unbeknown
And see his lady almost every day.
So, on the spot, he doffed his lord's array,
And dressed as a poor labourer seeking hire.
Then all alone, except for a young squire,
Who knew the secret of his misery
And was disguised as wretchedly as he,
He went to Athens by the shortest way
And came to Court. And on the following day
Arcita proferred at the gate for hire
To do what drudgery they might require.

And briefly (there is little to explain)
He fell in service with a chamberlain
Who had his dwelling there with Emily.
The man was cunning and was quick to see
What work the servants did and which were
    good.
Arcite could carry water or hew wood,
For he was young and powerfully grown,
A tall young fellow too, and big of bone,
Fit to do any work that was ordained.
    Thus, for a year or two, Arcite remained
With Emily the bright, her page-of-state,
And gave it out his name was Philostrate.
And half so well beloved a man as he
There never was at Court, of his degree.
He was so much a gentleman by breed
He grew quite famous through the Court in-
    deed,
And it would be a charitable notion
(They said) if Theseus offered him promotion
And put him to a service less despised
In which his virtues might be exercised.
Thus in a little while his fame had sprung
Both for goods deeds and for a courteous
    tongue,
And Theseus took him and advanced him
    higher,
Made him his personal and chamber-squire,
And gave him money to maintain his station.
There came, moreover, men of his own nation
Secretly, year by year, and brought his dues.
He spent them cunningly, these revenues,
But honestly; none wondered at his wealth.
Three years went by in happiness and health;
He bore himself so well in peace and war
That there was no one Theseus valued more.
I leave him there in bliss, though bliss is
    brittle,
And turn to speak of Palamon a little.
    In darkness horrible and prison tears
Poor Palamon has sat for seven years,
Pining away in sorrow and distress.
Who feels a two-fold grief and heaviness
But Palamon, whom love oppresses so
That he has lost his very wits for woe?
Added to which, he must lie prisoner there
Perpetually, not only for a year.
    Who could make rhymes in English fit
        to vie
With martyrdom like that? Indeed, not I.
Let me pass lightly over it and say
It happened in the seventh year, in May,
The third of May (my ancient sources give

This detail in their fuller narrative),
Whether by accident or destiny,
For as events are shaped they have to be,
Soon after midnight, ere the sun had risen,
Helped by a friend, Palamon broke from
    prison
And fled the town as fast as he could go.
A drink had proved his jailer's overthrow,
A kind of honeyed claret he had fixed
With Theban opium and narcotics mixed.
The jailer slept all night; had he been shaken
He would have been impossible to waken.
So off runs Palamon as best he may.
The night was short and it was nearly day,
So it was necessary he should hide.
Into a grove that flanked the city's side
Palamon stalked with terror-stricken feet.
Here was, in his opinion, a retreat
In which he could conceal himself all day
And whence at nightfall he could make
    his way
On towards Thebes and rally at his back
A host of friends all eager to attack
Duke Theseus. He would either lose his life
Or conquer and win Emily to wife.
That was his whole intention, fair and plain.
    I turn my story to Arcite again.
He little knew how close he was to care
Till Fortune brought him back into the snare.
    The busy lark, the messenger of day,
Sings salutation to the morning grey,
And fiery Phoebus rising up so bright
Sets all the Orient laughing with the light,
And with his streams he dries the dewy
    sheaves
And silver droplets hanging on the leaves.
And now Arcita, at the royal court,
Principal squire to Theseus, seeking sport
Has risen from bed and greets the merry day.
Thinking to do observances to May,
And musing on the point of his desires
He rode a courser full of flickering fires
Into the fields for pleasure and in play
A mile or two from where the palace lay,
And to the very grove you heard me mention
He chanced to hold his course, with the in-
    tention
To make himself a garland. There he weaves
A hawthorn-spray and honeysuckle leaves
And sings aloud against the sunny sheen,
"O Month of May, with all thy flowers and green,
Welcome be thou, O fairest, freshest May,
Give me thy green, in hope of happy day!"

Quickly dismounting from his horse, he
    started
To thrust his way into the grove, light-
    hearted,
And roamed along the pathway, on and on,
Until he came by chance where Palamon
Crouched in a bush, scarce daring to draw
    breath
Lest he be seen, in deadly fear of death.
He little knew it was Arcite he heard,
It would have seemed incredible, absurd;
Yet there's a saying, known these many years:
Fields have their eyes, and forests have their ears.
It's well to be upon one's guard, I mean,
Since all day long we meet the unforeseen.
And little knew Arcite that there, beside him,
Palamon lay, with but a bush to hide him,
So close to him, and hearing all he said
But keeping still and silent as the dead.

    Now when at last Arcite had roamed his fill
And sung his roundel with a lusty will
He felt of change of humour, for the nonce,
And fell into a study all at once,
As do these lovers in their quaint desires,
Now on the spray, now down among the
    briars,
Now up, now down, like buckets in a well,
Just as upon a Friday, truth to tell,
It shines one moment, and the next rains fast;
For thus can whimsical Venus overcast
The spirits of her folk, just as her day,
Friday is changeable, and so too are they,
Seldom is Friday like the rest of the week.
And, having sung, Arcite began to speak,
And sat him down, unutterably forlorn.
"Alas!" he said, "the day that I was born!
How long, O Juno, in thy cruelty,
Wilt thou make war and bring to misery
The city of Thebes, and those that played the
    lion,
The royal blood of Cadmus and Amphion!
Cadmus, the first of men to win renown
By building Thebes, or first in laying down
Her strong foundations, first to be crowned
    her king;
And I that share his lineage, I that spring
By right descent out of the royal stock,
Have fallen captive and am made a mock,
Slave to my mortal enemy, no higher
Than a contemptible, a menial squire!
Yet Juno does me even greater shame;
I dare no more acknowledge my own name.
Time was Arcita was my name by right;

Now I'm called Philostrate, not worth a mite!
Alas, fell Mars! Ah, Juno, stern of face,
You have undone our lineage and our race
Save for myself and Palamon, who dwells
In martyrdom, poor wretch, in Theseus' cells.
On top of this, to slay me utterly,
The fiery dart of love so burningly
Thrusts through my faithful heart with deadly
    hurt!
My death was shaped for me before my shirt.
You kill me with your eyes, my Emily,
You are the cause that brings my death on me!
All the remainder of my cares and needs
I'd rate no higher than a mound of weeds
Could I but please or earn a grateful glance!"
    And on the word he fell into a trance
A long, long time, then woke and moved
    apart.
    Palamon felt a cleaving in his heart
As of a cold sword suddenly gliding through.
He quaked with anger; hiding would not do
Now that he'd listened to Arcita's tale,
And with a madman's face, extinct and pale,
He started up out of his bushy thicket
And cried, "Arcita! Traitor! False and wicked,
Now you are caught that love my lady so,
For whom I suffer all this pain and woe,
And of my blood—sworn friend—for so we
    swore
As I have told you many times before,
And you have cheated Theseus with this
    game,
False as you are, of a pretended name!
Let it be death for you or death for me.
You shall not love my lady Emily.
I, no one else, will love her! Look and know
That I am Palamon your mortal foe.
And though I have no weapon in this place,
Having escaped from prison by God's grace,
I doubt it not you shall be slain by me
Or else yield up the love of Emily.
You shan't escape me, therefore choose your
    part!"
    Arcite, however, full of scorn at heart,
Knowing his face and hearing what he said,
Fierce as a lion drew his sword instead
And answered him, "By God that sits above,
Were you not sick, and lunatic for love,
And weaponless moreover in this place,
You never should so much as take a pace
Beyond this grove, but perish at my hand.
And I denounce all covenants that stand
Or are alleged, as between you and me.

Fool that you are, remember love is free
And I will love her! I defy your might.
Yet, as you are an honourable knight
Willing by battle to decide your claim,
Tomorrow, by the honour of my name
I will not fail you, nor will make it known
To anyone. To-morrow, here, alone
You'll find me as a knight, and on my oath
I shall bring arms and harness for us both;
And you shall have the right of choosing first,
Taking the best and leaving me the worst.
I'll bring you meat and drink, let that be said,
Enough for you, and clothes to make
    your bed.
As for my lady, should you chance to win
And kill me in this thicket we are in,
Then you can have your lady, as for me."
And Palamon gave answer, "I agree."
And thus they parted at the coppice-edge
Until the morning. Each had given pledge.
    O Cupid, Cupid, lost to charity!
O realm that brooks no fellow-king in thee!
Well is it said that neither love nor power
Admit a rival, even for an hour.
Arcite and Palamon had found that out.
    So back to town Arcite turned about,
And the next morning, ere the day was light,
He filched two suits of armour by a sleight,
Fully sufficient for the work in hand,
The battle in the fields, that they had planned.
Alone as at his birth Arcita rode
And carried all the armour in a load.
There in the grove where time and place
    were set
This Palamon and this Arcite are met.
    Then slowly changed the colour in
        each face
Just as when hunters in the realm of Thrace
That standing in the gap will poise a spear
And wait for bear or lion to appear,
Then hear him coming, breaking through the
    branches,
And hear the swish of leaves upon his
    haunches,
And think, "Here comes my mortal enemy!
It's either death for him or death for me.
For either I must slay him at this gap
Or he slay me, if I should have mishap."
Just so these knights changed colour when
    they met,
Knowing each other and the purpose set.
    There was no salutation, no "Good day,"
But without word or prelude straight away
Each of them gave his help to arm the other

As friendly as a brother with his brother;
And after that with spears of sharpened
    strength
They fought each other at amazing length.
You would have thought, seeing Palamon en-
    gage,
He was a lion fighting-mad with rage,
Arcite a cruel tiger, as they beat
And smote each other, or as boars that meet
And froth as white as foam upon the flood.
They fought till they were ankle-deep in
    blood.
And in this rage I leave them fighting thus
And turn once more to speak of Theseus.
    Now Destiny, that Minister-General
Who executes on earth and over all
What God, from everlasting, has foreseen,
Is of such strength, that though the world
    had been
Sure of the contrary, by Yea and Nay,
That thing will happen on a certain day,
Though never again within a thousand years.
And certainly our appetites and fears,
Whether in war or peace, in hate or love,
Are governed by a providence above.
    Thus must explain why mighty Theseus
        found
A sudden wish to hunt with horse and hound
Especially the hart in early May.
About his bed there never dawned a day
But he was up and ready dressed to ride
With horn and hound and hunter at his side.
Hunting to him was such a keen delight
It was his ruling joy and appetite
To be a stag's destroyer, for the stars
Ruled he should serve Diana after Mars.
    Clear was the day, as I have told ere this,
And Theseus, bathed in happiness and bliss,
With fair Hippolyta, his lovely Queen,
And Emily, who was arrayed in green,
Rode out to hunt; it was a royal band.
And to the coppice lying near at hand
In which a hart—or so they told him—lay,
He led his gathering by the shortest way.
And pressing on towards a glade in sight
Down which the hart most often took to
    flight
Over a brook and off and out of view,
The Duke had hopes to try a course or two
With certain hounds that he had singled out;
And when he reached the glade he looked
    about.
Glancing towards the sun he thereupon
Beheld Arcita fighting Palamon.

They fought like boars in bravery. There go
The shining swords in circle, to and fro,
So hideously that with their lightest stroke
It seemed as if they would have felled an oak.
What they could be he did not know, of
      course,
But he clapped spur at once into his horse
And, at a bound, he parted blow from blow,
And pulling out his sword he shouted, "Ho!
No more on pain of death! Upon your head!
By mighty Mars, he is as good as dead
That dares to strike a blow in front of me!
Tell me, what sort of fellows may you be
That have the impudence to combat here
Without a judge or other overseer,
Yet as if jousting at a royal tilt?"

Palamon answered quickly and in guilt,
"O Sir, what need of further word or breath?
Both of us have deserved to die the death,
Two wretched men, your captives, met in
      strife,
And each of them encumbered with his life.
If to judge righteously has been your fashion,
Show neither of us mercy nor compassion,
And kill me first for holy charity!
But kill my fellow too, the same as me.
Or kill him first, for little though you know,
This is Arcita and your mortal foe,
Banished by you on forfeit of his head,
For which alone he merits to be dead.
This is the man that waited at your gate
And told you that his name was Philostrate.
This is the man that mocked you many a year,
And you have made him chief equerry here.
This is the man who dares love Emily.
Now, since my day of death has come to me,
I will make full confession and go on
To say I am that woeful Palamon
That broke out of your jail feloniously.
And it is I, your mortal enemy,
That am in love with Emily the Bright
And glad to die this moment in her sight.
And so I ask for judgement and for death;
But slay my fellow in the self-same breath,
Since we have both deserved that we be slain!"

And noble Theseus answered back again,
"This is a short conclusion. It shall stand.
Your own confession damns you out of hand.
I shall record your sentence as it stood;
There needs no torturing to make it good.
Death you shall have, by mighty Mars the
      Red!"

On hearing this, the Queen began to shed
Her womanly tears, and so did Emily

And all the ladies in the company.
It seemed so very piteous to them all
That ever such misfortune should befall
For they were noblemen of great estate
And love the only cause of their debate.
They saw their bloody gashes gaping wide
And, from the greatest to the least, they cried,
"Have mercy, Lord, upon us women all!"
Down on their knees they then began to fall,
Ready to kiss his feet as there he stood.

Abated in the end his angry mood;
Pity runs swiftly in a noble heart.
Though he had quaked with anger at the start
He had reflected, having time to pause,
Upon their trespass and upon its cause,
And though his anger at their guilt was loth
To pardon either, reason pardoned both.
For thus he argued: almost any man
Will help himself to love, if so he can,
And anyone will try to break from prison;
And then compassion in his heart had risen
Seeing these ladies weeping there together,
And in his noble heart he wondered
      whether
He should not show his clemency, and "Fie,"
He thought, "on lords who show no
      mercy! Why,
To be a lion both in word and deed
To a penitent in fear, is not to heed
His change of heart, and equal him with one
Proudly persisting in an evil done.
A lord will lack discretion among his graces
Who does not make distinction in such cases,
But weighs humility and pride as one."
And, to be brief, his anger being done,
His eyes began to sparkle and uncloud
And having taken thought he said aloud:
"The God of Love! Ah, *Benedicite!*
How mighty and how great a lord is he!
No obstacles for him make any odds;
His miracles proclaim his power a God's.
Cupid can make of every heart and soul
Just what he pleases, such is his control.
Look at Arcita here and Palamon!
Both had escaped scot-free and could
      have gone
To Thebes and lived there royally; they know
That I have ever been their mortal foe;
Their lives are mine, they can make no de-
      fence;
Yet Cupid in the teeth of common sense
Has brought them here to die in melancholy!
Consider, is it not the height of folly?
What is so foolish as a man in love?

Look at them both! By God that sits above
See how they bleed! Are they not well ar-
    rayed?
Thus has their lord, the God of Love, repaid
Their services; these are his fees and wages!
And yet, in spite of that, they pose as sages,
These devotees of Love, as I recall.
But still this is the finest stroke of all,
That she, the cause of all these jolly pranks,
Has no more reason to return them thanks
Than I, and knows no more of this affair,
By God, than does a cuckoo or a hare!
Well, well, try anything once, come hot,
    come cold!
If we're not foolish young, we're foolish old.
I long have known myself what Love can do,
For, in my time, I was a lover too.
And therefore, knowing something of love's
    pain,
How violently it puts a man to strain,
As one so often caught in the same snare
I readily forgive the whole affair,
Both at the Queen's request, that on her knees
Petitions, and my sister Emily's.
But you shall swear to me and give your hands
Upon it never to attack my lands,
Or levy war on me by night or day,
But be my friends in everything you may.
I pardon you your fault. You are forgiven."
    They swore as he had asked, and, having
        striven
To gain his patronage and further grace,
Were satisfied, and Theseus summed the case:
    "So far as riches go, and nobleness,
Were she a queen in question, or princess,
You would be worthy when the moment
    came,
Either of you, to marry. All the same,
Speaking as for my sister Emily,
The cause of all your strife and jealousy,
You are aware yourselves that she can never
Wed both at once, though you should fight
    for ever.
And one of you, come joy to him or grief,
Must go pipe tunes upon an ivy-leaf;
That is to say she cannot have you both,
However jealous you may be, or loth.
And so, to put the matter in good order,
Let Destiny herself be your Awarder,
And shape your fortune. Listen to the close,
For here is the solution I propose.
    "My will is this, to make a flat conclusion
And end all counterpleading and confusion,

(And you will please to take it for the best)
That each shall take his freedom, east or
    west,
And without ransom or constraint of war;
And, a year later, neither less nor more,
Each shall return, bringing a hundred knights,
Armed for the lists and everything to rights,
Ready by battle to decide his claim
To Emily. To this I give my name,
My faith and honour, as I am a knight.
Whichever of you proves of greater might,
Or, more precisely, whether you or he,
Backed by the hundred knights allowed
    by me,
Can drive his foe to stake, or take his life,
To him I shall give Emily to wife,
To whom kind Fortune gives so fair a grace.
I'll build the lists upon this very place,
And God in wisdom deal my soul its due
As I shall prove an even judge and true.
There is no other way, let that be plain;
One of you must be taken or else slain.
And if this seems to you to be well said,
Think yourselves lucky, sirs, and nod your
    head.
That's the conclusion I've decided on."
    Who looks delighted now but Palamon?
And who springs up rejoicing but Arcite?
And who could tell, what poetry repeat
The joy of all those present in the place
That Theseus had vouchsafed so fair a grace?
Down on their knees went everyone in sight
Returning thanks with all their heart and
    might,
Especially the Thebans, time on time.
Thus in good hope, with beating heart
    a-climb,
Each took his leave, and they began to ride
To Thebes and to her ancient walls and wide.

PART III

I judge it would be held for negligence
If I forgot to tell of the dispense
Of money by the Duke who set about
To make the lists a royal show throughout.
A theatre more noble in its plan
I dare well say was never seen by man.
It had a circuit of a mile about,
Well walled with stone; there was a ditch
    without.
Shaped like a circle there it stood complete
In tier on tier, the height of sixty feet,
So that a man set in a given row

Did not obstruct his neighbour from below.
    Eastward there stood a gate of marble
        white,
And westward such another rose to sight;
Briefly, there never was upon the face
Of earth so much within so small a space.
No craftsmen in the land that had the trick
Of pure geometry, arithmetic,
Portraiture, carving and erecting stages,
But Theseus found him and supplied his
    wages
To build this theatre and carve devices.
And, to observe due rites and sacrifices,
Eastward he built upon the gate, above,
An oratory to the Queen of Love,
To Venus and her worship, and he dressed
An altar there; and like it, to the west,
In reverence to Mars he built a second;
The cost in gold was hardly to be reckoned.
Yet, northward, in a turret on the wall
He built a third, an oratory tall
And rich, of whitest alabaster, set
Within crimson coral, to discharge the debt
Of worship to Diana of Chastity.
And it was thus that Theseus built these three
Temples in great magnificence of style.
    But yet I have forgotten all this while
To tell you of the portraits that there were,
The shapes, the carvings and the figures there
To grace these temples high above the green.
    First, in the temple of Venus, you had seen
Wrought on the wall, and piteous to be-
    hold,
The broken sleeps and sighings manifold,
The sacred tears and the lamenting songs
And every fiery passion that belongs
To those that suffer love, the long-endured,
Their taken oaths, their covenants assured,
Pleasure and Hope, Desire, Foolhardiness,
Beauty and Youth, Lasciviousness, Largesse,
Philtres and Force, Falsehood and Flattery,
Extravagance, Intrigue and Jealousy
Gold-garlanded, with many a yellow twist,
That had a cuckoo sitting on her wrist.
Stringed instruments, and carols, feasts and
    dances,
Joy and display, and all the circumstances
Of love, as I have told you and shall tell,
Were in due order painted there as well,
And more than I can mention or recount.
Truly the whole of Citherea's Mount,
Where Venus has her dwelling above all
Her other playgrounds, figured on the wall

With all her garden in its joyful dress.
Nor was forgotten her porter, Idleness,
Nor yet Narcissus, beauty's paragon
In times gone by, nor doting Solomon,
Nor the unmastered strength of Hercules.
Medea and her enchantments next to these,
And Circe's too, and Turnus fierce and brave,
And rich King Croesus, captive and a slave,
That men might see that neither wit nor
    wealth,
Beauty or cunning, bravery or health
Can challenge Venus or advance their worth
Against that goddess who controls the earth.
And all these people captured in her noose
Cried out, "Alas!" but it was little use.
Suffice these few examples, but the score
Could well be reckoned many thousands
    more.
    Her statue, glorious in majesty,
Stood naked, floating on a vasty sea,
And from the navel down there were a mass
Of green and glittering waves as bright as
    glass.
In her right hand a cithern carried she
And on her head, most beautiful to see,
A garland of fresh roses, while above
There circles round her many a flickering
    dove.
    Cupid her son was standing to behold her
Fronting her statue, winged on either
    shoulder,
And he was blind, as it is often seen;
He bore a bow with arrows bright and keen.
    Why should I not go on tell you all
The portraiture depicted on the wall
Within the Temple of Mighty Mars the Red?
The walls were painted round and overhead
Like the recesses of that grisly place
Known as the Temple of Great Mars in
    Thrace,
That frosty region under chilling stars
Where stands the sovereign mansion of King
    Mars.
    First on the walls a forest with no plan
Inhabited by neither beast nor man
Was painted—tree-trunks, knotted, gnarled
    and old,
Jagged and barren, hideous to behold,
Through which there ran a rumble and a
    soughing
As though a storm should break the branches
    bowing
Before it. Downwards from a hill there went

A slope; the Temple of Armipotent
Mars was erected there in steel, and burnished.
The Gateway, narrow and forbidding, fur-
    nished
A ghastly sight, and such a rushing quake
Raged from within, the portals seemed to
    shake.
In at the doors a northern glimmer shone
Onto the walls, for windows there were none;
One scarce discerned a light, it was so scant.
The doors were of eternal adamant,
And vertically clenched, and clenched across
For greater strength with many an iron boss,
And every pillar to support the shrine
Weighed a full ton of iron bright and fine.
    And there I saw the dark imaginings
Of felony, the stratagems of kings,
And cruel wrath that glowed an ember-red,
The pick-purse and the image of pale Dread,
The smiler with the knife beneath his cloak,
The out-houses that burnt with blackened
    smoke;
Treason was there, a murder on a bed,
And open war, with wounds that gaped and
    bled;
Dispute, with bloody knife and snarling
    threat;
A screaming made the place more dread-
    ful yet.
The slayer of himself, I saw him there
With all his heart's blood matted in his hair;
The driven nail that made the forehead crack,
Cold Death, with gaping mouth, upon its
    back.
    And in the middle of the shrine Mischance
Stood comfortless with sorry countenance.
There I saw madness cackling his distress,
Armed insurrection, outcry, fierce excess,
The carrion in the undergrowth, slit-throated,
And thousands violently slain. I noted
The raping tyrant with his prey o'ertaken,
The levelled city, gutted and forsaken,
The ships on fire dancingly entangled,
The luckless hunter that wild bears had stran-
    gled,
The sow, munching the baby in the cradle,
The scalded cook, in spite of his long ladle—
Nothing forgotten of the unhappy art
Of Mars: the carter crushed beneath his cart,
Flung to the earth and pinned beneath the
    wheel;
Those also on whom Mars has set his seal,
The barber and the butcher and the smith

Who forges things a man may murder with.
And high above, depicted in a tower,
Sat Conquest, robed in majesty and power,
Under a sword that swung above his head,
Sharp-edged and hanging by a subtle thread.
    And Caesar's slaughter stood in effigy
And that of Nero and Mark Antony;
Though to be sure they were as yet unborn,
Their deaths were there prefigured to adorn
This Temple with the menaces of Mars,
As is depicted also in the stars
Who shall be murdered, who shall die for
    love;
Such were the portraits on the walls above.
Let these examples from the past hold good,
For all I cannot reckon, though I would.
    The statue of Mars was in a cart, and clad
In armour, grim and staring, like the mad,
Above his head there shone with blazing looks
Two starry figures, named in ancient books,
Puella one, the other Rubeus.
The God of Battles was encompassed thus:
There stood a wolf before him at his feet,
His eyes glowed red, he had a man to eat.
Subtle the pencil was that told this story
Picturing Mars in terror and in glory.
    To the temple of Diana, now, the Chaste,
I briefly turn, for I will use what haste
I can in trying to describe it all.
Here there were many paintings on the wall
Of hunting and of shamefast chastity.
There I perceived the sad Callisto, she
Whom in her rage Diana did not spare
But changed her from a woman to a bear,
Then to a star, and she was painted so
(She is the lode-star, that is all I know;
Her son, too, is a star, as one can see).
There I saw Dana, turned into a tree[1]
(No, not Diana, she was not the same,
But Penneus' daughter, Dana was her name).
I saw Actaeon turned into a stag;
This was Diana's vengeance, lest he brag
Of having seen her naked. There they
    show him
Caught and devoured—his own hounds did
    not know him.
Close by there was a painting furthermore
Of Atalanta hunting a wild boar,
And Meleager; there were others too
Diana chose to harry and undo,
And many other wonders on the wall
Were painted, that I need not now recall.
    High on a stag the Goddess held her seat,

And there were little hounds about her feet;
Below her feet there was a sickle moon,
Waxing it seemed, but would be waning soon.
Her statue bore a mantle of bright green,
Her hand a bow with arrows cased and keen;
Her eyes were lowered, gazing as she rode
Down to where Pluto has his dark abode.
A woman in her travail lay before her,
Her child unborn; she ceased not to im-
    plore her
To be delivered and with piteous call
Cried, "Help, Lucina, thou the best of all!"
It was a lively painting, every shade
Had cost the painter many a florin paid.
So now the lists were made, and Theseus
Who, at huge cost, had bidden them produce
These temples in a theatre so stately,
Saw it was finished, and it pleased him greatly.
No more of Theseus now; I must pass on
To speak of Arcite and of Palamon.

The day approached for trial of their rights
When each should bring with him a hundred
    knights
To settle all by battle, as I said;
So, back to Athens each of them had led
His hundred knights, all helmeted and spurred
And armed for war. They meant to keep their
    word.
And it was said indeed by many a man
That never since the day the world began
In all God's earth, wide seas and reach of land,
Had so few men made such a noble band
As in respect of knighthood and degree.
Everyone with a taste for chivalry
And keen (you bet!) to win a glorious name
Had begged to be allowed to join the game.
Lucky the man to whom they gave the word!
And if, tomorrow, such a thing occurred
You know quite well that every lusty knight
Who loved the ladies and had strength to
    fight,
Whether in England here, or anywhere,
Would wish—you cannot doubt it—to be
    there.
Fight for a lady? *Benedicite!*
That would be something for a man to see.

And that was just the case with Palamon.
With him there rode his comrades—many
    a one;
Some were in coat of mail and others wore
A breastplate and a tunic, little more.
Some carried heavy plating, front and back,
And some a Prussian shield to ward attack;

Some cased their legs in armour, thigh to heel,
Some bore an axe and some a mace of steel
—There's never a new fashion but it's old—
And so they armed themselves as I have told.
Each man according to his own opinion.

You might have seen arrive from his do-
    minion
Mighty Lycurgus, famous King of Thrace;
Black was his beard and manly was his face.
To see the circling eye-balls of the fellow
Set in his head and glowing red and yellow!
And like a gryphon he would stare and rouse
The shaggy hair upon his beetling brows.
Huge were his limbs, his muscles hard and
    strong,
His back was broad, his bulging arms were
    long.
True to his country's custom from of old
He towered in a chariot of gold
And four white bulls were harnessed in the
    traces.
Over his armour, which in many places
Was studded with bright nails of yellow gold,
He wore a coal-black bear-skin, fold on fold,
Instead of surcoat, and behind his back
His fell of hair was combed and shone as black
As raven's feather, and a golden wreath,
Thick as your arm, weighted the head beneath.
It was immensely heavy, and was bright
With many precious stones of fiery light,
With finest rubies and with diamonds.
About his chariot, white enormous hounds,
Twenty and more, each larger than a steer,
And trained to hunt the lion and the deer,
Went following him. Their muzzles were fast
    bound;
Their collars were of gold with rings set
    round.
He had a hundred nobles in his rout
Armed to the teeth; their hearts were stern and
    stout.

And with Arcita, so the poets sing,
Went great Emetrius the Indian king
On a bay steed whose trappings were of steel
Covered in cloth of gold from haunch to heel
Fretted with diaper. Like Mars to see,
His surcoat was in cloth of Tartary,
Studded with great white pearls; beneath
    its fold
A saddle of new-beaten, burnished, gold.
He had a mantle hanging from his shoulders,
Which, crammed with rubies, dazzled all be-
    holders.

His hair was crisped in ringlets, as if spun
Of yellow gold, and glittered like the sun.
Aquiline nose and eyes with lemon light
And rounded lips he had, his colour bright,
With a few freckles sprinkled here and there,
Some yellow and some black. He bore an air
As of a lion when he cast a glance.
He was some twenty-five years old, to chance
A guess at it; a healthy beard was springing.
His voice resounded like a trumpet ringing.
He had a wreath of laurel on his head
For he was freshly, greenly garlanded.
And on his hand he bore for his delight
An eagle; it was tame and lily-white.
He had a hundred lords beside him there,
In all their armour (though their heads were
        bare)
And sumptuously decked with furnishings.
For take my word for it that dukes and kings
Were gathered in this noble company
For love and for the spread of chivalry.
Many a lion tame and spotted pard
Gambolled about this king of stern regard.
And in this manner in their fine adorning
These lords came to the city on Sunday
        morning,
Round about nine o'clock, and lighted down.

    The noble Theseus led them through
        his town
(So it became him as a duke and knight),
And housed them each according to his right.
He feasted them and took great pains to please,
To honour and to set them all at ease,
And to this day it's said no human wit
However lofty could have bettered it.

    What minstrelsy, what service at the feast,
What gifts bestowed on greatest as on least,
How richly decked the palace, what the place
Ordained for first and last upon the dais,
What ladies loveliest in the dancing throng,
And which most exquisite in dance and song
And which to speak most feelingly of love,
Or what the falcons that were perched above,
And what the hounds that couched upon the
        floor—
Of all such questions I shall say no more
Than the result of it; I will not tease you,
Here comes the point, so listen if it please you

    That Sunday night ere day began to spring
There was a lark which Palamon heard sing
(although two hours before the day came on,
Yet the lark sang, and so did Palamon).
With holy heart and in a lofty mood

He rose on pilgrimage and he pursued
His path to Citherea, the benign
And blissful Venus, to her honoured shrine.
And in her hour, among the early mists,
He stepped towards her Temple in the lists
And down he knelt in humbleness and fear
With aching heart, and said as you shall hear:

    "Fairest of Fair, O Venus, Lady mine,
Consort of Vulcan, Daughter of Jove Divine,
Giver of joy upon the heights above
The Mount of Citherea, by that love
Thou gavest to Adonis, heal my smart
And take my humble prayer into thy heart.
Alas! I have no language that can tell
The ravages and torments of my hell,
Which heart is all unable to convey,
And I am so confused I cannot say
More than: 'O Lady bright, that art aware
Of all my thought and seest my despair,
Consider this, have pity on my pain
As I shall ever struggle to maintain
Thy service, in so far as it shall be
Within my power to combat chastity.'
This is my vow, if only thou wilt help!
I am not one of those who brag and yelp
Of victory, nor ask for it tomorrow,
Or for renown; I neither beg nor borrow
Vainglorious praise, nor do I make profession
Of prowess—but would fully have possession
Of Emily, and die thy worshipper.
Choose Thou the means for this, administer
The ways, I care not how, whether it be
By my defeat of them, or theirs of me,
So that I have my lady in my arms.
Though Mars be god of battles and alarms
Thy power is so great in Heaven above
That if thou please I well may have my love.
And I will worship at thy shrine for ever;
Ride where I may, to thee my whole en-
        deavour
Shall be in sacrifice and kindling fires
Upon thy altars. Yet if my desires,
Sweet lady, cannot please thee, end my sorrow
With death upon Arcita's spear to-morrow.
I shall not care when I have lost my life
Though he should win my Emily to wife.
This is the sum and purpose of my prayer,
Give me my love, sweet Goddess ever fair!"

    When Palamon had done his orison
He then did sacrifice with woe-begone
Devotion and with ceremonial rite
More than I now have leisure to recite.
And in the end the statue of Venus shook

And made a sign; and by that sign he took
His prayer had been accepted on that day,
For though the sign had hinted a delay
He knew for certain that his boon was
    granted,
And home he went at once, his soul en-
    chanted.
    In the third hour after Palamon
Had sought out Venus for his orison,
Up rose the sun, and up rose Emily
And hastened to Diana's sanctuary,
Taking such maidens as she might require,
And they were ready furnished with the fire,
The incense and the vestments and a throng
Of other necessaries that belong
To sacrifices, horns of brimming mead,
As was the custom, all that they could need.
The Temple smoked and the adornments
    there
Glittered in beauty. Emily the fair
Joyfully washed her body in a well,
But how she did her rite I dare not tell
Save in a general way, though I for one
Think that to hear the detail would be fun.
If one means well why bother to feel queasy?
It's good for people to be free and easy.
Her shining hair untressed upon her cloak
They combed and set a crown of cerrial oak
Green on her golden head with fitting grace.
Two fires she kindled in the proper place
And did her rites, as he will find who looks
In Statius' *Book of Thebes* and other books,
And when the fires were kindled she
    drew near
With piteous heart, and prayed as you shall
    hear:
    "O Goddess Chaste of all the woodlands
    green,
That seest earth and heaven and sea, O Queen
Of Pluto's kingdom, dark and deep below,
Goddess of virgins that from long ago
Hast known my heart, and knowest my desire,
As I may shun the vengeance of thine ire
Such as upon Actaeon once was spent,
Thou knowest well, O chaste omnipotent,
That I would be a virgin all my life
And would be neither mistress, no, nor wife.
I am, thou knowest, of thy company,
A huntress, still in my virginity,
And only ask to walk the woodlands wild,
And not to be a wife or be with child,
Nor would I know the company of man.
O help me, Goddess, for none other can,

By the three Forms that ever dwell in thee,[2]
And as for Palamon who longs for me
And for Arcita's passion, I implore
This favour of thy grace and nothing more;
Set them in amity and let them be
At peace, and turn their hearts away from me.
Let all their violent loves and hot desires,
Their ceaseless torments and consuming fires,
Be quenched, or turned towards another place.
Yet if thou wilt not do me so much grace,
Or if my destiny ordains it so
That one shall have me whether I will or no,
Then send me him that shall desire me most.
Clean Goddess of the chaste and virgin host,
Look down upon the bitter tears that fall
Upon my cheeks, O keeper of us all,
Keep thou my maidhood, prosper my en-
    deavour,
And while I live a maid I'll serve thee ever."
    The fires flamed up upon the altar fair
And clear while Emily was thus in prayer;
But all at once she saw a curious sight,
For suddenly one fire quenched its light
And then rekindled; as she gazed in doubt
The other fire as suddenly went right out;
As it was quenched it made a whistling sound
As of wet branches burning on the ground.
Then, from the faggot's tip, there ran a flood
Of many drops that had the look of blood.
    Now at the sight she was so terrified
It almost drove her from her wits, she cried,
Not knowing what it was to signify,
For it was fear alone that made her cry,
She wept and it was pitiful to hear.
And then began Diana to appear,
With bow in hand, garbed as a Hunteress,
And said, "My daughter, cease your heaviness.
For thee the Gods on high have set their term,
And by eternal word and writ confirm
That thou shalt be espoused to one of those
That have for thee endured so many woes.
But unto which of them I may not tell.
Longer I cannot tarry, fare thee well.
And yet the fires of sacrifice that glow
Upon my altar shall, before thou go,
Make plain thy destiny in this for ever."
    And on the word the arrows in her quiver
Clattered together and began to ring
And forth she went and made a vanishing.
    Wholly amazed at what had come to pass,
Emily thought, "What can this mean? Alas!
O take me, take me under thy protection,
Diana, for I yield to thy direction!"

Then she went homeward by the shortest way
And that was all, there is no more to say.
　Now in the hour of Mars next after this
Arcite rose up and sought the edifice
Of fiery Mars, to do beneath his banner
His sacrifice, as was the pagan manner,
In high devotion with a piteous heart,
And thus he said his orison apart:
"O thou strong God of War that art adored
In the cold realms of Thrace and held for
　Lord,
That hast of every monarchy and land
Of warlike men the bridle in thine hand,
And dealest them their fortunes by thy choice,
Accept my sacrifice and hear my voice.
And if my youth be such as to deserve
Thy favour, if my strength be fit to serve
Thy godhead, if I may be one of thine,
I pray thee then, pity this pain of mine.
　"By that same suffering and burning fire
That long ago consumed thee with desire,
Having in use the incomparable flesh
Of fair free-hearted Venus, young and fresh,
Holding her in thine arms and at thy will,
—Albeit that once the time was chosen ill,
Seeing that Vulcan caught thee in his net
And found thee lying with his wife—but yet
By all the pain and passion of thy heart
Pity me too that suffer the same smart!
Thou knowest I am ignorant and young
And, as I think, more passionately stung
By love than any creature dead or living;
Little she thinks, in all the grief she's giving,
Of me, or cares whether I swim or sink,
And well I know ere she can learn to think
Kindly of me that force must have its place,
And well I know without thy help or grace
The little strength I have is all too slight;
Then help me, Lord, tomorrow, in the fight,
Not only for the flames that burnt in thee
But for the fire that now is burning me.
Grant victory tomorrow to my sword!
Mine be the labour, thine the glory, Lord;
Thy sovereign temple I will honour above
All other places, it shall be my love
To work for thy delight, to use thy arts,
And hang my banner, yea, my heart of hearts
Above thy altar. All my Company
Shall do the same for ever, there shall be
Eternal fires burning before thy Shrine.
Nay, further to this binding vow of mine,
My beard and hair, whose length and excel-
　lence

Has never suffered yet from the offence
Of razor or of shear, to Thee I give,
And I'll be thy true servant while I live.
Now, Lord, have pity on a heart so sore;
And give me victory, I ask no more."
　His prayer was over, and the rings
　　that hung
Upon the portals of the Temple swung;
So did the doors and clattered far and near,
At which Arcita felt the touch of fear.
The fires blazed, the altar glistened bright,
So that the Temple was suffused with light,
A scented air rose upward from the ground.
Arcita lifted up his hand and found
More incense and he cast it on the flame
With other rituals. At last the frame
Of mighty Mars began to shake and ring
Its hauberk, and he heard a murmuring,
Low-voiced and dim, that answered "*Victory*";
And giving thanks and glorifying he,
Filled with the joyful hope that he would win,
Returned at once and went to seek his inn,
As happy as a bird is of the sun.
　Immediately an uproar was begun
Over this granted boon in Heaven above
As between Venus, fairest Queen of Love,
And the armipotent Mars; it did not cease,
Though Jupiter was busy making peace,
Until their father Saturn, pale and cold,
Who knew so many stratagems of old,
Searched his experience and found an art
To please the disputants on either part.
Age has a great advantage over youth
In wisdom and by custom, that's the truth.
The old may be out-run but not out-reasoned.
And Saturn stopped their argument and sea-
　soned
Their fears, although it's not his nature to,
And found a remedy for this to-do.
　"My dearest daughter Venus," said Old
　　Saturn,
"My heavenly orbit marks so wide a pattern
It has more power than anyone can know;
In the wan sea I drown and overthrow,
Mine is the prisoner in the darkling pit,
Mine are both neck and noose that strangles it,
Mine the rebellion of the serfs astir,
The murmurings, the privy poisoner;
And I do vengeance, I send punishment,
And when I am in *Leo* it is sent.
Mine is the ruin of the lofty hall,
The falling down of tower and of wall
On carpenter and mason, I their killer.

'Twas I slew Samson when he shook the
    pillar;
Mine are the maladies that kill with cold;
The dark deceits, the stratagems of old;
A look from me will father pestilence.
Then weep no more, for by my diligence
This Palamon, your dedicated knight,
Shall have his lady, as you swore he might.
Though Mars should help his champion, none
    the less
Peace must be made between you soon, I guess,
Although you do not share the same complex-
    ions;
That is what brings these daily insurrections.
I am your grandfather and, as before,
I'll do my best to please you; weep no more."
    Now I shall cease to speak of Gods above,
Of angry Mars and Venus Queen of Love,
And tell you all, as plainly as I can,
The grand result for which I first began.

PART IV

Great was the festival they held that day
In Athens, and the lusty time of May
Put everyone so well in countenance
They spent all Monday at a joust and dance
And the high services of Venus. Yet
Because they knew that up they'd have to get,
And early too, to witness the great fight,
They went to bed betimes on Monday night.
    Next morning when the day began to
    spring
Clattering horse and noise of harnessing
Echoed through all the hostelries about.
Up to the palace cantered rout on rout
Of lords on palfreys, stallions, many a steed;
And what device of harness too indeed,
So rich and so outlandish, what a deal
Of goldsmith work, embroidery and steel!
Bright shields and trappings, headpieces and
    charms,
Great golden helmets, hauberks, coats of arms,
Lords on apparelled coursers, squires too
And knights belonging to their retinue,
Spears being nailed and helmets buckled
    strong,
Strapping of shields and lacing up of thong,
The work was urgent, not a man was idle.
The foamy steeds gnawing the golden bridle,
The armourers up and down and round about
Racing with file and hammer through the
    rout,
Yeomen on foot and commonalty come

With pipe and clarion, trump and kettle-
    drum,
Armed with short sticks and making such a
    rattle
It sounded like the blast of bloody battle.
The palace full of people up and down,
Here three, there ten, in all the talk of town
And making bets about the Theban knights.
Says one, "He'll win"; another, "Not by
    rights";
Some backed the man whose beard was black
    and squared,
Some backed the skin-heads, some the
    shaggy-haired;
Said one, "There's a grim fellow, I'll be bound
He'll fight, his battle-axe weighs twenty
    pound!"
And prophecy went seething round the hall
Long after day had risen on them all.
    Great Theseus was awoken out of sleep
By minstrelsy and noise about the keep,
But kept his chamber—a resplendent room—
Till the two Theban knights, to both
    of whom
An equal honour was done, were brought in
    presence.
    Throned in a window giving on a pleasance
Sat Theseus like a god in panoply,
And all the people crowded there to see
The Duke and offer him their reverence
And hear what orders he might issue thence.
A herald on a scaffold shouted "Ho!"
Till all the noise was quieted below;
Seeing at last the people hushed and still
He thus declared the mighty Theseus' will:
    "Our Lord the Duke has in his high dis-
    cretion
Considered the destruction and suppression
Of gentle blood, were he to jeopardize
The lives of those engaging under guise
Of mortal battle. Wishing none to die,
His Grace now purposes to modify
His ordinance. On forfeit of your lives
No cross-bow darts, no poleaxes or knives
May pass into the lists or be conveyed
Thither, no stabbing-sword with pointed
    blade
Be drawn or even carried at the side.
Further, no pair of combatants shall ride
More than one course with spears, descending
    thence
To thrust on foot only in self-defence.
If any man be injured, none shall take

His life; he shall be carried to the stake
That is to be ordained on either side,
And there conveyed by force he shall abide.
And should the principal of either faction
Be taken to the stake, or killed in action,
All fighting shall determine thereupon.
God speed you all, go forward and lay on!
With mace and long-sword you may fight
   your fill.
Now go your ways. This is his Grace's will."

   The people rifted heaven with a shout
Of merriest good humour, crying out,
"God bless our Duke for doing what he can
To save the blood of many a gentleman!"

   Up go the trumpets and the melody,
Forth to the lists canter the company,
As they were bidden, to the city verge;
The streets were hung in cloth-of-gold, not
   serge.

   And like a lord the Duke began to ride
With him a Theban knight, on either side.
Behind them rode the Queen and Emily,
And behind them another company
Of one or other according to their rank,
Threading through the city with the clank
Of hoof and armour to the lists that lay
Beyond. It was not fully prime of day
When Theseus took his seat in majesty.
Hippolyta the Queen and Emily
Were with him, other ladies ranked about,
And round the scaffoldage a seething rout.

   And westward, look! Under the Mar-
   tian Gate
Arcita and his hundred knights await,
And now, under a banner of red, march on.
And at the self-same moment Palamon
Enters by Venus' Gate and takes his place
Under a banner of white, with cheerful face.
You had not found, though you had searched
   the earth,
Two companies so equal in their worth.
Never were two so splendidly arrayed
And there was none so wise as to have
   weighed
Which of them had the advantage of his foe
In valiance, age, degree or strength of show;
They were so equal one could only guess.

   In two formations they began to dress
And when the roll was called that all
   might see
Their number was not swelled by treachery,
The gates were shut, and then the herald
   cried:

"Young knights, now do your duty, show
   your pride!"
   The heralds then withdrew, their work was
   done;
Out blared the trumpet and the clarion.
There is no more to say, but east and west
In go the spears in readiness, at the "rest,"
In go the spurs into the horse's side.
It's easy seeing which can joust and ride.
There the shafts shiver on the shields so thick;
One through his breast-bone feels the thrust
   and prick.
Up spring the spears to twenty foot in height,
Out go the long-swords flashing silver-bright,
Hewing the helmets as they shear and shred;
Out bursts the blood in streams of sternest red,
The mighty maces swing, the bones are
   bashed,
One thrusting through the thickest throng
   has crashed,
There the strong steeds have stumbled, down
   goes all,
Man under foot and rolling like a ball.
Another on his feet with truncheon pound
Hurtles a rider and his horse to ground;
One's wounded in the body, whom they take,
Spite of his teeth, and bear him to the stake
As was ordained, and there he has to stay;
One more is carried off the other way.
From time to time the Duke decrees a rest
To drink and be refreshed as they think best.

   Many a time our Thebans in the flow
Of battle met and did each other woe,
And each unhorsed the other. There could be
No tiger in the vale of Galgophy
Raging in search after a stolen cub
So cruel as Arcite with spear and club
For jealousy of heart to Palamon.
No lion is so fierce to look upon
In all Benamarin, and none so savage
Being hunted, nor so hunger-mad in ravage
For blood of prey as Palamon for Arcite.
The blows upon their helmets bite and beat
And the red blood runs out on man and steed.

   There comes at last an end to every deed,
And ere into the west the sun had gone
Strong King Emetrius took Palamon
As he was fighting with Arcite, still fresh,
And made his sword bite deeply in his flesh;
It asked the strength of twenty men to take
The yet-unyielded Palamon to stake.
Seeking a rescue, King Lycurgus coursed
Towards Palamon but was himself unhorsed,

And King Emetrius for all his strength
Was flung out of the saddle a sword's length
By Palamon's last stroke in sweeping rake.
But all for nought, they brought him to the
    stake;
Nothing could help, however hard he fought,
His hardy heart must stay there, he was caught
By force and by the rules decided on.

    Who clamours now in grief but Palamon
That may no more go in again and fight?
And when the noble Theseus saw this sight
He rose and thundered forth to every one,
"Ho! Stop the fight! No more, for it is done!
I will be true judge and no partisan.
The Theban Prince Arcita is the man
And shall have Emily, won by Fortune's
    grace."

    A tumult of rejoicing filled tall space
From every throat in such a caterwaul
It seemed as if the very lists would fall.

    What now can lovely Venus do above?
What is she saying, hapless Queen of Love?
Wanting her will her eyes were filled with
    mists
And shining tears fell down upon the lists.
    She cried, "I am disgraced and put to
        shame!"
But Saturn said, "Peace, daughter, watch the
    game.
Mars has his will, his knight has had his boon,
But, by my head, it shall be your turn soon."

    The trumpeters with loudest minstrelsy
And the shrill heralds shouting frenziedly
Were in high joy for honour of Arcite.
But listen quietly and keep your seat,
See what a miracle happened thereupon!

    The fierce Arcita, with no helmet on,
Riding his courser round to show his face
Cantered the whole length of the jousting-
    place,
Fixing his eye on Emily aloft;
And her returning gaze was sweet and soft,
For women, speaking generally, are prone
To follow Fortune's favours, once they're
    known.
She was his whole delight, his joy of heart.
    Out of the ground behold a fury start,
By Pluto sent at the request of Saturn.
Arcita's horse in terror danced a pattern
And leapt aside and foundered as he leapt,
And ere he was aware Arcite was swept
Out of the saddle and pitched upon his head
Onto the ground, and there he lay for dead;

His breast was shattered by the saddle-bow.
As black he lay as any coal or crow
For all the blood had run into his face.
Immediately they bore him from the place
Sadly to Theseus' palace. What avail
Though he was carved out of his coat of mail
And put to bed with every care and skill?
Yet he was still alive, and conscious still,
And calling ceaselessly for Emily.

    Theseus, attended by his company,
Came slowly home to Athens in full state
Of joyous festival, no less elate
For this misfortune, wishing not to cast
A gloom upon them all for what had passed.
Besides they said Arcita would not die,
He would recover from his injury.
And then there was another thing that filled
All hearts with pleasure, no one had been
    killed,
Though some were badly hurt among the rest,
Especially the man with stoven breast.
As for the other wounds and broken arms
Some produced salves and some relied on
    charms,
Herb pharmacies and sage to make them trim;
They drank them off, hoping to save a limb.

    For such as these Duke Theseus did his best,
He comforted and honoured every guest
And ordered revelry to last the night
For all the foreign princes, as was right.
None were discouraged or in discontent;
It was a jousting, just a tournament.
Why should they be discouraged? After all,
It's only an accident to have a fall.
There is no shame in being borne by force,
Unyielded, to the stake by twenty horse,
Alone, with none to help—it must be so,
Harried away by arm and foot and toe,
And on a horse maddened by sticks and noise,
By men on foot, by yeomen and their boys—
There's nothing despicable in all this;
No one could ever call it cowardice.
And therefore Theseus made proclamation
To stop all rancour, grudge and emulation,
That each side was as valorous as the other
And both as like as brother is to brother.
He gave them gifts, to each in his degree,
And for three days they held festivity.
Then he conveyed the Kings in solemn state
Out of his city, far beyond the gate,
And home went everyone by various ways
With no more than "Good-bye!" and "Happy
    days!"

The battle done with, I may now go on
To speak of poor Arcite and Palamon.
Up swells Arcita's breast, the grievous sore
About his heart increases more and more;
The clotting blood, for all the doctor's skill,
Corrupts and festers in his body still,
That neither cupping, bleeding at a vein
Or herbal drink can make him well again.
The expulsive forces, known as "animal,"
Had lost their power to cleanse the "natural"
Of poison, and it could not be expelled.[3]
His lungs began to choke, the vessels swelled.
Clotted was every muscle of his chest
By poison and corruption in his breast.
Nor could he profit, in his will to live,
By upward vomit or by laxative.
All, all was shattered and beyond repair,
Nature no longer had dominion there,
And certainly, where nature will not work,
Physic, farewell! Go, bear the man to kirk!
This is the sum of all, Arcite must die.

And so he sent for Emily to be by,
And Palamon, the cousin of his heart,
And thus he spoke, preparing to depart:
"Nothing of all the sorrows in my breast
Can now declare itself or be expressed
To you, O lady that I love the most;
But I bequeath the service of my ghost
To you, above all creatures in the world,
Now that my life is done, and banner furled.
Alas the woe! Alas the pain, so strong,
That I have suffered for you, and so long!
Alas, O Death! Alas, my Emily!
Alas the parting of our company!
Alas, my heart's own queen, alas, my wife,
O lady of my heart that ends my life!
What is this world? What does man ask to
  have?
Now with his love, now in his cold, cold
  grave,
Alone, alone, with none for company!
Farewell, my sweetest foe, my Emily!
O softly take me in your arms, I pray,
For love of God, and hearken what I say.
"I have here, with my cousin Palamon,
Had strife and rancour many a day now gone,
For love of you, and for my jealousy.
And may Jove's wisdom touch the soul in me,
To speak of love and what its service means
Through all the circumstances and the scenes
Of life, namely good faith and knightly deed,
Wisdom, humility and noble breed,
Honour and truth and openness of heart,

For, as I hope my soul may have its part
With Jove, in all the world I know of none
So worthy to be loved as Palamon,
Who serves you and will serve you all his life.
And should you ever choose to be a wife,
Forget not Palamon, that great-hearted man."
Speech failed in him, the cold of death
  began
Its upward creeping from his feet to numb
The breast, and he was slowly overcome,
And further still as from his arms there went
The vital power; all was lost and spent.
Only the intellect, and nothing more,
That dwelt within his heart, so sick and sore,
Began to falter when the heart felt death.
Dusked his two eyes at last and failed his
  breath,
And yet he gazed at her while he could see
And his last word was "Mercy . . . Emily!"
His spirit changed its house and went away
Where I came never—where I cannot say,
And so am silent. I am no divine.
Souls are not mentioned in this tale of mine,
I offer no opinion, I can tell
You nothing, though some have written
  where they dwell.
Arcite is cold. Mars guide him on his way!
Something of Emily I have to say.
Palamon howls and Emily is shrieking,
And Theseus leads away his sister, seeking
To bear her from the corpse; she faints away.
Why tarry on her tears or spend the day
Telling you how she wept both eve and
  morrow?
For in these cases women feel such sorrow
When it befalls their husbands to be taken
The greater part seem utterly forsaken
And fall into a sickness so extreme
That many of them perish, it would seem.
Infinite were the sorrows and the tears
Of older folk and those of tender years
Throughout the town, all for this Theban's
  death.
Wept man and boy, and sure a wilder breath
Of lamentation never had been heard
Since Hector, freshly slaughtered, was in-
  terred
In Troy. Alas to see the mourning there,
The scrabbled faces, the dishevelled hair!
"Must you have died?" the women wailed.
  "For see,
Had you not gold enough—and Emily?"
No one could lighten Theseus of his care

Except his father, old Aegeus, there.
He knew the transmutations of the world
And he had seen its changes as it whirled
Bliss upon sorrow, sorrow upon bliss,
And gave his son instruction upon this:
  "Just as there never died a man," said he,
"But had in life some station or degree,
Just so there never lived a man," he said,
"In all the world but in the end was dead.
This world is but a thoroughfare of woe
And we are pilgrims passing to and fro.
Death is the end of every worldly sore."
On top of this he said a great deal more
To this effect, with wisest exhortation,
Heartening the people in their tribulation.
  In time the thoughts of Theseus were astir
To find a site and build a sepulchre
For good Arcite, and how it best might be
Ordained to fit his honour and degree.
And in the end the place decided on
Was where Arcite first met with Palamon
In battle for their love, and there between
The branches in that very grove of green
Where he had sung his amorous desire
In sad complaint, and felt love hot as fire,
He planned a fire to make, in funeral
Observances, and so accomplish all.
So he commanded them to hack and fell
The ancient oak-trees and to lay them well
In rows and bundles faggoted to burn.
  Forth ride his officers and soon return
On swiftest foot with his commandments
    done.
And after this, Theseus appointed one
To fetch a bier and had it fitly clad
In cloth-of-gold, the finest that he had.
And in the self-same cloth he clad Arcite
And on his hands white gauntlets, as was
    meet,
He placed, and on his head a laurel crown
And in his hand the sword of his renown.
He laid him, bare his face, upon the bier,
And wept upon him, pity was to hear.
And that his body might be seen by all,
When it was day he bore him to the hall
That roared with mourning sounds in unison.
  Then came that woeful Theban, Palamon,
With fluttering beard and ash-besprinkled
    hair,
In sable garments stained with many a tear.
Yet, passing all in weeping, Emily
Was the most sorrowful of the company.
And that the service to be held might be

The nobler, more befitting his degree,
Duke Theseus commanded them to bring
Three steeds, all trapped in steel and glittering
And mantled with the arms of Prince Arcite.
Upon these huge white steeds that paced the
    street
On these rode one who bore Arcita's shield,
A second bore the spear he used to wield;
His Turkish bow and quiver of burnished gold
Was given to the third of them to hold;
Slowly they paced, their countenances drear,
Towards the destined grove, as you shall hear.
Upon the shoulders of the noblest men
Among the Greeks there came the coffin then.
Their eyes were red with tears, their slack-
    ened feet
Paced through the city by the master-street;
The way was spread with black, and far
    on high
Black draperies hung downwards from
    the sky.
  The old Aegeus to the right was placed
With Theseus on his left, and so they paced
Bearing gold vessels of a rare design
Brimming with honey and milk, with blood
    and wine;
And then came Palamon with his company,
And after that came woeful Emily
With fire in her hand, the custom then
Used in the obsequies of famous men.
  High was the labour, rich was the attire
And service, at the making of the fire
That reached to heaven in a cone of green.
The arms were twenty fathoms broad—
    I mean
The boughs and branches heaped upon the
    ground—
And straw in piles had first been loaded round.
  But how they made the funeral fires flame,
Or what the trees by number or by name
—Oak, fir-tree, birch, aspen and poplar too,
Ilex and alder, willow, elm and yew,
Box, chestnut, plane, ash, laurel, thorn and
    lime,
Beech, hazel, whipple-tree—I lack the time
To tell you, or who felled them, nor can tell
How their poor gods ran up and down the dell
All disinherited of habitation,
Robbed of their quiet and in desolation,
The nymph and dryad of the forest lawn,
The hamadryad and the subtle faun,
These I pass over, birds and beasts as well
That fled in terror when the forest fell;

Nor shall I say how in the sudden light
Of the unwonted sun the dell took fright,
Nor how the fire first was couched in straw,
Then in dry sticks thrice severed with a saw,
Then in green wood with spice among the
    stems
And then in cloth-of-gold with precious gems
And many a flower-garland in the stir
Of breathing incense and the scent of myrrh;
Nor how Arcita lay among it all,
Nor of the wealth and splendour of his pall,
Nor yet how Emily thrust in the fire
As custom was and lit the funeral pyre,
Nor how she fainted when they fed the flame,
Nor what she said or thought; and I
    shall name
None of the jewels that they took and cast
Into the fire when it flamed at last,
Nor shall I tell how some threw shield and
    spear,
Or what their garments, by the burning bier,
Nor of the cups of wine and milk and blood
That others poured upon the fiery flood,
Nor tell you how the Greeks in mighty rout
Left-handedly went thrice and thrice about
The flaming pyre, and shouted as they drove,
And thrice they clashed their spears about the
    grove;
Nor yet relate how thrice the ladies wept
Nor who supported Emily and kept
Pace with her homeward, nor shall it be told
How Prince Arcita burnt to ashes cold;
Nor how the wake was held in the delight
Of funeral games that lasted all the night.
What naked wrestler, glistening with oil,
Made the best showing in his dangerous toil
I will not say, nor say how one by one
They all went home after the games were
    done;
But shortly to the point; for I intend
To bring my long narration to an end.
    In course of time, and after certain years,
Mourning had been accomplished and their
    tears
Were shed no more, by general consent.
And then it seems they held a parliament
At Athens touching certain points and cases;
And among these they dealt with certain
    places
With which to form alliances abroad
To keep the Thebans fully overawed,
And noble Theseus ordered thereupon
That summons should be sent for Palamon.

Not knowing for what reason ordered back,
And still in melancholy suit of black,
Palamon came on this authority
In haste. Then Theseus sent for Emily.
    When all were seated there and hushed the
        place,
The noble Duke kept silent for a space
And era he spoke the wisdom in his breast
He let his eyes fall where it pleased him best.
Then with a sober visage and the still
Sound of a sigh, he thus expressed his will:
    "The First Great Cause and Mover of all
        above
When first He made that fairest chain of love,
Great was the consequence and high the in-
    tent.
He well knew why He did, and what He
    meant.
For in that fairest chain of love He bound
Fire and air and water and the ground
Of earth in certain limits they may not flee.
And that same Prince and Mover then,"
    said he,
"Stablished this wretched world, appointing
    ways,
Seasons, durations, certain length of days,
To all that is engendered here below,
Past which predestined hour none may go,
Though they may have power to abridge
    those days.
I need not quote authority or raise
More proof than what experience can show,
But give opinion here from what I know.
    "Since we discern this order, we are able
To know that Prince is infinite and stable.
Anyone but a fool knows, in his soul,
That every part derives from this great whole.
For nature cannot be supposed to start
From some particular portion or mere part,
But from a whole and undisturbed perfection
Descending thence to what is in subjection
To change, and will corrupt. And there-
    fore He
In wise foreknowledge stablished the decree
That species of all things and the progression
Of seed and growth continue by succession
And not eternally. This is no lie,
As any man can see who has an eye.
    "Look at the oak; how slow a tree to nourish
From when it springs until it comes to
    flourish!
It has so long a life, and yet we see
That in the end it falls, a wasted tree.

"Consider too how hard the stone we tread
Under our feet! That very rock and bed
On which we walk is wasting as it lies.
Time will be when the broadest river dries
And the great cities wane and last descend
Into the dust, for all things have an end.

"For man and woman we can plainly see
Two terms appointed; so it needs must be
—That is to say, the terms of youth and age.
For every man will perish, king and page,
Some in their beds and some in the deep sea,
And some upon the battle-field, maybe.
There is no help for it, all take the track,
For all must die and there is none comes back.

"Who orders this but Jupiter the King,
The Prince and Cause of all and everything,
Converting all things back into the source
From which they were derived, to which they
    course?
And against this no creature here alive
Whatever his degree may hope to strive.

"Then hold it wise, for so it seems to me,
To make a virtue of necessity,
Take in good part what we may not eschew,
Especially whatever things are due
To all of us; his is a foolish soul
That's rebel against Him who guides the
    whole,
And it is honour to a man whose hour
Strikes in his day of excellence and flower,
When he is certain of his own good name
And never known in any act of shame.
And gladder should a friend be of his death
Where there is honour in the yielded breath,
Gladder than for a name by age made pale,
And all forgotten the heroic tale.
Then is the time, if you would win a name,
To die, upon the moment of your fame.

"The contrary of this is wilfulness;
Why do we murmur? Where is the distress
If good Arcite, the flower of chivalry,
Is gone in honour and in duty, free
Of the foul prison of this life?
Shall those he loved, his cousin and his wife,
Murmur against his welfare, or suppose
He can return them thanks? Not he, God
    knows.
Offending so against him, they offend
Themselves, and are no happier in the end.

"So what conclusion can I draw from this
Except that after grief there should be bliss
And praise to Jupiter for all his grace?
So, ere we make departure from this place,

I rule that of two sorrows we endeavour
To make one perfect joy, to last for ever.
Then let us look, and where we find herein
The greatest grief let happiness begin.

"Sister," he said, "it has my full assent,
And is confirmed by this my parliament,
That gentle Palamon, your own true knight,
Who loves and serves you, heart and soul and
    might,
And always has since first he saw your face,
Shall move you to feel pity, gain your grace
And so become your husband and your lord.
Give me your hand, for this is our award.
Let us now see your womanly compassion.
By God, he's a king's nephew! Were his
    fashion
No more than that of a knight-bachelor,
What with the years he served and suffered for
Your love (unless his sufferings deceive me)
He would be worth considering, believe me.
A noble mercy should surpass a right."

And then he said to Palamon the knight,
"I think there needs but little sermoning
To gain your own assent to such a thing.
Come near, and take your lady by the hand."
And they were joined together by the band
That is called matrimony, also marriage,
By counsel of the Duke and all his peerage.

And thus with every bliss and melody
Palamon was espoused to Emily,
And God that all this wide, wide world has
    wrought,
Send them his love, for it was dearly bought!
Now Palamon's in joy, amid a wealth
Of bliss and splendour, happiness and health.
He's tenderly beloved of Emily
And serves her with a gentle constancy,
And never a jealous word between them
    spoken
Or other sorrow in a love unbroken.
Thus ended Palamon and Emily,
And God save all this happy company!

                                        Amen.

THE MILLER'S TALE
Words between the Host and the Miller

When we had heard the tale the Knight had
    told,
Not one among the pilgrims, young or old,
But said it was indeed a noble story
Worthy to be remembered for its glory,

And it especially pleased the gentlefolk.
Our Host began to laugh and swore in joke:
"It's going well, we've opened up the bale;
Now, let me see. Who'll tell another tale?
Upon my soul the game has begun well!
Come on, Sir Monk, if you've a tale to tell,
Repay the Knight a little for his tale!"
	The Miller, very drunk and rather pale,
Was straddled on his horse half-on half-off
And in no mood for manners or to doff
His hood or hat, or wait on any man,
But in a voice like Pilate's he began[1]
To huff and swear. "By blood and bones and
		belly,
I've got a noble story I can tell 'ee,
I'll pay the Knight his wages, not the Monk."
	Our Host perceived at once that he was
		drunk
And said, "Now hold on, Robin, dear old
		brother;
We'll get some better man to tell another;
You wait a bit. Let's have some common
		sense."
"God's soul, I won't!" said he. "At all events
I mean to talk, or else I'll go my way."
Our Host replied, "Well, blast you then,
		you may.
You fool! Your wits have gone beyond recall."
	"Now listen," said the Miller, "one and all,
To what I have to say. But first I'm bound
To say I'm drunk, I know it by my sound.
And if the words get muddled in my tale
Just put it down to too much Southwark ale.
I will relate a legend and a life
Of an old carpenter and of his wife,
And how a student came and set his cap . . ."
	The Reeve looked up and shouted, "Shut
		your trap!
Give over with your drunken harlotry.
It is a sin and foolishness," said he,
"To slander any man or bring a scandal
On wives in general. Why can't you handle
Some other tale? There's other things beside."
	To this the drunken Miller then replied,
"My dear old brother Oswald, such is life.
A man's no cuckold if he has no wife.
For all that, I'm not saying you are one;
There's many virtuous wives, all said and done,
Ever a thousand good for one that's bad,
As well you know yourself, unless you're mad.
Why are you angry? What is this to-do?
I have a wife, God knows, as well as you,
Yet not for all the oxen in my plough

Would I engage to take it on me now
To think myself a cuckold, just because . . .
I'm pretty sure I'm not and never was.
One shouldn't be too inquisitive in life
Either about God's secrets or one's wife.
You'll find God's plenty all you could desire;
Of the remainder, better not enquire."
	What can I add? The Miller had begun,
He would not hold his peace for anyone,
But told his churl's tale his own way, I fear.
And I regret I must repeat it here,
And so I beg of all who are refined
For God's love not to think me ill-inclined
Or evil in my purpose. I rehearse
Their tales as told, for better or for worse,
For else I should be false to what occurred.
So if this tale had better not be heard,
Just turn the page and choose another sort;
You'll find them here in plenty, long and
		short;
Many historical, that will profess
Morality, good breeding, saintliness.
Do not blame me if you should choose amiss.
The Miller was a churl, I've told you this,
So was the Reeve, and other some as well,
And harlotry was all they had to tell.
Consider then and hold me free of blame;
And why be serious about a game?

The Miller's Tale

Some time ago there was a rich old codger
Who lived in Oxford and who took a lodger.
The fellow was a carpenter by trade,
His lodger a poor student who had made
Some studies in the arts, but all his fancy
Turned to astrology and geomancy,
And he could deal with certain propositions
And make a forecast under some conditions
About the likelihood of drought or showers
For those who asked at favourable hours,
Or put a question how their luck would fall
In this or that, I can't describe them all.
	This lad was known as Nicholas the
		Gallant,
And making love in secret was his talent,
For he was very close and sly, and took
Advantage of his meek and girlish look.
He rented a small chamber in the kip
All by himself without companionship.
He decked it charmingly with herbs and fruit
And he himself was sweeter than the root
Of liquorice, or any fragrant herb.
His astronomic text-books were superb,

He had an astrolabe to match his art
And calculating counters laid apart
On handy shelves that stood above his bed.
His press was curtained coarsely and in red;
Above there lay a gallant harp in sight
On which he played melodiously at night
With such a touch that all the chamber rang;
It was *The Virgin's Angelus* he sang,
And after that he sang *King William's Note,*
And people often blessed his merry throat.
And that was how this charming scholar spent
His time and money, which his friends had
   sent.

   This carpenter had married a new wife
Not long before, and loved her more than life.
She was a girl of eighteen years of age.
Jealous he was and kept her in the cage,
For he was old and she was wild and young;
He thought himself quite likely to be stung.

   He might have known, were Cato on his
   shelf,
A man should marry someone like himself;
A man should pick an equal for his mate.
Youth and old age are often in debate.
However, he had fallen in the snare,
And had to bear his cross as others bear.

   She was a fair young wife, her body as
   slender
As any weasel's, and as soft and tender;
She used to wear a girdle of striped silk;
Her apron was as white as morning milk
Over her loins, all gusseted and pleated.
White was her smock; embroidery repeated
Its pattern on the collar, front and back,
Inside and out; it was of silk, and black.
The tapes and ribbons of her milky mutch
Were made to match her collar to a touch;
She wore a broad silk fillet, rather high,
And certainly she had a lecherous eye.
And she had plucked her eyebrows into bows,
Slenderly arched they were, and black as sloes;
And a more truly blissful sight to see
She was than blossom on a cherry-tree,
And softer than the wool upon a wether;
And by her girdle hung a purse of leather,
Tasselled with silk and silver droplets, pearled;
If you went seeking up and down the world,
The wisest man you met would have to
   wrench
His fancy to imagine such a wench;
And her complexion had a brighter tint
Than a new florin from the Royal Mint.
As to her song, it was as loud and quick

As any swallow's chirping on a rick;
And she would skip or play some game or
   other
Like any kid or calf behind its mother.
Her mouth was sweet as mead or honey—say
A hoard of apples lying in the hay.
Skittish she was, and jolly as a colt,
Tall as a mast and upright as a bolt
Out of a bow. Her collaret revealed
A brooch as big as boss upon a shield.
High shoes she wore, and laced them to
   the top.
She was a daisy, O a lollypop
For any nobleman to take to bed
Or some good man of yeoman stock to wed.

   Now, gentlemen, this Gallant Nicholas
One day began to romp and make a pass
At this young woman, in a mood of play,
Her husband being out, down Osney way.
Students are sly, and giving way to whim,
He made a grab and caught her by the quim
And said, "Unless I have my will of you
I'll die of secret love—O, darling, do!"
Then held her haunches hard and gave a cry
"O love-me-all-at-once or I shall die!"
She gave a spring, just like a skittish colt
Boxed in a frame for shoeing, and with a jolt
Managed in time to wrench her head away,
And said, "Give over, Nicholas, I say!
No, I won't kiss you! Stop it! Let me go
Or I shall scream! I'll let the neighbours
   know!
Where are your manners? Take away your
   paws!"

   Then Nicholas began to plead his cause
And spoke so fair in proffering what he could
That in the end she promised him she would,
Swearing she'd love him, with a solemn
   promise
To be at his disposal, by St. Thomas,
When she could spy an opportunity.
"My husband is so full of jealousy,
Unless you watch your step and hold your
   breath
I know for certain it will be my death,"
She said, "So keep it well under your hat."
"Oh, never mind about a thing like that."
Said he; "A scholar doesn't have to stir
His wits so much to trick a carpenter."

   And so they both agreed to it, and swore
To watch their chance, as I have said before.
When things were settled thus as they
   thought fit,

And Nicholas had stroked her loins a bit
And kissed her sweetly, he took down his harp
And played away, a merry tune and sharp.

It happened later she went off to church,
This worthy wife, one holiday, to search
Her conscience and to do the works of Christ.
She put her work aside and she enticed
The colour to her face to make her mark;
Her forehead shone. There was a parish clerk
Serving the church, whose name was Absalon.
His hair was all in golden curls and shone;
Just like a fan it strutted outwards, starting
To left and right from an accomplished
        parting.
Ruddy his face, his eyes as grey as goose,
His shoes cut out in tracery, as in use
In old St. Paul's. The hose upon his feet
Showed scarlet through, and all his clothes
        were neat
And proper. In a jacket of light blue,
Flounced at the waist and tagged with
        laces too,
He went, and wore a surplice just as gay
And white as any blossom on the spray.
God bless my soul, he was a merry knave!
He knew how to let blood, cut hair and shave,
And draw up legal deeds; at other whiles
He used to dance in twenty different styles
(After the current school at Oxford though,
Casting his legs about him to and fro).
He played a two-stringed fiddle, did it proud,
And sang a high falsetto, rather loud;
And he was just as good on the guitar.
There was no public-house in town, or bar,
He didn't visit with his merry face
If there were saucy barmaids round the place.
He was a little squeamish in the matter
Of farting, and satirical in chatter.
This Absalon, so jolly in his ways,
Would bear the censer round on holy days
And cense the parish women. He would cast
Many a love-lorn look before he passed,
Especially at this carpenter's young wife;
Looking at her would make a happy life
She was so neat, so sweet, so lecherous!
And I dare say if she had been a mouse
And he a cat, she'd have been pounced upon.
    In taking the collection Absalon
Would find his heart was set in such a whirl
Of love, he would take nothing from a girl,
For courtesy, he said, it wasn't right.
    That evening, when the moon was shining
        bright

He ups with his guitar and off he tours
On the look-out for any paramours.
Larky and amorous, away he strode
Until he reached the carpenter's abode
A little after cock-crow, took his stand
Beside the casement window close at hand
(It was set low upon the cottage-face)
And started singing softly and with grace,
    "Now dearest lady, if thy pleasure be
    In thoughts of love, think tenderly of me!"
On his guitar he plucked a tuneful string.
    This carpenter awoke and heard him sing
And turning to his wife said, "Alison!
Wife! Do you hear him? There goes Absalon
Chanting away under our chamber wall."
And she, "Yes, John, God knows I hear it all."
If she thought more of it she didn't tell.
    So things went on. What's better than
        "All's well"?
From day to day this jolly Absalon,
Wooing away, became quite woe-begone;
He lay awake all night, and all the day,
Combed his thick locks and tried to pass
        for gay,
Wooed her by go-between and wooed by
        proxy,
Swore to be page and servant to his doxy,
Trilled and rouladed like a nightingale,
Sent her sweet wine and mead and spicy ale,
And wafers piping hot and jars of honey,
And, as she lived in town, he offered money.[2]
For there are some a money-bag provokes
And some are won by kindness, some by
        strokes.
    Once, in the hope his talent might engage,
He played the part of Herod on the stage.
What was the good? Were he as bold as brass,
She was in love with gallant Nicholas;
However Absalon might blow his horn
His labour won him nothing but her scorn.
She looked upon him as her private ape
And held his earnest wooing all a jape.
There is a proverb, true, as you may find,
That Out-of-Sight is also Out-of-Mind.
For Nigh-and-Sly has the advantage there;
And, much as Absalon might tear his hair,
And rage at being seldom in her sight,
Nicholas, nigh and sly, stood in his light.
Now, show your paces, Nicholas you spark!
And leave lamenting to the parish clerk.
    And so it happened that one Saturday,
When the old carpenter was safe away
At Osney, Nicholas and Alison

Agreed at last in what was to be done.
Nicholas was to exercise his wits
On her suspicious husband's foolish fits,
And, if so be the trick worked out all right,
She then would sleep with Nicholas all night,
For such was his desire and hers as well;
And even quicker than it takes to tell,
Young Nicholas, who simply couldn't wait,
Went to his room on tip-toe with a plate
Of food and drink, enough to last a day
Or two, and Alison was told to say,
In case her husband asked for Nicholas,
That she had no idea where he was,
And that she hadn't set eyes on him all day
And thought he must be ill, she couldn't say;
And more than once the maid had given a call
And shouted but no answer came at all.

So it continued, all that Saturday
Without a sound from Nicholas, who lay
Upstairs, and ate or slept as pleased him best
Till Sunday when the sun went down to rest.

This foolish carpenter was lost in wonder
At Nicholas; what could have got him under?
He said, "I can't help thinking, by the Mass,
Things can't be going right with Nicholas.
What if he took and died? God guard his
    ways!
A ticklish place the world is, nowadays.
I saw a corpse this morning borne to kirk
That only Monday last I saw at work.
Run up," he told the serving-lad, "be quick,
Shout at his door, or knock it with a brick.
Take a good look and tell me how he fares."

The serving-boy went sturdily upstairs,
Stopped at the door and, standing there,
    the lad
Shouted away and, hammering like mad,
Cried, "Ho! What's up? Hi! Master Nicholay!
How can you lie up there asleep all day?"

But all for nought, he didn't hear a soul.
He found a broken panel with a hole
Right at the bottom, useful to the cat
For creeping in by: so he looked through that,
And, in the end, he saw him through the
    crack.
This Nicholas lay gaping on his back
As if he'd caught a glimpse of the new moon.
Down went the boy and told his master soon
About the state in which he found the man.

On hearing this the carpenter began
To cross himself and said, "St. Frideswide
    bless us!
We little know what's coming to distress us.

The man has fallen, with this here 'astromy,'
Into a fit, or lunacy maybe.
I always thought that was how it would go.
God has some secrets that we shouldn't know.
How blessed are the simple, aye, indeed,
That only know enough to say their creed!
Happened just so with such another student
Of astromy and he was so imprudent
As to stare upwards while he crossed a field,
Busy foreseeing what the stars revealed;
And what should happen but he fell down flat
Into a marl-pit. He didn't foresee that!
But by the Saints we've reached a sorry pass;
I can't help worrying for Nicholas.
He shall be scolded for his studying
If I know how to scold, by Christ the King!
Get me a staff to prise against the floor.
Robin, you put your shoulder to the door.
We'll shake the study out of him, I guess!"

The pair of them began to heave and press
Against the door. Happened the lad was
    strong
And so it didn't take them very long
To heave it off its hinges; down it came.
Still as a stone lay Nicholas, with the same
Expression, gaping upwards into air.
The carpenter supposed it was despair
And caught him by the shoulders mightily,
Shook him and shouted with asperity:
"What, Nicholas! Hey! Look down! Is that a
    fashion
To act? Wake up and think upon Christ's
    passion.
I sign you with the cross from elves and
    sprites!"
And he began the spell for use at nights
In all four corners of the room and out
Across the threshold too and round about:
    Jesu Christ and Benedict Sainted
    Bless this house from creature tainted,
    Drive away night-hags, white Pater-noster,
    Where did you go, St. Peter's soster?
And in the end the dandy Nicholas
Began to sigh, "And must it come to pass?"
He said, "Must all the world be cast away?"
The carpenter replied, "What's that you say?
Put trust in God as we do, working men."
Nicholas answered, "Fetch some liquor then,
And afterwards, in strictest secrecy,
I'll speak of something touching you and me,
But not another soul must know, that's plain."

This carpenter went down and came again
Bringing some powerful ale—a largish quart.

When each had had his share of this support
Young Nicholas got up and shut the door
And, sitting down beside him on the floor,
Said to the carpenter, "Now, John, my dear,
My excellent host, swear on your honour here
Not to repeat a syllable I say,
For here are Christ's intentions, to betray
Which to a soul puts you among the lost,
And vengeance for it at a bitter cost
Shall fall upon you. You'll be driven mad!"
"Christ and His holy blood forbid it, lad!"
The silly fellow answered. "I'm no blab,
Though I should say it. I'm not given to gab.
Say what you like, for I shall never tell
Man, woman or child by Him that harrowed
    Hell!"³

    "Now, John," said Nicholas, "believe
        you me,
I have found out by my astrology,
And looking at the moon when it was bright,
That Monday next, a quarter way through
    night,
Rain is to fall in torrents, such a scud
It will be twice as bad as Noah's Flood.
This world," he said, "in just about an hour,
Shall all be drowned, it's such a hideous
    shower,
And all mankind, with total loss of life."
    The carpenter exclaimed, "Alas, my wife!
My little Alison! Is she to drown?"
And in his grief he very near fell down.
"Is there no remedy," he said, "for this?"
"Thanks be to God," said Nicholas, "there is,
If you will do exactly what I say
And don't start thinking up some other way.
In wise old Solomon you'll find the verse
'Who takes advice shall never fare the
    worse,'
And so if good advice is to prevail
I undertake with neither mast nor sail
To save her yet, and save myself and you.
Haven't you heard how Noah was saved too
When God forewarned him and his sons and
    daughters
That all the world should sink beneath the
    waters?"
"Yes," said the carpenter, "a long time back."
"Haven't you heard," said Nicholas, "what a
    black
Business it was, when Noah tried to whip
His wife (who wouldn't come) on board the
    ship?
He'd have been better pleased, I'll undertake,

With all that weather just about to break,
If she had had a vessel of her own.
Now, what are we to do? We can't postpone
The thing; it's coming soon, as I was saying,
It calls for haste, not preaching or delaying.
    "I want you, now, at once, to hurry off
And fetch a shallow tub or kneading-trough
For each of us, but see that they are large
And such as we can float in, like a barge.
And have them loaded with sufficient victual
To last a day—we only need a little.
The waters will abate and flow away
Round nine o'clock upon the following day.
Robin the lad mayn't know of this, poor
    knave,
Nor Jill the maid, those two I cannot save.
Don't ask me why; and even if you do
I can't disclose God's secret thoughts to you.
You should be satisfied, unless you're mad,
To find as great a grace as Noah had.
And I shall save your wife, you needn't
    doubt it,
Now off you go, and hurry up about it.
    "And when the tubs have been collected,
        three,
That's one for her and for yourself and me,
Then hang them in the roof below the
    thatching
That no one may discover what we're
    hatching.
When you have finished doing what I said
And stowed the victuals in them overhead,
Also an axe to hack the ropes apart,
So, when the water rises, we can start,
And, lastly, when you've broken out the
    gable,
The garden one that's just above the stable,
So that we may cast free without delay
After the mighty shower has gone away,
You'll float as merrily, I undertake,
As any lily-white duck behind her drake.
And I'll call out, 'Hey, Alison! Hey, John!
Cheer yourselves up! The flood will soon be
    gone.'
And you'll shout back, 'Hail, Master
    Nicholay!
Good morning! I can see you well. It's day!'
We shall be lords for all the rest of life
Of all the world, like Noah and his wife.
    "One thing I warn you of; it's only right.
We must be very careful on the night,
Once we have safely managed to embark,
To hold our tongues, to utter no remark,

No cry or call, for we must fall to prayer.
This is the Lord's dear will, so have a care.
   "Your wife and you must hang some way
      apart,
For there must be no sin before we start,
No more in longing looks than in the deed.
Those are your orders. Off with you! God
   speed!
To-morrow night when everyone's asleep
We'll all go quietly upstairs and creep
Into our tubs, awaiting Heaven's grace.
And now be off. No time to put the case
At greater length, no time to sermonize;
The proverb says, 'Say nothing, send the
   wise.'
You're wise enough, I do not have to
   teach you.
Go, save our lives for us, as I beseech you."
   This silly carpenter then went his way
Muttering to himself, "Alas the day!"
And told his wife in strictest secrecy.
She was aware, far more indeed than he,
What this quaint stratagem might have in
   sight,
But she pretended to be dead with fright.
"Alas!" she said. "Whatever it may cost,
Hurry and help, or we shall all be lost.
I am your honest, true and wedded wife,
Go, dearest husband, help to save my life!"
   How fancy throws us into perturbation!
People can die of mere imagination,
So deep is the impression one can take.
This silly carpenter began to quake,
Before his eyes there verily seemed to be
The floods of Noah, wallowing like the sea
And drowning Alison his honey-pet.
He wept and wailed, his features were all set
In grief, he sighed with many a doleful grunt.
He went and got a tub, began to hunt
For kneading-troughs, found two, and had
   them sent
Home to his house in secret; then he went
And, unbeknowns, he hung them from a
   rafter.
With his own hands he made three ladders
   after,
Uprights and rungs, to help them in their
   scheme
Of climbing where they hung upon the beam.
He victualled tub and trough, and made
   all snug
With bread and cheese, and ale in a large jug,
Enough for three of them to last the day,

And, just before completing this array,
Packed off the maid and his apprentice too
To London on a job they had to do.
And on the Monday when it drew to night
He shut his door and dowsed the candle-light
And made quite sure all was as it should be.
And shortly, up they clambered, all the three,
Silent and separate. They began to pray
And "*Pater Noster* mum," said Nicholay,
And "mum" said John, and "mum" said Al-
   ison.
The carpenter's devotions being done,
He sat quite still, then fell to prayer again
With one ear cocked, however, for the rain.
   The carpenter, with all the work he'd seen,
Fell dead asleep—round curfew, must have
   been,
Maybe a little later on the whole.
He groaned in sleep for travail of his soul
And snored because his head was turned awry.
   Down by their ladders, stalking from
      on high
Came Nicholas and Alison, and sped
Softly downstairs, without a word, to bed,
And where this carpenter was wont to be
The revels started and the melody.
And thus lay Nicholas and Alison
Busy in solace and the quest of fun,
Until the bell for lauds had started ringing
And in the chancel friars began their singing.
   This parish clerk, this amorous Absalon,
Love-stricken still and very woe-begone,
Upon the Monday was in company
At Osney with his friends for jollity,
And chanced to ask a resident cloisterer
What had become of John the carpenter.
The fellow drew him out of church to say,
"Don't know; not been at work since Saturday.
I can't say where he is; I think he went
To fetch the Abbot timber. He is sent
Often enough for timber, has to go
Out to the Grange and stop a day or so;
If not, he's certainly at home to-day,
But where he is I can't exactly say."
   Absalon was a jolly lad and light
Of heart; he thought, "I'll stay awake to-night;
I'm certain that I haven't seen him stirring
About his door since dawn; it's safe inferring
That he's away. As I'm alive I'll go
And tap his window softly at the crow
Of cock—the sill is low-set on the wall.
I shall see Alison and tell her all
My love-longing, and I can hardly miss

Some favour from her, at the least a kiss.
I'll get some satisfaction anyway;
There's been an itching in my mouth all day
And that's a sign of kissing at the least.
And all last night I dreamed about a feast.
I think I'll go and sleep an hour or two,
Then wake and have some fun, that's what I'll
    do."
    The first cock crew at last, and thereupon
Up rose this jolly lover Absalon
In gayest clothes, garnished with that and this;
But first he chewed a grain of liquorice
To charm his breath before he combed his hair.
Under his tongue the comfit nestling there
Would make him gracious. He began to roam
Towards the carpenter's; he reached their
    home
And by the casement window took his stand.
Breast-high it stood, no higher than his hand.
He gave a cough, it was a semi-sound;
"Alison, honey-comb, are you around?
Sweet cinnamon, my little pretty bird,
Sweetheart, wake up and say a little word!
You seldom think of me in all my woe,
I sweat for love of you wherever I go!
No wonder if I do, I pine and bleat
As any lambkin hungering for the teat,
Believe me, darling, I'm so deep in love
I croon with longing like a turtle-dove,
I eat as little as a girl at school."
"You go away," she answered, "you Tom-
    fool!
There's no come-up-and-kiss-me here
    for you.
I love another and why shouldn't I too?
Better than you, by Jesu, Absalon!
Take yourself off or I shall throw a stone.
I want to get some sleep. You go to Hell!"
"Alas!" said Absalon. "I knew it well;
True love is always mocked and girded at;
So kiss me, if you can't do more than that,
For Jesu's love and for the love of me!"
"And if I do, will you be off?" said she.
"Promise you, darling," answered Absalon.
"Get ready then; wait, I'll put something on,"
She said and then she added under breath
To Nicholas, "Hush . . . we shall laugh to
    death!"
    This Absalon went down upon his knees;
"I am a lord!" he thought, "And by degrees
There may be more to come; the plot may
    thicken."
"Mercy, my love!" he said, "Your mouth, my
    chicken!"

She flung the window open then in haste
And said, "Have done, come on, no time to
    waste,
The neighbours here are always on the spy."
    Absalon started wiping his mouth dry.
Dark was the night as pitch, as black as coal,
And at the window out she put her hole,
And Absalon, so fortune framed the farce,
Put up his mouth and kissed her naked arse
Most savorously before he knew of this.
    And back he started. Something was amiss;
He knew quite well a woman has no beard,
Yet something rough and hairy had appeared.
"What have I done?" he said. "Can that be
    you?"
"Teehee!" she cried and clapped the win-
    dow to.
Off went poor Absalon sadly through the dark.
"A beard! a beard!" cried Nicholas the Spark.
"God's body, that was something like a joke!"
And Absalon, overhearing what he spoke,
Bit on his lips and nearly threw a fit
In rage and thought, "I'll pay you back for it!"
    Who's busy rubbing, scraping at his lips
With dust, with sand, with straw, with cloth,
    with chips,
But Absalon? He thought, "I'll bring him
    down!
I wouldn't let this go for all the town.
I'd take my soul and sell it to the Devil
To be revenged upon him! I'll get level.
O God, why did I let myself be fooled?"
    The fiery heat of love by now had cooled,
For from the time he kissed her hinder parts
He didn't give a tinker's curse for tarts;
His malady was cured by this endeavour
And he defied all paramours whatever.
    So, weeping like a child that has been
    whipped,
He turned away; across the road he slipped
And called on Gervase. Gervase was a smith;
His forge was full of things for plough-
    ing with
And he was busy sharpening a share.
    Absalon knocked, and with an easy air
Called, "Gervase! Open up the door, come on!"
"What's that? Who's there?" "It's me, it's Ab-
    salon."
"What, Absalon? By Jesu's blessed tree
You're early up! Hey, *benedicite*,
What's wrong? Some jolly girl as like as not
Has coaxed you out and set you on the trot.
Blessed St. Neot! You know the thing I
    mean."

But Absalon, who didn't give a bean
For all his joking, offered no debate.
He had a good deal more upon his plate
Than Gervase knew and said, "Would it
  be fair
To borrow that coulter in the chimney there,
The hot one, see it? I've a job to do;
It won't take long, I'll bring it back to you."
Gervase replied, "Why, if you asked for gold,
A bag of sovereigns or of wealth untold,
It should be yours, as I'm an honest smith.
But, Christ, why borrow that to do it with?"
"Let that," said Absalon, "be as it may;
You'll hear about it all some other day."
    He caught the coulter up—the haft was
      cool—
And left the smithy softly with the tool,
Crept to the little window in the wall
And coughed. He knocked and gave a lit-
tle call
Under the window as he had before.
    Alison said, "There's someone at the door.
Who's knocking there? I'll warrant it's a
  thief."
"Why, no," said he, "my little flower-leaf,
It's your own Absalon, my sweety-thing!
Look what I've brought you—it's a
  golden ring
My mother gave me, as I may be saved.
It's very fine, and prettily engraved;
I'll give it to you, darling, for a kiss."
    Now Nicholas had risen for a piss,
And thought he could improve upon the jape
And make him kiss his arse ere he escape,
And opening the window with a jerk,
Stuck out his arse, a handsome piece of work,
Buttocks and all, as far as to the haunch.
    Said Absalon, all set to make a launch,
"Speak, pretty bird, I know not where thou
  art!"
This Nicholas at once let fly a fart
As loud as if it were a thunder-clap.
He was near blinded by the blast, poor chap,
But his hot iron was ready; with a thump
He smote him in the middle of the rump.
    Off went the skin a hand's breadth round
      about
Where the hot coulter struck and burnt it out.
Such was the pain, he thought he must be
  dying
And, mad with agony, he started crying,
"Help! Water! Water! Help! For Heaven's
  love!"
    The carpenter, startled from sleep above,

And hearing shouts for water and a thud,
Thought, "Heaven help us! Here comes
  Nowel's Flood!"
And up he sat and with no more ado
He took his axe and smote the ropes in two
And down went everything. He didn't stop
To sell his bread and ale, but came down flop
Upon the floor and fainted right away.
    Up started Alison and Nicholay
And shouted, "Help!" and "Murder!" in the
  street.
The neighbours all came running up in heat
And stood there staring at the wretched man.
He lay there fainting, pale beneath his tan;
His arm in falling had been broken double.
But still he was obliged to face his trouble,
For when he spoke he was at once borne down
By Nicholas and his wife. They told the town
That he was mad, there'd got into his blood
Some sort of nonsense about "Nowel's
  Flood,"
That vain imaginings and fantasy
Had made him buy the kneading-tubs, that he
Had hung them in the rafters up above
And that he'd begged them both for heav-
  en's love
To sit up in the roof for company.
    All started laughing at this lunacy
And streamed upstairs to gape and pry and
  poke,
And treated all his sufferings as a joke.
No matter what the carpenter asserted
It went for nothing, no one was converted;
With powerful oaths they swore the fel-
  low down
And he was held for mad by all the town;
The students all ganged up with one another
Saying: "The fellow's crazy, my dear
  brother!"
And every one among them laughed and
  joked.
And so the carpenter's wife was truly poked,
As if his jealousy to justify,
And Absalon has kissed her nether eye
And Nicholas is branded on the bum
And God bring all of us to Kingdom Come.

THE REEVE'S TALE
The Reeve's Prologue

When all had laughed at the preposterous lark
Of Absalon and Nicholas the Spark,
Various folk made various comment after;

But the majority dissolved in laughter,
Nor did I see a soul it seemed to grieve
Unless it might be Oswald, the old Reeve,
For, as he was a carpenter by trade,
He was a little angry still and made
Grumbling remarks and scolded for a bit.

"As I'm a man I'd pay you back for it,"
He said, "with how they bleared a Miller's eye,
If I liked dirt and wished to argufy.
But I am old. Dirt doesn't go with doddering,
Grass-time is done and I'm for winter fod-
    dering.
My hoary top-knot writes me down for old;
Same as my hair, my heart is full of mould,
Unless I be like them there medlar-fruit,
Them that gets rottener as they ripen to't,
Till they be rotted down in straw and dung.
That's how we get to be, no longer young.
Till we be rotten we can never ripe.
We hop along, as long as world will pipe;
Our will is always catching on the nail,
Wanting a hoary head and a green tail,
Like leeks have got; the strength to play
    that game
Is gone, though we love foolishness the same.
What we can't do no more we talk about
And rake the ashes when the fire is out.

"Yet we have four live coals, as I can show;
Lies, boasting, greed and rage will always
    glow.
Those are the sparks among the ancient
    embers
Though we be nigh unwelded in our mem-
    bers.
Desire never fails, and that's the truth,
For even now I have a coltish tooth,
Many as be the years now dead and done
Before my tap of life began to run.
Certain, when I was born, so long ago,
Death drew the tap of life and let it flow;
And ever since the tap has done its task,
And now there's little but an empty cask.
My stream of life's but drops upon the rim.
An old fool's tongue will run away with him
To chime and chatter of monkey-tricks that's
    past;
There's nothing left but dotage at the last!"

Our Host, on hearing all this sermoning,
Began to speak as lordly as a king,
And said, "What does it come to, all this wit?
What! Spend the morning talking Holy Writ?
The devil that makes a preacher of a Reeve
Turns cobblers into doctors, I believe.

Give us your story, if you've one in stock.
Why, look! Here's Deptford and it's nine
    o'clock!
And Greenwich too, with many a blackguard
    in it.
High time to tell your story, so begin it."

"Now, gentlemen," Oswald the Reeve
    replied,
"I hope as none will be dissatisfied
Though I should tweak the Miller by the cap,
For lawful 'tis to give him tap for tap.

"This drunken Miller we've had so much
    drool of,
Told how a carpenter was made a fool of,
Maybe to score off me, for I am one.
By y'r leave, I'll pay him back before I've done
In his own filthy words, you may expec'.
I hope to God he breaks his bloody neck.
He sees the mote in my eye, if there is un,
But cannot see the beam there is in his'n."

The Reeve's Tale

At Trumpington, not far from Cambridge
    town,
A bridge goes over where the brook runs
    down
And by that brook there stands a mill as well.
And it's God's truth that I am going to tell.

There was a miller lived there many a day
As proud as any peacock and as gay;
He could play bag-pipes too, fish, mend his
    gear,
And turn a lathe, and wrestle, and poach deer.
And at his belt he carried a long blade,
Trenchant it was as any sword that's made,
And in his pouch a jolly little knife.
No one dared touch him, peril of his life.
He had a Sheffield dagger in his hose.
Round was his face and puggish was his nose;
Bald as an ape he was. To speak more fully,
He was a thorough-going market bully
Whom none dared lay a hand on or come near
Without him swearing that they'd buy it dear.

He was a thief as well of corn and meal,
And sly at that; his habit was to steal.
Simpkin the Swagger he was called in scorn.
He had a wife and she was nobly born;
Her father was the parson of the town;
A dowry of brass dishes he put down
In order to have Simpkin his relation.
The nuns had given her an education.
Simpkin would take no woman, so he said,
Unless she were a virgin and well-bred,

To save the honour of his yeoman stock;
And she was proud, pert as a magpie cock.
  It was a proper sight to see the pair
On holidays, what with him strutting there
In front of her, his hood about his head,
And she behind him all decked out in red,
Like Simpkin's hose, for scarlet-red he had 'em.
No one dared call her anything but "Madam,"
No one who passed was bold enough to try
A bit of fun with her or wink an eye,
Unless indeed he wanted Sim the Swagger
To murder him with cutlass, knife or dagger,
For jealous folk are dangerous, you know,
At least they want their wives to think
    them so.
And then her birth was smirched to say the
    least;
Being the daughter of a celibate priest
She must maintain her dignity, of which
She had as much as water in a ditch.
She was a sneering woman and she thought
That ladies should respect her, so they ought,
What with her well-connected family,
And education in a nunnery.
  They had a daughter too between them
    both,
She was a girl of twenty summers' growth;
But that was all except a child they had
Still in the cradle, but a proper lad.
The wench was plump, well-grown enough
    to pass,
With a snub nose and eyes as grey as glass;
Her rump was broad, her breasts were round
    and high;
She'd very pretty hair, I will not lie.
The parson of the town, for she was fair,
Intended to appoint the girl as heir
To all his property in house and land
And he was stiff with suitors to her hand.
He purposed to bestow her if he could
Where blood and ancient lineage made it
    good.
For Holy Church's goods should be expended
On Holy Church's blood, so well-descended,
And holy blood should have what's proper
    to it
Though Holy Church should be devoured to
    do it.
  This miller levied toll beyond a doubt
On wheat and malt from all the land about,
Particularly from a large-sized College
In Cambridge, Solar Hall.[1] 'Twas common
    knowledge

They sent their wheat and malt to him to
    grind it.
Happened one day the man who ought to
    mind it,
The college manciple, lay sick in bed,
And some reported him as good as dead.
On hearing which the miller robbed
    him more
A hundred times than he had robbed before;
For up till then he'd only robbed politely,
But now he stole outrageously, forthrightly.
  The Warden scolded hard and made a
    scene,
But there! The miller didn't give a bean,
Blustered it out and swore it wasn't so.
  Two poor young Bible-clerks or students,
    though,
Lived in this College (that of which I spoke).
Headstrong they were and eager for a joke,
And simply for the chance of sport and play
They went and plagued the Warden night
    and day
Just for a little leave to spend the morn
Watching the miller grind their meal and
    corn,
And each was ready to engage his neck
The miller couldn't rob them half a peck
Of corn by trickery, nor yet by force;
And in the end he gave them leave, of course.
  One was called John and Alan was the
    other,
Both born in the same village, name of
    Strother,
Far in the north, I cannot tell you where.
  Alan collected all his gear with care,
Loaded it on a horse the warden had,
And off he went with John the other lad,
Each with his sword and buckler by his side.
John knew the way—he didn't need a
    guide—
Reaches the mill and down the sack he flings.
  Alan spoke first: "Well, Simon, lad, how's
    things?
And how's your canny daughter[2] and your
    wife?"
Says Simpkin, "Welcome, Alan! Odds my
    life,
It's John as well! What, are you in the se-
    quel?"
"By God," said John, "Needs-must has got no
    equal,
And it behoves a man that has nie servant
To work, as say the learned and observant.

Wor Manciple is like enough to dee,
Such aches and torments in his teeth has he;
So Alan here and I have brought wor sack
Of corn for grinding and to bring it back.
Help us get home as quickly as ye can."
"It shall be done," said he, "as I'm a man.
What'll you do while I've the job in hand?"
"By God," said John, "I have a mind to stand
Right by the hopper here and watch the corn
As it gans in. Never since I was born
Saw I a hopper wagging to and fro."
    Alan spoke up: "Eh, John, and will ye so?
Then I shall stand below a short way off
And watch the meal come down into the
    trough;
I need no more than that by way of sport,
For John, in faith, I'm one of the same sort
And diven't knaa nowt of milling, same as ye."
    The miller smiled at their simplicity
And thought, "It's just a trick what they're
    about,
They think that nobody can catch them out,
But by the Lord I'll blear their eyes a bit
For all their fine philosophy and wit.
The more they try to do me on the deal,
When the time comes, the more I mean to
    steal.
Instead of flour I will give them bran;
'The greatest scholar is not the wisest man,'
As the wolf said in answer to the mare.
Them and their precious learning! Much I
    care."
    And when he saw his chance he sidled out
Into the yard behind and looked about
Without their noticing until at last
He found their horse where they had made
    him fast
Under an arbour just behind the mill.
    Up to the horse he goes with quiet skill
And strips the bridle off him there and then.
And when the horse was loose, off to the fen
Through thick and thin, and whinneying
    "Weehee!"
He raced to join the wild mares running free.
    The miller then went back, and did not say
A word of this, but passed the time of day
With John and Alan till their corn was
    ground;
And when the meal was fairly sacked and
    bound,
John wandered out and found their horse was
    gone.
"Good Lord! Help! Help! Come quickly!"
    shouted John,

"Wor horse is lost, Alan! The devil's in it!
God's bones, man, use your legs! Come out
    this minute!
Lord save us all, the Warden's palfrey's lost."
    Alan forgot his meal and corn and cost,
Abandoning frugality and care.
"What's that?" he shouted. "Palfrey? Which
    way? Where?"
    The miller's wife ran clucking like a hen
Towards them, saying, "Gone off to the fen
To the wild mares as fast as he can go.
Curse on the clumsy hand that tied him so!
Should have known better how to knit the
    reins."
John said, "Bad luck to it. Alan, for Christ's
    pains,
Put down your sword, man; so will I; let's gan!
We'll rin him like a roe together, man!
God's precious heart! He cannot scape us all!
Why didn't you put the palfrey in the stall?
You must be daft, bad luck to you! Haway!"
And off ran John and Alan in dismay,
Towards the fen as fast as they could go.
    And when the miller saw that this was so,
A good half-bushel of their flour he took
And gave it over to his wife to cook.
"I think," he said, "these lads have had a
    fright.
I'll pluck their beards. Yes, let 'em read and
    write,
But none the less a miller is their match.
Look at them now! Like children playing
    catch.
Won't be an easy job to get him, though!"
    These foolish Bible-clerks ran to and fro
And shouted, "Woa, lad, stand! . . . Look out
    behind!
Whistle him up . . . I've got him . . . watch it
    . . . mind!"
But to be brief, it wasn't until night
They caught the palfrey, hunt him as they
    might
Over the fens, he ran away so fast;
But in a ditch they captured him at last.
    Weary and wet, like cattle in the rain,
Came foolish John and Alan back again.
Said John, "Alas the day that I was born!
We've earned nowt here but mockery and
    scorn.
Wor corn is stolen and they'll call us fools,
Warden and all wor meäts in the Schools,
And most of all the miller. What a day!"
    So back they went, John grousing all
    the way,

Towards the mill and put the horse in byre.
They found the miller sitting by the fire,
For it was night, too late for going home,
And, for the love of God, they begged a room
For shelter and they proffered him their
    penny.
"A room?" the miller said. "There isn't any.
There's this, such as it is; we'll share it then.
My house is small, but you are learned men
And by your arguments can make a place
Twenty foot broad as infinite as space.
Take a look round and see if it will do,
Or make it bigger with your parley-voo."
"Well, Simon, you must have your little joke
And, by St. Cuthbert, that was fairly spoke!
Well, people have a proverb to remind them
To bring their own, or take things as they find
    them,"
Said John. "Dear host, do get us out the cup;
A little meat and drink would cheer us up.
We'll give ye the full payment, on my word.
No empty-handed man can catch a bird;
See, here's the silver, ready to be spent."
    Down into Trumpington the daugh-
    ter went
For bread and ale; the miller cooked a goose,
And tied their horse up lest it should get loose
Again, and in his chamber made a bed
With clean white sheets and blankets fairly
    spread,
Ten foot from his, upon a sort of shelf.
His daughter had a bed all by herself
Quite close in the same room; they were to lie
All side by side, no help for it, and why?
Because there was no other in the house.
    They supped and talked and had a fine
    carouse
And drank a lot of ale, the very best.
Midnight or thereabout they went to rest.
    Properly pasted was this miller's head,
Pale-drunk he was, he'd passed the stage
    of red;
Hiccupping through his nose he talked and
    trolled
As if he'd asthma or a heavy cold.
To bed he goes, his wife and he together;
She was as jolly as a jay in feather,
Having well wet her whistle from the ladle.
And by her bed she planted down the cradle
To rock the baby or to give it sup.
    When what was in the crock had been
    drunk up,
To bed went daughter too, and thereupon
To bed went Alan and to bed went John.

That was the lot; no sleeping-draught was
    needed.
The miller had taken so much booze un-
    heeded,
He snorted like a cart-horse in his sleep
And vented other noises, loud and deep.
His wife joined in the chorus hot and strong;
Two furlongs off you might have heard their
    song.
The wench was snoring too, for company.
    Alan the clerk in all this melody
Gave John a poke and said, "Are ye awake?
Did ye ever hear sich sang for guidness sake?
There's family prayers for ye among they nod-
    dies!
Wild fire come doon and burn them up, the
    bodies!
Who ever heard a canny thing like that?
The devil take their souls for what they're at!
All this lang neet I shall na get nie rest.
    "But never ye mind, all shall be for the best;
I tell ye, John, as sure as I'm a man,
I'm going to have that wench there, if I can!
The law grants easement when things gan
    amiss,
For, John, there is a law that gans like this:
'If in one point a person be aggrieved,
Then in another he shall be relieved.'
    "Wor corn is stolen, nivvor doubt of that;
Ill-luck has followed us in all we're at,
And since no compensation has been offered
Against wor loss, I'll take the easement prof-
    fered.
God's soul, it shall be so indeed, none other!"
    John whispered back to him, "Be careful,
    brother,
The miller is a torble man for slaughter;
If he should wake and find ye with his
    daughter
He might do injury to you and me."
"Injury? Him! I coont him nat a flea!"
    Alan rose up; towards the wench he crept.
The wench lay flat upon her back and slept,
And ere she saw him, he had drawn so nigh
It was too late for her to give a cry.
To put it briefly, they were soon at one.
Now, Alan, play! For I will speak of John.
    John lay there still for quite a little while,
Complaining and lamenting in this style:
"A bloody joke . . . Lord, what a chance to
    miss!
I shall be made a monkey of for this!
My meät has got some comfort for his harms,
He has the miller's daughter in his arms;

He took his chance and now his needs are
  sped,
I'm but a sack of rubbish here in bed.
And when this jape is told in time to come
They'll say I was a softie and a bum!
I'll get up too and take what chance I may,
For God helps those that help theirsels, they
  say."
  He rises, steals towards the cradle, lifts it,
And stepping softly back again, he shifts it
And lays it by his bed upon the floor.
  The miller's wife soon after ceased to snore,
Began to wake, rose up, and left the room,
And coming back she groped about in gloom,
Missing the cradle John had snatched away.
"Lord, Lord," she said, "I nearly went astray
And got into the student's bed . . . How
  dreadful!
There would have been foul doings. What
  a bed-ful!"
  At last she gropes to where the cradle
  stands,
And so by fumbling upwards with her hands
She found the bed and thinking nought but
  good,
Since she was certain where the cradle stood,
Yet knew not where she was, for it was dark,
She well and fairly crept in with the clerk,
Then lay quite still and tried to go to sleep.
John waited for a while, then gave a leap
And thrust himself upon this worthy wife.
It was the merriest fit in all her life,
For John went deep and thrust away like mad.
It was a jolly life for either lad
Till the third morning cock began to sing.
  Alan grew tired as dawn began to spring;
He had been hard at work the long, long
  night.
"Bye-bye," he said, "sweet Molly. . . . Are ye
  a'right?
The day has come, I cannot linger here,
But ever mair in life and death, my dear,
I am your own true clerk, or strike me deid!"
"Good-bye, my sweet," she whispered, "take
  good heed . . .
But first I'll tell you something, that I will!
When you are riding homewards past the mill
By the main entrance-door, a bit behind it,
There's the half-bushel cake—you're sure to
  find it—
And it was made out of the very meal
You brought to grind and I helped father
  steal. . . .

And, dearest heart, God have you in his keep-
  ing!"
And with that word she almost burst out
  weeping.
  Alan got up and thought, "Dawn's com-
  ing on.
Better get back and creep in beside John."
But there he found the cradle in his way.
"By God," he thought, "I nearly went astray!
My heid is tottering with my work to-neet,
That'll be why I cannot gan areet!
This cradle tells me I have lost my tether;
Yon must be miller and his wife together."
  And back he went, groping his weary way
And reached the bed in which the miller lay,
And thinking it was John upon the bed
He slid in by the miller's side instead,
Grabbing his neck, and with no more ado
Said, "Shake yourself, wake up, you pig's-
  head, you!
For Christ's soul, listen! O such noble games
As I have had! I tell you, by St. James,
Three times the neet, from midnight into
  morn,
The miller's daughter helped me grind my
  corn,
While you've been lying in your cowardly
  way . . . "
"You scoundrel!" said the miller. "What
  d'you say?
You beast! You treacherous blackguard!
  Filthy rat!
God's dignity! I'll murder you for that!
How dare you be so bold as to fling mud
Upon my daughter, come of noble blood?"
  He grabbed at Alan by his Adam's apple,
And Alan grabbed him back in furious grapple
And clenched his fist and bashed him on the
  nose.
Down miller's breast a bloody river flows
Onto the floor, his nose and mouth all broke;
They wallowed like two porkers in a poke,
And up and down and up again they go
Until the miller tripped and stubbed his toe,
Spun round and fell down backwards on his
  wife.
  She had heard nothing of this foolish strife,
For she had fallen asleep with John the clerk,
Weary from all their labours in the dark.
The miller's fall started her out of sleep.
"Help!" she screamed. "Holy cross of
  Bromeholme[3] keep
Us! Lord! Into thy hands! To Thee I call!

Simon, wake up! The devil's among us all!
My heart is bursting, help! I'm nearly dead,
One's on my belly, and another's on my head.
Help, Simpkin, help! These nasty clerks are
　　fighting!"
　　Up started John, he needed no inciting,
And groped about the chamber to and fro
To find a stick; she too was on the go
And, knowing the corners better than
　　them all,
Was first to find one leaning by the wall;
And by a little shaft of shimmering light
That shone in through a hole—the moon was
　　bright—
Although the room was almost black as pitch
She saw them fight, not knowing which was
　　which;
But there was something white that caught
　　her eye
On seeing which she peered and gave a cry,
Thinking it was the night-cap of the clerk.
　　Raising her stick, she crept up in the dark
And, hoping to hit Alan, it was her fate
To smite the miller on his shining pate,
And down he went, shouting, "O God, I'm
　　dying!"
　　The clerks then beat him well and left him
　　lying
And throwing on their clothes they took their
　　horse
And their ground meal and off they went, of
　　course,
And as they passed the mill they took the cake
Made of their meal the girl was told to bake.
　　And thus the bumptious miller was well
　　beaten
And done out of the supper they had eaten,
And done out of the money that was due
For grinding Alan's corn, who beat him too.
His wife was plumbed, so was his daughter.
　　Look!
That comes of being a miller and a crook!
　　I heard this proverb when I was a kid,
"Do evil and be done by as you did."
Tricksters will get a tricking, so say I;
And God that sits in majesty on high
Bring all this company, great and small, to
　　Glory!
Thus I've paid out the Miller with my story!

THE COOK'S TALE
The Cook's Prologue

The Cook, in joy to hear the Miller pickled,
Laughed like a man whose back is being
　　tickled;
"Haha!" he roared. "Haha! Christ's blessed
　　passion!
That miller was paid out in proper fashion
For trying to argue that his house was small!
'Be careful who you bring into the hall,'
Says Solomon in Ecclesiasticus,
For guests who stay the night are dangerous.
A man can't be too careful when he brings
A stranger in among his private things.
May the Lord send me misery and care
If ever, since they called me Hodge of Ware,
I heard a miller scored off so completely!
That jest of malice in the dark came neatly.
　　"But God forbid that we should stop
　　at that,
So if you'll condescend to hear my chat,
I'll tell a tale, though only a poor man;
But I will do the very best I can,
A little joke that happened in our city."
　　"Well," said our Host, "let it be good and
　　witty;
Now tell on, Roger, for the word's with you.
You've stolen gravy out of many a stew,
Many's the Jack of Dover you have sold[1]
That has been twice warmed up and twice left
　　cold;
Many a pilgrim's cursed you more than
　　sparsely
When suffering the effects of your stale
　　parsley
Which they had eaten with your stubble-fed
　　goose;
Your shop is one where many a fly is loose.
Tell on, my gentle Roger, and I beg
You won't be angry if I pull your leg,
Many a true word has been said in jest."
　　"That's sure enough," said Roger, "for the
　　rest,
'True jest, bad jest' is what the Flemings say,
And therefore, Harry Bailey, don't give way
To temper either if I have a plan
To tell a tale about a publican
Before we part. Still, I won't tell it yet,
I'll wait until we part to pay my debt."
And then he laughed and brightened up a bit
And he began his story. This was it.

The Cook's Tale

There was a prentice living in our town
Worked in the victualling trade, and he was
    brown,
Brown as a berry; spruce and short he stood,
As gallant as a goldfinch in the wood.
Black were his locks and combed with fetch-
    ing skill;
He danced so merrily, with such a will,
That he was known as Revelling Peterkin.
He was as full of love, as full of sin
As hives are full of honey, and as sweet.
Lucky the wench that Peter chanced to meet.
At every wedding he would sing and hop,
And he preferred the tavern to the shop.

    Whenever any pageant or procession
Came down Cheapside, goodbye to his pro-
    fession!
He'd leap out of the shop to see the sight
And join the dance and not come back that
    night.
He gathered round him many of his sort
And made a gang for dancing, song and sport.
They used to make appointments where
    to meet
For playing dice in such and such a street,
And no apprentice had a touch so nice
As Peter when it came to casting dice.
Yet he was generous and freely spent
In certain secret places where he went.
Of this his master soon became aware;
Many a time he found the till was bare,
For an apprentice that's a reveller,
With music, riot, dice or paramour,
Will surely cost his shop and master dear;
Though little music will his master hear.
Riot and theft can interchange and are
Convertible by fiddle and guitar.
Revels and honesty among the poor
Are pretty soon at strife, you may be sure.

    This jolly prentice—so the matter stood
Till nearly out of his apprenticehood—
Stayed in his job, was scolded without fail,
And sometimes led with minstrelsy to jail.[2]

    But in the end his master, taking thought
While casting up what he had sold and
    bought,
Hit on a proverb, as he sat and pored:
"Throw out a rotten apple from the hoard
Or it will rot the others": thus it ran.
So with a riotous servant; sack the man,
Or he'll corrupt all others in the place;
Far wiser to dismiss him in disgrace.

His master, then, gave Peterkin the sack
With curses, and forbade him to come back;
And so this jolly apprentice left his shop.
Now let him revel all the night, or stop.

    As there's no thief but has a pal or plucker
To help him to lay waste, or milk the sucker
From whom he borrows cash, or steals instead,
Peter sent round his bundle and his bed
To a young fellow of the self-same sort
Equally fond of revelling, dice and sport,
Whose wife kept shop—to save her good
    repute;
But earned her living as a prostitute . . .

(Of the Cook's Tale Chaucer made no more)

THE MAN OF LAW'S TALE
Introduction to the Man of Law's Tale

Our Host perceived the sun upon its arc
Of artificial day[1] (from dawn to dark)
Quarter way up plus half an hour or more;
And though not deeply versed in heav-
    enly lore
He knew quite well it was the eighteenth day
Of April that is messenger to May,
And was aware the shadow of every tree
Was of the same extent and quantity
As the erected body casting it.
    So, by the shadow cast, he had the wit
To judge that Phoebus, shining clear and
    bright,
Had climbed some forty-five degrees in
    height;
So for that day, and in these latitudes,
It must be ten o'clock, our Host concludes.
And suddenly he plucked his horse about;
"My lords," he said, "I would inform
    the rout
A quarter of the day's already gone.
Now, for the love of God and by St. John,
Let us no longer waste the time, I say.
My lords, time wastes itself by night and day,
Steals from us secretly, sleep or waking,
If we are negligent. For time is making
Stealthy escape, a stream that never again
Turns to the hills, but glides on to the plain.

    "Seneca and philosophers of old
Bewail time's loss more than the loss of gold:
'Lost money is not lost beyond recall,
But loss of time brings on the loss of all.'
It can return to us again, once sped,
No more than can poor Molly's maidenhead,

When she has lost it in her wantonness.
Let us not moulder here in idleness;
You, sir, the Man of Law, since you con-
tracted
To tell a tale, that tale is now exacted.
You all submitted—your consent was free—
To put this case for judgement up to me.
Acquit yourself! You promised so for one,
And then at least your duty will be done."

   "Host," he replied, "I'm willing, make no
doubt.
I never had a thought of backing out;
Promise is debt, and as I am your debtor
I'd like to keep my word, I can't say better.
Laws are for all, and he who seeks to lay them
On others should by rights himself obey
them.
Our text demands it; but I make avow
I can't recall a pithy tale just now;
But Chaucer, clumsy as he is at times
In metre and the cunning use of rhymes,
Has told them in such English, I suppose,
As he commands; for everybody knows
That if he has not told them, my dear brother,
In one book, he has told them in another.
He has told more of lovers up and down
Than even Ovid honoured with renown
In his Epistles, which are very old.
Why tell them all again since they've been
told?

   "In youth he wrote of Ceix and Halcyon,[2]
And since has celebrated every one
Of all these noble women and their lovers
As who will seek his lengthy book discovers.
The work is called 'The Legend of Cupid's
Saints,'[3]
And there you may perceive how Chaucer
paints
Lucrece and her wide wounds, and Thisbe
gored
In Babylon, and Dido's faithful sword
Because of false Aeneas, or may view
The fate of Phyllis that was hapless too,
Turned to a tree for love of Demophon.
There you may also listen to the moan
Of Deianira and Hermione,
Or Ariadne and Hypsipyle;
The barren island in the foaming sound
Is there to see, and brave Leander drowned
For Hero's love, and you may count the woes
Of Briseis or see the tear that flows,
Helen, from thee and thee, Laodamia!
There too the cruelty of Queen Medea,
Her little children hanging by the neck,

When the false Jason turned her love to
wreck!
O Hypermnestra, true Penelope,
Faithful Alcestis, how he praises thee!
But certainly he never writes a word
Of Canace—that tale should not be heard,
She loved her brother in a sinful way,
Fie on such cursed tales as that, I say!—
Nor draws from Apollonius, him of Tyre,[4]
How King Antiochus in mad desire
Bereft his daughter of her maidenhead.
The tale's too horrible, it can't be read.
He flung her on the pavement for his wooing!
But Chaucer knew quite well what he was
doing
And would not soil his sermons with narration
Of such unnatural abomination.
No more will I; ignore them if we may.
What shall I do, then, for a tale to-day?
I'd rather not be likened, if you please,
To those old Muses called Pierides
—The Metamorphoses know what I mean[5]—
Nevertheless I do not care a bean
Though I plod on behind him, some-
what dim;
I speak plain prose and leave the rhymes to
him."

   And on the word, in sober-faced relation,
As you shall hear, he started this narration.

The Man of Law's Prologue

O hateful grief to suffer indigence!
By hunger, thirst and cold to be confounded,
To feel heart's shame at asking a few pence,
Or, asking none, to know yourself surrounded
By such necessity your need is sounded
In every ear and you are left to creep
About and borrow, beg or steal your keep!

   You lay the blame on Christ and bitterly
Reproach Him for misdealing wealth;
the haul
Your neighbour has sets you at enmity;
You say, "I have so little. He has all!"
"By God," you say, "a judgement's sure
to fall
Upon him. He will feel the burning coals
Under his tail for scanting us poor souls!"

   Then listen to the opinion of the wise:
"Better to die than live in indigence
Such as your next-door neighbours will
despise."
If you be poor, farewell to eminence!

Yet from the wise take this for common sense
That to the poor all times are out of joint
Therefore beware of reaching such a point.

If you are poor your very brother hates you
And all your friends avoid you, sad to say.
O, you rich merchant-men, how Fortune
    fêtes you!
Noble and prudent folk! You've won the day;
You throw no double-aces when you play,[6]
But fives and sixes! Yours is the main chance
And Christmas-time for you's a time to dance!

You scour land and sea to fill your purses
And, like sagacious men, you bargain for
The fall and rise of kingdoms, you are sources
Of information, news of peace and war!
But for a merchant I should have no store
Of tales to tell you now, yet one I know,
Told to me by a merchant long ago.

The Man of Law's Tale

PART I

In Syria once there dwelt a company
Of wealthy merchants, serious, straight and
    wise,
That had a far-flung trade in spicery
And cloth-of-gold and satins of rich dyes,
All serviceable stuff that could surprise
With novelty; and business was a pleasure
Dealing with them and bartering for their
    treasure.

It happened that some merchants of
    this sort
Made up their minds to venture out to Rome,
Whether for business dealings or for sport;
Nor were they satisfied to stay at home
And send a messenger, but crossed the foam
In person thither; and where their expectation
Of profit lay, they found accommodation.

And having made a sojourn in that town
At their good pleasure for a month or more,
It happened that the excellent renown
Of Constance, daughter of the Emperor,
Reached them with every detail answered for,
And fresh particulars from day to day
Came to these Syrians, as I shall say.

This was the common voice of every man:
"Our Emperor—God save his majesty!—
Has such a daughter, since the world began

There never was another such as she
For beauty and for goodness; she could be
The Queen of Europe with all eyes upon her.
May God sustain her long in health and
    honour!

"Peerless in beauty, yet untouched by pride,
Young, but untainted by frivolity,
In all her dealings goodness is her guide,
And humbleness has vanquished tyranny.
She is the mirror of all courtesy,
Her heart the very chamber of holiness,
Her hand the minister to all distress."

All this was true as God Himself is true;
But to our purpose: when their ships were
    laden
These Syrian merchants started off anew
For Syria, having seen this blissful maiden,
Happy in this as in the goods they trade in,
Pursued their business as they did before
And lived contented; I can say no more.

It happened that these merchants stood in
    grace
With the young Syrian Sultan. Their return
From Rome, or any other foreign place,
He met with a benevolent concern
And entertained them eagerly, to learn
The news from other kingdoms—any word
They had to tell of wonders seen and heard.

And, among other things, they made report
Of Lady Constance and with special mention
Of her nobility, in such a sort
As to entrap the Sultan's pleased attention.
Her features filled his fancy and invention
Till all the passion of his heart was cast
On loving her as long as life should last.

In that large book that overhangs the earth
And people call the heavens, it well may be
That it was written in his stars at birth
Love was to be his death; for certainly
The death of every man is there to see
Patterned in stars clearer than in glass,
Could one but read how all will come to pass.

For in the stars, and many years before
His birth, the death of proud Achilles stood,
Hector's and Pompey's, Caesar's too; the War
Of Thebes, shorn Samson's death, the
    hardihood

Of Hercules, and Socrates the Good
And Turnus murdered, all was written plain.
Man cannot read it, he is dull of brain.

And thus it was the Sultan, to be brief,
Summoned the Privy Council of his land
And said that of his purposes the chief
Was to obtain the Lady Constance' hand,
And that at once; for they must understand
That he must perish, lacking her for wife;
Let them take thought in haste to save his life.

Various councillors said various things,
They argued and conjectured in profusion,
They brought forth many subtle reasonings
And spoke of charms and magical illusion,
But finally were drawn to the conclusion
There was no knowing how to save his life
Except by taking Constance for his wife.

They saw great difficulties in the case,
Reasoning thus (to make their feelings plain)
That there were such discrepancies to face
Between their laws and customs; it was vain
To ask a Christian prince to entertain
Thoughts of alliance under the dispensation
Mahomet blessedly had given their nation.

And he replied, "Rather than that I lose
The Lady Constance, I will be baptized;
I must be hers, in this I cannot choose.
O leave your arguments and be advised,
Can you not see my life is jeopardized?
I have a sickness she alone can cure,
It is a grief I cannot long endure."

What need is there for further dilatation?
I say by treaties and by embassy,
And by the Holy Father's mediation
Backed by the Church and the Nobility
To work destruction on Mahometry
And to enlarge the blessed law of Christ
All were agreed; the arguments sufficed.

The Sultan with his Peers in all their pride
And all his lieges were to undergo
Their christening; Constance was to be his
    bride,
And certain gold—how much I do not
    know—
Determined for the party to bestow
In surety; oaths were sworn on either side.
Fair Constance, God Almighty be your guide!

Now some of you expect, if I may guess
That I should tell you all the preparation
Made by the Emperor in his nobleness
For Lady Constance at the celebration;
But you must know that the elaboration
Ordained for an occasion such as this
Cannot be told in a parenthesis.

For bishops were appointed to attend,
Ladies and lords and knights of high renown
And many others; let me make an end.
And all were notified throughout the town
To pray with great devotion, calling down
Christ's blessing on the match, and to implore
A prosperous journey to the Syrian shore.

At last the day of her departure came,
I say there came that day of fatal woe.
No longer might she tarry or exclaim,
For each and all were ready decked to go.
Pale Constance rose in sorrow, for the glow
Of colour left her cheek as she prepared her,
Knowing too well that nothing would be
    spared her.

Alas, what wonder is it if she wept
At being sent into a stranger-nation
And parted from the friends that long had kept
Her tenderly, to suffer subjugation
To one she scarcely knew by reputation?
"All husbands are good husbands"; heretofore
Wives have established this, I say no more.

She said in tears, "O father, your poor girl,
Your Constance, softly fostered in your love,
And O beloved mother, crown and pearl
Of all my joy, save only Christ above,
To your kind graces she that was your dove
Commends herself, and journeys to the shore
Of Syria and shall never see you more!

"Alas, alas! Forth to a barbarous nation
At once to go! But since it is your will,
May Jesus Christ that died for our salvation
Give me the strength of purpose to fulfil
His wishes! Wretched girl, to fare so ill!
And yet what matter? Woman is a thrall
Disposed and ruled over by men in all!"

No, not in Troy, when Pyrrhus broke
    the wall
And burnt down Ilium, nor in Thebes de-
    stroyed,

Nor yet in Rome when it was ripe to fall
To conquering Hannibal that had thrice en-
   joyed
The victory, was grief so unalloyed
As in her chamber when she made to go.
But go she must, whether she wept or no.

First cause of motion, cruel firmament,[7]
Driving the stars with thy diurnal sway
And hurling all from east to occident
That naturally would take another way,
Thy crowding force set heaven in such array
That this her first, fierce journey must mis-
   carry
And Mars will slay this marriage, if she marry.

O thou unfortunate oblique degree
Of the Ecliptic, whence the cadent Mars,
Thrust from his proper angle, helplessly
Falls into *Scorpio*,[8] darkest house of stars!
O lord of war, whose influence debars
All hope! O feeble Luna, vainly knit
To him, thrust forth from where thou
   shouldest sit!

And O imprudent Emperor of Rome,
Is one time like another in such case?
Haddest thou no astrologer at home
To choose the favourable time and place
For journeying? For one of such high race,
Whose hour of birth was known to thee?
   But O,
We are, alas, too ignorant, or too slow.

With solemn ceremonial, as was due,
The ship for this poor maid was brought to
   shore;
She only said, "Christ Jesus be with you!"
And they, "Farewell, fair Constance!"—noth-
   ing more.
How resolute a countenance she bore!
Forth in this manner then I let her sail
And turn to other matters in my tale.

The Sultan's mother was a well of vices;
She saw the course on which her son was bent
Of giving up their ancient sacrifices,
And so for certain councillors she sent
Who came to be apprised of her intent;
And when these men of mark were gath-
   ered near
She took her seat and said as you shall hear.

"My lords," she said, "you know it to a man

How that my son is purposed to abjure
The holy teaching of our *Alkoran*
And all Mahomet had from God the Pure.
And to that God I here make promise sure
Rather to die the death than to depart
From what that Faith has written in my heart.

"What could befall us from this newer Law
But thraldom of our bodies and remorse?
For to deny Mahomet can but draw
Our souls through everlasting Hell, perforce.
But, my good lords, will you pursue a course
I shall suggest and further my endeavour,
One that will surely make us safe for ever?"

They all assented, swearing to make good
Their oath to live and die with her and stand
In strength behind her; each as best he could,
Engaged to rally all his friends at hand.
This was the enterprise that she had planned
—I shall describe it to you if I may—
And thus addressing them went on to say:

"We first must make pretence to be bap-
   tized
—Cold water cannot hurt us very much—
And I shall have a banquet organized
To pay the Sultan out, if he should touch.
Though christened white, his wife and
   many such
Shall find there's blood to wash away!
   She'll want
More water than it takes to fill a font."

O Sultaness! Root of iniquity!
Virago, second Queen Semiramis!
O serpent masked in femininity![9]
The Serpent bound in Hell was like to this
Pretended woman that can wreck the bliss
Of innocence and virtue, through the spite
Bred in thy devil's nest of foul delight!

O Satan, ever envious since the day
On which they chased you out of Paradise,
Our heritage! How soon you found the way
Through Eve to woman! Our bondage is the
   price.
And now this Christian match by your
   advice
Shall be undone. Of woman you have made
The instrument by which we are betrayed!

This Sultaness (on whom my imprecation!),
Having dismissed her court in secrecy

—Why spin things out into a long narra-
tion?—
Rode round to see the Sultan presently
And told him she'd renounce Mahometry
And be baptized in Christ. She had been wrong
(She said) to be a heathen for so long.

And after that she begged him for the
honour
Of feasting him upon the wedding-day,
The Christians too; she'd take the work
upon her
To please them all. He answered, "As you
say,"
And knelt to thank her. Having got her way
She kissed her son, and he, with gladdened
heart
In speechless joy, allowed her to depart.

PART II

The company of Christians reached the coast
Of Syria, a great and solemn rout;
Immediately the Sultan sent a post
First to his mother, then to all about,
To say his wife had come beyond a doubt
And beg her to take horse to meet his bride
And do her honour, for his kingdom's pride.

Great was the throng and splendid the array
Of Syrians and Romans in their meeting.
The mother of the Sultan, rich and gay,
Received his lady with as fond a greeting
As any mother would have shown in treating
A well-beloved daughter; so they ride
Solemnly to the city side by side.

Not Caesar threading a triumphal arch
(Whom Lucan celebrates with such a boast)
Was royaller than this exotic march
At the assembly of this blissful host.
But yet this scorpion, at her wicked post,
The Sultaness, for all her flattering,
Gathered herself most mortally to sting.

The Sultan came himself a little after,
So royal he was wonderful to see,
And welcomed her with joy and happy
laughter
And in this merriment I let them be;
The fruit of it is what you'll get from me.
After a time they thought it for the best
To end their revelries and take their rest.

The day appointed came, the Sultaness,

Old harridan, fixed the feast of which I told;
Thither the host of Christian people press
In general assembly, young and old.
What a display there was of kingly gold,
What dainties in the dishes! As for those
They bought them all too dear before they
rose.

O sudden grief that ever art near neighbour
To worldly bliss! Sprinkled with bitterness
The ends of joy in all our earthly labour!
Grief occupies the goal to which we press.
For your own safety think it is no less,
And in your day of gladness bear in mind
The unknown evil forging on behind!

Briefly to tell my story as is fitting,
Sultan and Christians all were overthrown,
Hacked into pieces, stabbed where they were
sitting,
All but the Lady Constance, spared alone.
The ancient Sultaness, accursed crone,
Helped by her friends, did all as she had
planned,
Being resolved herself to rule the land.

For not a single one of those converted,
Not one of them that knew the Sultan's mind,
But he was hewn in pieces, ere alerted,
And Constance, as the Sultaness had designed,
Was hurried hot-foot off, and was confined
In an old rudderless vessel, and told to learn
Her way to Italy, and so return.

She had some store of treasure, let me add
For sake of truth, and full supplies of food
Were given her, with such garments as
she had,
And forth she sailed the ocean salt and rude.
O Constance, full of sweet solicitude,
O Emperor's daughter of a mighty realm,
He that is Lord of Fortune guide thy helm!

She crossed herself and with a piteous falter
Of voice, addressed the cross of Christ and
said:
"Holiest cross, O rich and shining altar
Bright with the blood of pity the Lamb bled
To wash the world's iniquity, O shed
Protection from the Fiend upon me! Keep
My soul the day I drown upon the deep!

"Victorious Tree, protection of the true,
Thou that wert only worthy to up-rear

The King of Heaven in His wounds all new,
That whitest Lamb, hurt with the cruel spear,
O blessed cross, that puts the fiend in fear
Of man or woman that is signed with thee,
Help me amend my life, and succour me!"

For many a year and day this creature fled
Upon the Grecian seas, and reached the strait
Beyond Morocco, so her fortunes led.
Many a time in grief she must abate
Her sorry meals, expecting death, and wait
Till in the raging waves her vessel reach
What shore soever in the end, and beach.

It might be questioned why she was not
    slain?
Who at that banquet could protect or save?
To that demand I answer back again
Who succoured Daniel in the horrible cave
When everyone but he, master and slave,
Fell to the lions and was torn apart?
No one but God, whom Daniel bore in heart.

God, to proclaim the wonders of His arm
By miracle through her, would have it so,
And Christ who is the honey to all harm
Has chosen instruments, as well we know,
To work his purposes, that darkly show
To human ignorance; our feeble sense
Grasps not the prudence of His providence.

And if not murdered at the feast, what law
Kept Constance then from drowning in
    the sea?
And who kept Jonah in the fish's maw
Till he was spouted up at Nineveh?
It was none other, certainly, than He
Who kept the Hebrew folk from being
    drowned,
Crossing the sea dry-footed, safe and sound.

And who commanded the tempestuous
    mouth
Of the four winds that trouble land and sea
Saying, "O west and east, O north and south,
Touch with no trouble ocean, land or tree!"?
There is no such commander if not He
That walked the water; He it was who kept
This woman safe, awake or when she slept.

Where, then, for some three years upon the
    wave,
Got she her food and drink? And who sufficed

To Mary the Egyptian in a cave[10]
And fed her there? Certainly none but Christ.
Five loaves and two small fishes overpriced
The needs of the five thousand; so indeed
God's foison came to Constance in her need.

Forth over ocean then she drove and came
Safe through our stormy channel till at last,
Under a castle that I cannot name,
Far in Northumberland, the billows cast
Her vessel on the sands and held it fast
From ebb of tide to the returning crest;
There by the will of Christ she came to rest.

This castle had a Constable-in-Chief
Who came to see the wreck and, as he ought,
He searched it through and found in all her
    grief
This woman and the treasure she had brought.
Him, in her foreign language, she besought
For mercy, begging him to take her life
And so deliver her from earthly strife.

Latin she spoke, of a degenerate kind,
But all the same she made him understand;
And he, assured there was no more to find
Upon the vessel, brought her safe to land.
She knelt to thank him, seeing in him God's
    hand.
But who she was she would not utter breath,
For hope of favour or the fear of death.

She said the seas had blotted out her life
And she in truth had lost her memory.
The Constable, together with his wife,
Moved to compassion, wept in sympathy.
And Constance showed such sweet alacrity
To serve and please all people in that place
They loved her that but looked upon her
    face.

This Constable and Hermengild his wife
Were pagans like their neighbours every-
    where;
Hermengild came to love her as her life
And Constance made so long a sojourn there,
Giving herself to weeping and to prayer,
That Jesus brought conversion, of His grace,
To Hermengild the lady of the place.

In all that land no Christians dared to meet
For worship, most had fled; for long before
A pagan army and a pagan fleet

Had made their conquest of this northern
   shore.
To Wales had therefore fled a Christian core
Of ancient Britons dwelling in our isle.
That was the refuge of the faith meanwhile.

   Not wholly so, for there were some be-
      lieved
And honoured Christ apart in secrecy,
So that their pagan rulers were deceived.
There happened, near the castle, to be three,
One among whom was blind and could
      not see,
Save with that inward eyesight of the mind
That still can shed its light upon the blind.

   Bright was the sun when, on a sum-
      mer's day,
The Constable suggested they might go,
He, Constance and his wife, along the way
Towards the sea for half a mile or so,
Just for the pleasure of roaming to and fro.
And on their walk it chanced they met at last
This old and crooked man, with eyes shut fast.

   The old, blind Briton cried, "For Jesus'
      sake,
My Lady Hermengild, restore my sight!"
Now she on hearing him began to quake
For fear her husband, should it come to light
She was of Christ, would have her slain out-
      right.
But Constance made her bold, bidding her
      search
And do Christ's will, as daughter of His
      Church.

   The Constable, abashed at what he saw,
Said, "What's all this about?" and stopped to
      stare.
And Constance answered, "Sir, the power
      and law
Of Christ can save us from the devil's snare."
Then she began so fully to declare
Our faith, that what she said to him sufficed
Ere evening fell to turn his heart to Christ.

   This Constable was not the over-lord
Where Constance had been found upon the
      strand,
But long had held the region with his sword
For Alla, king of all Northumberland.
He was a wise king with a powerful hand

Against the Scots, as everybody knows;
Let me turn back to how my story goes.

   Now Satan who is ever on our track
To trick us, seeing Constance's perfection
And casting round how he might pay her
      back,
Filled a young knight who lived in that di-
      rection
With foul desires of such a fierce complexion
The fellow thought he'd die, so sharp the spur
Of lust, unless he had his will of her.

   He wooed her fiercely; it availed him
      nought,
For she would yield to sin for no persuasion.
So, out of spite, he compassed in his thought
A shameful death for her by some evasion
Or stratagem, and when on some occasion
The Constable was absent, in he crept
Softly one night where Hermengilda slept.

   Weary with prayer and holy meditation
She lay near Constance. Little did she note
How he, o'ermastered by the Fiend's tempta-
      tion,
Had softly come upon her; then he smote
The Lady Hermengild and slit her throat,
Then laying the bloody knife beside the bed
Of Constance went his way. God strike him
      dead!

   Next day the Constable returned again
With Alla too, king of the country round,
To find his wife was pitilessly slain.
Wringing his hands he wept and fell to
      ground,
And there by Constance in the bed he found
The bloody knife; alas, what could she say,
Out of her wits with terror and dismay?

   They told the King of the unhappy deed
And also of the manner, time and place
In which they came on Constance in
      her need
Upon the ship, and brooding on the case
He felt a shock of pity; in her face
He saw benignity. Could such a glance
In one so lovely fall to such mischance?

   And so, as when a lamb is brought to
      slaughter,
She stood, this innocent, before the king,

And the false knight, the villain that had
    sought her
Destruction, swore that she had done the
    thing.
The rest stood weeping by, and clamouring
That it was unimaginable she
Had done so monstrous an iniquity.

For they had ever known her virtuous
And loving to her mistress Hermengild,
And the whole household gave its witness
    thus,
Except the knight by whom she had been
    killed.
Much moved by this the gentle King was
    filled
With a desire for stronger proof, to hit
By deeper questioning the truth of it.

Alas, my Constance! Champion hast thou
    none,
Nor canst defend thyself; what wilt thou say?
But He that died for our redemption, Son
Of God, who bound the fiend—and where
    he lay
There lies he still—shall champion thee
    this day!
Without an open miracle from on high
To save her she assuredly must die.

She fell upon her knees and thus she prayed:
"Immortal God, thou who didst save Susanna
Falsely accused, and thou, merciful maid
And mother, Mary, daughter of St. Anna,
Before whose Child the angels sing Hosanna,
If I be innocent of this felony
Let me not die, support and succour me!"

Have you not some time seen the paler face
Among a crowd, of one that has been led
Towards his death, having obtained no grace,
With such a colour in his face, so dead,
As to be singled out, beset by dread,
Among all other faces in that rout?
So also Constance stood, and gazed about.

O Queens, abiding in prosperity,
You Duchesses and Ladies, hearts of stone
Would have compassion on her misery;
An Emperor's daughter, there she stands,
    alone,
Without a soul to whom she can make moan!
O royal blood, standing in greatest need
And deadly fear, far are thy friends indeed!

King Alla felt compassion for her fears
—Fine hearts feel pity quickly—at a look—
And was unable to restrain his tears.
At last he said "Let someone fetch a book
And if this knight will swear an oath she took
The knife and killed this woman, we shall
    confer
And name a man for executioner."

They brought a British book in which were
    written
The Gospels, and the knight stood forth alone
And swore her guilt. And lo, the knight was
    smitten:
A hand appeared and struck him to the bone
Behind the neck and down he went like stone,
His eyes burst from their sockets in his face
In sight of all assembled in the place.

And as he fell a voice was heard to ring:
"Thou hast defamed the innocent and meek,
A daughter of the Church, before the King;
Thus hast thou done, and yet I did not speak."
Aghast at such a marvel, faces seek
Each other in amaze at the unknown,
Dreading a judgement, all but hers alone.

Great was their fear and great their peni-
    tence
For having made a wrongful accusation
And felt suspicion of her innocence.
And in the end the heavenly visitation,
With all that Constance spoke in mediation,
Converted Alla; many in that place
Were also turned to Christ, O blessed grace!

The treacherous knight was slain for his un-
    truth
By Alla's doom, there was no tarrying,
Though Constance felt deep pity for his
    youth.
Then Jesus in his mercy caused the King
To wed this holy maiden. Belfries ring
In solemn joy, and Constance the serene
By ordinance of Christ is made a queen.

Who grieved at this? Who was it took
    no part
In this rejoicing? Who but Donegild,
The mother of the King? Her tyrant heart
Felt it would burst in two, for she was filled
With raging spite at what her son had willed.
She thought it gross dishonour to his state
To take this foreign creature for his mate.

I do not choose to stuff with chaff and straw
My lengthy tale, I rather seek the corn.
Why then relate the majesty and awe
Of course on course upon the marriage morn?
Who blew upon a trumpet or a horn?
But let me pluck the fruit out of my story;
They ate, danced, drank, they sang and were
   in glory.

They went to bed, as reason was and right,
For wives, albeit very holy things,
Are bound to suffer patiently at night
Such necessary pleasures as the King's,
Or others' who have wedded them with rings.
Her holiness—well, she must do without it
Just for a little, and that's all about it.

He got a boy upon her then and there,
And to the Constable, and a Bishop too,
Entrusted Constance, being forced to fare
Once more to Scotland; there was work to do
Against his enemies. Constance, mild and true
And humble, heavy with her child, lay still
Within her chamber, waiting on Christ's will.

Time came to fullness and she bore a boy,
Maurice they christened him. In great content,
The Constable chose a man in his employ
And wrote the King a letter to be sent
By him with tidings of this glad event
And other news that brooked of no delay.
The envoy took the letter and went his way.

This man, upon a private calculation,
Rode quickly to the mother of the King
And proffered her a courteous salutation
In his own tongue: "Madam, rejoice! I bring
You news enough to make the heavens ring
A hundred thousand times in thankful joy;
The Queen has been delivered of a boy!

"Look, here are the sealed letters with
   the news
Which I must bear with all the speed I can
To greet your son the King, and should you
   choose
To write to him, I am your serving-man."
"Not at the moment," Donegild began,
"Stay here until to-morrow, take your rest."
And added, "Then I'll say as I think best."

The messenger drank deep of ale and wine,
And all the letters secretly were cheated
Out of his box; he slept there like a swine.

Another letter then was counterfeited,
But with the utmost skill, and when com-
   pleted,
Directed to King Alla, to appear
As from the Constable, as you shall hear.

The letter said the Queen had been deliv-
   ered,
But of some horrible fiend or creature lured
From Hell itself, and that the castle shivered
At sight of it, it could not be endured.
Its mother was an elf, they were assured,
A wandering witch of charms and sorcery.
None could abide her hateful company.

Great was King Alla's grief at what he read;
He spoke to no one of the woes he bore,
But wrote again in his own hand and said,
"Welcome the word of Christ for ever more
To me, that now am learned in His lore!
Lord, welcome be thy pleasure and thy will!
All mine I place at thy commandment still.

"Preserve this infant, be it foul or fair,
Until I come, and let my wife be nursed.
Christ, when He wills, can bless me with an
   heir,
One that can please me better than the first."
And sealing this in private, his tears burst
Forth from his eyes. The messenger
   went away
Bearing the letter; there's no more to say.

O messenger, sodden in drunkenness,
Strong is your breath, your limbs are all astray,
You blab the secrets that you should repress,
Your mind is gone, you chatter like a jay,
Your features are distorted, turned to clay!
Wherever there is drunkenness about
No secret can be hidden, make no doubt.

O Donegild, I have no English worthy,
Tyrant, of thy malignity and spying,
And therefore to the Devil I refer thee;
Let him make poems on your treacherous
   prying,
You man-shaped monster!—No, by God, I'm
   lying!—
You are a very fiend and I can tell,
Wherever you are, your spirit is in Hell.

The envoy left the King and once again
Reached the Queen-Mother's court to pass
   the night;

And Donegild was quick to entertain
The man as hospitably as she might.
He underpinned his girdle pretty tight
Boozing away, and snored with gummy eyes
All night, until the sun began to rise.

Again they stole his letters, and the pith
Of what they forged instead of them was now:
"King Alla bids the Constable forthwith,
On pain of hanging and the royal vow,
For no consideration to allow
Constance within his kingdom; let her bide
No longer than three days and half a tide.

"Into the very ship in which he found her
Let her be put and so thrust out to sea,
Her and her son, with all her gear around her,
And charge her never to return to me."
O Constance, tremble at the harsh decree!
What dreams will haunt your troubled sleep-
    ing, filled
With dread! All this was planned by
    Donegild.

On the next morning when the day was full
The envoy woke and took the shortest way
Towards the castle. To the Constable
He gave the letter, who in great dismay
Cried out repeatedly, "Alas, the day!
Lord Jesus Christ, how can the world go on
With such a mort of wickedness thereon?

"O mighty God! And can it be thy will?
Thou art a righteous Judge, how can it be
That Thou shouldst suffer innocence to spill
And leave the wicked in prosperity?
Ah kindest Constance! O the grief to me
To be thy executioner or pay
It with my life! There is no other way."

They wept, both young and old, through-
    out the place
At this accurst command the King had sent,
And Constance with a pale and deadly face
Arose the fourth day after; down she went
Towards the ship, fully obedient
To the will of Christ, and kneeling on the
    shore,
Said, "Welcome, Lord, thy word, for ever-
    more!

"He that protected me from unjust blame,
When first I came among you will allow

No shame or harm, will shield me just
    the same
In the salt sea, although I know not how.
As strong as ever He was, so is He now.
In Him I trust and in His mother dear,
My rudder and my sail! What need I fear?"

Her little child lay weeping in her arm,
And kneeling with him pityingly she said:
"Peace, little son, I will not do you harm!"
And then she took a kerchief from her head
And laid it on his little eyes instead;
She rocked him in her arms and lulled his cries
And up to Heaven's height she cast her eyes.

"Mary," she said, "O maid and mother
    bright,
Truth is that by a woman's egging on
Mankind was lost, condemned to death and
    night,
For which thy Son was rent and spit upon.
Thou sawest His torment; what comparison
Can ever be between thy sufferings there
And any other woe that man can bear?

"Thy Child thou sawest slain before thine
    eyes;
My little child lives still and seeks thy aid.
Thou to whom every woeful spirit cries,
Bright lady, glory of womanhood, fair maid,
Haven of refuge, star that cannot fade,
Have pity on my child! Thy gentleness
Pities all sorrowful creatures in distress.

"O little child, alas, what is thy guilt
That never sinned as yet, and couldst not do?
Why would thy hard-heart father have thee
    spilt?
O Constable, is there no mercy in you?
Keep my sweet child. . . . O, must he suf-
    fer too?
Let him but stay, or if you fear the blame,
Kiss him but once and in his father's name!"

And then she turned her gaze towards
    the land
And cried aloud, "Hard husband, ah, good-
    bye!"
And she arose and went along the strand
Towards the vessel (and the crowd drew nigh)
And still she begged her baby not to cry,
And took her leave, and with a holy heart
Crossing herself, made ready to depart.

The ship was victualled well enough, indeed
Abundantly for her in such a case,
With necessaries to supply her need
Sufficiently. Thank God for all His grace!
May He send light to shine upon her face
And waft her home! What better can I say?
Over the open sea she drove her way.

PART III

Alla the King came home, his warfare done,
And reached the castle—that of which I told—
And asked at once to see his wife and son.
The Constable, who felt his heart turn cold,
Began to tell him plainly and unfold
What you have heard—I cannot tell it better—
Ending by shewing him his seal and letter,

Saying, "My Lord, as you commanded me
On pain of death, I did. No less than that."
The messenger was tortured until he
Acknowledged all, confessing full and flat
Where he had been, what places rested at
By night, and how; and so, by questioning,
They guessed the author of this dreadful thing.

The hand was recognized that wrote the letter
And mixed the venom for this cursed deed,
But how I know not, I can say no better
Than that the outcome was the King decreed
His mother should be killed, as you may read,
For false allegiance, treason and dishonour.
Thus ends old Donegild, my curse upon her!

The sorrows of King Alla night and day
Consumed him for his wife and little child;
How great his sufferings were no tongue can say,
And so I turn to Constance on the wild
Paths of the sea, five years and more exiled
In grief and misery, but in the hand
Of Christ's protecting angel; she neared land.

Yes, by a heathen castle at long last
—What name it had, alas I cannot find
In my authorities—the sea upcast
Her and the child. O Saviour of mankind,
Think upon Constance, have her child in mind!

She's fallen among heathens dwelling near,
On point of perishing as you shall hear.

Down from the castle keep to see the sight
And stare at Constance many people came,
And from the castle also late that night
There came its steward, Heaven send him shame!
He was a thief that had renounced the name
Of Christ; he climbed the vessel, and made show
To lie with her, whether she would or no.

The wretched woman, overcome with grief,
Cried out for mercy, and her baby wept;
But Blessed Mary saved her from the thief,
For in the struggle, as the fellow leapt
In deadly grapple with her, he was swept
Over the side into the sea, and drowned;
And thus Christ kept her spotless, safe and sound.

Foul lust of lechery, behold thy due!
Not only dost thou darken a man's mind,
But bringst destruction on his body too.
In their beginning all thy works are blind
And in their end are grief. How many find
That not the act alone, but even the will
To set about it can deprave and kill!

How could this feeble woman have the strength
Against this scoundrel? Can you answer that?
Goliath, of immeasurable length,
How was it David came and knocked you flat,
So young and so unarmed and such a sprat?
How dared he look upon your dreadful face?
Only, one well can see, by Heaven's grace.

And who gave Judith heart and hardiness
To slay King Holofernes in his tent,
And to deliver out of their distress
The people of the Lord? My argument
Is this, that just as God Almighty sent
A spirit of vigour to them in their woe
He could send strength to Constance, even so.

Onwards her vessel through the narrow mouth
Of Ceuta and Gibraltar forged her way,
Sometimes to westward, sometimes north and south,

And sometimes east for many a weary day,
Until Christ's mother—blessed be she aye!—
Out of her endless goodness, to befriend
Poor Constance in her sorrow, made an end.

Now we turn to the Emperor of Rome
And say no more of Constance for a while;
From Syria the news had been brought home
About the Christians slaughtered, and the vile
Dishonour to his daughter by the guile
Of that foul Sultaness, accursed beast,
That had them murdered at the wedding-
        feast.

To take his vengeance then the Emperor
        chose
A Senator and many another lord
All royally appointed, and God knows
They took revenge upon that Syrian horde;
They smote and burnt and put them to the
        sword
For many a day, then, to be brief, turned home
—That was the end of it—and made for
        Rome.

And as this Senator returned in glory
Sailing in style, the laurel on his brow,
He met a vessel, driving, says the story,
With Constance, pale and piteous, at the
        prow.
Nothing he knew of who she was, or how
Brought down to such condition; nor
        would she
Tell, under threat of death, her history.

He brought her back to Rome, and to
        his wife
He gave her, with her little son, and so
Safe at the Senator's she lived her life.
Thus could Our Lady lift her out of woe
As she lifts many another here below.
There for a season Constance had her place
And lived in holy works, her gift of grace.

This Senator's wife, it happened, was her
        aunt;
But for all that she did not yet discern
Her niece, long-lost, in Constance. But I shan't
Delay my story longer; I return
To Alla. Long he felt his spirit yearn
And wept for Constance, who, for all his
        weeping,
Was safe enough in Rome, and in good
        keeping.

King Alla, who had doomed his mother's
        death,
One day was taken with a great remorse,
And, to relate the matter in a breath,
Set sail to Rome for whatsoever course
Of penance that the Pope might there enforce,
Little or great, and as he sailed besought
Christ to forgive the evils he had wrought.

The news at once was bandied through the
        town:
"Alla the King has come on pilgrimage!"
His harbingers were going up and down
And, by a custom common in that age,
The Senator and all his lineage
Rode out, as much to show magnificence
As to receive a King with reverence.

Splendid the welcome that these noblemen
Gave to King Alla; he, no less than due,
Did honour to him in return, and then,
After their meeting, in a day or two,
King Alla bade the Senator renew
Their meeting at a feast. And, truth to tell,
The little son of Constance came as well.

Some say it was at Constance's request
The little child was taken to this feast;
—I can't know everything, I do my best—
But be that as it may, I know at least
That he was there, and, by her wish, released
To stand in front of Alla after grace.
The child stood looking at the kingly face.

Seeing the child, the King began to ponder
And made remark a little later on:
"Who is that pretty infant standing yonder?"
The Senator said, "By God and by St. John,
He has a mother, but his father's gone
For all I know. . . . " He went on to expound
The circumstance in which the child was
        found.

"God knows," he then proceeded to de-
        clare,
"I never saw or heard in all my life
Of such a virtuous woman anywhere
As that boy's mother—woman, maid or wife.
And I'll be bound she'd rather have a knife
Thrust through her very heart than be impure;
No one could egg her on to that, for sure."

In this child's face there was as great resem-
        blance

To Constance as there possibly could be,
And Alla, bearing ever in remembrance
The beauty of his wife, bemusedly
Thought, "Could the mother of the child
    be she
That once I had to wife?" And in his heart
He sighed, and sought occasion to depart,

Thinking, "O Heaven! What phantoms in
    my head!
I should believe—unless all judgement's
    spent—
The seas have swallowed her and she is dead."
And then there came the further argument,
"How do I know that Christ may not
    have sent
My Constance hither safe, as once before,
He sent her safely to my northern shore?"

So, in the afternoon, the wondering King
Went with the Senator, upon the chance.
He took him home with honour, and made
    them bring
Constance in haste; he bade her to advance.
You may believe she had no thought to dance
When told the reason—whom she was to
    meet.
Faith, she could barely stand upon her feet.

When Alla saw his wife he greeted her
And wept. It was a moving thing to see
That first long look of recognition stir
Upon his face; he knew that it was she.
And she stood dumb in sorrow, like a tree;
Her heart was shut within its own distress
When she remembered his unnaturalness.

And twice she fell before him in a faint;
He wept and sought her pardon with the cry:
"As God above and every shining Saint
May show me mercy, dear, it was not I,
Who am as guiltless of the griefs that lie
On you as little Maurice here, whose look
Is so like yours—or blot me from God's book!"

Long was the sobbing, bitter was the pain
Before their troubled spirits came to peace,
And sad it was to hear them weep again
As if their weeping brought them an increase
Of sorrow, and I beg you to release
Me, for the task would take me till tomorrow
And I am weary now of so much sorrow.

But finally when all the truth was told

And when she knew him guiltless of her woes,
Their kisses fell, I think, a hundred-fold.
And such delight, such rapture then arose,
Save for the joys eternal, I suppose
Such joy as theirs has never been surpassed
Nor ever will be while the world may last.

Then, to repay her for her griefs, she
    pressed
Humbly upon her husband to agree
In sending a particular request
To beg her father, of his majesty,
To do him so much honour as to be
His guest one day at dinner, but to say
Nothing at all of her in any way.

Some men would have it that he sent
    his son,
Their little Maurice, to the Emperor;
But, as I think, King Alla was not one
To send a child as his ambassador
To greet the flower of Christian men,
    who bore
So sovereign an authority; I deem
He went himself, and so it well may seem.

The Emperor vouchsafed with courtesy
To come and dine with him as he besought.
I read he gazed at Maurice eagerly,
And Constance came at once into his thought.
Alla returned once more and, as he ought,
Made ready for the feast, and all his power
Was spent in preparation for the hour.

The morning came; King Alla and his
    Queen
Rose early and arrayed themselves to meet
The Emperor; they were of joyful mien.
And when she saw her father in the street
She lighted down and, falling at his feet,
Said, "Father, Constance was your child!
    O Sir,
Have you no thought or memory of her?

"I am your daughter Constance," then
    said she,
"That once you sent to Syria as to slaughter,
And it is I that on the salty sea
Was thrust alone, to perish on the water.
Now, father dear, have mercy on your
    daughter!
Send me no more to lands in heathen blindness,
But thank my husband here for all his kind-
    ness."

Who could describe the joys that seemed
    to rend
The hearts of all those three at such a meeting?
But I must bring my story to an end
And shall delay no more, the day is fleeting.
They then sat down to dine; I leave them
    eating,
These happy people, in their joyfulness
Greater a thousand times than you can guess.

Maurice in time became the Emperor,
Crowned by the Pope, and proved a very limb
Of Christ and lived to strive in honour for
His holy Church. My memories are dim;
This is a tale of Constance, not of him.
In ancient Roman histories you'll find
The life of Maurice—I have it not in mind.

His purpose ended, Alla chose the day
To bring his sweet and saintly wife and boy
To England, and they took the shortest way,
And there they lived in quietude and joy.
Not long it lasted; time, that can destroy
All happiness on earth, will never bide;
From day to night joy changes as the tide.

Who ever lived so happy for a day
As to have been unmoved by any sense
Of guilt or rage, unvexed by some affray,
By pride or envy, passion or offence?
And this I only say as evidence
That our felicities are of short life;
And so it was with Alla and his wife.

For death, that takes a rent from high
    and low,
After a year had passed, or even less,
Called for this king and Alla had to go;
He left his Constance full of heaviness.
God send a blessing on his soul, and bless
The Lady Constance, who returning home
Set sail on her last journey back to Rome.

To Rome she came, this holy soul, at last,
And found her friends again at home and well;
All her adventures now were safely past;
She found her father in the citadel
And weeping tears of tenderness she fell
Joyfully on her knees, pouring her praises
In thanks to God, a thousand eager phrases.

And so they lived in virtue and the giving
Of holy alms, never again to wend

Until by death divided from the living;
And so farewell! My tale is at an end.
May Jesus Christ, who in his might can send
Joy after sorrow, keep us in his grace,
Aye, every man and woman in this place!

                  Amen.

Epilogue to the Man of Law's Tale

Our Host, after the Man of Law had done,
Rose in his stirrups. "Listen, everyone,
Good value, that," he said, "to say the least,
A thrifty tale. God's bones, Sir Parish Priest,
Tell us a tale! You promised it before.
You learned men are full of ancient lore,
God's dignity! You know a lot, I see."
The Parson answered, "*Benedicite!*
What ails the man so sinfully to swear?"
Our Host retorted, "Ho! Is Johnny there?[11]
I smell a Lollard in the wind!" said he.
"Good men," our Host went on, "attend
    to me;
Don't run away! By Jesu's noble passion,
We're in for something done in sermon
    fashion.
This Lollard here would like to preach, that's
    what."
The Skipper said, "By thunder, he shall not!
He shan't come here to vex us with his
    preaching,
His commentaries and his Gospel-teaching.
We all believe in God round here," said he,
"And he'll go starting up some heresy
And sow his tares in our clean corn, per-
    chance;
And therefore, Host, I warn you in advance
This little body has a tale to tell
That ought to set you ringing like a bell;
I shall be waking up the company.
It won't be much about philosophy
Or *phislyas* or curious terms in law.[12]
There is but little Latin in my maw!"

THE SHIPMAN'S TALE

There was a merchant in St. Denys once
Who being rich was held to be no dunce.
He had a wife, unusually fair,
One of a gay, companionable air,
A thing which causes more pecunial dearth
Than all the foppish compliments are worth
That menfolk offer them at feasts and dances.
Such nods and becks and party countenances

Pass as a shadow passes on a wall.
But woe to him that has to pay for all!
The silly husband always has to pay,
He has to clothe us, he has to array[1]
Our bodies to enhance his reputation,
While we dance round in all this decoration.
And if he cannot pay, as it may chance,
Or won't submit to such extravagance,
Thinking his money thrown away and lost,
Then someone else will have to bear the cost
Or lend us money, and that's dangerous.

This noble merchant kept a splendid house
And all day long so many guests there were
—For he was generous and his wife was fair—
You would have been surprised; but to my
  tale.
His guests from up and down the social
  scale
Included a young monk, well-made and bold;
I judge he was some thirty winters old,
And he was always visiting the place.
Now this young monk, with his delightful
  face,
Was on such friendly terms with this good man
Ever since their acquaintance first began
That he was welcomed as familiarly
As it is possible for a friend to be.
And for as much as this good-natured man,
He and the monk, of whom my tale began,
Were born in the same village, the monk
  stated
That they were cousins, very near related;
The claim was neither questioned nor with-
  drawn;
Both were as glad of it as bird of dawn.
It pleased the merchant's heart, and his com-
  pliance
Had furthered this unbreakable alliance,
And each was happy to assure the other
He always would regard him as a brother.
This monk, Sir John, was very free in
  spending
Whenever he stayed there, carefully attending
To what should please; he poured out tips like
  wages,
Forgetting not the meanest of the pages
About the house; to each in his degree,
Master or man, he gave a gift or fee
Whenever he came—some honest kind of
  present—
And so, to them, his coming was as pleasant
As sunrise is to bird upon the nest.
I must have said enough, so let it rest.

The merchant, as it happened, one fine day,
Began to make arrangements for a stay
Somewhere near Bruges to further his affairs
And buy a fresh consignment of his wares.
And so he sent a message thereupon
To Paris, and invited good Sir John
Down to St. Denys, so as to give pleasure
To him and to his wife, and spend his leisure
With them agreeably, a day or two,
Before he left—as he would have to do—
For Bruges. This noble monk I am describing
Was glad enough, and needed little bribing;
He saw his Abbot and he got permission,
Being a man of prudence and position,
In fact a superintendent, one to ride
Inspecting abbey granges far and wide.
Off to St. Denys, then, the monk has gone.
Who was so welcome as my lord Sir John,
So full of courtesy and "cousin mine"?
He brought with him a jug of Malmsey wine
And also one of sweet Italian juice,
With these a brace of birds as was his use.
And thus I leave them at their meat and drink,
Merchant and monk, a day or two, I think.

On the third morning up the merchant gets
In serious thought about his needs and debts
And up into his counting house he goes
To reckon up, as you may well suppose,
All the past year and how things stood
  with him,
What he had spent, how the accounts would
  trim,
And whether his business had increased
  or not.
Many a ledger and money-bag he got
And laid them out upon his counting-board.
He had a deal of treasure in his hoard
And so he locked the door with an abrupt
Command that no one was to interrupt
His casting of accounts; he worked away
Sitting up there till past the prime of day.
Sir John had risen early too, to go
Into the garden. Walking to and fro
He said his office, courteous and devout.
This excellent wife then stealthily came out
Where he was walking softly in the sun
And greeted him, as she had often done.
A little girl was there for company
Beside her, under her authority,
Still subject to the rod; her mistress said:
"Ah, my dear cousin John! What, not in bed?
What's wrong with you that you are up so
  soon?"

"Niece," he replied, "a man can keep in tune
On five good hours of sleep, as I should judge,
Unless he is a poor old pallid drudge
Like all those married men who cower there
In bed, as in her form a weary hare
When she has had the hounds upon her tail.
But, my dear niece, why do you look so pale?
I cannot but imagine our good man
Has been at work with you since night began;
You really ought to go and take a rest."
And he laughed merrily at his little jest,
And for his private thoughts his face
    turned red.
    This pretty wife began to shake her head
And answered thus: "Ah, God knows all!"
    said she.
"No, cousin mine, things aren't like that
    with me;
For, by the Lord that gave me soul and life,
In all the realm of France there is no wife
That has less pleasure in that sorry play.
For I may sing 'Alas, and woe the day
That ever I was born!' I daren't," said she,
"Tell anyone how matters go with me.
If only I could get away, or end
It all—Oh, I could kill myself, dear friend,
I am so terrified, so full of care. . . . "
    On hearing this the monk began to stare
And said, "Alas, dear cousin, God forbid
That fear or grief, whatever else they did,
Should make you kill yourself! Unfold your
    grief;
It may be I can give you some relief,
Advice or help, perhaps; and therefore, come,
Tell me about your trouble, I'll keep mum.
Look, on this prayer-book I will take a vow
Never by chance or choice, no matter how,
To give away what you may say to me."
"I say the same again to you," said she,
"By God and by this prayer-book I can swear,
Though I were torn in pieces, to play fair
And never breathe syllable or tell
A living soul, not though I went to Hell;
Not on account of cousinship, but just
Out of affection for you, love the trust."
And having sworn, they kissed to seal the oath
And then conversed as impulse prompted both.
    "Cousin," she said, "if I had time and space
And I have none, especially in this place,
I could unfold a legend of my life
And what I've had to suffer as a wife.
As for my husband, though he's your rela-
    tion . . . "

"No!" said the monk. "By God and my salva-
    tion!
Cousin indeed! He's no more cousin to me
Than is this leaf, here hanging on the tree.
I call him so, but by the saints of France
I do so only for a better chance
Of seeing you—because I love you dearly,
Above all other women, most sincerely.
I swear it you on my profession, love!
Tell me your troubles while he's still above,
Quick, don't hang back! and then you can be
    gone."
"O my dear love," she answered, "sweet Sir
    John,
I hate to tell you. . . . O if I were stronger!
But it must out, I cannot bear it longer.
My husband is the very meanest man,
To me at any rate, since the world began.
It's unbecoming, since I am his wife,
To tell a soul about our private life,
Whether in bed or any other place,
And God forbid I sank to such disgrace!
I know a wife should only speak in honour
About her husband, or else fie upon her!
Only to you, the only one on earth,
This much I'll say. God help me, he's not
    worth
A fly upon the wall! In no respect.
But his worst fault is niggardly neglect.
For you must know that women naturally
Need to have sixty things, the same as me;
They want to have their husbands, to be
    candid,
Sturdy and prudent, rich and open-handed,
Obedient to their wives and fresh in bed.
But by the Lord that died for us and bled,
By Sunday next, if I am to look smart
And do my husband honour I must part
With—well, a hundred francs; or I'm undone.
Far better not be born than to be one
That people slander and say cheap things
    about.
Yet if my husband were to find it out
I were as good as lost—ah, don't deny!
Lend me this little sum or I shall die.
Sir John, I say, lend me these hundred francs!
Trust me I will not fail you in my thanks
If only you'll oblige me as I say.
I'll pay you back, and you shall name the day,
And if there's anything else—some little task
That I can do for you—well, only ask.
And if I don't, God send as foul mischance
To me as fell to Ganelon of France!"[2]

The monk gave answer in his well-
    bred way:
"My own dear lady, I can truly say
I weep in sympathy for what I've heard,
And here I promise you and plight my word
That when your husband has gone off to
    Flanders
I will deliver you from fear of slanders
For I will bring you down a hundred francs."
And on the word he caught her by the flanks
And clasped her closely, giving her a riot
Of kisses, saying softly, "Keep things
    quiet . . .
And now let's have some dinner if we may,
My dial says it's past the prime of day;
You'd best be off. And be as true to me
As I to you." "God forbid else!" said she.
    And off she went as jolly as a lark
And told the cooks to hurry off the mark
So that they all could dine without delay.
Up to her husband then she made her way
And boldly knocked upon the counter-door.
"*Qui là?*" he said. "It's me, dear. How
    much more
Have you to do up there," she said, "and
    fasting?
How long will you be reckoning up and
    casting
All those accounts of yours and books and
    things?
The devil run off with all such reckonings!
Heavens, you've had enough of it, my Own!
Come down and leave those money-bags
    alone.
Aren't you ashamed to leave that poor Sir John
Fasting all day while you go on and on?
What? . . . Let's hear Mass, and then go in to
    dine."
    "Dear wife," he said, "how little you divine
The complicated nature of affairs!
God save us all! Of such as deal in wares,
There's hardly two of us, as I'm alive,
Not two in twelve, I say, can hope to thrive[3]
Till they retire, showing a steady clearance.
All very well to make a good appearance,
To drive about the world and make a mark,
But our affairs must always be kept dark
Till we are dead, unless we are to play
At pilgrimage and keep out of the way
Of creditors. It's vital to consider
This curious world and find the highest bidder;
There's always chance to fear, and many a slip
Makes for anxiety in salesmanship.

"I have to go to Bruges at break of day;
I shall come home as quickly as I may.
Therefore, dear wife, I beg of you to be
Courteous and meek to all in place of me.
Look after all our property with care,
See to the house; here's plenty and to spare.
Govern it well. I'll see you have enough,
But still, be thrifty over household stuff.
You've all the clothes you need, and all the
    stores.
I'll put some silver in that purse of yours."
    And with that word he shut the
    counter-door
And came downstairs, he lingered there no
    more.
Quickly they all went off to Mass and prayed,
And quickly too the tables then were laid;
The merchant and his wife attacked the
    spread,
Sir John the monk was sumptuously fed.
    Soon after dinner, soberly, Sir John
Took him aside—this merchant—and
    went on
To say as follows: "Cousin, as I see,
You're off to Bruges for some commodity.
May God and St. Augustine be your guide!
Now do be careful, cousin, how you ride,
And moderate in your diet; in this heat
You should be temperate in what you eat.
Well, don't let's stand on ceremony!
    Good-bye,
Dear cousin! God protect you from on high!
And if there's anything by night or day
That I can do to help you, only say.
Command me, and whatever be the task
It shall be done exactly as you ask.
    "Oh . . . One thing. May I ask you as a
    friend
Before you go . . . Could you contrive to lend
A hundred francs? Just for a week or two?
I have to buy some cattle to renew
A farm of ours with animals and stores.
So help me God I wish the place were yours!
You may be sure I will not fail my day,
Not if it were a thousand francs, I say.
But please tell no one of this little debt.
—You see, I haven't bought the cattle yet.
And now, good-bye to you, my own dear
    cousin,
And for your kindness to me, thanks a dozen!"
    This noble-hearted merchant thereupon
Replied, "Good heavens, cousin! Dear Sir
    John,

This is indeed a very small request!
My gold is yours whenever you think best.
And not my gold alone, but all my stuff;
Take what you please, be sure you take
     enough.
Of course—I hardly need remind you now—
We merchants use our money like a plough.
We can get credit while our name will run,
But to be short of money is no fun;
So pay me back when you've the cash about.
Meanwhile I'm very glad to help you out."
     He fetched a hundred francs out of his
          trunk
And handed them in secret to the monk,
So secretly the deal was only known
To him—this merchant—and Sir John alone.
They drank and talked and loitered for a spell;
Sir John rode back then to his abbey cell.
     Day came; the merchant started on his ride
To Flanders with a prentice as his guide
And came at last to Bruges in good condition.
Once there he worked in haste without re-
     mission
And did his business, borrowed, made ad-
     vances,
And never turned aside for dice or dances,
But purely as a merchant, let me say,
He spent his time, and there I let him stay.
     The very Sunday after he had gone,
Back to St. Denys came the good Sir John
New-tonsured and with freshly-shaven face.
There was no little boy in all the place
Nor any other person, it was plain,
But was rejoiced to see Sir John again.
And to go shortly to the point indeed
This lovely woman readily agreed
To take his hundred francs and to requite
Sir John by lying in his arms all night.
And just as was agreed, so it was done.
All night they led a life of busy fun
Till dawn came up. Then with a kindly laugh
He left, wishing good luck to all the staff,
For not a soul, there or in town about,
Had formed the least suspicion or slightest
     doubt
Of what had happened. Homewards, or
     where whim
Directed, off he rode; no more of him.
     This merchant, having finished his affairs,
Turned for St. Denys; thither he repairs
And cheers his wife with fun and feast and
     such,
But said his merchandise had cost so much

That he must needs negotiate an advance
For he was bound by a recognisance
For twenty thousand crowns he had to pay.
He'd have to go to Paris the next day
To borrow certain sums among his friends
Which, with his ready cash, would meet his
     ends.
     No sooner had he come into the town
Than, out of pure affection, he got down
And called upon Sir John for simple pleasure
And not at all to claim the borrowed treasure,
But just to see him, ask how he was doing
And tell him what affairs he was pursuing
As friends will do on their occasional meet-
     ings.
Sir John was most effusive in his greetings
And he as blithely chatted back and told
How prosperously he had bought and sold,
Thanks be to God, in all his merchandise,
Save that it was incumbent to devise
The raising of a loan at interest;
That done, he could afford to take a rest.
     Sir John replied, "Indeed, I am delighted
That you are safely back with matters righted;
If I were rich—we all have ups and downs—
You should not lack for twenty thousand
     crowns,
You were so kind to me the other day
Lending me money; all I have to say
Is many, many thanks! God give you life!
But I returned the money to your wife
—The sum you lent—and put it in your till
At home. She'll know about it all, she will,
For it was all arranged by double entry.
Now I must go and leave you business gentry.
I have to join the Abbot here today,
He's going out of town—I cannot stay.
Best greetings to my pretty little niece,
Your wife! Good-bye, dear cousin, go in
     peace!
Let's hope it won't be long before we meet."
     This merchant, who was wary and discreet,
Soon managed to negotiate his loan;
The bond that he had signed became his own
For he paid down the money to a franc
To certain Lombards at their Paris Bank.
He left as merry as a popinjay
For home, his business done in such a way
That he was bound to make, to the extent
Of fully a thousand francs, more than he'd
     spent.
     His wife was there and met him at the gate
Just as she always did, and they sat late

That night and had a feast. He did not fret,
Knowing that he was rich and out of debt.
 At dawn this merchant started to embrace
His wife afresh, and kissed her on the face,
And up he went and made it pretty tough.
"No more!" she said. "By God, you've had
   enough!"
And wantonly she gambolled for a while,
Until at last the merchant with a smile
Said, "I'm a little cross with you, my dear,
Though I am loth to be so, never fear.
Do you know why? By God, or so I guess,
You've brought about a sort of awkwardness
Between myself, I say, and Cousin John.
You should have warned me, dear, before I'd
   gone,
That he had paid you back my hundred francs
By double entry.[4] It was little thanks
He gave me when I spoke of borrowing
   money.
His face showed plainly that it wasn't funny.
But all the same, by God our Heavenly King,
I had no thought to ask for anything!
I beg you not to do it any more.
When off on business I must know before
If any debtor has paid you back my pence
Unknown to me, in case your negligence
Should make me ask for what's been paid al-
   ready."
 So far from being frightened or unsteady,
This wife retorted boldly thereupon:
"Then I defy that treacherous monk Sir John!
Him and his entries! I don't care a bit!
He gave me a sum of money, I admit.
So what? A curse upon his monkish snout!
God knows I had imagined, out of doubt,
That he had given it me because of you,
To spend on looking smart, on what is due
To your position and the friendly cheer
You've always shown him as a cousin here!
But now it seems that things are out of joint.
Well then! I'll answer briefly to the point;
You've many slacker debtors than myself!
I'll pay you readily, and as for pelf,
If that should fail, from sunset to revally
I am your wife, so score it on my tally.
I'll pay you back as promptly as I may.
I promise you I spent it in the way
Of pretty clothes; it didn't go in waste,
But, I assure you, in the best of taste
To honour you; for goodness' sake I say
Don't be so angry, dear, let's laugh and play.
My jolly body's pledged to you instead;

By God I'll never pay except in bed.
Forgive me, dearest husband, just this while;
Turn round again and let me see you smile!"
 This merchant saw that there was no re-
   dress
And that to chide her was but foolishness
Since nothing could be done, and was content
To say, "Well, I forgive you what you spent,
But don't be so extravagant again;
You must economize, let that be plain."
 And now my story's done, and may God
   send us
Plenty of entries until death shall end us!
                                    Amen.

THE PRIORESS'S TALE

Words of the Host to the Shipman and
the Prioress

"Well said, by *Corpus Dominus!*" cried our
   Host.[1]
"Long life to you! And may you sail the coast
In safety, noble skipper! Don't get sunk.
A load of lousy luck upon that monk!
Hey, fellows, watch your step for such a jape!
He took the merchant's hood and put an ape
Inside, by St. Augustine, and what's more
Into his wife's hood too! Well, shut your door
Against all monks! . . . What next? . . . Well,
   let me see;
Who else shall entertain the company?"
 And turning round, he checked himself,
   displayed
A courtesy becoming to a maid,
And said, "My Lady Prioress, by your leave,
If I felt certain not to vex or grieve,
I'd judge it time for you to show your skill
By telling the next story, if you will.
Will you vouchsafe, dear lady, to comply?"
"Gladly," the Prioress answered, "I will try."

The Prioress's Prologue

Domine, dominus noster (Psalm viii)
"O Lord, our Lord, how marvellous Thy name,
Spread through the reaches of the earth!"
   said she,
"Nor only are Thy precious praise and fame
Found in the mouths of men of dignity,
For in the mouths of children, such maybe
As suck the breast, the bounty of Thy ways
Can be declared in worship and in praise.

"Wherefore in honour of Thee, as best I can,
Of Thee and of that whitest lily-flower
That bare Thee, all without the touch of man,
I tell my tale and will put forth my power,
Though all unable to increase her dower
Of honour, who is honour itself, and root
Of bounty, next to Thee, her body's fruit.

"O mother-maid, maid-mother, chaste and
    free!
O bush unburnt, burning in Moses' sight,
Thou that didst ravish down from Deity
Upon thy humbleness the Spirit's flight
That lit upon thy heart, and in whose might
The Word took flesh, help me to tell my story
In reverence of thee and of thy glory!

"No tongue or knowledge can have confi-
    dence,
Lady, to tell thy great humility,
Thy bounty, virtue and magnificence;
For sometimes, lady, ere men pray to thee
Thou goest before in thy benignity
And through thy prayer thou gettest for
    each one
Light that may guide them to thy blessed Son.

"Weak is my skill in speech, O blissful
    Queen;
How then shall I declare thy worthiness
Or how sustain the weight of what I mean?
For as a child, a twelvemonth old, or less,
That hardly has a word it can express,
Just so am I, and therefore pity me!
Guide thou the song that I shall sing for thee!"

The Prioress's Tale

In Asia once there was a Christian town
In which, long since, a Ghetto used to be
Where there were Jews, supported by the
    Crown
For the foul lucre of their usury,
Hateful to Christ and all his company.
And through this Ghetto one might walk
    or ride
For it was free and open, either side.

A little school stood for the Christian flock
Down at the further end, and it was here
A heap of children come of Christian stock
Received their early schooling year by year
And the instruction suited to their ear,
That is to say in singing and in reading

—The simple things of childhood and good
    breeding.

Among these children was a widow's son,
A little chorister of seven years old,
And day by day to school he used to run
And had the custom (for he had been told
To do so) should he happen to behold
An image of Christ's mother, to kneel and say
Hail Mary as he went upon his way.

Thus had this widow taught her little boy
To reverence the mother of Christ, our dear
And blissful lady, and it was his joy;
A happy child will always learn and hear.
When I remember this, the ever-near
Saint Nicholas stands in my presence, he
Who did Christ reverence in infancy.

This little child, while he was studying
His little primer, which he undertook,
Sitting at school, heard other children sing
O Alma Redemptoris from their book.
Close as he dared he drew himself to look,
And listened carefully to work and part
Until he knew the opening verse by heart.

He had no notion what this Latin meant
Being so young, so tender too, so green;
But in the end, one morning there, he went
And asked a comrade what the song
    might mean
And why it was in use. He was so keen
To know it that he went upon his knees
Begging the boy explain it if he please.

His schoolfellow—an older boy than he—
Answered him thus: "This song, I have
    heard say,
Is to salute Our Blessed Lady; she
Will hear us when we turn to her and pray
For help and comfort on our dying day.
I can explain no more—that's all I know;
I can learn singing, but my grammar's slow."

"And is this anthem made to reverence
Christ's mother?" said this innocent. "If I may,
I certainly will show my diligence
To learn it off by heart for Christmas Day.
Though they should scold me when I can-
    not say
My primer, though they beat me thrice an hour,
I'll learn it in her honour, to my power."

So every day his comrade secretly
As they went homewards taught it him by
      rote;
He sang it with a childlike clarity
And boldly, word by word and note by note;
And twice a day it filled his little throat,
Going to school and coming back again,
Praising Christ's mother with all his might
      and main.

As I have said, this child would go along
The Jewish street and, of his own accord,
Daily and merrily he sang his song
O Alma Redemptoris; as it soared,
The sweetness of the mother of our Lord
Would pierce his heart, he could not choose
      but pray
And sing as, to and fro, he went his way.

First of our foes, the Serpent Satan shook
Those Jewish hearts that are his waspish nest,
Swelled up and said. "O Hebrew people look!
Is this not something that should be redressed?
Is such a boy to roam as he thinks best
Singing to spite you, canticles and saws
Against the reverence of your holy laws?"

From that time forward all these Jews con-
      spired
To chase this innocent child from the earth's
      face.
Down a dark alley-way they found and hired
A murderer who owned that secret place;
And as the boy passed at his happy pace
This cursed Jew grabbed him and held
      him, slit
His little throat and cast him in a pit.

Cast him, I say, into a privy-drain,
Where they were wont to void their excre-
      ment.
O cursed folk of Herod come again,
Of what avail your villainous intent?
Murder will out, and nothing can prevent
God's honour spreading, even from such seed;
The blood cries out upon your cursed deed.

"O martyr wedded to virginity,
Now mayest thou sing and follow, on and on,
The white, celestial Lamb of Heaven,"
      said she,
"Of whom the great evangelist, St. John,
In Patmos wrote, who says that there they don

White robes before that Lamb, and sing afresh
That never have known woman in the flesh."

This wretched widow waited all that night,
She waited for her child, but all for nought;
And very early in the morning light,
All pale with sleepless dread and busy
      thought,
She searched his school, then up and down she
      sought
Elsewhere, and finally she got the news
That he was last seen in the street of Jews.

Within her breast her mother's pity closed,
She went about as one half out of mind
To every place in which, as she supposed,
There was some likelihood for her to find
Her child, and to Christ's mother, meek and
      kind,
She cried in heart, and in the end was brought
Among the accursed Jews, and there she
      sought.

She made enquiry with a piteous cry
Of every Jew inhabiting that place,
Asking if they had seen her child go by,
And they said, "No." But Jesus of His grace
Put in her thought, after a little space,
To come upon that alley as she cried,
Where, in a pit, he had been cast aside.

Great God, that to perform Thy praise hast
      called
The innocent of mouth, how great Thy
      might!
This gem of chastity, this emerald,
This jewel of martyrdom and ruby bright,
Lying with carven throat and out of sight,
Began to sing O Alma from the ground
Till all the place was ringing with the sound.

The Christian people going through the street
Came crowding up astonished at the thing,
And sent to fetch the Provost to entreat
His presence, and he came and heard him sing.
The Provost, praising Christ our heav-
      enly king
And His dear mother, honour of mankind,
Bade all the Jews be fettered and confined.

They took the child with piteous lamentation
And he was brought, still singing out his song,
In high solemnity and celebration

Towards the nearest abbey by the throng.
His mother, swooning as they went along
Beside the bier, could not be reconciled,
A second Rachel, weeping for her child.

The Provost then did judgement on the men
Who did the murder, and he bid them serve
A shameful death in torment there and then
On all those guilty Jews; he did not swerve.
"Evils shall meet the evils they deserve."
And he condemned them to be drawn apart
By horses. Then he hanged them from a cart.

Still lay this innocent child upon his bier
At the high altar while a Mass was said.
The abbot and his convent then drew near
To hasten on his burial, and spread
A rain of holy water on his head;
And as they let the holy water spill
He sang O *Alma Redemptoris* still.

This abbot then, who was a holy man
As abbots are, or else they ought to be,
In invocation of the boy began
To say aloud, "Dear child, I conjure thee
By virtue of the Holy Trinity
To say how singing is permitted thee
Although thy throat is cut, or seems to be."

"Through to the bone my neck is cut, I know,"
Answered the child; "and had I been confined
By natural law I should, and long ago,
Have died. But Christ, whose glory you
      may find
In books, wills it be also kept in mind.
So for the honour of his mother dear
I still may sing O *Alma* loud and clear.

"That well of mercy, sweetest mother of
      Christ,
I long have loved with all that I could bring;
This at the hour of my death sufficed
To draw her down to me. She bade me sing
This anthem till my time of burying
As you have heard; and when my song
      was sung
She seemed to lay a grain upon my tongue.

"And so I sing as I must sing again
For love of her, the blissful and the free,
Till from my tongue you take away the grain.
For after that, the Virgin said to me,
'My little child, behold I come for thee

When from thy tongue this grain of seed is
      taken.
And have no fear; thou shalt not be forsaken.' "

This holy monk, this abbot, even he,
Touched the child's tongue and took away the
      grain;
And he gave up the ghost so peacefully,
So softly, and the marvel was so plain,
Salt fell the abbot's tears in trickling rain,
And down he fell, prostrate upon the ground,
And lay as still as one who had been bound.

And all the weeping convent also bent
To earth and praised Christ's mother with
      many a tear,
And after that they rose, and forth they went
Taking this little martyr from his bier,
And in sepulchre of marble clear
Enclosed his little body, fair and sweet.
Where he now is, God grant we all may meet!

O Hugh of Lincoln, likewise murdered so
By cursed Jews, as is notorious
(For it was but a little time ago),
Pray mercy on our faltering steps, that thus
Merciful God may multiply on us
His mercy, though we be unstable and vary,
In love and reverence of His mother Mary.
                                          Amen.

THE TALE OF SIR TOPAZ
Words of the Host to Chaucer

Now when they heard this miracle every man
Was sobered; it was marvellous to see.
But in the end our Host again began
His jokes, and then he turned and looked
      at me,
And thus he spoke: "What man are you?"
      said he,
"You look as if you were trying to find a hare,
Scanning the ground with such a steady stare!

"Come nearer, man, look up, look merrily!
Make room there, gentlemen, let this man
      have place!
He's shaped about the waist the same as me;
He'd be a likely poppet to embrace
For any woman, small and fair of face!
There's something elvish in his countenance;
He never speaks a word in dalliance.

"Say something now, as other folk have
    done;
And let it be a tale of mirth; at once!"
"Host," I replied, "I hope you are not one
To take it in bad part if I'm a dunce;
I only know a rhyme which, for the nonce,
I learnt." "That's good," he said, "well, take
    your place;
It should be dainty, judging by your face."

Chaucer's Tale of Sir Topaz

THE FIRST FIT

Listen, lords, with all your might
And I will tell you, honour bright,
    A tale of mirth and game,
About a fair and gentle knight
In battle, tournament and fight,
    Sir Topaz was his name.

And he was born in far countree
In Flanders all beyond the sea,
    At Poperinghe in that place.
His father was of high degree
And lord of all the land was he,
    As God had given him grace.

Sir Topaz grew a doughty swain,
With face like bread of whitest grain.
    His lips were red as rose,
And his complexion like a stain
Of scarlet red, and I maintain
    He had a seemly nose.

He'd saffron hair and beard as well
That down below his girdle fell,
    His shoe-leather was Spanish;
Rich brown his hose (it so befell)
From Bruges, and rich his robe as well,
    It made the money vanish.

And he was great at hunting deer
And hawking down along the mere
    With goshawk on his hand;
He was an archer, never fear,
A wrestler too that had no peer,
    No peer in all the land.

Full many a maiden bright in bower
Lay longing for him hour by hour
    Who should have been asleep;
But he was chaste and fled the power
Of lechery, chaste as bramble-flower
    Where red the berries creep.

It so befell upon a day,
As I'll tell truly if I may,
    Sir Topaz went to ride.
He mounted on his steed of grey
And, lance in hand, he rode away,
    A long-sword by his side.

He spurred his way through forest fair
Where many a monster has its lair,
    Such as the hare and buck;
And as he went by east and north,
I tell you, and was riding forth
    He met with evil luck.

The herbs were springing in the vale;
Green ginger plants and liquorice pale
    And cloves their sweetness offered,
With nutmegs too, to put in ale
No matter whether fresh or stale,
    Or else to be kept coffered.

The birds were singing, let me say,
The sparrowhawk and popinjay,
    It was a joy to hear.
The throstlecock attuned his lay,
The turtle-dove upon the spray
    Sang very loud and clear.

Sir Topaz fell in love-longing
On hearing thus the throstle sing
    And spurred away like mad.
His steed was hot with galloping
And sweated so, a man could wring
    Him out, such sweat he had.

Sir Topaz, so it came to pass,
Wearied of spurring o'er the grass;
    So very fierce his courage
That down he lay as bold as brass
And eased his steed by a morass
    Where there was splendid forage.

"Saint Mary, *benedicite!*"
He said. "What love has done to me!
    It binds my heart, no joke.
By God I dreamt all night," said he,
"An Elf-Queen should my mistress be
    And sleep beneath my cloak.

"I'll have an Elf-Queen, I declare!
In all the world there's none so fair
    Or worthy to be mine
              In town;

All other women I resign,
An Elf shall be my Valentine
  By dell and dale and down!"

He climbed his saddle like a throne
And galloped over stile and stone
  To spy an Elfin Queen.
And soon, as fast as if he'd flown,
He found a secret place and lone,
  Sweet Fairy-land, I mean,
           So wild;
For not a soul in all that zone
There was and not a face was shown,
  No woman, not a child,

Until a mighty Giant came
On him, Sir Elephant by name,
  A perilous man indeed,
Who said, "Sir Knight, by fire and flame
Be off! By Termagent, I'll maim
  You and your sturdy steed
           With mace
Unless you go. The Queen of Faerie
With harp and pipe and music airy
  Has dwelling in this place."

The Knight replied, "By all that's blue,
To-morrow I will meet with you
  When I have got my armour;
And then I hope to make you dance
With this my slender little lance
  And you shall be the warmer.
           Your belly
Shall feel its prick as I advance
Ere prime of day, and it may chance
  That you'll be slain, I tell 'ee."

Sir Topaz quickly then retired;
The Giant took a sling and fired
  Fell stones, but greatly daring
Sir Topaz swiftly left the place
And got away by God's good grace
  And by his noble bearing.

My lords, still hearken to my tale
That's merrier than the nightingale,
  And let me whisper plain
How good Sir Topaz, small and pale,
By spurring over hill and dale
  Got back to town again.

He ordered all his merry throng
To cheer him up with sport and song,

For he would have to fight
A three-head giant, very strong,
To gain the transports that belong
  To love and lady bright.

"Come forth," he said, "my minstrels all,
You story tellers in my hall,
  And tell me while I arm
Romances such as may befall
To Prince and Pope and Cardinal
  And of a lover's charm."

They fetched him first the sweetest wine,
Then mead in mazers they combine
  With lots of royal spice,
And gingerbread, exceeding fine,
And liquorice and eglantyne
  And sugar, very nice.

They covered next his ivory flank
With cloth spun of the finest hank,
  With breeches and a shirt,
And over that (in case it fail)
A tunic, then a coat of mail,
  For fear he might be hurt,

And over that contrived to jerk
A hauberk (finest Jewish work
  And strong in every plate)
And over that his coat of arms,
White as a lily-flower's charms,
  In which he must debate.

His shield was of a golden red
Emblazoned with a porker's head,
  Carbuncles at the side;
And there he swore by ale and bread
That he would kill the giant dead,
  Betide what might betide!

Boiled leather on his shins had he,
His sword was sheathed in ivory,
  His helm was copper bright.
His saddle was of narwhal bone,
His bridle shone like precious stone,
  Or sun, or moon at night.

Of cypress was the spear he bore,
Not made for peace, but boding war,
  The head was sharply ground.
His palfrey was of dapple-grey
It wandered in an ambling way
  And softly trotted round

About.
My lords, this is the opening fit!
If you want any more of it
    I'll tell you more, no doubt.

THE SECOND FIT

Now hold your tongues for charity,
My noble knights and ladies free,
    And listen to my spell,
To battle and to chivalry
And making love in wantonry
    For such is what I tell.

Men tell romances such as this
About Sir Horn, Sir Hypotis,
    Sir Bevis and Sir Guy,
Sir Libeus and Sir Pleyndamour,
But our Sir Topaz will endure
    Above the lesser fry.

His worthy steed he then bestrode
And forth upon his way he glode
    Like sparkles from a flame.
And on his crest he bore a tower
And stuck thereon a lily-flower,
    God guard him from all shame!

And as he was a valiant knight
He sought no house at evening light
    But laid him down on earth,
Wrapped in his hood, his helm a pillow,
And tied his palfrey to a willow;
    It grazed to keep its girth.

But he drank water from the well,
As did the knight Sir Percivell,
    That worthy man-at-arms,
Till on a day . . .

The Host stops Chaucer's Tale of Sir Topaz

"No more of this for God's dear dignity!"
Our Host said suddenly. "You're weary-
    ing me
To death, I say, with your illiterate stuff.
God bless my soul! I've had about enough.
My ears are aching from your frowsty story!
The devil take such rhymes! They're purga-
    tory!
That must be what's called doggerel-rhyme,"
    said he.
    "Why so?" said I, "Why should you hin-
        der me

In telling my tale more than another man,
Since I am giving you the best I can?"
    "By God," he said, "put plainly in a word,
Your dreary rhyming isn't worth a turd!
You're doing nothing else but wasting time.
Sir, in a word, you shall no longer rhyme.
Let's see if you can tell us one of those
Old tales from history; and speak in prose.
Let it be gay or have a wholesome moral."
    "Gladly," I said, "Dear God, I hate a
        quarrel.
So let me tell a little thing in prose
That ought to give you pleasure, I suppose,
Or else it must be very hard to please you;
It has a virtuous moral to appease you;
It has been told again and yet again
By various writers; but I may explain
No one Evangelist would have sufficed
To tell us of the pains of Jesus Christ,
Nor does each tell it as the others do;
Nevertheless what each has said is true,
And all agree as to their general sense,
Though each with some degree of difference.
If some of them say more and some say less
About his piteous Passion, I should guess
—Speaking of Mark and Matthew, Luke and
    John—
Their meaning doubtless was agreed upon.
And therefore let me beg of you, my lords,
If you should think my story ill accords
With the original—if, for instance, more
Proverbial matter than you've heard before
Is thrust into my little treatise here
To enforce its meaning in the moral sphere,
Or if the words I use are not the same
As you have heard, I beg you not to blame
My variations; in my general sense
You won't find much by way of difference
Between the little treatise as it's known
And this, a merry story of my own.
So listen, please, to what I have to say,
And let me tell my tale as best I may."

CHAUCER'S TALE OF MELIBEE

Chaucer's prose Tale of Melibee (the tone of which is entirely serious throughout) here follows in the original. It is a dialectical homily or moral debate, exhibiting a learned store of ethical precept culled from many ancient authorities. It extends over a thousand lines or so. Among the authorities quoted are Job, Solomon, St. Paul, Jesus son of Sirach,

St. Augustine, St. Jerome, St. Gregory, Pope Innocent, Ovid, Cato, Seneca, Cicero, Cassiodorus, and
Petrus Alphonsus.

The principal character in the debate is Dame
Prudence, the wife of Melibee, but we also hear the
views of his acquaintances, doctors, lawyers, prudent
old men and hot-headed young ones. Melibee himself
offers some opinions, most of which are wisely and
modestly refuted by his wife. He is, however, more
talked against than talking, and is always won over,
in the end, to the right view.

The principal subject of the debate is whether we
should avenge a violent injury by violence, and the
subject arises because during his absence from home
Melibee's daughter, Sophia, has been assaulted and
wounded by three miscreants who have made a bur-
glarious entry. Should revenge be taken upon them?

In the course of the debate the following subjects
arise and are dealt with learnedly and logically, for
the most part by Dame Prudence:

· how to purify one's heart of anger, covetousness,
and impetuosity; how to keep one's opinions to
oneself and distinguish true friends from false
ones, fools, and flatterers; how to examine any advice proffered and when to change one's advisers;

· whether women are to be trusted, and whether
their advice can ever be good, and if so, whether
husbands ought to submit themselves to their direction (Dame Prudence wins heavily on this);

· whether to take a private revenge is (a) dangerous,
(b) justifiable morally, (c) in this case expedient
(in parentheses, why does God permit evil? No
one knows): the outcome of violence is uncertain,
one cannot be sure of success in vengeance. It is
better to agree or compound with one's enemies.
But would not this involve a loss of prestige?
Prestige considered;

· the importance of not making God your enemy,
to whom vengeance belongs. If you reconcile yourself with Him, He will reconcile your enemies
with you.

The enemies of Melibee are then sent for; Dame
Prudence sees them privately and points out the supe-
riority of a peaceful settlement. They are astonished
and delighted.

Melibee decides to let them off with a fine. Dame
Prudence persuades him to forgive them altogether.

His enemies then return before Melibee, who for-
gives them utterly, but not before he has rebuked
them severely and pointed out his own magnanimity. This is perhaps the only point he scores.

Nothing is said of what happened to Sophia or
whether she recovered from her injuries. The homily
is immediately followed by

THE MONK'S TALE
Words of the Host to the Monk

When I had done my tale of Melibee
And of Dame Prudence's benignity,
Our Host exclaimed, "As I'm an honest man,
And by the precious bones of Madrian,
I'd rather have had my wife to hear this tale,
Good soul, than have a barrelful of ale!
She never shows such patience when with me
As Prudence showed in handling Melibee.
God's bones! Whenever I go to beat those
   knaves
My tapsters, out she comes with clubs and
   staves,
'Go on!' she screams—and it's a caterwaul—
'You kill those dogs! Break back and bones
   and all!'
"If any of my neighbours when in church
Fails to acknowledge her, or gives a lurch
And bumps against her, as may be the case,
No sooner home, she's ramping in my face,
'You wretched coward,' she cries, 'avenge
   your wife!
By corpus bones,' she says, 'give me your knife
And you shall have my distaff and go spin!'
"That's how the evenings end and days
   begin.
'My word!' she says. 'Things are in pretty
   shape;
I've married a milksop or a cowardly ape
Who lets himself be downed by every sot
And daren't stand up to back his wife, that's
   what!'
"Such is my daily life; unless I fight,
By God, she turns me out of doors at night
Lost, if I show the slightest sign of tardiness
Or seem less than a lion in fool-hardiness!
Sooner or later, thanks to all her labours,
I shall be driven to murdering the neighbours;
For, knives out, I'm an ugly customer,
Though I confess I can't stand up to her.
Her arm is pretty tough as, by St. Victor,
You'd find were you to wound or contra-
   dict her!
But now let's drop the subject and pass on.
"My lord the Monk, don't look so woe-
   begone,
For it's your turn to tell a story, sir.
Why, look! We've almost got to Rochester!
Forward, my lord, and don't hold up our
   game.
But, on my honour, I don't know your name;

Sir John, perhaps? Why have you kept it
    from us?
Or should I say Sir Alban, or Sir Thomas?
What monastery have they shut you in?
I vow to God you have a pretty skin!
There was fine pasturage where you were sent,
You're nothing like a ghost or penitent!
My! You must surely be some officer,
Some worthy Sexton, or some Cellarer.
For by my father's soul, in my opinion,
When you're at home, you're in your own do-
    minion.
You are no novice, cloistered in retreat,
But in control, and wily as discreet.
Moreover when it comes to brawn and bone,
You seem to be well-cared-for, you must own.
God send confusion on the fellow who
First had the thought to make a monk of you!
You would have put a hen to pretty use,
Had you permission, as you have the juice,
To exercise your pleasure in procreation!
You could have done your part to build the
    nation.
Alas, who put you in so wide a cope?
Damnation take me, but if I were Pope,
Not only you but many a mighty man
Going about the world with tonsured pan
Should have a wife; for look, the world's for-
    lorn!
Religion has got hold of all the corn
Of procreation, laymen are but shrimps.
Weak trees make sorry seedlings! That's what
    skimps
Our heirs and children, makes them all so
    slender
And feeble that they hardly can engender.
And that's what makes our wives so apt
    to cope
Religious people; there they have some hope
Of honest coin to pay the debts of Venus;
We laymen hardly have a groat between us!
    "But don't be angry, sir, at what I say;
Many a true word has been said in play!"
    This worthy Monk took all without of-
    fence
And said, "Sir, I will do my diligence
To tell you all a tale or two, or three,
As far as may conform with decency.
And if you care to hear, as our assessor,
I'll tell the *Life of Edward the Confessor;*
Or else I have some tragedies to tell;
I have at least a hundred in my cell.
    " 'Tragedy' means a certain kind of story,
As old books tell, of those who fell from glory,

People that stood in great prosperity
And were cast down out of their high degree
Into calamity, and so they died.
Such tales are usually versified
In six-foot lines they call *Hexameter.*
Many are told in prose, if you prefer,
And other metres suited to the stuff;
This explanation ought to be enough.
    "Now listen, therefore, if you care to hear.
But first I beg you not to be severe
If my chronology in all these things,
Be they of popes, of emperors or kings,
Forsakes the order in which they fell of yore
And I put some behind and some before;
They come to my remembrance but by
    chance;
Accept excuses for my ignorance."

The Monk's Tale

In Tragic Manner I will now lament
The griefs of those who stood in high degree
And fell at last with no expedient
To bring them out of their adversity.
For sure it is, if Fortune wills to flee,
No man may stay her course or keep his hold;
Let no one trust a blind prosperity.
Be warned by these examples, true and old.

LUCIFER

With Lucifer, although an angel he
And not a man, I purpose to begin.
For notwithstanding angels cannot be
The sport of Fortune, yet he fell through sin
Down into hell, and he is yet therein.
O Lucifer, brightest of angels all,
Now thou art Satan, and canst never win
Out of thy miseries; how great thy fall!

ADAM

Consider Adam, made by God's own finger,
And not begotten of man's unclean seed,
He that in Eden was allowed to linger
—Now called Damascus—and had power
    at need
Over all Paradise, save that decreed
And single tree prohibited. Than he
None ever on earth stood higher, till his deed
Drove him to labour, Hell and misery.

SAMSON

Long ere his birth, by an annunciation,
Samson was heralded by an angel bright
Who marked him out for God in consecration.
He stood forth nobly while he had his sight;

There never was another of such might,
Or hardihood of mind for might to borrow;
And yet he let his secret come to light,
He told his wife, and killed himself for
    sorrow.

Samson, this noble warrior of Zion,
Having no weapon by him for the fray
But his bare hands, yet slew and tore a lion
While walking to his wedding, on the way.
His treacherous wife so pleased him with her
    play,
She coaxed his secrets forth; with double face
She then betrayed them to his foes that lay
In wait, and took another in his place.

And Samson took, in his avenging ire,
And lashed three hundred foxes in a band,
Tying their tails, then set the tails on fire
(To every tail he bound a fiery brand)
And burnt up every cornfield in the land
And every vine and olive in a mass
Of flame, and slew a thousand with his hand,
No weapon but the jaw-bone of an ass;

But having slain them was so parched with
    thirst
He was near lost, yet prayed the Lord on high
To show that favour He had showed at first
And send His servant water lest he die:
Then from that very jaw-bone which was dry
Out of a molar-tooth there sprang a well,
And there he drank enough to satisfy
His thirst; God sent His help, as *Judges* tell.

And then at Gaza on a certain night
By force he rent apart the city gate,
Bore off the pieces on his back, in spite
Of what the Philistines in fierce debate
Could do, and then he set them up in state
High on a hill. O Samson, dear thy worth!
Hadst thou not blabbed thy secrets to thy mate
None ever could have matched thee upon
    earth!

This Samson never drank of mead or wine,
His head no razor ever touched, or shear;
This precept was enjoined by the divine
Messenger-angel—all his strength lay here,
Lodged in his locks. And fully twenty year
He was a Judge and ruler of Israel;
Yet the day came to him for many a tear
And it was by a woman that he fell.

It was to Dálila, his lover, she
To whom he owned that all his power lay
Within his hair, and to the enemy
She sold her lover sleeping, as he lay
Upon her breast, and bade them cut away
His locks, revealed his secret to those spies,
And so they found him there an easy prey.
They bound him fast and put out both his
    eyes.

But yet before his hair was clipped and shaved
There was no thong or lashing that could bind
His arm; and now they took him and encaved
Him in a prison, set him there to grind
A quern! O Samson, strongest of mankind,
O sometime Judge in glory and in power,
Now mayst thou weep although thine eyes are
    blind!
Fled is thy joy and come thy bitter hour.

Perished this captive wretch as I shall say;
His foes prepared a feast, and for their jeers
Made him their fool and bade him to display
Amidst a temple, thronged in crowded tiers,
His strength; and yet he set them by the ears.
He grasped two pillars, shook and made them
    fall,
And the whole temple, shaken from its piers,
Crashed down and slew him, and his foe-
    men all.

That is to say, not Magistrates alone
But some three thousand others also slain
In the huge ruin of their temple of stone.
Of Samson I will say no more; but gain
A warning from his story, old and plain:
Men should keep counsel and not tell their
    wives
Secrets that it concerns them to retain,
Touching the safety of their limbs and lives.

HERCULES

For Hercules, victor of sovereign power,
His labours sing his praise and lasting fame,
Who in his time was human strength in
    flower.
He slew a lion and he skinned the same;
He robbed the Centaurs of their boasted
    name;
He slew the Harpies, cruel birds and fell;
He robbed the golden apples, overcame
Their dragon-guard, drove Cerberus from
    Hell,

And slew Busiris the tyrannical,
And made his horses eat him, flesh and bone;
He brought about the fiery serpent's fall,
Made one of Acheloüs' horns his own,
Killed the fierce Cacus in his cave of stone
And left Antaeus the Gigantic dead;
He met the grisly boar and laid it prone,
And last he shouldered heaven overhead.

Was never creature since the world began
That slew so many monsters as did he.
Throughout the world his reputation ran,
What with his strength and magnanimity.
All kingdoms of the earth he went to see,
None said him nay, none equalled him in
    worth,
And the Chaldean prophet named Trophee
Says he set pillars up to bound the earth.

He had a lover, this redoubted man,
Her name was Deianira, fresh as May;
And as the learned tell us, she began
To fashion him a shirt, to make him gay.
O fatal shirt! Alas, alas, I say!
Poison was subtly woven in its mesh;
Ere he had worn it scarcely half a day
From every bone there fell away his flesh.

But some authorities would thus excuse her,
Saying that Nessus made the shirt, not she;
Let that be as it may, I won't accuse her;
He wore it anyhow, and certainly
Blackness began to rot his flesh, and he
Raked burning coals upon himself and died,
Having perceived there was no remedy
And scorning death by poison, out of pride.

Thus fell the famous, mighty Hercules!
Who then may trust the dice, at Fortune's
    throw?
Who joins in worldly struggles such as these
Will be, when least prepared for it, laid low!
Wise is the man who well has learnt to know
Himself. Beware! When Fortune would elect
To trick a man, she plots his overthrow
By such a means as he would least expect.

NEBUCHADNEZZAR

The mighty throne, the precious stores of
    treasure,
The glorious sceptre and the diadem
That once belonged to King Nebuchadnezzar
Tongue cannot tell, hard to describe one gem

Among them! Twice he took Jerusalem
And, from the Temple, bore the vessels
    plighted
To God, and to his realm he carried them
In Babylon, where he gloried and delighted.

The fairest children of the royal line
Of Israel he gelded, and this done,
Made each of them a thrall and let them pine
In servitude. Daniel of these was one,
Wisest among them all, or under sun.
He could expound the dreams whose visitation
Troubled the King; Chaldean there was none
That could interpret their signification.

This proud king made an image out of gold;
Its height was sixty cubits and its frame
Seven in breadth. He ordered young and old
To bow before this idol and acclaim
Its glory; in a furnace of red flame
Any that disobeyed him should be flung.
But Daniel would not stoop to such a shame
Nor would his two companions. They were
    young.

This king of kings, so mighty and elate,
Supposed that God who sits in majesty
Could never rob him of his kingly state,
Yet he was cast from it, and suddenly.
Forth in the rain, thinking himself to be
An animal, he went and fed without
On hay as oxen do; and there dwelt he
Among the beasts till time had come about.

And like an eagle's feathers grew his hair,
His nails were like the talons of a bird,
Till God released him of his madness there
For certain years and the king's heart was
    stirred
In thanks to God; with many a tearful word
He swore to sin no more, until the hour
Of death when at the last he was interred,
He recognized God's mercy and his power.

BELSHAZZAR

He had a son, Belshazzar was his name,
Who held the throne after his father's day,
But took no warning from him all the same,
Proud in his heart and proud in his display,
And an idolater as well, I say.
His high estate on which he so had prided
Himself, by Fortune soon was snatched away,
His kingdom taken from him and divided.

He made a feast and summoned all his lords
A certain day in mirth and minstrelsy,
And called a servant, as the Book records,
"Go and fetch forth the vessels, those,"
    said he,
"My father took in his prosperity
Out of the Temple of Jerusalem,
That we may thank our gods for the degree
Of honour he and I have had of them."

His wife, his lords and all his concubines
Drank on, as long as appetite would last,
Out of these vessels, filled with sundry wines.
The king glanced at the wall; a shadow passed
As of an armless hand, and writing fast.
He quaked for terror, gazing at the wall;
The hand that made Belshazzar so aghast
Wrote *Mene, Tekel, Peres,* that was all.

In all the land not one magician there
Who could interpret what the writing meant;
But Daniel soon expounded it, "Beware,"
He said, "O king! God to your father lent
Glory and honour, kingdom, treasure, rent;
But he was proud and did not fear the Lord.
God therefore punished that impenitent
And took away his kingdom, crown and
    sword.

"He cast him from the company of men
To make his habitation in the dew
Among the beasts, eat grass and tread the fen
In rain and drought, until at last he knew
By grace and reason God alone is true
And has dominion over crowns and creatures.
Then God at last was minded to renew
His mercy and restored his realm and features.

"But you, his son, are proud, though well
    you know
The truth of all these things that I have told;
You are a rebel before God, his foe,
Having defiled his vessels of pure gold;
Your wife and all your wenches have
    made bold
To do the like and drink of many a wine
In honour of false gods, accurst of old.
But God will punish you, and this his sign!

"That hand was sent of God, that on the wall
Wrote *Mene, Tekel, Peres,* as you see;
Your reign is done, you have been weighed,
    and fall;

Your kingdom is divided and shall be
Given to Persians and to Medes," said he.
They slew the King Belshazzar the same
    night,
Darius took his throne and majesty,
Though taking them neither by law nor right.

My lords, from this the moral may be taken
That there's no lordship but is insecure.
When Fortune flees a man is left forsaken
Of glory, wealth and kingdom; all's past cure.
Even the friends he has will not endure,
For if good fortune makes your friends for you
Ill fortune makes them enemies for sure,
A proverb very trite and very true.

ZENOBIA[1]

Palmyra (say the Persians) had a queen,
Zenobia; one accounted to possess
A noble nature, and in arms so keen
And hardy, none could match her, they pro-
    fess.
Her lineage and her breeding were no less
Than of a Persian royally descended;
I will not call her first in loveliness
But say her beauty could not be amended.

I find that from her childhood she had fled
The offices of women, for she went
Off to the wildness of the woods to shed
The blood of forest deer, her bow she bent
On them, still swift of foot when they were
    spent;
And as she grew to woman she would kill
Leopard and lion too, and once she rent
A bear apart; she ruled the beasts at will.

She dared them all, would thrust into a den,
Or course upon the mountains through the
    night,
Taking her sleep in bushes; as for men
She was a wrestler and could win a fight
Against a stripling of whatever might;
None could resist her arm and none elude.
And she had kept her maiden honour bright,
Not deigning to be vanquished or subdued.

At last her friends prevailed and she was
    married
To one Prince Odenathus of that land,
Albeit that she long refused and tarried;
And yet it is as well to understand
He was reluctant too to give his hand,

Having like fantasies. When knit together
Nevertheless their union proved a bland
And happy one, they came to love each other,

Save for one thing: she never would consent
To let him lie with her, except it be
Once only, when it was her clear intent
To have a child, to leave posterity;
And therefore when she knew that certainly
She had conceived no child from such an act,
She then permitted him his fantasy
Again, but only once; and that is fact.

And when she was with child by him at last
She suffered no more toying at that game
Until the fortieth week was fully past,
Then she permitted him to do the same;
And Odenathus, whether wild or tame,
Could get no more of her. She would aver
It was no more than lechery and shame
To woman for a man to play with her.

Two sons she had by Odenathus then,
Whom she brought up in virtue and in
    learning.
Now let us turn back to our tale again;
I say once more a creature so discerning,
So much esteemed, so lavish and so burning
In warlike zeal, so courteous by her birth,
You never could have found although re-
    turning
From search in all the corners of the earth.

Her splendour of array may not be told,
Whether in clothing or in store of treasure,
For she was clad in jewelry and gold.
In spite of all her hunting she found leisure
For languages and learnt them in full measure
And she applied herself to many, feeling
The study of a book to be a pleasure
That taught the way to power and high
    dealing.

And briefly to continue with my story,
Her husband was as powerful as she;
They conquered many kingdoms of great
    glory
Far in the Orient, they held in fee
Cities belonging to the majesty
Of Rome itself, and made their conquests
    thrive.
They never fled before an enemy
So long as Odenathus was alive.

As for her battles (should you wish for
    reading)
Against Shapur the King, and more as well,
With all the details of the whole proceeding,
What title won, what captured citadel,
And how at length she came to grief and fell
Besieged, made captive—all that she en-
    dured—
Study my master Petrarch, he can tell;
He wrote enough about her, be assured.

When Odenathus died, she mightily
Held all those kingdoms in her sovereign
    hand,
And was so cruel to her enemy
There was no king or prince in all the land
But felt that it was grace enough to stand
In safety and secured from war and riot,
And treated with her, that they might dis-
    band;
Let her make wars so long as they had quiet.

And neither Claudius the Emperor
Nor his successor Gallienus ran
The danger of provoking her to war;
No, nor Armenian or Egyptian,
No Syrian either or Arabian
Dared take the field against her in a fight
Lest she should slay them, or her conquer-
    ing van
Put them in all its multitude to flight.

In royal robe her sons were wont to go,
Heirs of their father's kingdoms, one and all,
Their names Hermanno and Thymalaö,
Or such at least are what the Persians call
The pair. But Fortune's honey turns to gall;
Fortune withdrew her shining countenance
From this great queen and brought about her
    fall,
And she was plunged in sorrow and mis-
    chance.

For when Aurelian came upon the scene
With Rome beneath his government and
    sway,
He planned a mighty vengeance on the queen,
And, gathering his legions, took his way
Against Zenobia; to be brief, I say,
He routed her, enslaved and brought
    her home
In fetters with her children, there they lay!
And having conquered, he returned to Rome.

Amongst the other trophies of the war
There was her golden chariot, richly gemmed;
And great Aurelian, Roman emperor,
Returned with it in glory and condemned
The queen to walk before his Triumph,
  hemmed
By shouting crowds, gold chains about her
  throat,
And still, as rank allowed her, diademed,
And there were jewels crusted on her coat.

O alas, Fortune! She that once had been
Terror of kings and of imperial powers,
Jeered at and gaped upon! A noble queen
That oft had worn the helmet through long
  hours
Of battle, and had taken towns and towers,
Now wears a mob-cap on her royal head;
She that had held a sceptre wreathed with
  flowers
Carries a distaff in her hand instead!

KING PETER OF SPAIN[2]

O noble, worthy Peter, glory of Spain,
Whom Fortune held so high in majesty,
How bitterly should we lament thy pain,
Who, by thy brother driven forth to flee,
After a siege wert caught by treachery,
And thus betrayed wert taken to his tent
Where with his own bare hands he mur-
  dered thee
And gained succession to thy throne and
  rent!

Upon an argent field an eagle sable[3]
Caught on a lime-rod gules (if you can read
This riddle) brewed the treason and was able
—O "wicked nest"!—to do a wicked deed!
No Oliver of Charlemagne he, to heed
Honour and truth, but Brittany's mishap,
A Ganelon-Oliver corrupt in greed
It was that brought this King to such a trap!

KING PETER OF CYPRUS[4]

O Peter King of Cyprus, fine and true,
That conqueredst Alexandria by the right
Of arms, and didest woe on heathens too,
Thy very liegemen envied thee, and spite
(No other cause) against thy chivalrous might
Moved them to murder thee upon the morrow
There, on thy bed! Thus Fortune with a light
Turn of her wheel brings men from joy to
  sorrow.

BERNABO VISCONTI OF LOMBARDY[5]

Great Bernabo Visconti of Milan,
God of indulgence, scourge of Lombardy,
Should I not tell of thee, unhappy man,
That scaled the summit of felicity?
Thy brother's son, so doubly bound to thee,
Being thy nephew and thy son-in-law,
Yet in his prison wrought thy misery
And death, but how or why I never saw.

COUNT UGOLINO OF PISA

There is no tongue of pity that has power
To tell Count Ugolino's tragedy.
A little out of Pisa stands a tower;
There in that tower he was imprisoned, he
And all his little children. There were three,
Of whom the eldest-born was barely five.
O Fortune! It was grievous cruelty
To put such birds in such a cage, alive!

He was condemned to perish in that prison,
For Bishop Ruggieri had framed lies
Against him, and the city folk had risen,
Believing all the Bishop could devise,
And jailed him, as I said, without supplies
Save for some water and a little meat,
But these so scant and poor, you may surmise
That there was scarce enough for them to eat.

And on a certain day when came the hour
At which their food was usually brought,
The jailer shut the opening to the tower.
He heard it well enough, but he said nought;
There came into his heart at once the thought
That they were minded he should starve to
  death.
"Alas that I was born!" he said, and sought
In vain to check his tears and calm his breath.

His younger son—just three—ah, it is cruel
To think of him!—said, "Father dear, why
  weep?
When will the prison-jailer bring our gruel?
Is there no bread, a morsel, in the keep?
I am so hungry that I cannot sleep.
If only I could sleep till I were dead!
Hunger no more would then have power to
  creep.
There's nothing I should like so much as
  bread."

Thus day by day the little child would cry

Till on his father's bosom down he lay,
And said, "Farewell, dear father, I must die!"
And kissed him; and he died that very day.
Seeing him dead his father could but say,
Biting his arm and crying "Wretched me!
Bitterest Fortune, thou hast had thy way,
Thy false wheel turns against me, as I see!"

The other children thought it must be hunger
That made him bite upon his arm, not pain.
"Ah father, don't, don't do it!" cried the
    younger,
"But rather eat the flesh upon us twain;
Our flesh you gave us, take it back again
And eat enough!" Thus both the children
    cried,
But in a day or two, their grief in vain,
They crept into his lap and there they died.

He in despair sat on, and slowly starved.
Thus, mighty once, he met his end in jail;
Fortune foreclosed on his estate and carved
His greatness from him. Of this tragic tale,
Those who wish more, and on a nobler scale,
Should turn and read the great Italian poet[6]
Dante by name; they will not find him fail
In any point or syllable, I know it.

NERO

Though Nero was a vicious man who lusted
As fiercely as a fiend who treads the deep
(Says Suetonius, and he may be trusted),
He ruled the whole wide world; 'twas his to
    keep.
East, west, north, south, he scoured it o'er
    to reap
Its rubies, sapphires, pearls of orient white . . .
And his embroidered garments, heap on heap,
Blazed with them richly; gems were his de-
    light.

A prouder, more fastidious ostentation
Of pomp no emperor has ever shown;
A dress once worn he had no inclination
To see again, would scarcely seem to own.
His many nets of golden mesh were thrown
To fish the Tiber with, just to amuse him.
His pleasures were his laws, he made it known
That there was nothing Fortune could
    refuse him.

And Rome, to please his palate for sensations,
He burnt; he killed his senators in play,
Just for the fun of hearing lamentations
And shrieks of pain; with his own sister lay;
Murdered his brother; carved his dreadful way
Into his mother's womb, only to know
Where he had been conceived. Alas the day
That ever man should treat his mother so!

Yet at the sight of it he shed no tear
But "A fine woman once, she was," he said.
Wonder it is that he could so appear
To sit in judgement on her beauty dead.
And then he bade a table to be spread
And drank some wine but showed no other
    grief.
Where power and a cruel heart are wed
How deep the poison, challenging belief!

In youth they gave him an instructor; he
Taught him to read and taught him gentle
    breeding.
He was the flower of morality
At that far time, according to my reading.
And for a while he mastered him, succeeding
In putting his intelligence to use
With suppleness and wisdom. Tyranny
And vice in him were not as yet let loose.

This Seneca—the man of whom I speak—
Made Nero fear him, but he went in dread
Of Seneca because he chose to speak
In the rebuke of wickedness instead
Of punishing him. "An emperor," he said,
"Shuns tyranny and follow's virtue's path."
So Nero cut his veins for him and bled
The man to death, he killed him in a bath.

It had been Nero's practice, I should judge,
When he was young, to mutiny and rise
Against his master; he could bear a grudge
And killed him for it, so we may surmise.
Nevertheless this Seneca the wise
Preferred to perish thus lest worse disaster
Should overtake him in another guise.
Thus Nero murdered his beloved master.

But as it happened Fortune cared no longer
To cherish Nero in his soaring pride.
Though he was strong enough yet she was
    stronger
And thus she thought: "By God, I let
    him ride
Far too indulgently upon the tide
Of vice, and lend the title that protects

An emperor. By heaven, he shall slide
Out of his seat, and when he least expects."

One night the citizens of Rome revolted
Against his tyrannies and mad ambition
And, when he heard them mutiny, he bolted
Alone and sought his friends for coalition.
The more he knocked and begged them for
   admission
The more they shut their doors and said
   him nay.
And then he saw that of his own perdition
He was sole author and he fled away.

The people yelled for him and rumbled round
So that their shouts were dinning in his ear:
"Where's Nero? Where's the tyrant? Treach-
   erous hound!"
He almost went out of his mind for fear.
Pitifully he prayed the gods to hear
And succour him; in vain, they would not
   shield him.
Distraught, and knowing that his end was
   near,
He ran into a garden that concealed him.

He found two peasants in the garden there
Seated beside a bonfire glowing red
And he approached these peasants with a
   prayer
To kill him and by smiting off his head
To shield his body after he was dead
From mutilation or a shameful stroke.
And then he slew himself, for all was said.
And Fortune laughed, for she had had her
   joke.

HOLOFERNES[7]

There never was a captain served a king
Who brought so many countries in subjection
Or one more famous then for everything
Touching the fields of war and insurrection,
Or more presumptuous by predilection
Than Holofernes. Fortune ever fair
Kissed him with such a lecherous affection
He lost his head before he was aware.

It was not only that he made a wraith
Of the world's wealth and plundered liberty,
He made his enemies renounce their faith:
"Nebuchadnezzar is your God," said he,
"You shall adore none other that may be!"
There was no city dared stand up to him

Save one that proved a rebel to decree,
Bethulia, and her priest Eliachim.

But watch how Holofernes met his fate;
Drunken amid his host he lay one night
In his enormous barn-like tent of state.
For all his pomp, his majesty and might,
Judith, a woman, had the strength to smite.
Off went his sleepy head and from the tent
She crept away before the morning light
Bearing his head with her, and home she went.

KING ANTIOCHUS THE ILLUSTRIOUS[8]

What need to tell of King Antiochus
Or to describe his royal panoply,
His overweening pride, his venomous
Ill-doing? There was never such as he.
Read what is said of him in *Maccabee*,
Read those proud words so arrogantly spoken
And why he fell from his felicity
Upon a hill-side, festering and broken.

Fortune indeed had so enhanced his pride
That verily he thought to take his stand
Among the stars themselves or turn aside
To lift and weigh a mountain in his hand
Or warn the flood of ocean from the land.
But it was God's own people he most hated
And slew by torture, steel and firebrand.
He thought his pride could never be abated.

Because Nicanor once and Timothy
Had by the Jews been mightily defeated
His hatred swelled for Israel. Hastily
He made his chariot ready and when seated
He vowed and swore that they should all be
   treated
To something of his spite, that they should
   rue it;
Jerusalem he said should be deleted.
He was prevented ere he came to do it.

God smote him for these menacing recitals
With an invisible and cureless blain
That carved his guts and bit into his vitals.
Afflicted with intolerable pain
He yet had little reason to complain;
It was a just revenge, for he had often
Carved out the guts of other men to gain
His ends; their tortures did not make him
   soften.

He gave the word to summon all his hosts

When suddenly, before he was aware,
God daunted his presumption and his boasts,
And down he fell out of his chariot there.
It tore his limbs and flesh, the bone lay bare;
No longer could he either walk or ride
But only could be carried in a chair
All bruised and lacerated, back and side.

The vengeance of the Lord smote cruelly;
Pestilent worms within his body crept
So that he stank, and stank so horribly,
Not one of all the servants that he kept
To guard him when awake or when he slept
Could bear the stench or look upon his fea-
    tures.
And in this agony he wailed and wept
And knew that God was lord of all his crea-
    tures.

To all his host and to himself no less
The carrion stench that rose from every vent
Was unendurable in loathsomeness;
They could not carry him. In redolent
And agonizing pain within his tent
Upon a hill this thief and homicide
Who made so many suffer and lament
Wretchedly perished, the reward of pride.

ALEXANDER[9]

The story of Alexander is so famous
That it is known to everyone at least
In part, unless he be an ignoramus.
He conquered the wide world from west
    to east
By force of arms, and as his fame increased
Men gladly sued to have him for their friend.
He brought to naught the pride of man and
    beast
Wherever he came, as far as the world's end.

And never can comparison be made
Of him with any other; at his face
Kingdoms would quake, the whole world was
    afraid.
He was the flower of knighthood and of
    grace,
The heir of Fortune and in nothing base;
Save wine and women there was naught
    could part
Him from his high designs or take their place,
He was a man so leonine of heart.

What praise were it to him though I should tell

Of great Darius and a thousand more
Kings, princes, generals, dukes and earls
    as well
Conquered by him and brought to grief
    in war?
As far as men may ride from shore to shore
Of the wide world, the world was his to hold.
Though I should speak for ever on the score
Of knightly honour, his could not be told.

Twelve years he reigned, so say the *Maccabees,*
And was King Philip's son, of Macedon,
First to be king over the land of Greece.
Alas that Alexander, such a son,
So gentle, so magnanimous, were one
To die by poison from the men he kept!
But Fortune threw his aces for the run[10]
Of sixes thrown before. She little wept.

Who then will give me tears that I may plain
The death of greatness that was never rough,
Of generous feeling that had held domain
Over the world and thought it not enough?
His was a spirit brimming with the stuff
Of high design. Ah, help me to speak shame
Of poisoners and of the foul rebuff
Of fickle Fortune, whom alone I blame.

JULIUS CAESAR

By wisdom, manhood and the works of war
From humble bed to royal majesty
Arose great Julius Caesar, conqueror,
Who won the occident by land and sea
By strength of arms or by diplomacy
And made of each a Roman tributary
And last was emperor himself till he
Was picked by Fortune for her adversary.

O Caesar that in Thessaly excelled
Against your father-in-law great Pompey's
    sway,
The whole of orient chivalry was held
In whose command, far as the dawn of day!
Your valour was enough to take and slay
All but a few that fled with him, your spell
Held the whole east in terror and dismay.
Give thanks to Fortune for she served you
    well!

Yet for a little while I will bewail
This Pompey's fate, the noble governor
Of Rome who fled the battle, for the tale
Tells of a man of his, a perjurer,

Who smote his head off, for he hoped to stir
Some gratitude in Caesar, so he brought
The head to him. O Pompey, Justicer
Of all the east, alas that thou wert caught!

To Rome once more this Julius turned, to don
The laurel-wreath, triumphant and elate.
But Brutus Cassius[11] as time went on,
One that had ever envied his estate,
Made a conspiracy in subtle hate
Against this Julius, gave the treacherous vow,
And chose the place where he should meet
    his fate
By dagger-thrust, and I shall tell you how.

Up to the Capitol this Julius went
A certain day as he was wont to do.
There he was taken by the malcontent
False-hearted Brutus and his scheming crew,
They stabbed him there with daggers through
    and through,
Many the wounds, and there they let him die.
After one dagger-stroke or maybe two
He never groaned, unless the stories lie.

He was a soldier with a manly heart;
So dear to him was honest decency
That deeply as he felt his gashes smart
He sought to shroud his person, casting free
His cloak about his hips and privity,
And in the trance of dying, though he knew
It was his death, he held in memory
The things of seemliness and order due.

I recommend you Lucan for this story
And Suetonius and Valerius too.
They write of these two conquerors in their
    glory
And in their end, how both of them
    once knew
Fortune to be their friend, and how she grew
To be their foe. No man may trust her long,
Beware of her in everything you do
And think of these great leaders, once so
    strong.

CROESUS

Rich Croesus, King of Lydia long ago,
Whom even Persian Cyrus held in dread
Was yet cut short in all his pride and show
And led out to be burnt; but as they led
Him to the stake such rain from overhead
Came down it quenched the fire and he es-
    caped.

He failed to take the warning, be it said;
Fate kept him for the gallows, where he
    gaped.

For having thus evaded death by fire
Nothing would stop him making war again.
He thought that Fortune meant to raise him
    higher,
After his luck in being saved by rain,
And he presumed he never could be slain.
Moreover being favoured by a vision
That cockered up his heart, he felt so vain
He set himself to vengeance and derision.

He dreamt that he was perching in a tree
With Jupiter to wash him, back and side,
While Phoebus, with a towel fair to see,
Was drying him. This was what swelled his
    pride.
He told his daughter who was at his side,
Knowing her versed in mysteries, it would
    seem,
And asked her what the vision signified.
And thus she started to expound his dream:

"This tree," she told him, "signifies a gibbet
And Jupiter betokens snow and rain,
While Phoebus with his towel must exhibit
The streaming sun, to dry you off again.
You will be hanged, my father, that is plain;
The rain shall wash you and the sun shall
    bake."
And thus his daughter warned him, but in
    vain;
Her name Phanýa, if I not mistake.

Hanged, then, was Croesus, this tremendous
    king;
His royal sceptre was of no avail.
Tragedy is no other kind of thing
Nor tunes her song save only to bewail
How Fortune, ever fickle, will assail
With sudden stroke the kingdoms of the
    proud,
And when men trust in her she then will fail
And cover her bright face as with a cloud. . . .

Words of the Knight and the Host

"Ho, my good sir, no more!" exclaimed the
    Knight.
"What you have said so far no doubt is right,
And more than right, but still a little grief
Will do for most of us, in my belief.
As for myself, I take a great displeasure

In tales of those who once knew wealth and leisure
And then are felled by some unlucky hit.
But it's a joy to hear the opposite,
For instance tales of men of low estate
Who climb aloft and growing fortunate
Remain secure in their prosperity;
That is delightful as it seems to me
And is a proper sort of tale to tell."
　　"That's certain, by St. Paul's and by its bell!"
Our Host joined in. "This Monk, he talks too loud;
All about 'Fortune covered with a cloud'
—I don't know what—and as for 'Tragedy,'
You heard just now, what has to be must be.
It does no good to grumble and complain,
What's done is done. Moreover, it's a pain,
As you have said, to hear about disaster;
Let's have no more of it. God bless you, master,
It's an offence, you're boring us, that's why!
Such talk as that's not worth a butterfly,
Gives no enjoyment, doesn't help the game.
In short Sir Monk—Sir Peter—what's-your-name—
I heartily beg you'll talk of something else.
But for the clink and tinkle of those bells
That hang your bridle round on every side,
By my salvation, by the Lord that died,
I simply should have fallen down asleep
Into the mud below, however deep.
Your story then would have been told in vain,
For, quoting the authorities again,
'When lecturers find their audiences decrease
It does them little good to say their piece.'
Give us a word or two on hunting, say."
"No," said the Monk, "I'm in no mood today
For fun. Ask someone else, I've said enough."
　　Our Host, whose language was a little rough,
Seeing a Priest beside the Nun, went on:
"Come here, you priest, step forward, you, Sir John,
And tell a tale to make our troubles pack.
Cheer yourself up although you ride a hack.
What if your ugly horse is poor and thin?
If it will serve you, never care a pin!
And always keep your heart up—that's the test!"
"Yes," he replied, "yes, Host, I'll do my best,
Not to be merry would deserve reproach."
And he immediately began to broach

His story to us as we all rode on,
This charming priest and kindly man, Sir John.

THE NUN'S PRIEST'S TALE

Once, long ago, there dwelt a poor old widow
In a small cottage, by a little meadow
Beside a grove and standing in a dale.
This widow-woman of whom I tell my tale
Since the sad day when last she was a wife
Had led a very patient, simple life.
Little she had in capital or rent,
But still, by making do with what God sent,
She kept herself and her two daughters going.
Three hefty sows—no more—were all her showing,
Three cows as well; there was a sheep called Molly.
Sooty her hall, her kitchen melancholy,
And there she ate full many a slender meal;
There was no *sauce piquante* to spice her veal,
No dainty morsel ever passed her throat,
According to her cloth she cut her coat.
Repletion never left her in disquiet
And all her physic was a temperate diet,
Hard work for exercise and heart's content.
And rich man's gout did nothing to prevent
Her dancing, apoplexy struck her not;
She drank no wine, nor white, nor red had got.
Her board was mostly served with white and black,
Milk and brown bread, in which she found no lack;
Broiled bacon or an egg or two were common,
She was in fact a sort of dairy-woman.
　　She had a yard that was enclosed about
By a stockade and a dry ditch without,
In which she kept a cock called Chanticleer.
In all the land for crowing he'd no peer;
His voice was jollier than the organ blowing
In church on Sundays, he was great at crowing.
Far, far more regular than any clock
Or abbey bell the crowing of this cock.
The equinoctial wheel and its position[1]
At each ascent he knew by intuition;
At every hour—fifteen degrees of movement—
He crowed so well there could be no improvement.
His comb was redder than fine coral, tall

And battlemented like a castle wall,
His bill was black and shone as bright as jet,
Like azure were his legs and they were set
On azure toes with nails of lily white,
Like burnished gold his feathers, flaming
    bright.
    This gentlecock was master in some
        measure
Of seven hens, all there to do his pleasure.
They were his sisters and his paramours,
Coloured like him in all particulars;
She with the loveliest dyes upon her throat
Was known as gracious Lady Pertelote.
Courteous she was, discreet and debonair,
Companionable too, and took such care
In her deportment, since she was seven
    days old
She held the heart of Chanticleer controlled,
Locked up securely in her every limb;
O what a happiness his love to him!
And such a joy it was to hear them sing,
As when the glorious sun began to spring,
In sweet accord, *My Love is far from land*[2]
—For in those far off days I understand
All birds and animals could speak and sing.
    Now it befell, as dawn began to spring,
When Chanticleer and Pertelote and all
His wives were perched in this poor wid-
    ow's hall
(Fair Pertelote was next him on the perch),
This Chanticleer began to groan and lurch
Like someone sorely troubled by a dream,
And Pertelote who heard him roar and scream
Was quite aghast and said, "O dearest heart,
What's ailing you? Why do you groan and
    start?
Fie, what a sleeper! What a noise to make!"
"Madam," he said, "I beg you not to take
Offence, but by the Lord I had a dream
So terrible just now I had to scream;
I still can feel my heart racing from fear.
God turn my dream to good and guard all
    here,
And keep my body out of durance vile!
I dreamt that roaming up and down a while
Within our yard I saw a kind of beast,
A sort of hound that tried or seemed at least
To try and seize me . . . would have killed me
    dead!
His colour was a blend of yellow and red,
His ears and tail were tipped with sable fur
Unlike the rest; he was a russet cur.
Small was his snout, his eyes were glowing
    bright.

It was enough to make one die of fright.
That was no doubt what made me groan and
    swoon."
    "For shame," she said, "you timorous
        poltroon!
Alas, what cowardice! By God above,
You've forfeited my heart and lost my love.
I cannot love a coward, come what may.
For certainly, whatever we may say,
All women long—and O that it might be!—
For husbands tough, dependable and free,
Secret, discreet, no niggard, not a fool
That boasts and then will find his courage cool
At every trifling thing. By God above,
How dare you say for shame, and to your love,
That there was anything at all you feared?
Have you no manly heart to match your
    beard?
And can a dream reduce you to such terror?
Dreams are a vanity, God knows, pure error.
Dreams are engendered in the too-replete
From vapours in the belly, which compete
With others, too abundant, swollen tight.
    "No doubt the redness in your dream to-
        night
Comes from the superfluity and force
Of the red choler in your blood. Of course.
That is what puts a dreamer in the dread
Of crimsoned arrows, fires flaming red,
Of great red monsters making as to fight him,
And big red whelps and little ones to bite him;
Just so the black and melancholy vapours
Will set a sleeper shrieking, cutting capers
And swearing that black bears, black bulls as
    well,
Or blackest fiends are haling him to Hell.
And there are other vapours that I know
That on a sleeping man will work their woe,
But I'll pass on as lightly as I can.
    "Take Cato now, that was so wise a man,
Did he not say, 'Take no account of dreams'?
Now, sir," she said, "on flying from these
    beams,
For love of God do take some laxative;
Upon my soul that's the advice to give
For melancholy choler; let me urge
You free yourself from vapours with a purge.
And that you may have no excuse to tarry
By saying this town has no apothecary,
I shall myself instruct you and prescribe
Herbs that will cure all vapours of that tribe,
Herbs from our very farmyard! You will find
Their natural property is to unbind
And purge you well beneath and well above.

Now don't forget it, dear, for God's own love!
Your face is choleric and shows distension;
Be careful lest the sun in his ascension
Should catch you full of humours, hot and
    many.
And if he does, my dear, I'll lay a penny
It means a bout of fever or a breath
Of tertian ague. You may catch your death.
    "Worms for a day or two I'll have to give
As a digestive, then your laxative.
Centaury, fumitory, caper-spurge
And hellebore will make a splendid purge;
And then there's laurel or the blackthorn
    berry,
Ground-ivy too that makes our yard so merry;
Peck them right up, my dear, and swallow
    whole.
Be happy, husband, by your father's soul!
Don't be afraid of dreams. I'll say no more."
    "Madam," he said, "I thank you for your
    lore,
But with regard to Cato all the same,
His wisdom has, no doubt, a certain fame,
But though he said that we should take
    no heed
Of dreams, by God, in ancient books I read
Of many a man of more authority
Than ever Cato was, believe you me,
Who say the very opposite is true
And prove their theories by experience too.
Dreams have quite often been significations
As well of triumphs as of tribulations
That people undergo in this our life.
This needs no argument at all, dear wife,
The proof is all too manifest indeed.
    "One of the greatest authors one can read
Says thus: there were two comrades once
    who went
On pilgrimage, sincere in their intent.
And as it happened they had reached a town
Where such a throng was milling up and down
And yet so scanty the accommodation,
They could not find themselves a habitation,
No, not a cottage that could lodge them both.
And so they separated, very loth,
Under constraint of this necessity
And each went off to find some hostelry,
And lodge whatever way his luck might fall.
    "The first of them found refuge in a stall
Down in a yard with oxen and a plough.
His friend found lodging for himself
    somehow
Elsewhere, by accident or destiny,
Which governs all of us and equally.

"Now it so happened, long ere it was day,
This fellow had a dream, and as he lay
In bed it seemed he heard his comrade call,
'Help! I am lying in an ox's stall
And shall tonight be murdered as I lie.
Help me, dear brother, help or I shall die!
Come in all haste!' Such were the words he
    spoke;
The dreamer, lost in terror, then awoke.
But, once awake, he paid it no attention,
Turned over and dismissed it as invention,
It was a dream, he thought, a fantasy.
And twice he dreamt this dream successively.
    "Yet a third time his comrade came again,
Or seemed to come, and said, 'I have been
    slain!
Look, look! my wounds are bleeding wide and
    deep.
Rise early in the morning, break your sleep
And go to the west gate. You there shall see
A cart all loaded up with dung,' said he,
'And in that dung my body has been hidden.
Boldly arrest that cart as you are bidden.
It was my money that they killed me for.'
    "He told him every detail, sighing sore,
And pitiful in feature, pale of hue.
This dream, believe me, Madam, turned out
    true;
For in the dawn, as soon as it was light,
He went to where his friend had spent the
    night
And when he came upon the cattle-stall
He looked about him and began to call.
    "The innkeeper, appearing thereupon,
Quickly gave answer, 'Sir, your friend has
    gone.
He left the town a little after dawn.'
The man began to feel suspicious, drawn
By memories of his dream—the western gate,
The dung-cart—off he went, he would not
    wait,
Towards the western entry. There he found,
Seemingly on its way to dung some ground,
A dung-cart loaded on the very plan
Described so closely by the murdered man.
So he began to shout courageously
For right and vengeance on the felony,
'My friend's been killed! There's been a foul
    attack,
He's in that cart and gaping on his back!
Fetch the authorities, get the sheriff down
—Whosever job it is to run the town—
Help! My companion's murdered, sent to
    glory!'

"What need I add to finish off the story?
People ran out and cast the cart to ground,
And in the middle of the dung they found
The murdered man. The corpse was fresh
    and new.
    "O blessed God, that art so just and true,
Thus thou revealest murder! As we say,
'Murder will out.' We see it day by day.
Murder's a foul, abominable treason,
So loathsome to God's justice, to God's reason,
He will not suffer its concealment. True,
Things may lie hidden for a year or two,
But still 'Murder will out,' that's my conclu-
    sion.
    "All the town officers in great confusion
Seized on the carter and they gave him hell,
And then they racked the innkeeper as well,
And both confessed. And then they took the
    wrecks
And there and then they hanged them by
    their necks.
    "By this we see that dreams are to be
    dreaded.
And in the self-same book I find embedded,
Right in the very chapter after this
(I'm not inventing, as I hope for bliss)
The story of two men who started out
To cross the sea—for merchandise no doubt—
But as the winds were contrary they waited.
It was a pleasant town, I should have stated,
Merrily grouped about the haven-side.
A few days later with the evening tide
The wind veered round so as to suit them best;
They were delighted and they went to rest
Meaning to sail next morning early. Well,
To one of them a miracle befell.
    "This man as he lay sleeping, it would
    seem,
Just before dawn had an astounding dream.
He thought a man was standing by his bed
Commanding him to wait, and thus he said:
'If you set sail to-morrow, as you intend,
You will be drowned. My tale is at an end.'
    "He woke and told his friend what had oc-
    curred
And begged him that the journey be deferred
At least a day, implored him not to start.
But his companion, lying there apart,
Began to laugh and treat him to derision.
'I'm not afraid,' he said, 'of any vision,
To let it interfere with my affairs;
A straw for all your dreamings and your scares.
Dreams are just empty nonsense, merest japes;
Why, people dream all day of owls and apes,

All sorts of trash that can't be understood,
Things that have never happened and never
    could.
But as I see you mean to stay behind
And miss the tide for wilful sloth of mind
God knows I'm sorry for it, but good day!'
And so he took his leave and went his way.
    "And yet, before they'd covered half
    the trip
—I don't know what went wrong—there
    was a rip
And by some accident the ship went down,
Her bottom rent, all hands aboard to drown
In sight of all the vessels at her side,
That had put out upon the self-same tide.
    "So, my dear Pertelote, if you discern
The force of these examples, you may learn
One never should be careless about dreams,
For, undeniably, I say it seems
That many are a sign of trouble breeding.
    "Now, take St. Kenelm's life which I've
    been reading;
He was Kenulphus' son, the noble King
Of Mercia. Now, St. Kenelm dreamt a thing
Shortly before they murdered him one day.
He saw his murder in a dream, I say.
His nurse expounded it and gave her
    reasons
On every point and warned him against
    treasons
But as the saint was only seven years old
All that she said about it left him cold.
He was so holy how could visions hurt?
    "By God, I willingly would give my shirt
To have you read his legend as I've read it;
And, Madam Pertelote, upon my credit,
Macrobius wrote of dreams and can explain us
The vision of young Scipio Africanus,
And he affirms that dreams can give a due
Warning of things that later on come true.
    "And then there's the Old Testament—a
    manual
Well worth your study; see the *Book of Daniel*.
Did Daniel think a dream was vanity?
Read about Joseph too and you will see
That many dreams—I do not say that all—
Give cognizance of what is to befall.
    "Look at Lord Pharaoh, king of
    Egypt! Look
At what befell his butler and his cook.
Did not their visions have a certain force?
But those who study history of course
Meet many dreams that set them wondering.
    "What about Croesus too, the Lydian king,

Who dreamt that he was sitting in a tree,
Meaning he would be hanged? It had to be.
    "Or take Andromache, great Hector's wife;
The day on which he was to lose his life
She dreamt about, the very night before,
And realized that if Hector went to war
He would be lost that very day in battle.
She warned him; he dismissed it all as prattle
And sallied forth to fight, being self-willed,
And there he met Achilles and was killed.
The tale is long and somewhat overdrawn,
And anyhow it's very nearly dawn,
So let me say in very brief conclusion
My dream undoubtedly foretells confusion,
It bodes me ill, I say. And, furthermore,
Upon your laxatives I set no store,
For they are venomous. I've suffered by them
Often enough before, and I defy them.
    "And now, let's talk of fun and stop all this.
Dear Madam, as I hope for Heaven's bliss,
Of one thing God has sent me plenteous
    grace,
For when I see the beauty of your face,
That scarlet loveliness about your eyes,
All thought of terror and confusion dies.
For it's as certain as the Creed, I know,
Mulier est hominis confusio
(A Latin tag, dear Madam, meaning this:
'Woman is man's delight and all his bliss'),
For when at night I feel your feathery side,
Although perforce I cannot take a ride
Because, alas, our perch was made too narrow,
Delight and solace fill me to the marrow
And I defy all visions and all dreams!"
    And with that word he flew down from the
        beams,
For it was day, and down his hens flew all,
And with a chuck he gave the troupe a call
For he had found a seed upon the floor.
Royal he was, he was afraid no more.
He feathered Pertelote in wanton play
And trod her twenty times ere prime of day.
Grim as a lion's was his manly frown
As on his toes he sauntered up and down;
He scarcely deigned to set his foot to ground
And every time a seed of corn was found
He gave a chuck, and up his wives ran all.
Thus royal as a prince who strides his hall
Leave we this Chanticleer engaged on feeding
And pass to the adventure that was breeding.
    Now when the month in which the world
        began,
March, the first month, when God cre-
    ated man,

Was over, and the thirty-second day
Thereafter ended, on the third of May
It happened that Chanticleer in all his pride,
His seven wives attendant at his side,
Cast his eyes upward to the blazing sun,
Which in the sign of *Taurus* then had run
His twenty-one degrees and somewhat more,
And knew by nature and no other lore
That it was nine o'clock. With blissful voice
He crew triumphantly and said, "Rejoice,
Behold the sun! The sun is up, my seven.
Look, it has climbed forty degrees in heaven,
Forty degrees and one in fact, by this.
Dear Madam Pertelote, my earthly bliss,
Hark to those blissful birds and how they sing!
Look at those pretty flowers, how they spring!
Solace and revel fill my heart!" He laughed.
    But in that moment Fate let fly her shaft;
Ever the latter end of joy is woe,
God knows that worldly joy is swift to go.
A rhetorician with a flair for style
Could chronicle this maxim in his file
Of Notable Remarks with safe conviction.
Then let the wise give ear; this is no fiction.
My story is as true, I undertake,
As that of good Sir Lancelot du Lake
Who held all women in such high esteem.
Let me return full circle to my theme.
    A coal-tipped fox of sly iniquity
That had been lurking round the grove for
        three
Long years, that very night burst through and
        passed
Stockade and hedge, as Providence forecast,
Into the yard where Chanticleer the Fair
Was wont, with all his ladies, to repair.
Still, in a bed of cabbages, he lay
Until about the middle of the day
Watching the cock and waiting for his cue,
As all these homicides so gladly do
That lie about in wait to murder men.
O false assassin, lurking in thy den!
O new Iscariot, new Ganelon!
And O Greek Sinon,[3] thou whose treach-
    ery won
Troy town and brought it utterly to sorrow!
O Chanticleer, accursed be that morrow
That brought thee to the yard from thy high
        beams!
Thou hadst been warned, and truly, by thy
        dreams
That this would be a perilous day for thee.
    But that which God's foreknowledge can
        foresee

Must needs occur, as certain men of learning
Have said. Ask any scholar of discerning;
He'll say the Schools are filled with alter-
    cation
On this vexed matter of predestination
Long bandied by a hundred thousand men.
How can I sift it to the bottom then?
The Holy Doctor St. Augustine shines
In this, and there is Bishop Bradwardine's[4]
Authority, Boethius'[5] too, decreeing
Whether the fact of God's divine foreseeing
Constrains me to perform a certain act
—And by "constraint" I mean the simple fact
Of mere compulsion by necessity—
Or whether a free choice is granted me
To do a given act or not to do it
Though, ere it was accomplished, God
    foreknew it,
Or whether Providence is not so stringent
And merely makes necessity contingent.

But I decline discussion of the matter;
My tale is of a cock and of the clatter
That came of following his wife's advice
To walk about his yard on the precise
Morning after the dream of which I told.
    O woman's counsel is so often cold!
A woman's counsel brought us first to woe,
Made Adam out of Paradise to go
Where he had been so merry, so well at ease.
But, for I know not whom it may displease
If I suggest that women are to blame,
Pass over that; I only speak in game.
Read the authorities to know about
What has been said of women; you'll find out.
These are the cock's words, and not mine, I'm
    giving;
I think no harm of any woman living.
    Merrily in her dust-bath in the sand
Lay Pertelote. Her sisters were at hand
Basking in sunlight. Chanticleer sang free,
More merrily than a mermaid in the sea
(For *Physiologus* reports the thing[6]
And says how well and merrily they sing).
And so it happened as he cast his eye
Towards the cabbage at a butterfly
It fell upon the fox there, lying low.
Gone was all inclination then to crow.
"Cok cok," he cried, giving a sudden start,
As one who feels a terror at his heart,
For natural instinct teaches beasts to flee
The moment they perceive an enemy,
Though they had never met with it before.
    This Chanticleer was shaken to the core

And would have fled. The fox was quick
    to say
However, "Sir! Whither so fast away?
Are you afraid of me, that am your friend?
A fiend, or worse, I should be, to intend
You harm, or practise villainy upon you;
Dear sir, I was not even spying on you!
Truly I came to do no other thing
Than just to lie and listen to you sing.
You have as merry a voice as God has given
To any angel in the courts of Heaven;
To that you add a musical sense as strong
As had Boethius who was skilled in song.
My Lord your Father (God receive his soul!),
Your mother too—how courtly, what con-
    trol!—
Have honoured my poor house, to my great
    ease;
And you, sir, too, I should be glad to please.
For, when it comes to singing, I'll say this
(Else may these eyes of mine be barred from
    bliss),
There never was a singer I would rather
Have heard at dawn than your respected fa-
    ther.
All that he sang came welling from his soul
And how he put his voice under control!
The pains he took to keep his eyes tight shut
In concentration—then the tip-toe strut,
The slender neck stretched out, the delicate
    beak!
No singer could approach him in technique
Or rival him in song, still less surpass.
I've read the story in *Burnel the Ass*,[7]
Among some other verses, of a cock
Whose leg in youth was broken by a knock
A clergyman's son had given him, and for this
He made the father lose his benefice.
But certainly there's no comparison
Between the subtlety of such a one
And the discretion of your father's art
And wisdom. Oh, for charity of heart,
Can you not emulate your sire and sing?"
    This Chanticleer began to beat a wing
As one incapable of smelling treason,
So wholly had this flattery ravished reason.
Alas, my lords! there's many a sycophant
And flatterer that fill your courts with cant
And give more pleasure with their zeal for-
    sooth
Than he who speaks in soberness and truth.
Read what *Ecclesiasticus* records
Of flatterers. 'Ware treachery, my lords!

This Chanticleer stood high upon his toes,
He stretched his neck, his eyes began to close,
His beak to open; with his eyes shut tight
He then began to sing with all his might.

Sir Russel Fox leapt in to the attack,
Grabbing his gorge he flung him o'er his back
And off he bore him to the woods, the brute,
And for the moment there was no pursuit.

O Destiny that may not be evaded!
Alas that Chanticleer had so paraded!
Alas that he had flown down from the beams!
O that his wife took no account of dreams!
And on a Friday too to risk their necks!
O Venus, goddess of the joys of sex,
Since Chanticleer thy mysteries professed
And in thy service always did his best,
And more for pleasure than to multiply
His kind, on thine own day, is he to die?

O Geoffrey, thou my dear and sovereign
    master[8]
Who, when they brought King Richard to
    disaster
And shot him dead, lamented so his death,
Would that I had thy skill, thy gracious
    breath,
To chide a Friday half so well as you!
(For he was killed upon a Friday too.)
Then I could fashion you a rhapsody
For Chanticleer in dread and agony.

Sure never such a cry or lamentation
Was made by ladies of high Trojan station,
When Ilium fell and Pyrrhus with his sword
Grabbed Priam by the beard, their king and
    lord,
And slew him there as the *Aeneid* tells,
As what was uttered by those hens. Their yells
Surpassed them all in palpitating fear
When they beheld the rape of Chanticleer.
Dame Pertelote emitted sovereign shrieks
That echoed up in anguish to the peaks
Louder than those extorted from the wife
Of Hasdrubal, when he had lost his life
And Carthage all in flame and ashes lay.
She was so full of torment and dismay
That in the very flames she chose her part
And burnt to ashes with a steadfast heart.
O woeful hens, louder your shrieks and higher
Than those of Roman matrons when the fire
Consumed their husbands, senators of Rome,
When Nero burnt their city and their home;
Beyond a doubt that Nero was their bale!

Now let me turn again to tell my tale;
This blessed widow and her daughters two

Heard all these hens in clamour and halloo
And, rushing to the door at all this shrieking,
They saw the fox towards the covert streaking
And, on his shoulder, Chanticleer stretched
    flat.
"Look, look!" they cried, "O mercy, look at
    that!
Ha! Ha! the fox!" and after him they ran,
And stick in hand ran many a serving man,
Ran Coll our dog, ran Talbot, Bran and
    Shaggy,
And with a distaff in her hand ran Maggie,
Ran cow and calf and ran the very hogs
In terror at the barking of the dogs;
The men and women shouted, ran and cursed,
They ran so hard they thought their hearts
    would burst,
They yelled like fiends in Hell, ducks left the
    water
Quacking and flapping as on point of
    slaughter,
Up flew the geese in terror over the trees,
Out of the hive came forth the swarm of bees;
So hideous was the noise—God bless us all,
Jack Straw and all his followers in their brawl[9]
Were never half so shrill, for all their noise,
When they were murdering those Flemish
    boys,
As that day's hue and cry upon the fox.
They grabbed up trumpets made of brass
    and box,
Of horn and bone, on which they blew and
    pooped,
And therewithal they shouted and they
    whooped
So that it seemed the very heavens would fall.
    And now, good people, pay attention all.
See how Dame Fortune quickly changes side
And robs her enemy of hope and pride!
This cock that lay upon the fox's back
In all his dread contrived to give a quack
And said, "Sir Fox, if I were you, as God's
My witness, I would round upon these clods
And shout, 'Turn back, you saucy bump-
    kins all!
A very pestilence upon you fall!
Now that I have in safety reached the wood
Do what you like, the cock is mine for good;
I'll eat him there in spite of every one.' "
    The fox replying, "Faith, it shall be done!"
Opened his mouth and spoke. The nimble
    bird,
Breaking away upon the uttered word,

Flew high into the tree-tops on the spot.
And when the fox perceived where he
   had got,
"Alas," he cried, "alas, my Chanticleer,
I've done you grievous wrong, indeed I fear
I must have frightened you; I grabbed too hard
When I caught hold and took you from the
   yard.
But, sir, I meant no harm, don't be offended,
Come down and I'll explain what I intended;
So help me God I'll tell the truth—on oath!"
"No," said the cock, "and curses on us both,
And first on me if I were such a dunce
As let you fool me oftener than once.
Never again, for all your flattering lies,
You'll coax a song to make me blink my eyes;
And as for those who blink when they should
   look,
God blot them from his everlasting Book!"
"Nay, rather," said the fox, "his plagues be
   flung
On all who chatter that should hold their
   tongue."
   Lo, such it is not to be on your guard
Against the flatterers of the world, or yard,
And if you think my story is absurd,
A foolish trifle of a beast and bird,
A fable of a fox, a cock, a hen,
Take hold upon the moral, gentlemen.
   St. Paul himself, a saint of great discerning,
Says that all things are written for our
   learning;
So take the grain and let the chaff be still.
And, gracious Father, if it be thy will
As saith my Saviour, make us all good men,
And bring us to his heavenly bliss.
                          Amen.

Words of the Host to the Nun's Priest

"Sir Priest," our Host remarked in merry
   tones,
"Blest be your breeches and your precious
   stones,
That was a merry tale of Chanticleer!
If you had only been a secular
You would have trodden a pretty fowl, no
   doubt.
Had you the heart, your muscles would
   hold out;
You look as if you needed hens, I mean,
Yes, more than seven. Seven times seventeen!
Just look what brawn he has, this gentle priest,

And what a neck! His chest's not of the least.
As for his eyes, they're like a sparrow-hawk's,
And his complexion like a box of chalks;
He needs no dyes imported from the East
Or Portugal. Good luck to you, Sir Priest,
For telling a fine tale!" And saying thus
He turned, as you shall hear, to one of us.

Here follows the Physician's Tale.

THE PHYSICIAN'S TALE

Livy has handed down a tale to us
About a knight surnamed Virginius.
He was a man of honourable birth,
Rich, well-befriended and of sterling worth.
   This knight had had a daughter by his wife;
There were no other children in his life.
Of an excelling loveliness was she,
Above all others that a man might see.
Nature had shown a sovereign diligence
In forming her to such an excellence,
As if she wished to say, "Look! I am Nature,
And this is how I form and paint a creature
When so I choose. Who dares a counterfeit?
No, not Pygmalion, though he forge and beat,
Colour and carve for ever; I maintain
That Zeuxis or Apelles would work in vain
To colour or to carve, to forge or beat,
If they presumed to make a counterfeit.
For He that is the Maker-Principal
Appointed me His vicar-general
To fashion creatures, all that ever were,
And paint them as I please; for in my care
Lies all that's under moon and, wax or wane,
I form them all. I do not work for gain;
My Lord and I are leagued in close accord.
I made her for the worship of my Lord,
And so I do with all my other creatures
Whatever be their colour or their features."
This was, I think, what Nature meant to say.
   The maiden was fourteen on whose array
Nature had spent her care with such delight.
For just as she can paint a lily white,
Redden a rose and teach it to unfurl
Her petals, so she touched this noble girl
Ere she was born; her limbs so lissom she
Had touched with colour where they ought
   to be.
Phoebus her mass of tresses with a gleam
Had dyed in burnish from his golden stream,

And if her beauty was beyond compare,
Her virtue was a thousand times more rare;
There lacked no quality in her to move
The praises sober wisdom would approve.
Chaste of her body and her soul was she,
And so she flowered in her virginity
With all humility and abstinence
In temperate and patient innocence,
With modesty of bearing and of dress
And showed in speech a modesty no less.
Though I dare say as wise as Pallas, she
Was simple in her words, and womanly;
She used no fancy terms in affectation
Of learning, but according to her station
She spoke; in all and everything she said
She showed that she was good and gently
	bred.
Shamefast she was, in maiden shamefastness,
And constant in her heart. She was express
In conquering sloth to fill the busy hour;
Over her mouth had never Bacchus power,
For wine and youth swell Venus and desire,
Much as when oil is cast upon the fire.
Indeed her native goodness unconstrained
So prompted her that she had often feigned
Some sickness to escape from company
Where there was likelihood of ribaldry,
As well there may be; junketings and dances
Are good occasions for lascivious glances.
Such things as these may soon too easily
Make a child bold and ripe, as one can see;
That's very dangerous and long has been,
For all too soon she learns to play the queen
And show how bold she is, when she's a wife.

And all you ladies that in middle life
Are put in charge of younger gentlefolk,
Pray do not think I speak as to provoke
Your anger; think that your appointment
	springs
From either one or other of two things,
Either that you were chaste and did not fail
To guard your honour, or that you were frail,
And therefore, knowing well the ancient
	dance,
You have forsaken your intemperance
For ever. Teach them then for Jesu's sake
And never slacken; virtue is at stake.
Just as a poacher who forsakes his crimes
And leaves his trade in villainy betimes,
Makes the best gamekeeper—he's just
	the man—
Keep you your charges; if you will you can.

Never belittle or connive at vice
Lest you should pay damnation as the price;
For those who do are traitors, never doubt it,
And so give heed to what I say about it.
Top of all treason, sovereign pestilence,
Is the betrayal done on innocence.

You Fathers and you Mothers, let me add,
However many children you have had,
Yours is the duty of their supervision
As long as they are bound by your decision.
Beware lest the example you present
Or your neglect in giving chastisement
Cause them to perish; otherwise I fear,
If they should do so, you will pay it dear.
Shepherds too soft who let their duty sleep
Encourage wolves to tear the lambs and sheep.
One parable's enough, you understand;
Let me return to what I had in hand.

This girl who is the theme of my address
Was such as not to need a governess.
The way she lived, if other girls would look,
Could teach them more of goodness than a
	book.
In all that should concern a virtuous maid,
She was so prudent, bountiful and staid;
And common fame was eager to confess
Her matchless beauty and her kindliness.
Lovers of virtue praised her and gave proof
Of her deserts, though envy stood aloof,
Envy that glowers at favour like a thief
And gloats to see another come to grief
(A phrase that St. Augustine noted down).

This girl one morning went into the town
Towards the temple, with her mother too,
As one may see a girl will often do.
Now at that time there was a judge in charge
Over the city and the land at large,
And so it happened that he cast his eye
Upon this girl as she was passing by
And narrowly appraised her. As he viewed
Her loveliness, a sudden change of mood
Entered his heart and, feeling himself caught
By her attraction, secretly he thought,
"I'll have that girl whether I sink or swim!"
At once the devil entered into him,
Whose machinations then began to stir
And teach him how to have his will of her.
He knew quite well that neither force nor fee
Could suit his purpose in the least degree,
For she had powerful friends and what
	was more
Her sovereignty of goodness closed the door

On his desires, he could not hope to win
Her soul or body to an act of sin.
So, after much reflection, he sent down
For a known blackguard living in the town,
As low in cunning tricks as he was bold.
He came; in secret then the tale was told
And having heard it he was made to swear
Never to tell a soul, and should he dare
So much as whisper, he should lose his head.
When he agreed to all that had been said
Of his accursed plan the judge was glad
And gave him precious gifts, the best he had.
    When they had framed their whole con-
      spiracy
From point to point to suit the lechery
That was to be enacted on the sly
(Though you shall hear about it by and by)
Home went the fellow, Claudius was his
    name;
This treacherous judge that was so lost to
    shame
Was surnamed Appius—for the thing's no
    fable
But quite historical, and many able
Historians will vouch the gist of it—
This treacherous judge, I tell you, set his wit
To work and went about without delay
To gratify his lust. There came a day
When the false judge (authorities report)
As was his custom, took his seat in court
And gave his judgement upon various cases.
All of a sudden in this fellow races
Crying, "My Lord, I beg with your per-
    mission
For justice in my pitiful petition
Touching my suit against Virginius.
If he denies it, says it was not thus,
Then I shall prove it and produce good
    witness
To testify the truth of it, and fitness."
    "In absence," said the judge, "of the ac-
      cused
Definitive award must be refused.
Summon him, state your case, and I will
    hear it
Gladly; you shall have justice, never fear it."
    Virginius came to learn the judge's will,
And instantly they read the cursed bill;
These were the terms of it, as you shall hear:
    "To you, Lord Appius, it shall appear
On showing of your poor servant Claudius
How that a certain knight, Virginius,
Against the law, against all equity,

And an express injunction lodged by me
Retains a servant that is mine by right,
One that was stolen from my house by night
When she was very young. I can support
The charge on witness, may it please the
    court.
My lord the judge, whatever he may say
The girl is not his daughter and I pray
My slave may be restored, by your good will."
This was the tenor of his cursed bill.
    Virginius stared in horror at the churl,
But quickly, ere he could defend his girl
And prove it on his honour as a knight,
Or bring a host of witness, as he might,
That all was false his enemy had stated,
This cursed judge, who never so much as
    waited
To hear the answer of Virginius,
Spoke out at once and gave his judgement
    thus:
"I rule this fellow is to have his slave
Immediately. The case is very grave.
Your house shall not protect her. Fetch the girl.
I say the court awards her to the churl."
    And when Virginius, this excellent knight,
Had understood the judge's doom aright
And knew his daughter, on compulsion, must
Be handed over to the judge's lust,
Home he returned and seated in his hall
He sent a servant, bidding him to call
His daughter to him, and with ashen face
Deathly and cold, gazed on her lowly grace.
Fatherly pity pierced him to the heart
And yet he did not falter in his part.
    "Daughter," he said, "Virginia, I
      must name
The ways that lie before you, death or shame.
One you must take. Alas, that I was born!
O judgement undeserved! O my forlorn
And innocent girl to die upon the knife!
O my dear daughter, ender of my life,
You that I fostered up with such delight,
Whose thought has never left me day or night,
O daughter, you that are my last of woe
And last of any joy that I shall know,
Be patient, O my gem of chastity,
And take your death, for that is my decree.
And it is love, not hate, would have you dead;
My pitying hand must strike, and take your
    head.
Alas that ever Appius saw your face
To give false judgement in a treacherous
    case!"

He told her then all you have heard before
Of what had happened; I need say no more.
  "O mercy, dearest father!" said the maid
And as she spoke she came to him and laid
Her arms about his neck, as oft she did,
And the tears flooded under either lid.
Thus as she wept, "O father dear," said she,
"Am I to die? Is there no remedy?"
"None, none, my dearest daughter. Hope is
    dead."
"O give me time, dear father," then she said,
"Let me lament my death a little space,
For Jephtha gave his daughter so much grace
As to allow her time to sorrow in,
Before he slew her. She had done no sin,
God knows, but ran, the first among them all,
To welcome him in solemn festival."
And on the word she fell into a swoon;
But when her faintness passed she rose as soon
And thus addressed her father, unafraid,
"Blessed be God that I shall die a maid!
I take my death rather than take my shame,
So do your will upon me in God's name!"
  And having spoken thus the child implored
That he would smite her softly with his sword
And then once more she fainted and lay still.
Her father sorrowful in heart and will
Smote off her head and took it by the hair,
Sought out the judge and gave it to him there
Sitting in judgement, in the open court.
When he beheld it, Livy makes report,
He rose and gave the order to his men
To take the knight and hang him. There
    and then
A thousand men came surging from the city
Thrusting their way into the court, in pity
And hope to save the knight; the news had
    flown,
The treacherous iniquity was known,
For there had been suspicion of the thing
Bred from the way the churl had sought to
    bring
His charge against the knight with the
    consent
Of Appius. They knew his lecherous bent,
And so it was the people had arisen.
They took that judge and cast him into prison
And there he slew himself; and Claudius,
Him that was instrument to Appius,
They took and would have hanged upon a tree
But that Virginius in clemency
Begged for his exile. They could scarce refuse,
Else he would certainly have got his dues.

The rest were hanged, the greater and the less,
That had been party to this cursedness.
  Here one can see how sin is paid its wages;
Beware, for no one knows how God engages
Or when to smite the sinner, or how
    the worm
Of conscience will bring terror to the firm
In wickedness, however secretly,
Though none should know of it but God
    and he.
Be he illiterate or a man of learning,
How soon the blow will fall there's no dis-
    cerning.
I offer you this counsel; let it make you
Forsake your sins before your sins forsake you.

Words of the Host to the Physician and to the Pardoner

Our Host began a violent tirade.
"God's nails and blood," he said, "alas, poor
    maid!
What a low blackguard! What a treacherous
    judge!
Death to all lawyers that will bribe and fudge
To trap you, be they judge or advocate!
Well, the poor girl was killed at any rate.
Alas, her beauty cost her all too dear!
Just as I always say, it's pretty clear
The handsome gifts that fate and nature
    lend us
Are very often those that least befriend us.
Her beauty was her death as one might say;
How pitifully she was made away!
Those gifts that I was mentioning just now
Do us more harm than good, one must allow.
Well, my dear sir, if I may speak sincere,
Your tale was truly pitiful to hear.
Nevertheless, pass on. No sense in fretting.
God's blessing on you, Doctor, not forgetting
Your various urinals and chamber-pots,
Bottles, medicaments and cordial tots
And boxes brimming all with panaceas,
God's blessing on them all and St. Maria's!
You look a proper fellow! Pills and pellets!
St. Ronyan, you've a figure like a prelate's!
Don't I say well?—although I lack the art
To talk like you; your story touched my heart,
It gave me heart-disease, or very near.
By corpus bones! I'll need a dose, I fear,
Or else a good wet draught of malted ale
If someone doesn't tell a cheerful tale;
I'm lost in pity for that poor girl dead.
Come on, old chum and Pardoner," he said,

"Tell us a funny story, break a joke!"
"Right, by St. Ronyan! but I'll have a soak
First at this pub. I've got a thirst to slake,"
Said he, "I'll drink and eat a bit of cake."
    Outcry arose among the gentlefolk.
"No, no, don't let him tell a dirty joke!
Tell something with a moral, something clear
And profitable, and we'll gladly hear."
"Granted," he said, "but first I'll have to
    think;
I'll ponder something decent while I drink."

THE PARDONER'S TALE
The Pardoner's Prologue

"My lords," he said, "in churches where I
    preach
I cultivate a haughty kind of speech
And ring it out as roundly as a bell;
I've got it all by heart, the tale I tell.
I have a text, it always is the same
And always has been, since I learnt the game,
Old as the hills and fresher than the grass,
Radix malorum est cupiditas.
    "But first I make pronouncement whence I
        come,
Show them my bulls in detail and in sum.
And flaunt the papal seal for their inspection
As warrant for my bodily protection,
That none may have the impudence to irk
Or hinder me in Christ's most holy work.
Then I tell stories, as occasion calls,
Showing forth bulls from popes and cardinals,
From patriarchs and bishops; as I do,
I speak some words in Latin—just a few—
To put a saffron tinge upon my preaching
And stir devotion with a spice of teaching.
Then I bring all my long glass bottles out
Cram-full of bones and ragged bits of clout,
Relics they are, at least for such are known.
Then, cased in metal, I've a shoulder-bone,
Belonging to a sheep, a holy Jew's.
'Good men,' I say, 'take heed, for here is news.
Take but this bone and dip it in a well;
If cow or calf, if sheep or ox should swell
From eating snakes or that a snake has stung,
Take water from that well and wash its
    tongue,
And it will then recover. Furthermore,
Where there is pox or scab or other sore,
All animals that water at that well
Are cured at once. Take note of what I tell.

If the good man—the owner of the stock—
Goes once a week, before the crow of cock,
Fasting, and takes a draught of water too,
Why then, according to that holy Jew,
He'll find his cattle multiply and sell.
    " 'And it's a cure for jealousy as well;
For though a man be given to jealous wrath,
Use but this water when you make his broth,
And never again will he mistrust his wife,
Though he knew all about her sinful life,
Though two or three clergy had enjoyed her
    love.
    " 'Now look; I have a mitten here, a glove.
Whoever wears this mitten on his hand
Will multiply his grain. He sows his land
And up will come abundant wheat or oats,
Providing that he offers pence or groats.
    " 'Good men and women, here's a word of
        warning;
If there is anyone in church this morning
Guilty of sin, so far beyond expression
Horrible, that he dare not make confession,
Or any woman, whether young or old,
That's cuckolded her husband, be she told
That such as she shall have no power or grace
To offer to my relics in this place.
But those who can acquit themselves of blame
Can all come up and offer in God's name,
And I will shrive them by the authority
Committed in this papal bull to me.'
    "That trick's been worth a hundred marks
        a year
Since I became a Pardoner, never fear.
Then, priestlike in my pulpit, with a frown,
I stand, and when the yokels have sat down,
I preach, as you have heard me say before,
And tell a hundred lying mockeries more.
I take great pains, and stretching out my neck
To east and west I crane about and peck
Just like a pigeon sitting on a barn.
My hands and tongue together spin the yarn
And all my antics are a joy to see.
The curse of avarice and cupidity
Is all my sermon, for it frees the pelf.
Out come the pence, and specially for myself,
For my exclusive purpose is to win
And not at all to castigate their sin.
Once dead what matter how their souls may
    fare?
They can go blackberrying, for all I care!
    "Believe me, many a sermon or devotive
Exordium issues from an evil motive.
Some to give pleasure by their flattery

And gain promotion through hypocrisy,
Some out of vanity, some out of hate;
Or when I dare not otherwise debate
I'll put my discourse into such a shape,
My tongue will be a dagger; no escape
For him from slandering falsehood shall
    there be.
If he has hurt my brethren or me.
For though I never mention him by name
The congregation guesses all the same
From certain hints that everybody knows,
And so I take revenge upon our foes
And spit my venom forth, while I profess
Holy and true—or seeming holiness.

"But let me briefly make my purpose plain;
I preach for nothing but for greed of gain
And use the same old text, as bold as brass,
Radix malorum est cupiditas.
And thus I preach against the very vice
I make my living out of—avarice.
And yet however guilty of that sin
Myself, with others I have power to win
Them from it, I can bring them to repent;
But that is not my principal intent.
Covetousness is both the root and stuff
Of all I preach. That ought to be enough.

"Well, then I give examples thick and fast
From bygone times, old stories from the past.
A yokel mind loves stories from of old,
Being the kind it can repeat and hold.
What! Do you think, as long as I can preach
And get their silver for the things I teach,
That I will live in poverty, from choice?
That's not the counsel of my inner voice!
No! Let me preach and beg from kirk to kirk
And never do an honest job of work,
No, nor make baskets, like St. Paul, to gain
A livelihood. I do not preach in vain.
There's no apostle I would counterfeit;
I mean to have money, wool and cheese and
    wheat
Though it were given me by the poorest lad
Or poorest village widow, though she had
A string of starving children, all agape.
No, let me drink the liquor of the grape
And keep a jolly wench in every town!

"But listen, gentlemen; to bring
    things down
To a conclusion, would you like a tale?
Now as I've drunk a draught of corn-ripe ale,
By God it stands to reason I can strike
On some good story that you all will like.
For though I am a wholly vicious man

Don't think I can't tell moral tales. I can!
Here's one I often preach when out for win-
    ning;
Now please be quiet. Here is the beginning."

The Pardoner's Tale

In Flanders once there was a company
Of youngsters haunting vice and ribaldry,
Riot and gambling, stews and public-houses
Where each with harp, guitar or lute carouses,
Dancing and dicing day and night, and bold
To eat and drink far more than they can hold,
Doing thereby the devil sacrifice
Within that devil's temple of cursed vice,
Abominable in superfluity,
With oaths so damnable in blasphemy
That it's a grisly thing to hear them swear.
Our dear Lord's body they will rend and tear
As if the Jews had rent Him not enough;
And at the sin of others every tough
Will laugh, and presently the dancing-girls,
Small pretty ones, come in and shake their
    curls,
With youngsters, selling fruit, and ancient
    bawds,
And girls with cakes and music, devil's gauds
To kindle and blow the fires of lechery
That are so close annexed to gluttony.
Witness the Bible, which is most express
That lust is bred of wine and drunkenness.

    Look how the drunken and unnatural Lot
Lay with his daughters, though he knew
    it not;
He was too drunk to know what he was doing.

    Take Herod, too, his tale is worth pursuing.
Replete with wine and feasting, he was able
To give the order at his very table
To kill the innocent Baptist, good St. John.

    Seneca has a thought worth pondering on;
No difference, he says, that he can find
Between a madman who has lost his mind
And one who is habitually mellow
Except that madness when it takes a fellow
Lasts longer, on the whole, than drunkenness.
O cursed gluttony, our first distress!
Cause of our first confusion, first temptation,
The very origin of our damnation,
Till Christ redeemed us with his blood again!
O infamous indulgence! Cursed stain
So dearly bought! And what has it been
    worth?
Gluttony has corrupted all the earth.

    Adam, our father, and his wife as well,

From Paradise to labour and to Hell
Were driven for that vice, they were indeed.
While she and Adam fasted, so I read,
They were in Paradise; when he and she
Ate of the fruit of that forbidden tree
They were at once cast forth in pain and woe.
O gluttony, it is to thee we owe
Our griefs! O if we knew the maladies
That follow on excess and gluttonies,
Sure we would diet, we would temper
    pleasure
In sitting down at table, show some measure!
Alas the narrow throat, the tender mouth!
Men labour east and west and north and south
In earth, in air, in water—Why, d'you think?
To get a glutton dainty meat and drink!
How well of this St. Paul's Epistle treats!
"Meats for the belly, belly for the meats,
But God shall yet destroy both it and them."
Alas, the filth of it! If we contemn
The name, how far more filthy is the act!
A man who swills down vintages in fact
Makes a mere privy of his throat, a sink
For cursed superfluities of drink!

    So the Apostle said, whom tears could
        soften:
"Many there are, as I have told you often,
And weep to tell, whose gluttony sufficed
To make them enemies of the cross of Christ,
Whose ending is destruction and whose God
Their belly!" O thou belly! stinking pod
Of dung and foul corruption, that canst send
Thy filthy music forth at either end,
What labour and expense it is to find
Thy sustenance! These cooks that strain and
    grind
And bray in mortars, transubstantiate
God's gifts into a flavour on a plate,
To please a lecherous palate. How they batter
Hard bones to put some marrow on your
    platter,
Spicery, root, bark, leaf—they search and
    cull it
In the sweet hope of flattering a gullet!
Nothing is thrown away that could delight
Or whet anew lascivious appetite.
Be sure a man whom such a fare entices
Is dead indeed, though living in his vices.

    Wine is a lecherous thing and drunkenness
A squalor of contention and distress.
O drunkard, how disfigured is thy face,
How foul thy breath, how filthy thy embrace!
And through thy drunken nose a stertorous
    snort

Like "samson-samson"—something of the sort.
Yet Samson never was a man to swig.
You totter, lurch and fall like a stuck pig,
Your manhood's lost, your tongue is in a burr.
Drunkenness is the very sepulchre
Of human judgement and articulation.
He that is subject to the domination
Of drink can keep no secrets, be it said.
Keep clear of wine, I tell you, white or red,
Especially Spanish wines which they provide
And have on sale on Fish Street and Cheap-
    side.
That wine mysteriously finds its way
To mix itself with others—shall we say
Spontaneously!—that grow in neighbouring
    regions.[1]
Out of the mixture fumes arise in legions,
So when a man has had a drink or two
Though he may think he is at home with you
In Cheapside, I assure you he's in Spain
Where it was made, at Lepé I maintain,
Not even at Bordeaux. He's soon elate
And very near the "samson-samson" state.

    But seriously, my lords, attention, pray!
All the most notable acts, I dare to say,
And victories in the Old Testament,
Won under God who is omnipotent,
Were won in abstinence, were won in prayer.
Look in the Bible, you will find it there.

    Or else take Attila the Conqueror;
Died in his sleep, a manner to abhor,
In drunken shame and bleeding at the nose.
A general should live sober, I suppose.
Moreover call to mind and ponder well
What was commanded unto Lemuel
—Not Samuel, but Lemuel I said—
Read in the Bible, that's the fountain-head,
And see what comes of giving judges drink.
No more of that. I've said enough, I think.

    Having put gluttony in its proper setting
I wish to warn you against dice and betting.
Gambling's the very mother of robbed purses,
Lies, double-dealing, perjury, and curses,
Manslaughter, blasphemy of Christ, and
    waste
Of time and money. Worse, you are debased
In public reputation, put to shame.
"A common gambler" is a nasty name.
    The more exalted such a man may be
So much the more contemptible is he.
A gambling prince would be incompetent
To frame a policy of government,
And he will sink in general opinion
As one unfit to exercise dominion.

Stilbon, that wise ambassador whose
mission
Took him to Corinth, was of high position;
Sparta had sent him with intent to frame
A treaty of alliance. When he came,
Hoping for reinforcement and advice,
It happened that he found them all at dice,
Their very nobles; so he quickly planned
To steal away, home to his native land.
He said, "I will not lose my reputation,
Or compromise the honour of my nation,
By asking dicers to negotiate.
Send other wise ambassadors of state,
For on my honour I would rather die
Than be a means for Sparta to ally
With gamblers; Sparta, glorious in honour,
Shall take no such alliances upon her
As dicers make, by any act of mine!"
He showed his sense in taking such a line.

Again, consider King Demetrius;
The King of Parthia—history has it thus—
Sent him a pair of golden dice in scorn,
To show he reckoned him a gambler born
Whose honour, if unable to surmount
The vice of gambling, was of no account.
Lords can amuse themselves in other ways
Honest enough, to occupy their days.

Now let me speak a word or two of
swearing
And perjury; the Bible is unsparing.
It's an abominable thing to curse
And swear, it says; but perjury is worse.
Almighty God has said, "Swear not at all,"
Witness St. Matthew, and you may recall
The words of Jeremiah, having care
To what he says of lying: "Thou shalt swear
In truth, in judgement and in righteousness."
But idle swearing is a sin, no less.
Behold and see the tables of the Law
Of God's Commandments, to be held in awe;
Look at the third where it is written plain,
"Thou shalt not take the name of God in
vain."
You see He has forbidden swearing first;
Not murder, no, nor other thing accurst
Comes before that, I say, in God's commands.
That is the order; he who understands
Knows that the third commandment is just
that.
And in addition, let me tell you flat,
Vengeance on him and all his house shall fall
That swears outrageously, or swears at all.
"God's precious heart and passion, by God's
nails

And by the blood of Christ that is at Hailes,[2]
Seven's my luck, and yours is five and three;
God's blessed arms! If you play false with me
I'll stab you with my dagger!" Overthrown
By two small dice, two bitching bits of bone,
Their fruit is perjury, rage and homicide.
O for the love of Jesus Christ who died
For us, abandon curses, small or great!
But, sirs, I have a story to relate.

It's of three rioters I have to tell
Who, long before the morning service bell,
Were sitting in a tavern for a drink.
And as they sat, they heard the hand-bell clink
Before a coffin going to the grave;
One of them called the little tavern-knave
And said "Go and find out at once—look
spry!—
Whose corpse is in that coffin passing by;
And see you get the name correctly too."
"Sir," said the boy, "no need, I promise you;
Two hours before you came here I was told.
He was a friend of yours in days of old,
And suddenly, last night, the man was slain,
Upon his bench, face up, dead drunk again.
There came a privy thief, they call him Death,
Who kills us all round here, and in a breath
He speared him through the heart, he never
stirred.
And then Death went his way without a word.
He's killed a thousand in the present plague,
And, sir, it doesn't do to be too vague
If you should meet him; you had best be wary.
Be on your guard with such an adversary,
Be primed to meet him everywhere you go,
That's what my mother said. It's all I know."

The publican joined in with, "By St. Mary,
What the child says is right; you'd best be
wary,
This very year he killed, in a large village
A mile away, man, woman, serf at tillage,
Page in the household, children—all there
were.
Yes, I imagine that he lives round there.
It's well to be prepared in these alarms,
He might do you dishonour." "Huh, God's
arms!"
The rioter said, "Is he so fierce to meet?
I'll search for him, by Jesus, street by street.
God's blessed bones! I'll register a vow!
Here, chaps! The three of us together now,
Hold up your hands, like me, and we'll be
brothers
In this affair, and each defend the others,
And we will kill this traitor Death, I say!

Away with him as he has made away
With all our friends. God's dignity! Tonight!"
    They made their bargain, swore with ap-
      petite,
These three, to live and die for one another
As brother-born might swear to his born
    brother.
And up they started in their drunken rage
And made towards this village which the page
And publican had spoken of before.
Many and grisly were the oaths they swore,
Tearing Christ's blessed body to a shred;
"If we can only catch him, Death is dead!"
    When they had gone not fully half a mile,
Just as they were about to cross a stile,
They came upon a very poor old man
Who humbly greeted them and thus began,
"God look to you, my lords, and give you
    quiet!"
To which the proudest of these men of riot
Gave back the answer, "What, old fool? Give
    place!
Why are you all wrapped up except your face?
Why live so long? Isn't it time to die?"
    The old, old fellow looked him in the eye
And said, "Because I never yet have found,
Though I have walked to India, searching
    round
Village and city on my pilgrimage,
One who would change his youth to have
    my age.
And so my age is mine and must be still
Upon me, for such time as God may will.
    "Not even Death, alas, will take my life;
So, like a wretched prisoner at strife
Within himself, I walk alone and wait
About the earth, which is my mother's gate,
Knock-knocking with my staff from night
    to noon
And crying, 'Mother, open to me soon!
Look at me, mother, won't you let me in?
See how I wither, flesh and blood and skin!
Alas! When will these bones be laid to rest?
Mother, I would exchange—for that were
    best—
The wardrobe in my chamber, standing there
So long, for yours! Aye, for a shirt of hair
To wrap me in!' She has refused her grace,
Whence comes the pallor of my withered
    face.
    "But it dishonoured you when you began
To speak so roughly, sir, to an old man,
Unless he had injured you in word or deed.

It says in holy writ, as you may read,
'Thou shalt rise up before the hoary head
And honour it.' And therefore be it said
'Do no more harm to an old man than you,
Being now young, would have another do
When you are old'—if you should live till
    then.
And so may God be with you, gentlemen,
For I must go whither I have to go."
    "By God," the gambler said, "you shan't
    do so,
You don't get off so easy, by St. John!
I heard you mention, just a moment gone,
A certain traitor Death who singles out
And kills the fine young fellows hereabout.
And you're his spy, by God! You wait a bit.
Say where he is or you shall pay for it,
By God and by the Holy Sacrament!
I say you've joined together by consent
To kill us younger folk, you thieving swine!"
    "Well, sirs," he said, "if it be your design
To find out Death, turn up this crooked way
Towards that grove, I left him there today
Under a tree, and there you'll find him
    waiting.
He isn't one to hide for all your prating.
You see that oak? He won't be far to find.
And God protect you that redeemed mankind,
Aye, and amend you!" Thus that ancient man.
    At once the three young rioters began
To run, and reached the tree, and there they
    found
A pile of golden florins on the ground,
New-coined, eight bushels of them as they
    thought.
No longer was it Death those fellows sought,
For they were all so thrilled to see the sight,
The florins were so beautiful and bright,
That down they sat beside the precious pile.
The wickedest spoke first after a while.
"Brothers," he said, "you listen to what I say.
I'm pretty sharp although I joke away.
It's clear that Fortune has bestowed this
    treasure
To let us live in jollity and pleasure.
Light come, light go! We'll spend it as we
    ought.
God's precious dignity! Who would have
    thought
This morning was to be our lucky day?
    "If one could only get the gold away,
Back to my house, or else to yours, perhaps—
For as you know, the gold is ours, chaps—

We'd all be at the top of fortune, hey?
But certainly it can't be done by day.
People would call us robbers—a strong gang,
So our own property would make us hang.
No, we must bring this treasure back by night
Some prudent way, and keep it out of sight.
And so as a solution I propose
We draw for lots and see the way it goes;
The one who draws the longest, lucky man,
Shall run to town as quickly as he can
To fetch us bread and wine—but keep things
 dark—
While two remain in hiding here to mark
Our heap of treasure. If there's no delay,
When night comes down we'll carry it away,
All three of us, wherever we have planned."

He gathered lots and hid them in his hand
Bidding them draw for where the luck should
 fall.
It fell upon the youngest of them all,
And off he ran at once towards the town.

As soon as he had gone the first sat down
And thus began a parley with the other:
"You know that you can trust me as a brother;
Now let me tell you where your profit lies;
You know our friend has gone to get supplies
And here's a lot of gold that is to be
Divided equally amongst us three.
Nevertheless, if I could shape things thus
So that we shared it out—the two of us—
Wouldn't you take it as a friendly act?"

"But how?" the other said. "He knows
 the fact
That all the gold was left with me and you;
What can we tell him? What are we to do?"

"Is it a bargain," said the first, "or no?
For I can tell you in a word or so
What's to be done to bring the thing about."

"Trust me," the other said, "you needn't
 doubt
My word. I won't betray you, I'll be true."

"Well," said his friend, "you see that we
 are two,
And two are twice as powerful as one.
Now look; when he comes back, get up in fun
To have a wrestle; then, as you attack,
I'll up and put my dagger through his back
While you and he are struggling, as in game;
Then draw your dagger too and do the same.
Then all this money will be ours to spend,
Divided equally of course, dear friend.
Then we can gratify our lusts and fill
The day with dicing at our own sweet will."

Thus these two miscreants agreed to slay
The third and youngest, as you heard me say.

The youngest, as he ran towards the town,
Kept turning over, rolling up and down
Within his heart the beauty of those bright
New florins, saying, "Lord, to think I might
Have all that treasure to myself alone!
Could there be anyone beneath the throne
Of God so happy as I then should be?"

And so the Fiend, our common enemy,
Was given power to put it in his thought
That there was always poison to be bought,
And that with poison he could kill his friends.
To men in such a state the Devil sends
Thoughts of this kind, and has a full per-
 mission
To lure them on to sorrow and perdition;
For this young man was utterly content
To kill them both and never to repent.

And on he ran, he had no thought to tarry,
Came to the town, found an apothecary
And said, "Sell me some poison if you will,
I have a lot of rats I want to kill
And there's a polecat too about my yard
That takes my chickens and it hits me hard;
But I'll get even, as is only right,
With vermin that destroy a man by night."

The chemist answered, "I've a preparation
Which you shall have, and by my soul's sal-
 vation
If any living creature eat or drink
A mouthful, ere he has the time to think,
Though he took less than makes a grain of
 wheat,
You'll see him fall down dying at your feet;
Yes, die he must, and in so short a while
You'd hardly have the time to walk a mile,
The poison is so strong, you understand."

This cursed fellow grabbed into his hand
The box of poison and away he ran
Into a neighbouring street, and found a man
Who lent him three large bottles. He
 withdrew
And deftly poured the poison into two.
He kept the third one clean, as well he might,
For his own drink, meaning to work all night
Stacking the gold and carrying it away.
And when this rioter, this devil's clay,
Had filled his bottles up with wine, all three,
Back to rejoin his comrades sauntered he.

Why make a sermon of it? Why waste
 breath?
Exactly in the way they'd planned his death

They fell on him and slew him, two to one.
Then said the first of them when this was
    done,
"Now for a drink. Sit down and let's be
    merry,
For later on there'll be the corpse to bury."
And, as it happened, reaching for a sup,
He took a bottle full of poison up
And drank; and his companion, nothing loth,
Drank from it also, and they perished both.

    There is, in Avicenna's long relation[3]
Concerning poison and its operation,
Trust me, no ghastlier section to transcend
What these two wretches suffered at
    their end.
Thus these two murderers received their due,
So did the treacherous young poisoner too.

        O cursed sin! O blackguardly excess!
O treacherous homicide! O wickedness!
O gluttony that lusted on and diced!
O blasphemy that took the name of Christ
With habit-hardened oaths that pride began!
Alas, how comes it that a mortal man,
That thou, to thy Creator, Him that wrought
    thee,
That paid His precious blood for thee and
    bought thee,
Art so unnatural and false within?

    Dearly beloved, God forgive your sin
And keep you from the vice of avarice!
My holy pardon frees you all of this,
Provided that you make the right approaches,
That is with sterling, rings, or silver brooches.
Bow down your heads under this holy bull!
Come on, you women, offer up your wool!
I'll write your name into my ledger; so!
Into the bliss of Heaven you shall go.
For I'll absolve you by my holy power,
You that make offering, clean as at the hour
When you were born. . . . That, sirs, is how I
    preach.
And Jesu Christ, soul's healer, aye, the leech
Of every soul, grant pardon and relieve you
Of sin, for that is best, I won't deceive you.

    One thing I should have mentioned in my
    tale,
Dear people. I've some relics in my bale
And pardons too, as full and fine, I hope,
As any in England, given me by the Pope.
If there be one among you that is willing
To have my absolution for a shilling
Devoutly given, come! and do not harden

Your hearts but kneel in humbleness for
    pardon;
Or else, receive my pardon as we go.
You can renew it every town or so
Always provided that you still renew
Each time, and in good money, what is due.
It is an honour to you to have found
A pardoner with his credentials sound
Who can absolve you as you ply the spur
In any accident that may occur.
For instance—we are all at Fortune's beck—
Your horse may throw you down and break
    your neck.
What a security it is to all
To have me here among you and at call
With pardon for the lowly and the great
When soul leaves body for the future state!
And I advise our Host here to begin,
The most enveloped of you all in sin.
Come forward, Host, you shall be the first
    to pay,
And kiss my holy relics right away.
Only a groat. Come on, unbuckle your
    purse!"

    "No, no," said he, "not I, and may the curse
Of Christ descend upon me if I do!
You'll have me kissing your old breeches too
And swear they were the relic of a saint
Although your fundament supplied the paint!
Now by St. Helen and the Holy Land
I wish I had your ballocks in my hand
Instead of relics in a reliquarium;
Have them cut off and I will help to carry 'em.
We'll have them shrined for you in a hog's
    turd."

    The Pardoner said nothing, not a word;
He was so angry that he couldn't speak.
"Well," said our Host, "if you're for showing
    pique,
I'll joke no more, not with an angry man."

    The worthy Knight immediately began,
Seeing the fun was getting rather rough,
And said, "No more, we've all had quite
    enough.
Now, Master Pardoner, perk up, look cheerly!
And you, Sir Host, whom I esteem so dearly,
I beg of you to kiss the Pardoner.

    "Come, Pardoner, draw nearer, my dear sir.
Let's laugh again and keep the ball in play."
They kissed, and we continued on our way.

THE WIFE OF BATH'S TALE
The Wife of Bath's Prologue

"If there were no authority on earth
Except experience, mine, for what it's worth,
And that's enough for me, all goes to show
That marriage is a misery and a woe;
For let me say, if I may make so bold,
My lords, since when I was but twelve
    years old,
Thanks be to God Eternal evermore,
Five husbands have I had at the church door;
Yes, it's a fact that I have had so many,
All worthy in their way, as good as any.

    "Someone said recently for my persuasion
That as Christ only went on one occasion
To grace a wedding—in Cana of Galilee—
He taught me by example there to see
That it is wrong to marry more than once.
Consider, too, how sharply, for the nonce,
He spoke, rebuking the Samaritan
Beside the well, Christ Jesus, God and man.
'Thou hast had five men husband unto thee
And he that even now thou hast,' said He,
'Is not thy husband.' Such the words that fell;
But what He meant thereby I cannot tell.
Why was her fifth—explain it if you can—
No lawful spouse to the Samaritan?
How many might have had her, then, to wife?
I've never heard an answer all my life
To give the number final definition.
People may guess or frame a supposition,
But I can say for certain, it's no lie,
God bade us all to wax and multiply.
That kindly text I well can understand.
Is not my husband under God's command
To leave his father and mother and take me?
No word of what the number was to be,
Then why not marry two or even eight?
And why speak evil of the married state?

    "Take wise King Solomon of long ago;
We hear he had a thousand wives or so.
And would to God it were allowed to me
To be refreshed, aye, half so much as he!
He must have had a gift of God for wives,
No one to match him in a world of lives!
This noble king, one may as well admit,
On the first night threw many a merry fit
With each of them, he was so much alive.
Blessed be God that I have wedded five!
Welcome the sixth, whenever he appears.
I can't keep continent for years and years.

No sooner than one husband's dead and gone
Some other Christian man shall take me on,
For then, so says the Apostle, I am free
To wed, o' God's name, where it pleases me.
Wedding's no sin, so far as I can learn.
Better it is to marry than to burn.

    "What do I care if people choose to see
Scandal in Lamech for his bigamy?
I know that Abraham was a holy man
And Jacob too—I speak as best I can—
Yet each of them, we know, had several
    brides,
Like many another holy man besides.
Show me a time or text where God disparages
Or sets a prohibition upon marriages
Expressly, let me have it! Show it me!
And where did He command virginity?
I know as well as you do, never doubt it,
All the Apostle Paul has said about it;
He said that as for precepts he had none.
One may advise a woman to be one;
Advice is no commandment in my view.
He left it in our judgement what to do.

    "Had God commanded maidenhood to all
Marriage would be condemned beyond recall,
And certainly if seed were never sown,
How ever could virginity be grown?
Paul did not dare pronounce, let matters rest,
His Master having given him no behest.
There's a prize offered for virginity;
Catch as catch can! Who's in for it? Let's see!

    "It is not everyone who hears the call;
On whom God wills He lets His power fall.
The Apostle was a virgin, well I know;
Nevertheless, though all his writings show
He wished that everyone were such as he,
It's all mere counsel to virginity.
And as for being married, he lets me do it
Out of indulgence, so there's nothing to it
In marrying me, suppose my husband dead;
There's nothing bigamous in such a bed.
Though it were good a man should never
    touch
A woman (meaning here in bed and such)
And dangerous to assemble fire and tow
—What this allusion means you all must
    know—
He only says virginity is fresh,
More perfect than the frailty of the flesh
In married life—except when he and she
Prefer to live in married chastity.

    "I grant it you. I'll never say a word
Decrying maidenhood although preferred

To frequent marriage; there are those
    who mean
To live in their virginity, as clean
In body as in soul, and never mate.
I'll make no boast about my own estate.
As in a noble household, we are told,
Not every dish and and vessel's made of gold,
Some are of wood, yet earn their master's
    praise,
God calls His folk to Him in many ways.
To each of them God gave His proper gift,
Some this, some that, and left them to make
    shift.
Virginity is indeed a great perfection,
And married continence, for God's dilection,
But Christ, who of perfection is the well,
Bade not that everyone should go and sell
All that he had and give it to the poor
To follow in His footsteps, that is sure.
He spoke to those that would live perfectly,
And by your leave, my lords, that's not for me.
I will bestow the flower of life, the honey,
Upon the acts and fruit of matrimony.

    "Tell me to what conclusion or in aid
Of what were generative organs made?
And for what profit were those creatures
    wrought?
Trust me, they cannot have been made for
    naught.
Gloze as you will and plead the explanation
That they were only made for the purgation
Of urine, little things of no avail
Except to know a female from a male,
And nothing else. Did somebody say no?
Experience knows well it isn't so.
The learned may rebuke me, or be loth
To think it so, but they were made for both,
That is to say both use and pleasure in
Engendering, except in case of sin.
Why else the proverb written down and set
In books: 'A man must yield his wife her
    debt'?
What means of paying her can he invent
Unless he use his silly instrument?
It follows they were fashioned at creation
Both to purge urine and for propagation.

    "But I'm not saying everyone is bound
Who has such harness as you heard me ex-
    pound
To go and use it breeding; that would be
To show too little care for chastity.
Christ was a virgin, fashioned as a man,
And many of his saints since time began

Were ever perfect in their chastity.
I'll have no quarrel with virginity.
Let them be pure wheat loaves of maidenhead
And let us wives be known for barley-bread;
Yet Mark can tell that barley-bread sufficed
To freshen many at the hand of Christ.
In that estate to which God summoned me
I'll persevere; I'm not pernickety.
In wifehood I will use my instrument
As freely as my Maker me it sent.
If I turn difficult, God give me sorrow!
My husband, he shall have it eve and morrow
Whenever he likes to come and pay his debt,
I won't prevent him! I'll have a husband yet
Who shall be both my debtor and my slave
And bear his tribulation to the grave
Upon his flesh, as long as I'm his wife.
For mine shall be the power all his life
Over his proper body, and not he,
Thus the Apostle Paul has told it me,
And bade our husbands they should love us
    well;
There's a command on which I like to
    dwell . . . "

    The Pardoner started up, and thereupon
"Madam," he said, "by God and by St. John,
That's noble preaching no one could surpass!
I was about to take a wife; alas!
Am I to buy it on my flesh so dear?
There'll be no marrying for me this year!"

    "You wait," she said, "my story's not
    begun.
You'll taste another brew before I've done;
You'll find it doesn't taste as good as ale;
And when I've finished telling you my tale
Of tribulation in the married life
In which I've been an expert as a wife,
That is to say, myself have been the whip.
So please yourself whether you want to sip
At that same cask of marriage I shall broach.
Be cautious before making the approach,
For I'll give instances, and more than ten.
And those who won't be warned by
    other men,
By other men shall suffer their correction,
So Ptolemy has said, in this connection.[1]
You read his *Almagest;* you'll find it there."

    "Madam, I put it to you as a prayer,"
The Pardoner said, "go on as you began!
Tell us your tale, spare not for any man.
Instruct us younger men in your technique."
"Gladly," she said, "if you will let me speak,
But still I hope the company won't reprove me

Though I should speak as fantasy may
    move me,
And please don't be offended at my views;
They're really only offered to amuse.
    "Now, gentlemen, I'll on and tell my tale
And as I hope to drink good wine and ale
I'll tell the truth. Those husbands that I had,
Three of them were good and two were bad.
The three that I call 'good' were rich and old.
They could indeed with difficulty hold
The articles that bound them all to me;
(No doubt you understand my simile).
So help me God, I have to laugh outright
Remembering how I made them work at
    night!
And faith I set no store by it; no pleasure
It was to me. They'd given me their treasure,
And so I had no need of diligence
Winning their love, or showing reverence.
They loved me well enough, so, heavens
    above,
Why should I make a dainty of their love?
    "A knowing woman's work is never done
To get a lover if she hasn't one,
But as I had them eating from my hand
And as they'd yielded me their gold and land,
Why then take trouble to provide them
    pleasure
Unless to profit and amuse my leisure?
I set them so to work, I'm bound to say;
Many a night they sang, 'Alack the day!'
Never for them the flitch of bacon though
That some have won in Essex at Dunmow![2]
I managed them so well by my technique
Each was delighted to go out and seek
And buy some pretty thing for me to wear,
Happy if I as much as spoke them fair.
God knows how spitefully I used to scold
    them.
    "Listen, I'll tell you how I used to hold
    them,
You knowing women, who can understand,
First put them in the wrong, and out of hand.
No one can be so bold—I mean no man—
At lies and swearing as a woman can.
This is no news, as you'll have realized,
To knowing ones, but to the misadvised.
A knowing wife if she is worth her salt
Can always prove her husband is at fault,
And even though the fellow may have heard
Some story told him by a little bird
She knows enough to prove the bird is crazy
And get her maid to witness she's a daisy,

With full agreement, scarce solicited.
But listen. Here's the sort of thing I said:
    " 'Now, sir old dotard, what is that you say?
Why is my neighbour's wife so smart and gay?
She is respected everywhere she goes.
I sit at home and have no decent clothes.
Why haunt her house? What are you doing
    there?
Are you so amorous? Is she so fair?
What, whispering secrets to our maid? For
    shame,
Sir ancient lecher! Time you dropped that
    game.
And if I see my gossip or a friend
You scold me like a devil! There's no end
If I as much as stroll towards his house.
Then you come home as drunken as a mouse,
You mount your throne and preach, chapter
    and verse
—All nonsense—and you tell me it's a curse
To marry a poor woman—she's expensive;
Or if her family's wealthy and extensive
You say it's torture to endure her pride
And melancholy airs, and more beside.
And if she has a pretty face, old traitor,
You say she's game for any fornicator
And ask what likelihood will keep her straight
With all those men who lie about in wait.
    " 'You say that some desire us for our
    wealth,
Some for our shapeliness, our looks, our
    health,
Some for our singing, others for our dancing,
Some for our gentleness and dalliant glancing,
And some because our hands are soft and
    small;
By your account the devil gets us all.
    " 'You say what castle wall can be so strong
As to hold out against a siege for long?
And if her looks are foul you say that she
Is hot for every man that she can see,
Leaping upon them with a spaniel's airs
Until she finds a man to buy her wares.
Never was goose upon the lake so grey
But that she found a gander, so you say.
You say it's hard to keep a girl controlled
If she's the kind that no one wants to hold.
That's what you say as you stump off to bed,
You brute! You say no man of sense
    would wed,
That is, not if he wants to go to Heaven.
Wild thunderbolts and fire from the Seven
Planets descend and break your withered neck!

" 'You say that buildings falling into
    wreck,
And smoke, and scolding women, are the
    three
Things that will drive a man from home.
    Dear me!
What ails the poor old man to grumble so?
    " 'We women hide our faults but let
    them show
Once we are safely married, so you say.
There's a fine proverb for a popinjay!
    " 'You say that oxen, asses, hounds and
    horses
Can be tried out on various ploys and courses;
And basins too, and dishes when you buy
    them,
Spoons, chairs and furnishings, a man can
    try them
As he can try a suit of clothes, no doubt,
But no one ever tries a woman out
Until he's married her; old dotard crow!
And then you say she lets her vices show.
    " 'You also say we count it for a crime
Unless you praise our beauty all the time,
Unless you're always poring on our faces
And call us pretty names in public places;
Or if you fail to treat me to a feast
Upon my birthday—presents at the least—
Or to respect my nurse and her grey hairs,
Or be polite to all my maids upstairs
And to my father's cronies and his spies.
That's what you say, old barrelful of lies!
    " 'Then there's our young apprentice,
    handsome Johnny,
Because he has crisp hair that shines as bonny
As finest gold, and squires me up and down
You show your low suspicions in a frown.
I wouldn't have him, not if you died to-
    morrow!
    " 'And tell me this, God punish you with
    sorrow,
Why do you hide the keys of coffer doors?
It's just as much my property as yours.
Do you want to make an idiot of your wife?
Now, by the Lord that gave me soul and life,
You shan't have both, you can't be such a
    noddy
As think to keep my goods and have my body!
One you must do without, whatever you say.
And do you need to spy on me all day?
I think you'd like to lock me in your coffer!
"Go where you please, dear wife," you ought
    to offer,

"Amuse yourself! I shan't give ear to malice,
I know you for a virtuous wife, Dame Alice."
We cannot love a husband who takes charge
Of where we go. We like to be at large.
    " 'Above all other men may God confer
His blessing on that wise astrologer
Sir Ptolemy who, in his *Almagest,*
Has set this proverb down: "Of men, the best
And wisest care not who may have in hand
The conduct of the world." I understand
That means, "If you've enough, you
    shouldn't care
How prosperously other people fare."
Be sure, old dotard, if you call the bluff,
You'll get your evening rations right enough.
He's a mean fellow that lets no man handle
His lantern when it's just to light a candle;
He has lost no light, he hasn't felt the strain;
And you have light enough, so why complain?
    " 'And when a woman tries a mild display
In dress or costly ornament, you say
It is a danger to her chastity,
And then, bad luck to you, start making free
With Bible tags in the Apostle's name;
"And in like manner, chastely and with
    shame,
You women should adorn yourselves,"
    said he,
"And not with braided hair or jewelry,
With pearl or golden ornament." What next!
I'll pay as much attention to your text
And rubric in such things as would a gnat.
    " 'And once you said that I was like a cat,
For if you singe a cat it will not roam
And that's the way to keep a cat at home.
But when she feels her fur is sleek and gay
She can't be kept indoors for half a day
But off she takes herself as dusk is falling
To show her fur and go a-caterwauling.
Which means if I feel gay, as you suppose,
I shall run out to show my poor old clothes.
    " 'Silly old fool! You and your private spies!
Go on, beg Argus with his hundred eyes
To be my bodyguard, that's better still!
But yet he shan't, I say, against my will.
I'll pull him by the beard, believe you me!
    " 'And once you said that principally three[3]
Misfortunes trouble earth, east, west and
    north,
And no man living could endure a fourth.
My dear sir shrew, Jesu cut short your life!
You preach away and say a hateful wife
Is reckoned to be one of these misfortunes.

Is there no other trouble that importunes
The world and that your parables could con-
    demn?
Must an unhappy wife be one of them?
    " 'Then you compared a woman's love to
        Hell,
To barren land where water will not dwell,
And you compared it to a quenchless fire,
The more it burns the more is its desire
To burn up everything that burnt can be.
You say that just as worms destroy a tree
A wife destroys her husband and contrives,
As husbands know, the ruin of their lives.'
    "Such was the way, my lords, you under-
        stand
I kept my older husbands well in hand.
I told them they were drunk and their un-
    fitness
To judge my conduct forced me to take
    witness
That they were lying. Johnny and my niece
Would back me up. O Lord, I wrecked their
    peace,
Innocent as they were, without remorse!
For I could bite and whinney like a horse
And launch complaints when things were all
    my fault;
I'd have been lost if I had called a halt.
First to the mill is first to grind your corn;
I attacked first and they were overborne,
Glad to apologize and even suing
Pardon for what they'd never thought of doing.
    "I'd tackle one for wenching, out of hand,
Although so ill the man could hardly stand,
Yet he felt flattered in his heart because
He thought it showed how fond of him I was.
I swore that all my walking out at night
Was just to keep his wenching well in sight.
That was a dodge that made me shake with
    mirth;
But all such wit is given us at birth.
Lies, tears and spinning are the things God
    gives
By nature to a woman, while she lives.
So there's one thing at least that I can boast,
That in the end I always ruled the roast;
Cunning or force was sure to make them
    stumble,
And always keeping up a steady grumble.
    "But bed-time above all was their misfor-
        tune;
That was the place to scold them and im-
    portune

And baulk their fun. I never would abide
In bed with them if hands began to slide
Till they had promised ransom, paid a fee:
And then I let them do their nicety.
And so I tell this tale to every man,
'It's all for sale and let him win who can.'
No empty-handed man can lure a bird.
His pleasures were my profit; I concurred,
Even assumed fictitious appetite,
Though bacon never gave me much delight.
And that's the very fact that made me chide
    them.
And had the Pope been sitting there be-
    side them
I wouldn't have spared them at their very
    table,
But paid them out as far as I was able.
I say, so help me God Omnipotent,
Were I to make my will and testament
I owe them nothing, paid them word for word
Putting my wits to use, and they preferred
To give it up and take it for the best
For otherwise they would have got no rest.
Though they might glower like a maddened
    beast
They got no satisfaction, not the least.
    "I then would say, 'My dear, just take a
        peep!
What a meek look on Willikin our sheep!
Come nearer, husband, let me kiss your cheek;
You should be just as patient, just as meek;
Sweeten your heart. Your conscience needs a
    probe.
You're fond of preaching patience out of Job,
And so be patient; practise what you preach,
And if you don't, my dear, we'll have to teach
You that it's nice to have a quiet life.
One of us must be master, man or wife,
And since a man's more reasonable, he
Should be the patient one, you must agree.
    " 'What ails you, man, to grumble so and
        groan?
Just that you want my what-not all your own?
Why, take it all, man, take it, every bit!
St. Peter, what a love you have for it!
For if I were to sell my belle chose,
I could go walking fresher than a rose;
But I will keep it for your private tooth.
By God, you are to blame, and that's the
    truth.'
    "That's how my first three husbands were
        undone.
Now let me tell you of my last but one.

"He was a reveller, was number four;
That is to say he kept a paramour.
Young, strong and stubborn, I was full of rage
And jolly as a magpie in a cage.
Play me the harp and I would dance and sing,
Believe me, like a nightingale in spring,
If I had had a draught of sweetened wine.
    "Metellius, that filthy lout—the swine
Who snatched a staff and took his woman's life
For drinking wine—if I had been his wife
He never would have daunted me from drink.
Whenever I take wine I have to think
Of Venus, for as cold engenders hail
A lecherous mouth begets a lecherous tail.
A woman in her cups has no defence,
As lechers know from long experience.
    "But Christ! Whenever it comes back
        to me,
When I recall my youth and jollity,
It fairly warms the cockles of my heart!
This very day I feel a pleasure start,
Yes, I can feel it tickling at the root.
Lord, how it does me good! I've had my fruit,
I've had my world and time, I've had my fling!
But age that comes to poison everything
Has taken all my beauty and my pith.
Well, let it go, the devil go therewith!
The flour is gone, there is no more to say,
And I must sell the bran as best I may;
But still I mean to find my way to fun. . . .
Now let me tell you of my last but one.
    "I told you how it filled my heart with spite
To see another woman his delight,
By God and all His saints I made it good!
I carved him out a cross of the same wood,
Not with my body in a filthy way,
But certainly by seeming rather gay
To others, frying him in his own grease
Of jealousy and rage; he got no peace.
By God on earth I was his purgatory,
For which I hope his soul may be in glory.
God knows he sang a sorry tune, he flinched,
And bitterly enough, when the shoe pinched.
And God and he alone can say how grim,
How many were the ways I tortured him.
    "He died when I came back from Jordan
        Stream
And he lies buried under the rood-beam,
Albeit that his tomb can scarce supply us
With such a show as that of King Darius
—Apelles sculped it in a sumptuous taste—
Expensive funerals are just a waste.

Farewell to him, God give his spirit rest!
He's in his grave, he's nailed up in his chest.
    "Now of my fifth, last husband let me tell.
God never let his soul be sent to Hell!
And yet he was my worst, and many a blow
He struck me still can ache along my row
Of ribs, and will until my dying day.
    "But in our bed he was so fresh and gay,
So coaxing, so persuasive. . . . Heaven knows
Whenever he wanted it—my *belle chose*—
Though he had beaten me in every bone
He still could wheedle me to love, I own.
I think I loved him best, I'll tell no lie.
He was disdainful in his love, that's why.
We women have a curious fantasy
In such affairs, or so it seems to me.
When something's difficult, or can't be had,
We crave and cry for it all day like mad.
Forbid a thing, we pine for it all night,
Press fast upon us and we take to flight;
We use disdain in offering our wares.
A throng of buyers sends prices up at fairs,
Cheap goods have little value, they suppose;
And that's a thing that every woman knows.
    "My fifth and last—God keep his soul in
        health!
The one I took for love and not for wealth,
Had been at Oxford not so long before
But had left school and gone to lodge next
        door,
Yes, it was to my godmother's he'd gone.
God bless her soul! *Her* name was Alison.
She knew my heart and more of what I
        thought
Than did the parish priest, and so she ought!
She was my confidante, I told her all.
For had my husband pissed against a wall
Or done some crime that would have cost his
        life,
To her and to another worthy wife
And to my niece, because I loved her well,
I'd have told everything there was to tell.
And so I often did, and Heaven knows
It used to set him blushing like a rose
For shame, and he would blame his lack of
        sense
In telling me secrets of such consequence.
    "And so one time it happened that in Lent,
As I so often did, I rose and went
To see her, ever wanting to be gay
And go a-strolling, March, April and May,
From house to house for chat and village
        malice.

"Johnny (the boy from Oxford) and Dame
    Alice
And I myself, into the fields we went.
My husband was in London all that Lent;
All the more fun for me—I only mean
The fun of seeing people and being seen
By cocky lads; for how was I to know
Where or what graces Fortune might bestow?
And so I made a round of visitations,
Went to processions, festivals, orations,
Preachments and pilgrimages, watched the
    carriages
They use for plays and pageants, went to mar-
    riages,
And always wore my gayest scarlet dress.
    "These worms, these moths, these mites, I
        must confess,
Got little chance to eat it, by the way.
Why not? Because I wore it every day.
    "Now let me tell you all that came to pass.
We sauntered in the meadows through the
    grass
Toying and dallying to such extent,
Johnny and I, that I grew provident
And I suggested, were I ever free
And made a widow, he should marry me.
And certainly—I do not mean to boast—
I ever was more provident than most
In marriage matters and in other such.
I never think a mouse is up to much
That only has one hole in all the house;
If that should fail, well, it's good-bye the
    mouse.
    "I let him think I was as one enchanted
(That was a trick my godmother implanted)
And told him I had dreamt the night away
Thinking of him, and dreamt that as I lay
He tried to kill me. Blood had drenched
    the bed.
    " 'But still it was a lucky dream,' I said,
'For blood betokens gold as I recall.'
It was a lie. I hadn't dreamt at all.
'Twas from my godmother I learnt my lore
In matters such as that, and many more.
    "Well, let me see . . . what had I to ex-
        plain?
Aha! By God, I've got the thread again.
    "When my fourth husband lay upon
        his bier
I wept all day and looked as drear as drear,
As widows must, for it is quite in place,
And with a handkerchief I hid my face.
Now that I felt provided with a mate

I wept but little, I need hardly state.
    "To church they bore my husband on the
        morrow
With all the neighbours round him venting
    sorrow,
And one of them of course was handsome
    Johnny.
So help me God, I thought he looked so
    bonny
Behind the coffin! Heavens, what a pair
Of legs he had! Such feet, so clean and fair!
I gave my whole heart up, for him to hold.
He was, I think, some twenty winters old,
And I was forty then, to tell the truth.
But still, I always had a coltish tooth.
Yes, I'm gap-toothed; it suits me well I feel,
It is the print of Venus and her seal.
So help me God I was a lusty one,
Fair, young and well-to-do, and full of fun!
And truly, as my husbands said to me
I had the finest *quoniam* that might be.
For Venus sent me feeling from the stars
And my heart's boldness came to me from
    Mars.
Venus gave me desire and lecherousness
And Mars my hardihood, or so I guess,
Born under Taurus and with Mars therein.
Alas, alas, that ever love was sin!
I ever followed natural inclination
Under the power of my constellation
And was unable to deny, in truth,
My chamber of Venus to a likely youth.
The mark of Mars is still upon my face
And also in another privy place.
For as I may be saved by God above,
I never used discretion when in love
But ever followed on my appetite,
Whether the lad was short, long, black or
    white.
Little I cared, if he was fond of me,
How poor he was, or what his rank might be.
    "What shall I say? Before the month
        was gone
This gay young student, my delightful John,
Had married me in solemn festival.
I handed him the money, lands and all
That ever had been given me before;
This I repented later, more and more.
None of my pleasures would he let me seek.
By God, he smote me once upon the cheek
Because I tore a page out of his book,
And that's the reason why I'm deaf. But look,
Stubborn I was, just like a lioness;

As to my tongue, a very wrangleress.
I went off gadding as I had before
From house to house, however much he
    swore.
Because of that he used to preach and scold,
Drag Roman history up from days of old,
How one Simplicius Gallus left his wife,
Deserting her completely all his life,
Only for poking out her head one day
Without a hat, upon the public way.
    "Some other Roman—I forget his name—
Because his wife went to a summer's game
Without his knowledge, left her in the lurch.
    "And he would take the Bible up and
        search
For proverbs in Ecclesiasticus,
Particularly one that has it thus:
'Suffer no wicked woman to gad about.'
And then would come the saying (need you
    doubt?)
    A man who seeks to build his house of sallows,
    A man who spurs a blind horse over fallows,
    Or lets his wife make pilgrimage to Hallows,
    Is worthy to be hanged upon the gallows.
But all for naught. I didn't give a hen
For all his proverbs and his wise old men.
Nor would I take rebuke at any price;
I hate a man who points me out my vice,
And so, God knows, do many more than I.
That drove him raging mad, you may rely.
Nor more would I forbear him, I can promise.
    "Now let me tell you truly by St. Thomas
About that book and why I tore the page
And how he smote me deaf in very rage.
    "He had a book, he kept it on his shelf,
And night and day he read it to himself
And laughed aloud, although it was quite se-
    rious.
He called it *Theophrastus and Valerius.*[4]
There was another Roman, much the same,
A cardinal; St. Jerome was his name.
He wrote a book against Jovinian,
Bound up together with Tertullian,
Chrysippus, Trotula and Heloise,
An abbess, lived near Paris. And with these
Were bound the parables of Solomon,
With Ovid's *Art of Love* another one.
All these were bound together in one book
And day and night he used to take a look
At what it said, when he had time and leisure
Or had no occupation but his pleasure,
Which was to read this book of wicked wives;
He knew more legends of them and their lives

Than there are good ones mentioned in the
    Bible.
For take my word for it, there is no libel
On women that the clergy will not paint,
Except when writing of a woman-saint,
But never good of other women, though.
Who called the lion savage? Do you know?
By God, if women had but written stories
Like those the clergy keep in oratories,
More had been written of man's wickedness
Than all the sons of Adam could redress.
Children of Mercury[5] and we of Venus
Keep up the contrariety between us;
Mercury stands for wisdom, thrift and science,
Venus for revel, squandering and defiance.
Their several natures govern their direction;
One rises when the other's in dejection.
So Mercury is desolate when halted
In *Pisces,* just where Venus is exalted,
And Venus falls where Mercury is raised,
And women therefore never can be praised
By learned men, old scribes who cannot do
The works of Venus more than my old shoe.
These in their dotage sit them down to frowse
And say that women break their marriage-
    vows!
    "Now to my purpose as I told you; look,
Here's how I got a beating for a book.
One evening Johnny, glowering with ire,
Sat with his book and read it by the fire.
And first he read of Eve whose wickedness
Brought all mankind to sorrow and distress,
Root-cause why Jesus Christ Himself was
    slain
And gave His blood to buy us back again.
Aye, there's the text where you expressly find
That woman brought the loss of all mankind.
    "He read me then how Samson as he slept
Was shorn of all his hair by her he kept,
And by that treachery Samson lost his eyes.
And then he read me, if I tell no lies,
All about Hercules and Deianire;
She tricked him into setting himself on fire.
    "He left out nothing of the miseries
Occasioned by his wives to Socrates.
Xantippe poured a piss-pot on his head.
The silly man sat still, as he were dead,
Wiping his head, but dared no more complain
Than say, 'Ere thunder stops, down comes the
    rain.'
    "Next of Pasiphaë the Queen of Crete;[6]
For wickedness he thought that story sweet;
Fie, say no more! It has a grisly sting,

Her horrible lust. How could she do the thing!
  "And then he told of Clytemnestra's
    lechery
And how she made her husband die by
  treachery.
He read that story with a great devotion.
  "He read me what occasioned the com-
    motion
By which Amphiaraüs lost his life;
My husband had a legend about his wife
Eriphyle, who for a gaud in gold
Went to the Greeks in secret, and she told
Them where to find him, in what hiding-
  place.
At Thebes it was; he met with sorry grace.
  "Of Livia and Lucilia then he read,
And both of course had killed their husbands
  dead,
The one for love, the other out of hate.
Livia prepared some poison for him late
One evening and she killed him out of spite,
Lucilia out of lecherous delight.
For she, in order he might only think
Of her, prepared an aphrodisiac drink;
He drank it and was dead before the morning.
Such is the fate of husbands; it's a warning.
  "And then he told how one Latumius
Lamented to his comrade Arrius
That in his orchard-plot there grew a tree
On which his wives had hanged themselves,
  all three,
Or so he said, out of some spite or other;
To which this Arrius replied, 'Dear brother,
Give me a cutting from that blessed tree
And planted in my garden it shall be!'
  "Of wives of later date he also read,
How some had killed their husbands when
  in bed,
Then night-long with their lechers played the
  whore,
While the poor corpse lay fresh upon the
  floor.
  "One drove a nail into her husband's brain
While he was sleeping, and the man was slain;
Others put poison in their husbands' drink.
He spoke more harm of us than heart can
  think
And knew more proverbs too, for what they're
  worth,
Than there are blades of grass upon the earth.
  " 'Better,' says he, 'to share your habitation
With lion, dragon, or abomination
Than with a woman given to reproof.

Better,' says he, 'take refuge on the roof
Than with an angry wife, down in the house;
They are so wicked and cantankerous
They hate the things their husbands like,'
  he'd say.
'A woman always casts her shame away
When she casts off her smock, and that's in
  haste.
A pretty woman, if she isn't chaste,
Is like a golden ring in a sow's snout.'
  "Who could imagine, who could figure out
The torture in my heart? It reached the top
And when I saw that he would never stop
Reading this cursed book, all night no doubt,
I suddenly grabbed and tore three pages out
Where he was reading, at the very place,
And fisted such a buffet in his face
That backwards down into our fire he fell.
  "Then like a maddened lion, with a yell
He started up and smote me on the head,
And down I fell upon the floor for dead.
  "And when he saw how motionless I lay
He was aghast and would have fled away,
But in the end I started to come to.
'O have you murdered me, you robber, you,
To get my land?' I said. 'Was that the game?
Before I'm dead I'll kiss you all the same.'
  "He came up close and kneeling gent-
    ly down
He said, 'My love, my dearest Alison,
So help me God, I never again will hit
You, love; and if I did, you asked for it.
Forgive me!' But for all he was so meek,
I up at once and smote him on the cheek
And said, 'Take that to level up the score!
Now let me die, I can't speak any more.'
  "We had a mort of trouble and heavy
    weather
But in the end we made it up together.
He gave the bridle over to my hand,
Gave me the government of house and land,
Of tongue and fist, indeed of all he'd got.
I made him burn that book upon the spot.
And when I'd mastered him, and out of
  deadlock
Secured myself the sovereignty in wedlock,
And when he said, 'My own and truest wife,
Do as you please for all the rest of life,
But guard your honour and my good estate,'
From that day forward there was no debate.
So help me God I was as kind to him
As any wife from Denmark to the rim
Of India, and as true. And he to me.

And I pray God that sits in majesty
To bless his soul and fill it with his glory.
Now, if you'll listen, I will tell my story."

Words between the Summoner and the Friar

The Friar laughed when he had heard all this.
"Well, Ma'am," he said, "as God may send
    me bliss,
This is a long preamble to a tale!"
But when the Summoner heard the Friar rail,
"Just look!" he cried, "by the two arms
    of God!
These meddling friars are always on the prod!
Don't we all know a friar and a fly
Go prod and buzz in every dish and pie!
What do you mean with your 'preambulation'?
Amble yourself, trot, do a meditation!
You're spoiling all our fun with your commo-
    tion."
The Friar smiled and said, "Is that your mo-
    tion?
I promise on my word before I go
To find occasion for a tale or so
About a summoner that will make us laugh."
"Well, damn your eyes, and on my own be-
    half,"
The Summoner answered, "mine be damned
    as well
If I can't think of several tales to tell
About the friars that will make you mourn
Before we get as far as Sittingbourne.
Have you no patience? Look, he's in a huff!"
    Our Host called out, "Be quiet, that's
        enough!
Shut up, and let the woman tell her tale.
You must be drunk, you've taken too
    much ale.
Now, Ma'am, you go ahead and no demur."
"All right," she said, "it's just as you prefer,
If I have licence from this worthy friar."
"Nothing," said he, "that I should more de-
    sire."

The Wife of Bath's Tale

When good King Arthur ruled in ancient days
(A king that every Briton loves to praise)
This was a land brim-full of fairy folk.
The Elf-Queen and her courtiers joined and
    broke
Their elfin dance on many a green mead,
Or so was the opinion once, I read,
Hundreds of years ago, in days of yore.

But no one now sees fairies any more.
For now the saintly charity and prayer
Of holy friars seem to have purged the air;
They search the countryside through field and
    stream
As thick as motes that speckle a sun-beam,
Blessing the halls, the chambers, kitchens,
    bowers,
Cities and boroughs, castles, courts and
    towers,
Thorpes, barns and stables, outhouses and
    dairies,
And that's the reason why there are no fairies.
Wherever there was wont to walk an elf
To-day there walks the holy friar himself
As evening falls or when the daylight springs,
Saying his mattins and his holy things,
Walking his limit round from town to town.
Women can now go safely up and down
By every bush or under every tree;
There is no other incubus but he,
So there is really no one else to hurt you
And he will do no more than take your virtue.

    Now it so happened, I began to say,
Long, long ago in good King Arthur's day,
There was a knight who was a lusty liver.
One day as he came riding from the river
He saw a maiden walking all forlorn
Ahead of him, alone as she was born.
And of that maiden, spite of all she said,
By very force he took her maidenhead.

    This act of violence made such a stir,
So much petitioning to the king for her,
That he condemned the knight to lose
    his head
By course of law. He was as good as dead
(It seems that then the statutes took that view)
But that the queen, and other ladies too,
Implored the king to exercise his grace
So ceaselessly, he gave the queen the case
And granted her his life, and she could choose
Whether to show him mercy or refuse.

    The queen returned him thanks with all her
        might,
And then she sent a summons to the knight
At her convenience, and expressed her will:
"You stand, for such is the position still,
In no way certain of your life," said she,
"Yet you shall live if you can answer me:
What is the thing that women most desire?
Beware the axe and say as I require.

    "If you can't answer on the moment,
        though,

I will concede you this: you are to go
A twelvemonth and a day to seek and learn
Sufficient answer, then you shall return.
I shall take gages from you to extort
Surrender of your body to the court."
     Sad was the knight and sorrowfully sighed,
But there! All other choices were denied,
And in the end he chose to go away
And to return after a year and day
Armed with such answer as there might
     be sent
To him by God. He took his leave and went.
     He knocked at every house, searched every
          place,
Yes, anywhere that offered hope of grace.
What could it be that women wanted most?
But all the same he never touched a coast,
Country or town in which there seemed to be
Any two people willing to agree.
     Some said that women wanted wealth and
          treasure,
"Honour," said some, some "Jollity and plea-
     sure,"
Some "Gorgeous clothes" and others "Fun in
     bed,"
"To be oft widowed and remarried," said
Others again, and some that what most mat-
     tered
Was that we should be cossetted and flattered.
That's very near the truth, it seems to me;
A man can win us best with flattery.
To dance attendance on us, make a fuss,
Ensnares us all, the best and worst of us.
     Some say the things we most desire are
          these:
Freedom to do exactly as we please,
With no one to reprove our faults and lies,
Rather to have one call us good and wise.
Truly there's not a woman in ten score
Who has a fault, and someone rubs the sore,
But she will kick if what he says is true;
You try it out and you will find so too.
However vicious we may be within
We like to be thought wise and void of sin.
Others assert we women find it sweet
When we are thought dependable, discreet
And secret, firm of purpose and controlled,
Never betraying things that we are told.
But that's not worth the handle of a rake;
Women conceal a thing? For Heaven's sake!
Remember Midas? Will you hear the tale?
     Among some other little things, now stale,
Ovid relates that under his long hair

The unhappy Midas grew a splendid pair
Of ass's ears; a subtly as he might,
He kept his foul deformity from sight;
Save for his wife, there was not one that knew.
He loved her best, and trusted in her too.
He begged her not to tell a living creature
That he possessed so horrible a feature.
And she—she swore, were all the world
     to win,
She would not do such villainy and sin
As saddle her husband with so foul a name;
Besides to speak would be to share the shame.
Nevertheless she thought she would have died
Keeping this secret bottled up inside;
It seemed to swell her heart and she, no doubt,
Thought it was on the point of bursting out.
     Fearing to speak of it to woman or man,
Down to a reedy marsh she quickly ran
And reached the sedge. Her heart was all
     on fire
And, as a bittern bumbles in the mire,
She whispered to the water, near the ground,
"Betray me not, O water, with thy sound!
To thee alone I tell it: it appears
My husband has a pair of ass's ears!
Ah! My heart's well again, the secret's out!
I could no longer keep it, not a doubt."
And so you see, although we may hold fast
A little while, it must come out at last,
We can't keep secrets; as for Midas, well,
Read Ovid for his story; he will tell.
     This knight that I am telling you about
Perceived at last he never would find out
What it could be that women loved the best.
Faint was the soul within his sorrowful breast,
As home he went, he dared no longer stay;
His year was up and now it was the day.
     As he rode home in a dejected mood
Suddenly, at the margin of a wood,
He saw a dance upon the leafy floor
Of four and twenty ladies, nay, and more.
Eagerly he approached, in hope to learn
Some words of wisdom ere he should return;
But lo! Before he came to where they were,
Dancers and dance all vanished into air!
There wasn't a living creature to be seen
Save one old woman crouched upon the
     green.
A fouler-looking creature I suppose
Could scarcely be imagined. She arose
And said, "Sir knight, there's no way on from
     here.
Tell me what you are looking for, my dear,

For peradventure that were best for you;
We old, old women know a thing or two."
   "Dear Mother," said the knight, "alack
     the day!
I am as good as dead if I can't say
What thing it is that women most desire;
If you could tell me I would pay your hire."
"Give me your hand," she said, "and
   swear to do
Whatever I shall next require of you
—If so to do should lie within your might—
And you shall know the answer before night."
"Upon my honour," he answered, "I agree."
"Then," said the crone, "I dare to guarantee
Your life is safe; I shall make good my claim.
Upon my life the queen will say the same.
Show me the very proudest of them all
In costly coverchief or jewelled caul
That dare say no to what I have to teach.
Let us go forward without further speech."
And then she crooned her gospel in his ear
And told him to be glad and not to fear.
   They came to court. This knight, in full
     array,
Stood forth and said, "O Queen, I've kept
   my day
And kept my word and have my answer
   ready."
   There sat the noble matrons and the heady
Young girls, and widows too, that have the
   grace
Of wisdom, all assembled in that place,
And there the queen herself was throned
   to hear
And judge his answer. Then the knight
   drew near
And silence was commanded through the hall.
   The queen gave order he should tell
     them all
What thing it was that women wanted most.
He stood not silent like a beast or post,
But gave his answer with the ringing word
Of a man's voice and the assembly heard:
   "My liege and lady, in general," said he
"A woman wants the self-same sovereignty
Over her husband as over her lover,
And master him; he must not be above her.
That is your greatest wish, whether you kill
Or spare me; please yourself. I wait your will."
   In all the court not one that shook her head
Or contradicted what the knight had said;
Maid, wife and widow cried, "He's saved his
   life!"

And on the word up started the old wife,
The one the knight saw sitting on the green,
And cried, "Your mercy, sovereign lady
   queen!
Before the court disperses, do me right!
'Twas I who taught this answer to the knight,
For which he swore, and pledged his honour
   to it,
That the first thing I asked of him he'd do it,
So far as it should lie within his might.
Before this court I ask you then, sir knight,
To keep your word and take me for your wife;
For well you know that I have saved your life.
If this be false, deny it on your sword!"
   "Alas!" he said, "Old lady, by the Lord
I know indeed that such was my behest,
But for God's love think of a new request,
Take all my goods, but leave my body free."
"A curse on us," she said, "if I agree!
I may be foul, I may be poor and old,
Yet will not choose to be, for all the gold
That's bedded in the earth or lies above,
Less than your wife, nay, than your very
   love!"
   "My love?" said he. "By heaven, my
     damnation!
Alas that any of my race and station
Should ever make so foul a misalliance!"
Yet in the end his pleading and defiance
All went for nothing, he was forced to wed.
He takes his ancient wife and goes to bed.
   Now peradventure some may well suspect
A lack of care in me since I neglect
To tell of the rejoicings and display
Made at the feast upon their wedding-day.
I have but a short answer to let fall;
I say there was no joy or feast at all,
Nothing but heaviness of heart and sorrow.
He married her in private on the morrow
And all day long stayed hidden like an owl,
It was such torture that his wife looked foul.
   Great was the anguish churning in his head
When he and she were piloted to bed;
He wallowed back and forth in desperate style.
His ancient wife lay smiling all the while;
At last she said "Bless us! Is this, my dear,
How knights and wives get on together here?
Are these the laws of good King Arthur's
   house?
Are knights of his all so contemptuous?
I am your own beloved and your wife,
And I am she, indeed, that saved your life;
And certainly I never did you wrong.

Then why, this first of nights, so sad a song?
You're carrying on as if you were half-witted
Say, for God's love, what sin have I com-
     mitted?
I'll put things right if you will tell me how."
     "Put right?" he cried. "That never can
          be now!
Nothing can ever be put right again!
You're old, and so abominably plain,
So poor to start with, so low-bred to follow;
It's little wonder if I twist and wallow!
God, that my heart would burst within my
          breast!"
     "Is that," said she, "the cause of your un-
          rest?"
     "Yes, certainly," he said, "and can you
          wonder?"
     "I could set right what you suppose a
          blunder,
That's if I cared to, in a day or two,
If I were shown more courtesy by you.
Just now," she said, "you spoke of gentle
          birth,
Such as descends from ancient wealth and
          worth.
If that's the claim you make for gentlemen
Such arrogance is hardly worth a hen.
Whoever loves to work for virtuous ends,
Public and private, and who most intends
To do what deeds of gentleness he can,
Take him to be the greatest gentleman.
Christ wills we take our gentleness from Him,
Not from a wealth of ancestry long dim,
Though they bequeath their whole estab-
          lishment
By which we claim to be of high descent.
Our fathers cannot make us a bequest
Of all those virtues that became them best
And earned for them the name of gentlemen,
But bade us follow them as best we can.
     "Thus the wise poet of the Florentines,
Dante by name, has written in these lines,
For such is the opinion Dante launches:
'Seldom arises by these slender branches
Prowess of men, for it is God, no less,
Wills us to claim of Him our gentleness.'
For of our parents nothing can we claim
Save temporal things, and these may hurt and
          maim.
     "But everyone knows this as well as I;
For if gentility were implanted by
The natural course of lineage down the line,
Public or private, could it cease to shine

In doing the fair work of gentle deed?
No vice or villainy could then bear seed.
     "Take fire and carry it to the darkest house
Between this kingdom and the Caucasus,
And shut the doors on it and leave it there,
It will burn on, and it will burn as fair
As if ten thousand men were there to see,
For fire will keep its nature and degree,
I can assure you, sir, until it dies.
     "But gentleness, as you will recognize,
Is not annexed in nature to possessions.
Men fail in living up to their professions;
But fire never ceases to be fire.
God knows you'll often find, if you enquire,
Some lording full of villainy and shame.
If you would be esteemed for the mere name
Of having been by birth a gentleman
And stemming from some virtuous, noble
          clan,
And do not live yourself by gentle deed
Or take your father's noble code and creed,
You are no gentleman, though duke or earl.
Vice and bad manners are what make a churl.
     "Gentility is only the renown
For bounty that your fathers handed down,
Quite foreign to your person, not your own;
Gentility must come from God alone.
That we are gentle comes to us by grace
And by no means is it bequeathed with place.
     "Reflect how noble (says Valerius)
Was Tullius surnamed Hostilius,
Who rose from poverty to nobleness.
And read Boethius, Seneca no less,
Thus they express themselves and are agreed:
'Gentle is he that does a gentle deed.'
And therefore, my dear husband, I conclude
That even if my ancestors were rude,
Yet God on high—and so I hope He will—
Can grant me grace to live in virtue still,
A gentlewoman only when beginning
To live in virtue and to shrink from sinning.
     "As for my poverty which you reprove,
Almighty God Himself in whom we move,
Believe and have our being, chose a life
Of poverty, and every man or wife
Nay, every child can see our Heavenly King
Would never stoop to choose a shameful
          thing.
No shame in poverty if the heart is gay,
As Seneca and all the learned say.
He who accepts his poverty unhurt
I'd say is rich although he lacked a shirt.
But truly poor are they who whine and fret

And covet what they cannot hope to get.
And he that, having nothing, covets not,
Is rich, though you may think he is a sot.
  "True poverty can find a song to sing.
Juvenal says a pleasant little thing:
'The poor can dance and sing in the relief
Of having nothing that will tempt a thief.'
Though it be hateful, poverty is good,
A great incentive to a livelihood,
And a great help to our capacity
For wisdom, if accepted patiently.
Poverty is, though wanting in estate,
A kind of wealth that none calumniate.
Poverty often, when the heart is lowly,
Brings one to God and teaches what is holy,
Gives knowledge of oneself and even lends
A glass by which to see one's truest friends.
And since it's no offence, let me be plain;
Do not rebuke my poverty again.
  "Lastly you taxed me, sir, with being old.
Yet even if you never had been told
By ancient books, you gentlemen engage
Yourselves in honour to respect old age.
To call an old man 'father' shows good
    breeding,
And this could be supported from my reading.
  "You say I'm old and fouler than a fen.
You need not fear to be a cuckold, then.
Filth and old age, I'm sure you will agree,
Are powerful wardens over chastity.
Nevertheless, well knowing your delights,
I shall fulfil your worldly appetites.
  "You have two choices; which one will
    you try?
To have me old and ugly till I die,
But still a loyal, true, and humble wife
That never will displease you all her life,
Or would you rather I were young and pretty
And chance your arm what happens in a city
Where friends will visit you because of me,
Yes, and in other places too, maybe.
Which would you have? The choice is all
    your own."
      The knight thought long, and with a
        piteous groan
At last he said, with all the care in life,
"My lady and my love, my dearest wife,
I leave the matter to your wise decision.
You make the choice yourself, for the pro-
    vision
Of what may be agreeable and rich
In honour to us both, I don't care which;
Whatever pleases you suffices me."

  "And have I won the mastery?" said she,
"Since I'm to choose and rule as I think fit?"
"Certainly, wife," he answered her, "that's
    it."
"Kiss me," she cried. "No quarrels! On
    my oath
And word of honour, you shall find me both,
That is, both fair and faithful as a wife;
May I go howling mad and take my life
Unless I prove to be as good and true
As ever wife was since the world was new!
And if to-morrow when the sun's above
I seem less fair than any lady-love,
Than any queen or empress east or west,
Do with my life and death as you think best.
Cast up the curtain, husband. Look at me!"
      And when indeed the knight had looked
        to see,
Lo, she was young and lovely, rich in charms.
In ecstasy he caught her in his arms,
His heart went bathing in a bath of blisses
And melted in a hundred thousand kisses,
And she responded in the fullest measure
With all that could delight or give him plea-
    sure.
  So they lived ever after to the end
In perfect bliss; and may Christ Jesus send
Us husbands meek and young and fresh in bed,
And grace to overbid them when we wed.
And—Jesu hear my prayer!—cut short the
    lives
Of those who won't be governed by their
    wives;
And all old, angry niggards of their pence,
God send them soon a very pestilence!

THE FRIAR'S TALE
The Friar's Prologue

Our worthy limiter, the noble Friar,
Kept glancing with a lowering sort of ire
Towards the Summoner, but, to keep polite,
As yet had said no ugly word outright.
At last he turned towards the Wife of Bath,
"Madam," he said, "God be about your path!
You here have touched on many difficult rules
Debated, I assure you, in the Schools.
Much you advanced was excellent, I say!
But, Madam, as we ride along the way
We're only called upon to speak in game.
Let's leave the authorities, in Heaven's name,
To preachers and to schools for ordinands.

"But if it meets the company's demands,
I'll talk about a summoner, for a game,
Lord knows, one can be certain from the name
A summoner isn't much to be commended.
I hope that none of you will be offended.
     "A summoner's one who runs about the
          nation
Dealing out summonses for fornication,
Is beaten up by every villager
At the town's end . . . " "Now, mind the
     manners, sir,"
Our Host called out, "befitting your estate.
In company we do not want debate.
You tell your tale and let the Summoner be."
"Nay," said the Summoner, "makes no odds
     to me.
Say what he likes, and when my turn's
     to come
I'll pay him back, by God! I'll strike him
     dumb!
I'll tell him what an honour it is, none higher,
To be a limiter, a flattering friar!
I'll tell him all about that job of his."
     Our Host replied, "Let's have no more of
          this."
Then turning to the Friar, "We prefer,"
He said, "to hear your story, my dear sir."

The Friar's Tale

In my own district once there used to be
A fine archdeacon, one of high degree,
Who boldly did the execution due
On fornication and on witchcraft too,
Bawdry, adultery and defamation,
Breaches of wills and contract, spoliation
Of church endowment, failure in the rents
And tithes and disregard of sacraments,
All these and many other kinds of crime
That need have no rehearsal at this time,
Usury, simony too. But he could boast
That lechery was what he punished most.
They had to sing for it if they were caught,
Like those who failed to pay the tithes they
     ought.
As for all such, if there was an informant,
Nothing could save them from pecunial tor-
     ment.
For those whose tithes and offerings were
     small
Were made to sing the saddest song of all,
And ere the bishop caught them with his
     crook
They were all down in the archdeacon's book,

And he had jurisdiction, on inspection,
And powers to administer correction.
     He had a summoner ready to his hand.
There was no slyer boy in all the land,
For he had subtly formed a gang of spies
Who taught him where his profit might arise,
And he would spare one lecher from his store
To teach the way to four-and-twenty more.
Though it may drive him mad as a March
     hare,
Our Summoner here, I mean, I will not spare
His harlotries. He has no jurisdiction
On friars and he cannot make infliction
Upon us, now or ever, or take dues
From friars . . . "Nor from women of the
     stews!"
The Summoner shouted, "We have no
     control
On either lot." "The devil take your soul!"
Called out the Host, "I say I won't have
     squalls.
On with your story, sir, and if it galls
The Summoner, spare him not, my worthy
     master! . . . "
     This treacherous thief (the Friar said) was
          pastor
To certain bawds that ate out of his hand,
Lures for a hawk, none such in all the land.
They told him all the secret things they drew
From sinners; their acquaintance was not new.
Each was his agent, say, his private spy;
He drew large profits to himself thereby.
Even the archdeacon didn't always know
How much he got. He didn't have to show
A warrant when he chose to make things hot
For some obscure, uneducated sot;
For he could summon under threat of curse
And they were glad enough to fill his purse
Or give him banquets at the *Lamb and Flag*.
     And just as Judas kept a little bag
And was a thief, just such a thief was he.
His master got no more than half the fee.
To give the man his due and not to skimp,
He was a thief, a summoner, and a pimp.
     And he had wenches in his retinue,
So when the Reverend Robert or Sir Hugh
Or Jack or Ralph, whoever it was, drew near
And lay with them, they told it in his ear.
He and these wenches made a gang at it.
Then he would fetch forth a fictitious writ,
Summon them both before the Chapter-
     bench
And skin the man while letting off the wench,

Saying, "Dear friend, I know you would
    prefer
Her name were struck from our black register;
Trouble yourself no further, my good man,
On her account. I'll help you all I can."
    He knew so much of bribery and blackmail
I should be two years telling you the tale.
There is no sporting dog that's more expert
At knowing a wounded deer from one unhurt
Than was this summoner who could spot
    for sure
Lecher, adulterer or paramour.
Indeed on that his whole attention went
Because it was the source of all his rent.
    So it befell that on a certain day
This summoner rode forth to catch his prey,
A poor old fiddle of the widow-tribe
From whom, on a feigned charge, he hoped a
    bribe.
Now as he rode it happened that he saw
A gay young yeoman under a leafy shaw;
He bore a bow with arrows bright and keen
And wore a little jacket of bright green
And had a black-fringed hat upon his head.
"Hail, welcome and well met!" the summoner
    said.
"Welcome to you and all good lads," said he.
"Whither away under the greenwood tree?"
Pursued the yeoman, "Have you far to go?"
    The summoner paused a moment and said,
    "No,
Just here, close by. In fact I'm only bent
On going for a ride, to raise a rent
That's owing to my lord, a little fee."
"Why then you are a bailiff?" "Yes," said he.
He did not dare, for very filth and shame,
Say that he was a summoner, for the name.
    "Well, I'll be damned!" the yeoman said.
        "Dear brother,
You say you are a bailiff? I'm another.
But I'm a stranger round about this part.
I'll beg acquaintance with you for a start,
And brotherhood, if that is fair to offer.
I have some gold and silver in my coffer
And should you chance to cross into our shire
All shall be yours, as much as you desire."
"My word!" the summoner answered,
        "Thanks a lot!"
The pair of them shook hands upon the spot,
Swore to be brothers to their dying day
And, chatting pleasantly, rode on their way.
    This summoner, always ready with a word,
As full of venom as a butcher-bird,

And sticking his nose into one thing or other
Went on, "And where do you live at home,
    dear brother?
I might come calling there some other day."
    The yeoman said in his soft-spoken way,
"O, far away up north; I'll tell you where.
I hope that some time I shall see you there.
Before we part I shall be so explicit
About my home I'm sure you'll never miss it."
    "Brother," the summoner said, "I'd like
        to know
If you can teach me something as we go.
Since you're a bailiff just the same as me,
Tell me your subtler tricks. Now, seriously,
How can I win most money at the game?
Keep nothing back for conscience, or from
    shame.
Talk like a brother. How do you make out?"
    "Well, I break level, brother, just about.
I'll tell a truthful story; all in all
My wages are extremely tight and small.
My master's hard on me and difficult,
My job laborious and with poor result,
And so it's by extortion that I live.
I take whatever anyone will give.
At any rate by tricks and violences
From year to year I cover my expenses.
I can't say better, speaking truthfully."
    The summoner said, "It's just the same
        with me.
I'm ready to take anything, God wot,
Unless it is too heavy or too hot.
What I can get out of a little chat
In private—why should conscience boggle at
    that?
Without extortion, how could I make a
    living?
My little jokes are hardly worth forgiving.
Bowels of pity, conscience, I have none.
Plague on these penance-fathers every one!
We make a pair, by God and by St. James!
But, brother, what do you say to swopping
    names?"
    The summoner paused; the yeoman all the
        while
The summoner spoke had worn a little smile.
"Brother," he answered, "would you have me
    tell?
I am a fiend, my dwelling is in Hell.
I ride on business and have so far thriven
By taking anything that I am given.
That is the sum of all my revenue.
You seem to have the same objective too,

You're out for wealth, acquired no mat-
    ter how,
And so with me. I'll go a-riding now
As far as the world's end in search of prey."
    "Lord!" said the summoner. "What did I
        hear you say?
I thought you were a yeoman, certainly
You have the body of a man like me.
And have you, then, another shape as well
Appointed for your high estate in Hell?"
    "No," he replied, "for Hell admits of none.
But when we like we can appropriate one,
Or rather make you think we have a shape;
Sometimes it's like a man, sometimes an ape,
Even an angel riding into bliss.
There's nothing very wonderful in this;
A lousy conjuror can trick your eye,
And he, God knows, has far less power than I."
    "But why," pursued the summoner, "track
        your game
In various shapes? Why don't you stay the
    same?"
"Just to appear," he said, "in such a way
As will enable us to snatch our prey."
"But why do you have to go to all this
    bother?"
"For very many reasons, my dear brother;
You shall know all about it in good time.
The day is short and it is long past prime,
And yet I've taken nothing the whole day,
And I must think of business, if I may,
Rather than air my intellectual gift;
Besides, you lack the brains to catch my drift.
If I explained you wouldn't understand;
Yet since you ask why we're a busy band,
It's thus: at times we are God's instruments,
A means of forwarding divine events,
When He so pleases, that concern His crea-
    tures,
By various arts, disguised by various features.
We have no power without Him, that's a fact,
If it should please Him to oppose some act.
Sometimes, at our request, He gives us leave
To hurt the body, though we may not grieve
The soul. Take Job; his is a case in point.
At other times the two are not disjoint,
That is to say, the body and the soul.
Sometimes we are allowed to take control
Over a man and put his soul to test,
But not his body; all is for the best;
For every time a man withstands temptation
It is a partial cause of his salvation,
Though our intention is, when we beset him,

Not that he should be saved, but we should
    get him.
At times we slave for men without complaint
As on Archbishop Dunstan, now a saint;
Why, I was servant to the apostle once."
    "Tell me," the summoner said, "—I'm just
        a dunce—
But do you make new bodies as you go
Out of the elements?" The fiend said, "No;
We just create illusions, or we raise
A corpse and use it; there are many ways.
And we can talk as trippingly and well
As, to the Witch of Endor, Samuel.
And yet some people say it wasn't he;
I have no use for your theology.
    "One thing I warn you of, it is no jape;
You will be learning all about our shape
In any case, hereafter, my dear brother,
Where you'll not need me, no, nor yet an-
    other,
To teach you; for your own experience
Will furnish you sufficient evidence
To give a lecture on it, and declare
As well as from a professorial chair,
Better than Virgil when he was alive,
Or Dante either. Now, if we're to thrive
Let's hurry on; I'll keep you company
Unless it chance that you abandon me."
    "What?" said the summoner, "Leave you
        on your own?
I am a yeoman, pretty widely known;
I'll hold to my engagement, on the level,
Though you were Satan's self, the very Devil!
I keep my word of honour to a brother,
As I have sworn, and so shall each to other;
True brothers we shall be; the bargain's made
And both of us can go about our trade.
You take your share—whatever people
    give—
And I'll take mine, and that's our way to live.
If either should do better than the other,
Let him be true and share it with his brother."
    "Agreed," the devil answered. "As you
        say."
And on the word they trotted on their way.
Just at the entry of the very village
The summoner had it in his mind to pillage
They saw a farm-cart loaded up with hay.
There was a carter driving, but the way
Was deep and muddy and the cart stood still.
The carter lashed and shouted with a will,
"Hey, Brock! Hup, Scottie! Never mind for
    stones!

The foul fiend come and fetch you, flesh and
   bones,
As sure as you were foaled! Mud, ruts and
   rubble!
Lord, what a team! I've never known such
   trouble!
The devil take all, cart, horse and hay in one!"
   The summoner said, "Now we shall have
     some fun!"
And, as if nothing were happening, he
   drew near
And whispered softly in the devil's ear:
   "Listen to that, dear brother, use your head!
Didn't you hear what the old carter said?
Take it at once, he gave them all to you,
His hay, his cart and his three horses too."
   "Don't you believe it!" said the fiend. "I
     heard,
But he meant nothing by it, take my word.
Go up and ask him if you don't trust me,
Or else keep quiet for a bit and see."
   The carter thwacked his horses, jerked the
     rein,
And got them moving; as they took the strain,
"Hup, there!" he shouted, "Jesus bless you,
   love,
And all His handiwork! Hey! Saints above!
Well tugged, old fellow, that's the stuff,
   Grey Boy!
God save you all, my darlings, send you joy!
That's lifted the old cart out of the slough!"
   "What did I tell you," said the fiend,
     "just now?
That ought to make it clear to you, dear
   brother,
The chap said one thing but he meant another.
So let's go on a bit. You mustn't scoff,
But here there's nothing I can carry off."
   When they were out of town a little way
The summoner whispered to the fiend to say,
"There's an old fiddle here, an ancient wreck,
Dear brother, who would rather break
   her neck
Than lose a penny of her goods. Too bad,
She'll have to pay me twelve-pence. She'll
   be mad,
But if she doesn't pay she'll face the court.
And yet, God knows there's nothing to report,
She has no vices. But as you failed just now
To earn your keep, I'd like to show you how."
   The summoner battered at the widow's
     gate.
"Come out," he said, "you old inebriate!

I'll bet you've got a friar or priest inside!"
   "Who's knocking? Bless us, Lord!" the
     widow cried,
"God save you, sir, and what is your sweet
   will?"
   "Here!" said the summoner. "I've a sum-
     mons-bill.
On pain of excommunication, see
That you're at court at the archdeacon's knee
To-morrow morning. There are certain
   things
To answer for." "Christ Jesus, King of
   Kings,"
She said, "have mercy! What am I to say?
I can't! I'm ill, and have been many a day.
I couldn't walk so far, nor even ride,
'Twould kill me. There's a pricking in my
   side.
Couldn't you write it down and save a
   journey,
And let me answer it through my attorney,
The charge I mean, whatever it may be?"
   "Yes, if you pay at once," he said.
     "Let's see.
Twelve pence to me and I'll secure acquittal.
I get no profit from it—very little.
My master gets the profit and not me.
Come off it, I'm in haste. It's got to be.
Give me twelve pence. No time to wait, old
   fairy."
   "Twelve pence!" said she. "O blessed Vir-
     gin Mary,
Help me and keep me clear of sin and dearth!
Why, if you were to offer me the earth
I couldn't! There's not twelve pence in
   my bag!
You know I'm nothing but a poor old hag,
Show kindness to a miserable wretch!"
   "If I excuse you may the devil fetch
Me off! Though it should break you! Come
   along,
Pay up!" he said. "But I've done nothing
   wrong!"
   "You pay at once, or by the sweet St. Anne,"
He said, "I'll carry off your frying-pan
For debt, the new one, owed me since the day
You cuckolded your husband. Did I pay
For the correction then or did I not?"
   "You lie!" she said. "On my salvation!
     What?
Correction? Whether as widow or as wife
I've never had a summons in my life;
I never cuckolded my poor old man!

And as for you and for your frying-pan
The hairiest, blackest devil out of Hell
Carry you off and take the pan as well!"
    Seeing her kneel and curse, the devil spoke:
"Now, Mother Mabel, is this all a joke,
Or do you really mean the things you say?"
    "The devil," she said, "can carry him away
With pan and all unless he will repent!"
"No, you old cow, I have no such intent,"
The summoner said, "there's no repen-
    tance due
For anything I ever had of you.
I'd strip you naked, smock and rag and clout!"
    The devil said, "What are you cross about,
Dear brother? You and this pan are mine by
    right.
You yet shall be in Hell with me tonight,
Where you'll know more about our mystery
Than any Doctor of Divinity."
    And on the word this foul fiend made a
    swoop
And dragged him, body and soul, to join the
    troupe
In Hell, where summoners have their special
    shelf.
And God, who in the image of Himself
Created man, guide us to Abraham's lap,
And make this Summoner here a decent chap!
    My lords, I could have told you, never fear,
Had I the time to save this Summoner here,
Following texts from Christ and Paul
    and John
And many teachers who are dead and gone,
Of torments that are fit to terrorize
Your hearts, though tongue of man can scarce
    devise
Such things, or in a thousand winters tell
The pain of that accursed house of Hell.
Watch therefore, and pray Jesus of his grace
To keep us out of that accursed place
And ward off Satan, tempting us from glory;
Ponder my words, reflect upon my story.
The lion's always on the watch for prey
To kill the innocent, if so he may;
And so dispose your heart that it withstand
The fiend who would enslave you in his band.
He may not tempt you, though, above your
    might,
For Christ will be your champion and your
    knight.
And, Summoners, flee the sins that so be-
    set you,
And learn repentance ere the devil get you.

THE SUMMONER'S TALE
The Summoner's Prologue

The Summoner rose in wrath against the Friar
High in his stirrups, and he quaked with ire.
He stood there trembling like an aspen leaf.
"I've only one desire," he said, "it's brief,
And one your courtesy will not deny;
Since you have heard this filthy friar lie,
Let me refute him. I've a tale to tell!
This friar boasts his knowledge about Hell,
And if he does, God knows it's little wonder;
Friars and fiends are seldom far asunder.
Lord knows you must have often heard
    them tell
Of how a friar was ravished down to Hell
Once in a vision, taken there in spirit.
An angel led him up and down to ferret
Among the torments—various kinds of fire—
And yet he never saw a single friar,
Though he saw plenty of other kinds of folk
In pain enough. At last this friar spoke:
'Sir, are the friars in such a state of grace,'
He said, 'none ever come into this place?'
'Why, yes,' the angel answered, 'many a mil-
    lion!'
And led him down to Lucifer's pavilion.
'Satan,' the angel said, 'has got a tail
As broad or broader than a barge's sail.
Hold up thy tail, thou Satan!' then said he,
'Show forth thine arse and let the friar see
The nest ordained for friars in this place!'
Ere the tail rose a furlong into space
From underneath it there began to drive,
Much as if bees were swarming from a hive,
Some twenty thousand friars in a rout
And swarmed all over Hell and round about,
And then came back as fast as they could run
And crept into his arse again, each one.
He clapped his tail on them and then
    lay still.
And after when the friar had looked his fill
On all the torments in that sorry place
His spirit was restored by Heaven's grace
Back to his body again and he awoke.
But all the same the terror made him choke,
So much the devil's arse was in his mind,
The natural heritage of all his kind.
God save you all except this cursed Friar,
For that is all the prologue I require."

The Summoner's Tale

My lords, there lies—in Yorkshire, as I
     guess—
A marshy district known as Holderness,
In which a friar, a limiter, went about
To preach his sermons and to beg, no doubt.
And on a certain day it so befell,
When he had preached in church, and cast his
     spell
With one main object, far above the rest,
To fire his congregation with a zest
For buying trentals,[1] and for Jesu's sake
To give the wherewithal for friars to make
Their holy houses, where the Lord is dowered
With truest honour, not to be devoured
By those to whom there is no need to give
Like those endowed already, who can live,
Thanks be to God, in affluence and glory.
"Trentals," he said, "can fetch from Pur-
     gatory
The souls of all your friends, both old and
     young,
Yes, even when they're very quickly sung
—Not that a priest is frivolous or gay
Because he only sings one mass a day—
Release the souls," he thundered, "from
     the pit,
Deliver them from the flesh-hook and the
     spit!
What agony to be clawed, to burn, to bake!
Be quick, exert yourselves, for Jesu's sake!"
     When he had finished all he had to say,
With *qui cum Patre*[2] off he went his way.
When folk had put their pennies in the plate
He used to go away, he wouldn't wait.
With scrip and pointed staff uplifted high
He went from house to house to poke and pry
And beg a little meal and cheese, or corn.
His comrade had a staff was tipped with horn,
And bore two ivory tablets, wax-anointed,
Also a stylus elegantly pointed.
He always wrote the names down as he stood
Of those who gave him offerings or food
(Pretence of praying for them by and by).
     "Give us a bushel of barley, malt or rye,
A wee God's cookie, then, a slice of cheese,
It's not for us to choose, but as you please;
A penny to say mass, or half a penny,
Some of your brawn perhaps—you haven't
     any?—
Well then, a bit of blanket, worthy dame,
Our well-beloved sister! There's your name,

It's down. Beef? Bacon? Anything you can
     find!"
A sturdy varlet followed them behind—
The servant for their guests, and bore a sack,
What they were given he carried on his back.
Once out of doors again and business done,
He used to plane the names out, every one
That he had written on his waxen tables.
He'd served them all with fairy-tales and fa-
     bles.
"No, there you lie, you Summoner!" cried the
     Friar;
"Peace!" said our Host. "Who cares if he's a
     liar?
Tell on your story! Let the Friar keep still
Never you spare him, Summoner!" "Nor I
     will."
     On went this friar from house to house
     till he
Came upon one where he was wont to be
Better refreshed than anywhere in town.
The householder was sick and lying down.
Bedridden on a couch the fellow lay.
"*Deus hic!* Friend Thomas, how are we to-
     day?"
The Friar said, taking pains to soften
His voice politely; "God protect you! Often—
How often!—I've sat upon this very bench to
     steal
Your kindness and enjoyed a merry meal!"
And, from the bench, he drove away the cat,
And, laying down his pointed staff, his hat,
And then his scrip, he settled softly down.
     His comrade was off walking in the town;
He and his varlet had gone off to see
The hostel where they aimed, that night,
     to be.
     "O my dear master," said this ailing man,
"How have things been with you since March
     began?
Ain't seen you this last fortnight now, or
     more."
"God knows," he answered, "I have
     laboured sore
And, more especially, have said in care
Of your salvation many a precious prayer,
And for our other friends, but let that pass.
I went this morning to your church for Mass,
And preached according to my simple wit;
It wasn't all on texts from Holy Writ,
For that's too hard for you as I suppose,
And I prefer to paraphrase or gloze.
Glozing's a glorious thing, and anyway

'The letter killeth' as we clerics say.
And so I taught them to be charitable
And spend their goods where it is reasonable;
And there I saw your wife—Ah, where is she?"
"Out in the yard, I think, or ought to be,"
The fellow said; "she'll come, she can't be far."
"Why, sir, you're welcome, by St. John you are!"
The woman said, "I hope you're keeping sprightly?"
Up from his bench the friar rose politely
Embracing her—the clasp was somewhat narrow—
And kissed her sweetly, chirping like a sparrow
As his lips parted. "Ma'am," he said, "I'm fine.
Your servant, Ma'am," he said, "in all that's mine.
Thanks be to God that gave you soul and life
I haven't seen a prettier little wife
In all the church today, upon my word!"
"Well, God amend defects!" the woman purred.
"At any rate you're welcome, I'll be bound."
"My warmest thanks! That's what I've always found.
If I may trespass—you're so very kind—
On your good nature; if you wouldn't mind,
I want to talk to Thomas here; you know
These curates are so negligent and slow
At groping consciences with tenderness.
I study how to preach and to confess,
Earnestly read St. Peter and St. Paul
And walk about to fish and make a haul
Of Christian souls, pay Christ his proper rent,
And if I spread His word I am content."
   "Now, my dear master, by your leave," said she,
"Scold the man well, for by the Trinity,
He is as irritable as an ant,
Though he has everything a man can want.
I try to keep him warm at night, I squeeze him,
Put my leg over him, or arm, to please him,
And all he does is grunt, like boar in sty!
I get no other sport of him, not I.
No way of pleasing him at all, I promise."
   "O Thomas, *je vous dis,* O Thomas, Thomas!
That is the devil's work and must be chidden.
Anger's a thing by Heavenly God forbidden;

I mean to speak of that, a word or so."
   "Now, master," said the wife, "before I go,
What would you like for dinner? What would suit?"
"Well, Ma'am," he answered, "*je vous dis sans doute,*
If I could have a little chicken-liver
And some of your soft bread—the merest shiver—
And then a pig's head roasted—but, do you see?
I won't have any creature killed for me—
It would be homely and sufficient fare.
The sustenance I take is very spare;
You see, my spirit draws its nourishment
Out of the Bible, and my body's spent
In pains and prayers; my stomach is destroyed.
   "However, Ma'am, you mustn't be annoyed
To hear me speak as frankly as I do,
For these are things I tell to very few."
   "Before I leave you, sir, you ought to know,"
She said, "my baby died two weeks ago,
Just after you left town on visitation."
   "I know. I saw his death by revelation,"
Replied the friar, "in our dormitory.
I saw the little fellow borne to glory,
I dare say it was less than half an hour
After his death indeed. To God the power!
Our sexton and our infirmarian,
They saw it too, both friars, boy and man,
These fifty years, thank God. They now are free
To walk alone, they've reached their jubilee.[3]
I rose at once, in fact the entire place
Rose, and the tears were trickling down my face;
There was no noise, no clattering bells were rung,
But a *Te Deum*—nothing else—was sung,
Save that I made an act of adoration
To Christ, to thank Him for His revelation.
For I assure you both, believe me well,
Our orisons are more effectual
And we see more of Christ's most secret things
Than common people do, or even kings.
We live in poverty and abstinence
But common folk in riches and expense
On food and drink, and other foul delight;
But we contemn all worldly appetite.
   "Dives and Lazarus lived differently,
And different their guerdon had to be.

Whoever prays must fast, he must keep clean,
Fatten his soul and make his body lean.
We follow the Apostle; clothes and food
Suffice us though they may be rough and rude,
Our purity and fasting have sufficed
To make our prayers acceptable to Christ.

"Moses had fasted forty days and nights
Before Almighty God, upon the heights
Of Sinai, came down to speak with him,
And with an empty stomach, frail of limb,
Moses received the law Jehovah drew
With his own finger; and Elijah too
When in Mount Horeb, ere he could have
      speech
With that Almighty Lord, who is the leech
Of life, had fasted long on contemplation.

"Aaron no less, under whose domination
The temple was, and other Levites too,
When they approached the temple to renew
Their services and supplications, they
Refrained from drinking—drinking, that's
      to say,
That might have made them drunk—attend-
      ing there
In abstinence, in watching and in prayer
Lest they should die. Take heed of what I say;
Unless the priest is sober who would pray
For you—but there! I've said enough of it.

"Jesus our Lord, it says in Holy Writ,
Fasted and prayed, and patterned our desires,
And so we mendicants, we simple friars
Have wedded poverty and continence,
Charity, humbleness and penitence,
And persecution too for righteousness;
Pure, merciful, austere, but quick to bless
Though weeping often. Therefore our desires
—I'm speaking of ourselves, mendicant
      friars—
Are more acceptable to God, more able
Than yours, with all your feasts upon the
      table.

"I speak the truth; gluttony was the vice
That first flung Adam out of Paradise;
And man was chaste in Eden, I may mention.

"But listen to me, Thomas, pay attention.
Though there's no text exactly, I suppose,
Yet in a manner of speaking, if I gloze
A little, you will see our Lord referred
Especially to friars in the word
'Blessed are the poor in spirit.' Think and
      look,
Study the gospels, search the Holy Book,
And see if it be liker our profession

Than theirs who swim in riches and posses-
      sion.
Fie on their pomp! Fie on their gluttony!
Their ignorance is a disgrace to see.

"Jovinian makes a good comparison,
'Fat as a whale and waddling like a swan,'
They stink of wine like bottles in a bar;
How reverent their supplications are!
When they say prayers for souls their psalm of
      David
Is just a 'Burp! *Cor meum eructavit!*'[4]
Who follows on the gospel, tracks the spoor
Of Christ, but we the humble, chaste and poor,
The doers of the word, not hearers only?
And as a hawk springs up into the lonely
Regions of heaven, so the prayer aspires
Of charitable, chaste and busy friars,
Takes flight and enters in at God's two ears.
O Thomas, Thomas! Let me say with tears
And by that patron who is called St. Ives,
Where were your hope to be as one that
      thrives
If you were not our brother? Day and night
Our Chapter prays the Lord to send you
      might,
Strengthen your body, girdle it and belt it!"
"God knows," the fellow said, "I haven't
      felt it.
So help me Christ, I've spent a lot in hire,
These last few years, on various kinds of friar,
Aye, many a pound; and yet I'm none the
      better.
I've poured it out. I'm very near a debtor.
Farewell my gold, it's gone; no more to go!"

"O Thomas!" said the friar. "Did you so?
What need to seek out 'various kinds of friar'?
Who, with a perfect doctor, could require
To seek out other doctors in the town?
Your own inconstancy has let you down.
Do you suppose our convent, and I too,
Are insufficient, then, to pray for you?
Thomas, that joke's not good. Your faith is
      brittle.
You're ill because you've given us too little.
'Ah! give that convent half a quarter of oats!'
'Ah! give that convent four and twenty
      groats!'
'Ah! give that friar a penny and let him go?'
No, Thomas, Thomas, it should not be so!
What is a farthing worth if split in twelve?
An undivided thing is (if you delve
Into your wits) stronger than when it's scat-
      tered.

Thomas, by me you never shall be flattered.
You're trying to get our work for nothing, eh?
What does Almighty God who made us say?
'The labourer is worthy of his hire.'
Thomas, you know it's not that I desire
Your treasure for myself; it should be spent,
Seeing our convent is so diligent
In prayer for you, to build the church of
    Christ.
Thomas! If you would learn or be enticed
To learn what good there is in building
    churches,
Your namesake's life will further your re-
    searches,
St. Thomas of India. There you lie in ire,
The devil having set your heart on fire,
And chide this foolish, innocent woman here,
Your wife, so meek, so patient, so sincere.
So, Thomas, please let this be understood:
No wrangling with your wife! It's for your
    good.
And take this thought away to fill your head
Touching this matter; wisely was it said:
'Then be not as a lion in thy house,
A terror to thy household, tyrannous,
Nor such that thine acquaintance flees away.'
I charge you, Thomas, once again and say,
Beware of her that in your bosom sleeps;
Beware the serpent that so slyly creeps
Amidst the grass and stings with subtlety.
Beware, my son, and listen patiently,
For twenty thousand men have lost their lives
For wrangling with their lovers and their
    wives.
And since you have so holy and meek a wife,
What, Thomas, is the need for all this strife?
No serpent is so cruel, truth to tell,
If one should tread upon his tail, so fell
As women who have given way to ire.
Vengeance is then the sum of their desire.
Ire is a sin, one of the deadly seven,
Abominable unto God in Heaven,
And a destruction to yourself, none quicker.
Every illiterate parson, every vicar
Can tell that ire engenders homicide.
For ire is the executor of pride.
Were I to say what ire can bring in sorrow
To man, my tale would last until tomorrow.
So day and night I pray as best I can
God send no power to an angry man!
Great harm can come of it, great misery,
When angry men are set in high degree.
    "Once on a time an angry potentate,

Seneca says, bore rule over a state.
A certain day two knights went riding out
And fortune willed that it should come about
That one of them returned, the other not.
The knight was brought to judgement on the
    spot;
This judge gave sentence: 'You have killed
    your friend.
You are condemned to death and that's the
    end.'
And to another knight was standing by
He turned and said, 'Go, lead him out to die.'
And so it happened as they went along
To the appointed place, towards the throng
There came the knight that was reported dead.
So it seemed best that both of them be led
Together back before the judge again.
'My lord,' they said, 'the knight has not been
    slain;
His friend is guiltless. As you see, they thrive.'
'You all shall die,' said he, 'as I'm alive!
You first, the second, you, and you the third!'
And turning to the first he said this word:
'I have condemned you. You must therefore
    die.'
Then to the next, 'You too, and this is why:
Your comrade clearly owes his death to you.'
Then to the third he turned and said,
    'You too;
You had my orders; they were not fulfilled.'
And so it was the three of them were killed.
    "An angry man and drunken was Cam-
        byses,
Who took great joy in showing off his vices.
A knight, it happened, in his company,
Given to virtue and morality,
In private conference with him began:
'A lord is lost if he's a vicious man,
And drunkenness is filthy to record
Of any man, especially a lord.
Many the eye and ear that takes good care
To spy on lords, they can't be certain where.
For God's love be more temperate in your
    drink.
For wine will rob you of your power to think
And incapacitate your members too.'
    " 'You'll see,' said he, 'the opposite is true,
And prove it by your own experience
That wine has no such power of offence.
There is no wine so strong as to deny
Strength to my hand or foot or sight of eye.'
    "And out of spite he drank as much,
        nay, more

A hundred times than he had drunk before
And right away this angry, cursed wretch
Gave an immediate command to fetch
This noble's son, and there he made him
    stand;
Then snatching up a bow into his hand
Drew string to ear, and aiming it with care
He shot him with an arrow then and there.
'Now have I got a steady hand or not?
Now have my mental powers gone to rot?'
The tyrant said, 'Has wine destroyed my
    sight?'
    "Why should I tell the answer of the
        knight?
His son was slain, there is no more to say.
Dealing with lords be careful in your play;
You sing *Placebo*! I shall if I can,
Except when talking to some poor old man.
To tell their vices to the poor is well,
But not to lords, though they should go to Hell.
    "Cyrus the Persian was an evil-liver
And given to anger; he destroyed the river
Gyson in which his horse was drowned, upon
His expedition to take Babylon.
That river in his rage was so diminished
Women could wade it by the time he'd fin-
    ished.
    "Solomon teaches us as no one can:
'Make thou no friendship with an angry man;
And with a furious man take not thy way,
Lest thou repent it'; there's no more to say.
    "Leave anger, Thomas; brother, have a
        care!
You'll find me just. I'm like a joiner's square.
That devil's knife, O draw it from your heart!
It is your anger causes you to smart.
Make your confession to me if you can."
    "No, by St. Simon," said the ailing man,
"The curate came and shrived me here today.
I told him everything I had to say.
There's no more need to speak of it," said he,
"Unless I care to, from humility."
    "Then give me of your gold to make our
        cloister,"
Said he, "for many a mussel, many an oyster,
When other men eat well and fill their cup,
Has been our food, to build our cloister up.
And yet we've hardly finished the foundation.
There's not a tile as yet or tessellation
Upon the pavement that we hope to own,
And forty pound is owing still for stone.
    "Now, Thomas, help, for Him that har-
        rowed Hell,

For otherwise we shall be forced to sell
Our books, and if you lacked our predication
The world would quickly fall to desolation.
To cheat it of our sermons and bereave
The world of us, dear Thomas, by your leave,
Were worse than to bereave it of the sun.
Who teaches and who works as we have done?
And for a long, long time," he said, "because
There have been friars since Elijah was;
Elisha too was one (the books record)
In charity with us, I thank our Lord.
Now Thomas, help, for holy charity!"
And down at once he went upon his knee.
    The ailing man was nearly mad with ire;
He would have very gladly burnt the friar,
Him and his lying speech and false profession.
    "I'll give you what I have in my possession,
Such as it is," he said, "I have none other.
You said a moment back I was your brother?"
    "Believe it," said the friar, "and none better;
I brought your wife our sealed Fraternal Let-
        ter!"
    "Well now," he said, "there's something I
        can give
Your holy convent, if I am to live.
And you shall have it in your hand to own
On one condition and on one alone,
That you divide it equally, dear brother,
And every friar to have as much as other.
But swear by your profession to the thing,
And without fraudulence or cavilling."
    "I swear it by my faith!" the friar said,
Clasping the hand of the poor man in bed.
"My hand on it! In me shall be no lack."
    "Well, then, reach down your hand along
        my back,"
The sick man said, "and if you grope behind,
Beneath my buttocks you are sure to find
Something I've hidden there for secrecy."
    "Ah!" thought the friar, "that's the thing
        for me!"
And down he launched his hand and searched
        the cleft
In hope of profiting by gift or theft.
When the sick man could feel him here and
        there
Groping about his fundament with care,
Into that friar's hand he blew a fart.
There never was a farmhorse drawing cart
That farted with a more prodigious sound.
    Mad as a lion then the friar spun round,
"You treacherous lout!" he cried, "God's
        bones and blight!

You did it on purpose! It was done for spite!
You shall pay dearly for that fart, I say!"
•   The sick man's servants, hearing the affray,
Came leaping in and chased away the friar,
And off he went still spluttering with ire
To find his comrade where he kept his goods.
He looked like a wild boar out of the woods,
Gnashing his teeth, he was so furious.

He strode along towards the manor-house
Where lived a man of honour and possession
Who used to seek the friar in confession.
This worthy man was the manorial lord;
As he was sitting eating at his board
In came the friar in a towering rage
Almost past speech for anger by that stage,
But in the end "God bless you, sir," said he.
The lord stared back. "Hey, *benedicite!*
It's Friar John! What sort of world is this?
It's easy seen that something is amiss!
You look as if the thieves were in the wood;
Sit down and say if I can do you good;
I'll settle matters for you, if I can!"

   "I have received an insult," said the man.
"God give you joy—below here, in your vil-
   lage,
In all the world there is no serf at tillage
So poor but would have held in execration
And counted it as an abomination
The affront that I've been offered in your
   town.
And yet, what grieves me most, this hoary
   clown
Blasphemed against our holy convent too!"
   "Now, master," said the lord, "I beg of
   you—"
"No master, sir," he said, "your servitor!
Although the Schools did me that honour, sir,
But still God wishes not that men should call
Us 'Rabbi' either here in your large hall
Or in the market." "Never mind," said he,
"Tell me your trouble." "Sir, there was done
   to me,
And to my Order too, an odious wrong;
Per consequens to all that may belong
To Holy Church itself. May God amend it."
   "Sir," said the lord, "you know the way to
   end it.
Keep calm, you're my confessor; I know your
   worth.
You are the salt and savour of the earth.
For love of God be patient and unfold
The matter of your grief." So then he told
The story (you have heard it) with a will.

The lady of the house sat very still
Till she had heard the friar's whole tirade.
"Mother of God," she said, "O blessed Maid!
And is there nothing else? Now tell me true."
   "Madam," he answered, "May I hear your
   view?"
"My view?" she said. "God help us! What's
   the need?
I say a churl has done a churlish deed.
What should I say? May God deny him ease!
His poor sick head is full of vanities.
I think he must have had some kind of fit."
   "Madam," said he, "I'll pay him out for it,
By God I will! There are within my reach
Several ways; for instance I can preach,
I can defame him! I won't be derided
Or bidden divide what cannot be divided
In equal parts—God damn his ignorance!"
   The lord had sat like someone in a trance,
Rolling in heart the problem up and down,
How the imagination of a clown
Had hit on this conundrum for the friar.
"I never before heard such a thing transpire;
I think the devil put it in his mind.
In all arithmetic you couldn't find
Until today so tricky an equation.
How could one set about a demonstration
Where every man alike should have his part
Both of the sound and savour of a fart?
Proud churl! O nice distinction! Damn his
   nerve!"
He then went on more gravely to observe,
"Who ever heard of such a thing till now!
'To every man alike?' Good Lord, but how?
It is impossible, it cannot be!
Aha, nice churl! God send him misery!
The rumbling of a fart or any sound
Is only air reverberating round,
What's more, diminishingly, bit by bit.
Upon my word! No one could have the wit
To see it was divided equally.
To think a churl, a churl of mine, could be
So shrewd, and to my own confessor too!
He's certainly demoniac in my view!
Now eat your food and leave the churl alone
And let the devil hang him for his own!"
   Now the lord's squire was standing by and
   heard
The tale as he was carving, word for word,
And saw the problem you have heard defined.
"My lord," he said, "I hope you will not
   mind,
But, for a piece of cloth to make a gown,

I'd tell the friar—but he mustn't frown—
How such a fart could equally be shared
Between him and his convent, if I cared."

His lord replied, "Well, tell us then, go on,
And you shall have your gown-cloth, by St.
John."

"Well, when the weather, sir," he said, "is
fair,
When there's no wind or movement in
the air,
Then have a cart-wheel brought into this hall,
But see the spokes are fitted—twelve in all,
A cartwheel has twelve spokes—then, by
and by,
Bring me twelve friars. You will ask me why?
Well, thirteen make a convent, as I guess.
And this confessor here, for worthiness,
Shall bring the number to thirteen, my lord.
Then they shall all kneel down with one ac-
cord;
To each spoke's end a friar, I propose,
Shall very seriously lay his nose.
Your excellent confessor, whom God save,
Shall put his nose right up under the nave.
And then the churl, with belly stiff and taut
As drum or tabor, hither shall be brought,
Set on the wheel thus taken from the cart
Above the nave, and made to let a fart.
Then you will see, as surely as I live,
And by a proof that is demonstrative,
That equally the sound of it will wend,
Together with the stink, to the spokes' end,
Save that this worthy friar, your confessor,
Being of great honour, they of lesser,
Shall have the first-fruits, as is only right.
A noble custom, in which friars unite,
Is that a worthy man should first be served
And certainly it will be well-deserved.
Today his preaching did us so much good,
Being beneath the pulpit where he stood,
That I'd allow him, if it fell to me,
First smell of every fart, say up to three,
And so would all his convent I am sure,
His bearing is so holy, fair and pure."

The lord and lady—all except the friar—
Thought Jacky's answer all they could
desire,
As wise as Euclid or as Ptolemy.
As for the churl, it was his subtlety,
His wit, they said, to think of such a crack.
"He is no fool, he's no demoniac!"
And Jacky has acquired a new gown.
My tale is done; we've almost come to town.

THE CLERK'S TALE
The Clerk's Prologue

"You, sir, from Oxford!" said the Host.
"God's life!
As coy and quiet as a virgin-wife
Newly espoused and sitting mum at table!
You haven't said a word since we left stable.
Studying, I suppose? On wisdom's wing?
Says Solomon, 'There's a time for everything.'

"For goodness' sake cheer up, show anima-
tion!
This is no time for abstruse meditation.
Tell us a lively tale in Heaven's name;
For when a man has entered on a game
He's bound to keep the rules, it's by consent.
But don't you preach as friars do in Lent,
Dragging up all our sins to make us weep,
Nor tell a tale to send us all to sleep.

"Let it be brisk adventure, stuff that nour-
ishes
And not too much of your rhetorical flour-
ishes.
Keep the 'high style' until occasion brings
A use for it, like when they write to kings,
And for the present put things plainly, pray,
So we can follow all you have to say."

This worthy cleric left the land of nod
And said benignly, "Sir, I kiss the rod!
Our company is under your control
And I am all obedience heart and soul,
That is, as far as reason will allow.

"I heard the story I shall tell you now
In Padua, from a learned man now dead,
Of proven worth in all he did and said.
Yes, he is dead and nailed up in his chest,
And I pray God his spirit may have rest.

"Francis Petrarch,[1] the poet laureate,
They called him, whose sweet rhetoric of
late
Illumined Italy with poesy,
As Lynian[2] did with his philosophy
And law, and other special kinds of learning.
Death that allows no lingering or returning
In, as it were, the twinkling of an eye
Has slain them both; and we must also die.

"But, to return to this distinguished man
From whom I learnt the tale, as I began,
Let me say first he starts it by enditing
A preface in the highest style of writing,
Ere coming to the body of his tale,
Describing Piedmont, the Saluzzo vale,

And the high Apennines that one may see
Bounding the lands of western Lombardy;
And he is most particular to tell
Of Monte Viso, where, from a little well,
The river Po springs from its tiny source.
Eastwards it runs, increasing on its course,
Towards the Aemilian Way; Ferrara past,
It reaches Venice and the sea at last,
Which is not only far too long to tell
But, as I think, irrelevant as well,
Except to set the tale and engineer it
A frame-work. This is it, if you will hear it."

The Clerk's Tale

PART I

Upon the western shores of Italy
Where Monte Viso lifts into the cold,
There lies a plain of rich fertility
With many a town and tower to behold,
Built by their forefathers in days of old,
And other lovely things to see in legion.
Saluzzo it is called, this splendid region.

There was a marquis once who ruled that land,
As had his ancestors in days gone by.
His vassals were obedient at his hand
Ready to serve, the lowly and the high.
Honoured and dreaded, under fortune's eye
He long had lived and found the living
    pleasant,
Beloved alike by nobleman and peasant.

He was, moreover, speaking of descent,
The noblest-born of all in Lombardy,
Handsome and young and strong; in him were
    blent
High honour and a gentle courtesy.
He was discreet in his authority,
Though in some things he was indeed to
    blame,
As you shall hear, and Walter was his name.

I blame his failure in consideration
Of what the distant future might provide.
He always fed his present inclination,
Hawking and hunting round the countryside.
As to more serious cares, he let them slide,
And worst of all, whatever might miscarry,
He could not be prevailed upon to marry.

This was the only point that really stung them,
And so one day a deputation went
To wait on him. The wisest man among them,

Or else the least unwilling to consent
To give the marquis their admonishment,
The ablest there to touch on such a head,
Boldly addressed the marquis thus and said:

"My noble lord, your great humanity
Gives us assurance; we are therefore bold
To speak on any point of urgency
Or heavy care of which you should be told.
Then, sir, let not your clemency withhold
A hearing to our pitiful petition;
Do not disdain my voice or our position.

"Though what I ask concerns me no more
    nearly
Than any of your subjects in this place,
Yet forasmuch as you have loved me dearly
And ever shown the favours of your grace,
I dare the better beg in such a case
For gentle audience; here is our request,
And you, my lord, must do as you think best.

"We love you well, sir, are indeed rejoiced
In all you do or ever did, and we
Scarce can imagine thoughts that could be
    voiced
To lap us round in more felicity
Save one thing only, would that it might be!
Did you but choose, my lord, to take a wife,
What sovereign comfort to your country's
    life!

"O bow your neck under that blessed yoke!
It is a kingdom, not a slavery;
Espousal, wedlock, it is called. Invoke
Your wisdom, ponder carefully and see
How variously days pass; the seasons flee
Away in sleeping, waking, roaming, riding.
Time passes on and there is no abiding.

"Still in the flower of your youth's delights
Age creeps upon you, silent as a stone.
Death menaces all ages and he smites
The high and low, the known and the un-
    known;
.We see for certain, are obliged to own
That we must die, but we are ignorant all
Of when the hour's to come, the blow to fall.

"Incline to our petition for protection,
Hear us that never crossed your least behest,
And we, with your consent, will make
    election

Immediately and choose a wife possessed
Of gentlest quality and birth, the best
In all the land, beseeming to her place,
An honour both to God and to your Grace.

"Deliver us from anxious fears and rid
Our hearts of care, for blessed Jesu's sake;
For if it so befell—which God forbid!—
Your line should end, then might not for-
    tune rake
Some strange successor in to come and take
Your heritage? Should we not all miscarry?
Therefore we beg you speedily to marry."

Their humble prayer and their imploring fea-
    tures
Made much impression on his clemency
And he replied, "My people, fellow-creatures,
Married's a thing I never thought to be.
I go rejoicing in my liberty,
And that and marriage seldom go together;
Where I was free, am I to take the tether?

"Yet, since your offer is sincerely meant,
And since I trust you now as in the past,
I freely will admit myself content
To humour you and take a wife at last.
But as for the suggestion you should cast
About to find me a bride, I must remit
That duty; kindly say no more of it.

"God knows it's true that children in the main
Are much unlike their elders gone before,
Natural goodness comes of God, no strain
Of blood can give it, no, nor ancestor;
I trust in God's good bounty; say no more.
My marriage, my condition, rank and ease
I lay on Him. Do He as He may please.

"Leave me alone to choose myself a wife,
That is my burden, my prerogative.
But I command you, charge you, on your life,
That whomsoever I choose, you are to give
All honour to her, long as she may live,
In word and deed, here and elsewhere, no less
Than to an emperor's daughter or princess.

"And over this you furthermore shall swear
Never to grumble, never to check or strive
Against my choice, if I am to impair
My personal liberty that you may thrive.
Where I have set my heart I mean to wive;
If you withhold consent as to this latter
I beg you'll speak no more upon the matter."

With heart's goodwill they gave him their
    assent
To this demand, not one that made objection,
But begged the princely favour ere they went
That he would name a day for the election
Of his espoused and quickly, for a section
Among his folk were yet uneasy, dreading
The marquis had no real thought of wedding.

He granted them a day of their own choosing
When he would wed in sober certainty;
He said he did so not to seem refusing
Their reasonable request, and reverently
In grave obedience then they bent the knee
Thanking him one and all, and were content,
Having achieved their aim, and home they
    went.

And thereupon he bade his ministers
To make such preparations as were fit
Against a feast, giving his officers
And squires such orders as he pleased for it,
And they obeyed him, setting all their wit
With diligence, the greatest and the least,
To make provision for a solemn feast.

PART II

Not far from where the noble palace stood
In which this marquis set about his wedding
There was a pretty village near a wood
Where the poor folk, each in his little steading,
Tended their animals with food and bedding
And took what sustenance they could from
    toil,
According to the bounty of the soil.

Among these poorer folk there dwelt a man
Who was esteemed the poorest of them all;
Yet there are times when God in Heaven can
Send grace into a little ox's stall.
Janicula the village used to call
This poor old man; his daughter was a pearl.
Griselda was the name of this young girl.

But in the virtuous beauty of her heart
She was among the loveliest man could ask,
For being poorly bred, no sensual part
Had learnt to use her beauty as a mask.
More often from the well than from the cask
She drank, and loving virtue, sought to please
By honest labour, not by idle ease.

And though as yet a girl of tender age,
Yet in the breast of her virginity

There was a ripeness, serious and sage.
With fostering love and reverent constancy
Her poor old father in his poverty
She tended, spun her wheel and watched his
    sheep
At pasture, never idle save asleep.

When she came homeward she would often
    bring
Roots, herbs and other grasses to the croft;
These she would shred and seethe for
    flavouring,
Then make her bed that was in nothing soft.
And thus she kept her father's heart aloft
With all the obedience, all the diligence
By which a child can show her reverence.

Griselda, though among his poorest creatures,
Walter had often seen, for, riding by,
Hunting perhaps, a something in her features
Caught his regard, not that he sought to try
The frivolous glance of wantonness; his eye
Fell on her with a serious awareness
And he would often ponder on her fairness.

Her womanliness was what his heart com-
    mended,
Her goodness too, far passing the condition
Of one so young, was beautifully blended
In looks and deeds. A vulgar intuition
Lacks insight into virtue; his position
Taught him to recognize it and decide,
Were he to marry, she should be his bride.

The day appointed for his wedding came
But no one knew what woman it should be,
In wonder at which his people would exclaim,
Talking among themselves in privacy,
"When will the marquis quit his vanity
And take a wife? Alas to see him thus!
Why does he try to fool himself and us?"

Nevertheless the marquis bade prepare
Brooches and rings, all for Griselda, lit
With jewels, gold and lapis; he took care
Her wedding-garment should be made to fit,
But by another girl they measured it,
Who was of equal stature; gems were sewn
On it to grace a wedding like his own.

And as the morning opened on the day
Appointed when the wedding was to be,
They decked the palace out in full array,
The hall, the chambers, each in its degree:

The store-rooms, bulging with a quantity
Of delicate viands, held in plenteous strength
Italy's best from all its breadth and length.

The royal marquis in his richest dress
With lords and ladies in a company
Invited to the banquet, and no less
His household officers and soldiery,
Rode off with many a sound of minstrelsy
Towards the little thorpe I spoke about
And by the shortest road, in sumptuous rout.

How could the innocent Griselda tell
That all this pomp was levelled at her head?
She had gone off for water to the well
And having drawn it, home she quickly sped,
For she had heard the marquis was to wed;
She knew it was the day and hoped she might
Be present as he passed, and see the sight.

She thought, "I'll stand among the other girls,
My own companions, by our door and see
The marchioness, the marquis and his earls.
I'll hurry home as quickly as can be
And finish off the work that's there for me,
So that I can have leisure then to wait
And watch her riding to the castle gate."

She reached the threshold with her water-pot
And as she did the marquis called her name.
She, putting down her vessel on the spot
Beside the cattle-stall, returned and came
Before him, falling on her knees, the same
Serious-looking girl; she knelt quite still
And waited quietly to hear his will.

The thoughtful marquis, speaking with an air
Of sober gravity, said thus to her:
"Tell me, Griselda, is your father there?"
In all humility, without demur,
She answered, "He is here and ready, sir."
She rose at once and of her own accord
Fetched out her father to his overlord.

He took the poor old fellow by the hand,
Leading him off to speak with him apart.
"Janicula, I can no more withstand,
No, nor conceal, the pleasures of my heart.
If you consent, accepting from the start
Whatever follows, I will take to wife
Your daughter and will love her all my life.

"You love me as I know and would obey,
Being my liege-man born and faithful too;

Whatever pleases me I dare to say
May well succeed in also pleasing you.
Yet in this point I specially pursue:
Tell me, I beg you, can my purpose draw
Consent to take me for your son-in-law?"

Wholly astounded at the news he heard
The old man turned deep red and stood there
    quaking,
So troubled he could hardly say a word,
Except "My lord, my will is in your making;
What you desire in any undertaking
Let me not hinder; I am bound to do,
My dear, dear master, what best pleases you."

The marquis answered softly, "None the less
In your own cottage you and I and she
Must have a conference. Why? You cannot
    guess?
I have to ask her if her will may be
To marry and submit herself to me.
This must be done while you are by to hear,
I will not speak unless I have you near."

While they were in the chamber and about
The treaty, which you presently shall hear,
The throng pressed round their dwelling-
    place without
And wondered at its decency and cheer,
How well she tended on her father dear.
But she, Griseld, might wonder even more,
For such a sight she'd never seen before.

Nor is it strange Griselda was astounded
To see so great a guest in such a place,
She was not used to being so surrounded
By noble visitors. How pale her face . . .
But let me keep my story up to pace;
These are the words in which her lord con-
    veyed
His will to this benign, true-hearted maid:

"Griselda, I would have you understand
As pleasing to your father and to me
That I should marry you, and here's my hand
If, as I may conjecture, you agree.
But I would rather ask you first," said he,
"Since all is done in such a hasty way,
Will you consent, or pause before you say?

"I warn you to be ready to obey
My lightest whim and pleasure; you must show
A willing heart, ungrudging night or day,

Whether I please to offer joy or woe.
When I say 'Yes' you never shall say 'No'
Either by word or frowning a defiance.
Swear this and I will swear to our alliance."

In wonder at these words, quaking for dread,
She answered, "Lord, unworthy though I be
Of so much honour, so unmerited,
If it seems good to you it is to me.
And here I promise never willingly
To disobey in deed or thought or breath
Though I should die, and yet I fear my death."

"That is enough, Griselda mine!" said he.
He left the chamber then with sober tread
And reached the door; and after him came she.
And to the throng of people there he said:
"Here stands the wife it is my choice to wed.
Give her your reverence and love, I pray,
Whoever loves me. There's no more to say."

And that she might not take the smallest bit
Of her old gear into his house, he bade
His women strip her there, and I admit
Those ladies of the court were scarcely glad
To touch the rags in which the girl was clad.
Yet the bright beauty of her natural glow
Was clothed anew at last from top to toe.

They combed her hair that fell but rudely
    tressed
With slender hands as if preparatory
To coronation, and a crown was pressed
Upon her head with gems of changeful glory.
Why should I let her raiment stay my story?
She stood transfigured in her gorgeous dress
Scarce recognizable for loveliness.

The marquis then espoused her with a ring
Brought for the purpose; on a horse he set her,
It was a nobly-pacing snow-white thing.
And to the palace next with those that met her,
Leading the way with joyful heart he let her
Be brought in triumph, and the day had end
In revel till they saw the sun descend.

Shortly, to let my story quicken pace,
I say this young, new marchioness so stood
In favour with the Lord and Heaven's grace
It could not seem by any likelihood
That she was born and bred in servitude,
As in a cottage or an oxen-stall,
But rather nourished in an emperor's hall.

To all that looked on her she grew so dear,
So much to be revered, where she was born
Those who had watched her childhood year
   by year
Could hardly credit it, and dared have sworn
That she had never laboured in the corn
Nor was Janicula's child, for by her feature
Fancy would think she was some other crea-
   ture.

Virtuous ever, as had long been known,
She had increased to such an excellence
Of grace she was as bounty on a throne,
Wise, and so lovely in her eloquence,
So grave and so benign, she charmed the sense
And gathered every heart in her embrace,
They loved her all that looked upon her face.

Nor only was Griselda thus renowned
Within Saluzzo, for her bounteous name
Was published forth in all the region round.
If one said well another said the same;
Indeed her goodness had so wide a fame,
Men, women too, the younger and the older,
Went to Saluzzo only to behold her.

And thus in humble, nay, in royal kind,
Walter espoused a love as fortunate
As it was fair. God's peace was in his mind
And he enjoyed the outward gifts of fate;
And in that he had seen in low estate
The hidden grace, men held him to have been
A prudent man, and that is seldom seen.

Nor was it only that by natural wit
She could accomplish all a woman should
In homely ways, for, were there call for it,
She also could advance the public good;
There was no rancour, no discordant mood
In all that country that she did not ease
Or use her grace and wisdom to appease.

She, in her husband's absence, did not cease
Her labours; if the nobles of the land
Fell into enmity she made their peace.
So wise and ripe the words at her command,
Her heart so equitable and her hand
So just, they thought that Heaven had sent
   her down
To right all wrongs and to protect the town.

And it was not long after, to her joy,
Griselda bore a daughter fine and fair,

And though she would have rather borne
   a boy,
Walter was glad and so his people were,
For though it was a girl, perchance an heir
Might yet be born to them and likely so,
Seeing she was not barren. Time would show.

PART III

It happened, as it often does in life,
While yet the child was sucking at her breast
The marquis, in obsession for his wife,
Longed to expose her constancy to test.
He could not throw the thought away or rest,
Having a marvellous passion to assay her;
Needless, God knows, to frighten and dis-
   may her,

He had assayed her faith enough before
And ever found her good; what was the need
Of heaping trial on her, more and more?
Though some may praise the subtlety, indeed
For my part I should say it could succeed
Only in evil; what could be the gain
In putting her to needless fear and pain?

But this was how he fed his prepossession;
He came alone one night to where she lay
With troubled features and a stern expression
And said, "Griseld, do you recall the day
I came and took you from your poor array
And raised you to the height of nobleness?
You've not forgotten that, or so I guess.

"I say, Griseld, this present dignity
To which I raised you cannot have, I know,
Made you forgetful of your debt to me
Who took you up from what was poor and low,
For all the little wealth that you could show.
Take heed of every word I say to you;
No one is here to hear it but us two.

"You may remember your arrival here
Into this house, it's not so long ago;
And though I love you much and hold you
   dear,
My noblemen are far from doing so.
They say it is a scandal and a show
That they should serve you, lifted from the
   tillage
As you have been, born in a little village.

"And now you've borne your daughter, all
   the more

No doubt they murmur phrases such as these.
But I desire, as I did before,
To live my life among them and in ease.
I cannot then ignore contingencies
And must dispose your daughter as is best,
Not as I wish to, but as they suggest.

"But still God knows it's painful to me too;
Yet without your full knowledge and consent
I will do nothing, but it is for you
To acquiesce and show no discontent.
Summon your patience, show that they were
     meant,
Those promises you gave me to obey,
Down in your village on our wedding-day."

Apparently unmoved as she received
What he had said, no change in her expression
Or tone of voice, Griselda unaggrieved
Replied, "My child and I are your possession
And at your pleasure; on my heart's profession
We are all yours and you may spare or kill
What is your own. Do therefore as you will.

"Nor is there anything, as God may save
My soul, that pleasing you displeases me,
Nor is there anything that I could crave
To have, or dread to lose, but you," said she.
"This is my heart's will and shall ever be;
This may no length of time, no death deface;
My heart will never turn or change its place."

If he were gladdened at her mild reply
There was no sign upon his face to show,
But gravely and with unrelenting eye
He gazed at her. At last he turned to go.
Soon after this, within a day or so,
He told a man in secret what he held
Was needful, and he sent him to Griseld.

He was a sort of secret agent, one
That had been ever faithful in pursuing
Important tasks. When wickedness is done
Such men are very useful in the doing.
He loved and feared his master, and reviewing
What was commanded of him, made his way
With silent stalk to where Griselda lay.

"Madam," the fellow said, "I must be par-
     doned
For doing that to which I am constrained;
You are too wise to let your heart be hardened,
You know a lord's command must be sus-
     tained

And not refused, although it be complained
Against and wept for. Servants must obey,
And so will I. There is no more to say.

"It is commanded that I take this child."
He said no more but grabbed the innocent
Despitefully, his countenance as wild
As if he would have slain it ere he went.
Griselda had to suffer and consent,
And like a lamb she lay there, meek and still,
And let the cruel fellow do his will.

He was a man of ominous ill-fame,
In voice and feature ominous, as are such,
And ominous the hour at which he came.
Alas, her daughter that she loved so much
Would, as she thought, be murdered at his
     touch.
Nevertheless she wept not nor lamented;
It was her husband's will and she consented.

She found her voice at last and she began
Humbly imploring not to be denied
This mercy, as he was a gentleman,
To let her kiss the child before it died;
She took it to her breast, with terrified
And stricken face, and lulled it in her loss;
She kissed it then and signed it with the cross,

Saying with love, "Farewell, O sacrificed
And blessed child that I shall never see;
Look, I have marked thee with the cross of
     Christ.
He is thy Father, may He comfort thee,
Who died, for sake of us, upon a tree;
Thy little soul I offer in His sight
Since thou shalt die, for sake of me, tonight."

And had there been a nurse with her, God
     knows
She would have thought it pitiful to see;
Well might a mother then have wept her
     woes.
Yet she was grave, and gazing steadfastly
As one who suffers all adversity
In meek submission, turned with sorrow-
     laden
Spirit and said, "Take back your little maiden.

"Go now," she said, "and do as you are
     bidden.
But one thing let me beg of you your grace;
Bury the little body, be it hidden,
Unless my lord forbade it, in some place

That beasts and birds of prey can never trace."
Yet not a word in answer would he say;
He took the little child and went his way,

Reporting to the marquis once again
What she had said, how looked, if reconciled,
As briefly point by point he made all plain
And having done he gave him up the child.
And though some touch of tenderness be-
    guiled
His master, yet he held his purpose still
As lords will do that mean to have their will.

He bade the fellow secretly to take
The child and wrap the softest winding
    round
Her little form and carefully to make
A chest to bear it in; and then he bound
The man on pain of death that not a sound
Of his intention should be uttered, dumb
On whither he was going or whence come.

But to Bologna, to the marquis' sister,
The Countess of Panaro, he must go,
Taking the child, and he must there enlist her
To help him in this matter and bestow
All fostering care, so that the child
    might grow
In nobleness—and yet that none might trace
Or tell whose child she was, in any case.

The man went off and did as he was bidden.
Now let us watch the marquis as he ranged
In quick imagination for some hidden
Sign in his wife whether she were estranged;
Was there a chance word showing she had
    changed
Towards him? But he still could never find
Her anything but serious and kind,

As glad, as humble and as quick to serve,
And in her love as she was wont to be;
In everything the same, she did not swerve,
And of her daughter not a word said she.
There was no sign of that adversity
To see upon her; and her daughter's name
She never used, in earnest or in game.

PART IV

Four years went by in this unaltered state
Before Griselda was with child once more,
And then she bore a boy as delicate
In grace and beauty as the child before.
The marquis, being told, set greatest store

On it; nor only he but the whole country,
And all gave thanks and honour to God's
    bounty.

When it was two years old, weaned from the
    breast
And taken from its nurse, there came a day
When Walter yet again was moved to test
The patience of his wife in the same way.
O needless, needless was the test, I say!
But married men too often use no measure
That have some patient creature at their plea-
    sure.

"Wife," said the marquis, "as I said at first,
My people take it ill that we were married.
Now that my son is born they think the
    worst;
Never were things so bad, for I am harried
By murmurings and rumours that are carried
About my ears; I feel a deadly smart
That has indeed almost destroyed my heart.

"For now they say, 'When Walter's reign
    is done
Old Janicle's descendants will succeed
And be our masters, either that or none.'
Such is the common talk, it is indeed.
Murmurs like that a ruler has to heed,
And certainly I dread all such opinions,
Though secretly advanced, in my dominions.

"I mean to live in quiet if I may,
And so am utterly disposed in mind
To serve the brother in the self-same way
As I have served his sister. I designed
To give this warning lest you were inclined
To do some outrage in your violent grief;
I beg you to be patient then, in brief."

"I long have said," she answered, "Oh, be-
    lieve me,
Nothing I will, nor yet would have unwilled,
But as it pleases you. It does not grieve me
At all, though son and daughter both be killed
At your commandment; let it be fulfilled.
In my two children I have had no part
But sickness first, then pain and grief of heart.

"You are our sovereign, do with what is yours
Just as you please and do not bid me frame
Advice for you; for at my father's doors
I left my clothing. Was it not the same
To leave my will and freedom when I came?

I took your clothing and I therefore pray
Your pleasure may be done. I will obey.

"And surely had I had the prescience
To know your will before you told it me
I had performed it without negligence.
But knowing what your pleasure is to be,
I hold to it with firmest constancy.
For if I knew my death itself would ease you,
Then I would die, and gladly die, to
    please you.

"For death can never make comparison
Beside your love." And when the marquis saw
Her faithfulness he could not look upon
Her face and dropped his eyes in wonder-
    ing awe,
Thinking, "What patience to endure the law
Of my caprices!" and he left the room
Happy at heart, but set his face in gloom.

The ugly officer as brutally
As he had snatched her daughter, or
    with more
Brutality if more in man could be,
Seized on her son, so beautiful, and tore
Him from her arms; she, patient as before,
Gave him no sign of suffering in her loss
But kissed her son and signed him with the
    cross.

But yet she begged the fellow, if he might,
To close the little body in a grave.
His tender limbs so delicate to sight
She sought in her extremity to save
From birds and beasts, but not a sign he gave
And snatched the child with careless cruelty,
But bore it to Bologna tenderly.

The marquis wondered ever more and more
At so much patience in her misery;
Had he not known for certain long before
How perfectly she loved her children, he
Would have supposed some cunning devilry
Of malice, some heart's cruelty or base
Indifference beneath her constant face.

But well the marquis knew it was no mask,
For she had ever loved her children best,
Next to himself. Now, I would like to ask
Of women, had he made sufficient test?
Could stubborn husband fancy or suggest
More that would prove a steadfast wifeliness
To one continuing stubborn to excess?

But there are folk in such a state of mind
That, if they finally resolve to take
Some certain course to which they feel in-
    clined,
Cannot hold back, but fettered to their stake,
Hold to their purposes and cannot slake
Their fevered wills. So too this marquis nursed
His purposes, to test her as at first.

And so he waited for a word or glance
To show her change of heart, but there was
    none,
No variation in her countenance
Could he discover; face and heart were one.
And as she aged the love in her begun
Continued even truer, made addition,
If that could be, in love and true submission.

Therefore there seemed to be between
    these two
One undivided will; if Walter pressed
For something, it became her joy to do;
And God be thanked all happened for the best.
And she gave proof that in whatever test
A wife, as of herself, in nothing should
Direct her will but as her husband would.

Walter's ill-fame began to mount and spread;
His cruel soul had led him to embark
For having wed a pauper, people said,
On murdering both his children in the dark.
Such was the common murmur and remark.
No wonder; common rumours all concurred:
He'd murdered them. There came no other
    word.

And so the love his people felt of yore
Turned into hatred; scandal and ill-fame
Are things a man may well be hated for;
To be called murderer is a hateful name.
Yet he, in game or earnest, with the same
Cruel device drove on to what he sought;
To test her further was his only thought.

Now when his daughter was some twelve
    years old
He sent to Rome, long cunningly apprised
Of his intentions, and the court was told
That such a papal bull should be devised,
That his fell purpose might be realized,
And that the Pope, to set all minds at rest,
Should bid him wed again, as he thought best.

I say he ordered them to counterfeit

A papal bull declaring approbation
Of a divorce, for Walter then could meet
Objection with a papal dispensation
And calm the rancour and the indignation
Between his people and him. They framed
    the bull
And published the whole forgery in full.

The common people, and no wonder, held,
Or else supposed, that things were even so.
But when these tidings came to poor Griseld
I deem her heart was weighted down
    with woe.
But she, and now no less than long ago,
Was ready, humble creature, faithfully
To meet misfortune and adversity.

And still she waited on his will and pleasure
To whom she had been given, heart and soul,
As to her one unfailing worldly treasure.
Yet to be brief about it and control
My tale, the marquis now to reach his goal
Devised a letter that declared his aim,
And to Bologna secretly it came.

It was for Lord Panaro, for the earl
Who had espoused his sister, and requested
That he would send him home his boy
    and girl
In public state and openly invested
With every honour, but it still protested
That upon no account should he declare,
Even if questioned, whose the children were,

But say the maid was shortly to espouse
The Marquis of Saluzzo; and thereto
The earl agreed. As day began to rouse
He started on the journey and he drew
Towards Saluzzo with a retinue
Of many lords in rich array, to guide
This maiden and the brother at her side.

All in her wedding-dress and fresh as heaven,
She rode in pearl and gold without alloy.
Her brother too, a little lad of seven,
Looked freshly, in the tunic of a boy;
So with great splendour, every face in joy,
They shaped their journey, riding all the way;
And thus they neared Saluzzo day by day.

PART V

Meanwhile, according to his cruel bent,
The Marquis sought to test his wife yet more.
And by the uttermost experiment

To prove her spirit to the very core,
Whether she still were steadfast as before;
And so in open audience one day
And in a blustering voice he chose to say:

"It was agreeable enough, forsooth,
To marry you, Griselda, in the flower
Of your obedient love and simple truth,
And not for lineage or for worldly dower;
But now I know in very truth that power,
If one reflects, is nothing much to praise;
It is a servitude in many ways.

"I may not do as any ploughman may:
My subjects are constraining me to take
Another wife, they clamour day by day.
Even the Pope has thought it fit to slake
Their rancour by consenting, you need make
No doubt of that; indeed I have to say
My second wife is now upon her way.

"Strengthen your heart to give her up your
    place.
As for the dowry that you brought of old,
Take it again, I grant it as a grace;
Go home, rejoin you father in his fold.
No one can count upon his luck to hold,
And I enjoin you to endure the smart
Of fortune's buffets with an even heart."

She answered patiently without pretence:
"My lord, I know as I have always done
That, set against your high magnificence,
My poverty makes no comparison.
It cannot be denied, and I for one
Was never worthy, never in my life,
To be your chambermaid, much less your wife.

"And in this house whose lady you have
    made me,
As God's my witness whom I love and fear,
And as His power may gladden me and aid me,
I never thought myself the mistress here,
Rather a servant, humble and sincere,
To your high honour; so I shall think for ever
Of you, above all creatures whatsoever.

"That you so long of your benignity
Have held me high in honour and display,
Whereas I was not worthy so to be,
I thank my God and you; and now I pray
Revoke it, for there is no more to say.
Gladly I seek my father and will live
My life with him, whatever life may give.

"For I was fostered there when I was small,
Only a child, and there I'll live and die
A widow clean in body, heart and all;
I gave my maidenhead to you, and I
Am still your faithful wife, I do not lie.
And God forbid a wife to one so great
Should take another man to be her mate.

"Touching your second wife, may God in
     grace
Grant you both joy and long prosperity,
For I will gladly yield her up my place
That once was such a happiness to me.
But since it pleases you, my lord," said she,
"In whom was formerly my whole heart's
     rest,
Then I will go when you shall think it best.

"But as you proffer me what first I brought,
Such dowry as I had, it's in my mind
It was my wretched clothing and worth
     nought,
And would indeed be hard for me to find.
O blessed God, how noble and how kind
You seemed in speech, in countenance, in car-
     riage,
That day, the day on which we made our mar-
     riage!

"It's truly said, at least I find it true
For the effect of it is proved in me,
'A love grown old is not the love once new.'
And yet whatever the adversity,
Though it were death, my lord, it cannot be
That ever I should repent, though I depart,
For having wholly given you my heart.

"My lord, you know that in my father's place
You stripped me of my rags and in their stead
Gave me rich garments, as an act of grace.
I brought you nothing else it may be said
But faith and nakedness and maidenhead.
Here I return your garments and restore
My wedding-ring as well, for evermore.

"And the remainder of the gems you lent
Are in your chamber I can safely say.
Naked out of my father's house I went
And naked I return again today;
Gladly I'll do your pleasure, if I may.
But yet I hope you will not make a mock
Of me or send me forth without a smock.

"So infamous a thing you could not do

As let the womb in which your children lay
Be seen in nakedness, bare to the view
Of all your people, let me not I pray
Go naked as a worm upon the way.
Bethink yourself, my own dear lord, because
I was your wife, unworthy though I was.

"Therefore in guerdon of my maidenhead
Which, hither brought, returns with me no
     more,
Vouchsafe a payment, give to me instead
Just such a simple smock as once I wore
To hide the womb of one that heretofore
Has been your wife; and here at last I leave you
And bid farewell, dear lord, lest I should
     grieve you."

"The smock," he said, "you have upon
     your back
You may retain; remove it to your stall."
Yet as he spoke his voice began to crack
For pity, and he turned and left the hall.
She stripped her garments in the sight of all
And in her smock, head bare and feet unshod,
Home to her father and his house she trod.

Folk followed weeping when she passed
     them by,
They railed on fate for all that had occurred.
Her eyes withheld their weeping and were dry
And at this time she did not speak a word.
The news soon reached her father; when he
     heard
He cursed the day and hour of his birth
That fashioned him a man to live on earth.

He, never doubt it, though so old and poor,
Had ever been suspicious of the match,
Had always thought it never could endure,
In that the marquis, having had the snatch
Of his desires, would feel disgrace attach
To his estate in such a low alliance
And when he could would set it at defiance.

At her approach he hastened forth to meet her
Led by the sound of many a beholder
That wept to see her pass, and he to greet her
Brought her old cloak and cast it on her
     shoulder
And wept. It fitted not, for it was older
By many a day than was her wedding-dress;
The cloth was coarsely woven, comfortless.

Thus with her father for a certain space

This flower of love and wifely patience stayed.
Never a word or look upon her face
In front of others, or alone, conveyed
A hint that she had suffered, or betrayed
Any remembrance of her former glory;
Her countenance told nothing of her story.

And that's no wonder; in her high estate
Her spirit had a full humility,
No tender mouth for food, no delicate
Heart's hungering after royal brilliancy
Or show of pomp; benignly, patiently,
She had lived wise in honour, void of pride,
Meek and unchanging at her husband's side.

They speak of Job and his humility,
For clerics when they wish to can endite
Its praises nobly, and especially,
In men—they praise few women when they
     write;
Yet none can reach a humbleness as white
As women can, nor can be half so true
As women are, or else it's something new.

PART VI

Now from Bologna he of whom I spoke,
The earl, arrived. The greater and the less
Got wind of it and all the common folk
Buzzed with the news a second mar-
     chioness
Was being brought in all the loftiness
Of pomp and splendour. Such a sight to see
Had never been known in all west Lombardy.

The marquis, who had planned and knew
     it all,
Before the earl had fully reached his place,
Sent down for poor Griselda in her stall;
And she with humble heart and happy face
Came at his bidding, all without a trace
Of swelling thought, and went upon her
     knees
And greeted him with reverence and at ease.

"Griseld," said he, "my will is firmly set.
This maiden hither brought to be my bride
Tomorrow shall as royally be met
As possible, with all I can provide
That's in my house. My servants, side by side
According to their rank, shall wait upon her
As may be best arranged in joy and honour.

"I have no woman of sufficient skill
To decorate the chambers as I hold

They should be decorated. If you will,
I should be glad to see it all controlled
By you who know me and my tastes of old.
And though your dress is not a thing of
     beauty,
I hope at least that you will do your duty."

"Not only, lord, would I be glad," said she,
"To do your will; I long and shall endeavour
To serve and please you in my own degree
And not to faint in service, now or ever.
For neither grief or happiness can sever
My love from me. My heart can never rest
Save in the ceaseless will to love you best."

And she began upon the decorations;
There were the boards to set, the beds to
     make.
All she could do in many occupations
She did, and begged the maids for good-
     ness' sake
To hurry and to sweep and dusk and shake,
While she, most serviceable of them all,
Went garnishing the chambers and the hall.

The earl arrived, beginning to alight
With the two children early in the day,
And all the people ran to see the sight
Of so much opulence and rich array.
And soon among them there were those to say
That Walter was no fool, and though obsessed
To change his wife, it might be for the best.

"For she is lovelier," they all agreed,
"And younger than Griselda. Put the case
That fruit will fall to them; a fairer breed
Will issue from such lineage and grace."
Her brother had so beautiful a face
It caught them with delight, opinion changed.
They now applauded what had been arranged.

"O stormy people, frivolous and fickle,
Void of true judgement, turning like a vane,
Whom every novelty and rumour tickle,
How like the moon you are to wax and wane,
Clapping your praises, shouting your disdain,
False judges, dear at a penny as a rule,
Who trusts to your opinion is a fool."

So said the serious people of the city
Who watched the throng go gazing up
     and down
Glad merely for the novelty, the pretty
New lady that had come to grace the town.

But let me leave the pleasure-seeking clown
And turn to my Griselda, in the press
Of all her labours, in her steadfastness.

Busy in all, she worked, disposed and settled,
Laboured and strove to cater and adorn,
Nor did she seem at all abashed or nettled
Although her clothes were coarse and some-
    what torn,
But with a face as cheerful as the morn
Went to the gate with all her retinue
To greet the marchioness, and then withdrew.

She met the guests so cheerfully and
    greeted them
With so much skill according to their rank
That none could find a fault in how she
    treated them
And all were wondering whom they had to
    thank,
For how could such a pauper, to be frank,
Know all the rules of honour and degree?
They praised her prudence as a rarity.

And in the meanwhile ceaselessly she still
Praised the young bride and praised her
    brother too
With so much heart, with such benign
    goodwill
That no one could have given them bet-
    ter due.
And in the end when all the retinue
Sat down to meat, Walter began to call
Griselda who was busy in his hall.

"Griseld," he said to her as if in jest,
"How do you like the beauty of my wife?"
"Indeed, my lord," she said, "I must protest
I never saw a lovelier in my life.
God give her joy and may there be no strife
Between you, and I pray that He may send
Your fill of happiness to your lives' end!

"One thing I beg of you, and warn you too,
Never to goad her, never put on trial
This tender girl as I have known you do;
For she was fostered preciously, a vial
More delicate. I think the self-denial
Adversity might force on her would be
Harder for her to suffer than for me."

When Walter saw this patience in Griseld,

Her happy face, no malice there at all,
And thought of his offences long upheld
To test her, ever constant as a wall,
Grave, innocent and ever at his call,
The stubborn marquis could no more repress
His pity for such wifely steadfastness.

"It is enough," he said, "Griselda mine!
Have no more fears, let not your heart be sore.
Your faith and gentleness as far outshine
All other faith as you were tested more,
In wealth and want, than any wife before.
Dear wife, I know your steadfastness by this."
He took her up into his arms to kiss.

She, lost in wonder, did not seem to grasp
Or even hear the words he uttered thus,
But as a sleeper breaking from the clasp
Of an amazement, woke incredulous.
"Griseld," said he, "by Him that died for us
You are my wife and I have none but you,
Nor ever had as God may judge me true!

"This is your daughter whom you so com-
    mended
As wife for me; the other on my oath
Shall be my heir as I have long intended,
They are the children of your body, both.
Bologna nourished them and fed their growth
In secret; take them back and never say
Your children have been lost or snatched
    away.

"Let those that otherwise have talked of me
Know that I did this, be it bad or good,
Neither in malice nor in cruelty
But for the trial of your womanhood.
What! Slay my children? God forbid I should!
Rather I kept them privately apart
Till I had proved the purpose of your heart."

On hearing this Griselda fell aswoon
In piteous joy, but made recovery
And called her children to her and they soon
Were folded in her arms. How tenderly
She kissed them as the salt tears falling free
Bathed them and glistened on their face and
    hair;
How like a mother stood Griselda there!

And Oh how pitiful it was to see
Her fainting and to hear her humble tone!

"All thanks to you, my dearest lord," said she,
"For you have saved my children, you alone!
Were I to die this moment I have known
Your love and have found favour in your
    sight,
And death were nothing, though I died
    tonight.

"O dear, O tender ones, so long away,
Your sorrowing mother steadfastly had
    thought
That some foul vermin, hound or beast of prey
Had eaten you. But God in mercy brought
You back to me and your kind father sought
In tender love to keep you safe and sound."
She suddenly swooned again and fell to
    ground.

Though she had fainted, sadly, clingingly
She held her children in that first embrace,
And it was difficult for skill to free
Them from her arms, and touching to unlace.
O many a tear on many a pitying face
Ran down among those standing at her side,
Scarce able in her presence to abide.

Walter caressed her, loosed her from her grief,
And up she rose bewildered from her trance,
While all the rest in joy at her relief
Made much of her and cleared her counte-
    nance;
And Walter showed such loving vigilance
It was a dainty thing to see the air
Of new-found happiness between the pair.

The ladies round her, when the moment
    came,
Led her towards her chamber; there the old
Poor rags she wore, though never worn in
    shame,
They stripped and set on her a gown of gold;
A coronet of jewels manifold
They crowned her with and led her into hall
There to receive the homage of them all.

Thus to a piteous day a blissful close,
And every man and woman, as they might,
Gave themselves up to revelry; there rose
The stars and all the welkin shone with light.
Greater the glad solemnities that night,
Greater the joy in feasting and defray
In treasure than upon their wedding-day.

For many a year in high prosperity
These two lived on in concord to the close;
Their daughter too they married worthily
And richly to a lord, best among those
In Italy. They also found repose
For old Janicula whom Walter kept
Safe at his court till soul from body crept.

Their son succeeded to the inheritance
After his father's day in peace and rest;
He married happily but did not chance
To put his wife to such a searching test.
This world of ours, it has to be confessed,
Is not so sturdy as it was of old.
Hear how my author ends the tale he told:

"This story does not mean it would be good
For wives to ape Griseld's humility,
It would be unendurable they should.
But everybody in his own degree
Should be as perfect in his constancy
As was Griselda." That is why Petrarch chose
To tell her story in his noble prose.

For since a woman showed such patience to
A mortal man, how much the more we ought
To take in patience all that God may do!
Reason He has to test what He has wrought,
Yet never tempts the souls that He has bought
Above what they are able, and St. James
Tells us He tests us daily, and reclaims.

He will permit, to exercise our virtue,
The sharper scourges of adversity
To lash us often, not that they may hurt you,
Nor yet to test the will, for certainly
No one can know our frailty more than He
Who knew it ere our birth, and all is best;
Then let our virtues learn to suffer test.

But one word more, my lords, before I go.
It isn't very easy nowadays
To find Griseldas round the town, you know.
And if you try imposing these assays,
What gold they have is mixed with such allays
Of brass, that though the coin looks right per-
    haps,
When you begin to bend the thing, it snaps.

So, from affection for the Wife of Bath,
Whose life and all her sect may God maintain
In high authority upon their path

—And pity else—I sing you this refrain
With lusty heart, to gladden you again,
Dropping the note of earnest emphasis.
So listen to my song, it goes like this:

Chaucer's Envoy to the Clerk's Tale[3]

Griselda and her patience both are dead
And buried in some far Italian vale.
So let it then in open court be said,
Husbands, be not so hardy as to assail
The patience of your wives in hope to find
Griseldas, for you certainly will fail.

O noble wives, in highest prudence bred,
Allow no such humility to nail
Your tongues, nor give a scholar cause to
    shed
Such light on you as this astounding tale
Sheds of Griselda, patient still, and kind,
Lest Chichevache[4] engulf you like a whale.

Imitate Echo, she that never fled
In silence, but returns you hail for hail,
Never let innocence besot your head,
But take the helm yourselves and trim the sail.
And print this lesson firmly in your mind
For common profit; it can never stale.

Arch-wives, stand up, defend your board
    and bed!
Stronger than camels as you are, prevail!
Don't swallow insults, offer them instead.
And all you slender little wives and frail,
Be fierce as Indian tigers, since designed
To rattle like a windmill in a gale.

Never revere them, never be in dread,
For though your husband wears a coat of mail
Your shafts of crabbed eloquence will thread
His armour through and drub him like a flail.
Voice your suspicions of him! Guilt will bind
Him down, he'll couch as quiet as a quail.

If you are beautiful, advance your tread,
Show yourself off to people, blaze the trail!
If you are ugly, spend and make a spread,
Get friends, they'll do the business of a male;
Dance like a linden-leaf if so inclined,
Leave him to weep and wring his hands and
    wail!

THE MERCHANT'S TALE
The Merchant's Prologue

"Weeping and wailing, care and other sorrow,
I know them well enough by eve and mor-
    row,"
The Merchant said; "like others I suppose
That have been married, that's the way it goes;
I know too well that's how it goes with me.
I have a wife, the worst that there could be;
For if a fiend were coupled to my wife,
She'd overmatch him, you can bet your life.
Why choose a special instance to recall
Her soaring malice? She's a shrew in all.
There's wide difference I'm bound to say
Between Griselda's patience and the way
My wife behaves; her studied cruelty
Surpasses everything. If I were free,
Never again, never again the snare!
We married men, our life is grief and care.
Try it who will, and he will find, I promise
That I have spoken truly, by St. Thomas,
For most of us—I do not say for all,
And God forbid that such a thing befall.
    "Ah, my good Host, I have been wed-
    ded now
These two months past, no more than that,
    I vow,
Yet I believe no bachelor alive,
Not if you were to take a knife and rive
Him to the heart, could tell of so much grief
As I could tell you of; beyond belief,
The curst malignity I get from her!"
    Our Host replied, "God bless you, my
    dear sir!
But since you know so much about the art
Of marriage, let me beg you to impart."
    "With pleasure," he said, "but on the per-
    sonal score
I'm so heart-scalded I shall say no more."

The Merchant's Tale

There was a knight one time of good renown
In Lombardy, Pavia was the town.
He'd lived there very prosperously for more
Than sixty years and was a bachelor,
Though always taking bodily delight
On women, such as pleased his appetite,
As do these foolish worldlings, never fear.
Now when this knight had passed his sixti-
    eth year
—Whether for holiness, or from a surge

Of dotage, who can say?—he felt an urge
So violent to be a wedded man
That day and night his eager fancies ran
On where and how to spy himself a bride,
Praying the Lord he might not be denied
Once to have knowledge of that blissful life
There is between a husband and his wife,
And live within the holy bond and tether
In which God first bound woman and man to-
    gether.
"No other life," he said, "is worth a bean;
For wedlock is so easy and so clean
It is a very paradise on earth."
Thus said this ageing knight, so full of worth.

    And certainly, as sure as God is King,
To take a wife is a most glorious thing,
Especially if a man is old and hoary;
Then she's the fruit of all his wealth and
    glory.
It's then he ought to take her, young and fair,
One upon whom he might beget an heir,
And lead a life of rapture and content,
Whereas these bachelors can but lament
And suffer, when in some adversity
From love, which is but childish vanity.
And it's no more than right it should be so
If bachelors are beset by grief and woe:
On brittle ground they build, so all is ready
For brittle love though they expect a steady.
Their liberty is that of bird or beast,
They've no restraint, no discipline at least,
Whereas a married man achieves a state
Of bliss that's orderly and fortunate.
Under the yoke of matrimony bowed,
The heart, in bliss abounding, sings aloud.
For who is so obedient as a wife?
Who is so true, so careful for his life
Whether in health or sickness, as his mate?
For weal or woe she tends upon his state,
In service, and in love, she never tires,
Though he lie bedridden till he expires.

    And yet some writers say this isn't so;
One such was Theophrastus long ago.
Who cares if Theophrastus was a liar?
"Don't take a wife," he said, "from a desire
To make economies and spare expense.
A faithful servant shows more diligence
In guarding your possessions than a wife
For she claims half you have throughout her
    life;
And if you're sick, as God may give me joy,
Your very friends, an honest serving-boy,
Do more than she, who's watching for a way

To corner your possessions night and day.
And if you take a wife into your bed
You're very likely to be cuckolded."

    Opinions such as these and hundreds worse
This fellow wrote, God lay him under curse!
But take no heed of all such vanity,
Defy foul Theophrastus and hear me.

    A wife is verily the gift of God.
All other kinds of gift, the fruitful sod
Of land, fair pastures, movables in store,
Rents—they're the gifts of Fortune, nothing
    more,
That pass as does a shadow on a wall.

    Still, if I must speak plainly, after all
A wife does last some time, and time may lapse
A good deal slower than one likes, perhaps.

    Marriage is a momentous sacrament,
Bachelordom contemptible, and spent
In helpless desolation and remorse
—I'm speaking of the laity, of course.
I don't say this for nothing; listen why.
Woman was made to be a man's ally.
When God created Adam, flesh and bone,
And saw him belly-naked and alone,
He of His endless goodness thus began:
"Let us now make a help-meet for this man
Like to himself." And He created Eve.
Here lies the proof of what we all believe,
That woman is man's helper, his resort,
His earthly paradise and his disport.
So pliant and so virtuous is she
They cannot but abide in unity.
One flesh they are; one flesh as I suppose
Has but a single heart in joys and woes.

    A wife! Saint Mary, what a benediction!
How can a man be subject to affliction
Who has a wife? Indeed I cannot say.
There is a bliss between them such as may
No tongue tell forth, such as no heart can
    judge.
If he be poor she helps her man to drudge,
Sets guard upon his goods and checks the
    waste;
All that her husband likes is to her taste,
She never once says "no" when he says "yes."
"Do this," says he; "already done," she says.
O blissful state of wedlock, no way vicious
But virtuous and merry, nay, delicious,
And so commended and approved withal
That any man who's worth a leek should fall
On his bare knees, to thank God, all his life,
For having ordained and given him a wife,
Or else to pray that he vouchsafe to send

A wife to last him to the very end.
   Then he can count upon security
And not be tricked, as far as I can see,
Provided that he works by her advice:
Jacob, the learned tell us, was precise
In following the good counsel of his mother,
And won his father's blessing from his
   brother,
By binding round his neck a pelt of kid.
Or Judith, one can read of what she did:
Her wisdom held God's people in its keeping
By slaying Holofernes, who was sleeping.
   Take Abigail, what good advice she gave!
It saved her husband Nabal from the grave.
Take Esther too, whose wisdom brought relief
To all God's people, saved them from their
   grief
And made Ahasuerus grant promotion
To Mordecai for his true devotion.
There's no superlative that ranks in life,
Says Seneca, above a humble wife.
"The tongue of wife," so Cato was to say,
"Commands the husband: suffer and obey."
And yet she will obey by courtesy.
A wife is guardian of your husbandry;
Well may a man in sickness wail and weep
Who has no wife to nurse him and to keep
His house for him; do wisely then and search
For one and love her as Christ loves His
   Church.
For if you love yourself you love your wife,
For no one hates his flesh, nay all his life
He fosters it, and so I bid you wive
And cherish her, or you will never thrive.
Husband and wife, whatever the worldly say
In ribald jest, are on the straight, sure way.
They are so knit no accident or strife
Harms them, particularly not the wife.
   So January thought, of whom I told,
Deeply considering as he grew old
The life of lusty joy and virtuous quiet
That marriage offers in its honey-diet.
And so one day he sent for all his friends
To ask their views on what he now intends.
   With serious face he spoke, and solemn
      tongue.
"My friends," he said, "I am no longer young;
God knows, I'm near the pit, I'm on the brink:
I have a soul, of which I ought to think.
   "My body I have foolishly expended;
Blessed be God, that still can be amended.
I have resolved to be a wedded man,
And that at once, in all the haste I can,

To some fair virgin; one of tender years.
Prepare yourselves to help as overseers
Against my wedding, for I will not wait.
I for my own part will investigate
And find a hasty match, if there be any:
But in as much as you, my friends, are many,
You may discern more readily than I
Where it would most befit me to ally.
   "But, my dear friends, you may as well
      be told
The woman must on no account be old,
Certainly under twenty, and demure.
Flesh should be young though fish should be
   mature;
As pike, not pickerel, makes the tastier meal,
Old beef is not so good as tender veal.
I'll have no woman thirty years of age;
That's only fodder, bean-straw for a cage.
Old women are as tricky in their trade
Of making trouble as the Boat of Wade[1]
And when they choose, they can be such a
   pest—
It's clear I'd never have a moment's rest.
Subtle is the scholar taught in several schools;
And women taught in many are no fools,
Half-scholars one might say; but when they're
   young
A man can still control them with his tongue
And guide them, should their duty seem
   too lax
Just as a man may model in warm wax.
So let me sum the matter in a clause;
I will have no old woman, for this cause.
For were I so unlucky as to marry
Where I could take no pleasure, I'd miscarry,
I should commit adultery and slide
Straight downwards to the devil when I died.
I could beget no child on her to greet me,
Yet I had rather that the dogs should eat me
Than that my fine inheritance should fall
Into strange hands, that let me tell you all.
   "I'm not a fool, I know the reason why
One ought to wed, though I could specify
Many who prate of it, but I engage
They know about as little as my page
Touching the reasons why to take a wife.
A man unable to be chaste in life
Should take a wife in holy dedication
And for the sake of lawful procreation
Of children, to the honour of God above,
Not as a paramour or lady-love,
But to curb lechery, which he should eschew,
Paying his debt whenever it falls due,

Or each a willing helper to the other
In trouble, like a sister to a brother
And live a life of holy chastity;
But, by your leave, sirs, that would not
    suit me,
For, God be thanked, I dare to make the claim,
I feel my limbs sufficient, strong and game
For all that is belonging to a man,
And am my own best judge in what I can.
I may seem hoary, but I'm like a tree
That blossoms white before the fruit can be;
Blossoming trees are neither dry nor dead
And I am only hoary on my head.
My heart and all my members are as green
As laurel is; all the year round, I mean.
And now you are informed of my intention
I beg you to agree without dissension."
    Various men gave various examples
Of classic marriages, convincing samples;
Some praised it certainly, some reprehended,
But at the last (to get the matter ended),
As altercation happens every day
Among good friends who mean to say
    their say,
An argument was presently begun
Between two friends of his, Placebo one,
Justinus, as I recollect, the other.
    Placebo said, "O January, dear brother,
You have no need, sweet lord, it must appear,
To take advice from anybody here,
Save that your sapience, after meditation,
Would prudently resist the inclination
To set aside the word of Solomon,
For this is what he said for everyone:
'Do all things by advice,' his saying went,
'And then you'll have no reason to repent.'
Though that may be what Solomon com-
    mends,
Dear lord, my brother, nay, my best of friends,
As surely as the Lord may give me rest
I think your own opinion is the best.
Take it from me—if I can find the phrase—
You know I've been a courtier all my days,
God knows unworthily, I make admission,
Yet I have stood in quite a high position
And among lords of very great estate;
But I have never joined in a debate
With them, or offered contradiction. Why?
Well, obviously, my lord knows more than I,
And what he says I hold as firm and stable;
I echo it as far as I am able.
No counsellor is such a fool as he
That, serving on a lord of high degree,

Dares to presume or even thinks it fit
To be superior to him in wit.
Lords are no fools, believe me . . . May I say
That you have also shown yourself today
A man of lofty views, an eloquent,
A holy-minded man, and I consent
To all you said. It should be written down.
A speech like that—there isn't one in town,
No, nor all Italy, able to supply it!
Christ holds himself more than rewarded
    by it.
In anyone at all advanced in age
It shows a lively spirit to engage
In taking a young wife. Ah, Lord of grace!
You've pinned your heart up in a jolly place;
Follow your inclination; I protest
Whatever you decide on will be best."
    Justinus who sat silent, having heard
Placebo speaking, then took up the word.
"Brother," he said, "be patient with me, pray;
You spoke your mind, now hear what I
    would say;
Seneca gave a lot of sound advice;
He says it's always better to think twice
Before you give away estate or pelf.
And therefore if you should advise yourself
In giving property away or land,
If it's important you should understand
Who is to get your goods, how much
    the more
You ought to think things over well before
You give away your body. If I may
I'd like to warn you; it is no child's play
Choosing a wife. It needs consideration,
In fact it asks a long investigation.
"Is she discreet and sober? Or a drinker?
Or arrogant? Or, in other ways, a stinker?
A scolder? Or extravagant? Too clannish?
Too poor? Too rich? Unnaturally mannish?
Although we know there isn't to be found
In all the world one that will trot quite sound,
Whether it's man or beast, the way we'd
    like it,
It were sufficient bargain, could we strike it,
In any woman, were one sure she had
More good among her qualities than bad.
    "But all this asks some leisure to review;
God knows that many is the tear I too
Have wept in secret since I had a wife.
Praise whoso will the married state of life
I find it a routine, a synthesis
Of cost and care, and wholly bare of bliss.
And yet the neighbours round about, by God,

Especially the women—in a squad—
Congratulate me that I chose to wive
The constantest, the meekest soul alive.
I know where the shoe pinches; but for you,
Why, you must please yourself in what
    you do.
You're old enough—that's not what I dis-
    parage—
To think before you enter into marriage,
Especially if your wife is young and fair.
By Him that made earth, water, fire and air,
The youngest man in this distinguished rout
Will have a busy task—you need not doubt—
To keep a woman to himself. Trust me,
You will not please her more than for, say,
    three
Years—that is, please her to the point of fer-
    vence.
Wives ask a lot in matters of observance.
I beg you not to take it the wrong way."
    "Well," said old January, "have you said
        your say?
Straw for your Seneca and proverbial tags;
Not worth a basketful of weeds and rags,
Your pedant-jargon! Wiser men than you,
As you have heard, take quite another view
Of my proposal. What would you reply,
Placebo?" "An accursed man, say I,
It is that offers an impediment,"
Said he, and so, by general consent,
His friends then rose, declaring it was good
That he should marry when and where he
    would.
    Busy imaginations, strange invention
And soaring fantasy obsessed the attention
Of January's soul, about his wedding.
Came many a lovely form and feature
    shedding
A rapture through his fancies night by night.
As who should take a mirror polished bright
And set it in the common market-place,
And watch the many figures pause and pace
Across his mirror; in the self-same way,
Old January allowed his choice to play
Mirroring all the girls that lived nearby,
Still undetermined where his thought
    should lie.
For were there one with beauty in her face
There was another standing high in grace
With people, for her grave benignity,
Whose voices gave her the supremacy.
Others were rich, but had a tarnished name.
    At last, and half in earnest, half in game,

He fixed on one, and setting her apart,
He banished all the others from his heart.
He chose her on his own authority,
For love is always blind and cannot see,
And when he lay in bed at night his thought
Pictured her in his heart, for he was caught
By her fresh beauty and her age so tender,
Her little waist, her arms so long and slender,
Her wise self-discipline, her gentle ways,
Her womanly bearing and her serious gaze.
His thought, descending on her thus, was fet-
    tered,
It seemed to him choice could not be bettered.
Once he was satisfied in this decision,
He held all other judgement in derision:
It was impossible to disagree
With him in taste, such was his fantasy.
    He sent his friends a very strong request
Begging the pleasure—would they do their
    best?—
Of an immediate visit. In his belief
They needn't be kept long; he would be brief,
For there was no more need to cast around;
His mind made up, he would not shift his
    ground.
    Placebo came and so did all the rest,
And January began with the request
That none should offer any argument
Against the purpose "which was his intent,
Pleasing to God Almighty, and," said he,
"The very ground of his prosperity."
    He said there was a maiden in the town
Whose beauty was indeed of great renown;
Her rank was not so great, to tell the truth,
But still she had her beauty and her youth;
She was the girl he wanted for his wife,
To lead a life of ease, a holy life.
And he would have her all—thank God for
    this!—
There would be shares for no one in his bliss.
He begged them then to labour in his need
And help to make his enterprise succeed,
For then, he said, his mind would be at rest
"With nothing to annoy me or molest,
But for one thing which pricks my conscience
    still,
So listen to me kindly if you will.
    "I've often," he continued, "heard ere this
That none may have two perfect kinds of bliss,
Bliss in this world, I mean, and bliss in
    Heaven;
Though he keep clear of sin—the deadly
    seven

And all the branches of their dreadful tree—
Yet there's so perfect a felicity
In marriage, so much pleasure, so few tears,
That I keep fearing, though advanced in years,
I shall be leading such a happy life,
So delicate, with neither grief nor strife,
That I shall have my heaven here in earth,
And may not that cost more than it is worth?
Since that true heaven costs a man so dear
In tribulation and in penance here,
How should I then, living in such delight,
As every married man, by day and night,
Has with his wife, attain to joys supernal
And enter into bliss with Christ Eternal?
That is my terror. Have you a suggestion,
My worthy brothers, to resolve the question?"

Justinus, who despised his nonsense, said,
Jesting as ever, what came into his head;
And wishing not to spin things out in chatter
Used no authorities to support the matter.
"If there's no obstacle," he said, "but this,
God by some mighty miracle of His
May show you mercy as He is wont to do,
And long before they come to bury you
May cause you to bewail your married life
In which you say there never can be strife,
And God forbid that there should not be sent
A special grace that husbands may repent,
And sent more often than to single men.
This, sir, would be my own conclusion then;
Never despair! You still may go to glory,
For she perhaps may prove your purgatory,
God's means of grace, as one might say, 'God's whip,'
To send your soul to Heaven with a skip
And swifter than an arrow from the bow!

"I hope to God that you will shortly know
There's no such paramount felicity
In marriage, nor is ever like to be,
As to disqualify you for salvation,
Provided you observe some moderation,
Tempering down the passions of your wife
With some restriction of your amorous life,
Keeping yourself, of course, from other sin.
My tale is done, but there! My wit is thin.
Be not afraid, dear brother, that's the moral.
Let us wade out, however, of this quarrel;
The Wife of Bath, if you can understand
Her views in the discussion now on hand,
Has put them well and briefly in this case:
And now, farewell, God have you in His Grace!"
He then took leave of January his brother

And they had no more speech with one another.
And when his friends saw that it needs must be
They made a careful marriage-treaty. She,
The girl agreed upon, whose name was May,
(And with the smallest possible delay)
Was to be married to this January.

And I assume there is no need to tarry
Over the bonds and documents they planned
To give her the possession of his land.
Or make you listen to her rich array,
But finally there came the happy day
And off at last to church the couple went
There to receive the holy sacrament.

Out came the priest, with stole about his neck,
And bade her be like Sarah at the beck
Of Abraham in wisdom, truth and grace,
Said all the prayers were proper to the case,
Then signed them with the cross and bade God bless
Them both, and made all sure in holiness.

Thus they were wedded in solemnity,
And at the wedding-banquet he and she
Sat with their worthier guests upon the dais.
Joy and delight filled the entire place,
Stringed instruments, victuals of every kind,
The daintiest all Italy could find.
Music broke forth as with the sound of Zion,
Not Orpheus nor the Theban king Amphion
Ever achieved so sweet a melody.

At every course there came loud minstrelsy
And Joab's trumpets never took the ear
So forcefully as this, nor half so clear
Those of Theodamas when Thebes held out.
Bacchus himself was pouring wine about
And Venus smiled on everyone in sight,
For January had become her knight
And wished to try his courage in the carriage
Of his new liberty combined with marriage.
Armed with a fire-brand she danced about
Before the bride and all the happy rout;
And certainly I'll go as far as this.
And say that Hymen, God of wedded bliss,
Never beheld so happy a wedded man.

Hold thou thy peace, O poet Martian,
Give us no more thy marital doxology
For Mercury on wedding with Philology!
Silence the song the Muses would have sung,
Thine is too small a pen, too weak a tongue,
To signalize this wedding or engage
To tell of tender youth and stooping age,
Such joy it is as none may write about:

Try it yourself and you will soon find out
If I'm a liar or not in such a case.

    For there sat May with so benign a face
That but to see her was a fairy-tale.
Queen Esther's eye could never so assail
Ahasuerus, never looked so meek;
Of so much loveliness I dare not speak,
Yet thus much of her beauty I will say
That she was like the brightest morn of May
With every grace and pleasure in her glance.
This January sat ravished, in a trance,
And every time he gazed upon her face
His heart began to menace her and race;
That night his arms would strain her with the
    ardour
That Paris showed for Helen, aye, and harder.
And yet he felt strong qualms of pity stir
To think he soon must do offence to her,
That very night, and thought, "O tender crea-
    ture!
Alas, God grant you may endure the nature
Of my desires, they are so sharp and hot.
I am aghast lest you sustain them not.
God hinder me from doing all I might!
But O I wish to God that it were night,
And the night last for ever! Oh, how slow . . .
I wish these guests would hurry up and go!"

    So he began to dedicate his labours
To getting rid politely of his neighbours,
And to detaching them from food supplies.
At last their reason told them they should rise;
They danced and drank and, left to their de-
    vices,
They went from room to room to scatter
    spices
About the house. Joy rose in every man
Except in one, a squire called Damian,
Who carved for January every day.

    He was so ravished by the sight of May
As to be mad with suffering; he could
Almost have died or fainted where he stood,
So sorely Venus burnt him with the brand
Which, as she danced, she carried in her hand.
And hastily the boy went off to bed;
No more of him at present need be said.
I leave him there to weep and to complain
Till fresh young May have pity on his pain.

    O perilous fire kindled in the bedding,
Domestic traitor, with the danger spreading!
O adder in the bosom, false of hue,
So sly, so homely-seeming, so untrue!
God shield us all from your acquaintanceship!
O January, drunk upon the lip

Of marriage, see your servant, Damian,
Who was your very squire, born your man,
Even now is meditating villainy.
O God unmask your household enemy!
Over the world no pestilence can roam
That is so foul as treachery at home.

    The sun had traced his arc with golden
    finger
Across the sky, caring no more to linger
On the horizon in that latitude.
Night with her mantel which is dark and rude
Had overspread the hemisphere about,
And gone were all the merry-making rout
Of January's guests, with hearty thanks,
And homeward each convivially spanks
To undertake such business as will keep
Him happy, till it should be time for sleep.

    Soon after this the restive January
Demanded bed; no longer would he tarry
Except to quaff a cordial for the fire
That claret laced with spice can lend desire;
For he had many potions, drugs as fine
As those that monk, accursed Constantine,
Has numbered in his book *De Coitu*.
He drank them all; not one did he eschew,
And to his private friends who lingered on
He said, "For God's love, hurry and be gone,
Empty the house politely if you can."
And presently they did so to a man.
A toast was drunk, the curtains back were
    thrown;
The bride was borne to bed as still as stone.
And when the priest had blessed the wed-
    ding-bed
The room was emptied and the guests were
    sped.

    Fast in the arms of January lay
His mate, his paradise, his fresh young May.
He lulled her, sought to kiss away all trouble;
The bristles of his beard were thick as stubble,
Much like a dog-fish skin, and sharp as briars,
Being newly shaved to sweeten his desires.
He rubbed his chin against her tender cheek
And said, "Alas, alas that I should seek
To trespass—yet I must—and to offend
You greatly too, my spouse, ere I descend.
Nevertheless consider this," said he,
"No workman, whatsoever he may be,
Can do his work both well and in a flurry;
This shall be done in perfect ease, no hurry.
It's of no consequence how long we play,
We are in holy wedlock, and we may.
And blessed be the yoke that we are in

For nothing we can do will count as sin.
A man is not a sinner with his wife,
He cannot hurt himself with his own knife;
We have the law's permission thus to play."
And so he laboured till the break of day,
Then took a sop of claret-sodden toast,
Sat up in bed as rigid as a post,
And started singing very loud and clear.
He kissed his wife and gave a wanton leer,
Feeling a coltish rage towards his darling
And chattering in the jargon of a starling.
The slack of skin about his neck was shaking
As thus he fell a-chanting and corn-cracking.

God knows what May was thinking in her
        heart,
Seeing him sit there in his shirt apart,
Wearing his night-cap, with his scrawny
        throat.
She didn't think his games were worth a groat.
    At last he said, "I think I'll take a rest;
Now day has come a little sleep were best."
And down he lay and slept till half-past eight;
Then he woke up, and seeing it was late,
Old January arose; but fresh young May
Kept her apartment until the fourth day
As women will, they do it for the best.
For every labourer must have time to rest,
For otherwise he can't keep labouring;
And that is true of every living thing,
Be it a fish, a bird, a beast, or man.

Now I will speak of woeful Damian
Languishing in his love, as will appear.
I would address him thus, if he could hear:
"O silly Damian! Alas, alas!
Answer my question; in your present pass
How are you going to tell her of your woe?
She's absolutely bound to answer no,
And if you speak, she's certain to betray you;
I can say nothing. God be your help, and stay
        you!"

Sick-hearted Damian in Venus' fire
Is so consumed, he's dying with desire;
And so he took his courage in his hand
To end a grief he could no longer stand
And with a pen that he contrived to borrow
He wrote a letter pouring out his sorrow,
After the fashion of a song or lay,
Indited to his lady, dazzling May,
And wrapped it in a purse of silk apart
To hang inside his shirt, upon his heart.
The moon, that stood in Taurus on the day
When January had wedded lovely May,
Had glided into Cancer; she of whom

I speak, fresh May, had meanwhile kept her
        room,
As is the custom among nobles all.
A bride of course should never eat in hall
Till four days afterwards, or three at least,
But when they're over, let her go and feast.

On the fourth day, from noon to noon
        complete,
And when high mass was over, in his seat
Sat January in his hall with May,
As fresh and bright as is a summer's day.
And it so happened that this good old man
Exclaimed, as he remembered Damian,
"Blessed St. Mary! How can such things be?
Why isn't Damian here to wait on me?
Is he still sick? What's happened? Is he up?"

The squires standing there to fill his cup
Excused him on the grounds that he was ill,
He was in bed, unfit for duty still;
No other reason could have made him tarry.
"I'm very sorry for it," said January,
"And he's a gentleman, to tell the truth,"
The old man said, "and if he died, poor youth,
It were a pity; he's a lad of worth.
I don't know anyone of equal birth
So wise, discreet and secret, and so able;
Thrifty and serviceable too at table.
As soon as possible after meat to-day
I'll visit him myself; and so shall May.
We'll give him all the comfort that we can."

Then everybody blessed the kind old man
So eager in his bounty and good breeding
To offer anything that might be needing
To comfort a sick squire; a gentle deed.

"Madam," said January, "take good heed
That after meat you and your women all,
When you have sought your room and left the
        hall,
Go up and have a look at Damian
And entertain him; he's a gentleman.
And tell him too that I shall do my best
To visit him myself, after my rest.
Now hurry on, be quick, and I shall bide me
Here, until you return to sleep beside me."
And on the word he rose and gave a call
To fetch a squire (the marshal of the hall)
And gave him some instructions. Fresh
        young May
With all her women took the shortest way
To Damian's room and sat beside his bed;
A warmth of comfort was in all she said,
Benignity and beauty in her glance.
And Damian, when at last he saw his chance,

Secretly took his purse and billet-doux,
Couched in the sweetest phrases that he knew,
And put it in her hand with nothing more
Than a long sigh, as deep as to the core;
But in a whisper he contrived to say,
"Mercy, have mercy! Don't give me away!
I should be killed if this were ever known."
The purse slid from his bosom to her own
And off she went. You get no more of me.
Back to old January then went she;
He was reclining on his bed by this.
He drew her to his arms with many a kiss,
Then settled back to sleep at once; and so
She then pretended that she had to go
Where everybody has to go at times.
There, after memorizing Damian's rhymes,
She tore them into pieces and she cast
Them softly down the privy-drain at last.

    Who fell into a study then but May?
And down beside old January she lay
Who slept until awoken by his cough.
He begged her then to strip her garments off
For he would have some pleasure of her, he
    said,
Her clothes were an encumbrance, to be shed.
And she obeyed, whether she would or no.
Lest I offend the precious, I will go
No further into what he did, or tell
Whether she thought it paradise or hell.
I leave them working thus as I suppose
Till it was evensong, and then they rose.

    Whether by destiny or accident,
By starry influence or natural bent,
Or whether some constellation held its state
In heaven to make the hour fortunate
For giving billet-doux and lending wing
To Venus—there's a time for everything,
The learned say—and get a lady's love,
I cannot tell. But God who sits above
And knows that every action has a cause,
Let Him decide, for I can only pause
In silence; this at least is true of May
That such was the impression made that day
And such her pity for that sick young man
She could not rid her heart of Damian,
Or of the wish to see his troubles ended.
"Whoever else," she thought, "may be of-
    fended,
I do not care; but I can promise this,
To love him more than anyone there is,
Though he mayn't have a shirt. I will be
    kind."
Pity flows swiftly in a noble mind.

    Here one may see how excellently free
In bounty women, on taking thought, can be.
Some female tyrants—many I have known—
Are pitiless, their hearts are made of stone
And would have rather let him die the death
Than yield their grace or favour by a breath,
And they exult in showing cruel pride,
Calmly indifferent to homicide.

    Soft May felt pity, you must understand.
She wrote a letter in her own fair hand
In which she granted him her very grace.
There needed nothing but the time and place
To grant the satisfaction he desired;
He was to have whatever he required.

    So when she saw occasion one fine day
To visit him, off went the lovely May
And thrust this letter down with subtle skill
Under his pillow, read it if he will.
She took him by the hand and squeezed it hard
(But secretly, for she was on her guard),
Bade him get well, then went without demur
To January who had called for her.

    And up rose happy Damian on the morrow;
Gone was all trace of malady and sorrow.
He preens himself and prunes and combs his
    curls
To take the fancy of this queen of girls.
To January his master, in addition
He was a very spaniel in submission,
And was so pleasant in his general drift
(Craft's all that matters if you have the gift),
That people spoke him well in every way,
But above all he stood in grace with May.
Thus I leave Damian, busy with his needs,
And turn once more to how my tale proceeds.

    Some writers argue that felicity
Wholly consists in pleasure; certainly
This noble January, as best he might
In all that was befitting to a knight,
Had planned to live deliciously in pleasure;
His house and all his finery and treasure
Were fashioned to his rank as are a king's,
And among other of his handsome things
He had a garden, walled about with stone;
So fair a garden never was there known.
For out of doubt I honestly suppose
That he who wrote the *Romance of the Rose*
Could not have pictured such magnificence;
Priapus never had the eloquence,
Though he be god of gardens, to re-tell
The beauty of this garden and the well
Under a laurel, standing ever-green.
Many a time King Pluto and his Queen

Prosérpina and all her fairy rout
Disported and made melody about
That well and held their dances, I am told.
This January, so noble, and so old,
Found walking in it such felicity
That no one was allowed to have the key
Except himself, and for its little wicket
He had a silver latch-key to unclick it
Or lock it up, and when his thought was set
Upon the need to pay his wife her debt
In summer season, thither would he go
With May his wife when there was none to
    know,
And anything they had not done in bed
There in the garden was performed instead,
So in this manner many a merry day
Was spent by January and lovely May.
But worldly joys, alas, may not endure
For January or anyone, be sure.

    Changeable Fortune, O unstable Chance,
Thine is the scorpion's treacherous advance!
Thy head all flattery, about to sting,
Thy tail a death, and death by poisoning.
O brittle joy, O venom sweet and strange,
O monster that so subtly canst arrange
Thy gifts and colour them with all the dyes
Of durability to catch the wise
And foolish too! Say, why hast thou deceived
Old January, thy friend, as he believed?
Thou hast bereft him of his sight, his eye
Is dark, and in his grief he longs to die.

    Alas this noble January, he
So generous once in his prosperity
Went blind; quite suddenly he lost his sight.
Pitiful loss! He wept it day and night,
While fires of jealousy seared his melancholy,
For fear his wife might fall into some folly.
His heart burned hot; he had been nothing
    loth,
Nay glad, if one had come to slay them both.
For neither on his death nor in his life
Was she to be the mistress or the wife
Of any other, but in weeds of state,
True as a turtle that has lost her mate,
She was to live, the garments on her back
A widow's, never anything but black.

    But in the end, after a month or two,
His sorrows cooled a little, it is true,
For when he saw there was no remedy
He took in patience his adversity,
Save that the ineradicable sting
Of jealousy embittered everything,
For so outrageous are the thoughts it rouses

That neither when at home nor in the houses
Of his acquaintance, no, nor anywhere
Would he allow his wife to take the air
Unless his hand were on her, day and night.
    Ah, how she wept, fresh as she was, and
        bright,
Who loved her Damian, and with so benign
A love that sudden death was her design
Unless she could enjoy him; so at first
She wept and waited for her heart to burst.

    And Damian too, upon the other part,
Became in turn so sorrowful of heart
That none was ever like him: night or day
There never was a chance to speak to May
As to his purpose, no, nor anything near it,
Unless old January was there to hear it,
Holding her hand and never letting go.
Nevertheless by writing to and fro
And private signals, Damian knew her mind;
And she was well aware what he designed.
O January, what might it thee avail
Though thou couldst see as far as ship can sail?
As well be blind and be deceived as be
Deceived as others are that still can see.
Consider Argus with his hundred eyes
Poring and prying, yet for all these spies
He was deceived, and many more I know,
God wot, who sagely think they are not so.
Least said is soonest mended; say no more.

    Now this fresh May of whom I spoke
        before
Took some warm wax and fashioned an im-
        pression
Of that same key (in January's possession)
Into the garden, where he often went.
Damian, who knew exactly what she meant,
Secretly forged a counterfeited key.
That's all there is to say, but presently
A wonder will befall, if you will wait,
Thanks to this key and to the wicket-gate.

    O noble Ovid, that was truly spoken
When you affirmed there was no cunning
        token
Or trickery, however long or hot,
That lovers could not find. For did they not
When Pyramus and Thisbe, I recall,
Though strictly watched, held converse
        through a wall?
There was a trick that none could have fore-
        cast!
But to our purpose; ere a week had passed,
Before July was on them, it befell
That January's thoughts began to swell,

Incited by his wife, with eager wishes
To be at play with her among the bushes
In his walled garden, he and she alone,
And so at last one morning he made moan
To May with this intention: "Ah," said he,
"Rise up, my wife, my love, my lady free!
The turtle's voice is heard, my dove, my pet.
Winter is gone with all its rain and wet;
Come out with me, bright-eyes, my
    columbine,
O how far fairer are thy breasts than wine!
Our garden is enclosed and walled about;
White spouse, come forth to me; ah, never
    doubt
But I am wounded to the heart, dear wife,
For love of you, unspotted in your life
As well I know. Come forth to take our
    pleasures,
Wife of my choice and treasure of my trea-
    sures!"
    He got these lewd old words out of a book.
And May at once gave Damian a look
Signalling he should go before and wait;
So Damian ran ahead, unlocked the gate
And darted in as swiftly as a bird,
He managed to be neither seen nor heard,
And crouched beneath the bushes on his own.
    And then this January, blind as stone,
Came hand in hand with May, but unat-
    tended,
And down into the garden they descended
And having entered clapped the wicket to.
    "Now wife," he said, "none's here but I
        and you,
And you are she, the creature I best love.
For by the Lord that sits in Heaven above,
Believe me I would die upon the knife
Rather than hurt you, truest, dearest wife.
Remember how I chose you, for God's sake;
Not covetously nor in hope to make,
But only for the love I had to you.
And though I may be old and sightless too,
Be true to me and I will tell you why.
    "Three things for certain you shall win
        thereby:
First, love of Christ; next, honour to yourself;
Last, your inheritance, my lands and pelf,
Towers and towns; draw the agreement up,
They're yours, it shall be signed before we sup.
But first, as God may bring my soul to bliss,
I pray you seal the covenant with a kiss.
And though I may be jealous, blame me not;
You are so deeply printed in my thought

That when I see your beauty, and engage
That thought with my dislikable old age,
I cannot—though it might be death to me—
Forbear a moment of your company
For very love; I say it with no doubt.
Now kiss me, wife, and let us roam about."
    Fresh-hearted May on hearing what he said
Benignly answered him with drooping head,
But first and foremost she began to weep.
"Indeed," she said, "I have a soul to keep
No less than you, and then there is my honour
Which for a wife is like a flower upon her.
I put it in your hands for good or ill
When the priest bound my body to your will,
So let me answer of my own accord
If you will give me leave, beloved lord;
I pray to God that never dawn the day
—Or let me die as foully as I may—
When I shall do my family that shame
Or bring so much dishonour on my name
As to be false. And if my love grow slack,
Take me and strip me, sew me in a sack
And drop me in the nearest lake to drown.
I am no common woman of the town,
I am of gentle birth, I keep aloof.
So why speak thus to me, for what reproof
Have I deserved? It's men that are untrue
And women, women ever blamed anew.
I think it a pretence that men profess;
They hide behind a charge of faithlessness."
    And as she spoke she saw a short way off
Young Damian in his bush. She gave a cough
And signalled with a finger quickly where
He was to climb into a tree—a pear—
Heavily charged with fruit, and up he went,
Perfectly understanding what she meant,
Or any other signal, I may state,
Better than January could, her mate.
For she had written to him, never doubt it,
Telling him all and how to set about it.
And there I leave him sitting, by your pardon,
While May and January roamed the garden.
    Bright was the day and blue the firmament,
Down fell the golden flood that Phoebus sent
To gladden every flower with his beams;
He was in Gemini at the time, it seems,
And but a little from his declination
In Cancer, which is Jupiter's exaltation.
And so it happened through the golden tide
Into the garden from the further side
Came Pluto who is king of Fairyland
And many a lady of his elfin band
Behind his queen, the lady Proserpine,

Ravished by him from Aetna, I incline
To think it is in Claudian you can read
How she was gathering flowers in a mead
And how he fetched her in his grisly cart.
The King of Faery sat him down apart
Upon a little bench of turfy green,
And then he turned and thus addressed his
    queen:
    "Dear wife," he said, "what no one can
      gainsay
And what experience shows us every day
Are the foul treacheries women do to men.
Ten thousand tales, and multiply by ten,
Record your notable untruth and lightness.
O Solomon in thy wisdom, wealth and bright-
    ness,
Replete in sapience as in worldly glory,
How memorable are thy words and story
To every creature capable of reason!
Of man's true bounty and of woman's treason
Thou saidst, 'Among a thousand found I one,
And yet among all women found I none.'
    "So said the king who knew your wicked-
      ness;
And Jesus son of Sirach,[2] as I guess,
Seldom says much of you in reverence—
Wild fire and a corruptive pestilence
Fall down upon you all to burn and blight!
Do you not see that honourable knight
Who, being blind and old and unobservant,
Is to be cuckolded by his own servant?
Look, there he sits, that lecher in the tree!
Now will I grant it of my majesty
To this blind, old and estimable knight
That he shall instantly receive his sight
Whenever his wife begins her villainy.
He shall know all about her harlotry
Both in rebuke of her and others too."
    "So that," the queen replied, "is what
      you'll do!
Now, by my grandsire's soul, though she is
    young
I'll put a ready answer on her tongue
And every woman's after, for her sake.
Though taken in their guilt they yet
    shall make
A bold-faced explanation to excuse them
And bear down all who venture to accuse them;
For lack of answer none of them shall die.
Though a man saw things with his naked eye
We'll face it out, we women, and be bold
To weep and swear, insinuate and scold
As long as men are gullible as geese.

"What do I care for your authorities?
I'm well aware this Jew, this Solomon,
Found fools among us women, many a one;
But if he never found a woman true,
God knows that there are many men who do,
Who find them faithful, virtuous and good.
Witness all those in Christian sisterhood
Who proved their constancy by martyrdom.
And Roman history has mentioned some,
Aye many, women of exceeding truth.
Now keep your temper, sir, though he, for-
    sooth,
Said there were no good women, if you can.
Consider the opinion of this man.
He meant it thus, that sovereign constancy
Is God's alone who sits in Trinity.
Hey! God knows Solomon is only one;
Why do you make so much of Solomon?
What though he built God's temple in the
    story?
What though he were so rich, so high in
    glory?
He made a temple for false gods as well,
And what could be more reprehensible?
Plaster him over as you may, dear sir,
He was a lecher and idolater,
And in his latter days forsook the Lord;
Had God not spared him, as the books record,
Because He loved his father, surely he would
Have lost his kingdom, rather than that he
    should.
And all the villainous terms that you apply
To women, I value at a butterfly!
I am a woman and I needs must speak
Or swell until I burst. Shall I be meek
If he has said that we were wrangleresses?
As ever I may hope to flaunt my tresses,
I will not spare for manners or politeness
To rail at one who rails at woman's lightness."
    "Madam," he said, "be angry now no more;
I give it up. But seeing that I swore
Upon my oath to grant him sight again,
I'll stand by what I said, I tell you plain.
I am a king, it fits me not to lie."
"And I'm the Queen of Fairyland, say I!
Her answer she shall have, I undertake.
Let us have no more words, for goodness' sake.
Indeed I don't intend to be contrary."
    Now let us turn again to January
Who walked the garden with his airy May
And sang more merrily than a popinjay,
"I love you best, and ever shall, my sweet!"
So long among the paths had strayed their feet

That they at last had reached the very tree
Where Damian sat in waiting merrily,
High in his leafy bower of fresh green.
And fresh young May, so shiningly serene,
Began to sigh and said "Oh! I've a pain!
Oh Sir! Whatever happens, let me gain
One of those pears up there that I can see,
Or I shall die! I long so terribly
To eat a little pear, it looks so green.
O help me for the love of Heaven's Queen!
I warn you that a woman in my plight
May often feel so great an appetite
For fruit that she may die to go without."
    "Alas," he said, "that there's no boy about,
Able to climb. Alas, alas," said he,
"That I am blind." "No matter, sir," said she,
"For if you would consent—there's nothing
      in it—
To hold the pear-tree in your arms a minute
(I know you have no confidence in me),
Then I could climb up well enough," said she,
"If I could set my foot upon your back."
    "Of course," he said, "why, you shall
      never lack
For that, or my heart's blood to do you good."
And down he stooped; upon his back she
      stood,
Catching a branch, and with a spring she
      thence
—Ladies, I beg you not to take offence,
I can't embellish, I'm a simple man—
Went up into the tree, and Damian
Pulled up her smock at once and in he thrust.
    And when King Pluto saw this shame-
      ful lust
He gave back sight to January once more
And made him see far better than before.
Never was man more taken with delight
Than January when he received his sight.
And his first thought was to behold his love.
He cast his eyes into the tree above
Only to see that Damian had addressed
His wife in ways that cannot be expressed
Unless I use a most discourteous word.
He gave a roaring cry, as might be heard
From stricken mothers when their babies die.
"Help! Out upon you!" He began to cry.
"Strong Madam Strumpet! What are you up
      to there?"
"What ails you, sir?" said she, "what makes
      you swear?
Have patience, use the reason in your mind,
I've helped you back to sight when you were
      blind!

Upon my soul I'm telling you no lies;
They told me if I wished to heal your eyes
Nothing could cure them better than for me
To struggle with a fellow in a tree.
God knows it was a kindness that I meant."
"Struggle?" said he, "Yes! Anyhow, in it
      went!
God send you both a shameful death to die!
He had you, I saw it with my very eye,
And if I did not, hang me by the neck!"
    "Why then," she said, "my medicine's
      gone to wreck,
For certainly if you could really see
You'd never say such words as those to me;
You caught some glimpses, but your sight's
      not good."
"I see," he said, "as well as ever I could,
Thanks be to God! And with both eyes, I do!
And that, I swear, is what he seemed to do."
    "You're hazy, hazy, my good sir," said she;
"That's all I get for helping you to see.
Alas," she said, "that ever I was so kind!"
    "Dear wife," said January, "never mind,
Come down, dear heart, and if I've slan-
      dered you
God knows I'm punished for it. Come
      down, do!
But by my father's soul, it seemed to me
That Damian had enjoyed you in the tree
And that your smock was pulled up over your
      breast."
"Well, think," she said, "as it may please you
      best,
But, Sir, when suddenly a man awakes,
He cannot grasp a thing at once, it takes
A little time to do so perfectly,
For he is dazed at first and cannot see.
Just so a man who has been blind for long
Cannot expect his sight to be so strong
At first, or see as well as those may do
Who've had their eyesight back a day or two.
Until your sight has settled down a bit
You may be frequently deceived by it.
Be careful then, for by our heavenly King
Many a man feels sure he's seen a thing
Which was quite different really, he may
      fudge it;
Misapprehend a thing and you'll misjudge it."
    And on the word she jumped down from
      the tree.
And January—who is glad but he?—
Kissed her and clasped her in his arms—how
      often!—
And stroked her womb caressingly to soften

Her indignation. To his palace then
He led her home. Be happy, gentlemen,
That finishes my tale of January;
God and his Mother guard us, blessed Mary!

Epilogue to the Merchant's Tale

"Ey, mercy of God!" our Host exclaimed
       thereat,
"May God preserve me from a wife like that!
Just look what cunning tricks and subtleties
There are in woman! Busy little bees
They are, deceiving silly men like us!
They're always sliding and evading thus,
Dodging the truth; the Merchant's tale has
       shown it
And it's as true as steel—I have to own it.
I have a wife myself, a poor one too,
But what a tongue! She is a blabbing shrew,
And she has other vices, plenty more.
Well, let it go! No sense to rub a sore.
But, d'you know what? In confidence,
       good sir,
I much regret that I am tied to her.
Were I to reckon her vices one by one,
I'd only be a fool when I had done;
And why? Because it would be sure to be
Reported back to her, by two or three
Among us here; by whom I needn't say;
In all such matters women find a way.
And anyhow my brains would hardly run
To telling you, and so my story's done."

THE SQUIRE'S TALE
The Squire's Prologue

"Squire, come up and if you feel disposed
Say something about love—it is supposed
You know as much of that as any man."
"O no, sir," he replied, "but what I can
I'll do with all my heart. I won't rebel
Against your pleasure; I've a tale to tell.
Have me excused if I should speak amiss,
My will is good and, look, my tale is this."

The Squire's Tale
PART I

At Tzarev in the land of Tartary
There dwelt a king at war with Muscovy
Which brought the death of many a
       doughty man.
This noble king was known as Cambuskan[1]
And in his time enjoyed such great renown
That nowhere in that region up or down

Was one so excellent in everything;
Nothing he lacked belonging to a king.
    As to the faith in which he had been born
He kept such loyalties as he had sworn,
Then he was powerful and wise and brave,
Compassionate and just, and if he gave
His word he kept it, being honourable,
The same to all, benevolent, and stable
As is a circle's centre; and in a fight
As emulous as any squire or knight,
Young, personable, fresh and fortunate,
Maintaining such a kingliness of state
There never was his match in mortal man.
    This noble king, this Tartar Cambuskan,
Begat two sons of Elpheta his wife.
The elder bore the name of Algarsyf,
The other son, the younger, Cambalo.
He had another child, a daughter though,
Youngest of all; her name was Canace.
To tell her beauty is too much for me,
Lying beyond what tongue of mine can sing;
I dare not undertake so high a thing.
My English too is insufficient for it,
It asks a rhetorician to explore it,
A poet in the colours of that art,
To give a fair account of every part.
I am none such, I speak as best I can.
    Now it so happened that when Cambuskan
Had borne his diadem for twenty years,
As was his usual custom it appears,
He had the feast of his nativity
Proclaimed throughout the land of Tartary.
It was the Ides of March, in the new year;
Phoebus the sun shone happily and clear
For he was near his point of exaltation
In face of Mars, and there he held his station
In *Aries,* and that's a sultry sign.
Cheerful the weather, vigorous and benign,
And all the birds against the sunny sheen,
What with the season and the early green,
Sang the loud canticles of their affection,
For, as it seemed, at last they had protection
Against the sword of winter, keen and cold.
    This noble Cambuskan of whom I told
Sat on his dais in a royal robe,
High on his throne with diadem and globe,
And there held feast in all his power enfurled,
And there was nothing like it in the world.
If I should pause to tell of his array
The task would occupy a summer's day,
Nor is there any need I should enforce
Attention to his banquet, course on course,
Or number the quaint dishes they put on,
The heron-chick, the richly roasted swan,

For in that country veteran knights report
There are some meats esteemed the dainti-
    est sort
Though in this country their esteem is small,
But there is none who could report it all,
So let me not delay you—it is prime
Of day, it would be fruitless loss of time.

Let me retrace my footsteps to their source.
It happened, close upon the second course,
As the king sat with his nobility
Listening to instruments of minstrelsy
That made delicious music in the hall,
Suddenly at the door in sight of all
There came a knight upon a steed of brass
Bearing a mirror, broad and made of glass.
Upon his thumb he had a golden ring
And at his side a naked sword a-swing,
And up he rode and reached the royal table.
In all that hall not one of them was able
To speak a word for wonder at this knight;
They waited, young and old, and watched the
    sight.

This stranger-knight so suddenly pre-
    sented,
Bare-headed, armed and richly ornamented,
Saluted king and queen and nobles all
In order as they sat about the hall
With such deep reverence and comely grace
Not only in his speech but in his face,
That Gawain,[2] ever courteous, ever bland,
Though he were come again from fairyland
A greater courtesy could not have shown.
And thus before High Table and the throne
He gave his message in a manly voice
In his own language, with a perfect choice
Of phrase, faultless in syllable or letter;
And, that his story might appear the better,
Gesture and word were fitted each to each,
As taught to those that learn the art of speech,
And though I lack his talent to beguile
And cannot climb over so tall a stile,
I say, as to their general content,
The words I use amount to what he meant,
So far as I can trust my memory.

"The King of India and Araby,
Who is my sovereign lord, this solemn day
Salutes your Majesty as best he may
And sends you here in honour of your feast,
Through me who am your servant, though
    the least,
This steed of brass that easily may run
Within the natural circuit of the sun,
That is to say in four and twenty hours,

Wherever you may wish, in drought or
    showers,
And bear your body to whatever place
Your heart desires, at a gentle pace
And without hurt to you through foul or fair.
If you should wish to fly, and mount the air
As does an eagle when it seeks to soar,
This very steed will bear you as before
In perfect safety on your chosen track,
Though you should fall asleep upon his back,
And, when you twist this pin, return again.

"He that devised it had a cunning brain;
He watched through many a change of con-
    stellation
Ere finding one to suit his operation,
And he knew many a magic seal and spell.

"This mirror that I have in hand as well
Is such that those who look in it may see
The coming shadow of adversity
Upon yourself and kingdom, it will show
You plainly who is friend and who is foe.
More than all this, if any lady bright
Has set on any man her heart's delight,
If he be false she shall perceive his shady
And treacherous conduct, and the other lady,
So openly, nothing will hide his treason.
And so, against this lusty summer season,
This mirror and this ring are sent by me,
As you behold, to Lady Canace
Your excellent and lovely daughter here.

"The virtue of the ring, as will appear,
Stands in this point; if she be not averse
To wear it on her thumb or in her purse,
There is no bird that flies beneath the reach
Of heaven but she will understand its speech
And know its meaning openly and plain
And in its language answer it again.
Of every rooted grass that grows on earth
She shall have knowledge too and test its
    worth
In sickness, or on wounds, however wide.

"This naked sword here hanging at my side
Retains the property to cut and bite
The armour of whatever man you smite,
Though it were thicker than a branching oak;
And when a man is wounded by its stroke,
Nothing can heal him till the sword is laid
In mercy flat upon the wound it made,
Where he was hurt. This is as much to say
Lay the blade flat, turning the edge away,
And stroke the wound, and you will see it
    close;
This is the very truth in sober prose.

While it is in your hold it cannot fail."
    The stranger-knight, thus having told his
      tale,
Rode out of hall, dismounted and had done.
His steed of brass that glittered like the sun
Stood in the courtyard still as any stone.
They gave the knight a chamber of his own,
Unarmed and feasted him, and in a while
His gifts were carried forth in royal style,
That is to say the mirror and the sword,
And brought to the high tower under ward
Of certain officers appointed for it.
    As for the ring, in solemn pomp they
      bore it
To Canace herself who sat at table.
But I assure you all it is no fable,
That horse of brass could not be raised or
    slewed
But stood its ground as if it had been glued.
It was of no avail to drive or bully,
Use windlass, engine, artifice or pulley;
And why? Because they didn't know the
    dodge.
And so they were obliged to let it lodge
Below until the knight had shown them how
To shift him; you shall hear it, but not now.
    Great was the crowd that swarmed about in
      force
To gaze upon the stationary horse.
It was as tall, as broad, and of a length
Just as proportionable to its strength
As any courser bred in Lombardy,
Quick-eyed, as horsely as a horse can be,
Like an Apulian steed, as highly bred.
And I assure you that from tail to head
Nothing could be improved by art or nature,
So they supposed at least who saw the crea-
    ture.
But yet the wonder nothing could surpass
Was how it went if it were made of brass.
Some thought it came from fairyland's domin-
    ions.
    Various men gave various opinions,
As many heads, so many fallacies.
They murmured round it like a swarm of bees
And guessed according to their fantasy,
Or quoted snatches of old poetry
Saying it was like Pegasus of old,
The fabled horse that flew on wings of gold,
Or it was Sinon's horse by whose employ
The Greeks had brought destruction upon
    Troy,
As one may read in those old epic tales.

Said one of them, "My spirit fairly quails
To think there may be men-of-arms within it
Plotting to take our town this very minute.
It would be well if such a thing were known."
Another, whispering to his friend alone,
Muttered, "He's wrong. More like some ap-
    parition
Or trick-illusion made by a magician,
Like what these jugglers do at feasts of state."
    Thus they kept up the jangle of debate
As the illiterate are wont to do
When subtler things are offered to their view
Than their unletteredness can comprehend;
They reach the wrong conclusions in the end.
    Some wondered at the mirror and its power
(It had been taken to the master-tower)
And how such things could be foreseen in it.
Another said that such a thing could fit
Quite naturally by the skilled direction
Of angles, by the laws of light-reflection,
And said there was another such in Rome.
Then they referred to many a learned tome
By Aristotle and by Alhazen
And Witelo and other learned men[3]
Who when alive had written down directives
For use of cunning mirrors and perspectives,
As anyone can tell who has explored
These authors. Others wondered at the sword
That had the power to pierce through any-
    thing,
And spoke of Telephus the Mysian king,
And of Achilles and his marvellous spear,
Able to heal no less than it could shear,
Exactly like this sword, that at a word
Could wound a man or heal him, as you heard.
    They spoke of sundry ways of hardening
      metal
By various ointments, and they tried to settle
The times and methods for this mystery,
Which are unknown, at any rate to me.
    And then they spoke about the magic ring
Given to Canace, a marvellous thing,
Concluding thus: "None such, as one sup-
    poses,
Was ever known; but Solomon and Moses
Were said to have been cunning in that art."
Thus people spoke in little groups apart;
And others said how strange it was to learn
That glass is made out of the ash of fern,
Though bearing no resemblances to glass;
But being used to this they let it pass,
The argument declined, they ceased to
    wonder,

Like those who speculate on what makes
    thunder,
Ebb, flood or mist, how gossamer is blown,
Or anything until the cause is known.
And so they guessed and judged as they
    were able
Until the king began to rise from table.
    Phoebus was over the meridian line;
It was the hour of the ascending sign
Of royal *Leo* with his Aldiran,[4]
And this great Tartar king, this Cambuskan,
Rose from the board in all his majesty.
Before him went a blare of minstrelsy
Until he reached the presence-room sur-
    rounded
By divers instruments, and these were sounded
So sweetly it was heaven to those that listened.
Children of Venus glided there and glistened
In happy dance, for she was mounted high
In *Piscis,* and looked down with friendly eye.
    The noble king was seated on his throne;
The stranger-knight was fetched and he alone
Was chosen forth to dance with Canace.
Great was the revelling and jollity,
It went beyond all dull imagination;
Only a man who knows the exaltation
Of serving love, a man as fresh as May,
A gamesome one, could tell of their array.
    For who could paint the circling of their
      dances,
So foreign to us, or the countenances
So subtle-smooth in their dissimulations
For fear of jealousy's insinuations?
No one but Launcelot and he is dead.
Pass over them and leave them there to tread
Their long delight, beyond all words of mine.
So on they danced till it was time to dine.
    The steward bids them hurry with the
      spices
And fetch the wine, the minstrelsy entices,
The ushers and the squires in a pack
Run off and bring the wines and spices back.
They ate and drank, and having left the table
They sought the temple, as was reasonable.
The service done, they feasted all day long.
Why should I tell you what they served the
    throng?
Everyone knows that at a royal feast
There's plenty for the greatest and the least,
And delicacies more than I would know.
    His supper done, the king proposed to go
And see this horse of brass, with all his rout
Of lords and ladies standing round about.

Such the amazement at this brazen horse,
Not since the siege of Troy had run its course,
At which another horse amazed her men,
Had there been such astonishment as then.
The king at last put question to the knight
As to this courser's properties and might,
Begging him to explain the beast's control.
    This horse began to dance and caracole
Under its master's hand that held the rein;
He answered, "Sir, there's nothing to
    explain,
But this; if you would ride it far or near,
Just twirl this pin that's standing in its ear,
As when we are alone I soon can show,
Then name the country where you would
    wish to go,
Or else the place, wherever you would ride,
And having reached it, if you so decide,
Bid him descend and twirl another pin,
For all the mechanism lies therein,
And down he'll go to carry out your will
And having reached the ground will stand
    stock-still.
Whatever then the world may do or say
He cannot thence be dragged or borne away.
    "To make him move or seek some other
      place
Twirl *this* pin and he'll vanish into space,
Yes, disappear completely out of sight,
Yet will return to you by day or night
If you should please to summon him again
After a manner that I shall explain
To you alone, and that without delay;
Ride when you will, there is no more to say."
    The king, informed by what the knight had
      said,
And once he had it firmly in his head
How to control the beast in everything,
How blithe, how happy was this doughty
    king!
And he returned to revel as before.
Then they took off the bridle that it wore
And laid it with his treasures in the tower.
The horse then vanished; it's beyond my
    power
To tell you how, you get no more from me.
And thus I leave, in joy and jollity,
This Cambuskan, feasting with all his train
Till dawn of day had almost sprung again.

PART II

The nourisher of all digestion, Sleep,
Began to wink upon them. "Drinking deep,"

He said, "and heavy toil, for slumber call."
And with a yawning mouth he kissed
    them all,
Saying, "To bed, to bed, it is the hour
Of my dominion, blood is in its power.
Cherish your blood," he whispered, "nature's
    friend."
    They thanked him yawningly and in
        the end
By twos and threes they wandered off to rest
As sleep ordained, they took it for the best.
What dreams they had shall not be told,
    for me;
Their heads were full of the fumosity
That causes dreams which are of no account.
And so they lay and slept until the fount
Of day filled heaven, all but Canace;
For she was temperate and womanly
And having kissed her father, had departed
And sought her rest before the evening
    started.
She had no wish to pale her lovely cheek
Or greet the morrow colourless and bleak.
    She slept her beauty sleep and then awoke,
And at her waking, in her heart there spoke
Such joy about her glass and magic ring
That twenty times she felt her colour spring.
She had dreamed visions from the deep im-
    pression
Made by the magic glass, her new possession.
    So ere the sun began its upward glide
She called the waiting-woman at her side
And told her that it was her wish to rise.
    Like all old women, glad to be as wise
As are their mistresses, the crone replied,
"What, madam, do you mean to go outside
So early? Everyone is still asleep."
"I will arise," she said, "I cannot keep
In bed or sleep, I want to walk about."
    Her woman called the servants in a rout
And up they got—some ten or twelve there
    were—
And up rose Canace as fresh and fair,
As bright and ruddy as the early sun
When by some four degrees it has begun
To rise into the *Ram*. It was no higher
When she was ready; forth at her desire
With easy pace, and gowned to greet the May,
She lightly went to walk on foot and play.
Some five or six were with her, and, content,
Forth by an alley through the park she went.
    There was a mist that glided from the earth
And gave the sun a huge and ruddy girth,

And yet it was so beautiful a sight
That all their hearts were lifted in delight,
What with the season and the dawn-light
    springing
And noise of all the birds in heaven singing,
For instantly she knew what they were saying
And understood the meaning in their maying.
    The knot and gist of every tale that's told,
If lingered out till all desire be cold
In those that listen and the moment's past,
Savours the less the longer it may last
By fulsomeness of its prolixity,
And for that reason as it seems to me
I ought to reach that knot of which I'm
    talking
And make an end, and quickly, of her
    walking.
    Amidst a tree so parched it seemed of chalk
Where Canace came dallying in her walk
Above her head a falcon sat on high.
This bird began so piteously to cry
That all the woods re-echoed her distress.
And she had scourged herself with pitiless
Beatings of her wings; a crimson flood
Poured down and painted all the tree with
    blood,
As ever and again with scream and shriek
She bent and tore her body with her beak.
There is no tiger, no, nor cruel beast
That dwells in wood or forest, west or east,
But would have wept if weep indeed it could
In pity of her, shrieking as she stood.
And never yet has been a man to tell
—If only I could describe a falcon well!—
Of such another bird, as fair to see
Both in its plumage and nobility
Of form and attribute, or find her twin.
    It seemed this falcon was a peregrine
From foreign country; bleeding there she
    stood,
Fainting from time to time from loss of blood,
Till she had nearly fallen from the tree.
    This beautiful king's daughter, Canace,
That on her finger bore the curious ring
By which she understood whatever thing
Birds in their language said, and which could
    teach
Her how to answer in their natural speech,
Had understood the words the falcon said;
The pity of it almost struck her dead.
    Up to the tree she hastened at her cries
And looking with compassion in her eyes
Held out her lap towards it, knowing well

The bird was like to faint, and if she fell
For lack of blood, she would be there at hand
Below the branches. Long she seemed to stand
And wait, and then at last began to talk,
As you shall hear, and thus addressed the
    hawk.
    "What is the cause, if you are free to tell,
That puts you to the furious pain of Hell?"
Said Canace to the poor bird above.
"Is it for grief in death, or loss of love?
For as I think these have the greatest part
Among the sorrows of a noble heart.
Other misfortunes one may well contemn,
The way is open for avenging them,
So that it must be either love or loss
That is occasion for your cruel cross,
For none, I see, has hunted you today.
God's love, have pity on yourself, or say
How I can help you. Neither east nor west
Was ever bird or beast so sore distressed
That ever I saw, or in such piteous plight;
It kills my heart to witness such a sight.
I feel such great compassion, come to me,
Come down for love of God and leave the
    tree,
For as I am the daughter of a king,
If I knew verily the cause and spring
Of your misfortunes, were it in my power
I would make all things well this very hour.
Great God of nature, help me so to do!
I shall find herbs enough and salves for you
To heal your wounds, and quickly if you
    will."
    The falcon gave a shriek more piteous still
Than any yet and fell to earth; she lay
Stone-still for she had fainted dead away,
Till, lifted up by Canace and taken
Into her lap, the bird began to waken,
And, being recovered, had the strength to talk,
Answering in the language of a hawk:
    "That pity is swift to course in noble heart,
Feeling the likeness of another's smart,
Is daily proved, as anyone can see,
Both by experience and authority,
For gentleness of birth and breeding shows
Itself in gentleness; you feel my woes
As I can see, and sure it is a fashion
Well fitting a princess to show compassion
As you have done, my lovely Canace,
In true and womanly benignity
That nature planted in your disposition.
And in no hope to better my condition
But to obey your generosity,

Also that others may be warned by me,
As lions may take warning when a pup[5]
Is punished, I will therefore take it up
And make a full confession of my woe
While yet there is the time before I go."
    And ever while the falcon said her say
The other wept as she would melt away
Until the falcon bade her to be still
And sighing spoke according to her will.
    "Where I was bred—alas, the cruel day!—
And fostered in a rock of marble grey
So tenderly that nothing troubled me,
I never knew the word adversity
Till I could wing aloft into the sky.
    "There was a tercelet[6] that lived nearby
Who seemed a very well of gentle breeding;
Yet he was filled with treachery, exceeding
In all that's false. He wore the humble cloak
And colour of true faith in all he spoke,
An eagerness to please me and to serve.
Who could think such a hawk had power to
    swerve?
Dyed in the grain they were, those treacher-
    ous powers,
Just as a serpent hides itself in flowers,
Ready to strike, and waits the moment fit,
Just so this god of love, this hypocrite,
Kept up all ceremonious obligations,
The sweet observances and protestations
That make the music of a gentle love.
    "But as a sepulchre is white above
The rotting corpse within, as we are told,
Just so this hypocrite blew hot and cold
And in this way pursued his treacherous bent;
None knew, unless the devil, what he meant.
    "So long I heard his weeping and com-
    plaining,
So long beheld the service he was feigning,
My heart, too foolish-pitiful to sound him,
All innocent of the treachery that
    crowned him,
Fearing his death (for so it seemed to me),
Believed his oaths, believed him trustworthy,
And granted him my love, on this condition,
That my good name, my honour and position
In public and in private had no hurt;
That is to say according to desert
In him, my heart and thought were his for
    ever,
But otherwise God knows, and he knew,
    never.
I took his heart, exchanging it for mine.
    "How true the saying in the ancient line,

'Thieves' thoughts are not the thoughts of
  honest men,'
For seeing things had gone so far by then,
That I had fully granted him my love
In such a way as I have told above
And had as freely given my heart as he
Had sworn his own was given up to me,
Straightway this tiger with his double heart
Fell on his knees and played the humble part
With such devout and bashful reverence
He seemed a noble lover, one whose sense
Was ravished, one would think, for very joy.

"Not Jason, no, nor Paris, Prince of Troy
—Did I say Jason? Sure, no other man
Since Lamech was, Lamech who first began,
So it is said, the game of loving two,
Has ever, since the world itself was new,
Thought or contrived the twenty thou-
  sandth part
Of counterfeited sophistry and art
As did my love. None fit to tie his shoe
Where there was doubled-faced deceit to do,
Not one to pay the thanks he paid to me!
And yet his manner was a heaven to see
For any woman, be she ne'er so wise,
Painted and trim and barbered to the eyes
Both in his words and in his countenance.

"I loved him, then, for his obedient glance
And for the truth I judged was in his heart,
So that at any time he felt the smart
Of pain, were it so little as a breath,
And I was told, it seemed the twist of death
Tore at my heart. And so it grew to this,
My will became the instrument of his,
That is to say my will obeyed his mood
In everything, as far as reason would,
Within the bounds of honour; nearer, nearer
We grew together, none so dear, none dearer
Than he, God knows, and none shall ever be!

"This lasted for two years perhaps, or three,
And I supposed nothing of him but good.
But at its final ending thus it stood:
As fortune willed, he had to leave the land
In which I lived. Ah, never make demand
Of what I felt in sorrow, ask no question,
I cannot picture it, for no suggestion
Would paint the truth, but this I boldly say,
I knew the pain of death that fatal day,
Such was my grief because he had to go.

"He took his leave with such a world
  of woe,
So sorrowfully, that I felt assured
His feelings were no less than I endured

Hearing him speak, seeing his change of hue.
I was so certain he was wholly true,
So certain he would come to me again
And very soon, if ever truth were plain.

"And there were reasons too for him to go,
Reasons of honour; it is often so.
I made a virtue of necessity
And took it well, knowing it had to be.
I sought to hide my sorrow, as in fitness
I should, and took his hand—St. John my wit-
  ness!—
And said, 'Lo, I am yours, and though we
  sever,
Be such as I have been and shall be ever.'

"What he replied I need not now rehearse;
For who could have said better, or done
  worse?
Yes, what he said was well enough, and soon
The thing was done. Ah, 'long should be your
  spoon
When supping with the devil!' so they say.

"And so at last he went upon his way
And forth he flew, whither it seemed him
  best.
Yet later, when he had a mind to rest,
I think he must have had the text in mind
That 'everything, according to its kind,
Seeks its own pleasure,' so they say, I guess.
Man by his nature seeks new-fangledness,
As do those birds that people keep in cages;
One cares for them day-long and one engages
To get them straw as fair and soft as silk
And gifts of sugar, honey, bread and milk,
Yet on the instant that the slide is up,
The foot will spurn away the proffered cup
And to the woods they fly for worms to eat,
Such is their longing for new-fangled meat.
The love for novelty their natures gave them;
No royalty of blood has power to save them.

"So with this tercelet falcon, woe the day!
Although of gentle birth, though fresh
  and gay,
Handsome, adoring, good in everything,
One day he saw a kite upon the wing
And suddenly he felt a love so hot
For this same kite my love was clean forgot,
And thus he broke his faith in foul delight
And thus my love is servant to a kite
And I am lost and there's no remedy!"

She ceased and with a scream of agony
She swooned away in her protectress' arms.
Great the lamenting for her falcon's harms
That Canace and all her ladies made,

Not knowing how to soothe her or persuade.
　Canace bore her homeward in her lap;
In softest plasters she began to wrap
The falcon's wounds that her own beak had
　torn,
And Canace went delving eve and morn
For herbs out of the ground; new salves
　she made
From precious grasses of the finest shade
To heal her hawk, indeed both day and night
She lavished on her all the care she might.
　Beside her bed she made a little mew
To house the falcon, hung with velvet blue[7]
To signify fair faith, so often seen
In women, and the mew was painted green
Without, with pictures of these treacherous
　fowls
Like tytyfers and tercelets and owls,
And there were magpies painted too, to chide
Them spitefully, to chatter and deride.
　Thus I leave Canace to nurse her hawk
And of her ring at present I will talk
No more, till I return to make it plain
How the poor falcon got her love again
Repentant, as the tale I tell will show,
Through the good offices of Cambalo,
Son of the king of whom I have made men-
　tion.
But for the moment it is my intention
To tell adventures and the feats of war,
Such marvels as you never heard before.
　First I will tell you about Cambuskan
And all the cities that he overran;
Then I shall speak of Algarsyf his son
And next of Theodora whom he won
To wife, and of the perils he must pass
On her account, helped by the steed of brass.
And after of another Cambalo
Who fought her brothers in the lists and so
At last won Canace by might and main.
And where I stopped I shall begin again.

PART III

Apollo whirled his chariot on high
Up through the house of Mercury, the sly—

Words of the Franklin to the Squire
and of the Host to the Franklin

"Well! you have done yourself great credit,
　Squire,
Most like a gentleman! I do admire
Your powers," said the Franklin. "For a
　youth,

You speak most feelingly, and that's the truth;
In my opinion there is no one here
Will equal you in eloquence, or near,
If you should live. God prosper all that's
　in you
And may your talents flourish and continue!
It's all so dainty, it delighted me.
　"I have a son, and by the Trinity
I'd rather than have twenty pounds' worth
　land,
Though it should fall right now into my hand
That he could show the excellent discretion
That you have shown. A plague upon posses-
　sion!
What use is property if you're a dunce?
I've spoken to him sharply, more than once
And shall again. He doesn't like advice,
All he can do is squander and play dice
And lose his money, at his present stage.
He'd rather romp and chatter with a page
Than entertain a serious conversation
Or learn to be a gentleman. Vocation—"
"Franklin, a straw for your gentility!"
Remarked our Host, "You know as well as me
That each must tell a tale or two at least
Or break his word and miss the final feast."
　"I know it well," the Franklin said again,
"I beg you not to hold me in disdain,
Just for a word or two to this young man."
　"Well, no more words, and tell us if
　　you can
Some story of your own." "Glad to obey,
Since it's your wish; here's what I have to say.
Nothing could move me to oppose your will,
Save in so far as I may lack the skill;
I hope you may take pleasure in my stuff,
And if you do, I'll know it's good enough."

THE FRANKLIN'S TALE
The Franklin's Prologue

Of old the noble Bretons in their days
Delighted in adventures and made lays
In rhyme, according to their early tongue,
Which to the sound of instruments were sung,
Or read in silence for their own delight.
And I remember one, if I am right,
Which I will render you as best I can.
　But, sirs, I'm not a cultivated man,
And so from the beginning I beseech
You to excuse me my untutored speech.
They never taught me rhetoric, I fear,

So what I have to say is bare and clear.
I haven't slept on Mount Parnassus, no.
Nor studied Marcus Tullius Cithero.[1]
I can't give colouring to my words—indeed
Such colours as I know adorn the mead,
Or else are those they use in dyes or paint.
"Colours of rhetoric" to me seem quaint,
I have no feeling for such things; but still
Here is my story, listen if you will.

The Franklin's Tale

In Brittany, or as it then was called,
Armorica, there was a knight enthralled
To love, who served his lady with his best
In many a toilsome enterprise and quest,
Suffering much for her ere she was won.
     She was among the loveliest under sun
And came from kindred of so high a kind
He scarce had the temerity of mind
To tell her of his longing and distress.
But in the end she saw his worthiness
And felt such pity for the pains he suffered,
Especially for the meek obedience offered,
That privately she fell into accord
And took him for her husband and her lord
—The lordship husbands have upon their
     wives.
And to enhance the bliss of both their lives
He freely gave his promise as a knight
That he would never darken her delight
By exercising his authority
Against her will or showing jealousy,
But would obey in all with simple trust
As any lover of a lady must;
Save that his sovereignty in name upon her
He should preserve, lest it should shame his
     honour.
     She thanked him, and with great humility
Replied, "Sir, since you show a courtesy
So fair in proffering me so free a rein,
God grant there never be betwixt us twain,
Through any fault of mine, dispute or strife.
Sir, I will be your true and humble wife,
Accept my truth of heart, or break, my
     breast!"
Thus were they both in quiet and at rest.
     For there's one thing, my lords, it's safe
          to say;
Lovers must each be ready to obey
The other, if they would long keep company.
Love will not be constrained by mastery;
When mastery comes the god of love anon
Stretches his wings and farewell! he is gone.

Love is a thing as any spirit free;
Women by nature long for liberty
And not to be constrained or made a thrall,
And so do men, if I may speak for all.
     Whoever's the most patient under love
Has the advantage and will rise above
The other; patience is a conquering virtue.
The learned say that, if it not desert you,
It vanquishes what force can never reach;
Why answer back at every angry speech?
No, learn forbearance or, I'll tell you what,
You will be taught it, whether you will or not.
No one alive—it needs no arguing—
But sometimes says or does a wrongful
     thing;
Rage, sickness, influence of some malign
Star-constellation, temper, woe or wine
Spur us to wrongful words or make us trip.
One should not seek revenge for every slip,
And temperance from the times must take her
     schooling
In those that are to learn the art of ruling.
     And so this wise and honourable knight
Promised forbearance to her that he might
Live the more easily, and she, as kind,
Promised there never would be fault to find
In her. Thus in this humble, wise accord
She took a servant when she took a lord,
A lord in marriage in a love renewed
By service, lordship set in servitude;
In servitude? Why no, but far above
Since he had both his lady and his love,
His lady certainly, his wife no less,
To which the law of love will answer "yes."
     So in the happiness that they had planned
He took his wife home to his native land
With joyful ease and reached his castle there
By Penmarch Point, not far from Finisterre,
And there they lived in amity unharried.
     Who can recount, unless he has been mar-
          ried,
The ease, the prosperous joys of man and wife?
A year or more they lived their blissful life
Until it chanced the knight that I have thus
Described and who was called Arvéragus
Of Caer-rhud, planned to spend a year or so
In Britain (no, not Brittany), to go
And seek high deeds of arms and reputation
In honour; that was all his inclination.
He stayed two years, at least the book says
     thus.
     Now I will pause about Arvéragus
And turn to speak of Dorigen his wife

Who loved her husband as her own heart's
  life.
    She wept his absence, sighed for him and
      pined
As noble wives will do when so inclined;
She mourned, lay wakeful, fasted and
  lamented,
Strained by a passion that could be contented
Only by him, and set the world at naught.
Her friends who knew the burden of her
  thought
Brought her such consolations as they might;
They preached to her, they told her day and
  night,
"You'll kill yourself for nothing." Such relief
And comfort as is possible to grief
They fuss about to find, and finding, press
Upon her to relieve her heaviness.
    Slow is the process, it is widely known,
By which a carver carves his thought in stone,
Yet cuts at last the figure he intended;
And slowly too, thus soothed and thus be-
  friended,
Her soul received the print of consolation
Through hope and reason, and her long pros-
  tration
Turned to recovery, she ceased to languish;
She couldn't be always suffering such anguish.
    Besides, Arvéragus as it befell
Sent letters to her saying all was well
And that he shortly would be home again;
Only for that her heart had died of pain.
    Her friends, seeing her grief began to ease,
Begged her for heaven's sake and on their
  knees
To come and roam about with them and play
And drive her darker fantasies away,
And finally she granted their request
And clearly saw it would be for the best.
    Her husband's castle fronted on the sea
And she would often walk in company
High on the ramparts, wandering at large.
Many a ship she saw and many a barge
Sailing such courses as they chose to go;
But these made part and parcel of her woe
And she would often say, "Alas for me,
Is there no ship, so many as I see,
To bring me home my lord? For then my
  heart
Would find a cure to soothe its bitter smart."
    At other times she used to sit and think
With eyes cast downward to the water's brink
And then her heart endured a thousand shocks

To see such jagged, black and grisly rocks,
So that she scarce could stand upon her feet.
Then she would refuge in some green retreat,
Lie on a lawn, and looking out to sea
With long, cold sighs, would murmur
  piteously:
    "Eternal God that by Thy providence
Guidest the world in wise omnipotence,
They say of Thee that Thou hast noth-
  ing made
In vain; but, Lord, these fiendish rocks are laid
In what would rather seem a foul confusion
Of work than the creation and conclusion
Of One so perfect, God the wise and stable;
Why madest Thou thy work unreasonable?
These rocks can foster neither man nor beast
Nor bird, to north or south, to west or east;
They are a menace, useless, to my mind.
Lord, seest Thou not how they destroy
  mankind?
A hundred thousand bodies dead and rotten
Have met their death on them, though now
  forgotten;
Thy fairest work, wrecked on a rocky shelf,
Mankind, made in the image of Thyself.
It seemed that then Thou hadst great charity
Towards mankind; how therefore may it be
That Thou hast fashioned means as these to
  harm them
That do no good, but injure and alarm them?
    "I know it pleases scholars to protest
In argument that all is for the best,
Though what their reasons are I do not know.
    "But O Thou God that madest wind to
    blow,
Preserve my husband, that is my petition!
I leave the learned to their disquisition.
But would to God these rocks so black, so
  grim,
Were sunk in Hell itself for sake of him!
They are enough to kill my heart with fear."
Thus she would speak with many a piteous
  tear.
    Her friends could see it gave her no relief
To roam the shore, but added to her grief,
And so they sought amusement somewhere
  else.
They led her by the water-ways and wells
And many another scene of loveliness;
They danced, they played backgammon, they
  played chess.
    And so one sunny morning, as they'd
    planned,

They went into a garden near at hand
Where they had staged a picnic and supplied
Victuals enough and other things beside,
And there they lingered out the happy day.

It was the morning of the sixth of May
And May had painted with her softest showers
A gardenful of leafiness and flowers;
The hand of man with such a cunning craft
Had decked this garden out in pleach and
    graft.
There never was a garden of such price
Unless indeed it were in Paradise.
The scent of flowers and the freshening sight
Would surely have made any heart feel light
That ever was born, save under the duress
Of sickness or a very deep distress;
Pleasure and beauty met in every glance.

And after dinner they began to dance
And there was singing; Dorigen alone
Made her continual complaint and moan
For never among the dancers came to view
Her husband, he that was her lover too.
Nevertheless she had to pass the day
In hope and let her sorrows slide away.

Now in this dance, among the other men,
There danced a squire before Dorigen,
Fresher and jollier in his array,
In my opinion, than the month of May.
He sang and danced better than any man
There is or has been since the world began.
He was, what's more, if I could but contrive
To picture him, the handsomest man alive,
Young, strong and wealthy, mettlesome, dis-
    creet,
And popular as any you could meet;
And shortly, if I am to tell the truth,
All unbeknown to Dorigen, this youth
—A lusty squire and servant in the game
Of Venus, and Aurelius was his name—
Had loved her best of any for two years
And longer so it chanced, but still his fears
Had never let him bring the matter up;
He drank his penance down without a cup.[2]

He had despaired of her and dared not say
More of his passion than he might convey
In general terms, by saying that he burned
With love but that his love was not returned;
On all such themes he fashioned many a
    phrase,
Wrote songs, complaints, roundels and
    virelays
Saying his griefs were more than he dared tell,
He languished as a fury did in Hell,

And he must die, he said, as Echo did
For young Narcissus and the love she hid.
But in no other way, as said above,
Had he the courage to confess his love,
Save that perhaps from time to time at dances,
Where youth pays love's observances, his
    glances
It well may be would linger on her face
Beseechingly, as is the common case;
But she was unaware of what he meant.

Nevertheless it happened, ere they went
Out of the garden, since he lived nearby
And was of good position, standing high
In honour and had known her from of old,
They fell in speech and he at last grew bold
And drew towards the purpose in his head.
Taking his opportunity he said:

"Madam, by God's green earth and all its
    treasure,
Had I imagined it could give you pleasure
That day, on which your lord Arvéragus
Went over sea, then I, Aurelius
Would have gone too, and never come again.
I know the service of my love is vain,
My recompense is but a bursting heart.

"Madam, have pity on the pain and smart
Of love; a word from you can slay or save.
Would God your little feet stood on my
    grave!
There is no time to say what I would say;
Have mercy, sweetheart, chase me not away."

She looked at him with closer scrutiny
And answered, "Are you saying this to me?
Can you intend it? Never," she said, "till now
Had I suspected that—what you avow.
But by the Lord that gave me soul and life
I never mean to prove a faithless wife
In word or deed if I can compass it.
I will be his to whom I have been knit.
Take that for final answer, as for me."

But after that she added playfully,
"And yet, Aurelius, by the Lord above
I might perhaps vouchsafe to be your love,
Since I perceive you groan so piteously.
Look; on the day the coasts of Brittany
Are stone by stone cleared of these hateful
    rocks
By you, so that no ship or vessel docks
In danger, when, I say, you clear the coast
So clean there's not a single stone to boast,
I'll love you more than any man on earth;
Accept my word in truth for all it's worth."

"Is there no other way than this?" said he.

"No, by the Lord," she said, "that fash-
      ioned me.
For it will never happen; that I know.
So clear your heart of fancies, let them go.
How can a man find daintiness in life
Who goes about to love another's wife,
That can enjoy her body when he pleases?"

      Aurelius sighed again. The long uneases
Of lovers' woe returned on hearing this
And he replied with sorrowing emphasis,
"Madam, it is impossible to do,
So I must die a sudden death, for you."
And on the word he turned and went away.

      Her many other friends came up to play
And wander with her through the leafy walk
Of alleys pleached, but of her lover's talk
They did not know. Revels began anew,
Until the dazzling sun had lost its hue
For the horizon reft it of its light;
This is as much to say that it was night.
So they went home delighted, all in joy
Except, alas, Aurelius, wretched boy.

He sought his house, a sigh at every breath,
And could see no way of avoiding death.
Within himself he felt his heart turn cold
And falling on his knees began to hold
His hands to heaven and the upper air
In raving madness, and he said a prayer.
Excessive suffering had turned his head,
He knew not what he spoke, but this he said,
With pleading heart and pitiful, to one
And all the gods, beginning with the sun:

      "Apollo, God and Governor, whose power
Tends over every plant and herb and flower
And tree, appointing unto each by reason
Of thy celestial course, his time and season,
According as thy arc is low or high,
Lord Phoebus, in thy mercy cast an eye
On sad Aurelius, wretched and forlorn.
Look on me, Lord! My lady-love has sworn
To prove my death, though for no fault in me,
Unless, O Lord, in thy benignity
Thou pity a dying heart; for well I know,
Shouldest thou please, Lord Phoebus, to
      bestow
Thy mercy, thou canst help me best of all
Except my lady; listen to my call,
Vouchsafe to hear me, Lord, if I expound
A means of help and how it may be found.

      "Thy blissful sister, Luna the Serene,
Chief goddess of the ocean and its queen,
Though Neptune have therein his deity,
Is over him and empress of the sea.

Thou knowest, Lord, that just as her desire
Is to be lit and quickened by thy fire,
For busily she follows after thee,
Just so the natural longing of the sea
Follows on her and so is bound to do;
She is its goddess and the rivers' too.

      "And so, Lord Phoebus, this is my request,
Do me this miracle—or burst, my breast!—
That even now at thy next opposition
Which is to be in *Leo,* thou petition
Thy sister to bring floods so much increased
That they shall rise five fathom at the least
Above the highest rock that now appears
In Brittany, and let this last two years.
Then to my lady I can safely say,
'Keep truth with me, the rocks are all away.'

      "Lord Phoebus, do this miracle for me now!
Beg her to go no faster, Lord, than thou;
I say, beseech thy sister that she go
No faster than thyself two years or so,
Then she will stay at full, and at their height
The spring floods will continue, day and
      night.
And should she not vouchsafe in such a way
The granting of my lady, then I pray
That she may sink the rocks, that they be
      drowned
Within her own dark region underground
Where Pluto dwells, for while they are above
I cannot hope to win my lady-love.

      "Barefoot to Delphi will I go and seek
Thy temple! See the tears upon my cheek,
Lord Phoebus, have compassion, grant my
      boon!"
And on the word he fell into a swoon
And long he lay upon the ground in trance.

      His brother who had heard of his mis-
      chance
Found him and caught him up, and off to bed
He carried him. With torment in his head,
I leave this woeful creature, if to die
In desperation, he must choose, not I.

      Meanwhile Arvéragus in health and power
Came honourably home, the very flower
Of chivalry, with other noble men.
How art thou blissful now, my Dorigen!
Thou has a lusty husband for thy charms,
Thine own fresh knight, thy honoured man-
      at-arms
That loves thee as his life, in whom there
      springs
No inclination to imagine things
Or ask if anyone while he was out

Has talked to thee of love. But not a doubt
Entered his head; he had no thought in life
Except to dance and joust and cheer his wife
In blissful joy; and so I leave him thus
And turn again to sick Aurelius.

In furious torment, languishing away,
Two years and more wretched Aurelius lay
Scarce with the strength to put his foot to
    ground.
No comfort during all that time he found
Except his brother, who had been a scholar,
And who knew all about his woes and dolour,
For to no other could Aurelius dare
Ever to say a word of his affair.
More secretly he guarded his idea
Than Pamphilus his love for Galatea.[3]
To all appearances his breast was whole,
But a keen arrow stuck within his soul.
A wound that's only surface-healed can be
A perilous thing, you know, in surgery,
Unless the arrow-head be taken out.

His brother wept for him and fell in doubt
Of his recovery until by chance
It came to him that when he was in France
At Orleans—he was a student then—
He lusted in his heart like all young men
To study things prohibited, to read
In curious arts of magic, and indeed
Search every hole and corner with defiance
To learn the nature of that special science.
And he remembered how he took a look
One morning, in his study, at a book
On natural magic which it chanced he saw
Because a friend, then bachelor-at-law
Though destined later to another trade,
Had hidden it in his desk. This book displayed
The workings of the moon; there were expan-
    sions
In detail on the eight-and-twenty mansions
Belonging to her—nonsense such as that,
For nowadays it isn't worth a gnat,
Since holy church has managed to retrieve us
And suffers no illusion now to grieve us.

And so, remembering this book by chance,
His heart as suddenly began to dance
For joy within him; quickly reassured,
He said, "My brother surely shall be cured
For I am certain that there must be sciences
By which illusions can be made, appliances
Such as these subtle jugglers use in play
At banquets. Very often, people say,
These conjurors can bring into a large
And lofty hall fresh water and a barge

And there they seem to row it up and down;
Sometimes a lion, grim and tawny-brown,
Sometimes a meadow full of flowery shapes,
Sometimes a vine with white and purple
    grapes,
Sometimes a castle which by some device,
Though stone and lime, will vanish in a trice,
Or seem at least to vanish, out of sight.

"So I conclude that if I only might
Discover some old fellow of the kind
Who has these moony mansions in his mind
At Orleans, or has some power above
All this, my brother might enjoy his love.
A learned man could hoodwink all beholders
With the illusion that the rocks and boulders
Of Brittany had vanished one and all
And ships along the brink could safely call,
Coming and going, and, if this could but last
A day or two, the danger would be past.
She will be forced to recognize his claim
Or else she will at least be put to shame."

Why draw my story out? What need be
    said?
He went to where his brother lay in bed
And brought him so much comfort with
    his plot
To visit Orleans, that up he got
And started off at once upon the road
High in the hope of lightening his load.

They neared the city; when it seemed to be
About two furlongs off, or maybe three,
They met a youngish scholar all alone
Who greeted them in Latin, in a tone
Of friendly welcome, and he struck
    them dumb
In wonder with "I know why you have
    come."
And ere they went a step upon their way
He told them all they had in mind to say.

The Breton scholar wanted to be told
About the friends that they had known of old
And he replied that they were all now dead;
He spoke with feeling, many tears were shed.

Down from his horse Aurelius soon
    alighted
To follow the magician, who invited
Him and his brother home, set them at ease
And served them victuals; nothing that could
    please
Was lacking and Aurelius soon decided
He'd never seen a house so well provided.

And the magician caused there to appear
Before their supper, parks of forest deer

And he saw stags among them, antlered high,
The greatest ever seen by human eye.
He saw a hundred of them killed by hounds
And others, arrow-wounded, lay in mounds.
Next, when the deer had vanished, he was
    shown
A river bank and there a hawk was flown
By falconers; they saw a heron slain.

    Then he saw knights at joust upon a plain
And after that Aurelius was entranced
At seeing his beloved as she danced
And he, it seemed, was dancing with her too.
And when the master of this magic view
Saw it was time he clapped his hands and ban-
    ished
The figures, and farewell! our revels vanished.
Yet all the time they had not left the house
While being shown these sights so marvel-
    lous,
But sat within his study where there lay
His books about them; there were none but
    they.

    The master called the squire who was to set
Their meal, and said, "Is supper ready yet?
It's very near an hour I could swear,"
He added, "since I told you to prepare,
When these two gentlemen came in with me
To see my study and my library."

    "Sir," said the squire, "it's ready, and
    you may
Begin, if it so please you, right away."
"Then let us eat," he said; "that will be best;
These amorous people sometimes need a rest."

    After they'd eaten, bargaining began;
What payment should this master-artisan
Have to remove the rocks of Brittany
From the Gironde to where the Seine
    meets sea?
He made it difficult and roundly swore
He'd take a thousand pounds for it or more,
He wasn't too eager even at that price.
Aurelius with his heart in paradise
Readily answered, "Fie on a thousand pound!
I'd give the world, which people say is round,
The whole wide world, if it belonged to me;
Call it a bargain then, for I agree.
You shall be truly paid it, on my oath.
But look, be sure no negligence or sloth
Delay us here beyond tomorrow, now!"
The scholar gave him answer "That I vow."

    Aurelius went to bed in high delight
And rested soundly, pretty well all night.
Tired by his journey and with hope retrieved
He slept, the troubles of his heart relieved.

And morning came; as soon as it was day
They made for Brittany by the nearest way,
The brothers with the wizard at their side,
And there dismounted having done their ride.
It was—so say the books, if I remember—
The cold and frosty season of December.
Phoebus grew old, his coppered face was
    duller
Than it had been in *Cancer* when his colour
Shone with the burnished gold of streaming
    morn,
But now descending into *Capricorn*
His face was very pale, I dare maintain.
The bitter frosts, the driving sleet and rain
Had killed the gardens; greens had disap-
    peared.
Now Janus by the fire with double beard,
His bugle-horn in hand, sits drinking wine;
Before him stands a brawn of tusky swine,
And "*Sing Noël!*" cries every lusty man.

    Aurelius, using all the means he can,
Gives welcome to the master, shows respect
And begs his diligence, that no neglect
Or sloth delay the healing of his smart,
Lest he should kill himself, plunge sword in
    heart.

    This subtle sage had pity on the man
And night and day went forward with
    his plan
Watching the hour to favour the conclusion
Of his experiment, that by illusion
Or apparition—call it jugglery,
I lack the jargon of astrology—
She and the world at large might think and say
The rocks had all been spirited away
From Brittany or sunk under the ground.

    And so at last the favouring hour was
    found
To do his tricks and wretched exhibition
Of that abominable superstition.
His calculating tables were brought out
Newly corrected (he made sure about
The years in series and the single years
To fix the points the planets in their spheres
Were due to reach and so assessed their "root"
In longitude) and other things to suit,
Such as his astrolabe, and argument
From arc and angle, and was provident
Of fit proportionals for the minor motion
Of planets, and he studied with devotion,
Measuring from the point where
    Alnath[4] swam
In the eighth sphere, to where the head of
    the *Ram*

Stood in the ninth, in its eternal station
(As we suppose), and made his calculation.
And finding the first mansion of the moon,
He calculated all the rest in tune
With that. He worked proportionally,
  knowing
How she would rise and whither she was
  going
Relative to which planets and their place,
Equal or not, upon the zodiac face.
And thus according to his calculations
He knew the moon in all her operations
And all the relevant arithmetic
For his illusion, for the wretched trick
He meant to play, as in those heathen days
People would do. There were no more delays
And by his magic for a week or more
It seemed the rocks were gone; he'd cleared
  the shore.
    Aurelius, still despairing of the plot,
Nor knowing whether he'd get his love
  or not,
Waited for miracles by night and day
And when he saw the rocks were cleared
  away,
All obstacles removed, the plot complete,
He fell in rapture at his master's feet.
"Wretch as I am, for what has passed be-
  tween us,
To you, my lord, and to my lady Venus
I offer thanks," he said, "for by your care,
As poor Aurelius is well aware,
He has been rescued from a long dismay."
    And to the temple then he took his way
Where, as he knew, his lady was to be;
And when he saw his opportunity
With terror in his heart, and humbled face,
He made obeisance to her sovereign grace.
    "My truest lady," said this woeful man,
"Whom most I dread and love—as best
  I can—
Last in the world of those I would displease,
Had I not suffered many miseries
For love of you, so many I repeat
That I am like to perish at your feet,
I would not dare approach you, or go on
To tell you how forlorn and woebegone
I am for you; but I must speak or die.
You kill me with your torture; guiltless, I.
Yet if my death could never so have stirred
Your pity, think before you break your
  word.
Repent, relent, remember God above you
Before you murder me because I love you.

You know what you have promised to requite
—Not that I challenge anything of right,
My sovereign lady, only of your grace—
Yet in a garden yonder, at such a place
You made a promise which you know must
  stand
And gave your plighted troth into my hand
To love me best, you said, as God above
Knows, though I be unworthy of your love.
It is your honour, madam, I am seeking;
It's not to save my life that I am speaking.
I have performed what you commanded me
As if you deign to look you soon will see.
Do as you please but think of what you said
For you will find me here alive, or dead.
It lies in you to save me or to slay—
But well I know the rocks are all away!"
He took his leave of her and left the place.
    Without a drop of colour in her face
She stood as thunderstruck by her mishap.
"Alas," she said, "to fall in such a trap!
I never had thought the possibility
Of such a monstrous miracle could be,
It goes against the processes of nature."
And home she went, a very sorrowful
  creature
In deadly fear, and she had much to do
Even to walk. She wept a day or two,
Wailing and swooning, pitiful to see,
But why she did so not a word said she,
For her Arvéragus was out of town.
But to herself she spoke and flinging down
In pitiable pallor on her bed
She voiced her lamentation and she said:
    "Alas, of thee, O Fortune, I complain,
That unawares hast wrapped me in thy chain,
Which to escape two ways alone disclose
Themselves, death or dishonour, one of those,
And I must choose between them as a wife.
Yet I would rather render up my life
Than to be faithless or endure a shame
Upon my body, or to lose my name.
My death will quit me of a foolish vow;
And has not many a noble wife ere now
And many a virgin slain herself to win
Her body from pollution and from sin?
    "Yes, surely, many a story we may trust
Bears witness; thirty tyrants full of lust
Slew Phido the Athenian[5] like a beast,
Then had his daughters carried to their feast,
And they were brought before them in despite
Stark naked, to fulfil their foul delight,
And there they made them dance upon the
  floor,

God send them sorrow, in their father's gore.
And these unhappy maidens, full of dread,
Rather than they be robbed of maidenhead,
Broke from their guard and leapt into a well
And there were drowned, so ancient authors
    tell.

"The people of Messina also sought
Some fifty maidens out of Sparta, brought
Only that they might work their lechery
Upon them, but in all that company
Not one that was not slain; they were content
To suffer death itself than to consent
To be despoiled of their virginity;
What then's the fear of death, I say, to me?

"Consider Aristoclides for this,
A tyrant lusting after Stymphalis
Who, when her father had been slain one
    night,
Fled for protection to Diana's might
Into her temple, clung to her effigy
With both her hands and from it could not be
Dragged off, they could not tear her
    hands away
Till they had killed her. If a virgin may
Be seen to have so loath an appetite
To be defiled by filthy man's delight,
Surely a wife should kill herself ere she
Were so defiled, or so it seems to me.

"And what of Hasdrubal? Had he not a wife
At Carthage who had rather take her life?
For as she watched the Romans win the town
She took her children with her and leapt down
Into the fire; there she chose to burn
Rather than let them do their evil turn.

"Did not Lucrece choose death for her
    escape
In Rome of old when she had suffered rape
For Tarquin's lust? Did not she think it shame
To live a life that had been robbed of name?

"The seven virgins of Miletus too
Took their own lives—were they not bound
    to do?—
Lest they be ravished by their Gaulish foes.
More than a thousand stories I suppose
Touching this theme were easy now to tell.

"Did not his wife, when Abradates fell,
Take her own life and let the purple flood
Glide from her veins to mingle with his blood,
Saying, 'My body shall at least not be
Defiled by man, so far as lies in me'?

"Since there are found so many, if one
    delves,
That gladly have preferred to kill themselves

Rather than be defiled, need more be sought
For my example? Better were the thought
To kill myself at once than suffer thus.
I will be faithful to Arvéragus
Or slay myself as these examples bid,
As the dear daughter of Demotion did
Who chose to die rather than be defiled.

"O Skedasus, thou also hadst a child
That slew herself, and sad it is to read
How she preferred her death to such a deed.

"As pitiable or even more, I say,
The Theban maid who gave her life away
To foil Nichanor and a like disgrace.

"Another virgin at that very place
Raped by a Macedonian, it is said,
Died to repay her loss of maidenhead.

"What shall I say of Niceratus' wife
Who, being thus dishonoured, took her life?

"And O how true to Alcibiades
His lover was! She died no less than these
For seeking to give burial to her dead.

"See what a wife Alcestis was," she said,
"And what says Homer of Penelope?
All Greece can celebrate her chastity.

"Laodamia, robbed of all her joy,
Protesilaus being killed at Troy,
Would live no longer, seeing that he was
    slain.

"Of noble Portia let me think again;
She could not live on being forced to part
From Brutus whom she loved with all her
    heart.

"And Artemisia, faithful to her man,
Is honoured, even by the barbarian.

"O Teuta, queen! Thy wifely chastity
Should be a mirror for all wives to see;
I say the same of Bilia and as soon
Of chaste Valeria and Rhodogoun."

Thus for a day or two she spent her breath,
Poor Dorigen, and ever purposed death.

On the third day, however, of her plight,
Home came Arvéragus, that excellent knight,
And questioned her; what was she crying for?
But she continued weeping all the more.
"Alas," she said, "that ever I was born!
Thus have I said," she answered, "thus have
    sworn—"
She told him all as you have heard before.
It need not be repeated here once more.

Her husband, gladly smiling, with no fuss,
But with a friendly look, made answer thus:
"And is there nothing, Dorigen, but this?"
"No, no, so help me God!" with emphasis

She answered. "Is it not enough, too much?"
"Well, wife," he said, "it's better not to touch
A sleeping dog, so I have often heard;
All may be well, but you must keep your
    word.
For, as may God be merciful to me,
I rather would be stabbed than live to see
You fail in truth. The very love I bear you
Bids you keep truth, in that it cannot
    spare you.
Truth is the highest thing in a man's keep-
    ing."
And on the word he suddenly burst out
    weeping
And said, "But I forbid on pain of death,
As long as you shall live or draw your breath,
That you should ever speak of this affair
To living soul; and what I have to bear
I'll bear as best I may; now wash your face,
Be cheerful. None must guess at this dis-
    grace."
    He called a maidservant and squire then
And said, "Go out with Lady Dorigen;
Attend upon her, whither she will say."
They took their leave of him and went
    their way
Not knowing why their mistress was to go.
It was his settled purpose none should know.
    Perhaps a heap of you will want to say,
"Lewd, foolish man to act in such a way,
Putting his wife into such jeopardy!"
Listen before you judge them, wait and see.
She may have better fortune, gentlemen,
Than you imagine; keep your judge-
    ments then
Till you have heard my story which now turns
To amorous Aurelius as he burns
For Dorigen; they happened soon to meet
Right in the town, in the most crowded street
Which she was bound to use, however loth,
To reach the garden and to keep her oath.
    Aurelius gardenwards was going too;
A faithful spy on all she used to do,
He kept close watch whenever she went out
And so by accident or luck no doubt
They met each other; he, his features glowing,
Saluted her and asked where she was going,
And she replied as one half driven mad,
"Why, to the garden, as my husband bade
To keep my plighted word, alas, alas!"
    Aurelius, stunned at what had come to pass,
Felt a great surge of pity that arose
At sight of Dorigen in all her woes

And for Arvéragus the noble knight
That bade her keep her word of honour white,
So loth he was that she should break her truth.
And such a rush of pity filled the youth
That he was moved to think the better course
Was to forgo his passion than to force
An act on her of such a churlish kind,
And against such nobility of mind.
So, in few words, the squire addressed her thus:
    "Madam, say to your lord Arvéragus
That since I well perceive his nobleness
Towards yourself, and also your distress,
Knowing the shame that he would rather take
(And that were pity) than that you should
    break
Your plighted word, I'd rather suffer too
Than seek to come between his love and you.
    "So, Madam, I release into your hand
All bonds or deeds of covenant that stand
Between us, and suppose all treaties torn
You may have made with me since you were
    born.
I give my word never to chide or grieve you
For any promise given, and so I leave you,
Madam, the very best and truest wife
That ever yet I knew in all my life.
Let women keep their promises to men,
Or at the least remember Dorigen.
A squire can do a generous thing with grace
As well as can a knight, in any case."
    And she went down and thanked him on
        her knees.
Home to her husband then with heart at ease
She went and told him all as I've recorded.
You may be sure he felt so well rewarded
No words of mine could possibly express
His feelings. Why then linger? You may
    guess.
    Arvéragus and Dorigen his wife
In sovereign happiness pursued their life,
No discord in their love was ever seen,
He cherished her as though she were a queen,
And she stayed true as she had been before;
Of these two lovers you will get no more.
    Aurelius, all whose labour had been lost,
Cursing his birth, reflected on the cost.
"Alas," he said, "alas that I am bound
To pay in solid gold a thousand pound
To that magician! What am I to do?
All I can see is that I'm ruined too.
There's my inheritance; that I'll have to sell
And be a beggar. Then there's this as well;
I can't stay here a shame and a disgrace

To all my family; I must leave the place.
And yet he might prove lenient; I could pay
A yearly sum upon a certain day
And thank him gratefully, I can but try.
But I will keep my truth, I will not lie."

And sad at heart he went to search his coffer
And gathered up what gold he had to offer
His master, some five hundred pound I guess,
And begged him as a gentleman, no less,
To grant him time enough to pay the rest.

"Sir, I can boast, in making this request,"
He said, "I've never failed my word as yet,
And I will certainly repay this debt
I owe you, master, ill as I may fare,
Yes, though I turn to begging and go bare.
If you'd vouchsafe me, on security,
A little respite, say two years or three,
All would be fine. If not I'll have to sell
My patrimony; there's no more to tell."

Then this philosopher in sober pride,
Having considered what he'd said, replied,
"Did I not keep my covenant with you?"
"You did indeed," he said, "and truly too."
"And did you not enjoy your lady then?"
"No . . . no . . . " he sighed, and thought of
    Dorigen.
"What was the reason? Tell me if you can."

Reluctantly Aurelius then began
To tell the story you have heard before,
There is no need to tell it you once more.
He said: "Her husband, in his nobleness,
Would have preferred to die in his distress
Rather than that his wife should break her
    word."
He told him of her grief, as you have heard,
How loth she was to be a wicked wife
And how she would have rather lost her life;
"Her vow was made in innocent confusion,
She'd never heard of magical illusion.
So great a sense of pity rose in me,
I sent her back as freely then as he
Had sent her to me; I let her go away.
That's the whole story, there's no more to
    say."

Then the magician answered, "My dear
    brother,
Each of you did as nobly as the other.
You are a squire, sir, and he a knight,
But God forbid in all His blissful might
That men of learning should not come as near
To nobleness as any, never fear.

"Sir, I release you of your thousand pound
No less than if you'd crept out of the ground

Just now, and never had had to do with me.
I will not take a penny, sir, in fee
For all my knowledge and my work to rid
The coast of rocks; I'm paid for what I did,
Well paid, and that's enough. Farewell, good-
    day!"
He mounted on his horse and rode away.

My lords, I'll put a question: tell me true,
Which seemed the finest gentleman to you?
Ere we ride onwards tell me, anyone!
I have no more to say, my tale is done.

THE SECOND NUN'S TALE
The Second Nun's Prologue

That nourisher and servant to our vices
Known in our English tongue as Idleness,
The portress at the gateway that entices
To self-abandonment, we should oppress
By her own contrary, a measureless
And lawful industry, with all our power,
Lest the fiend snatch us in an idle hour.

For he with many a cunning cord and bridle
Continually watches us to clap
All whomsoever of us that are idle
And so easy to be taken, in his trap.
Not till a man is tossed into his lap
Does he perceive the fiend; let us be loth
To slacken in our work and yield to sloth.

And though we dreaded not what is to be,
That is, our death, reason would teach us keep
From idleness that rots in sluggardry
From whence no harvest comes, which none
    can reap;
We see that sloth can leash us in a sleep,
To pass the time in sleeping, eating, drinking,
Devouring other people's work, unthinking.

So, to put all such idleness away,
The cause of so much ruin and stagnation,
I have, as diligently as I may,
Followed the legend in my own translation
Touching thy sufferings and exaltation,
Made of thy garlands, rose and lily-laden,
Cecilia, thine, O martyr, Saint and maiden!

Invocacio ad Mariam

And thou that art the flower of virgins all,
Of whom St. Bernard had such skill to write
To thee at my beginning first I call;

Comfort of sinners, teach me to endite
Thy maiden's death who put the fiend to
    flight
And won by merit an eternal glory,
As all may find in following her story.

Thou maid and mother, daughter of thy Son,
Thou well of mercy, balm to sinful nature,
In whom God chose His dwelling, as in one
Humblest and highest over every creature,
Who gav'st such nobleness to human feature
That God had no disdain to clothe and wind
His Son in flesh and blood of human kind.

Within the blissful cloister of thy womb
There took man's shape the eternal love and
    peace,
Lord and guide of the trinal circle, whom
The heavens and earth and sea shall never
    cease
To glorify, pure virgin, the increase
Of whose fair body, never by man mated,
Was the Creator of all things created.

In thee assembled are magnificence,
Mercy and goodness, with such clemency
That thou, who art the sun of excellence,
Not only helpest those that pray to thee,
But many a time in thy benignity
Thou goest before them freely ere they speak,
O leech of life, and grantest what they seek.

Help me then, fair and meek and blissful maid,
Me, banished in the desert, in the street
Of gall; remember who was not afraid
To say in Cana, "Lo, the dogs may eat
The crumbs that fall about their masters' feet";
Though I be an unworthy son of Eve,
Accept me for my faith, for I believe.

Since faith is dead that does not live in works,
O therefore give me power to work apace.
Save me from darkness and the fiend that
    lurks
In darkness, O thou fair and full of grace!
Be thou my advocate in that high place
Where endlessly the angels sing "Hosanna,"
Mother of Christ, dear daughter of St. Anna!

Shed thou thy light upon my soul in prison,
Troubled by the contagion of the flesh,
Weighed down by lusts of earth that have
    arisen

Of false affection, tangled in their mesh;
Haven of refuge, O salvation fresh
And comforting to all by sorrow shaken,
Help me in that which I have undertaken!

And you, all you that read what I shall write,
Forgive me if I show no diligence
To ornament my story or endite
A subtle style; I take the words and sense
From one who held in holiest reverence
The saint of whom he wrote, and tell her tale,
Begging you to amend it where I fail.

Interpretatio Nominis Ceciliae

First let me tell you whence her name has
    sprung,
Cecilia, meaning, as the books agree,[1]
"Lily of Heaven" in our English tongue,
To signify her chaste virginity;
Or for the whiteness of her constancy,
The greenness of her conscience, of her fame
The scent and sweetness, "lily" was her name.

Cecilia may betoken "path to the blind"
From the example given in her story;
Or in Cecilia some would have us find
A union as it were of "Heaven's glory"
And Leah, the Active Life, in allegory;
"Heaven" is set for thoughts of holiness
And "Leah" for ceaseless labour and address.

Cecilia may be also said to mean
"Wanting in blindness," as she had the light
Of sapience and a bearing calm and clean;
Or, as the maiden was beloved and bright,
To say from "Heaven" and "leos" would be
    right
And mean "a Heaven for people," so to call
The good example of her works to all.

For "leos" means "people" in the English
    tongue,
And just as one may look to heaven and see
The sun and moon, and where the stars are
    hung,
So in this maiden, spiritually,
We see her faith and magnanimity
And the whole clarity of her wisdom thence
In many works of shining excellence.

And just as these philosophers will write
To prove that heaven is swift and round and
    burning,

Just so was fair Cecilia the White,
As swift and ceaseless, turning and returning
To works of mercy, and round in her dis-
    cerning
And perseverance, burning with the flame
Of charity, and so I read her name.

The Second Nun's Tale

This maiden, bright Cecilia, so I read,
Was Roman born and came of noble kind
And from her cradle fostered in the creed
Of Christ, and bore His gospel in her mind;
She never ceased in prayer, or so I find
It written of her, to God in love and dread,
Beseeching Him to guard her maidenhead.

And when this maid was given to a man
In wedlock—he was young and bore the name
(Her legend tells us) of Valerian—
Upon the day of marriage, when it came,
She was devout and humble, still the same;
For there, beneath her robe of golden mesh,
She wore a shirt of hair upon her flesh.

And while the organs made their melody,
To God alone within her heart there sounded
This prayer, "Lord, keep my soul and
    body free
From all defilement, lest I be confounded."
On Him who died upon a tree she grounded
Her faith in love, and every second day
Or every third she fasted and would pray.

Yet the night came and she must go to bed
Beside her husband, as is oft the way,
And turning to him privately she said,
"Sweet and beloved husband, if I may,
There is a thing I dearly wish to say
If you will hear, and yet I would conceal it;
Swear to me, then, you never will reveal it."

Firmly Valerian on his honour swore
That for no cause, whatever it might be,
Would he betray her, he could say no more.
And she began to speak. "I have," said she,
"A guardian angel, one that tenders me
So great a love, that whether awake or
    sleeping
My body is committed to his keeping.

"Were he to feel—and O, believe it true—
That you had touched me either in love or lust
He instantly would bring your death on you;
Young as you are you would go down to dust."

But if you love me cleanly, as you must,
He will love you, even as he loves me,
And show the glory of his ecstasy."

Valerian, corrected by God's grace,
Answered again, "That I may trust in you,
Show me that angel, let me see his face,
And if indeed he be an angel true
Then I will do as you have begged me to,
But if you love another man, on oath
I say this sword of mine shall slay you both."

Cecilia answered, "You are well advised,
And you shall see the angel if you will,
But first believe in Christ and be baptized.
Go by the Appian way," she said, "until
You reach, some three miles hence upon a hill,
A village where the poorer people live.
Go up to them and speak the words I give.

"Tell them that I, Cecilia, sent you there
That they might show you Urban,[2] old and
    good,
For secret needs and say your thoughts are fair.
And when you met Saint Urban, as you
    should,
Repeat my words; they will be understood
And when he has confessed and purged your
    heart
You then shall see the angel, ere you part."

Valerian went out to seek the place
And just as she had told him there he found
Holy Saint Urban, met him face to face
At work upon a Christian burial ground,
And told him on what errand he was bound.
And Urban, when his message had been given,
Was filled with joy and raised his hands to
    heaven.

And from his eyes the tears began to fall.
"Almighty Lord, O Jesu Christ," said he,
"Sower of chaste thought, shepherd of us all,
Take thou the fruit, whose seed of chastity
Thou sowedst in Cecilia, unto Thee!
Lo, like a busy bee that knows no guile
Thy thrall Cecilia serves thee all the while!

"Her very spouse, that she but now has taken
Fierce as a lion, hither has she sent
Meek as a lamb, his violence forsaken
For Thee, dear Lord!" Now, as he spoke,
    there went
A man before them clad in white and bent

With age; a golden book was in his hand.
Before Valerian he took his stand.

Valerian fell down for very dread
On seeing him. He raised him from his fall,
Opened the golden book and thus he read:
"One Lord, one Faith, one God above us all,
One Christendom, and One that we may call
Father, supreme both here and everywhere."
These were the words in golden letters there.

Thus having read, then said this ancient man,
"Believest thou these sayings? Yes or no?"
"All this I do believe," Valerian
Replied. "For nothing is more truly so
In Heaven above or in the earth below."
The ancient vanished then, he knew not
    where;
Urban the Pope baptized him then and there.

Home to Cecilia then he went and found
Her standing with an angel in his room;
The angel held two coronals that were bound
With lily-flowers and roses in full bloom
And to Cecilia then he turned, to whom
He gave the first, the second with its weight
Of roses to Valerian, her mate.

"With a clean body and with spotless
    thought
Cherish these coronals for ever. They,"
The angel said, "from Paradise were brought
For you, and they shall never rot away
Or lose their savour, trust to what I say.
And they are such as none shall see, unless
His heart is chaste and hates all filthiness.

"And thou, Valerian, that wert so soon
Glad to pursue what good advice began,
Say what thou wouldest; thou shalt have thy
    boon."
"I have a brother," said Valerian,
"In all the world there is no other man
I love so well. I pray he may find grace
To know the truth as I do, in this place."

The angel said, "God liketh thy request;
You both shall bear the palm of martyrdom
And come hereafter to His blissful rest."
Now while the angel spoke, Tiburce had
    come,
Valerian's brother, and aware of some
Sweet savour which the rose and lily cast
About the chamber, felt his heart beat fast,

And "Where, I wonder, at this time of year
Can such a fragrance come from? Can you
    tell?
The scent," he said, "of rose and lily here—
Why, if I had them in my hands their smell
Could pierce no deeper, could not pierce so
    well.
I find a savour in my heart, and seeing
Nothing, I know that it has changed my be-
    ing."

Valerian said, "Two coronals have we,
Snow-white and rosy-red and shining fair,
Such as your eye has never learnt to see;
As you have smelt their savour at my prayer
So, dearest brother, you shall see them there,
If without tardiness you will receive
The very truth, and knowing it, believe."

Tiburce replied, "Do you say this to me
In truth or do I hear it in a dream?"
"Dreaming," Valerian said, "we used to be,
Till now we were in sleep, so it must seem,
But now awake, in truth." "Yet how to
    deem,"
Tiburce replied, "Whether we're dreaming
    now?"
Valerian answered, "I will tell you how.

"The angel of God has taught me truth.
    Your eyes
Shall also see if you renounce the power
Of idols and be clean, not otherwise."
(As to the miracle of these crowns of flower,
St. Ambrose speaks of it to strengthen our
Belief, commends it solemnly indeed;
The noble Doctor's preface, if you read,

Says thus, "To gain the palm of martyrdom,
Cecilia, being filled with Heaven's grace,
Forsook the world, her chamber and her
    groom,
Witness Valerian and Tiburce, in face
Of whose conversion we may judge her case,
Which God in bounty honoured with a crown
Of flowers for each, brought by an angel
    down.

"This maiden brought these men to bliss
    above:
The world well knows the worth, you may be
    sure,
Of a devoted chastity in Love.
This St. Cecilia showed him, and secure

In faith he held all idols as impure,
Vain, dumb and deaf, even as those that make
  them;
And so it was she charged him to forsake
  them.")

"Who thinks not so is but a brute at best,"
Tiburce gave answer, "if I do not lie."
Cecilia turned and kissed him on the breast
In joy that he beheld with inward eye
And saw the truth. Said she, "Though we
  should die
For it, let us ally ourselves today."
Blissful and lovely she went on to say:

"Just as the love of Christ has fashioned me
To be your brother's wife, that love devised
A new alliance as for you and me,
And so I take you now that have despised
Your idols; therefore go and be baptized,
Make yourself clean and then you shall behold
The angel's face of which your brother told."

Tiburce for answer turned and said, "Dear
  brother,
First tell me whom I am to seek and where?"
"Whom you should seek? Be happy," said the
  other.
"None but Pope Urban; I will take you
  there."
"Urban, my brother?" He began to stare.
"Is that where you will take me, then?"
  said he.
"That would be very strange, it seems to me.

"You cannot mean that Urban," he went on,
"That has so often been condemned to die
And lives in holes and corners, here and gone,
And daren't put forth his head if one goes by?
People would burn him, they would have
  him fry
If he were seen and caught. To seek him thus
Would surely make them do the same to us.

"So, in our search after the Deity
That Heaven in her secrecies may hide,
We shall be burnt on earth, most certainly."
To which Cecilia valiantly replied:
"Men might fear death and would be justified
In seeking to preserve their lives, dear brother,
If there were only this life and no other.

"But there's a better in another place
That never shall be lost. Be not afraid;

God's Son has told us of it, by His grace,
The Father's Son, by whom all things were
  made;
Those creatures in whom reason is displayed
The Holy Ghost proceeding from the Father
Dowers with a living soul, believe it rather.

"By word and miracle the Son of God,
When in this world, declared and we have
  learned
There was an after-life for all who trod
The path He chose." "Dear sister," he re-
  turned,
"Did you not say just now, in what concerned
The Being of God, there was but One, and He
Was Lord in truth? Yet now you speak of
  three."

"That too I shall explain," she said, "in
  season.
Just as the wisdom in a man is three,
Having invention, memory and reason,
So also in God's nature there can be
Three Persons that are One in Deity."
And she began to preach in eager fashion
Of Christ's first coming and His pain and pas-
  sion,

And all He underwent in our condition,
And how the Son of God had been withheld
On earth from making man a full remission,
Bound as he is in sinfulness and quelled
By many cares, and when she had dispelled
His lingering doubt, Tiburce in eager hope
Went with Valerian to seek the Pope.

Urban thanked God; with happy heart and
  light
He christened him and within little space
Perfected him in learning as God's knight;
And after that Tiburce was filled with grace
And every day thereafter saw the face
Of God's bright angel, and if he was stirred
To ask of God a boon, his prayer was heard.

It would be hard to tell in order due
How many wonders for them Jesus wrought,
But lastly, if I may be brief with you,
The officers of Rome went out and sought
These brothers. To the prefect they were
  brought,
Almachius named. He questioned them and
  strove
To search their will, and to the idol of Jove

He sent them. "Make them sacrifice," he said,
"Or strike their heads off; so my orders are."
One Maximus, his officer, the head
Among the prefects and his registrar,
Took these two saints together, whom so far
I have described, and brought them through
    the city,
And as he led them forth he wept for pity.

When Maximus had listened to their teaching
He got the torturers to give him leave
To take them to his house, and by their
    preaching
He was converted ere the fall of eve.
Their faith was found sufficient to retrieve
The torturers too and bring them to disown
Their false beliefs and trust in God alone.

Cecilia came when evening drew to night
With priests who christened all with one ac-
    cord,
And afterwards when morning had grown
    light
She gravely said, "O you that are restored
In Christ and are the soldiers of the Lord,
Cast off the works of darkness and put on
The armour of righteousness, the night is
    gone.

"You have done battle greatly and prevail,
Your course is done, your faith has never
    swerved;
Go to the crown of life that cannot fail.
The righteous Judge and Saviour you have
    served
Shall give it you, for you have well deserved."
And then they led them forth to sacrifice
As I have told you, or to pay the price.

But, taken to the temple, no advice
—To tell the matter briefly—could persuade
These men to offer incense, sacrifice
Or bow to Jove, but on their knees they
    prayed
To God with humble hearts and unafraid.
Their heads were severed in that very place;
Their souls went upward to the King of
    Grace.

And Maximus who saw it testified
With piteous tears that he had seen the sight;
High into Heaven he saw their spirits glide
With angels, full of clarity and light.
His words converted many before night.

And when Almachius heard what he had said
He had him scourged to death with whips of
    lead.

Cecilia buried him beside her own,
Beside Tiburce, beside Valerian,
In her own burial-place beneath a stone.
Almachius therefore hastily began
To issue orders; officer and man
Were sent to fetch Cecilia before him
To honour Jove with incense and adore him.

But they, converted by her holy lore,
Wept and affirmed their fullest confidence
In all she said, and cried out, more and more,
"Christ is God's Son, without a difference,
Verily God; we cite in evidence
That He has saints to serve him, such as these,
And, though we die, proclaim it on our
    knees."

Almachius (for these doings made a stir)
Ordered her to be fetched that he might see
Cecilia for himself and question her.
"What sort of woman, then, are you?" said he.
"I am a gentlewoman born," said she.
"I'm asking you," he said, "of your belief,
About your faith, though it may cause you
    grief."

"You have begun your questions foolishly,"
Answered Cecilia, "seeking to conclude
Two points in one, which shows stupidity."
He, vexed at her rejoinder, then pursued,
"How is it that your answer is so rude?"
"How!" she replied on being thus arraigned,
"Of conscience and pure heart and faith un-
    feigned."

Almachius answered, "Do you take no heed
Of my authority?" And she returned,
"Your power is little to be feared indeed;
Power of mortal man is soon discerned
To be a bladder full of wind and spurned;
For prick it with a needle when it's blown
And the inflated boast is overthrown."

"Well, you began most contumaciously,"
He said, "and you continue turbulent.
Do you not know the Principality
Has given ordinance to this intent
That every Christian shall have punishment
Unless he will deny his Christian creed,
And that denying it he shall be freed?"

"Your princes err, and so your nobles do,"
Cecilia said, "and by some crazy law
Would make us guilty, but it is not true.
You know us innocent; because you saw
That we held Christ in reverence and awe
And bore the name of Christians, down
  you sat
And put a crime upon us, just for that.

"But we, that know the name for virtuous,
Renounce it not, whatever be the price."
Almachius answered her, "The choice stands
  thus;
Abjure your Christendom, or sacrifice!
There's no escaping; follow my advice."
At this the beautiful and blessed maid
Began to laugh and answered, unafraid,

"O Judge, confused for all your subtlety,
Would you that I denied my innocence?
Is it your wish to make a sinner of me?
Look at him there upholding this pretence
In open court, a madman lost to sense
In his endeavours!" He answered, "Sorry
  wretch,
Do you know how far my power may stretch?

"Is there no force or power in my breath?
Have not our mighty princes given to me
Authority and power of life and death?
Why do you speak so proudly then?" said he.
"I do not speak in pride but steadfastly,"
She answered; "I, and those upon my side,
Have deadly hatred for the sin of pride.

"If you are not afraid to hear the truth
I will be open and expose to view
Your monstrous lies. Authority forsooth!
You say your princes have bestowed on you
Power of life and death; but that's not true.
You can take life, have power to destroy,
But that's the only power you enjoy.

"But you may say your princes in their might
Made you death's minister. Say more than so
And you will lie. Your power is very slight."
"Muzzle your boldness," said Almachius, "go!
And pay our gods the sacrifice you owe.
Your insults to myself can be endured,
I'm a philosopher and am inured.

"But there are insults that I will not swallow
That you have levelled at our gods," said he.

Cecilia cried, "Your sophistries are hollow,
There's not a word in what you've said to me
That did not publish your obliquity
And prove yourself, I say it without grudge,
An ignorant official, a vain judge.

"Nothing you lack to make your outward eye
Totally blind, for what is seen by all
To be a stone you seek to glorify,
A senseless piece of stone that you would call
A god! Put out your hand and let it fall
Upon it, touch it, taste it! You will find
Your hand says 'Stone!' although your eyes are
  blind.

"People will laugh at you to hear such stuff
As you have uttered, they will think you mad,
For it is known, and commonly enough,
That God Almighty is in Heaven, clad
In glory, and these idols—if you had
The eyes to see it—offer no delight
To you or to themselves; not worth a mite."

All this she said and more it well may be,
Till he grew angry. "Take her whence
  she came
Home to her house, and in her house,"
  said he,
"Burn her to ashes in a bath of flame."
Thus he commanded and they did the same,
They shut her in a bath and set alight
A mighty fire beneath it. Day and night

They stoked it and from night to day again,
And yet in spite of all the flame and heat
She sat there cool and neither feeling pain
Nor sweating, not a drop from head to feet.
Yet it was in that bath she was to meet
Her death, for this Almachius in his wrath
Sent a man down to kill her in the bath.

Three grievous strokes upon her neck he
  smote,
This torturer, but by no circumstance
Could he succeed in cutting through her
  throat;
Now at that time there was an ordinance
Forbidding executioners to chance
Smiting a fourth stroke, whether soft or sore,
And so this torturer dared do no more.

Half dead with carven neck she perished
  there;

He left her lying and he went his way.
But all the Christian folk, or such as were
About her then, bound her with sheets to stay
The flow of blood, and she, to the third day,
Lingered in pain yet never ceased in teaching
The faith she fostered, and continued
    preaching.

Goods, movables, her rights in everything
She then bequeathed to Urban, saying, "Lo,
There was a boon I asked of Heaven's King;
Three days of respite I desired that so
I might commend these souls before I go
To you that you may guide them in their
    search
And build my house for a perpetual church."

St. Urban and his deacons secretly
Fetched forth her body and buried it by night
Among his saints. Her mansion came to be
The Church of St. Cecilia, hers by right;
St. Urban hallowed it, as well he might.
And in that Church in every noble way
Christ and his saint are honoured to this day.

THE CANON'S YEOMAN'S TALE
The Canon's Yeoman's Prologue

When St. Cecilia's life had reached the close,
Some five miles further on, as I suppose,
At Boughton-under-Blean we saw a hack
Come galloping up. Its rider was in black
And under that a dingy surplice lay.
The hackney horse he rode was dappled grey
And sweating hard, it was a sight to see;
It must have galloped miles, it seemed to me.
His yeoman's horse was also puffed and
    blowing,
And sweated so it hardly could keep going.
The foam stood high upon its collar, flecked
Just like a magpie—that was the effect.
    A wallet on the crupper, doubled tight,
Was fastened and it seemed he travelled light
To suit a summer day, this worthy man.
And as he came towards us I began
Wondering about him till I understood
His cloak was sewn together with his hood,
And pondering this it needed no research
To write him down a canon of the church.[1]
    His hat hung down behind him on a lace
As he had ridden at more than trotting-pace,
In fact he had been galloping like mad.

To keep him cool and catch the sweat, he had
Beneath his hood a dock-leaf, dripping wet.
It was a joy to see that canon sweat!
His forehead dropped down moisture like a
    still
For plantain, pellitory-juice or squill.
When he came up with us he gave a hearty
Shout and he said, "God bless this jolly party!
How fast I've spurred," he said, "all for your
    sake;
I was determined I would overtake
Your happy crowd and ride in company."
    His man was just as full of courtesy
And said, "My lords, I saw the day begin
With your departure, when you left the inn,
And so I warned my lord and master, who
Is very eager, sir, to ride with you
Just for enjoyment; he is fond of fun."
    "God bless you, friend, for warning him.
        Well done!"
Our Host rejoined. "And one may well
    suppose
Your lord is wise, he looks it, goodness
    knows;
I'll wager he's high-spirited as well.
D'you think he has a tale or two to tell
To brighten up our company this morning?"
    "Who? He? My lord? Rather! I give you
        warning
He's a great joker, all for jollity,
Not half he is, you can rely on me.
If you had studied him as well as I,
You'd be amazed how capable and sly
When he gets down to work my master is.
All sorts of enterprise! Those jobs of his
Are more than any of you here and now
Could bring about unless he showed you how.
Homely as he may look among your crowd,
If you but knew him you would all be proud;
You wouldn't forgo acquaintance with my
    lord,
Not for a fortune; if I could afford
To bet, I'd wager all in my possession.
He is a man of very great discretion,
I warn you, sir, he's a superior being."
    "Well," said our Host, "while I'm not dis-
        agreeing,
What is he then? A clerical? Or what?"
    "Only a cleric? Him? I should say not!"
The Yeoman said. "Much more, or else I'm
    daft.
Let me inform you briefly of his craft.
    "I say my master has such subtle powers

—Although I help him in this work of ours
I can't explain them all, he's so far on—
That all this blessed road we ride upon
From here as far as Canterbury town,
Why, he could turn it all clean upside down
And pave it all with silver and with gold!"
     The Yeoman paused as if his tale was told.
Our thoughtful Host said, "*Benedicite!*
All that you say sounds wonderful to me,
For if your lord is truly so sagacious,
So much to be respected, goodness gracious,
Why does he take his dignity so light?
That gabardine is hardly worth a mite
—Well, for a man like that; God bless my
     wits,
It isn't even clean, it's torn to bits!
Why is your lord so sluttish, may I say?
With all those magic powers can't he pay
For better cloth, if what you say is so?
Answer me that, that's what I'd like to know."
     "Why?" said the Yeoman. "Need you ask
     me that?
God help us all, the thing he's working at
Can never be successful—this remark
I can't make openly, so keep it dark—
He knows too much, I think. Easy to scoff,
But things when overdone just don't
     come off,
The learned tell us, it's a waste endeavour;
That's why he's such a fool—he's far too
     clever.
Often enough a man with too much brain
Is likely to misuse it. What's the gain?
I'm very sorry for it, but that's his way,
God help him! I have nothing more to say."
     "Well, never mind, my man," replied our
     Host,
"But what's this subtlety of his you boast,
If I may ask? What does he do all day,
If he's as sly and crafty as you say?
Where do you live now, if you don't mind
     telling?"
"In slums," he answered, "suburbs are our
     dwelling;
We lurk in holes and corners and blind alleys,
Places where every thief and robber rallies
By nature, fear-stricken and secret places
Where those reside who dare not show their
     faces;
That, to tell truth, is where we go a-walking."
     "Now," said the Host, "if I may go on
     talking,
Why are you so discoloured round the face?"

"God was unkind to it, that's about the case,"
He said; "I'm used to blowing up the fire
And that's what changed my colour. I don't
     enquire
Into complexions, mirrors leave me cold.
I work like mad at learning to make gold.
We're always blundering, spilling things in
     the fire,
But for all that we fail in our desire
For our experiments reach no conclusion,
Yet we keep plenty under that illusion
And borrow money, say a pound or two,
Or ten or twelve and even more, we do,
And make them think that at the very least
Their money will be doubled or increased.
Yet it's a lie, but still we live in hope
It might be managed somehow; on we grope.
But the whole science lies so far ahead
It can't be overtaken, though we said
On oath it could, it slides away so fast.
It will make beggars of us all at last."
     Now while his Yeoman was enlarg-
     ing thus
In came the Canon, hearing him discuss,
To listen closer; his suspicious head
Distrusted anything that people said.
Cato has said a guilty conscience delves;
The guilty think all talk is of themselves.
That was the cause the Canon drew in near
His Yeoman; he was very keen to hear,
And he addressed his Yeoman, having heard,
"You hold your tongue, don't speak an-
     other word
Or if you do you'll pay for it, d'you see?
You're slandering me before this company.
What's more, you're telling things that should
     be hidden."
     "Yeah?" said our Host. "Go on, don't be
     forbidden,
I wouldn't mind his threats if I were you,
They're not worth anything." "No more I
     do,"
He answered. When the Canon realized
That all his secrets were to be surprised
He fled away in very grief and shame.
"Ha!" said the Yeoman. "Now we'll have a
     game,
Now I can talk, and I've a lot to tell.
He's gone, the foul fiend carry him off to
     Hell!
We'll never meet again, I'll tell you flat,
For pound or penny, I can promise that.
He was the one first brought me to the game,

Grief strike him down, before he dies, in
   shame!
For it's a serious thing to me I say,
As I am well aware, think as you may.
And yet for all my misery and grief,
Long hours and injuries without relief,
I never could leave the business, any price.
O that I had a brain that would suffice
To tell you all that's proper to that art!
Nevertheless I'll try to tell you part,
And since my master's gone I will not spare;
All that I know about it I'll declare."

The Canon's Yeoman's Tale

PART I

I've served this canon seven years and more,
Yet am no nearer science than before.
All that I ever had I've lost thereby,
And so, God knows, have many more than I.
Time was when I was fresh and fond of cheer,
Liked decent clothes and other handsome
   gear;
Now I might wear my hose upon my head,
And where my colour was a lively red
My face is wan and wears a leaden look;
If you try science you'll be brought to book.
My eyes are bleared with work on preparations,
That's all the good you get from transmuta-
   tions.
That slippery science stripped me down
   so bare
That I'm worth nothing, here or anywhere.
Added to that I am so deep in debt
From borrowing money, you can lay a bet
Long as I live I'll never pay it, never!
   Let every man be warned by me for ever;
Whoever tries his hand at such behavings,
If he goes on I say will lose his savings.
What's more, so help me God, his only gains
Are empty money-bags and addled brains.
And by the time the man's gone raging mad
And risked and lost whatever goods he had,
He then eggs others on and off they run
To lose their goods, as he himself has done.
   A spiteful wretch takes pleasure when
   he sees
That others suffer from the same disease,
So I was told once by a learned man.
But what's the odds? I'll on as I began.
   When we had fixed a place to exercise
Our esoteric craft, we all looked wise;
Our terms were highly technical and quaint.
I blew the fire up till fit to faint.

As for proportions, why should I rattle on
About the substances we worked upon,
The six or seven ounces it may be
Of silver, or some other quantity,
Or bother to name the things that we were
   piling
Like orpiment,[2] burnt bones and iron filing
Ground into finest powder, all the lot,
Or how we poured them in an earthen pot?
(You put in salt and pepper, be it stated,
Before these powders I enumerated,
Securely covered by a sheet of glass,
And plenty of other things, but let them
   pass.)
And how the pot and glass were daubed
   with clay
For fear the gases might escape away,
And then the fire, whether slow or brisk,
We had to make, the trouble and the risk
We took to sublimate the preparation
Or in the amalgaming and calcination
Of quicksilver, crude mercury that is?
   We always failed, for all those tricks of his.
Our orpiment, our mercury sublimate,
Our lead protoxide ground on a porphyry
   plate
And measured out in ounces, grain by grain,
Gave us no help. Our labour was in vain.
Neither the gas that rose as things grew hot
Nor solids at the bottom of the pot
Were the least use in what we tried to do,
Lost was our trouble, lost our labour too,
And all the money, in the name of Hell,
That we'd laid out on it was lost as well.
   And there was also many another thing
Pertaining to the trade we had to bring,
Though I can't name them in an ordered plan
Because I'm an uneducated man;
Yet I will list them as they come to mind,
Though not distinguishing their class and
   kind:
Armenian clay, borax and verdigris,
Earthen and glass-ware vessels piece by piece,
Our urinals, our pots for oil-extraction,
Crucibles, pots for sublimative action,
Phial, alembic, beaker, gourd-retort,
And other useless nonsense of the sort
Not worth a leek, needless to name them all;
Water in rubefaction,[3] bullock's gall,
Arsenic, brimstone, sal ammoniac,
And herbs that I could mention by the sack,
Moonwort, valerian, agrimony and such,
Which I could number if it mattered much.

Our lamps—we had them burning day and
    night
To help us to succeed, if we but might!
Our furnace too for calcifying action,
Our waters in a state of albefaction,
Chalk, quicklime, ashes and the white of eggs,
Various powders, clay, piss, dung and dregs,
Waxed bags, saltpetre, vitriol and a whole
Variety of fires of wood and coal;
Alkali, tartar, salt in preparation,
Matters combust or in coagulation,
Clay mixed with horse-hair, sometimes with
    my own,
Crystallized alum, oil of tartar thrown
With tartar crude and unfermented beer,
Yeast and a dozen more than you shall hear,
Realgar,[4] various absorbent batters
And, I may add, incorporative matters;
Our silver in a state of citrination,[5]
Things sealed in wax and things in fermenta-
    tion,
Our moulds, our vessels for assaying metal
And many other things I learnt to settle
I'll tell as I was taught, if you want more.
    There were the bodies seven and the spir-
      its four
Which my instructor frequently rehearsed;
Among the spirits quicksilver came first
And orpiment came second, then he passed
To sal ammoniac and brimstone last.
As for the seven bodies I should mention,
Here they all are, if they are worth attention:
Gold for the sun and silver for the moon,
Iron for Mars and quicksilver in tune
With Mercury, lead which prefigures Saturn
And tin for Jupiter. Copper takes the pattern
Of Venus if you please! This cursed trade
Robs one of all the money one has made,
And all one spends on it or round about it
Will certainly be lost, I cannot doubt it.
    If you would publish your infatuation
Come on and try your hand at transmutation;
If one of you has money in his fist
Step up and make yourself an alchemist.
Perhaps you think the trade is easy learnt?
Why then, come on and get your fingers
    burnt;
Monk, friar, priest, canon, let them come
    who may,
And study books and papers night and day
To learn the weird directions verse by verse,
They'll find it's all in vain, God knows, and
    worse.

And as for trying to teach a simpleton,
Pooh! No use talking of it; can't be done.
Whether you know your alphabet or not,
All's one for all the good that may be got.
Learned and simple by my soul's salvation
Achieve the same results from transmutation
Equally well when all is said and done;
They all fail absolutely, every one.
    And still I have forgotten my intention
To speak of iron filings and to mention
Corrosive liquids, ways of mollifying
Or hardening substances, or of supplying
Oils and ablutions, stores of fusible metal,
And so on. It's beyond a book to settle
These matters, any book; it would be best
To give this catalogue and myself a rest,
For I imagine I have said enough
To raise the devil, be he never so rough.
    Ah no, let be! For the Philosopher's Stone,
Called the Elixir, never can be known.
We seek and seek, and were it once discovered
We should be safe enough—expenses cov-
    ered.
But there's no way; whatever paths we trod
The search was useless and I swear to God,
For all our cunning, when all's tried and done
That stone won't yield itself to anyone.
It's made us squander all we ever had,
Losses enough to drive us nearly mad
But for the hope that crept about our heart
Always supposing, when we felt the smart,
It would relieve us of our sad condition;
Sharp was the hope and hard the supposition.
    I give fair warning you may search for ever;
A golden future lures one on to sever
Oneself from all one ever had, and trust
An art for which one cannot lose the lust;
People will always find it bitter-sweet,
Or so it seems. With nothing but a sheet
To cover one at night, with no array
Other than some outlandish cloak by day
One yet would sell them both and be bereft.
No one can stop until there's nothing left.
    Go where they may a man can always tell
Such people by their pungent brimstone smell;
For all the world they stink as will a goat,
A hot and ram-like smell that seems to float
About them, and a man a mile away
Will catch the foul infection, I dare say.
See? By the smell and by the threadbare cloak
You're pretty sure to recognize these folk.
    If privately you ask them to confess
Why they go round in such a shabby dress,

They'll turn at once and whisper in your ear
That if they should be spotted they must fear
Death for their learning, such is their pretence.
That's how these people trade on innocence.

Well, pass on to the story you require;
Before the pot is placed upon the fire
My master takes a certain quantity
Of metals which he tempers, none but he
—I can speak boldly now he's gone away—
For he's a cunning worker as they say,
At any rate he's made himself a name;
He blundered very often just the same.
And how, d'you think? It happens, like as not,
There's an explosion and good-bye the pot!
These metals are so violent when they split
Our very walls can scarce stand up to it,
Unless well-built and made of stone and
    lime—
Bang go the metals through them every time.
And some are driven down into the ground
—That way we used to lose them by the
    pound—
And some are scattered all about the floor;
Some even jump into the roof, what's more.
Although the devil didn't show his face
I'm pretty sure he was about the place.
In Hell itself where he is lord and master
There couldn't be more rancour in disaster
Than when our pots exploded as I told you;
All think they've been let down and start to
    scold you.
Some said the way the fire was made was
    wrong;
Others said, "No—the bellows. Blown too
    strong."
That frightened me, I blew them as a rule.
"Stuff!" said a third. "You're nothing but a
    fool,
It wasn't tempered as it ought to be."
"No!" said a fourth. "Shut up and listen to me;
I say it should have been a beech-wood fire
And that's the real cause, or I'm a liar."
    I cannot tell you why the thing went wrong;
Recriminations though were hot and strong.
"Well," said my lord, "there's nothing more
    to do.
I'll note these dangers for another brew;
I'm pretty certain that the pot was cracked.
Be that as may, don't gape! We've got to act.
Don't be alarmed, help to sweep up the floor
Just as we always do, and try once more.
Pluck up your hearts!" The muck was gath-
    ered up,

A canvas then was laid to form a cup
And all the muck was thrown into a sieve;
He sifted it for what it yet might give.
    "By God," says one, "I saw some metal fall,
Some's saved although we haven't got it all.
If things went wrong just now and acted
    tough,
Another time they may go well enough.
We've got to risk our goods if we're to gain.
What about merchants? Lord! They don't
    maintain
A fixed prosperity, believe you me.
Sometimes their goods are swallowed by
    the sea,
And sometimes they come safely back to
    port."
"Well, calm yourself," my master would re-
    tort;
"Next time I shall have things in proper
    frame,
I'll see our ship comes home, or take the
    blame.
Something went wrong I know, I'll find out
    what."
    Another said the fire was too hot.
But whether hot or cold you may depend
We always met with failure in the end.
Yet, though we never reached the wished
    conclusion
We still went raving on in our illusion,
Sitting together, arguing on and on
And every one as wise as Solomon.
    However, all that glitters is not gold,
And that's the truth as we're so often told.
It isn't every apple on the spray
Is good to eat, lament it how you may.
It's just the same with us. Though it may
    please us
To think we're wise, the wisest one, by Jesus,
Will prove the biggest fool, that's my belief,
And he that seems the honestest, a thief.
That will be clear enough to you, my friends,
Before I leave you and my story ends.

PART II

There is a canon going up and down
Amongst us, one who could infect a town
As large as Nineveh and Rome spread flat
With Troy and three or four on top of that.
The endless tricks and cunning of this crook
Are more than could be written in a book
Though you sat down and wrote a thousand
    years;

He has no equal in this vale of tears.
The terms he uses wriggle, wind and scuttle
In tones of voice so infinitely subtle,
A man engaged with him in conversation
Soon finds his brain is dizzy with rotation,
Unless the man's a devil like himself.
Many a man he's cozened of his pelf
And will again, if he should live awhile.
Yet there are men will travel mile on mile
To seek this canon out and be acquainted,
Not knowing everything he does is tainted.
So if you care to listen to what I say
You shall hear all about it right away.

    If, holy canons of the church, it rouses
The thought that I am slandering your houses,
Since it is of a canon I am speaking,
Reject the thought! God knows, there is some
    sneaking
Rascal in every house and God forbid
That all were judged by what one mad-
    man did.
Slandering you's no part of my intention,
But to set right the evils that I mention.
    Nor is my tale aimed specially at you;
It will apply to many others too.
Among the twelve apostles our Creator
Found faith in all but one, who was a traitor.
Then why should the remainder be to blame
That stood in innocence? I say the same
Of you, except for this, if you will hear:
If any lurking Judas should appear
Among you, fling him out I say betimes,
Before you're shamed and beggared by his
    crimes.
And therefore take no umbrage, sirs, I pray,
And in this instance listen to what I say.

    There was a chantry priest, it would appear,
One who had lived in London many a year,
So pleasant in his manner and so able,
The lady in whose house he sat at table
Refused to take a farthing's worth of pay
For board and clothes, whatever his display,
And she allowed him pocket-money as well.
No matter for that; I shall proceed to tell
My story of the canon, whose intrusion
Brought this unhappy priest to his confusion.
    This treacherous canon, then, came in
        one day,
Entered the priest's apartment where he lay
And begged him to advance a certain sum,
Which was to be repaid him, saying, "Come,
Lend me a mark, it's only for three days,

I'll pay you on the nail—I'm one who pays.
And if I fail you when you come to check,
Another time just hang me by the neck!"
    This priest produced the money on the
        spot;
The canon, after thanking him a lot,
Took leave of him and went upon his way
And brought his money back the proper day.
When it had been paid back and matters
    righted
This foolish priest of course was quite de-
    lighted
And said, "Trust me, I never take offence
If someone comes to borrow a few pence
Or anything I have in my possession
When he's an honest man of good profession
And doesn't break his day if he should owe;
To such a man I never can say no."
    "What!" said the canon. "I not pay
        when due?
That would be something altogether new!
My honour is a thing I hope to keep
For ever till the moment when I creep
Into my grave. God send I do indeed;
You can trust that as surely as the creed.
And I thank God—in good hour be it
    spoken—
No one can say my word was ever broken
For any gold or silver I was lent;
I never stole a farthing with intent.
    "Now, sir," he said, "to speak of my con-
        cerns,
Since you are fond of doing kindly turns
And were particularly kind to me,
To pay you back the coin of charity
I'll tell you something, if you care to learn,
In simple language how I came to turn
My talents towards alchemy and science.
Watch! You can place an absolute reliance
On seeing me work a miracle ere I go."
    "What!" said the priest. "Can that be re-
        ally so?
Mother of God! I beg you to proceed!"
    "At your commandment, sir, I will in-
        deed,"
He answered, "God forbid that I should not."
D'you see? This thief's kind service was a plot.
How true it is that proffered service stinks!
So say the wise, and anyone who thinks.
I'll verify that saying in a while
Upon this canon, root of fraud and guile.
He took a special pleasure and delight,
Such was his fiendish heart, and appetite

For bringing Christian people to destruction;
God keep us from his treacherous seduction!
    The priest had no idea with whom he
        dealt,
And what was coming to him never felt.
O foolish priest! O innocent in bliss,
Soon to be blinded, and by avarice!
O God-abandoned, blind in a complete
And thoughtless ignorance of the deceit
This wily fox is putting into shape!
You're in the snare, there will be no escape;
And therefore to press on to a conclusion
That only can refer to your confusion,
Unhappy man, I hurry on to volley
Anathemas upon your witless folly
And on the treachery of that other wretch
As far as my abilities will stretch.
    You think this canon was my master, eh?
Sir Host, by Mary of Heaven let me say
It was another canon and not he,
A hundred times more skilled in trickery.
His frauds have cozened people many a time;
It dulls my wits to speak of it in rhyme.
Whenever I think of them it brings a rush
Of blood for very shame, I have to blush
—At any rate my cheeks begin to glow
Though there's no colour in them, well I
        know;
My face is tarnished, fumes of the diverse
Metals you heard me latterly rehearse
Have wasted and consumed and turned it
        yellow.
Now take account of this accursed fellow:
    "Sir," he addressed the priest, "send out
        your man
For quicksilver, as quickly as you can;
Let him bring several ounces, two or three,
And when he's back I promise you shall see
A miracle you never saw before."
    "Certainly," said the priest, "he's at the
        door,
It shall be done at once." The man was sent,
Ready to do his bidding; off he went
And, to tell truth, returned immediately
Bringing three ounces of the mercury,
And gave them to the canon for a start.
    The canon laid them carefully apart
And sent the servant out again for coal,
In order to start work towards his goal.
    The man came back and brought a scut-
        tleful;
This canon then drew forth a crucible
Out of his bosom, showed it to his dupe,

"And now," he said, "be good enough to
        stoop
And measure out an ounce of mercury.
This is our instrument, as you can see.
Open your hand; now put the mercury in,
That's it . . . and in the name of Christ begin
The study of science, be an alchemist!
    "Few, very few indeed, I would enlist
With those who share the secrets of my sci-
        ence.
But you shall watch me, using this appliance,
Do an experiment. I shall reduce
Or mortify this metal—no abuse
Of your good faith—before your very eyes.
Yes, you shall watch it as it mortifies
And changes into silver just as fine
And good as any in your purse or mine
Or anywhere else, and just as malleable.
If not, call me a liar and unable
To show my face, a subject for your mirth!
    "I have a powder here that cost the earth
And it will make all good, for it's the basis
Of all my power—I'll show you—in these
        cases.
Send your man off, tell him to wait outside,
And shut the door on him. I won't be spied
Upon at work, for no one else must see
The way we set to work in alchemy."
    He gave his orders and the thing was done,
The servant was sent packing at a run,
The chamber door was bolted with a jerk
And these philosophers got down to work.
    At the accursed canon's fell desire
The priest then set the thing upon the fire
And grabbed the bellows busily and blew.
Into the crucible the canon threw
This powder—what it was I cannot tell;
Possibly chalk, or glass would do as well,
Or anything else indeed, not worth a fly
To hoodwink him—and urged him to
        look spry
And cover up the crucible with coal.
    "To demonstrate my love for you, dear
        soul,"
The canon said, "in what we're going to do,
I'll leave the handling of it all to you."
    "Oh, thank you!" said the priest, who was
        delighted,
And couched the coals just as he was invited.
And while he busied himself this fiendish
        wretch,
This treacherous canon, whom the devil fetch,
Produced a bit of beech-wood, charred to coal,

In which there had been subtly bored a hole
That held an ounce of silver filings, stopped
With wax securely, lest a filing dropped.
Please understand this treacherous invention
Was not made then, but made of long inten-
tion;
The canon had devised it all before,
And other dodges too. I'll tell you more
Hereafter of those other things he brought,
For long before he came he had the thought
Of tricking him. So he did before they parted.
He couldn't wait to skin him, having started.
It dulls my wits, I say, to speak of him.
Oh, to take vengeance on this treacher-
ous, trim
Liar! If only I knew how! But there,
He's slippery—here and there and every-
where.
    Now listen, gentlemen, for God's dear love.
He took this coal of which I spoke above
And palmed it dexterously, while the priest,
Still busy as I said, had nearly ceased
Poking, as I have told you, with a prong
Among the coals. "You're doing it all
wrong!"
The canon said, "Here's how it ought to be,
Dear chap, I'll fix it; give the thing to me,
Just let me interfere a little. There!
St. Giles, I'm sorry for you! I declare
You've got quite hot—why, man, you're
pouring sweat,
Here, take this cloth and wipe yourself, you're
wet."
    And while the priest was mopping up
his face
The canon took his coal—the damned dis-
grace!—
And stuck it in the middle, somewhat higher
Than was the crucible, and blew the fire
Till up it flamed and all the coals were red.
    "And now let's have a drink," the canon
said;
"All will be well quite soon, I'll undertake.
Sit down, let's cheer ourselves for goodness'
sake."
    After a while this canon's beechen coal
Burnt up; out came the silver from the hole
Into the crucible and began to run
As you'd expect. What else could it have
done?
Couched well above the flames it couldn't
miss.
The priest, alas, knew nothing of all this,

Thinking the coals were all alike and good;
It was a trick he had not understood.
    And when this alchemist saw all was ready
"Rise up," he said, "Sir priest, beside me—
steady,
We haven't got a mould. Let's take a walk
For we shall need to buy ourselves some chalk
Which I can carve, if I may make so bold,
Into the shape required for a mould.
And you must get me out a bowl or pan
With water in it, for I tell you, man,
Our business here is just about to sprout.
And just to disabuse you of all doubt,
While you're away, to clear me of suspicion
I shall go with you on your expedition
And stay with you till we return once more."
    And to be brief he then unlocked the door,
Went out and shut it, turning to re-lock it,
And off they went. The key was in his pocket.
Presently back they came with no delay.
Why should I drag my story out all day?
He took the chalk when they got back again
And made a mould of it. Let me explain:
Out of his sleeve I say he took a rod
Of silver—pour thy vengeance on him,
God!—
Which weighed an ounce exactly; this he took
(Watch for the tricks of this accursed crook),
And carved his mould to make a perfect fit
For this same silver rod, depend on it,
So furtively the priest, you may believe,
Saw nothing. Then he tucked it up his sleeve,
Turned to the fire, took out the preparation
And poured it in the mould with great elation.
He cast the mould into the water-pan
When ready, saying to the priest, poor man,
"Look what we've got, put in your hand and
grope
And you will find some silver there, I hope."
    Hell's devils! What else could have been
the stuff?
Silver filings are silver right enough.
    The priest put in his hand and took a scoop
And out he brought the metal with a whoop,
Thrilled to the veins to see this silver rod.
"God's blessing on you, and the Mother
of God
And all his saints preserve you, worthy mas-
ter!"
He cried. "And may they bring me to disaster
Unless you will vouchsafe your kind com-
pliance
In teaching me this noble art and science."

I'll work for you with all my might and
  main!"
  "Well," said the canon, "let me try again;
We'll have a second shot; pay careful heed
And you'll become an expert, and at need
Can try it in my absence, once you're in
The ways of scientific discipline.
Let's take another ounce of mercury,
This is no time for chattering," said he,
"And do the same with it as we have done
Already with the first, our silver one."

  The priest then set to business and began
To do precisely what this cursed man
Commanded of him, puffing at the fire
In the mad hope of reaching his desire.
Meanwhile the canon, if I need explain,
Stood ready by, to gull the priest again,
Dandling, to give him countenance in this,
A hollow stick—observe the artifice!—
Into the end of which an ounce, no more,
Of silver filings had been stuffed before,
As in the beech-wood coal, with wax no
  doubt,
To stop the silver filings falling out.

  And while the priest was busy at his job
The canon came and touched him with
  the knob
And with a flourish cast the powder in
Just as before—the devil scrape his skin,
Hear me, O God, and flay him for the trick!—
And stirred the crucible with this same stick
Primed in the treacherous way that you have
  heard;
He always was a crook in deed and word.

  He stirred the coals until the wax began
To melt over the flame, as any man
Except a fool of course would know it must.
Out of the stick slid all the silver dust
And down into the crucible it fell.

  What can be better, gentlemen, than well?
For when this priest had been deceived again
And taken it all for gospel, right as rain,
He was so happy that I can't express
In words his ecstasy of happiness.
He proffered to the canon on the spot
Body and soul. "Eh," said the canon. "What?
I have some powers, though I seem poor to
  some,
But let me tell you there is more to come.
D'you happen to have some copper here?"
  said he.
"Yes," said the priest, "I think I have,
  maybe."

"If not you'll have to buy some right away,
Be off with you, dear sir, be quick I say."
  He went away and came back with the
  copper;
The canon took it from him as was proper,
And carefully weighed out a measured ounce.

  My tongue is all too simple to pronounce
Words that could serve my thoughts or match
  my feelings
About his bloody-minded double-dealings.
Friendly he seemed to those he hadn't caught
But was a fiend in what he felt and thought.
It wearies me to say how false he was,
Yet I must try to speak of it because
It may help others to beware his treason
In time, and truly that's my only reason.

  Within the crucible the canon placed
His ounce of copper, set it then in haste
Among the flames and cast the powder in,
Telling the priest to stoop down and begin
Blowing the fire, and it was all a hoax;
He made a monkey of him with his jokes.

  He cast the molten copper in his mould
And put it in the water to get cold;
Leaning above it, in he put his hand.
Now in his sleeve—as you will understand,
You heard me say so—was a silver rod.
He took it slyly out, the filthy sod,
—The priest knew nothing of his treacherous
  plan—
And left it in the bottom of the pan.
He fumbled in the water, groped about
And with amazing sleight-of-hand took out
And hid the copper rod. With friendly charm
He took the unsuspecting victim's arm
And said to him, as if it were a joke,
"By God, you're much to blame! Stoop down
  and poke;
Help me as I helped you. That's only fair;
Come on, put in your hand and see what's
  there."
  The priest took out the silver there and
  then.
The canon said, "We must go out again
Taking these rods, all three, that we have
  made,
And ask some fellow in the goldsmith trade
Whether they're anything. I should be dis-
  tressed
To find them less than silver of the best.
Well, it's a thing that can be proved forth-
  with."
  So off they went to find a silversmith

And gave their metal to the man to try it
With fire and hammer; no one could deny it,
All were as should be, silver unalloyed.

Was that besotted cleric overjoyed?
Never was bird gladder to greet the day,
Never was nightingale in depth of May
More joyful in her eagerness to sing,
Nor lady lustier in carolling
Or in her talk of love and womanhood,
Nor knightly soul more eager to do good
In deeds of arms to please his chosen lady
Than was the priest to learn that graceless,
    shady
Business; and he addressed the canon thus:
"For love of God who died for all of us,
And if I may deserve so much of you,
What will that powder cost me? Tell me, do!"

    "By our Lady," said the canon, "for a buyer
I warn you it's expensive; save one friar
And I myself there's no one who can make it,
Not in all England." "Never mind, I'll take
    it,"
The priest replied; "for God's sake, what's the
    price?"
"It's dear," he said, "but at a sacrifice,
Since you're a friend and really want to bid,
God help me, it is yours for forty quid.
But for the kindness that you showed before
In lending me a mark it would be more."

    This priest at once collected forty pound
In golden pieces and he took them round
To give the canon for his recipe,
Whose work in life was fraud and treachery.

    "Sir priest," he said, "I look for no renown
In this my art; in fact I play it down.
So, if you love me keep the matter quiet;
If people knew my skill there'd be a riot.
By God, there'd be such envy and defiance
Against me for philosophy and science,
I should be killed; there'd be no other way."

    "Why God forbid!" the priest said. "Killed,
    you say?
Better to squander all the wealth I had
To save you—if I didn't, send me mad,
Dear God!—than see you suffer such an ill."
"You have a solid reason for good will,"
The canon said. "Good-bye and many
    thanks!"
And off he went, this prince of mountebanks;
The priest never set eyes on him again
After that day. I hardly need explain
That when he tried experiments the priest
Had no success whatever, not the least.

The powder wouldn't work, it was a mock;
He had been tricked and made a laughing-
    stock.
That was the canon's way of introduction
When bringing down poor people to destruc-
    tion.

    Gentlemen, think, there has been strife
    of old
In every class waged between men and gold,
So fierce there's hardly any to be had.
Alchemy has made many people mad
And on my word I think it may well be
The greatest reason for its scarcity.
    Their scientific jargon is so woolly
No one can hope to understand it fully,
Not as intelligence goes nowadays.
And they may go on chattering like jays
And take delight and trouble in their chatter
But for all that they'll never solve the matter.
If you are rich it's easy to be taught
How to transmute and bring your wealth to
    naught.
    There's so much lucre in this fine affair
One's joy can be transmuted to despair.
It can impoverish the heaviest purses,
Yet all it does for one is buy the curses
Of those that lend their goods before they've
    learnt.
Oh fie, for shame! When people have been
    burnt
Cannot they learn, alas, to shun the fire?
And you that use it, master your desire
Lest you lose all; for better late than never.
Long is the ruin that can last for ever!
  · Prowl as you may, the secret can't be found,
Though you're as bold as Dobbin blundering
    round;
Poor blind old horse, in dangers all unknown,
He's just as liable to hit a stone
As keep along the highway, and I hold
It's just the same transmuting into gold.
    Should, then, your outward eye see incor-
    rectly
Let the mind's eye behold more circum-
    spectly.
You may be wide awake, but though you stare
You will make nothing of that business there,
Rather will waste all you can grab or earn.
Slacken a fire that is quick to burn;
Meddle no more with alchemy, I mean,
For if you do all thrift will be swept clean.
    I should at once inform you if I may

What genuine philosophers would say.
Arnold[6] is one of those that make the quorum;
He wrote *Rosarium Philosophorum*
And came from Villa Nova. Thus says he:
"There is no mortifying mercury
Without the use of sulphur, brother to it."
The first of all philosophers that knew it
Was Hermes Trismegistus and he said:
"Doubtless the dragon never can be dead
Or mortify, unless you also slay
His brother with him. Put another way,
The dragon stands for Mercury, none other,
And sulphur, known as brimstone, is his
brother,
And these are drawn from *Luna* and from *Sol*.
Therefore," he said, "observe this protocol:
Let no man busy himself to seek this art
Unless he knows the language and the heart
Of science, both in aim and technical term,
For, without these, he is an ignorant worm.
This is a craft and science that is furled
As secrets of the secrets of the world."

Plato had a disciple once, and he
Said to his master—if you care to see,
It is recorded in the *Chimica
Senioris Zadith Tabula*—[7]
"Tell me the name, sir, of the Secret Stone?"
And Plato said in answer, "It is known
As Titan Stone upon the tongues of men."
"And what is that?" said the disciple then.
"Magnesia," answered Plato. "Is it thus?
Then it's *ignotum per ignotius!*[8]
What then may be Magnesia, master, pray?"
"Magnesia is the liquid, I would say,
Composed of the Four Elements," he said.
"What's its root-principle or fountain-head?
Will you be pleased to indicate that fount?"
"No, no," said Plato then, "on no account.
Philosophers are under strict control
Never to tell that secret to a soul
Or write it in a book; it is unpriced,
Being a secret very dear to Christ.
It is His will that no discovery
Be made of it, save where His Deity
Wills to inspire His servants, else forbidden.
No more; from whom He wills He keeps it
hidden."
So I conclude; since God will not allow
Philosophers to tell their pupils how
To find this stone, no doubt it's better so,
And my advice would be to let it go.
Make God your adversary for a whim
And work at what is contrary to Him

And to His will, and you will never thrive
Though you transmute as long as you're alive.
Aye, there's the point for which my tale
began,
And may God prosper every honest man!
                                        Amen.

THE MANCIPLE'S TALE
The Manciple's Prologue

Don't you all know where stands a little town,
The one that people call Bob-up-and-down,
Near Blean Woods on the way to Canterbury?
Well, it was thereabouts our Host turned
merry.
"Dun's in the mire!"[1] he said. "Behold
King Log;
For love of money drag him from his bog!
Will no one wake our friend asleep behind?
A thief could rob him and he wouldn't mind.
Look at him napping . . . Forty winks? Cock's
bones!
He'll tumble off his horse and hit the stones.
Is that the London Cook, the devil take him?
Make him come here, he knows the fine, we'll
make him
Tell us a story, though I'm bound to say
It won't be worth a barrow-load of hay.
Wake up, you Cook!" he said. "God give you
sorrow,
What's up with you to sleep this sunny
morrow?
Have you had fleas all night, or else got drunk,
Or spent the night in toiling with a punk,
And haven't got the strength to raise your
head?"
The Cook was drunk, pale-drunk, no touch
of red,
And answered from a stupor, "Bless my soul!
I feel all heavy, haven't got control;
I'd rather sleep," he said, "I don't know why,
Than drink a gallon of wine, the best you buy
In all Cheapside." The Manciple said, "Well,
If I can make things easier for a spell
For you, and not offend the company,
And if the Host extends his courtesy
To let me, I'll excuse you from your tale.
"Upon my word, your face is pretty pale,
Your eyes are somewhat dazed, I can't help
thinking,
As for your breath, I'm bound to say it's
stinking,

Which shows you indisposed for such a matter.
Blunt words are best, I never was one to
flatter.
   "Look at him yawning there, the
     drunken sot!
You'd think he meant to swallow us on the
   spot.
Keep your mouth shut, man! Mercy, what a
   socket!
The devil of Hell's own hoof would hardly
   block it;
Your cursed breath may well infect us all.
You stinking swine, fie, how you gape and
   sprawl!
(Look out, take care, sir, he's a powerful man)
I'd like to see a punch-ball hit his pan!
He's about ripe for trouble in that line;
You'd think he had been drinking monkey-
   wine,[2]
And that's when one goes playing with a
   straw!"
   This speech annoyed the Cook who, turn-
     ing raw,
Craned at the Manciple with so much force
For want of speech, he tumbled off his horse
And there he lay for all the care they took;
Fine cavalry performance for a cook!
Pity he couldn't have held on by his ladle.
   They got him back at last into the cradle
After a deal of shoving to and fro;
To lift him up, it was a sorry show;
Poor, pallid soul, unwieldier than most!
   But to the Manciple at last our Host
Turned and remarked, "Drink is in domi-
     nation
Over the fellow; by my soul's salvation
I think he'd only tell a lousy tale.
Whether it's wine or maybe new-brewed ale
That's in him, he is talking through his nose;
Like someone with a cold, one would suppose,
Snuffling like that. I think he's going to spew.
It's just about as much as he can do
To keep his horse from falling in the ditch
And if his horse should fall, he'll follow,
   which
Gives us as much as we can do to strain
And lift his drunken body up again.
Carrying corpses would be just as grim.
Tell on your tale, I've had enough of him.
   "But, Manciple, it wasn't very nice
Of you to scold the fellow for his vice.
Another day those chickens you have loosed
May very likely all return to roost.

I mean he might allude to small amounts
That could be criticized in your accounts
As not quite honest, if it came to proof."
   "That might be awkward; I shall keep aloof.
He easily could catch me in the snare,"
The other said, "I'd rather buy the mare
Between his drunken legs than start a row,
I mustn't make him angry anyhow.
The things I said were only meant in jest.
   "Do you know what? I've something of
     the best
Here in this gourd, wine of the ripest grape;
Just watch and we shall have another jape.
I'll give the Cook some liquor if I may,
On pain of death he shall not say me nay!"
   And certainly, to tell you what occurred,
The Cook, alas, drank freely from the gourd.
What was the need? He'd had enough before,
Yet spluttered in the mug and drank some
   more,
Giving it back when he had had enough.
The Cook, who was delighted with the stuff
Thanked him as best he could for some time
   after.
   Our Host went off into a roar of laughter
And said "Well, now I see how necessary
It is to bring one's drink to keep us merry,
For it can turn all rancour and dissension
To love and harmony and stop contention.
   "O Bacchus, thou! A blessing on thy name
That so convertest earnest into game;
Our thanks and worship to thy deity!
My prayers are done, you get no more of me."
   "Now, Manciple, on with your story,
     pray."
"Well, sir," he said, "attend to what I say."

The Manciple's Tale

When Phoebus had his dwelling here on earth
As ancient books report, for what they're
   worth,
He was a paladin of lustiest marrow,
Better than anyone with bow and arrow.
He slew the serpent Python as it lay
Coiled in the sunshine and asleep one day,
And many a noble and distinguished deed
His bow performed for him, as you can read.
   And every instrument of minstrelsy
He well knew how to play, while melody
Poured from his throat, clear joy to hear him
   sing.
Even Amphion, famous Theban King
Who built the town's defences by his singing,

Was not so skilled in setting echoes ringing.
Added to that he was the handsomest man
That ever was heard of since the world began.
Why should I make description of his features?
He was the fairest living of earthly creatures.
And therewithal he was of noblest bearing,
Filled with high honour, excellence and daring.

This Phoebus, flower in the cap of youth,
Renowned for bounty, chivalry and truth,
To please himself and signalize his glory
In having vanquished Python, says my story,
Was wont to carry in his hand a bow.

It happened that this Phoebus kept a crow
Lodged in a cage, and there for many a day
He taught it speech, as one can teach a jay,
And fostered it with care. This crow was white,
White as a snowy swan; it could recite
With perfect mimicry of tone and word
What any man had uttered, and the bird
Would use this talent when it told a tale.
In all the world there was no nightingale,
Moreover, with a hundred thousandth part
Of what it had in merriness and art.

Now in his house this Phoebus had a wife
Who lived with him; he loved her more than life
And night and day he gave his diligence
To pleasing her and showing reverence,
Except for this, if it's the truth they tell us,
I have to say he was extremely jealous
And wished to guard her, lest an exhibition
Be made of him, as those in his condition
Commonly do—in vain, it can't succeed.
A good wife who is pure in thought and deed
Should not be checked and spied on, that is plain,
And truly it is labour all in vain
To check a wicked wife; it can't be done.
It's imbecility, say I for one,
For men to waste their labour checking wives,
And so the ancients say who wrote their lives.

But to my purpose, as I first began;
This excellent Phoebus does the best he can
To please her, thinking by his kind address
And by his management and manliness
That no one could extrude him from her graces.
But God knows, none can compass in such cases
The power to restrain a thing which nature
Has naturally implanted in a creature.
Take any bird and put it in a cage
And let your heart's intention then engage
To foster it tenderly with food and drink,
With every dainty mess that thought can think,
And keep it clean as nearly as you may,
Caged in a cage of gold however gay,
That bird would rather twenty thousand fold
Be in a forest which is rough and cold,
Feeding on worms and other wretched trash.
It's on the watch, and ready in a flash
To escape out of the cage and to be gone.
Freedom is what it sets its heart upon.

Or take a cat, nourish it well with milk
And tender meat, make it a couch of silk,
But let it see a mouse along the wall
And it abandons milk and meat and all,
Aye, every other dainty in the house,
Such is its appetite to eat a mouse.
You see, a natural lust is in possession
And appetite has banished its discretion.

She-wolves are also of this baser kind;
They choose the lowest wolf that they can find,
The least in reputation, to be mated,
When the time comes to have their passion sated.

These parallels are all produced to show
The faithlessness of men, they do not go
For women, not at all. The foul delight
Of men is wreaking lecherous appetite
On lower things than wives however fair,
However true, however debonair;
Flesh pines for the new-fangled, curse upon it,
And nothing with the stamp of virtue on it
Will pleasure us for more than a short while.

This Phoebus who was innocent of guile
Was well deceived, for all his excellent features.
She had a man, one of the lowest creatures
Beneath him and of little reputation,
Worth nothing next a man of Phoebus' station.
And more's the harm it happens often so
And is a common source of human woe.

It chanced his wife, when Phoebus was away,
Sent for her bully—bully, did I say?
Tut-tut, that was a very knavish speech!
Your pardon, lords and ladies, I beseech.

Wise Plato says, as those who can may read,
Words should be in accordance with the deed.

In tales told properly a word should bring
The sense of being cousin to the thing.
I'm a blunt, boisterous man and tell you all
There is no real difference at all
Between a lady-wife of high degree
Dishonest of her body, if she be,
And some poor wench, no difference but this
—That's if so be they both should go amiss—
That since the gentlewoman ranks above
She therefore will be called his "lady-love,"
Whereas that other woman, being poor,
Will be referred to as his wench or whore.
And as God knows (and so do you, dear
    brother),
One name is just as low as is the other.

    Nor is there difference in my belief
Between a tyrant and an arrant thief
Or outlaw, when the tyrant has no claim.
They told great Alexander just the same,
That just because a tyrant has the might
By force of arms to murder men downright
And burn down house and home and leave all
    flat,
They call the man a captain, just for that.
But since an outlaw with his little band
Cannot bring half such mischief on a land
Or be the cause of so much harm and grief,
He only earns the title of a thief.

    Well, I'm no scholar and you shan't be vexed
By hearing me enlarge on any text;
Back to the tale I started, but more fully.

    When Phoebus' wife had notified her bully
They wrought their will in all its transient
    rage.
Now the white crow, still hanging in its cage,
Beheld their work and never said a word.
But once Lord Phoebus had returned, the bird
Unlocked its throat and sang, "Cuckoo!
    Cuckoo!"
    "What, bird!" said Phoebus, "That's no
        song for you!
Were you not wont to sing your songs so gaily
That it rejoiced my heart to hear you daily
In tuneful voice? Alas, what song is this?"
    "By God," it said, "I do not sing amiss.
Phoebus," it said, "in spite of all your worth,
Of all your beauty and your gentle birth,
Of all your minstrelsy and singing too,
And all your watching, someone's hood-
    winked you,
Has bleared your eyes—a man whose repu-
    tation
Compared with yours has little estimation,

Not worth a gnat indeed; upon my life,
On your own bed I saw him plumb your
    wife."
    What more d'you want? The crow, in his
        behoof,
Boldly informed him, giving serious proof,
Of how his wife had done her lechery
And had put shame on him and villainy;
He swore he had seen it with his very eyes.
    Phoebus fell backward at the crow's replies;
It seemed to him his sorrowful heart was
    breaking.
Setting an arrow to his bow and taking
Aim as he bent it in his rage to slay,
He killed his wife; there is no more to say.
    And all his instruments of minstrelsy
He broke in sorrow for it, psaltery,
Lute, harp, guitar, and then he broke his bow
And arrows, and he thus addressed the crow:
    "Traitor," he said, "it was thy scorpion-
        tongue
Brought my confusion. Oh, my heart is
    wrung
With grief! Why was I born? Would I were
    dead!
O dearest wife, O gem of joy that shed
So grave, so true a light upon our love!
Now thou art dead and pale of face, O dove
Of innocence, that I can swear! O speed
Of hand too rash, to do so foul a deed!
O mind confused, O thoughtless rage sur-
    prised
That smote a guiltless creature unadvised!
O fainting trust, O prompting to suspect,
Where was your thought and wisdom to di-
    rect?
O every man, beware how you are moved,
Never believe but what is strongly proved!
Strike not too soon, ere you can reason why,
Be soberly advised before you try
To execute your justice and assuage
Suspicion by the acting of your rage.
Alas, a thousand in their hasty ire
Have been undone and brought into the mire.
O sorrow! I shall kill myself for grief!"
    And to the crow he said, "O wicked thief,
Now I shall pay you for your lying tale!
Once you sang sweetly like a nightingale,
But now, false thief, your liquid song is done
And all your snowy feathers, every one;
Never in all your life to utter word,
Vengeance shall fall upon you, traitor-bird.
You and your issue ever shall be black;

Their sweetest music, like your own, shall
    crack
And you shall croak, foretelling storm and rain
In token that through you my wife was slain."
    And up he started at the crow and tore
The fair white feathers out that once it bore
And made it black, and took away its song
And power of speech, and flung it forth
    headlong
Down to the devil, nor do I wish it back.
And that's the reason why all crows are black.
    My lords, this is a parable conveying
A moral; pray take heed of what I'm saying.
Never tell anyone in all your life
That any other has enjoyed his wife,
For he will hate you mortally, believe it.
    Solomon said—the learned so receive it—
"Teach every man how to refrain his tongue."
But as I said, you won't find me among
The scholars, but my mother long ago
Would say, "My son, reflect upon the crow;
My son, you hold your tongue and hold your
    friends.
A wicked tongue but serves the devil's ends.
My son, the cross can save you from his net;
My son, God in His endless goodness set
A wall about the tongue of teeth and lip:
Take counsel ere you speak, let nothing slip.
My son, too often by some babbling speech
Many are blasted, so the scholars teach.
A little wisely spoken as a rule
Will save a man from being cursed for fool.
My son, restrain your tongue in self-denial
On all occasions, save in making trial
Of prayer or speaking in the honour of God.
The first of virtues, if you will kiss the rod,
My son, is to restrain and guard your tongue;
So teach your children this when they are
    young.
My son, superfluous, unthinking speech,
When to say less is still within your reach
And would suffice, will harm you, I was
    taught.
Much chatter is the food of sinful thought.
Are you aware what hasty tongues can do?
Just as a sword can cut an arm in two
Or slice it into bits, dear son, just so
A tongue can sever friendship at a blow.
    "A chatterbox is hateful to the Lord;
Here Solomon the wise is in accord
With David in his psalms, and Seneca too.
My son, say nothing when a nod will do.
Feign to be deaf if you should hear the chatter

Of any fool that broaches dangerous matter.
And add this Flemish proverb to your diet
If you will learn it, 'Little speech, much
    quiet.'
My son, if you have said no wicked word
You need not fear to have been overheard,
Whereas a wicked word, I tell you plain,
Once said can never be recalled again.
What's said is said and goes upon its way,
Like it or not, repent it as you may.
    "He is a slave to any that has heard
Him tell a tale, he'll suffer for that word.
My son, be cautious, fashion nothing new
By way of tidings, whether false or true;
Wherever you may be, with high or low,
Refrain your tongue and think upon the
    crow."

THE PARSON'S TALE
The Parson's Prologue

The story of the Manciple had ended.
From the south line the sun had now de-
    scended
So low, it stood—so far as I had sight—
At less than twenty-nine degrees in height.
Four o' the clock it was, to make a guess;
Eleven foot long, or little more or less,
My shadow was, as at that time and place,
Measuring feet by taking in this case
My height as six, divided in like pattern[1]
Proportionally; and the power of Saturn[2]
Began to rise with *Libra* just as we
Approached a little thorpe. Our referee,
Our Host, that is, and trusted guide,
    who made
Decisions for our happy cavalcade,
Turned round and said, "Matters, my lords,
    stand thus;
There's but one story lacking now to us.
We've carried out my sentence and decree.
We've heard a tale from each in his degree,
What I ordained is nearly done, I say,
God send the best of fortune, so I pray,
On whomsoever is last to pour the liquor.
Sir Priest," he said, "are you by chance a vicar?
Or else the parson? Tell the truth, I say;
Don't spoil our sport though, be you what
    you may,
For every man but you has told his tale.
Unbuckle now and show what's in your bale,
For honestly, to judge you by your looks,

You could knit mighty matters out of books.
So up and tell a story, by cock's bones!"

The parson said at once in level tones,
"You'll get no fable or romance from me,
For Paul in his Epistle to Timothy
Reproves all those who waive aside the truth
For fables that are wretched and uncouth.
And why unclench my fist on your behalf,
I that can scatter wheat, to give you chaff?
And therefore if you care to hear my
    preaching
I'll offer virtuous matter, moral teaching.
So if you'll hear me, granting that sufficed,
I would be glad in reverence of Christ
To give you lawful pleasure if I can.

"But trust me truly, I'm a southern man,
I can't romance with rum-ram-ruf by letter,[3]
And rhyme, God knows, I hold but little
    better;
I won't embellish things with tricks like those
If you'll excuse me, but I'll speak in prose,
A happy thing, to knit and make an end
Of all our feast. Jesu in mercy send
Me wit to guide your way one further stage
Upon that perfect, glorious pilgrimage
Called the celestial, to Jerusalem.
These are my thoughts; if you approve
    of them
I'll start my tale at once, so tell me pat
If you agree. I can't say more than that.

"Nevertheless I put this meditation
In full submission to the castigation
Of learned men. I am not skilled in texts,
I only take, as each of you expects,
The moral of it, and for your protection
As I protest, submit it to correction."

These words had gained assent from ev-
    eryone,
For that, we thought, was just what should be
    done,
To close upon a virtuous persuasion
And give him both an audience and occasion;
Our Host was then requested to prevail
On our behalf with him to tell his tale.

Our Host was ready and found words
    for all,
And said, "Now, master Parson, fair befall
Your reverent meditation! But I'm thinking
You'd better hurry, for the sun is sinking.
Be fructuous and brief in what you tell
And may God send you grace to do it well!
Say what you please; you will be gladly
    heard."
So he began his sermon, on the word.

The Parson's Tale

*The Parson's tale is a prose sermon on the proper
preparation for Confession and the true nature of
the Seven Deadly Sins. It seems therefore to lead
naturally to Chaucer's Retractions which follow it.
On the literal plane of meaning it seems to be offered
as an appropriate ending to a pilgrimage before the
Saint's shrine is reached. On the allegorical plane,
referred to by the Parson when first called upon for
a story, it may be deemed a preparation for a last
confession to be made on "that perfect, glorious pilgrimage" that is called the celestial, to the Heavenly
Jerusalem.*

*A brief summary of the Parson's sermon here
follows:*

· *God desires no man to perish and there are many
   spiritual ways to the celestial city. One noble way
   is Penitence, the lamenting for sin and the will to
   sin no more. The root of the tree of Penitence is
   contrition, the branches and the leaves are confession, the fruit satisfaction, the seed grace,
   and the heat in that seed the Love of God.*

· *Contrition is the heart's sorrow for sin. Sin may
   be venial or deadly. Venial sin is for one to love
   Christ less than he ought. Deadly sin is to love a
   creature more than the Creator. Venial sin may
   lead to deadly sin. There are seven deadly sins of
   which the first is pride.*

· *Pride is shown in many forms: arrogance, impudence, boasting, hypocrisy, joy in having done
   harm, etc. It may be inward or outward. Outward pride is like a tavern sign that shows there is
   wine in the cellar. It may show itself in too many
   clothes or too few, or in the carriage of the body,
   as when the buttocks jut as it were the hinder
   parts of a she-ape in the full of the moon. One
   can show sinful pride in retinue, in ostentatious
   hospitality, in one's strength, in one's gentility.
   The remedy for Pride is Humility or true self-
   knowledge.*

· *Envy is sorrow at the prosperity of others and
   joy in their hurt. It is the worst of sins as it
   sets itself against all other virtues and goodness,
   and is flatly against the Holy Ghost, source of
   Bounty. Backbiting and grumbling are the Devil's Paternoster.*

· *The remedy for Envy is to love God, your neighbor, and your enemy.*

· *Anger is the wicked will to vengeance. Anger
   against wickedness, however, is good, wrath
   without bitterness. Wicked anger is either sudden
   or premeditated; the latter is the worse. Malice
   aforethought chases the Holy Ghost out of the*

soul. It is the devil's furnace and heats hatred, manslaughter, treachery, lies, flattery, scorn, discord, menaces, and curses. *The remedy for Anger is Patience.*

· Accidie *does all tasks with vexation, slackly and without joy, and is encumbered by doing good. It restrains one from prayer. It is the rotten-hearted sin of Sloth. It leads to despair.* The remedy is Fortitude.

· Avarice *is a lecherous desire for earthly things, a kind of idolatry. Every florin in one's coffer is a mommet, an idol. It leads to feudal extortions by lords from their villeins, to fraud, to simony, gambling, theft, false-witness, sacrilege.* The remedy is Mercy *or "pity largely taken."*

· Gluttony *is an immeasurable appetite to eat or drink. Drunkenness is the horrible sepulchre of man's reason.* The remedy is Abstinence, Temperance, and Sobriety.

· Lechery *is near cousin to Gluttony. It has many forms and is the greatest sin of theft there is, for it steals body and soul.* The remedy is Chastity and Continence, *and not to eat or drink too much. When the pot boils strongly the best remedy is to withdraw the fire.*

· Confession *must be freely willed and made in full faith. A man must only confess his own sins, and truthfully with his own mouth, not painted with subtle words. It must be a considered, not a hasty act, and frequent.*

· Satisfaction *consists generally in alms-giving, penance, fasting, and bodily pains. Its fruit is endless bliss in Heaven.*

CHAUCER'S RETRACTIONS
The Maker of this Book here takes his Leave

Now I beg all those that listen to this little treatise, or read it, that if there be anything in it that pleases them, they thank Our Lord Jesu Christ for it, from whom proceeds all understanding and goodness.

And if there be anything that displeases them, I beg them also to impute it to the fault of my want of ability, and not to my will, who would very gladly have said better if I had had the power. For our Book says "all that is written is written for our doctrine"; and that is my intention. Wherefore I beseech you meekly for the mercy of God to pray for me, that Christ have mercy on me and forgive me my sins: and especially for my translations and enditings of worldly vanities, which I revoke in my retractions: as are the book of *Troilus;* also the book of *Fame;* the book of *The Nineteen Ladies;* the book of *The Duchess;* the book of *St. Valentine's Day of the Parliament of Fowls; The Tales of Canterbury,* those that tend towards sin; the book of *The Lion;*[1] and many another book, if they were in my memory; and many a song and many a lecherous lay; that Christ in his great mercy forgive me the sin.

But the translation of Boethius *De Consolatione,* and other books of Saints' legends, of homilies, and morality and devotion, for them I thank our Lord Jesu Christ and His blissful Mother, and all the Saints of Heaven; beseeching them that they henceforth, to my life's end, send me grace to bewail my sins and to study the salvation of my soul; and grant me the grace of true penitence, confession and satisfaction, that I may perform them in this present life, through the benign grace of Him that is King of kings and Priest over all priests, who bought us with the precious blood of His heart; so that I may be one of those that at the Day of Judgement shall be saved. *Qui cum Patre,* etc.

Here ends the book of the *Tales of Canterbury* compiled by Geoffrey Chaucer, on whose soul Jesu Christ have mercy.

Amen.

Notes

THE CANTERBURY TALES

In preparing this translation I have used the texts as they appear in the standard editions by W.W. Skeat in seven volumes (Oxford 1894–7) and by F. N. Robinson in one volume (Cambridge, Mass., 1933; also Oxford). The texts in these two editions are naturally not identical. I have generally referred to both, and where there seemed to be a discrepancy that could affect a translation I have made my own choice. I have followed the order of the tales as it is given by Skeat rather than that given by Robinson.

The notes which follow derive very largely from both these authorities and from other works of reference I have from time to time consulted.

THE PROLOGUE

1. *Martyr.* St. Thomas à Becket of Canterbury.
2. *The Knight's campaigning: Alexandria.* Taken and immediately after abandoned by Pierre de Lusignan, King of Cyprus, in 1365. *Algeciras.* Besieged and taken from the Moorish King of Granada in 1344. *Ayas* in Armenia, taken from the Turks by Pierre de Lusignan in about the year 1367. *Attalia,* on the south coast of Asia Minor, taken by Pierre de Lusignan soon after 1352. *Tramissene,* now called Tlemcen or Tremessen in western Algeria. *Balat* is a conjecture for the original *Palatye* and occupies the former site of Miletus.
3. *Gaudies.* Every eleventh bead in a rosary stands for a *paternoster* and is called a "gaudy."
4. *A Limiter.* A begging friar who was granted a district to beg in, to limit his activities.
5. *Four Orders.* The four Orders of mendicant friars, the Dominicans, the Franciscans, the Carmelites, and the Austin Friars.
6. *St. Paul's.* Lawyers used to meet for consultation at the portico of St. Paul's cathedral.
7. *A Franklin.* A class of landowner, a freeholder, who is also free by birth, but not noble. It is noteworthy that his self-conscious chatter about gentility when he politely interrupts the Squire is contemptuously interrupted by the Host.
8. *Images.* The Doctor worked by what Chaucer calls "Natural Magic" (here translated as "the powers of favourable planets"). Small images or effigies, moulded, probably in wax, to represent the patient, or other sorts of talisman or text, would be hung on the patient at hours when his horoscope indicated that the planets were favourably placed for him, in relation to the zodiac; at such hours (as if by what we call "cosmic rays") virtue was believed to descend into these images, etc., and thence to the patient, with healing effect. Faith is a great healer.
9. *Dry, cold, moist or hot.* A man's body was conceived as being composed of the four elements, earth, water, air, and fire in due proportions. *Earth* was thought to be cold and dry, *water* cold and moist, *air* hot and moist, *fire* hot and dry. Diseases were thought to be due to an imbalance in one or more of these qualities. A man's character could be roughly defined by reference to them, and their proportion decided his "humour," e.g. a *sanguine* man (like the Franklin) was held to be hot and moist, which

gave him the character of being a laughing, amorous, high-coloured, fleshy, good-natured fellow, with many desires and capacities. A *choleric* man (like the Reeve) was thought to be hot and dry. There were also *melancholy* men (cold and dry) and *phlegmatic* men (cold and moist).

10. *Aesculapius* and other medical authorities: *Aesculapius,* mythical son of Apollo and Coronis, who learnt the art of medicine from Cheiron the Centaur, and whom Zeus struck by lightning for having restored too many people to life. He had a daughter called Hygieia and a temple was built to him, when after death he was deified as the god of medicine, at Epidaurus. *Hippocrates,* the most famous physician of antiquity, born at Cos about 460 B.C. *Dioscorides,* a Greek physician who lived in Cilicia in the first century A.D., with some of whose opinions Chaucer appears, in the *Nun's Priest's Tale* and elsewhere, to have been familiar. *Galen,* a physician and a voluminous author on medical subjects, born at Pergamus in Mysia, who studied at Smyrna, Corinth, and Alexandria and practised in Rome. Approximate dates 130–201 A.D. *Rhazes,* a Spanish Arab doctor of the tenth century. *Hali, Serapion and Avicenna* were Arabian physicians and astronomers of the tenth and eleventh centuries. *Averroes,* a Moorish medical author who lived in Morocco in the twelfth century. *Scotch Bernard.* Bernard Gordon, professor of medicine at Montpellier about the year 1300. *John of Gaddesden,* a medical authority educated at Merton College, Oxford, who died in 1361. *Gilbertine,* supposed to be Gilbertus Magnus, an Englishman who flourished towards the middle of the thirteenth century, wrote books about medicine, and is said to have been Chancellor at Montpellier.
11. *A Reeve.* A steward or minor official on an estate, generally an intermediary between a lord and his serfs.
12. *A Summoner.* One paid to summon sinners to trial before an ecclesiastical court. For further details of his profession see the opening of the *Friar's Tale.*
13. *Cherubin.* In medieval art the Cherubim are generally depicted with flame-coloured faces.
14. *Questio quid juris.* "The question is, what is the point in law?"
15. *A Pardoner.* As the name implies, one who has authority (from the Pope) to sell pardons and indulgences, though not necessarily in holy orders.

THE KNIGHT'S TALE

1. *Dana,* a modernization of the name *Dane* as it is here found in Chaucer. He meant Daphne of course, who, being so inhuman as to flee the embraces of Apollo, was turned into a laurel. Her preserved virginity qualifies her for representation in Diana's temple.
2. *By the three forms:* in Heaven, *Luna.* On earth, *Diana.* In Hell, *Proserpina.* As in Keats' sonnet on Homer:
   > Such seeing hadst thou as it once befell
   > To Dian, Queen of earth and heaven and hell.
3. *Could not be expelled.* Chaucer is airing his technical knowledge of contemporary physiology. Three forces or "virtues" were believed to control the life in a human body: the "animal" virtues in the brain, the "natural"

in the liver, and the "vital" in the heart. The "animal" controlled all muscles, and therefore should have been able to expel the poison from Arcita's liver. But he was too far gone.

THE MILLER'S TALE

1. *A voice like Pilate's.* Miracle plays represented Herod and Pilate as huffing roarers and braggarts. Their lines generally carry heavy alliteration.

2. *Money.* More useful in a town than in the country, where there are fewer things to buy.

3. *Him that harrowed Hell.* When Christ descended into Hell He led away therefrom Adam, Eve, the Patriarchs, St. John the Baptist, and others, redeemed and at last released. This act was commonly called "The harrowing of Hell" in the middle ages and was the subject of several miracle-plays. The original story comes from the *Gospel of Nicodemus* in the Apocryphal New Testament.

THE REEVE'S TALE

1. *Solar Hall.* So called because of its large sunny windows. Its official name was King's Hall, having been founded by Edward III. Later it was merged in what is now called Trinity College.

2. *And how's your canny daughter?* In Chaucer's original the two young northerners from Strother, Alan and John, are made to talk in northern dialect and idiom, for instance, the forms *swa* for *so, bathe* for *both, raa* for a *roe* are used by them. So far as I know this is the first time dialect occurs for comic effect in English fiction.

3. *Bromeholme.* A piece of wood, said to be of the true cross, known as the Rood of Bromeholme, much venerated in Norfolk.

THE COOK'S TALE

1. *Jack of Dover.* The authorities disagree as to what this expression means. Some think it is a fish, others that it is a pie that has been cooked, allowed to cool, and then has been cooked again to freshen it up when rather stale.

2. *Led with minstrelsy to jail.* Skeat notes that in those days when disorderly persons were carried to prison they were preceded by *minstrels*, in order to call public attention to their disgrace.

THE MAN OF LAW'S TALE

1. *Artificial day*, that is, from dawn to sunset, as opposed to the "natural day" of twenty-four hours.

2. *Ceix and Halcyon.* Their story occurs in Chaucer's first long original poem, *The Book of the Duchess, c.* 1369.

3. *The Legend of Cupid's Saints.* Better known as *The Legend of Good Women,* composed towards 1386 by Chaucer at the command of the Queen in expiation for his supposed defamation of women in the person of Criseyde in *Troilus and Criseyde.* The list of these tender creatures as given by the Man of Law does not precisely tally with those whose tales are told in the *Legend,* but is near enough for the Man of Law.

4. *Apollonius.* This horror, whether real or pretended on Chaucer's part, is supposed by some to be a dig at his close friend the poet John Gower, who relates this tale in his *Confessio Amantis,* but he says nothing about "pavement-wooing."

5. *Metamorphoses.* There is an account in this work of Ovid, Bk. v, where the daughters of Pierus vied with the Muses and were transformed into magpies for their presumption.

6. *Double-aces.* There was a game called *Hazard* in which dice were thrown. Double-aces was the lowest throw, fives and sixes a high one.

7. *First cause of motion,* etc. Skeat notes that the old, Ptolemaic astronomy supposed the earth stationary and central with nine spheres revolving about it. The seven innermost each carried a planet with it (Moon, Venus, Mercury, Sun, Mars, Jupiter, Saturn). The eighth sphere contained the fixed stars and was believed to have a slow motion from west to east. The ninth and outermost sphere was called the *primum mobile* or sphere of first motion, which was held to make a diurnal revolution from east to west that carried all else with it in the same direction, which is opposite to the "natural" motion of the sun, which advances along the signs of the zodiac.

8. *Scorpio.* These contrary motions are suggested by Chaucer as the cause of the failure of Constance's marriage because of the evil influence of Mars in *Scorpio,* which is the house of death, battle, travail, and harm.

9. *O serpent masked in femininity.* Medieval poets and illuminators constantly represent Satan in Eden as a snake with a woman's face. This was perhaps because the serpent in Eden was a fallen angel, and, being an angel, had long hair, and having long hair looked like a woman.

10. *St. Mary the Egyptian.* It is said that this St. Mary, whose day is April 9th, was in early life loose in her morals, but being converted fled into the desert and lived forty-seven years there, beyond Jordan. She belonged to the fifth century.

11. *Johnny.* Sir John was a common name for a priest; *Lollards* were the strict but heretical followers of Wycliffe.

12. *Phislyas.* This word or, as it appears in some MSS., *phillyas* is thought by Skeat to be a corruption of some technical word in philosophy. It may be so, but perhaps the word is a deliberate piece of nonsense to underline the unlearnedness of the Skipper.

THE SHIPMAN'S TALE

1. *He has to clothe us.* It is obvious that this passage was meant for a woman speaker, presumably the Wife of Bath. It is likely that Chaucer had at first designed the tale for her, then changed his mind (having found one that suited her even better) and unloaded this one on the Skipper without remembering these tell-tale lines.

2. *Ganelon of France.* The villain of the *Chanson de Roland* that betrayed Roland and Oliver who, with Archbishop Turpin, formed Charlemagne's rearguard at Roncesvalles against the Moors. Ganelon was torn asunder by four horses.

3. *Two in twelve.* The MSS. differ as to the proportion; some say ten in twelve, some twelve in twenty.

4. *Double entry.* In Chaucer's original the Merchant rebukes his wife for not having told him that the monk had repaid (which of course he had not) this trifling debt of 100 francs "by redy token"; and she, quite unabashed, says he has many slacker debtors than she is, and, if she fails, let him score it on her tally:

> and if so be I faille
> I am youre wyf; score it upon my taille.

making thereby a very obvious sexual jest, which is repeated in the last line of the Shipman's Tale:

> and God us sende
> Taylynge unough unto our lyves ende.

It is one of Chaucer's rare puns: the word *taille* equals *tail* and tail equals *tail-end* or *backside,* and taille equals *tally.*

Payment by tally consisted in the interchange of a notched stick, split in half, of which the debtor and creditor each retained half, and if the two halves "tallied" the amount due was in no doubt because of the notches.

THE PRIORESS'S TALE

1. *Corpus Dominus.* The Host was no Latinist. He meant

corpus Domini, the body of our Lord. He makes the same blunder later on.

THE MONK'S TALE

1. *Zenobia* flourished A.D. 264 as Queen of Palmyra and was married to Odenathus, a Bedouin. Recognized by the Emperor Gallienus, she was attacked and defeated and led in triumph by the Emperor Aurelian, but survived to live in comfort.

2. *King Peter of Spain.* Skeat notes: "He reigned over Castille and Leon from 1350 to 1362 and his conduct was marked by numerous acts of unprincipled atrocity."

3. *Upon an argent field.* The second stanza of this "tragedy" is written as a sort of heraldic riddle intermixed with puns. The arms described (argent, a double-headed eagle sable, displayed, debruised by a bend gules) are those of Bertrand Du Guesclin who "brewed" the treason by luring King Peter into his brother's tent. The "wicked nest" is a pun on the name of Sir Oliver Mauny (*Mau* is Old French for *wicked, nid* for *nest*), who was an accomplice according to Chaucer. Chaucer continues that this was not such an Oliver as that in the *Chanson de Roland,* loyal soldier of Charlemagne, but much more like Ganelon (the villain of the *Chanson*).

4. *King Peter of Cyprus.* Pierre de Lusignan, ascended to the throne of Cyprus in 1352 and was assassinated in 1369. Chaucer's Knight seems to have seen service with him.

5. *Bernabo Visconti,* Duke of Milan, was deposed and died in prison in 1385. Chaucer knew him personally, though this does not show from what the Monk has to say. He went on the King's business to treat with him in 1378. The death of Bernabo is the most recent historical event mentioned in the *Canterbury Tales.*

6. *Dante.* See *Inferno* xxxii–xxxiii.

7. *Holofernes,* and

8. *Antiochus.* For both of these see the *Book of Judith* and 2 *Maccabees* ix in the *Apocrypha.*

9. *Alexander of Macedon,* the Great, 356–323 B.C. His dazzling career, high intelligence, and astounding magnanimity made him a legendary ideal of knightly soldiership in the middle ages.

10. *Aces.* The lowest possible throw of the dice in the game of *Hazard.*

11. *Brutus Cassius.* Chaucer supposed these two famous assassins to be one and the same.

THE NUN'S PRIEST'S TALE

1. *The equinoctial wheel.* I quote from Professor Robinson: "A great circle of the heavens in the plane of the equator. According to the old astronomy it made a complete daily revolution so that 15 degrees would 'ascend' every hour." It was a popular belief in the time of Chaucer that cocks crew punctually on the hour.

2. *My Love is far from land.* The original, probably the refrain of a popular song, reads "my life is faren in londe" and means "my love has gone away into foreign parts" but I could not resist the allusion to a song of our own, "She is far from the land where her young hero sleeps."

3. *Greek Sinon.* The Greek who tricked King Priam into admitting the Trojan Horse to Troy.

4. *Bishop Bradwardine,* a famous contemporary theologian, Proctor of Oxford University in 1325, and later Professor of Divinity and Chancellor.

5. *Boethius,* author of *De Consolatione Philosophiae* which Chaucer translated, was esteemed not only as a philosopher but also as a musician. Boethius lived *c.* A.D. 470–525.

6. *Physiologus.* I quote from Tyrwhitt, "a book in Latin metre entitled *Physiologus de Naturis xii Animalium,* by one

Theobaldus, whose age is not known. The Chapter *De Sirenis* begins thus:

Sirenae sunt monstra resonantia magnis vocibus, etc."

7. *Burnel the Ass.* A poem by Nigel Wireker of the twelfth century. The tale alluded to is that of a priest's son who broke a rooster's leg by throwing a stone at it. In revenge the bird declined to crow in the morning on the day when the priest was to be ordained and receive a benefice, so the priest failed to wake up in time and being late for the ceremony lost his preferment.

8. *Geoffrey* is Geoffrey de Vinsauf, an author on the art of Rhetoric who flourished in the twelfth century. Chaucer, who derived a great deal of his stylistic manner from a sane use of the rules of rhetoric as laid down by his "dear and sovereign master," is here poking gentle fun at him. It may be observed that the whole of the *Nun's Priest's Tale* is a farrago of rhetorical fireworks which must have made the poem far funnier to the fourteenth century, trained in such matters, than it is to us.

9. *Jack Straw* was one of the leaders of the riots in London during the Peasants' Revolt of 1381, according to Walsingham's Chronicle. He and his gang massacred a number of Flemings in the Vintry, and he was later captured and decapitated.

THE PARDONER'S TALE

1. *In neighbouring regions.* There were regulations against the mixture of wines. Lepe wine is light by nature, but may have been fortified with spirit for export. He is ironically suggesting that—as one cannot, of course, suspect an honest Fish Street vintner of deliberately mixing his wines—one can only suppose the mixture to occur spontaneously, thanks to the geographical proximity of Spain and France.

2. *Hailes.* In Gloucestershire; the abbey ruins can still be seen. It formerly possessed a phial of Christ's blood; later publicly destroyed at St. Paul's Cross by order of Henry VIII.

3. *Avicenna.* An Arabian physician (A.D. 980–1037) who wrote a work on medicines that includes a chapter on poisons.

THE WIFE OF BATH'S TALE

1. *Ptolemy.* Claudius Ptolemacus, an astronomer of the second century whose chief work was known as his *Almagest,* an Arabic corruption of its title in Greek. His astronomical theories are those on which all medieval astronomy was based. His general wisdom also was proverbial.

2. *Dunmow.* The prize of a flitch of bacon for the married pair that can swear, after a year and a day of matrimony, that they have never had a quarrel, or regretted their marriage, and that if they were both free to choose again, would make the same choice. This is said to have been an annual event.

3. *Three misfortunes.* She is alluding to Proverbs xxx, 21–3. "For three things the earth is disquieted, and for four which it cannot bear; for a servant when he reigneth; and a fool when he is filled with meat; for an odious woman when she is married; and an handmaid that is heir to her mistress."

4. *Theophrastus and Valerius.* A work attributed to Walter Map, a wit and cynic who flourished about A.D. 1200. The subject of the work here referred to is *De non ducenda uxore,* a satire on matrimony.

5. *Children of Mercury.* Learning was held to be under the protection of Mercury; his "children" are scholars, who in those days were generally celibate.

6. *Pasiphaë.* Wife of Minos, King of Crete. She fell